Classic World *Atlas*

TABLE OF CONTENTS

Introductory Section
Using the Atlas . . . . iii-iv
Natural Wonders: Masterpieces of Nature . . . . v-xvi

Maps
Index Map and Legend 1

World 2-5
World, Political 2-3
World, Physical 4-5

Europe 6-29
Europe, Political 6-7
Northern Europe and Scandinavia 8-9
Baltic Regions and Moscow 10-11
British Isles 12-13
Northern France, Belgium, and the Netherlands 14-15
Germany, Czech Republic, Slovakia, and Poland 16-17
Southern France and Switzerland 18-19
Spain and Portugal 20-21
Northern Italy, Austria, and the Balkans 22-23
Southern Italy 24-25
Hungary, Serbia and Montenegro, Romania, and Bulgaria 26-27
Greece and Western Turkey 28-29

Asia 30-59
Asia, Political 30-31
Northwestern Asia 32-33
Northeastern Asia 34-35
China, Korea, and Japan 36-37
Japan, Korea, and Northeastern China 38-39
Central and Southern Japan 40-41
Eastern China 42-43
Southeast Asia 44-45
Southern Asia 46-47
Myanmar, Thailand, and Singapore 48-49
Borneo, Java, and Sumatra 50-51
Philippines 52
Southern India 53
Northern India 54-55
Southwestern Asia 56-57
Israel, Lebanon, and Jordan 58-59

Africa 60-71
Africa, Political 60-61
Northeastern Africa 62-63
Northwestern Africa 64-65
Central Africa 66-67
Southern Africa 68-69
South Africa 70-71

Australia and Oceania 72-80
Australia and Oceania, Political 72-73
Australia 74-75
Southeastern Australia 76-77
Islands of the Pacific 78-79
New Zealand 80

Antarctica 81

South America 82-93
South America, Political 82-83
Northern South America 84-85
Venezuela and Colombia 86-87
Eastern Brazil 88-89
Southern South America 90-91
Central Argentina and Chile 92-93

North America 94-141
North America, Political 94-95
Mexico, Central America, and the Caribbean 96-97
Northwestern Mexico and Southwestern United States 98-99
Central Mexico 100-101
Central America 102-103
Islands of the Caribbean 104-105
Canada 106-107
United States 108-109
Northeastern United States and Southeastern Canada 110-111
Great Lakes 112-113
Central Atlantic States 114-115
Southeastern United States 116-117
Northern Midwest 118-119
Midwest 120-121
Mississippi Delta 122-123
Northern Great Plains 124-125
Central Great Plains 126-127
Southern Great Plains 128-129
Southern Texas 130-131
Arizona and Utah 132-133
California, Nevada, and Hawaii 134-135
Northwestern United States 136-137
Southwestern Canada 138-139
Alaska and the Aleutians 140
Greenland 141

Oceans 142-144
Pacific and Indian Oceans 142-143
Atlantic Ocean 144

Index
Index to the Reference Maps . . . . I•1-I•64

Editors
Brett R. Gover
Anne Ford

Art Direction and Design
Rand McNally Art and Design

Writers
Donald V. Beaulieu
Catherine C. VanPatten

Cartography
Robert K. Argersinger
Gregory P. Babiak
Barbara Benstead-Strassheim
Kerry B. Chambers
Marzee L. Eckhoff
Susan K. Hudson
Brian M. Lash
Nina Lusterman
David R. Simmons
Raymond Tobiaski
Howard Veregin
Thomas F. Vitacco
Richard A. Wanzo

Photo Credits   (l=left, r=right, c=center, t=top, b=bottom)

Jacket
© 2004 PhotoDisc, Inc.

Contents
© Ken Ross/FPG International, v (t); © William Wheeler/Dave Houser Photography, v (t c); © Telegraph Colour Library/FPG International, v (b l); © C. Bowman/Picture Perfect, v (b c); © Jerry Sieve/Adstock Photos, v (b r); © Bob Grant/Comstock, vi (t); © Dave Bartruff/Artistry International, vi (b); © Franco Salmoiraghi/Photo Resource Hawaii Stock Photography, vii; © Dewitt Jones/Tony Stone Images, viii (t); © Robert Frerck/Odyssey Productions, viii (b); © Chad Ehlers/International Stock, ix (t); © James Strachan/Tony Stone Images, ix (b); © Arakaki-Argelia/International Stock, x (t); © Galen Rowell/Mountain Light, x (b); © Eye Ubiquitous/Art Directors & TRIP Photo Library, xi (t); © Tom Till/Tom Till Photography, xi (b); © David Muench/David Muench Photography, xii (t); © Tom Till/Tom Till Photography, xii (b); © David Muench/David Muench Photography, xiii (t); © Galen Rowell/Mountain Light, xiii (b); © Greg Vaughn/Tom Stack & Associates, xiv (t); © Boyd Norton, xiv (b); © TravelPix/FPG International, xv (t); © Kevin Schafer/Kevin Schafer Photography, xv (b); © Blaine Harrington, xvi (t); © Brian Lawrence/Uniphoto, xvi (b)

HOW TO USE THE ATLAS

What is an Atlas?

A set of maps bound together is called an atlas. Abraham Ortelius' *Theatrum orbis terrarum*, published in 1570, is considered to be the first modern "atlas," although it was not referred to as such for almost 20 years. In 1589, Gerardus Mercator *(figure 1)* coined the term when he named his collection of maps after Atlas, the mythological Titan who carried Earth on his shoulders as punishment for warring against Zeus. Since then, the definition of "atlas" has been expanded, and atlases often include additional geographic information in diagrams, tables, and text.

figure 1

Latitude and Longitude

The terms "latitude" and "longitude" refer to the grid of horizontal and vertical lines found on most maps and globes. Any point on Earth can be located by its precise latitude and longitude coordinates.

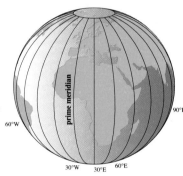

figure 2

The imaginary horizontal line that circles Earth halfway between the North and South poles is called the equator; it represents 0° latitude and lies 90° from either pole. The other lines of latitude, or parallels, measure distances north or south from the equator *(figure 2)*. The imaginary vertical line that measures 0° longitude runs through the Greenwich Observatory in the United Kingdom, and is called the prime meridian. The other lines of longitude, or meridians, measure distances east or west from the prime meridian *(figure 3)*, up to a maximum of 180°. Lines of latitude and longitude cross each other, forming a grid *(figure 4)*.

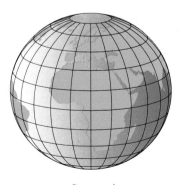

figure 3

Map Projections

Every cartographer is faced with the problem of transforming the curved surface of Earth onto a flat plane with a minimum of distortion. The systematic transformation of locations on Earth (a spherical surface) to locations on a map (a flat surface) is called projection.

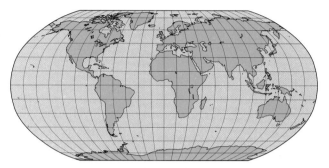

figure 4

It is not possible to represent on a flat map the spatial relationships of angle, distance, direction, and area that only a globe can show faithfully. As a result, projections inevitably involve some distortion. On large-scale maps representing a few square miles, the distortion is generally negligible. But on maps depicting large countries, continents, or the entire world, the amount of distortion can be significant. On maps which use the Mercator Projection *(figure 5)*, for example, distortion increases with distance from the equator. Thus the island of Greenland appears larger than the entire continent of South America,

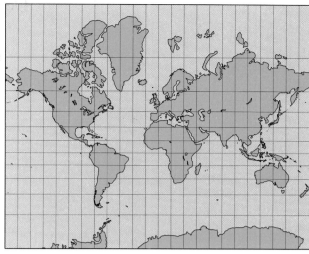

figure 5

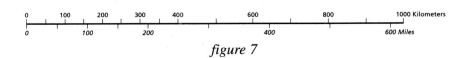

figure 6

although South America is in fact nine times larger. In contrast, the Robinson Projection *(figure 6)* renders the world's major land areas in generally correct proportion to one another, although distortion is still apparent in areas such as Antarctica, which is actually smaller than all of the continents except Europe and Australia.

There are an infinite number of possible map projections, all of which distort one or more of the characteristics of the globe in varying degrees. The projection that a cartographer chooses depends on the size and location of the area being projected and the purpose of the map. In this atlas, most of the maps are drawn on projections that give a consistent or only slightly distorted area scale, good land and ocean shape, parallels that are parallel, and as consistent a linear scale as possible throughout the projection.

Map Scale

The scale of a map is the relationship between distances or areas shown on the map and the corresponding distances or areas on Earth's surface. Large-scale maps show relatively small areas in greater detail than do small-scale maps, such as those of individual continents or of the world.

There are three different ways to express scale. Most often scale is given as a fraction, such as 1:10,000,000, which means that the ratio of distances on the map to actual distances on Earth is 1 to 10,000,000. Scale can also be expressed as a phrase, such as "One inch represents approximately ten million miles." Finally, scale can be illustrated via a bar scale on which various distances are labeled *(figure 7)*. Any of these three scale expressions can be used to calculate distances on a map.

0	100	200	300	400		600		800		1000 Kilometers
0		100		200			400			600 Miles

figure 7

Measuring Distances

Using a bar scale, it is possible to calculate the distance between any two points on a map. To find the approximate distance between São Paulo and Rio de Janeiro, Brazil, for example, follow these steps:

1) Lay a piece of paper on the right-hand page of the "Eastern Brazil" map found on pages 88-89, lining up its edge with the city dots for São Paulo and Rio de Janeiro. Make a mark on the paper next to each dot (figure 8).

2) Place the paper along the scale bar found below the map, and position the first mark at 0. The second mark falls about a quarter of the way between the 200-mile tick and the 300-mile tick, indicating that the distance separating the two cities is approximately 225 miles (figure 9).

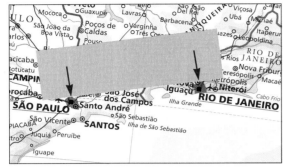

figure 8

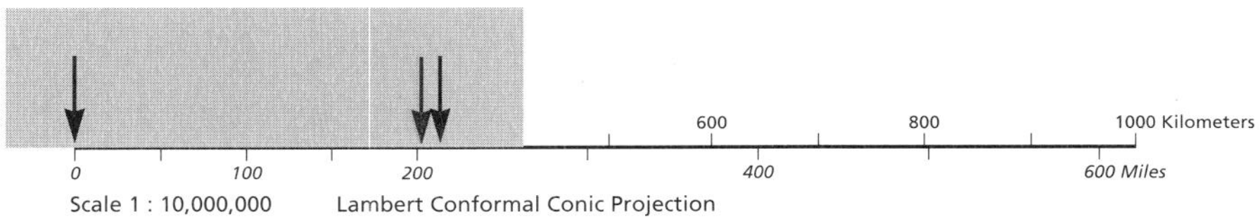

figure 9

3) To confirm this measurement, make a third pencil mark (shown in red in figure 9) at the 200-mile tick. Slide the paper to the left so that this mark lines up with 0. The Rio de Janeiro mark now falls about halfway between the 0 tick and the 50-mile tick. Thus, São Paulo and Rio de Janeiro are indeed approximately 225 (200 + 25) miles apart.

Using the Index to Find Places

One of the most important purposes of an atlas is to help the reader locate cities, towns, and geographic features such as rivers, lakes, and mountains. This atlas uses a "bingo key" indexing system. In the index, found on pages I•1 through I•64, every entry is assigned an alpha-numeric code that consists of a letter and a number. This code relates to the red letters and numbers that run along the perimeter of each map. To locate places or features, follow the steps outlined in this example for the city of Bratsk, Russia.

1) Look up Bratsk in the index. The entry (figure 10) contains the following information: the place name (Bratsk), the name of the country (Russia) in which Bratsk is located, the map reference key (C18) that corresponds to Bratsk's location on the map, and the page number (32) of the map on which Bratsk can be found.

Brassey, Banjaran, mts., Malay	A10	50
Brass Islands, is., V.I.U.S.	o7	104 b
Brasstown Bald, mtn., Ga., U.S.	B2	116
Bratca, Rom.	C9	26
Bratislava, Slov.	H13	16
Bratislava, state, Slov.	H13	16
Bratsk, Russia	C18	32
Bratskoe vodohranilisce, res., Russia	C18	32

figure 10

figure 11

2) Turn to the Northwestern Asia map on pages 32-33. Look along either the left or right-hand margin for the red letter "C"—the letter code given for Bratsk. The "C" denotes a band that arcs horizontally across the map, between the grid lines representing 55° and 60° North latitude. Then, look along either the top or bottom margin for the red number "18"—the numerical part of the code given for Bratsk. The "18" denotes a widening vertical band, between the grid lines representing 100° and 105° East longitude, which angles from the top center of the map to right-hand edge.

3) Using your finger, follow the horizontal "C" band and the vertical "18" band to the area where they overlap (figure 11). Bratsk lies within this overlap area.

Physical Maps and Political Maps

Most of the maps in the *Classic World Atlas* are physical maps, like the one shown in *figure 12*, emphasizing terrain, landforms, and elevation. Political maps, as in *figure 13*, emphasize countries and other political units over topography. The atlas includes political maps of the world and each of the continents except Antarctica.

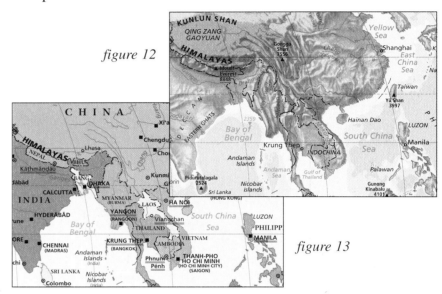

figure 12

figure 13

How Maps Show Topography

The physical maps in this atlas use two techniques to depict Earth's topography. Variations in elevation are shown through a series of colors called hypsometric tints. Areas below sea level appear as a dark green; as the elevation rises, the tints move successively through lighter green, yellow, and orange. Similarly, variations in ocean depth are represented by bathymetric tints. The shallowest areas appear as light blue; darker tints of blue indicate greater depths. The hypsometric/bathymetric scale that accompanies each map identifies, in feet and meters, all of the elevation and depth categories that appear on the map.

Principal landforms, such as mountain ranges and valleys, are rendered in shades of gray, a technique known as shaded relief. The combination of hypsometric tints and shaded relief provides the map reader with a three-dimensional picture of Earth's surface (figure 14).

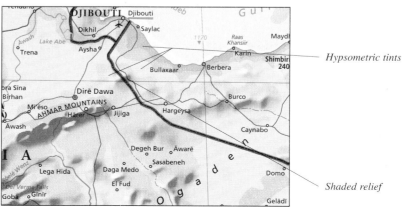

figure 14

Masterpieces of Nature

A landscape artist would have a difficult time painting a single portrait that captures the essence of our planet. From the thunderous tumble of Africa's Victoria Falls to the iridescent coral of Australia's Great Barrier Reef to the cake-layered mesas of the United States' Grand Canyon, the world's geographic terrain is infinitely varied, multi-hued, and wondrous—and impossible to capture at a glance.

An intimate, close-up portrait of Earth must include such vast expanses as Asia's mighty Himalayas and such singularly unique sites as Northern Ireland's fantastic Giant's Causeway, the biggest or tallest or longest natural wonders along with those that are simply stunningly unique. While no listing of the world's wonders is complete, certain geographic features on each continent stand out for their magnificent beauty and enormity—not just as geographic marvels but as important places in the human culture and mythology of the people who experience them. Together these great mountains, rivers, lakes, deserts, canyons, waterfalls, fjords, volcanic craters, reefs, and rock formations—pinpointed on the maps within this atlas—create a detailed portrait of our planet's landscape and represent its greatest works of art.

A pyramid-shaped colossus serrated by glaciers and blasted by wind and snow, Mount Everest is the pinnacle of the planet, actually jutting into the jet stream, marked by a ribbon of ice particles whirling eastward off the summit. The 29,028-foot (8,848-meter) peak crowns the world's

Mount Everest

youngest and highest mountains, Asia's mighty Himalayas, which means "abode of snow" in the Sanskrit language. Glaciers carved severe features into Everest and other megaliths of the Himalayan Range, forming along the Nepal-Tibet border a massive skyline of dramatic peaks that seem to be cleaved from Earth like chiseled shards of ice.

The summit of Everest was actually once the seafloor. The Himalayas today separate the Indian subcontinent from the rest of Asia, but until 180 million years ago an ocean divided the two land masses. The Indo-Australian crustal plate on which India sits migrated northward, where it collided with the Eurasian plate, crushing the seafloor and buckling it—along with rocky layers of the ocean bottom—toward the skies.

Everest has always been venerated: The mountain is Chomolungma, "goddess mother of the world," to Tibetans in the north, while Nepalis to the south call it Sagarmatha, "goddess of the sky." But Everest is never so revered as by climbers, for whom the tallest mountain in the world is an irresistible lure. Mere mortals have climbed two thirds of the way up through Earth's atmosphere: Edmund Hillary and Tenzing Norgay are credited with the first ascent in 1953, though it's widely held that George Mallory and Andrew Irvine summited in 1924 before disappearing on their descent. Since then, adventurers have conquered the peak in new and creative ways. Japanese climber Yuichiro Miura summited in 1970 and then descended the mountain on skis, breaking many bones. Reinhold Messner and Peter Habeler first scaled the peak without bottled oxygen in 1978. In 1990 Australian Tim McCartney-Snape repeated the feat, but began from sea level, at the Bay of Bengal.

More than 700 people have reached Everest's summit, but for every five who have succeeded, one has died in the attempt. Some die from falls or avalanches; others succumb to cold, altitude sickness, and oxygen deprivation above 25,000 feet in the Death Zone. "Life of mountains," said Anatoli Boukreev, a Kazakhstani guide who narrowly survived a deadly 1996 Everest storm, but died on Annapurna in 1997, "is stronger than life of people." *(page 55)*

Other Remarkable Mountains

1 Cerro Aconcagua, Argentina: The tallest peak in the Western Hemisphere, this steep, 22,831-foot (6,959-meter) glacially sculpted massif in the central Andes was a sacred burial site in Pre-Colombian times. *(page 90)*

2 K2, Pakistan/China: Teetering above the Karakoram Range, the world's second-tallest mountain (28,251 feet, 8,611 meters) has claimed the lives of almost as many climbers as have reached its summit. *(page 57)*

3 Kilimanjaro, Tanzania: The almost perfect cone of this snowcapped volcanic peak (19,340 feet, 5,895 meters), the highest in Africa, soars above the Serengeti Plain. *(page 67)*

4 Mount Elbrus, Russia: Europe's highest point, Elbrus' twin-peaked volcanic cone (18,510 feet, 5,642 meters) is 5,000 feet taller than neighboring peaks. *(page 56)*

5 Mount Fuji, Japan: Rising majestically from almost sea level to 12,388 feet (3,776 meters), Japan's highest mountain, Fuji-san, is a stratovolcano built on the remains of older volcanoes. *(page 41)*

6 Mount McKinley, United States: Known as the Great One, or "Denali," to the Athabascan people of Alaska, the tallest peak in North America rises dramatically from 2,000 feet (610 meters) at its lowlands base to 20,320 feet (6,194 meters) at its summit. *(page 140)*

At 13,796 feet (4,260 meters) above sea level, the snow-capped crown of Mauna Kea floats like a mirage over the balmy valhalla of the Big Island of Hawaii. A paradox of fire and ice, Mauna Kea was the only glaciated spot in the tropical Pacific during the last Ice Age, and even today Lake Waiau, located inside a volcanic cinder cone near the peak, is fed entirely by permafrost, a frozen Ice Age remnant still melting below the surface. Starkly beautiful, this dormant volcano's rounded slopes were molded into an inverted bowl by repeated eruptions of fast-flowing lava. Its peak is flanked by an arresting moonscape of cinder cones and red lava fields—the Apollo astronauts actually test-drove the lunar rover here in a crater called Moon Valley.

These cinder cones near the summit, representing smaller volcanoes, are an ideal site for the world's largest astronomy telescopes. At the Mauna Kea Observatories the atmosphere is extremely dry and stable, making for accurate measurements of infrared radiation. The skies are dark and cloud-free, with one of the world's best proportions of clear nights. A tropical inversion cloud layer near the summit separates the atmosphere atop the peak from the wetter maritime air at lower elevations and from atmospheric pollutants.

Many consider Mauna Kea the tallest mountain on Earth: It measures nearly 32,000 feet (9,750 meters) from base to summit, but 18,200 of those feet are below sea level. Ancient Hawaiians believed Mauna Kea was the home of the snow goddess Poliahu, whose tempestuous sister Pele resided in Mauna Loa, an active volcano across the island. The sister goddesses sparred perpetually over a human love interest, and the saddle between the two mountains became their battlefield. Prudently, islanders avoided that area and settled on the coast below.

In a precursor of the Ironman Triathlon, natives would run up Mauna Kea, grab as much snow as they could carry, and race back down to the ocean. The runner who arrived with enough snow to make a snowball was declared the winner. Today, visitors

Mauna Kea

pay homage to the mountain by skiing its snowy summit, then sunbathing on its beaches below, in the shadow of this volcanic peak forged by fire from below and shaped by ice from above. *(page 78)*

Canyons

Grand Canyon

Each year, five million pilgrims gape at the Grand Canyon's labyrinthine landscape of mesas and spires, its cathedrals of sandstone and shale. They marvel at its pink, red, white, and gold terraces of cake-layered strata a mile (1.6 kilometers) deep. But this intricately eroded chasm was not initially destined to become a tourist mecca. Early explorers of the U.S. Southwest deemed the impassable gorge a "horrible abyss" and "grave of the world." Until a local miner offered in an 1886 Flagstaff, Arizona, newspaper ad to "conduct parties thereto at any time," very few people had any good reason to travel there. But John Hance's modest advertisement opened up to tourists two billion years of geological history laid bare as the Colorado River sliced through northern Arizona's Kaibab Plateau. At the rate of about one inch (2.5 centimeters) every 80 years, the river eroded red Mesozoic mudstone, then creamy Paleozoic limestone, down to dark Precambrian schist in the lower gorge. Side tributaries, along with rain, wind, and frost, gradually broadened the gorge to 18 miles (29 kilometers) wide and 277 miles (446 kilometers) long.

Visitors today—up to 20,000 each day in the summer—descend the Grand Canyon's hiking paths on foot or muleback, soar over the canyon by plane, or merely peer over the precarious edge in an attempt to comprehend its magnificence. Since 1919, most of the canyon has been designated a national park, whose directors work diligently to cope with growing numbers of tourists while fulfilling the mandate of Theodore Roosevelt: "Keep it for your children...and for all who come after you, as the one great sight which every American...should see." *(page 133)*

An immense landscape of steep gorges and rugged badlands isolated from the rest of Mexico for many centuries, Copper Canyon, or "Barranca del Cobre," is the homeland of the Tarahumara Indians. In the seventeenth century, the Tarahumara fled northwestern Mexico's desert plains near present-day Chihuahua to escape enslavement by the Spanish. They settled in Copper Canyon, which burrows along the western slope of the Sierra Madre Occidental Range. Here the Urique River has sculpted sinuous ravines and veined ridges of red volcanic rock into a series of boulder-strewn trenches deeper than the Grand Canyon in places and four times the area. The canyon's arid upper slopes stand in marked contrast with tropical

Copper Canyon

vegetation in its lower depths, and it is named for its rich resources—ancient copper mines that pockmark the region. The land has also yielded, over the course of four centuries, more than a billion dollars' worth of gold.

The only practical means of entering Copper Canyon is a railroad that has traversed the area since the 1960s. There are no paved roads, and the Tarahumara travel the canyon by running along hundreds of miles of switchback trails (their traditional means of hunting deer is running the animals to death). Copper Canyon remains today a harsh, intractable wilderness that retains a mystic hold on the Mexican imagination. "This great Mexican abyss," wrote author Carlos Fuentes, "bears witness to the two extremes of creation, birth and death." *(page 100)*

Other Impressive Canyons and Gorges

1 Black Canyon of the Gunnison River, United States: Even its river's namesake, Captain John Gunnison, never entered this gloomy, 2,000-foot-deep (608-meter-deep) canyon in southwestern Colorado, which is deeper in places than it is wide. *(page 132)*

2 Colca Canyon, Peru: More than 10,000 feet (3,222 meters) deep, the Andes' Colca is the world's deepest canyon and home of the Andean condor, the world's largest bird, with a wingspan of ten feet (three meters). *(page 84)*

3 Daryal Gorge, Georgia: The 5,900-foot-tall (1,794-meter-tall) granite cliffs of this gorge, called the Gates of the Caucasus in Roman times, frame the major pass through the imposing Caucasus Mountains. Greek mythology claims that Prometheus was chained to the mountain above it. *(page 56)*

4 Grand Canyon of the Verdon River, France: Carving through limestone pocked with subterranean caves and sinkholes, the Verdon River has created France's longest, deepest, and most scenic canyon, with walls only 650 feet (200 meters) apart in places. *(page 18)*

5 Tiger Leaping Gorge, China: This narrow, 9,850-foot (2,994-meter) gorge along the Jinsha River (the Upper Yangtze) in Yunnan Province was named for a hunted tiger of Chinese legend who escaped death by leaping across the chasm. *(page 36)*

6 Vikos Canyon, Greece: Its sheer, almost vertical cliffs of brilliant white limestone rise 4,000 feet (1,216 meters) above the Voidomatis River in the Pindus Mountains of northwestern Greece. *(page 28)*

Amazon River

When the Spanish conquistadors explored this South American waterway in 1541, they allegedly encountered a fierce tribe of giant female warriors, which they likened to the Amazons of Greek myth. Truth or exaggeration, the Spanish could not have bestowed a more apt name upon this formidable body of water, artery of the South American continent. The Amazon is unrivaled in physical magnitude among all rivers in the world: More than six million cubic feet (168,000 cubic meters) of water—one fifth of all the flowing water on Earth—discharge through the river's mouth every second. The drainage basin of the Amazon and its thousand tributaries covers 2.7 million square miles (6.9 million square kilometers). Through Brazil the river runs so wide and deep that ocean-going freighters can sail upriver thousands of miles to Iquitos, Peru.

The Amazon's waters originate just below the peaks of the Andes in northern Peru, where small streams cascade down steep gorges and eventually form a flow a mile (1.6 kilometers) wide. From there the river moves languidly through dense jungle; during the rainy season it spills into secondary channels and lakes, drenching an enormous floodplain. This abundant ecosystem supports some truly Amazonian species, including the 30-foot-long (nine-meter-long) anaconda, the 110-pound (50-kilogram) capybara rodent, and a giant water lily that spans up to six feet (two meters) across. The Amazon rain forest has also been home to hundreds of indigenous groups of people, though many have been displaced by logging, farming, and cattle-grazing. The subsequent harm from these activities on the rain forest, river, and even on the global environment and climate suggests that the Amazon is not just the artery of a continent but of Earth itself. *(pages 84-85)*

Nile River

Other Great Rivers

1 ***Congo River, Central Africa:*** Its drainage basin, the second largest in the world, straddles the equator and draws on such diverse sources that the river's output into the Atlantic is constant year-round. *(page 66)*

2 ***Ganges River, India:*** Considered sacred by Hindus, the Ganges flows from the Himalayas to create the world's largest delta, which forms 250 miles (400 kilometers) inland and fans 200 miles (320 kilometers) wide. *(page 55)*

3 ***Mississippi River, United States:*** Combined with its major tributary, the Missouri River, the Mississippi is the fourth-longest river in the world, with a catchment that collects four-fifths of the rainfall between North America's Rocky and Appalachian Mountain Ranges. *(pages 108-109)*

4 ***Ob-Irtysh Rivers, Russia:*** The sixth-longest river system in the world, western Siberia's Ob and Irtysh Rivers descend from ancient glaciers and alpine lakes high in the Altay (Altaj) Mountains to converge and flow into the Gulf of Ob at the Arctic Circle. *(page 32)*

5 ***Volga River, Russia:*** The longest river in Europe, the Volga forms a busy waterway with a network of canals connecting the Caspian, Baltic, and Black Seas. *(page 32)*

6 ***Yangtze River, China:*** The longest river in Asia and the deepest river in the world is 600 feet (183 meters) deep in the spectacular Yichang Gorges. One in 13 people in the world lives within the basin of the Yangtze, and the Three Gorges Dam, scheduled for completion in 2009, will displace more than a million people. *(page 42)*

The longest river in the world, the fabled Nile stretches 4,145 miles (6,671 kilometers) across Africa, a distance greater than the span between Chicago and London. From Khartoum, Sudan, where the White Nile (issuing from Lake Victoria) and the Blue Nile (flowing from Lake Tana on the Ethiopian Plateau) meet, the river flows north through Egypt to the Mediterranean Sea, creating a verdant floodplain of dark, rich soil and lush vegetation up to 20 miles (32 kilometers) wide through the Nubian and Arabian Deserts.

But the true source of the Nile's legend is its delta—the seedbed of Egyptian culture and nurturer of one of the world's most ancient civilizations. Here desert nomads settled 7,000 years ago to escape the advancing sands and arid climate. They farmed, raised animals, fished, and, around 3,000 B.C., founded the city of Memphis, capital of the ancient Egyptian civilization that flourished for three millennia. "Egypt," wrote the ancient Greek historian Herodotus, "is the gift of the Nile."

Little wonder that the Egyptians worshiped the Nile as a god, albeit a mercurial one. Every year the retreating floodwaters deposited a layer of nutrient-rich mud that fertilized their crops, but occasional high floods threatened their settlements, and droughts provoked famines. Modern Egyptians have averted some of the river's wrath by building the Aswan High Dam in the 1960s; its reservoir, Lake Nasser, provides year-round irrigation. But the dam also prevents silt from fertilizing the soil of the floodplain, which only emphasizes the godlike powers of this ribboned oasis bisecting an otherwise barren, arid land. *(page 63)*

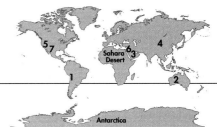

Arabs call the sterile sun-seared terrain of the Sahara Desert "bahr bila maa," or "ocean without water." Covering a third of the African continent, the desert receives less than three inches (7.6 centimeters) of rainfall a year. Other environments may be drier, but at 3.5 million square miles (9.1 million square kilometers) the Sahara is by far the largest hot desert on Earth.

Sahara Desert

Great expanses of shifting, rippled sand dunes known as ergs cover only 20 percent of the Sahara, although the Grand Erg de Bilma, which straddles the Niger and Chad border, is almost the size of Spain. The rest of the desert comprises rock-and-gravel plateaus and plains corrugated with wind-scoured mountains and craggy gorges. The Sahara raises millions of tons of dust clouds a year, which are carried away on atmospheric winds as far as the Southeastern United States; these dust clouds make for blinding windstorms and magnify heat like a greenhouse. A person walking the long distances between oases in the summer sun would need four gallons of water a day to replenish lost fluids in temperatures that have soared to 130 degrees Fahrenheit (54 degrees Celsius).

The Sahara is not uninhabited. Nomadic Tuaregs, desert-dwelling camel drivers who once controlled the trans-Saharan caravan trade between the Mediterranean and Central Africa, make their home here. Tuareg men wear cotton veils across their faces to shield themselves from desert winds and from evil spirits—the Muslim Tuaregs believe that their breath is the gateway to the soul. "The desert is the Garden of Allah," an Arab saying goes, "from which the Lord of the Faithful removed all superfluous human and animal life, so that there might be one place where he could walk in peace." *(page 64)*

Other Magnificent Deserts

1 ***Atacama Desert, Chile:*** Where the slopes of the Andes Mountains meet the Pacific Ocean is one of the driest places on Earth. Arica, Chile, receives an average .03 inches (.08 centimeters) of moisture a year, mostly brought by ocean fogs. *(page 92)*

2 ***Australian Interior:*** In the "Red Heart" interior of the most desertified continent besides Antarctica, enormous expanses of parallel sand ridges shift with the winds and small clumps of porcupine grass survive on 0.4 inches (one centimeter) of rain a year. *(pages 74-75)*

3 ***The Empty Quarter, Southwest Asia:*** Acclaimed by T. E. Lawrence of Lawrence of Arabia fame, the roughly 250,000 square miles (640,000 square kilometers) of Ar-rub al-Khali on the Arabian Peninsula contain the world's largest continual tract of sand dunes. *(page 56)*

4 ***Gobi Desert, Mongolia/China:*** This rocky plateau in Central Asia—home of the two-humped Bactrian camel ridden by Mongol nomads—has one of the world's harshest climates, with temperatures ranging from -40 degrees Fahrenheit (-40 degrees Celsius) to 113 degrees Fahrenheit (45 degrees Celsius). *(page 36)*

5 ***Mojave Desert, United States:*** Mostly a high plateau, 560 square miles (1,450 square kilometers) of this desert are below sea level. In Death Valley, California, soil temperatures get so hot that early natives called the land "Ground Afire." *(page 135)*

6 ***Negev Desert, Israel:*** The Negev's 4,700 square miles (12,200 square kilometers) of undulating ridges and basins bisected by dry riverbeds was the site of four thousand years of Biblical history, including Moses' exodus out of Egypt. *(page 59)*

7 ***White Sands National Monument, United States:*** Not technically a desert, this milky white sea of billowing sand represents the world's largest gypsum dune field. *(page 130)*

Antarctica

Antarctica brings to mind endless seas of snow and ice, a vast sheet of frost up to three miles (4,775 meters) thick and deep enough to bury the Alps. This pristine frozen wilderness contains three quarters of the world's fresh water—enough, if melted, to raise all the oceans by 200 feet (61 meters). But Antarctica is also the world's largest desert. Less than two inches (five centimeters) of precipitation fall annually on the continent, and water vapor is literally frozen out of the air by extreme cold temperatures that average -40 degrees Fahrenheit (-40 degrees Celsius).

In the Dry Valleys along the Ross Sea in East Antarctica no rain has fallen at all for more than a million years. The air is too dry in these expansive lowlands for snow and ice to exist; the ice sheet has thinned to expose gigantic areas of rock that absorb radiation from the sun. The strongest winds on Earth—with speeds up to 199 miles per hour (320 kilometers per hour)—sweep dense, colder air down from the polar plateau, sculpting and polishing fantastic rock boulders and fins called "ventrifacts" while essentially freeze-drying any forms of life. Scientists believe this desolately beautiful terrain is quite similar to that of Mars.

Explorer Robert Scott deemed the valleys a "very wonderful place" when he discovered them during a 1903 expedition. "We have seen all the indications of colossal ice action and considerable water action, and yet neither of these agents is now at work," he wrote in *The Voyage of the Discovery.* "It is certainly a valley of the dead; even the great glacier which once pushed through it has withered away." *(page 81)*

Angel Falls

In 1933 an American bush pilot scouting Venezuela's Guiana Highlands for a lost cache of gold came upon a treasure greater than he had imagined. Banking his single-engine transport plane around a flat-topped mountain, or *tepuí*, Jimmy Angel saw something incredible: an iridescent column of water 17 times the height of Niagara Falls, plunging in solemn magnificence down the mesa's cliff wall into a dense green jungle shrouded in mist. "Biggest damn waterfall in the world," Angel boasted later to a bartender in Ciudad Bolívar. He was right: The cascade that now bears his name is the tallest on Earth, spanning 3,212 feet (979 meters) from the top of the escarpment to the floor of the gorge.

Angel Falls begins its dramatic descent where the Churun River spills down Auyán-Tepuí (or "Devil's Mountain"), one of many reddish sandstone plateaus that lay like titans' footstools above the high grasslands of the Gran Sabana. Before reaching the plateau's edge, the river disappears underground into a vertical fissure and then springs forth from gashes in the cliff wall, as if emanating from some inner mystical source. It falls in a single unbroken plume for the first 2,648 feet (807 meters) before hitting rock, then tumbles down to a churning plunge pool below.

Tens of thousands of tourists journey to Angel Falls each year, mostly by plane or motorized dugout canoe. But the national park land surrounding the falls is still a wild and remote place where rare species of flora and fauna flourish, red howler monkeys emit plaintive wails, and morpho butterflies dance in slow, jagged serpentines, glinting metallic blue in the sun. *(page 87)*

Other Wondrous Waterfalls

1 ***Iguassu Falls, Argentina/Brazil:*** Some 275 dramatic cascades spanning two and a half miles (four kilometers) thunder down from the Iguassu River over the lip of a half-moon-shaped plateau into a lush jungle of bamboos and tree ferns. *(page 93)*

2 ***Khone Falls, Laos:*** More than six miles (9.6 kilometers) wide, this spectacular chain of waterfalls and islands boasts the greatest volume of all the world's waterfalls. One of its largest cascades, Khong Phapheng Falls, is known as "the voice of the Mekong." *(page 44)*

3 ***Mardalsfossen, Norway:*** These two-tiered falls crest over a granite ridge and drop more than 2,150 feet (655 meters) down a glacier-carved hanging valley in Norway's breathtaking fjord country. *(page 8)*

4 ***Niagara Falls, United States/Canada:*** Actually two enormous cataracts flanking a central island, 2,200-foot-wide (670-meter-wide) Horseshoe Falls and 1,060-foot-wide (325-meter-wide) American Falls are slowly devouring the dolomite escarpment and receding upstream from Lake Ontario to Lake Erie. *(page 113)*

5 ***Tugela Falls, South Africa:*** Descending from the Drakensberg Mountains, the world's second-highest waterfall jumps down several small cataracts, then plunges 2,014 feet (614 meters) in a single cascade for a total drop of 3,110 feet (948 meters). *(page 71)*

Natives called this series of spectacular cataracts Mosi-oa-Tunya, "The Smoke That Thunders." The collective roar of Victoria Falls, located along the border of Zambia and Zimbabwe, clatters window panes a mile away, and its thousand-foot-high (300-meter-high) cloud of vapor refracts rainbows even from the full moon. David Livingstone, the Scottish missionary-explorer escorted down the Zambezi River via dugout canoe by Makololo tribesmen in 1855, named the falls for his queen, concluding that "scenes so lovely must have been gazed upon by angels in their flight."

The breadth of this wall of water—5,500 feet (1,675 meters)—is dramatic, but the narrowness of its gorge is even more astonishing. At the falls, the Zambezi River dives into a steep chasm of black basaltic lava, bottlenecks through a canyon cleft only 200 feet (60 meters) wide, and roils into behemoth Class-V rapids known to kayakers and rafters as the Boiling Pot. From there the river caroms through 45 miles (72 kilometers)

Victoria Falls

of pulse-revving whitewater. Above the falls' crest is an archipelago of palm-shaded islands deemed sacred by tribal chieftains, who, according to Dr. Livingstone's journal, gathered there "with reverential awe" to worship their deities. Here in the flat, hot bushland of southern Africa the mist from the falls nurtures a lush enclave of fig trees, ilala palms, and ferns, and small, striped antelopes called bushbucks live alongside the irascible hippos known to charge Zambezi paddlers above the falls.

The chasm and waterfall were created as erosion enlarged deep fractures in the bedrock of sandstone and basaltic lava. The canyon is growing still larger today as powerful Devil's Cataract at the end of the falls erodes another upstream fracture, which will eventually shift the line of the falls. *(page 68)*

NATURAL WONDERS
Rock Formations

Framing a brilliant backdrop of red rock and azure desert sky in southern Utah, the weathered sandstone of the largest natural bridge in the world reflects an earthy rainbow of colors, from rusty reds to deep salmons to burnished golds. Iron oxide has glazed on the span of Rainbow Bridge a patina of dark, vertical streaks, called "desert varnish." The bridge's proportions are massive: 290 feet (88 meters) high—as high as the United States Capitol Building—and 275 feet (84 meters) wide—nearly the length of a football field. At its highest point, the bridge is 42 feet (13 meters) thick and 33 feet (10 meters) wide, awesome in its symmetry as it spans the creek that carved it.

The bridge's formation is linked to the sudden and rapid uplifting of the Colorado Plateau some five million years ago. The land, which had been relatively level, broke and buckled, creating peaks such as Utah's Navajo Mountain. Regional watercourses steepened, and rivers began carving the canyons that today define the U.S. Southwest. One of these rivers, now known as Bridge Creek, rushed down the north flank of Navajo Mountain, cutting a deep canyon and boring its way through a fin of salmon-pink Navajo and reddish-gold Kayenta sandstone to form Rainbow Bridge.

Traces of ancient ceremonial fires indicate that the bridge has been a holy place for hundreds, perhaps thousands of years. The modern Navajo, Hopi, Ute, and Paiute nations continue to regard the awe-inspiring span of rock as a sacred site and a cathedral of nature; pilgrims come to make spiritual offerings and pray in its shadow. The U.S. government designated Rainbow Bridge a national monument in 1910. *(page 132)*

Rainbow Bridge

Along the Antrim coast of Northern Ireland stretches the bizarre and fascinating Giant's Causeway, an uneven 300-yard (275-meter) expanse of vertical, polygonal pillars of rock fitted together as if by a superhuman mason.

Local lore has it that the causeway was indeed the work of a giant. Legendary Irish warrior Finn MacCool assembled the pillars to reach the tiny Scottish island of Staffa, 75 miles (120 kilometers) north, and challenge a rival giant, Finn Gall. After driving the last pillar into place, MacCool went home to nap before the big battle. Finn Gall, however, crossed over the causeway to Ireland, where MacCool's wife convinced him that the snoring form beneath the bedclothes was not her husband but her baby son. Finn Gall, thinking himself no match for the father of such an enormous infant, fled back to Staffa, tearing up the causeway behind him. All that remains is the stretch of shattered pillars on the Antrim coast and similar pillars underpinning Staffa.

In fact, the rock formations were produced 50 to 60 million years ago, when basaltic lava flowed out of great fissures in the Earth's crust, then slowly cooled, shrank, and cracked. At least 40,000 of these mostly hexagonal columns make up the Giant's Causeway. The constant hammering of waves has broken off the columns at varying heights; some groups rise in fantastic formations, others form a surface as smooth as pavement.

There was no easy access to the Giant's Causeway until 1830, when a celebrated coast road was opened. Prior to that, visitors often fortified themselves at the Bushmills distillery before making the difficult journey on horseback to the site. *(page 12)*

Giant's Causeway

Other Fascinating Rock Formations

1 Arches National Park, United States: Shaped by water, ice, and wind, these 2,000 sandstone arches in eastern Utah include breathtaking Delicate Arch and graceful Landscape Arch, at 291 feet (89 meters) the longest natural rock span on Earth. *(page 132)*

2 Ayers Rock, Australia: One of the largest monoliths in the world, Ayers Rock (also known by its aboriginal name, Uluru) rises 1,100 feet (335 meters) above the surrounding plains of central Australia. Its iron-rich sandstone flanks, reflecting the sun in crimson and purple hues, are visible 60 miles (96 kilometers) away. *(page 74)*

3 Cones of Cappadocia, Turkey: Swift streams slicing through a plateau of solidified volcanic ash capped by basalt and limestone created this strange, fairy-tale landscape of 100-foot-tall (30-meter-tall) cones. During the Middle Ages, Christian monks and hermits carved hundreds of churches and monasteries into the cones' soft flanks. *(page 56)*

4 Stolby Nature Reserve, Russia: On the banks of Siberia's Yenisey (Enisej) River lies a rock-climber's paradise: a concentration of granite and syenite pinnacles that tower as high as 300 feet (92 meters) over the surrounding forest and have been sculpted by wind, rain, and ice into fanciful shapes such as "The Feathers" and "The Kiss." *(pages 34-35)*

5 Stone Forests of Guilin, China: The limestone pinnacles of Guangxi province have inspired Chinese artists and poets for centuries. These stone "trees"—the world's prime examples of tower karst—are nearly as spectacular within as without: Hundreds of caverns, shimmering with calcite formations, honeycomb the pinnacles. *(page 43)*

Lakes

Lake Superior & the Great Lakes

Gaze across the deep, cold, vast waters of Lake Superior and you'll get the sense that you're on the shore of something much more imposing than a lake. Superior seems like an ocean. Towering crags and cliffs, besieged by wind and waves, abut the shore like stone fortresses. Winters are particularly long and severe, but in any season Superior is known for its fierce gales and deadly storms; more than 350 vessels rest at the bottom.

Appropriately, the Ojibwa people called the lake Kitchi Gami, the Great Lake. With a surface area of 31,700 square miles (82,100 square kilometers), it is the largest of the five glacially carved North American inland seas known as the Great Lakes, and the greatest expanse of fresh water on Earth. Scotland could fit neatly within its shores. Superior is also the deepest of the Great Lakes. Its maximum depth of 1,332 feet (406 meters) is not just the work of glaciers: Volcanic rock lining the lake suggests that Superior sits over an ancient rift system, an area where tectonic forces ripped the Earth's crust apart. Molten rock, rising from the planet's fiery mantle and carrying an abundance of minerals, spread across the landscape. Iron, nickel, copper, silver, and gold mined near the lake have long been mainstays of the region's economy.

Scoured out of North America's surface by massive glaciers during the ice ages, the Great Lakes are among the continent's defining features. Lakes Superior, Michigan, Huron, Erie, and Ontario cover an area of 94,450 square miles (244,620 square kilometers) and hold 18 percent of the world's fresh water. They spread across landscapes varying from rolling farmland to unadulterated forests to shifting mountains of sand to the skyscrapered shores of Detroit, Toronto, Cleveland, and Chicago. Since the earliest days of settlement by Europeans, the Great Lakes have been conduits of commerce between the eastern seaboard and the mines and granaries of the central plains. *(pages 108-109)*

Other Wondrous Lakes

1 *Caspian Sea, Europe/Asia:* The largest inland body of water on Earth, the salty Caspian Sea is 750 miles (1,210 kilometers) long and has a surface area of 143,240 square miles (370,900 square kilometers). *(page 32)*

2 *Dead Sea, Israel/Jordan:* The lowest point on the planet's surface, at 1,339 feet (408 meters) below sea level, the Dead Sea is eight times saltier than any ocean, making it extremely buoyant. *(page 59)*

3 *Lake Tanganyika, East Africa:* The longest freshwater lake in the world, Tanganyika is so deep that its water layers do not mix: The cold bottom layers are nearly devoid of life, while the warmer upper layers teem with fish. *(page 67)*

4 *Lake Titicaca, Bolivia/Peru:* Lying on the Andean altiplano at 12,500 feet (3,810 meters), Titicaca is the highest navigable lake on Earth and the birthplace of the pre-Incan Tiahuanaco culture. *(page 84)*

5 *Lake Victoria, East Africa:* Africa's largest lake and the second-largest body of fresh water in the world (after Lake Superior) is situated in a shallow depression between the arms of the Rift Valley. *(page 67)*

Lake Baikal

Chill, clear, and cradled in a basin of evergreen forests and snowcapped granite peaks in southern Siberia, Lake Baikal is the oldest, deepest, and most voluminous body of fresh water on Earth. Although lakes generally have life spans of less than one million years, Baikal has existed for perhaps 25 million years. It was born of tectonic forces, which tore open a rift in the Earth's crust. As the Baikal Rift grew, so did the lake; the still-active rift widens approximately one inch (2.5 centimeters) per year. Today the lake is 395 miles (636 kilometers) long and an average of 30 miles (48 kilometers) wide.

Lake Baikal reaches a greatest depth of more than a mile (1.6 kilometers). The lake bed sits atop sediment that lies some four miles (6.4 kilometers) thick, the accumulation of 25 million years.

Baikal's tremendous volume—5,500 cubic miles (23,000 cubic kilometers)—represents a fifth of the fresh water in the world, and more than the five Great Lakes combined. It would take all of Earth's rivers together a year to fill Baikal. More than 300 rivers do feed the lake but only one, the Angara, drains it; if all 300 tributaries were suddenly to run dry, it would take Lake Baikal four centuries to empty.

Revered by Russians as "the Pearl of Siberia," and sacred to the local Buryat tribespeople, Baikal shelters more endemic species than any other habitat on Earth. Naturalists come to catch a glimpse of some of these roughly 1,500 species, including a pink, transparent oilfish known as the *golom-yanka* and the Baikal seal, or *nerpa*, prized for its sleek coat of fur. *(page 35)*

Crater Lake

Formed in the wake of one of the most powerful volcanic events of the last 10,000 years, Crater Lake is today a serene jewel set high in the mountains of North America's Cascade Range. Circular and stunningly cobalt blue, the lake is fringed with windblown evergreens and surrounded by the steep, sloping sides of the caldera that contains it. Six miles (ten kilometers) wide and 1,932 feet (589 meters) deep, Crater Lake is the deepest lake in the United States and the seventh deepest in the world. The lake has no inlet or outlet; seepage and evaporation keep the water level steady.

Where Crater Lake lies today in southwestern Oregon, a cluster of stratovolcanoes once rose approximately 12,000 feet (3,650 meters) above sea level. Roughly 7,000 years ago, this ancient mountain, now referred to as Mount Mazama, blew its top, spewing ash over much of the continent. Eventually, rainfall and snowmelt filled the caldera that remained, producing Crater Lake. Wizard Island, near the lake's western shore, is the youngest and tallest of three cinder cones that formed after the catastrophic explosion; the other two lie below the surface. Hot spots in the lake's depths and the fact that the water almost never freezes despite huge snowfalls point to continued volcanic activity beneath the lake.

In the legends of the Klamath Indians, Mount Mazama was the throne of Llao, ruler of the underworld; Mount Shasta, a hundred miles south, was the domain of Skell, who ruled the "above world." An ongoing feud manifested itself in thunderous eruptions and rivers of molten lava that destroyed villages. The final battle raged for a week before Llao's ruined mountain collapsed upon him, sealing him forever beneath the Earth.

Crater Lake National Park was established in 1902, and today half a million people come each year to drive around the lake, hike along the rim, cross-country ski, or catch a boat to Wizard Island. *(page 136)*

Within the 2,000-foot-high (610-meter-high) walls of Ngorongoro Crater, a great profusion of animals vie for space and nourishment amidst the swamps, springs, lakes, and low forests that cover the level crater floor. Almost every animal species common to eastern Africa ranges the crater's 100 square miles (260 square kilometers). Whereas wildlife living in other African savanna habitats must migrate with the seasons in search of water, the springs and swamps of Ngorongoro Crater provide water year-round. Lions, elephants, hippos, zebras, gazelles, wildebeests, baboons, leopards, cheetahs, and hyenas—an estimated 25,000 to 30,000 animals in all—make their permanent homes here. The crater is the only remaining habitat of the severely endangered black rhinoceros, and Lake Magadi, an alkaline lake in the middle of the basin, supports thousands of dazzling pink flamingos and throngs of other water birds.

Ngorongoro Crater is the largest volcanic caldera of its type in the world. A volcanic mountain rivaling the height of nearby Kilimanjaro once stood on the site of Ngorongoro. Around 2.5 million years ago, shifting tectonic activity in Africa's Rift Valley caused the huge magma chamber beneath the volcano to drain away, and the mountain caved in upon itself.

Ngorongoro is sacred to the Masai people. Several centuries ago, the tribe took the crater from its original inhabitants, the Datoga, and claimed it as cattle-grazing land. As the Masai made their way down the slopes, bells they were wearing rang out "ngoro, ngoro," and thus the crater was named. Ngorongoro Crater Conservation Area was established in the 1950s, and in 1974 the Tanzanian government ruled that the Masai had to leave. Today Ngorongoro has no permanent human inhabitants. *(page 67)*

Ngorongoro Crater

Other Remarkable Craters and Volcanoes

1 **Kilauea Crater, United States:** The legendary home of the fire goddess Pele and currently Earth's most active volcano, Kilauea has erupted steadily since 1983. Its lava produces a spectacular explosion of steam as it meets the Pacific Ocean. *(page 134)*

2 **Meteor Crater, United States:** This immense crater, 575 feet (176 meters) deep and .8 mile (1.25 kilometers) in diameter, marks the spot in the Arizona desert where a huge meteor slammed into Earth between 5,000 and 50,000 years ago. *(page 133)*

3 **Mount Tambora, Indonesia:** Its cataclysmic 1815 eruption was the most forceful ever recorded. Ash blown into the upper atmosphere screened the sun's rays, lowered temperatures globally for two years, and caused widespread crop failures in 1816, the famous "year without a summer." *(page 51)*

4 **Surtsey, Iceland:** The world's youngest island, tiny one-square-mile (2.5-square-kilometer) Surtsey formed between 1963 and 1967 as magma poured from a volcanic vent on the seafloor off the southern coast of Iceland. *(page 8)*

5 **Vesuvius, Italy:** Vesuvius' eruption in A.D. 79 destroyed Pompeii and Herculaneum, killing more than 3,500 people. Vesuvius is considered one of the most dangerous volcanoes on Earth today: More than 2,000,000 people live in its shadow. *(page 24)*

Barrier Reefs

The turquoise waters of Australia's 1,250-mile-long (2,010-kilometer-long) Great Barrier Reef teem with life. Schools of brilliant tropical fish shimmer amid forests of anemones, sheltered by multi-hued walls and glowing outcroppings of live coral, while palm-shaded cays of sparkling coral sand are home to myriad birds. In all, some 400 species of coral, 1,500 varieties of vividly colored fish and crustaceans, and more than 200 bird species live in and around the reef.

Great Barrier Reef

The largest structure ever built by living creatures, the Great Barrier Reef is the work of countless tiny animals, most no larger than an inch (2.5 centimeters) long. With the symbiotic help of algae, coral polyps secrete skeletons of calcium carbonate, or limestone, to protect themselves and attach themselves to the remains of dead coral. Core samples reveal that the reef has been forming for at least 25 million years: As the continental shelf slowly subsided, the living corals built the reef ever higher to keep within the extent of the sun's rays. Then, during the ice ages when much of Earth's water was frozen, the reef was exposed as limestone cliffs lining the coast of Australia. It's likely that Aborigines lived amidst these cliffs before the ice receded and the reef was again submerged. Today the reef covers an area exceeding 100,000 square miles (270,000 square kilometers) along the continental shelf off Australia's northeastern coast.

Vast portions of the Great Barrier Reef are protected from poachers and oil companies by the Great Barrier Reef Marine Park, the largest marine reserve in the world. Close to five million tourists visit the park annually and take reef excursions ranging from glass-bottom boat rides to hot-air balloon flights. Scuba diving and snorkeling are favorite pastimes on the reef, but they are carefully regulated to keep this exquisite and delicate ecosystem healthy for generations to come. *(page 75)*

Belizean Reef

Other Spectacular Reefs and Sea Caves

1 **Blue Grotto, Italy:** Sunlight streaming in through an underwater aperture casts a brilliant azure reflection on the walls of this marine cave on the island of Capri. The ancient Romans worshiped here, though locals considered the grotto a lair of witches and monsters. *(page 24)*

2 **Blue Holes of Andros, Bahamas:** More than 400 of these circular entrances to submerged limestone caverns dot the continental shelf off the largest island in the Bahamas. The holes appear to "breathe," sucking the sea into ferocious whirlpools, then disgorging it in a roiling frenzy. *(page 104)*

3 **Florida Coral Reef, United States:** Lying about six miles (ten kilometers) offshore, this coral reef parallels the Florida Keys for almost 130 miles (209 kilometers) within a protected marine sanctuary. *(page 117)*

4 **Maldives:** Comprising 26 individual atolls that contain some 1,200 small coral islands—not one larger than five square miles (13 square kilometers)—the Maldives stretch for more than 500 miles (820 kilometers) across the Indian Ocean. *(page 142)*

5 **Racine Formation, United States:** This "reef" in what is now southeastern Wisconsin was alive with coral, sponges, and trilobites about 425 million years ago. Today it has metamorphosed into dolomite; stone quarried from the formation built the cities of Chicago and Milwaukee. *(page 119)*

6 **Red Sea Reefs:** Sheltered from the open ocean, these coral reefs harbor many endemic species, including brilliant butterfly fish. The reefs grow so fast near the Bab el Mandeb strait that they are routinely blasted away to keep the shipping channel clear. *(pages 62-63)*

From the air, the largest barrier reef in the Western Hemisphere—and the second largest on Earth—appears to be a white crest riding the deep blue Caribbean toward mainland Belize. Between the 185-mile-long (296-kilometer-long) reef and the mainland stretch aquamarine waters noted for resplendent red and purple and green corals—colors that are mirrored by fish, anemones, and sponges. At Rocky Point, the northern edge of the reef meets the continental shoreline in one of the only places in the world where a barrier reef and a coastline converge.

Hundreds of cays dot the surface, and on the eastward side of the reef lie three large atolls, circular coral formations common in the South Pacific but extremely rare in the Caribbean. The atolls—Turneffe Islands, Lighthouse Reef, and Glovers Reef—shelter spectacular reef life and are favorite diving destinations due to the extraordinary clarity of their azure waters. Jacques Cousteau's celebrated 1970s exploration of the Blue Hole—a submerged, 300-foot-deep (100-meter-deep) sinkhole in the shallow lagoon of the Lighthouse Reef atoll— revealed that the entire Belizean reef system is riddled with submarine caverns adorned with massive stalactites and stalagmites.

The reef and atolls are also home to large game fish and aquatic mammals such as dolphins and the world's largest population of West Indian manatees. Relics and middens found in the region reveal that the reef served as a Maya fishing ground and transportation and trading corridor, while the cays were used as ceremonial sites and burial places. Once Europeans discovered the reef, it became a favorite hideout for pirates. Today tourism is Belize's economic mainstay, and the reef was recently designated a United Nations World Heritage Site—a move that many hope will protect this beautiful, fragile natural wonder. *(page 102)*

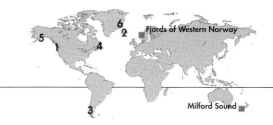

Fjords of Western Norway

Milford Sound

Milford Sound

With its steep walls, hanging waterfalls, and Mitre Peak, a 5,551-foot (1,692-meter) sculpted monolith standing perpetual guard, glacier-carved Milford Sound is the northernmost and most spectacular of all of New Zealand's stunning South Island fjords. Only 180 feet (55 meters) deep at its mouth, the fjord plunges to maximum depths exceeding 1,300 feet (396 meters). Some of the highest sea cliffs in the world rise abruptly from the water's edge, soaring nearly a mile (1.6 kilometers) into a sky often shrouded in low mist and rain. One of the rainiest places on Earth, Milford Sound receives in excess of 250 inches (635 centimeters) of precipitation each year.

The aboriginal Maori people knew Milford Sound as Piopiotahi, or "the place of the thrush." According to legend, Maui, the first man, kept a thrush as a companion to sing to him as he wandered the island's coast. After Maui died, the desolate thrush remained beside the sound, its lament ringing off Milford's sheer walls. The Maori came thereafter to hunt, fish, and collect the region's beautiful nephrite jade, which they believed could take on the *mana*, or spiritual power, of its owners. Weapons and ornaments carved from nephrite have passed through families for generations.

Fiordland National Park's 14 fjords, and Milford Sound in particular, harbor a wide range of wildlife, from bottlenose dolphins to the flightless takahe, a blue-plumaged bird once thought to be extinct. Before migrating to Antarctica for the summer, Fiordland crested penguins nest in Milford Sound. The unusual composition of the sound accounts for a stunning variety of sea creatures clinging to the granite walls below the surface: A layer of fresh water, darkened by organic materials leached from the surrounding soil, floats over a deep, clear, warm base of saltwater from the Tasman Sea. Sheltered by the fresh water, colorful reef life—similar to that of Hawaii or the Caribbean—thrives beneath the brackish zone. *(page 80)*

Other Wondrous Fjords

1 **Desolation Sound and the Fjords of British Columbia, Canada:** Riddled with deep sounds, remote inlets, glacial fjords, and cascading waterfalls, the stunningly rugged coasts of British Columbia and western Vancouver Island were forbidding even to explorer Captain George Vancouver, who gave Desolation Sound its name. *(page 138)*

2 **Fjords of Iceland:** Both the east and west coasts of Iceland are incised by classic fjords with sheer cliffs adorned with lacy ribbons of falling water. The fjords along the east coast are often blanketed in *Austfjardapoka*, the Eastern Fjord Fog. *(page 8)*

3 **Fjords of Southern Chile and Argentina:** Along the heavily glaciated western coast at the southern tip of South America, ice has excavated remote and daunting fjords that reach into the very heart of the Andes and attract adventurous sea kayakers from around the globe. *(page 90)*

4 **Gros Morne National Park, Canada:** The fjords of Newfoundland's Gros Morne are renowned both for beauty and geologic legacy: The strata of their walls harbor volcanic rock and fossils dating back 600 million years. *(page 107)*

5 **Kenai Fjords National Park, United States:** Glaciers once etched steep-sided valleys into the flanks of Alaska's Kenai Mountains; today these valleys are inundated and transformed into breathtaking fjords, framed by the dramatic backdrop of the vast Harding Icefield. *(page 140)*

6 **Scoresby Sund, Greenland:** This sound and its tributaries comprise the world's largest fjord system, extending 196 miles (314 kilometers). Carved into the periphery of granite and basalt mountains, Scoresby presents a strikingly varied cliffside panorama. *(page 141)*

Etched deeply into Norway's western coastline are hundreds of inundated, U-shaped valleys. Farms and tiny hamlets cling to ledges on their nearly vertical walls, and streams plummet into the still waters from hanging valleys hundreds of feet above. The spectacular fjords of Norway are known the world over for their beautiful scenery and their profound depths—positive proof of the power of the ice-age glaciers that sculpted them.

In the last two to three million years, vast ice sheets have advanced and retreated over Northern Europe at least 40 times. On the western coast of present-day Norway, these glaciers followed and filled existing river valleys. So great were the thickness and weight of these glaciers that they scoured the valleys to depths far below sea level. Sogne Fjord, the longest and deepest of Norway's fjords, extends more than 125 miles (200 kilometers) inland and reaches a maximum depth of 4,291 feet (1,308 meters) in Lustra Fjord, its longest branch. For a single glacier to carve such a deep valley, it would have to be approximately 6,000 feet (1,850 meters) thick.

The earliest thriving cultures in Norway's fjord region date back to A.D. 400–600. Nevertheless, the population of the region has always been sparse, due to the scarcity of flat land on which to build and farm. The largest towns are built on river deltas at the heads of the fjords. The most picturesque human habitations, however, are the small farms built on ledges in the sheer valley walls. Farmers who settled on these aeries built systems of ropes and pulleys to bring supplies, building materials, and even farm animals up the cliffs to their homesteads. A series of ladders connected their farms with their boat docks far below. Even today, boats are the best form of fjordland transportation and Sogne Fjord can be crossed only by ferry. *(page 8)*

Fjords of
Western Norway

INDEX MAP AND LEGEND

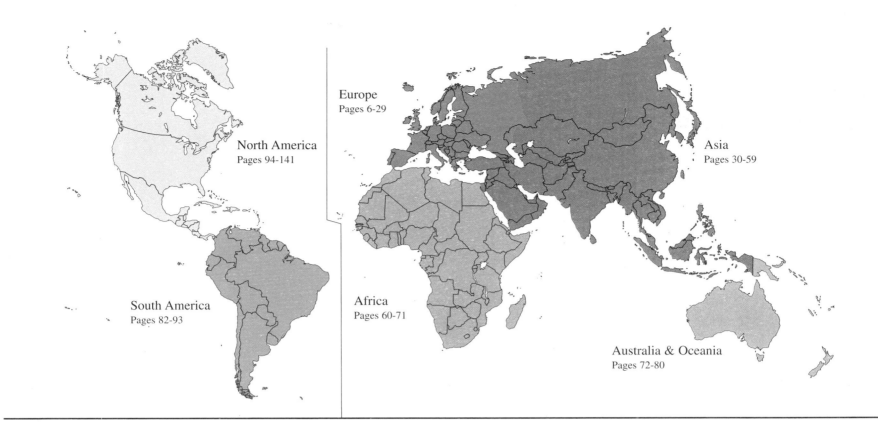

Europe
Pages 6-29

North America
Pages 94-141

Asia
Pages 30-59

South America
Pages 82-93

Africa
Pages 60-71

Australia & Oceania
Pages 72-80

Hydrographic Features

	Perennial river
	Seasonal river
	Dam
	Falls
	Aqueduct
	Lake, reservoir
	Seasonal lake
	Salt lake
	Seasonal salt lake
	Dry lake
395	Lake surface elevation
	Swamp, marsh
	Reef
	Glacier/ice sheet

Aswan High Dam (Dam)
Salto Ángel (Falls)
Los Angeles Aqueduct (Aqueduct)

Topographic Features

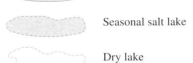

764 ▽	Depth of water
2278 ▲	Elevation above sea level
1700 ▼	Elevation below sea level
⊰	Mountain pass
Huo Shan 1774	Mountain peak/elevation

The highest elevation on each continent is underlined.
The highest elevation in each country is shown in boldface.

Transportation Features

	Motorway/special highway
	Major road
	Other road
	Trail
	Major railway
	Other railway
	Navigable canal
	Tunnel
	Ferry
✈	International airport
⊀	Other airport

Political Features

International boundaries (First-order political unit)

	Demarcated
	Disputed (de facto)
	Disputed (de jure)
	Indefinite/undefined
	Demarcation line

Internal boundaries

	State/province
	Third-order (counties, oblasts, etc.)

NORMANDIE
(Denmark)
Cultural/historic region
Administering country

Cities and Towns

The size of symbol and type indicates the relative importance of the locality.

■	**LONDON**
▣	**CHICAGO**
◉	**Milwaukee**
◎	Tacna
⊙	Iquitos
○	Old Crow
○	Mettawa
	Urban area

Capitals

MEXICO CITY Bratislava	Country, dependency
RIO DE JANEIRO Perth	State, province
MANCHESTER Chester	County

Cultural Features

or ▪	National park, reservation
▪	Point of interest
⌁	Wall
∴	Ruins
	Military installation
•	Polar research station

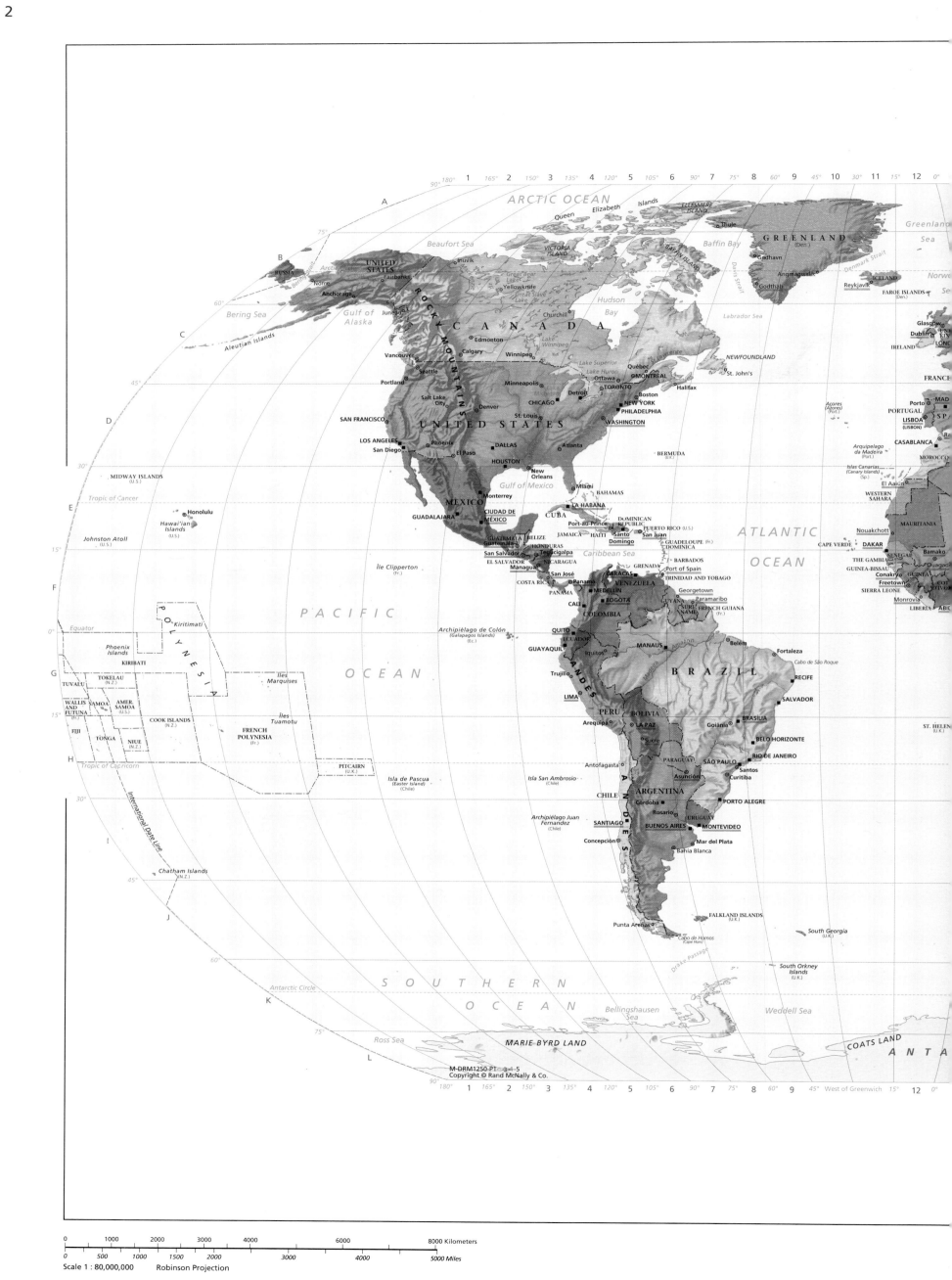

ARCTIC OCEAN

Zemlja Franca-Iosifa

Barents Sea

Novaja
Zemlja

more Laptevyh

Novosibirskie
ostrova

Vostočno-Sibirskoe
more

Karskoe more

A

B

Spitsbergen

...BARD

Narvik

Hammerfest Murmansk

Arhangel'sk

Igarka

Vorkuta

Tiksi

Jakutsk

Arctic Circle

75°

SWEDEN

FINLAND Helsinki

SANKT-PETERBURG
(ST. PETERBURG)

RUSSIA

Magadan

Bering Sea

60°

Stockholm

ESTONIA

LATVIA

NIŽNIJ
NOVGOROD

MOSKVA
(MOSCOW)

Perm

Ekaterinburg

Omsk

Novosibirsk

Krasnojarsk

Cita

Habarovsk

Sea of
Okhotsk

ostrov
Sahalin

Petropavlovsk-
Kamčatskij

C

BERLIN

POLAND

BELARUS

WARSZAWA

KYÏV

UKRAINE

Samara

Celjabinsk

KAZAKHSTAN

Astana
(Aqmola)

Aral

ALTAI

Irkutsk

Ulaanbaatar

MONGOLIA

GOBI DESERT

Kuril'skie
ostrova

Sapporo

Hokkaidō

45°

LITH.

CZECH
REP.

WIEN

SLOVA.

HUNG.

ROMANIA

Volgograd

ALMATY

Ürümqi

TIEN SHAN

BEIJING

SHENYANG

Vladivostok

MILANO

CRO.

BOSS.

SERB.

BULGARIA

Black Sea

GEORGIA

UZBEKISTAN

TAŠKENT

TIANJIN

Dalian

NORTH
KOREA

Pyongyang

Sea of
Japan

Sendai

JAPAN

ROMA

ITALY

ALB.

Beograd

Sofija

ISTANBUL

ANKARA

AZER.

BAKI

TURKMENISTAN

DUŠANBE

KABOL

Hohhot

Xi'an

CHINA

Nanjing

SHANGHAI

SŎUL

SOUTH
KOREA

PUSAN

Fukuoka

HONSHU

ŌSAKA

TŌKYŌ

D

Napoli

GREECE

ATHINA
(ATHENS)

TURKEY

Izmir

CYPRUS

SYRIA

TEHRAN

AFGHANISTAN

Chengdu

Chongqing

WUHAN

Changsha

Nansei-
shotō

PACIFIC

OCEAN

30°

TUNISIA

Tarabulus

Mediterranean Sea

LEBANON

ISRAEL

BAGHDAD

IRAQ

Esfahan

IRAN

Islamabad

Rawalpindi

LAHORE

HIMALAYAS

Lhasa

Kunming

GUANGZHOU

T'AIPEI

TAIWAN

Tropic of Cancer

E

...RIA

LIBYA

Banghazi

EGYPT

EL-ISKANDARIYA
(ALEXANDRIA)

EL-QAHIRA
(CAIRO)

AMMAN

JORDAN

KUWAIT

BAHRAIN

AR-RIYAD
(RIYADH)

QATAR

U.A.E.

Masqat

PAKISTAN

KARACHI

DELHI

New
Delhi

Kathmandu

Ahmadabad

KOLKATA
(CALCUTTA)

DHAKA

MYANMAR
(BURMA)

YANGON
(RANGOON)

LAOS

HA NOI

XIANGGANG
(HONG KONG)

WAKE ISLAND
(U.S.)

NORTHERN
MARIANA
ISLANDS
(U.S.)

NIGER

CHAD

Al-Khartum
(Khartoum)

ERITREA

Şan'a'

YEMEN

Arabian
Sea

MUMBAI
(BOMBAY)

Pune

HYDERABAD

INDIA

Bay of
Bengal

Andaman
Islands
(India)

KRUNG THEP
(BANGKOK)

THAILAND

Viangchan

CAMBODIA

VIETNAM

MANILA

South China
Sea

Philippine
Sea

GUAM (U.S.)

LUZON

MARSHALL
ISLANDS

15°

KANO

NIGERIA

Abuja

N'Djamena

Lake Chad

ADĪS ABEBA

Djibouti

DJIBOUTI

Aden

'Adan

BANGALORE

Kochi

CHENNAI
(MADRAS)

SRI LANKA

Nicobar
Islands
(India)

Phnum
Pénh

THANH-PHO
HO CHI MINH
(HO CHI MINH CITY)
(SAIGON)

Davao

MINDANAO

FEDERATED STATES OF MICRONESIA

MICRONESIA

F

LAGOS

...VO

CAMEROON

Yaoundé

CENTRAL AFRICAN
REPUBLIC

Bangui

ETHIOPIA

SOMALIA

Gees Gwardafuy

Colombo

MALDIVES

BRUNEI

MALAYSIA

Medan

Kuala Lumpur

SINGAPORE

BORNEO
(KALIMANTAN)

PALAU

NAURU

Equator

0°

EQUAT.
GUINEA

GABON

...reville

Brazzaville

Congo DEM. REP.
OF THE
CONGO

KINSHASA

UGANDA

Kampala

Kigali

RWANDA

BURUNDI

Bujumbura

KENYA

NAIROBI

SEYCHELLES

BRITISH INDIAN
OCEAN TERRITORY

SUMATERA
(SUMATRA)

JAKARTA

Banjarmasin

SULAWESI
(CELEBES)

Ujungpandang

INDONESIA

Surabaya

JAWA
(JAVA)

EAST TIMOR

PAPUA NEW
GUINEA

NEW
GUINEA

Port Moresby

Cape York

MELANESIA

SOLOMON
ISLANDS

KIRIBATI

TUVALU

G

LUANDA

Lobito

ANGOLA

Lubumbashi

ZAMBIA

Lusaka

TANZANIA

Dodoma

Dar es Salaam

Zanzibar

INDIAN

OCEAN

Darwin

15°

NAMIBIA

Windhoek

Walvis Bay

BOTSWANA

Gaborone

ZIMBABWE

Harare

MALAWI

Lilongwe

MOZAMBIQUE

Mozambique Channel

COMOROS

MADAGASCAR

Antananarivo

MAURITIUS

REUNION
(Fr.)

Cairns

Coral Sea

NEW
CALEDONIA
(Fr.)

Nouméa

VANUATU

FIJI

Suva

H

SOUTH
AFRICA

JOHANNESBURG

Pretoria

Maputo

SWAZILAND

LESOTHO

Durban

Alice Springs

Rockhampton

AUSTRALIA

Tropic of Capricorn

Cape Town

Cape of Good Hope

Port Elizabeth

Perth

Darling

Brisbane

SYDNEY

30°

Adelaide

Canberra

MELBOURNE

Tasman Sea

Auckland

NORTH ISLAND

I

TASMANIA

Hobart

SOUTH ISLAND

NEW ZEALAND

Wellington

Christchurch

45°

Îles Kerguélen
(Fr.)

J

SOUTHERN OCEAN

60°

Antarctic Circle

ENDERBY LAND

WILKES LAND

75°

K

...TICA

L

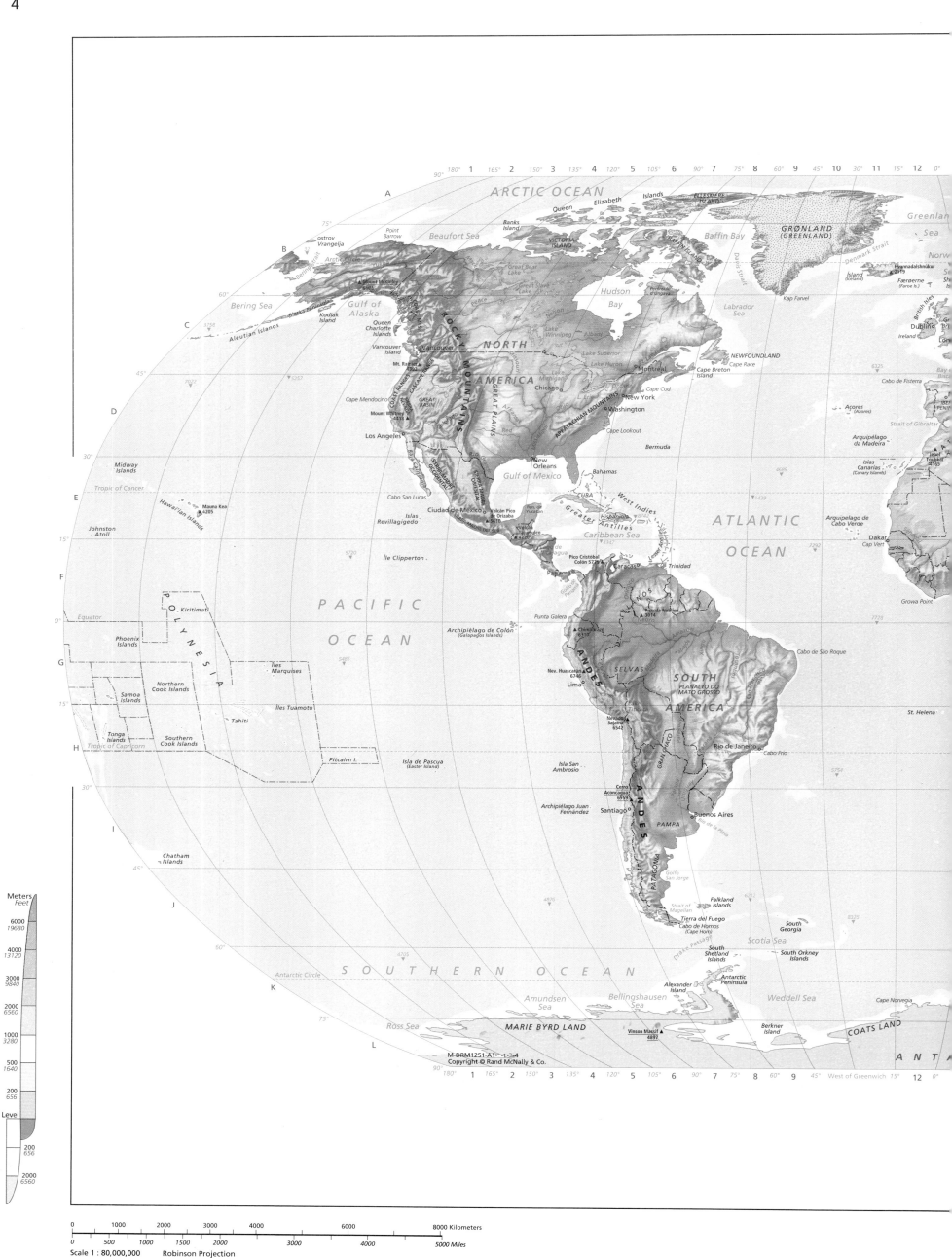

ARCTIC OCEAN

GRØNLAND
(GREENLAND)

Greenland
Sea

Baffin Bay

Hudson
Bay

Labrador
Sea

Denmark Strait

Ísland
(Iceland)

Færøerne
(Faroe Is.)

British Isles

Dublin

Ireland

Beaufort Sea

Banks
Island

Queen   Elizabeth   Islands

ELLESMERE
ISLAND

VICTORIA
ISLAND

Point
Barrow

ostrov
Vrangelja

Bering Sea

Great Bear
Lake

Great Slave
Lake

Mount McKinley

Gulf of
Alaska

Kodiak
Island

Aleutian Islands

Queen
Charlotte
Islands

Vancouver
Island

Vancouver

Mt. Rainier

NORTH

AMERICA

ROCKY MOUNTAINS

Lake
Winnipeg

Lake Superior

Lake Huron

Lake
Michigan

Chicago

Montreal

Cape Breton
Island

NEWFOUNDLAND

Cape Race

Kap Farvel

Cape Cod

New York

Washington

Cape Lookout

Bermuda

Acores
(Azores)

Cabo de Fisterra

Strait of Gibraltar

IBERIAN
PENINSULA

Cape Mendocino

Mount Whitney
4418

GREAT
BASIN

COAST RANGE

CASCADE RANGE

GREAT   PLAINS

APPALACHIAN MOUNTAINS

Ohio

Red

Los Angeles

Cabo San Lucas

New
Orleans

Gulf of Mexico

Bahamas

CUBA

Hispaniola

West Indies

Greater
Antilles

ATLANTIC

OCEAN

Islas
Canarias
(Canary Islands)

Jebel
Toubkal
4165

Tropic of Cancer

Midway
Islands

Hawaiian Islands

Mauna Kea
4205

Johnston
Atoll

Islas
Revillagigedo

Ciudad de México

Volcán Pico
de Orizaba

Acapulco

SIERRA MADRE OCCIDENTAL

SIERRA MADRE ORIENTAL

Pen. de
Yucatán

Caribbean Sea

Arquipélago de
Cabo Verde

Dakar
Cap Vert

Île Clipperton

Pico Cristóbal
Colón 5775

Panamá

Caracas

Trinidad

Growa Point

PACIFIC

OCEAN

POLYNESIA

Kiritimati

Equator

Archipiélago de Colón
(Galápagos Islands)

Punta Galera

NOS

Pico da Neblina
3014

Phoenix
Islands

Chimborazo
6310

ANDES

SELVAS

SOUTH

AMERICA

St. Helena

Northern
Cook Islands

Îles
Marquises

Nev. Huascarán
6746

Lima

PLANALTO DO
MATO GROSSO

Cabo de São Roque

Samoa
Islands

Îles Tuamotu

Tahiti

Nevado
Sajama
6542

GRAN CHACO

Rio de Janeiro

Cabo Frio

Tonga
Islands

Southern
Cook Islands

Tropic of Capricorn

Pitcairn I.

Isla de Pascua
(Easter Island)

Isla San
Ambrosio

Cerro
Aconcagua
6959

Santiago

ANDES

Buenos Aires

Río de la Plata

PAMPA

Archipiélago Juan
Fernández

Chatham
Islands

PATAGONIA

ANDES

Golfo
San Jorge

Falkland
Islands

Strait of
Magellan

Tierra del Fuego

Cabo de Hornos
(Cape Horn)

South
Georgia

Scotia Sea

Drake Passage

South
Shetland
Islands

South Orkney
Islands

Antarctic Circle

SOUTHERN   OCEAN

Amundsen
Sea

Bellingshausen
Sea

Alexander
Island

Antarctic
Peninsula

Weddell Sea

Cape Norvegia

Ross Sea

MARIE BYRD LAND

Vinson Massif
4897

Berkner
Island

COATS LAND

ANTA

Meters
Feet

6000
19680

4000
13120

3000
9840

2000
6560

1000
3280

500
1640

200
656

Sea Level

200
656

2000
6560

0   1000   2000   3000   4000   6000   8000 Kilometers

0   500   1000   1500   2000   3000   4000   5000 Miles

Scale 1 : 80,000,000   Robinson Projection

14   *30°*   15   *45°*   16   *60°*   17   *75°*   18   *90°*   19   *105°*   20   *120°*   21   *135°*   22   *150°*   23   *165°*   24   *180°*   *90°*

ARCTIC OCEAN

Barents Sea

Zemlja Franca-Iosifa
Severnaja Zemlja
Novosibirskie ostrova
Nordkapp
Novaja Zemlja
Karskoe more
Vostočno-Sibirskoe more
more Laptevyh

A

B

Bering Sea

Koŕskij poluostrov
gora Kamen 1701 ▲

ZAPADNO-SIBIRSKAJA RAVNINA (WEST SIBERIAN PLAIN)
Nižnjaja Tunguska
S I B I R' (SIBERIA)
gora Pobeda 3147 ▲

Arctic Circle

URAĽSKIE GORY
Ekaterinberg
Sea of Okhotsk
ostrov Sahalin

Moskva (Moscow)
Berlin
Ladožskoe ozero

Irkutsk
Ulaanbaatar
mys Lopatka
Kuriľskie ostrova

C

EUROPE
CARPATHIANS
ALPS
APPENNINO
Roma
Sicilia (Sicily)
Kriti
Black Sea
Istanbul
CAUCASUS
gora Eľbrus 5642
Balqaš köli
ALTAI
GOBI DESERT
Beijing
Hokkaidō
HONSHŪ
Sea of Japan
SICHOTE ALIN

D

Mediterranean Sea
Cyprus
Tehran
DASHT-E KAVIR
Golleh-ye Damavand 5604
KŪHHĀ-YE ZAGROS
TIEN SHAN
HINDU KUSH
Pik Pobedy 7439
Pik Ismail Samani
KUNLUN SHAN
QING ZANG GAOYUAN (Qing Zang)
HIMALAYAS
Mount Everett 8848
Qognga Shan 7590
Shanghai
East China Sea
Fuji-san 3776 ▲ Tōkyō
Shikoku
Kyūshū
Yellow Sea
Nansei-shotō

E

PACIFIC OCEAN

Tropic of Cancer

SAHARA
TIBESTI
HOGGAR
Tahat 2908
Emi Koussi 3415
NUBIAN DESERT
ARABIAN PENINSULA
AR-RUB' AL-KHALI
Red Sea
Persian Gulf
Gulf of Oman
Delhi
WESTERN GHATS
EASTERN GHATS
Godavari
Taiwan
Yü Shan 3997
Hainan Dao
Wake Island

F

AFRICA
Lake Chad
Ras Dashen Terara 4620
Adis Abeba
Gulf of Aden
Suqutrā
Gees Gwardafuy
Arabian Sea
Mumbai (Bombay)
Cape Comorin
Piduruttalagala 2524
Sri Lanka
Bay of Bengal
Andaman Islands
Andaman Sea
Nicobar Islands
Maldive Islands
Gulf of Thailand
Krung Thep
INDOCHINA
Malay Peninsula
South China Sea
Gunong Kinabalu 4101
Palawan
Manila
LUZON
PHILIPPINES
Philippine Sea
Mariana Islands
Guam
MINDANAO
Palau Islands
MICRONESIA
Marshall Islands
Caroline Islands

G

Margherita Peak 5109
CONGO BASIN
RIFT VALLEY
Lake Victoria
Kirinyaga 5199
Kilimanjaro 5895
Lake Tanganyika
Zanzibar
Les Amirantes
Seychelles
BORNEO (KALIMANTAN)
SUMATERA (SUMATRA)
Greater Sunda Islands
Jakarta
JAWA (JAVA)
SULAWESI (CELEBES)
Celebes Sea
Halmahera
Seram
Laut Banda
NEW GUINEA
Mount Wilhelm 4509
New Britain
Solomon Islands
MELANESIA

Equator

INDIAN OCEAN
MADAGASCAR
Tanjona Bobaomby
Maromokotro 2876
Réunion
Mauritius
Timor
Arafura Sea
Timor Sea
Cape York
New Hebrides
Fiji Islands

H

Cape Fria
NAMIB DESERT
KALAHARI DESERT
Mozambique Channel
Tanjona Vohimena
North West Cape
Kimberley Plateau
GREAT SANDY DESERT
Tanami Desert
Gulf of Carpentaria
CAPE YORK PENINSULA
Coral Sea
Nouvelle-Calédonie

Tropic of Capricorn

Cape of Good Hope
Cape Town
Thabana-Ntlenyana 3482
DRAKENSBERG
Orange
Mount Meharry 1253
AUSTRALIA
Mount Woodroffe 1435
GREAT VICTORIA DESERT
Great Australian Bight
Cape Leeuwin
Darling
GREAT DIVIDING RANGE
Sydney
Mount Kosciuszko 2229
Tasman Sea
North Cape

I

Île Amsterdam
Melbourne
Mount Ossa 1617 ▲
TASMANIA
NORTH ISLAND
Mount Ruapehu 2797
SOUTH ISLAND
Aoraki (Mount Cook) 3754

Prince Edward Islands
Îles de Crozet
Îles Kerguélen
South East Cape
South West Cape

J

Heard Island
Macquarie Island

SOUTHERN OCEAN

K

Cape Poinsett
Antarctic Circle

ENDERBY LAND
WILKES LAND
Cape Adare
VICTORIA LAND
Ross Sea

QUEEN MAUD LAND
ANTARCTICA

L

East of Greenwich   *45°*   16   *60°*   17   *75°*   18   *90°*   19   *105°*   20   *120°*   21   *135°*   22   *150°*   23   *165°*   24   *180°*

ICELAND

Reykjavik

Hvannadalshnúkur
2119

ATLANTIC
OCEAN

FAROE ISLANDS
(Den.) Tórshavn

SHETLAND
ISLANDS
(U.K.)

Rockall
(U.K.)

ORKNEY
ISLANDS

HEBRIDES

Thurso

Inverness

Aberdeen

GLASGOW
EDINBURGH

UNITED
KINGDOM

Belfast
Carlisle

NEWCASTLE
UPON TYNE

Middlesbrough

Londonderry

Sligo

Galway

DUBLIN

IRELAND

Limerick

Cork

Waterford

LIVERPOOL

LEEDS
MANCHESTER
Sheffield

Nottingham

BIRMINGHAM

Leicester

Swansea

Cardiff

Bristol

Oxford

LONDON

Norwich

Ipswich

Southampton

Brighton

Dover

Plymouth

Penzance

ISLES OF
SCILLY

English Channel

Strait of Dover

GREENLAND SEA

NORWEGIAN SEA

Arctic Circle

NORWAY

SWEDEN

VESTERÅLEN

LOFOTEN

Tromsø

Narvik

Bodø

Mo i Rana

Namsos

Storuman

Galdhøpiggen
2469

Kristiansund

Trondheim

Dombås

Ålesund

Molde

Bergen

Hamar

Haugesund

Oslo

Stavanger

Drammen

Skien

Moss

Kristiansand

Lindesnes

Östersund

Härnösand

Sundsvall

Hudiksvall

Falun

Gävle

Uppsala

Västerås

STOCKHOLM

Norrköping

Linköping

Örebro

Karlstad

NORTH SEA

DENMARK

Frederikshavn

Göteborg

Jönköping

Växjö

Halmstad

Helsingborg

Esbjerg

Odense

Århus

Kolding

KØBENHAVN
(COPENHAGEN)

MALMÖ

GOTLAND

ÖLAND

Kalmar

Karlskrona

BALTIC

Kiel

Flensburg

Holstebro

Skagerrak

Kattegat

Gdynia

Gdańsk

Kaliningrad

Bornholm
(Den.)

Bremerhaven

HAMBURG

Lübeck

Rostock

Stralsund

Szczecin

Bydgoszcz

Groningen

Bremen

NETHERLANDS

's-Gravenhage
(The Hague)

AMSTERDAM

Utrecht

Münster

Hannover

Magdeburg

BERLIN

Poznań

POLAND

ROTTERDAM

ANTWERPEN

ESSEN

Dortmund

GERMANY

Leipzig

Dresden

Wrocław

Łódź

BRUXELLES

BELGIUM

LILLE

Liège

KÖLN

DÜSSELDORF

Bonn

Wiesbaden

FRANKFURT
AM MAIN

Erfurt

Chemnitz

Plzeň

PRAHA

CZECH REP

Ostrava

Olomouc

Brno

Częstochowa

Katowice

Kraków

SLOVAKIA

Amiens

Le Havre

Rouen

Reims

Luxembourg

MANNHEIM

Würzburg

Nürnberg

Regensburg

Cherbourg

GUERNSEY
(U.K.)

JERSEY
(U.K.)

Caen

Saint-
Malo

Brest

Rennes

Angers

Nantes

La Rochelle

Poitiers

Tours

Bourges

Orléans

PARIS

Troyes

Metz

Nancy

Strasbourg

Mulhouse

Basel

Bern

Dijon

Besançon

STUTTGART

Augsburg

MÜNCHEN
(MUNICH)

Linz

WIEN
(VIENNA)

Bratislava

Salzburg

Innsbruck

AUSTRIA

Graz

Klagenfurt

BUDAPEST

HUNGARY

Győr

FRANCE

Limoges

Clermont-
Ferrand

LYON

Saint-
Étienne

Grenoble

Genève

Lausanne

SWITZ.

Zürich

LIECHT.

Vaduz

Mont Blanc
4807

Bolzano

SLOVENIA

Ljubljana

Zagreb

Pécs

Szeged

Saarbrücken

Pointe de
Saint-Mathieu

Girond...

Bordeaux

Bayonne

Toulouse

PYRENEES

ANDORRA

Andorra
la Vella

Montpellier

Nîmes

Avignon

MARSEILLE

Toulon

Nice

MONACO

SAN
MARINO

Brescia

TORINO

MILANO

Verona

Padova

Parma

GENOVA

La Spezia

Bologna

Firenze

Livorno

Pisa

VENÉZIA
(Venice)

Trieste

Rijeka

CROATIA

Zadar

BOSNIA AND
HERZEGOVINA

Sarajevo

Split

ADRIATIC SEA

Dubrovnik

Beograd

Podgorica

LIGURIAN SEA

CORSE
(CORSICA)
(Fr.)

Bastia

Ajaccio

APPENNINO

Perugia

Ancona

Pescara

L'Aquila

ROMA
(ROME)

VATICAN CITY

ITALY

NAPOLI
(NAPLES)

Salerno

Bari

Foggia

Brindisi

Taranto

Lecce

Tirana

ALBANIA

A Coruña

Cabo de Fisterra

Gijón

Vigo

Oviedo

Santander

Bay of Biscay

Braga

León

Bilbao

Donostia-
San Sebastián

Gasteiz

Pamplona

Ourense

PORTUGAL

Burgos

Zaragoza

Lleida

Valladolid

Salamanca

Duero

SPAIN

MADRID

Segovia

LISBOA
(LISBON)

Setúbal

Coimbra

Évora

Badajoz

Toledo

Castelló
de la Plana

VALÉNCIA

Tarragona

BARCELONA

ILLES BALEARS
(BALEARIC ISLANDS)

Menorca

Palma de
Mallorca

MALLORCA

Eivissa

Cabo de
São Vicente

Faro

Huelva

Córdoba

Sevilla

Granada

Jaén

Albacete

Murcia

Elx

Alacant

Lorca

Mulhacén
3482

Cartagena

Cádiz

Málaga

Strait of Gibraltar

GIBRALTAR
(U.K.)

Ceuta (Sp.)

Isla de
Alborán
(Sp.)

SARDEGNA
(SARDINIA)
(It.)

Sassari

Olbia

Nuoro

Cagliari

TYRRHENIAN
SEA

MEDITERRANEAN

Palermo

Trapani

Messina

Reggio
di Calabria

Catanzaro

Cosenza

IONIAN SEA

Monte Etna
3323

SICILIA
(SICILY)

Catania

Siracusa

Agrigento

Isola di
Pantelleria
(It.)

Isole
delle Correnti

MALTA

Valletta

ISOLE
PELAGIE

Tanger

Larache

Tetouan

Al Hoceima

Melilla (Sp.)

EL DJAZAÏR
(ALGIERS)

Tizi
Ouzou

Béjaïa

Skikda

Annaba

Bizerte

Cap Bon

TUNIS

Nabeul

Sousse

CASABLANCA

Rabat

Salé

El-Jadida

Meknès

Fès

Oujda

Wahran

Mestghanem

Ech Cheliff

Bouïra

Qacentina

La Galite

Béja

Kairouan

Sfax

MOROCCO

Safi

Essaouira

Khouribga

Taza

Sidi bel
Abbès

Tihert

ATLAS MOUNTAINS

ALGERIA

Tébessa

Batna

Sétif

TUNISIA

Gafsa

Agadir

Jebel Toubkal
4165

Marrakech

Er-Rachidia

Oued Guir

Laghouat

Beskra

Chott el
Jerid

Chott
Melrhir

NORWEGIAN SEA

IRISH SEA

M-DRM3302-P1- 3-3-5
Copyright © Rand McNally & Co.

West of Greenwich 0° East of Greenwich

0   200   400   800
                        1200 Kilometers

0   100   200   400   600   800 Miles

Scale 1 : 12,500,000   Conic Equidistant Projection

BARENTS SEA

Nordkapp
Hammerfest
Vadsø
Kirkenes
Nikel'
Murmansk

ostrov Kolguev

POLUOSTROV KANIN

Naryan-Mar

ZAPADNO-SIBIRSKAJA RAVNINA
(WEST SIBERIAN PLAIN)

Ob'

Nižnevartovsk

Surgut

Inari
Muonio
Rovaniemi
Kemi
Kokkola

Apatity

Kandalakša

KOL'SKIJ POLUOSTROV
(KOLA PENINSULA)

Ponoj

BELOE MORE
(WHITE SEA)

mys Kanin Nos

Mezen'

Pečora

Ust'ilimsk
Inta

Arctic Circle

Pečora

gora Narodnaja
1895

URAĽSKIE GORY (URAL MOUNTAINS)

Konda

Ob'

Hanty-Mansijsk
Demjanskoje

Irtyš

Tara

Oulu
Kuusamo
Oulujärvi

Belomorsk

Onega

Arhangel'sk

Severodvinsk

Severnaja Dvina

Uhta

Sosnogorsk

Serov

Tavda

Tjumen'

Kamensk-Ural'skij

Tobol

Petropavlovsk

Kökshetau

Serganiski
Ivdel'

FINLAND

Kuopio
Iisalmi
Varkaus
Mikkeli
Imatra
Lahti

Segeža

Onežskoe ozero

Petrozavodsk

Vel'sk

Vologda

Kotlas

Velikij Ustjug

Syktyvkar

Kirov

Berezniki

gora Konžakovskij Kamen'
1569

Nižnij Tagil

Pervoural'sk

EKATERINBURG

Kurgan

KAZAKHSTAN

Tampere
Jyväskylä

RUSSIA

Kostroma

Glazov

PERM'

Zlatoust

ČELJABINSK

Troick

Kostanaj

Makinsk

HELSINKI

Gulf of Finland

SANKT-PETERBURG
(ST. PETERSBURG)

Tallinn

Vyborg

Volhov

Čerepovec

Rybinskoe vodohranilišče

Jaroslavl'

Ivanovo

Votkinsk

Sarapul

Čeboksary

KAZAN'

Iževsk

Naberežnye Čelny

UFA

gora Jamantau
1640

Sterlitamak

Magnitogorsk

Karталy

Rudnyj

Arqalyq

ESTONIA

Narva

Pärnu

Tartu

Novgorod

Bologoe

Tver'

Vladimir

Sergiev Posad

Murom

Kujbyševskoe vodohranilišče

Uljanovsk

NIŽNIJ NOVGOROD

Gor'kovskoe vodohranilišče

Gulf of Riga

RĪGA

LATVIA

Pskov

Velikie Luki

MOSKVA
(MOSCOW)

Orehovo-Zuevo

Kolomna

Rjazan'

Saransk

Penza

Kuzneck

Syzran'

Toljatti

SAMARA

Saratovskoe vodohranilišče

Orenburg

Sol'-Ileck

Aqtöbe

Šalqar

Aral

LITHUANIA

Rēzekne

Daugavpils

Šiauliai

Vicebsk

Ržev

Vjaz'ma

Serpuhov

Tula

Mičurinsk

Tambov

Balakovo

Engel's

Oral

Inderbor

Torghay

Yrghyz

Zhangaqazaly

Kaunas

Vilnius

Hrodna

MINSK

Mahilëu

Smolensk

Kaluga

Novomoskovsk

Rjažsk

Penza

SARATOV

Kamyšin

Volgogradskoe vodohranilišče

Maqat

Zhympity

BELARUS

Baranavičy

Babrujsk

Homel'

Brjansk

Orel

Elec

Lipeck

Voronež

Borisoglebsk

Kalač

Caspian Depression

ŠARŠA WARSAW

Brèst

Lublin

Pripjat'

Pripet

Černihiv

Konotop

Sumy

Kursk

Staryj Oskol

List

Mihajlovka

Volžskij

PRIKASPIJSKAJA NIZMENNOST'

Atyrau

Beyneü

Žetibaj

UZBEKISTAN

Kungrad

Rzeszów

L'viv

Ternopil'

Rivne

Korosten'

Kyïv's'ke vodoshovyšče

KYÏV (KIEV)

Bila Cerkva

Poltava

Belgorod

Izjum

Sloviansk

Kremenčuk

Kremenčuc'ke vodoshovyšče

Slavjansk

Severskij Donec

Millerovo

Volgodonsk

Atyrau

Aqtau

Zhangaözen

Beyneü

UKRAINE

Ivano-Frankivs'k

Černivci

Vinnycja

Kirovohrad

Kryvyj Rih

DNIPROPETROVS'K

Zaporizhzhia

Horlivka

DONETS'K

Luhans'k

Kakhovs'ke vodoshovyšče

VOLGOGRAD

Ahtubinsk

Cimljanskoe vodohranilišče

Astrahan'

Caspian Depression

CASPIAN SEA

zaliv Kara Bogaz Gol

TURKMENISTAN

Nebitdag

MOLDOVA

Chişinău

Iaşi

Bălți

Târgu Mureş

Vârful Pietrosu
2303

Mykolaïv

Kherson

Taganrog

ROSTOV-NA-DONU

Melitopol'

Tihoreck

Elista

Stavropol'

Pjatigorsk

Majkop

Čerkessk

Terek

Groznyj

Mahačkala

Derbent

ROMANIA

Oradea

Cluj-Napoca

Braşov

Bacău

Galaţi

Brăila

Izmail

ODESA

KRYMS'KYI PIVOSTRIV
(CRIMEAN PENINSULA)

Simferopol'

Sevastopol'

Kerč'

Krasnodar

Novorossijsk

Tuapse

Armavir

Soči

gora El'brus
5642

CAUCASUS

Vladikavkaz

GEORGIA

Tbilisi

BAKI (BAKU)

Sibiu

Piteşti

BUCUREŞTI
(BUCHAREST)

Constanţa

Sea of Azov

BLACK SEA

Suhumi

Kutaisi

Poti

Batumi

Kars

ARMENIA

Yerevan

Ağrı Dağı
5137

Gäncä

Xankändi

Länkäran

Gorgān

Craiova

Pleven

Ruse

BALKAN PENINSULA

Varna

Burgas

İnce Burun

Şinop

Samsun

Trabzon

AZERBAIJAN

Ardabil

Bandar-e Anzali

Rasht

RESHTEH-YE KÜHHĀ-YE ALBORZ

BULGARIA

SOFIJA
(SOFIA)

Stara Zagora

Plovdiv

Edirne

Zonguldak

Kastamonu

Ordu

Erzurum

Van

Gölü Van

Orūmiyeh

Daryācheh-ye Orūmiyeh
(Lake Urmia)

Tabriz

Zanjān

Qazvin

dolleh ye Damāvand
5604

Semnān

TEHRĀN

Skopje

Plovdiv

İSTANBUL

İzmit

Sakarya

Çankırı

Çorum

Sivas

Erzincan

Elazığ

K U R D I S T A N

Miāneh

MAKEDONIJA

Kavala

Alexandroupoli

Marmara Denizi

ANKARA

Kırıkkale

Kızılırmak

Kayseri

Malatya

Diyarbakır

Tigris

Arbil

Sanandaj

Kermānshāh

Qom

Arāk

Kāshān

Thessaloniki

Olympos
2917

Çanakkale

Bursa

Eskişehir

Kütahya

Afyon

TURKEY

Tuz Gölü

Niğde

Kahramanmaraş

Gaziantep

Şanlıurfa

Al-Ḥasakah

Al-Mawṣil

Karkūk

KÜHHĀ-YE ZĀGROS

Lárisa

Vólos

İZMIR

Manisa

Aydın

Denizli

ANADOLU
(ANATOLIA)

Isparta

Konya

Adana

Tarsus

İçel

İskenderun

TOROS DAĞLARI
(TAURUS MOUNTAINS)

Antalya

Gaziantep

Halab (Aleppo)

Euphrates

Dayr az-Zawr

Al-Qāmishlī

Khorramābād

Kermānshāh

Dezfūl

Ahvāz

ESFAHĀN

Zard Kūh
4547

PELOPÓNNISOS

KIKLÁDES

KRITI
(CRETE)

Chaniá

Irákleio

Ákra Taínaron

AEGEAN SEA

Lésvos

Chíos

DODEKANISOS

Ródos

Rhodes

NORTH CYPRUS

Nicosia

CYPRUS

LEBANON

Al-Lādhiqīyah

Tarābulus (Tripoli)

Ḥimṣ

Ḥamāh

Tudmur

SYRIA

Abū Kamāl

BAGHDAD

Al-Kūt

Karbalā'

An-Najaf

Abū Ghraib

Ar-Ruṭbah

IRAQ

MESOPOTAMIA

Tigris

Euphrates

An-Nāṣirīyah

Al-'Amārah

Dezfūl

Kāzerūn

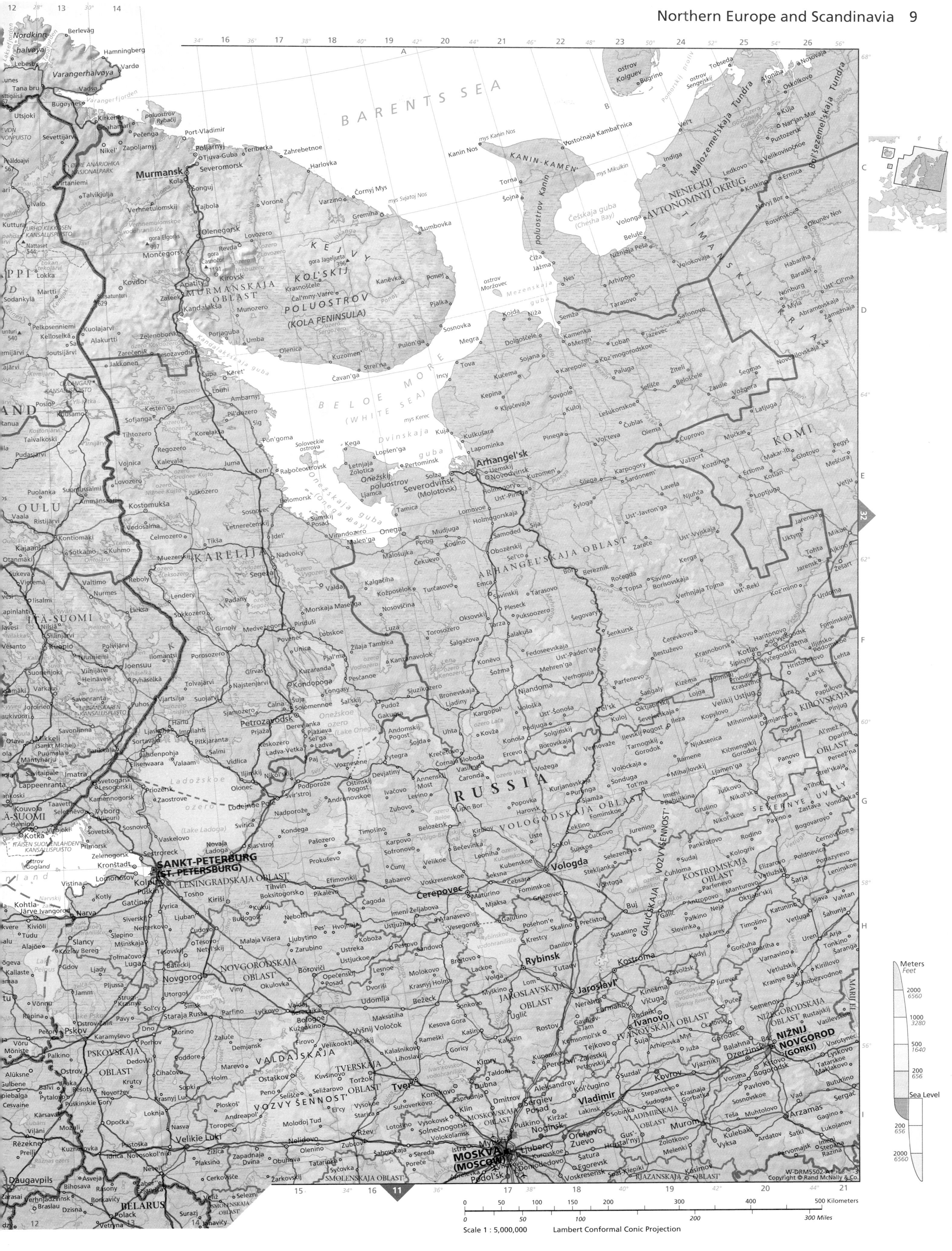

BARENTS SEA

KANIN-KAMEN'

NENECKIJ AVTONOMNYJ OKRUG

poluostrov Kanin

Čёšskaja guba (Chesha Bay)

Mezenskaja guba

KOL'SKIJ POLUOSTROV (KOLA PENINSULA)

KEJVY

Murmansk

Severodvinsk (Molotovsk)

Arhangel'sk

BELOE MORE (WHITE SEA)

Dvinskaja guba

Onežskij poluostrov

Onežskaja guba (Onega Bay)

ARHANGEL'SKAJA OBLAST

KOMI

KARELIJA

MURMANSKAJA OBLAST

OULU

ITÄ-SUOMI

Petrozavodsk

Onežskoe ozero (Lake Onega)

Ladožskoe ozero (Lake Ladoga)

RUSSIA

VOLOGODSKAJA OBLAST

KIROVSKAJA OBLAST

SANKT-PETERBURG (ST. PETERSBURG)

LENINGRADSKAJA OBLAST

Vologda

Čerepovec

KOSTROMSKAJA OBLAST

GALIČSKAJA VOZVYŠENNOST'

SEVERNYE UVALY

OBLAST

Novgorod

NOVGORODSKAJA OBLAST

Rybinsk

Jaroslavl'

JAROSLAVSKAJA OBLAST

Kostroma

Ivanovo

IVANOVSKAJA OBLAST

NIŽNIJ NOVGOROD (GORKI)

NIŽEGORODSKAJA OBLAST

MARIJ EL

Pskov

PSKOVSKAJA OBLAST

VALDAJSKAJA VOZVYŠENNOST'

TVERSKAJA OBLAST

Tver'

Vladimir

VLADIMIRSKAJA OBLAST

Murom

MOSKVA (MOSCOW)

MOSKOVSKAJA OBLAST

SMOLENSKAJA OBLAST

RJAZANSKAJA OBLAST

BELARUS

DAUGAVPILS

Meters Feet	
2000	6560
1000	3280
500	1640
200	656
Sea Level	
200	656
2000	6560

Scale 1 : 5,000,000   Lambert Conformal Conic Projection

0 50 100 150 200 300 400 500 Kilometers

0 50 100 150 200 300 Miles

Copyright © Rand McNally & Co.

W-DRM5502

Scale 1 : 2,500,000
Lambert Conformal Conic Projection

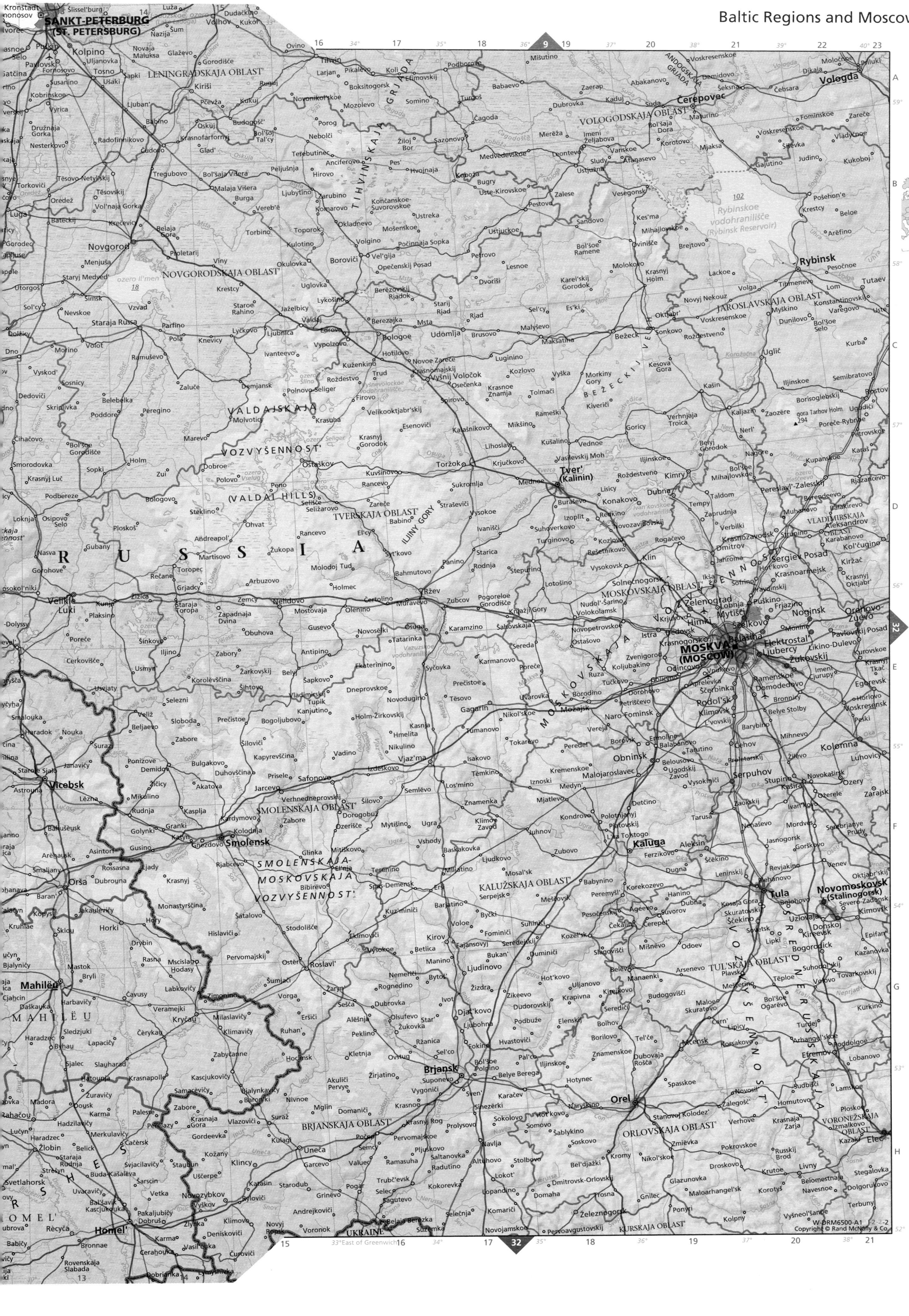

SANKT-PETERBURG
(ST. PETERSBURG)

LENINGRADSKAJA OBLAST'

Novgorod

NOVGORODSKAJA OBLAST'

Staraja Russa

VALDAJSKAJA

VOZVYŠENNOST'

(VALDAI HILLS)

TVERSKAJA OBLAST'

R U S S I A

Velikie Luki

Tver'
(Kalinin)

MOSKOVSKAJA OBLAST'

MOSKVA
(MOSCOW)

Elektrostal'
Ljubercy

Vicebsk

SMOLENSKAJA OBLAST'

Smolensk

SMOLENSKAJA-
MOSKOVSKAJA
VOZVYŠENNOST'

Obninsk

KALUŽSKAJA OBLAST'

Kaluga

Serpuhov

Tula

Novomoskovsk
(Stalinogorsk)

TUL'SKAJA OBLAST'

Mahilëu

MAHILËU

Brjansk

BRJANSKAJA OBLAST'

Orel

ORLOVSKAJA OBLAST'

KURSKAJA OBLAST'

UKRAINE

Homel'

HOMEL'

Čerepovec

VOLOGODSKAJA OBLAST'

Rybinskoe
vodohranilišče
(Rybinsk Reservoir)

Rybinsk

JAROSLAVSKAJA OBLAST'

VLADIMIRSKAJA
OBLAST'

Sergiev Posad

Vologda

Copyright © Rand McNally & Co.

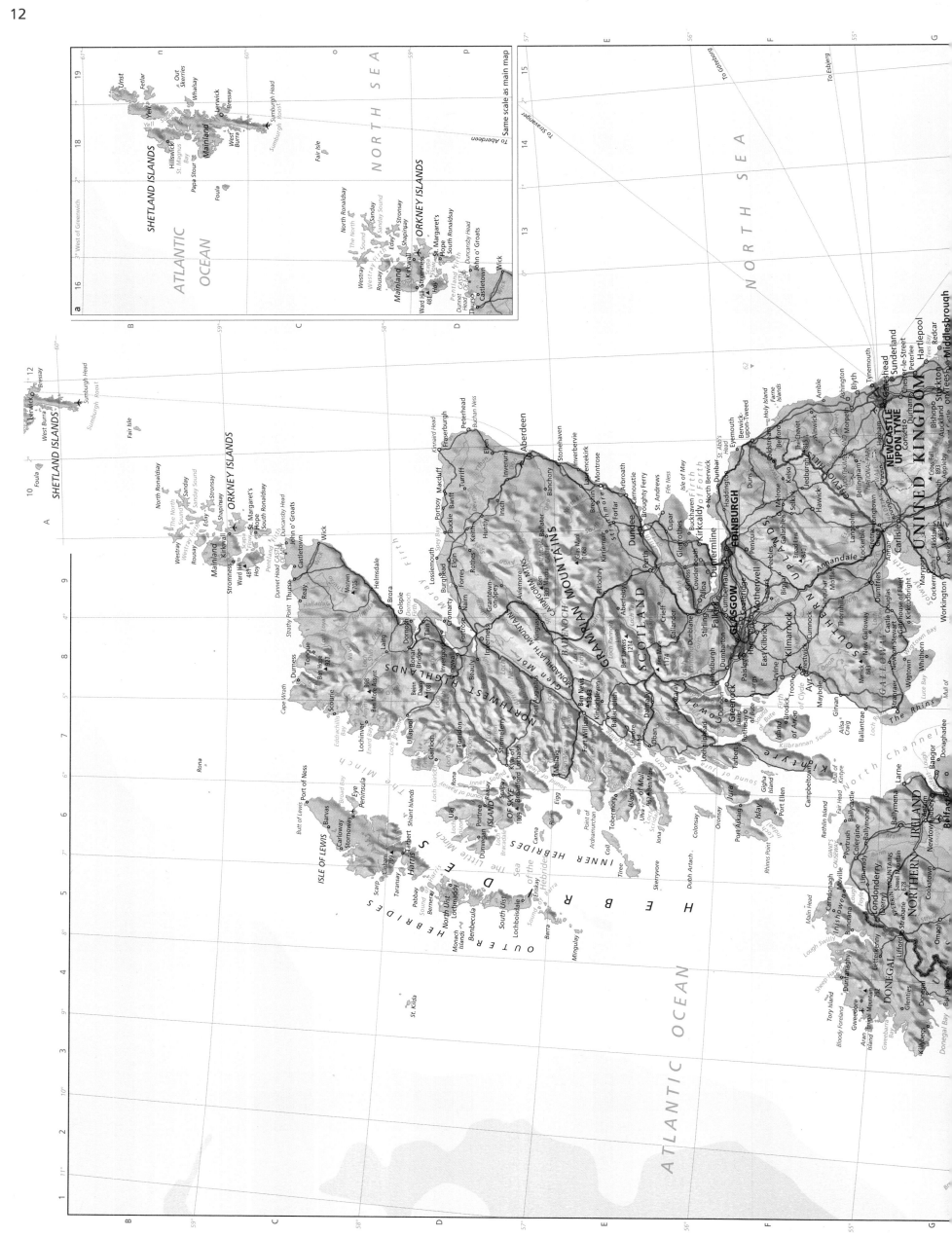

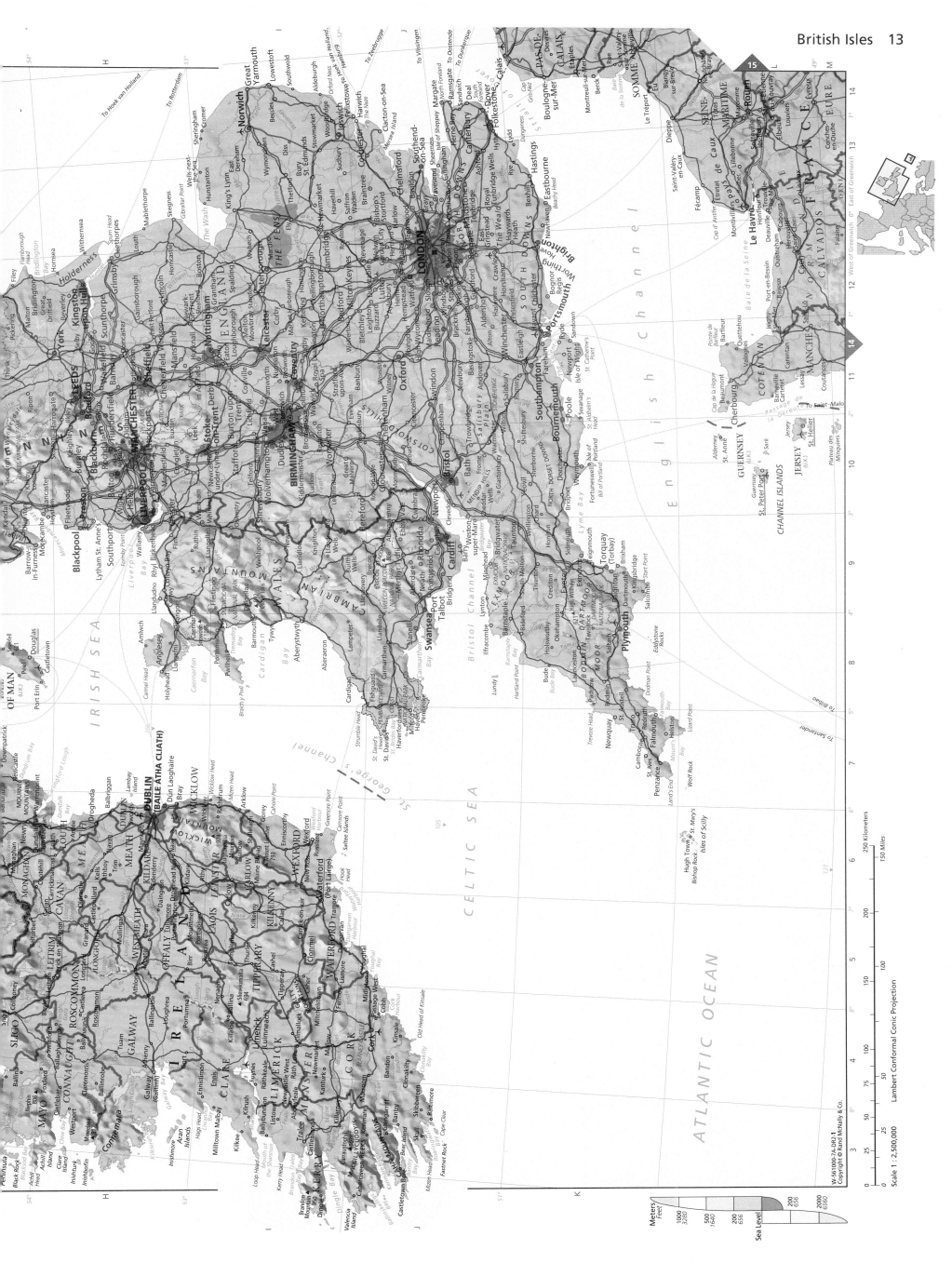

Scale 1 : 2,500,000

Lambert Conformal Conic Projection

W-561000-7A-DR2.1
Copyright © Rand McNally & Co.

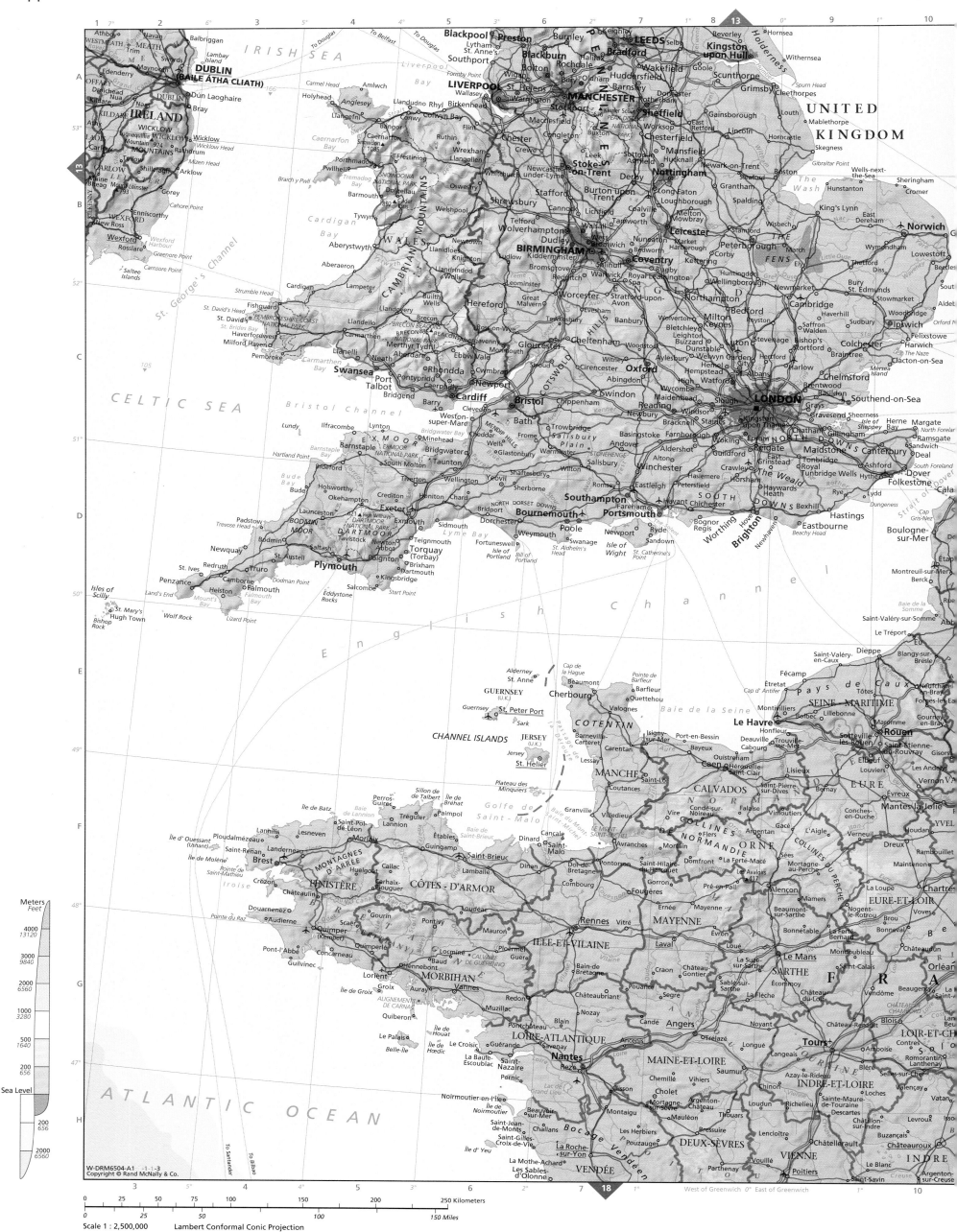

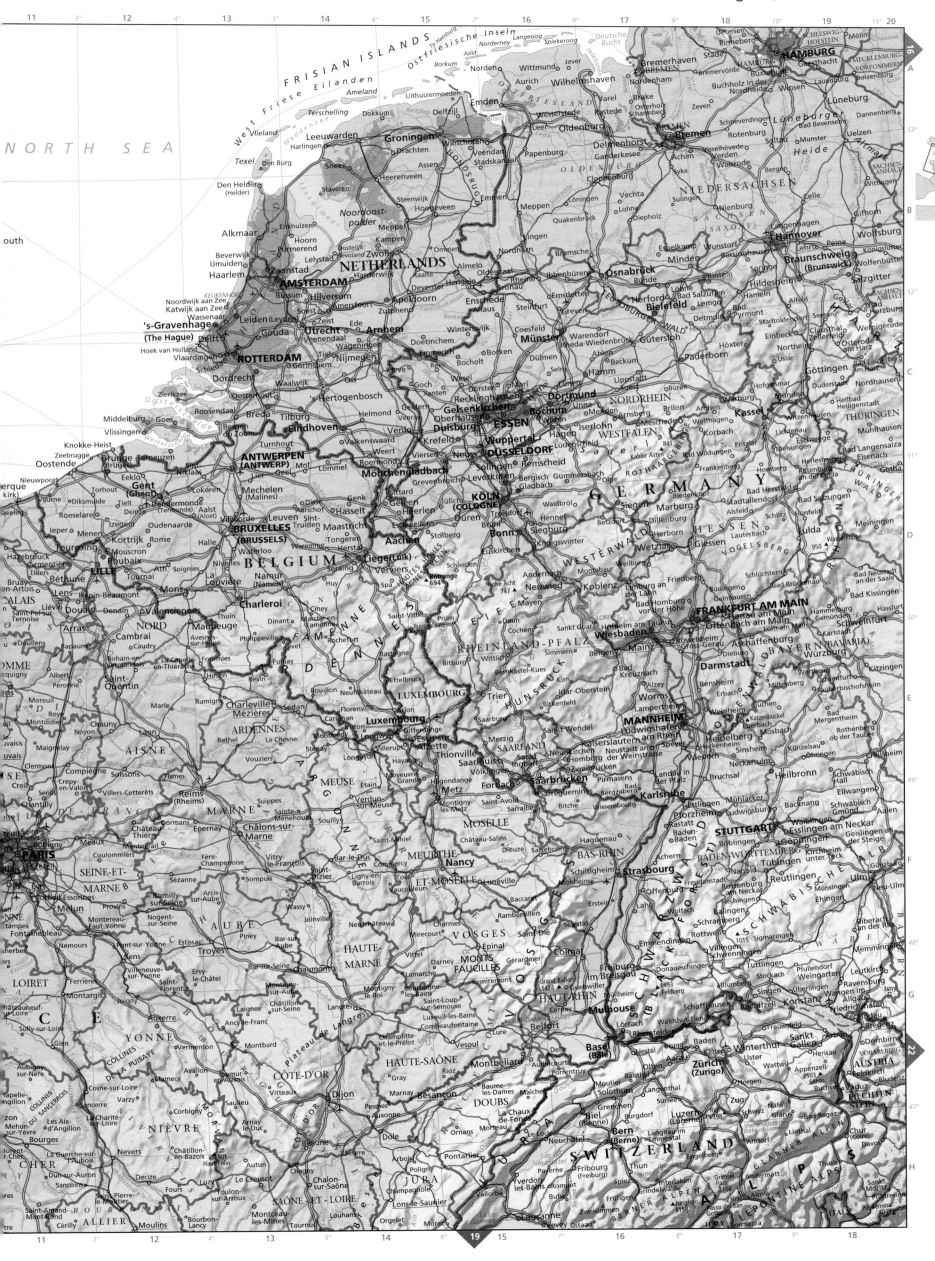

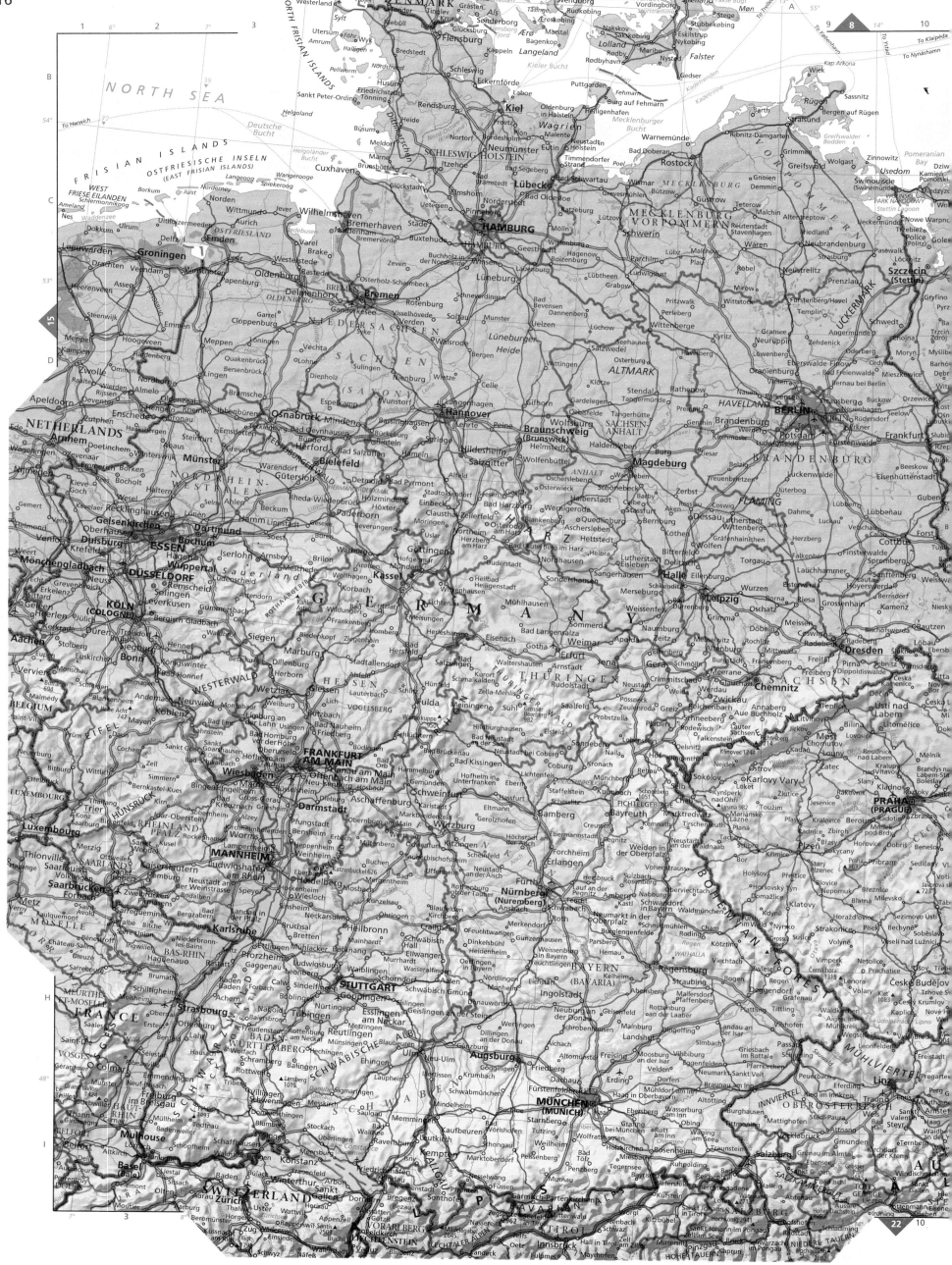

Bay of Biscay

ATLANTIC OCEAN

ALBORAN SEA

Golfo de Cádiz

Baía de Setúbal

PORTUGAL

SPAIN

GALICIA

ASTURIAS

CANTABRIA

CASTILLA Y LEÓN

CORDILLERA CANTÁBRICA

TRÁS-OS-MONTES

VILA REAL

BRAGANÇA

MINHO

VIANA DO CASTELO

BRAGA

PORTO

AVEIRO

VISEU

GUARDA

BEIRA

CASTELO BRANCO

LEIRIA

ESTREMADURA

SANTARÉM

PORTALEGRE

ÉVORA

EXTREMADURA

BADAJOZ

CÁCERES

ALENTEJO

SETÚBAL

BEJA

FARO

ALGARVE

ANDALUCÍA

HUELVA

SEVILLA

CÓRDOBA

JAÉN

GRANADA

SIERRA MORENA

SIERRA NEVADA

CORDILLERA

CAMPIÑA

LA MANCHA

CIUDAD REAL

CASTILLA–LA MANCHA

MONTES DE TOLEDO

SISTEMA CENTRAL

SIERRA DE GREDOS

SIERRA DE GUADARRAMA

LA ALCARRIA

OLD CASTILE

SALAMANCA

ZAMORA

VALLADOLID

SEGOVIA

PALENCIA

BURGOS

A Coruña (Corunna)

Ferrol

Santiago de Compostela

Pontevedra

Vigo

Ourense

Lugo

León

Ponferrada

Oviedo

Gijón

Avilés

Santander

Bilbao

Valladolid

Zamora

Salamanca

Ávila

Segovia

MADRID

Guadalajara

Alcalá de Henares

Toledo

Cáceres

Mérida

Badajoz

Córdoba (Cordova)

Jaén

Granada

Sevilla (Seville)

Huelva

Cádiz

Jerez de la Frontera

Málaga

Algeciras

GIBRALTAR (U.K.)

Porto

Coimbra

Aveiro

Viseu

Guarda

Leiria

LISBOA (LISBON)

Setúbal

Évora

Beja

Faro

Braga

Cabo Ortegal

Cabo de Peñas

Cabo Finisterre

Cabo de São Vicente

Cabo de Santa Maria

Cabo Trafalgar

Europa Point

Strait of Gibraltar

Estrecho de Gibraltar

To Islas Canarias (Canary Islands)

MOROCCO

Ceuta (Sp.)

Meters / Feet
3000 / 9840
2000 / 6560
1000 / 3280
500 / 1640
200 / 656
Sea Level
200 / 656
2000 / 6560

0   25   50   75   100   150   200 Kilometers
0   25   50   100 Miles

Scale 1 : 2,500,000   Lambert Conformal Conic Projection

W-DRM6503-A1
Copyright © Rand McNally & Co.

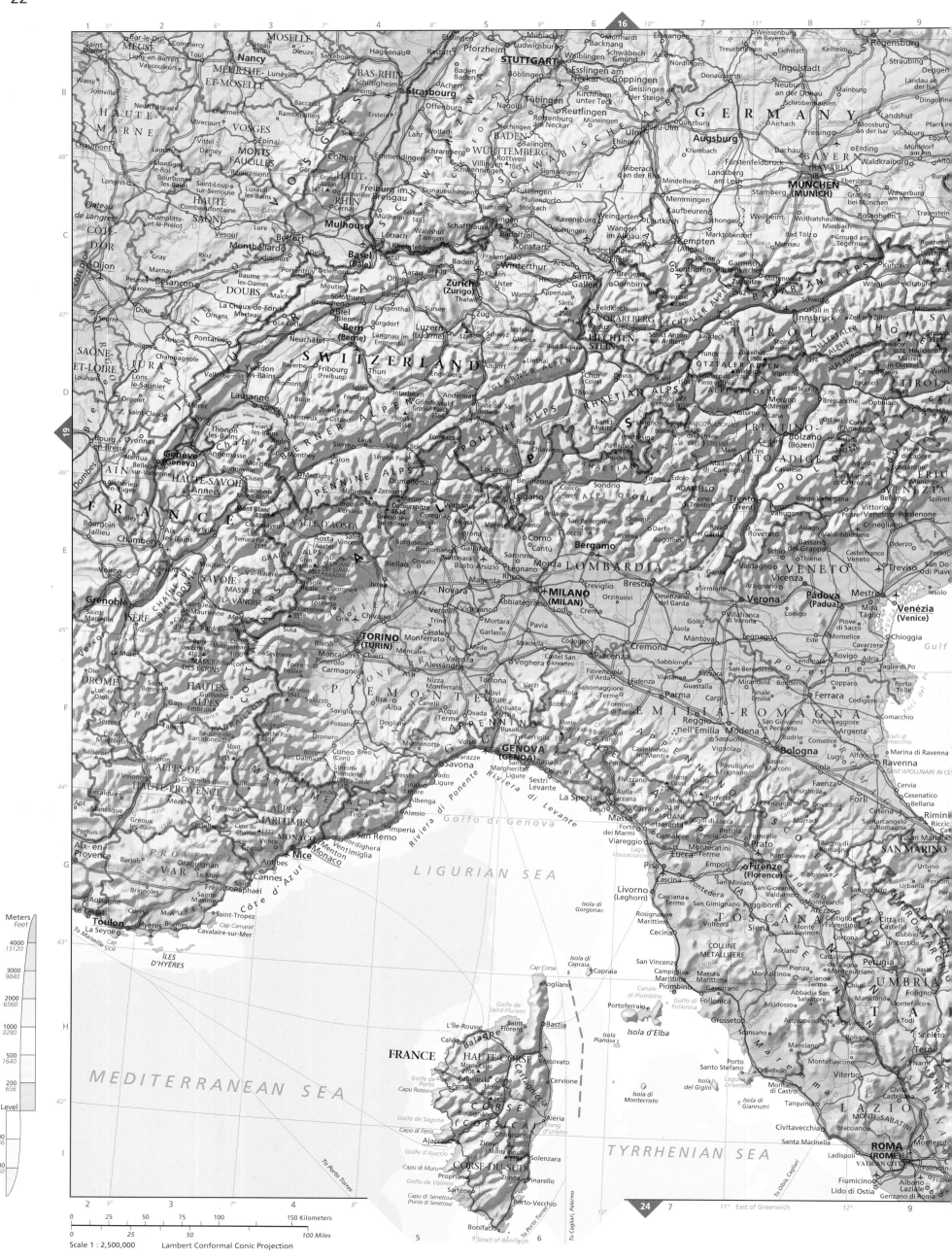

MEDITERRANEAN SEA

LIGURIAN SEA

TYRRHENIAN SEA

Meters / Feet
4000 / 13120
3000 / 9840
2000 / 6560
1000 / 3280
500 / 1640
200 / 656
Sea Level
200 / 656
2000 / 6560

0 25 50 75 100 150 Kilometers
0 25 50 100 Miles
Scale 1 : 2,500,000   Lambert Conformal Conic Projection

FRANCE

HAUTE-CORSE

CORSE (CORSICA)

CORSE-DU-SUD

ITALY

SARDEGNA (SARDINIA)

SARDEGNA

TOSCANA

UMBRIA

MARCHE

LAZIO

ROMA (ROME)

ABRUZZO

MOLISE

NAPOLI (NAPLES)

TYRRHENIAN SEA

ISOLE PONZIANE (PONTINE ISLANDS)

ISOLE EOLIE (ISOLE LIPARI)

MEDITERRANEAN

SICILIA

Palermo

ISOLE EGADI

TUNIS

ALGERIA

TUNISIA

MONTS DE TÉBOURSOUK

DORSALE

Isola di Pantelleria

ISOLE PELAGIE (Italy)

MALTA

Valletta

Meters / Feet

3000 / 9840
2000 / 6560
1000 / 3280
500 / 1640
200 / 656
Sea Level
200 / 656
2000 / 6560

0   25   50   75   100   150   200   250 Kilometers
0   25   50   100   150 Miles

Scale 1 : 2,500,000   Lambert Conformal Conic Projection

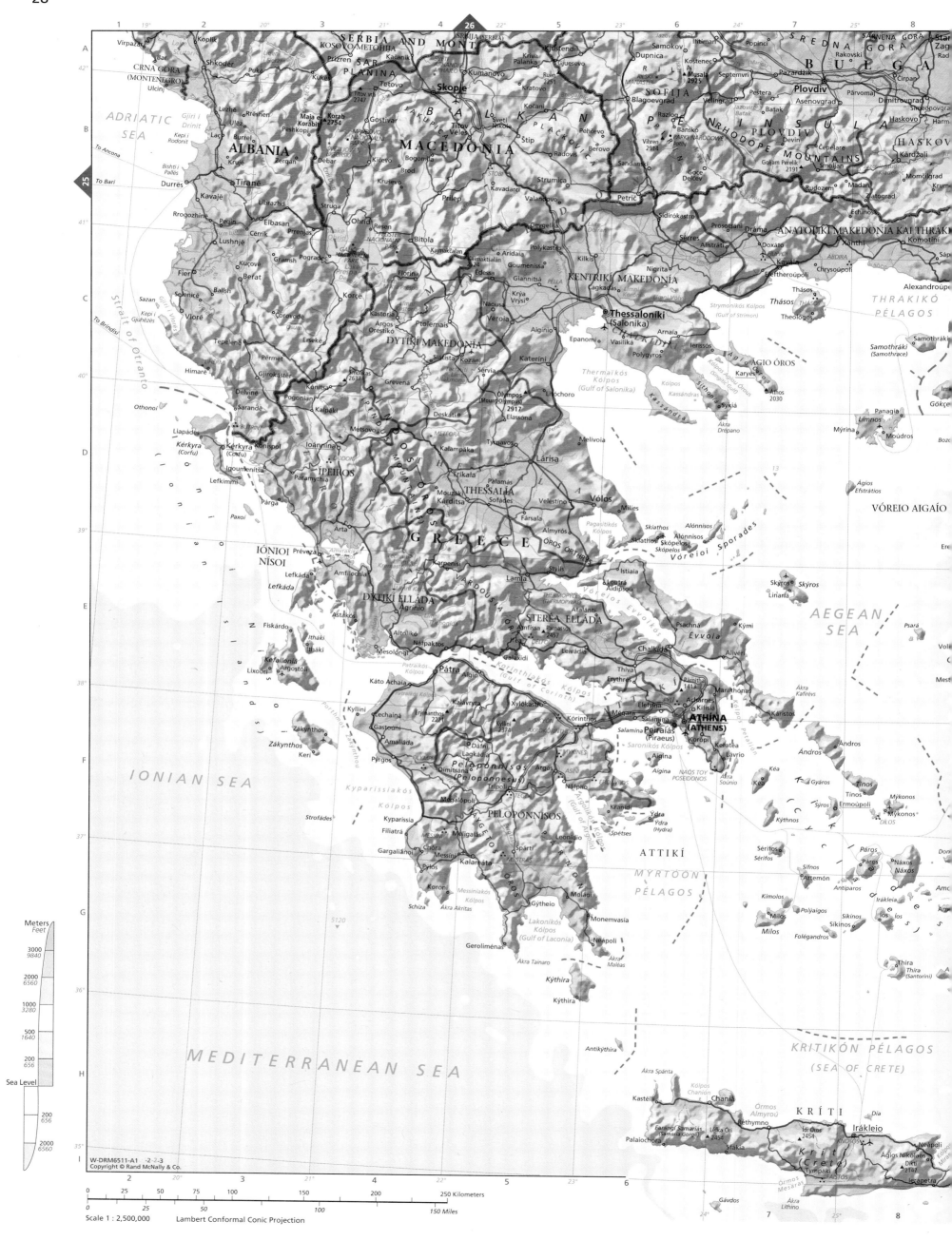

MEDITERRANEAN SEA

IONIAN SEA

ADRIATIC SEA

AEGEAN SEA

ALBANIA

MACEDONIA

GREECE

SERBIA AND MONT.

BULGARIA

PELOPONNISOS
(Peloponnesus)

Thessaloníki
(Salonika)

ATHÍNA
(ATHENS)

KRÍTI
(Crete)

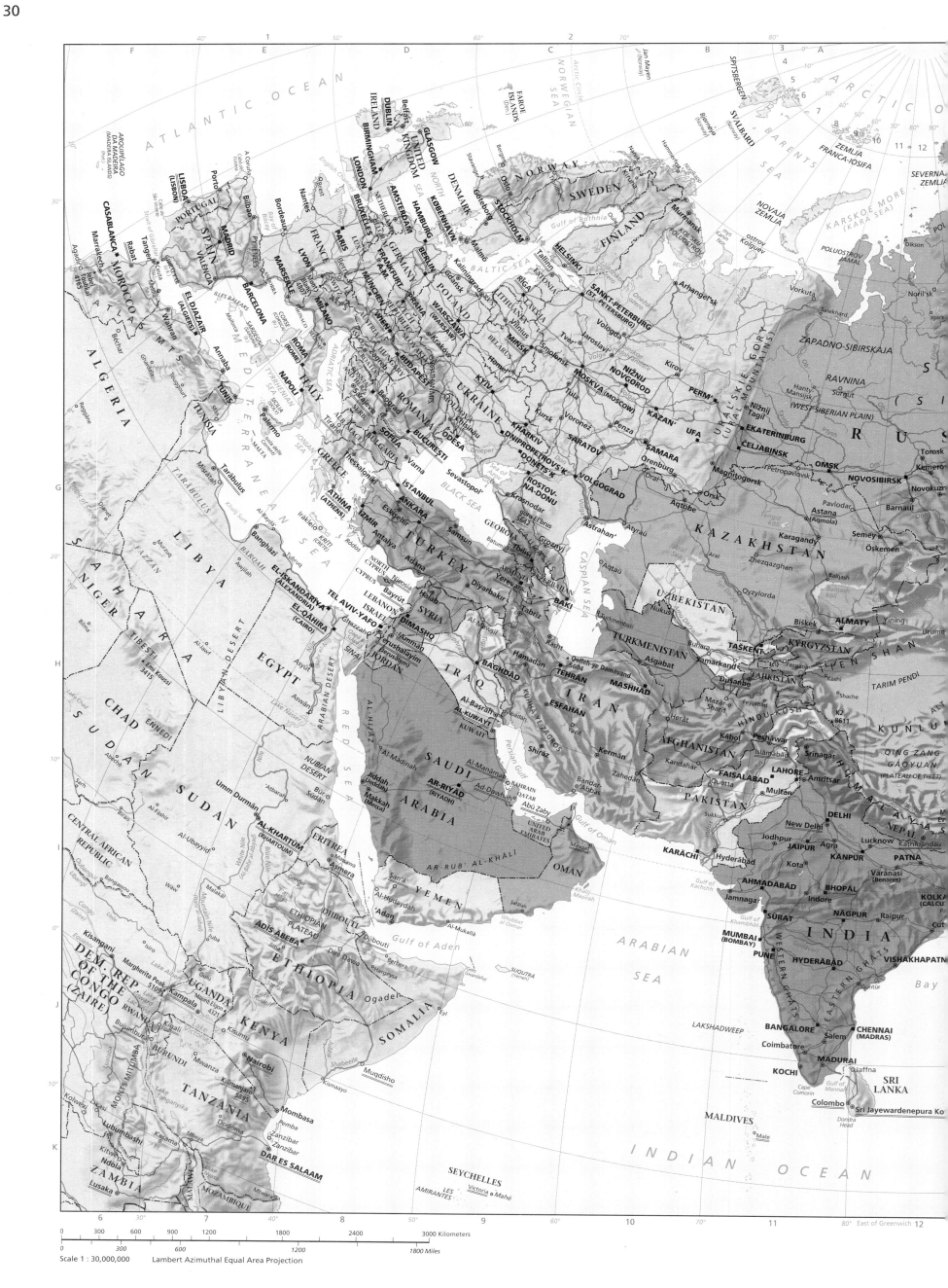

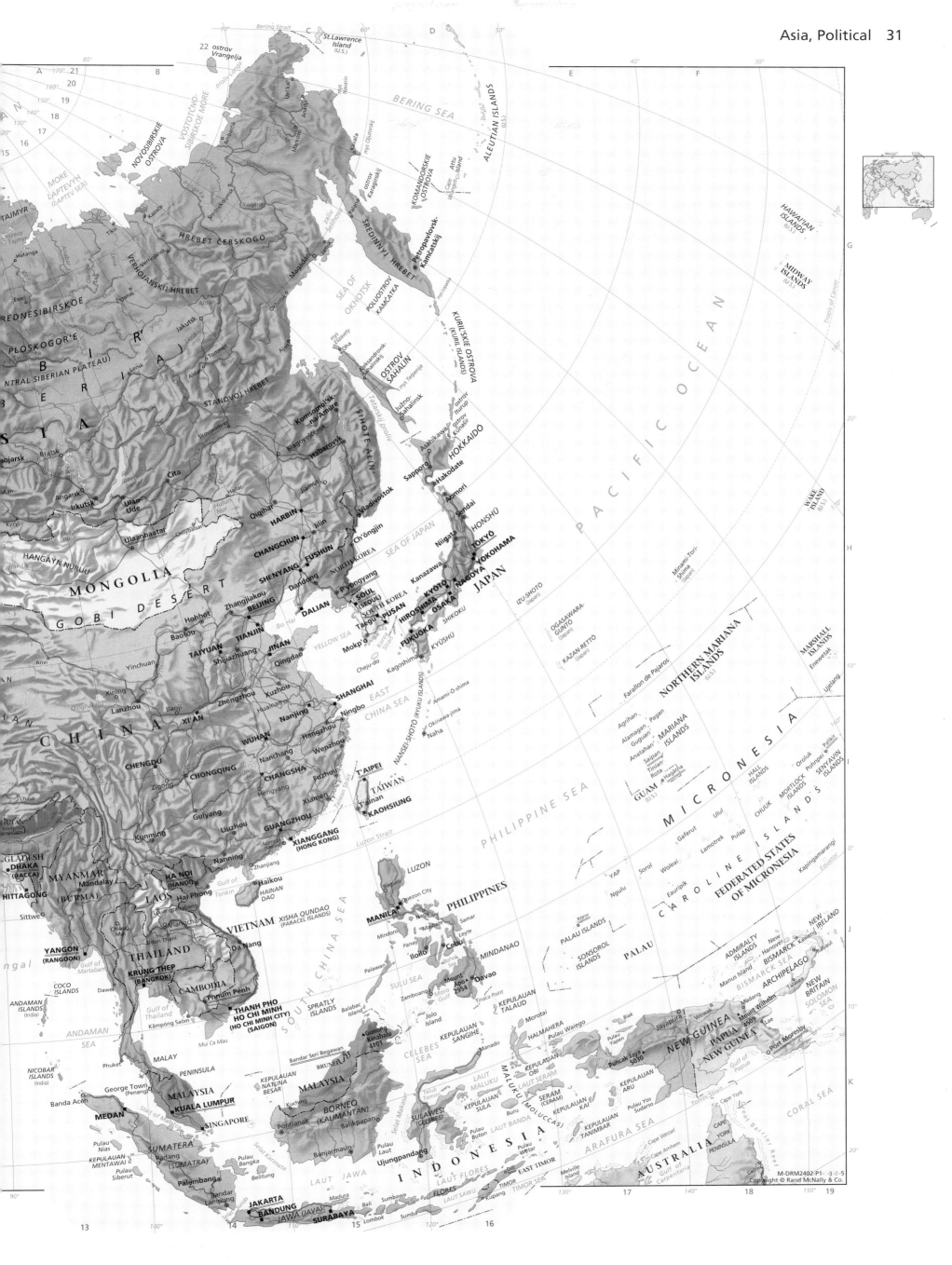

A 170° 21
80° 20
160° 19
150° 18
130° 17
16
15

22 ostrov
Vrangelja

C St.Lawrence
Island
(U.S.)

D

Bering Strait

BERING SEA

ALEUTIAN ISLANDS
(U.S.)

E

40°

30°

F

G

MORE
LAPTEVYH
(LAPTEV SEA)

TAJMYR

Tozero
Tajmyr

Hatanga

NOVOSIBIRSKIE
OSTROVA

VOSTOCNO-
SIBIRSKOE MORE

mys Olutorskij

ostrov
Karaginskij

KOMANDORSKIE
OSTROVA

Attu
Island

Attu

HAWAI'IAN
ISLANDS
(U.S.)

MIDWAY
ISLANDS
(U.S.)

REDNESIBIRSKOE
PLOSKOGOR'E

NTRAL SIBERIAN PLATEAU)

HREBET CERSKOGO

VERHOJANSKIJ HREBET

SREDINNYJ HREBET

Petropavlovsk-
Kamčatskij

SEA OF
OKHOTSK

POLUOSTROV
KAMČATKA

PACIFIC OCEAN

Angara

ojarsk

Bratsk

Angarsk

Irkutsk

Kyzyl

Ulan-
Ude

Ulaanbaatar

Cita

STANOVOJ HREBET

Blagoveščensk

Komsomol'sk-
na-Amure

Habarovsk

OSTROV
SAHALIN

mys Terpenija

ostrov
Iturup

ostrov
Kunašir

KURIL'SKIE OSTROVA
(KURIL ISLANDS)

Tatarskij proliv

zaliv
Seliihova

Magadan

HANGAYN NURUU

MONGOLIA

GOBI DESERT

Hohhot

Zhangjiakou

BEIJING

Baotou

Jiamusi

Jilin

HARBIN

CHANGCHUN

SHENYANG
FUSHUN

Dandong

Pyongyang

NORTH KOREA

SOUL
(SEOUL)

DALIAN

Bo Hai

Vladivostok

Ch'ŏngjin

SEA OF JAPAN

SIHOTE-ALIN'

Asahikawa

Sapporo

HOKKAIDO

Hakodate

Aomori

Sendai

Niigata

HONSHŪ

Kanazawa

PUSAN

SOUTH KOREA

Taegu

KYOTO

HIROSHIMA OSAKA

FUKUOKA

TOKYO
YOKOHAMA

NAGOYA

JAPAN

IZU-SHOTO
(Japan)

Minami-Tori-
Shima
(Japan)

WAKE
ISLAND
(U.S.)

TAIYUAN

Yinchuan

Shijiazhuang

JINAN

Qingdao

YELLOW SEA

Mokpo

SHIKOKU

KYŪSHŪ

Cheju-do

Kagoshima

OGASAWARA-
GUNTO
(Japan)

KAZAN-RETTO
(Japan)

NORTHERN MARIANA
ISLANDS
(U.S.)

MARSHALL
ISLANDS

Enewetak

Ujelang

Xining

Lanzhou

Baoji

Zhengzhou

Xuzhou

Huainan

SHANGHAI

Ningbo

EAST
CHINA SEA

Amami-Ō-shima

NANSEI-SHOTO (RYUKYU ISLANDS)

Okinawa-jima

Naha

Farallon de Pajaros

Agrihan

Alamagan Pagan

Guguan

Anatahan MARIANA
Saipan ISLANDS

Tinian
Rota

MICRONESIA

CHINA

XI'AN

WUHAN

Nanjing

Hangzhou

Nanchang

CHENGDU

CHONGQING

CHANGSHA

Wenzhou

T'AIPEI

TAIWAN

Tainan

KAOHSIUNG

Hengyang

PHILIPPINE SEA

Gaferut

Faraulep

Lamotrek

Pulap

CHUUK

Oroluk

Pohnpei

HALL
ISLANDS

MORTLOCK
ISLANDS

PALIKIR

SENYAVIN
ISLANDS

Zigong

Guiyang

Xiamen

GUAM
(U.S.)

Hagåtña

Guilin

Liuzhou

GUANGZHOU

XIANGGANG
(HONG KONG)

YAP

Ngulu

Sorol

Woleai

Eauripik

Ifalik

CAROLINE ISLANDS

FEDERATED STATES
OF MICRONESIA

Kapingamarangi

Equator

Kunming

Nanning

Zhanjiang

LUZON

Baguio

GLADESH

DHAKA
(DACCA)

HITTAGONG

MYANMAR

Mandalay

(BURMA)

Sittwe

HA NOI
(HANOI)

LAOS

Hai Phong

Haikou

HAINAN
DAO

Gulf of
Tonkin

XISHA QUNDAO
(PARACEL ISLANDS)

SOUTH CHINA SEA

Quezon City

MANILA

PHILIPPINES

Naga

Samar

PALAU ISLANDS

Koror

PALAU

SONSOROL
ISLANDS

ADMIRALTY
ISLANDS

NEW
HANOVER

NEW
IRELAND

Kavieng

Manus Island

New

BISMARCK

Rabaul

BISMARCK SEA

ARCHIPELAGO

NEW
BRITAIN

VIETNAM

Da Nang

Mindoro

Panay

Iloilo

Cebu

Leyte

MINDANAO

YANGON
(RANGOON)

THAILAND

COCO
ISLANDS

KRUNG THEP
(BANGKOK)

CAMBODIA

Phnum Penh

THANH PHO
HO CHI MINH
(HO CHI MINH CITY)
(SAIGON)

SPRATLY
ISLANDS

Palawan

Zamboanga

Jolo
Island

Moro
Gulf

Davao

Mount
Apo
2954

Tinaca Point

KEPULAUAN
TALAUD

Morotai

SOLOMON
SEA

ANDAMAN
ISLANDS
(India)

Dawei

Gulf of
Martaban

Kâmpóng Saôm

Balabac
Island

SULU SEA

Gunung
Kinabalu
4101

Bandar Seri Begawan

BRUNEI

CELEBES
SEA

Manado

KEPULAUAN
SANGIHE

HALMAHERA

Pulau Waigeo

KEPULAUAN
OBI

LAUT
MALUKU

LAUT SERAM

Biak

Pulau
Yapen

Jayapura

Wewak

Madang

Mount Wilhelm
4509

NEW GUINEA

PAPUA
NEW GUINEA

Lae

Port Moresby

Gulf of
Papua

Mui Ca Mau

MALAY

PENINSULA

Phuket

KEPULAUAN
NATUNA
BESAR

MALAYSIA

Kuching

SULAWESI
(CELEBES)

Teluk
Tomini

KEPULAUAN
SULA

Buru

SERAM
(CERAM)

KEPULAUAN
KAI

Pulau Yos
Sudarso

Puncak Jaya
5030

NICOBAR
ISLANDS
(India)

George Town
(Penang)

Banda Aceh

MEDAN

MALAYSIA

KUALA LUMPUR

SINGAPORE

Pontianak

BORNEO
(KALIMANTAN)

Balikpapan

Selat Makassar

MALUKU (MOLUCCAS)

LAUT BANDA

Pulau
Buton

KEPULAUAN
ARU

Cape Wessel

Cape York

Cape Arnhem

YORK
PENINSULA

Great Barrier Reef

CORAL SEA

ANDAMAN
SEA

Pulau Nias

KEPULAUAN
MENTAWAI

Padang

Pulau
Siberut

SUMATERA
(SUMATRA)

Pulau
Bangka

Pulau
Laut

Banjarmasin

Ujungpandang

Pulau
Wetar

Melville
Island

Gulf of
Carpentaria

AUSTRALIA

Palembang

Bandar
Lampung

Belitung

LAUT JAWA

Madura

Bali

Lombok

Sumbawa

Sumba

FLORES

East Timor

TIMOR SEA

ARAFURA SEA

JAKARTA

BANDUNG

JAWA (JAVA)

SURABAYA

INDONESIA

LAUT FLORES

LAUT SAWU

Kupang

13

14

15

16

17

18

19

M-DRM2402-P1- -3-3-5
Copyright © Rand McNally & Co.

POLUOSTROV JAMAL

Obskaja guba
Tazovskij poluostrov

Novyj Port
Nahodka
Nyda
Nori
Jar-Sale
Nadym

Tarko-Sale
Numto
Samburg
Sidorovsk
Urengoj
Krasnosel'kup

Igarka
Serkovo
Turuhansk
Farkovo
Kostino

Arctic Circle

SREDNESIBIRSKOE PLOSKOGOR'E
(CENTRAL SIBERIAN PLATEAU)

Tura

Jukta
Nakanno
Inarigda

CENTRALNO-
TUNGUSSKOE PLATO

S I B I R '   (S I B E R I A)

Z A P A D N O -

Haljasavėj
Harampur
Tol'ka
Ratta

Verhneimbatsk
Kellog
Bahta

Podkamennaja Tunguska

Poligus
Balkit
Kujumba

S I B I R S K A J A

Surgut
Hanty-Mansijsk
Megion
Neftejugansk
Nižnevartovsk
Aleksandrovskoe
Larjak
Nazina
Altaj

Kargasok
Berëzovka
Kljukvenka
Maksimkin Jar
Losinoborskaja

Ust'-Ozërnoe
Ždanova
Eniseisk
Lesosibirsk
Novoenisejsk

A
R A V N I N A
(WEST SIBERIAN PLAIN)

Krasnojarsk

Tomsk
Kemerovo
NOVOSIBIRSK
Novokuzneck

Abakan
Minusinsk

VOSTOČNYJ SAJAN

Bratsk
Irkutsk
Angarsk
BURJATIJA

SAYAN MOUNTAINS

HAKASIA
ZAPADNYJ SAJAN
T U V A
TANNU-OLA
HREBET SANGILEN

OMSK

Step'

Barabinskaja

Kulundinskaja
ravnina

Pavlodar

Barnaul

Gorno-Altajsk

A L T A J

MONGOLIA
HANGAYN NURUU

Astana
(Aqmola)
Semey
(Semipalatinsk)
Öskemen

Mount Belukha
4374

Mount Kujtun
4374

M O N G O L   A L T A Y N   N U R U U

Karagandy
(Karaganda)

QAZAQTYNG
USAQSHOQYLYGHY
(KAZAKH HILLS)

KHREBET TARBAGATAJ

JUNGGAR PENDI

BOGDA SHAN

Balqash köli
(Lake Balkhash)

DZHUNGARIAN ALATAU MTS.

BOROHORO SHAN

Ürümqi
Turpan
Turpan Pendi
(Turfan Depression)

MOYYNQUM QUMY

ALMATY

Biškek

Pik Pobedy
7439

KURUKTAG

Lop Nur

GANSU

Taraz (Žambyl)
Shymkent

KIRGIZ RANGE
HREBET TERSKEJ-ALATAU

T   I   E   N   S   H   A   N

XINJIANG

C   H   I   N   A

ALTUN SHAN

QAIDAM PENDI

TAŠKENT

KYRGYZSTAN

TARIM PENDI

Tarim

Taklimakan Shamo
(Takla Makan Desert)

QINGHAI

TAJIKISTAN

pik Ismail Samani
7495

P A M I R

KUNLUN SHAN

AFG

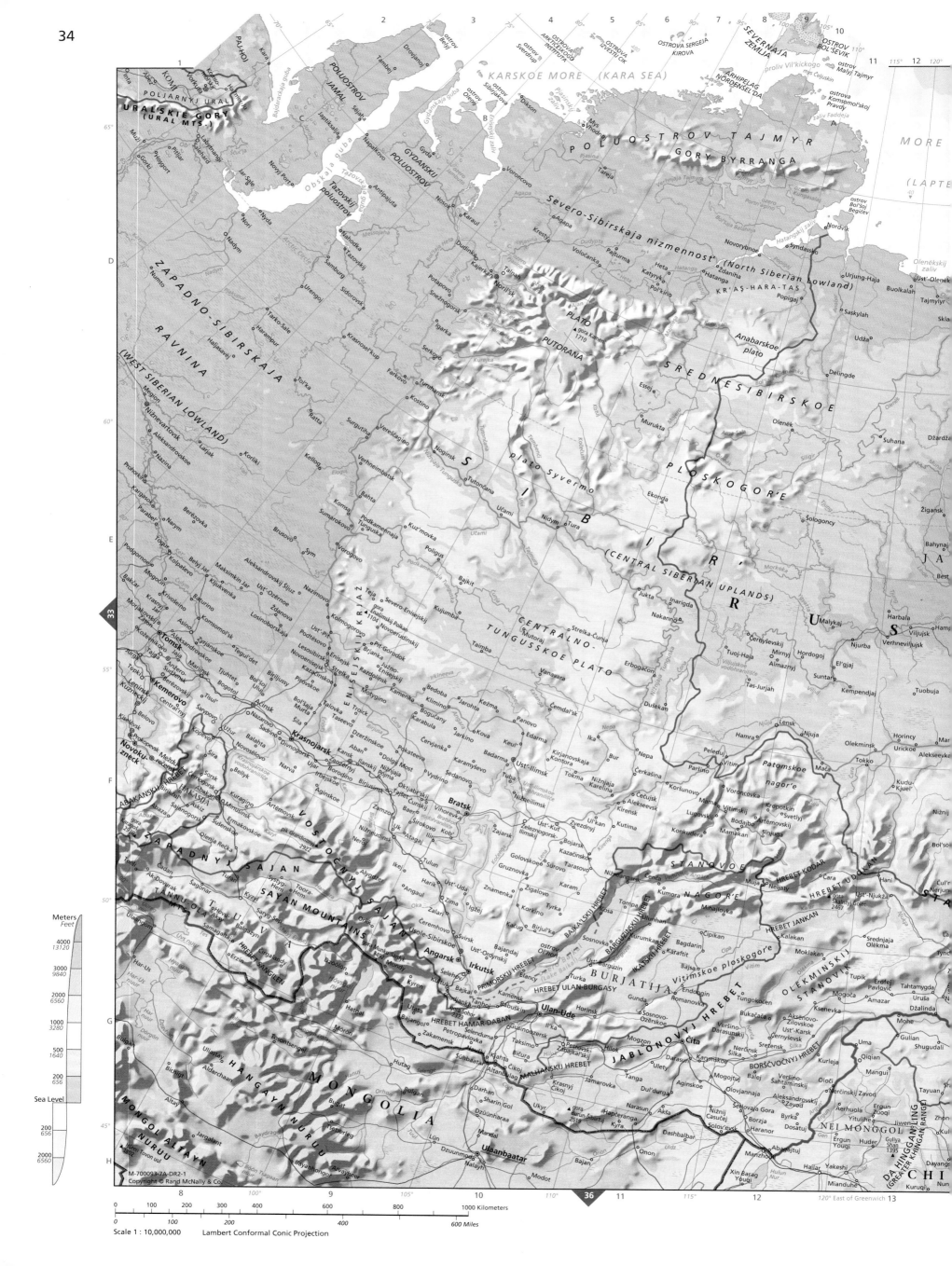

NOVOSIBIRSKIE
OSTROVA
OSTROVA
ANŽU

ostrov
Genrietty
OSTROVA DE-LONGA
ostrov
Žannetty
ostrov
Bennetta
ostrov
Žohova

OSTROV
KOTEL'NYJ

ostrov
Bel'kovskij

ostrov
Vil'kickogo

OSTROV
FADDEEVSKIJ

LJAHOVSKIJE
OSTROV

OSTROV
NOVAJA SIBIR'

OSTROV BOL'ŠOJ
LJAHOVSKIJ

ostrov
Stolbovoj

proliv Sannikova

LJAHOVSKIJE OSTROVA

proliv Dmitrija Lapteva

mys
Svjatoj Nos

VOSTOČNO-SIBIRSKOE MORE
(EAST SIBERIAN SEA)

OSTROV VRANGELJA
(WRANGEL ISLAND)

proliv Longa

CHUKCHI
SEA

ČUKOTSKIJ
POLUOSTROV
(CHUKOTSK PEN.)

U.S.
ALASKA

Bering Strait
proliv Beringa
Cape Prince
of Wales

Teller

Arctic Circle

ČUKOTSKOE

MEDVEŽJI
OSTROVA

ostrov
Aen

Ambarčik

Tabor

Logašino

Pohodsk

Kolymskaja

Čerskij

Anjujsk

Malyj Anjuj

Bol'šoj Anjuj

Malyj Anjuj

ANJUJSKIJ HREBET

ANADYRSKOE
PLOSKOGOR'E

HREBET PEKUL'NEJ

Anadyrskij liman

Anadyrskij
zaliv
(Gulf of Anadyr)

BERING
SEA

KORJAKSKOE NAGOR'E

PENŽINSKIJ HREBET

KOMANDORSKIE
OSTROVA

SREDINNYJ HREBET

KAMČATSKIJ
POLUOSTROV

VOSTOČNYJ HREBET

POLUOSTROV
KAMČATKA

Petropavlovsk-
Kamčatskij

SEA OF OKHOTSK

OSTROV SAHALIN
(SAKHALIN)

KURIL'SKIE OSTROVA (KURIL ISLANDS)

ŠANTARSKIE
OSTROVA

POLUOSTROV
SMIDTA

HREBET DŽAGDY

ZAPADNYJ HREBET

SIHOTE ALIN'

Komsomol'sk-
na-Amure

Habarovsk

Jano-Indigirskaja nizmennost'

Kolymskaja nizmennost'
(Kolyma Plain)

Jukagirskoe
ploskogor'e

VERHOJANSKIJ HREBET
(VERHOYANSK MOUNTAINS)

HREBET ČERSKOGO
(CHERSKIJ MOUNTAINS)

MOMSKIJ HREBET

gora Pobeda
3147

HREBET SUNTAR-HAJATA

gora Mus-Haja
2959

HREBET SETTE-DABAN

HREBET DŽUGDŽUR

Jakutsk

OSTROV SAHALIN

Južno-Sahalinsk

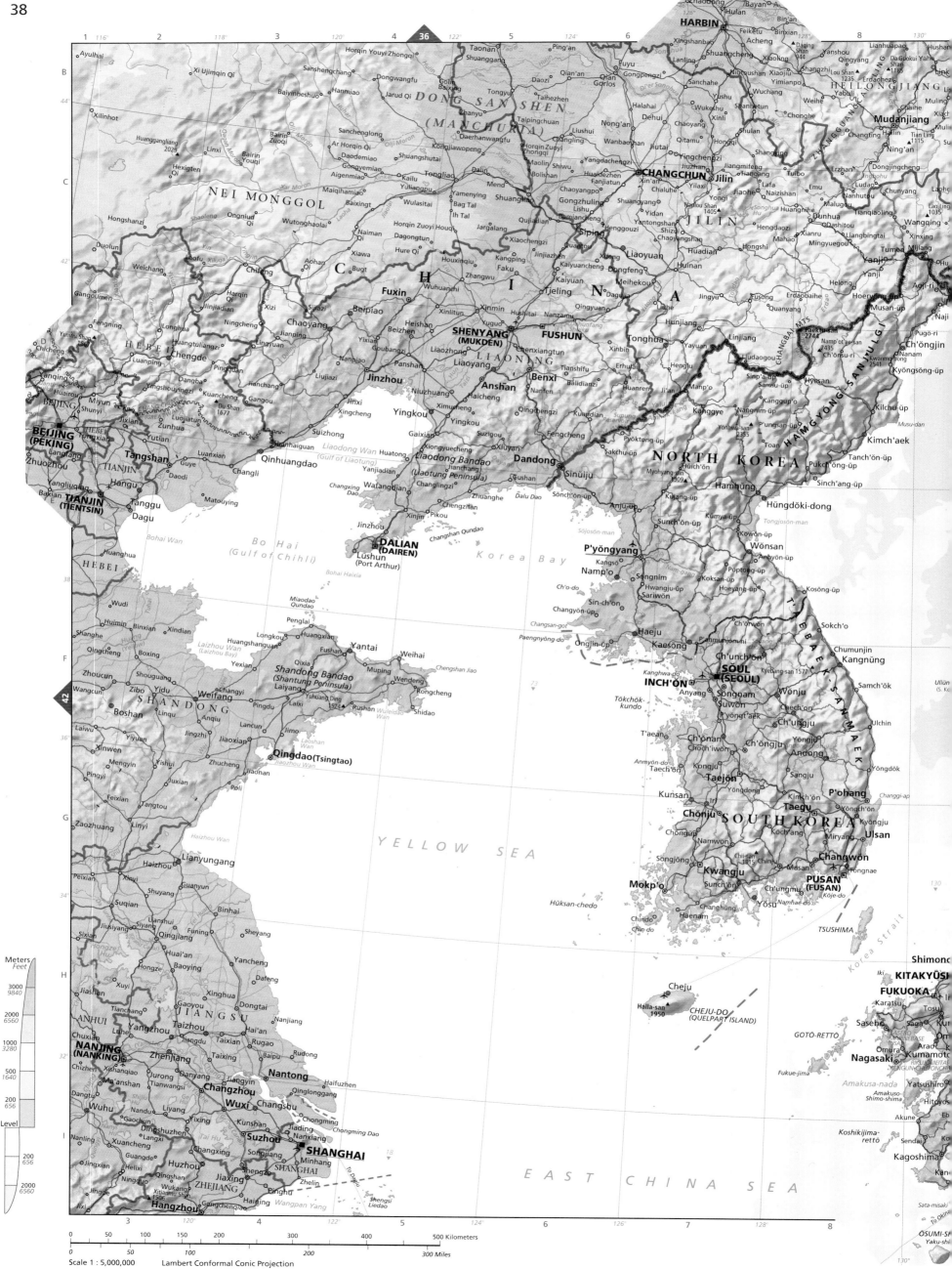

36

42

HARBIN

HEILONGJIANG

Mudanjiang

CHANGCHUN Jilin

JILIN

NEI MONGGOL

C H I N A

Fuxin

Chaoyang

Beipiao

**SHENYANG
(MUKDEN)** **FUSHUN**

Liaoyang

HEBEI

Chengde

Jinzhou

Anshan Benxi

Yingkou

NORTH KOREA

Dandong

**BEIJING
(PEKING)**

Tangshan

Qinhuangdao

Liaodong Wan
(Gulf of Liaotung)

Liaotung Peninsula

P'yŏngyang

Hamhŭng

**TIANJIN
(TIENTSIN)**

**DALIAN
(DAIREN)**
Lüshun
(Port Arthur)

Bo Hai
(Gulf of Chihli)

Korea Bay

Namp'o

Wŏnsan

HEBEI

Penglai

Yantai
Weihai

Shandong Bandao
(Shantung Peninsula)

SHANDONG

Weifang

Haeju

Kaesŏng

**SŎUL
(SEOUL)**
INCH'ŎN

T'AEBAEK SANMAEK

Kangnŭng

Wŏnju

Qingdao(Tsingtao)

Taejŏn

SOUTH KOREA

Taegu
Chŏnju

P'ohang

YELLOW SEA

Lianyungang

Kwangju

**PUSAN
(FUSAN)**

Mŏkp'o

TSUSHIMA

Korea Strait

ANHUI

**NANJING
(NANKING)**

JIANGSU

Nantong

Cheju
Halla-san
1950

CHEJU-DO
(QUELPART ISLAND)

KITAKYŪSHI

FUKUOKA

Nagasaki

Changzhou
Wuxi

Suzhou

SHANGHAI

ZHEJIANG

Hangzhou

EAST CHINA SEA

Meters
Feet

3000
9840

2000
6560

1000
3280

500
1640

200
656

Sea Level

200
656

2000
6560

0   50   100   150   200   300   400   500 Kilometers

0   50   100   200   300 Miles

Scale 1 : 5,000,000   Lambert Conformal Conic Projection

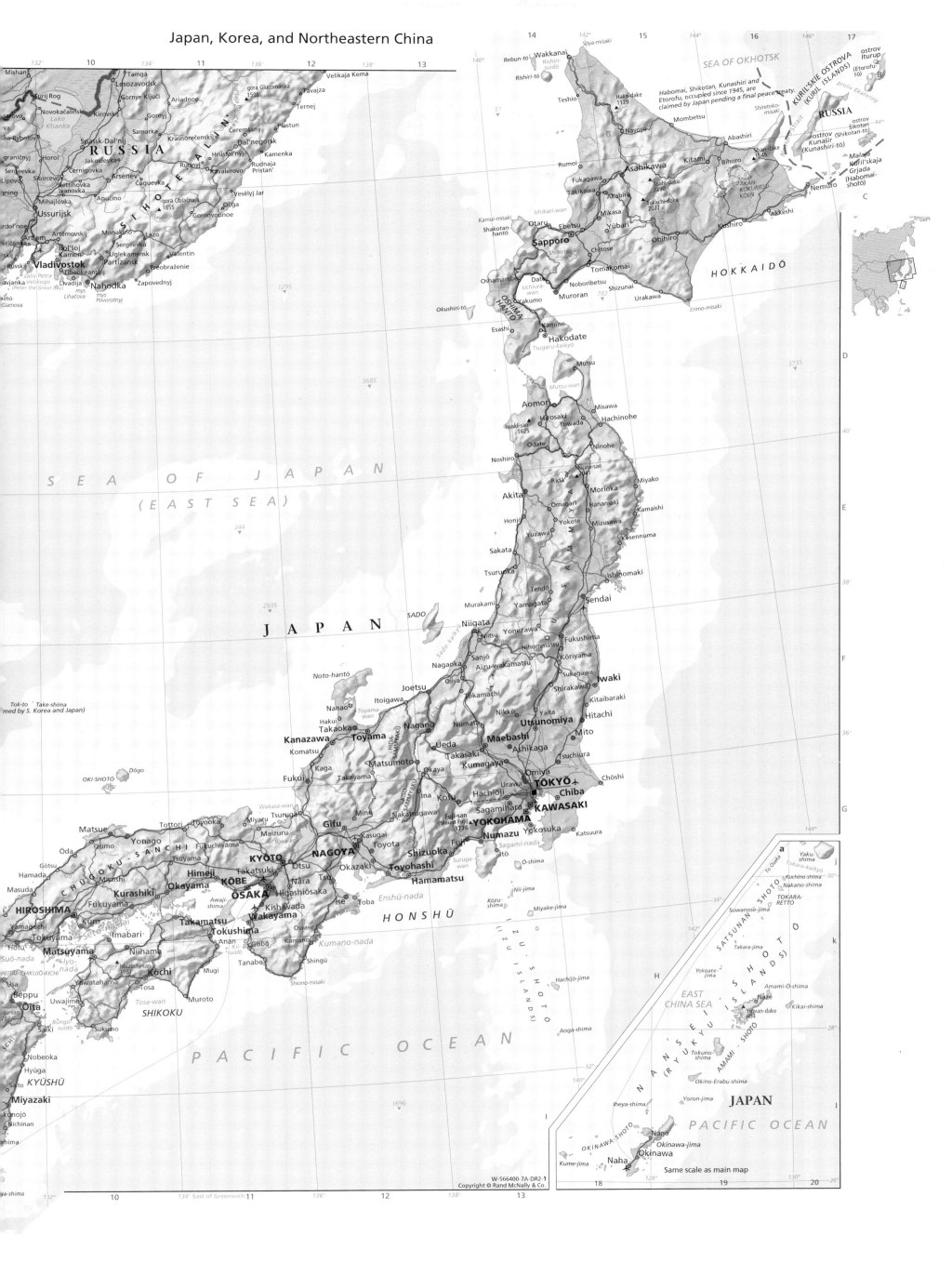

Japan, Korea, and Northeastern China

SEA OF JAPAN

(EAST SEA)

JAPAN

NORTH KOREA

SOUTH KOREA

TSUSHIMA

Korea Strait

Western Channel

Tsushima-kaikyō (Eastern Channel)

EAST CHINA SEA

KYŪSHŪ

SHIKOKU

OKI-SHOTŌ

Tok-to ° Take-shima
(Claimed by S. Korea and Japan)

GOTŌ-RETTŌ

Danjo-guntō

Uji-guntō

Koshikijima-rettō

Amakusa-nada

To Okinawa

KIRISHIMA-YAKU-KOKURITSU-KŌEN

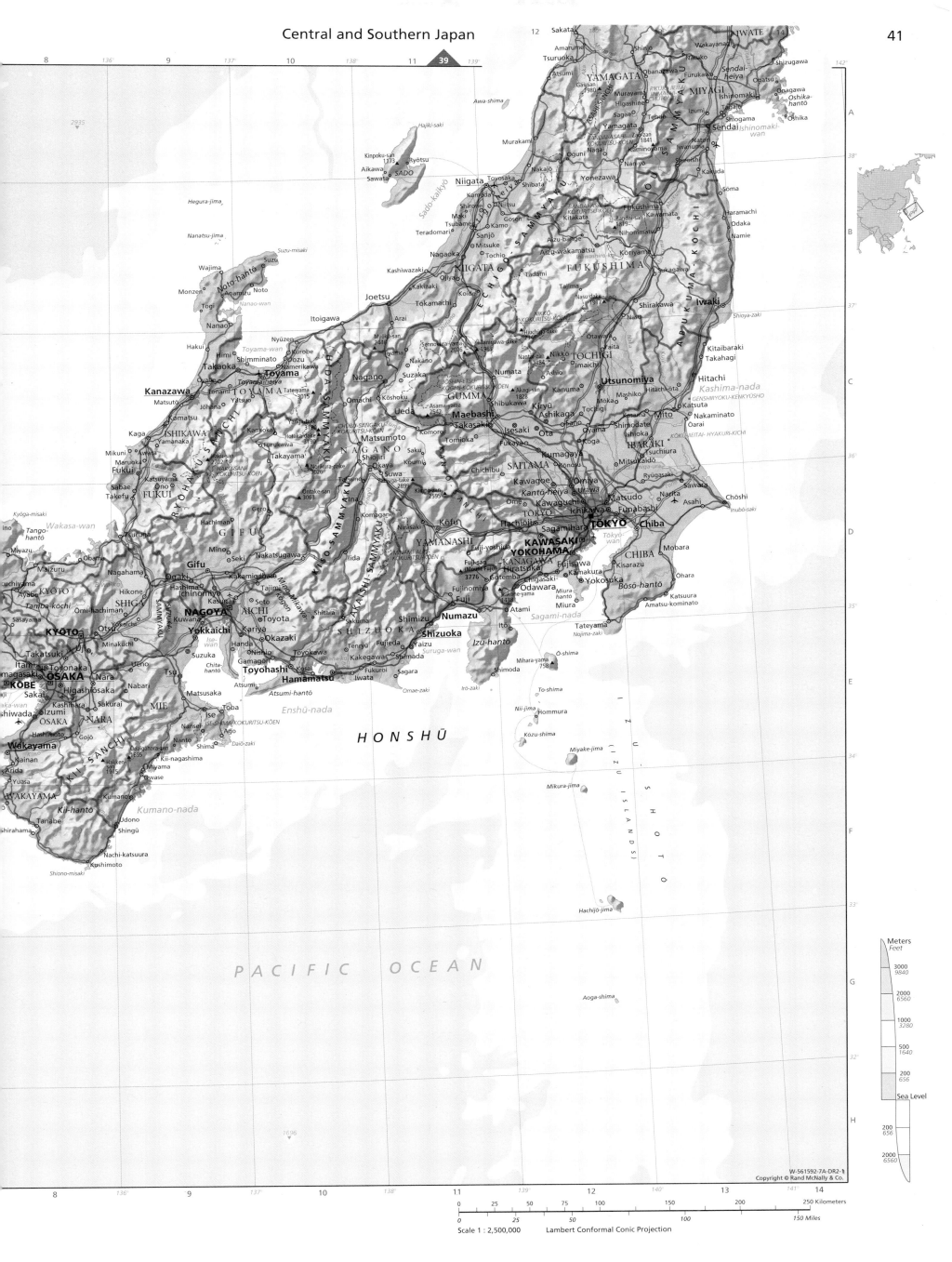

HONSHŪ

PACIFIC OCEAN

Sakata

Tsuruoka

YAMAGATA

MIYAGI

Sendai

Ishinomaki-wan

Niigata

SADO

NIIGATA

FUKUSHIMA

Iwaki

Kashima-nada

Joetsu

TOCHIGI

Utsunomiya

Hitachi

IBARAKI

Mito

Kanazawa

Toyama

GUMMA

Maebashi
Takasaki

SAITAMA

Kawagoe
Omiya

Narita

Chōshi

ISHIKAWA

NAGANO

Matsumoto

TŌKYŌ

KAWASAKI
YOKOHAMA

KANAGAWA

CHIBA

Bōsō-hantō

Fukui

FUKUI

GIFU

YAMANASHI

Fuji-yoshida

Odawara

Yokosuka

Gifu

Mino

AICHI

Fuji
Numazu

Izu-hantō

Sagami-nada

KYŌTO

SHIGA

NAGOYA

Yokkaichi

SHIZUOKA
Shizuoka

Ō-shima

IZU ISLANDS

KYŌTO

OSAKA

NARA

MIE

Hamamatsu

Enshū-nada

To-shima

Nii-jima

KŌBE

WAKAYAMA

Kii-hantō

Kumano-nada

Miyake-jima

Mikura-jima

Hachijō-jima

Aoga-shima

W-561592-7A-DR2-1
Copyright © Rand McNally & Co.

Meters
Feet

3000
9840

2000
6560

1000
3280

500
1640

200
656

Sea Level

200
656

2000
6560

0 25 50 75 100   150   200   250 Kilometers

0   25   50   100   150 Miles

Scale 1 : 2,500,000   Lambert Conformal Conic Projection

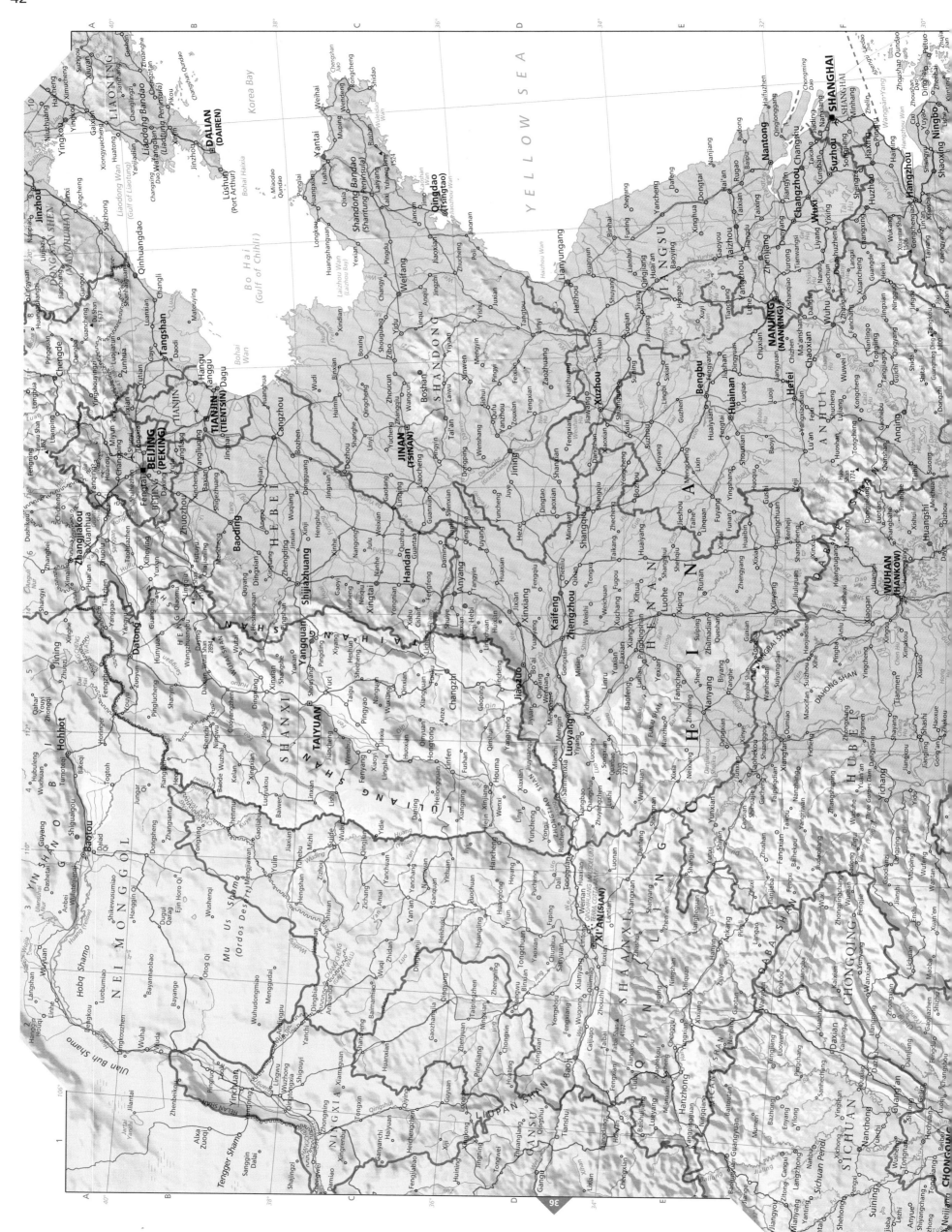

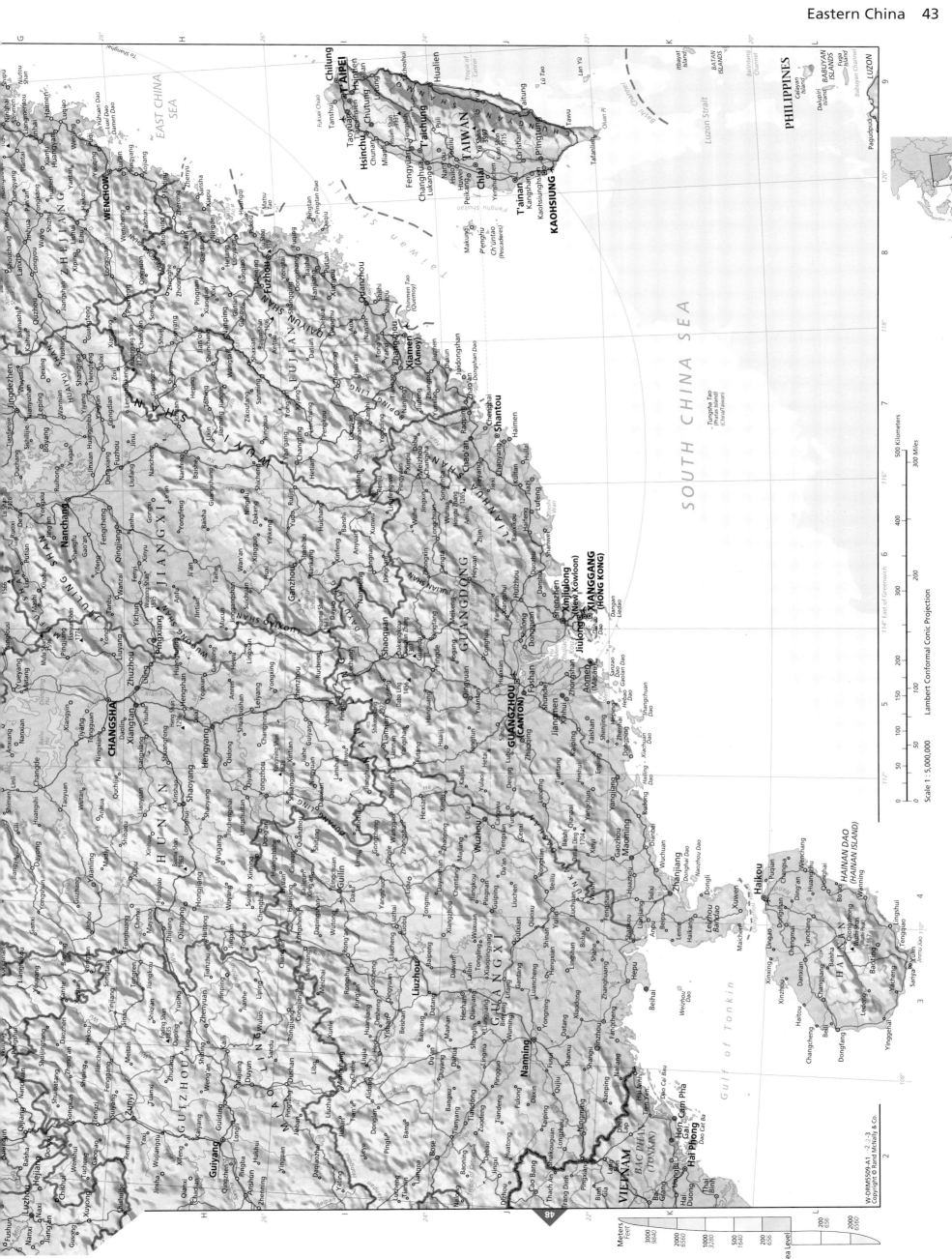

47 1 95° 2 3 Mong Hsat 4 Gulf of Tonkin 5 A 36 6

HA NOI
Hai Phong
Thai Binh
Nam Dinh
Ninh Binh
Thanh Hoa
Sam Son

CHINA
Xuwen Leizhou Bandao
Lingang
Qiongzhou Haixia
Haikou Wenchang
Changjiang Chengmai
Danxian
Dongfang Wuzhi Shan 1867 Baoting
Sanya Lingshui
HAINAN DAO
(HAINAN ISLAND)

PEGU YOMA
Allanmyo
Thayetmyo
Prome
Paungde
Sandoway
Kyeintali
Gwa
Kyaunggon
Pathein
Myaungmya
Bogale
Wakema
Pyapon
Mouths of the Ayeyarwady

Pyinmana
Loi-kaw
Ela
Toungoo
Oktwin
Nattalin
Pyu
Kyaukkyi
Papun
Thandaung
Nyaunglebin
Tharrawaddy
Thonze
Bago
YANGON (RANGOON)
Syriam
Thongwa
Thaton
Pha-an
Mawlamyine
Gulf of Martaban
Myittar
Dawei
Myinmoletkat Taung 2075
Palaw
Kadan Kyun
Tenasserim
Daung Kyun
MERGUI
Bentinck Island
Letsôk-aw Kyun
Kanmaw Kyun
ARCHIPELAGO
Lanbi Kyun
Mergui

MYANMAR (BURMA)

Chiang Rai
Hsipaw
Hsuphang
Mae Hong Son
Doi Inthanon 2600
Chiang Mai
Lamphun
Phayao
Nan
Lampang
Thoen
Uttaradit
Sukhothai
Sawankhalok
Phitsanulok
Phichit
Kamphaeng Phet
Tak
Nakhon Sawan
Taphan Hin
Chum Saeng
Chai Nat
Uthai Thani
Nakhon Ratchasima
Chaiyaphum
Bua Yai
Nakhon Chedi
Phra Nakhon Si Ayutthaya
Suphan Buri
Lop Buri
Saraburi
Nakhon Pathom
KRUNG THEP (BANGKOK)
Samut Prakan
Samut Songkhram
Chon Buri
Si Racha
Phetchaburi
Cha-am
Hua Hin
Prachuap Khiri Khan
Chumphon
Ranong
Ko Tao
Ko Phangan
Ko Samui
Surat Thani
Nakhon Si Thammarat
Pak Phanang
Trang
Kantang
Ko Phuket
Phuket
Phangnga
Phatthalung
Songkhla
Hat Yai
Yala
Narathiwat
Pattani
Alor Setar
Sungai Petani
Kangar
Pulau Langkawi

THAILAND
Maha Sarakham
Kalasin
Roi Et
Surin
Ubon
Ratchathani
Si Sa Ket
Buri Ram
Chaturat
Khon Kaen
Nakhon Phanom
Udon Thani
Sakon Nakhon
Nong Khai

LAOS
Louangphrabang
Viangchan (Vientiane)
Ban Nahin
Muang Pakxan
Muang Khammouan
Savannakhét
Muang Phalan
Muang Xépôn
Saravan
Pakxe
Champasak
Attapu

VIETNAM
Vinh
Ha Tinh
Cam Lo
Hue
Da Nang
Hoi An
Tam Ky
Quang Ngai
Sa Huynh
Tam Quan
An Nhon
Quy Nhon
Song Cau
Tuy Hoa
Nha Trang
Cam Ranh
Phan Rang
Phan Thiet
Da Lat
Di Linh
Bao Loc
Buon Ma Thuot
Play Ku
Kon Tum
Virochey

INDOCHINA

CAMBODIA
Phumĭ Kântuŏt
Sâmrâong
Bătdâmbâng
Poŭthĭsăt
Krâkôr
Kâmpóng Thum
Kâmpóng Cham
Phnum Aôral 1813
Phnum Pénh (Phnom Penh)
Kâmpóng Chhnăng
Kâmpóng Spœ
Tăkêv
Kâmpôt
Svay Riêng
Kracheh
Stœ̆ng Trêng
Lumphăt
Loc Ninh
Tay Ninh
Tan An
My Tho
Bien Hoa
THANH PHO HO CHI MINH (HO CHI MINH CITY) (SAIGON)
Long Xuyen
Rach Gia
Can Tho
Vinh Long
Tra Vinh
Soc Trang
Bac Lieu
Ca Mau
Mui Ca Mau

SOUTH CHINA SEA

XISHA QUNDAO (PARACEL ISLANDS) (Claimed by China, Taiwan and Vietnam)

Nanshan Island

SPRATLY ISLANDS (Claimed by Brunei, China, Malaysia, Philippines, Taiwan and Vietnam)

Con Son
Hon Khoai
Dao Phu Quoc
Quan Dao Nam Du
Îles Catwick

Andaman Sea
Isthmus of Kra

Gulf of Thailand
Ko Chang
Ko Kut
Krŏng Kaôh Kong
Phumĭ Kaôh Kong
Phumĭ Chămbâk
Phnum
Kaôh Rŭng

Strait of Malacca
Pulau We
Banda Aceh
Lhokseumawe
Gunung Abongabong 2985
Meulaboh
Blangpidie
Tapaktuan
Gunung Leuser 3381
Binjai
MEDAN
Tebingtinggi
Pematangsiantar
Gunung Sinabung 2451
Kisaran
Tanjungbalai
Bagansiapiapi
Rantauprapat
Sibolga
Padangsidempuan
Pulau Simeulue
Sinabang
Pulau Babi
Pulau Tuangku
Pulau Mursala
Gunungsitoli
Pulau Nias

SUMATERA (SUMATRA)
Bukittinggi
Payakumbuh
Padangpanjang
Pariaman
Padang
Talu
Bangkinang
Pekanbaru
Taluk
Tembilahan
Rengat
Jambi
Bangko
Muarabungo
Gunung Kerinci 3800
Sungaidareh
Painan
Muaraenim
Lubuklinggau
Lahat
Gunung Dempo 3159
Baturaja
Manna
Palembang
Kayuagung
Perabumulih
Martapura
Menggala
Kotabumi
Bintuhan
Bengkulu
Lais

PEGUNUNGAN BARISAN

MALAY PENINSULA
Kota Bharu
Pasir Mas
Kuala Krai
Kuala Terengganu
Betong
Kuala Lipis
Gunong Tahan 2187
Kuala Kangsar
Taiping
Ipoh
Kampar
Teluk Intan
Raub
Bentung
Gunong Benum 2107
Kuantan
Cukai
SEMENANJUNG MALAYSIA
Shah Alam
KUALA LUMPUR
Klang
Kajang
Kuala Pilah
Seremban
Segamat
Labis
Keluang
Mersing
Muar
Batu Pahat
Johor Bahru
SINGAPORE
Melaka
Pulau Rupat
Dumai
Pulau Bengkalis

MALAYSIA
Ko Samui

KEPULAUAN NATUNA BESAR
Pulau Laut
Natuna Besar
KEPULAUAN ANAMBAS
Pulau Midai
Pulau Jemaja
KEPULAUAN NATUNA SELATAN
Pulau Subi
Pulau Serasan
KEPULAUAN TAMBELAN

Selat Serasan

Pulau Tioman
Pulau Batam
Pulau Bintan
Tanjungpinang
Pulau Lingga
KEPULAUAN RIAU
Pulau Singkep
KEPULAUAN LINGGA
Pulau Sebangka
Pulau Pejantan

BRUNEI
Bandar Seri Begawan
Seria
Miri
Niah
Gunong Mulu 2377
Mukah
Bintulu
Sibu
Sarikei
Kapit
Kuching
Serian
Betong
Sambas
Singkawang
Semitau
Sintang
Putussibau
Sanggau
Mempawah
Pontianak

MALAYSIA
SARAWAK
UPPER KAPUAS MTS.
IRAN MTS.
Gunong Murud 2422
Kota Kinabalu
Kota Belud
SABAH
Gunong Kinabalu 4101
Pulau Labuan
Labuan
Kudat
Pulau Balambangan
Pulau Balabangan
Balabac Island
Balabac Strait
Mount Mantalingajan 2085

BORNEO (KALIMANTAN)
PEG. MÜLLER
Gunung Menyapa 2000
Bukit Raya 2278
Gunung Saran 1758
Nangatayap
Sukadana
Ketapang
Pulau Karimata
KEPULAUAN KARIMATA
Sukaraja
Kendawangan
Palangkaraya
Pangkalanbun
Kumai
Sampit
Kualakapuas
Buntok
Banjarmasin
Martapura
Amuntai
Kandangan
Pulau Sebuku
Pulau Laut

GREATER SUNDA
IND

Equator
Pulau Tanahmasa
KEPULAUAN BATU
Pulau Tanahbala
Pulau Pini
KEPULAUAN MENTAWAI
Pulau Sipura
Pulau Siberut
Pulau Pagai Utara
Pulau Pagai Selatan
Mukomuko
Surulangun
Belitung
Muntok
Pangkalpinang
Pulau Bangka
Tanjungpandan
Tanjung Lumut
Pulau Lepar
Teluk Kumai
Teluk Sampit
Tanjung Puting
Tanjung Selatan
Selat Laut

LAUT JAWA (JAVA SEA)
Pulau Bawean
Pulau Masalembu Besar

Krui
Pulau Enggano
Kotaagung
Bandar Lampung
Panjang
Kotabumi
Selat Sunda
Tanjung Cina
Serang
Karawang
Indramayu
Cirebon
Tegal
Pekalongan
Kudus
Rembang
Tuban
Madura
Bangkalan
Sumenep
Pamekasan
Pulau Kangean
Pulau Sepanjang

JAKARTA
Bogor
Sukabumi
Cianjur
Purwakarta
Sumedang
BANDUNG
Garut
Ujunggenteng
Sindangbarang
Cilacap
Purwokerto
Magelang
Yogyakarta
Gunung Slamet 3428
Surakarta
SEMARANG
SURABAYA
Gresik
Kediri
Pasuruan
Probolinggo
Malang
Jember
Blitar
Tulungagung
Banyuwangi
Gunung Semeru 3676
Selat Madura
Laut Bali (Bali Sea)
Bali
Denpasar
Gunung Agung 3142m
Mataram
Praya
Gunung Rinjani 3726
Lombok
Nusa Penida
Tanjung Cangkuang

JAWA (JAVA)

INDIAN OCEAN

Meters / Feet
4000 / 13120
3000 / 9840
2000 / 6560
1000 / 3280
500 / 1640
200 / 656
Sea Level
200 / 656
2000 / 6560
6000 / 6560

M-DRM4708-A1- -2-2-4
Copyright © Rand McNally & Co.

0 100 200 300 400 600 800 1000 Kilometers
0 100 200 400 600 Miles
Scale 1 : 10,000,000 Sinusoidal Projection

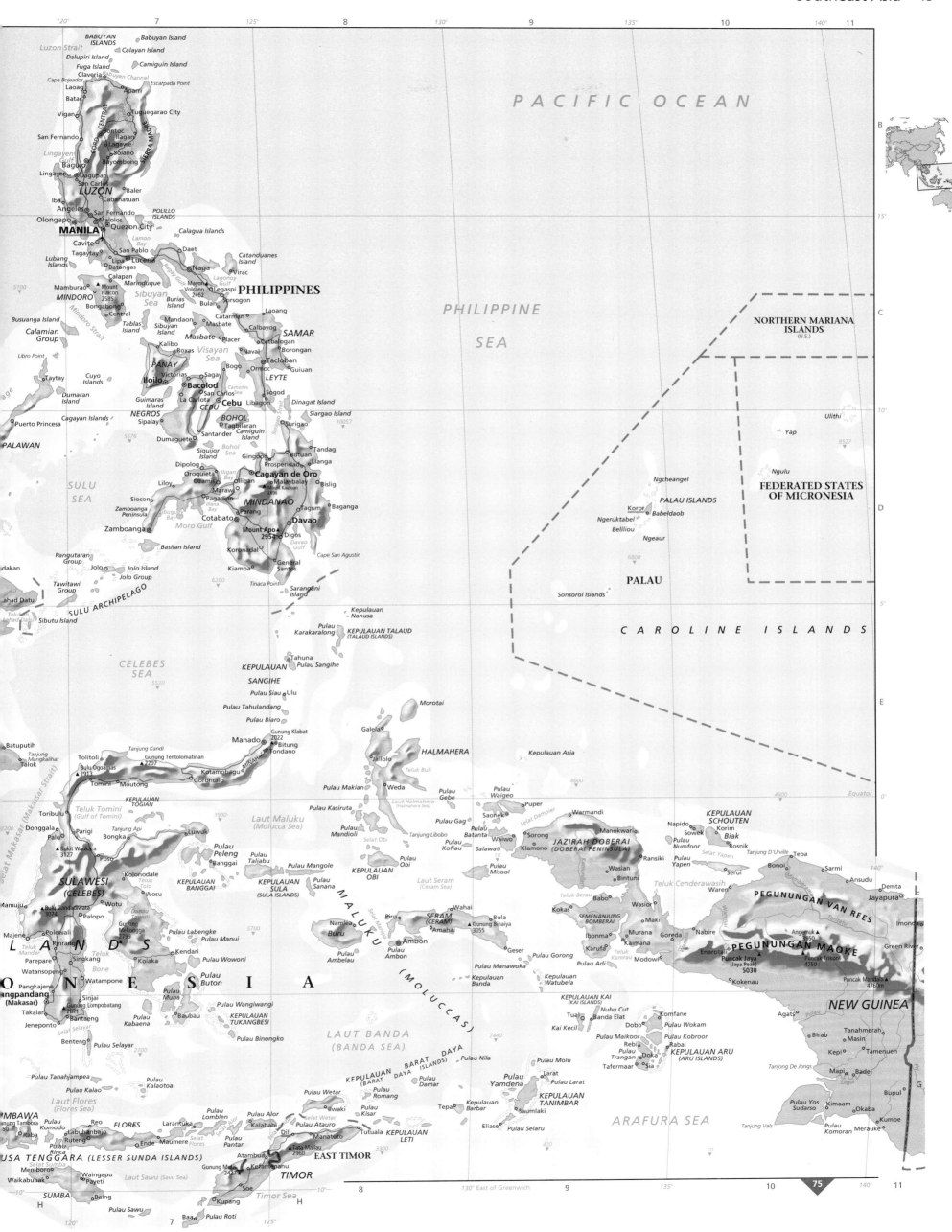

PACIFIC OCEAN

Luzon Strait
BABUYAN
ISLANDS
Babuyan Island
Dalupiri Island   Calayan Island
Fuga Island   Camiguin Island
Claveria   Abuyan Channel
Cape Bojeador   Escarpada Point
Laoag   Aparri   Tuguegarao City
Batac   Vigan
San Fernando   Ilagan   Bayombong
Baguio   Lagawe   Solano
Lingayen   Dagupan   Bontoc
Lingayen   San Carlos   LUZON
Iba   Cabanatuan
Angeles   Baler
Olongapo   San Fernando   Malolos
MANILA   Quezon City
Cavite   San Pablo   POLILLO
ISLANDS
Tagaytay   Lucena   Calagua Islands
Lipa   Daet
Lubang   Batangas   Naga   Catanduanes
Islands   Calapan   Virac   Island
Mamburao   Marinduque   Legaspi   PHILIPPINES
Mount   Mayon
MINDORO   Halcon   Volcano 2462
2585   Sibuyan   Burias   Sorsogon
Bongabong   Sea   Island
Central   Mandaon   Catarman   Laoang
Tablas   Masbate   SAMAR
Busuanga Island   Sibuyan   Kalibo   Catbalogan
Calamian   Island   Roxas   Calbayog   Borongan
Group   Cuyo   PANAY   Victorias   Naval   Tacloban
Libro Point   Islands   Iloilo   Bogo   Ormoc   Guiuan
Taytay   La Carlota   San Carlos   LEYTE
Dumaran   Guimaras   Cebu   Libagon   Dinagat Island
Island   Island   Bacolod   CEBU   Siargao Island
NEGROS   BOHOL   Sogod
Cagayan Islands   Sipalay   Tagbilaran   Surigao
PALAWAN   Dumaguete   Camiguin   Tandag
Puerto Princesa   Siquijor   Bohol   Island
Island   Dipolog   Prosperidad   Bislig
SULU   Liloy   Oroquieta   Ozamiz   Iligan   Butuan   Gingoog
SEA   Siocon   Marawi   Malaybalay
Zamboanga   Pagadian   MINDANAO   Tagum
Peninsula   Cotabato   Parang   Baganga
Zamboanga   Davao
Basilan Island   Koronadal   Mount Apo
2954   Digos
Pangutaran   Kiamba   General   Cape San Agustin
Group   Jolo   Santos
Jolo Island   Tinaca Point   Sarangani
Tawitawi   Jolo Group   Island
Group
Sibutu Island   SULU ARCHIPELAGO
Kepulauan
Nanusa
Pulau
Karakaralong   KEPULAUAN TALAUD
(TALAUD ISLANDS)
CELEBES   Tahuna
SEA   Pulau Sangihe
KEPULAUAN   Ulu
SANGIHE   Pulau Siau
Pulau Tahulandang
Pulau Biaro
Morotai
Batuputih   Galela
Tanjung   Manado   Bitung
Mangkalihat   Gunung Klabat   Jailolo
Talok   2022   Tondano
Tolitoli   Gunung Tentolomatinan   Weda   HALMAHERA   Kepulauan Asia
Bulu Ogoamas   2207   Kotamobagu   MINAHASSA
2911   Moutong   Gorontalo   Pulau Makian
Tomini   Pulau Kasiruta   Laut Halmahera
KEPULAUAN   (Halmahera Sea)
Toribulu   TOGIAN   Pulau Gebe
Teluk Tomini   Pulau Waigeo   Puper
Donggala   (Gulf of Tomini)   Tanjung Api   Luwuk   Pulau Gag   Saonek   Warmandi
Parigi   Bongka   KEPULAUAN   Tanjung Libobo   Selat Dampier   Napido   KEPULAUAN
Palu   Poso   BANGGAI   Pulau   Pulau   Sorong   Manokwari   Sowek   SCHOUTEN
Bukit Waukura   Pulau Peleng   Mandioli   Selat Obi   Batanta   Waiwo   Klamono   Numfoor   Korim
3127   Banggai   Pulau   Pulau   Salawati   JAZIRAH DOBERAI   Biak
Pulau Taliabu   Mangole   Obi   Pulau   (DOBERAI PENINSULA)   Bosnik
SULAWESI   KEPULAUAN   Pulau Sanana   Pulau   Kofiau   Ransiki   Serui
(CELEBES)   SULA   Kofiau   Misool   Wasian   Teba
Wotu   (SULA ISLANDS)   KEPULAUAN   Bintuni   Bonoi
Mamuju   Gunung Gandadiwata   Palopo   OBI   Laut Seram   Babo   Teluk Cenderawasih   Ansudu
3074   Pulau Labengke   (Ceram Sea)   Kokas   SEMENANJUNG   Waren   Sarmi
Majene   Pulau Manui   Namlea   Wahai   BOMBERAI   Demta
Teluk   Pinrang   Kendari   Buru   SERAM   Bula   Ibonma   Murana   PEGUNUNGAN VAN REES
Mandar   Singkang   (CERAM)   Gunung Binaiya   Kaimana   Goreda   Jayapura
I S L A N D S   Kolaka   Ambon   3055   Amahai   Karufa   Nabire   Imonda
Parepare   Pulau Ambon   Geser   Modowi   Angemuk   Green River
Watansoppeng   Teluk   Pulau   Pulau Gorong   Pulau Adi   3950   PEGUNUNGAN MAOKE
Bone   Ambelau   Enarotali   Puncak Trikora
Pangkajene   Watampone   Kepulauan   Puncak Jaya   4750   Puncak Mandala
Ujungpandang   Pulau Wowoni   Manawoka   (Jaya Peak)   4760m
(Makasar)   Sinjai   Kepulauan   5030   Kokenau
I N D O N E S I A   Pulau Buton   Banda
Takalar   Gunung Lompobatang   KEPULAUAN KAI
Jeneponto   2871   Pulau Muna   (KAI ISLANDS)   NEW GUINEA
Benteng   Baubau   Tual   Nuhu Cut   Komfane   Agat
KEPULAUAN   Banda Elat   Tanahmerah
Pulau Selayar   TUKANGBESI   Kai Kecil   Dobo   Pulau Wokam   Birab   Masin
Pulau   Wangiwangi   Rebia   Pulau Kobroor   Kepi
Kabaena   LAUT BANDA   Pulau Maikoor   Rabal   Tamenuen
Pulau Tanahjampea   (BANDA SEA)   7440   Trangan   KEPULAUAN ARU   Mapi
Pulau Binongko   Pulau Nila   Doka   (ARU ISLANDS)   Bade
Pulau Kalao   Tafermaar   Sia   Bupul
BARAT DAYA   Larat   Pulau Yos
Pulau Kalaotoa   KEPULAUAN   BARAT   (ISLANDS)   Pulau Yamdena   Pulau Larat   Sudarso   Kimaam   Okaba
BARAT DAYA   DAYA   KEPULAUAN   Merauke
Laut Flores   Pulau Damar   TANIMBAR
(Flores Sea)   Pulau Wetar   Pulau Romang   Tepa   ARAFURA SEA   Tanjung Vals   Pulau
MBAWA   Pulau Alor   Ilwaki   Pulau Kisar   Kepulauan   Saumlaki   Komoran
Gunung Tambora   Komodo   Larantuka   Kalabahi   Selat Wetar   Barbar   Eliase
Reo   Pulau Atauro   Tata Mailau   Pulau Selaru
Labuanbajo   FLORES   Maumere   Dili   2960   Pulau   Tuluala   KEPULAUAN
Ruteng   Ende   Manatuto   LETI
Raba   Pulau Pantar   EAST TIMOR
NUSA TENGGARA (LESSER SUNDA ISLANDS)   Gunung Mutis   Kefamenanu
Waingapu   Pulau Lomblen   2427   TIMOR
Memboro   Atambua
Waikabubak   Laut Sawu   Soe   Timor Sea
SUMBA   Payeti   (Savu Sea)   Kupang
Waing   Baing
Pulau Sawu   Baa   Pulau Roti

CAROLINE ISLANDS

NORTHERN MARIANA
ISLANDS
(U.S.)

PHILIPPINE
SEA

Ulithi

Yap

Ngcheangel   FEDERATED STATES
OF MICRONESIA
PALAU ISLANDS
Korot   Babeldaob
Ngeruktabel
Beliliou
Ngeaur

PALAU

Sonsorol Islands

57

AFGHANISTAN

SELSELEH-YE SAFĪD KOH

HINDU KUSH

KARAKORAM RANGE

JAMMU AND KASHMIR

XINJIANG

KUN LUN

QING ZANG (PLATEAU)

XIZANG (TIBET)

PAKISTAN

IRAN

BALUCHISTAN

RĪGESTĀN

DASHT-E MĀRGOW

CENTRAL MAKRĀN RANGE

CHĀGAI HILLS

TOBA KĀKAR RANGE

SULAIMAN RANGE

KIRTHAR RANGE

THAR DESERT

GREAT INDIAN DESERT

Karāchi

Hyderābād

HIMACHAL PRADESH

Srīnagar

Jammu

Rāwalpindi

Islāmābād

Peshāwar

Kābol

Herāt

Kandahār

Quetta

FAISALABAD

LAHORE

Amritsar

LUDHIANA

PUNJAB

Chandīgarh

Shimla

Multān

HARYANA

DELHI

New Delhi

UTTARANCHAL

Dehra Dūn

Meerut

NEPAL

Kāthmāndu (Kathmandu)

Mount Everest 8848

RĀJASTHĀN

JAIPUR

UTTAR PRADESH

KĀNPUR (CAWNPORE)

LUCKNOW

Gorakhpur

BIHĀR

PATNA

VĀRĀNASI (BENARES)

Allahābād

JHARKHAND

Rānchī

Dhanbād

Jamshedpur

Bīkāner

Jodhpur

Udaipur

Kota

Gwalior (Lashkar)

Āgra

Jhānsi

GUJARĀT

AHMADĀBĀD

Vadodara

SŪRAT

Rājkot

Jāmnagar

Bhuj

Gulf of Kachchh

Kāthiāwār Peninsula

GĪR RANGE

Gulf of Khambhāt

MADHYA PRADESH

BHOPĀL

INDORE

Jabalpur

VINDHYA RA.

SĀTPURA RANGE

MAHĀDEO HILLS

CHHATTISGARH

Raipur

Bilāspur

ORISSA

Cuttack

Bhubaneshwar

Puri

MAHĀRĀSHTRA

NĀGPUR

MUMBAI (BOMBAY)

Pune (Poona)

Nāshik

Solāpur

AJANTA RANGE

BALĀGHĀT RANGE

I N D I A

ANDHRA PRADESH

HYDERĀBĀD

VISHĀKHAPATNAM

Warangal

Rājahmundry

Kākināda

KARNĀTAKA

BANGALORE

Hubli-Dhārwār

Belgaum

Gulbarga

Mangalore

Mysore

WESTERN GHĀTS

EASTERN GHĀTS

GOA

Panaji

TAMIL NĀDU

CHENNAI (MADRAS)

MADURAI

Salem

Coimbatore

Tiruchchirāppalli

PONDICHERRY

Pondicherry

Tirunelveli

Tuticorin

KERALA

KOCHI (COCHIN)

Kozhikode (Calicut)

Quilon

Thiruvananthapuram (Trivandrum)

Cape Comorin

Coromandel Coast

Malabar Coast

ARABIAN SEA

Tropic of Cancer

LAKSHADWEEP

Kavaratti

Amindivi Islands

MALDIVES

Male'

Male' Atoll

Ari Atoll

Miladummadulu Atoll

Suvadiva Atoll

Addu Atoll

Equator

INDIAN OCEAN

Lakshadweep Sea

Nine Degree Channel

Eight Degree Channel

Bay of ...

SRI LANKA

Colombo

Sri Jayewardenepura Kotte

Kandy

Jaffna

Pidurutalagala 2524

Trincomalee

Gulf of Mannar

Palk Strait

The boundary between India and Pakistan through the disputed state of Jammu and Kashmir follows the "line of control" agreed upon by both countries in 1972.

(A) Area occupied by Pakistan and claimed by India.
(B) Area claimed and occupied by India; status disputed by Pakistan.
(C) Area occupied by China and claimed by India.
(D) Area occupied by India and claimed by China.

Meters / Feet
6000 / 19680
4000 / 13120
3000 / 9840
2000 / 6560
1000 / 3280
500 / 1640
200 / 656
Sea Level
200 / 656
2000 / 6560

MALDIVES

LAKSHADWEEP

Nine Degree Channel

Minicoy Island (Ind.)

Lakshadweep Sea

Eight Degree Channel

Tiladummati Atoll

Miladummadulu Atoll

Fadiffolu Atoll

Mulaku Atoll

Addu Atoll

Same scale as main map

Amindivi Islands

Chettlatt Island

Killtān Island

Kavaratti

Kavaratti Island

Andrott Island

Minicoy Island

0 100 200 300 400 600 800 1000 Kilometers
0 100 200 300 400 600 Miles

Scale 1 : 10,000,000   Lambert Conformal Conic Projection

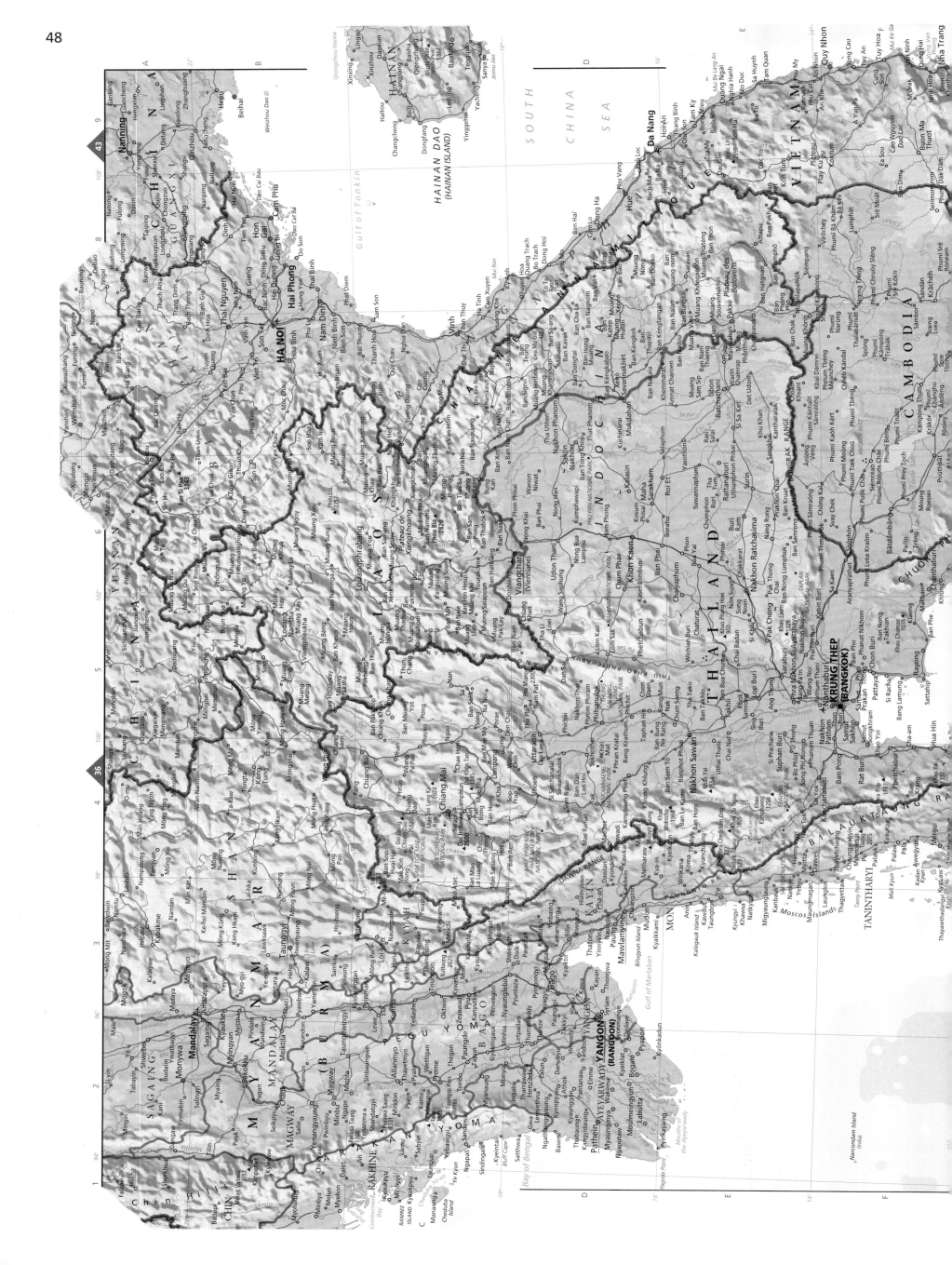

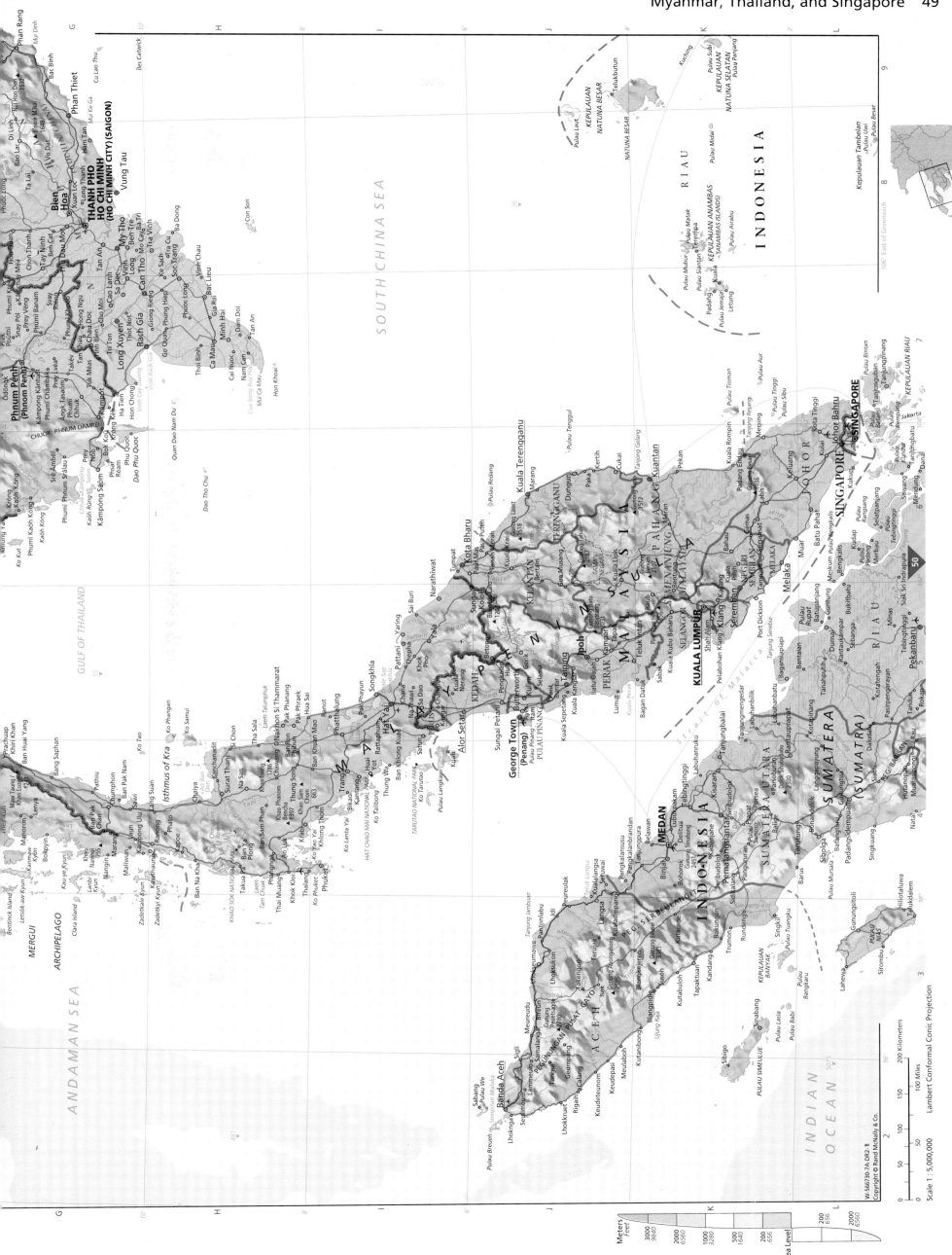

SOUTH CHINA SEA

INDONESIA

R I A U

KEPULAUAN ANAMBAS
(TANAMBAS ISLANDS)

NATUNA BESAR

KEPULAUAN
NATUNA SELATAN

Kepulauan Tambelan

106° East of Greenwich

GULF OF THAILAND

ANDAMAN SEA

MERGUI

ARCHIPELAGO

Isthmus of Kra

KHAO SOK NATIONAL PARK

HAT CHAO MAI NATIONAL PARK

TARUTAO NATIONAL PARK

Phan Rang

Phan Thiet

Vung Tau

THANH PHO
HO CHI MINH
(HO CHI MINH CITY) (SAIGON)

Bien
Hoa

Phnum Pénh
(Phnom Penh)

CHUOR PHNUM DAMREI

MALAYSIA

KEDAH

PERLIS

KELANTAN

TERENGGANU

PERAK

PAHANG

SELANGOR

NEGERI
SEMBILAN

MELAKA

JOHOR

PULAU PINANG

KUALA LUMPUR

George Town
(Penang)

SINGAPORE

Kota Bharu

Kuala Terengganu

Kuantan

Ipoh

Johor Bahru

INDONESIA

SUMATERA
UTARA

RIAU

SUMATERA
(SUMATRA)

ACEH

MEDAN

Pekanbaru

Banda Aceh

INDIAN
OCEAN

PULAU SIMEULUE

PULAU
NIAS

Straits of Malacca

Strait of Malacca

Meters / Feet

Meters	Feet
3000	9840
2000	6560
1000	3280
500	1640
200	656
Sea Level	

200
656
2000
6560

200 Kilometers

100 Miles

W-566730-7A-DR2-1

Copyright © Rand McNally & Co.

Scale 1 : 5,000,000   Lambert Conformal Conic Projection

50

Meters
Feet

3000
9840

2000
6560

1000
3280

500
1640

200
656

Sea Level

200
656

2000
6560

0   50   100   150   200   300 Kilometers
0   50   100   200   300 Miles

Scale 1 : 5,000,000

Sinusoidal Projection

CELEBES SEA

SULU SEA

SULU ARCHIPELAGO

PHILIPPINES

TAWITAWI GROUP

SABAH

MALAYSIA

SARAWAK

BRUNEI
Bandar Seri Begawan

BORNEO

KALIMANTAN TIMUR

(KALIMANTAN)

KALIMANTAN BARAT

KALIMANTAN TENGAH

KALIMANTAN SELATAN

Palangkaraya

Banjarmasin

Samarinda

Balikpapan

SULAWESI
TENGAH

Palu

SULAWESI
(CELEBES)

SULAWESI
SELATAN

SULAWESI
TENGGARA

Ujungpandang
(Makasar)

Teluk Tomini
(Gulf of Tomini)

Teluk Bone
(Gulf of Bone)

Selat at Makasar
(Makassar Strait)

DA ISLANDS

NESIA

AWA (JAVA SEA)

KEPULAUAN
LAUT KECIL

Laut Flores
(Flores Sea)

SEMARANG

SURABAYA

Surakarta

MADURA

JAWA TIMUR

Malang

Denpasar

BALI BALI

Mataram

LOMBOK

NUSA TENGGARA BARAT

SUMBAWA

Laut Bali
(Bali Sea)

FLORES

NUSA TENGGARA TIMUR
NUSA TENGGARA
(LESSER SUNDA ISLANDS)

SUMBA

Laut Sawu
(Savu Sea)

Sumba

Equator

Equator

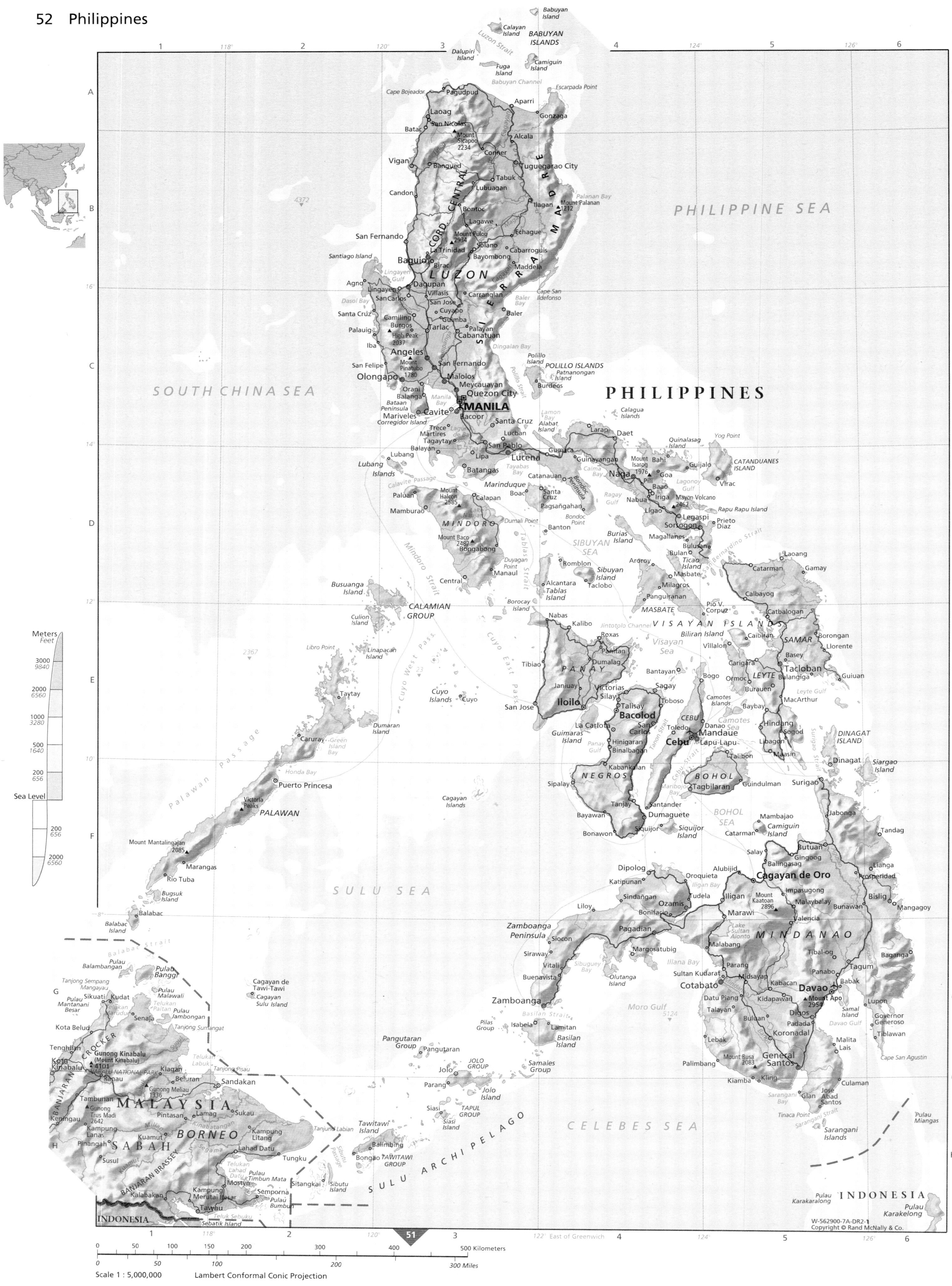

Map labels

Seas and waters

PHILIPPINE SEA
SOUTH CHINA SEA
SULU SEA
CELEBES SEA
SIBUYAN SEA
VISAYAN SEA
BOHOL SEA
Luzon Strait
Babuyan Channel
Lingayen Gulf
Dasol Bay
Santa Bay
Manila Bay
Ragay Gulf
Tayabas Bay
Lamon Bay
Palanan Bay
Baler Bay
Dingalan Bay
Polillo Strait
Tablas Strait
Mindoro Strait
Calavite Passage
Cuyo West Pass.
Cuyo East Pass
Palawan Passage
Honda Bay
Green Island Bay
Panay Gulf
Guimaras
Leyte Gulf
Camotes Sea
Dinagat
Surigao Strait
Maqueda Bay
Iligan Bay
Lake Sultan Alonto
Moro Gulf
Illana Bay
Sibuguey Bay
Davao Gulf
Sarangani Bay
Basilan Strait
Balabac Strait
Sibutu Passage
Telukan Labuk
Teluk Sebuku
Lagonoy Gulf
Sorsogon
Bernardino Strait
Cagayan Islands
Yog Point
Escarpada Point
Cape San Ildefonso
Cape San Ildefonso
Prieto Diaz
Jintotolo Channel
Borocay Island

Luzon and northern islands

BABUYAN ISLANDS
Babuyan Island
Calayan Island
Dalupiri Island
Fuga Island
Camiguin Island
Cape Bojeador
Pagudpud
Laoag
San Nicolas
Batac
Vigan
Bangued
Candon
San Fernando
Santiago Island
Agno
Palauig
Santa Cruz
Iba
Angeles
San Felipe
Olongapo
Orani
Balanga
Bataan Peninsula
Mariveles
Corregidor Island
Cavite
Trece Martires
Tagaytay
Balayan
Lubang
Lubang Islands
Aparri
Gonzaga
Alcala
Conner
Mount Sicapoo 2234
Tuguegarao City
Tabuk
Lubuagan
Bontoc
Lagawe
Echague
Ilagan
Mount Palanan 1212
Maddela
Cabarroguis
Bayombong
Solano
Mount Pulog 2934
Trinidad
Baguio
Birac
Dagupan
Villasis
San Carlos
San Jose
Cuyapo
Camiling
Burgos
High Peak 2037
Tarlac
Gerona
Palayan
Cabanatuan
San Fernando
Carranglan
Baler
Mount Pinatubo 1780
Malolos
Meycauayan
Quezon City
MANILA
Bacoor
Santa Cruz
Lucban
Lucena
San Pablo
Lipa
Batangas
Calamba
LUZON
CORD. CENTRAL
SIERRA MADRE
Polillo
POLILLO ISLANDS
Patnanongan Island
Burdeos
Alabat Island
Santa Cruz
Gumaca
Daet
Larap
Calagua Islands
Quinalasag Island
CATANDUANES ISLAND
Virac
Bahi
Mount Isarog 1976
Naga
Goa
Pili
Baao
Iriga
Nabua
Ligao
Mayon Volcano 2462
Rapu Rapu Island
Legaspi
Magallanes
Bulusan
Bulan
Ticao Island
Aroroy

Mindoro, Marinduque and central

MINDORO
Mamburao
Paluan
Calapan
Boac
Santa Cruz
Pagsanghan
Bondoc Point
Banton
Dumali Point
Mount Halcon 2585
Mount Baco 2482
Bongabong
Central
Duyagan Point
Manaul
Marinduque
Catanauan
Romblon
Sibuyan Island
Alcantara
Tablas Island
Taclobo
Milagros
Panguiranan
Masbate
MASBATE
Pio V. Corpuz
Catbalogan

Palawan / Calamian

CALAMIAN GROUP
Busuanga Island
Culion Island
Linapacan Island
Libro Point
Taytay
Cuyo Islands
Cuyo
Caruray
Dumaran Island
Puerto Princesa
Victoria Peaks
PALAWAN
Mount Mantalingajan 2085
Marangas
Rio Tuba
Bugsuk Island
Balabac
Balabac Island

Visayas

VISAYAN ISLANDS
PANAY
Nabas
Kalibo
Roxas
Pandan
Tibiao
Januiay
Dumalag
Bantayan
Bogo
Camotes Islands
SAMAR
Catarman
Gamay
Laoang
Borongan
Llorente
Guiuan
MacArthur
Baybay
LEYTE
Ormoc
Carigara
Tacloban
Balangiga
Basey
Villalon
Caibiran
Biliran Island
Calbayog
Sagay
Victorias
Silay
Talisay
ILOILO
San Jose
La Carlota
San Carlos
Hinigaran
Binalbagan
Kabankalan
NEGROS
Sipalay
Bayawan
Bonawon
Tanjay
Santander
Dumaguete
Siquijor
Siquijor Island
Guimaras Island
BOHOL
Tagbilaran
Guindulman
Jagna
CEBU
Toledo
Danao
Mandaue
Cebu
Lapu-Lapu
Talibon
Hindang
Sogod
Libagon
Maasin
Dinagat Island
Dinagat
Siargao Island
Surigao
Bacolod
Tibiao
Toboso
Buruauen
Camotes

Mindanao

MINDANAO
Dipolog
Katipunan
Sindangan
Liloy
Siraway
Ozamis
Tudela
Bonifacio
Oroquieta
Alubijid
Cagayan de Oro
Balingasag
Salay
Camiguin Island
Mambajao
Jabonga
Butuan
Gingoog
Lianga
Prosperidad
Bislig
Mangagoy
Tandag
Iligan
Mount Kaatoan 2896
Malaybalay
Impasugong
Marawi
Valencia
Bunawan
Baganga
Zamboanga Peninsula
Siocon
Pagadian
Vitali
Buenavista
Margosatubig
Malabang
Parang
Sultan Kudarat
Olutanga Island
Zamboanga
Isabela
Lamitan
Basilan Island
Pilas Group
Samales Group
Cotabato
Datu Piang
Lebak
Talayan
Kabacan
Midsayap
Kidapawan
Buluan
Palimbang
Kiamba
Kling
Kabacan
Mount Busa 2083
General Santos
Koronadal
Pada da
Digos
Mount Apo 2954
Davao
Babak
Panabo
Tagum
Tibal-og
Samal Island
Lupon
Governor Generoso
Tiblawan
Malita
Lais
Glan
Culaman
Jose Abad Santos
Cape San Agustin
Tinaca Point

Sulu Archipelago

SULU ARCHIPELAGO
Pangutaran Group
Pangutaran
Cagayan de Tawi-Tawi
Cagayan Sulu Island
JOLO GROUP
Jolo
Jolo Island
Parang
Siasi
Siasi Island
TAPUL GROUP
TAWITAWI GROUP
Tawitawi Island
Bongao
Balimbing
Sitangkai
Sibutu Island

Malaysia / Borneo

MALAYSIA
BORNEO
SABAH
Kudat
Pulau Banggi
Pulau Malawali
Tanjong Sempang Mangayau
Pulau Balambangan
Sikuati
Telukan Marudu
Pulau Jambongan
Tenghilan
Tanjong Sumangat
Kota Belud
Gunong Kinabalu (Mount Kinabalu) 4101
KINABALU NATIONAL PARK
BANJARAN CROCKER
Kota Kinabalu
Penampang
Klagan
Beluran
Gunong Meliau 1536
Sandakan
Tambunan
Trus Madi 2642
Keningau
Tenom
Pinangah
Kampung Litang
Tungku
Lahad Datu
Telukan Darvel
Pulau Timbun Mata
Kunak
Semporna
Pulau Bumbum
INDONESIA
Tawau
Sebatik Island
BANJARAN BRASSEY
Kuamut
Mostyn
Senaja
Paitan
Lamag
Sukau
Kampung Kudat

Indonesia (southeast)

INDONESIA
Pulau Karakaralong
Pulau Karakelong
Pulau Miangas

Labels and text

PHILIPPINES
Manila Bay

Elevation scale (left margin)

Meters
Feet
3000 / 9840
2000 / 6560
1000 / 3280
500 / 1640
200 / 656
Sea Level
200 / 656
2000 / 6560

Scale information (bottom)

Scale 1 : 5,000,000
Lambert Conformal Conic Projection

0 50 100 150 200 300 400 500 Kilometers
0 50 100 200 300 Miles

East of Greenwich

Scale 1 : 5,000,000   Lambert Conformal Conic Projection

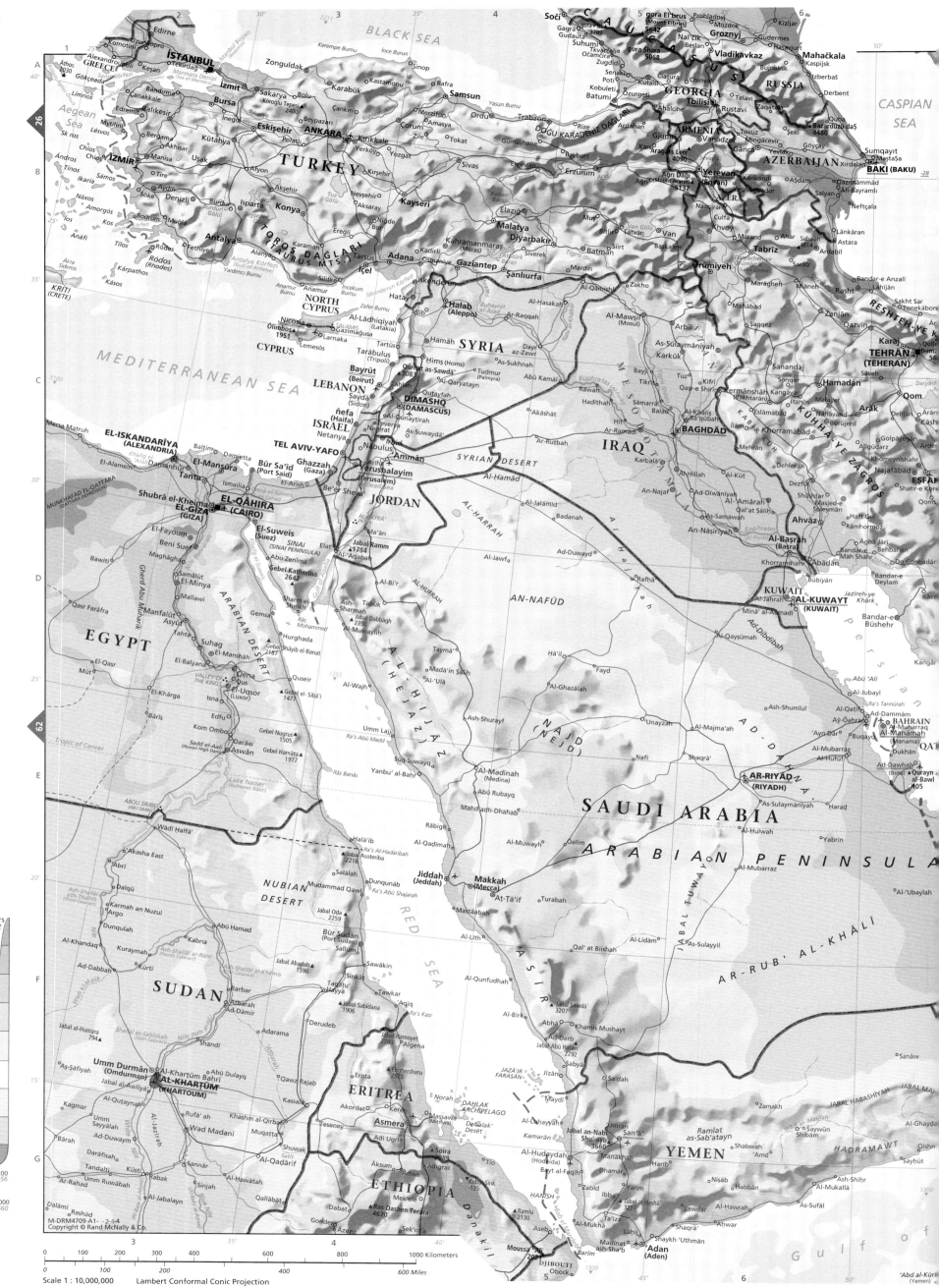

Meters
Feet

6000
19680

4000
13120

3000
9840

2000
6560

1000
3280

500
1640

200
656

Sea Level

200
656

2000
6560

0   100   200   300   400   600   800   1000 Kilometers
0   100   200   400   600 Miles
Scale 1 : 10,000,000   Lambert Conformal Conic Projection

M-DRM4709-A1- - 2-4-4
Copyright © Rand McNally & Co.

The boundary between India and Pakistan through the disputed state of Jammu and Kashmir follows the "line of control" agreed upon by both countries in 1972.

Ⓐ Area occupied by Pakistan and claimed by India.

Ⓑ Area claimed and occupied by India; status disputed by Pakistan.

Ⓒ Area occupied by China and claimed by India.

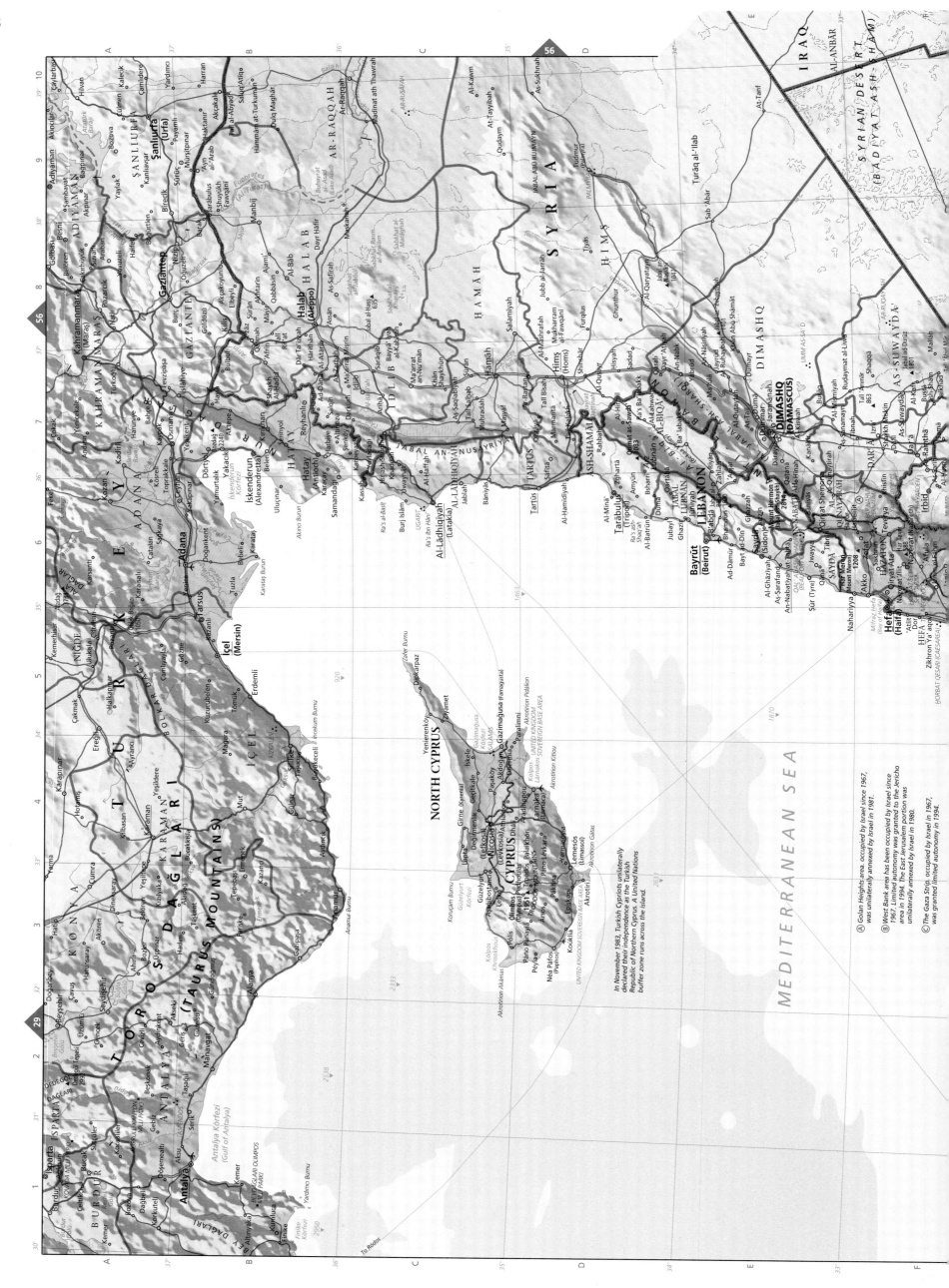

MEDITERRANEAN SEA

NORTH CYPRUS

CYPRUS

In November 1983, Turkish Cypriots unilaterally declared their independence as the Turkish Republic of Northern Cyprus. A United Nations buffer zone runs across the island.

Ⓐ Golan Heights area, occupied by Israel since 1967, was unilaterally annexed by Israel in 1981.

Ⓑ West Bank area has been occupied by Israel since 1967. Limited autonomy was granted to the Jericho area in 1994. The East Jerusalem portion was unilaterally annexed by Israel in 1980.

Ⓒ The Gaza Strip, occupied by Israel in 1967, was granted limited autonomy in 1994.

S Y R I A

IRAQ

SYRIAN DESERT
(BADIYAT ASH-SHAM)

LEBANON

DAMASCUS
DIMASHQ

Bayrūt
(Beirut)

Ḥimṣ
(Homs)

Ḥamāh

Ḥalab
(Aleppo)

TURKEY

Adana

Gaziantep

Şanlıurfa
(Urfa)

Kahramanmaraş

Antalya

İçel
(Mersin)

TOROS DAĞLARI
(TAURUS MOUNTAINS)

Tarābulus
(Tripoli)

Ṭarṭūs

Al-Lādhiqīyah
(Latakia)

Hefa
(Haifa)

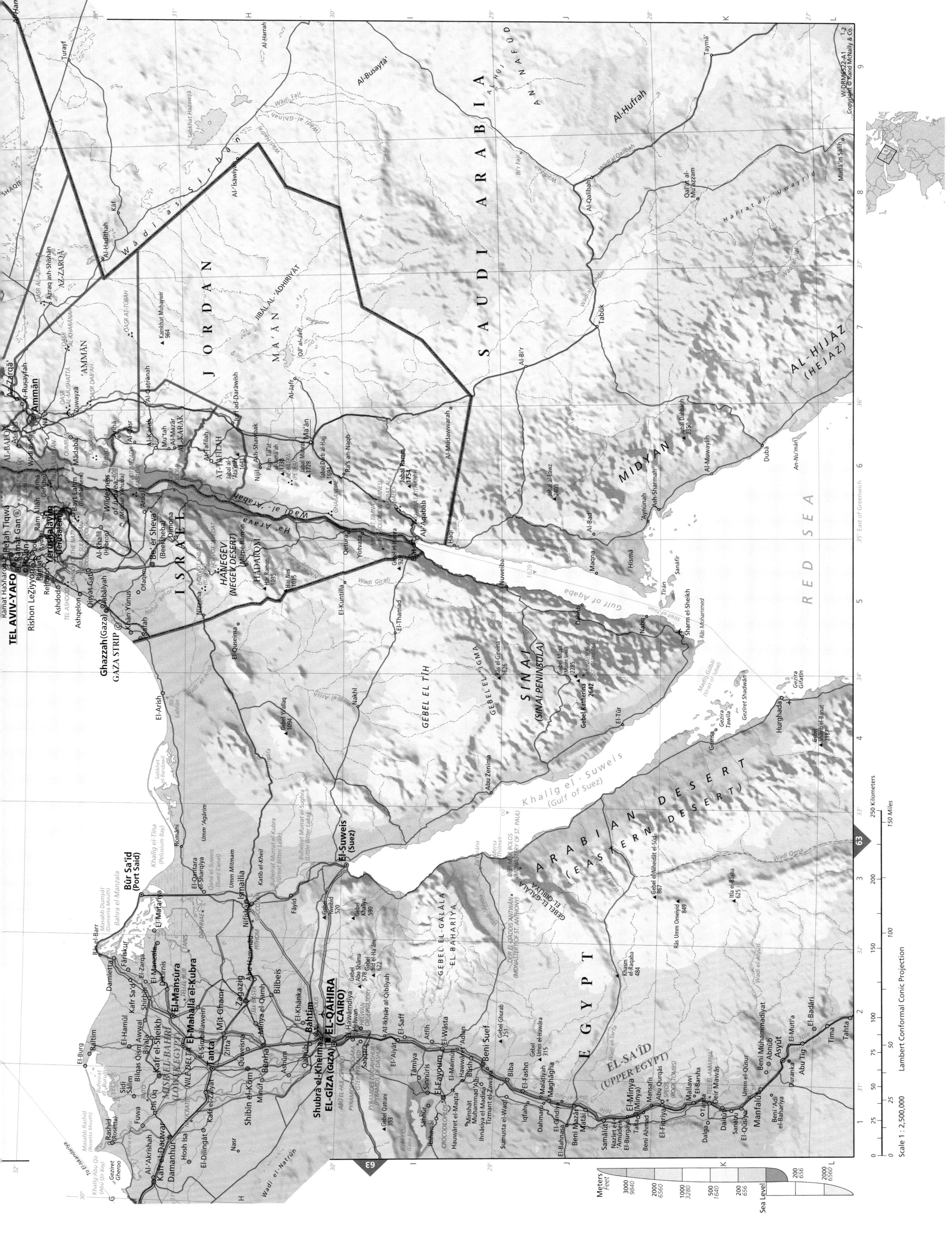

SAUDI ARABIA

JORDAN

ISRAEL

EGYPT

SINAI (SINAI PENINSULA)

RED SEA

Gulf of Aqaba

Khalig el-Suweis (Gulf of Suez)

ARABIAN DESERT (EASTERN DESERT)

AL-ḤIJĀZ (HEJAZ)

MIDYAN

AN NAFŪD

MA'ĀN

AMMĀN

TEL AVIV-YAFO

Yerushalayim / Jerusalem

EL-QAHIRA (CAIRO)

EL-GIZA (GIZA)

El-Iskandariya (Alexandria)

Bûr Sa'îd (Port Said)

El-Suweis (Suez)

Ismailia

Ghazzah (Gaza)

GAZA STRIP

HANEGEV (NEGEV DESERT)

Al-'Aqaba

Tabūk

EL-SA'ÎD (UPPER EGYPT)

MISR EL-BAHRI (LOWER EGYPT)

NILE DELTA

Gebel Katherîna 2642

Gebel Mûsa (Mount Sinai) 2285

Jabal Ramm 1754

35° East of Greenwich

Scale 1 : 2,500,000

Lambert Conformal Conic Projection

Copyright © Rand McNally & Co.

250 kilometers

150 Miles

Meters / Feet
3000 / 9840
2000 / 6560
1000 / 3280
500 / 1640
200 / 656
Sea Level

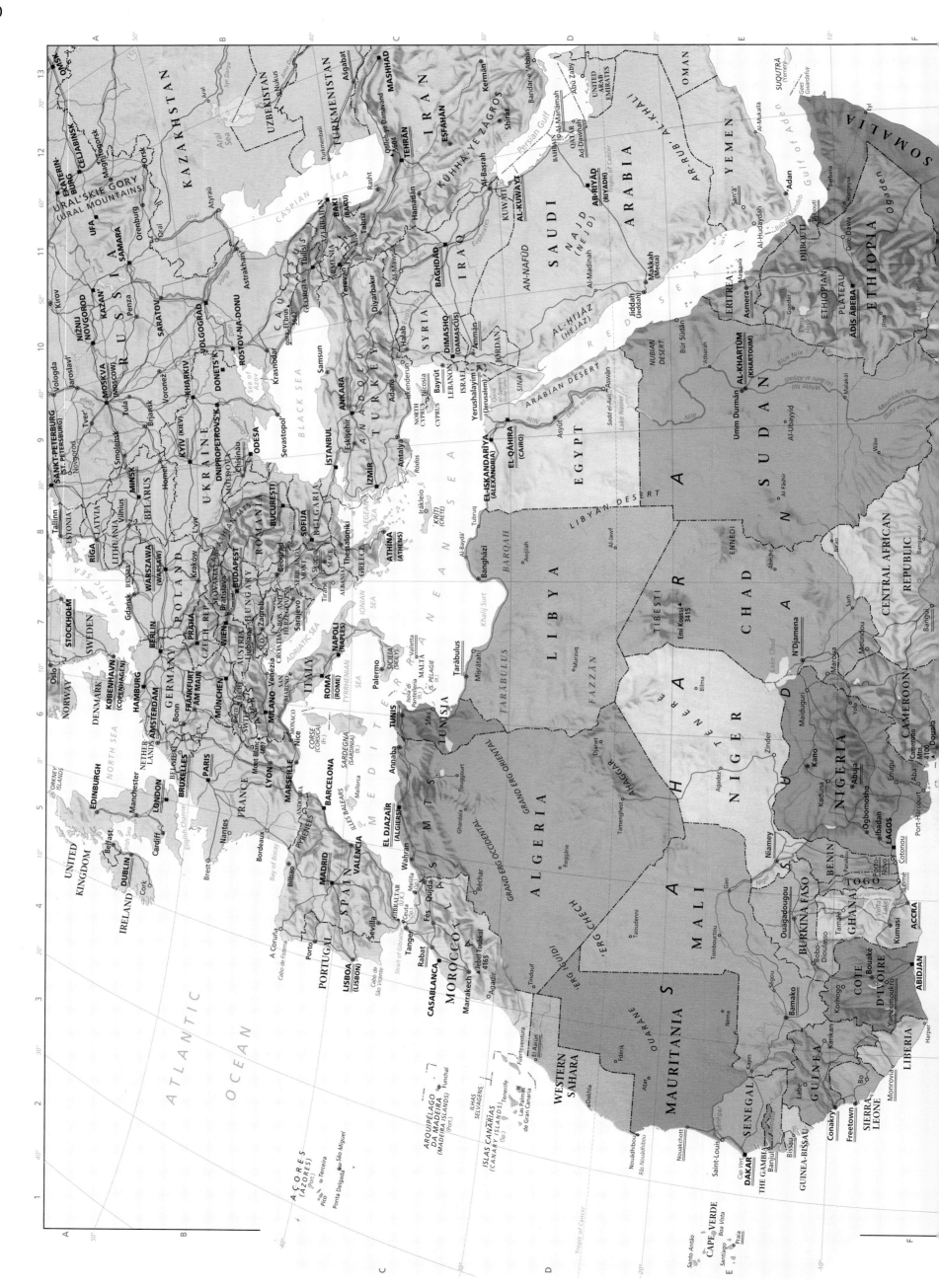

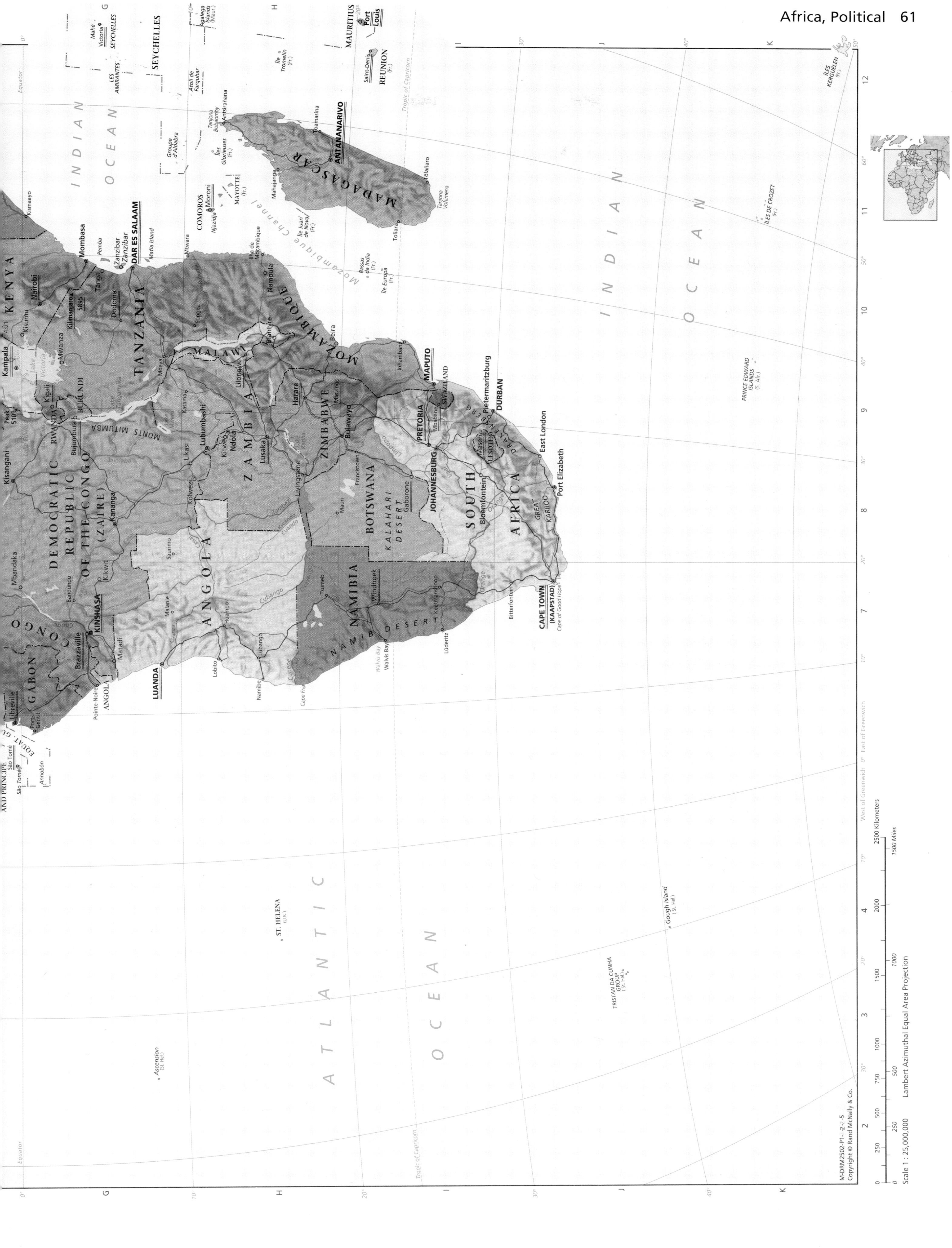

INDIAN OCEAN

SEYCHELLES

Mahé
Victoria
SEYCHELLES

LES AMIRANTES

Atoll de Farquhar

Groupe d'Aldabra

Îles Glorieuses (Fr.)

Aldabra Islands (Maur.)

MAURITIUS
Port Louis

Saint-Denis
RÉUNION (Fr.)

Île Tromelin (Fr.)

Tropic of Capricorn

ÎLES KERGUÉLEN

Toamasina
Antsirañana
Mahajanga
ANTANANARIVO
MADAGASCAR
Toliara
Tanjona Vohimena

Mozambique Channel

COMOROS
Moroni
Nzazidja
MAYOTTE (Fr.)

Île Juan de Nova (Fr.)
Bassas da India (Fr.)
Île Europa (Fr.)

Mombasa
Pemba
Zanzibar
Zanzibar
DAR ES SALAAM
Mafia Island

KENYA
Kismaayo
Nairobi
Kisumu
Mwanza
Kilimanjaro
Tanga
Dodoma
TANZANIA
Mtwara
Songea

MALAWI
Lilongwe
Blantyre

MOZAMBIQUE
Nampula
Mozambique
Beira
Inhambane
Pemba
MAPUTO

Kampala
Lake Victoria
Kigali
RWANDA
BURUNDI
Bujumbura
Lake Tanganyika

Peak 5110
MONTS MITUMBA

Kisangani
DEMOCRATIC REPUBLIC OF THE CONGO (ZAÏRE)
Kananga
Mbandaka
KINSHASA
Bandundu
Kikwit
Matadi

Lubumbashi
Likasi
Kolwezi
Kitwe
Ndola
ZAMBIA
Lusaka
Livingstone
Kabwe
Lake Kariba

Harare
ZIMBABWE
Bulawayo
Masvingo

Francistown
BOTSWANA
Maun
Gaborone
KALAHARI DESERT

ANGOLA
Luanda
Lobito
Benguela
Namibe
Lubango

NAMIBIA
Windhoek
Tsumeb
Swakopmund
Walvis Bay
Lüderitz
NAMIB DESERT

SOUTH AFRICA
PRETORIA
JOHANNESBURG
Bloemfontein
SWAZILAND
Mbabane
LESOTHO
Maseru
Pietermaritzburg
DURBAN
East London
Port Elizabeth
Keetmanshoop
GREAT KARROO
DRAKENSBERG
CAPE TOWN (KAAPSTAD)
Cape of Good Hope
Bitterfontein

GABON
CONGO
Brazzaville
Libreville
Pointe-Noire
Port-Gentil

SÃO TOMÉ AND PRÍNCIPE
São Tomé
Annobón

ST. HELENA (U.K.)
Ascension (St. Hel.)

ATLANTIC OCEAN

TRISTAN DA CUNHA GROUP (St. Hel.)

Gough Island (St. Hel.)

PRINCE EDWARD ISLANDS (S. Afr.)

ÎLES DE CROZET (Fr.)

INDIAN OCEAN

Equator

West of Greenwich   0°   East of Greenwich

M-DRM2SR2-P1-2-3-5
Copyright © Rand McNally & Co.

Scale 1 : 25,000,000

Lambert Azimuthal Equal Area Projection

2500 Kilometers
1500 Miles

0   250   500   750   1000   1500   2000   2500

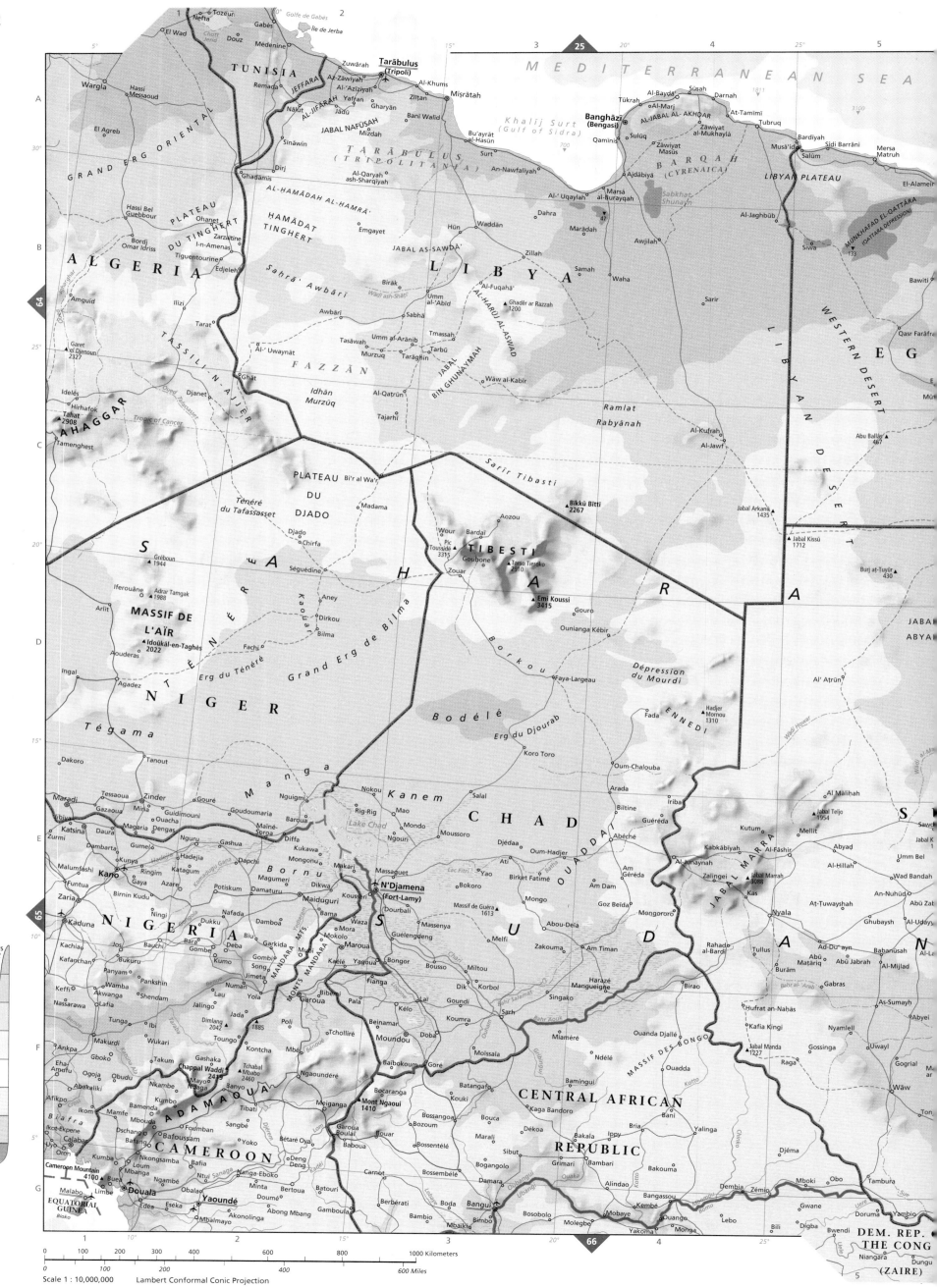

MEDITERRANEAN SEA

TUNISIA

ALGERIA

LIBYA

NIGER

CHAD

SUDAN

NIGERIA

CAMEROON

CENTRAL AFRICAN
REPUBLIC

EQUATORIAL
GUINEA

DEM. REP.
THE CONGO
(ZAIRE)

S A H A R A

Meters
Feet
4000
13120
3000
9840
2000
6560
1000
3280
500
1640
200
656
Sea Level
200
656
2000
6560

0   100   200   300   400   600   800   1000 Kilometers
0   100   200   400   600 Miles
Scale 1 : 10,000,000   Lambert Conformal Conic Projection

LEBANON
Şaydā (Sidon)
DIMASHQ SYRIA (DAMASCUS)
Hefa (Haifa)
Teverya
Nazerat
Irbid
JORDAN
'Ajlūn
'Ammān
TEL AVIV-YAFO
ISRAEL
Netanya
O Nābulus
Ghazzah (Gaza)
Yerushalayim (Jerusalem)
Be'ér Sheva'
Al-'Arish
Ma'ān
SINAI (SINAI PENINSULA)
Jabal Ramm 1754
Elat
Al-'Aqabah
El-'Arish
'Ismailia
Bür Sa'īd (Port Said)
Damietta
Baltim
El-Mansûra
Tanta
Shubra
El-Kheima
EL-QÂHIRA (CAIRO)
EL-GÎZA (GIZA)
El-Suweis (Suez)
ayoum
Beni Suef
Abu Zenîma
Gemsa
Sharm el-Sheikh
Ra's Mohammed
Hurghada
Gebel Shâyib el-Banat 2187

IRAQ
Ar-Ramādi
Ar-Rutbah
BAGHDĀD
Al-Qā'im
MESOPOTAMIA
Tigris
Al-Hillah
Karbalā'
Al-Kūt
Al-'Amārah
Qal'at Sālih
An-Najaf
An-Nāsiriyah
Ad-Dīwānīyah
As-Samāwah
AL-BASRAH (Basra)
Dezfūl
Ahvāz
Masjed-e Soleymān
Rāmhormoz
Āghā Jārī
Behbahān
EŞFAHĀN
Najafābād
Shahr-e Kord
KŪHHĀ-YE ZAGROS
Qomsheh
Ardakān
Yazd
Ābādeh
Eqlīd
Sīr Kūh 4077
Shīr Kūh

Badanah
Al-Jalāmid
Ar-Rafḥa
Ad-Duwayd
Al-Jawf
SYRIAN DESERT
AL-HARRAH
AL-HUFRAH
AN-NAFŪD
Al-Bi'r
Tabūk
Ash-Sharmah
Al-Muwaylih
Taymā'
Hā'il
Fayd
Al-Ghazālah
'Unayzah
Al-Majma'ah
Shaqrā'
Nafí
'Afīf
Al-Madīnah (Medina)
Abū Rubayq
Mahd adh-Dhahab
AR-RIYĀD (RIYADH)
As-Sulaymānīyah
Harad
Al-Hulwah
Yabrīn

KUWAIT
AL-KUWAYT (KUWAIT)
Al-Jahrah
Mīnā' al-Ahmadī
Jazīreh-ye Khārk
Bandar-e Māh Shahr
Khorramshahr
Ābādān
Bandar-e Deylam
Bandar-e Büshehr
Kāzerūn
Shīrāz
Fīrūzābād
Jahrom
Dārāb
Fasā
Neyrīz
Kangān
Lār
Jazīreh-ye Kīsh
Abū 'Ali
Al-Jubayl
Ad-Dammām
Aÿ-Ṣaḥrān
Al-Qatīf
Ra's Tannūrah
BAHRAIN
Al-Muharraq
Al-Manamah (Manama)
QATAR
Ad-Dawhah (Doha)
Dukhān
Qurayn Abā al-Bawl 105
Şīr Banī Yās
Jazīreh-ye Kīsh
Marv Dasht
Persian Gulf

SAUDI ARABIA
NEJD
AD-DAHNĀ
JABAL TUWAYQ
Al-Mubarraz
Al-Hufūf
Ash-Shumlul
Al-Qaysūmah
'Ayn Dār
Al-Mubarraz
Buqayq
Al-'Ubaylah
Harad
Tropic of Cancer
UNITED ARAB EMIRATES
OMAN
AR-RUB' AL-KHĀLĪ

ARABIAN DESERT
Mallawi
Minya
anfalūt
Asyūt
Tahta
Suhag
El-Balyana
Qena
Qus
VALLEY OF THE KINGS
El-Uqsor (Luxor)
Gebel el-Sibā'i 1477
Isna
Edfu
Kom Ombo
Darāw
Gebel Nugrus 1505
Aswān
Sadd el-'Āli (Aswan High Dam)
First Cataract
El-Khārga
Bârîs
ABOU SIMBEL (ABU SIMBEL)
Lake Nasser (Buheirat Nâsir)
Wādī Halfā'
'Akasha East
Abrī
Dalqū
Karmah an Nuzul
Kuraymah
Ash-Shallāl ar-Rābi' (Fourth Cataract)
Kabna
NUBIAN DESERT
'Aqīq
Muhammad Qawl
Jabal Oda 2259
Jabal Asoteriba 2216
Ra's al-Hadārbah
Halā'ib
Ra's Banās
Gebel Hamâta 1977
Al-Qadīmah
Al-Wajh
Yanbu' al-Bahr
AL-'ARAB (HEJAZ)
Umm Lajj
Ra's Abū Madd
Rābigh
Al-Muwayh
Jiddah (Jeddah)
Makkah (Mecca)
At-Tā'if
Turabah
Qal'at Bīshah
As-Sulayyil
Al-Lidām
'Alim
ARABIAN PENINSULA
'A S I R
Al-Lith
Al-Qunfudhah
Jabal Sawdā' 3207
Abhā
Khamīs Mushayt
Al-Birk
Ad-Darb
Jabal Abū Hasan 2292
Sabyā
Sa'dah
Zamakh
Shibām
Saywūn
'Amd
Al-Ghaydah
RED SEA

BŪR SŪDĀN (Port Sudan)
Sallūm
Sawākin
Tawkar
Jabal Abadab 1596
Sinkāt
Ra's Kasar
Tagatu Hayyā
Jabal Sabdana 1906
Jabal Hamoyet
Algena
Derudeb
Togni
Barbar
Shandi
Adarama
'Aṭbara
Ad-Dāmir
Kürti
al-Humara 794
'Abū Dulayq
Qawz Rajab
Kassalā
Khashm al-Qirbah
Derudeb
Enghershatu 2575
Erota
ERITREA
Akordat
Keren
Massawa (Mitsiwa)
Dahlak Deset
Norah
DAHLAK ARCHIPELAGO
JAZĀ'IR FARASĀN
Jizān
Al-Luhayyah
Kamarān
'Umran
Şan'ā'
Jabal an-Nabi Shu'ayb 3660
Ma'rib
Nisāb
Shabwah
YEMEN
HADRAMAWT
Ramlat as-Sab'atayn
JABAL HABASHIYAH
Wādī al-Masīlah
Ash-Shihr
Al-Mukallā
As-Sufāl
JABAL MAHRĀT
Qishn
Ra's Fartak
Sayhūt

Asmera
Adi Ugri
Soira 2989
Teseney
Muqatta'
Shuwak
Al-Qadārif
Adwa
Aksum
Adigrat
Mek'elē
Kobar Sink
Ramlu 2130
Asmera
HANISH
Al-Hudaydah (Hodeida)
Bayt al-Faqīh
Zabīd
Dhamār
Yarīm
Ibb
Ta'izz
Jabal al-Hashā' 3227
Lawdar
Ahwar
Al-Hawrah
AL-KHARTŪM (KHARTOUM)
Umm Durmān (Omdurman)
Al-Khartūm Baḥrī
Jabal al-Awliyā'
Al-Qutaynah
Rufā'ah
Wad Madanī
AL-JAZĪRAH
Sinjah
Sannār
Al-Hawātah
Qallābāt
Gedaref
Dabat
Azezo
Gonder
Ras Dashen Terara 4620
Sek'ot'a
K'obo
Lalibela
Debre Tabor
T'ana Hāyk'
Bahir Dar
Weldiya
Serdo
Tendaho
Moussa 'Ali 2021
Dikhil
DJIBOUTI
Tadjoura
Obock
Saylac
Zeila
Barbara
DANAKIL
Aseb
Al-Mukhā
Madīnat ash-Sha'b
Shaykh 'Uthmān
ADAN (Aden)
Lahij
Shaqrā'
Gulf of Aden
Bāb el-Mandeb
Bārīm
Abd al-Kūrī (Yemen)
Raas Gwardafuy
Caluula
Gees Gwardafuy
Boosaaso
Qandala
Bargaal
Baxaya 2200
Hurdiyo
Raas Xaafuun
Meeladeen
Ceerigaabo
Qardho
Bandarbeyla
Eyl

Kaka
Talawdi
Tungaru
Abū Jubayah
Ar-Rahad
Rashād
JIBĀL AN-NŪBAH
Dilling
Kadugli
Kologi
Talodi
ETHIOPIAN PLATEAU
CHOK'E
Mendi
Bambesi
Asosa
Kurmuk
Guba
Dangila
Mot'a
Amba Farit 3975
Debre Mark'os
Debre Sīna
Fiche
Debre Birhan
ĀDĪS ĀBEBA (ADDIS ABABA)
Ak'ak'i Beseka
Giyon
Mojo
Nazrēt
Welk'īt'ē
Jima
Hosa'ina
AMHAR MOUNTAINS
Harer
Jijiga
Dirē Dawa
Awash
Mī'eso
Degeh Bur
Āwarē
Sasabaneh
Jijiga
Hargeysa
Caynabā
Burco
Garoowe
SOMALIA
ETHIOPIA
RIFT VALLEY
Tulu Welel 3001
Neĵemtē
Gambēla
Gorē
Dembi
Dembi Dolo
Bedelē
Mizan Teferi
Majī
Maji
Mai Gudo 3100
Shambu
Waka
Shashemenē
Awasa
Yirga 'Alem
Sodo
Dila
Gidole
Kibre Mengist
El Kere
Goba
Ginir
Lega Hida
El Fud
Denan
Domo
Werder
Beyra
Gaalkacyo
Daborow
Qooriga Neegro
MENDEBO
Guge 4200
Abela
Ch'amo Hāyk'
Arba Minch
INDIAN OCEAN
SUDAN
Fangak
Bentiu
Abwong
Nyerol
Mogogh
Ayod
Duk Fadiat
Nāşir
Sobat
Kodok
Malakāl
Daga Post
Tombe
Pibor Post
Akōbō
Gīmbi
Tor
Beigi
Dembi Dolo
Kaka
Talawdi
UGANDA
KENYA
Lake Rudolf (Lake Turkana)
Lake Stefanie
Moyale
Filtu
Negēlē
Mega
Ramu
Dolo
Luuq
Waajid
Buulobarde
Totiyas
Mandera
El Wak
Buna
Mereeg
Ceelbuur
Xarardheere
Hobyo
Dhuusamarreeb
Shilabo
K'elafo
Mustahil
Wabe Shebele
Beledweyne
Lema Shilindi
Jabal Laūke 2963
Kinyeti 3187
Lokichokio
Kaabong
Loyoro
Kapoeta
Loki taung
Lodwar
North Horr
El Wak

M-DRM4713-A1- -3-3-3
Copyright © Rand McNally & Co.

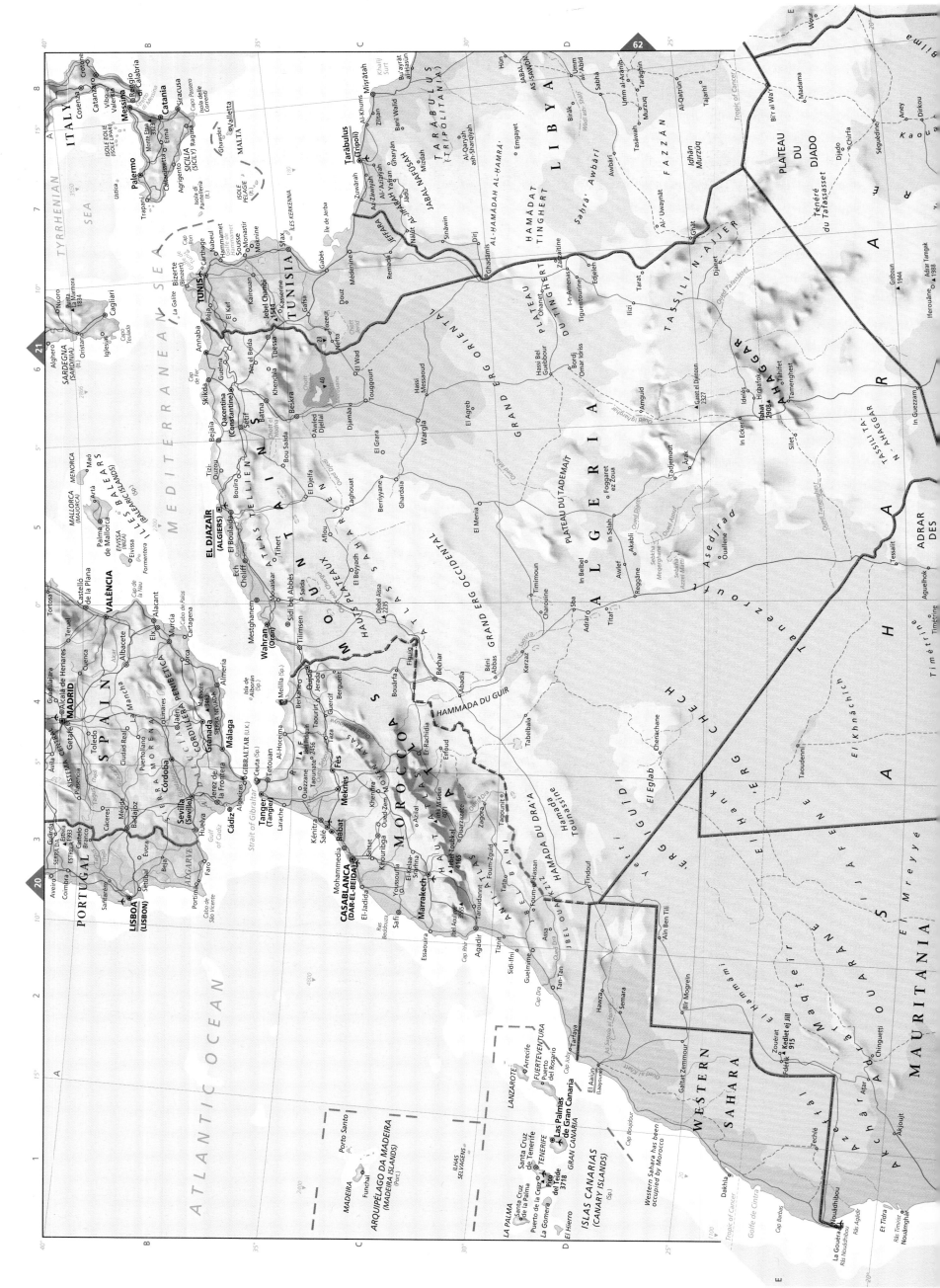

Western Sahara has been occupied by Morocco

66

Countries and regions:

CHAD

NIGER

N I G E R I A

CAMEROON

ADAMAWA

CONGO

GABON

EQUATORIAL GUINEA

SAO TOME AND PRINCIPE

SÃO TOMÉ

Príncipe

BIOKO

Annobón (Eq. Guinea)

M A L I

BURKINA FASO

BENIN

TOGO

G H A N A

COTE D'IVOIRE

Ashanti

LIBERIA

SIERRA LEONE

G U I N E A

GUINEA-BISSAU

THE GAMBIA

S E N E G A L

D A H O M E Y

FOUTA DJALON

CAPE VERDE

SANTO ANTÃO

SÃO NICOLAU

SANTIAGO

Capitals / major cities:

N'Djamena

Niamey

Ouagadougou

Abuja

LAGOS

Porto-Novo

Cotonou

Lomé

ACCRA

Tema

Kumasi

ABIDJAN

Yamoussoukro

Bamako

Conakry

Freetown

Monrovia

Bissau

BANJUL

DAKAR

Yaoundé

Douala

Libreville

Malabo

Water bodies:

Gulf of Guinea

Bight of Biafra

Bight of Benin

ATLANTIC OCEAN

Lake Chad

Lake Volta

White Volta

Black Volta

Niger Delta

Slave Coast

Gold Coast

Ivory Coast

Grain Coast

Mountains / elevations:

Cameroon Mtn. 4100

Pico de Santa Isabel 3008

Pico de São Tomé 2024

Chappal Waddi 2419

Hombori Tondo 1155

Tema Kourou 747

Bintimani 1945

Mount Nimba 1752

Pic de Tibé 1443

Scale / projection info:

Scale 1 : 10,000,000

Lambert Conformal Conic Projection

M-DRM4714-A1-·1-·2

Copyright © Rand McNally & Co.

1000 Kilometers

600 Miles

Equator

West of Greenwich   0°   East of Greenwich

25° West of Greenwich

Elevation legend:

Meters	Feet
4000	13120
3000	9840
2000	6560
1000	3280
500	1640
200	656
Sea Level	
200	656
2000	6560

a Same scale as main map

Meters
Feet

4000
13120

3000
9840

2000
6560

1000
3280

500
1640

200
656

Sea Level

200
656

2000
6560

M-DRM4712-A1- -2-2-2
Copyright © Rand McNally & Co.

0   100   200   400   600   800   1000 Kilometers
0   200   400   600 Miles
Scale 1 : 10,000,000   Sinusoidal Projection

RED SEA

ERITREA
Asmera Adi Ugri Soira 2989 Teseney Adigrat Tio Ramlu 2130 Kamarān Qishn Sayhūt

YEMEN
Jabal an-Nabī Shu'ayb 3660 San'ā' Shabwah 'Amd Ash-Shihr Al-Mukallā As-Sufāl Ahwar Shaqrā' Lawdar Lahij Shaykh 'Uthmān Adan (Aden) Al-Hawrah Nisāb Habbān Harib Dhamār Yarim Ibb Ta'izz Zabid Bayt al-Faqīh Al-Hudaydah (Hodeida) Jabal al Nashā' 3227 Barim

ETHIOPIA
ADĪS ABEBA (ADDIS ABEBA) Aksum Ādwa Mek'elē Ras Dashen Terara 4620 Gonder Dabat Azezo Bahir Dar Dangila Guba Debre Tabor Lalibela Weldiya Dese Amba Farit 3975 Debre Mark'os CHOK'Ē PLATEAU Mot'a Fichē Debre Birhan Debre Sīna Giyon Mojo Nazrēt Awash Dirē Dawa Harer Jijiga ETHIOPIAN PLATEAU Nek'emtē Welk'itē Ak'ak'ī Besek'a Jima Hosa'ina Shashemenē Waka Sodo Yirga'Alem Agere Selam Dila Abaya Hāyk' Goba Ginīr Adaba Batu 4307 MENDEBO Kibre Mengist Negēle Filtu El Kerē Imi Wabera Denan K'ebrī Dehar Shilabo K'elafo Gelādī Beyra Geladī Werdēr Gol Dhuusamarreeb Hobyo

SOMALIA
Boosaaso Qandala Caluula Gees Gwardafuy Bargaal Hurdiyo Raas Xaafuun Bandarbeyla Qardho Garoowe Eyl Laascaanood Domo Gaalkacyo Daborow Beledweyne Ceelbuur Xarardheere Mereeg Totiyas Waajid Buulobarde Ceeldheere Baydhabo (Baidoa) Buurhakaba Weyne Jawhar Balcad Afgooye Muqdisho (Mogadiscio) Marka Baraawe Diinsor Dhoomadheere Baardheere Jilib Dujuuma Jamaame Kamsuuma Kismaayo Jumba Buur Gaabo Kiunga Burco Hargeysa Berbera Bullaxaar Caynabo Shimbiris 2407 Xalin Eyl Qooriga Neegro

DJIBOUTI
Djibouti Dikhil Obock Tadjoura Serdo Aysha Saylac Maydh Karin Ceerigaabo Baxaya 2200

DANAKIL
Moussa 'Alī 2021 Asebo

SUDAN
Al-Qadārif Wad Madanī Sannar Sinjah Al-Hawātah Rufā'ah Khashm al-Qirbah Ad-Duwaym Kūstī Rabak Tandalti Ar-Rahad Rashād Dilāmī Talawdī Kāka Kaduqli Kurmuk Āsosa Malakāl Kodok Fangak Abwong Nyerol Daga Post Bentiu Ayod Duk Fadiat Nāsir Pibor Post Nelichu 1740 Mongalla Juba Bor Yirol Tombe Yei Torit Kapoeta

UGANDA
KAMPALA Entebbe Jinja Tororo Soroti Lira Gulu Pakwach Hoima Masindi Mbale Mount Elgon 4321 Kitgum Moroto 3084 Kaabong Loyoro Kotido Amudat Kabalega Falls Margherita Peak 5109 Fort Portal Kasese Mubende Masaka

KENYA
NAIROBI Nakuru Naivasha Gilgil Nyeri Thika Embu Kirinyaga (Mount Kenya) 5199 Meru Isiolo Nanyuki Maralal Baragoi South Horr Marsabit North Horr Moyale Buna El Wak Wajir Garissa Mado Gashi Archer's Post Merti Kitui Machakos Kajiado Ngong Magadi Narok Konza Makindu Voi Mackinnon Road Mariakani Mombasa Malindi Lamu Garsen Kipini Bura Kolbio Dif Lake Rudolf (Lake Turkana) Lokitaung Lodwar Lokichar Lokichokio Sabarei Mega Ramu Mandera Doolow Luuq Laisamis Ng'iro 2805 Chalbi Desert Kericho Kisumu Kakamega Busia Butere Eldoret Kitale Cherangani 3370 Solai Lake Baringo Kaniido Kaningo Thomson's Falls Kisii Homa Bay Migori Amboseli National Park

TANZANIA
DODOMA DAR ES SALAAM Tanga Pemba Zanzibar Mombasa Bagamoyo Morogoro Kilosa Mikumi Kidatu Iringa Mbeya Tukuyu Songea Tunduru Masasi Newala Mtwara Lindi Kilwa Masoko Kilwa Kivinje Mafia Island Utete Mpwapwa Manyoni Singida Shinyanga Mwanza Musoma Tabora Kahama Nzega Kondoa Babati Arusha Moshi Same Korogwe Lushoto Pangani Njombe Mahenge Mbinga Chunya Makongolosi Sumbawanga Mpanda Uvinza Kigoma Kibondo Kasulu Biharamulo Bukoba Ngara Nyakanazi Geita Kilimanjaro 5895 Ngorongoro Crater 2648 Ol Doinyo Lengai Olduvai Gorge Lake Natron Lake Eyasi Lake Manyara Serengeti Plain SERENGETI NATIONAL PARK MASAI MARA GAME RESERVE NGORONGORO CRATER CONSERVATION AREA Masai Steppe Masai Steppe Ukerewe Island Rubondo Island Mafia Island Lake Kitangiri Great Ruaha Kilombero Rufiji Kipembawe Rungwa Sao Hill Mikumi Mgeta Ifakara Liwale Nachingwea Nyamtumbo Kilindoni

MALAWI
LILONGWE Mzuzu Nkhata Bay Nkhotakota Salima Dedza Mchinji Lichinga Chilumba Livingstonia Rumphi Mzimba Karonga Lake Nyasa Nyika Plateau 2606

MOZAMBIQUE
Metangula Lichinga Nantulo Mueda Montepuez Pemba Mecula Marrupa Balama Chamba Diaca Quiterajo Palma Mocímboa Cabo Delgado Macomia Mucojo Quissanga Ancuabe Namapa Lúrio Nampula Nacala Muite Maúa Mecanhelas Balama Cuamba Metarica Mandimba

COMOROS
MORONI Njazidja Kartala 2361 Nzwani Mwali Fomboni Mutsamudu Domoni

MAYOTTE (Fr.)
Dzaoudzi

SEYCHELLES
Groupe d'Aldabra Assomption Atoll de Cosmoledo Astove Atoll de Providence St. Pierre Atoll de Farquhar Îles Glorieuses (Fr.)

MADAGASCAR
Antsiranana Nosy Be Ambilobe Ambanja Andoany Iharaña Maromokotro 2876 Tanjona Bobaomby

Gulf of Aden

INDIAN OCEAN

Lake Victoria

Lake Tanganyika

Lake Nyasa

ARCHIPEL DES COMORES

RIFT VALLEY

MUCHINGA MOUNTAINS

KIPENGERE RANGE

AHMAR MOUNTAINS

Equator

INDIAN OCEAN

SEYCHELLES

Groupe d'Aldabra
Assomption   Atoll de Cosmoledo   St. Pierre   Atoll de Providence
Astove 4030

Atoll de Farquhar

COMOROS
Njazidja
Moroni ✈ Kartala 2361
Mwali   Nzwani   Mutsamudu
Fomboni
Dzaoudzi
MAYOTTE (Fr.)

Îles Glorieuses (Fr.)

ARCHIPEL DES COMORES

TANZANIA
Dodoma   Mpwapwa
Zanzibar   Zanzibar
Bagamoyo   Kizimkazi
DAR ES SALAAM

Kilosa   Morogoro
Kimokulu   Kidatu   Kisiju
Iringa   Mafia Island
Ifakara   Kilindoni
Sao Hill   Utete
Mahenge   Kilwa Kivinje
Mdandu   Njombe   Kilwa Masoko
Songea   Zinga Muliku
Nachingwea   Liwale
Lindi
Masasi   Mtama   Mikindani   Mtwara
Newala   Cabo Delgado
Palma
Diaca
Mueda   Quiterajo
Mecula   Mucojo
Macomia
Nantulo   Quissanga   Pemba
Marrupa   Montepuez   Ancuabe
Maua   Balama
Catur   Belém
Lúrio   Namapa
Namialo   Memba
Cuamba   Nacala-a-Velha   Nacala
Malema   Ribáuè   Monapo
Murrupula   Lumbo   Ilha de Moçambique
Nampula
Nametil   Mogincual

MALAWI
Nkhata Bay 474
Olivença
Mzimba
Lichinga
Niassa
Metangula
Lake Nyasa
Lake Chilwa
Zomba
Blantyre Sapitwa 2002
Thyolo   Milange
Chiperone 2054
Mandimba   Namarrói
Serra Namúli 2419
Lugela   Mocuba
Mulevala   Moma
Angoche
Larde
Pebane

MOZAMBIQUE
Tete   Moatize
Chimoio   Chemba
Changara   Doa   Nsanje
Morrumbala
Vila de Sena
Mopeia   Quelimane
Marromeu   Chinde
Serra da Gorongosa 1856
Manica
Monte Binga 2437
Dondo   Beira
Chibabava   Sofala
Espungabera
Nova Mambone
Inhassoro
Ilha do Bazaruto
Massangena   Vilankulo   Ponta São Sebastião
Mabote   Mapinhane
Funhalouro   Massinga
Morrumbene
Chigubo   Maxixe   Ponta da Barra
Panda   Inhambane
Chibuto   Inharrime
Xinavane   Quissico
Macia   Chidenguele
Xai-Xai
Moamba   Baía de Maputo
MAPUTO
Ilha da Inhaca
Bela Vista
Zitundo

Mozambique Channel

MADAGASCAR
Antsiranana
Tanjona Bobaomby
Nosy Mitsio
Nosy Be   Ambohitra 1476
Andoany   Ambilobe   Iharaña
Maromandia   TSARATANANA
Maromokotro 2876   Sambava
Analalava   Andapa
Antsohihy   Antalaha
Bealanana
Mandritsara   Rantabe
Mahajanga   Maroantsetra
Mampikony   Tsaratanana
Soalala   Marovoay   Nosy Sainte Marie
Maevatanana   Mananara Avaratra
Tanjona Vilanandro   Madirovalo
Besalampy   Andriamena   Andilamena   Fenoarivo Atsinanana
Farihy Alaotra   Ambatondrazaka
Tambohorano   Mahabe
Morafenobe   Kandreho   Ambodifototra
Ankazobe   Moramanga
Maintirano   Tsiroanomandidy
Analatsoa   Ankavandra
Nosy Barren   Bekopaka   Ariovonimamo   Toamasina
ANTANANARIVO
Soavinandriana   Ampasimanolotra
Belo-Tsiribihina   Miandrivazo   Tsiafajavona 2642   Ambatolampy   Vatomandry
Morondava   Antsirabe   Manjakandriana
Betafo   Ambatofinandrahana   Ambositra   Mahanoro
Mahabo   Malaimbandy   Ambohimahasoa   Nosy-Varika
Belo-sur-Mer   Mandabe
Andranopasy   Manja   Mananjary
Morombe   Beroroba   Fianarantsoa   Ifanadiana
Tanjona Ankaoa   Befandriana Avaratra
Ankazoabo   Ambalavao   Manakara
Ihosy   Boby 2658   Ivohibe   Vohipeno
Manombo Atsimo   Ranohira   Farafangana
Sakaraha   Betroka
Toliara   Bezaha   Vondrozo
Bekily   Vangaindrano
Ejeda   Beraketa
Itampolo   Ampanihy   Midongy Atsimo
Androka   Manantenina
Tsiombe   Ambovombe   Tôlañaro
Tanjona Vohimena

Bassas da India (Fr.)
Île Juan de Nova (Fr.)
Île Europa (Fr.)

INDIAN OCEAN

Tropic of Capricorn

SEYCHELLES
Praslin   La Digue
Silhouette   Victoria
Mahé

Poivre Atoll   Desroches   Île Plate
LES AMIRANTES
Alphonse
Coëtivy

a Same scale as main map
INDIAN OCEAN
MAURITIUS
Port Louis
Piton de la Petite Rivière Noire 828   Curepipe
Saint-Denis   Mahébourg
Piton des Neiges 3070
Saint-Paul
Saint-Pierre   RÉUNION (Fr.)
MASCARENE ISLANDS
East of Greenwich

b Same scale as main map
INDIAN OCEAN
SEYCHELLES
Groupe d'Aldabra
St. Pierre   Atoll de Providence
Assomption   Atoll de Cosmoledo
Astove 4030   Atoll de Farquhar
Agalega Islands (Maur.)
East of Greenwich

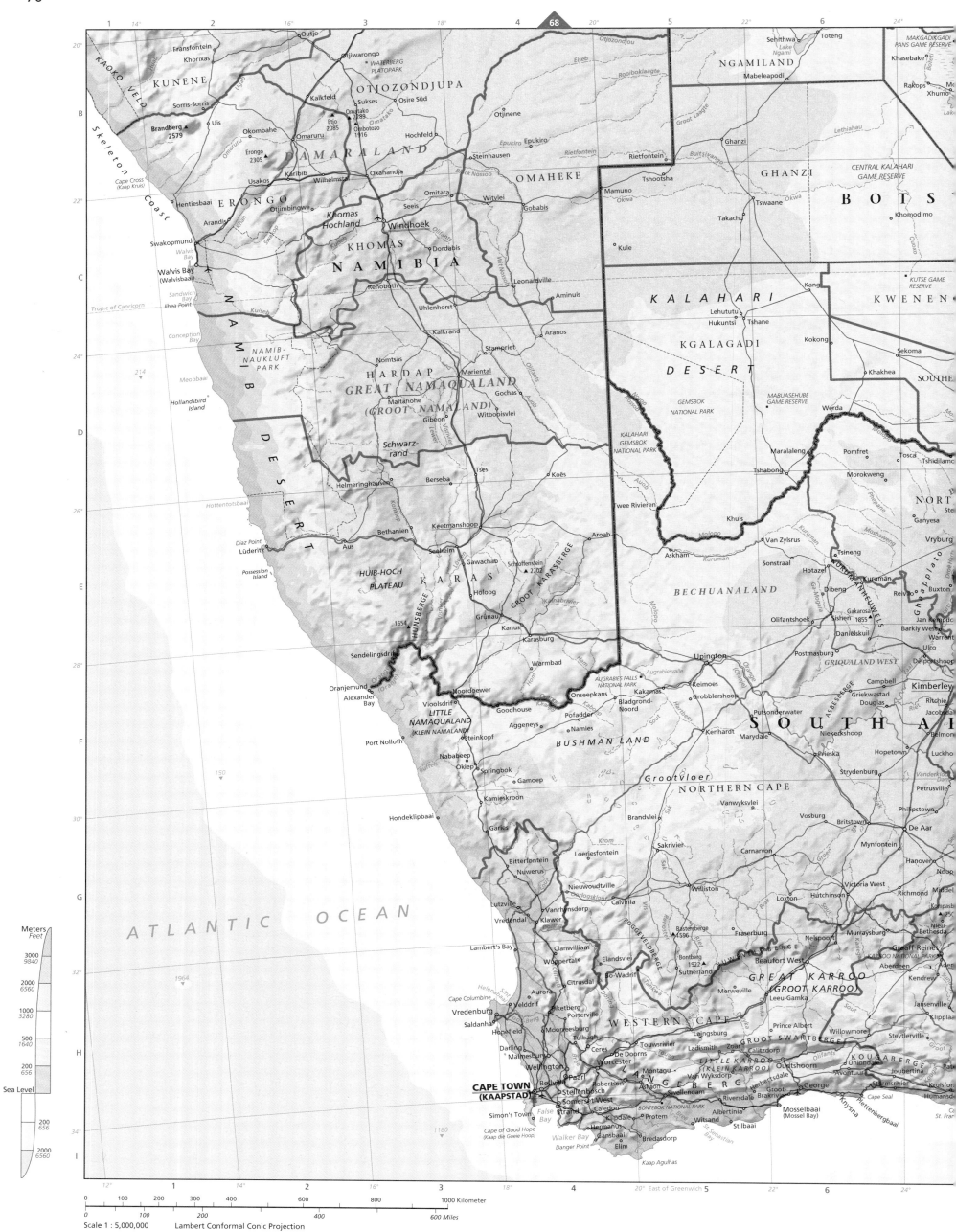

68

KUNENE
Fransfontein
Khorixas
Sorris-Sorris
Kalkfeld
Outjo
Otjiwarongo
WATERBERG PLATOPARK
Brandberg 2579
Uis
Okombahe
Omaruru
Etjo 2085
Omatako 2289
Ombotozo 1916
Hochfeld
Otjinene
Epukiro Epukiro
Rietfontein
Rietfontein
Ghanzi
Steinhausen

KAOKO VELD
DAMARALAND
Erongo 2305
Karibib
Usakos
Wilhelmstal
Okahandja
Omitara
Witvlei
Gobabis
OMAHEKE

NGAMILAND
Mabeleapodi
Tshootsha
Mamuno
Okwa
GHANZI
Tswaane
Takachu
Kule

BOTS
Sehithwa
Lake Ngami
Toteng
Khasebake
Rakops
Xhumo
MAKGADIKGADI PANS GAME RESERVE
Khomodimo
CENTRAL KALAHARI GAME RESERVE

ERONGO
Hentiesbaai
Arandis
Otjimbingwe
Seeis
Khomas Hochland
Windhoek
KHOMAS
NAMIBIA
Rehoboth
Dordabis
Leonardville
Aminuis

Cape Cross (Kaap Kruis)
Swakopmund
Walvis Bay
Walvis Bay (Walvisbaai)
Sandwich Bay
Ilhea Point
Trop.c of Capricorn

KALAHARI
Lehututu
Hukuntsi
Tshane
Kang
Kokong
Sekoma
Khakhea
KUTSE GAME RESERVE
KWENEN
KGALAGADI
DESERT
Werda
SOUTHE

Conception Bay
214
Meobbaai
Hollandbird Island

NAMIB
NAMIB-NAUKLUFT PARK
Nomtsas
HARDAP
GREAT NAMAQUALAND (GROOT NAMALAND)
Maltahöhe
Mariental
Gochas
Stampriet
Aranos

Schwarz-rand
Gibeon
Witbooisvlei
GEMSBOK NATIONAL PARK
MABUASEHUBE GAME RESERVE
Maralaleng
Pomfret
Tosca
Tshidilamo
DESERT
KALAHARI GEMSBOK NATIONAL PARK
Tshabong
Morokweng

Hottentotsbaai
Helmeringhausen
Berseba
Tses
Koës
Twee Rivieren
Khuis
Van Zylsrus
Askham
Kuruman
Tsineng
Ganyesa
Vryburg

Diaz Point
Lüderitz
Bethanien
Aus
Seeheim
Gawachab
Schoffenstein 2202
GROOT KARASBERGE
Aroab
Sonstraal
Hotazel
Kuruman
1855
Reivilo
Buxton

Possession Island
HUIB-HOCH PLATEAU
KARAS
Holoog
Kalabrivier
BECHUANALAND
Olifantshoek
Sishen
Jan Kempd
Barkly West
Warrent

1654
HUNSBERGE
Grünau
Kanus
Karasburg
Molopo
Upington
Postmasburg
Danielskuil
Uleo
GRIQUALAND WEST
Delportshoop

Sendelingsdrif
Warmbad
Ham
Augrabiesvalle
Keimoes
Grobblershoop
Putonderwater
Campbell
Kimberley
Griekwastad
Douglas
Ritchie
Jacobsdal

Oranjemund
Noordoewer
AUGRABIES FALLS NATIONAL PARK
Kakamas
SOUTH A
Belmon

Alexander Bay
Vioolsdrif
Goodhouse
Onseepkans
Bladgrond-Noord
Pofadder
Namies
Kenhardt
Marydale
Niekerkshoop
NORTHERN CAPE

LITTLE NAMAQUALAND (KLEIN NAMALAND)
Aggeneys
BUSHMAN LAND
Phieska
Hopetown
Luckho

Port Nolloth
Steinkopf
Nababeep
Okiep
Springbok
Gamoep
Groot vloer
Strydenburg
Vanderkli
Petrusville

150
Kamieskroon
Brandvlei
Vanwyksvlei
Vosburg
Britstown
De Aar
Mynfontein
Hanover
Noup

Hondeklipbaai
Garies
Loeriesfontein
Sak
Sakrivier
Carnarvon
Victoria West
Richmond
Middel
Philipstown

Nieuwoudtville
Williston
Loxton
Hutchinson
Kompasb
Nieu Bethesda
Graaff-Reinet

ATLANTIC OCEAN
Lutzville
Vanrhynsdorp
Calvinia
Fraserburg
Nelspoort
Murraysburg
Aberdeen

Vredendal
Klawer
Clanwilliam
Bastersberge 1596
ROGGEVELDBERGE
Beaufort West
GREAT KARROO (GROOT KARROO)
Kendrew

Lambert's Bay
Wuppertal
Elandsvlei
Bontberg 1922
Sutherland
NUWEVELDBERGE
Merweville
Aberdeen

1964
Citrusdal
Aurora
To Wadrif
Prince Albert
Willowmore
Steytlerville
Klipplaa
Jansenville

Cape Columbine
Vredenburg
Velddrif
Piketberg
Porterville
Tulbagh
WESTERN CAPE
GROOT-SWARTBERG
KOUGABERGE
Joubertina

Saldanha
Hopefield
Moorreesburg
LITTLE KARROO (KLEIN KARROO)
Ladismith
Calitzdorp
Oudtshoorn
Uniondale
Avontuur
Pat

Darling
Malmesbury
Ceres
De Doorns
Touwsrivier
Laingsburg
Van Wyksdorp
Groot
Herbertsdale
George
Cape Seal

Wellington
Paarl
Worcester
Montagu
LANGEBERG
Riversdale
Brakrivier
Knysna
St. Fra

CAPE TOWN (KAAPSTAD)
Bellville
Stellenbosch
Somerset West
Strand
Robertson
Ashton
Swellendam
Witsand
Mosselbaai (Mossel Bay)
Kruisfon

Simon's Town
False Bay
Caledon
Klipdale
Protem
Albertinia
Stilbaai
St. Sebastian Bay
St. Fra

Cape of Good Hope (Kaap die Goeie Hoop)
Walker Bay
Hermanus
Danger Point
Bredasdorp
Elim
Kaap Agulhas

1180
BONTEBOK NATIONAL PARK

Meters / Feet
3000 / 9840
2000 / 6560
1000 / 3280
500 / 1640
200 / 656
Sea Level
200 / 656
2000 / 6560

0   100   200   300   400   600   800   1000 Kilometer
0   100   200   400   600 Miles
Scale 1 : 5,000,000   Lambert Conformal Conic Projection
East of Greenwich

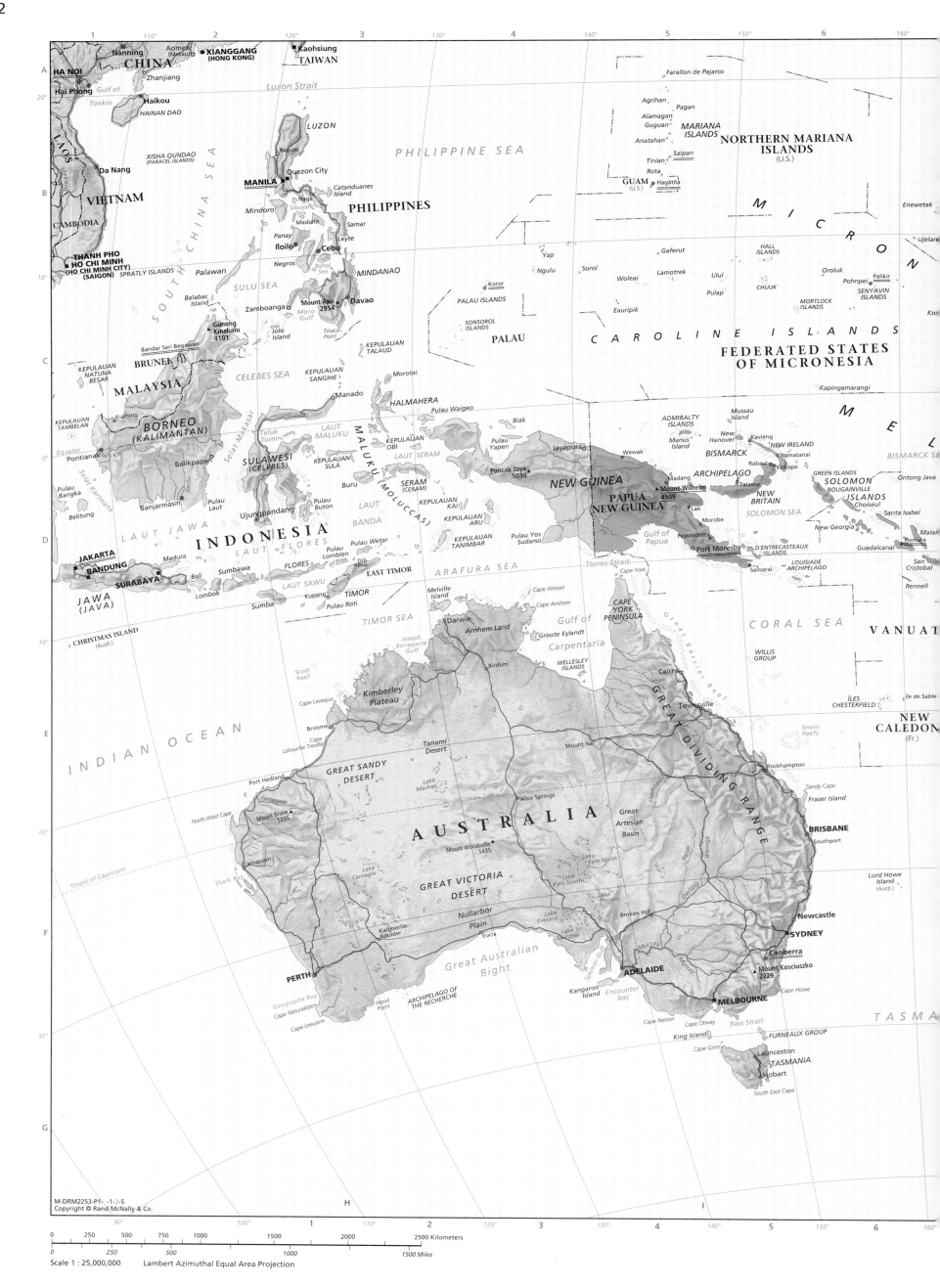

0   250   500   750   1000   1500   2000   2500 Kilometers

0   250   500   1000   1500 Miles

Scale 1 : 25,000,000   Lambert Azimuthal Equal Area Projection

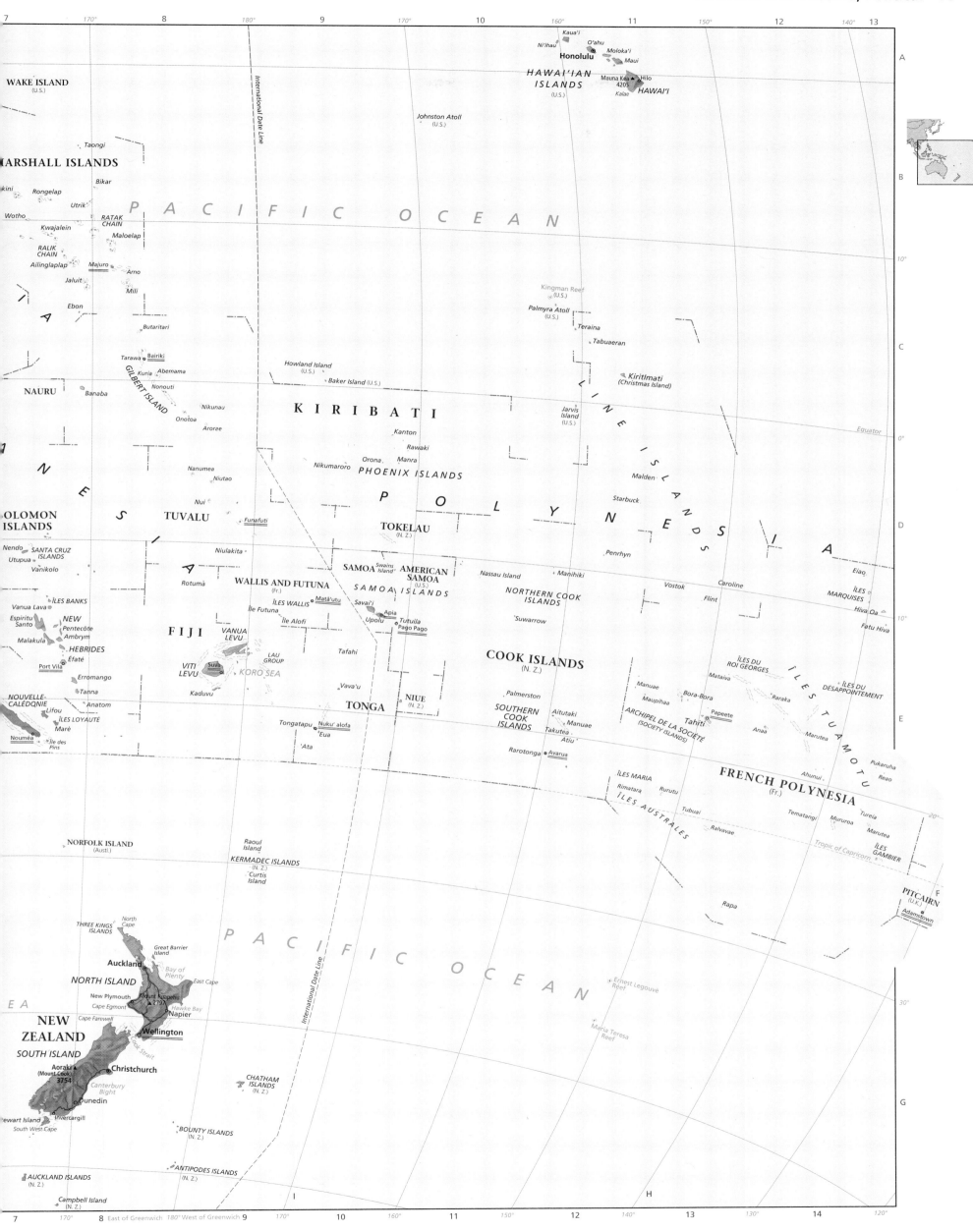

7   170°   8   180°   9   170°   10   160°   11   150°   12   140°   13

WAKE ISLAND
(U.S.)

Taongi

MARSHALL ISLANDS

Bikar

Bikini   Rongelap   Utrik

Wotho

RATAK
CHAIN

Kwajalein   Maloelap

RALIK
CHAIN

Ailinglaplap   Majuro   Arno

Jaluit   Mili

Ebon

Butaritari

Tarawa   Bairiki
Kuria   Abemama

NAURU   Banaba   Nonouti

GILBERT ISLAND

Nikunau

Onotoa
Aroræ

Nanumea

Niutao

Nui

TUVALU   Funafuti

Niulakita

SOLOMON
ISLANDS

Nendo   SANTA CRUZ
ISLANDS

Utupua   Vanikolo

Rotumà

ÎLES BANKS

Vanua Lava

Espíritu   NEW
Santo   Pentecôte
Ambrym

Malakula   HEBRIDES
Éfaté

Port Vila

Erromango

Tanna

NOUVELLE-
CALÉDONIE

Anatom

ÎLES LOYAUTÉ

Lifou

Maré

Nouméa

Île des
Pins

PACIFIC   OCEAN

Johnston Atoll
(U.S.)

Kingman Reef
(U.S.)

Palmyra Atoll
(U.S.)   Teraina

Tabuaeran

Howland Island
(U.S.)

Baker Island (U.S.)

KIRIBATI

Kanton

Rawaki

Orona   Manra

Nikumaroro   PHOENIX ISLANDS

P   O   L   Y

TOKELAU
(N. Z.)

Niu'ihau   O'ahu   Moloka'i
Honolulu   Maui
Kaua'i

HAWAI'IAN
ISLANDS
(U.S.)   Mauna Kea   Hilo
4205
Kalae   HAWAI'I

Kiritlmati
(Christmas Island)

Jarvis
Island
(U.S.)   Equator   0°

Malden

Starbuck

N   E   S

Penrhyn

SAMOA   Swains
Island   AMERICAN
SAMOA
(U.S.)

Nassau Island   Manihiki

SAMOA ISLANDS   Vostok   Caroline

Savai'i   NORTHERN COOK
ISLANDS   Flint

WALLIS AND FUTUNA
(Fr.)

ÎLES WALLIS   Matá'utu

Île Futuna

Île Alofi

Upolu   Apia
Tutuila
Pago Pago

FIJI   VANUA
LEVU

Tafahi

'Suwarrow

COOK ISLANDS
(N. Z.)

VITI
LEVU   Suva   LAU
GROUP

KORO SEA

Kaduvu

Vava'u

Palmerston

Manuae   Bora-Bora

Maupihaa

NIUE
(N. Z.)

SOUTHERN
COOK
ISLANDS   Aitutaki
Manuae

TONGA

Tongatapu   Nuku' alofa

'Eua

Takutea
Atiu

'Ata

Rarotonga   Avarua

ÎLES MARIA

Rimatara   Rurutu

FRENCH POLYNESIA
(Fr.)

ÎLES AUSTRALES

Tubuai

Ralvavae

Rapa

L   I   N   E   I   S   L   A   N   D   S

P   O   L   Y   N   E   S   I   A

ÎLES
MARQUISES

Hiva Oa

Fatu Hiva

ÎLES DU
ROI GEORGES

Mataiva   Raraka

Anaa   Marutea

Papeete   ÎLES DU
DÉSAPPOINTEMENT

Tahiti

ARCHIPEL DE LA SOCIÉTÉ
(SOCIETY ISLANDS)

Ahunui   Pukaruha
Reao

Tematangi   Mururoa   Tureia

Marutea

ÎLES
GAMBIER

Tropic of Capricorn   20°

PITCAIRN
(U.K.)

Adamstown

NORFOLK ISLAND
(Austl.)

Raoul
Island

KERMADEC ISLANDS
(N. Z.)

Curtis
Island

THREE KINGS
ISLANDS   North
Cape

Great Barrier
Island

Auckland   Bay of
Plenty

NORTH ISLAND   East Cape

New Plymouth   Mount Ruapehu
Cape Egmont   2797

Napier
Hawke Bay

NEW
ZEALAND   Cape Farewell

SOUTH ISLAND   Wellington

Cook Strait

Aoraki
(Mount Cook)   Christchurch
3754

Canterbury
Bight

Dunedin

Stewart Island

Invercargill

South West Cape

AUCKLAND ISLANDS
(N. Z.)

Campbell Island
(N. Z.)

BOUNTY ISLANDS
(N. Z.)

ANTIPODES ISLANDS
(N. Z.)

CHATHAM
ISLANDS
(N. Z.)

PACIFIC   OCEAN

Ernest Legouvé
Reef

Maria Teresa
Reef

International Date Line

30°

7   170°   8   East of Greenwich   180°   West of Greenwich   9   170°   10   160°   11   150°   12   13   130°   14   120°

INDONESIA

SUMBA · Baing · Kupang · TIMOR
Pulau Sawu · Seba · Baa · Pulau Roti
Nembara · Sedah

TIMOR SEA

INDIAN OCEAN

Ashmore Islands · Cartier Islands

Cape Van Diemen · Coburg Peninsula · Cape Croker · Croker Island · ARAFU
Bathurst Island · Dundas Strait · Goulburn Islands
Melville Island · Van Diemen Gulf
Beagle Gulf · Clarence Strait · Oenpelli · Maning
Charles Point · Darwin · Humpty Doo · Jabiru
Rum Jungle · Batchelor · Adelaide River · Arnhem Land
Ansons Bay · Tipperary · Pine Creek
Cape Londonderry · Katherine · Roper Va

Admiralty Gulf · Kalumburu
Scott Reef · Browse Island
Adèle Island · BUCCANEER ARCHIPELAGO · Collier Bay · Wyndham · Kununurra · Auvergne · Willeroo · Mataranka · Larrimah · Birdum
Cape Leveque · King Sound · KING LEOPOLD RANGES · Gibb River · Karunjie · Kildurk · Victoria River Downs · Montejinni · Top Springs · Dunmarra
Beagle Bay · Dampier Land · Derby · Kimberley Downs · Kimberley Plateau · Mount Ord 947 · Mount Lush 781 · Ord River · Mount Napier 487 · Waterloo · Turner · Wave Hill · Camfield · Newcastle Wat
Broome · Roebuck Bay · Yeeda · Liveringa · Fitzroy Crossing · Halls Creek · Gordon Downs · Inverway · Hooker Creek · Eva Dow
Thangoo · Noonkanbah · Christmas Creek · Banka Banka
Cape Latouche Treville · LaGrange · EDGAR RANGES · Billiluna · Tanami · Mount Samuel 433 · Tanami
Lagrange Bay · Anna Plains · Tanami Desert · The Granites · The Granites 436 · Wauchope
Eighty Mile Beach · Mandora · GREAT SANDY DESERT · Lake Gregory · Lake White · NORTHERN TER
Wallal Downs · Lake Hazlett · Willowra · Murray Downs
Port Hedland · Goldsworthy · Shay Gap · Warrawagine · Percival Lakes · Mount Singleton 808 · Barrow Creek
Dampier · Wickham · Roebourne · Marble Bar · Lake Auld · AUSTRA · Stirling
Barrow Island · Karratha · Millstream · Nullagine · Lake Dora · Lake Mackay · Mount Cockburn 846 · Utopia · Aileron · Mount Riddock
North West Cape · Glenroy · Yarraloola · Pannawonica · Mount Brockman 1132 · Wittenoom · Ethel Creek · Lake George · Mount Liebig 1274 · Narwietooma · Mount Zeil 1531 · Mount Brasse
Exmouth · Onslow · Minderoo · Boolaloo · HAMERSLEY RANGE · Mount Bruce 1235 · Mount Meharry 1253 · Lake Disappointment · Mount Leisler 897 · MACDONNELL RANGES · Alice Spr
Learmonth · Giralia · Tom Price · Paraburdoo · Newman · Lake Macdonald · Henbury · Deep V
Ningaloo · Winning · BARLEE RANGE · Gibson Desert · WESTERN AUSTRALIA · Lake Neale · Mount Olga 1066 · Angas Downs · Erldunda
Chabjuwardoo Bay · Cape Farquhar · Gnaraloo · Gifford Creek · Mount Vernon · Lake Amadeus · PETERMANN RANGES · Uluru (Ayers Rock) 863 · Curtin Springs · Finke
Cape Cuvier · Mount Augustus 1105 · Mount Augustus · Mount Essendon 910 · Mount Salvado 738 · Mount Jenkins · Kulgera
Bernier Island · Gascoyne Junction · Granite Peak · Lake Burnside · Mount Squires 705 · Mount Aloysius 982 · Mount Cockburn 1134 · Sundown
Dorre Island · Carnarvon · Mount Fraser 770 · Peak Hill · Lake Gregory · Carnegie · Lake Gillen · TOMKINSON RANGES · Mount Woodroffe 1435
Cape Inscription · Carey Downs · Karalundi · Lake Nabberu · Lake Carnegie · Baker Lake
Dirk Hartog Island · Byro · Meekatharra · Wiluna · Lake Wells · Mount Sir Thomas 805
Denham · Hamelin · Mount Murchison 520 · Nannine · Lake Way · Lake Throssel · Wintinna
Tamala · Meeberrie · Cue · Wondinong · Agnew · Mount Darlot · Yeo Lake · GREAT VICTORIA DESERT · Mount Willoughby
Mount Shenton 520 · Serpentine Lakes · Lake Meramangye · Cooper Pe
Kalbarri · Bluff Point · Wooramel · Sandstone · Melrose · White Cliffs · Lake Darlot · Lake Gidgi · Lake Dey-Dey
Northampton · Mount Magnet · Mount Redcliffe 562 · Laverton · Rason Lake · Lake Maurice · SOUTH
Houtman Abrolhos · Geraldton · Yalgoo · Youanmi · Gwalia · Leonora · Malcolm · Lake Carey · Plumridge Lakes · Maralinga
Mullewa · Mongers Lake · Paynes Find · Kookynie · Lake Minigwal · Nullarbor Plain
Greenough · Mingenew · Morawa · Mount Singleton 678 · Menzies · Lake Ballard · Lake Rebecca · Seemore Downs · Forrest · Deakin · Cook · Ooldea · Malbooma · Mount 361
Dongara · Carnamah · Three Springs · Lake Moore · Goongarrie · Haig · Loongana · Rawlinna · Hampton Tableland · Nullarbor · Colona · Penong
Coorow · Dalwallinu · Mount Jackson 617 · Kalgoorlie-Boulder · Karonie · Zanthus · Eucla · Madura · Mundrabilla · Fowlers Bay · Ceduna
Mount Lesueur 313 · Watheroo · Beacon · Bonnie Rock · Lake Deborah · Coolgardie · Kambalda · Head of Bight · Streaky Bay
Moora · New Norcia · Pithara · Mukinbudin · West Lake Seabrook · Southern Cross · Widgiemooltha · Eyre · Pooche
Lancelin · Gingin · Toodyay · Bencubbin · Bullfinch · Lake Lefroy · Fraser Range · Anxious Bay
Wanneroo · Stirling · New Norcia · Trayning · Higginsville · Lake Cowan · Madura · Elli
Merredin · Kellerberrin · Lake Johnston · Norseman · Balladonia · Ca
PERTH · Northam · York · Bruce Rock · Lake Dundas · RUSSELL RANGE · Great Australian Bight
Fremantle · Gosnells · Corrigin · Hyden · Peak Charles 651 · Salmon Gums
Rockingham · Armadale · Pingelly · Kondinin · Lake King · Gibson · Point Dempster
Pinjarra · Narrogin · Wagin · Newdegate · Ravensthorpe · Esperance · Cape Arid
Yarloop · DARLING RANGE · Wickepin · Lake Grace · Nyabing · Hopetoun
Bunbury · Collie · Darkan · Katanning · Gnowangerup · Hood Point · Bremer Bay · ARCHIPELAGO OF THE RECHERCHE
Geographe Bay · Donnybrook · Kojonup · Cranbrook · Cheyne Bay
Cape Naturaliste · Busselton · Nannup · Bridgetown · Mount Barker · Bremer Bay
Margaret River · Augusta · Pemberton · Denmark · Albany · King George Sound
Cape Leeuwin · Flinders Bay · Northcliffe · West Cape Howe · Bald Head
Point D'Entrecasteaux · Walpole

Meters
Feet
2000 / 6560
1000 / 3280
500 / 1640
200 / 656
Sea Level
200 / 656
2000 / 6560

M-DRM4717-A1- -1- -2
Copyright © Rand McNally & Co.

0 100 200 300 400 600 800 1000 Kilometers
0 200 400 600 Miles
Scale 1 : 10,000,000 · Lambert Conformal Conic Projection

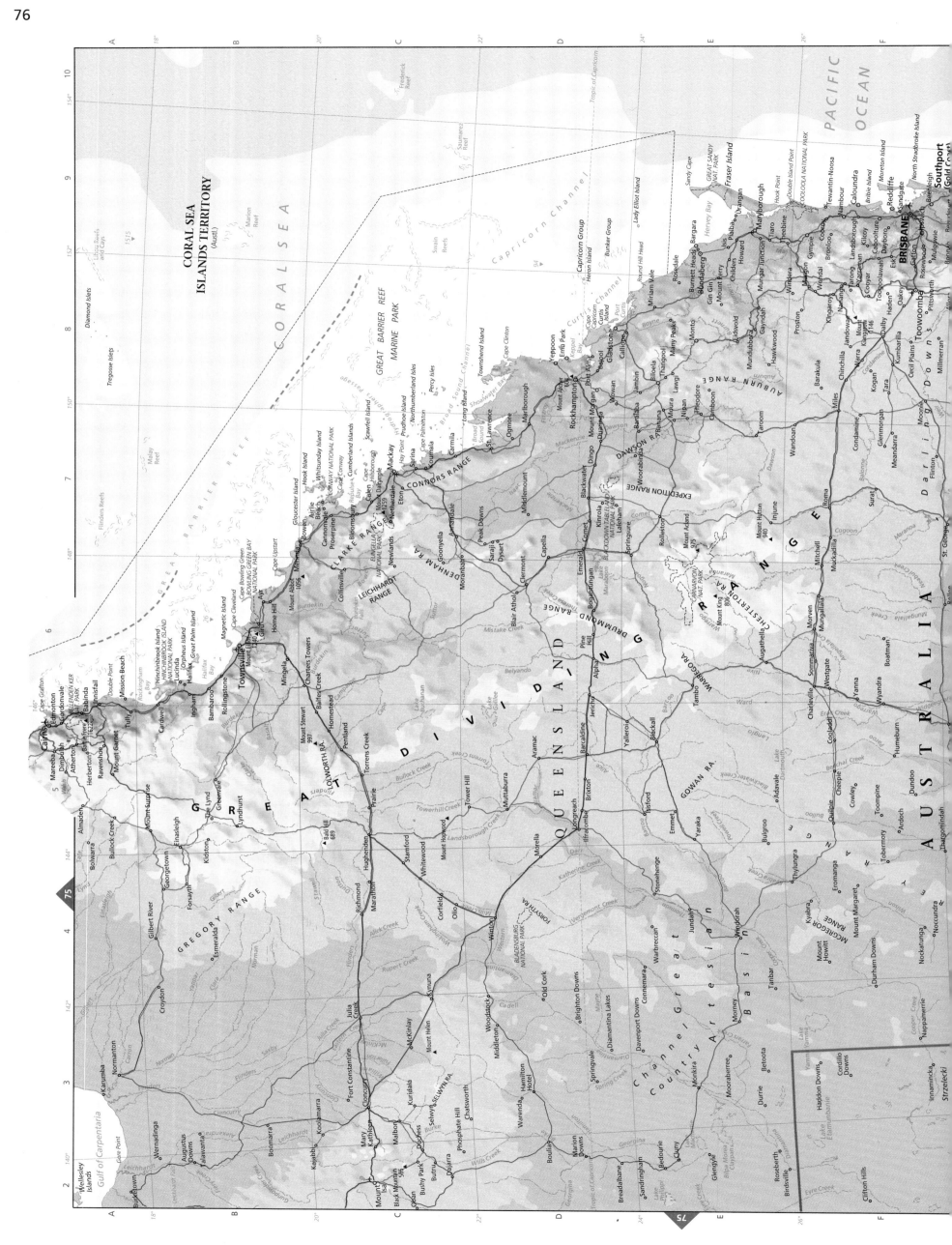

CORAL SEA
ISLANDS TERRITORY
(Aust.)

PACIFIC OCEAN

C O R A L   S E A

QUEENSLAND

AUSTRALIA

Gulf of Carpentaria

BRISBANE

Southport
(Gold Coast)

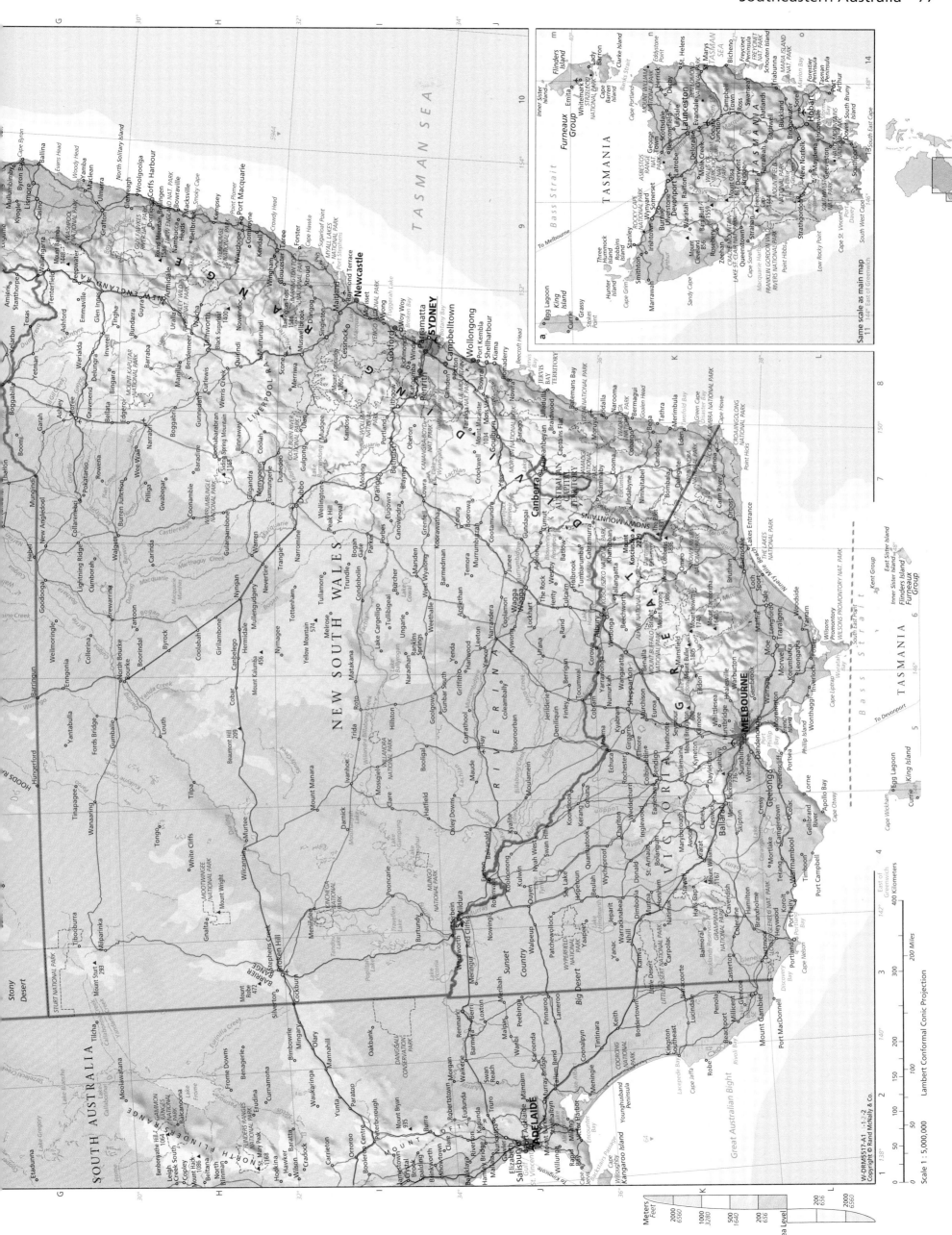

Same scale as main map

TASMANIA

TASMAN SEA

Bass Strait

To Melbourne

To Devonport

NEW SOUTH WALES

SYDNEY

Newcastle

Wollongong

Canberra
AUSTRALIAN CAPITAL TERRITORY

VICTORIA

MELBOURNE

SOUTH AUSTRALIA

ADELAIDE

RIVERINA

SNOWY MOUNTAINS

Great Australian Bight

Scale 1 : 5,000,000

Lambert Conformal Conic Projection

W-DRM5517-A1 .1.2.2
Copyright © Rand McNally & Co.

Meters Feet
2000 6560
1000 3280
500 1640
200 656
Sea Level
200 656
2000 6560

400 Kilometers
200 Miles

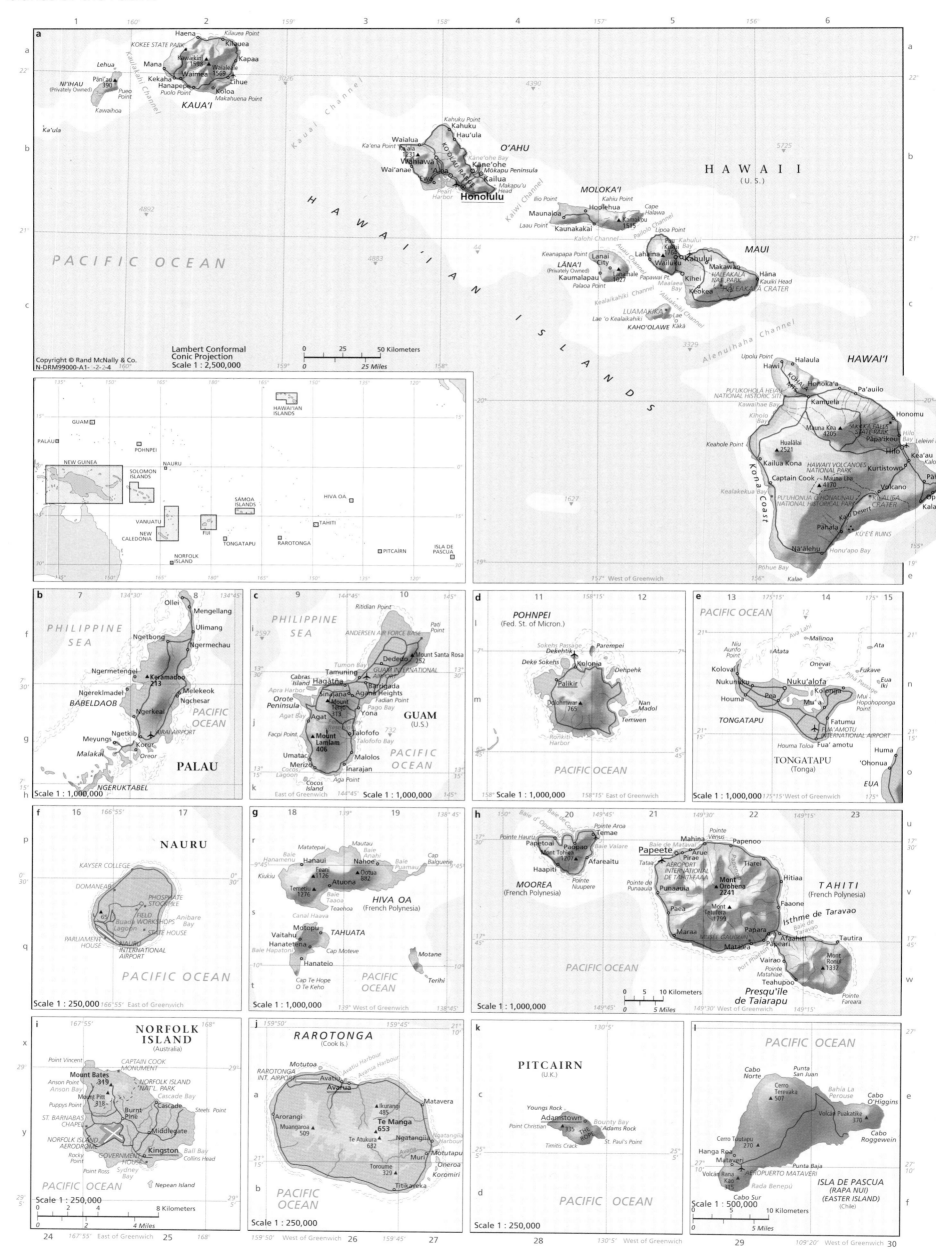

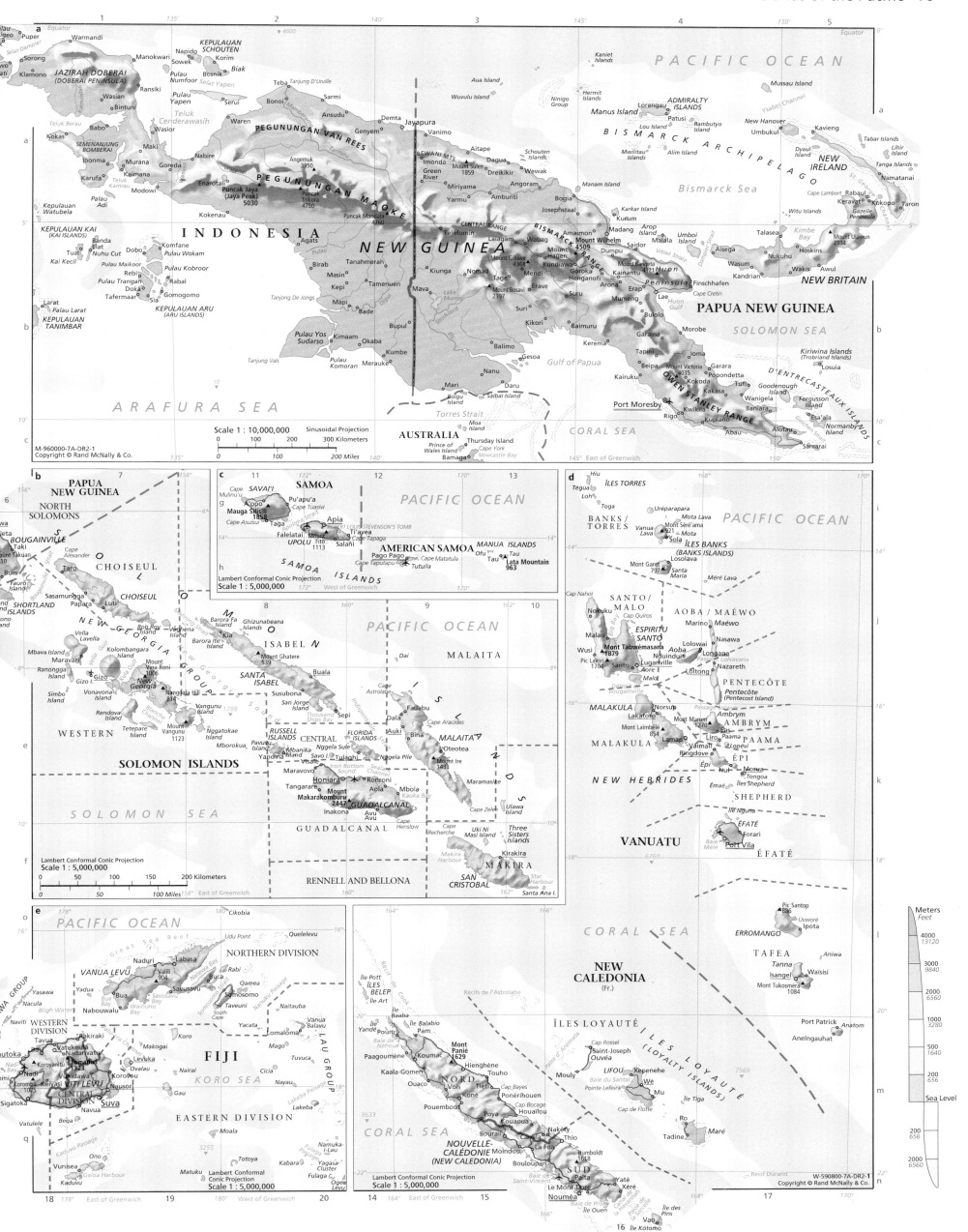

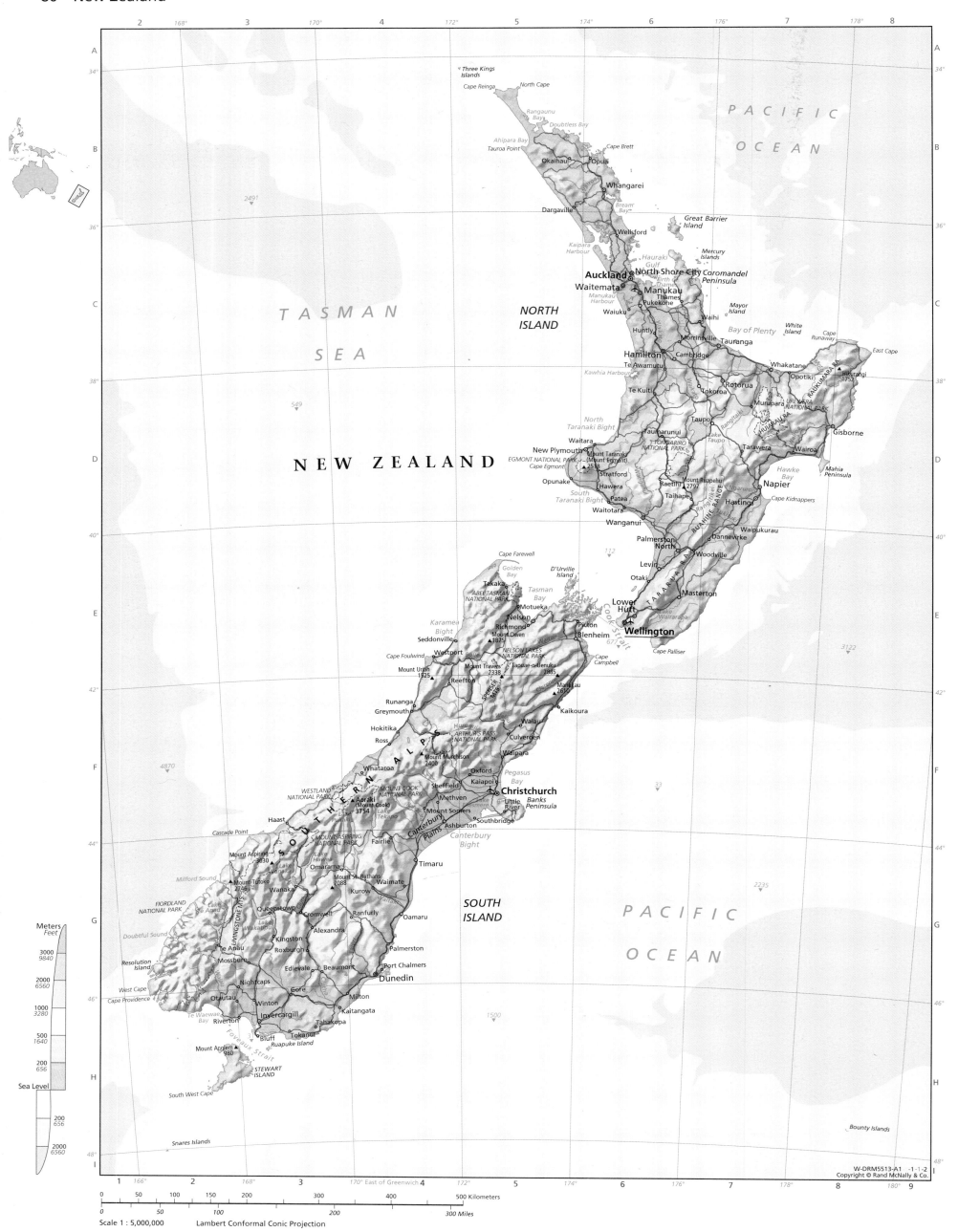

NEW ZEALAND

TASMAN SEA

PACIFIC OCEAN

NORTH ISLAND

SOUTH ISLAND

PACIFIC OCEAN

Scale 1 : 5,000,000
Lambert Conformal Conic Projection

W-DRM5513-A1 -1-1-2
Copyright © Rand McNally & Co.

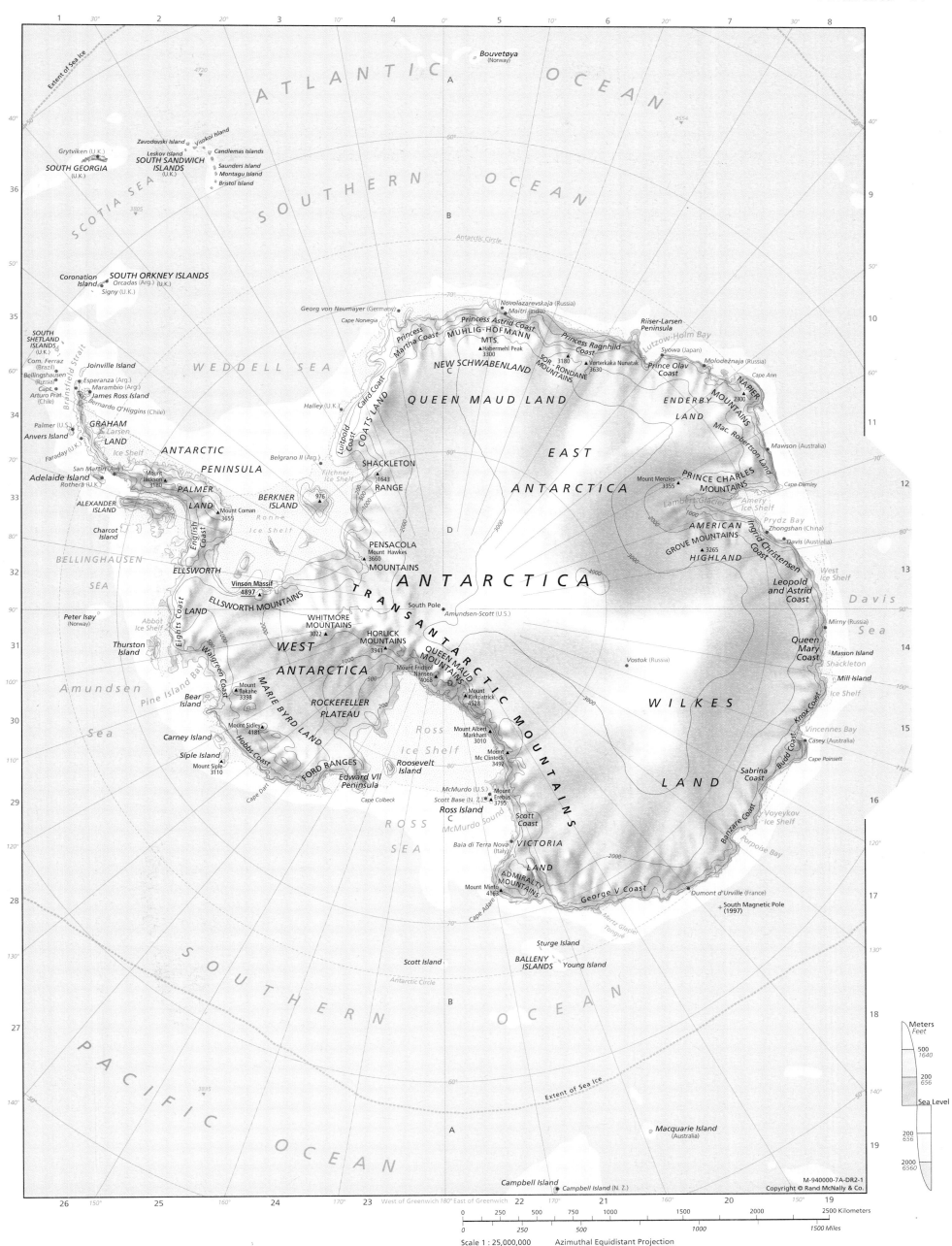

Scale 1 : 25,000,000 Azimuthal Equidistant Projection

M-940000-7A-DR2-1
Copyright © Rand McNally & Co.

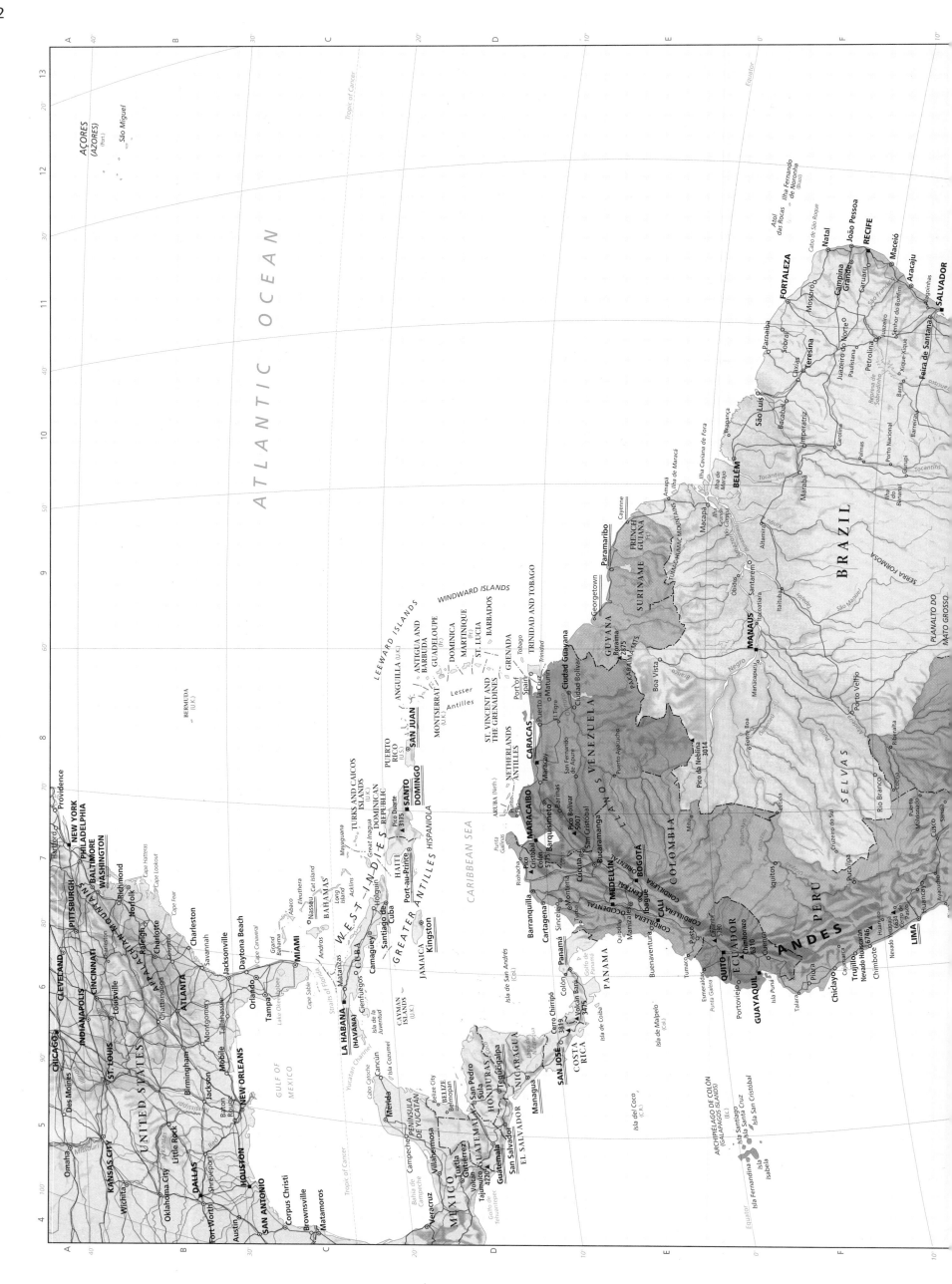

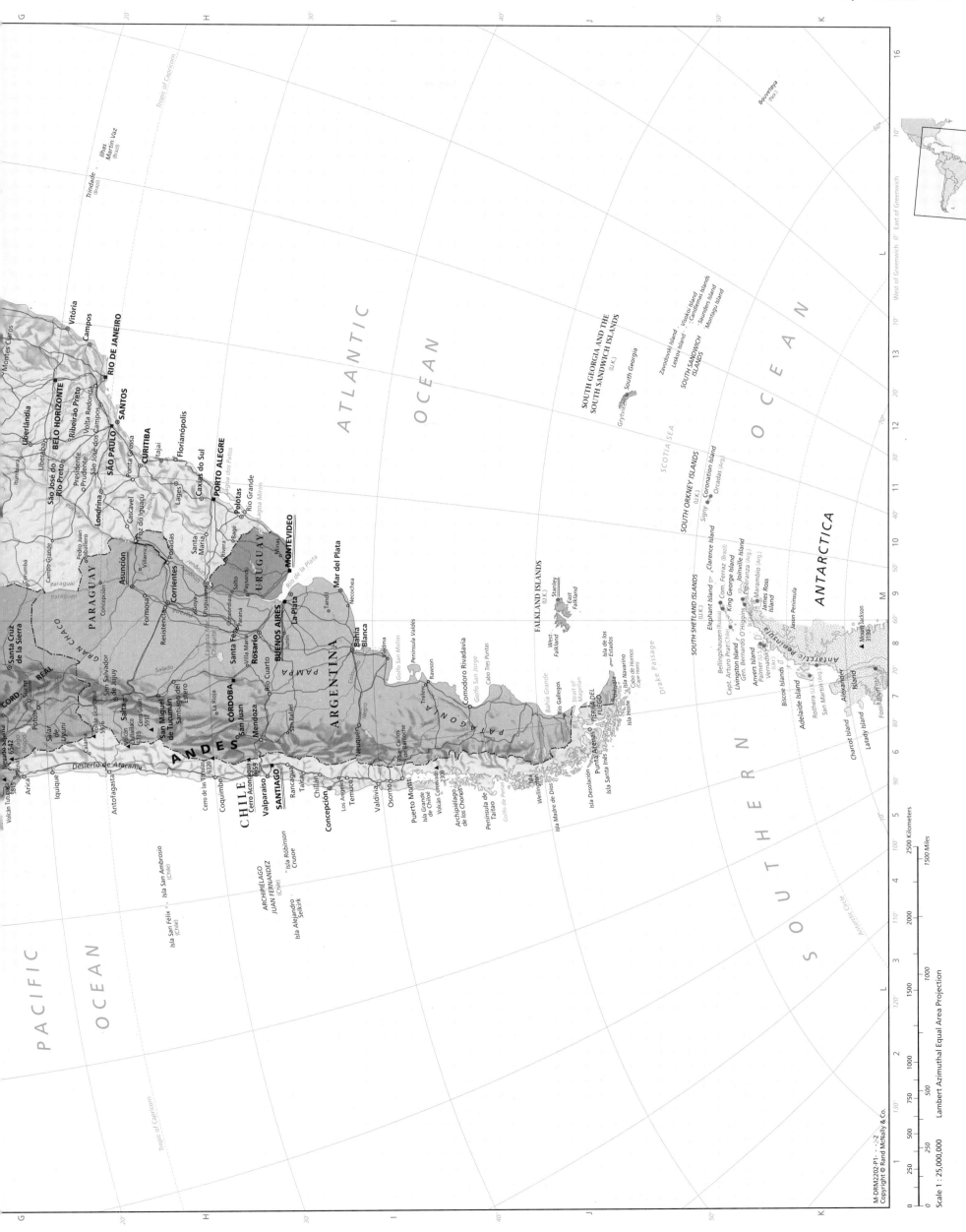

PACIFIC

OCEAN

ATLANTIC

OCEAN

SCOTIA SEA

SOUTHERN

OCEAN

Tropic of Capricorn

ANDES

CORD. REAL

GRAN CHACO

PAMPA

PATAGONIA

ARGENTINA

CHILE

PARAGUAY

URUGUAY

ANTARCTICA

Antarctic Peninsula

ARCHIPIÉLAGO
JUAN FERNÁNDEZ
(Chile)

Isla Alejandro
Selkirk

Isla Robinson
Crusoe

Isla San Félix
(Chile)

Isla San Ambrosio
(Chile)

FALKLAND ISLANDS
(U.K.)

SOUTH GEORGIA AND THE
SOUTH SANDWICH ISLANDS
(U.K.)

SOUTH ORKNEY ISLANDS
(U.K.)

SOUTH SHETLAND ISLANDS
(U.K.)

Bouvetøya
(Nor.)

Trindade
(Brazil)

Ilhas
Martin Vaz
(Brazil)

Drake Passage

TIERRA DEL
FUEGO

Cities and places:
Vitória
Campos
RIO DE JANEIRO
SANTOS
SÃO PAULO
São José dos Campos
Volta Redonda
Ribeirão Preto
BELO HORIZONTE
Uberlândia
Uberaba
Ituiutaba
São José do
Rio Preto
Presidente
Prudente
Londrina
Ponta Grossa
CURITIBA
Itajaí
Florianópolis
Lages
Caxias do Sul
PORTO ALEGRE
Pelotas
Rio Grande
Cascavel
Foz do Iguaçu
Posadas
Corrientes
Resistencia
Formosa
Asunción
Concepción
Villarrica
Paraguaí
Campo Grande
Corumbá
Santa Cruz
de la Sierra
Sucre
Potosí
Oruro
Salar de
Uyuni
Arica
Iquique
Antofagasta
Volcán Tutupaca
5815
Volcán
Llullaillaco
6739
Cerro Galán
5912
San Salvador
de Jujuy
Salta
San Miguel
de Tucumán
Santiago del
Estero
La Rioja
San Juan
Cerro Aconcagua
6959
Mendoza
CÓRDOBA
Río Cuarto
San Rafael
Cerro de las Tórtolas
6320
Coquimbo
Valparaíso
SANTIAGO
Rancagua
Talca
Chillán
Concepción
Los Ángeles
Temuco
Valdivia
Osorno
Volcán Corcovado
2300
Puerto Montt
Isla Grande
de Chiloé
Archipiélago
de los Chonos
Península de
Taitao
Golfo de Penas
Wellington
Isla Madre de Dios
Isla Desolación
Isla Santa Inés
Punta Arenas
Isla Navarino
Isla Hoste
Cabo de Hornos
(Cape Horn)
Río Gallegos
Bahía Grande
Strait of Magellan
Isla de los
Estados
Golfo San Jorge
Comodoro Rivadavia
Cabo Tres Puntas
Trelew
Rawson
Golfo San Matías
Península Valdés
Viedma
Neuquén
San Carlos
de Bariloche
Colorado
Negro
Salado
Santa Fe
Rosario
Paraná
BUENOS AIRES
La Plata
Junín
Tandil
Necochea
Mar del Plata
Bahía
Blanca
MONTEVIDEO
Río de la Plata
Minas
Salto
Paysandú
Rivera
Bagé
Santa
Maria
Lagoa dos Patos
Lagoa Mirim
Montes Claros

Stanley
West
Falkland
East
Falkland

South Georgia
Grytviken

Zavodovski Island
Visokoi Island
Leskov Island
Candlemas Islands
Saunders Island
Montagu Island

Signy
Coronation Island
Orcadas (Arg.)

Elephant Island (Russia)
Com. Ferraz (Brazil)
King George Island
Capt. Arturo Prat (Chile)
Bellingshausen (Russia)
Livingston Island
Gen. Bernardo O'Higgins (Chile)
Joinville Island
Esperanza (Arg.)
Marambio (Arg.)
Clarence Island
James Ross
Island
Jason Peninsula
Anvers Island
Palmer (U.S.)
Vernadskiy (Ukr.)
Biscoe Islands
Adelaide Island
Rothera (U.K.)
San Martín (Arg.)
Charcot Island
Latady Island
Fossil Bluff
Alexander
Island
Mouth Jackson
3190

Tropic of Capricorn

Antarctic Circle

West of Greenwich   0°   East of Greenwich

ATLANTIC

OCEAN

SURINAME

**FRENCH
GUIANA**

New Amsterdam
Nieuw
Nickerie
Totness
Paramaribo
Nieuw Amsterdam
Groningen
Onverwacht
Moengo
Brokopondo
Albina
Kwakoegron
Saint-Laurent
du Maroni
Iracoubo
Sinnamary
Kourou
Île du Diable
Tonate
Cayenne
Saint-Élie
Rémiré

Brokopondo Stuwmeer

WILHELMINA
GEBERGTE
Juliana Top
1230

Guisan Bourg
Cabo Orange
Ouanary
Saint-Georges
Cabo Cacipore
Clevelândia
do Norte
Oiapoque

ORANJE GEBERGTE

Saül
Vila Velha

Cunani
Calçoene

TUMUC-HUMAC MOUNTAINS

AMAPÁ
Amapá
Ilha de Maracá
Cabo Norte
Sucuriju

Lago Novo

Aporema
Serra do Navio
Porto Grande
Ferreira
Gomes
Ilha Bailique
Ilha do Curuá
Ilha Janaucu
Ilha Caviana de Fora
Ilha Mexiana

Macapá
Porto Santana
Mazagão

Cabo Maguari

ILHA DE MARAJÓ
Itatupã
Soure
Salinópolis
Ilha Grande
do Gurupá
Joanes
Curuçá
Maracanã
Igarapé-Açu
Boca do Jari
Anajás
Mosqueiro
Bragança
Oriximiná
Óbidos
Alenquer
Prainha
Monte Alegre
Gurupá
Curumu
Ilha da
Laguna
Breves
São Miguel
dos Macacos
BELÉM
Muaná
São Domingos do Capim
Capanema
Carutapera
Faro
Terra Santa
Juriti
Carrazedo
Porto de
Moz
Portel
Curralinho
Abaetetuba
Acará
Irituia
Camiranga
Cururupu
Cametá
Tomé-Açu
Santa
Helena
Guimarães
Veiros
Juaba
Carapajó
Itamataré
Alcântara
Anil
Paulino
Neves
Tutóia
Ararú
Balão
Pinheiro
São Luís
Rosário
Barreirinhas
Parnaíba
Camocim
Granja
Marco
Paracuru
Vitória
Viana
Monção
Urbano Santos
Brejo
Luzilândia
Sobral
Itapipoca
FORTALEZA
Altamira
Pindaré-Mirim
Itapecuru-Mirim
Piracuruca
Tianguá
Ipu
Maranguape
Maracanaú
Pacajus
Beberibe
Aracati
Tucuruí
Bacabal
Chapadinha
Miguel Alves
Piripiri
Pedro II
Canindé
Batuité
Quixadá
Russas
Areia Branca
São Bento
do Norte
Cabo
de
São Roque
Cantanhede
Coroatá
Barras
União
Campo Maior
Tamboril
Itapuã
Mossoró
Tabuleiro
do Norte
Macau
Touros

Itaituba

PARÁ
Itupiranga
Açailândia
São João
do Araguaia
Imperatriz
Amarante do
Maranhão
Sitio
Novo
Grajaú
Colinas
Mirador
Teresina
Crateús
Valença
do Piauí
Oeiras
Floriano
Senador Pompeu
Piquet Carneiro
Elesbão Veloso
Taua
Jaguaribe
Acopiara
Jucás
Iguatu
Sousa
Pombal
Caicó
Currais Novos
Ceará-Mirim
**RIO GRANDE
DO NORTE**
Natal
Assu

Marabá
Araguatins
Santa Isabel
do Araguaia
Montes Altos
Nazaré
Tocantinópolis
Xambioá
Carajás
MARANHÃO
Presidente
Dutra
São Miguel do Tapuio
Agua Branca
Caxias
Timon
Bacabal
Barra do Corda
Bacaúba
Amarante
São João dos Patos
Pastos Bons
São Raimundo
das Mangabeiras
Riachão
Carolina
Balsas
Benedito Leite
Picos
Campos Sales
Crato
Juazeiro
do Norte
Cajazeiras
Patos
Itaporanga
**Campina
Grande**
Timbaúba
Goiana
Paulista
Olinda
**João
Pessoa**
PARAÍBA
RECIFE

Gradaús
Araguaína
Itaporã
de Goiás
Itacajá
PIAUÍ
São Raimundo
Nonato
Simplício Mendes
Paulistana
Parnamirim
Salgueiro
Arcoverde
Belém de
São Francisco
PERNAMBUCO
Caruaru
Garanhuns
Brejo da
Madre de Deus

Conceição do Araguaia
Pequizeiro
Canto do Buriti
Cristino Castro
Alto Parnaíba
São Raimundo
Nonato
Santa Maria da Boa Vista
Chorrochó
Petrolândia
União dos
Palmares
Porto
de Pedras

BRAZIL
SERRA DOS CARAJÁS

Araguacema
Cachimbo
Dois Irmãos de Goiás
Pedro Afonso
Miracema do
Tocantins
Tocantinia
Curupá
Bom Jesus
Caracol
Casa Nova
Petrolina
Juazeiro
Paulo Afonso
Palmeira
dos Indios
ALAGOAS
Rio Largo
Maceió

Pium
Cristalândia
Palmas
Monte Alegre
do Piauí
Gilbués
Curimatá
Remanso
Uauá
Arapiraca
Jundiaré
Corurupe
Propriá
Penedo

Ilha do
Bananal
Duerê
Porto Nacional
Brejinho de Nazaré
Parnaguá
Barra
Xique-Xique
Jaguarari
Jeremoabo
Euclides da
Cunha
Brejo Grande
SERGIPE

TOCANTINS
Natividade
Dianópolis
Gurupi
Peixe
Barreiras
Irecê
Jacobina
Queimadas
Tucano
Itabaiana
Lagarto
Aracaju
Estância

MATO GROSSO
*PLANALTO DO
MATO GROSSO*
Ponte Alta do
Bom Jesus
Taguatinga
Paranã
Morro do Chapéu
Riachão do Jacuípe
Serrinha
Inhambupe
Rio Real
Esplanada

Parecis
Alto Araguaia
Arraias
Ibotirama
Ruy Barbosa
BAHIA
Feira de Santana
Santo Amaro
Alagoinhas

Diamantino
Nobres
São Miguel
do Araguaia
São Domingos
Santana
Barreiras
Correntina
Ibitiara
Itaberaba
Iaçu
Candeias
Santo Antônio
de Jesus
Valença
SALVADOR

Rosário Oeste
Porangatu
Cavalcante
Nova Roma
Posse
Santana
Riacho de Santana
Bom Jesus
da Lapa
Paratinga
Mucujé
Pico das Almas
1836
Maracás
Itiruçu
Jaguaquara
Ilha de Tinharé

Acorizal
Bandeirantes
Colinas
Cocos
Guanambi
Carinhanha
Caetité
Brumado
Poções
Jequié
Ubatã
Itacaré
Coaraci
Ilhéus

Cuiabá
Várzea Grande
GOIÁS
Pilar de Goiás
São João
da Aliança
Manga
Caculé
Vitória da
Conquista
Ibicaraí
Itabuna

Cáceres
Mozarlândia
Itapaci
São Gabriel
de Goiás
Formosa
Cabeceiras
Januária
Monte Azul
Itambé
Itapetinga
Una

Barão de Melgaço
Poconé
Rosário Oeste
Aruanã
Britânia
Jeroaquara
Ceres
Uruana
Jaraguá
Goianésia
BRASÍLIA
*DISTRITO
FEDERAL*
São Francisco
São João
do Paraíso
Salinas
Coronel
Murta
Pedra Azul
Jordânia
Salto da Divisa
Canavieiras
Belmonte

General Carneiro
Poxoréu
Itapirapuã
Jussara
Iaciara
Haberaí
GOIÂNIA
Anápolis
Silvânia
Luziânia
Cristalina
São Romão
MINAS GERAIS
Grão Mogol
Itaobim
Águas
Formosas
Itamaraju
Porto Seguro

Jaciara
Barra do
Garças
Jaraguá
Inhumas
Cristianópolis
Pirapora
Minas Novas
Capelinha
Ponta da Baleia

Guiratinga
Piranhas
Aurilândia
Pires do Rio
Campo Alegre de Goiás
Paracatu
Caatinga
Montes Claros
Bocaiúva
Alcobaça

Rondonópolis
Alto Garças
Rio Verde
Jandaia
Pontalina
Ipameri
João Pinheiro
Pirapora
Carlos
Chagas
Caravelas

MATO GROSSO DO SUL
Pedro Gomes
Jataí
Santa Helena
de Goiás
Morrinhos
Campo Alegre de Goiás
Teófilo Otoni
Nanuque

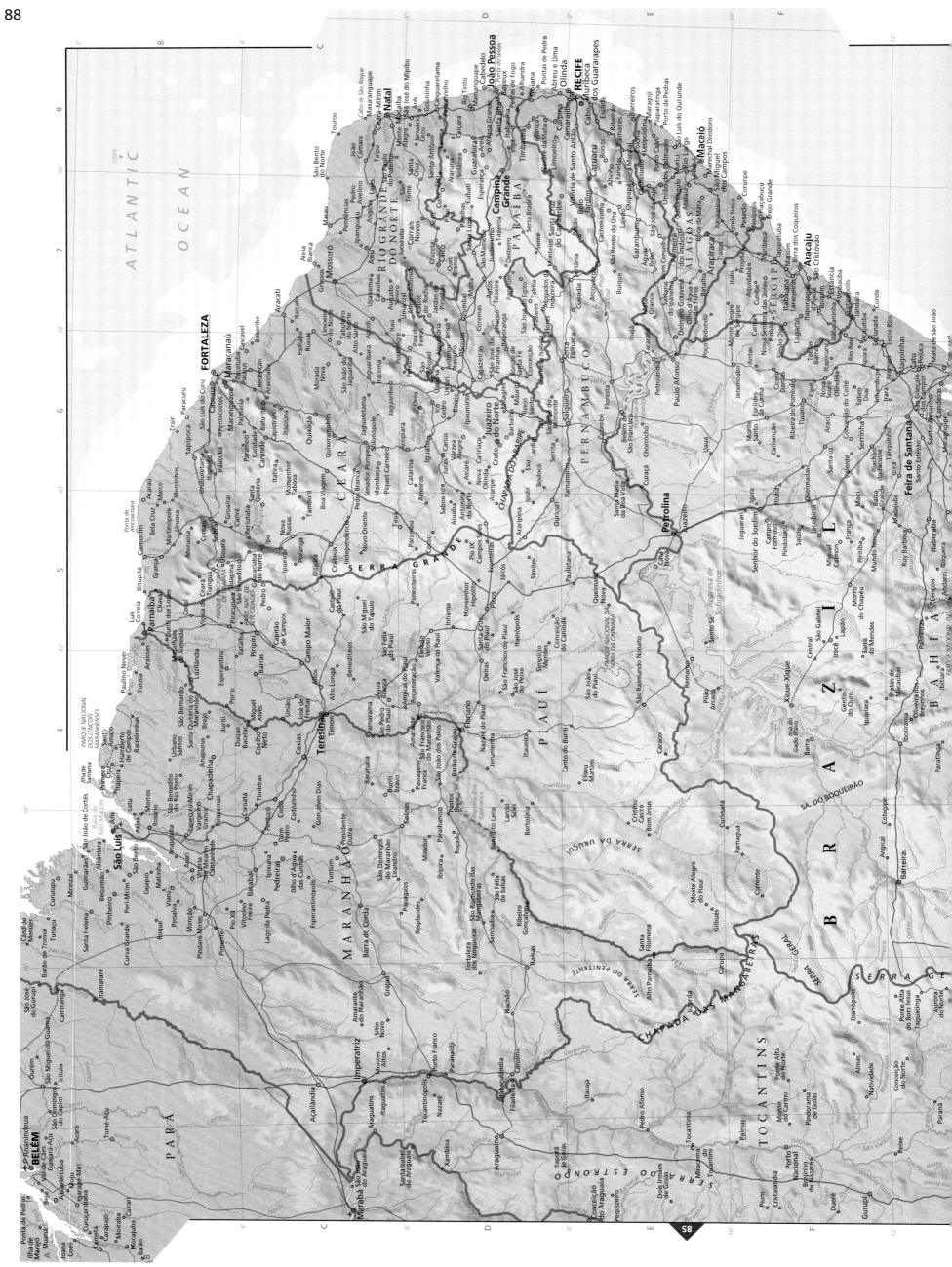

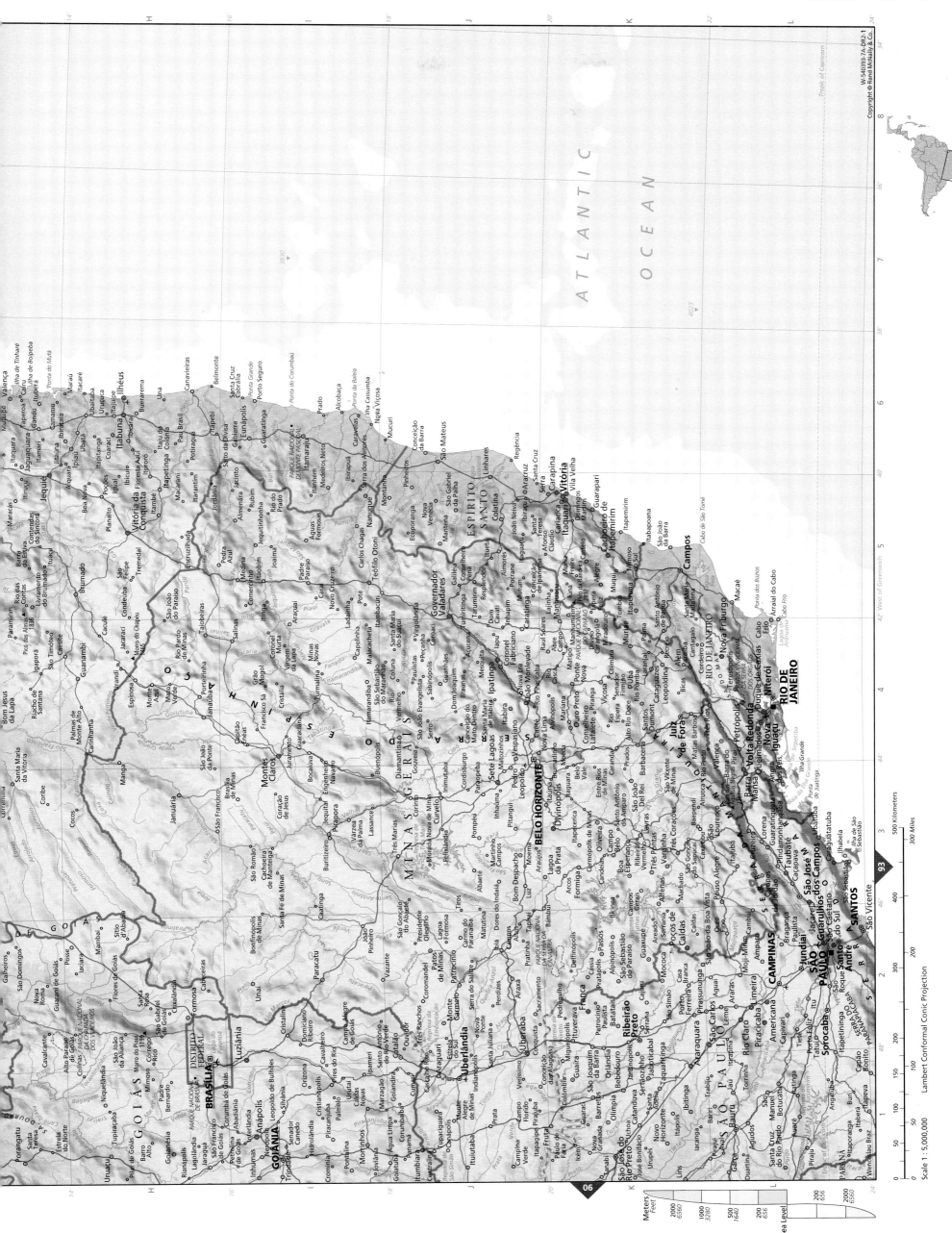

ATLANTIC

OCEAN

Tropic of Capricorn

RIO DE JANEIRO

RIO DE JANEIRO

Niterói

Campos

Vitória

ESPÍRITO SANTO

MINAS GERAIS

BELO HORIZONTE

Governador
Valadares

Juiz de Fora

Volta Redonda

Nova Iguaçu

Petrópolis

Duque de Caxias

SÃO PAULO

SÃO PAULO

CAMPINAS

Santo André

Osasco

SANTOS

São Vicente

Guarulhos

São José
dos Campos

Taubaté

Jundiaí

Sorocaba

Ribeirão Preto

Franca

Uberaba

Uberlândia

Araraquara

Piracicaba

Americana

GOIÁS

BRASÍLIA

GOIÂNIA

Anápolis

**DISTRITO
FEDERAL**

Luziânia

Formosa

Montes
Claros

Diamantina

Sete Lagoas

Divinópolis

Ipatinga

Teófilo Otoni

Vitória da
Conquista

Jequié

Ilhéus

Itabuna

Valença

Porto Seguro

Ilha de São
Sebastião

Cabo
Frio

PARANÁ

MAR

Meters
Feet
2000   6560
1000   3280
500   1640
200   656
Sea Level
200   656
2000   6560

Scale 1 : 5,000,000   Lambert Conformal Conic Projection

500 Kilometers

300 Miles

0   50   100   150   200   300   400   500

0   50   100   200   300

14°   16°   18°   20°   22°   24°

34°   36°   38°   40°   42° West of Greenwich   44°   46°   48°

H   I   J   K   L

1   2   3   4   5   6   7   8

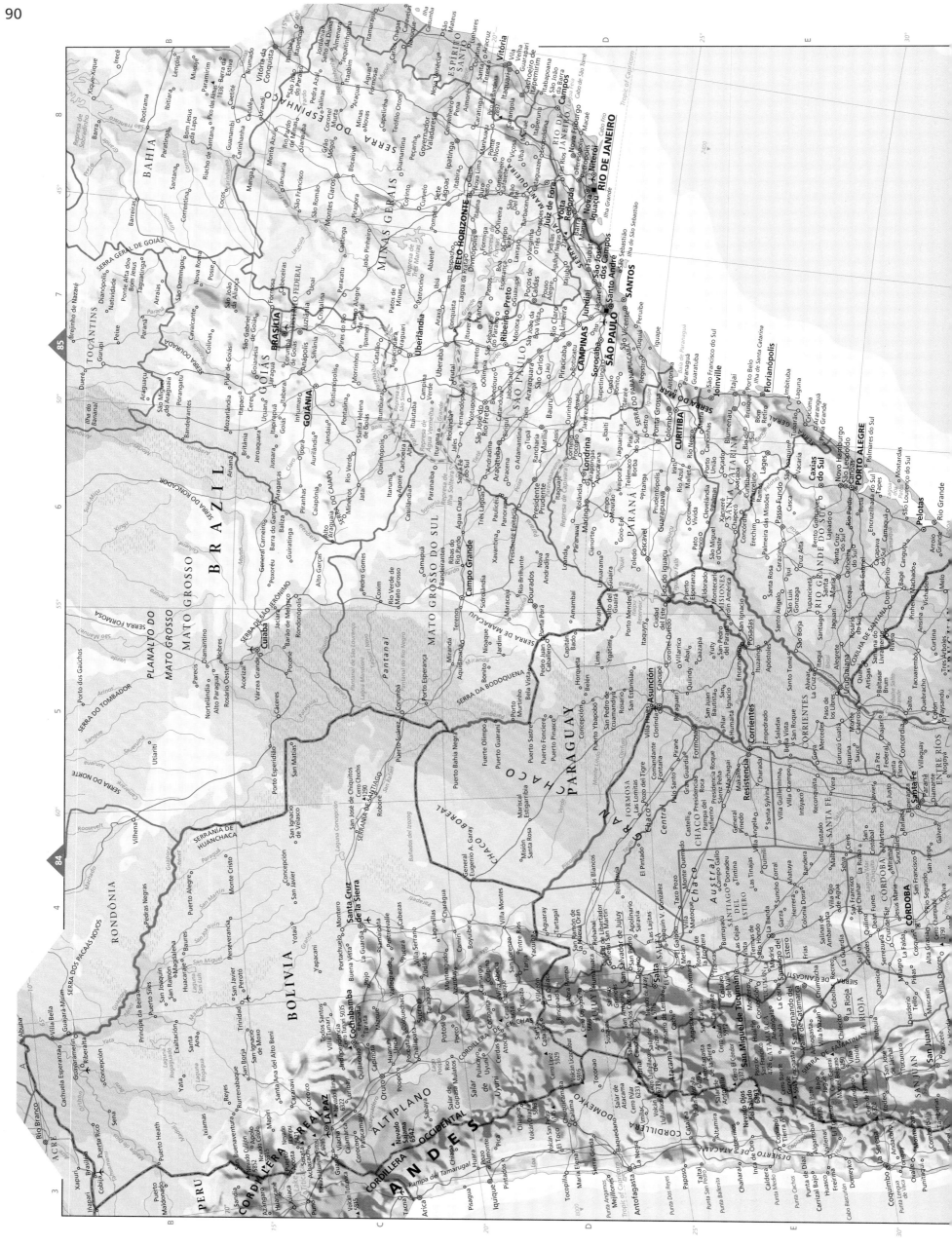

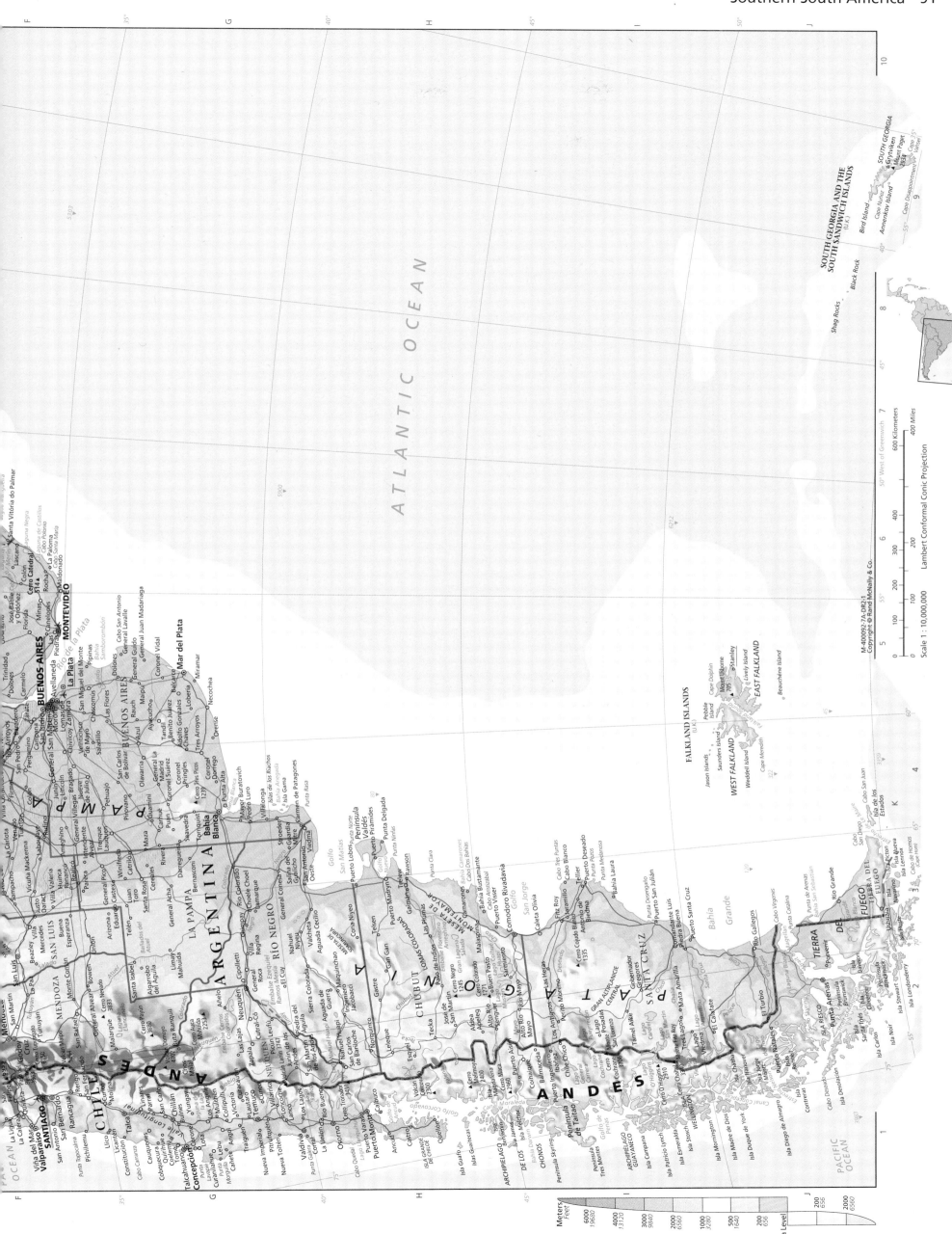

ATLANTIC OCEAN

SOUTH GEORGIA AND THE
SOUTH SANDWICH ISLANDS
(U.K.)

SOUTH GEORGIA

Grytviken
Mount Paget
2934

FALKLAND ISLANDS
(U.K.)

WEST FALKLAND

EAST FALKLAND
Stanley

PACIFIC OCEAN

M-400092-7A-DR21
Copyright © Rand McNally & Co.

Scale 1 : 10,000,000

Lambert Conformal Conic Projection

CHILE

ARGENTINA

ANDES

PAMPA

LA PAMPA

PATAGONIA

TIERRA DEL FUEGO

SANTA CRUZ

CHUBUT

RIO NEGRO

NEUQUEN

BUENOS AIRES

MENDOZA

SAN LUIS

BUENOS AIRES

MONTEVIDEO

La Plata

Mar del Plata

Bahía Blanca

Comodoro Rivadavia

SANTIAGO

Valparaíso

Concepción

Punta Arenas

Río Gallegos

Meters
Feet
6000 19680
4000 13120
3000 9840
2000 6560
1000 3280
500   1640
200   656
Sea Level

200   656
2000 6560

PARAGUAY

BRAZIL

PARANÁ

SANTA CATARINA

RIO GRANDE DO SUL

URUGUAY

CORRIENTES

ATLANTIC OCEAN

Asunción
CURITIBA
Florianópolis
PORTO ALEGRE
MONTEVIDEO
BUENOS AIRES
La Plata
Mar del Plata
Pelotas
Rio Grande

Scale 1 : 5,000,000   Lambert Conformal Conic Projection

W-540195-7A-DR2-1
Copyright © Rand McNally & Co.

Meters
Feet
6000
19680
4000
13120
3000
9840
2000
6560
1000
3280
500
1640
200
656
Sea Level
200
656
2000
6560

0   50   100   150   200   300   400   500 Kilometers
0   50   100   200   300 Miles

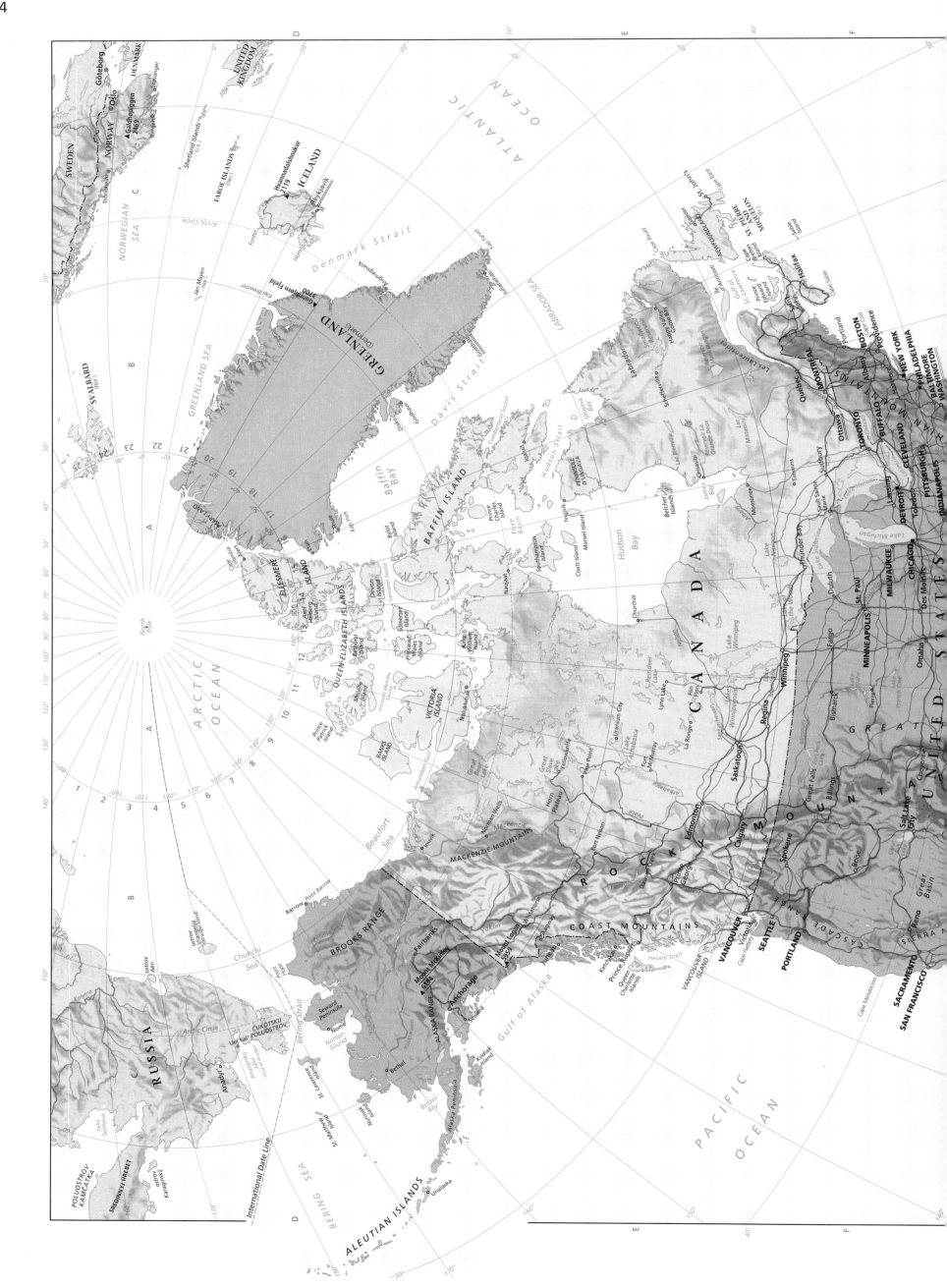

G   20°   H   10°   0°   I   10°   J   20°   K   30°   L

ATLANTIC OCEAN

BERMUDA (U.K.)

Cape Hatteras
Cape Lookout
Cape Fear
Raleigh
Charlotte
Charleston
Columbia
Savannah
Jacksonville
Daytona Beach
Orlando
Tampa
Tallahassee
MIAMI

Cape Canaveral

WEST INDIES

BAHAMAS
Nassau
Grand Bahama
Abaco
Eleuthera
Andros
Cat Island
Long Island
Great Inagua

TURKS AND CAICOS ISLANDS (U.K.)

LEEWARD ISLANDS
ANGUILLA (U.K.)
ANTIGUA AND BARBUDA
GUADELOUPE (Fr.)
DOMINICA
ST. KITTS AND NEVIS
MONTSERRAT (U.K.)
MARTINIQUE (Fr.)
ST. LUCIA
BARBADOS
ST. VINCENT AND THE GRENADINES
GRENADA

PUERTO RICO (U.S.)
SAN JUAN

DOMINICAN REPUBLIC
SANTO DOMINGO
Pico Duarte 3175
HISPANIOLA

HAITI
Port-au-Prince

CUBA
LA HABANA (HAVANA)
Matanzas
Cienfuegos
Isla de la Juventud
Camagüey
Holguín
Santiago de Cuba
Guantánamo

JAMAICA
Kingston

CAYMAN ISLANDS (U.K.)

Yucatán Channel
Straits of Florida

GREATER ANTILLES
LESSER ANTILLES

CARIBBEAN SEA

NETHERLANDS ANTILLES
ARUBA (Neth.)
Curaçao Bonaire

TRINIDAD AND TOBAGO
Port of Spain

CARACAS
Barquisimeto
Maracaibo
VENEZUELA
Ciudad Guayana
Ciudad Bolívar
Roraima 2875
GUYANA

Punta Gallinas
Riohacha
Barranquilla
Cartagena
Sincelejo

COLOMBIA
Medellín
BOGOTÁ
Bucaramanga
Cúcuta
CORDILLERA ORIENTAL
CORDILLERA CENTRAL
CORDILLERA OCCIDENTAL

Cali
Buenaventura
Quibdó
Manizales
Pasto

PANAMÁ
Colón
Volcán Barú 3475
Golfo de Panamá
Isla de Coiba

COSTA RICA
SAN JOSÉ
Cerro Chirripó 3819
Bluefields
Managua
NICARAGUA

Golfo de San Andrés (Col.)

Isla del Coco (C.R.)

Isla de Malpelo (Col.)

ECUADOR
QUITO
GUAYAQUIL
Golfo de Guayaquil
Portoviejo
Chimborazo 6310
Cuenca

PERÚ
LIMA
Chiclayo
Trujillo
Chimbote
Talara
Piura
Cajamarca
Iquitos

BRAZIL

SELVAS

BOLIVIA
LA PAZ
Cochabamba
Arequipa
Sucre
Potosí
CORD. REAL
Nevado Sajama 6542
Nevado Illimani 6485
Desierto de Atacama
CHILE
Arica
Iquique

GRAN CHACO
PARAGUAY

Pico da Neblina 3014

Amazonas
Rio Negro
Rio Branco
Porto Velho
Boa Vista

ATLANTIC OCEAN

70°   15   80°   14   90° West of Greenwich   13   100°   12   110°   11   120°   10   130°

ATLANTIC OCEAN
Tropic of Cancer

Raleigh
Charlotte
Knoxville
Chattanooga
Atlanta
Montgomery
Birmingham
Nashville
Memphis
Jackson
Mobile
NEW ORLEANS
Baton Rouge
Shreveport
Little Rock
Tulsa
Oklahoma City
Wichita
Amarillo
Fort Worth
DALLAS
Austin
SAN ANTONIO
HOUSTON
Corpus Christi
Brownsville
Matamoros
Laredo

Ozark Plateau

GULF OF MEXICO

Cabo Catoche
Cancún
Isla Cozumel
Mérida
PENÍNSULA DE YUCATÁN
Campeche
Bahía de Campeche
Villahermosa
Tuxtla Gutiérrez
Volcán Tajumulco 4220
GUATEMALA
Guatemala
BELIZE
Belize City
Belmopan
San Pedro Sula
HONDURAS
Tegucigalpa
EL SALVADOR
San Salvador
Volcán de Orizaba 5610
CIUDAD DE MÉXICO
Veracruz
Tampico
MÉXICO
Acapulco
MONTERREY
Saltillo
Torreón
Monclova
GUADALAJARA
Aguascalientes
SIERRA MADRE ORIENTAL
SIERRA MADRE OCCIDENTAL
Chihuahua
Ciudad Juárez
El Paso
Hermosillo
Culiacán
Mazatlán
Tepic

Juchitán de Zaragoza
Golfo de Tehuantepec

Santa Fe
Albuquerque
PHOENIX
Tucson
LOS ANGELES
SAN DIEGO
Tijuana
Mexicali

BAJA CALIFORNIA
Golfo de California
La Paz
Cabo San Lucas
Islas Tres Marías
Cabo Corrientes
Isla Guadalupe

Islas Revillagigedo

Archipiélago de Colón (Galápagos Islands) (Ec.)
Isla Fernandina
Isla Isabela
Isla Santiago
Isla Santa Cruz
Isla San Cristóbal
Isla San Salvador

PACIFIC OCEAN

Equator

Tropic of Cancer

Scale 1 : 25,000,000
Lambert Azimuthal Equal Area Projection
M-DRMZ241-P1--1-1-2
Copyright © Rand McNally & Co.

250   0   250   500   750   1000   1500   2000   2500 Kilometers
250   0   250   500   1000   1500 Miles

Meters
Feet

4000
13120

3000
9840

2000
6560

1000
3280

500
1640

200
656

Sea Level

200
656

2000
6560

0   100   200   300   400   600   800   1000 Kilometers

0   100   200   400   600 Miles

Scale 1 : 10,000,000   Lambert Conformal Conic Projection

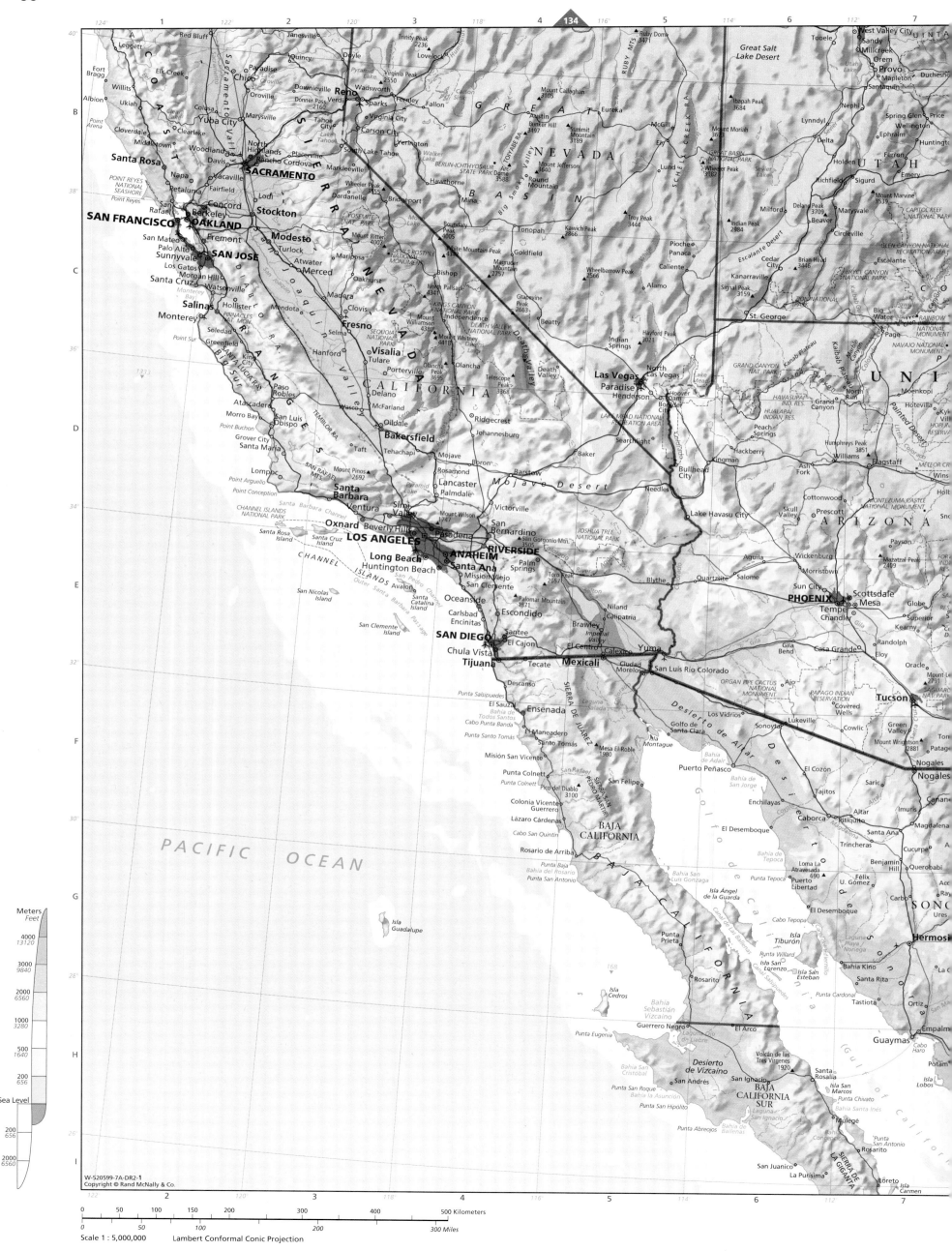

Scale 1 : 5,000,000   Lambert Conformal Conic Projection

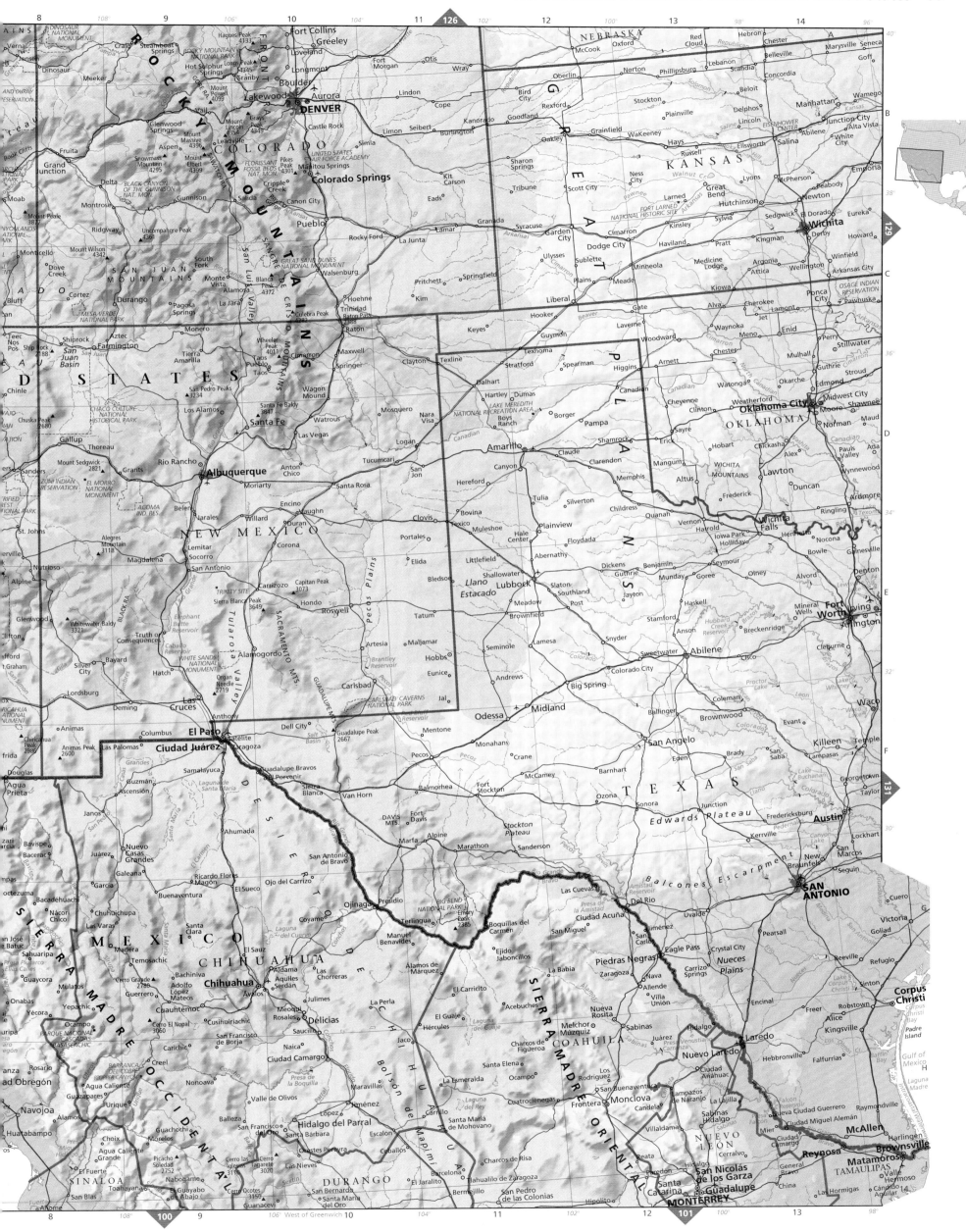

Meters
Feet

4000
13120

3000
9840

2000
6560

1000
3280

500
1640

200
656

Sea Level

200
656

2000
6560

W-532095-7A-DR2-1
Copyright © Rand McNally & Co.

Scale 1 : 5,000,000   Lambert Conformal Conic Projection

0   50   100   150   200   300   400   500 Kilometers
0   50   100   200   300 Miles

Scale 1 : 5,000,000   Lambert Conformal Conic Projection

W-536000-7A-DR2-1
Copyright © Rand McNally & Co.

Canal de San Nicolás
Canal Viejo de Bahama

BAHAMAS

CUBA

Deadman's Cay
Long Cay
Clarence Town
Cape Verde
Crooked Island
North East Point
Samana Cay
Mayaguana
Acklins
Bight of Acklins
Ragged Island
Ragged Island Range
Salina Point
Matthew Town
Great Inagua
Little Inagua
Palacca Point
Lake Rosa

TURKS AND CAICOS ISLANDS (U.K.)

Kew
Providenciales
North Caicos
Middle Caicos
East Caicos
West Caicos
CAICOS ISLANDS
Grand Turk
TURKS ISLANDS
Seal Cays
Silver Bank Passage
Mouchoir Passage

ATLANTIC OCEAN

Caibarién
Yaguajay
Cayo Coco
Cayo Romano
Cayo Guajaba
Placetas
Morón
Bahía de
Cayo Lobos
Cayo Sabinal
Sancti Spíritus
Ciego de Ávila
Esmeralda
Nuevitas
Puerto Padre
Trinidad
de Zaza
Júcaro
Florida
Minas
Puerto Manatí
Jesús Menéndez
Rafael Freyre
Punta de Mulas
Camagüey
Vertientes
Las Tunas
Holguín
Gibara
Banes
Bahía de Nipe
Antilla
Santa Cruz del Sur
Bayamo
Jiguaní
Alto Cedro
Mayarí
Sagua de Tánamo
Baracoa
Campechuela
Manzanillo
Palma Soriano
San Luis
Tiguabos
Guantánamo
Cueto
Niquero
Marea del Portillo
SIERRA MAESTRA
Caimanera
GUANTANAMO BAY NAVAL STATION (U.S.)
Punta de Quemado
Cabo Cruz
Pico Turquino 1972
Santiago de Cuba

Cayman Brac

GREATER ANTILLES

HISPANIOLA

HAITI

Île de la Tortue
Monte Cristi
Cabo Isabela
Cap-Haïtien
Cap du Môle
Limbé
SANS SOUCI
Fort-Liberté
Puerto Plata
Cabo Macorís
Pico Diego de Ocampo 1249
Cabo Francés Viejo
Port-de-Paix
LA CITADELLE
Dajabón
Mao
Moca
Nagua
Bahía Escocesa
Cabo Samaná
Cap à Foux
Gonaïves
Desdunes
Santiago de los Caballeros
La Vega
San Francisco de Macorís
Sabana de la Mar
Miches
Golfe de la Gonâve
Île de la Gonâve
Pico Duarte 3175
Bonao
Alto Bandera 2630
Samaná
Bahía de Samaná
Morne Bonhomme 1788
Comendador
San Juan de la Maguana
SANTO DOMINGO
Jérémie
Grande Cayemite
Canal du Sud
Baie de Port-au-Prince
Port-au-Prince
Pétion-Ville
Neiba
Lago Enriquillo
Azua
San Cristóbal
Hato Mayor del Rey
El Seibo
Higüey
Cabo Engaño
Pic Macaye 2347
Anse-d'Hainault
Léogâne
Aquin
Petit-Goâve
Jacmel
Morne La Selle 2674
Barahona
Baní
San Pedro de Macorís
La Romana
Bahía de Yuma
Isla Saona
Coteaux
Les Cayes
Île à Vache
Pointe Abacou
Pedernales
Enriquillo
Cabo Falso
Isla Beata
Cabo Beata

DOMINICAN REPUBLIC

JAMAICA

Montego Bay
Falmouth
Ocho Rios
Saint Ann's Bay
Port Maria
Port Antonio
South Negril Point
Mount Denham 986
Savanna-la-Mar
Mandeville
Kingston
Spanish Town
Blue Mountain Peak 2256
Morant Bay
Morant Point
Portland Point
Portland Bight

Navassa Island (U.S.)
Pointe Fanchon
Jamaica Channel
Windward Passage
Caicos Passage
Windward Passage
Mona Passage

GREATER ANTILLES

2184
Morant Cays

Pedro Cays

Cayo de Serranilla (Col.)
Bajo Nuevo (Col.)

CARIBBEAN SEA

5102

LESSER ANTILLES

ARUBA (Neth.)
Oranjestad
NETHERLANDS ANTILLES (Neth.)
Bonaire
Curaçao
Willemstad

Punta Gallinas
Bahía Honda
Cabo de La Vela
Punta Espada
Cabo San Román
Pueblo Nuevo
Península de Paraguaná
Puerto Bolívar
Punta Espada
Golfo de Venezuela
Punta Cardón
Puerto Cumarebo
Punta Zamuro
Península de La Guajira
Los Taques
Punto Fijo
Coro
La Vela de Coro
Cabure
Uribia
Ensenada de Calabozo
Golfete de Coro
Pedregal
San Luis
Churuguara
Ríohacha
Maicao
Paraguaipoa
Capatárida
Dabajuro
FALCÓN
Cabo de La Aguja
Santa Marta
Ciénaga
Pico Cristóbal Colón 5775
LA GUAJIRA
Barrancas
Albania
Sinamaica
San Rafael
Altagracia
Mene de Mauroa
YARACUY
PARQUE NACIONAL YURUBÍ
Barranquilla
Soledad
Fonseca
San Juan del César
Villanueva
MARACAIBO
Santa Rita
Cerro Cerrón
San Felipe
ATLÁNTICO
Baranoa
Malambo
La Paz
Cabimas
VENEZUELA
Cartagena
Sabanalarga
Manatí
Valledupar
Villa del Rosario
Ciudad Ojeda
LARA
Barquisimeto
Islas del Rosario
Turbaco
Piojó
Fundación
Aracataca
Agustín Codazzi
Tía Juana
Mene Grande
Carora
Quíbor
Arjona
Pivijay
Machiques
Lago de Maracaibo
El Piñón
Calamar
Mahates
Pedraza
CESAR
El Banco
Cerro Mu 2610
ZULIA
La Ceiba
Bachaquero
Mene Grande
Sabana de Mendoza
Bobures
TRUJILLO
Valera
María La Baja
San Juan Nepomuceno
San Jacinto
MAGDALENA
Magangué
Chimichagua
San Carlos del Zulia
Timotes
TÁCHIRA
Islas de San Bernardo
San Onofre
El Carmen de Bolívar
Ovejas
San Pedro
Encontrados
MÉRIDA
Mucuchíes
Guanare
Istmo de Panamá (Isthmus of Panama)
Tolú
Corozal
Guamal
Tamalameque
Casigua
El Vigía
Pico Bolívar 5007
PORTUGUESA
Nombre de Dios
El Porvenir
San Blas
Sincelejo
Lorica
Corozal
BOLÍVAR
La Gloria
Petróleo
Santa Bárbara
BARINAS
Barinas
Manzanillo
Niatupu
SUCRE
Sahagún
Cerité
Pinillos
El Carmen
NORTE DE SANTANDER
Tovar
Santa Rosa
Panamá
SERRANÍA DE SAN BLAS
Punta Mosquito
Mansucum
Ciénaga de Oro
Majagual
Gamarra
Abrego
CORDILLERA DE MÉRIDA
Ciudad Bolivia
Libertad
de Nutrias
Arboletes
Montería
Planeta Rica
San Marcos
La Jagua
Ocaña
San Cayetano
LLANOS
APURE
CHOCÓ
ANTIOQUIA
CÓRDOBA
Ayapel
Tierralta
Montelíbano
Nechí
Aguachica
Río de Oro
El Carmen
San Juan de Colón
Cúcuta
Palmarito
Apure
ARCHIPIÉLAGO DE LAS PERLAS
Isla del Rey
San Miguel
Yaviza
El Real de Santa María
Turbo
Simití
Caucasia
San Antonio del Táchira
Rubio
San Cristóbal
Golfo de Panamá
Apartadó
PARQUE NACIONAL DARIÉN
COLOMBIA

a

ATLANTIC OCEAN

Punta Aguijereada
Punta Las Tunas
Punta Puerto Nuevo
Poblado Cerro Gordo
SAN JUAN
Bahía de San Juan
AEROPUERTO INT. LUIS MUÑOZ MARIN
To Charlotte Amalie
Virgin Passage

Isabela
Camuy Hatillo
San Antonio
Feliciano Quebradillas
Arecibo
Vega Baja
Toa Baja
Levittown
Loíza Aldea
Poblado Mediania Alta
Punta Picúa

Aguadilla
Moca
Pueblo de Ponce
El Coto
Pueblo Nuevo
Barceloneta
Manati
Vega Alta
Toa Alta
Río Piedras
Bayamón
Carolina
Canóvanas
Palmer
Luquillo
Cabezas de San Juan
Isla de Culebra
Cayo Norte
Culebra

Aguada
Contro Puntas
Rincón
La Cuesta
Charco Hondo
Palo Blanco
El Campamento
Corozal
La Esperanza
Guaynabo
El Minao
Cidra
El Yunque 1065
Sabana
Punta de Fajardo
Isla Piñeros
Isla de Culebra
Culebrita

Córcega
Punta Cadena
Anasco
San Sebastián
Perchas
Lares
OBSERVATORIO DE ARECIBO
Dos Bocas
Florida
Morovis
Naranjito
Aguas Buenas
Gurabo
Las Piñas
Ceiba
Florida
Quebrada Seca
Sonda de Vieques

Mona Passage
Mayagüez
Mani
AEROPUERTO MAYAGÜEZ
Las Marias
Villa Perez
Utuado
Jayuya
Orocovis
Caguas
San Lorenzo
Daguao
Naguabo
Punta Puerca
Vieques

PUERTO RICO (U.S.)

Bahía de Mayagüez
Punta Guanajibo
Las Vegas
Maricao
Los Rábanos
Indiera Alta
Cerro de Punta
Monte Guilarte 1205
Adjuntas 1338
Barranquitas
La Torrecilla 943
Comerío
Aibonito
Cerro La Santa 903
Humacao
Las Piedras
Punta Lima
Pasaje de Vieques
Punta Mulas
Vieques
Santa María
Esperanza

Joyuda
San Germán
Sabana Grande
Villalba
Coamo
Cayey
SIERRA DE CAYEY
Cerro de la Tabla 890
Playa de Guayanés
Punta Arenas
Monte Pirata 301
Isla de Vieques
Punta Este

Puerto Real
Cabo Rojo
Lajas
Palmarejo
Yauco
Peñuelas
Poblado Jacaguas
Juana Diaz
Las Flores
Vertederos
Salinas
Yabucoa
Maunabo

Las Arenas
Guanábana
Guánica
Barinas
El Faro
Guayanilla
Playa de Guayanilla
Ponce
AEROPUERTO PONCE
Paso Seco
Arenal
Guayama
Patillas
Palmas

Ensenada
Pastillo
Boca Chica
Santa Isabel
Coquí
Jobos
Arroyo
Colonia Providencia

Cabo Rojo
Bahía Fosforescente
Punta Brea
Punta Cabullones
Punta Petrona
Bahía de Rincón
Bahía de Jobos
Las Mareas

Isla Caja de Muertos

CARIBBEAN SEA

Scale 1 : 1,000,000

b

ATLANTIC OCEAN

VIRGIN ISLANDS

Great Camanoe
Necker Island
Mosquito Island
Pájaros Point
Virgin Gorda Peak 414
South Sound
VIRGIN GORDA
Spanish Town
Copper Mine Point

Great Tobago
West End Point
Little Harbour
Jost Van Dyke
Little Tobago
TORTOLA
Guana Island
Scrub Island
Dog Islands
Beef Island
Fallen Jerusalem

Brass Islands
Hans Lollick Island
Great Thatch Island
Road Town
Mount Sage 521
Long Swamp
Sir Francis Drake Channel
Ginger Island

Crown Mountain 474
ST. THOMAS
Thatch Cay
Coral Bay
East End
Cooper Island

Fortuna
CYRIL E. KING AIRPORT
Charlotte Amalie
Lind Point
VIRGIN IS. NAT. PARK
Bordeaux Mtn. 390
Peter Island
Salt Island

To San Juan
Hassel Island
Nadir
Cruz Bay
St. James Islands
ST. JOHN
Norman Island
BRITISH VIRGIN ISLANDS (U.K.)

Saba Island
Water Island
Long Point
Ram Head

Capella Islands
VIRGIN ISLANDS (U.S.)

CARIBBEAN SEA

Frenchcap Cay

0   5   10 Kilometers
0   5 Miles

Scale 1 : 500,000

c

ST. CROIX (Virgin Islands-U.S.)

To San Juan
Baron Bluff
BUCK ISLAND REEF NATIONAL MONUMENT
Buck Island
East Point

Hams Bluff
Mount Eagle 354
Christiansted

Frederiksted
Kingshill
ALEXANDER HAMILTON AIRPORT

Southwest Cape

CARIBBEAN SEA

Scale 1 : 500,000

d

4891

Montego Bay
Duncans
St. Ann's Bay
Galina Point
2711

Lucea
Dolphin Head 545
Falmouth
Clark's Town
Cockpit Country
Browns Town
Ocho Rios
Port Maria

Montpelier
Whithorn
Savanna-la-Mar
Mount Denham 986
Frankfield
Linstead
Annotto Bay

South Negril Point
Little London
Christiana
Porus
Chapelton
Catherines Peak
BLUE MTS.
Blue Mtn. Peak 2256
Port Antonio

Bluefields Bay
Black River
Mandeville
Spanish Town
Kingston
Manchioneal

Mount Ida 725
May Pen
Lionel Town
Portmore
Old Harbour
Port Royal
Morant Bay
Port Morant

JAMAICA

Alligator Pond
Portland Point
Portland Bight

Jamaica Channel

CARIBBEAN SEA

Scale 1 : 2,500,000

e

ATLANTIC OCEAN

St. George's Island
FORT VICTORIA
St. George
KINDLEY FIELD
St. David's Island

Ireland Island North
Harrington Sound
Castle Harbour

Somerset Island
Spanish Point
Flatts
Town Hill 79

Great Sound
Hamilton

Little Sound

High Point
BERMUDA (U.K.)

Scale 1 : 500,000

f

ATLANTIC OCEAN

Northeast Providence Channel

North Cay
Long Cay
Paradise Island
Salt Cay

Delaport Point
Nassau
Athol Island
East End Point

Old Fort Point
NASSAU INTERNATIONAL AIRPORT
Lake Killarney
Sandilands Village

Adelaide
South West Bay
Coral Harbour
Cay Point
Long Point

NEW PROVIDENCE (Bahamas)

Scale 1 : 500,000

g

Westpunt
ARUBA (Neth.)

Druif
Bushiribana
Hooiberg 167
Oranjestad
Jamanota 188
Sint Nicolaas
Lago Kolonie
Punt Basora

CARIBBEAN SEA

Noordpunt
Savonet
Sint Christoffelberg 375
Sint Kruis
Soto
Bocht van Hato

CURAÇAO

Malmok
Brandaris 240
Dos Pos
BONAIRE
Wekoewa Punt
Montagne
Klein Bonaire
Kralendijk
Wanapa

Cabo San Román
Puerto Escondido
Bullenbaai
Julianadorp
Willemstad

NETHERLANDS ANTILLES (Neth.)

San Lorenzo
Salina de Bariqua
Las Cumaraguas
El Vínculo
Santa Rita
Nieuwpoort
Tafelberg 194
Oostpunt

VENEZUELA
Península de Paraguaná
FALCON
La Sirena
San José
Asaro
Klein Curaçao
Lacre Punt

To La Vela de Coro

Scale 1 : 1,000,000

W-537000-7A-DR2-1
Copyright © Rand McNally & Co.

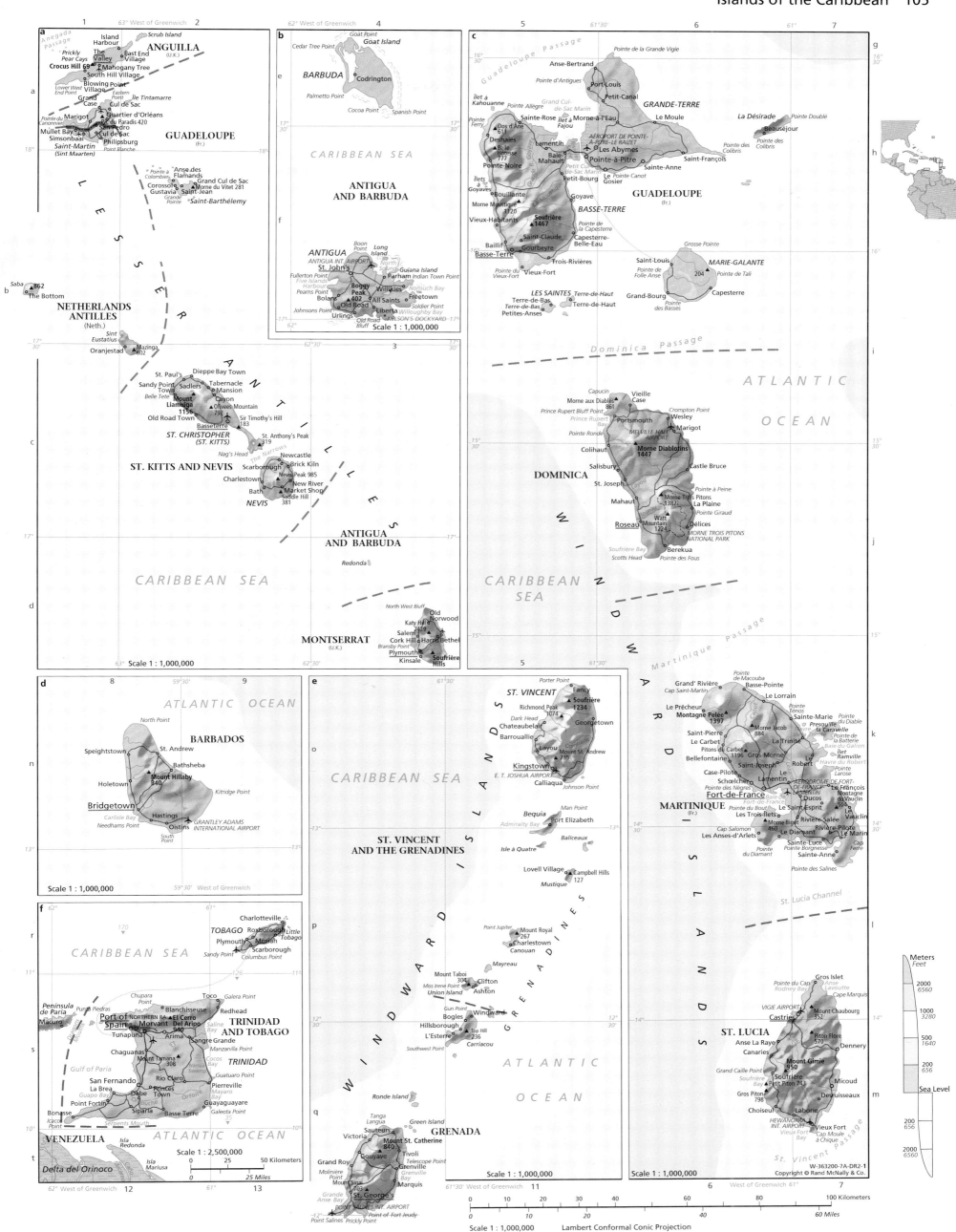

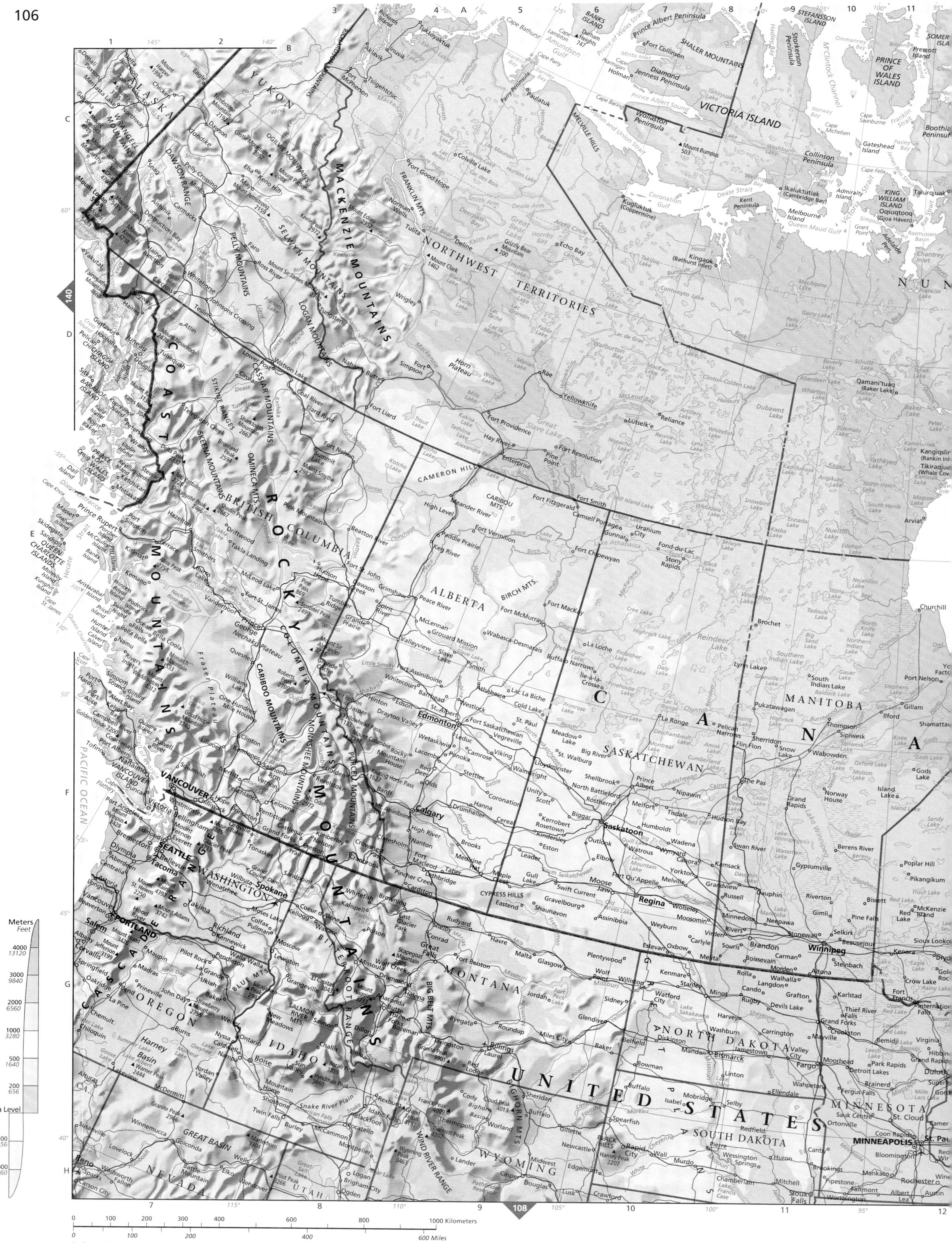

ALASKA

YUKON

MACKENZIE MOUNTAINS

SELWYN MOUNTAINS

NORTHWEST TERRITORIES

VICTORIA ISLAND

SHALER MOUNTAINS

PRINCE OF WALES ISLAND

BANKS ISLAND

STEFANSSON ISLAND

SOMERSET ISLAND

KING WILLIAM ISLAND

NUNAVUT

BRITISH COLUMBIA

ALBERTA

SASKATCHEWAN

MANITOBA

CANADA

ROCKY MOUNTAINS

COAST MOUNTAINS

CASSIAR MOUNTAINS

OMINECA MTS.

COLUMBIA MOUNTAINS

CARIBOO MOUNTAINS

MONASHEE MOUNTAINS

PURCELL MOUNTAINS

QUEEN CHARLOTTE ISLANDS

VANCOUVER ISLAND

PACIFIC OCEAN

WASHINGTON

OREGON

IDAHO

MONTANA

WYOMING

NEVADA

UTAH

GREAT BASIN

CASCADE RANGE

BLUE MTS.

BITTERROOT RANGE

SALMON RIVER MTS.

BIG BELT MTS.

WIND RIVER RANGE

BIGHORN MTS.

BLACK HILLS

CYPRESS HILLS

NORTH DAKOTA

SOUTH DAKOTA

MINNESOTA

UNITED STATES

Edmonton
Calgary
Saskatoon
Regina
Winnipeg
Vancouver
Victoria
SEATTLE
Tacoma
Bellevue
Spokane
PORTLAND
Salem
MINNEAPOLIS
St. Paul
Yellowknife
Whitehorse
Prince Rupert
Fort Smith
Churchill
Reno

Meters / Feet
4000 / 13120
3000 / 9840
2000 / 6560
1000 / 3280
500 / 1640
200 / 656
Sea Level
200 / 656
2000 / 6560

0   100   200   300   400   600   800   1000 Kilometers
0   100   200   400   600 Miles
Scale 1 : 10,000,000   Lambert Conformal Conic Projection

QUÉBEC
NEWFOUNDLAND AND LABRADOR
NEWFOUNDLAND
SAINT PIERRE AND MIQUELON (Fr.)
CAPE BRETON ISLAND
NOVA SCOTIA
ATLANTIC OCEAN

St. John's

Same scale as main map

BAFFIN ISLAND
GREENLAND (Den.)
Davis Strait
Cumberland Peninsula
Hudson Strait
Hudson Bay
James Bay
Ungava Bay
PÉNINSULE D'UNGAVA
LABRADOR SEA
ATLANTIC OCEAN
NEWFOUNDLAND AND LABRADOR
Labrador
QUÉBEC
ONTARIO
NOVA SCOTIA
PRINCE EDWARD ISLAND
MAINE
NEW YORK
MICHIGAN
WISCONSIN
VERMONT
N.H.
MASS.
CONN.
R.I.

Gulf of St. Lawrence
Gulf of Maine

MONTRÉAL
Ottawa
TORONTO
Kitchener
Hamilton
BUFFALO
DETROIT
Windsor
BOSTON
Albany
Québec
Halifax

All islands within Hudson Bay, James Bay, and Ungava Bay lie within Nunavut

West of Greenwich

M-DRM4701-A1- -2- -3
Copyright © Rand McNally & Co.

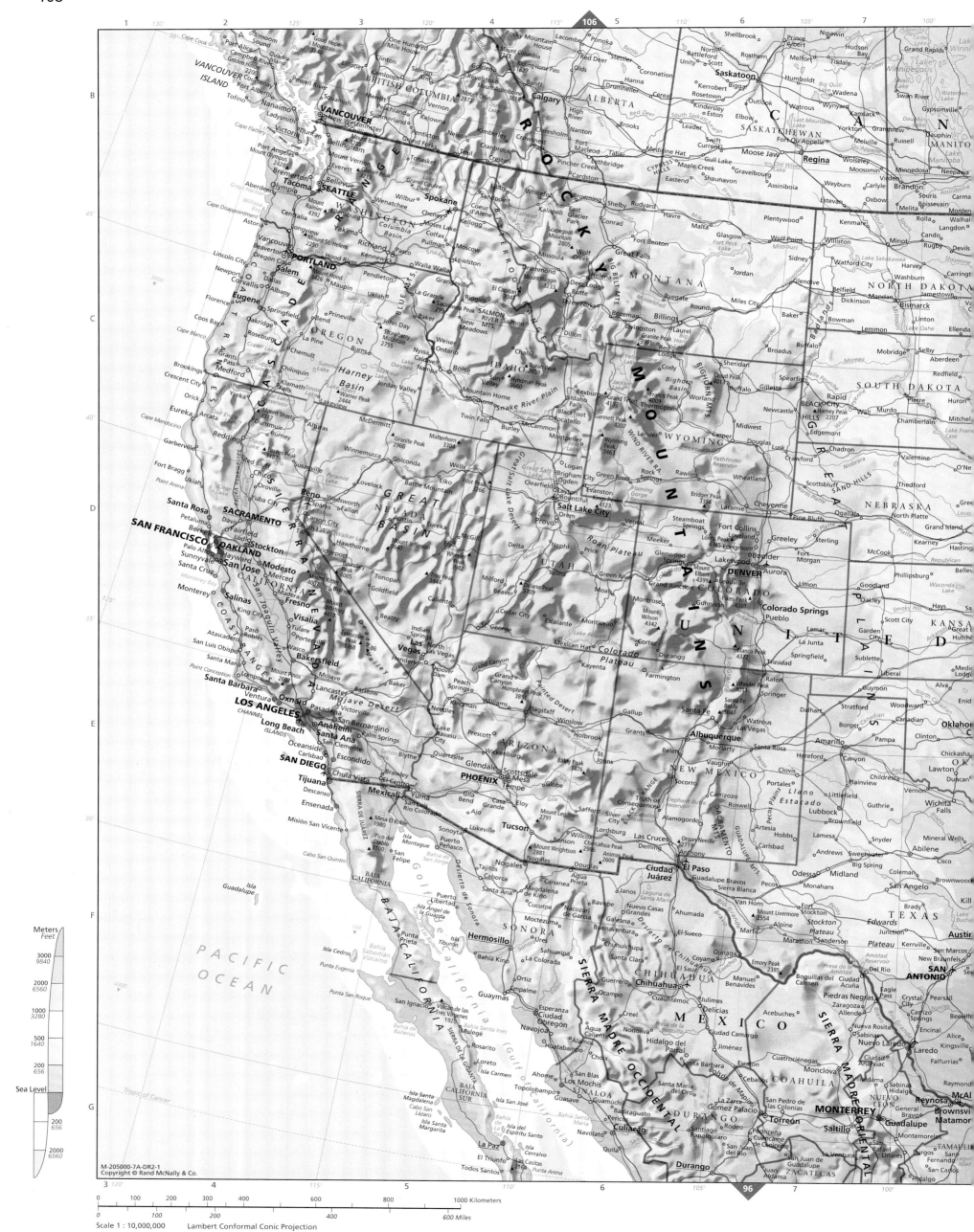

Meters
Feet

3000
9840

2000
6560

1000
3280

500
1640

200
656

Sea Level

200
656

2000
6560

M-205000-7A-DR2-1
Copyright © Rand McNally & Co.

0   100   200   300   400   600   800   1000 Kilometers

0   100   200   400   600 Miles

Scale 1 : 10,000,000   Lambert Conformal Conic Projection

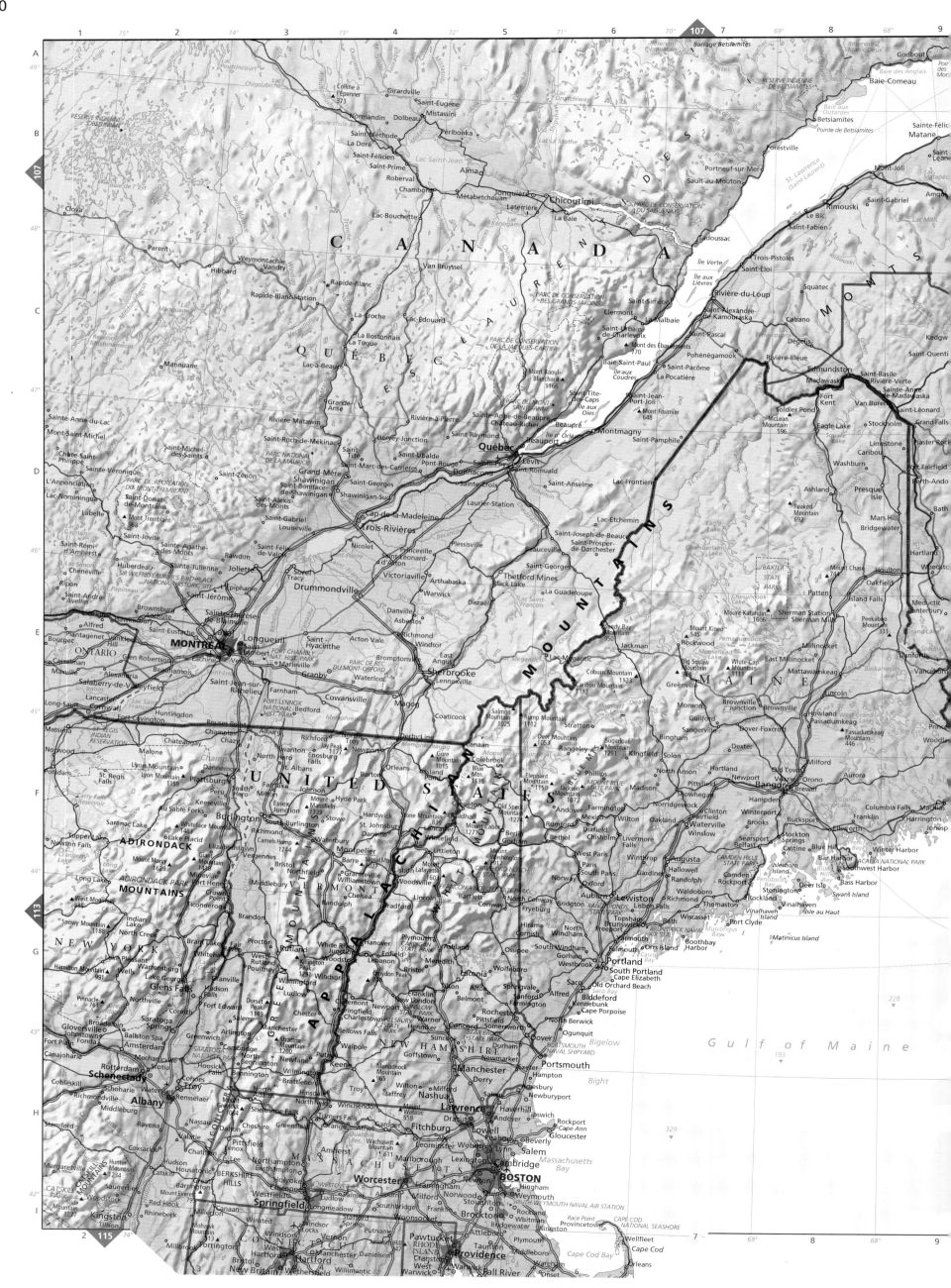

ÎLE D'ANTICOSTI

Gulf of St. Lawrence

NEWFOUNDLAND AND LABRADOR

NEWFOUNDLAND

Cabot Strait

PÉNINSULE DE LA GASPÉSIE
(GASPE PENINSULA)

MONTS NOTRE DAME

CHIC-CHOCS

NEW BRUNSWICK

PRINCE EDWARD ISLAND

NOVA SCOTIA

CAPE BRETON ISLAND

Bay of Fundy

ATLANTIC OCEAN

Sable Island
(N.S.)

Halifax

Fredericton

Saint John

Moncton

Charlottetown

Sydney

Yarmouth

Meters	Feet
1000	3280
500	1640
200	656
	Sea Level
200	656
2000	6560

W-DRM6518-A1   -2-3
Copyright © Rand McNally & Co.

0   25   50   75   100   150   200   250 Kilometers

0   25   50   100   150 Miles

Scale 1 : 2,500,000   Lambert Conformal Conic Projection

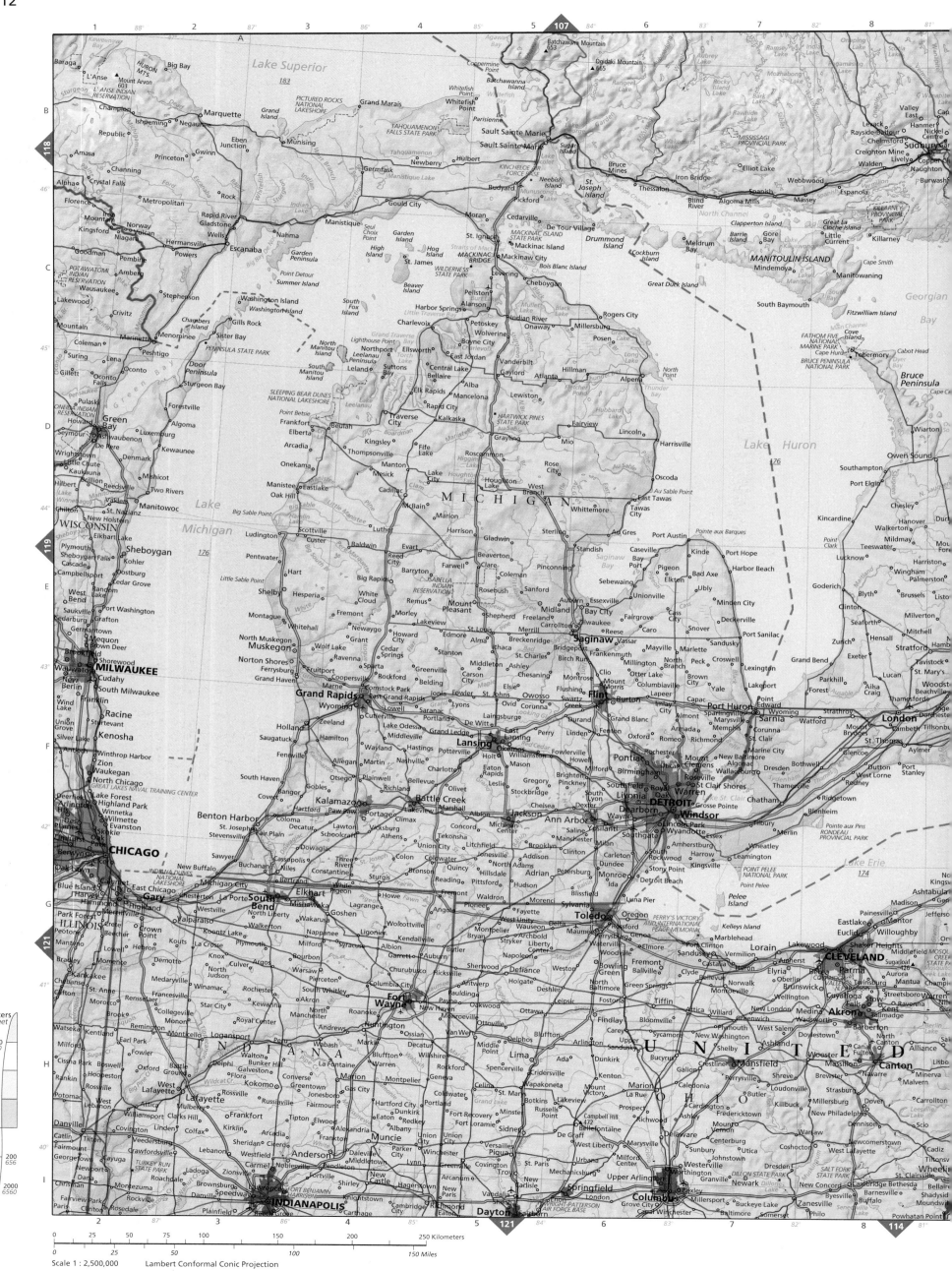

Meters
Feet

1000
3280

500
1640

200
656

Sea Level

200
656

2000
6560

0   25   50   75   100   150   200   250 Kilometers

0   25   50   100   150 Miles

Scale 1 : 2,500,000   Lambert Conformal Conic Projection

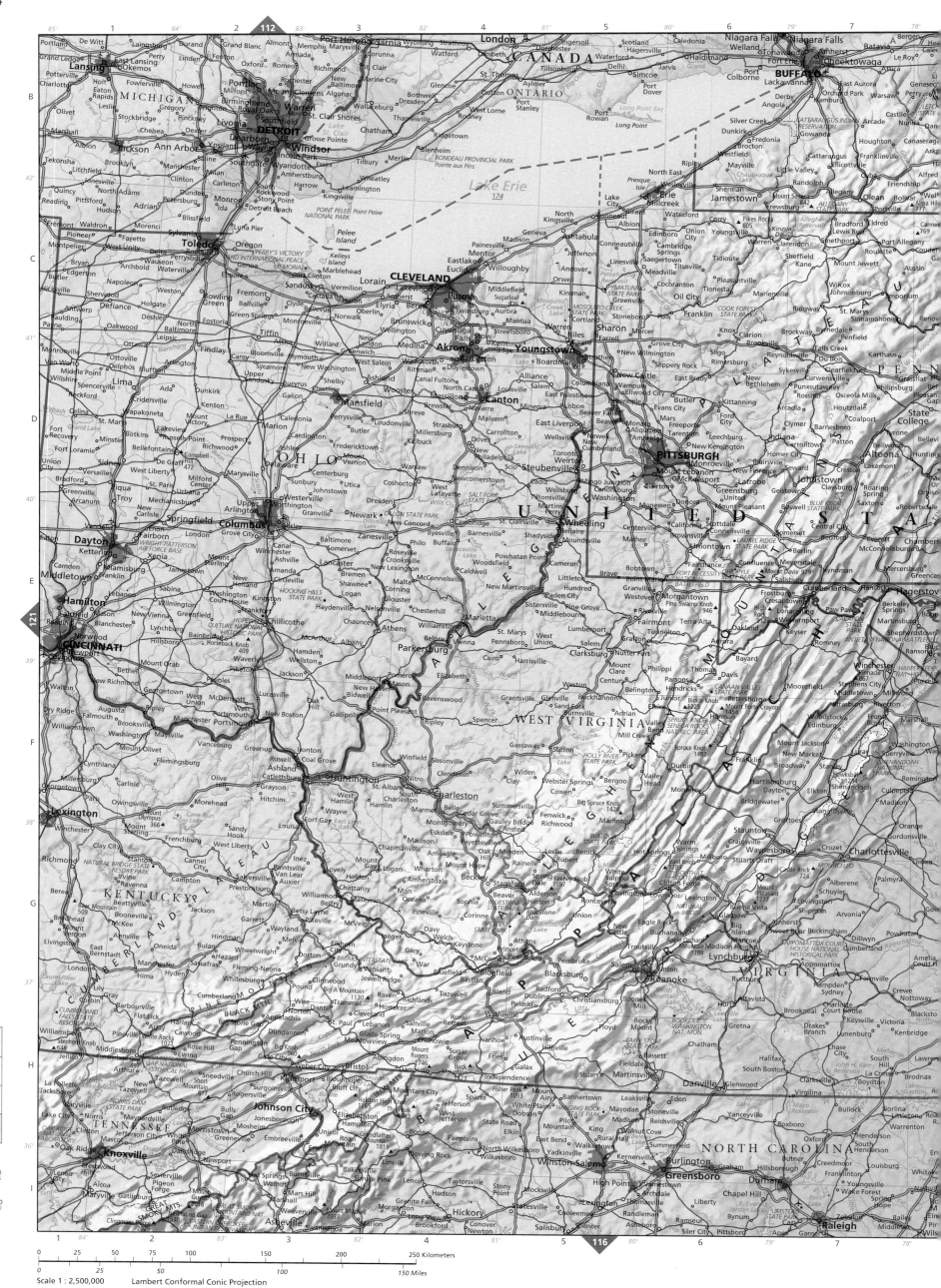

Scale 1 : 2,500,000 Lambert Conformal Conic Projection

NEW YORK

VERMONT

NEW HAMPSHIRE

MASSACHUSETTS

CONNECTICUT

RHODE ISLAND

NEW JERSEY

DELAWARE

MARYLAND

Syracuse · Auburn · Ithaca · Binghamton · Elmira · Scranton · Wilkes-Barre · Albany · Schenectady · Kingston · Poughkeepsie · Newburgh · Springfield · Worcester · **BOSTON** · Hartford · New Haven · Bridgeport · Providence · Warwick · Pawtucket · Fall River · New Bedford · Cape Cod · Nantucket · Martha's Vineyard

NEWARK · Jersey City · **NEW YORK** · LONG ISLAND · Trenton · Princeton · Allentown · Bethlehem · Reading · Lancaster · York · **PHILADELPHIA** · Camden · Wilmington · Cherry Hill · Atlantic City

BALTIMORE · **WASHINGTON** · Alexandria · Annapolis · Dover · Salisbury · Ocean City

Delmarva Peninsula · Chesapeake Bay

Richmond · Newport News · Hampton · **Virginia Beach** · Norfolk · Portsmouth · Chesapeake · Suffolk

CATSKILL MOUNTAINS · POCONO MTS. · BERKSHIRE HILLS

Long Island Sound · Rhode Island Sound · Nantucket Sound · Cape Cod Bay · Gulf of Maine

ATLANTIC OCEAN

CAPE COD NAT. SEASHORE · ASSATEAGUE ISLAND NATIONAL SEASHORE · FIRE ISLAND NATIONAL SEASHORE

Albemarle Sound · Pamlico Sound · Currituck Sound

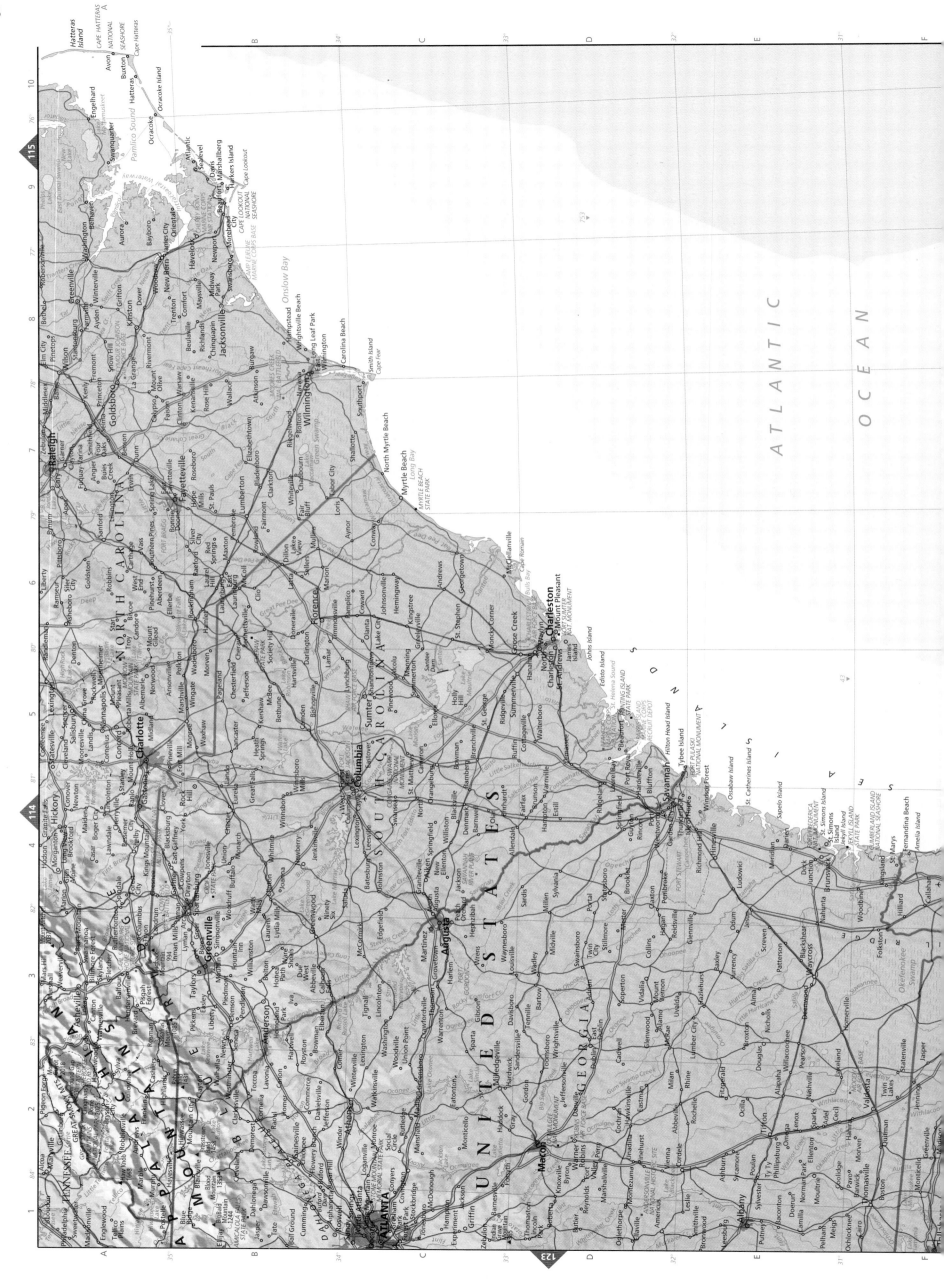

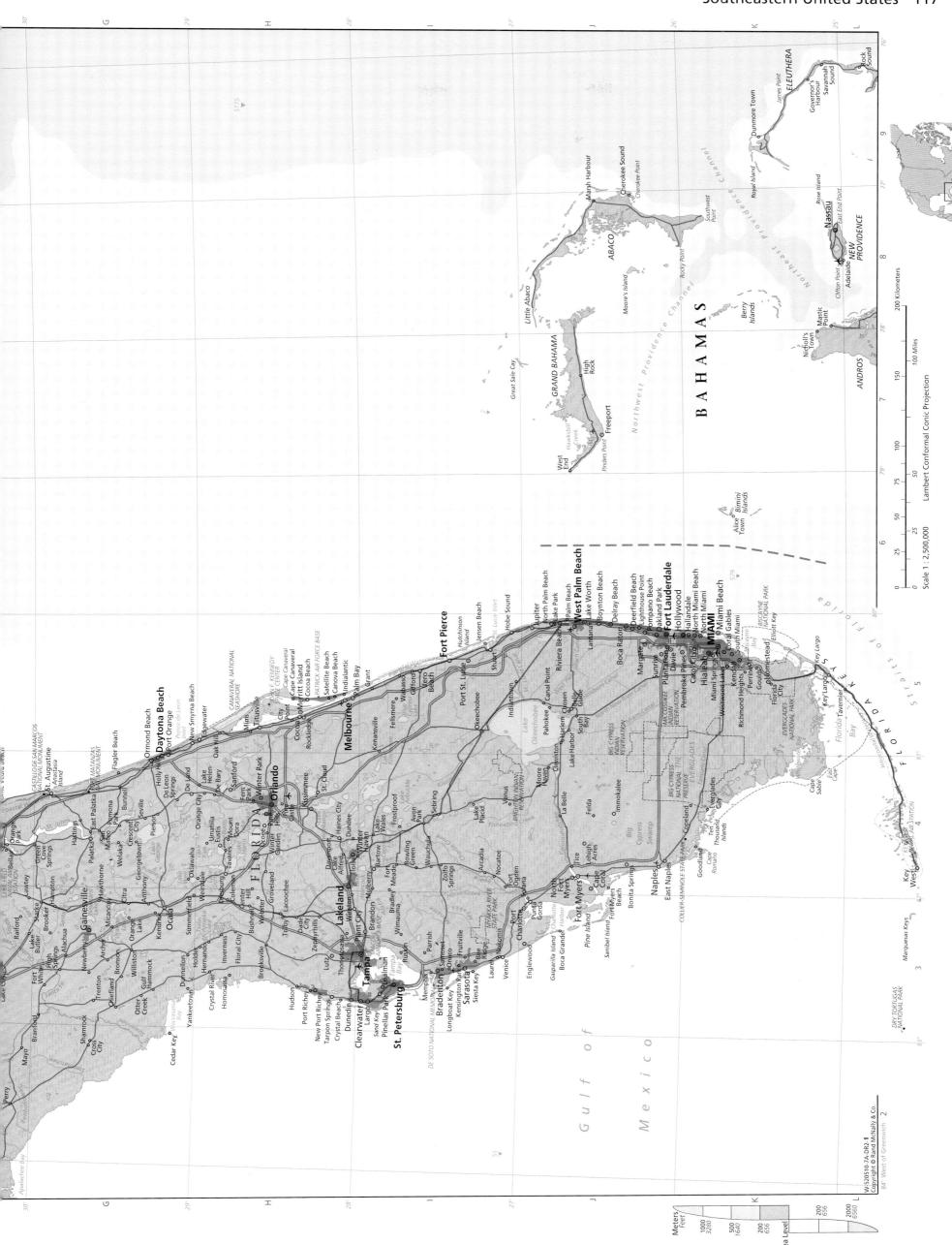

BAHAMAS

ELEUTHERA

Rock Sound

Governor's Harbour

Savannah Sound

James Point

Royal Island

Rose Island

Nassau

East End Point

NEW PROVIDENCE

Adelaide

Clifton Point

Mastic Point

Nicholl's Town

ANDROS

Berry Islands

Mangrove Cay

Dunmore Town

ABACO

Marsh Harbour

Cherokee Sound

Cherokee Point

Southwest Point

Rocky Point

Moore's Island

Little Abaco

GRAND BAHAMA

Great Sale Cay

High Rock

Hawksbill Creek

Freeport

West End

Pinders Point

Northwest Providence Channel

Northeast Providence Channel

Bimini Islands

Alice Town

200 Kilometers

100 Miles

Scale 1 : 2,500,000

Lambert Conformal Conic Projection

150

100

75

50

50

25

25

0

0

W-520510-7A-DR2.1
Copyright © Rand McNally & Co.

FLORIDA

Daytona Beach

Ormond Beach

St. Augustine

New Smyrna Beach

Titusville

Melbourne

Orlando

Fort Pierce

West Palm Beach

Fort Lauderdale

MIAMI

Miami Beach

Hollywood

Tampa

St. Petersburg

Clearwater

Lakeland

Sarasota

Bradenton

Fort Myers

Naples

Key West

FLORIDA KEYS

Key Largo

EVERGLADES NATIONAL PARK

BIG CYPRESS NATIONAL PRESERVE

Gulf of Mexico

Straits of Florida

Gainesville

Ocala

Meters Feet

2000 6560

1000 3280

500 1640

200 656

Sea Level

200 656

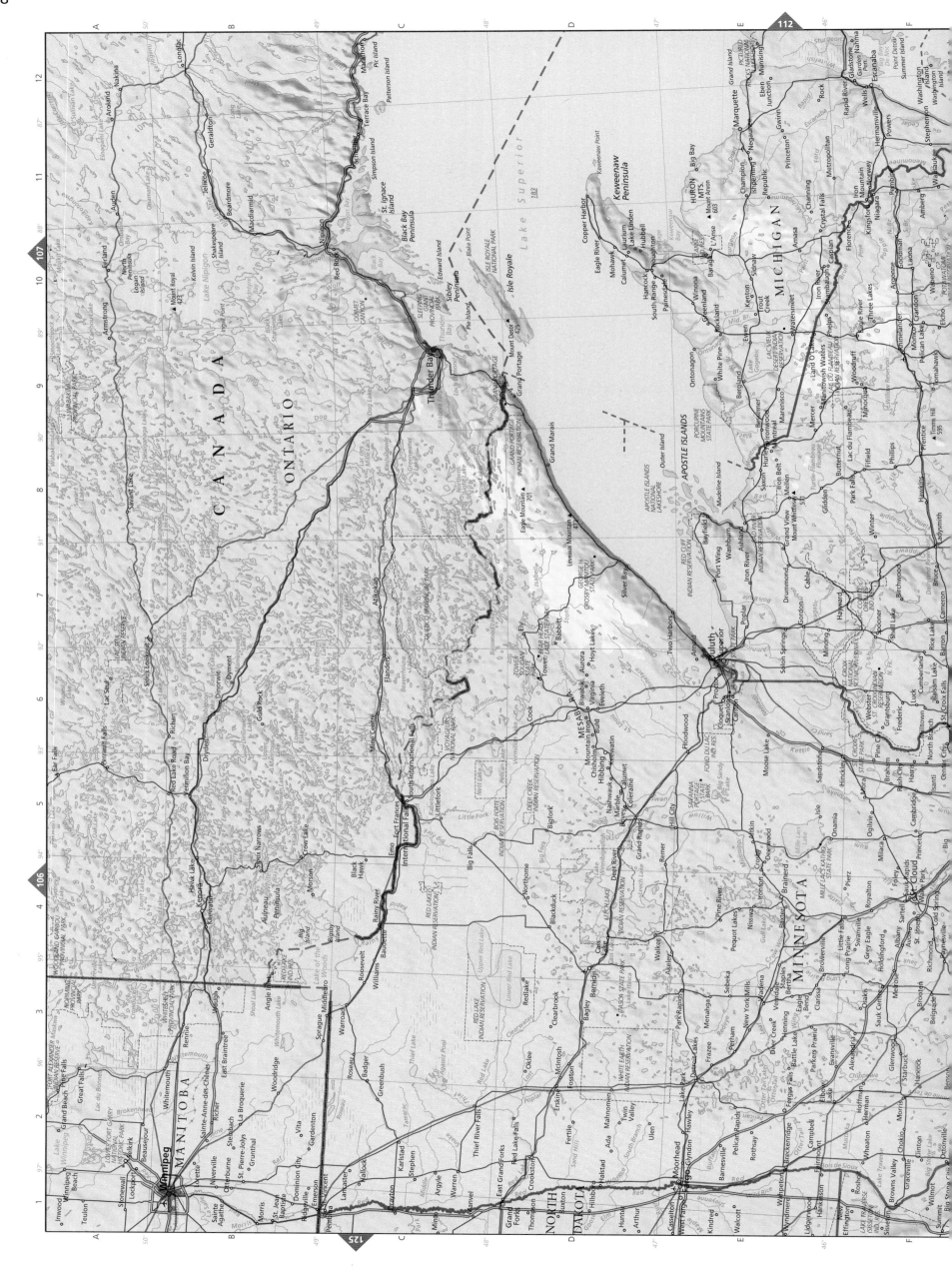

112
107
106
125

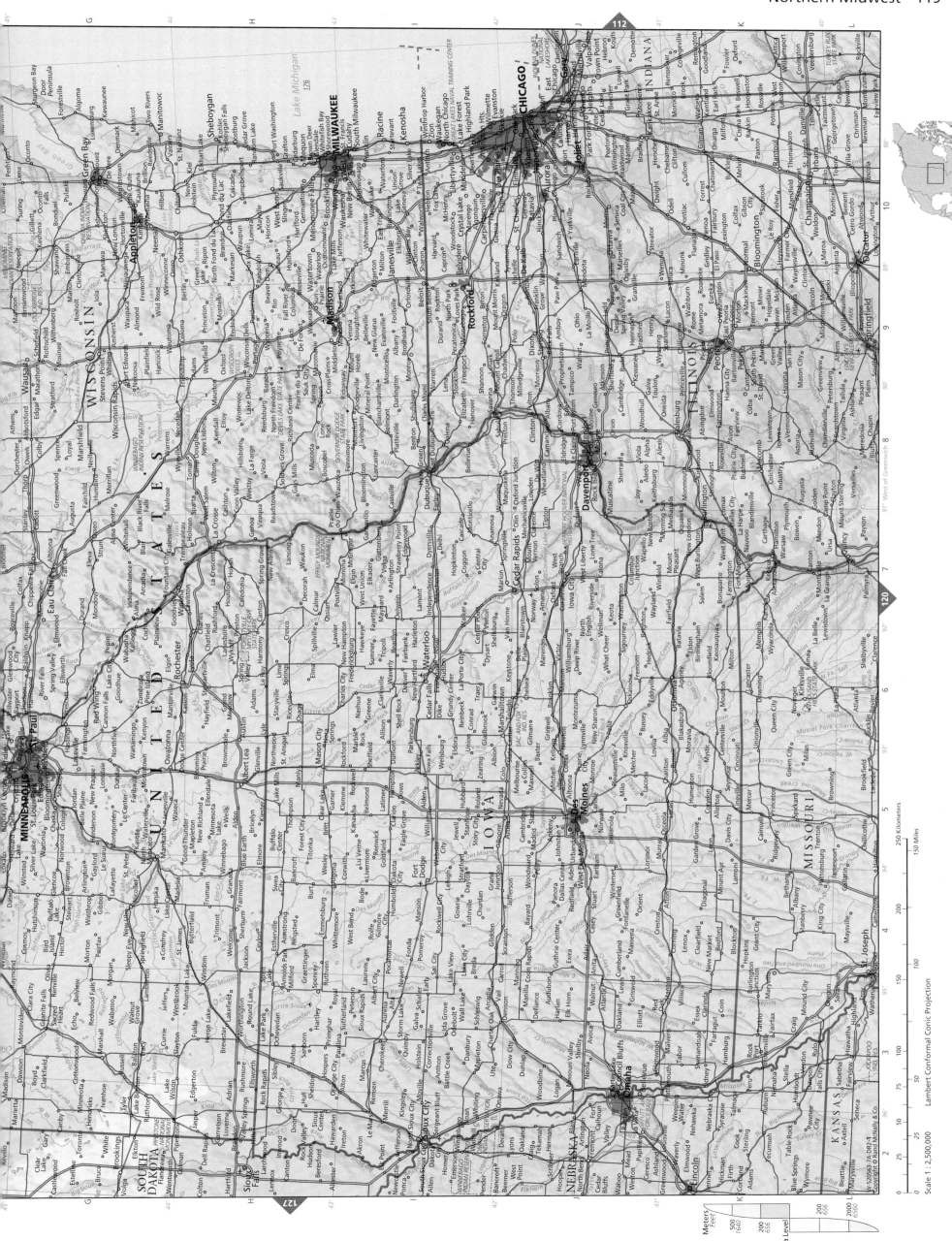

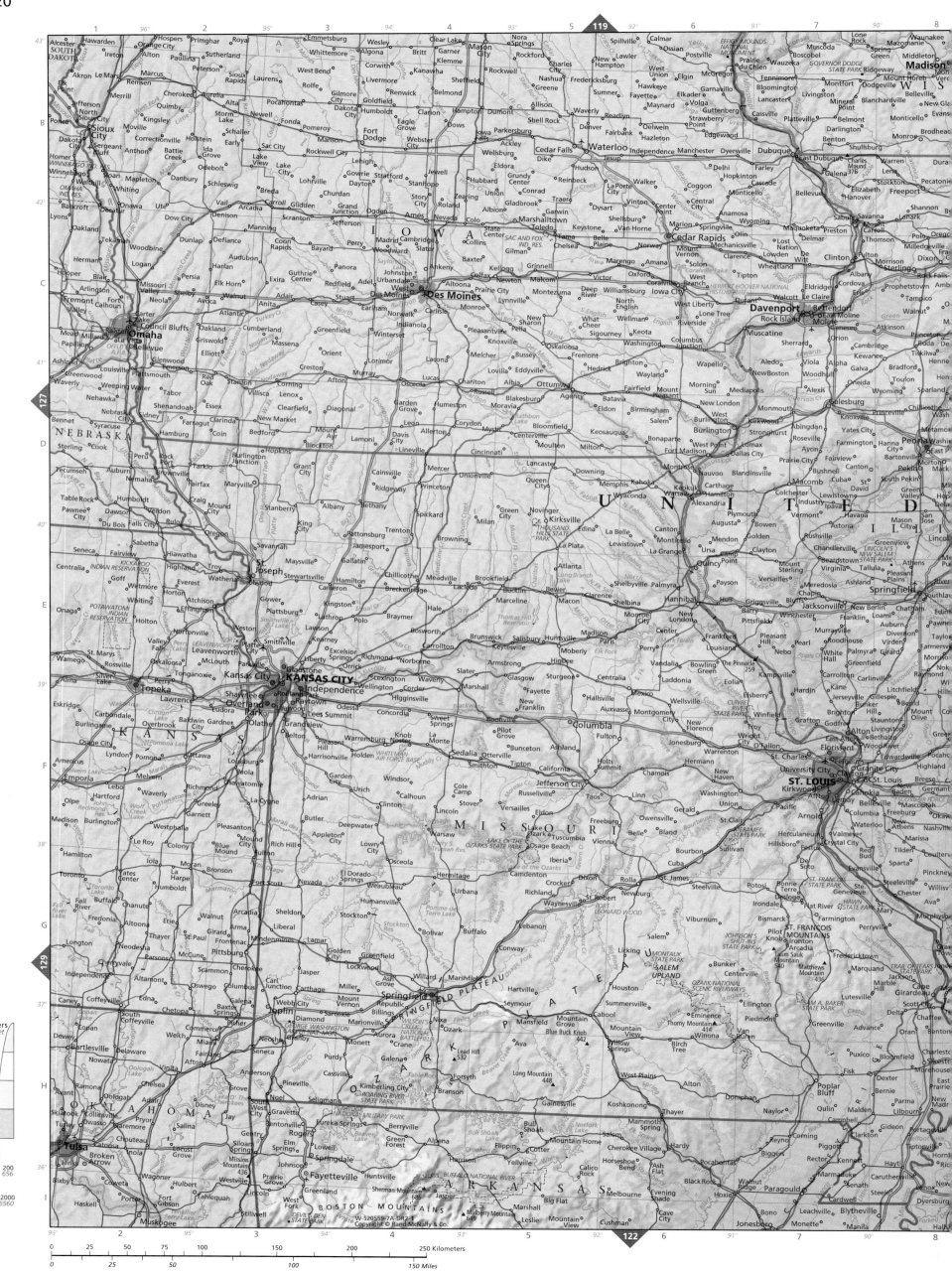

Meters
Feet

1000
3280

500
1640

200
656

Sea Level

200
656

2000
6560

0   25   50   75   100   150   200   250 Kilometers

0   25   50   100   150 Miles

Scale 1 : 2,500,000   Lambert Conformal Conic Projection

W-520559-7A-DR2-1
Copyright © Rand McNally & Co.

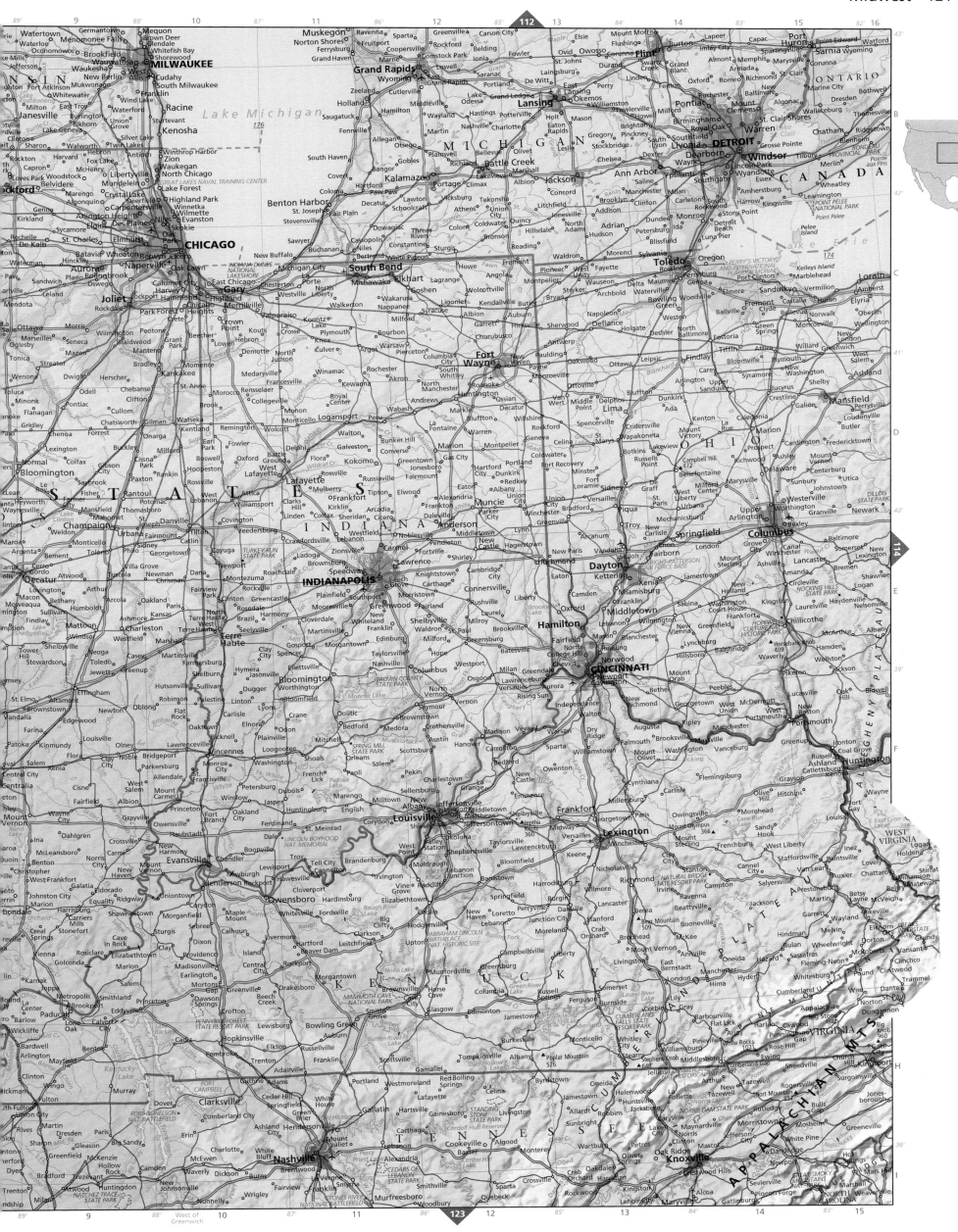

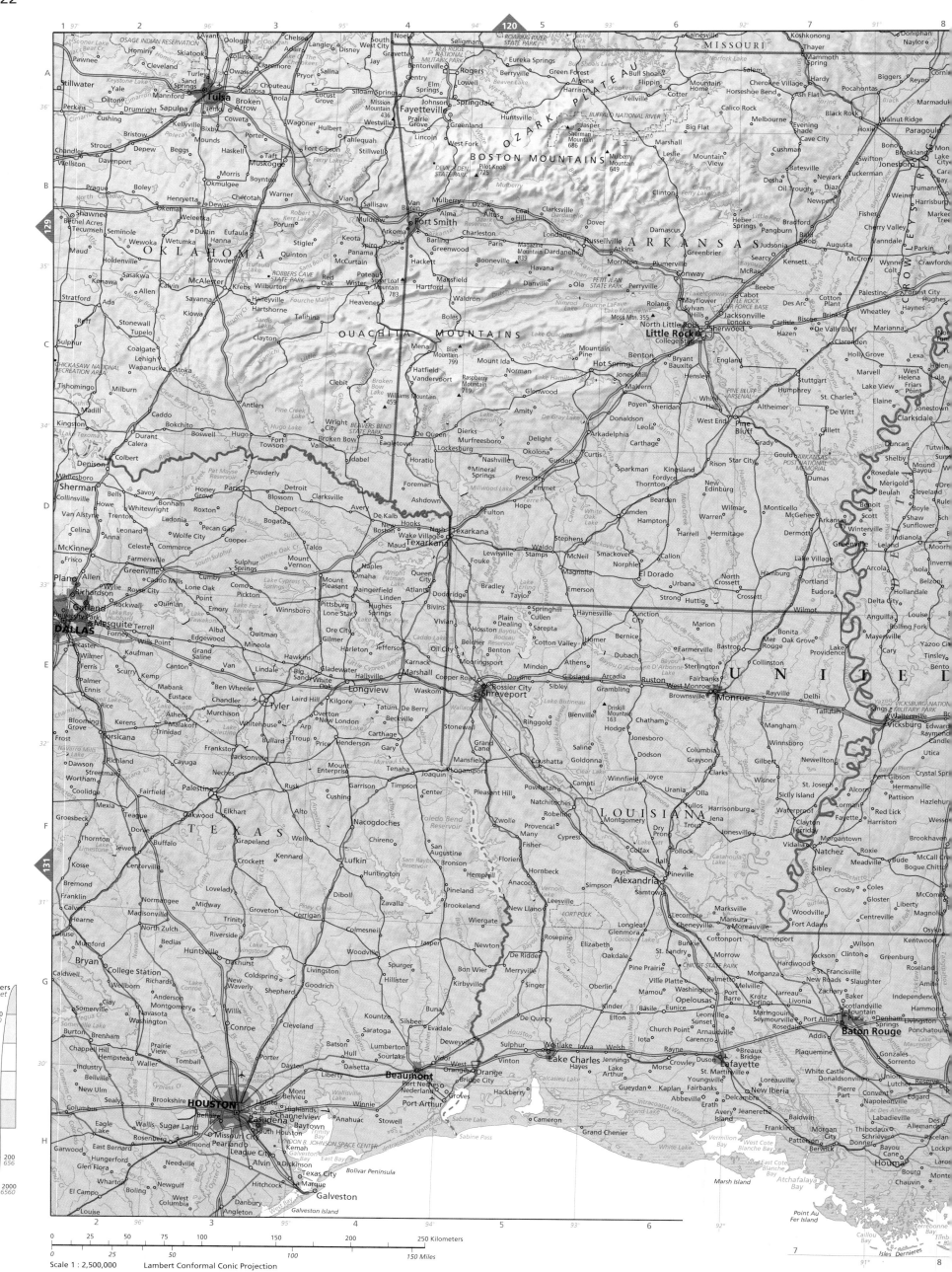

Scale 1 : 2,500,000   Lambert Conformal Conic Projection

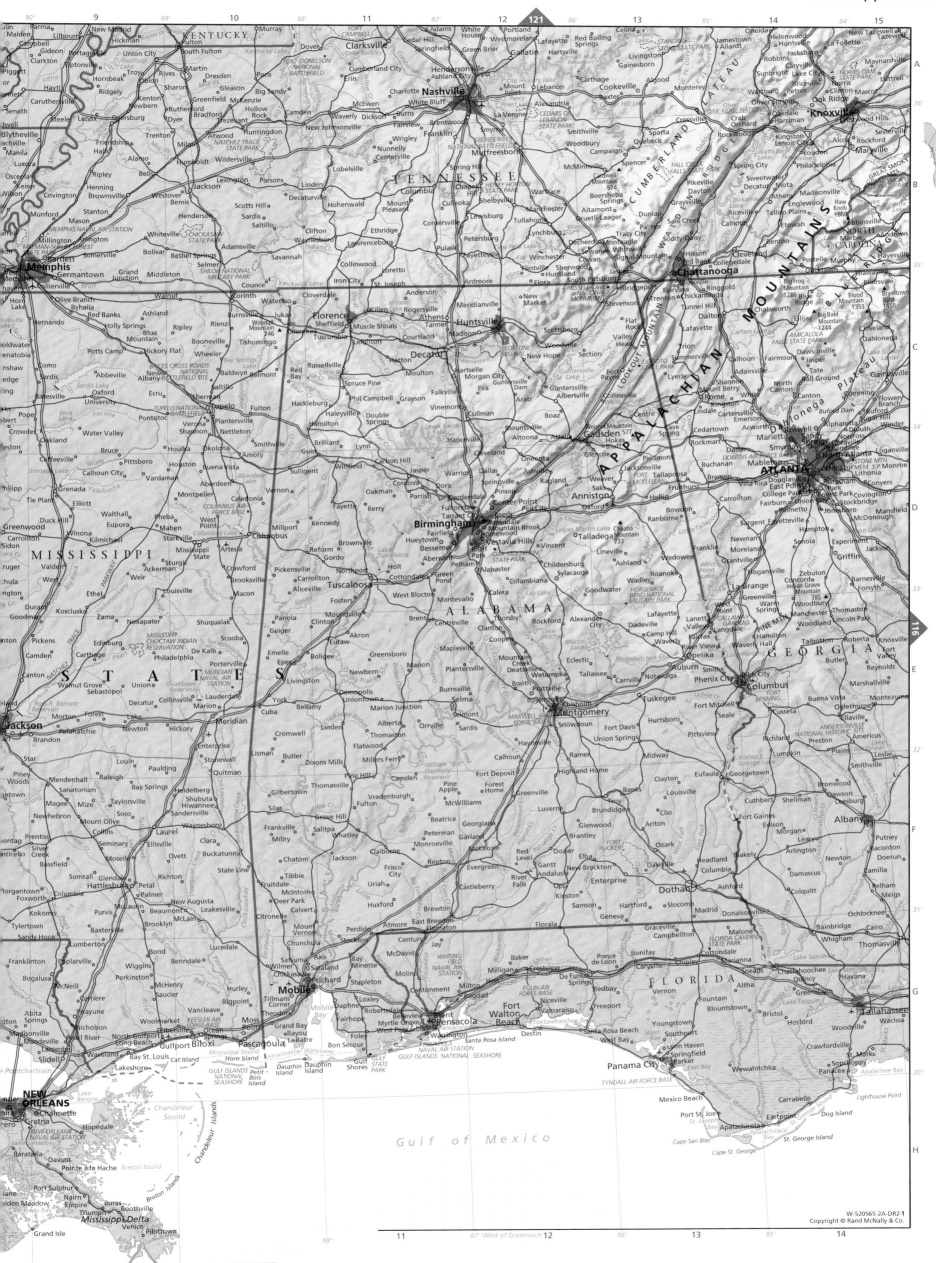

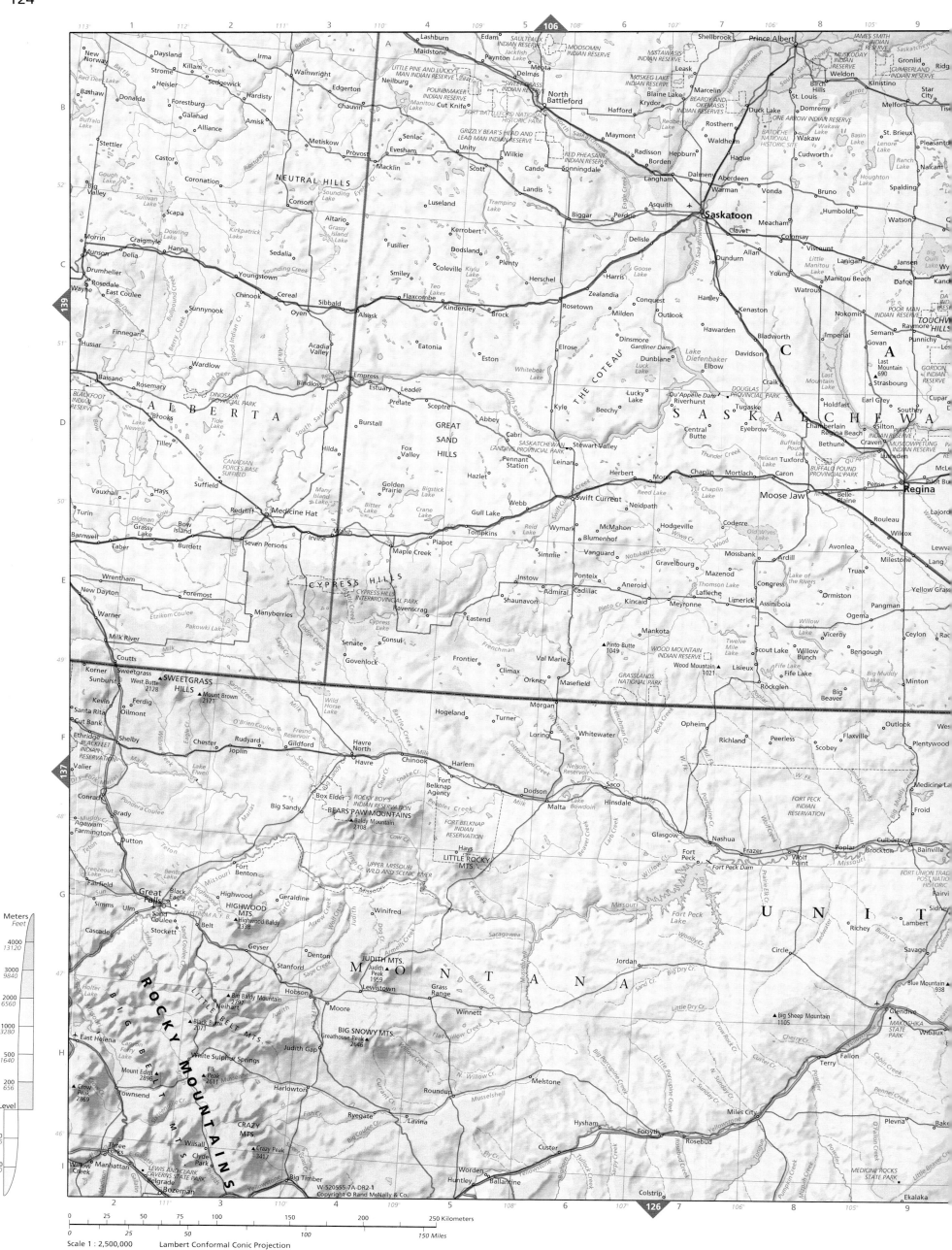

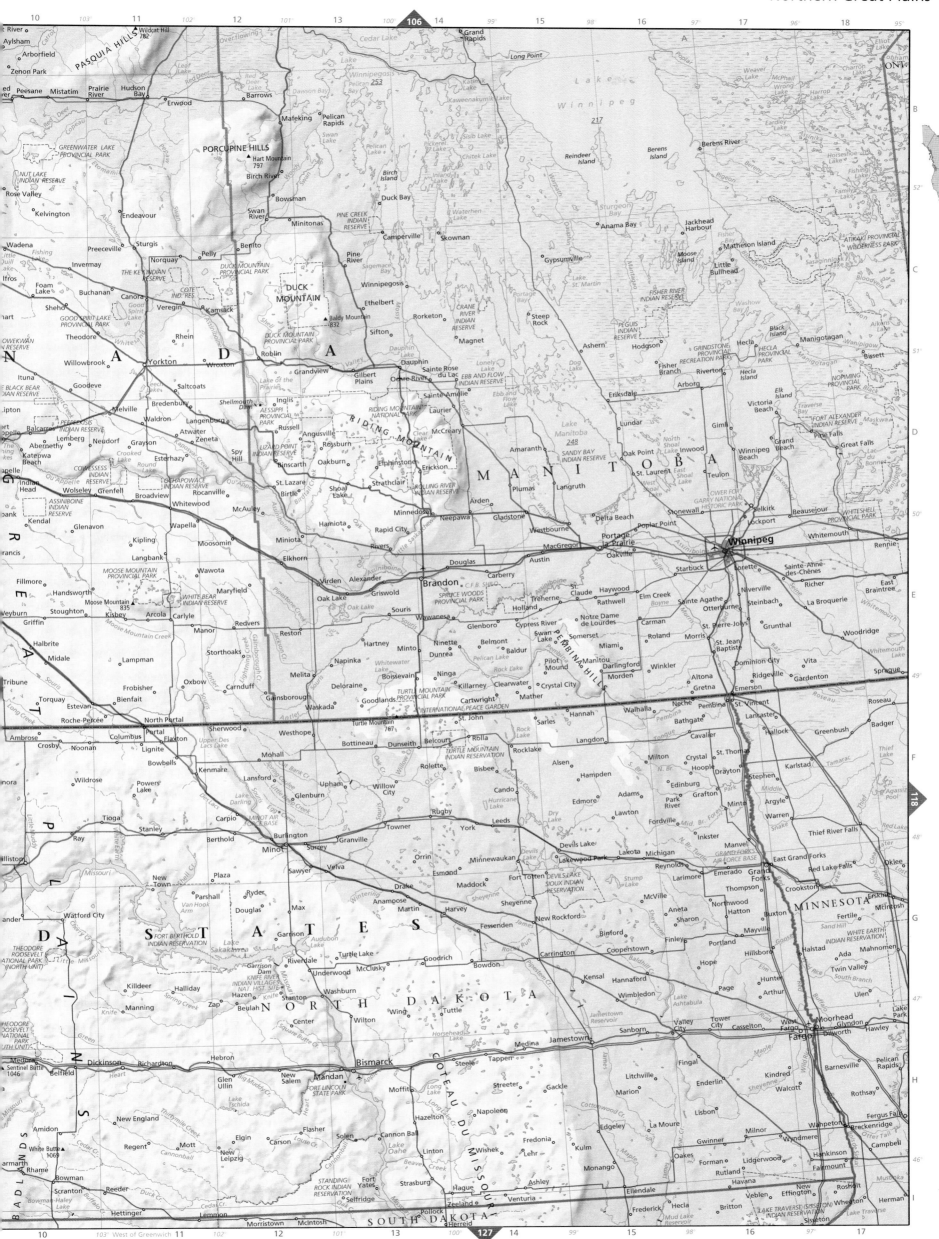

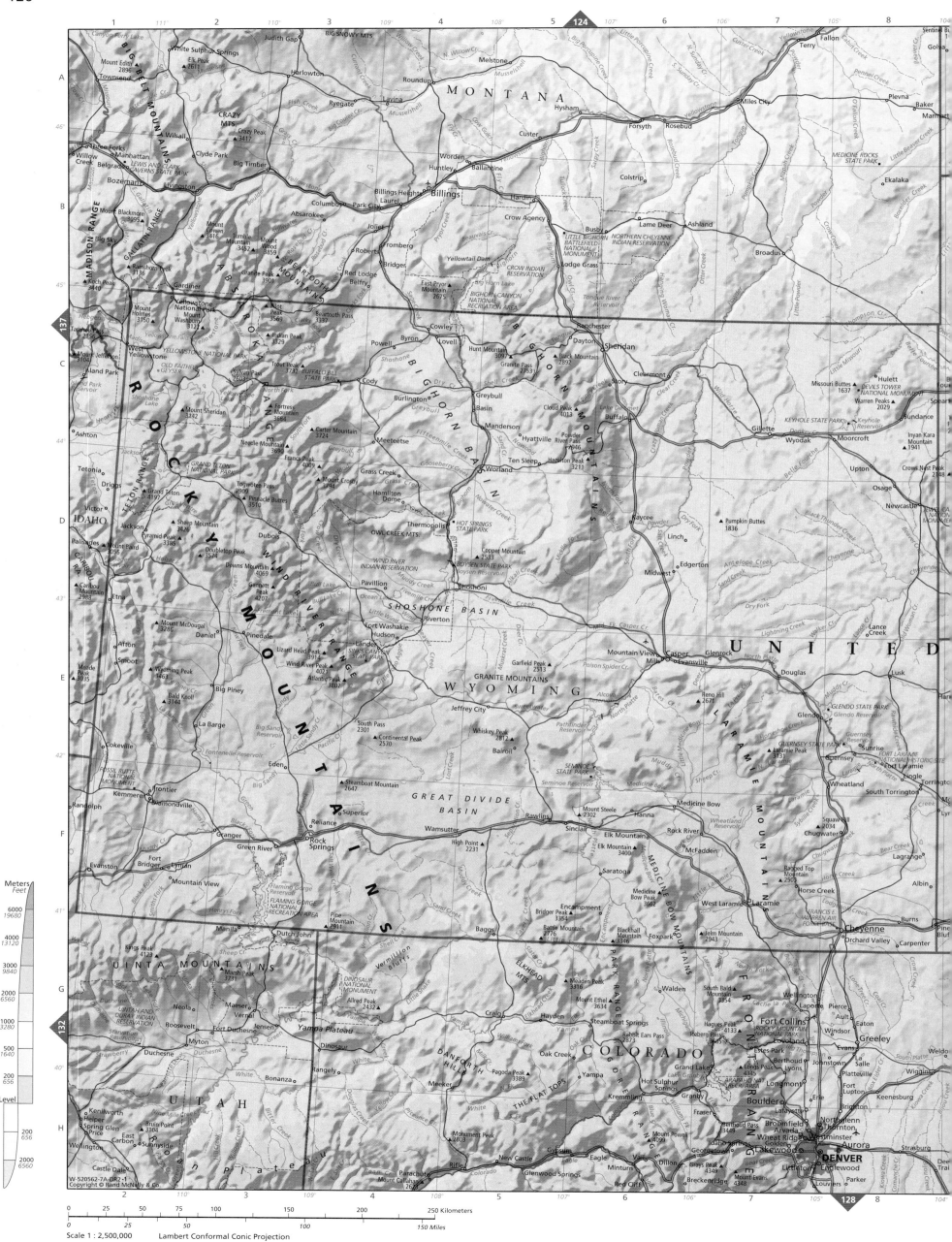

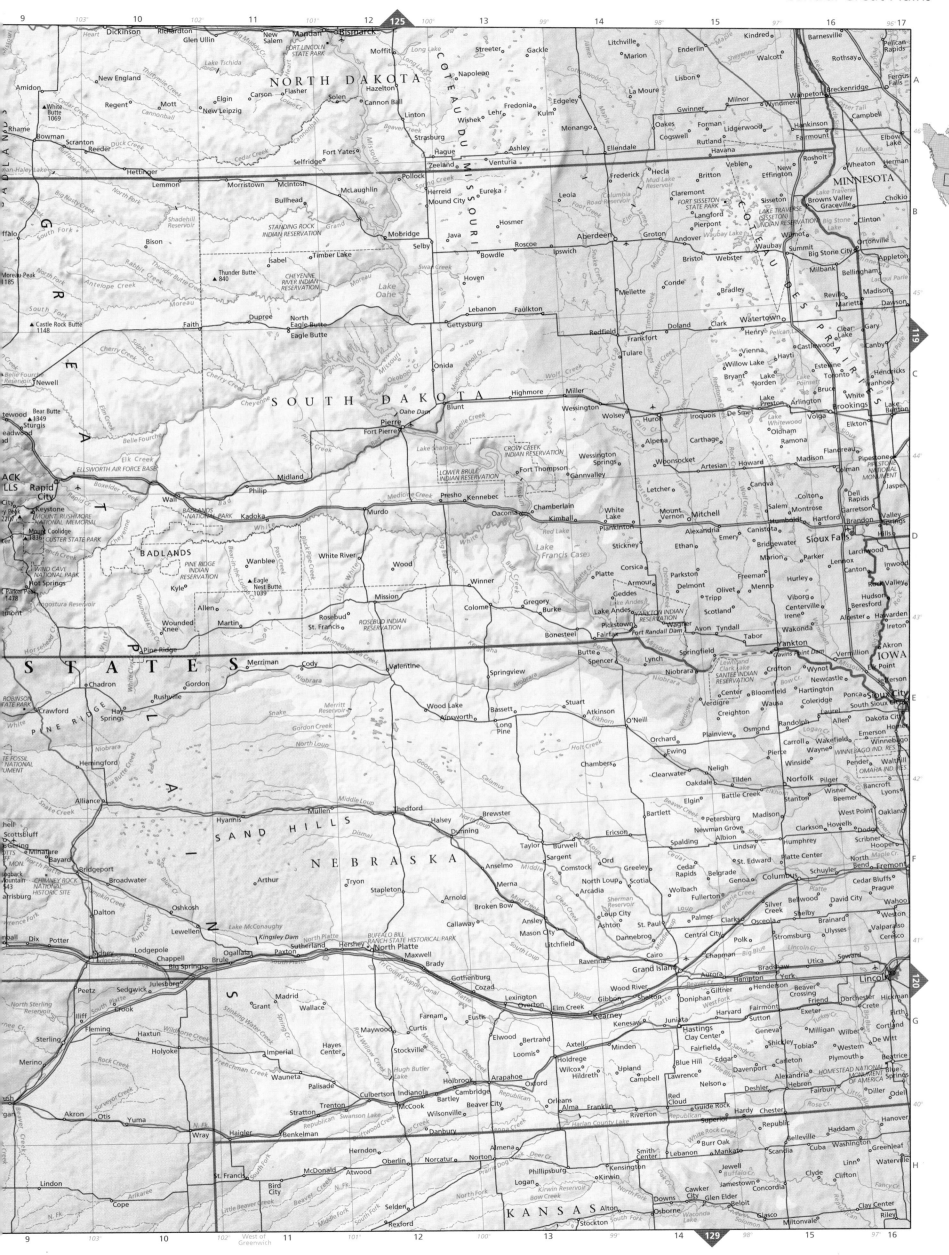

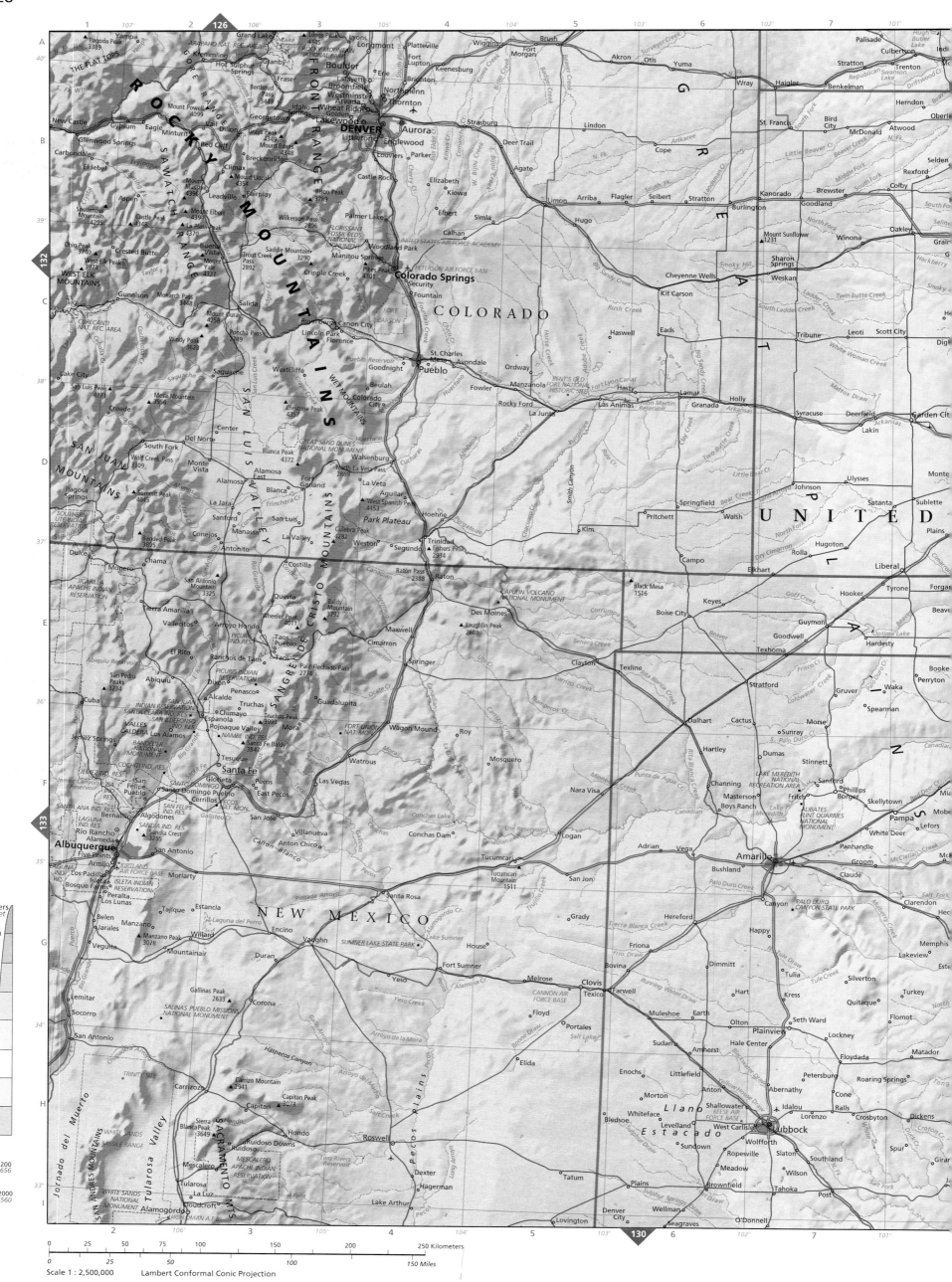

Meters
Feet

6000
19680

4000
13120

3000
9840

2000
6560

1000
3280

500
1640

200
656

Sea Level

200
656

2000
6560

0   25   50   75   100   150   200   250 Kilometers

0   25   50   100   150 Miles

Scale 1 : 2,500,000   Lambert Conformal Conic Projection

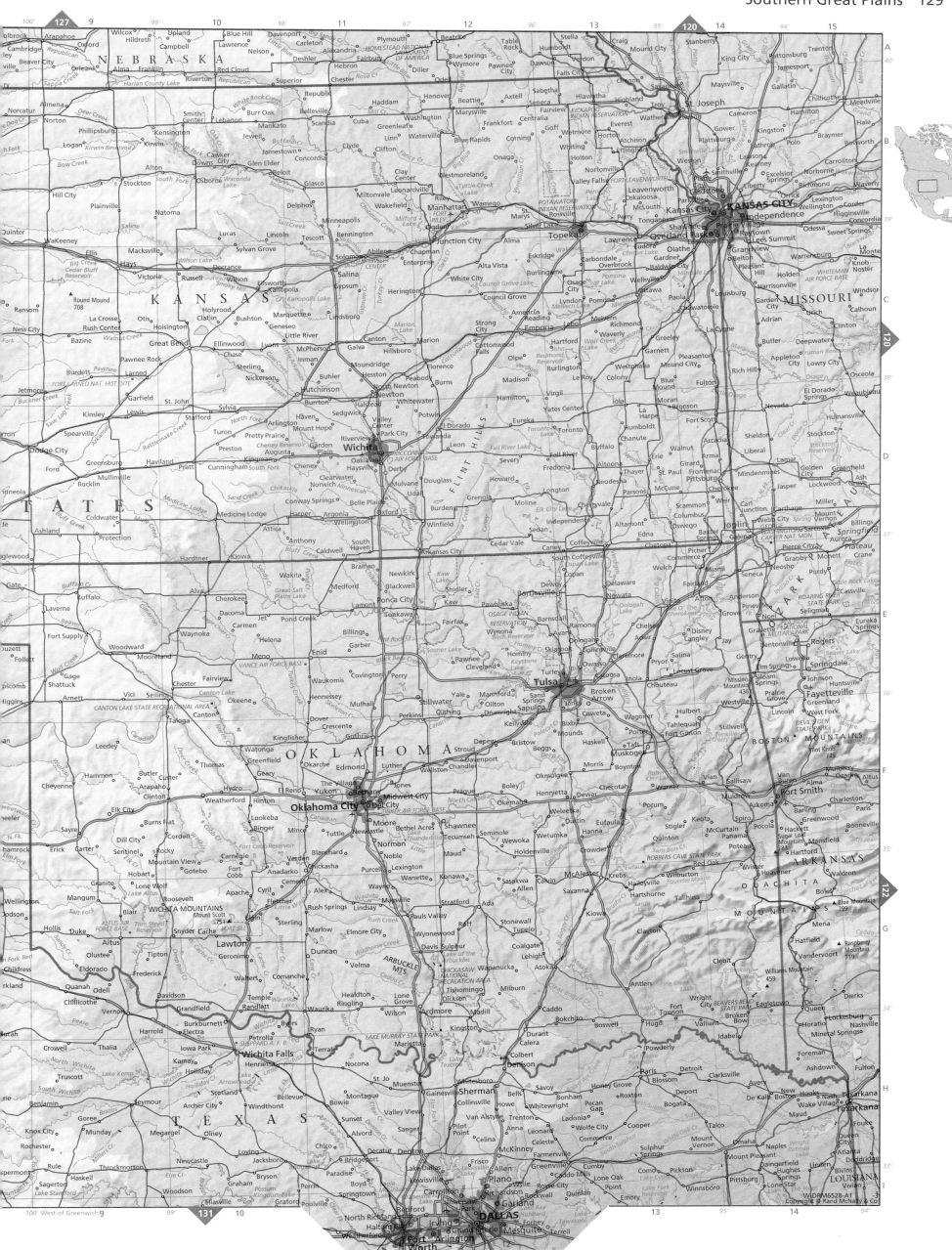

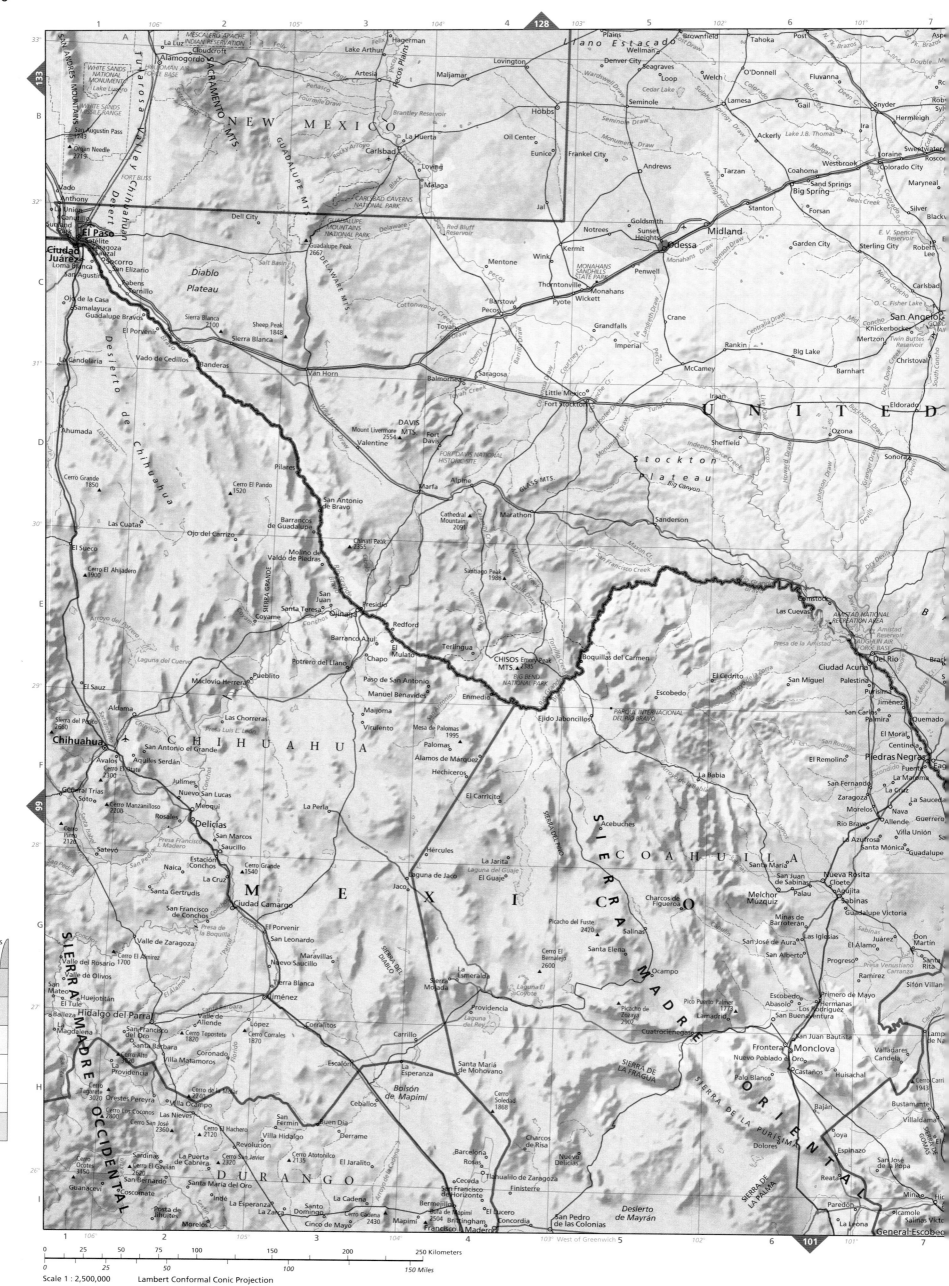

Meters
Feet

4000
13120

3000
9840

2000
6560

1000
3280

500
1640

200
656

Sea Level

200
656

2000
6560

0   25   50   75   100   150   200   250 Kilometers

0   25   50   100   150 Miles

Scale 1 : 2,500,000   Lambert Conformal Conic Projection

Gulf of Mexico

LOUISIANA

TEXAS

TAMAULIPAS

PADRE ISLAND
NATIONAL
SEASHORE

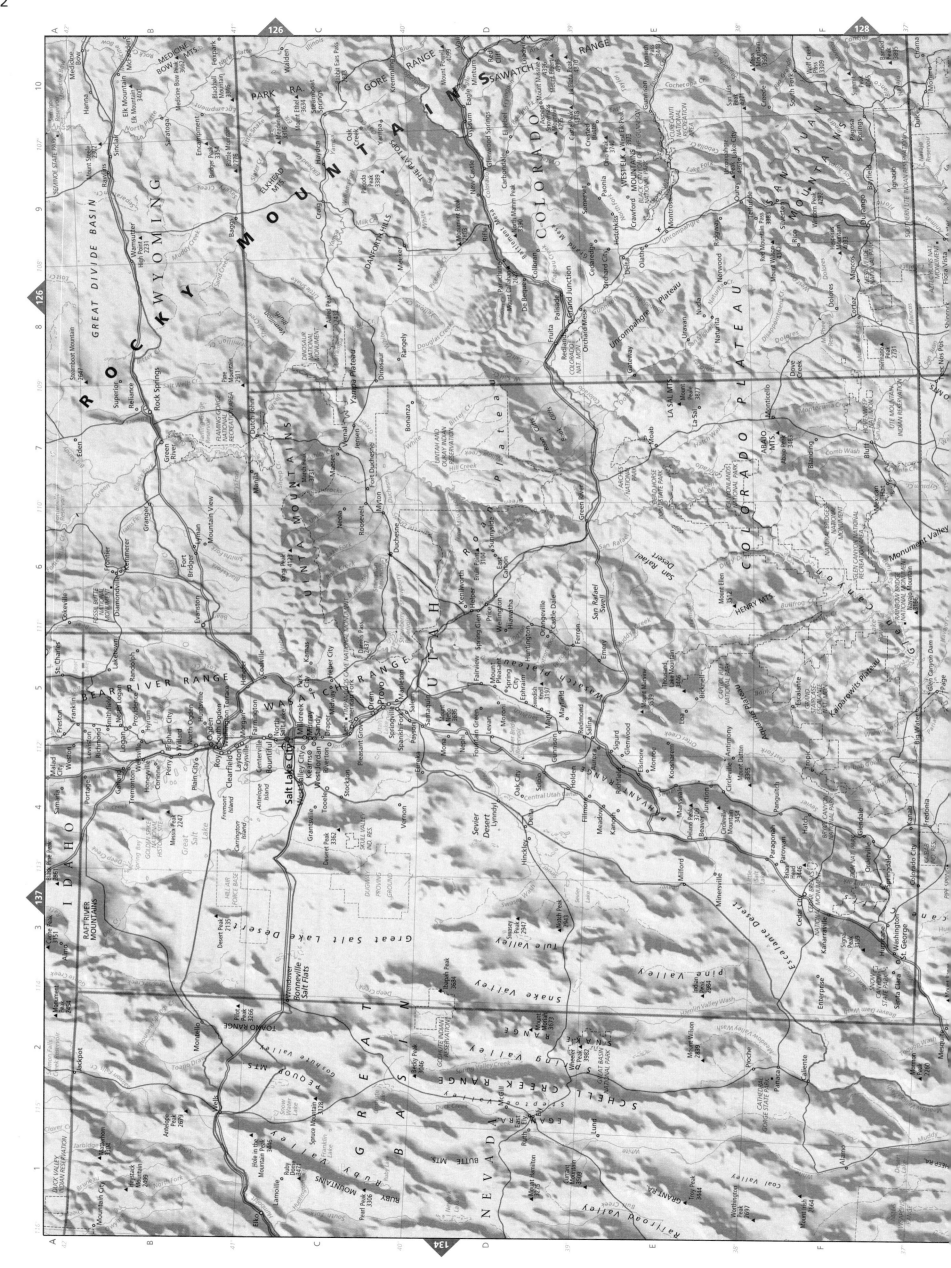

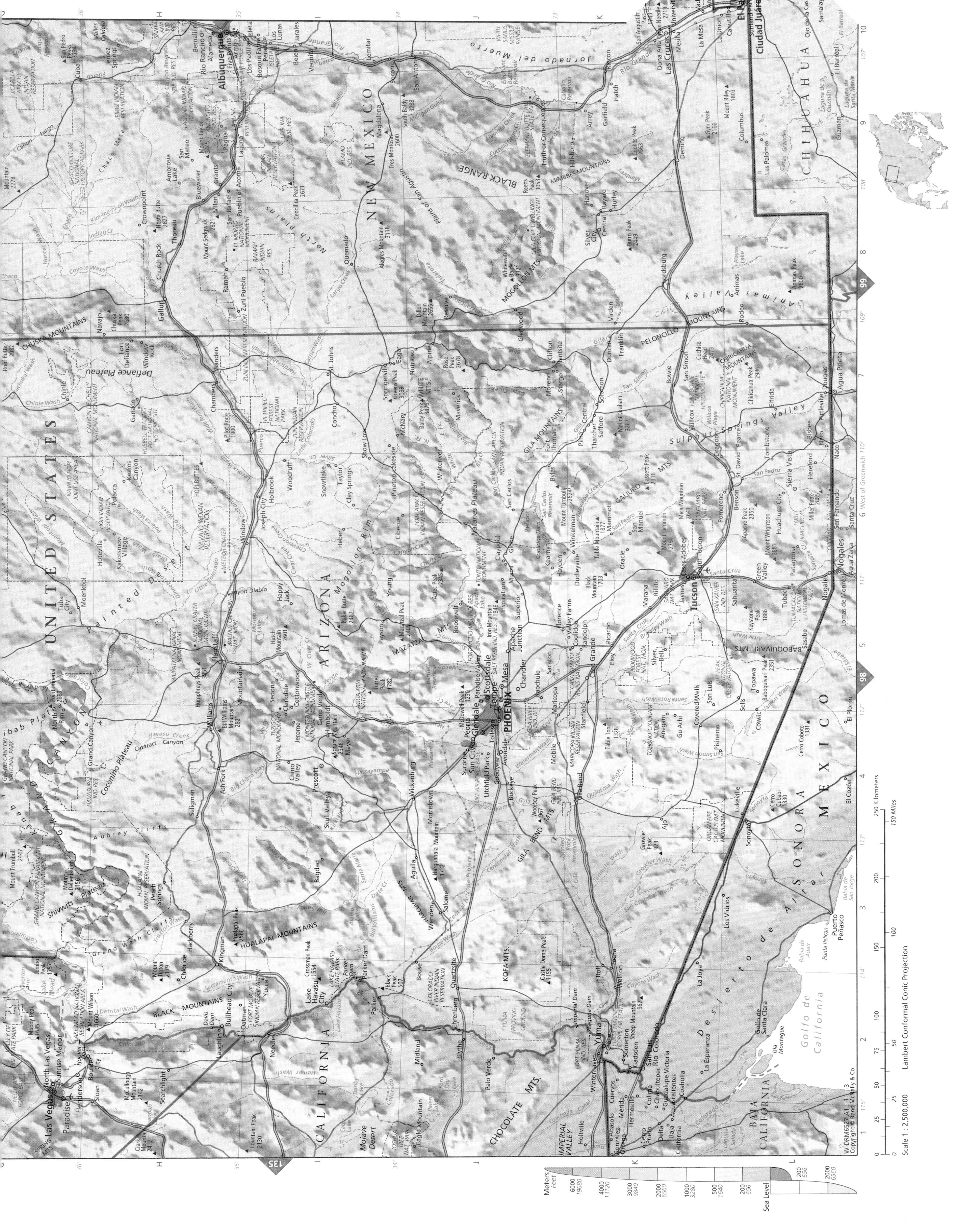

Arizona and Utah

NEW MEXICO

ARIZONA

UNITED STATES

CALIFORNIA

MEXICO

SONORA

BAJA CALIFORNIA

CHIHUAHUA

Albuquerque

Las Vegas
North Las Vegas
Paradise
Henderson
Boulder City

Flagstaff

Phoenix
Mesa
Tempe
Scottsdale
Glendale
Chandler
Peoria
Surprise

Tucson

Yuma

El Paso
Ciudad Juárez
Las Cruces

Gallup
Grants
Kingman
Prescott
Sedona
Williams
Cottonwood
Jerome
Wickenburg
Payson
Globe
Safford
Willcox
Benson
Sierra Vista
Bisbee
Douglas
Nogales
Casa Grande
Coolidge
Florence
Buckeye
Gila Bend
Ajo
Blythe
Needles
Parker
Lake Havasu City
Bullhead City

GRAND CANYON NATIONAL PARK
PETRIFIED FOREST NATIONAL PARK
SAGUARO NATIONAL PARK
ORGAN PIPE CACTUS NAT. MON.

NAVAJO INDIAN RESERVATION
HOPI INDIAN RESERVATION
HUALAPAI INDIAN RESERVATION
FORT APACHE INDIAN RES.
SAN CARLOS INDIAN RESERVATION
TOHONO O'ODHAM INDIAN RESERVATION

Colorado River
Rio Grande
Gila River
Little Colorado

Mojave Desert
Painted Desert
Coconino Plateau
Defiance Plateau
Kaibab Plateau
Mogollon Rim

Golfo de California

Scale 1 : 2,500,000
Lambert Conformal Conic Projection

Copyright © Rand McNally & Co.

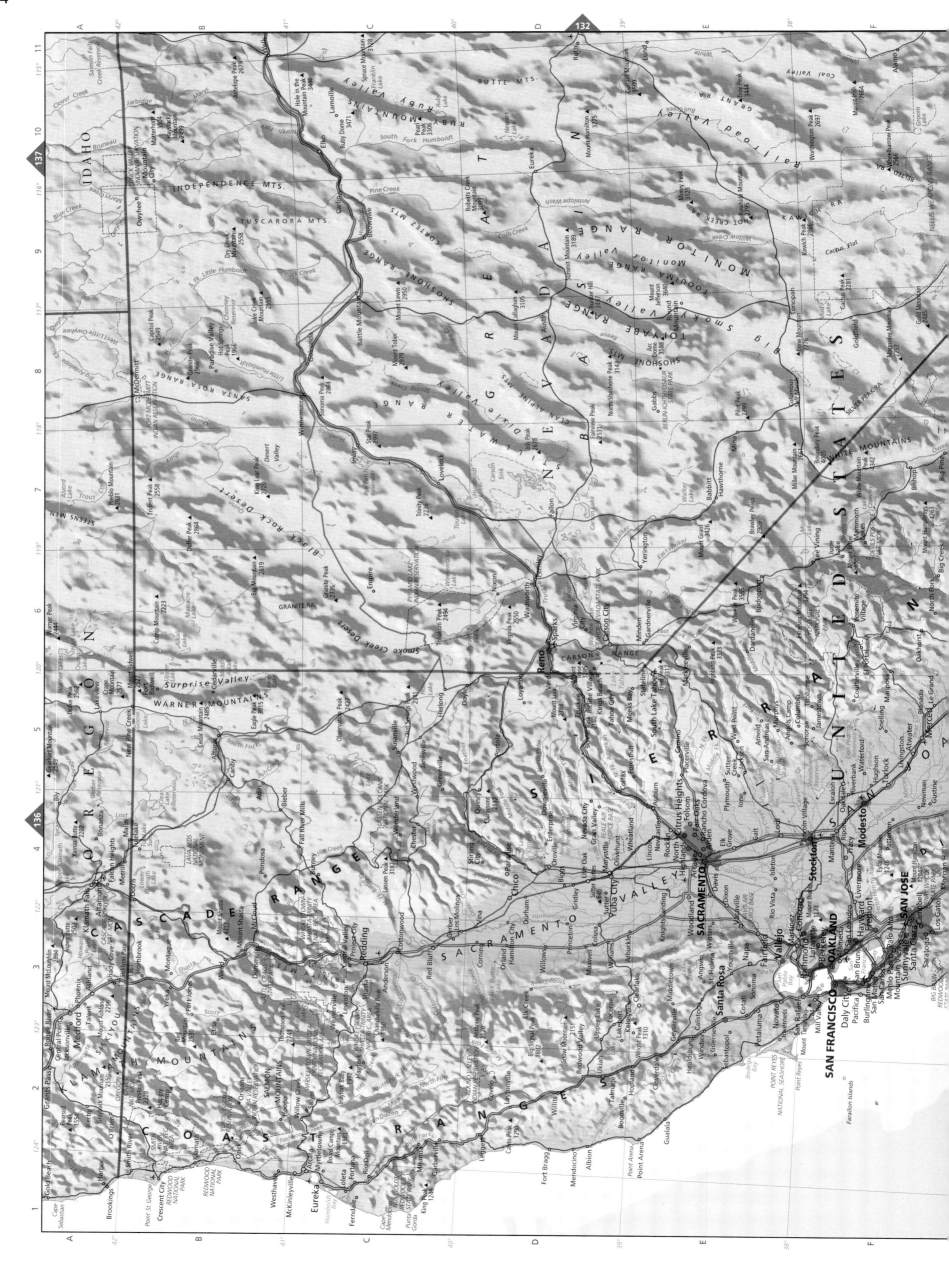

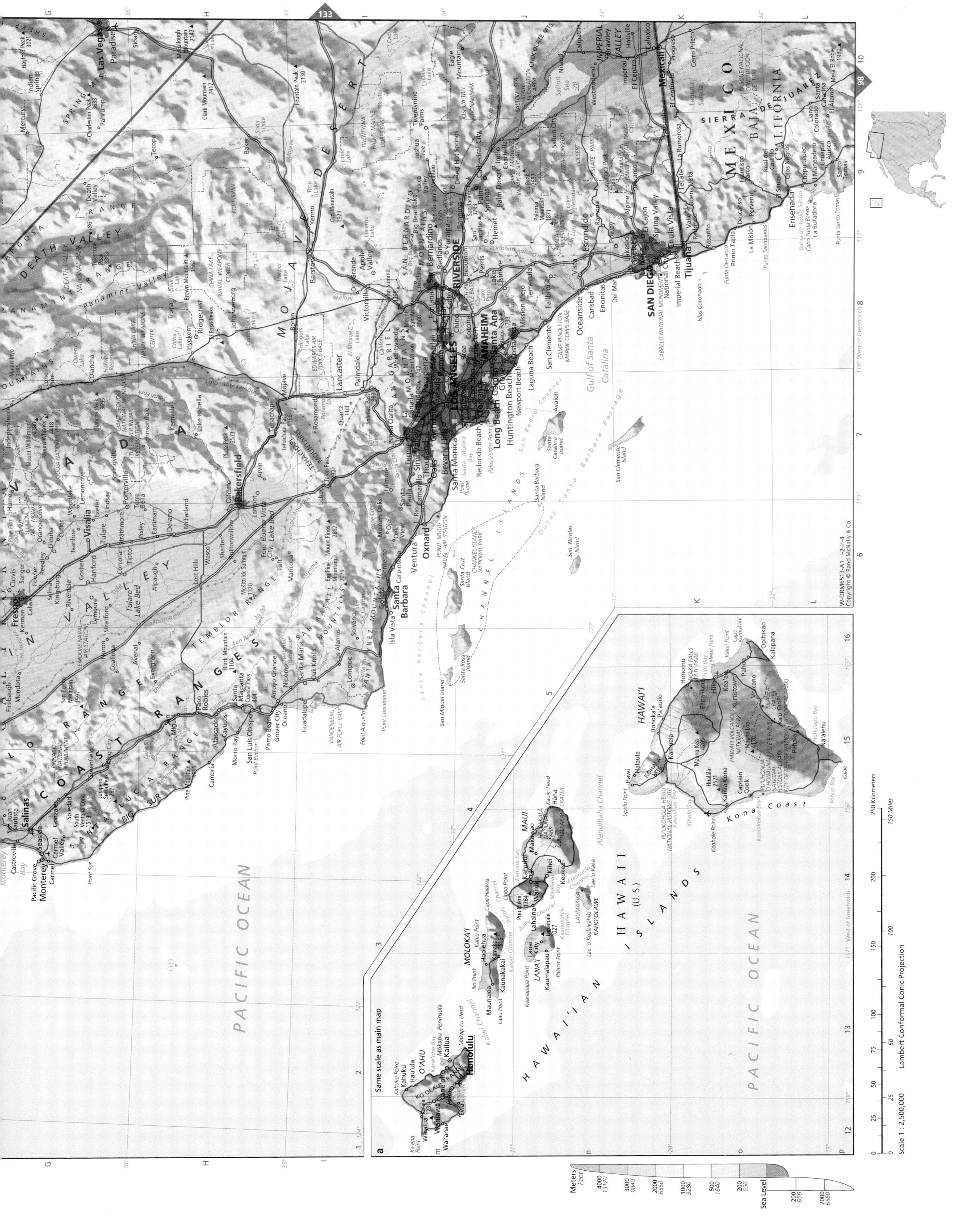

PACIFIC OCEAN

DEATH VALLEY

MOJAVE DESERT

Las Vegas
Paradise

Bakersfield
Visalia
Tulare
Fresno

Lancaster
Palmdale
Victorville
Barstow
Baker

LOS ANGELES
ANAHEIM
Santa Ana
Long Beach
Huntington Beach
Newport Beach
Beverly Hills
Santa Monica
Redondo Beach
Laguna Beach

RIVERSIDE
San Bernardino
Redlands
Hemet
Perris
Temecula

Oxnard
Ventura
Santa Barbara
Carpinteria
Isla Vista

Oceanside
Carlsbad
Encinitas
Escondido
Del Mar

SAN DIEGO
Imperial Beach
National City
Chula Vista
El Cajon

Tijuana
Mexicali
Ensenada
Tecate

MEXICO
BAJA CALIFORNIA
SIERRA JUAREZ

Salton Sea
IMPERIAL VALLEY
Brawley
El Centro
Calexico

San Luis Obispo
Morro Bay
Pismo Beach
Arroyo Grande
Santa Maria
Lompoc
Guadalupe

Paso Robles
Atascadero
Cambria
Big Sur

Salinas
Monterey
Pacific Grove
Carmel
Seaside

Santa Catalina Island
San Clemente Island
Santa Barbara Island
San Nicolas Island
Santa Cruz Island
Santa Rosa Island
San Miguel Island
Anacapa Island

Gulf of Santa Catalina
Santa Barbara Channel
CHANNEL ISLANDS

COAST RANGES
SIERRA NEVADA
TEHACHAPI MOUNTAINS
SANTA LUCIA RANGE
TEMBLOR RANGE
SAN GABRIEL MOUNTAINS
SAN BERNARDINO MOUNTAINS

Point Conception
Point Arguello

CAMP PENDLETON MARINE CORPS BASE
VANDENBERG AIR FORCE BASE
EDWARDS AIR FORCE BASE
FORT IRWIN
JOSHUA TREE NATIONAL PARK

HAWAIIAN ISLANDS (U.S.)

PACIFIC OCEAN

OʻAHU
Honolulu
Kahuku
Kailua
Waiʻanae
Waipahu

MOLOKAʻI
Kaunakakai
Hoolehua

LĀNAʻI
Lānaʻi City

MAUI
Kahului
Lahaina
Kihei
Makawao
Hāna

KAHOʻOLAWE

HAWAIʻI
Hilo
Kailua Kona
Captain Cook
Honokaʻa
Pāpaʻikou

Mauna Kea 4205
Mauna Loa
Hualālai
Kīlauea

HAWAII VOLCANOES NATIONAL PARK
HALEAKALĀ NATIONAL PARK

Kona Coast

Alenuihaha Channel
ʻAlalākeiki Channel
Kalohi Channel
Kaʻiwi Channel
Kaʻulakahi Channel
Auau Channel
Pailolo Channel

Same scale as main map

Scale 1 : 2,500,000

Lambert Conformal Conic Projection

W-DRM6513-A1 -2-2-4
Copyright © Rand McNally & Co.

Meters   Feet
4000   13120
3000   9840
2000   6560
1000   3280
500   1640
200   656
Sea Level
200   656
2000   6560

0   25   50   75   100   150   200   250 Kilometers
0   25   50   75   100   150 Miles

Meters / Feet

6000 / 19680
4000 / 13120
3000 / 9840
2000 / 6560
1000 / 3280
500 / 1640
200 / 656
Sea Level
200 / 656
2000 / 6560

0 25 50 75 100 150 200 250 Kilometers
0 25 50 100 150 Miles

Scale 1 : 2,500,000   Lambert Conformal Conic Projection

ALBERTA
SASKATCHEWAN
MONTANA
IDAHO
WYOMING
UTAH
NEVADA
STATES
ROCKY MOUNTAINS
BITTERROOT RANGE
CLEARWATER MOUNTAINS
SALMON RIVER MOUNTAINS
LEWIS RANGE
SWAN RANGE
MISSION RA.
SALISH MOUNTAINS
WHITEFISH RA.
LEWIS AND CLARK RANGE
BIG BELT MOUNTAINS
LITTLE BELT MTS.
HIGHWOOD MOUNTAINS
BEARS PAW MOUNTAINS
CRAZY MTS.
BIG SNOWY MTS.
JUDITH MTS.
GARNET RANGE
SAPPHIRE MTS.
FLINT CREEK RANGE
ANACONDA RANGE
PIONEER MTS.
BEAVERHEAD MOUNTAINS
LEMHI RANGE
LOST RIVER RANGE
TOBACCO ROOT MTS.
MADISON RANGE
GALLATIN RANGE
ABSAROKA RANGE
BEARTOOTH MTS.
CENTENNIAL MTS.
TETON RANGE
CARIBOU RANGE
BEAR RIVER RANGE
SUBLETT RA.
RAFT RIVER MOUNTAINS
PURCELL MOUNTAINS
CABINET MOUNTAINS
Snake River
Great Falls
Helena
Missoula
Butte
Bozeman
Billings
Kalispell
Coeur d'Alene
Lewiston
Boise
Nampa
Caldwell
Idaho Falls
Pocatello
Twin Falls
Havre
Livingston
Salmon
Dillon
West Yellowstone
Jackson
YELLOWSTONE NATIONAL PARK
GRAND TETON NATIONAL PARK
IDAHO NATIONAL ENGINEERING LABORATORY
CRATERS OF THE MOON NATIONAL MONUMENT
FORT HALL INDIAN RESERVATION
BLACKFEET INDIAN RESERVATION
FLATHEAD INDIAN RESERVATION
NEZ PERCE INDIAN RESERVATION
COEUR D'ALENE INDIAN RESERVATION
ROCKY BOY'S INDIAN RESERVATION
DUCK VALLEY INDIAN RESERVATION
MOUNTAIN HOME AIR FORCE BASE
MALMSTROM A.F.B.
WATERTON-GLACIER INTERNATIONAL PEACE PARK
West of Greenwich
WLDRM6520-A1
Copyright © Rand McNally & Co.

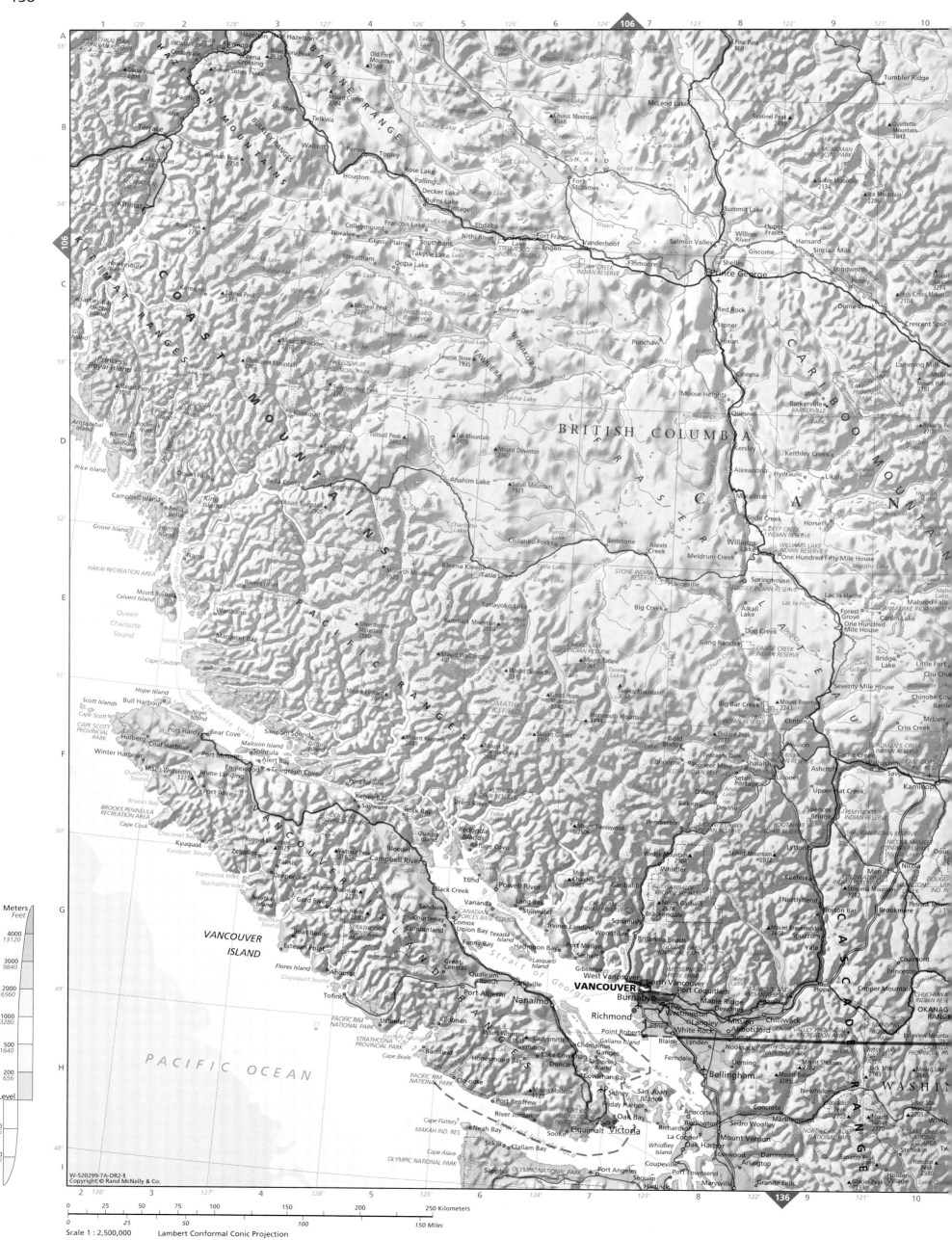

PACIFIC OCEAN

BRITISH COLUMBIA

VANCOUVER ISLAND

VANCOUVER

Victoria

WASHINGTON

Meters
Feet

4000
13120

3000
9840

2000
6560

1000
3280

500
1640

200
656

Sea Level

200
656

2000
6560

W-520299-7A-DR2-1
Copyright © Rand McNally & Co.

0   25   50   75   100   150   200   250 Kilometers

0   25   50   100   150 Miles

Scale 1 : 2,500,000   Lambert Conformal Conic Projection

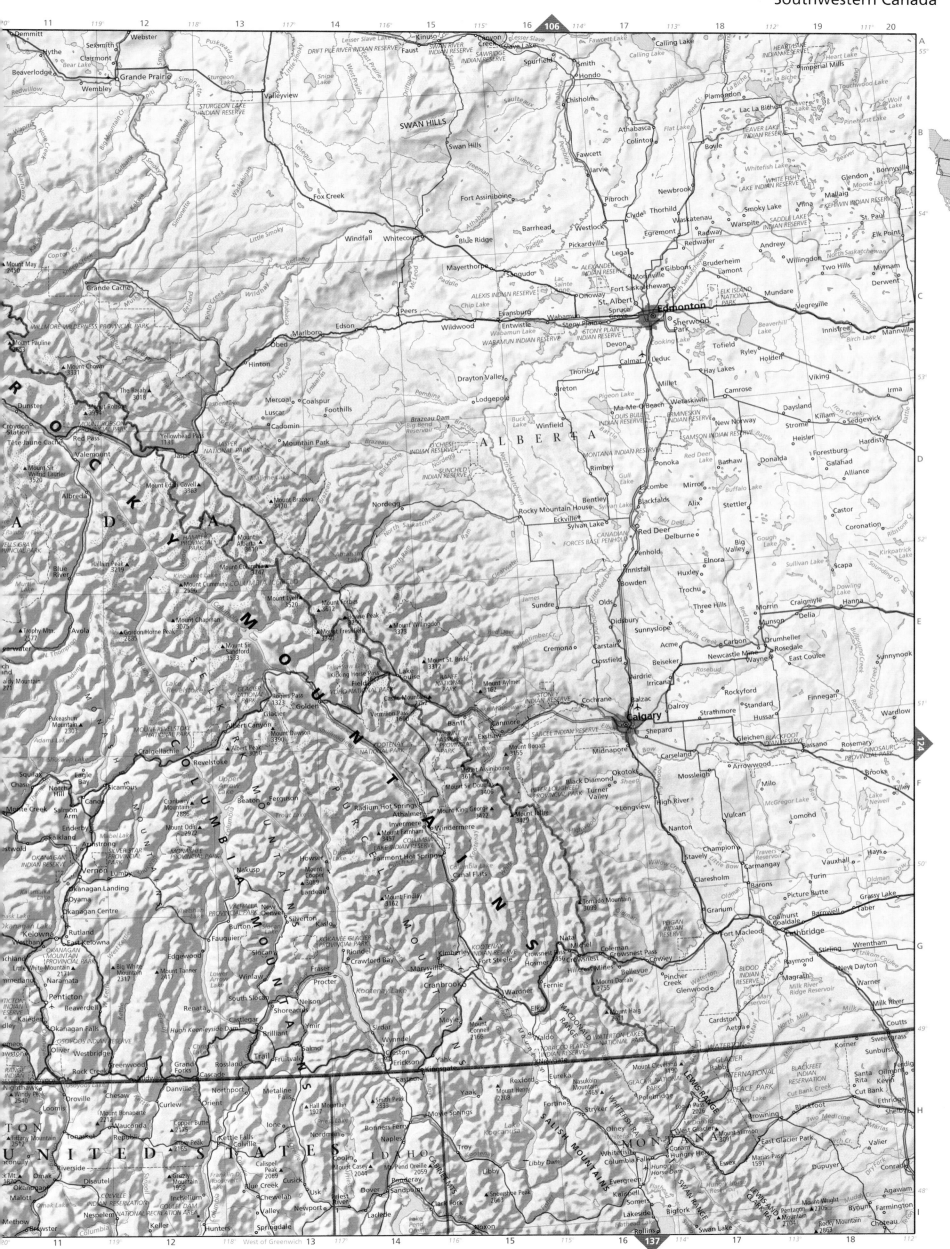

A   B   C   D   E   F

Meters / Feet

4000 / 13120
3000 / 9840
2000 / 6560
1000 / 3280
500 / 1640
200 / 656
Sea Level
200 / 656
2000 / 6560

ARCTIC OCEAN

BEAUFORT SEA

CHUKCHI SEA

International Date Line

OSTROV VRANGELJA (WRANGEL ISLAND)
mys Blossom

NUNAVUT

PRINCE PATRICK ISLAND
Heda and Griper Bay

MELVILLE ISLAND

BANKS ISLAND
Cape Prince Alfred
Sachs Harbour

VICTORIA ISLAND

M'Clure Strait
Viscount Melville Sound
Prince of Wales Strait
Amundsen Gulf
Dolphin and Union Strait

Cape Bathurst
Cape Parry
Baillie Islands
MELVILLE HILLS

NORTHWEST TERRITORIES

Barrow   Point Barrow
Wainwright
Icy Cape
Smith Bay   Cape Halkett
Harrison Bay
Teshekpuk Lake
Prudhoe Bay
Deadhorse
Kaktovik
Camden Bay
Demarcation Point
Herschel Island
Richards Island
Tuktoyaktuk
Mackenzie Bay

Point Hope
Cape Lisburne
LOOKOUT RIDGE
DE LONG MTS.
Mount Michelson 2699
Mount Isto 2761
BRITISH MTS.
ROMANZOF MTS.
PHILIP SMITH MTS.
Arctic Village
DAVIDSON MTS.
Old Crow
RICHARDSON MOUNTAINS
Fort McPherson

NORTHWEST TERRITORIES
Tsiigehtchic
Inuvik
Aklavik
Colville Lake
Lac Belot
FRANKLIN MOUNTAINS
Fort Good Hope
Great Bear Lake
Norman Wells
Tulita

RUSSIA
Cukotskij poluostrov (Chukotka Peninsula)
Vankarem
Enurmino
Uelen
Ostrov Ratmanova
Providenija

Kivalina
Noatak
BAIRD MTS.
SCHWATKA MTS.
Mount Doonerak 2273
Anaktuvik Pass
ENDICOTT MOUNTAINS
Wiseman
Chandalar
Venetie
Fort Yukon
YUKON FLATS
Black
Beaver
Circle
YUKON

CANADA

BROOKS RANGE

CHUKCHI SEA
Cape Lisburne

Shishmaref
Wales
Cape Prince of Wales
Teller
Nome
Gambell
ST. LAWRENCE ISLAND
Northeast Cape

Kotzebue
Kotzebue Sound
Selawik
Selawik Lake
Noorvik
Shungnak
Kobuk
Kiana
Deering
Buckland

Koyuk
Moses Point
Elim
Golovin
White Mountain
Koyukuk
Nulato
Galena
Ruby
Tanana
Rampart
Livengood

Huslia
Hughes
Allakaket
Bettles Field

UNITED STATES

Manley Hot Springs
College   Fairbanks
Nenana
Eagle
OGILVIE MOUNTAINS
Dawson
Klondike
Elsa
Mayo
Keno Hill

Norton Sound
Unalakleet
Shaktoolik
St. Michael
Kaltag

KAIYUH MTS.
Von Frank Mountain 1374
Lake Minchumina
ALASKA
Big Delta
Delta Junction
Mount Hayes 4216
Tanacross
Tok
Mount Kimball 3155
Northway
Mentasta Lake
Snag

Mount Harper 1994
Chicken
Klondike
DAWSON RANGE
Pelly Crossing
Minto
Faro
Ross River
SELWYN MOUNTAINS

MACKENZIE MOUNTAINS
Mount Eduni 2357

Mount Patterson 2057
Mount Armstrong 2159
Yeda Peak 2972
Mount James 2103
LOGAN MTS.
Tungsten
Macmillan

SEWARD PENINSULA
Cape Rodney

Seward Peninsula

Emmonak
Sheldon Point
Alakanuk
Mountain Village
St. Marys
Scammon Bay
Hooper Bay
Anvik
Shageluk
Flat
Holy Cross
McGrath
Ophir
Farewell

Cape Romanzof

KUSKOKWIM MTS.

Mount Foraker 5304
Mount McKinley 6194
Denali National Park
Cantwell
Denali
Talkeetna
Paxson
TALKEETNA MOUNTAINS
Gulkana
Gakona
Glennallen
Copper Center

WRANGELL MOUNTAINS
Mount Sanford 4949
Mount Drum 3661
Mount Blackburn 4996
McCarthy
Mount Bona 5044
Mount Churchill
Mount Kennedy

ST. ELIAS MOUNTAINS
Mount Logan 5959
Mount St. Elias 4256
Mount Lucania 5226
Mount Vancouver

Kantishna

Nunivak Island
Mekoryuk
Dall Lake
Kuskokwim Bay
Kipnuk
Kwigillingok
Tununak
Bethel
Kwethluk
Peek
Tuluksak
Aniak
Red Devil
Crooked Creek
Stony River

KILBUCK MTS.
Kalskag
Marshall
Russian Mission

Mount Gerdine 3431
Mount Torbert 3479
Redoubt Volcano 3108
Kenai

ALASKA RANGE

Skwentna
Willow
Sutton
Palmer
Anchorage
CHUGACH MOUNTAINS
Mount Marcus Baker 4016
Valdez
Cordova
Cordova Peak

Prince William Sound

Whittier
Hinchinbrook Island

Goodnews Bay
Quinhagak
Togiak
Aleknagik
Dillingham
New Stuyahok
Igiugig
Koliganek
Nondalton
Iliamna
Lake Iliamna

Nonvianuk
Naknek
Kvichak Bay
Egegik
BRISTOL BAY
Ugashik
Pilot Point
Port Heiden

BERING SEA

St. Paul
Pribilof Islands
St. George Island

St. Matthew Island

Cape Mohican

Cape Newenham
Hagemeister Island
Cape Constantine

Homer
Soldotna
Seldovia
KENAI PENINSULA
Port Graham
Moose Pass
Seward

Barren Islands
Shuyak Island
Afognak Island
Kodiak
KODIAK ISLAND
Karluk
Old Harbor
Sitkalidak Island

Mount Katmai 2047
Mount Denison 2304
Becharof Lake

ALASKA PENINSULA

Mount Veniaminof 2507
Chignik
Perryville
Cape Alitak
Trinity Islands
Sutwik Island

Chirikof Island

Pavlof Volcano 2714
Port Moller
Cold Bay
False Pass
Sand Point
Unga Island
Popof Island
Nagai Island
Shumagin Islands
Sanak Islands
Tigalda Island

Shishaldin Volcano 2857
Akun Island
Akutan Island
FOX ISLANDS
Umnak Island
Makushin Volcano 2036
Unalaska Island
Mount Vsevidof 2109
Nikolski

Gulf of Alaska

Montague Island
Cape St. Elias
Kayak Island
Middleton Island

Yakataga
Yakutat
Yakutat Bay
Dry Bay
Ocean Cape

BRITISH COLUMBIA

Fairweather Mountain 4663
Gustavus
Glacier Bay
Cross Sound
CHICHAGOF ISLAND
Pelican
Hoonah
Juneau
Douglas

Cape Yakataga

Haines
Skagway
Tulsequah
COAST MOUNTAINS
Atlin
Carcross
Teslin
Whitehorse
Johnsons Crossing
CASSIAR MOUNTAINS
Cedar River

STIKINE RANGES

BARANOF ISLAND
Sitka
ADMIRALTY ISLAND
Kake
Kupreanof Island
Petersburg
Kuiu Island
ALEXANDER ARCHIPELAGO
Wrangell
Etolin Island
Port Protection
PRINCE OF WALES ISLAND
Craig
Hydaburg
Dall Island
Klawock
Ketchikan
Metlakatla
Revillagigedo Island

SKEENA MOUNTAINS
Telegraph Creek

Dixon Entrance
Prince Rupert
Port Simpson
Cape Knox
Masset
QUEEN CHARLOTTE ISLANDS
Graham Island
Skidegate
Sandspit
Moresby Island

Bering Strait

SKEENA MOUNTAINS

RAT ISLANDS

Inset (a):

BERING SEA

ALEUTIAN   ISLANDS

Cape Wrangell
Attu
Attu Island
NEAR ISLANDS
Semichi Islands
Agattu Island
Buldir Island
Kiska Volcano 1220
Kiska Island
Little Sitkin Island
Garloi Island
Amchitka Island
Delarof Islands
Tanaga Island
Kanaga Island
Adak Island
Kagalaska Island
Great Sitkin Island
ANDREANOF ISLANDS
Atka
Atka Island
Amlia Island
Seguam Island

International Date Line

ISLANDS OF FOUR MOUNTAINS
Korovin Volcano 1478
Yunaska Island
Chuginadak Island

FOX ISLANDS
Umnak Island
Mount Vsevidof 2109
Nikolski
Unalaska
Makushin Volcano 2036
Akutan Island
Akun Island
Unimak Pass
Tigalda Island

PACIFIC OCEAN

Same scale as main map

M-DRM4700-A1-_-2-2-2
Copyright © Rand McNally & Co.

International Date Line
East of Greenwich   180°   West of Greenwich

0   100   200   300   400   600   800   1000 Kilometers
0   100   200   300   400   600 Miles
Scale 1 : 10,000,000
Lambert Conformal Conic Projection

ARCTIC OCEAN

SVALBARD

SPITSBERGEN

GREENLAND SEA

Peary Land

Kong Frederik VIII Land

ELLESMERE ISLAND

Knud Rasmussen Land

NORDGRØNLAND
(AVANERSUAQ)

Kong Christian X Land

Thule (Qaanaaq)

Lauge Koch Kyst

DEVON ISLAND

BAFFIN BAY

GREENLAND
(Den.)

Upernavik

ØSTGRØNLAND
(TUNU)

Gunnbjørn Field 3700

DISKO

Godhavn (Qeqertarsuaq)

Jakobshavn (Ilulissat)

Kong Christian IX Land

Mont Forel 3360

BAFFIN ISLAND

CANADA

Davis Strait

Denmark Strait

ICELAND

Reykjavik

VESTGRØNLAND
(KITAA)

Godthåb (Nuuk)

J.A.D. Jensens
Nunatakker 1680

Frederikshåb (Paamiut)

Kong Frederik VI Kyst

ATLANTIC OCEAN

NEWFOUNDLAND AND LABRADOR

QUÉBEC

LABRADOR SEA

Kap Farvel

Meters / Feet
3000 / 9840
2000 / 6560
1000 / 3280
500 / 1640
200 / 656
Sea Level

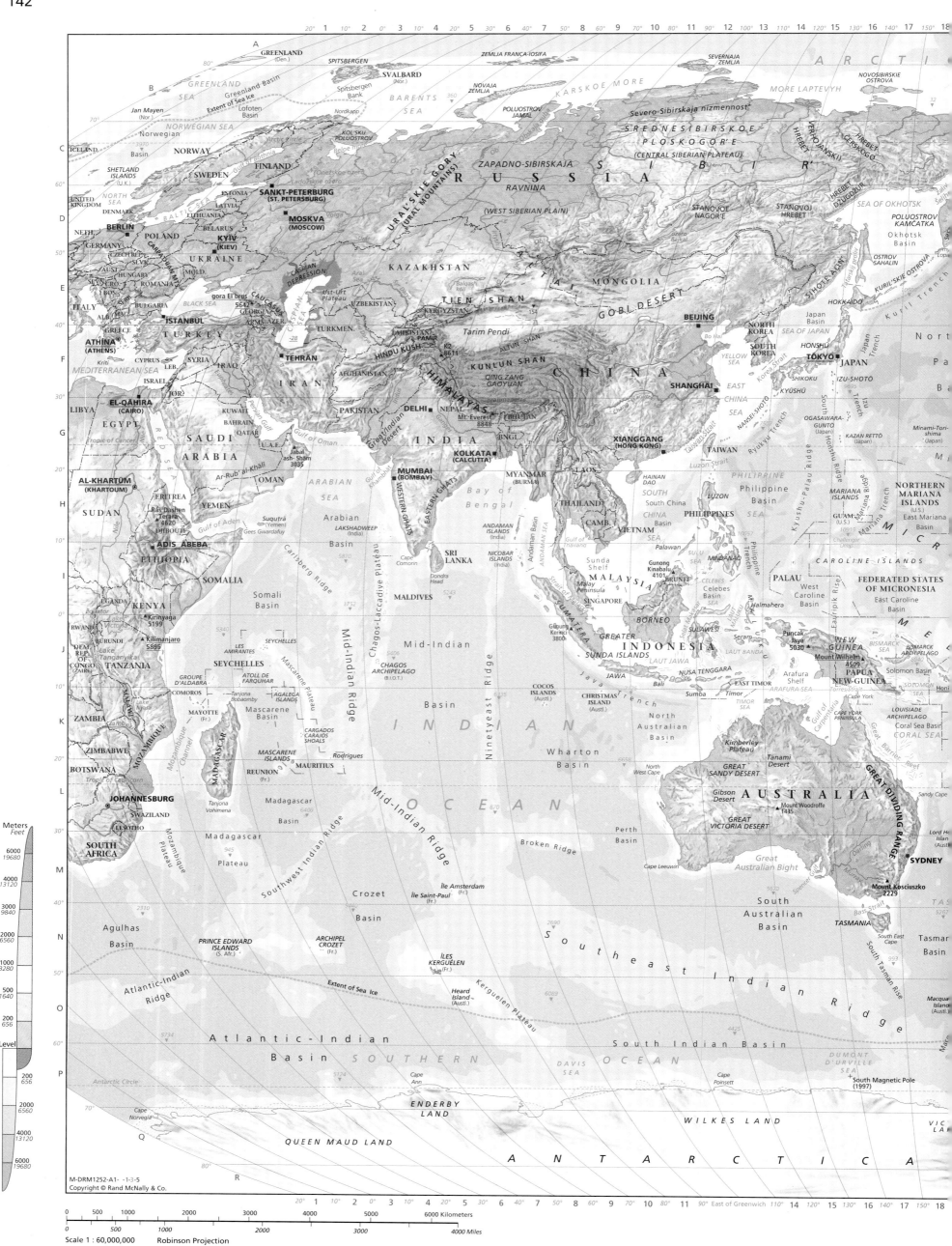

Meters
Feet

6000
19680

4000
13120

3000
9840

2000
6560

1000
3280

500
1640

200
656

Sea Level

200
656

2000
6560

4000
13120

6000
19680

0   500   1000   2000   3000   4000   5000   6000 Kilometers

0   500   1000   2000   3000   4000 Miles

Scale 1 : 60,000,000   Robinson Projection

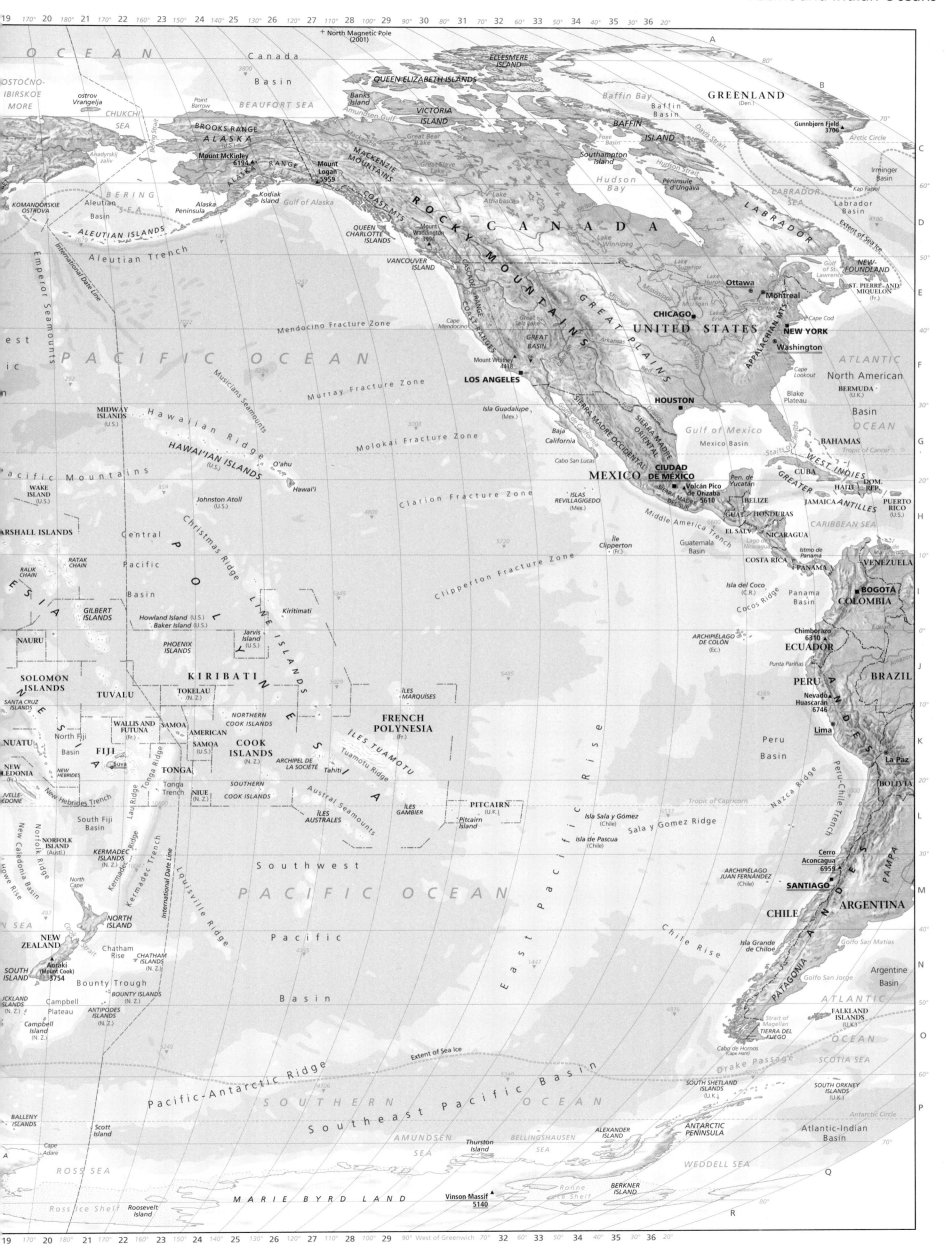

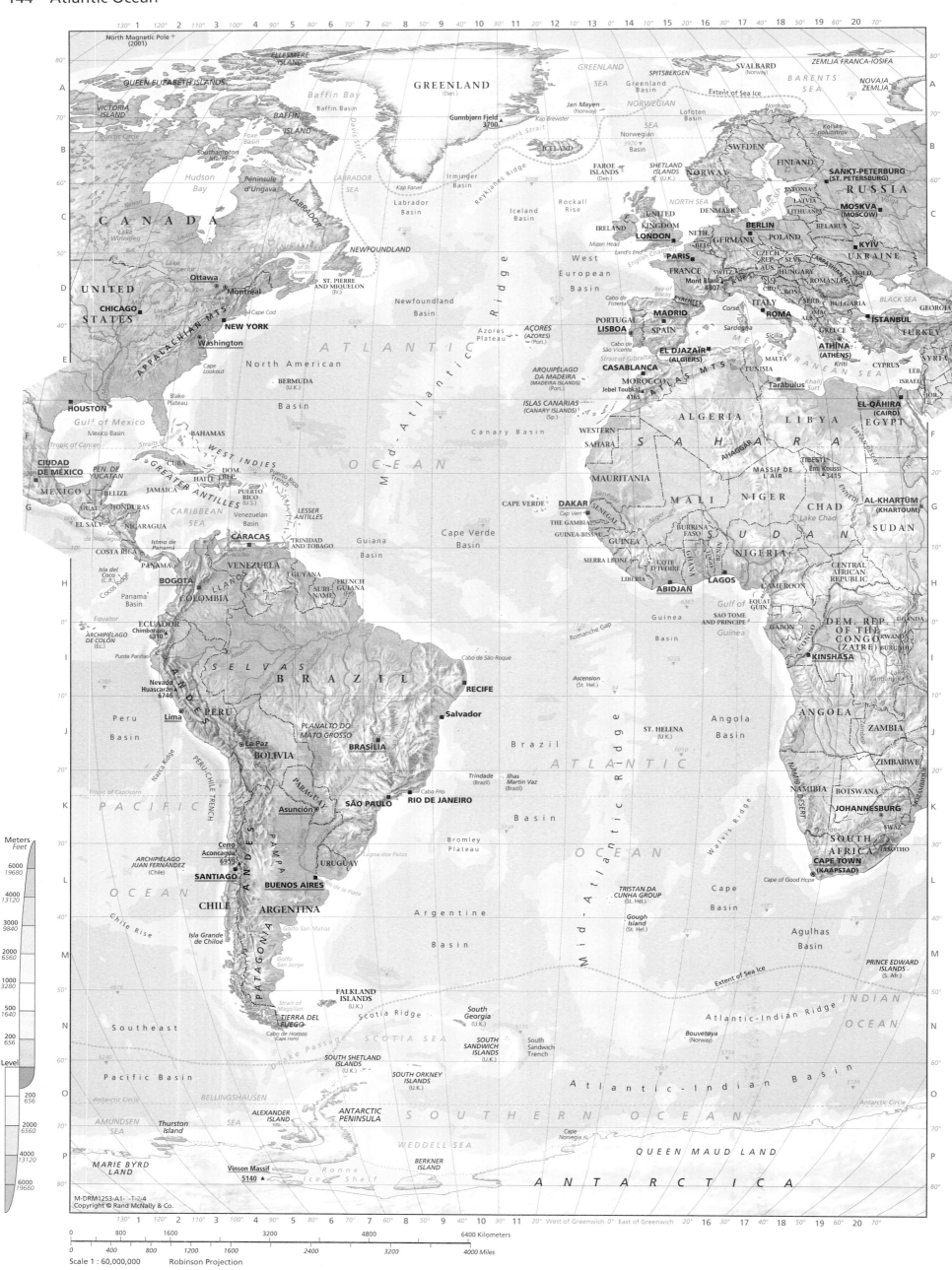

Meters
Feet

6000
19680

4000
13120

3000
9840

2000
6560

1000
3280

500
1640

200
656

Sea Level

200
656

2000
6560

4000
13120

6000
19680

0   800   1600   3200   4800   6400 Kilometers

0   400   800   1200   1600   2400   3200   4000 Miles

Scale 1 : 60,000,000   Robinson Projection

Index to World Reference Maps

Introduction to the Index

This index includes in a single alphabetical list approximately 54,000 names of places and geographical features that appear on the reference maps. Each name is followed by the name of the country or continent in which it is located, an alpha-numeric map reference key and a page reference.

Names The names of cities and towns appear in the index in regular type. The names of all other features appear in *italics*, followed by descriptive terms (hill, mtn., state) to indicate their nature.

Abbreviations of names on the maps have been standardized as much as possible. Names that are abbreviated on the maps are generally spelled out in full in the index.

Country names and names of features that extend beyond the boundaries of one country are followed by the name of the continent in which each is located. Country designations follow the names of all other places in the index. The locations of places in the United States, Canada, and the United Kingdom are further defined by abbreviations that indicate the state, province, or other political division in which each is located.

All abbreviations used in the index are defined in the List of Abbreviations to the right.

Alphabetization Names are alphabetized in the order of the letters of the English alphabet. Spanish *ll* and *ch*, for example, are not treated as distinct letters. Furthermore, diacritical marks are disregarded in alphabetization — German or Scandinavian *ä* or *ö* are treated as *a* or *o*.

The names of physical features may appear inverted, since they are always alphabetized under the proper, not the generic, part of the name, thus: "Gibraltar, Strait of". Otherwise every entry, whether consisting of one word or more, is alphabetized as a single continuous entity. "Lakeland", for example, appears after "La Crosse" and before "La Salle". Names beginning with articles (Le Havre, Den Helder, Al-Manāmah) are not inverted. Names beginning "St.", "Ste." and "Sainte" are alphabetized as though spelled "Saint".

In the case of identical names, towns are listed first, then political divisions, then physical features. Entries that are completely identical are listed alphabetically by country name.

Map Reference Keys and Page References The map reference keys and page references are found in the last two columns of each entry.

Each map reference key consists of a letter and number. The letters correspond to letters along the sides of the maps. Lowercase letters refer to inset maps. The numbers correspond to numbers that appear across the tops and bottoms of the maps.

Map reference keys for point features, such as cities and mountain peaks, indicate the locations of the symbols for these features. For other features, such as countries, mountain ranges, or rivers, the map reference keys indicate the locations of the names.

The page number generally refers to the main map for the country in which the feature is located. Page references for two-page maps always refer to the left-hand page.

List of Abbreviations

Ab., Can.	Alberta, Can.
Afg.	Afghanistan
Afr.	Africa
Ak., U.S.	Alaska, U.S.
Al., U.S.	Alabama, U.S.
Alb.	Albania
Alg.	Algeria
Am. Sam.	American Samoa
anch.	anchorage
And.	Andorra
Ang.	Angola
Ant.	Antarctica
Antig.	Antigua and Barbuda
aq.	aqueduct
Ar., U.S.	Arkansas, U.S.
Arg.	Argentina
Arm.	Armenia
at.	atoll
Aus.	Austria
Austl.	Australia
Az., U.S.	Arizona, U.S.
Azer.	Azerbaijan
b.	bay, gulf, inlet, lagoon
B.C., Can.	British Columbia, Can.
Bah.	Bahamas
Bahr.	Bahrain
Barb.	Barbados
bas.	basin
Bdi.	Burundi
Bel.	Belgium
Bela.	Belarus
Ber.	Bermuda
Bhu.	Bhutan
B.I.O.T.	British Indian Ocean Territory
Blg.	Bulgaria
Bngl.	Bangladesh
Bol.	Bolivia
Bos.	Bosnia and Hercegovina
Bots.	Botswana
Braz.	Brazil
Bru.	Brunei
Br. Vir. Is.	British Virgin Islands
Burkina	Burkina Faso
c.	cape, point
Ca., U.S.	California, U.S.
Cam.	Cameroon
Camb.	Cambodia
Can.	Canada
can.	canal
C.A.R.	Central African Republic
Cay. Is.	Cayman Islands
Christ. I.	Christmas Island
C. Iv.	Cote d'Ivoire
clf.	cliff, escarpment
Co., U.S.	Colorado, U.S.
co.	county, district, etc.
Cocos Is.	Cocos (Keeling) Islands
Col.	Colombia
Com.	Comoros
cont.	continent
Cook Is.	Cook Islands
C.R.	Costa Rica
crat.	crater
Cro.	Croatia
cst.	coast, beach
Ct., U.S.	Connecticut, U.S.
ctry.	independent country
C.V.	Cape Verde
cv.	cave
Cyp.	Cyprus
Czech Rep.	Czech Republic
D.C., U.S.	District of Columbia, U.S.
De., U.S.	Delaware, U.S.
Den.	Denmark
dep.	dependency, colony
depr.	depression
des.	desert
Dji.	Djibouti
Dom.	Dominica
Dom. Rep.	Dominican Republic
D.R.C.	Democratic Republic of the Congo
Ec.	Ecuador
El Sal.	El Salvador
Eng., U.K.	England, U.K.
Eq. Gui.	Equatorial Guinea
Erit.	Eritrea
Est.	Estonia
est.	estuary
Eth.	Ethiopia
E. Timor	East Timor
Eur.	Europe
Falk. Is.	Falkland Islands
Far. Is.	Faroe Islands
Fin.	Finland
Fl., U.S.	Florida, U.S.
for.	forest, moor
Fr.	France
Fr. Gu.	French Guiana
Fr. Poly.	French Polynesia
Ga., U.S.	Georgia, U.S.
Gam.	The Gambia
Gaza	Gaza Strip
Geor.	Georgia
Ger.	Germany
Gib.	Gibraltar
Golan	Golan Heights
Grc.	Greece
Gren.	Grenada
Grnld.	Greenland
Guad.	Guadeloupe
Guat.	Guatemala
Guern.	Guernsey
Gui.	Guinea
Gui.-B.	Guinea-Bissau
Guy.	Guyana
gysr.	geyser
Hi., U.S.	Hawaii, U.S.
hist.	historic site, ruins
hist. reg.	historic region
Hond.	Honduras
Hung.	Hungary
i.	island
Ia., U.S.	Iowa, U.S.
Ice.	Iceland
ice	ice feature, glacier
Id., U.S.	Idaho, U.S.
Il., U.S.	Illinois, U.S.
In., U.S.	Indiana, U.S.
Indon.	Indonesia
I. of Man	Isle of Man
Ire.	Ireland
is.	islands
Isr.	Israel
isth.	isthmus
Jam.	Jamaica
Jer.	Jericho Area
Jord.	Jordan
Kaz.	Kazakhstan
Kir.	Kiribati
Kor., N.	Korea, North
Kor., S.	Korea, South
Ks., U.S.	Kansas, U.S.
Kuw.	Kuwait
Ky., U.S.	Kentucky, U.S.
Kyrg.	Kyrgyzstan
l.	lake, pond
La., U.S.	Louisiana, U.S.
Lat.	Latvia
lav.	lava flow
Leb.	Lebanon
Leso.	Lesotho
Lib.	Liberia
Liech.	Liechtenstein
Lith.	Lithuania
Lux.	Luxembourg
Ma., U.S.	Massachusetts, U.S.
Mac.	Macedonia
Madag.	Madagascar
Malay.	Malaysia
Mald.	Maldives
Marsh. Is.	Marshall Islands
Mart.	Martinique
Maur.	Mauritania
May.	Mayotte
Mb., Can.	Manitoba, Can.
Md., U.S.	Maryland, U.S.
Me., U.S.	Maine, U.S.
Mex.	Mexico
Mi., U.S.	Michigan, U.S.
Micron.	Micronesia, Federated States of
Mid. Is.	Midway Islands
misc. cult.	miscellaneous cultural
Mn., U.S.	Minnesota, U.S.
Mo., U.S.	Missouri, U.S.
Mol.	Moldova
Mon.	Monaco
Mong.	Mongolia
Monts.	Montserrat
Mor.	Morocco
Moz.	Mozambique
Mrts.	Mauritius
Ms., U.S.	Mississippi, U.S.
Mt., U.S.	Montana, U.S.
mth.	river mouth or channel
mtn.	mountain
mts.	mountains
Mwi.	Malawi
Mya.	Myanmar
N.A.	North America
N.B., Can.	New Brunswick, Can.
N.C., U.S.	North Carolina, U.S.
N. Cal.	New Caledonia
N. Cyp.	North Cyprus
N.D., U.S.	North Dakota, U.S.
Ne., U.S.	Nebraska, U.S.
Neth.	Netherlands
Neth. Ant.	Netherlands Antilles
Nf., Can.	Newfoundland and Labrador, Can.
ngh.	neighborhood
N.H., U.S.	New Hampshire, U.S.
Nic.	Nicaragua
Nig.	Nigeria
N. Ire., U.K.	Northern Ireland, U.K.
N.J., U.S.	New Jersey, U.S.
N.M., U.S.	New Mexico, U.S.
N. Mar. Is.	Northern Mariana Islands
Nmb.	Namibia
Nor.	Norway
Norf. I.	Norfolk Island
N.S., Can.	Nova Scotia, Can.
N.T., Can.	Northwest Territories, Can.
Nu., Can.	Nunavut, Can.
Nv., U.S.	Nevada, U.S.
N.Y., U.S.	New York, U.S.
N.Z.	New Zealand
Oc.	Oceania
Oh., U.S.	Ohio, U.S.
Ok., U.S.	Oklahoma, U.S.
On., Can.	Ontario, Can.
Or., U.S.	Oregon, U.S.
p.	pass
Pa., U.S.	Pennsylvania, U.S.
Pak.	Pakistan
Pan.	Panama
Pap. N. Gui.	Papua New Guinea
Para.	Paraguay
P.E., Can.	Prince Edward Island, Can.
pen.	peninsula
Phil.	Philippines
Pit.	Pitcairn
pl.	plain, flat
plat.	plateau, highland
p.o.i.	point of interest
Pol.	Poland
Port.	Portugal
P.R.	Puerto Rico
Qc., Can.	Quebec, Can.
r.	rock, rocks
reg.	physical region
rel.	religious facility
res.	reservoir
Reu.	Reunion
rf.	reef, shoal
R.I., U.S.	Rhode Island, U.S.
Rom.	Romania
Rw.	Rwanda
s.	sea
S.A.	South America
S. Afr.	South Africa
sand	sand area
Sau. Ar.	Saudi Arabia
S.C., U.S.	South Carolina, U.S.
sci.	scientific station
Scot., U.K.	Scotland, U.K.
S.D., U.S.	South Dakota, U.S.
Sen.	Senegal
Serb.	Serbia and Montenegro
Sey.	Seychelles
S. Geor.	South Georgia
Sing.	Singapore
Sk., Can.	Saskatchewan, Can.
S.L.	Sierra Leone
Slov.	Slovakia
Slvn.	Slovenia
S. Mar.	San Marino
Sol. Is.	Solomon Islands
Som.	Somalia
Sp. N. Afr.	Spanish North Africa
Sri L.	Sri Lanka
state	state, province, etc.
St. Hel.	St. Helena
St. K./N.	St. Kitts and Nevis
St. Luc.	St. Lucia
stm.	stream (river, creek)
S. Tom./P.	Sao Tome and Principe
St. P./M.	St. Pierre and Miquelon
strt.	strait, channel, etc.
St. Vin.	St. Vincent and the Grenadines
Sur.	Suriname
sw.	swamp, marsh
Swaz.	Swaziland
Swe.	Sweden
Switz.	Switzerland
Tai.	Taiwan
Taj.	Tajikistan
Tan.	Tanzania
T./C. Is.	Turks and Caicos Islands
Thai.	Thailand
Tn., U.S.	Tennessee, U.S.
Tok.	Tokelau
Trin.	Trinidad and Tobago
Tun.	Tunisia
Tur.	Turkey
Turkmen.	Turkmenistan
Tx., U.S.	Texas, U.S.
U.A.E.	United Arab Emirates
Ug.	Uganda
U.K.	United Kingdom
Ukr.	Ukraine
unds.	undersea feature
Ur.	Uruguay
U.S.	United States
Ut., U.S.	Utah, U.S.
Uzb.	Uzbekistan
Va., U.S.	Virginia, U.S.
val.	valley, watercourse
Vat.	Vatican City
Ven.	Venezuela
Viet.	Vietnam
V.I.U.S.	Virgin Islands (U.S.)
vol.	volcano
Vt., U.S.	Vermont, U.S.
Wa., U.S.	Washington, U.S.
Wake I.	Wake Island
Wal./F.	Wallis and Futuna
W.B.	West Bank
well	well, spring, oasis
Wi., U.S.	Wisconsin, U.S.
W. Sah.	Western Sahara
wtfl.	waterfall, rapids
W.V., U.S.	West Virginia, U.S.
Wy., U.S.	Wyoming, U.S.
Yk., Can.	Yukon Territory, Can.
Zam.	Zambia
Zimb.	Zimbabwe

Index

A

Name	Map Ref.	Page

Å, Nor. — C5 8
Aabenraa, Den. — I3 8
Aachen, Ger. — F1 16
Aalborg, Den. — H4 8
Aalborg Bugt, b., Den. — H4 8
Aalen, Ger. — H6 16
Aali, Sadd el- (Aswan High Dam), dam, Egypt — C6 62
Aalst (Alost), Bel. — D13 14
Äänekoski, Fin. — E11 8
Aarau, Switz. — C4 22
Aare, stm., Switz. — C5 22
Aarlen see Arlon, Bel. — E14 14
Aarschot, Bel. — D14 14
Aasiaat see Egedesminde, Grnld. — D15 141
Aat see Ath, Bel. — D12 14
Aba, China — E5 36
Aba, D.R.C. — D6 66
Aba, Nig. — H6 64
Abā al-Bawl, Qurayn, hill, Qatar — E7 56
Abacaxis, stm., Braz. — E6 84
Abaco, i., Bah. — B9 96
Abacou, Pointe, c., Haiti — D10 102
Abadab, Jabal, mtn., Sudan — D7 62
Ābādān, Iran — C6 56
Ābādeh, Iran — C7 56
Abadla, Alg. — C4 64
Abaeté, Braz. — J3 88
Abaeté, stm., Braz. — A1 88
Abaetetuba, Braz. — A1 88
Abag Qi, China — C7 36
Abaí, Para. — C10 92
Abaj see Abay, Kaz. — E12 32
Abakaliki, Nig. — H6 64
Abakan, Russia — C17 32
Abakan, stm., Russia — D15 32
Abakanovo, Russia — A20 10
Abakanskij hrebet, mts., Russia — D15 32
Abala, Niger — G5 64
Abalak, Niger — F6 64
Aban, Russia — C17 32
Abancay, Peru — F3 84
Abashiri, Japan — B16 38
Abasolo, Mex. — C6 100
Abasolo, Mex. — I7 100
Abasolo, Mex. — G6 130
Abau, Pap. N. Gui. — c4 79a
Abay, Kaz. — E12 32
Abay see Blue Nile, stm., Afr. — E6 62
Abaya, Lake see Ābaya Hāyk', l., Eth. — F7 62
Ābaya Hāyk', l., Eth. — F7 62
Abaza, Russia — D15 32
Abbadia San Salvatore, Italy — H8 22
Abbé, Lac see Abe, Lake, l., Afr. — E8 62
Abbeville, Fr. — D10 14
Abbeville, Ga., U.S. — D2 116
Abbeville, La., U.S. — H6 122
Abbeville, S.C., U.S. — B3 116
Abbey, Sk., Can. — D5 124
Abbeyfeale, Ire. — I3 12
Abbiategrasso, Italy — E5 22
Abbot, Mount, mtn., Austl. — B6 76
Abbot Ice Shelf, ice, Ant. — C31 81
Abbotsford, B.C., Can. — G8 138
Abbottābād, Pak. — A4 54
'Abd al-Kūrī, i., Yemen — G7 56
Ābdīra, sci., Grc. — B7 28
Abdulino, Russia — D8 32
Abe, Lake, l., Afr. — E8 62
Abéché, Chad — E4 62
Abel Tasman National Park, p.o.i., N.Z. — E5 80
Abemama, at., Kir. — C8 72
Abengourou, C. Iv. — H4 64
Abenójar, Spain — F6 20
Abensberg, Ger. — H7 16
Abeokuta, Nig. — H5 64
Aberdare, Wales, U.K. — J9 12
Aberdeen, S. Afr. — H6 70
Aberdeen, Scot., U.K. — D10 12
Aberdeen, Id., U.S. — H14 136
Aberdeen, Md., U.S. — E9 114
Aberdeen, Ms., U.S. — D10 122
Aberdeen, N.C., U.S. — A6 116
Aberdeen, S.D., U.S. — B14 126
Aberdeen, Wa., U.S. — D3 136
Aberdeen, Wn., i., Nu., Can. — C10 106
Aberdeen Lake, res., Ms., U.S. — D10 122
Aberfeldy, Scot., U.K. — E9 12
Abergavenny, Wales, U.K. — J11 12
Abernant, Al., U.S. — D11 122
Abernathy, Tx., U.S. — H7 128
Abernethy, Sk., Can. — D10 124
Abert, Lake, l., Or., U.S. — H6 136
Aberystwyth, Wales, U.K. — I8 12
Abez', Russia — A10 32
Abhā, Sau. Ar. — F5 56
Abidjan, C. Iv. — H4 64
Abilene, Tx., U.S. — B8 130
Abingdon, Eng., U.K. — J11 12
Abingdon, Il., U.S. — D7 120
Abingdon, Va., U.S. — H4 114
Abiquiu, N.M., U.S. — E2 128
Abiquiu Reservoir, res., N.M., U.S. — E2 128
Abisko, Swe. — B8 8
Abitibi, stm., On., Can. — E14 106
Abitibi, Lake, l., Can. — F15 106
Abja-Paluoja, Est. — B8 10
Abo see Turku, Fin. — F9 8
Abohar, India — C5 54
Abomey, Benin — H5 64
Abong Mbang, Cam. — D2 66
Abony, Hung. — B6 26
Aborigen, pik, mtn., Russia — D18 34
Abou-Deïa, Chad — E3 62
Abou Simbel (Abu Simbel), sci., Egypt — C6 62
Abraham Lake, res., Ab., Can. — D14 138
Abra Pampa, Arg. — D3 90
Abre Campo, Braz. — K4 88
Abreu e Lima, Braz. — D8 88
Abring, India — B6 54
Abrud, Rom. — C10 26
Abruzzo, state, Italy — H10 22
Abruzzo, Parco Nazionale d', p.o.i., Italy — C7 24
Absaroka Range, mts., U.S. — E17 136
Absarokee, Mt., U.S. — E17 136
Absecon, N.J., U.S. — E11 114
Abū 'Alī, i., Sau. Ar. — D6 56
Abū Ballāş, mtn., Egypt — C5 62
Abu Dhabi see Abū Zaby, U.A.E. — E7 56
Abū Dulayq, Sudan — D6 62
Abū al-Hul (Sphinx), hist., Egypt — I1 58
Abufari, Braz. — E5 84
Abū Hamad, Sudan — D6 62
Abū Jabrah, Sudan — E5 62
Abuja, Nig. — H6 64
Abū Jubayhah, Sudan — E6 62

Abū Kamāl, Syria — C5 56
Abukuma, stm., Japan — B13 40
Abukuma-kōchi, plat., Japan — B13 40
Abū Madd, Ra's, c., Sau. Ar. — E4 56
Abu Mendi, Eth. — E7 62
Abunã, Braz. — E4 84
Abū Qīr, Khalīj, b., Egypt — G1 58
Abū Qurqāş, Egypt — K1 58
Abū Road, India — F4 54
Abū Rubayq, Sau. Ar. — E4 56
Abū Shajarah Ra's, c., Sudan — C7 62
Abu Simbel see Abou Simbel, sci., Egypt — C6 62
Abu Tig, Egypt — K2 58
Abū Zabad, Sudan — E5 62
Abū Zaby (Abu Dhabi), U.A.E. — E7 56
Abwong, Sudan — F6 62
Abyei, Sudan — F5 62
Abyssinia see Ethiopia, ctry., Afr. — F7 62
Acacias, Col. — E5 86
Acadia National Park, p.o.i., Me., U.S. — F8 110
Açailândia, Braz. — C2 88
Acajutiba, Braz. — F7 88
Acámbaro, Mex. — E8 100
Acandí, Col. — C3 86
Acaponeta, Mex. — D6 100
Acaponeta, stm., Mex. — D6 100
Acapulco de Juárez, Mex. — G8 100
Acará, Braz. — A1 88
Acará, stm., Braz. — A1 88
Acarai Mountains, mts., S.A. — C6 84
Acará-Mirim, stm., Braz. — B1 88
Acaraú, Braz. — B5 88
Acaray, stm., Para. — B10 92
Acari, Peru — G3 84
Acari, Braz. — H3 88
Acarigua, Ven. — C7 86
Acatlán de Osorio, Mex. — F9 100
Acay, Nevado de, mtn., Arg. — B4 92
Acayucan, Mex. — F11 100
Acceglio, Italy — F3 22
Accomac, Va., U.S. — G10 114
Accra, Ghana — H5 64
Acebuches, Mex. — A7 100
Aceguá, Braz. — E10 92
Aceh, state, Indon. — J3 48
Acerra, Italy — D8 24
Achacachi, Bol. — C3 90
Achaguas, Ven. — D7 86
Achalpur, India — H6 54
Achao, Chile — H2 92
Acharnés, Grc. — E6 28
Achelóos, stm., Grc. — E4 28
Acheng, China — B7 38
Achern, Ger. — H4 16
Achill Head, c., Ire. — G2 12
Achill Island, i., Ire. — H2 12
Achiras, Arg. — F5 92
Achit nuur, l., Mong. — E16 32
Achwa, stm., Afr. — D6 66
Acı Göl, l., Tur. — F12 28
Ačinsk, Russia — C16 32
Acıpayam, Tur. — F12 28
Acireale, Italy — G9 24
Ackerly, Tx., U.S. — B6 130
Ackley, Ia., U.S. — B5 120
Acklins, i., Bah. — C10 96
Acklins, Bight of, b., Bah. — A10 102
Acme, Ab., Can. — E17 138
Aconcagua, Cerro, mtn., Arg. — F3 92
Aconchi, Mex. — G7 98
Acopiara, Braz. — D6 88
Açores (Azores), is., Port. — C3 60
Acoyapa, Nic. — G6 84
A Coruña (Corunna), Spain — A2 20
A Coruña, co., Spain — A2 20
Acquasanta Terme, Italy — H10 22
Acqui Terme, Italy — F5 22
Acre see 'Akko, Isr. — F6 58
Acre, state, Braz. — E4 84
Acre, stm., S.A. — E4 84
Acri, Italy — E10 24
Acton Vale, Qc., Can. — E4 110
Actopan, Mex. — E9 100
Açucena, Braz. — J4 88
Acuña, Arg. — D8 92
Ada, Mn., U.S. — D2 118
Ada, Oh., U.S. — D2 114
Ada, Ok., U.S. — C2 122
Adaba, Eth. — F7 62
Adair, Bahía de, b., Mex. — A1 98
Adair, Cape, c., Nu., Can. — A16 106
Adairsville, Ga., U.S. — C14 122
Adairville, Ky., U.S. — H11 120
Adaja, stm., Spain — C6 20
Adak Island, i., Ak., U.S. — g23 140a
Adam, Oman — E8 56
Adamantina, Braz. — D6 90
Adamaoua, Afr. — C2 66
Adamclisi, Rom. — E14 26
Adamello, mts., Italy — D7 22
Adaminaby, Austl. — K7 76
Adams, Mn., U.S. — H6 118
Adams, N.D., U.S. — F15 124
Adams, Ne., U.S. — K2 118
Adams, N.Y., U.S. — E13 112
Adams, stm., B.C., Can. — E11 138
Adams, Mount, vol., Wa., U.S. — D5 136
Adam's Bridge, rf., Asia — G4 53
Adams Lake, l., B.C., Can. — E11 138
Adams Peak, mtn., Sri L. — H5 53
Adams Rock, r., Pit. — c28 78k
Adamstown, Pit. — c28 78k
Adamsville, Tn., U.S. — B10 122
Adana, Tur. — A6 58
Adana, state, Tur. — A6 58
Adanero, Spain — C6 20
Adarama, Sudan — D6 62
Adare, Cape, c., Ant. — C22 81
Adavale, Austl. — E5 76
Adda, stm., Italy — E6 22
Ad-Dabbah, Sudan — D6 62
Ad-Dahnā', des., Sau. Ar. — D6 56
Ad-Dammām, Sau. Ar. — D7 56
Ad-Dammān, Sau. Ar. — D7 56
Ad-Dānā, Syria — B7 58
Ad-Dawḥah (Doha), Qatar — D7 56
Ad-Dibdibah, reg., Sau. Ar. — D6 56
Addis, La., U.S. — G7 122
Addis Ababa see Ādīs Ābeba, Eth. — F7 62
Ādīs Ābeba, Eth. — F7 62
Addison, Mi., U.S. — C7 66
Addison, N.Y., U.S. — F5 112
Ad-Dīwānīyah, Iraq — C5 56
Addo Elephant National Park, p.o.i., S. Afr. — H7 70
Addu Atoll, at., Mald. — j12 46a
Ad-Duwayd, Sau. Ar. — C5 62
Ad-Duwaym, Sudan — E6 62
Adel, Ga., U.S. — E2 116
Adel, Ia., U.S. — C3 120
Adelaide, Austl. — J2 76
Adelaide, Bah. — n18 104f
Adelaide Island, i., Ant. — B33 81
Adelaide Peninsula, pen., Nu., Can. — B11 106
Adelaide River, Austl. — B6 74
Adèle, Island i., Austl. — C4 74
Adélie, Côte, cst., Ant. — B18 81

Adelie Coast see Adélie, Terre, cst., Ant. — B18 81
Adelong, Austl. — J6 76
Aden see 'Adan, Yemen — G6 56
Adendorp, S. Afr. — H7 70
Adi, Pulau, i., Indon. — F9 44
Adiaké, C. Iv. — H4 64
Adige (Etsch), stm., Italy — E8 22
Adīgrat, Eth. — E7 62
Adıgüzel Baraji, res., Tur. — E12 28
Adilābād, India — B4 53
Adiri, Russia — G16 34
Adin, Ca., U.S. — B5 134
Adirondack Mountains, mts., N.Y., U.S. — E15 112
Ādīs Ābeba (Addis Abeba), Eth. — F7 62
Adi Ugri, Erit. — E7 62
Adıyaman, Tur. — A9 58
Adıyaman, state, Tur. — A9 58
Adjuntas, Presa de las see Vicente Guerrero, Presa, res., Mex. — D9 100
Admiral, Sk., Can. — E5 124
Admiralty Gulf, b., Austl. — B5 74
Admiralty Inlet, b., Nu., Can. — A13 106
Admiralty Island, i., Nu., Can. — B10 106
Admiralty Island, i., Ak., U.S. — E13 140
Admiralty Islands, is., Pap. N. Gui. — a4 79a
Admiralty Mountains, mts., Ant. — C21 81
Ado, Nig. — H5 64
Ado-Ekiti, Nig. — H6 64
Adolfo Gonzales Chaves, Arg. — H7 92
Adolfo López Mateos, Mex. — A5 100
Adolfo López Mateos, Presa, res., Mex. — C5 100
Adolfo Rodriguez Sáa see Santa Rosa del Conlara, Arg. — F5 92
Adoni, India — D3 53
Adour, stm., Fr. — F4 18
Adra, India — G11 54
Adra, Spain — H7 20
Adrano, Italy — G8 24
Adrar, Alg. — D4 64
Adrar, reg., Maur. — E2 64
Adrar, Tassili n-, plat., Alg. — D6 64
Adré, Chad — E4 62
Adria, Italy — E9 22
Adrian, Mi., U.S. — C1 114
Adrian, Mo., U.S. — F3 120
Adrian, Or., U.S. — G10 136
Adrian, Tx., U.S. — F6 128
Adrian, W.V., U.S. — F5 114
Adriatic Sea, s., Eur. — G11 22
A Dun, Viet. — F9 48
Adutiškis, Lith. — E9 10
Advance, Mo., U.S. — G7 120
Advocate Harbour, N.S., Can. — E11 110
Ādwa, Eth. — E7 62
Adyča, stm., Russia — C16 34
Adygea, state see Adygeja, state, Russia — F6 32
Adygejsk, Russia — F5 32
Adygeja, state, Russia — F6 32
Adygheya see Adygeja, state, Russia — F6 32
Adzópé, C. Iv. — H4 64
Aegean Sea, s., Eur. — E7 28
Aegina see Aígina, i., Grc. — F6 28
Aegviidu, Est. — A8 10
Aen, ostrov, i., Russia — B22 34
Aerku Hu, l., China — C9 54
Ærø, i., Den. — I4 8
Ærøskøbing, Den. — I4 8
A Estrada, Spain — B2 20
Aetna, Ab., Can. — G17 138
Afaahiti, Fr. Poly. — v22 78h
Afadjoto, mtn., Ghana — H5 64
Afareaitu, Fr. Poly. — v20 78h
Afars and Issas see Djibouti, ctry., Afr. — E8 62
Afghanistan, ctry., Asia — C9 56
Afgooye, Som. — D8 66
Afikpo, Nig. — H6 64
Aflou, Alg. — C5 64
Afmadow, Som. — D8 66
Afogados da Ingazeira, Braz. — D7 88
Afognak Island, i., Ak., U.S. — E9 140
Afoniha, Russia — B25 8
A Fonsagrada, Spain — A3 20
Africa, cont. — F14 4
'Afrīn, Syria — B7 58
Afton, N.Y., U.S. — B10 114
Afton, Ok., U.S. — H2 120
Afton, Wy., U.S. — H16 136
Afula, Isr. — F6 58
Afyon, Tur. — E13 28
Afyon, state, Tur. — E13 28
Agadez, Niger — F6 64
Agadir, Mor. — C2 64
Agadyr', Kaz. — E12 32
Agalak, Sudan — E6 62
Agalega Islands, is., Mrts. — K8 142
Agan, stm., Russia — B13 32
Agana see Hagåtña, Guam — j10 78c
Agana Heights, Guam — j10 78c
Agano, stm., Japan — B12 40
Agapa, Russia — B6 34
Aga Point, c., Guam — k10 78c
Agar, India — G5 54
Agartala, India — G13 54
Agassiz, B.C., Can. — G9 138
Agassiz Pool, res., Mn., U.S. — D2 118
Agate, Co., U.S. — B5 128
Agate Fossil Beds National Monument, p.o.i., Ne., U.S. — E9 126
Agattu Island, i., Ak., U.S. — g21 140a
Agawa Bay, b., On., Can. — A5 112
Agawam, Mt., U.S. — B14 136
Agboville, C. Iv. — H4 64
Ağdam, Azer. — B6 56
Agdz, Mor. — C3 64
Ageevo, Russia — F19 10
Agen, Fr. — E6 18
Agency, Ia., U.S. — C5 120
Agency Lake, l., Or., U.S. — H5 136
Agha Jārī, Iran — C6 56
Āghā Jārī see Agha Jārī, Iran — C6 56
Agía Marina, Grc. — F9 28
Agiásos, Grc. — D9 28
Aginskoe, Russia — F11 34
Ágio Óros, state, Grc. — C7 28
Ágio Óros, pen., Grc. — C7 28
Agios Nikólaos, Grc. — H8 28
Agíou Órous, Kólpos (Singitic Gulf), b., Grc. — C6 28
Aglasun, Tur. — F13 28
Agnew, Austl. — E4 74
Agnibilékrou, C. Iv. — H4 64
Agno, Phil. — C3 52
Agno, stm., Phil. — C3 52
Agnone, Italy — C8 24
Agogna, stm., Italy — E5 22
Agou, Mont, mtn., Togo — H5 64
Agra, India — E6 54
Agradada, Ur. — F8 92
Agreda, Spain — C8 20
Agri, Italy — D10 24
Agri, stm., Italy — D9 24
Ağrı, i., N. Mar. Is. — B5 72
Ağrı Dağı (Ararat, Mount), mtn., Tur. — B5 56
Agrigento, Italy — G7 24
Agrihan, i., N. Mar. Is. — B5 72
Aïssa, Djebel, mtn., Alg. — C4 64
Agrínio, Grc. — E4 28

Agrio, stm., Arg. — H2 92
Agrópoli, Italy — D9 24
Agro Pontino, reg., Italy — C6 24
Agto, Grnld. — D15 141
Agua Branca, Braz. — C4 88
Agua Caliente, Mex. — B4 100
Agua Caliente Grande, Mex. — B4 100
Aguachica, Col. — C5 86
Água Clara, Braz. — D6 90
Aguada Cecilio, Arg. — H3 90
Aguada de Guerra, Arg. — H3 90
Aguada de Pasajeros, Cuba — A7 102
Aguadas, Col. — E4 86
Aguadilla, P.R. — B1 104a
Água Doce, Braz. — C12 92
Aguadulce, Pan. — H7 102
Agua Dulce, Tx., U.S. — G9 130
Agua Fria, stm., Az., U.S. — I4 132
Agua Fria National Monument, p.o.i., Az., U.S. — I5 132
Aguaí, Braz. — L2 88
Agualeguas, Mex. — H8 130
Aguán, stm., Hond. — E4 102
Aguanaval, stm., Mex. — C7 100
Aguapey, stm., Arg. — D9 92
Agua Preta, Igarapé, stm., Braz. — H9 86
Agua Prieta, Mex. — F8 98
Aguaray Guazú, stm., Para. — A9 92
Aguaro-Guariquito, Parque Nacional, p.o.i., Ven. — C8 86
Aguasabon, stm., On., Can. — C11 118
Águas Belas, Braz. — E7 88
Aguas Buenas, P.R. — B3 104a
Aguascalientes, Mex. — E7 100
Aguascalientes, state, Mex. — D7 100
Água Vermelha, Represa de, res., Braz. — C6 90
Aguayo, Arg. — E4 92
Agu Bay, b., Nu., Can. — A13 106
Agudos, Braz. — L1 88
Águeda, stm., Eur. — D4 20
Aguelhok, Mali — F5 64
Aguilar, Co., U.S. — D4 128
Aguilar de la Frontera, Spain — G6 20
Aguilares, Arg. — C5 92
Águilas, Spain — G9 20
Aguililla, Mex. — F7 100
Aguijereada, Punta, c., P.R. — A1 104a
Agujita, Mex. — H6 130
Agulhas, Kaap, c., S. Afr. — I5 70
Agulhas Basin, unds. — M15 144
Agulhas Negras, Pico das, mtn., Braz. — L3 88
Agung, Gunung, vol., Indon. — G6 44
Agusan, stm., Phil. — F5 52
Agustín Codazzi, Col. — C5 86
Āgwa, Tur. — B12 28
Ahaggar, mts., Alg. — E6 64
Ahaggar, Tassili ta-n-, plat., Alg. — E5 64
Ahalcihe, Geor. — F6 32
Aḥar, Iran — B6 56
Ahaus, Ger. — D3 16
Ahipara Bay, b., N.Z. — B5 80
Ahlen, Ger. — E3 16
Ahmadābād, India — G4 54
Ahmadnagar, India — B2 53
Ahmadpur Siāl, Pak. — C3 54
Ahmar Mountains, mts., Eth. — F8 62
Ahmeti, Tur. — E10 28
Ahmic Lake, l., On., Can. — C10 112
Ahoskie, N.C., U.S. — H9 114
Ahousat, B.C., Can. — G4 138
Ahraura, India — F9 54
Ahtuba, stm., Russia — E7 32
Ahtubinsk, Russia — E7 32
Ahuacatlán, Mex. — E6 100
Ahumada, Mex. — D1 130
Ahunui, at., Fr. Poly. — E12 72
Aḥvāz, Iran — C6 56
Ahvenanmaa see Åland, state, Fin. — F9 8
Ahvenanmaa see Åland, is., Fin. — F8 8
Ahwar, Yemen — G6 56
Ahwa-ri, Kor., S. — D2 40
Åi Åfjord, Nor. — D4 8
Aibonito, P.R. — B3 104a
Aichi, state, Japan — D10 40
Aidong, China — I2 42
Āiea, Hi., U.S. — B3 78a
Aigialoúsa, N. Cyp. — C5 58
Aigina, Grc. — F6 28
Aígina, i., Grc. — F6 28
Aígio, Grc. — E5 28
Aigle, Switz. — D3 22
Aigle, stm., Qc., Can. — A11 110
Aiguá, Ur. — G10 92
Aigüestortes i Estany Sant Maurici, Parque Nacional d', p.o.i., Spain — B11 20
Aigüestortes i Llac de Sant Maurici, Parc Nacional d' see Aigüestortes i Esta, p.o.i., Spain — B11 20
Aiken, S.C., U.S. — C4 116
Aikens Lake, l., Mb., Can. — C18 124
Ailao Shan, mts., China — G5 36
Aileron, Austl. — D6 74
Aililngaplap, at., Marsh. Is. — C7 72
Ailsa Craig, On., Can. — E8 112
Ailsa Craig, i., Scot., U.K. — F7 12
Ain, state, Fr. — D11 18
Ain, stm., Fr. — D11 18
Aïn Benian, Alg. — H13 20
Aïn Bessem, Alg. — H14 20
Aïn Defla, Alg. — H12 20
Aïn el Beïda, Alg. — B6 64
Ainslie Lake, l., N.S., Can. — D15 110
Aïn Taya, Alg. — H13 20
Aïr, Massif de l', mts., Niger — F6 64
Air Airport, Palau — g8 78b
Airbangis, Indon. — C1 50
Airdrie, Ab., Can. — E16 138
Aire, stm., Eng., U.K. — H11 12
Aire-sur-l'Adour, Fr. — F5 18
Air Force Island, i., Nu., Can. — B16 106
Airhaji, Indon. — D2 50
Airolo, Switz. — D5 22
Airuoca, Braz. — L3 88
Aishihik Lake, l., Yk., Can. — C3 106
Āīslingen, India —
Aisne, state, Fr. — E12 14
Aisne, stm., Fr. — E12 14
Aitape, Pap. N. Gui. — a3 79a

Alakol, ozero see Alaköl köli, l., Kaz. — E14 32
Alaköl köli, l., Kaz. — E14 32
Al-'Akrishah, Egypt — G1 58
Alaktara, India — H9 54
Alakurtti, Russia — C13 8
'Alalakeiki Channel, strt., Hi., U.S. — c5 78a
Alalaú, stm., Braz. — H11 86
Alamagan, i., N. Mar. Is. — B5 72
Al-'Amārah, Iraq — C6 56
Alameda, Ca., U.S. — F3 134
Alameda, N.M., U.S. — H10 132
Alamo, Ga., U.S. — D3 116
Alamo, Tn., U.S. — B9 122
Alamo, Ca., U.S. — K1 132
Alamogordo, N.M., U.S. — H3 128
Alamo Heights, Tx., U.S. — E9 130
Alamo Lake, res., Az., U.S. — I3 132
Álamos, Mex. — A8 100
Álamos, Mex. — B4 100
Alamosa, Co., U.S. — D3 128
Álamos de Márquez, Mex. — A7 100
Alamos de India — C3 53
Åland, state, Fin. — F9 8
Åland (Ahvenanmaa), is., Fin. — F8 8
Åland Islands see Åland, is., Fin. — F8 8
Åland Sea, s., Eur. — G8 8
Alandur, India — E5 53
Alanya, Tur. — G15 28
Alaotra, Farihy, l., Madag. — D8 68
Alapaevsk, Russia — C10 32
Alapaha, Ga., U.S. — E2 116
Alapaha, stm., U.S. — F2 116
Alaplı, Tur. — B14 28
Alappuzha see Alleppey, India — G3 53
Al-'Aqabah, Jord. — I6 58
Alarcón, Spain — E8 20
Alarcón, Embalse de, res., Spain — E9 20
Alas, Selat, strt., Indon. — H10 50
Alaşehir, Tur. — E11 28
Alashanyouqi, China — C5 36
Alaska, state, U.S. — D9 140
Alaska, Gulf of, b., Ak., U.S. — E10 140
Alaska Peninsula, pen., Ak., U.S. — E7 140
Alaska Range, mts., Ak., U.S. — D9 140
Alassio, Italy — F5 22
Alatan'aola see Xin Barag Youqi, China — B8 36
Alatri, Italy — I10 22
Alatyr', Russia — D7 32
Alausí, Ec. — I2 86
Alava, Cape, c., Wa., U.S. — B2 136
Álava, co., Spain — B8 20
Al-'Ayn, U.A.E. — E8 56
Alayor see Alaior, Spain — E15 20
Alazeja, stm., Russia — B19 34
Al-'Azīzīyah, Libya — A2 62
Alba, Italy — F5 22
Alba, Mi., U.S. — D5 112
Alba, Tx., U.S. — E3 122
Alba, state, Rom. — C10 26
Al-Bāb, Syria — B8 58
Albacete, Spain — F9 20
Albacete, co., Spain — F9 20
Al-Bad', Sau. Ar. — J6 58
Alba de Tormes, Spain — D5 20
Albaida, Spain — F10 20
Alba Iulia, Rom. — C10 26
Al-Balqā', state, Jord. — F6 58
Al-Bālū'ah, l., Syria — C7 58
Albanel, Lac, l., Qc., Can. — E16 106
Albania, Col. — B5 86
Albania, ctry., Eur. — C14 24
Albano Laziale, Italy — I9 22
Albany, Austl. — G3 74
Albany, In., U.S. — H4 112
Albany, Ky., U.S. — H12 120
Albany, Mn., U.S. — F4 118
Albany, Mo., U.S. — D3 120
Albany, N.Y., U.S. — B12 114
Albany, Oh., U.S. — E3 114
Albany, Or., U.S. — F3 136
Albany, Tx., U.S. — B8 130
Albany, Wi., U.S. — B8 120
Albany, stm., On., Can. — E14 106
Al-Başrah (Basra), Iraq — C6 56
Al-Batrā' (Petra), sci., Jord. — H6 58
Albatross Bay, b., Austl. — B8 74
Al-Baydā', Libya — A4 62
Albemarle, N.C., U.S. — A5 116
Albemarle Island see Isabela, Isla, i., Ec. — i11 84a
Albemarle Sound, strt., N.C., U.S. — H9 114
Albenga, Italy — F5 22
Alberche, stm., Spain — D6 20
Alberdi, Para. — C8 92
Alberga Creek, stm., Austl. — E6 74
Alberni Inlet, b., B.C., Can. — G6 138
Alberobello, Italy — D11 24
Alberta, Al., U.S. — E11 122
Albert, Fr. — D11 14
Albert, Lake, l., Afr. — D6 66
Albert, Lake, l., Austl. — J2 76
Alberta, state, Can. — E8 106
Alberta, Mount, mtn., Ab., Can. — D13 138
Albert Canyon, B.C., Can. — E13 138
Albert City, Ia., U.S. — I3 118
Albert Edward Bay, b., Nu., Can. — B10 106
Alberti, Arg. — G7 92
Albertirsa, Hung. — B6 26
Albertkanaal, can., Bel. — D14 14
Albert Lea, Mn., U.S. — H5 118
Albert Markham, Mount, mtn., Ant. — D21 81
Albert Nile, stm., Afr. — D6 66
Alberton, P.E., Can. — D12 110
Albertville, Al., U.S. — C12 122
Albi, Fr. — E8 18
Albia, Ia., U.S. — C5 120
Albin, Wy., U.S. — F8 126
Albina, Sur. — B7 84
Albina, Ponta, c., Ang. — D1 68
Albion, Ca., U.S. — E2 134
Albion, Id., U.S. — H13 136
Albion, Il., U.S. — F9 120
Albion, In., U.S. — G4 112
Albion, Mi., U.S. — B1 114
Albion, Ne., U.S. — F15 126
Albion, N.Y., U.S. — E11 112
Albion, Pa., U.S. — C5 114
Al-Biqā', state, Leb. — D7 58
Al-Biqā' (Bekaa Valley), val., Leb. — D7 58
Al-Birk, Sau. Ar. — F5 56
Albocàsser, Spain — D10 20
Alborán, Sea, s., — B4 64
Alborz, Reshteh-ye Kühhā-ye, mts., Iran — B7 56
Albuñol, Spain — H7 20
Albuquerque, N.M., U.S. — H10 132
Albuquerque, Cayos de, is., Col. — F6 102
Alburg, Vt., U.S. — F3 110
Alburquerque, Spain — E3 20
Albury, Austl. — J6 76
Alcains, Port. — E3 20
Alcalá de Guadaira, Spain — G5 20
Alcalá de Henares, Spain — D7 20
Alcalá la Real, Spain — G7 20
Alcalde, N.M., U.S. — E2 128

Name	Map Ref.	Page
Alcamo, Italy	G6	24
Alcanar, Spain	D11	20
Alcañices, Spain	C4	20
Alcañiz, Spain	C10	20
Alcántara, Braz.	B3	88
Alcántara, Spain	E3	20
Alcantarilla, Spain	G9	20
Alcaraz, Spain	F8	20
Alcaudete, Spain	G6	20
Alcázar de San Juan, Spain	E7	20
Alcester, S.D., U.S.	A1	120
Alcira, Arg.	F5	92
Alcira see Alzira, Spain	E10	20
Alcobaça, Braz.	I6	88
Alcobendas, Spain	D7	20
Alcoi, Spain	F10	20
Alcolea del Pinar, Spain	C8	20
Alcolu, S.C., U.S.	C5	116
Alcorn, Ms., U.S.	F7	122
Alcorta, Arg.	F7	92
Alcoutim, Port.	G3	20
Alcoy see Alcoi, Spain	F10	20
Alcúdia, Spain	E14	20
Alcúdia, Badia d', b., Spain	E14	20
Aldabra, Groupe d', is., Sey.	k11	69b
Aldama, Mex.	A5	100
Aldama, Mex.	D9	100
Aldan, Russia	E14	34
Aldan, stm., Russia	D15	34
Aldan Plateau see Aldanskoe nagor'e, plat., Russia	E14	34
Aldanskoe nagor'e (Aldan Plateau), plat., Russia	E14	34
Aldarchaan, Mong.	B4	36
Aldeia Nova de São Bento, Port.	G3	20
Alden, Mn., U.S.	H5	118
Alderney, i., Guern.	E6	14
Aldershot, Eng., U.K.	J12	12
Alderson, W.V., U.S.	G5	114
Aledo, Il., U.S.	C7	120
Aleg, Maur.	F2	64
Alegre, Braz.	K5	88
Alegrete, Braz.	D10	92
Alej, stm., Russia	D14	32
Alejandro Roca, Arg.	F5	92
Alejandro Selkirk, Isla, i., Chile	I6	82
Alejsk, Russia	D14	32
Aleksandrov, Russia	D21	10
Aleksandrovkij Zavod, Russia	F12	34
Aleksandrovsk, Russia	B13	32
Aleksandrovsk-Sahalinskij, Russia	F17	34
Aleksandrów Kujawski, Pol.	D14	16
Alekseevka, Kaz.	D12	32
Alekseevka, Kaz.	E14	32
Alekseevka, Russia	D5	32
Alekseevka, Russia	C19	32
Aleksejevka see Alekseevka, Kaz.	D12	32
Alekseyevka see Alekseevka, Kaz.	D12	32
Aleksin, Russia	F19	10
Aleksinac, Serb.	F8	26
Alemania, Arg.	B5	92
Além Paraíba, Braz.	K4	88
Alençon, Fr.	F9	14
Alenquer, Braz.	D7	84
Alentejo, hist. reg., Port.	F3	20
Alenuihaha Channel, strt., Hi., U.S.	c5	78a
Aleppo see Ḩalab, Syria	B8	58
Aleria, Fr.	G15	18
Alert, Nu., Can.	A13	141
Alert Bay, B.C., Can.	F4	138
Alert Point, c., Nu., Can.	A8	141
Alès, Fr.	E10	18
Alešnja, Russia	G16	10
Alessândria, Italy	F5	22
Alesund, Nor.	E1	8
Aleutian Basin, unds.	D20	142
Aleutian Islands, is., Ak., U.S.	g22	140a
Aleutian Range, mts., Ak., U.S.	E8	140
Aleutian Trench, unds.	E21	142
Aleutka, Russia	G19	34
Alevina, mys, c., Russia	E19	34
Alex, Ok., U.S.	G11	128
Alexander, Mb., Can.	E13	124
Alexander, N.D., U.S.	G10	124
Alexander, Kap, c., Grnld.	B11	141
Alexander Archipelago, is., Ak., U.S.	E12	140
Alexander Bay, S. Afr.	F3	70
Alexander City, Al., U.S.	E12	122
Alexander Island, i., Ant.	B33	81
Alexandra, N.Z.	G3	80
Alexandra, stm., Austl.	B3	76
Alexandra Falls, wtfl., N.T., Can.	C7	106
Alexandretta see İskenderun, Tur.	B6	58
Alexandretta, Gulf of see İskenderun Körfezi, b., Tur.	B6	58
Alexandria, Braz.	D6	88
Alexandria, B.C., Can.	D8	138
Alexandria, On., Can.	E2	110
Alexandria see El-Iskandarîya, Egypt	A6	62
Alexandria, Rom.	F12	26
Alexandria, La., U.S.	F6	122
Alexandria, Mn., U.S.	F3	118
Alexandria, Mo., U.S.	D6	120
Alexandria, S.D., U.S.	D15	126
Alexandria, Tn., U.S.	H11	120
Alexandria, Va., U.S.	F8	114
Alexandria Bay, N.Y., U.S.	D14	112
Alexandrina, Lake, l., Austl.	J2	76
Alexandroúpoli, Grc.	C8	28
Alexis, Il., U.S.	C7	120
Alfambra, Spain	D9	20
Alfaro, Spain	B9	20
Alfarràs, Spain	C11	20
Alfarràs see Alfarràs, Spain	C11	20
Al-Fāshir, Sudan	E5	62
Alfeiós, stm., Grc.	F4	28
Alfeld, Ger.	D5	16
Alfenas, Braz.	K3	88
Alföld, pl., Hung.	C7	26
Alfonsine, Italy	F9	22
Alfred, On., Can.	E2	110
Alfred, Me., U.S.	G6	110
Alfred, N.Y., U.S.	B8	114
Al-Fujayrah, U.A.E.	D8	56
Al-Fuqahā', Libya	B3	62
Al-Furāt see Euphrates, stm., Asia	C6	56
Ålgård, Nor.	G1	8
Algarrobal, Chile	D2	92
Algarrobo, Chile	G2	92
Algarrobo del Aguila, Arg.	H4	92
Algarve, hist. reg., Port.	G2	20
Algeciras, Col.	F4	86
Algeciras, Spain	H5	20
Algemesí, Spain	E10	20
Algeria, ctry., Afr.	D5	64
Algha, Kaz.	E9	32
Al-Ghāb, sw., Syria	C6	58
Al-Ghaydah, Yemen	F7	56
Al-Ghāziyah, Leb.	E6	58
Alghero, Italy	D2	24
Algiers see El Djazaïr, Alg.	B5	64
Alginet, Spain	E10	20
Algoabaai, b., S. Afr.	H7	70
Algoa Bay see Algoabaai, b., S. Afr.	H7	70
Algodón, stm., Peru	I5	86
Algodones, N.M., U.S.	F2	128
Algoma Mills, On., Can.	B7	112
Algona, Ia., U.S.	A3	120
Algonac, Mi., U.S.	B3	114
Algonquin, Il., U.S.	B9	120
Algorta, Spain	A7	20
Algorta, Ur.	F9	92
Al-Ḩaffah, Syria	C6	58
Al-Ḩajarah, reg., Asia	C5	56
Al-Ḩamād, pl., Sau. Ar.	C4	56
Alhama de Murcia, Spain	G9	20
Alhandra, Braz.	D8	88
Al-Ḩarrah, lav., Sau. Ar.	C4	56
Al-Ḩarūj al-Aswad, hills, Libya	B3	62
Al-Ḩasakah, Syria	B5	56
Alhaurín el Grande, Spain	H6	20
Al-Ḩawātah, Sudan	E7	62
Al-Ḩawrah, Yemen	G6	56
Al-Ḩijāz (Hejaz), reg., Sau. Ar.	D4	56
Al-Ḩillah, Iraq	C5	56
Al-Ḩirmil, Leb.	D7	58
Al-Hoceima, Mor.	B4	64
Al-Hudaydah (Hodeida), Yemen	G5	56
Al-Ḩufrah, reg., Sau. Ar.	J9	58
Al-Ḩufūf, Sau. Ar.	D6	56
Al Ḩūj, hills, Sau. Ar.	J9	58
Al-Ḩulwah, Sau. Ar.	E6	56
Alia, Spain	E5	20
Aliaga, Tur.	E9	28
Aliákmonas, stm., Grc.	C4	28
Aliança, Braz.	D8	88
Alībāg, India	B1	53
Alibates Flint Quarries National Monument, p.o.i., Tx., U.S.	F7	128
Ali Bayramlı, Azer.	B6	56
Alibei, ozero, l., Ukr.	D17	26
Alibey Adası, i., Tur.	D9	28
Alibunar, Serb.	D7	26
Alicante see Alacant, Spain	F10	20
Alicante, co., Spain	F10	20
Alice, S. Afr.	H8	70
Alice, Tx., U.S.	G9	130
Alice, stm., Austl.	D5	76
Alice, Punta, c., Italy	E11	24
Alice Springs, Austl.	D6	74
Alice Town, Bah.	K6	116
Aliceville, Al., U.S.	D10	122
Alick Creek, stm., Austl.	C4	76
Alīgarh, India	E6	54
Alignements de Carnac, hist., Fr.	G5	14
Aligūdarz, Iran	C6	56
'Alī Kheyl, Afg.	B2	54
Al-Ikhṣās al-Qiblīyah, Egypt	I2	58
Alima, stm., Congo	E3	66
Alim Island, i., Pap. N. Gui.	a4	79a
Alindao, C.A.R.	C4	66
Alingsås, Swe.	G5	8
Alīpur, Pak.	D3	54
Alīpur Duār, India	E12	54
Aliquippa, Pa., U.S.	D5	114
Alīrājpur, India	G5	54
Aliseda, Spain	E4	20
Alitak, Cape, c., Ak., U.S.	E9	140
Alivéri, Grc.	E7	28
Aliwal North, S. Afr.	G8	70
Alix, Ab., Can.	D17	138
Al-Jabalayn, Sudan	E6	62
Al-Jafr, Jord.	H7	58
Al-Jaghbūb, Libya	B4	62
Al-Jahrah, Kuw.	D6	56
Al-Jawārah, Oman	F8	56
Al-Jawf, Libya	C4	62
Al-Jawf, Sau. Ar.	D4	56
Al-Jazair see El Djazaïr, Alg.	B5	64
Al-Jazīrah, reg., Sudan	E6	62
Al-Jifārah (Jeffara), pl., Afr.	C7	64
Al-Jubayl, Sau. Ar.	D6	56
Al-Junaynah, Sudan	E4	62
Aljustrel, Port.	G2	20
Al-Kafr, Syria	F7	58
Al-Karak, Jord.	G6	58
Al-Karak, state, Jord.	G6	58
Al-Khalīl (Hebron), W.B.	G5	58
Al-Khālis, Iraq	C5	56
Al-Khandaq, Sudan	D6	62
Al-Kharṭūm Bahrī, Sudan	D6	62
Al-Kharṭūm (Khartoum), Sudan	D6	62
Al-Khaṣab, Oman	D8	56
Al-Khums, Libya	A2	62
Alkmaar, Neth.	B13	14
Al-Kufrah, Libya	C4	62
Al-Kūt, Iraq	C6	56
Al-Kuwayt (Kuwait), Kuw.	D6	56
Al-Labwah, Leb.	D7	58
Al-Lādhiqīyah (Latakia), Syria	C6	58
Al-Lādhiqīyah, state, Syria	C6	58
Allagash, stm., Me., U.S.	D7	110
Allahābād, India	F8	54
Allah-Jun', Russia	D16	34
Allakaket, Ak., U.S.	C9	140
Allan, Sk., Can.	C7	124
Allanmyo, Mya.	C2	48
Allanridge, S. Afr.	E8	70
Allatoona Lake, res., Ga., U.S.	C14	122
Alldays, S. Afr.	C9	70
Allegan, Mi., U.S.	F4	112
Allegany, N.Y., U.S.	B7	114
Allegheny, stm., U.S.	D6	114
Allegheny Mountains, mts., U.S.	E6	114
Allegheny Plateau, plat., U.S.	D5	114
Allegheny Reservoir, res., U.S.	C7	114
Allemands, Lac des, l., La., U.S.	H8	122
Allen, Ne., U.S.	I2	118
Allen, Ok., U.S.	C2	122
Allen, Lough, l., Ire.	G4	12
Allendale, Il., U.S.	F10	120
Allendale, S.C., U.S.	C4	116
Allende, Mex.	A8	100
Allenstein see Olsztyn, Pol.	C16	16
Allentown, Pa., U.S.	D10	114
Alleppey, India	G3	53
Aller, stm., Ger.	D5	16
Alliance, Ab., Can.	D19	138
Alliance, Ne., U.S.	E10	126
Alliance, Oh., U.S.	D4	114
Al-Lidām, Sau. Ar.	E5	56
Allier, state, Fr.	C9	18
Allier, stm., Fr.	D9	18
Alligator Pond, Jam.	j13	104d
Allinagaram, India	F3	53
Allison, Ia., U.S.	B5	120
Al-Lith, Sau. Ar.	E5	56
Alloa, Scot., U.K.	E9	12
Allos, Fr.	E12	18
Allouez, Wi., U.S.	G11	118
Allred Peak, mtn., Co., U.S.	F4	105b
Al-Luḩayyah, Yemen	F5	56
Allumette Lake, l., Can.	C12	112
Allumettes, Île aux, i., Qc., Can.	C12	112
Alma, N.B., Can.	E12	110
Alma, Qc., Can.	B5	110
Alma, Ar., U.S.	B4	122
Alma, Ga., U.S.	E3	116
Alma, Ks., U.S.	E1	120
Alma, Mi., U.S.	E5	112
Alma, Wi., U.S.	G7	118
Almada, Port.	F1	20
Almaden, Austl.	A5	76
Almadén, Spain	F6	20
Al-Madīnah (Medina), Sau. Ar.	E4	56
Al-Mafraq, Jord.	F7	58
Al-Mafraq, state, Jord.	F8	58
Almafuerte, Arg.	F5	92
Almagro, Spain	F7	20
Al Māliḩah, Sudan	D5	62
Almalyk, Uzb.	F11	32
Al-Manāmah (Manama), Bahr.	D7	56
Almanor, Lake, res., Ca., U.S.	C4	134
Almansa, Spain	F9	20
Almanza, Spain	B5	20
Almanzor, mtn., Spain	D5	20
Al-Marj, Libya	A4	62
Almas, Braz.	F2	88
Almas, Pico das, mtn., Braz.	G4	88
Al-Mashrafah, Syria	D7	58
Almaty, Kaz.	F13	32
Al-Mawṣil (Mosul), Iraq	B5	56
Almeida, Port.	D3	20
Almejas, Bahía, b., Mex.	C3	100
Almelo, Neth.	B15	14
Almena, Ks., U.S.	B9	128
Almenara, Braz.	I5	88
Almendra, Embalse de, res., Spain	C4	20
Almendralejo, Spain	F4	20
Almería, Spain	H8	20
Almería, co., Spain	G8	20
Almería, Golfo de, b., Spain	H8	20
Al'metevsk, Russia	D8	32
Al-Miqdādīyah, Sudan	E5	62
Al-Mīnā', Leb.	D6	58
Almira, Wa., U.S.	C7	136
Almirante, Pan.	H6	102
Almirante Latorre, Chile	D2	92
Almo, Id., U.S.	A3	132
Almodóvar del Campo, Spain	F6	20
Almont, Mi., U.S.	B2	114
Almonte, On., Can.	C13	112
Almonte, Spain	G4	20
Almonte, stm., Spain	E4	20
Almora, India	D7	54
Al-Mubarraz, Sau. Ar.	E6	56
Al-Mubarraz, Sau. Ar.	D6	56
Al-Mudawwarah, Jord.	I6	58
Almudévar, Spain	B10	20
Al-Muḩarraq, Bahr.	D7	56
Al-Mukallā, Yemen	G6	56
Al-Mukhā, Yemen	G5	56
Almuñécar, Spain	H7	20
Al-Muwaylih, Sau. Ar.	K6	58
Almyrós, Grc.	D5	28
Almyroú, Órmos, b., Grc.	H7	28
Alnwick, Eng., U.K.	F11	12
Alónnisos, Grc.	D6	28
Alónnisos, i., Grc.	D6	28
Alor, Pulau, i., Indon.	G7	44
Alor, Selat, strt., Indon.	G7	44
Alor Setar, Malay.	I5	48
Alosno, Spain	G3	20
Alost see Aalst, Bel.	D13	14
Alotau, Pap. N. Gui.	c5	79a
Aloysius, Mount, mtn., Austl.	E5	74
Alpachiri, Arg.	H5	92
Alpaugh, Ca., U.S.	H6	134
Alpena, Mi., U.S.	C6	112
Alpena, S.D., U.S.	C14	126
Alpercatas, stm., Braz.	D3	88
Alpes-de-Haute-Provence, state, Fr.	E12	18
Alpha, Austl.	D6	76
Alpha, Il., U.S.	C7	120
Alpha, Mi., U.S.	B1	112
Alpharetta, Ga., U.S.	B1	116
Alphonse, i., Sey.	k12	69b
Alpine, Ca., U.S.	K9	134
Alpine, Tx., U.S.	D4	130
Alpine National Park, p.o.i., Austl.	K6	76
Alpinópolis, Braz.	K2	88
Alps, mts., Eur.	D6	22
Al-Qadārif, Sudan	E7	62
Al-Qadīmah, Sau. Ar.	E4	56
Al-Qāmishlī, Syria	B5	56
Al-Qaryah ash-Sharqīyah, Libya	A2	62
Al-Qaryatayn, Syria	D8	58
Al-Qaṭīf, Sau. Ar.	D6	56
Al-Qaṭrānī, Jord.	G7	58
Al-Qaṭrūn, Libya	C2	62
Al-Qaysūmah, Sau. Ar.	D6	56
Al-Qunayṭirah, Syria	E6	58
Al-Qunayṭirah, state, Syria	E6	58
Al-Qunfudhah, Sau. Ar.	F5	56
Al-Quṭayfah, Syria	E7	58
Al-Quṭaynah, Sudan	E6	62
Als, i., Den.	I3	8
Alsace, hist. reg., Fr.	F16	14
Al'šany, Bela.	H10	10
Alsask, Sk., Can.	C4	124
Alsasua, Spain	B8	20
Alsea, Or., U.S.	F3	136
Alsek, stm., N.A.	D3	106
Alsen, N.D., U.S.	F15	124
Alsfeld, Ger.	F5	16
Alta, Nor.	B10	8
Alta, Ia., U.S.	B10	8
Altaelva, stm., Nor.	E5	92
Alta Gracia, Arg.	B6	86
Altagracia, Ven.	C8	86
Altagracia de Orituco, Ven.	E15	32
Altai, mts., Asia	D15	32
Altaj, state, Russia	D14	32
Altaiskij, Russia	E3	116
Altamaha, stm., Ga., U.S.	D7	84
Altamira, Braz.	B3	92
Altamira, Chile	I10	130
Altamirano, Mex.	G2	120
Altamont, Ks., U.S.	A4	134
Altamont, Or., U.S.	B13	122
Altamont, Tn., U.S.	D10	24
Altamura, Italy	C4	100
Altamura, Isla, i., Mex.	A6	36
Altanbulag, Mong.	F7	98
Altar, Mex.	F7	98
Altar, stm., Mex.	F6	98
Altar, Desierto de, des., Mex.	D2	102
Altar de Los Sacrificios, sci., Guat.	C4	124
Altario, Ab., Can.	C12	128
Alta Vista, Ks., U.S.	E15	32
Altay, China	B4	36
Altay, Mong.	D15	32
Altay see Altaj, state, Russia	E15	32
Altay Mountains see Altai, mts., Asia	D5	22
Altdorf, Switz.	E8	16
Altenburg, Ger.	G8	120
Altenburg, Mo., U.S.	C9	16
Altentreptow, Ger.	E3	20
Alter do Chão, Port.	B8	8
Altevatnet, l., Nor.	G13	122
Altha, Fl., U.S.	C7	122
Altheimer, Ar., U.S.	E15	28
Altınekin, Tur.	H9	132
Altinho, Braz.	E7	88
Altınova, Tur.	D9	28
Altıntaş, Tur.	D13	28
Altiplano, plat., S.A.	G4	84
Altmark, reg., Ger.	D7	16
Altmühl, stm., Ger.	G6	16
Alto, Tx., U.S.	F3	122
Alto Araguaia, Braz.	G7	84
Alto Chicapa, Ang.	C2	68
Alto Garças, Braz.	G7	84
Alto Longá, Braz.	C4	88
Alton, Eng., U.K.	J11	12
Alton, Ia., U.S.	B1	120
Alton, Il., U.S.	F7	120
Alton, Ks., U.S.	B9	128
Alton, N.H., U.S.	G5	110
Altona, Mb., Can.	E16	124
Altoona, Al., U.S.	C12	122
Altoona, Ia., U.S.	C4	120
Altoona, Pa., U.S.	D7	114
Altoona, Wi., U.S.	G7	118
Alto Paraguai, Braz.	F6	84
Alto Paraíso de Goiás, Braz.	G2	88
Alto Paraná, state, Para.	B10	92
Alto Parnaíba, Braz.	E2	88
Alto Rio Mayo, Arg.	I2	90
Alto Rio Senguer, Arg.	I2	90
Altos, Braz.	C4	88
Alto Santo, Braz.	C6	88
Altötting, Ger.	H8	16
Altun Shan, mts., China	D2	36
Alturas, Ca., U.S.	B5	134
Altus, Ar., U.S.	B5	122
Altus, Ok., U.S.	G9	128
Alu see Shortland Island, i., Sol. Is.	d6	79b
Al-'Ubaylah, Sau. Ar.	E7	56
Al-Ubayyid, Sudan	E6	62
Alubijid, Phil.	F5	52
Al-Uḍayyah, Sudan	E5	62
Alūksne, Lat.	D9	10
Al-'Ulā, Sau. Ar.	D4	56
Al-'Uqaylah, Libya	A3	62
Al-'Uwaynāt, Libya	B2	62
Alva, Ok., U.S.	E10	128
Alvaiázere, Port.	E2	20
Alvarado, Mex.	F11	100
Alvarado, Tx., U.S.	B10	130
Álvaro Obregón, Presa, res., Mex.	B4	100
Alvear, Arg.	D9	92
Alverca, Port.	F1	20
Alvernia, Mount, hill, Bah.	C10	96
Alvesta, Swe.	H6	8
Alvin, Tx., U.S.	H3	122
Alvinópolis, Braz.	K4	88
Älvkarleby, Swe.	F7	8
Alvord, Tx., U.S.	H11	128
Alvord Desert, des., Or., U.S.	H8	136
Al-Wajh, Sau. Ar.	D4	56
Alwar, India	E6	54
Alwaye, India	F3	53
Alxa Zuoqi, China	B1	42
Alytus, Lith.	F6	10
Alzey, Ger.	G4	16
Alzira, Spain	E10	20
Amacuro (Amakura), stm., S.A.	C11	86
Amadeus, Lake, l., Austl.	D6	74
Amadjuak Lake, l., Nu., Can.	B16	106
Amagasaki, Japan	E8	40
Amagi, Japan	F3	40
Amahai, Indon.	F8	44
Amaichá del Valle, Arg.	C4	92
Amaimon, Pap. N. Gui.	b4	79a
Amajac, stm., Mex.	E9	100
Amakura (Amacuro), stm., S.A.	D11	86
Amakusa-nada, s., Japan	G2	40
Amakusa-shotō, is., Japan	G2	40
Amaliáda, Grc.	F4	28
Amalner, India	H5	54
Amambaí, Braz.	D5	90
Amami Islands see Amami-Ō-shima, i., Japan	k19	39a
Amami-Ō-shima, i., Japan	k19	39a
Amami-shotō, is., Japan	I19	39a
Amana, Ia., U.S.	C6	120
Amanã, Lago, l., Braz.	I9	86
Amana, stm., Ven.	C10	86
Amapá, Braz.	C7	84
Amapá, state, Braz.	C7	84
Amarante, Braz.	D4	88
Amaranth, Mb., Can.	D15	124
Amarapura, Mya.	B3	48
Amārāstii de Jos, Rom.	F11	26
Amaravati, India	F3	53
Amares, Port.	C2	20
Amargosa, stm., U.S.	H9	134
Amarillo, Tx., U.S.	F7	128
Amarkantak, India	G8	54
Amaro, Monte, mtn., Italy	H11	22
Amasra, Tur.	B15	28
Amasya, Tur.	A4	56
aMatikulu, S. Afr.	F10	70
Amatsu-kominato, Japan	D13	40
Amawbia Awka, Nig.	H6	64
Amazar, Russia	F13	34
Amazon (Amazonas) (Solimões), stm., S.A.	D7	84
Amazonas, state, Col.	H6	86
Amazonas, state, Braz.	D4	84
Amazonas, state, Ven.	F8	86
Ambajōgai, India	B3	53
Ambāla, India	C6	54
Ambalangoda, Sri L.	H4	53
Ambalavao, Madag.	E8	68
Ambam, Cam.	D2	66
Ambanja, Madag.	C8	68
Ambardah, Russia	C21	34
Ambargasta, Salinas de, pl., Arg.	D5	92
Ambato, Ec.	H2	86
Ambatofinandrahana, Madag.	D8	68
Ambatolampy, Madag.	D8	68
Ambatondrazaka, Madag.	D8	68
Ambelau, Pulau, i., Indon.	F8	44
Amberg, Ger.	G7	16
Ambérieu-en-Bugey, Fr.	D11	18
Ambgaon, India	H7	54
Ambidédi, Mali	G2	64
Ambikāpur, India	G9	54
Ambilobe, Madag.	C8	68
Amble, Eng., U.K.	F11	12
Ambo, Peru	F2	84
Ambodifototra, Madag.	D8	68
Ambohimahasoa, Madag.	E8	68
Amboise, Fr.	G10	14
Ambon, Indon.	F8	44
Ambon, Pulau, i., Indon.	F8	44
Amboseli, Lake, l., Afr.	E7	66
Amboseli National Park, p.o.i., Kenya	E7	66
Ambositra, Madag.	D8	68
Ambovombe, Madag.	F8	68
Amboy, Il., U.S.	C8	120
Amboy, Mn., U.S.	H4	118
Ambriz, Ang.	B1	68
Ambrolauri, Geor.	F6	32
Ambrosia Lake, N.M., U.S.	H9	132
Ambrym, state, Vanuatu	k17	79d
Ambrym, i., Vanuatu	k17	79d
Ambuntentimur, Indon.	G8	50
Ambunti, Pap. N. Gui.	a3	79a
Āmbūr, India	E4	53
Amchitka Island, i., Ak., U.S.	g22	140a
Amchitka Pass, strt., Ak., U.S.	g22	140a
Am Dam, Chad	E4	62
Amdo, China	B13	54
Ameagle, W.V., U.S.	G4	114
Ameca, Mex.	E6	100
Ameca, stm., Mex.	E6	100
Ameghino, Arg.	G6	92
Ameland, i., Neth.	A14	14
Amelia Court House, Va., U.S.	G8	114
Amelia Island, i., Fl., U.S.	F4	116
Amelia, India	E5	54
American, North Fork, stm., Ca., U.S.	D5	134
American, South Fork, stm., Ca., U.S.	E5	134
Americana, Braz.	L2	88
American Falls Reservoir, res., Id., U.S.	H13	136
American Fork, Ut., U.S.	C5	132
American Highland, plat., Ant.	C12	81
Americanos, Barra de los, i., Mex.	C10	100
American Samoa, dep., Oc.	h12	79c
Americus, Ga., U.S.	D1	116
Americus, Ks., U.S.	F1	120
Amersfoort, Neth.	B14	14
Amery, Wi., U.S.	F6	118
Amery Ice Shelf, ice, Ant.	B12	81
Ames, Ia., U.S.	B4	120
Amesbury, Ma., U.S.	B14	114
Amfilochía, Grc.	E4	28
Ámfissa, Grc.	E5	28
Amga, stm., Russia	D15	34
Amga, stm., Russia	D15	34
Amguema, stm., Russia	C24	34
Amguid, Alg.	D6	64
Amgun', stm., Russia	F16	34
Amherst, N.S., Can.	E12	110
Amherst, Ma., U.S.	B13	114
Amherst, N.Y., U.S.	A7	114
Amherst, Oh., U.S.	C3	114
Amherst, Tx., U.S.	G6	128
Amherst, Wi., U.S.	G9	118
Amherstburg, On., Can.	F6	112
Amherstdale, W.V., U.S.	G4	114
Amherst Island, i., On., Can.	D13	112
Amherstview, On., Can.	D13	112
Amiens, Austl.	G8	76
Amiens, Fr.	E11	14
Amindivi Islands, is., India	F3	46
Amino, Japan	D8	40
Aminuis, Nmb.	C4	70
Amirantes, Les, is., Sey.	k12	69b
Amisk, Ab., Can.	B2	124
Amisk Lake, l., Sk., Can.	E10	106
Amistad, Parque Internacional de la, p.o.i., C.R.	H6	102
Amistad National Recreation Area, p.o.i., Tx., U.S.	E6	130
Amistad Reservoir (Amistad, Presa de la), res., N.A.	E6	130
Amite, La., U.S.	G8	122
Amite, stm., La., U.S.	G8	122
Amity, Ar., U.S.	C5	122
Amla, India	H7	54
Âmli, Nor.	G3	8
'Ammān, Jord.	G6	58
'Ammān, state, Jord.	G7	58
'Ammānsaari, Fin.	D13	8
'Ammār, Tall, hill, Syria	F7	58
Ammassalik see Angmagssalik, Grnld.	D18	141
Ammon, Id., U.S.	G15	136
Amnat Charoen, Thai.	E7	48
Amnok-kang (Yalu), stm., Asia	D7	38
Amo (Torsa), stm., Asia	E12	54
Amo, stm., China	A5	48
Amol, Iran	B7	56
Amorgós, i., Grc.	G8	28
Amory, Ms., U.S.	D10	122
Amos, Qc., Can.	F15	106
Åmot, Nor.	G2	8
Amoy see Xiamen, China	I7	42
Ampanihy, Madag.	E8	68
Amparo, Braz.	L2	88
Ampasimanolotra, Madag.	D8	68
Amposta, Spain	D11	20
Amqui, Qc., Can.	B9	110
Amrāvati, India	H6	54
Amreli, India	H3	54
Amritsar, India	C5	54
Amroha, India	D7	54
Amrum, i., Ger.	B4	16
Amsterdam, Neth.	B13	14
Amsterdam, S. Afr.	E10	70
Amsterdam, N.Y., U.S.	B11	114
Amsterdam, Île, i., Afr.	M11	142
Am Timan, Chad	E4	62
Amu Darya, stm., Asia	F10	32
Amugulang see Xin Barag Zuoqi, China	B8	36
Amundsen Gulf, b., Can.	B14	140
Amundsen-Scott, sci., Ant.	D19	81
Amundsen Sea, s., Ant.	P27	142
Amuntai, Indon.	E9	50
Amur (Heilong), stm., Asia	F16	34
Amursk, Russia	F16	34
Amuzhong, China	C10	54
Amvrakikós Kólpos, b., Grc.	E3	28
An, Mya.	C2	48
Anabar, stm., Russia	B11	34
Anaco, Ven.	C9	86
Anaconda, Mt., U.S.	D14	136
Anaconda Range, mts., Mt., U.S.	E13	136
Anacortes, Wa., U.S.	B4	136
Anadarko, Ok., U.S.	F10	128
Anadolu (Anatolia), hist. reg., Tur.	H15	6
Anadyr', Russia	C23	34
Anadyr', Gulf of see Anadyrskij zaliv, b., Russia	C21	142
Anadyrskij liman, b., Russia	C23	34
Anadyrskij zaliv, b., Russia	C21	142
Anadyrskoe ploskogor'e, plat., Russia	C23	34
Anáfi, i., Grc.	G8	28
Anagni, Italy	C7	24
Anaheim, Ca., U.S.	J8	134
Anáhuac, Mex.	H6	130
Anáhuac, Mex.	B8	100
Anahola, Hi., U.S.	a2	78a
Anai Mudi, mtn., India	F3	53
Anaiza see 'Unayzah, Sau. Ar.	D5	56
Anaka, Ug.	D6	66
Anakāpalle, India	C6	53
Anaktuvuk Pass, Ak., U.S.	C9	140
Analalava, Madag.	C8	68
Anamã, Braz.	D5	84
Anama Bay, Mb., Can.	C15	124
Ana María, Golfo de, b., Cuba	B8	102
Anambas, Kepulauan (Anambas Islands), is., Indon.	B5	50
Anambas Islands see Anambas, Kepulauan, is., Indon.	B5	50
Anamizu, Japan	B9	40
Anamoose, N.D., U.S.	G13	124
Anamur, Tur.	B3	58
Anamur Burnu, c., Tur.	B3	58
Anan, Japan	F7	40
Anand, India	H11	54
Anandapur, India	H11	54
Anan'iv, Ukr.	B16	26
Anantapur, India	D3	53
Anantnāg, India	B5	54
Anápolis, Braz.	I1	88
Anapurus, Braz.	B4	88
Añasco, P.R.	B1	104a
Anastasia Island, i., Fl., U.S.	G4	116
Anatahan, i., N. Mar. Is.	B5	72
Anatolia see Anadolu, hist. reg., Tur.	H15	6
Anatoliki Makedonía kai Thráki, state, Grc.	B8	28
Anatom, i., Vanuatu	m17	79d
Añatuya, Arg.	D6	92
Anauá, stm., Braz.	G11	86
Anavilhanas, Arquipélago das, is., Braz.	I11	86
Anbei, China	F17	32
Anbianbu, China	C2	42
Anbyŏn-ŭp, Kor., N.	E7	38
Ancaster, On., Can.	E9	112
Áncash, Sierra de, mts., Arg.	D5	92
Anchang see Qianyang, China	H3	42
Anch'ing see Anqing, China	F7	42
Anchorage, Ak., U.S.	D10	140
Anchuras, Spain	E6	20
Ancona, Italy	G10	22
Ancón de Sardinas, Bahía de, b., S.A.	G2	86
Ancuabe, Moz.	C6	68
Ancud, Chile	H2	90
Ancy-le-Franc, Fr.	G13	14
Anda, China	B10	36
Andacollo, Arg.	H2	92
Andahuaylas, Peru	F3	84
Andalgalá, Arg.	C4	92
Andalucía, state, Spain	G6	20
Andalusia see Andalucía, state, Spain	G6	20
Andalusia, Al., U.S.	F12	122
Andaman and Nicobar Islands, state, India	F7	46
Andaman Basin, unds.	H12	142
Andaman Islands, is., India	F7	46
Andaman Sea, s., Asia	G8	46
Andamooka, Austl.	F7	74
Andapa, Madag.	C8	68
Andenes, Nor.	B6	8
Andéramboukane, Mali	F5	64
Andernach, Ger.	F3	16
Anderson, Ca., U.S.	C3	134
Anderson, In., U.S.	H4	112
Anderson, Mo., U.S.	H3	120
Anderson, S.C., U.S.	B3	116
Anderson, Tx., U.S.	G3	122
Anderson, stm., N.T., Can.	B5	106
Anderson, Mount, mtn., Wa., U.S.	C3	136
Anderson Dam, Id., U.S.	G11	136
Andes, Col.	E4	86
Andes, mts., S.A.	F2	82
Andfjorden, strt., Nor.	B7	8
Andhra Lake, res., India	B1	53
Andhra Pradesh, state, India	C4	53
Andilamena, Madag.	D8	68
Andimeshk, Iran	B6	56
Andirlang, China	A5	46
Andižan, Uzb.	F12	32
Andkhvoy, Afg.	B10	56
Andoany, Madag.	C8	68
Andoga, stm., Russia	A19	10
Andong, Kor., S.	C1	40
Andong-chōsuji, res., Kor., S.	C1	40
Andorra, ctry., Eur.	B12	20
Andorra-la-Vella, And.	B12	20
Andover, Eng., U.K.	J11	12
Andover, Ma., U.S.	B14	114
Andover, N.Y., U.S.	B8	114
Andover, Oh., U.S.	C5	114
Andover, S.D., U.S.	B15	126
Andøya, i., Nor.	B6	8
Andradina, Braz.	D6	90
Andreanof Islands, is., Ak., U.S.	g23	140a
Andreápol', Russia	D15	10
Andrews, In., U.S.	H4	112
Andrews, N.C., U.S.	A2	116
Andrews, S.C., U.S.	C6	116
Andrews, Tx., U.S.	B5	130
Andria, Italy	C10	24
Andriamena, Madag.	D8	68
Andriivka, Ukr.	B17	26
Andros, i., Grc.	F7	28
Andros, i., Bah.	C9	96
Androscoggin, stm., Me., U.S.	F6	110
Andrott Island, i., India	F3	53
Andrupene, Lat.	D10	10
Andudu, D.R.C.	D5	66
Anduze, Fr.	E9	18
Anegada Passage, strt., N.A.	h15	96a
Aného, Togo	H5	64
Añelo, Arg.	I3	92
Anemata, Passe d', strt., N. Cal.	m16	79d
Anenii Noi, Mol.	C16	26
Aneroid, Sk., Can.	E6	124
Anétis, Mali	F5	64
Aneto, mtn., Spain	B11	20
Anfu, China	H6	42
Angamos, Punta, c., Chile	B2	90
Angara, stm., Russia	C18	32
Angarsk, Russia	D18	32
Angas Downs, Austl.	D6	74
Angastaco, Arg.	B4	92
Ånge, Swe.	E6	8
Ángel, Salto (Angel Falls), wtfl., Ven.	E10	86
Ángel de la Guarda, Isla, i., Mex.	G6	98
Angeles, Phil.	C3	52
Angel Falls see Ángel, Salto, wtfl., Ven.	E10	86
Ängelholm, Swe.	H5	8
Angellala Creek, stm., Austl.	F6	76
Angels Camp, Ca., U.S.	E5	134
Angemuk, mtn., Indon.	F10	44

Name	Map Ref.	Page
Ångermanälven, stm., Swe.	E7	8
Angermünde, Ger.	C9	16
Angers, Fr.	G8	14
Angical, Braz.	F3	88
Angical do Piauí, Braz.	D4	88
Angicos, Braz.	C4	88
Angijak Island, i., Nu., Can.	D13	141
Angikuni Lake, l., Nu., Can.	C11	106
Angkor Wat, sci., Camb.	F6	48
Angle Tasaôm, Camb.	G7	48
Angle Inlet, Mn., U.S.	B3	118
Anglem, Mount, mtn., N.Z.	H2	80
Anglesey, i., Wales, U.K.	H8	12
Anglet, Fr.	F4	18
Angleton, Tx., U.S.	H3	122
Anglona, reg., Italy	D2	24
Angmagssalik (Ammassalik), Grnld.	D18	141
Angoche, Moz.	D6	68
Angol, Chile	H1	92
Angola, In., U.S.	G5	112
Angola, N.Y., U.S.	B6	114
Angola, ctry., Afr.	C2	68
Angola Basin, unds.	J14	144
Angora see Ankara, Tur.	D15	28
Angoram, Pap. N. Gui.	a3	79a
Angostura, Presa de la, res., Mex.	H12	100
Angoulême, Fr.	D6	18
Angoumois, hist. reg., Fr.	D5	18
Angra dos Reis, Braz.	L3	88
Angren, Uzb.	F12	32
Anguilla, Cuba.	B10	102
Anguilla, Ms., U.S.	E8	122
Anguilla, dep., N.A.	h15	96a
Anguli Nur, l., China	A6	42
Anguo, China.	B6	42
Angus, On., Can.	D10	112
Angusville, Mb., Can.	D13	124
Anhalt, hist. reg., Ger.	D7	16
Anholt, i., Den.	H4	8
Anhua, China.	G4	42
Anhui, China	F7	42
Anhwei see Anhui, state, China	F7	42
Aniak, Ak., U.S.	D8	140
Anibare Bay, b., Nauru	q17	78f
Anie, Pic d', mtn., Fr.	F5	18
Anil, Braz.	B3	88
Animas, N.M., U.S.	L8	132
Animas, stm., U.S.	G9	132
Animas Valley, val., N.A.	L8	132
Anina, Rom.	D8	26
Anita, Ia., U.S.	C3	120
Antrkaya, Tur.	E13	28
Aniva, mys, c., Russia	B13	36
Aniva, zaliv, b., Russia.	G17	34
Aniwa, i., Vanuatu	I17	79d
Anjangaon, India.	H6	54
Anjār, India.	G2	54
'Anjar, Leb.	E6	58
Anjou, hist. reg., Fr.	G8	14
Anjouan see Nzwani, i., Com.	C7	68
Anjudin, Russia	B9	32
Anjujsk, Russia	C21	34
Anjujskij hrebet, mts., Russia	C21	34
Anju-ŭp, Kor., N.	E6	38
Anka, Nig.	G6	64
Ankaboa, Tanjona, c., Madag.	E7	68
Ankang, China.	E3	42
Ankara, Tur.	D15	28
Ankara, state, Tur.	D15	28
Ankavandra, Madag.	D8	68
Ankazoabo, Madag.	E7	68
Ankazobe, Madag.	D8	68
Ankeny, Ia., U.S.	C4	120
Anking see Anqing, China.	F7	42
Ankleshwar, India	H4	54
Ankoro, D.R.C.	F5	66
Anlong, China	F6	36
Ânlông Vêng, Camb.	E7	48
Anlu, China	F5	42
An Muileann gCearr see Mullingar, Ire.	H5	12
Ånn, l., Swe.	E5	8
Ann, Cape, c., Ant.	B10	81
Ann, Cape, c., Ma., U.S.	H6	110
Anna, Il., U.S.	G8	120
Anna, Lake, res., Va., U.S.	F8	114
Annaba, Alg.	B6	64
An-Nabatīyah, state, Leb.	E6	58
An-Nabatīyah at-Tahtā, Leb.	E6	58
Annaberg-Buchholz, Ger.	F9	16
An-Nabk, Syria	D7	58
An-Nafūd, des., Sau. Ar.	D5	56
An-Najaf, Iraq.	C5	56
Annam see Trung Phan, hist. reg., Viet.	D8	48
Annamitique, Chaîne, mts., Asia.	D8	48
Annan, Scot., U.K.	G9	12
Annandale, Austl.	C7	76
Annandale, Mn., U.S.	F4	118
Annandale, val., Scot., U.K.	F9	12
Anna Plains, Austl.	C4	74
Annapolis, Md., U.S.	F9	114
Annapolis Royal, N.S., Can.	F11	110
Annapūrṇa, mtn., Nepal	D9	54
Ann Arbor, Mi., U.S.	B2	114
An Nás see Naas, Ire.	H6	12
An-Nāsirīyah, Iraq	C6	56
An-Nāsiriyah, Syria	E7	58
An-Nawfalīyah, Libya	A3	62
Annecy, Fr.	D12	18
Annecy, Lac d', l., Fr.	D12	18
Annemasse, Fr.	C12	18
Annenkov Island, i., S. Geor.	J9	90
An Nhon, Viet.	F9	48
Anning, China.	G5	36
Anniston, Al., U.S.	D13	122
Annobón, i., Eq. Gui.	J6	64
Annonay, Fr.	D10	18
An-Nuhūd, Sudan	E5	62
Annville, Ky., U.S.	G2	114
Annville, Pa., U.S.	D9	114
Anoka, Mn., U.S.	F5	118
Anori, Braz.	D5	84
Anpu, China.	K3	42
Anqing, China	F7	42
Anren, China.	H5	42
Ansai, China.	C3	42
Ansbach, Ger.	G6	16
Anse-d'Hainault, Haiti	C10	102
Anse La Raye, St. Luc.	m6	105c
Anselmo, Ne., U.S.	F13	126
Anserma, Col.	E4	86
Anshan, China.	D5	38
Anshun, China.	H1	42
Ansina, Ur.	E10	92
Ansley, Ne., U.S.	F13	126
Anson, Tx., U.S.	B8	130
Anson Bay, b., Austl.	B6	74
Anson Bay, b., Norf. I.	y24	78i
Ansongo, Mali	F5	64
Ansonville, N.C., U.S.	A6	116
Ansted, W.V., U.S.	F4	114
Antakya see Hatay, Tur.	B7	58
Antalaha, Madag.	C9	68
Antalieptė Lith.	E8	10
Antalya, Tur.	G13	28
Antalya, state, Tur.	F14	28
Antalya, Gulf of see Antalya Körfezi, b., Tur.	G14	28
Antalya Körfezi (Antalya, Gulf of), b., Tur.	G14	28
Antananarivo, Madag.	D8	68
An tAonach see Nenagh, Ire.	I4	12
Antarctica, cont.	D11	81
Antarctic Peninsula, pen., Ant.	C35	81
Antas, Braz.	F6	88
Antas, stm., Braz.	D12	92
Antelope Island, i., Ut., U.S.	C4	132
Antelope Mine, Zimb.	B9	70
Antelope Peak, mtn., Nv., U.S.	B1	132
Antenor Navarro, Braz.	D6	88
Antequera, Para.	A9	92
Antequera, Spain	H6	20
Anthon, Ia., U.S.	B2	120
Anthony, Ks., U.S.	D10	128
Anthony, N.M., U.S.	K10	132
Anthony, Tx., U.S.	E9	98
Anti-Atlas, mts., Mor.	D3	64
Anticlsa, India	F13	18
Anticosti, Île d', i., Qc., Can.	F18	106
Antifer, Cap d', c., Fr.	E8	14
Antigonish, N.S., Can.	E14	110
Antigua, i., Antig.	f4	105b
Antigua and Barbuda, ctry., N.A.	h15	96a
Antigua International Airport, Antig.	f4	105b
Antiguo Morelos, Mex.	D9	100
Antikýthira, i., Grc.	H6	28
Anti-Lebanon (Sharqī, Al-Jabal ash-), mts., Asia	E7	58
Antilla, Cuba.	B10	102
Antillen, Nederlandse see Netherlands Antilles, dep., N.A.	i14	96a
Antimony, Ut., U.S.	E5	132
Antioch see Hatay, Tur.	B7	58
Antioch, Il., U.S.	F1	112
Antioquia, Col.	D4	86
Antioquia, state, Col.	D4	86
Antipayuta, Russia	C4	34
Antipodes Islands, is., N.Z.	H9	72
Antisana, vol., Ec.	H2	86
Antler, stm., N.A.	E12	124
Antofagasta, Chile.	A2	92
Antofagasta, state, Chile	B3	92
Antofagasta de la Sierra, Arg.	C4	92
Antofalla, Salar de, pl., Arg.	C3	92
Antofalla, Volcán, vol., Arg.	B4	92
Antón, Pan.	H7	102
Anton, Tx., U.S.	H6	128
Anton Chico, N.M., U.S.	F3	128
Antongila, Helodrano, b., Madag.	D8	68
Antonina, Braz.	B13	92
Antonina do Norte, Braz.	D5	88
Antônio Prado, Braz.	D12	92
Antonito, Co., U.S.	D2	128
Antón Lizardo, Punta, c., Mex.	F10	100
Antopal', Bela.	H7	10
Antrim, N. Ire., U.K.	G6	12
Antropovo, Russia	G20	8
Antsalova, Madag.	D7	68
Antsirabe, Madag.	D8	68
Antsirañana, Madag.	C8	68
Antsohihy, Madag.	C8	68
Antulai, Gunong, mtn., Malay.	A10	50
Antun', Russia	G16	34
Antung see Dandong, China.	D5	38
Antwerp see Antwerpen, Bel.	C13	14
Antwerp, Oh., U.S.	C1	114
Antwerpen (Antwerp), Bel.	C13	14
An Uaimh see Navan, Ire.	H6	12
Anugul, India	H10	54
Anūpgarh, India	D4	54
Anūpshahr, India	G5	53
Anvers see Antwerpen, Bel.	C13	14
Anvers Island, i., Ant.	B34	81
Anvik, Ak., U.S.	D7	140
Anxi, China	I8	42
Anxi, China	C4	36
Anxious Bay, b., Austl.	F6	74
Anyang, China	C6	42
Anyang, Kor., S.	F7	38
A'nyêmaqên Shan, mts., China	D4	36
Anyer Kidul, Indon.	G4	50
Anykščiai, Lith.	E7	10
Anyuan, China	I6	42
Anyuanji see Tianzhu, China.	D5	36
Anyue, China	F1	42
Anzá, Col.	C5	42
Anzero-Sudžensk, Russia	C15	32
Anzio, Italy	C6	24
Anzoátegui, state, Ven.	C9	86
Anžu, ostrova, is., Russia	A17	34
Aoba, i., Vanuatu	j16	79d
Aoba-i Madewo, state, Vanuatu	j17	79d
Aoga-shima, i., Japan	G12	40
Aohan Qi, China	C3	38
Aojiang, China	H9	42
Aoji-ri, Kor., N.	C9	38
Ao Luk, Thai.	H4	48
Aomar, Alg.	H14	20
Aomen (Macau), China.	J5	42
Aomori, Japan	D14	38
Aonla, India	D7	54
Aóós (Vjosés), stm., Eur.	D13	24
A'opo, Samoa	g11	79c
Aoraki (Cook, Mount), mtn., N.Z.	F4	80
Aoral, Phnum, mtn., Camb.	F7	48
Aore, i., Vanuatu	j16	79d
Aosta (Aoste), Italy	E4	22
Aoste see Aosta, Italy	E4	22
Aouderas, Niger	F6	64
Aouk, Bahr, stm., Afr.	F3	62
Aoukâr, reg., Maur.	F3	64
Aoya, Japan	D7	40
Aozou, Chad	C3	62
Apache Junction, Az., U.S.	J5	132
Apache Peak, mtn., Az., U.S.	L6	132
Apalachee, stm., Ga., U.S.	C2	116
Apalachee Bay, b., Fl., U.S.	H13	122
Apalachicola, Fl., U.S.	H14	122
Apalachicola, stm., Fl., U.S.	H13	122
Apalachicola Bay, b., Fl., U.S.	H13	122
Apaporis, stm., S.A.	H7	86
Aparados da Serra, Parque Nacional de, p.o.i., Braz.	D12	92
Aparri, Phil.	A3	52
Apatin, Serb.	D3	26
Apatity, Russia	C15	8
Apatzingán de la Constitución, Mex.	F7	100
Apaxtla de Castrejón, Mex.	F8	100
Apeldoorn, Neth.	B15	14
Apennines see Appennino, mts., Italy	G11	6
Apex, N.C., U.S.	I7	114
Api, mtn., Nepal.	D8	54
Apia, Col.	E4	86
Apia, Samoa	g12	79c
Apiacás, Serra dos, plat., Braz.	E6	84
Apiaí, Braz.	B13	92
Apiaú, stm., Braz.	F11	86
Apizaco, Mex.	F9	100
Apo, Mount, mtn., Phil.	G5	52
Apodi, Braz.	C7	88
Apodi, stm., Braz.	C7	88
Apolakkiá, Grc.	G10	28
Apolda, Ger.	E7	16
Apolinario Saravia, Arg.	B6	92
Apopngas, Braz.	D6	90
Apolo, Bol.	B3	90
Aponguao, stm., Ven.	E11	86
Apopka, Lake, l., Fl., U.S.	H4	116
Aporá, Braz.	F6	88
Aporé, Braz.	C6	90
Apóstoles, Arg.	C10	92
Apostle Islands, is., Wi., U.S.	E8	118
Apostle Islands National Lakeshore, p.o.i., Wi., U.S.	D8	118
Apostolove, Ukr.	E4	32
Appalaches, Les see Appalachian Mountains, mts., N.A.	D12	108
Apalachia, Va., U.S.	H3	114
Appalachian Mountains, mts., N.A.	D12	108
Appennino (Apennines), mts., Italy	G11	6
Appennino Calabro, mts., Italy	E10	24
Appennino Abruzzese, mts., Italy	B7	24
Appennino Ligure, mts., Italy	F6	22
Appennino Lucano, mts., Italy	D9	24
Appennino Tosco-Emiliano, mts., Italy.	F8	22
Appennino Umbro-Marchigiano, mts., Italy	G11	6
Appenzell, Switz.	C6	22
Apple Orchard Mountain, mtn., Va., U.S.	G6	114
Appleton, Mn., U.S.	F3	118
Appleton, Wi., U.S.	G10	118
Appleton City, Mo., U.S.	F3	120
Apple Valley, Ca., U.S.	I8	134
Appomattox, Va., U.S.	G7	114
Appomattox, stm., Va., U.S.	G7	114
Aprelevka, Russia	E20	10
Aprilia, Italy	C6	24
Apşeronsk, Russia	F5	32
Apt, Fr.	F11	18
Apucarana, Braz.	A12	92
Apulia see Puglia, state, Italy	C10	24
Apure, state, Ven.	D7	86
Apure, stm., Ven.	D8	86
Apurímac, stm., Peru	F3	84
Apurito, Ven.	D7	86
Aqaba, Gulf of, b.	J5	58
Aqaba see 'Aqaba, Jord.	B5	56
Āqchah, Afg.	B10	56
'Aqīq, Sudan	D7	62
Aqkŏl, Kaz.	F12	32
Aqkŏl, Kaz.	E13	32
Aqmola see Astana, Kaz.	D12	32
Aqsū, Kaz.	D13	32
Aqsū, Kaz.	D12	32
Aqsū, stm., Kaz.	E13	32
Aqsūat, Kaz.	E14	32
Aqsūat, Kaz.	E14	32
Aqtaū, Kaz.	D12	32
Aqtaū, Kaz.	F8	32
Aqtöbe, Kaz.	D9	32
Aquidabá, Braz.	D5	90
Aquidauana, Braz.	D6	90
Aquila, Mex.	F7	100
Aquiles Serdán, Mex.	A6	100
Aquiles Serdán, Mex.	C9	100
Aquin, Haiti	C11	102
Aquio, stm., Col.	F8	86
Ara, India.	F10	54
Ara, stm., Japan	D12	40
Arab, Al., U.S.	C12	122
'Arab, Bahr al-, stm., Sudan	E5	62
'Araba, Wadi ('Arabah, Wādī), stm., Egypt	I3	58
'Arabah, Wādī al- (Ha'Arava), val., Asia	H6	58
Arabako, co., Spain	A8	58
Araban, Tur.	A8	58
Arabian Basin, unds.	H9	142
Arabian Gulf see Persian Gulf, b., Asia	D7	56
Arabian Peninsula, pen., Asia	E6	56
Arabian Sea, s.	G10	36
Aracaju, Braz.	F7	88
Aracataca, Col.	B4	86
Aracati, Braz.	C7	88
Aracena, Spain	G4	20
Aracides, Cape, c., Sol. Is.	e9	79b
Aracoiaba, Braz.	C6	88
Aracruz, Braz.	J5	88
Araçuaí, Braz.	I4	88
Araçuaí, stm., Braz.	I4	88
Araguaia, stm., Braz.	D1	88
Araguaiana, Braz.	G7	84
Araguaína, Braz.	E1	88
Araguao, Caño, stm., Ven.	C11	86
Araguari, Braz.	J1	88
Araguari, stm., Braz.	J1	88
Araguatins, Braz.	C1	88
Arai, Japan.	B11	40
Araioses, Braz.	B4	88
Arāk, Alg.	D5	64
Arāk, Iran.	C6	56
Arak, stm., Alg.	D5	64
Arakan Yoma, mts., Mya.	C1	48
Arakan see Rakhine, state, Mya.	C1	48
Arakkonam, India	E4	53
Araks see Aras, stm., Asia	B6	56
Araks see Araz, stm., Asia	B6	56
Aral, Kaz.	E10	32
Aral Sea, l., Asia	E9	32
Aral'sk see Aral, Kaz.	E10	32
Aramac, Austl.	D5	76
Aramberri, Mex.	C8	100
Arana, Mex.	F9	98
Aranda de Duero, Spain	C7	20
Arandis, Nmb.	C2	70
Arandu, Pak.	A11	54
Aranjuez, Spain	D7	20
Arani, India	E4	53
Aranos, Nmb.	C3	70
Aransas, stm., Tx., U.S.	F10	130
Arantãngi, India	F4	53
Aranyaprathet, Thai.	F6	48
Arao, Japan	G3	40
Araouane, Mali	F4	64
Arapaho, Ok., U.S.	F9	128
Arapahoe, Ne., U.S.	A9	128
Arapey Grande, stm., Ur.	E9	92
Arapiraca, Braz.	E7	88
Arapongas, Braz.	D6	90
Arapoti, Braz.	B12	92
Araquara, Braz.	K1	88
Araras, Braz.	L2	88
Araras, Açude, res., Braz.	C5	88
Ararat, Austl.	K4	76
Ararat, Mount see Ağrı Dağı, mtn., Tur.	B5	56
Arara, Braz.	B3	88
Araripe, Braz.	D5	88
Araripe, Chapada do, plat., Braz.	D6	88
Araripina, Braz.	D5	88
Araripina, stm., Braz.	H10	86
Araruama, Lagoa de, b., Braz.	L4	88
Araruna, Braz.	D8	88
Aras (Araz), stm., Asia	B6	56
Aratuípe, Braz.	G6	88
Arauca, Col.	D6	86
Arauca, state, Col.	D6	86
Arauca, stm., S.A.	D8	86
Araucária, Braz.	B13	92
Arauquita, Col.	D6	86
Araure, Ven.	C7	86
Arāvalli Range, mts., India	C4	54
Arawa, Pap. N. Gui.	d6	79b
Araxá, Braz.	J2	88
Araya, Ven.	B9	86
Araya, Punta de, c., Ven.	B9	86
Araz (Aras), stm., Asia	B6	56
Árba Minch', Eth.	F7	62
Arbatax, Italy	E3	24
Arbil, Iraq.	B5	56
Arboga, Swe.	G6	8
Arboledas, Arg.	H7	92
Arbon, Switz.	C6	22
Arborea, reg., Italy	E2	24
Arborfield, Sk., Can.	A10	124
Arbroath, Scot., U.K.	E10	12
Arbuckle, Ca., U.S.	D3	134
Arc, stm., Fr.	D12	18
Arcachon, Fr.	E4	18
Arcachon, Bassin d', b., Fr.	E4	18
Arcade, Ca., U.S.	E4	134
Arcadia, N.Y., U.S.	B2	120
Arcadia, Fl., U.S.	I4	116
Arcadia, Ks., U.S.	G3	120
Arcadia, La., U.S.	E6	122
Arcadia, Mi., U.S.	D3	112
Arcadia, S.C., U.S.	B3	116
Arcadia, Wi., U.S.	G7	118
Arcadia, reg., Grc.	F4	28
Arcanum, Oh., U.S.	D1	114
Arcas, Cayos, is., Mex.	E12	100
Arcata, Ca., U.S.	C1	134
Arc Dome, mtn., Nv., U.S.	E8	134
Arcelia, Mex.	F8	100
Arcevia, Italy	G9	22
Archangel see Arhangel'sk, Russia.	D19	8
Archbold, Oh., U.S.	C1	114
Archer, Fl., U.S.	G3	116
Archer, stm., Austl.	B8	74
Archer, Mount, mtn., Austl.	D8	76
Archer City, Tx., U.S.	H10	128
Arches National Park, p.o.i., Ut., U.S.	E7	132
Archiac, Fr.	D5	18
Archidona, Spain	G6	20
Arco, Il., U.S.	G13	136
Arcola, Il., U.S.	E9	120
Arcola, Ms., U.S.	D8	122
Arcos, Braz.	K3	88
Arcos de la Frontera, Spain	H5	20
Arcot, India	E4	53
Arcoverde, Braz.	E7	88
Arctic Bay see Tununirusiq, Nu., Can.	A14	106
Arctic Ocean	A21	4
Arctic Red, stm., N.T., Can.	B4	106
Arctic Village, Ak., U.S.	C10	140
Arda, stm., Eur.	H12	26
Ardabīl, Iran	B6	56
Ardahan, Tur.	A5	56
Ardakān, Iran	C7	56
Ardatov, Russia	I20	8
Ardèche, state, Fr.	E10	18
Arden, Ca., U.S.	E4	134
Ardennes, state, Fr.	E13	14
Ardennes, reg., Fr.	D14	14
Ardennes, Canal des, can., Fr.	E13	14
Ardestān, Iran	C7	56
Ardila, stm., Eur.	F3	20
Ardill, Sk., Can.	E8	124
Ardlethan, Austl.	J6	76
Ardmore, Al., U.S.	B12	122
Ardmore, Ok., U.S.	G11	128
Ardmore, S.D., U.S.	D10	114
Ardno, Braz.	K2	88
Åre, Swe.	E5	8
Areado, Braz.	K2	88
Arecibo, P.R.	B2	104a
Arecibo, Observatorio de sci., P.R.	B2	104a
Arecibo Observatory see Arecibo, Observatorio de, sci., P.R.	B2	104a
Arèbąusk, Bela.	F13	10
Areia, Braz.	D8	88
Areia, stm., Braz.	H3	88
Areia Branca, Braz.	C7	88
Arena, Point, c., Ca., U.S.	E2	134
Arena, Punta, c., Mex.	D4	100
Arena de la Ventana, Punta, c., Mex.	C4	100
Arenal, P.R.	C4	104a
Arenápolis, Braz.	F6	84
Arenas, Cayo, i., Mex.	D13	100
Arenas, Mex.	K2	88
Arenas de San Pedro, Spain	D5	20
Arendal, Nor.	G3	8
Arenys de Mar, Spain	C13	20
Arequipa, Peru	G3	84
Arequito, Arg.	F7	92
Arévalo, Spain	C6	20
Arezzo, Italy.	G8	22
Arga, stm., Spain	B9	20
Argadargada, Austl.	D7	74
Argamasilla de Alba, Spain	E7	20
Arganda del Rey, Spain	D7	20
Arga-Sala, stm., Russia	C11	34
Argelès-Gazost, Fr.	F5	18
Argens, stm., Austl.	F11	18
Argenta, Italy	F8	22
Argenteuil, Fr.	F11	14
Argentan, Fr.	F8	14
Argentat, Fr.	D7	18
Argentera, Italy	F4	22
Argentina, ctry., S.A.	G3	90
Argentine Basin, unds.	L10	144
Argentino, Lago, l., Arg.	J2	90
Argenton-sur-Creuse, Fr.	H10	14
Arges, state, Rom.	E11	26
Argeş, stm., Rom.	E13	26
Arghandāb, stm., Afg.	C10	56
Arghastān, stm., Afg.	C10	56
Argolikós Kólpos (Argolis, Gulf of), b., Grc.	F6	28
Argolís, Gulf of see Argolikós Kólpos, b., Grc.	F6	28
Argonia, Ks., U.S.	D11	128
Argonne, Wi., U.S.	F10	118
Argonne, reg., Fr.	E14	14
Argos, Grc.	F5	28
Argos, In., U.S.	G3	112
Argostóli, Grc.	E3	28
Arguello, Point, c., Ca., U.S.	I5	134
Argun' (Ergun), stm., Asia	F12	34
Argungu, Nig.	G5	64
Argyle, Lake, l., Austl.	C5	74
Arhangel'skaja oblast', co., Russia	E20	8
Arhangel'skoe, Russia	G20	10
Arhara, Russia	G15	34
Arhipovo, Russia	C21	8
Århus, Den.	H4	8
Århus, state, Den.	H4	8
Ariake-kai, b., Japan	F3	40
Ariana, Tun.	H4	24
Ariano Irpino, Italy	C9	24
Ariari, stm., Col.	F5	86
Arias, Arg.	F6	92
Ari Atoll, at., Mald.	i12	46a
Arica, Chile	C2	90
Arica, Col.	I6	86
Arichat, N.S., Can.	E16	110
Arichuna, Ven.	D8	86
Arid, Cape, c., Austl.	F4	74
Arida, Japan.	E8	40
Aridaia, Grc.	C5	28
Ariège, state, Fr.	G7	18
Ariège, stm., Fr.	F6	18
Arïguaní, stm., Col.	B5	86
Arīḥā (Jericho), Gaza	G6	58
Arīḥā, Syria.	C7	58
Arikaree, stm., U.S.	B6	128
Arima, Trin.	s12	105f
Arinos, stm., Braz.	F6	84
Arinos, stm., Braz.	F7	84
Ariogala, Lith.	E6	10
Ariporo, stm., Col.	D6	86
Aripuanã, Braz.	E5	84
Aripuanã, stm., Braz.	E5	84
Ariquemes, Braz.	E5	84
Arīsh, Wadi el- ('Arīsh, Wādī al-), stm., Egypt	H4	58
Aristazabal Island, i., B.C., Can.	E5	106
Ariton, Al., U.S.	F13	122
Arivonimamo, Madag.	D8	68
Ariyalūr, India	F4	53
Arīzaro, Salar de, pl., Arg.	B4	92
Arizgoiti, Spain	A8	20
Arizona, Arg.	G5	92
Arizona, state, U.S.	I5	132
Arizpe, Mex.	F7	98
Arjasa, Indon.	G9	50
Arjona, Col.	B4	86
Arjona, Spain	G7	20
Arjonilla, Spain	F7	20
Arka, Russia	D17	34
Arkadelphia, Ar., U.S.	C5	122
Arkalyk see Arqalyq, Kaz.	D11	32
Arkansas, state, U.S.	B6	108
Arkansas, stm., U.S.	D7	122
Arkansas, Salt Fork, stm., U.S.	D12	128
Arkansas City, Ar., U.S.	D7	122
Arkansas City, Ks., U.S.	D11	128
Arkanū, Jabal, mtn., Libya	C4	62
Arkhara see Arhara, Russia	G15	34
Arklow, Ire.	I6	12
Arkoma, Ok., U.S.	B4	122
Arkona, Kap, c., Ger.	B9	16
Arkport, N.Y., U.S.	B8	114
Arktičeskogo Instituta, ostrova, is., Russia	A5	34
Arlanza, stm., Spain	B7	20
Arlanzón, stm., Spain	B7	20
Arles, Fr.	F10	18
Arlington, S. Afr.	E8	70
Arlington, Ga., U.S.	F14	122
Arlington, Ks., U.S.	D10	128
Arlington, Ky., U.S.	H9	120
Arlington, Oh., U.S.	C1	120
Arlington, Or., U.S.	E6	136
Arlington, Tn., U.S.	B10	130
Arlington, Va., U.S.	F8	114
Arlington, Vt., U.S.	G3	110
Arlington, Wa., U.S.	B4	136
Arlington Heights, Il., U.S.	F2	112
Arlit, Niger	F6	64
Arlon, Bel.	E14	14
Arm, stm., Sk., Can.	D8	124
Arma, Ks., U.S.	G3	120
Armada, Mi., U.S.	B3	114
Armadale, Austl.	F3	74
Armageddon see Tel Megiddo, sci., Isr.	F6	58
Armagh, N. Ire., U.K.	G6	12
Armançon, stm., Fr.	G13	14
Armavir, Russia	E6	32
Armavir, Arm.	A5	56
Armenia, Col.	E4	86
Armenia, ctry., Asia	A5	56
Armenia see Armenia, ctry., Asia	A5	56
Armenistís, Fr.	F9	28
Armenia, Mex.	F6	100
Armería, Mex.	F6	100
Armidale, Austl.	H8	76
Armijo, N.M., U.S.	H10	132
Armour, S.D., U.S.	D14	126
Armstrong, Arg.	F7	92
Armstrong, B.C., Can.	F11	138
Armstrong, On., Can.	A9	118
Armstrong, Mo., U.S.	E5	120
Armstrong, Mount, mtn., Yk., Can.	C4	106
Armūr, India	B4	53
Arnaía, Tur.	C11	28
Arnaudville, La., U.S.	G6	122
Arnay-le-Duc, Fr.	G13	14
Arnedo, Spain	B8	20
Arnes, Nor.	F4	8
Arnett, Ok., U.S.	E9	128
Arnhem, Neth.	B14	14
Arnhem, Cape, c., Austl.	B7	74
Arnhem Land, reg., Austl.	B6	74
Arno, stm., Italy	G7	22
Arno, atoll, Marsh. Is.	C7	72
Arnold, Ca., U.S.	E5	134
Arnold, Mn., U.S.	E6	118
Arnold, Mo., U.S.	F7	120
Arnolds Park, Ia., U.S.	H3	118
Arnprior, On., Can.	C13	112
Arnsberg, Ger.	E4	16
Arnstadt, Ger.	F6	16
Aro, stm., Ven.	D9	86
Aroa, Pointe, c., Fr. Poly.	u20	78h
Aroab, Nmb.	E4	70
Aroland, On., Can.	A12	118
Arolsen, Ger.	E5	16
Arona, Pap. N. Gui.	b4	79a
Aroostook, stm., N.A.	D8	110
Arop Island (Long Island), i., Pap. N. Gui.	b4	79a
Arorae, i., Kir.	D8	72
Arosa, Ría de see Arousa, Ría de, est., Spain	B1	20
Arousa, Ría de, est., Spain	B1	20
Arp, Tx., U.S.	E3	122
Arqalyq, Kaz.	D11	32
Arquata Scrivia, Italy	F5	22
Arraga, Arg.	D5	92
Ar-Rahad, Sudan	E6	62
Arraial do Cabo, Braz.	L5	88
Arraias, Braz.	G2	88
Ar-Ramādī, Iraq	C5	56
Ar-Ramthā, Jord.	F7	58
Arran, Island of, i., Scot., U.K.	F7	12
Ar-Rank, Sudan	E6	62
Ar-Raqqah, Syria	B9	58
Ar-Raqqah, state, Syria.	B9	58
Arras, Fr.	D11	14
Ar-Rastan, Syria	D7	58
Arrecifes, Arg.	G7	92
Arrey, N.M., U.S.	K9	132
Ar-Riyāḍ (Riyadh), Sau. Ar.	E6	56
Arroio Grande, Braz.	F11	92
Arrojado, stm., Braz.	G3	88
Arronches, Port.	E3	20
Arros, stm., Fr.	F6	18
Arroux, stm., Fr.	B10	18
Arrowhead, Lake, res., Tx., U.S.	H10	128
Arrowwood, Ab., Can.	F17	138
Arroyito, Arg.	E6	92
Arroyo, P.R.	C3	104a
Arroyo de la Luz, Spain	E4	20
Arroyo Grande, Ca., U.S.	H5	134
Arroyo Hondo, N.M., U.S.	E3	128
Arroyo Seco, Arg.	F7	92
Arroyos y Esteros, Para.	B9	92
Ar-Rub' al-Khālī, des., Asia	E6	56
Ar-Ruqayyah, sci., Syria	F8	58
Ar-Rusāfah, sci., Syria	C9	58
Ar-Ruşayfah, Jord.	F7	58
Ar-Ruṣayriş, Sudan	E6	62
Ar-Ruṭbah, Iraq	C5	56
Arsenev, Russia	B10	38
Arsen'evka, stm., Russia	B10	38
Arsikere, India	E3	53
Arsos, Cyp.	D3	58
Art, Île, i., N. Cal.	I14	79d
Árta, Grc.	D3	28
Artà see Artà, Spain	E14	20
Arteaga, Mex.	F7	100
Artem, Russia	C10	38
Artemisa, Cuba	A6	102
Artëmovsk, Russia	D16	32
Artëmovskij, Russia	C10	38
Artëmovskij, Russia	E12	34
Artesia, Ms., U.S.	D10	122
Artesia, N.M., U.S.	B3	130
Arthabaska, ngh., Qc., Can.	D5	110
Arthal, India.	B6	54
Arthur, On., Can.	E9	112
Arthur, Il., U.S.	E9	120
Arthur, N.D., U.S.	D1	118
Arthur, Tn., U.S.	H2	114
Arthur's Pass National Park, p.o.i., N.Z.	F5	80
Arthur's Town, Bah.	C9	96
Artibonite, stm., Haiti	C11	102
Artigas, Ur.	E9	92
Artillery Lake, l., N.T., Can.	C9	106
Artois, hist. reg., Fr.	D11	14
Artsyz, Ukr.	D16	26
Artyk, Russia.	D18	34
Aru, Kepulauan (Aru Islands), is., Indon.	G10	44
Aru, Tanjung, b., Indon.	E10	50
Arua, Ug.	D6	66
Aruanã, Braz.	F7	84
Aruba, dep., N.A.	F12	102
Aru Islands see Aru, Kepulauan, is., Indon.	G10	44
Arunāchal Pradesh, state, India.	C7	46
Aruppukkottai, India	G4	53
Arurandeua, stm., Braz.	C1	88
Arusha, Tan.	E7	66
Arut, stm., Indon.	E7	50
Aruvi, stm., Sri L.	G4	53
Aruwimi, stm., D.R.C.	D4	66
Arvada, Co., U.S.	B3	128
Arvayheer, Mong.	B5	36
Arvi, India	H7	54
Arviat, Nu., Can.	C12	106
Arvidsjaur, Swe.	D8	8
Arvika, Swe.	G5	8
Arvin, Ca., U.S.	H7	134
Arvon, Mount, mtn., Mi., U.S.	B1	112
Arvorezinha, Braz.	D12	92
Arxan, China.	B8	36
Arys, Kaz.	F11	32
Arys köli, l., Kaz.	E11	32
Arzachena, Italy.	C3	24
Arzamas, Russia	I20	8
Arzgir, Russia	E7	32
Aš Lubnān, for., Leb.	D7	58
Aš, Czech Rep.	F8	16
Arzignano, Italy	E8	22
As, Russia	D9	32
Aša, stm., Ven.	D10	86
Asaba, Nig.	H6	64
Asad, Buhayrat al- (Assad, Lake), res., Syria	B9	58
Aşağıdağ, Afg.	C11	56
Aşağıbostancı, N. Cyp.	C3	58
Asahan, stm., Indon.	B1	50
Asahi, Japan	D13	40
Asahi, Japan	C15	38
Asahi-dake, vol., Japan	C15	38
Asahikawa see Asahikawa, Japan	C15	38
Asama-yama, vol., Japan	C11	40
Asan-man, b., Kor., S.	F7	38
Asansol, India.	G11	54
Asarna, Swe.	E5	8
Asbe, Ven.	q20	104g
Asbestos, Qc., Can.	C10	32
Asbestos Range National Park, p.o.i., Austl.	n13	77a
Asbury Park, N.J., U.S.	D12	114
Ascensión, Mex.	F9	98
Ascension, i., St. Hel.	G4	60
Aschaffenburg, Ger.	G5	16
Aschersleben, Ger.	E7	16
Ascoli Piceno, Italy.	H10	22
Ascoli Satriano, Italy	C9	24
Àscor (Oster), stm., Eur.	G14	10
Aseb, Erit.	E8	62
Åsele, Swe.	D7	8
Åsele, Swe.	D7	8
Asela, Eth.	F7	62
Asendabo, Eth.	F7	62
Asenovgrad, Blg.	G11	26
Aseri, Est.	A9	10
Asgabat, Turkmen.	B8	56
Asgārdr, Jabal al-, hills, Jord.	F6	58
Ashburton, N.Z.	F4	80
Ashburton, stm., Austl.	D3	74
Ashchysay, Kaz.	F11	32
Ashcroft, B.C., Can.	F9	138
Ashdod, Isr.	G5	58
Ashdown, Ar., U.S.	D4	122
Asheboro, N.C., U.S.	I6	114
Ashern, Mb., Can.	C16	124
Asheville, N.C., U.S.	I3	114
Ash Flat, Ar., U.S.	H6	120
Ashford, Eng., U.K.	J13	12
Ashford, Al., U.S.	F13	122
Ash Fork, Az., U.S.	H4	132
Ash Grove, Mo., U.S.	G4	120
Ashibe, Japan.	F2	40

Ashikaga – Baku I • 5

Name | Map Ref. | Page

Ashikaga, Japan C12 40
Ashington, Eng., U.K. F11 12
Ashio, Japan C12 40
Ashizuri-misaki, c., Japan G6 40
Ashland, Al., U.S. D13 122
Ashland, Il., U.S. E7 120
Ashland, Ks., U.S. D9 128
Ashland, Ky., U.S. F3 114
Ashland, Mo., U.S. F5 120
Ashland, Mt., U.S. B6 126
Ashland, Ne., U.S. C1 120
Ashland, N.H., U.S. G5 110
Ashland, Oh., U.S. D3 114
Ashland, Or., U.S. A3 134
Ashland, Va., U.S. G8 114
Ashland, Wi., U.S. E7 118
Ashland, Mount, mtn., Or., U.S. A3 134
Ashley, Austl. G7 76
Ashley, Il., U.S. F8 120
Ashley, Mi., U.S. E5 112
Ashley, Oh., U.S. D3 114
Ashmore, Il., U.S. E9 120
Ashmore Islands, is., Austl. B4 74
Ashoknagar, India F6 54
Ashqelon, Isr. G5 58
Ash-Shamāl, state, Leb. D7 58
Ash-Shaqrā' see Shaqrā', Sau. Ar. D6 56
Ash-Shāriqah, U.A.E. D8 56
Ash-Shawbak, Jord. H6 58
Ash-Shiḥr, Yemen G6 56
Ash-Shurayf, Sau. Ar. D4 56
Ashta, India C2 53
Ashta, India G6 54
Ashtabula, Oh., U.S. C5 114
Ashtabula, Lake, res., N.D., U.S. G16 124
Ashton, S. Afr. H5 70
Ashton, St. Vin. p11 105e
Ashton, Id., U.S. F15 136
Ashton, Il., U.S. C8 120
Ashton, Ne., U.S. F14 126
Ashuanipi Lake, l., Nf., Can. E17 106
Ashuapmushuan, stm., Qc., Can. B3 110
Ashûm, Egypt H1 58
Ashville, Al., U.S. D12 122
Ashwaubenon, Wi., U.S. D1 112
Asi see Orontes, stm., Asia B7 58
Asia, cont. C19 4
Asia, Kepulauan, is., Indon. E9 44
Asia Minor, hist. reg., Tur. E13 28
Āsika, India I10 54
Asinara, Golfo dell', b., Italy D2 24
Asinara, Isola, i., Italy C2 24
Asíni, sci., Grc. F5 28
Asino, Russia C15 32
Asintorf, Bela. F13 10
Asipovičy, Bela. G11 10
'Asīr, reg., Sau. Ar. F5 56
Askham, S. Afr. E5 70
Askiz, Russia D16 32
Askja, vol., Ice. k31 8a
Aslanapa, Tur. D12 28
Aslantaş Barajı, res., Tur. A7 58
Asmara see Asmera, Erit. D7 62
Asmera, Erit. D7 62
Ašmjany, Bela. F8 10
Asola, Italy E7 22
Asomante, P.R. B2 104a
Āsosa, Eth. E6 62
Asoteriba, Jabal, mtn., Sudan C7 62
Asotin, Wa., U.S. D9 136
Asouf, Oued, stm., Alg. D5 64
Asp, Spain F10 20
Aspe see Asp, Spain F10 20
Aspen, Co., U.S. D10 132
Aspendos, sci., Tur. G14 28
Aspermont, Tx., U.S. A7 130
Aspiring, Mount, mtn., N.Z. G3 80
Assad, Lake see Asad, Buḥayrat al-, res., Syria B9 58
As-Safīrah, Syria B8 58
Aş-Şāfiyah, Sudan D6 62
As-Salṭ, Jord. F6 58
Assam, state, India C7 46
As-Samāwah, Iraq C6 56
Aş-Şanamayn, Syria E7 58
Aş-Şarafand, Leb. E6 58
Assaré, Braz. D6 88
Assateague Island, i., U.S. F10 114
Assateague Island National Seashore, p.o.i., U.S. G10 114
Assemini, Italy E2 24
Assen, Neth. A15 14
Asseria, sci., Cro. F12 22
Assiniboia, Sk., Can. E8 124
Assiniboine, stm., Can. E16 124
Assiniboine, Mount, mtn., Can. F15 138
Assis, Braz. D6 90
Assis Chateaubriand, Braz. B11 92
Assisi, Italy G9 22
Assomption, i., Sey. k11 69b
Assu, Braz. C7 88
As-Sudd, reg., Sudan F6 62
As-Sufāl, Yemen G6 56
As-Sulaymānīyah, Iraq B6 56
As-Sulaymānīyah, Sau. Ar. E6 56
As-Sulayyil, Sau. Ar. E6 56
Assumption, Il., U.S. E8 120
As-Suwaydā', Syria F7 58
As-Suwaydā', state, Syria F7 58
Astakós, Grc. E3 28
Astana (Aqmola), Kaz. D12 32
Astara, Azer. B6 56
Asti, Italy F5 22
Astica, Arg. E4 92
Astola Island, i., Pak. D9 56
Astorga, Spain B4 20
Astoria, Il., U.S. D7 120
Astoria, Or., U.S. D3 136
Astove, i., Sey. I11 69b
Astrahan', Russia E7 32
Astrakhan see Astrahan', Russia E7 32
Astrašycki Haradok, Bela. F10 10
Astrolabe, Cape, c., Sol. Is. e9 79b
Astrolabe, Récifs de l', rf., N. Cal. I15 79d
Astrolabe Reefs see Astrolabe, Récifs de l', rf., N. Cal. I15 79d
Astrouna, Bela. E12 10
Astudillo, Spain B6 20
Asturias, state, Spain A5 20
Astypálaia, i., Grc. G9 28
Asunción, Para. B9 92
Asunción, Bahía la, b., Mex. B1 100
Asunción Nochixtlán, Mex. G10 100
Åsunden, l., Swe. H5 8
Asveja, Bela. E11 10
Asvejskae, vozero, l., Bela. D10 10
Aswân, Egypt C6 62
Aswan High Dam see Aali, Sadd el-, dam, Egypt C6 62
Asyût, Egypt K2 58
Asyûti, Wadi el- (Asyūṭī, Wādī al-), stm., Egypt K2 58
'Ata, i., Tonga F9 72
Atabapo, stm., S.A. F8 86
Atacama, state, Chile C3 92
Atacama, Desierto de, des., Chile E2 90
Atacama, Puna de, plat., S.A. B4 92
Atacama, Salar de, pl., Chile D3 90
Atacama Desert see Atacama, Desierto de, des., Chile B3 92
Ataco, Col. F4 86
Atagaj, Russia C17 32
Atakpamé, Togo H5 64
Atalaia, Braz. E7 88
Atambua, Indon. G7 44
Atami, Japan D12 40
Atangmik, Grnld. E15 141
Aṭar, Maur. E2 64
Atascadero, Ca., U.S. H5 134
Atascosa, stm., Tx., U.S. F9 130
Atasū, Kaz. E12 32
Atata, i., Tonga n14 78e
Atatürk Barajı, res., Tur. A9 58
Atauro, Pulau, i., E. Timor G8 44
'Aṭbarah, Sudan D6 62
'Aṭbarah, stm., Afr. D7 62
Atbasar, Kaz. D11 32
Atchafalaya, stm., La., U.S. G7 122
Atchafalaya Bay, b., La., U.S. H7 122
Atchison, Ks., U.S. E2 120
Ateca, Spain C9 20
Aterno, stm., Italy H10 22
Atfîh, Egypt I2 58
Ath, Bel. D12 14
Athabasca, Ab., Can. B17 138
Athabasca, stm., Ab., Can. D8 106
Athabasca, Lake, l., Can. D9 106
Athalmer, B.C., Can. F14 138
Athboy, Ire. H6 12
Athena, Or., U.S. E8 136
Athens, On., Can. D14 112
Athens see Athína, Grc. E6 28
Athens, Al., U.S. C11 122
Athens, Ga., U.S. C2 116
Athens, Il., U.S. E8 120
Athens, La., U.S. E5 122
Athens, Mi., U.S. F4 112
Athens, Oh., U.S. E3 114
Athens, Pa., U.S. C9 114
Athens, Tn., U.S. B14 122
Athens, Tx., U.S. E3 122
Athens, W.V., U.S. G5 114
Atherton, Austl. A5 76
Athi, stm., Kenya E7 66
Athiaínou, Cyp. C4 58
Athína (Athens), Grc. E6 28
Athlone, Ire. H4 12
Athni, India C2 53
Athok, Mya. D2 48
Athol, Ma., U.S. B13 114
Áthos, mtn., Grc. C7 28
Athos, Mount see Áthos, mtn., Grc. C7 28
Ati, Chad E3 62
Atiak, Ug. D6 66
Atico, Peru G3 84
Atienza, Spain C8 20
Atikokan, On., Can. C7 118
Atirāmpattinam, India F4 53
Atiu, i., Cook Is. F11 72
Atka, Russia D19 34
Atka Island, i., Ak., U.S. g24 140a
Atkarsk, Russia D6 32
Atkins, Ar., U.S. B6 122
Atkinson, Il., U.S. C8 120
Atkinson, N.C., U.S. B7 116
Atlanta, Ga., U.S. C1 116
Atlanta, Il., U.S. D8 120
Atlanta, Mi., U.S. C5 112
Atlanta, Mo., U.S. E5 120
Atlantic, Ia., U.S. C2 120
Atlantic, N.C., U.S. B9 116
Atlantic Beach, Fl., U.S. F4 116
Atlantic City, N.J., U.S. E11 114
Atlantic-Indian Basin, unds. O5 142
Atlantic-Indian Ridge, unds. N15 144
Atlántico, state, Col. B4 86
Atlantic Ocean E9 144
Atlantic Peak, mtn., Wy., U.S. E3 126
Atlas Mountains, mts., Afr. C4 64
Atlasova, ostrov, i., Russia F20 34
Atlas Saharien, mts., Alg. C4 64
Atlin, B.C., Can. D4 106
Atlin Lake, l., Can. D4 106
'Atlit, Isr. F5 58
Ātmakūr, India D4 53
Atmore, Al., U.S. F11 122
Atnarko, stm., B.C., Can. D5 138
Atocha, Bol. D3 90
Atoka, Ok., U.S. C2 122
Atotonilco, Cerro, mtn., Mex. H3 130
Atoyac, stm., Mex. F9 100
Atoyac de Álvarez, Mex. G8 100
Atrak (Atrek), stm., Asia B7 56
Ätran, stm., Swe. H5 8
Atrato, stm., Col. D3 86
Atrauli, India D7 54
Atrek (Atrak), stm., Asia B7 56
Atri, Italy H10 22
Atsumi, Japan E10 40
Atsumi-hantō, pen., Japan E10 40
Aṭ-Ṭafīlah, Jord. H6 58
Aṭ-Ṭafīlah, state, Jord. H6 58
Aṭ-Ṭā'if, Sau. Ar. E5 56
At-Tall, Syria E7 58
Attalla, Al., U.S. C12 122
Attapu, Laos E8 48
Attawapiskat, On., Can. E14 106
Attawapiskat, stm., On., Can. E13 106
Attawapiskat Lake, l., On., Can. E13 106
Aṭ-Ṭawīl, mts., Sau. Ar. D4 56
Aṭ-Ṭayyibah, Syria C9 58
Attendorn, Ger. E3 16
Attersee, l., Aus. C10 22
Attica, In., U.S. H2 112
Attica, Ks., U.S. D10 128
Attica, N.Y., U.S. B7 114
Attica see Attikí, hist. reg., Grc. E6 28
Attikí, state, Grc. F6 28
Attikí, hist. reg., Grc. E6 28
Attleboro, Ma., U.S. C14 114
Attock, Pak. B4 54
Attu, Ak., U.S. g21 140a
Attu Island, i., Ak., U.S. g21 140a
Āttūr, India F4 53
Aṭ-Ṭuwayshah, Sudan E5 62
Atuel, stm., Arg. G3 92
Atuel, Bañados del, sw., Arg. H4 92
Atuntaqui, Ec. G2 86
Atuona, Fr. Poly. s18 78g
Atwater, Ca., U.S. F5 134
Atwater, Mn., U.S. F4 118
Atwood, Il., U.S. E9 120
Atwood, Ks., U.S. B7 128
Atwood, Tn., U.S. I9 120
Atyraū, Kaz. E8 32
Aua Island, i., Pap. N. Gui. a3 79a
Auari, stm., Braz. F9 86
Auau Channel, strt., Hi., U.S. c5 78a
Aubagne, Fr. F11 18
Aube, state, Fr. F13 14
Aube, stm., Fr. F13 14
Aubigny-sur-Nère, Fr. G11 14
Aubinadong, stm., On., Can. A6 112
Aubrey Cliffs, clf., Az., U.S. H3 132
Aubrey Lake, res., On., Can. A6 112
Aubry Lake, l., N.T., Can. B5 106
Auburn, Al., U.S. E13 122
Auburn, Ca., U.S. E4 134
Auburn, Il., U.S. E8 120
Auburn, In., U.S. G4 112
Auburn, Ky., U.S. H11 120
Auburn, Ma., U.S. B14 114
Auburn, Me., U.S. F6 110
Auburn, Mi., U.S. E5 112
Auburn, N.Y., U.S. B9 114
Auburn, Wa., U.S. C4 136
Auburn, stm., Austl. E8 76
Aubusson, Fr. D8 18
Auca Mahuida, Cerro, mtn., Arg. H3 92
Auce, Lat. D5 10
Auch, Fr. F6 18
Auchi, Nig. H6 64
Aucilla, stm., U.S. F2 116
Auckland, N.Z. C6 80
Auckland Islands, is., N.Z. I7 72
Aude, state, Fr. F8 18
Aude, stm., Fr. F9 18
Auden, On., Can. A11 118
Audenarde see Oudenaarde, Bel. D12 14
Audierne, Fr. F4 14
Audincourt, Fr. G15 14
Audubon Lake, res., N.D., U.S. G12 124
Aue, Ger. F8 16
Augathella, Austl. E6 76
Augrabies Falls National Park, p.o.i., S. Afr. F4 70
Augrabiesvalle, wtfl., S. Afr. F5 70
Augsburg, Ger. H6 16
Augusta, Austl. F2 74
Augusta, Italy G9 24
Augusta, Ar., U.S. B7 122
Augusta, Ga., U.S. C3 116
Augusta, Il., U.S. D6 120
Augusta, Ky., U.S. F1 114
Augusta, Me., U.S. F7 110
Augusta, Mt., U.S. C14 136
Augusta, Wi., U.S. G7 118
Augusto Severo, Braz. C7 88
Augustów, Pol. C18 16
Augustowski, Kanał, can., Eur. C19 16
Augustus, Mount, mtn., Austl. D3 74
Auki, Sol. Is. e9 79b
Aukstaitijos nacionalnis parkas, p.o.i., Lith. E8 10
Aulander, N.C., U.S. H8 114
Auld, Lake, l., Austl. D4 74
Aulla, Italy F6 22
Aulne, stm., Fr. F5 14
Aulneau Peninsula, pen., On., Can. B4 118
Aumale, Fr. E10 14
Auna, Nig. G5 64
Auob, stm., Afr. E5 70
Auraiya, India E7 54
Aurangābād, India B2 53
Aurangābād, India F10 54
Aure, Nor. E3 8
Aurelia, Ia., U.S. B2 120
Aurich, Ger. C3 16
Aurilândia, Braz. G7 84
Aurillac, Fr. E8 18
Aurine, Alpi (Zillertaler Alpen), mts., Eur. C8 22
Aurora, On., Can. D10 112
Aurora, Co., U.S. B4 128
Aurora, Il., U.S. C9 120
Aurora, In., U.S. E13 120
Aurora, Me., U.S. F8 110
Aurora, Mn., U.S. D6 118
Aurora, N.C., U.S. A9 116
Aurora, N.Y., U.S. B9 114
Aurora, Oh., U.S. C4 114
Aurora, Ut., U.S. E4 132
Aurora, W.V., U.S. E6 114
Aurora do Norte, Braz. G2 88
Aursunden, l., Nor. E4 8
Aurukun, Austl. B8 74
Aus, Nmb. E3 70
Ausable, stm., On., Can. E8 112
Au Sable, stm., Mi., U.S. D6 112
Au Sable Forks, N.Y., U.S. F3 110
Au Sable Point, c., Mi., U.S. D6 112
Auschwitz see Oświęcim, Pol. F15 16
Aust-Agder, state, Nor. G3 8
Austin, In., U.S. F12 120
Austin, Mn., U.S. H6 118
Austin, Nv., U.S. D8 134
Austin, Pa., U.S. C7 114
Austin, Tx., U.S. D10 130
Austin, Lake, l., Austl. E3 74
Australes, Îles, is., Fr. Poly. F11 72
Australia, ctry., Oc. D5 74
Australian Capital Territory, state, Austl. J7 76
Austral Islands see Australes, Îles, is., Fr. Poly. F11 72
Austral Seamounts, unds. L24 142
Austria, ctry., Eur. C11 22
Austvågøya, i., Nor. B6 8
Ausuittuq (Grise Fiord), Nu., Can. B9 141
Autlán de Navarro, Mex. F6 100
Autun, Fr. H13 14
Auvergne, hist. reg., Fr. D8 18
Auxerre, Fr. G12 14
Auxier, Ky., U.S. G3 114
Auxi-le-Château, Fr. D11 14
Auxvasse, Mo., U.S. E6 120
Auyán Tepuy, mtn., Ven. E10 86
Auzances, Fr. C8 18
Auzangate, Nevado, mtn., Peru F3 84
Ava, Mo., U.S. H5 120
Avaí, Braz. L1 88
Avala, hist., Serb. E7 26
Avallon, Fr. G12 14
Avalon, Ca., U.S. J7 134
Ávalos, Mex. A5 100
Avanersuaq see Nordgrønland, state, Grnld. B14 141
Avant, Ok., U.S. H1 120
Avaré, Braz. L1 88
Avarua, Cook Is. a26 78j
Avarua Harbour, b., Cook Is. a26 78j
Avatiu Harbour, b., Cook Is. a26 78j
'Avedat, Ḥorvot, sci., Isr. H5 58
Aveiro, Port. D2 20
Aveiro, state, Port. D2 20
Aveiro, Ria de, mth., Port. D1 20
Avellaneda, Arg. G8 92
Avellaneda, Arg. D8 92
Avellino, Italy D8 24
Averøya, i., Nor. E2 8
Aversa, Italy D8 24
Avery, Id., U.S. C11 136
Avery, Tx., U.S. D4 122
Avery Island, La., U.S. H6 122
Aves, Islas de, is., Ven. B8 86
Avesnes-sur-Helpe, Fr. D12 14
Avesta, Swe. F6 8
Aveyron, state, Fr. E8 18
Aveyron, stm., Fr. E7 18
Avezzano, Italy H10 22
Avigliano, Italy D9 24
Avignon, Fr. F10 18
Ávila, Spain D6 20
Ávila, co., Spain D6 20
Ávila, Sierra de, mts., Spain D5 20
Avilés, Spain A4 20
Aviño, Spain A2 20
Avinurme, Est. B9 10
Avispa, Cerro, mtn., Ven. G9 86
Avoca, Austl. K4 76
Avoca, Ia., U.S. C2 120
Avoca, N.Y., U.S. B8 114
Avoca, stm., Austl. K4 76
Avola, B.C., Can. E11 138
Avola, Italy H9 24
Avon, Il., U.S. D7 120
Avon, Mn., U.S. F4 118
Avon, N.C., U.S. A10 116
Avon, N.Y., U.S. B8 114
Avon, stm., Eng., U.K. I11 12
Avon, stm., Eng., U.K. K11 12
Avon, stm., Eng., U.K. J10 12
Avondale, Az., U.S. J4 132
Avondale, Co., U.S. C4 128
Avon Downs, Austl. D7 74
Avon Park, Fl., U.S. I4 116
Avontuur, S. Afr. H6 70
Avranches, Fr. F7 14
Awaaso, Ghana H4 64
Awaji, Japan E8 40
Awaji-shima, i., Japan E7 40
Awara, Japan C9 40
Āwarē, Eth. F8 62
Āwasa, Eth. F7 62
Āwash, Eth. F8 62
Āwash, stm., Eth. E8 62
Awa-shima, i., Japan A12 40
Awbārī, Libya B2 62
Awbārī, Ṣaḥrā', reg., Libya B2 62
Awe, Loch, l., Scot., U.K. E7 12
Awegyun, Mya. F4 48
Awjilah, Libya B4 62
Awled Djellal, Alg. C6 64
Awlef, Alg. D5 64
Awul, Pap. N. Gui. b5 79a
Axel Heiberg Island, i., Nu., Can. A7 141
Axim, Ghana I4 64
Axiós (Vardar), stm., Eur. C5 28
Axis, Al., U.S. G10 122
Axixá, Braz. B3 88
Axtell, Ks., U.S. L2 118
Axtell, Ne., U.S. G13 126
Ayabe, Japan D8 40
Ayacucho, Arg. H8 92
Ayacucho, Peru F3 84
Ayakkum Hu, l., China D2 36
Ayaköz, Kaz. E13 32
Ayaköz, stm., Kaz. E13 32
Ayam, C. Iv. H4 64
Ayamonte, Spain G3 20
Ayapel, Col. C4 86
Ayaş, Tur. C15 28
Ayaviri, Peru F3 84
Aydın, Tur. F10 28
Aydın, state, Tur. F11 28
Aydınkent, Tur. F14 28
Ayer, Ma., U.S. B14 114
Ayers Rock see Uluru, mtn., Austl. E6 74
Ayeyarwady, state, Mya. D2 48
Ayeyarwady (Irrawaddy), stm., Mya. E8 46
Ayeyarwady, Mouths of the, mth., Mya. E7 46
Aylesbury, Eng., U.K. J12 12
Aylmer, On., Can. F8 112
Aylmer, Qc., Can. C14 112
Aylmer Lake, l., N.T., Can. C9 106
Aylsham, Sk., Can. A10 124
'Ayn Dār, Sau. Ar. D6 56
Aynor, S.C., U.S. B6 116
'Aynūnah, Sau. Ar. J6 58
Ayon Island see Aën, ostrov, i., Russia B22 34
Ayora see Aiora, Spain E9 20
Ayorou, Niger G5 64
'Ayoûn el 'Atroûs, Maur. F3 64
Ayr, Austl. B6 76
Ayr, Scot., U.K. F8 12
Ayrancı, Tur. A4 58
Ayre, Point of, c., I. of Man G8 12
Āysha, Eth. E8 62
Aytos see Ajtos, Blg. G14 26
Ayutla, Mex. E6 100
Ayutla de los Libres, Mex. G9 100
Ayvacık, Tur. D9 28
Ayvalık, Tur. D9 28
Azaila, Spain C10 20
Āzamgarh, India E9 54
Azángaro, Peru F3 84
Azaouâd, reg., Mali F4 64
Azare, Nig. G6 64
Azaryčy, Bela. H12 10
A'zāz, Syria B8 58
Azdavay, Tur. B16 28
Azeffâl, sand, Afr. E2 64
Azerbaijan, ctry., Asia A6 56
Azëry, Bela. G7 10
Āzezo, Eth. E7 62
Azhikode, India F2 53
Azilal, Mor. C3 64
Azogues, Ec. I2 86
Azores see Açores, is., Port. C3 60
Azores Plateau, unds. E10 144
Azov, Russia E5 32
Azov, Sea of, s., Eur. E5 32
Azovskoje more see Azov, Sea of, s., Eur. E5 32
Azraq, Al-Baḥr al- see Blue Nile, stm., Afr. E6 62
Aztec, N.M., U.S. G9 132
Aztec Peak, mtn., Az., U.S. J5 132
Aztec Ruins National Monument, p.o.i., N.M., U.S. G8 132
Azua, Dom. Rep. C12 102
Azuaga, Spain F5 20
Azuay, state, Ec. I2 86
Azuer, stm., Spain F7 20
Azuero, Península de, pen., Pan. D1 86
Azufre, Volcán, vol., S.A. B3 92
Azuga, Rom. D12 26
Azul, Arg. H8 92
Azur, Côte d', cst., Fr. F13 18
Azurduy, Bol. C4 90
Azure Lake, l., B.C., Can. D10 138
Aẓ-Ẓahrān, Sau. Ar. D6 56
Az-Zarqā', Jord. F7 58
Az-Zarqā', state, Jord. G8 58
Az-Zāwiyah, Libya A2 62
Azzel Matti, Sebkha, pl., Alg. D5 64

B

Ba, Fiji p18 79e
Ba, stm., China F6 42
Ba, stm., China F2 42
Ba, stm., Viet. F9 48
Baa, Indon. H7 44
Baaba, Île, i., N. Cal. I14 79d
Baao, Phil. D4 52
Baardheere, Som. D8 66
Baba Burnu, c., Tur. D9 28
Babadağ, Tur. F11 28
Babaeski, Tur. B10 28
Babaevo, Russia A18 10
Babahoyo, Ec. H2 86
Babak, Phil. G5 52
Babanango, S. Afr. F10 70
Babanūsah, Sudan E5 62
Babar, Kepulauan, is., Indon. G8 44
Babbitt, Mn., U.S. D7 118
Babbitt, Nv., U.S. E7 134
B'abdā, Leb. E6 58
Babeldaob, i., Palau g7 78b
Bab el Mandeb see Mandeb, Bab el, strt. E8 62
Babia, Arroyo de la, stm., Mex. F5 130
Babian, stm., China A5 48
Babičy, Bela. H12 10
Babīna, India F7 54
Babinda, Austl. A5 76
Babine, stm., B.C., Can. D5 106
Babine Lake, l., B.C., Can. B5 138
Babine Range, mts., B.C., Can. B4 138
Babino, Russia A14 10
Babiogórski Park Narodowy, p.o.i., Pol. G15 16
Babo, Indon. F9 44
Bābol, Iran B7 56
Baboquivari Peak, mtn., Az., U.S. L5 132
Baborów, Pol. F13 16
Babrujsk, Bela. G12 10
Babuškin, Russia F10 34
Babuyan Channel, strt., Phil. A3 52
Babuyan Island, i., Phil. A4 52
Babuyan Islands, is., Phil. A3 52
Bacabal, Braz. C3 88
Bacadéhuachi, Mex. G8 98
Bacatuba, Braz. C4 88
Bacău, Rom. C13 26
Bacău, state, Rom. C13 26
Bac Binh, Viet. G9 48
Baccarat, Fr. F15 14
Bačèjkava, Bela. F12 10
Bac Giang, Viet. B8 48
Bachaquero, Ven. B6 86
Bachiniva, Mex. A5 100
Bach Ma, Viet. D8 48
Bach Thong, Viet. A7 48
Bachu, China B12 56
Back, stm., Nu., Can. B11 106
Bačka, reg., Eur. E16 22
Bačka Palanka, Serb. D6 26
Bačka Topola, Serb. D6 26
Back Creek, stm., Va., U.S. F6 114
Backnang, Ger. H5 16
Backstairs Passage, strt., Austl. J1 76
Bac Lieu, Viet. H7 48
Bac Ninh, Viet. B8 48
Baco, Mount, mtn., Phil. D3 52
Bacoachi, Mex. F8 98
Bacolod, Phil. E4 52
Baconton, Ga., U.S. E1 116
Bacoor, Phil. C3 52
Bac Phan, hist. reg., Viet. A7 48
Bács-Kiskun, state, Hung. C6 26
Bâcu, stm., Mol. C15 26
Bacuri, Lago do, l., Braz. B4 88
Bād, Iran C7 56
Bad, stm., Mi., U.S. E5 112
Bad, stm., S.D., U.S. C12 126
Badagara, India F2 53
Badajós, Lago, l., Braz. D5 84
Badajoz, Spain F4 20
Badajoz, co., Spain F4 20
Badalona, Spain C13 20
Bādāmi, India D2 53
Badanah, Sau. Ar. C5 56
Badarīnāth, India C7 54
Badas, Bru. A9 50
Badas, Kepulauan, is., Indon. C5 50
Bad Axe, Mi., U.S. E7 112
Bad Bergzabern, Ger. G3 16
Bad Bevensen, Ger. C6 16
Bad Bramstedt, Ger. C5 16
Baddeck, N.S., Can. D16 110
Bad Doberan, Ger. B7 16
Bad Dürrenberg, Ger. E8 16
Bad Ems, Ger. F3 16
Baden, Switz. C5 22
Baden-Baden, Ger. H4 16
Badenoch, hist. reg., Scot., U.K. E8 12
Badenweiler, Ger. I3 16
Baden-Württemberg, state, Ger. H4 16
Bad Freienwalde, Ger. D9 16
Badgastein, Aus. C10 22
Badger, Mn., U.S. C3 118
Bad Hall, Aus. B11 22
Bad Harzburg, Ger. E6 16
Bad Hersfeld, Ger. F5 16
Bad Homburg vor der Höhe, Ger. F4 16
Bad Honnef, Ger. F3 16
Badin Lake, res., N.C., U.S. A5 116
Bad Ischl, Aus. C10 22
Bad Kissingen, Ger. F6 16
Bad Kreuznach, Ger. G3 16
Badlands, hills, S.D., U.S. D10 126
Badlands, hills, U.S. A9 126
Badlands National Park, p.o.i., S.D., U.S. D10 126
Bad Langensalza, Ger. E6 16
Bad Lauterberg im Harz, Ger. E6 16
Bad Mergentheim, Ger. G5 16
Bad Muskau, Ger. E10 16
Bad Nauheim, Ger. F4 16
Badnera, India H6 54
Bad Neustadt an der Saale, Ger. F6 16
Bad Oeynhausen, Ger. D4 16
Bad Oldesloe, Ger. C6 16
Badong, China F4 42
Bad Orb, Ger. F5 16
Bad Pyrmont, Ger. E5 16
Bad Reichenhall, Ger. I8 16
Bad Salzuflen, Ger. D4 16
Bad Salzungen, Ger. F6 16
Bad Schwalbach, Ger. F3 16
Bad Schwartau, Ger. C6 16
Bad Segeberg, Ger. C6 16
Bādshāhpur, India F9 54
Bad Tölz, Ger. I7 16
Badulla, Sri L. H5 53
Badvel, India D4 53
Bad Vöslau, Aus. C13 22
Bad Waldsee, Ger. I5 16
Bad Wildungen, Ger. E4 16
Bad Wörishofen, Ger. I6 16
Badžalskij hrebet, mts., Russia F15 34
Baena, Spain G6 20
Baependi, Braz. K3 88
Baer, Russia C17 32
Baeza, Spain G7 20
Baezaeko, stm., B.C., Can. D7 138
Bafang, Cam. C1 66
Bafatá, Gui.-B. G2 64
Baffin Basin, unds. A7 144
Baffin Bay, b., N.A. C12 141
Baffin Bay, b., Tx., U.S. G10 130
Baffin Island, i., Nu., Can. B16 106
Bafia, Cam. D2 66
Bafing, stm., Afr. G2 64
Bafoulabé, Mali G2 64
Bafoussam, Cam. C2 66
Bafra, Tur. A4 56
Bāft, Iran D8 56
Bafwaboli, D.R.C. D5 66
Bafwasende, D.R.C. D5 66
Bagaces, C.R. G5 102
Bagagem, stm., Braz. H1 88
Bagaha, India E9 54
Bāgalkot, India C2 53
Bagamoyo, Tan. F7 66
Bagan Datuk, Malay. K5 48
Baganga, Phil. G6 52
Bagansiapiapi, Indon. B2 50
Bagasra, India H3 54
Bagdad, Az., U.S. I3 132
Bagdad, Fl., U.S. G11 122
Bagdarin, Russia F11 34
Bagé, Braz. E10 92
Bagenkop, Den. B6 16
Bāgerhāt, Bngl. G12 54
Bāgevādi, India C2 53
Baghdād, Iraq C5 56
Bagheria, Italy F7 24
Baghlān, Afg. B10 56
Bagley, Mn., U.S. D3 118
Bagnères-de-Luchon, Fr. G6 18
Bagni di Lucca, Italy F7 22
Bagnols-sur-Cèze, Fr. E10 18
Bago (Pegu), Mya. D3 48
Bago, state, Mya. C2 48
Bagodar, India F10 54
Bagoé, stm., Afr. G3 64
Bağpınar, Tur. A9 58
Baguio, Phil. B3 52
Bāh, India E7 54
Bahādurgarh, India D6 54
Bahama, Canal Viejo de, strt., N.A. A8 102
Bahamas, ctry., N.A. C9 96
Baharampur, India F11 54
Bahau, Malay. K6 48
Bahau, stm., Indon. B9 50
Bahāwalnagar, Pak. C4 54
Bahāwalpur, Pak. D3 54
Bahçe, Tur. A7 58
Baheri, India D7 54
Bahi, Phil. D4 52
Bahia see Salvador, Braz. G6 88
Bahia, state, Braz. G4 88
Bahía, Islas de la, is., Hond. D4 102
Bahía Blanca, Arg. I6 92
Bahía Bustamante, Arg. I3 90
Bahía de Caráquez, Ec. H1 86
Bahía Kino, Mex. A3 100
Bahir Dar, Eth. E7 62
Bahraich, India E8 54
Bahrain, ctry., Asia D7 56
Bahta, Russia B15 32
Bahtîm, Egypt H2 58
Bahušèusk, Bela. F13 10
Bai, stm., China A7 42
Bai, stm., China E5 42
Baia de Aramă, Rom. E9 26
Baia di Terra Nova, sci., Ant. C21 81
Baía Farta, Ang. C1 68
Baia Mare, Rom. B10 26
Baião, Braz. B1 88
Baicheng, China F14 32
Baicheng, China B9 36
Baidoa see Baydhabo, Som. D8 66
Baie-Comeau, Qc., Can. A8 110
Baiersbronn, Ger. H4 16
Baie-Saint-Paul, Qc., Can. C6 110
Baie-Trinité, Qc., Can. A9 110
Baie Verte, Nf., Can. j22 107a
Baihe, China B11 46
Baijnāth, India D7 54
Baikal, Lake see Bajkal, ozero, l., Russia F10 34
Baikal Mountains see Bajkal'skij hrebet, mts., Russia F10 34
Baikonur see Bayqongyr, Kaz. E11 32
Bailadores, Ven. C6 86
Baile Átha Cliath see Dublin, Ire. H6 12
Baile Átha Luain see Athlone, Ire. H4 12
Băile Govora, Rom. D11 26
Bailén, Spain F7 20
Băilești, Rom. F10 26
Bailey, N.C., U.S. I7 114
Bail Hongal, India D2 53
Bailicun, China I4 42
Bailique, Ilha, i., Braz. C8 84
Baillie Islands, is., N.T., Can. B14 140
Baillif, Guad. h5 105c
Bailong, stm., China E1 42
Bailu Hu, l., China G5 42
Bailundo, Ang. C2 68
Baimamiao, China C2 42
Baima Shan, mtn., China H4 42
Baimuru, Pap. N. Gui. b3 79a
Bainbridge, Ga., U.S. G14 122
Bainbridge, N.Y., U.S. B10 114
Bain-de-Bretagne, Fr. G7 14
Baing, Indon. I12 50
Bainville, Mt., U.S. F9 124
Baio Grande, Spain A2 20
Baiona, Spain B2 20
Baipeng, China I3 42
Baipu, China E9 42
Baiquan, China B10 36
Baird, Tx., U.S. B8 130
Baird Mountains, mts., Ak., U.S. C7 140
Baird Peninsula, pen., Nu., Can. B15 106
Bairiki, Kir. C8 72
Bairin Zuoqi, China C8 36
Bairnsdale, Austl. K6 76
Baïse, stm., Fr. F6 18
Baisha, China G2 42
Baisha, China L3 42
Baisha, China I8 42
Baishe, China H7 42
Baishuijiang, China E2 42
Baisogala, Lith. E6 10
Baiwang, China I3 42
Baixingt, China C4 38
Baixio, Braz. D6 88
Baiyan Shan, mtn., China H8 42
Baiyin, China D5 36
Baiyü, China E4 36
Baja, Hung. C5 26
Baja, Punta, c., Chile e29 78l
Baja California, state, Mex. F5 98
Baja California, pen., Mex. B2 96
Baja California Sur, state, Mex. C2 100
Bajada del Agrio, Arg. I2 92
Baján, Mex. H6 130
Bajan, Mong. B7 36
Bajangol, Russia F9 34
Bajánsenye, Hung. C3 26
Bajawa, Indon. H12 50
Bajdarackaja guba, b., Russia C2 34
Bajestān, Iran C8 56
Bajkal, Russia F9 34
Bajkal, ozero (Baikal, Lake), l., Russia F10 34
Bajkal'skij hrebet, mts., Russia F10 34
Bajkit, Russia B17 32
Bajkonur see Bayqongyr, Kaz. E11 32
Bajmak, Russia D9 32
Bajmok, Serb. D6 26
Bajo, Indon. H11 50
Bajo Boquete, Pan. H6 102
Bajool, Austl. D8 76
Bajramaly, Turkmen. B9 56
Bajsun, Uzb. G11 32
Bakacak, Tur. C10 28
Bakala, C.A.R. C4 66
Bake, Indon. E2 50
Bakel, Sen. G2 64
Baker, Ca., U.S. H9 134
Baker, Fl., U.S. G12 122
Baker, La., U.S. G7 122
Baker, Mt., U.S. A8 126
Baker, Or., U.S. F9 136
Baker, Mount, vol., Wa., U.S. B5 136
Baker Butte, mtn., Az., U.S. I5 132
Baker Island, i., Oc. C9 72
Baker Lake see Qamani'tuaq, Nu., Can. C11 106
Baker Lake, l., Austl. E5 74
Baker Lake, l., Nu., Can. C11 106
Bakersfield, Ca., U.S. H7 134
Bâ Kêv, Camb. F8 48
Bakharden, Turkmen. B8 56
Bakhardok, Turkmen. B8 56
Bakhtegān, Daryācheh-ye, l., Iran D7 56
Bakı (Baku), Azer. A6 56
Bakkafjörður, Ice. j32 8a
Bakkaflói, b., Ice. j32 8a
Baklan, Tur. F12 28
Bako, C. Iv. H3 64
Bako, Eth. F7 62
Bakony, mts., Hung. C4 26
Bakouma, C.A.R. C4 66
Baku see Bakı, Azer. A6 56

I·6 Bakumpai – Bayano

Name	Map Ref.	Page
Bakumpai, Indon.	D8	50
Bakung, Pulau, i., Indon.	C4	50
Bakungan, Indon.	K3	48
Bakwanga see Mbuji-Mayi, D.R.C.	F4	66
Balâ, Tur.	D16	28
Balabac, Phil.	F1	52
Balabac Island, i., Phil.	G1	52
Balabac Strait, strt., Asia	G1	52
Ba'labakk, Leb.	D7	58
Balabalagan, Kepulauan, is., Indon.	E10	50
Balabanovo, Russia	E19	10
Balabio, Île, i., N. Cal.	m15	79d
Balad, Iraq	C5	56
Baladěk, Russia	F15	34
Bālāghāt, India	H8	54
Bālāghāt Range, mts., India	B3	53
Balagne, reg., Fr.	G14	18
Balaguer, Spain	C11	20
Balahna, Russia	H20	8
Balaikarangan, Indon.	C7	50
Balaisepuah, Indon.	C7	50
Balakirevo, Russia	D21	10
Balaklava, Austl.	J2	76
Balakovo, Russia	D7	32
Balama, Moz.	C6	68
Balambangan, Pulau, i., Malay.	G1	52
Bālā Morghāb, Afg.	B9	56
Balanga, Phil.	C3	52
Balāngīr, India	H9	54
Balapulang, Indon.	G6	50
Balarāmpur, India	G11	54
Balašiha, Russia	E20	10
Balašov, Russia	D6	32
Balassagyarmat, Hung.	A6	26
Balatina, Mol.	B14	26
Balaton, Mn., U.S.	G3	118
Balaton, l., Hung.	C4	26
Balayan, Phil.	D3	52
Balbieriškis, Lith.	F6	10
Balbina, Represa, res., Braz.	H12	86
Balcanoona, Austl.	H2	76
Balcarce, Arg.	H8	92
Balcarres, Sk., Can.	D10	124
Bălceşti, Rom.	E10	26
Balcones Escarpment, clf., Tx., U.S.	D9	130
Balde, Arg.	F4	92
Bald Knob, Ar., U.S.	B7	122
Bald Knob, mtn., Va., U.S.	G6	114
Bald Mountain, mtn., Or., U.S.	G5	136
Bald Mountain, mtn., Or., U.S.	F3	136
Baldock Lake, l., Mb., Can.	D11	106
Baldone, Lat.	D7	10
Baldwin, La., U.S.	H7	122
Baldwin, Mi., U.S.	E4	112
Baldwin, Wi., U.S.	G6	118
Baldwinsville, N.Y., U.S.	E13	112
Baldwyn, Ms., U.S.	C10	122
Baldy Mountain, mtn., Mb., Can.	C13	124
Baldy Mountain, mtn., N.M., U.S.	E3	128
Baldy Peak, mtn., Az., U.S.	J7	132
Bâle see Basel, Switz.	C4	22
Baleares see Balears, state, Spain	E13	20
Baleares, Islas see Balears, Illes, is., Spain	E12	20
Balearic Islands see Balears, state, Spain	E13	20
Balearic Islands see Balears, Illes, is., Spain	E12	20
Balears, state, Spain	E13	20
Balears, Illes (Balearic Islands), is., Spain	E12	20
Balease, Gunung, mtn., Indon.	E12	50
Baleh, stm., Malay.	C8	50
Baleia, Ponta da, c., Braz.	I6	88
Baleine, stm., Qc., Can.	D17	106
Baleine, Grande rivière de la, stm., Qc., Can.	D15	106
Baleine, Petite rivière de la, stm., Qc., Can.	D15	106
Balej, Russia	F12	34
Baler, Phil.	C3	52
Baler Bay, b., Phil.	C3	52
Bāleshwar, India	H11	54
Balezino, Russia	C8	32
Balfate, Hond.	E4	102
Balfour, N.C., U.S.	A3	116
Balgazyn, Russia	D17	32
Balhaš, ozero see Balqash köli, l., Kaz.	E13	32
Bāli, India	F4	54
Bali, state, Indon.	G9	50
Bali, i., Indon.	G9	50
Bali, Laut (Bali Sea), s., Indon.	G9	50
Bali, Selat, strt., Indon.	H9	50
Bali Barat National Park, p.o.i., Indon.	H9	50
Baliceaux, i., St. Vin.	p11	105e
Balige, Indon.	B1	50
Balıkesir, Tur.	D10	28
Balıkesir, state, Tur.	D10	28
Balīkh, stm., Syria	B10	58
Balikpapan, Indon.	D10	50
Balimbing, Indon.	F4	50
Balimbing, Phil.	H2	52
Balimo, Pap. N. Gui.	b3	79a
Balingen, Ger.	H4	16
Balingian, Malay.	B8	50
Balintang Channel, strt., Phil.	K9	42
Bali Sea see Bali, Laut, s., Indon.	G9	50
Bali Strait see Bali, Selat, strt., Indon.	H9	50
Baliza, Braz.	G7	84
Balkan Mountains, mts., Eur.	G11	26
Balkan Peninsula, pen., Eur.	B6	28
Balkaria see Kabardino-Balkarija, state, Russia	F6	32
Balkh, Afg.	B10	56
Balkhash, Lake see Balqash köli, l., Kaz.	E13	32
Ballachulish, Scot., U.K.	E7	12
Balladonia, Austl.	F4	74
Ballālpur, India	B4	53
Ballangen, Nor.	B7	8
Ballantine, Mt., U.S.	B4	126
Ballarat, Austl.	K4	76
Ballard, Lake, l., Austl.	E4	74
Ballater, Scot., U.K.	D9	12
Ball Bay, b., Norf. I.	y25	78i
Ballenas, Bahía de, b., Mex.	B2	100
Ballenita, Punta, c., Chile	B2	92
Balleny Islands, is., Ant.	B21	81
Balleza, Mex.	B5	100
Balleza, stm., Mex.	B5	100
Ball Ground, Ga., U.S.	B1	116
Ballia, India	F10	54
Ballina, Austl.	G9	76
Ballina, Ire.	G3	12
Ballina, Ire.	I4	12
Ballinrobe, Ire.	H3	12
Ballston Spa, N.Y., U.S.	G2	110
Ballville, Oh., U.S.	C2	114
Ballybunnion, Ire.	I3	12
Ballyhaunis, Ire.	H4	12
Ballymena, N. Ire., U.K.	G6	12
Ballymoney, N. Ire., U.K.	F6	12
Ballyrogan, Lake, l., Austl.	I6	76
Balmaceda, Chile	I2	90
Balmoral, Austl.	K3	76
Balmorhea, Tx., U.S.	C4	130
Balnearia, Arg.	E6	92
Baloda Bāzār, India	H9	54
Balombo, Ang.	C1	68
Balong, Indon.	G7	50
Balonne, stm., Austl.	G7	76
Bālotra, India	F4	54
Balphakram National Park, p.o.i., India	F13	54
Balqash köli (Balkhash, Lake), l., Kaz.	E13	32
Balrāmpur, India	E8	54
Balranald, Austl.	J4	76
Balş, Rom.	E11	26
Balsam Lake, Wi., U.S.	F6	118
Balsam Lake, l., On., Can.	D11	112
Balsas, Braz.	D2	88
Balsas, stm., Braz.	F2	88
Balsas, stm., Braz.	D3	88
Balsas, stm., Mex.	F8	100
Balsas, stm., Pan.	C3	86
Balsthal, Switz.	C4	22
Balta, Ukr.	B16	26
Baltasar Brum, Ur.	E9	92
Bălţi, Mol.	B14	26
Baltic Sea, s., Eur.	D12	6
Baltijsk, Russia	F2	10
Baltijskaja kosa, spit, Eur.	F2	10
Baltijskoje more see Baltic Sea, s., Eur.	D12	6
Baltim, Egypt	G2	58
Baltimore, Ire.	J3	12
Baltimore, Md., U.S.	E9	114
Baltimore, Oh., U.S.	E3	114
Ba Lu, stm., Viet.	E9	48
Baluchistān, state, Pak.	C2	54
Baluchistan, hist. reg., Asia	D9	56
Balui, stm., Malay.	B8	50
Bālurghāt, India	F12	54
Balvi, Lat.	C10	10
Balygyčan, Russia	D19	34
Balyqshy, Kaz.	E8	32
Balzac, Ab., Can.	E16	138
Balzar, Ec.	H2	86
Bam, Iran	D8	56
Bama, China	I2	42
Bama, Nig.	G7	64
Bamaga, Austl.	B8	74
Bamako, Mali	G3	64
Bamba, Mali	F4	64
Bambamarca, Peru	E2	84
Bambana, stm., Nic.	F6	102
Bambari, C.A.R.	C4	66
Bambaroo, Austl.	B6	76
Bamberg, Ger.	G6	16
Bamberg, S.C., U.S.	C4	116
Bambio, C.A.R.	D3	66
Bambuí, Braz.	K2	88
Bam Co, l., China	C13	54
Bamenda, Cam.	C1	66
Bami, Turkmen.	B8	56
Bāmīān, Afg.	C10	56
Bamingui, C.A.R.	C4	66
Bampūr, Iran	D9	56
Bāmra Hills, hills, India	H10	54
Bamumo, China	B14	54
Banaba, i., Kir.	D7	72
Banabuiú, stm., Braz.	C6	88
Banabuiú, Açude, l., Braz.	C6	88
Banalia, D.R.C.	D5	66
Banamba, Mali	G3	64
Banana Islands, is., S.L.	H2	64
Bananal, stm., Braz.	E1	88
Bananal, Ilha do, i., Braz.	F7	84
Banarlı, Tur.	B10	28
Banās, stm., India	E6	54
Banâs, Râs, c., Egypt	C7	62
Banat, hist. reg., Eur.	D7	26
Banaz, Tur.	E12	28
Ban Ban, Laos	C6	48
Ban Bouang-nom, Laos	E8	48
Banbridge, N. Ire., U.K.	G6	12
Ban Bung Na Rang, Thai.	D5	48
Banbury, Eng., U.K.	I11	12
Ban Cha La, Laos	D7	48
Bancroft, On., Can.	C12	112
Bancroft, Ia., U.S.	H4	118
Bancroft, Id., U.S.	H15	136
Bancroft, Ne., U.S.	C1	120
Bānda, India	F8	54
Banda, Kepulauan, is., Indon.	F9	44
Banda, Laut (Banda Sea), s., Indon.	G8	44
Banda Aceh, Indon.	J2	48
Bānda Dāūd Shāh, Pak.	B3	54
Banda del Río Salí, Arg.	C5	92
Bandai-Asahi-kokuritsu-kōen, p.o.i., Japan	B12	40
Bandai-san, vol., Japan	B13	40
Bandama, stm., C. Iv.	H3	64
Bandama Blanc, stm., C. Iv.	H3	64
Ban Dan, Thai.	E7	48
Ban Dangtai, Laos	D7	48
Bandar Beheshtī, Iran	D9	56
Bandarbeyla, Som.	C10	66
Bandar-e 'Abbās, Iran	D8	56
Bandar-e Anzalī, Iran	B6	56
Bandar-e Būshehr, Iran	D7	56
Bandar-e Deylam, Iran	D7	56
Bandar-e Lengeh, Iran	D7	56
Bandar-e Māh Shahr, Iran	C6	56
Bandar-e Moghūyeh, Iran	D7	56
Bandar-e Torkeman, Iran	B7	56
Bandar Lampung, Indon.	F4	50
Bandar Seri Begawan, Bru.	A9	50
Banda Sea see Banda, Laut, s., Indon.	G8	44
Bandeira, Pico da, mtn., Braz.	K5	88
Bandeirantes, Braz.	F7	84
Bandelier National Monument, p.o.i., N.M., U.S.	F2	128
Bandera, Arg.	D6	92
Bandera, Alto, mtn., Dom. Rep.	C12	102
Banderas, Mex.	C2	130
Banderas, Bahía de, b., Mex.	E6	100
Bandhavgarh National Park, p.o.i., India	G8	54
Bāndhi, Pak.	E2	54
Bandiagara, Mali	G4	64
Bandiantaolehai, China	C5	36
Bāndīkūi, India	E6	54
Bandipura, India	A5	54
Bandipur Tiger Reserve, India	F3	53
Bandırma, Tur.	C11	28
Bandon, Or., U.S.	G2	136
Ban Don, Ao, b., Thai.	H4	48
Ban Donhiang, Laos	C5	48
Bandundu, D.R.C.	E3	66
Bandung, Indon.	G5	50
Banes, Cuba	B10	102
Banff, Ab., Can.	E15	138
Banff, Scot., U.K.	D10	12
Banff National Park, p.o.i., Ab., Can.	E15	138
Banfora, Burkina	G4	64
Banga, D.R.C.	F4	66
Banga, India	C6	54
Banga, stm., Phil.	G5	52
Bangalore, India	E3	53
Bangaon, India	G12	54
Bangassou, C.A.R.	D4	66
Bangdag Co, l., China	A8	54
Banggai, Indon.	F7	44
Banggai, Kepulauan, is., Indon.	F7	44
Banggi, Pulau, i., Malay.	G1	52
Banggong Co, l., China	B7	54
Banghāzī (Bengasi), Libya	A3	62
Banghiang, stm., Laos	D7	48
Bangil, Indon.	G8	50
Bangka, Pulau, i., Indon.	E5	50
Bangka, Selat, strt., Indon.	E4	50
Bangkalan, Indon.	G8	50
Bangkaru, Pulau, i., Indon.	L3	48
Bangkinang, Indon.	C2	50
Bangkir, Indon.	C12	50
Bangko, Indon.	E3	50
Bangkog Co, l., China	C12	54
Bangkok see Krung Thep, Thai.	F5	48
Bangladesh, ctry., Asia	G13	54
Bang Lamung, Thai.	F5	48
Bang Mun Nak, Thai.	D5	48
Bangor, N. Ire., U.K.	G7	12
Bangor, Wales, U.K.	H8	12
Bangor, Me., U.S.	F8	110
Bangor, Pa., U.S.	D10	114
Bangriposi, India	G11	54
Bangs, Tx., U.S.	C8	130
Bangs, Mount, mtn., Az., U.S.	G3	132
Bang Saphan, Thai.	G4	48
Bangued, Phil.	B3	52
Bangui, C.A.R.	D3	66
Bangweulu, Lake, l., Zam.	C4	68
Bangweulu Swamps, sw., Zam.	C5	68
Bangxu, China	J2	42
Ban Hatgnao, Laos	E8	48
Ban Hèt, Laos	E8	48
Ban Hom, Thai.	E4	48
Ban Hong Muang, Laos	D7	48
Ban Houayxay, Laos	B5	48
Bani, C.A.R.	C4	66
Baní, Dom. Rep.	C12	102
Bani, Jbel, mts., Mor.	D3	64
Baniara, Pap. N. Gui.	b4	79a
Bani Bangou, Niger	F5	64
Banihāl Pass, p., India	B4	46
Banī Walīd, Libya	A2	62
Bāniyās, Golan	E6	58
Bāniyās, Syria	C6	58
Banja Luka, Bos.	E4	26
Banjarmasin, Indon.	E9	50
Banjul (Bathurst), Gam.	G1	64
Bānka, India	F11	54
Banka Banka, Austl.	C6	74
Ban Katèp, Laos	D7	48
Ban Kèngkabao, Laos	D7	48
Ban Kèngtangan, Laos	D7	48
Ban Kheun, Laos	B5	48
Ban Khuan Mao, Thai.	I4	48
Ban Kruat, Thai.	E6	48
Banks, Al., U.S.	F13	122
Banks, Îles (Banks Islands), is., Vanuatu	i16	79d
Banks Island, i., B.C., Can.	E4	106
Banks Island, i., N.T., Can.	B15	140
Banks Islands see Banks, Îles, is., Vanuatu	i16	79d
Banks Lake, res., Wa., U.S.	C7	136
Banks Peninsula, pen., N.Z.	F5	80
Banks Strait, strt., Austl.	n13	77a
Banks / Torres, state, Vanuatu	i16	79d
Bānkura, India	G11	54
Ban Mae La Luang, Thai.	C3	48
Ban Mit, Laos	C5	48
Ban Muangngat, Laos	C6	48
Bann, stm., N. Ire., U.K.	F6	12
Ban Nadou, Laos	E7	48
Ban Nahin, Laos	C7	48
Ban Nalan, Laos	E7	48
Ban Nam Chan, Thai.	C6	48
Ban Namnga, Laos	B6	48
Ban Nam Thaeng, Thai.	E7	48
Ban Naxouang, Laos	C7	48
Bannertown, N.C., U.S.	H5	114
Banning, Ca., U.S.	J9	134
Ban Nong Lumphuk, Thai.	E6	48
Bannu, Pak.	B3	54
Bañolas see Banyoles, Spain	B13	20
Baños, Ec.	H2	86
Banow, Afg.	B10	56
Ban Pak Bong, Thai.	C4	48
Ban Pakkhop, Laos	C5	48
Ban Pak Nam, Thai.	G4	48
Ban Phai, Thai.	D6	48
Ban Phai, Thai.	D6	48
Ban Pho, Thai.	F5	48
Ban Phông Pho, Laos	E7	48
Ban Pong, Thai.	F4	48
Ban Sa-ang, Laos	D7	48
Ban Salik, Thai.	C5	48
Ban Sam Pong, Laos	C6	48
Ban Samrong, Thai.	E6	48
Bānsda, India	H4	54
Banshadhāra, stm., India	B6	53
Banská Bystrica, Slov.	H15	16
Banská Štiavnica, Slov.	H14	16
Bansko, Blg.	H10	26
Ban Songkhon, Laos	C7	48
Bānswāra, India	G5	54
Bantaeng, Indon.	F11	50
Ban Takhlo, Thai.	E5	48
Bantarkawung, Indon.	G6	50
Bantayan, Phil.	E4	52
Ban Thabôk, Laos	C6	48
Ban Thapayi, Laos	D7	48
Ban Tian Sa, Laos	C6	48
Bantry, Ire.	J3	12
Bantry Bay, b., Ire.	J3	12
Ban Van Hom, Laos	C7	48
Ban Xènkhalôk, Laos	C5	48
Banya, Testa de la, c., Spain	D11	20
Banyak, Kepulauan, is., Indon.	K3	48
Ban Ya Plong, Thai.	H4	48
Banyo, Cam.	C2	66
Banyoles, Spain	B13	20
Banyuwangi, Indon.	H9	50
Banzare Coast, cst., Ant.	B17	81
Baode, China	B4	42
Baoding, China	B6	42
Baofeng, China	E5	42
Bao Ha, Viet.	A7	48
Baoji, China	D2	42
Baojing, China	G3	42
Bao Lac, Viet.	G8	48
Bao Lac, Viet.	A7	48
Baolunyuan, China	E1	42
Baoqing, China	B11	36
Baoshan, China	F4	36
Baoting, China	L3	42
Baotou, China	A4	42
Baoulé, stm., Mali	G3	64
Baowei, China	A8	48
Baoyi, China	E7	42
Baoying, China	E8	42
Bāpatla, India	D5	53
Bapaume, Fr.	D11	14
Baptiste Lake, res., On., Can.	C12	112
Bāqa el Gharbiyya, Isr.	F6	58
Baqanas, Kaz.	F13	32
Baqing, China	B14	54
Baqty, Kaz.	E14	32
Ba'qūbah, Iraq	C5	56
Baquedano, Chile	A3	92
Bar, Serb.	G6	26
Bara, Nig.	G7	64
Baraawe, Som.	D8	66
Barabinsk, Russia	C13	32
Barabinskaja step', pl., Russia	C13	32
Baraboo, Wi., U.S.	H9	118
Baraboo, stm., Wi., U.S.	H8	118
Baracaldo see Barakaldo, Spain	A8	20
Baracoa, Cuba	B10	102
Baradero, Arg.	F8	92
Baradine, Austl.	H7	76
Baraga, Mi., U.S.	B1	112
Bārah, Sudan	E6	62
Barahona, Dom. Rep.	C12	102
Barak, Tur.	B8	58
Barāk, stm., India	F14	54
Barakaldo, Spain	A8	20
Barakī Barak, Afg.	B2	54
Barakula, Austl.	F8	76
Baralaba, Austl.	E7	76
Baram, stm., Malay.	A9	50
Barama, stm., Guy.	D12	86
Bārāmati, India	B2	53
Bāramūla, India	A5	54
Baran', Bela.	F13	10
Bārān, India	F6	54
Baranagar, India	G12	54
Baranavičy, Bela.	G9	10
Barangbarang, Indon.	G12	50
Baranoa, Col.	B4	86
Baranof Island, i., Ak., U.S.	E12	140
Barany, Russia	C12	10
Baranya, state, Hung.	D5	26
Barão de Grajaú, Braz.	D4	88
Barão de Melgaço, Braz.	G6	84
Barão de Tromaí, Braz.	A3	88
Baraški, Russia	D24	8
Barataria, La., U.S.	H8	122
Barataria Bay, b., La., U.S.	H8	122
Barat Daya, Kepulauan (Barat Daya Islands), is., Indon.	G8	44
Barat Daya Islands see Barat Daya, Kepulauan, is., Indon.	G8	44
Barauana, stm., Braz.	G11	86
Barauni, India	F10	54
Baraut, India	D6	54
Baraya, Col.	F4	86
Barbacena, Braz.	K4	88
Barbacoas, Col.	G2	86
Barbadillo del Mercado, Spain	B7	20
Barbados, ctry., N.A.	h16	96a
Barbalha, Braz.	D6	88
Barbar, Sudan	D6	62
Barbaria, Cap de, c., Spain	F12	20
Barbas, Cap, c., W. Sah.	E1	64
Barbaši, Russia	C11	10
Barbastro, Spain	B10	20
Barbate, Spain	H4	20
Barbeau Peak, mtn., Nu., Can.	A10	141
Barberena, Guat.	E2	102
Barberton, S. Afr.	D10	70
Barberton, Oh., U.S.	C4	114
Barbil, India	G10	54
Barbosa, Col.	E5	86
Barbuda, i., Antig.	e4	105b
Barby, Ger.	E7	16
Bârca, Rom.	F10	26
Barcaldine, Austl.	D5	76
Barcău (Berettyó), stm., Eur.	B8	26
Barcellona Pozzo di Gotto, Italy	F9	24
Barcelona, Mex.	B7	100
Barcelona, Spain	C13	20
Barcelona, Ven.	B9	86
Barcelona, co., Spain	C13	20
Barceloneta, P.R.	B2	104a
Barcelos, Braz.	H10	86
Barcelos, Port.	C2	20
Barcin, Pol.	D13	16
Barcoo, stm., Austl.	E4	76
Barczewo, Pol.	C16	16
Barda del Medio, Arg.	I3	92
Bardaï, Chad	C3	62
Bardawîl, Sabkhet el-, b., Egypt	G4	58
Barddhamān, India	G11	54
Bardejov, Slov.	G17	16
Bardeskan, Iran	B8	56
Bardīyah, Libya	A5	62
Bardo, Tun.	H4	24
Bārdoli, India	H4	54
Bardstown, Ky., U.S.	G12	120
Bardwell Lake, res., Tx., U.S.	E2	122
Bareilly, India	D7	54
Barentsburg, Nor.	B29	141
Barentsøya, i., Nor.	B30	141
Barents Sea, s., Eur.	B7	30
Bareta, India	D5	54
Barfleur, Fr.	E7	14
Bargaal, Som.	B10	66
Bargara, Austl.	E9	76
Bargarh, India	D5	46
Barguzin, stm., Russia	F11	34
Barguzinskij hrebet, mts., Russia	F11	34
Bar Harbor, Me., U.S.	F8	110
Barharwa, India	F11	54
Barhi, India	F10	54
Bāri, India	E6	54
Bari, Italy	C10	24
Baria, stm., Ven.	G8	86
Barī Gāv, Afg.	B1	54
Barigua, Salina de, pl., Ven.	p20	104g
Barillas, Guat.	E2	102
Barīm, i., Yemen	G5	56
Barima, stm., S.A.	C12	86
Barima-Waini, state, Guy.	D12	86
Barinas, P.R.	B2	104a
Barinas, Ven.	C6	86
Barinas, state, Ven.	C7	86
Baring, Cape, c., N.T., Can.	A7	106
Baringo, Lake, l., Kenya	D7	66
Bāripada, India	H11	54
Bariri, Braz.	L1	88
Bârîs, Egypt	C6	62
Bari Sādri, India	F5	54
Barisāl, Bngl.	G13	54
Barisāl, state, Bngl.	G13	54
Barisan, Pegunungan, mts., Indon.	E2	50
Barito, stm., Indon.	E9	50
Barjols, Fr.	F11	18
Barkam, China	E5	36
Barkava, Lat.	D9	10
Barkerville, B.C., Can.	C9	138
Bark Lake, l., On., Can.	C12	112
Barkley, Lake, res., U.S.	H10	120
Barkley Sound, strt., B.C., Can.	H5	138
Barkly East, S. Afr.	G8	70
Barkly Tableland, plat., Austl.	C7	74
Barkly West, S. Afr.	F7	70
Barkol, China	C3	36
Bârlad, Rom.	C14	26
Bârlad, stm., Rom.	D14	26
Bar-le-Duc, Fr.	F14	14
Barlee, Lake, l., Austl.	E3	74
Barletta, Italy	C10	24
Barlinek, Pol.	D11	16
Barling, Ar., U.S.	B4	122
Barlow, Ky., U.S.	G8	120
Barmedman, Austl.	J6	76
Bārmer, India	F3	54
Barmera, Austl.	J3	76
Barnagar, India	G5	54
Barnard Castle, Eng., U.K.	G11	12
Barnaul, Russia	D14	32
Barn Bluff, mtn., Austl.	n12	77a
Barnegat, N.J., U.S.	E11	114
Barnegat Bay, b., N.J., U.S.	E11	114
Barnes Ice Cap, ice, Nu., Can.	A16	106
Barnesville, Ga., U.S.	C1	116
Barnesville, Mn., U.S.	E2	118
Barnesville, Oh., U.S.	E4	114
Barneville-Carteret, Fr.	E7	14
Barnsdall, Ok., U.S.	E12	128
Barnsley, Eng., U.K.	H11	12
Barnstable, Ma., U.S.	C15	114
Barnstaple, Eng., U.K.	J8	12
Barnstaple Bay, b., Eng., U.K.	J8	12
Barnwell, Ab., Can.	G18	138
Barnwell, S.C., U.S.	C4	116
Baro, stm., Afr.	F7	62
Baron Bluff, clf., V.I.U.S.	g10	104c
Baron'ki, Bela.	G15	10
Barora Fa Island, i., Sol. Is.	d8	79b
Barora Ite Island, i., Sol. Is.	d8	79b
Baroua, Niger	G7	64
Barpeta, India	E13	54
Barqah (Cyrenaica), hist. reg., Libya	A4	62
Barques, Pointe aux, c., Mi., U.S.	D7	112
Barquisimeto, Ven.	B7	86
Barra, Braz.	F4	88
Barra, i., Scot., U.K.	D5	12
Barra, Ponta da, c., Moz.	C12	70
Barraba, Austl.	H8	76
Barra da Estiva, Braz.	G5	88
Barra del Colorado, C.R.	G6	102
Barra de Rio Grande, Nic.	F6	102
Barra do Corda, Braz.	C3	88
Barra do Cuanza, Ang.	B1	68
Barra do Garças, Braz.	G7	84
Barra do Mendes, Braz.	F4	88
Barra do Piraí, Braz.	L3	88
Barra do Ribeiro, Braz.	E12	92
Barra Falsa, Ponta da, c., Moz.	C12	70
Barra Mansa, Braz.	L3	88
Barranca, Peru	F2	84
Barrancabermeja, Col.	D4	86
Barrancas, Ven.	C10	86
Barrancas, Ven.	C7	86
Barrancas, stm., Arg.	H2	92
Barranco Azul, Mex.	E3	130
Barranco do Velho, Port.	G3	20
Barranqueras, Arg.	C8	92
Barranquilla, Col.	B4	86
Barranquitas, P.R.	B3	104a
Barras, Braz.	C4	88
Barre, Vt., U.S.	F4	110
Barreal, Arg.	E3	92
Barreiras, Braz.	G3	88
Barreirinha, Braz.	D6	84
Barreiro, Port.	F1	20
Barreiros, Braz.	E8	88
Barren, stm., Ky., U.S.	H11	120
Barren, Nosy, is., Madag.	D7	68
Barren Islands, is., Ak., U.S.	E9	140
Barren River Lake, res., Ky., U.S.	H11	120
Barretos, Braz.	K1	88
Barrhead, Ab., Can.	B16	138
Barrie, On., Can.	D10	112
Barrie Island, i., On., Can.	C7	112
Barrière, B.C., Can.	E10	138
Barrier Range, mts., Austl.	H3	76
Barrigada, Guam	j10	78c
Barrington, N.S., Can.	G11	110
Barrington Tops National Park, p.o.i., Austl.	I8	76
Barringun, Austl.	G5	76
Barrouallie, St. Vin.	o11	105e
Barrow, Arg.	I7	92
Barrow, Ak., U.S.	B8	140
Barrow, stm., Ire.	I5	12
Barrow, Point, c., Ak., U.S.	B8	140
Barrow Creek, Austl.	D6	74
Barrow-in-Furness, Eng., U.K.	G9	12
Barrow Island, i., Austl.	D2	74
Barrows, Mb., Can.	B12	124
Barrow Strait, strt., Nu., Can.	C6	141
Barry, Wales, U.K.	J9	12
Barry, Il., U.S.	E6	120
Barryton, Mi., U.S.	E4	112
Barsalpur, India	D4	54
Bārsi, India	B2	53
Barsinghausen, Ger.	D5	16
Barstow, Ca., U.S.	I8	134
Barstow, Tx., U.S.	C4	130
Bar-sur-Seine, Fr.	F13	14
Bartang, Taj.	B11	56
Barth, Ger.	B8	16
Barthélemy, Deo, p., Viet.	C6	48
Bartholomew, Bayou, stm., U.S.	E7	122
Bartibougou, Burkina	G5	64
Bartica, Guy.	B6	84
Bartın, Tur.	B15	28
Bartın, state, Tur.	B15	28
Bartle Frere, mtn., Austl.	A5	76
Bartlesville, Ok., U.S.	H2	120
Bartlett, N.H., U.S.	F5	110
Bartlett, Tn., U.S.	B9	122
Bartlett, Tx., U.S.	D10	130
Bartley, Ne., U.S.	A8	128
Barton, Vt., U.S.	F4	110
Bartoszyce, Pol.	B16	16
Bartow, Fl., U.S.	I4	116
Bartow, Ga., U.S.	D3	116
Barú, Volcán, vol., Pan.	H6	102
Bārūk, Jabal al-, mtn., Leb.	E6	58
Barumini, Italy	E2	24
Barumun, stm., Indon.	C2	50
Barung, Nusa, i., Indon.	H8	50
Barus, Indon.	L4	48
Baruun-Urt, Mong.	B7	36
Barvas, Scot., U.K.	C6	12
Barview, Or., U.S.	G2	136
Barwāh, India	G5	54
Barwāni, India	H5	54
Barwick, Ga., U.S.	F2	116
Barwon, stm., Austl.	H6	76
Barybino, Russia	E20	10
Barycz, stm., Pol.	E13	16
Barysau, Bela.	F11	10
Basail, Arg.	C8	92
Basalt, stm., Austl.	B5	76
Basankusu, D.R.C.	D3	66
Basarabeasca, Mol.	C15	26
Basatongwula Shan, mtn., China	B13	54
Basavakalyān, India	C3	53
Basavilbaso, Arg.	F8	92
Bāsawul, Afg.	A3	54
Bascuñán, Cabo, c., Chile	D2	92
Basel (Bâle), Switz.	C4	22
Basella see Bassella, Spain	B12	20
Basey, Phil.	E5	52
Bashi Channel, strt., Asia	K9	42
Bashkortostan see Baškirija, state, Russia	D9	32
Basilan Island, i., Phil.	G4	52
Basilan Strait, strt., Phil.	G4	52
Basildon, Eng., U.K.	J13	12
Basile, La., U.S.	G6	122
Basilicata, state, Italy	D10	24
Basin, Mt., U.S.	D14	136
Basin, Wy., U.S.	C4	126
Basingstoke, Eng., U.K.	J11	12
Basin Lake, l., Sk., Can.	B8	124
Basīrhāt, India	G12	54
Baskahegan Lake, l., Me., U.S.	E8	110
Baskakovka, Russia	F17	10
Başkale, Tur.	B5	56
Baskatong, Réservoir, res., Qc., Can.	B13	112
Basket Lake, l., On., Can.	B6	118
Baškirija, state, Russia	D9	32
Baskomutan Milli Parkı, p.o.i., Tur.	E13	28
Basmat, India	B3	53
Bāsoda, India	G6	54
Basoko, D.R.C.	D4	66
Basora, Punt, c., Aruba	p20	104g
Basque Provinces see Euskal Herriko, state, Spain	A8	20
Basra see Al-Başrah, Iraq	C6	56
Bas-Rhin, state, Fr.	F16	14
Bassano, Ab., Can.	F18	138
Bassano del Grappa, Italy	E8	22
Bassari, Togo	H5	64
Bassas da India, rf., Reu.	E6	68
Bassein, stm., Mya.	D2	48
Bassella, Spain	B12	20
Basse Santa Su, Gam.	G2	64
Basse-Terre, Guad.	i5	105c
Basseterre, St. K./N.	C2	105a
Basse Terre, Trin.	s12	105f
Basse-Terre, i., Guad.	h5	105c
Bassett, Ne., U.S.	E13	126
Bassett, Va., U.S.	H6	114
Bassfield, Ms., U.S.	F9	122
Bassikounou, Maur.	F3	64
Bassila, Benin	H5	64
Bass River, N.S., Can.	E13	110
Bass Strait, strt., Austl.	L6	76
Basswood Lake, l., N.A.	C6	118
Båstad, Swe.	H5	8
Bastenaken see Bastogne, Bel.	D14	14
Bastersberge, hill, S. Afr.	G5	70
Basti, India	E9	54
Bastia, Fr.	G15	18
Bastogne, Bel.	D14	14
Bastrop, La., U.S.	E6	122
Bastrop, Tx., U.S.	D10	130
Basu, Pulau, i., Indon.	D3	50
Basutoland see Lesotho, ctry., Afr.	F9	70
Bata, Eq. Gui.	I6	64
Bataan Peninsula, pen., Phil.	C3	52
Batabanó, Golfo de, b., Cuba	A6	102
Batac, Phil.	A3	52
Batagaj, Russia	C15	34
Batagaj-Alyta, Russia	C15	34
Batak, Blg.	H11	26
Batala, India	C5	54
Batalha, Braz.	E7	88
Batalha, Port.	E2	20
Batam, Pulau, i., Indon.	C3	50
Batamaj, Russia	D14	34
Batang, China	E4	36
Batangafo, C.A.R.	C3	66
Batangas, Phil.	D3	52
Batangtoru, Indon.	C1	50
Batan Islands, is., Phil.	K9	42
Batanta, Pulau, i., Indon.	F9	44
Batatais, Braz.	K2	88
Batavia, Arg.	G5	92
Batavia see Jakarta, Indon.	G5	50
Batavia, Ia., U.S.	D5	120
Batavia, Il., U.S.	C9	120
Batavia, N.Y., U.S.	A7	114
Batchelor, Austl.	B6	74
Bătdâmbâng, Camb.	F6	48
Bateckij, Russia	B13	10
Batemans Bay, Austl.	J8	76
Bates, Mount, mtn., Norf. I.	y24	78i
Batesburg, S.C., U.S.	C4	116
Batesville, Ar., U.S.	B7	122
Batesville, Ms., U.S.	C9	122
Batesville, Tx., U.S.	F8	130
Bath, N.B., Can.	D9	110
Bath, Eng., U.K.	J10	12
Bath, Me., U.S.	G7	110
Bath, N.Y., U.S.	B8	114
Batha, stm., Chad	E3	62
Bathgate, N.D., U.S.	F16	124
Bathinda, India	C5	54
Bathsheba, Barb.	n8	105d
Bathurst, Austl.	I7	76
Bathurst, N.B., Can.	C11	110
Bathurst see Banjul, Gam.	G1	64
Bathurst, Cape, c., N.T., Can.	A5	106
Bathurst Inlet see Kingaok, Nu., Can.	B9	106
Bathurst Island, i., Austl.	B5	74
Bathurst Island, i., Nu., Can.	B5	141
Batlow, Austl.	J6	76
Batman, Tur.	B5	56
Batna, Alg.	B6	64
Ba To, Viet.	E9	48
Baton Rouge, La., U.S.	G7	122
Batouri, Cam.	D2	66
Batson, Tx., U.S.	G4	122
Batterie, Pointe de la, c., Mart.	k7	105c
Batticaloa, Sri L.	H5	53
Battipaglia, Italy	D8	24
Battle, stm., Can.	D19	138
Battle Creek, Mi., U.S.	F4	112
Battle Creek, Ne., U.S.	F15	126
Battle Creek, stm., N.A.	F4	124
Battle Ground, In., U.S.	H3	112
Battle Ground, Wa., U.S.	E4	136
Battle Harbour, Nf., Can.	i22	107a
Battle Mountain, Nv., U.S.	C8	134
Battle Mountain, mtn., Wy., U.S.	B9	132
Batu, mtn., Eth.	F7	62
Batu, Kepulauan, is., Indon.	F2	44
Batu-Batu, Indon.	F11	50
Batu Berincang, Gunong, mtn., Malay.	J5	48
Batubrok, Bukit, mtn., Indon.	C9	50
Batu Gajah, Malay.	J5	48
Batukelau, Indon.	C9	50
Batumi, Geor.	F6	32
Batu Pahat, Malay.	L6	48
Batupanjang, Indon.	C2	50
Baturaja, Indon.	F3	50
Baturino, Russia	C15	32
Baturité, Braz.	C6	88
Baturusa, Indon.	D5	50
Batusangkar, Indon.	D2	50
Batz, Île de, i., Fr.	F4	14
Bau, Malay.	C7	50
Baubau, Indon.	G7	44
Bauchi, Nig.	G6	64
Bauda, India	H10	54
Baudette, Mn., U.S.	C4	118
Baudó, stm., Col.	E3	86
Bauld, Cape, c., Nf., Can.	i22	107a
Bauman Fiord, b., Nu., Can.	B8	141
Baume-les-Dames, Fr.	G15	14
Baures, Bol.	B4	90
Bauru, Braz.	L1	88
Bauska, Lat.	D7	10
Bautzen, Ger.	E10	16
Bauxite, Ar., U.S.	C6	122
Bavaria see Bayern, state, Ger.	H7	16
Bavarian Alps, mts., Eur.	I7	16
Båven, l., Swe.	G7	8
Bavispe, Mex.	F8	98
Bavispe, stm., Mex.	F8	98
Bawang, Indon.	G6	50
Bawdwin, Mya.	A3	48
Bawean, Pulau, i., Indon.	F8	50
Bawiti, Egypt	B5	62
Bawmi, Mya.	D2	48
Baxaya, mtn., Som.	B9	66
Baxian, China	G2	42
Baxian, China	B7	42
Baxter, Ia., U.S.	C4	120
Baxter, Mn., U.S.	E4	118
Baxter, Tn., U.S.	H12	120
Baxterville, Ms., U.S.	F9	122
Bay, Ar., U.S.	B8	122
Bay, Laguna de, l., Phil.	C3	52
Bayamo, Cuba	B9	102
Bayamón, P.R.	B3	104a
Bayan, China	A7	38
Bayan, Indon.	H10	50
Bayāna, India	E6	54
Bayanaūyl, Kaz.	D13	32
Bayan Har Shan, mts., China	E4	36
Bayanhongor, Mong.	B5	36
Bayannaobao, China	B2	42
Bayano, Lago, res., Pan.	H8	102

Bayan Obo – Big Gull Lake I • 7

Name | Map Ref. | Page

Bayan Obo, China C7 36
Bayard, Ia., U.S. C3 120
Bayard, N.M., U.S. K8 132
Bayard, W.V., U.S. E6 114
Bayawan, Phil. F4 52
Baybay, Phil. E5 52
Bayboro, N.C., U.S. A9 116
Bayburt, Tur. A5 56
Bay City, Mi., U.S. E6 112
Bay City, Or., U.S. E3 136
Bay City, Tx., U.S. F12 130
Baydhabo (Baidoa), Som. D8 66
Baydrag, stm., Mong. B4 36
Bayern (Bavaria), state, Ger. H7 16
Bayeux, Braz. D8 88
Bayeux, Fr. E8 14
Bayfield, Co., U.S. F9 132
Bayfield, Wi., U.S. E8 118
Bayındır, Tur. E10 28
Bayjī, Iraq C5 56
Baykonur *see* Bayqongyr, Kaz. E11 32
Bay Minette, Al., U.S. G11 122
Bayombong, Phil. B3 52
Bayona *see* Baiona, Spain B2 20
Bayonne, Fr. F4 18
Bayou Bodcau Reservoir, res., La., U.S. E5 122
Bayou Cane, La., U.S. H8 122
Bayou D'Arbonne Lake, res., La., U.S. E6 122
Bayovar, Peru E1 84
Bay Port, Mi., U.S. E6 112
Bayport, Mn., U.S. F6 118
Bayqongyr, Kaz. E11 32
Bayramiç, Tur. D9 28
Bayreuth, Ger. G7 16
Bayrūt (Beirut), Leb. E6 58
Bays, Lake of, l., On., Can. C10 112
Bay Saint Louis, Ms., U.S. G9 122
Bay Shore, N.Y., U.S. D12 114
Bayside, On., Can. D12 112
Bay Springs Lake, res., Ms., U.S. C10 122
Bayt ad-Dīn, Leb. E6 58
Bayt al-Faqīh, Yemen G5 56
Bayt Laḥm (Bethlehem), W.B. G6 58
Baytown, Tx., U.S. H4 122
Bayyā'īyah al-Kabīrah, Syria C8 58
Baza, Spain G8 20
Bazardüzü dağ, mtn., Azer. A6 56
Bazaruto, Ilha do, i., Moz. B12 70
Bazhong, China F2 42
Baziège, Fr. F7 18
Bazine, Ks., U.S. C9 128
Be, stm., Viet. G8 48
Be, Nosy, i., Madag. C8 68
Beach Haven, N.J., U.S. E11 114
Beachport, Austl. K3 76
Beachville, On., Can. E9 112
Beachy Head, c., Eng., U.K. K13 12
Beacon, Austl. F3 74
Beacon, N.Y., U.S. C12 114
Beacon Hill, Wa., U.S. D3 136
Beaconsfield, Austl. n13 77a
Beagle Gulf, b., Austl. B5 74
Bealanana, Madag. C8 68
Bealdoaivi see Peäldoajvi, mtn., Fin. B12 8
Beale, Cape, c., B.C., Can. H5 138
Beals Creek, stm., Tx., U.S. B7 130
Bear, stm., Ca., U.S. D4 134
Bear, stm., U.S. I14 136
Bear Bay, b., Nu., Can. B8 141
Bear Creek, stm., U.S. C10 122
Bear Creek, stm., U.S. D6 128
Bearden, Ar., U.S. D6 122
Beardmore, On., Can. B11 118
Bear Island, i., Ant. C29 81
Bear Island, i., Ire. J3 12
Bear Island see Bjørnøya, i., Nor. B5 30
Bear Lake, l., Ab., Can. A11 138
Bear Lake, l., U.S. A5 132
Bear Mountain, mtn., Or., U.S. G3 136
Béarn, hist. reg., Fr. F5 18
Bear River, N.S., Can. F11 110
Bear River Range, mts., U.S. B5 132
Beartooth Pass, p., Wy., U.S. C3 126
Bear Town, Ms., U.S. F8 122
Beās, stm., India C6 54
Beasain, Spain A8 20
Beata, Cabo, c., Dom. Rep. D12 102
Beata, Isla, i., Dom. Rep. D12 102
Beaton, B.C., Can. F13 138
Beatrice, Al., U.S. F11 122
Beatrice, Ne., U.S. A12 128
Beatrice, Cape, c., Austl. B7 74
Beattie, Ks., U.S. L2 118
Beatton, stm., B.C., Can. D6 106
Beatty, Nv., U.S. G9 134
Beattyville, Ky., U.S. G2 114
Beaucaire, Fr. F10 18
Beauce, reg., Fr. F10 14
Beauceville, Qc., Can. D6 110
Beauchêne, Lac, l., Qc., Can. B11 112
Beauchêne Island, i., Falk. Is. J5 90
Beaudesert, Austl. F9 76
Beaufort, Malay. A9 50
Beaufort, S.C., U.S. D5 116
Beaufort Castle see Qal'at ash-Shaqīf, sci., Leb. E6 58
Beaufort Sea, s., N.A. B12 140
Beaufort West, S. Afr. H6 70
Beaugency, Fr. G10 14
Beauharnois, Qc., Can. E2 110
Beaujolais, hist. reg., Fr. C10 18
Beaumont, Fr. E7 14
Beaumont, N.Z. G3 80
Beaumont, Ca., U.S. J8 134
Beaumont, Ms., U.S. F9 122
Beaumont, Tx., U.S. G4 122
Beaumont Hill, hill, Austl. H5 76
Beaune, Fr. G13 14
Beauport, Qc., Can. D5 110
Beaupré, Qc., Can. C6 110
Beaurepaire, Fr. D11 18
Beausejour, Mb., Can. D17 124
Beauséjour, Guad. h6 105c
Beauvais, Fr. E11 14
Beauvoir-sur-Mer, Fr. H6 14
Beaver, Ak., U.S. C10 140
Beaver, Ok., U.S. E8 128
Beaver, Pa., U.S. D5 114
Beaver, Ut., U.S. E4 132
Beaver, stm., Can. C6 106
Beaver, stm., Can. D9 106
Beaver, stm., Ut., U.S. E3 132
Beaver, stm., U.S. E9 128
Beaver Creek, stm., Co., U.S. G9 126
Beaver Creek, stm., Mt., U.S. F6 124
Beaver Creek, stm., Ne., U.S. G14 126
Beaver Creek, stm., Ne., U.S. F14 126
Beaver Creek, stm., Ok., U.S. G10 128
Beaver Creek, stm., Tx., U.S. H9 128
Beaver Creek, stm., U.S. A8 128
Beaver Creek, stm., U.S. G9 124
Beaver Creek, stm., U.S. D8 126
Beaver Crossing, Ne., U.S. G15 126
Beaver Dam, Ky., U.S. G11 120
Beaver Dam, Wi., U.S. H9 118
Beaverdell, B.C., Can. G11 138
Beaver Falls, Pa., U.S. D5 114
Beaverhead, stm., Mt., U.S. E14 136
Beaverhead Mountains, mts., U.S. E13 136
Beaverhill Lake, l., Ab., Can. C18 138
Beaverhouse Lake, l., On., Can. C6 118
Beaver Island, i., Mi., U.S. C4 112
Beaver Lake, l., Ab., Can. B19 138
Beaver Lake, res., Ar., U.S. H4 120
Beaverlodge, Ab., Can. A11 138
Beaverton, On., Can. D10 112
Beaverton, Mi., U.S. E5 112
Beaverton, Or., U.S. E4 136
Beāwar, India E5 54
Beazley, Arg. F4 92
Bebedouro, Braz. K1 88
Becal, Mex. B2 102
Bécancour, stm., Qc., Can. D5 110
Beccles, Eng., U.K. I14 12
Bečej, Serb. D6 26
Beceni, Rom. D13 26
Bečevinka, Russia G17 8
Béchar, Alg. C4 64
Becharof Lake, l., Ak., U.S. E8 140
Bechevin Bay, b., Ak., U.S. E7 140
Bechuanaland see Botswana, ctry., Afr. E3 68
Bechuanaland, hist. reg., S. Afr. E5 70
Bechyně, Czech Rep. G10 16
Beckley, W.V., U.S. G4 114
Beckum, Ger. E4 16
Bédarieux, Fr. F9 18
Bedelē, Eth. F7 62
Bedford, Qc., Can. E4 110
Bedford, S. Afr. H8 70
Bedford, Eng., U.K. I12 12
Bedford, Ia., U.S. D3 120
Bedford, In., U.S. F11 120
Bedford, Ky., U.S. F12 120
Bedford, Pa., U.S. D7 114
Bedford, Tx., U.S. B10 130
Bedi, India G3 54
Bedoba, Russia C17 32
Bedourie, Austl. E2 76
Bedworth, Eng., U.K. I11 12
Beebe, Ar., U.S. B7 122
Beechal Creek, stm., Austl. F5 76
Beech Creek, Ky., U.S. G10 120
Beech Fork, stm., Ky., U.S. G12 120
Beech Grove, In., U.S. I3 112
Beechworth, Austl. K6 76
Beechy, Sk., Can. D6 124
Beecroft Head, c., Austl. J8 76
Beemer, Ne., U.S. J2 118
Beenleigh, Austl. F9 76
Bee Ridge, Fl., U.S. I3 116
Beersheba *see* Be'ér Sheva', Isr. G6 58
Beersheba Springs, Tn., U.S. B13 122
Be'ér Sheva' (Beersheba), Isr. G6 58
Beeskow, Ger. D10 16
Beeville, Tx., U.S. F10 130
Befale, D.R.C. D4 66
Befandriana Avaratra, Madag. E7 68
Bega, Austl. K7 76
Bega, stm., Eur. D9 26
Begamganj, India G7 54
Begur, Cap de, c., Spain C14 20
Begusarai, India F11 54
Behbahān, Iran C7 56
Behshahr, Iran B7 56
Bei, stm., China J5 42
Bei'an, China B10 36
Beibei, China G2 42
Beicheng, China G5 36
Beigi, Eth. F6 62
Beihai, China K3 42
Beijing (Peking), China B7 42
Beijing, state, China B6 42
Beili, China L3 42
Beiliu, China J4 42
Beinamar, Chad F3 62
Beipa, Pap. N. Gui. b4 79a
Beipan, stm., China I1 42
Beipiao, China D4 38
Beira, Moz. A12 70
Beira, hist. reg., Port. E3 20
Beiru, stm., China D5 42
Beirut *see* Bayrūt, Leb. E6 58
Beiseker, Ab., Can. E17 138
Beishan, China I3 42
Bei Shan, mts., China C4 36
Beitbridge, Zimb. C10 70
Beizhen, China D4 38
Beja, Port. G3 20
Béja, Tun. H3 24
Beja, state, Port. G3 20
Bejaïa, Alg. B6 64
Béjar, Spain D5 20
Bejhi, stm., Pak. D2 54
Bejuco, Pan. H8 102
Bekaa Valley see Al-Biqā', val., Leb. D7 58
Bekabad, Uzb. F11 32
Bekdaš, Turkmen. A7 56
Békés, Hung. C8 26
Békés, state, Hung. C7 26
Békéscsaba, Hung. C7 26
Bekilli, Tur. E12 28
Bekily, Madag. E8 68
Bekodoka, Madag. D7 68
Bekopaka, Madag. D7 68
Bela, India F9 54
Bela, Pak. D10 56
Belaazërsk, Bela. H8 10
Bela Crkva, Serb. E8 26
Belaga, Malay. B8 50
Bel Air, Md., U.S. E9 114
Belaja, stm., Russia C8 32
Belaja Gora, Russia B14 10
Belambanganumpu, Indon. F4 50
Belampalli, India B4 53
Bela Palanka, Serb. F9 26
Belarus, ctry., Eur. E14 6
Belaruskaja hrada, mts., Bela. F10 10
Belau see Palau, ctry., Oc. g8 78b
Bela Vista, Braz. D5 90
Bela Vista, Moz. E11 70
Belawan, Indon. B1 50
Belayan, stm., Indon. C10 50
Bełchatów, Pol. E15 16
Belcher, La., U.S. E5 122
Belcherāgh, Afg. B10 56
Belcher Channel, strt., Nu., Can. B6 141
Belcher Islands, is., Nu., Can. D14 106
Belding, Mi., U.S. E4 112
Belebelka, Russia C13 10
Beledweyne, Som. D8 66
Belém, Braz. A1 88
Belém, Moz. C6 68
Belém de São Francisco, Braz. E6 88
Belén, Arg. C4 92
Belén, Nic. G4 102
Belén, Para. D5 90
Belen, Tur. B7 58
Belén, Ur. E9 92
Belen, N.M., U.S. I10 132
Belén, stm., Arg. C4 92
Belep, Îles, is., N. Cal. I14 79d
Belesar, Embalse de, res., Spain B3 20
Belëv, Russia G19 10
Belfast, S. Afr. D9 70
Belfast, N. Ire., U.K. G6 12
Belfast, Me., U.S. F7 110
Belfield, N.D., U.S. H10 124
Belford, Eng., U.K. F11 12
Belfort, Fr. G15 14
Belfry, Mt., U.S. B3 126
Belgaum, India D2 53
Belgium, ctry., Eur. D13 14
Belgorod, Russia D5 32
Belgrade, Mt., U.S. E15 136
Belgrade, Ne., U.S. F14 126
Belgrade *see* Beograd, Serb. E7 26
Belgrano II, sci., Ant. C36 81
Belhaven, N.C., U.S. A9 116
Belick, Bela. H13 10
Beliliou, i., Palau D9 44
Belin, Fr. E5 18
Belin-Béliet *see* Belin, Fr. E5 18
Belington, W.V., U.S. E5 114
Belinyu, Indon. D4 50
Belitung, i., Indon. E5 50
Belize, ctry., N.A. D3 102
Belize, stm., Belize D3 102
Belize City, Belize D3 102
Belkovski, ostrov see Bel'kovskij, ostrov, i., Russia A16 34
Bel'kovskij, ostrov, i., Russia A16 34
Bella Bella, B.C., Can. D2 138
Bellac, Fr. C7 18
Bella Coola, B.C., Can. D4 138
Bella Coola, stm., B.C., Can. D4 138
Bellair, Fl., U.S. F4 116
Bellaire, Oh., U.S. D5 114
Bellaire, Tx., U.S. H3 122
Bellamy, Al., U.S. E10 122
Bellaria, Italy F9 22
Bellary, India D3 53
Bellata, Austl. G7 76
Bella Unión, Ur. E9 92
Bella Vista, Arg. D8 92
Bella Vista, Arg. C5 92
Bellavista, Peru E2 84
Bellbrook, Austl. H9 76
Belle, W.V., U.S. F4 114
Bellefontaine, Mart. k6 105c
Bellefontaine, Oh., U.S. D2 114
Bellefonte, Pa., U.S. D8 114
Belle Fourche, S.D., U.S. C9 126
Belle Fourche, stm., U.S. C10 126
Bellegarde-sur-Valserine, Fr. C11 18
Belle Glade, Fl., U.S. J5 116
Belle Hôtesse, mtn., Guad. h5 105c
Belle-Île, i., Fr. G5 14
Belle Isle, i., Nf., Can. i22 107a
Belle Isle, Strait of, strt., Nf., Can. i22 107a
Bellenden Ker National Park, p.o.i., Austl. A5 76
Belle Plaine, Ia., U.S. C5 120
Belle Plaine, Ks., U.S. D11 128
Belle Plaine, Mn., U.S. G5 118
Belleview, Fl., U.S. G11 122
Belleville, On., Can. D12 112
Belleville, Il., U.S. F8 120
Belleville, Ks., U.S. B11 128
Belleville, Pa., U.S. D8 114
Belleville-sur-Saône, Fr. C10 18
Bellevue, Ab., Can. G16 138
Bellevue, Ia., U.S. B7 120
Bellevue, Id., U.S. G12 136
Bellevue, Mi., U.S. F4 112
Bellevue, Ne., U.S. C2 120
Bellevue, Oh., U.S. C3 114
Bellevue, Wa., U.S. C4 136
Belley, Fr. D11 18
Bellingham, Mn., U.S. F2 118
Bellingham, Wa., U.S. B4 136
Bellinghausen, sci., Ant. B35 81
Bellingshausen Sea, s., Ant. P29 142
Bellinzona, Switz. D6 22
Bell Lake, l., On., Can. B7 118
Bellmead, Tx., U.S. C10 130
Bello, Col. D4 86
Bellot Strait, strt., Nu., Can. A12 106
Bell Peninsula, pen., Nu., Can. C14 106
Bells, Tn., U.S. B9 122
Bells, Tx., U.S. D2 122
Bells Corners, On., Can. C14 112
Belluno, Italy D9 22
Bell Ville, Arg. F6 92
Bellville, S. Afr. H4 70
Bellwood, Ne., U.S. F15 126
Bellwood, Pa., U.S. D7 114
Belly, stm., N.A. G17 138
Bellyk, Russia D16 32
Belmond, Ia., U.S. B4 120
Belmont, N.S., Can. E13 110
Belmont, S. Afr. F7 70
Belmont, N.H., U.S. G5 110
Belmont, Wi., U.S. B7 120
Belmonte, Braz. H6 88
Belmonte, Port. D3 20
Belmonte, Spain A4 20
Belmopan, Belize D3 102
Beloe, Russia B22 10
Beloe, ozero, l., Russia F17 8
Beloe more (White Sea), s., Russia D18 8
Belogorsk, Russia F14 34
Belo Horizonte, Braz. J3 88
Beloit, Ks., U.S. B10 128
Beloit, Wi., U.S. B8 120
Belo Jardim, Braz. E7 88
Belomestnaja, Russia H20 10
Belomorsk, Russia D16 8
Beloreck, Russia D9 32
Belören, Tur. F15 28
Belorussia see Belarus, ctry., Eur. E14 6
Beloščele, Russia D22 8
Belo sur Mer, Madag. E7 68
Belot, Lac, l., N.T., Can. B5 106
Belo Tsiribihina, Madag. D7 68
Belousovo, Russia E19 10
Belovo, Russia D15 32
Belozërsk, Russia F17 8
Belpre, Oh., U.S. E4 114
Belt, Mt., U.S. C16 136
Beltana, Austl. H2 76
Belt Creek, stm., Mt., U.S. C16 136
Belton, Mo., U.S. F3 120
Belton, Tx., U.S. C10 130
Belton Lake, res., Tx., U.S. C10 130
Beltrán, Arg. C5 92
Belukha, Mount, mtn., Asia E15 32
Belūr, India E2 53
Beluran, Malay. H1 52
Belvedere Marittimo, Italy E9 24
Belvidere, Il., U.S. B9 120
Belvidere, N.J., U.S. D10 114
Belview, Mn., U.S. G3 118
Belvoir see Kokhav HaYarden, sci., Isr. F6 58
Belyando, stm., Austl. D6 76
Belye Berega, Russia G17 10
Belye Stolby, Russia E20 10
Belyj Gorodok, Russia C20 10
Belyj Jar, Russia C15 32
Bełżec, Pol. F19 16
Belzig, Ger. D8 16
Belzoni, Ms., U.S. D8 122
Bement, Il., U.S. E9 120
Bemidji, Mn., U.S. D3 118
Benaco see Garda, Lago di, l., Italy E7 22
Bena-Dibele, D.R.C. E4 66
Benagerie, Austl. H3 76
Benalla, Austl. K6 76
Benares *see* Vārānasi, India F9 54
Ben Arous, Tun. H4 24
Benavarri, Spain B11 20
Benavente, Spain B5 20
Benbecula, i., Scot., U.K. D5 12
Ben Bolt, Tx., U.S. G9 130
Ben Cat, Viet. G8 48
Bencha, Khao Phanom, mtn., Thai. H4 48
Ben-Chicao, Col de, p., Alg. H13 20
Bencubbin, Austl. F3 74
Bend, Or., U.S. F5 136
Bendemeer, Austl. H8 76
Bender Cassim *see* Boosaaso, Som. B9 66
Bendigo, Austl. K5 76
Bēne, Lat. D6 10
Benedito Leite, Braz. D3 88
Benepú, Rada, anch., Chile f29 78l
Benevento, Italy C8 24
Bèng, stm., Laos B5 48
Bengal, Bay of, b., Asia F6 46
Bengara, Indon. B10 50
Bengasi *see* Banghāzī, Libya A3 62
Bengbu, China E7 42
Benghazi *see* Banghāzī, Libya A3 62
Bengkalis, Indon. C3 50
Bengkalis, Pulau, i., Indon. C3 50
Bengkayang, Indon. C6 50
Bengkulu, Indon. E3 50
Bengkulu, state, Indon. E3 50
Bengough, Sk., Can. E8 124
Benguela, Ang. C1 68
Benguerua, Ilha, i., Moz. B12 70
Benha, Egypt H2 58
Beni, D.R.C. D5 66
Beni, stm., Bol. B3 90
Béni Abbas, Alg. C4 64
Beni 'Adi el-Baharîya, Egypt K1 58
Beni Ahmad, Egypt J1 58
Benicarló, Spain D11 20
Benidorm, Spain F10 20
Beni Mazâr, Egypt J1 58
Beni Muhammadîyat, Egypt K2 58
Benin, ctry., Afr. G5 64
Benin, Bight of, b., Afr. I5 64
Benin City, Nig. H6 64
Benisa *see* Benissa, Spain F11 20
Benissa, Spain F11 20
Beni Suef, Egypt I2 58
Benito, Mb., Can. C12 124
Benito Juárez, Arg. H8 92
Benito Juárez, Presa, res., Mex. G10 100
Benjamin, Tx., U.S. H9 128
Benjamín, Isla, i., Chile H2 90
Benjamin Constant, Braz. D3 84
Benkelman, Ne., U.S. A7 128
Benkovac, Cro. F12 22
Benld, Il., U.S. E8 120
Ben Lomond, Ca., U.S. F3 134
Ben Lomond National Park, p.o.i., Austl. n13 77a
Benndale, Ms., U.S. G10 122
Bennetta, ostrov, i., Russia A18 34
Bennett Island see Bennetta, ostrov, i., Russia A18 34
Bennettsville, S.C., U.S. B6 116
Bennington, Ks., U.S. B11 128
Bennington, Vt., U.S. B12 114
Benoit, Ms., U.S. D7 122
Benoni, S. Afr. E9 70
Ben Sekka, Rass, c., Tun. G3 24
Bensheim, Ger. G4 16
Benson, Az., U.S. L6 132
Benson, Mn., U.S. F3 118
Benson, N.C., U.S. A7 116
Benteng, Indon. G12 50
Ben Thuy, Viet. C7 48
Bentinck Island, i., Austl. C7 74
Bentinck Island, i., Mya. G3 48
Bentiu, Sudan F6 62
Bento Gonçalves, Braz. D12 92
Benton, Ar., U.S. C6 122
Benton, Il., U.S. F9 120
Benton, Ky., U.S. H9 120
Benton, La., U.S. E5 122
Benton, Mo., U.S. G8 120
Benton, Tn., U.S. B14 122
Benton, Wi., U.S. B7 120
Benton Harbor, Mi., U.S. F3 112
Bentonia, Ms., U.S. E8 122
Bentonville, Ar., U.S. H3 120
Ben Tre, Viet. G8 48
Bentung, Malay. K5 48
Benua, Pulau, i., Indon. C5 50
Benue, stm., Afr. H6 64
Ben Wheeler, Tx., U.S. E3 122
Benxi, China D5 38
Beograd (Belgrade), Serb. E7 26
Beohāri, India F8 54
Béoumi, C. Iv. H3 64
Beowawe, Nv., U.S. C9 134
Beppu, Japan F4 40
Bequia, i., St. Vin. o11 105e
Bequimão, Braz. B3 88
Berat, Alb. D13 24
Berati *see* Berat, Alb. D13 24
Berau, stm., Indon. B10 50
Berau, Teluk, b., Indon. F9 44
Berazino, Bela. G11 10
Berazino, Bela. F11 10
Berbera, Som. B9 66
Berbérati, C.A.R. D3 66
Berchtesgaden, Ger. I8 16
Berck, Fr. D10 14
Berclair, Tx., U.S. F10 130
Berdians'k, Ukr. E5 32
Berdigestjah, Russia D14 34
Berdsk, Russia D14 32
Berea, Oh., U.S. C4 114
Berea, S.C., U.S. B3 116
Berehomet, Ukr. A12 26
Berehove, Ukr. A9 26
Berekua, Dom. j6 105c
Berekum, Ghana H4 64
Berens, stm., Can. B17 124
Berens Island, i., Mb., Can. B16 124
Berens River, Mb., Can. B16 124
Beresford, N.B., Can. C11 110
Beresford, S.D., U.S. H2 118
Bereşti, Rom. C14 26
Berettyó (Barcău), stm., Eur. B8 26
Berettyóújfalu, Hung. B8 26
Berezivka, Ukr. B17 26
Bereznik, Russia E20 8
Berezniki, Russia C9 32
Berëzovo, Russia B10 32
Berëzovskij, Russia C15 32
Berëzovskij Rjadok, Russia B17 10
Berga, Spain B12 20
Bergama, Tur. D10 28
Bergamo, Italy E6 22
Bergantín, Ven. C9 86
Bergby, Swe. F7 8
Bergen *see* Mons, Bel. D12 14
Bergen, Ger. D5 16
Bergen, Nor. F1 8
Bergen, N.Y., U.S. A7 114
Bergen auf Rügen, Ger. B9 16
Bergen op Zoom, Neth. C13 14
Bergerac, Fr. E6 18
Bergisch Gladbach, Ger. F3 16
Bergoo, W.V., U.S. F5 114
Bergsjö, Swe. E7 8
Berguent, Mor. C4 64
Bergville, S. Afr. F9 70
Berhala, Selat, strt., Indon. D4 50
Beringa, ostrov, i., Russia F22 34
Bering Glacier, ice, Ak., U.S. D11 140
Beringovskij, Russia D24 34
Bering Sea, s. D21 142
Bering Strait, strt. C6 140
Berja, Spain H8 20
Berkåk, Nor. E4 8
Berkakit, Russia E14 34
Berkane, Mor. C4 64
Berkeley, Ca., U.S. F3 134
Berkeley Springs, W.V., U.S. E7 114
Berkner Island, i., Ant. C35 81
Berkshire Hills, hills, Ma., U.S. B12 114
Berland, stm., Ab., Can. B13 138
Berlevåg, Nor. A13 8
Berlin, Ger. D9 16
Berlin, N.H., U.S. F5 110
Berlin, N.J., U.S. E11 114
Berlin, Pa., U.S. E7 114
Berlin, Wi., U.S. H9 118
Berlin, state, Ger. D9 16
Berlinguet Inlet, b., Nu., Can. A14 106
Bermagui, Austl. K8 76
Bermejillo, Mex. C7 100
Bermejito, stm., Arg. B7 92
Bermejo, stm., Arg. E4 92
Bermejo, stm., S.A. C8 92
Bermejo, Paso del, p., S.A. F2 92
Bermen, Lac, l., Qc., Can. E17 106
Bermeo, Spain A8 20
Bermuda, dep., N.A. k16 104e
Bern (Berne), Switz. C4 22
Bernalda, Italy D10 24
Bernasconi, Arg. H5 92
Bernau bei Berlin, Ger. D9 16
Bernay, Fr. E9 14
Bernburg, Ger. E7 16
Berndorf, Aus. C12 22
Berne *see* Bern, Switz. C4 22
Berner Alpen, mts., Switz. D4 22
Berneray, i., Scot., U.K. D5 12
Bernese Alps see Berner Alpen, mts., Switz. D4 22
Bernice, La., U.S. E6 122
Bernie, Mo., U.S. H8 120
Bernier Bay, b., Nu., Can. A12 106
Bernier Island, i., Austl. D2 74
Bernina, Piz, mtn., Eur. H18 14
Bernkastel-Kues, Ger. G3 16
Bernsdorf, Ger. E10 16
Berón de Astrada, Arg. C9 92
Beroroha, Madag. E8 68
Beroun, Czech Rep. G9 16
Berounka, stm., Czech Rep. F9 16
Berre, Étang de, l., Fr. F11 18
Berri, Austl. J3 76
Berriyyane, Alg. C5 64
Berry, Al., U.S. D11 122
Berry, hist. reg., Fr. H11 14
Berry, Canal du, can., Fr. G10 14
Berry Creek, stm., Ab., Can. E19 138
Berryessa, Lake, res., Ca., U.S. E3 134
Berry Islands, is., Bah. B9 96
Berseba, Nmb. D3 70
Bersenbrück, Ger. D3 16
Bershad', Ukr. A16 26
Bertha, Mn., U.S. E3 118
Berthold, N.D., U.S. F12 124
Berthoud, Co., U.S. G7 126
Berthoud Pass, p., Co., U.S. B3 128
Bertoua, Cam. D2 66
Bertrand, Mi., U.S. G3 112
Bertrand, Ne., U.S. G13 126
Beruri, Braz. D5 84
Berwick, La., U.S. H7 122
Berwick, Pa., U.S. C9 114
Berwick-upon-Tweed, Eng., U.K. F11 12
Berwyn, Il., U.S. G2 112
Besalampy, Madag. D7 68
Besançon, Fr. G14 14
Bešankovičy, Bela. E12 10
Besar, Gunong, mtn., Malay. K6 48
Besar, Gunung, vol., Indon. E9 50
Besedz', stm., Eur. H14 10
Beskid Mountains see Beskids, mts., Eur. G15 16
Beskids, mts., Eur. G15 16
Beskra, Alg. C6 64
Beslan, Russia F6 32
Besni, Tur. A8 58
Bessarabia, hist. reg., Eur. C15 26
Bessemer, Al., U.S. D11 122
Bessemer, Mi., U.S. E8 118
Bessemer City, N.C., U.S. A4 116
Bestjah, Russia D15 34
Bestöbe, Kaz. D12 32
Bestuževo, Russia F20 8
Betafo, Madag. D8 68
Betanzos, Spain A2 20
Bétaré Oya, Cam. C2 66
Bétera, Spain E10 20
Bethal, S. Afr. E9 70
Bethalto, Il., U.S. F7 120
Bethanien, Nmb. E3 70
Bethany, Mo., U.S. D3 120
Bethany, Ok., U.S. F11 128
Bethel, Monts. D3 105a
Bethel, Ak., U.S. D7 140
Bethel, Me., U.S. F6 110
Bethel, N.C., U.S. I8 114
Bethel Acres, Ok., U.S. B2 122
Bethel Springs, Tn., U.S. B10 122
Bethlehem, S. Afr. F9 70
Bethlehem, Pa., U.S. D10 114
Bethlehem, W.V., U.S. H9 112
Bethlehem *see* Bayt Laḥm, W.B. G6 58
Bethune, Sk., Can. D8 124
Béthune, Fr. D11 14
Bethune, S.C., U.S. B5 116
Betong, Malay. C7 50
Betong, Thai. J5 48
Betoota, Austl. E3 76
Betpaqdala, des., Kaz. E11 32
Betroka, Madag. E8 68
Bet She'arim, Ḥorbat, sci., Isr. F6 58
Betsiamites, stm., Qc., Can. A8 110
Betsiamites, Barrage, dam, Qc., Can. A7 110
Betsiamites, Pointe de, c., Qc., Can. B8 110
Betsiboka, stm., Madag. D8 68
Betsie, Point, c., Mi., U.S. D3 112
Betsy Layne, Ky., U.S. G3 114
Bettendorf, Ia., U.S. C7 120
Bettiah, India E10 54
Bettles Field, Ak., U.S. C9 140
Bettola, Italy F6 22
Betūl, India H6 54
Betung, Indon. E4 50
Betwa, stm., India F7 54
Betzdorf, Ger. F3 16
Beulah, Austl. J4 76
Beulah, Co., U.S. C4 128
Beulah, Mi., U.S. D3 112
Beulah, Ms., U.S. D8 122
Beulaville, N.C., U.S. B8 116
Beuvron, stm., Fr. G11 14
B. Everett Jordan Lake, res., N.C., U.S. I6 114
Beverley, Eng., U.K. H12 12
Beverly, Ma., U.S. B15 114
Beverly Hills, Ca., U.S. I7 134
Beverly Lake, l., Nu., Can. C10 106
Beverungen, Ger. E5 16
Beverwijk, Neth. B13 14
Bewani Mountains, mts., Pap. N. Gui. a3 79a
Bexhill, Eng., U.K. K13 12
Bexley, Oh., U.S. E3 114
Bey Dağları, mts., Tur. G13 28
Beydagları Olimpos Milli Parkı, p.o.i., Tur. G13 28
Beyla, Gui. H3 64
Beyneū, Kaz. E9 32
Beypazarı, Tur. C14 28
Beypore, India F2 53
Beyra, Som. C9 66
Beyşehir, Tur. F14 28
Beyşehir Gölü, l., Tur. F14 28
Bežanickaja vozvyšennost', plat., Russia D12 10
Bežanicy, Russia D12 10
Bežeck, Russia C19 10
Béziers, Fr. F9 18
Bezmein, Turkmen. B8 56
Bhadohi, India F9 54
Bhādra, India D5 54
Bhadrāchalam, India C5 53
Bhadrak, India H11 54
Bhadra Reservoir, res., India E2 53
Bhadrāvati, India E2 53
Bhāgalpur, India F11 54
Bhainsa, India B3 53
Bhāi Pheru, Pak. C4 54
Bhairab Bāzār, Bngl. F13 54
Bhaironghāti, India C7 54
Bhakkar, Pak. C3 54
Bhaktapur (Bhādgāon), Nepal E10 54
Bhālki, India C3 53
Bhalwāl, Pak. B4 54
Bhamo, Mya. D8 46
Bhandāra, India H7 54
Bhanvad, India H2 54
Bharatpur, India E6 54
Bharatpur, Nepal E10 54
Bharthana, India E7 54
Bharūch, India H4 54
Bhātāpāra, India H8 54
Bhātghar Lake, res., India B1 53
Bhatkal, India E2 53
Bhātpāra, India G12 54
Bhattiprolu, India C5 53
Bhavāni, India F3 53
Bhāvnagar, India H4 54
Bhawani Mandi, India F5 54
Bhawānipatna, India I9 54
Bhera, Pak. B4 54
Bhīkangaon, India H5 54
Bhilai, India H8 54
Bhīlwāra, India F5 54
Bhīma, stm., India C3 53
Bhīmavaram, India C5 53
Bhind, India E7 54
Bhīnmāl, India F4 54
Bhiwandi, India B1 53
Bhiwāni, India D6 54
Bhojpur, Nepal E11 54
Bhokardan, India H5 54
Bhongīr, India C4 53
Bhopāl, India G6 54
Bhuban, India H10 54
Bhubaneshwar, India H10 54
Bhuj, India G2 54
Bhusāwal, India H5 54
Bhutan, ctry., Asia E13 54
Bia, Phou, mtn., Laos C6 48
Biafra, Bight of, b., Afr. I6 64
Biak, i., Indon. F10 44
Biała Piska, Pol. C18 16
Biała Podlaska, Pol. D19 16
Biała Podlaska, state, Pol. E19 16
Białobrzegi, Pol. E16 16
Białogard, Pol. B12 16
Białowieski Park Narodowy, p.o.i., Pol. D19 16
Białystok, Pol. C19 16
Białystok, state, Pol. C19 16
Bianco, Monte see Blanc, Mont, mtn., Eur. D12 18
Biankouma, C. Iv. H3 64
Biaora, India F6 54
Biaro, Pulau, i., Indon. E8 44
Biarritz, Fr. F4 18
Biasca, Switz. D5 22
Biba, Egypt J2 58
Bibala, Ang. C1 68
Bibb City, Ga., U.S. E14 122
Bibbiena, Italy G8 22
Bibémi, Cam. C2 66
Bicas, Braz. K4 88
Bicaz, Rom. C13 26
Biche, Lac la, l., Ab., Can. B18 138
Bichigt, Mong. B4 36
Bicknell, In., U.S. F10 120
Bicknell, Ut., U.S. E5 132
Bicudo, stm., Braz. J3 88
Bičura, Russia F10 34
Bīd, India B2 53
Bida, Nig. H6 64
Bīdar, India C3 53
Biddeford, Me., U.S. G6 110
Bideford, Eng., U.K. J8 12
Bieber, Ca., U.S. B4 134
Biebrza, stm., Pol. C18 16
Biebrzański Park Narodowy, p.o.i., Pol. C18 16
Biecz, Pol. G17 16
Biedenkopf, Ger. F4 16
Biel (Bienne), Switz. C4 22
Bielawa, Pol. F12 16
Bielefeld, Ger. D4 16
Bieler Lake, l., Nu., Can. A15 106
Biella, Italy E4 22
Bielsko-Biała, Pol. G14 16
Bielsko-Biała, state, Pol. G15 16
Bielsk Podlaski, Pol. D19 16
Bienfait, Sk., Can. E11 124
Bien Hoa, Viet. G8 48
Bienne *see* Biel, Switz. C4 22
Bien Son, Viet. B7 48
Bienville, La., U.S. E5 122
Bienville, Lac, l., Qc., Can. D16 106
Bierutów, Pol. E13 16
Bieszczadzki Park Narodowy, p.o.i., Pol. G18 16
Bifoun, Gabon E2 66
Big, stm., Mo., U.S. F7 120
Biga, Tur. C10 28
Bigadiç, Tur. D11 28
Big A Mountain, mtn., Va., U.S. G3 114
Big Bald Mountain, mtn., Ga., U.S. B1 116
Big Baldy Mountain, mtn., Mt., U.S. D16 136
Big Bay, Mi., U.S. B2 112
Big Bay, b., Vanuatu j16 79d
Big Bay De Noc, b., Mi., U.S. C3 112
Big Bear Lake, Ca., U.S. I9 134
Big Beaver, Sk., Can. E8 124
Big Belt Mountains, mts., Mt., U.S. D15 136
Big Bend, Swaz. E10 70
Big Bend National Park, p.o.i., Tx., U.S. E4 130
Big Bend Reservoir, res., Ab., Can. D15 138
Big Black, stm., Ms., U.S. E8 122
Big Blue, stm., U.S. G16 126
Big Blue, West Fork, stm., Ne., U.S. G15 126
Big Bonito Creek, stm., Az., U.S. J7 132
Big Canyon, p., Tx., U.S. D5 130
Big Chino Wash, stm., Az., U.S. H4 132
Big Creek, B.C., Can. E7 138
Big Creek, Ca., U.S. F6 134
Big Creek, stm., B.C., Can. E8 138
Big Creek, stm., Ar., U.S. C8 122
Big Creek, stm., Ks., U.S. C9 128
Big Cypress National Preserve, Fl., U.S. J4 116
Big Cypress Swamp, sw., Fl., U.S. J4 116
Big Delta, Ak., U.S. D10 140
Big Desert, des., Austl. J3 76
Big Diomede Island see Ratmanova, ostrov, i., Russia C27 34
Big Dry Creek, stm., Mt., U.S. G7 124
Bigelow Bight, b., U.S. G6 110
Big Flat, Ar., U.S. I5 120
Bigfork, Mn., U.S. D5 118
Big Fork, stm., Mn., U.S. C5 118
Big Frog Mountain, mtn., Tn., U.S. C14 122
Biggar, Sk., Can. B6 124
Biggers, Ar., U.S. H7 120
Biggs, Ca., U.S. D4 134
Big Gull Lake, l., On., Can. D12 112

I·8 Big Hole – Boqueirão

Name	Map Ref.	Page
Big Hole, stm., Mt., U.S.	E14	136
Bighorn, stm., U.S.	A5	126
Bighorn Basin, bas., U.S.	C4	126
Bighorn Canyon National Recreation Area, p.o.i., U.S.	B4	126
Bighorn Lake, res., U.S.	B4	126
Bighorn Mountains, mts., U.S.	C5	126
Bight, Head of, b., Austl.	F6	74
Big Island, Va., U.S.	G6	114
Big Island, i., Nu., Can.	C17	106
Big Lake, Mn., U.S.	F5	118
Big Lake, l., Me., U.S.	E9	110
Big Lookout Mountain, mtn., Or., U.S.	F9	136
Big Lost, stm., Id., U.S.	G13	136
Big Muddy, stm., Il., U.S.	G8	120
Big Muddy Creek, stm., Mt., U.S.	F9	124
Big Nemaha, North Fork, stm., Ne., U.S.	K2	118
Bignona, Sen.	G1	64
Big Pine, Ca., U.S.	F7	134
Big Pine Mountain, mtn., Ca., U.S.	I6	134
Big Piney, Wy., U.S.	H16	136
Big Piney, stm., Mo., U.S.	G6	120
Bigpoint, Ms., U.S.	G10	122
Big Porcupine Creek, stm., Mt., U.S.	H6	124
Big Prairie Creek, stm., Al., U.S.	E11	122
Big Quill Lake, l., Sk., Can.	C9	124
Big Raccoon Creek, stm., In., U.S.	I2	112
Big Rapids, Mi., U.S.	E4	112
Big Rideau Lake, l., On., Can.	D13	112
Big River, Sk., Can.	E9	106
Big Sable Point, c., Mi., U.S.	D3	112
Big Sand Lake, l., Mb., Can.	D11	106
Big Sandy, Tn., U.S.	H9	120
Big Sandy, Tx., U.S.	E3	122
Big Sandy, stm., Wy., U.S.	F3	126
Big Sandy, stm., U.S.	F3	114
Big Sandy Creek, stm., Co., U.S.	C6	128
Bigsby Island, i., On., Can.	B4	118
Big Signal Peak, mtn., Ca., U.S.	D2	134
Big Sioux, stm., U.S.	E16	126
Big Sky, Mt., U.S.	E15	136
Big Smoky Valley, val., Nv., U.S.	E8	134
Big Spring, Tx., U.S.	B6	130
Big Spruce Knob, mtn., W.V., U.S.	F5	114
Big Stone City, S.D., U.S.	F2	118
Big Stone Gap, Va., U.S.	H3	114
Big Stone Lake, l., U.S.	F2	118
Big Sunflower, stm., Ms., U.S.	D8	122
Big Sur, reg., Ca., U.S.	H4	134
Big Timber, Mt., U.S.	E16	136
Big Trout Lake, l., On., Can.	E12	106
Biguaçu, Braz.	C13	92
Big Water, Ut., U.S.	F5	132
Big Wells, Tx., U.S.	F8	130
Big White Mountain, mtn., B.C., Can.	G12	138
Big Wood, stm., Id., U.S.	G12	136
Bihać, Bos.	E2	26
Bīhar, India	F10	54
Bihār, state, India	E10	54
Biharamulo, Tan.	E6	66
Bihor, state, Rom.	C9	26
Bihor, Vârful, mtn., Rom.	C9	26
Bihoro, Japan	C16	38
Bihosava, Bela.	E10	10
Bihu, China	G8	42
Bija, stm., Russia	D15	32
Bijagós, Arquipélago dos, is., Gui.-B.	G1	64
Bijainagar, India	F5	54
Bijaipur, India	E6	54
Bijāpur, India	C2	53
Bījāpur, India	B5	53
Bijeljina, Bos.	E6	26
Bijelo Polje, Serb.	F6	26
Bijie, China	F6	36
Bijnor, India	D7	54
Bijsk, Russia	D15	32
Bīkāner, India	D4	54
Bikar, at., Marsh. Is.	B8	72
Bikeqi, China	A4	42
Bikin, Russia	B11	36
Bikini, at., Marsh. Is.	B7	72
Bīkkū Bīttī, mtn., Libya	C3	62
Bikoro, D.R.C.	E3	66
Bilāra, India	E4	54
Bilāri, India	D7	54
Bilāsipāra, India	E13	54
Bilāspur, India	C6	54
Bilāspur, India	G9	54
Bila Tserkva, Ukr.	F15	6
Bilauktaung Range, mts., Asia	F4	48
Bilbao, Spain	A7	20
Bilbeis, Egypt	H2	58
Bilbilis, sci., Spain	C9	20
Bileća, Bos.	G5	26
Bilecik, Tur.	C12	28
Bilecik, state, Tur.	C13	28
Biłgoraj, Pol.	F18	16
Bilgrām, India	E8	54
Bilhorod-Dnistrovs'kyi, Ukr.	C17	26
Bili, D.R.C.	D5	66
Biliaïvka, Ukr.	C17	26
Bīliköl köli, l., Kaz.	F12	32
Bīlīmora, India	H4	54
Bilin, Mya.	D3	48
Bilin, stm., Mya.	D3	48
Bílina, Czech Rep.	F9	16
Biliran Island, i., Phil.	E5	52
Billabong Creek, stm., Austl.	J5	76
Billings, Mo., U.S.	G4	120
Billings, Mt., U.S.	B4	126
Billings Heights, Mt., U.S.	B4	126
Billiton see Belitung, i., Indon.	E5	50
Bill Williams, stm., Az., U.S.	I3	132
Billy Chinook, Lake, res., Or., U.S.	F5	136
Bilma, Niger	F7	64
Biloela, Austl.	E8	76
Biloxi, Ms., U.S.	G10	122
Bilpa Morea Claypan, l., Austl.	E2	76
Bilqas Qism Awwal, Egypt	G2	58
Biltine, Chad	E4	62
Biltmore Forest, N.C., U.S.	A3	116
Bilugyun Island, i., Mya.	D3	48
Bimbo, C.A.R.	D3	66
Bimbowrie, Austl.	H3	76
Bimini Islands, is., Bah.	B9	96
Bīna-Etāwa, India	F7	54
Binaiya, Gunung, mtn., Indon.	F9	44
Binalbagan, Phil.	E4	52
Bin'an, China	B7	38
Bindki, India	E8	54
Bindloss, Ab., Can.	D3	124
Bindura, Zimb.	D5	68
Binéfar, Spain	C11	20
Binford, N.D., U.S.	G15	124
Binga, D.R.C.	D4	66
Binga, Monte, mtn., Afr.	D5	68
Bingara, Austl.	G8	76
Bingen, Ger.	G3	16
Binger, Ok., U.S.	F10	128
Binghamton, N.Y., U.S.	B10	114
Bin Ghunaymah, Jabal, mts., Libya	B3	62
Binhai, China	D8	42
Binh Gia, Viet.	B8	48
Binjai, Indon.	K4	48
Binnaway, Austl.	H7	76
Binongko, Pulau, i., Indon.	G7	44
Binscarth, Mb., Can.	D12	124
Bintan, Pulau, i., Indon.	C4	50
Bintimani, mtn., S.L.	H2	64
Bintuhan, Indon.	F3	50
Bintulu, Malay.	B8	50
Bintuni, Indon.	F9	44
Binxian, China	D3	42
Binxian, China	C7	42
Binxian, China	B7	38
Binyang, China	J3	42
Bin-Yauri, Nig.	G5	64
Biobío, state, Chile	H1	92
Biobío, stm., Chile	G2	90
Biogradska Gora Nacionalni Park, p.o.i., Serb.	G6	26
Bioko, i., Eq. Gui.	I6	64
Bira, Russia	G15	34
Birac, Phil.	B3	52
Birāk, Libya	B2	62
Birakan, Russia	G15	34
Bi'r al Wa'r, Libya	C2	62
Birao, C.A.R.	B4	66
Birch, stm., Ab., Can.	D8	106
Birch Creek, stm., Mt., U.S.	B14	136
Birch Hills, Sk., Can.	B8	124
Birch Island, B.C., Can.	E10	138
Birch Island, i., Mb., Can.	B13	124
Birch Mountains, hills, Ab., Can.	D8	106
Birch Run, Mi., U.S.	E6	112
Birch Tree, Mo., U.S.	H6	120
Birchwood, Wi., U.S.	F7	118
Bird Creek, stm., Ok., U.S.	E13	128
Bird Island, Mn., U.S.	G4	118
Bird Island, sci., S. Geor.	J9	90
Birdsville, Austl.	E2	76
Birdtail Creek, stm., Mb., Can.	D13	124
Birdum, Austl.	C6	74
Birecik, Tur.	A9	58
Bireun, Indon.	J3	48
Bir Ghbalou, Alg.	H14	20
Birigui, Braz.	D6	90
Biriljussy, Russia	C16	32
Bīrjand, Iran	C8	56
Birjul'ka, Russia	D19	32
Birjusa, stm., Russia	C17	32
Birjusinsk, Russia	C17	32
Birken, B.C., Can.	F8	138
Birkenfeld, Ger.	G3	16
Birkenhead, Eng., U.K.	H9	12
Birmingham, Eng., U.K.	I10	12
Birmingham, Al., U.S.	D11	122
Birmingham, Ia., U.S.	D6	120
Birmingham, Mi., U.S.	B2	114
Birmitrapur, India	G10	54
Bîr Mogreïn, Maur.	D2	64
Birnin Gaouré, Niger	G5	64
Birnin-Kebbi, Nig.	G5	64
Birnin Konni, Niger	G5	64
Birnin Kudu, Nig.	G6	64
Birobidžan, Russia	G15	34
Birrie, stm., Austl.	G6	76
Birsk, Russia	C9	32
Birštonas, Lith.	F7	10
Birtle, Mb., Can.	D12	124
Birūr, India	E2	53
Biržai, Lith.	D7	10
Birżebbuġa, Malta	I8	24
Bisaccia, Italy	C9	24
Bīsalpur, India	D7	54
Bisbee, Az., U.S.	L7	132
Bisbee, N.D., U.S.	F14	124
Biscarrosse et de Parentis, Étang de, l., Fr.	E4	18
Biscay, Bay of, b., Eur.	E2	18
Biscayne Bay, b., Fl., U.S.	K5	116
Biscayne National Park, p.o.i., Fl., U.S.	K5	116
Bisceglie, Italy	C10	24
Bischofshofen, Aus.	C10	22
Bischofswerda, Ger.	E10	16
Biscoe, N.C., U.S.	A6	116
Bishnupur, India	G11	54
Bisho, S. Afr.	H8	70
Bishop, Ca., U.S.	F7	134
Bishop, Tx., U.S.	G10	130
Bishop Auckland, Eng., U.K.	G11	12
Bishop Rock, r., Eng., U.K.	L6	12
Bishop's Falls, Nf., Can.	j22	107a
Bishop's Stortford, Eng., U.K.	J13	12
Bishopville, S.C., U.S.	B5	116
Biškek, Kyrg.	F12	32
Biskupiec, Pol.	C16	16
Bislig, Phil.	F6	52
Bismarck, Mo., U.S.	G7	120
Bismarck, N.D., U.S.	A12	126
Bismarck Archipelago, is., Pap. N. Gui.	a4	79a
Bismarck Range, mts., Pap. N. Gui.	b3	79a
Bismarck Sea, s., Pap. N. Gui.	a4	79a
Bismark, Kap, c., Grnld.	B22	141
Bissa, Djebel, mtn., Alg.	H12	20
Bissau, Gui.-B.	G1	64
Bissett, Mb., Can.	C18	124
Bissikrima, Gui.	G2	64
Bistcho Lake, l., Ab., Can.	D7	106
Bistineau, Lake, res., La., U.S.	E5	122
Bistrica, Slvn.	D13	22
Bistrița, Rom.	B11	26
Bistrița, stm., Rom.	C13	26
Bistrița-Năsăud, state, Rom.	B11	26
Biswān, India	E8	54
Bitam, Gabon	D2	66
Bitburg, Ger.	G2	16
Bitche, Fr.	E16	14
Bitlis, Tur.	B5	56
Bitola, Mac.	B4	28
Bitolj see Bitola, Mac.	B4	28
Bitonto, Italy	C10	24
Bitou, Burkina	G4	64
Bitter Creek, stm., Wy., U.S.	B8	132
Bitterfeld, Ger.	E8	16
Bitterfontein, S. Afr.	G4	70
Bitterroot, stm., Mt., U.S.	D13	136
Bitterroot, West Fork, stm., Mt., U.S.	E12	136
Bitterroot Range, mts., U.S.	C11	136
Bitung, Indon.	E8	44
Bitupitá, Braz.	B5	88
Biu, Nig.	G7	64
Bivins, Tx., U.S.	E4	122
Biwabik, Mn., U.S.	D6	118
Biwa-ko, l., Japan	D8	40
Bixby, Ok., U.S.	I2	120
Biyala, Egypt	G2	58
Biyang, China	E5	42
Bizana, S. Afr.	G9	70
Bizen, Japan	E7	40
Bizerte (Binzert), Tun.	G3	24
Bizerte, Lac de, l., Tun.	G3	24
Bizkaiko, co., Spain	A8	20
Bjahoml', Bela.	F10	10
Bjala, Blg.	G14	26
Bjala Slatina, Blg.	F10	26
Bjalyničy, Bela.	F12	10
Bjarèzina, stm., Bela.	H13	10
Bjarèzina, stm., Bela.	G9	10
Bjaroza, Bela.	H7	10
Bjarozauka, Bela.	G8	10
Bjelovar, Cro.	E13	22
Björna, Swe.	E8	8
Björneborg see Pori, Fin.	F9	8
Bjorne Peninsula, pen., Nu., Can.	B8	141
Bjørnøya, i., Nor.	B5	30
Bla, Mali	G3	64
Blace, Serb.	F8	26
Black (Da, Song) (Lixian), stm., Asia	D9	46
Black, stm., Mb., Can.	D18	124
Black, stm., Ak., U.S.	C11	140
Black, stm., Az., U.S.	J6	132
Black, stm., La., U.S.	F7	122
Black, stm., Mi., U.S.	E7	112
Black, stm., N.Y., U.S.	E14	112
Black, stm., Wi., U.S.	G7	118
Black, stm., U.S.	I6	120
Blackall, Austl.	E5	76
Black Bay, b., On., Can.	C10	118
Black Bay Peninsula, pen., On., Can.	C10	118
Black Bear Creek, stm., Ok., U.S.	E11	128
Blackburn, Eng., U.K.	H10	12
Blackburn, Mount, mtn., Ak., U.S.	D11	140
Black Butte, mtn., Mt., U.S.	D15	136
Black Canyon of the Gunnison National Park, p.o.i., Co., U.S.	E9	132
Black Creek, stm., Ms., U.S.	G9	122
Black Creek, stm., S.C., U.S.	B6	116
Black Diamond, Ab., Can.	F16	138
Black Diamond, Wa., U.S.	C5	136
Blackdown Tableland National Park, p.o.i., Austl.	D7	76
Blackduck, Mn., U.S.	D4	118
Black Eagle, Mt., U.S.	C15	136
Blackfoot, Id., U.S.	G14	136
Blackfoot, Mt., U.S.	B14	136
Blackfoot, stm., Id., U.S.	G15	136
Blackfoot, stm., Mt., U.S.	D13	136
Blackfoot Reservoir, res., Id., U.S.	H15	136
Black Forest see Schwarzwald, mts., Ger.	H4	16
Black Hills, mts., U.S.	C9	126
Black Island, i., Mb., Can.	C17	124
Black Lake, Qc., Can.	D5	110
Black Lake, l., Sk., Can.	D10	106
Black Lake, l., Mi., U.S.	C5	112
Black Lake, l., N.Y., U.S.	D14	112
Black Mesa, mtn., U.S.	E6	128
Blackmore, Mount, mtn., Mt., U.S.	E15	136
Black Mountain, N.C., U.S.	A3	116
Black Mountain, mtn., Az., U.S.	K5	132
Black Mountain, mtn., Ca., U.S.	H5	134
Black Mountain, mtn., Mt., U.S.	D14	136
Black Mountain, hill, Austl.	C2	76
Black Mountain, mts., U.S.	H2	114
Black Nossob, stm., Nmb.	C4	70
Black Pine Peak, mtn., Id., U.S.	A3	132
Blackpool, Eng., U.K.	H9	12
Black Range, mts., N.M., U.S.	J9	132
Black River, N.Y., U.S.	D14	112
Black River Falls, Wi., U.S.	G8	118
Black Rock, Ar., U.S.	H6	120
Black Rock, r., Ire.	G2	12
Black Rock, r., S. Geor.	J8	90
Black Rock Desert, des., Nv., U.S.	B7	134
Blacksburg, S.C., U.S.	A4	116
Blacksburg, Va., U.S.	G5	114
Black Sea, s.	G15	6
Blacks Fork, stm., U.S.	B7	132
Blackshear, Lake, res., Ga., U.S.	D2	116
Blackstone, Va., U.S.	G8	114
Black Sturgeon Lake, l., On., Can.	B9	118
Blackville, S.C., U.S.	C4	116
Black Volta (Volta Noire) (Mouhoun), stm., Afr.	H4	64
Blackwater, Austl.	D7	76
Blackwater, stm., Ire.	I4	12
Blackwater, stm., Mo., U.S.	E4	120
Blackwater Creek, stm., Austl.	E5	76
Blackwater Draw, stm., Tx., U.S.	H7	128
Blackwater Lake, l., N.T., Can.	C6	106
Blackwell, Tx., U.S.	B7	130
Bladenboro, N.C., U.S.	B7	116
Bladensburg National Park, p.o.i., Austl.	D4	76
Bladgrond-Noord, S. Afr.	F4	70
Bladworth, Sk., Can.	C7	124
Bláfell, mtn., Ice.	k30	8a
Blagoevgrad, Blg.	G10	26
Blagoveščensk, Russia	D16	34
Blaine, Mn., U.S.	F5	118
Blaine, Wa., U.S.	B4	136
Blair, Ne., U.S.	C1	120
Blair, Ok., U.S.	G9	128
Blair, Wi., U.S.	G7	118
Blair Athol, Austl.	D6	76
Blairsville, Ga., U.S.	B2	116
Blairsville, Pa., U.S.	D6	114
Blaj, Rom.	C10	26
Blakely, Ga., U.S.	F13	122
Blake Plateau, unds.	E6	144
Blake Point, c., Mi., U.S.	C10	118
Blalock Island, i., Wa., U.S.	E7	136
Blanc, Mont, mtn., Eur.	D12	18
Blanca, Co., U.S.	D3	128
Blanca, Bahía, b., Arg.	G4	90
Blanca, Laguna, l., Chile	J2	90
Blanca, Punta, c., Chile	B2	92
Blanca, Sierra, mtn., Tx., U.S.	C2	130
Blanca Peak, mtn., Co., U.S.	D3	128
Blanchard, Ok., U.S.	F11	128
Blanchard, stm., Oh., U.S.	D2	114
Blanche, Lake, l., Austl.	G2	76
Blanche Channel, strt., Sol. Is.	e7	79b
Blanchester, Oh., U.S.	E1	114
Blanchisseuse, Trin.	s12	105f
Blanco, Tx., U.S.	D9	130
Blanco, stm., Arg.	D3	92
Blanco, stm., Ec.	G2	86
Blanco, stm., Tx., U.S.	E9	130
Blanco, Cabo, c., C.R.	H5	102
Blanco, Cañon, p., N.M., U.S.	F3	128
Blanco, Cape, c., Or., U.S.	H2	136
Blanco, Lago, l., Chile	J3	90
Blanc-Sablon, Qc., Can.	i22	107a
Bland, Va., U.S.	G4	114
Blanda, stm., Ice.	k30	8a
Blanding, Ut., U.S.	F7	132
Blandinsville, Il., U.S.	D7	120
Blanes, Spain	C13	20
Blangkejeren, Indon.	K3	48
Blangy-sur-Bresle, Fr.	E10	14
Blankenburg, Ger.	E6	16
Blanquilla, Isla, i., Ven.	B9	86
Blansko, Czech Rep.	G12	16
Blantyre, Mwi.	D6	68
Blarney Castle, sci., Ire.	J4	12
Błaszki, Pol.	E14	16
Blaubeuren, Ger.	H5	16
Blaufelden, Ger.	G5	16
Błażowa, Pol.	G18	16
Bledsoe, Tx., U.S.	H5	128
Blega, Indon.	G8	50
Bleik see Andenes, Nor.	B6	8
Blekinge, state, Swe.	H6	8
Blenheim, On., Can.	F8	112
Blenheim, N.Z.	E5	80
Blessing, Tx., U.S.	F11	130
Bletchley, Eng., U.K.	J12	12
Bligh Water, strt., Fiji	p18	79e
Blind River, On., Can.	B6	112
Blissfield, Mi., U.S.	C2	114
Blitar, Indon.	H8	50
Block Island, i., R.I., U.S.	C14	114
Blockton, Ia., U.S.	D3	120
Bloedel, B.C., Can.	F5	138
Bloemfontein, S. Afr.	F8	70
Bloemhof, S. Afr.	E7	70
Bloemhofdam, res., S. Afr.	E7	70
Blois, Fr.	G10	14
Blönduós, Ice.	k29	8a
Bloodvein, stm., Can.	E11	106
Bloody Foreland, c., Ire.	F4	12
Bloomer, Wi., U.S.	F7	118
Bloomfield, On., Can.	E12	112
Bloomfield, Ky., U.S.	G12	120
Bloomfield, Mo., U.S.	H8	120
Bloomfield, Ne., U.S.	E15	126
Bloomfield, N.M., U.S.	G9	132
Blooming Grove, Tx., U.S.	E2	122
Blooming Prairie, Mn., U.S.	H5	118
Bloomington, Il., U.S.	D9	120
Bloomington, In., U.S.	E11	120
Bloomington, Mn., U.S.	G5	118
Bloomington, Tx., U.S.	F11	130
Bloomington, Wi., U.S.	B7	120
Bloomsburg, Pa., U.S.	C9	114
Bloomsbury, Austl.	C7	76
Bloomville, Oh., U.S.	C2	114
Blora, Indon.	G7	50
Blosseville Kyst, cst., Grnld.	D20	141
Blossom, Tx., U.S.	D3	122
Blouberg, mtn., S. Afr.	C9	70
Blountstown, Fl., U.S.	G13	122
Blountsville, Al., U.S.	C12	122
Blowering Reservoir, res., Austl.	J6	76
Blowing Point Village, Anguilla	A1	105a
Blowing Rock, N.C., U.S.	H4	114
Bludenz, Aus.	C6	22
Blue, stm., Az., U.S.	J7	132
Blue, stm., Ok., U.S.	C2	122
Blue Creek, Wa., U.S.	B8	136
Blue Cypress Lake, l., Fl., U.S.	I5	116
Blue Earth, Mn., U.S.	H4	118
Blue Earth, stm., U.S.	H4	118
Bluefield, Va., U.S.	G4	114
Bluefield, W.V., U.S.	G4	114
Bluefields, Nic.	F6	102
Blue Hill, Ne., U.S.	A10	128
Blue Hill Bay, b., Me., U.S.	F8	110
Blue Island, Il., U.S.	G2	112
Blue Mound, Ks., U.S.	F3	120
Blue Mountain, Ms., U.S.	C9	122
Blue Mountain, mtn., Ar., U.S.	C4	122
Blue Mountain, mtn., Mt., U.S.	G9	124
Blue Mountain, mts., Pa., U.S.	D8	114
Blue Mountain Peak, mtn., Jam.	i14	104d
Blue Mountains, mts., Jam.	i14	104d
Blue Mountains, mts., Me., U.S.	F6	110
Blue Mountains, mts., U.S.	E8	136
Blue Mountains National Park, p.o.i., Austl.	J8	76
Blue Mud Bay, b., Austl.	B7	74
Blue Nile (Azraq, Al-Baḩr al-) (Ābay), stm., Afr.	E6	62
Bluenose Lake, l., Nu., Can.	B6	106
Blue Ridge, Ab., Can.	B15	138
Blue Ridge, Ga., U.S.	B1	116
Blue Ridge, mts., U.S.	H4	114
Blue River, B.C., Can.	D11	138
Bluestone Dam, dam, W.V., U.S.	G5	114
Bluestone Lake, res., W.V., U.S.	G5	114
Bluewater, N.M., U.S.	H9	132
Bluff, N.Z.	H3	80
Bluff, Ut., U.S.	F7	132
Bluff Cape, c., Mya.	D2	48
Bluff Creek, stm., U.S.	D11	128
Bluff Dale, Tx., U.S.	B9	130
Bluff Park, Al., U.S.	D12	122
Bluffs, Il., U.S.	E7	120
Bluffton, In., U.S.	H4	112
Bluffton, S.C., U.S.	D5	116
Blumberg, Ger.	I4	16
Blumenau, Braz.	C13	92
Blumenhof, Sk., Can.	D6	124
Bly, Or., U.S.	A4	134
Blyth, On., Can.	E8	112
Blyth, Eng., U.K.	F11	12
Blythe, Ca., U.S.	J2	132
Blytheville, Ar., U.S.	I7	120
Bø, Nor.	G3	8
Bo, S.L.	H2	64
Boac, Phil.	D3	52
Boaco, Nic.	F5	102
Boa Esperança, Braz.	K3	88
Boa Esperança, Represa, res., Braz.	D3	88
Bo'ai, China	D5	42
Boane, Moz.	E11	70
Board Camp Mountain, mtn., Ca., U.S.	C2	134
Boardman, Oh., U.S.	C5	114
Boatman, Austl.	F6	76
Boa Viagem, Braz.	C5	88
Boa Vista, Braz.	F11	86
Boa Vista, i., C.V.	k10	65a
Boawai, Indon.	H12	50
Boaz, Al., U.S.	C12	122
Bobai, China	J3	42
Bobaomby, Tanjona, c., Madag.	C8	68
Bobbili, India	B6	53
Bobcaygeon, On., Can.	D11	112
Bobigny, Fr.	F11	14
Böblingen, Ger.	H4	16
Bobo-Dioulasso, Burkina	G4	64
Bobolice, Pol.	C12	16
Bobonaza, stm., Ec.	H3	86
Bobonong, Bots.	B9	70
Bobr, Bela.	F12	10
Bobtown, Pa., U.S.	E5	114
Bobures, Ven.	C6	86
Boby, mtn., Madag.	E8	68
Bôca da Mata, Braz.	E7	88
Boca do Acre, Braz.	E4	84
Boca do Jari, Braz.	D7	84
Bocage, Cap, c., N. Cal.	m15	79d
Boca Grande, Fl., U.S.	J3	116
Bocaiúva, Braz.	I3	88
Bocaranga, C.A.R.	C3	66
Boca Raton, Fl., U.S.	J5	116
Bocas del Toro, Pan.	H6	102
Bocay, Nic.	E5	102
Bochnia, Pol.	G16	16
Bocholt, Ger.	E2	16
Bochum, Ger.	E3	16
Bocón, Caño, stm., Col.	F7	86
Boconó, Ven.	C6	86
Bocșa, Rom.	D8	26
Boda, C.A.R.	D3	66
Bodajbo, Russia	E11	34
Bodalla, Austl.	K8	76
Bodcau Creek, stm., Ar., U.S.	D5	122
Bode, Ia., U.S.	I4	118
Bodélé, reg., Chad	D3	62
Boden, Swe.	D9	8
Bodensee see Constance, Lake, l., Eur.	I5	16
Bodhan, India	B3	53
Bodh Gaya, India	F10	54
Bodināyakkanūr, India	G3	53
Bodmin, Eng., U.K.	K8	12
Bodø, Nor.	C6	8
Bodoquena, Serra da, plat., Braz.	D5	90
Bodrum, Tur.	F10	28
Bodzentyn, Pol.	F16	16
Boende, D.R.C.	E4	66
Bœng Lvea, Camb.	F7	48
Boeo, Capo, c., Italy	G6	24
Boesmans, stm., S. Afr.	H7	70
Boeuf, stm., U.S.	E7	122
Boffa, Gui.	G2	64
Bogale, Mya.	D2	48
Bogalusa, La., U.S.	G9	122
Bogan, stm., Austl.	H6	76
Bogan Gate, Austl.	I6	76
Bogangolo, C.A.R.	C3	66
Bogata, Tx., U.S.	D3	122
Bogcang, stm., China	C11	54
Bogda Shan, mts., China	C2	36
Bogen, Ger.	H8	16
Boger City, N.C., U.S.	A4	116
Boggabilla, Austl.	G8	76
Boggabri, Austl.	H7	76
Boggy Peak, mtn., Antig.	f4	105b
Bogles, Gren.	p11	105e
Bognor Regis, Eng., U.K.	K12	12
Bogo, Phil.	E5	52
Bogoljubovo, Russia	E15	10
Bogong, Mount, mtn., Austl.	K6	76
Bogor, Indon.	G5	50
Bogorodick, Russia	G21	10
Bogorodsk, Russia	H20	8
Bogorodskoe, Russia	F17	34
Bogotá, Col.	E4	86
Bogotol, Russia	C15	32
Bogra, Bngl.	F12	54
Bogučany, Russia	C17	32
Bogué, Maur.	F2	64
Bogue Chitto, stm., U.S.	G8	122
Bogue Phalia, stm., Ms., U.S.	D8	122
Böğürtlen, Tur.	A8	58
Bo Hai (Chihli, Gulf of), b., China	B8	42
Bohai Haixia, strt., China	B9	42
Bohain-en-Vermandois, Fr.	D12	14
Bohai Wan, b., China	B8	42
Bohemian Forest, mts., Eur.	G8	16
Böhmer Wald see Bohemian Forest, mts., Eur.	G8	16
Bohol, i., Phil.	F4	52
Bohol Sea, s., Phil.	F5	52
Boiaçu, Braz.	H11	86
Boiano, Italy	C8	24
Boiestown, N.B., Can.	D10	110
Boipeba, Ilha de, i., Braz.	G6	88
Bois, stm., Braz.	C6	90
Bois, Lac des, l., N.T., Can.	B6	106
Bois Blanc Island, i., Mi., U.S.	C5	112
Bois de Sioux, stm., U.S.	F2	118
Boise, Id., U.S.	G10	136
Boise, stm., Id., U.S.	G10	136
Boise, Middle Fork, stm., Id., U.S.	G11	136
Boise, South Fork, stm., Id., U.S.	G11	136
Boise City, Ok., U.S.	E6	128
Boissevain, Mb., Can.	E13	124
Boistfort Peak, mtn., Wa., U.S.	D3	136
Boizenburg, Ger.	C6	16
Boja, Indon.	G7	50
Bojadła, Pol.	E11	16
Bojeador, Cape, c., Phil.	A3	52
Bojnūrd, Iran	B8	56
Bojonegoro, Indon.	G7	50
Bojuru, Braz.	E12	92
Bokāro Steel City, India	G10	54
Bokchito, Ok., U.S.	C2	122
Boké, Gui.	G2	64
Bokhara, stm., Austl.	G6	76
Bok Koŭ, Camb.	G6	48
Boknafjorden, strt., Nor.	G1	8
Boko, Congo	E2	66
Bokoro, Chad	E3	62
Bokote, D.R.C.	E4	66
Boksitogorsk, Russia	A16	10
Bokungu, D.R.C.	E4	66
Bol, Cro.	G13	22
Bolama, Gui.-B.	G1	64
Bolaños, stm., Mex.	E7	100
Bolaños de Calatrava, Spain	F7	20
Bolān Pass, p., Pak.	D10	56
Bolayır, Tur.	C9	28
Bolbec, Fr.	E9	14
Bole, China	F14	32
Bole, Ghana	H4	64
Boles, Ar., U.S.	C4	122
Bolesławiec, Pol.	E11	16
Boley, Ok., U.S.	B2	122
Bolgatanga, Ghana	G4	64
Bolhov, Russia	G18	10
Bolhrad, Ukr.	D15	26
Boli, China	B11	36
Boligee, Al., U.S.	E10	122
Bolingbrook, Il., U.S.	C9	120
Bolishan, China	C5	38
Bolívar, Col.	G3	86
Bolívar, Col.	G3	86
Bolivar, Mo., U.S.	G4	120
Bolivar, N.Y., U.S.	B7	114
Bolivar, Tn., U.S.	B9	122
Bolívar, state, Col.	C4	86
Bolívar, state, Ec.	H2	86
Bolívar, state, Ven.	D10	86
Bolívar, Cerro, mtn., Ven.	D10	86
Bolívar, Pico (La Columna), mtn., Ven.	C6	86
Bolivar Peninsula, pen., Tx., U.S.	H4	122
Bolivia, ctry., S.A.	G5	84
Bollnäs, Swe.	F7	8
Bollon, Austl.	G6	76
Bolmen, l., Swe.	H5	8
Bolobo, D.R.C.	E3	66
Bologna, Italy	F8	22
Bolognesi, Peru	F3	84
Bologoe, Russia	C17	10
Bologovo, Russia	D14	10
Bolohovo, Russia	F20	10
Bolomba, D.R.C.	D3	66
Bolon', ozero, l., Russia	G16	34
Bolotnoe, Russia	C14	32
Bolovens, Plateau des, plat., Laos	E8	48
Bol'šaja Balahnja, stm., Russia	B9	34
Bol'šaja Heta, stm., Russia	C5	34
Bol'šaja Kuonamka, stm., Russia	C10	34
Bol'šaja Murta, Russia	C16	32
Bol'šaja Ussurka, stm., Russia	B11	38
Bol'šaja Višera, Russia	B15	10
Bol'šakovo, Russia	F4	10
Bolsena, Italy	H8	22
Bolsena, Lago di, l., Italy	H9	22
Bol'šereče, Russia	C13	32
Bol'šereck, Russia	F20	34
Bol'ševik, Russia	D18	34
Bol'ševik, ostrov, i., Russia	A10	34
Bol'šezemel'skaja Tundra, reg., Russia	A9	32
Bolshevik see Bol'ševik, ostrov, i., Russia	A10	34
Bol'šie Uki, Russia	C12	32
Bol'šoe Mihajlovskoe, Russia	D20	10
Bol'šoe Polpino, Russia	G17	10
Bol'šoe Selo, Russia	C21	10
Bol'šoj Anjuj, stm., Russia	C21	34
Bol'šoj Begičev, ostrov, i., Russia	B11	34
Bol'šoj Jugan, stm., Russia	B12	32
Bol'šoj Kamen', Russia	C10	38
Bol'šoj Ljahovskij, ostrov, i., Russia	B17	34
Bol'šoj Tal'cy, Russia	A15	10
Bolton, On., Can.	E10	112
Bolton, Eng., U.K.	H10	12
Bolton, Ms., U.S.	E8	122
Bolton, N.C., U.S.	B7	116
Bolu, Tur.	C14	28
Bolu, state, Tur.	C14	28
Bolva, stm., Russia	G17	10
Bolvadin, Tur.	E13	28
Bóly, Hung.	C5	26
Bolzano (Bozen), Italy	D8	22
Boma, D.R.C.	F2	66
Bomaderry, Austl.	J8	76
Bombala, Austl.	K7	76
Bombay see Mumbai, India	B1	53
Bomberai, Semenanjung, pen., Indon.	F9	44
Bomboma, D.R.C.	D3	66
Bom Conselho, Braz.	E7	88
Bom Despacho, Braz.	J3	88
Bomdila, India	E14	54
Bom Jesus, Braz.	E3	88
Bom Jesus da Lapa, Braz.	G4	88
Bomnak, Russia	F14	34
Bomokandi, stm., D.R.C.	D5	66
Bomongo, D.R.C.	D3	66
Bom Retiro, Braz.	C13	92
Bomu, stm., Afr.	D4	66
Bon, Cap, c., Tun.	G5	24
Bon Air, Va., U.S.	G8	114
Bonaire, i., Neth. Ant.	p23	104g
Bonampak, sci., Mex.	D2	102
Bonandolok, Indon.	C1	50
Bonanza, Or., U.S.	A4	134
Bonanza, Ut., U.S.	C7	132
Bonanza Peak, mtn., Wa., U.S.	B5	136
Bonao, Dom. Rep.	C12	102
Bonaparte, Ia., U.S.	D6	120
Bonaparte, stm., B.C., Can.	F9	138
Bonaparte, Mount, mtn., Wa., U.S.	B7	136
Bonaparte Lake, l., B.C., Can.	E10	138
Bonar Bridge, Scot., U.K.	D8	12
Bonasse, Trin.	s12	105f
Bonaventure, Qc., Can.	B11	110
Bonaventure, stm., Qc., Can.	B11	110
Bonaventure, Île, i., Qc., Can.	B12	110
Bonavista, Nf., Can.	j23	107a
Bonavista Bay, b., Nf., Can.	j23	107a
Bondeno, Italy	F8	22
Bondo, D.R.C.	D4	66
Bondo, D.R.C.	E4	66
Bondoc Peninsula, pen., Phil.	D4	52
Bondoukou, C. Iv.	H4	64
Bondowoso, Indon.	G8	50
Bonduel, Wi., U.S.	G10	118
Bone, Teluk, b., Indon.	F7	44
Bonebone, Indon.	E12	50
Boneogeh, Indon.	G12	50
Bonerate, Pulau, i., Indon.	G12	50
Bonesteel, S.D., U.S.	D13	126
Bonete Chico, Cerro, mtn., Arg.	D3	92
Bonete Grande, Cerro, mtn., Arg.	C3	92
Bongabong, Phil.	D3	52
Bongaigaon, India	E13	54
Bongandanga, D.R.C.	D4	66
Bongka, Indon.	F7	44
Bongo, Gabon	E2	66
Bongo, Massif des, mts., C.A.R.	C4	66
Bongor, Chad	E3	62
Bonham, Tx., U.S.	D2	122
Bonhomme, Morne, mtn., Haiti	C11	102
Bonifacio, Fr.	H15	18
Bonifacio, Strait of, strt., Eur.	H15	18
Bonifati, Capo, c., Italy	E9	24
Bonin Islands see Ogasawara-guntō, is., Japan	G18	30
Bonita, La., U.S.	E7	122
Bonita Springs, Fl., U.S.	J4	116
Bonito, Braz.	D5	90
Bonito, Braz.	E8	88
Bonito de Santa Fé, Braz.	D6	88
Bonn, Ger.	F2	16
Bonners Ferry, Id., U.S.	B10	136
Bonnet, Lac du, res., Mb., Can.	D17	124
Bonnétable, Fr.	F9	14
Bonne Terre, Mo., U.S.	G7	120
Bonnet Plume, stm., Yk., Can.	B3	106
Bonneville, Fr.	C12	18
Bonneville Peak, mtn., Id., U.S.	H14	136
Bonneville Salt Flats, pl., Ut., U.S.	C2	132
Bonney SE, Lake, l., Austl.	K3	76
Bonnie Rock, Austl.	F3	74
Bonny, Nig.	I6	64
Bonnyville, Ab., Can.	B20	138
Bono, Ar., U.S.	I7	120
Bonoi, Indon.	F10	44
Bonshaw, P.E., Can.	D13	110
Bontang, Indon.	C10	50
Bontebok National Park, p.o.i., S. Afr.	I5	70
Bonthe, S.L.	H2	64
Bontoc, Phil.	B3	52
Bon Wier, Tx., U.S.	G5	122
Booker, Tx., U.S.	E8	128
Booker T. Washington National Monument, p.o.i., Va., U.S.	H6	114
Boola, Gui.	H3	64
Boolaloo, Austl.	D3	74
Booleroo Centre, Austl.	I2	76
Boologooro, Austl.	D2	74
Boomarra, Austl.	B3	76
Boonah, Austl.	F9	76
Boone, Ia., U.S.	I5	118
Boone, N.C., U.S.	H4	114
Boone, stm., Ia., U.S.	B4	120
Booneville, Ar., U.S.	B5	122
Booneville, Ky., U.S.	G2	114
Booneville, Ms., U.S.	C10	122
Böön Tsagaan nuur, l., Mong.	B4	36
Boonville, Ca., U.S.	D2	134
Boonville, Mo., U.S.	F5	120
Boonville, N.Y., U.S.	E14	112
Boorindal, Austl.	H6	76
Booroorban, Austl.	J5	76
Boosaaso, Som.	B9	66
Booth, Al., U.S.	E12	122
Boothbay Harbor, Me., U.S.	G7	110
Boothia, Gulf of, b., Nu., Can.	A12	106
Boothia Peninsula, pen., Nu., Can.	A12	106
Boothville, La., U.S.	H9	122
Booué, Gabon	E2	66
Bophuthatswana, hist. reg., S. Afr.	E7	70
Boping Ling, mts., China	I7	42
Bopolu, Lib.	H2	64
Boqueirão, Serra do, hills, Braz.	F4	88

Name	Map Ref.	Page
Boquilla, Presa de la, res., Mex.	B6	100
Boquim, Braz.	F7	88
Bor, Russia	H20	8
Bor, Russia	E20	8
Bor, Sudan	F6	62
Bor, Tur.	B3	56
Bor, Serb.	E9	26
Bor, Lak, stm., Kenya	D7	64
Bora-Bora, i., Fr. Poly.	E11	72
Borabu, Thai.	E6	48
Borah Peak, mtn., Id., U.S.	F13	136
Borås, Swe.	H5	8
Borba, Braz.	D6	84
Bordeaux, Fr.	E5	18
Bordeaux Mountain, hill, V.I.U.S.	e8	104b
Borden, Sk., Can.	B6	124
Borden Peninsula, pen., Nu., Can.	A14	106
Bordertown, Austl.	K3	76
Bordesholm, Ger.	B6	16
Bordighera, Italy	G4	22
Bordj Menaïel, Alg.	H14	20
Bordj Omar Idriss, Alg.	D6	64
Bordoy, i., Far. Is.	m34	8b
Borgå see Porvoo, Fin.	F11	8
Borgarnes, Ice.	k28	8a
Børgefjell Nasjonalpark, p.o.i., Nor.	D5	8
Borger, Tx., U.S.	F7	128
Borgholm, Swe.	H7	8
Borgne, Lake, b., La., U.S.	G9	122
Borgnesse, Pointe, c., Mart.	I7	105c
Borgomanero, Italy	E5	22
Borgo San Dalmazzo, Italy	F4	22
Borgosesia, Italy	E5	22
Borgo Val di Taro, Italy	F6	22
Borgworm see Waremme, Bel.	D14	14
Borikhan, Laos	C6	48
Borisoglebsk, Russia	D6	32
Borisoglebskij, Russia	C21	10
Borjas Blancas see Les Borges Blanques, Spain	C11	20
Borkavičy, Bela.	E11	10
Borken, Ger.	E2	16
Borkou, reg., Chad	D3	62
Borkum, i., Ger.	C2	16
Borlänge, Swe.	F6	8
Bormes, Fr.	F12	18
Borna, Ger.	E9	16
Borneo (Kalimantan), i., Asia	E5	44
Bornholm, state, Den.	I6	8
Bornholm, i., Den.	I6	8
Borocay Island, i., Phil.	E3	52
Borodino, Russia	C17	32
Borogoncy, Russia	D15	34
Borohoro Shan, mts., China	F14	32
Boromo, Burkina	G4	64
Boron, Ca., U.S.	H8	134
Boronga Islands, is., Mya.	I14	54
Borongan, Phil.	E5	52
Borovan, Blg.	F10	26
Borovići, Russia	B16	10
Borovljanka, Russia	D14	32
Borovsk, Russia	E19	10
Borovskij, Russia	C11	32
Borovskoy, Kaz.	D10	32
Borrachudo, stm., Braz.	J3	88
Borrazópolis, Braz.	A12	92
Borriana, Spain	E10	20
Borroloola, Austl.	C7	74
Borş, Rom.	B8	26
Borşa, Rom.	B11	26
Borsad, India	G4	54
Boršćovочný hřebet, mts., Russia	F12	34
Borsod-Abaúj-Zemplén, state, Hung.	A8	26
Bort-les-Orgues, Fr.	D8	18
Borüjerd, Iran	C6	56
Borzja, Russia	F12	34
Borzya, Italy	D2	24
Bosa, Italy	D2	24
Bosanska Dubica, Bos.	D3	26
Bosanska Gradiška, Bos.	D4	26
Bosanska Krupa, Bos.	E3	26
Bosanski Novi, Bos.	D3	26
Bosanski Šamac, Bos.	D5	26
Bosavi, Mount, mtn., Pap. N. Gui.	b3	79a
Boscobel, Wi., U.S.	A7	120
Bose, China	J2	42
Boshan, China	C7	42
Boshof, S. Afr.	F7	70
Bosilegrad, Serb.	G9	26
Bosna, stm., Bos.	E5	26
Bosnia and Herzegovina, ctry., Eur.	E3	26
Bosnik, Indon.	F10	44
Bošnjakovo, Russia	G17	34
Bosobolo, D.R.C.	D3	66
Bōsō-hantō, pen., Japan	D13	40
Bosporus see İstanbul Boğazı, strt., Tur.	B12	28
Bossangoa, C.A.R.	C3	66
Bossembélé, C.A.R.	C3	66
Bossey Bangou, Niger	G5	64
Bossier City, La., U.S.	E5	122
Bosten Hu, l., China	C2	36
Boston, Eng., U.K.	H12	12
Boston, Ga., U.S.	F2	116
Boston, Ma., U.S.	B14	114
Boston Bar, B.C., Can.	G9	138
Boston Mountains, mts., Ar., U.S.	B5	122
Boswell, In., U.S.	H2	112
Boswell, Ok., U.S.	C3	122
Bosworth, Mo., U.S.	E4	120
Botād, India	G3	54
Botany Bay, b., Austl.	J8	76
Boteti, stm., Bots.	E3	68
Bothaville, S. Afr.	E8	70
Bothnia, Gulf of, b., Eur.	F8	112
Bothwell, On., Can.	F8	112
Boticas, Port.	C3	20
Botna, stm., Mol.	C15	26
Botoşani, Rom.	B13	26
Botoşani, state, Rom.	B13	26
Bo Trach, Viet.	D8	48
Botrange, mtn., Bel.	D15	14
Botswana, ctry., Afr.	E3	68
Botte Donato, Monte, mtn., Italy	E10	24
Bottineau, N.D., U.S.	F13	124
Botucatu, Braz.	L1	88
Botwood, Nf., Can.	j22	107a
Bouaflé, C. Iv.	H3	64
Bouaké, C. Iv.	H3	64
Bouar, C.A.R.	C3	66
Bouârfa, Mor.	C4	64
Bouca, C.A.R.	C3	66
Boucher, stm., Qc., Can.	A7	110
Bouches-du-Rhône, state, Fr.	F11	18
Bouctouche, N.B., Can.	D12	110
Boufarik, Alg.	H13	20
Bou Ficha, Tun.	H4	24
Bougainville, i., Pap. N. Gui.	d7	79b
Bougainville, Détroit de, strt., Vanuatu	j16	79d
Bougainville Strait, strt., Oc.	d7	79b
Bougouni, Mali	G3	64
Bouillante, Guad.	h5	105c
Bouillon, Fr.	E14	14
Bouïra, Alg.	B5	64
Boujdour, Cap, c., W. Sah.	D2	64
Boulardierie Island, i., N.S., Can.	D16	110
Boulder, Co., U.S.	A3	128
Boulder, Mt., U.S.	D14	136
Boulder, stm., Mt., U.S.	D15	136
Boulder City, Nv., U.S.	H2	134
Boulia, Austl.	D2	76
Boulogne-sur-Mer, Fr.	D10	14
Bouloupari, N. Cal.	m15	79d
Boulsa, Burkina	G4	64
Bou Medfaa, Alg.	H13	20
Bouna, C. Iv.	H4	64
Boundary Peak, mtn., Nv., U.S.	F7	134
Boundiali, C. Iv.	H3	64
Boun Nua, Laos	B5	48
Bountiful, Ut., U.S.	C4	132
Bounty Bay, b., Pit.	c28	78k
Bounty Islands, is., N.Z.	H8	80
Bounty Trough, unds.	N20	142
Bourail, N. Cal.	m15	79d
Bourbeuse, stm., Mo., U.S.	F6	120
Bourbon, Il., U.S.	G3	112
Bourbonnais, hist. reg., Fr.	C9	18
Bourbonne-les-Bains, Fr.	G14	14
Bourem, Mali	F4	64
Bourg, La., U.S.	H8	122
Bourg-en-Bresse, Fr.	C11	18
Bourges, Fr.	G11	14
Bourget, Fr.	E1	110
Bourget, Lac du, l., Fr.	D11	18
Bourgogne (Burgundy), hist. reg., Fr.	B10	18
Bourgogne, Canal de, can., Fr.	G13	14
Bourgoin-Jallieu, Fr.	D11	18
Bournemouth, Eng., U.K.	K11	12
Bou Saâda, Alg.	B5	64
Bouse Wash, stm., Az., U.S.	J3	132
Bou Smail, Alg.	H13	20
Bousso, Chad	E3	62
Boutilimit, Maur.	F2	64
Boutveøya, i., Ant.	A5	81
Bouza, Niger	G6	64
Bøvågen, Nor.	F1	8
Bovec, Slvn.	D10	22
Bovey, Mn., U.S.	D5	118
Bovill, id., U.S.	D10	136
Bovina, Tx., U.S.	G6	128
Bow, stm., Ab., Can.	G19	138
Bo-Wadrif, S. Afr.	H4	70
Bowbells, N.D., U.S.	F11	124
Bow Creek, stm., Ks., U.S.	B9	128
Bowden, Ab., Can.	E16	138
Bowden, S.D., U.S.	B13	126
Bowdon, N.D., U.S.	G14	124
Bowen, Arg.	G4	92
Bowen, Austl.	C7	76
Bowen, Il., U.S.	D7	120
Bowen, stm., Austl.	C6	76
Bowie, Az., U.S.	K7	132
Bowie, Md., U.S.	F9	114
Bowling Green, Fl., U.S.	I4	116
Bowling Green, Ky., U.S.	H11	120
Bowling Green, Mo., U.S.	E6	120
Bowling Green, Oh., U.S.	C2	114
Bowling Green, Va., U.S.	F8	114
Bowling Green, Cape, c., Austl.	B6	76
Bowling Green Bay National Park, p.o.i., Austl.	B6	76
Bowman, N.D., U.S.	A9	126
Bowman, S.C., U.S.	C5	116
Bowman, Mount, mtn., B.C., Can.	E9	138
Bowmanville, On., Can.	E11	112
Bowral, Austl.	J8	76
Bowraville, Austl.	H9	76
Bowron, stm., B.C., Can.	C9	138
Bowsman, Mb., Can.	B12	124
Box Elder Creek, stm., Mt., U.S.	G5	124
Boxelder Creek, stm., S.D., U.S.	C10	126
Boxelder Creek, stm., U.S.	C8	124
Boxing, China	C8	42
Boyacá, state, Col.	E5	86
Boyang, China	G7	42
Boyce, La., U.S.	F6	122
Boyceville, Wi., U.S.	F6	118
Boyd, Tx., U.S.	A10	130
Boyd, stm., Austl.	G9	76
Boyer, stm., Ia., U.S.	D10	114
Boyertown, Pa., U.S.	D10	114
Boykins, Va., U.S.	H8	114
Boyle, Ms., U.S.	D8	122
Boylston, Al., U.S.	E12	122
Boyne, stm., Austl.	E8	76
Boyne, stm., Mb., Can.	E16	124
Boyne, stm., Ire.	H5	12
Boyne City, Mi., U.S.	C5	112
Boynton Beach, Fl., U.S.	J5	116
Boysen Reservoir, res., Wy., U.S.	D4	126
Boys Ranch, Tx., U.S.	F6	128
Bozburun, Tur.	G11	28
Bozburun Yarımadası, pen., Tur.	G11	28
Boz Dağ, mtn., Tur.	E11	28
Boz Dağlar, mts., Tur.	E10	28
Bozdoğan, Tur.	F11	28
Bozeman, Mt., U.S.	E15	136
Bozen see Bolzano, Italy	D8	22
Bozhen, China	B7	42
Bozhou, China	E6	42
Bozkurt, Tur.	F12	28
Bozoum, C.A.R.	C3	66
Bozova, Tur.	A9	58
Bozovici, Rom.	D8	26
Bozshakōl, Kaz.	D12	32
Bozüyük, Tur.	D13	28
Bra, Italy	F4	22
Brač, Otok, i., Cro.	G13	22
Bracciano, Italy	H9	22
Bracciano, Lago di, l., Italy	H9	22
Bracebridge, On., Can.	C10	112
Brackendale, B.C., Can.	G7	138
Brackettville, Tx., U.S.	E7	130
Bracknell, Eng., U.K.	J12	12
Braço do Norte, Braz.	D13	92
Brad, Rom.	C9	26
Bradano, stm., Italy	D10	24
Bradenton, Fl., U.S.	I3	116
Bradford, Eng., U.K.	H11	12
Bradford, Ar., U.S.	B7	122
Bradford, Pa., U.S.	C7	114
Bradford, Tn., U.S.	H9	120
Bradford, Vt., U.S.	G4	110
Bradford West Gwillimbury, On., Can.	D10	112
Bradley, Ar., U.S.	D5	122
Bradley, Fl., U.S.	I3	116
Bradley, Il., U.S.	G2	112
Bradley, S.D., U.S.	B15	126
Brady, Mt., U.S.	B15	136
Brady, Ne., U.S.	F12	126
Brady, Tx., U.S.	C8	130
Brady Creek, stm., Tx., U.S.	C8	130
Braga, Port.	C2	20
Braga, state, Port.	C2	20
Bragado, Arg.	G7	92
Bragança, Braz.	D8	84
Bragança, Port.	C4	20
Bragança, state, Port.	C4	20
Bragança Paulista, Braz.	L2	88
Brāhmanbāria, Bngl.	F13	54
Brāhmani, stm., India	H10	54
Brahmapur, India	B7	53
Brahmaputra (Yarlung), stm., Asia	C7	46
Braich y Pwll, c., Wales, U.K.	I8	12
Braidwood, Austl.	J7	76
Braidwood, Il., U.S.	C9	120
Brăila, Rom.	D14	26
Brăila, state, Rom.	D14	26
Brainard, Ne., U.S.	F15	126
Brainerd, Mn., U.S.	E4	118
Braintree, Eng., U.K.	J13	12
Brak, stm., S. Afr.	G6	70
Brake, Ger.	C4	16
Brakorne, B.C., Can.	F8	138
Brampton, On., Can.	E10	112
Bramsche, Ger.	D3	16
Branchville, S.C., U.S.	C5	116
Branco, stm., Braz.	H11	86
Branco, stm., Braz.	F3	88
Brandaris, hill, Neth. Ant.	p23	104g
Brandberg, mtn., Nmb.	B2	70
Brandbu, Nor.	F4	8
Brandenburg, Ger.	D8	16
Brandenburg, Ky., U.S.	G11	120
Brandenburg, state, Ger.	D9	16
Brandfort, S. Afr.	F8	70
Brandon, Mb., Can.	E14	124
Brandon, Fl., U.S.	I3	116
Brandon, Ms., U.S.	E9	122
Brandon, S.D., U.S.	H2	118
Brandon, Vt., U.S.	G3	110
Brandsen, Arg.	G8	92
Brandvlei, S. Afr.	H5	70
Brandy Peak, mtn., Or., U.S.	H3	136
Brandys nad Labem-Stará Boleslav, Czech Rep.	F10	16
Branford, Fl., U.S.	G2	116
Braniewo, Pol.	B15	16
Bransby, Austl.	G4	76
Bransby Point, c., Monts.	D3	105a
Bransfield Strait, strt., Ant.	B35	81
Branson, Mo., U.S.	H4	120
Brantford, On., Can.	E9	112
Brantley, Al., U.S.	F12	122
Brantley Tank, res., N.M.	B3	130
Brantôme, Fr.	D6	18
Brantville, N.B., Can.	C12	110
Bras d'Or Lake, l., N.S., Can.	E16	110
Brasiléia, Braz.	F4	84
Brasília, Braz.	H1	88
Brasília, Parque Nacional de, p.o.i., Braz.	H1	88
Braslau, Bela.	E9	10
Braşov, Rom.	D12	26
Braşov, state, Rom.	D12	26
Brassey, Banjaran, mts., Malay.	A10	50
Brass Islands, is., V.I.U.S.	e7	104b
Brasstown Bald, mtn., Ga., U.S.	B2	116
Bratca, Rom.	C9	26
Bratislava, Slov.	H13	16
Bratislava, state, Slov.	H13	16
Bratsk, Russia	C18	32
Bratskoe vodohranilišče, res., Russia	C18	32
Bratsk Reservoir see Bratskoe vodohranilišče, res., Russia	C18	32
Brattleboro, Vt., U.S.	B13	114
Braulio Carrillo, Parque Nacional, p.o.i., C.R.	G5	102
Braunas, Braz.	J4	88
Braunau am Inn, Aus.	B10	22
Braunschweig (Brunswick), Ger.	D6	16
Brava, i., C.V.	l10	65a
Brava, Costa, cst., Spain	C14	20
Brava, Laguna, l., Arg.	D3	92
Brava, Punta, c., Ur.	G9	92
Brave, Pa., U.S.	E5	114
Bravo (Rio Grande), stm., N.A.	H13	98
Bravo, Cerro, mtn., Peru	E2	84
Bravo del Norte see Bravo, stm., N.A.	H13	98
Brawley, Ca., U.S.	K10	134
Bray, Ire.	H6	12
Bray Island, i., Nu., Can.	B15	106
Brazeau, stm., Ab., Can.	D15	138
Brazeau, Mount, mtn., Can.	C15	138
Brazeau Dam, dam, Ab., Can.	C15	138
Brazil, In., U.S.	E10	120
Brazil, ctry., S.A.	F9	82
Brazil Basin, unds.	J11	144
Brazoria, Tx., U.S.	E12	130
Brazos, stm., Tx., U.S.	E8	108
Brazos, Clear Fork, stm., Tx., U.S.	B8	130
Brazos, Double Mountain Fork, stm., Tx., U.S.	H8	128
Brazos, North Fork, stm., Tx., U.S.	H3	122
Brazzaville, Congo	E2	66
Brčko, Bos.	E5	26
Brda, stm., Pol.	C13	16
Bré see Bray, Ire.	H6	12
Brea, Ca., U.S.	J8	134
Bream Bay, b., N.Z.	B6	80
Brea Pozo, Arg.	D6	92
Breaux Bridge, La., U.S.	G7	122
Brebes, Indon.	G6	50
Brechin, Scot., U.K.	E10	12
Breckenridge, Mi., U.S.	E5	112
Breckenridge, Mn., U.S.	E2	118
Breckenridge, Tx., U.S.	B9	130
Brecknock, Peninsula, pen., Chile	J2	90
Břeclav, Czech Rep.	H12	16
Brecon, Wales, U.K.	J9	12
Brecon Beacons, hills, Wales, U.K.	J9	12
Brecon Beacons National Park, p.o.i., Wales, U.K.	J9	12
Breda, Neth.	C13	14
Breda, Ia., U.S.	B3	120
Bredasdorp, S. Afr.	I5	70
Bredenbury, Sk., Can.	D11	124
Bredy, Russia	D9	32
Bree, stm., S. Afr.	I5	70
Breese, Il., U.S.	F8	120
Bregalnica, stm., Mac.	A5	28
Bregenz, Aus.	C6	22
Bregovo, Blg.	E9	26
Bréhat, Île de, i., Fr.	F6	14
Breidhafjördhur, b., Ice.	k28	8a
Brejinho de Nazaré, Braz.	F1	88
Brejo, Braz.	B4	88
Brejo Grande, Braz.	F7	88
Brejo Santo, Braz.	D6	88
Brekstad, Nor.	E3	8
Bremen, Ger.	C4	16
Bremen, state, Ger.	C4	16
Bremen, Ga., U.S.	D13	122
Bremen, In., U.S.	G3	112
Bremen, Oh., U.S.	E3	114
Bremer Bay, Austl.	F3	74
Bremer Bay, b., Austl.	F3	74
Bremerhaven, Ger.	C4	16
Bremerton, Wa., U.S.	C4	136
Bremervörde, Ger.	C5	16
Bremond, Tx., U.S.	F2	122
Brenham, Tx., U.S.	G2	122
Brenner Pass, p., Eur.	C8	22
Brentford, Eng., U.K.	J12	12
Brenta, stm., Italy	D8	22
Brentwood, Eng., U.K.	J13	12
Brentwood, N.Y., U.S.	D12	114
Brentwood, Tn., U.S.	H11	120
Breo, Italy	F4	22
Bréscia, Italy	E7	22
Bressanone (Brixen), Italy	E13	16
Bressanone, Italy	D8	22
Bressay, i., Scot., U.K.	n18	12a
Bresse, reg., Fr.	C11	18
Bressuire, Fr.	H8	14
Brest, Bela.	H6	10
Brest, Fr.	F4	14
Brest, state, Bela.	H8	10
Bretagne (Brittany), hist. reg., Fr.	F5	14
Bretenoux, Fr.	E7	18
Breton, Ab., Can.	C16	138
Breton Islands, is., La., U.S.	H9	122
Breton Sound, strt., La., U.S.	H9	122
Brett, Cape, c., N.Z.	B6	80
Brett, Ger.	G4	16
Breueh, Pulau, i., Indon.	J2	48
Breuil-Cervinia, Italy	E4	22
Brevard, N.C., U.S.	A3	116
Breves, Braz.	D7	84
Brevoort Island, i., Nu., Can.	E13	141
Brewarrina, Austl.	G6	76
Brewer, Me., U.S.	F8	110
Brewster, Mn., U.S.	H3	118
Brewster, Wa., U.S.	B7	136
Brewster, Kap, c., Grnld.	C21	141
Brewton, Al., U.S.	F11	122
Breyten, S. Afr.	E10	70
Breznice, Slov.	H15	16
Brezno, Slov.	H15	16
Bria, C.A.R.	C4	66
Brian Boru Peak, mtn., B.C., Can.	A3	138
Briançon, Fr.	E12	18
Brian Head, mtn., Ut., U.S.	F4	132
Briare, Canal de, can., Fr.	G11	14
Bribie Island, i., Austl.	H5	118
Briceln, Mol.	A14	26
Briceville, Tn., U.S.	H1	114
Bri Chuallan see Bray, Ire.	H6	12
Bridge, stm., B.C., Can.	F7	138
Bridge City, Tx., U.S.	G5	122
Bridge Lake, B.C., Can.	E10	138
Bridgend, Wales, U.K.	J9	12
Bridgeport, Ca., U.S.	E6	134
Bridgeport, Ct., U.S.	C12	114
Bridgeport, Mi., U.S.	E6	112
Bridgeport, Ne., U.S.	F9	126
Bridgeport, Tx., U.S.	A9	130
Bridgeport, Wa., U.S.	B7	136
Bridgeport, Lake, res., Tx., U.S.	H10	128
Bridger, Mt., U.S.	B4	126
Bridger Peak, mtn., Wy., U.S.	B9	132
Bridgeton, N.J., U.S.	E10	114
Bridgetown, Austl.	F3	74
Bridgetown, Barb.	n8	105d
Bridgeville, De., U.S.	F10	114
Bridgewater, N.S., Can.	F12	110
Bridgewater, Ma., U.S.	B15	114
Bridgewater, S.D., U.S.	D15	126
Bridgewater, Va., U.S.	F6	114
Bridgwater, Eng., U.K.	J9	12
Bridgwater Bay, b., Eng., U.K.	J9	12
Bridlington, Eng., U.K.	G12	12
Bridport, Eng., U.K.	K10	12
Brie, reg., Fr.	F12	14
Brier Creek, stm., Ga., U.S.	C3	116
Brig, Switz.	D5	22
Briggs, Tx., U.S.	D10	130
Brigham City, Ut., U.S.	B4	132
Bright, Austl.	K6	76
Brighton, On., Can.	D12	112
Brighton, Eng., U.K.	K12	12
Brighton, Co., U.S.	A4	128
Brighton, Ia., U.S.	C6	120
Brighton, Mi., U.S.	B2	114
Brighton, N.Y., U.S.	E12	112
Brignoles, Fr.	F12	18
Brilhante, stm., Braz.	D5	90
Brilliant, B.C., Can.	G13	138
Brilliant, Al., U.S.	C11	122
Brillion, Wi., U.S.	D1	112
Brilon, Ger.	E4	16
Brindisi, Italy	D11	24
Brinkworth, Austl.	I2	76
Brion, Île, i., Qc., Can.	C15	110
Brioude, Fr.	D9	18
Brisbane, Austl.	F9	76
Brisighella, Italy	F8	22
Bristol, Eng., U.K.	J10	12
Bristol, Ct., U.S.	C12	114
Bristol, Fl., U.S.	G14	122
Bristol, N.H., U.S.	G5	110
Bristol, Pa., U.S.	D11	114
Bristol, R.I., U.S.	C14	114
Bristol, Tn., U.S.	H3	114
Bristol, Vt., U.S.	F3	110
Bristol Bay, b., Ak., U.S.	E7	140
Bristol Channel, strt., U.K.	J8	12
Bristol Island, i., S. Geor.	A2	81
Bristol Lake, l., Ca., U.S.	I10	134
Bristow, Ok., U.S.	B2	122
Britannia Beach, B.C., Can.	G7	138
British Columbia, state, Can.	E5	106
British Guiana see Guyana, ctry., S.A.	C6	84
British Honduras see Belize, ctry., N.A.	D3	102
British Indian Ocean Territory, dep., Afr.	G17	2
British Isles, is., Eur.	C12	4
British Mountains, mts., N.A.	C11	140
British Solomon Islands see Solomon Islands, ctry., Oc.	D7	72
British Virgin Islands, dep., N.A.	h15	96a
Brits, S. Afr.	D8	70
Britstown, S. Afr.	G6	70
Britt, Ia., U.S.	A4	120
Brittany see Bretagne, hist. reg., Fr.	F5	14
Britton, S.D., U.S.	B15	126
Brive-la-Gaillarde, Fr.	D7	18
Brixen see Bressanone, Italy	K9	12
Brixham, Eng., U.K.	D5	76
Brixton, Austl.	C16	32
Brjanka, stm., Mac.	G17	10
Brjansk, Russia	H16	10
Brjanskaja oblast', co., Russia	G12	16
Brno, Czech Rep.	A5	128
Broa, Ensenada de la, b., Cuba	A6	102
Broad, stm., Ga., U.S.	B2	116
Broad, stm., S.C., U.S.	B4	116
Broadalbin, N.Y., U.S.	G2	110
Broad Sound, b., Austl.	D7	76
Broad Sound Channel, strt., Austl.	B7	126
Broadus, Mt., U.S.	F10	114
Broadwater, Ne., U.S.	B7	126
Broadway, Va., U.S.	D10	106
Broceni, Lat.	D10	136
Brochet, Mb., Can.	C5	124
Brock, Sk., Can.	D3	74
Brockman, Mount, mtn., Austl.	B14	114
Brockton, Mt., U.S.	F9	124
Brockville, On., Can.	D14	112
Brockway, Pa., U.S.	C7	114
Brodeur Peninsula, pen., Nu., Can.	A13	106
Brodhead, Wi., U.S.	B8	120
Brodick, Scot., U.K.	F7	12
Brodnax, Va., U.S.	H7	114
Brodnica, Pol.	C15	16
Brogan, Or., U.S.	F9	136
Brok, Pol.	D17	16
Broken Arrow, Ok., U.S.	I2	122
Broken Bow, Ne., U.S.	F13	126
Broken Bay, b., Austl.	I8	76
Broken Bow, Ok., U.S.	C3	122
Broken Bow Lake, res., Ok., U.S.	C4	122
Broken Hill, Austl.	H3	76
Broken Hill see Kabwe, Zam.	C4	68
Broken Ridge, unds.	M12	142
Brokopondo, Sur.	B6	84
Brokopondo Stuwmeer, res., Sur.	C6	84
Bromley Plateau, unds.	K10	144
Bromptonville, Qc., Can.	E4	110
Bromsgrove, Eng., U.K.	I10	12
Bronkhorstspruit, S. Afr.	D9	70
Bronlund Peak, mtn., B.C., Can.	D5	106
Bronnae, Bela.	H13	10
Bronnicy, Russia	E21	10
Bronson, Fl., U.S.	G3	116
Bronson, Ks., U.S.	G2	120
Bronson, Mi., U.S.	G4	112
Bronte, Italy	G8	24
Bronte, Tx., U.S.	C7	130
Brook, In., U.S.	H2	112
Brookeland, Tx., U.S.	F5	122
Brooker, Fl., U.S.	G3	116
Brookfield, N.S., Can.	E13	110
Brookfield, Wi., U.S.	E1	112
Brookfield, Mo., U.S.	D4	120
Brookford, N.C., U.S.	I4	114
Brookhaven, Ms., U.S.	F8	122
Brookings, Or., U.S.	A1	134
Brookings, S.D., U.S.	G2	118
Brookland, Ar., U.S.	B8	122
Brooklyn, N.S., Can.	F12	110
Brooklyn, Ia., U.S.	J6	118
Brooklyn, Mi., U.S.	B1	114
Brooklyn Center, Mn., U.S.	F5	118
Brookmere, B.C., Can.	G10	138
Brookneal, Va., U.S.	G7	114
Brookport, Il., U.S.	G9	120
Brooks, Ab., Can.	E19	138
Brooks Bay, b., B.C., Can.	F2	138
Brookshire, Tx., U.S.	H3	122
Brooks Range, mts., Ak., U.S.	C8	140
Brooksville, Fl., U.S.	H3	116
Brooksville, Ms., U.S.	D10	122
Brookville, In., U.S.	E12	120
Brookville, Pa., U.S.	C6	114
Brookville Lake, res., In., U.S.	E13	120
Brookston, Austl.	C4	74
Broomfield, Co., U.S.	B3	128
Brooten, Mn., U.S.	F3	118
Brora, Scot., U.K.	C9	12
Brora, stm., Scot., U.K.	C9	12
Brosna, stm., Ire.	H5	12
Brotas de Macaúbas, Braz.	G4	88
Brou, Fr.	F10	14
Broughton, Austl.	K5	76
Broughton Island, i., Nu., Can.	A11	106
Brown, Mount, mtn., Mt., U.S.	B15	136
Brown, Point, c., Wa., U.S.	D2	136
Brown Deer, Wi., U.S.	E2	112
Browne Bay, b., Nu., Can.	A11	106
Brownfield, Tx., U.S.	A5	130
Browning, Mo., U.S.	D4	120
Browning, Mt., U.S.	B13	136
Brownlee Reservoir, res., U.S.	F9	136
Brownsburg, In., U.S.	I3	112
Brownsdale, Mn., U.S.	H5	118
Browns Town, Jam.	i13	104d
Brownstown, In., U.S.	F11	120
Brownsville, Ky., U.S.	G11	120
Brownsville, La., U.S.	E6	122
Brownsville, Or., U.S.	F4	136
Brownsville, Pa., U.S.	D5	114
Brownsville, Tn., U.S.	B9	122
Brownsville, Tx., U.S.	I10	130
Brownton, Mn., U.S.	G4	118
Brownville, Ne., U.S.	D2	120
Brownville Junction, Me., U.S.	E7	110
Brownwood, Tx., U.S.	C8	130
Brownwood, Lake, res., Tx., U.S.	C9	130
Browse Island, i., Austl.	B4	74
Broxton, Ga., U.S.	E3	116
Broža, Bela.	H12	10
Bruay-en-Artois, Fr.	D11	14
Bruce, S.D., U.S.	F7	118
Bruce, Wi., U.S.	F7	118
Bruce, Mount, mtn., Austl.	D3	74
Bruce Mines, On., Can.	B6	112
Bruce Peninsula, pen., On., Can.	C8	112
Bruce Peninsula National Park, p.o.i., On., Can.	C8	112
Bruce Rock, Austl.	F3	74
Bruchsal, Ger.	G4	16
Bruck an der Leitha, Aus.	B13	22
Bruck an der Mur, Aus.	C12	22
Bruges see Brugge, Bel.	C12	14
Bruges, Bel.	C12	14
Brugg, Switz.	C5	22
Brugge (Bruges), Bel.	C12	14
Brühl, Ger.	F2	16
Brûk, Pulau, i., Malay.	B7	50
Brule, Ne., U.S.	F10	126
Brumado, Braz.	G4	88
Brundidge, Al., U.S.	F13	122
Bruneau, Id., U.S.	H11	136
Bruneau, stm., U.S.	H11	136
Bruneck see Brunico, Italy	D8	22
Brunei, ctry., Asia	A9	50
Brunico, Italy	D8	22
Brunsbüttel, Ger.	C5	16
Brunson, S.C., U.S.	D4	116
Brunswick see Braunschweig, Ger.	D6	16
Brunswick, Ga., U.S.	E4	116
Brunswick, Me., U.S.	G6	110
Brunswick, Mo., U.S.	E4	120
Brunswick, Oh., U.S.	C4	114
Brunswick, Península, pen., Chile	J2	90
Bruntál, Czech Rep.	F13	16
Brus, Laguna de, b., Hond.	E5	102
Brusovo, Russia	C18	10
Brusque, Braz.	C13	92
Brussel see Bruxelles, Bel.	D13	14
Brussels see Bruxelles, Bel.	D13	14
Bruthen, Austl.	K6	76
Bruxelles (Brussels), Bel.	D13	14
Bruzual, Ven.	D7	86
Bryan, Oh., U.S.	C1	114
Bryan, Tx., U.S.	G2	122
Bryan, Mount, mtn., Austl.	I2	76
Bryce Canyon National Park, p.o.i., Ut., U.S.	F4	132
Bryli, Bela.	G13	10
Bryson, Qc., Can.	C13	112
Bryson City, N.C., U.S.	A2	116
Brzeg, Pol.	F13	16
Brześć Kujawski, Pol.	D14	16
Brzesko, Pol.	F16	16
Brzeziny, Pol.	E15	16
Bsharri, Leb.	D7	58
Bua, Fiji	p19	79e
Bua Bay, b., Fiji	p19	79e
Buada Lagoon, b., Nauru	q17	78f
Bua Yai, Thai.	E6	48
Buavao, Solomon Is.	e8	79b
Buba, Gui.-B.	G1	64
Bubanza, Bur.	E5	66
Bubaque, Gui.-B.	G1	64
Bubi, stm., Zimb.	B10	70
Būbiyān, i., Kuw.	D6	56
Bucak, Tur.	F13	28
Bucaramanga, Col.	D5	86
Buccaneer Archipelago, is., Austl.	C4	74
Buchanan, Sk., Can.	C11	124
Buchanan, Lib.	H2	64
Buchanan, Ga., U.S.	D13	122
Buchanan, Mi., U.S.	G3	112
Buchanan, Lake, l., Tx., U.S.	D9	130
Buchanan, Lake, l., Austl.	C5	76
Buchanan, Lake, l., Tx., U.S.	D9	130
Buchan Ness, c., Scot., U.K.	D11	12
Buchans, Nf., Can.	j22	107a
Bucharest see Bucureşti, Rom.	E13	26
Buchen, Ger.	G5	16
Buchholz in der Nordheide, Ger.	C5	16
Buchloe, Ger.	H6	16
Buchon, Point, c., Ca., U.S.	H4	134
Buchs, Switz.	C6	22
Buckatunna Creek, stm., Ms., U.S.	F10	122
Bückeburg, Ger.	D5	16
Buckeye, Az., U.S.	J4	132
Buckeye Lake, Oh., U.S.	I7	112
Buckhaven, Scot., U.K.	E9	12
Buckholts, Tx., U.S.	D10	130
Buckhorn Draw, stm., Tx., U.S.	D7	130
Buckie, Scot., U.K.	D10	12
Buckingham, Qc., Can.	C14	112
Buckingham, Va., U.S.	G7	114
Buckingham Bay, b., Austl.	B7	74
Buck Island, i., V.I.U.S.	g11	104c
Buck Island Reef National Monument, p.o.i., V.I.U.S.	g11	104c
Buckland, Ak., U.S.	C7	140
Buckland, Wa., U.S.	C4	136
Buckley, Il., U.S.	D9	128
Bucklin, Ks., U.S.	D9	128
Bucklin, Mo., U.S.	E5	120
Buck Mountain, mtn., B.C., Can.	B7	136
Bucovăț, Mol.	B15	26
Buco Zau, Ang.	A1	68
Bucureşti (Bucharest), Rom.	E13	26
Bucureşti, state, Rom.	E13	26
Bucyrus, Oh., U.S.	D3	114
Buda, Tx., U.S.	C8	120
Buda, Tx., U.S.	D10	130
Budalin, Mya.	A2	48
Budapest, Hung.	B6	26
Budapest, state, Hung.	B6	26
Budaun, India	D7	54
Budd Coast, cst., Ant.	B16	81
Buddh Gaya, India see Bodh Gaya, India	F10	54
Buddusò, Italy	D3	24
Bude, Ms., U.S.	F8	122
Bude, Eng., U.K.	K8	12
Bude Bay, b., Eng., U.K.	K8	12
Budënnovsk, Russia	F6	32
Budeşti, Rom.	E13	26
Büdingen, Ger.	F5	16
Budišov nad Budišovkou, Czech Rep.	G13	16
Budjala, D.R.C.	D3	66
Budogošč', Russia	G19	10
Budrio, Italy	F8	22
Budweis see České Budějovice, Czech Rep.	H10	16
Buea, Cam.	D1	66
Buena Esperanza, Arg.	G5	92
Buenaventura, Col.	F3	86
Buenaventura, Mex.	G9	98
Buena Vista, Bol.	C4	90
Buena Vista, Mex.	K9	134
Buenavista, Phil.	G4	52
Buena Vista, Co., U.S.	C2	128
Buena Vista, Ga., U.S.	E14	122
Buena Vista, Va., U.S.	G6	114
Buena Vista Lake Bed, reg., Ca., U.S.	H6	134
Buendía, Embalse de, res., Spain	D8	20
Buenópolis, Braz.	I3	88
Buenos Aires, Arg.	G8	92
Buenos Aires, Col.	F3	86
Buenos Aires, state, Arg.	G5	90
Buenos Aires, Lago see General Carrera, Lago, l., S.A.	I2	90
Buen Pasto, Arg.	I3	90
Buererema, Braz.	H6	88
Buffalo, Ks., U.S.	G2	120
Buffalo, Mn., U.S.	F5	118
Buffalo, Mo., U.S.	G4	120
Buffalo, N.Y., U.S.	B7	114
Buffalo, Oh., U.S.	E4	114
Buffalo, S.C., U.S.	B4	116
Buffalo, S.D., U.S.	B9	126
Buffalo, Tx., U.S.	F3	122
Buffalo, Wy., U.S.	C6	126
Buffalo, stm., Can.	C8	106
Buffalo, stm., Ar., U.S.	H4	120
Buffalo, stm., Tn., U.S.	B11	122
Buffalo Creek, stm., Mn., U.S.	G4	118
Buffalo Lake, Mn., U.S.	G4	118
Buffalo Lake, l., Ab., Can.	D18	138
Buffalo Lake, l., N.T., Can.	C7	106
Buffalo Narrows, Sk., Can.	D9	106
Buffalo Pound Lake, l., Sk., Can.	D8	124
Buffels, stm., S. Afr.	F10	70
Buffels, stm., S. Afr.	H3	70
Buford Dam, dam, Ga., U.S.	B1	116
Buftea, Rom.	E12	26
Bug (Buh) (Zakhidnyy Buh), stm., Eur.	D17	16
Buga, Col.	F3	86
Bugala Island, i., Ug.	E6	66
Bugeat, Fr.	D7	18
Bugiri, Ug.	D6	66
Bugojno, Bos.	E4	26
Bugrino, Russia	B23	8
Bugsuk Island, i., Phil.	F1	52
Bugt, China	B8	36
Bugul'ma, Russia	D8	32
Buguias, Russia	D8	32
Buguma, Nig.	I6	64
Buh, stm., China	D4	36
Buh (Bug) (Zakhidnyy Buh), stm., Eur.	D19	16
Buhara, Uzb.	G10	32
Buhl, Mn., U.S.	D6	118
Buhl, Id., U.S.	H12	136
Buhler, Ks., U.S.	C11	128
Buhusi, Rom.	C13	26
Buies Creek, N.C., U.S.	A7	116
Builth Wells, Wales, U.K.	I9	12
Buin, Pap. N. Gui.	d7	79b
Buin, Pap. N. Gui.	d6	79b
Buitsivango (Rietfontein), stm., Afr.	B4	70
Buj, Russia	G19	8
Bujalance, Spain	G6	20
Bujanovac, Serb.	E10	22
Bujaraloz, Spain	E7	20
Bujnaksk, Russia	F7	32
Bujumbura, Bur.	E5	66
Bukačača, Russia	F12	34
Bukama, D.R.C.	F5	66
Bukan', Russia	G18	10
Bukavu, D.R.C.	E5	66
Bukeya, D.R.C.	F5	66
Bukhara see Buhara, Uzb.	G10	32
Bükittinggi, Indon.	D2	50
Bükki Nemzeti Park, p.o.i., Hung.	A7	26
Bukoba, Tan.	E6	66
Bukovica, reg., Cro.	F12	22
Bukovina, hist. reg., Rom.	B12	26
Bukuru, Nig.	H6	64
Bûlaevo, Kaz.	C12	32
Bulajevka see Bûlaevo, Kaz.	C12	32
Bulan, Phil.	D4	52

Name	Map Ref.	Page
Bulandshahr, India	D6	54
Bulawayo, Zimb.	B9	70
Bulbul, Syria	B7	58
Buldan, Tur.	E11	28
Buldāna, India	H6	54
Buldir Island, i., Ak., U.S.	g22	140a
Bulgan, Mong.	B5	36
Bulgan, Mong.	B3	36
Bulgaria, ctry., Eur.	G12	26
Bulkley, stm., B.C., Can.	B3	138
Bullard, Tx., U.S.	E2	122
Bulla Regia, sci., Tun.	H2	24
Bullas, Spain	F9	20
Bullaxaar, Som.	B8	66
Bulle, Switz.	D4	22
Buller, stm., N.Z.	E5	80
Buller, Mount, mtn., Austl.	K6	76
Bull Harbour, B.C., Can.	F2	138
Bullhead, S.D., U.S.	B11	126
Bullhead City, Az., U.S.	H2	132
Bullock, N.C., U.S.	H7	114
Bullock Creek, Austl.	A5	76
Bullock Creek, stm., Austl.	C5	76
Bulloo, stm., Austl.	G4	76
Bullpound Creek, stm., Ab., Can.	E19	138
Bulls Gap, Tn., U.S.	H2	114
Bull Shoals, Ar., U.S.	H5	120
Bull Shoals Lake, res., U.S.	H5	120
Bulnes, Chile	H1	92
Buldar, India	H4	54
Buluan, Phil.	F12	50
Bulukumba, Indon.	F12	50
Bululawang, Indon.	H8	50
Bumba, D.R.C.	D4	66
Bumpus, Mount, hill, Nu., Can.	B8	106
Bumu Hu, l., China	C13	54
Buna, Kenya	D7	66
Bunawan, Phil.	F5	52
Bunbury, Austl.	F3	74
Bunceton, Mo., U.S.	F5	120
Bundaberg, Austl.	E9	76
Bundarra, Austl.	H8	76
Bünde, Ger.	D4	16
Bündi, India	F5	54
Bundoran, Ire.	G4	12
Bûndu, India	G11	54
Bungamas, Indon.	E3	50
Bungo-suidō, strt., Japan	G5	40
Bungo-takada, Japan	F4	40
Bungtlang, India	G14	54
Bunia, D.R.C.	D6	66
Bunker, Mo., U.S.	G6	120
Bunker Group, is., Austl.	D9	76
Bunker Hill, In., U.S.	H3	112
Bunker Hill, Il., U.S.	G2	136
Bunker Hill, mtn., Nv., U.S.	D8	134
Bunkie, La., U.S.	G6	122
Bunnell, Fl., U.S.	G4	116
Buñol see Bunyola, Spain	E10	20
Buntok, Indon.	D9	50
Bunyola, Spain	E10	20
Bunyu, Pulau, i., Indon.	B10	50
Buolkalah, Russia	B12	34
Buolkalakh see Buolkalah, Russia	B12	34
Buon Ma Thuot, Viet.	F9	48
Buor-Haja, guba, b., Russia	B15	34
Buor-Haja, mys, c., Russia	B15	34
Bupul, Indon.	G11	44
Buqayq, Sau. Ar.	D6	56
Bura, Kenya	E7	66
Burām, Sudan	E5	62
Burang, China	C8	54
Buranhém, stm., Braz.	I6	88
Burāq, Syria	E7	58
Burauen, Phil.	E5	52
Burbank, Wa., U.S.	D8	136
Burç, Tur.	A8	58
Burcher, Austl.	I6	76
Burco, Som.	C9	66
Burdekin, stm., Austl.	C6	76
Burdekin Falls, wtfl., Austl.	C6	76
Burden, Ks., U.S.	D12	128
Burdett, Ks., U.S.	C9	128
Burdur, Tur.	F13	28
Burdur, state, Tur.	F13	28
Burdur Gölü, l., Tur.	F12	28
Bureinskij hrebet, mts., Russia	G15	34
Bureja, Russia	G15	34
Bureja, stm., Russia	F15	34
Büren, Ger.	E4	16
Bürenhayrhan, Mong.	B3	36
Burford, On., Can.	E9	112
Burg, Ger.	D7	16
Burg, Den see Den Burg, Neth.	A13	14
Burgas, Blg.	G14	26
Burgas, state, Blg.	G13	26
Burgas, Gulf of see Burgaski Zaliv, b., Blg.	G14	26
Burgaski Zaliv, b., Blg.	G14	26
Burg auf Fehmarn, Ger.	B7	16
Burgaw, N.C., U.S.	B8	116
Burgdorf, Switz.	C4	22
Burgenland, state, Aus.	C13	22
Burgeo, Nf., Can.	j22	107a
Burgersdorp, S. Afr.	G8	70
Burghausen, Ger.	H8	16
Burghead, Scot., U.K.	D9	12
Burgin, Ky., U.S.	G13	120
Burgo de Osma, Spain	C7	20
Burgos, Mex.	C9	100
Burgos, Phil.	C3	52
Burgos, Spain	B7	20
Burgos, co., Spain	B7	20
Burgstädt, Ger.	F8	16
Burgundy see Bourgogne, hist. reg., Fr.	G14	18
Burhan Budai Shan, mts., China	D4	36
Burhaniye, Tur.	D9	28
Burhānpur, India	H5	54
Burias Island, i., Phil.	D4	52
Burica, Punta, c., N.A.	I6	102
Burien, Wa., U.S.	C4	136
Burila Mare, Rom.	E9	26
Buri Ram, Thai.	E6	48
Buriti, Braz.	B4	88
Buriti Bravo, Braz.	C4	88
Buriticupu, stm., Braz.	C2	88
Buriti dos Lopes, Braz.	B5	88
Buritizeiro, Braz.	I3	88
Burjasot see Burjassot, Spain	E10	20
Burjassot, Spain	E10	20
Burjatija, state, Russia.	F11	34
Burkburnett, Tx., U.S.	G10	128
Burke, S.D., U.S.	D13	126
Burke, stm., Austl.	A2	76
Burketown, Austl.	A2	76
Burkina Faso, ctry., Afr.	G4	64
Burleson, Tx., U.S.	B10	130
Burley, Id., U.S.	H13	136
Burlingame, Ca., U.S.	F3	134
Burlingame, Ks., U.S.	F2	120
Burlington, On., Can.	E10	112
Burlington, Co., U.S.	B6	128
Burlington, Ia., U.S.	D6	120
Burlington, Ks., U.S.	F2	120
Burlington, N.C., U.S.	H6	114
Burlington, Vt., U.S.	F3	110
Burlington, Wa., U.S.	B4	136
Burlington, Wi., U.S.	B9	120
Burlington, Wy., U.S.	C5	126
Burlington Junction, Mo., U.S.	D2	120
Burma see Myanmar, ctry., Asia	D8	46
Burnaby, B.C., Can.	G7	138
Burnet, Tx., U.S.	D9	130
Burnett, stm., Austl.	E8	76
Burnett Bay, b., N.T., Can.	B14	140
Burney, Ca., U.S.	C4	134
Burnie, Austl.	n12	77a
Burnley, Eng., U.K.	H10	12
Burns, Ks., U.S.	C12	128
Burns, Or., U.S.	G7	136
Burns, Tn., U.S.	H10	120
Burns, Wy., U.S.	F8	126
Burnside, Ky., U.S.	G13	120
Burnside, Lake, l., Austl.	E4	74
Burns Lake, B.C., Can.	B5	138
Burnsville, Ms., U.S.	C10	122
Burnsville, N.C., U.S.	I3	114
Burnsville, W.V., U.S.	F5	114
Burnt, stm., Or., U.S.	G9	136
Burnt Pine, Norf. I.	y25	78i
Burntwood, stm., Mb., Can.	D11	106
Burqin, China	B2	36
Burra, Austl.	I2	76
Burragorang, Lake, res., Austl.	J7	76
Burrel, Alb.	C13	24
Burreli see Burrel, Alb.	C13	24
Burrendong, Lake, res., Austl.	I7	76
Burren Junction, Austl.	H7	76
Burriana see Borriana, Spain.	E10	20
Burrinjuck Reservoir, res., Austl.	J7	76
Burr Oak, Ks., U.S.	B10	128
Burrton, Ks., U.S.	C11	128
Burruyacú, Arg.	C4	90
Bursa, Tur.	C11	28
Bursa, state, Tur.	C11	28
Bûr Sa'îd (Port Said), Egypt	G3	58
Burstall, Sk., Can.	D4	124
Bûr Sûdân (Port Sudan), Sudan	D7	62
Burt, Ia., U.S.	H4	118
Burt Lake, l., Mi., U.S.	C5	112
Burtnieks ezers, l., Lat.	C8	10
Burton, Mi., U.S.	E6	112
Burton, Tx., U.S.	G2	122
Burton upon Trent, Eng., U.K.	I11	12
Buru, i., Indon.	F8	44
Burullus, Buheirat el-, l., Egypt	G1	58
Burundi, ctry., Afr.	E6	66
Burun-Sibertuj, gora, mtn., Russia	G10	34
Bururi, Bdi.	E5	66
Burwash, On., Can.	B9	112
Burwell, Ne., U.S.	F13	126
Bury, Eng., U.K.	H10	12
Buryatia see Burjatija, state, Russia	F11	34
Bury Saint Edmunds, Eng., U.K.	I13	12
Burzil, Pak.	A5	54
Busa, Mount, mtn., Phil.	G5	52
Busan see Pusan-jikhalsi, state, Kor., S.	D2	40
Busanga, D.R.C.	E4	66
Busby, Mt., U.S.	B5	126
Bûsh, Egypt	I2	58
Bushire see Bandar-e Büshehr, Iran.	D7	56
Bushland, Tx., U.S.	F6	128
Bushman Land, reg., S. Afr.	F4	70
Bushnell, Fl., U.S.	H3	116
Bushnell, Il., U.S.	D7	120
Bushtyna, Ukr.	A10	26
Busia, Ug.	D6	66
Businga, D.R.C.	D4	66
Busira, stm., D.R.C.	E3	66
Buskerud, state, Nor.	F3	8
Busko-Zdrój, Pol.	F16	16
Busra ash-Shām, Syria	F7	58
Busselton, Austl.	F3	74
Bussey, Ia., U.S.	C5	120
Bussum, Neth.	B14	14
Bustamante, Mex.	B8	100
Busto Arsizio, Italy	E5	22
Busuanga Island, i., Phil.	D2	52
Busu-Djanoa, D.R.C.	D4	66
Büsum, Ger.	B4	16
Buta, D.R.C.	D4	66
Buta Ranquil, Arg.	H2	92
Butare, Rw.	E5	66
Butaritari, at., Kir.	C8	72
Bute, Island of, i., Scot., U.K.	F7	12
Bute Inlet, b., B.C., Can.	F5	138
Buterbo, D.R.C.	D5	66
Butera, Italy	G8	24
Butere, Kenya	D6	66
Butha-Buthe, Leso.	F9	70
Buthidaung, Mya.	D7	46
Butiá, Braz.	E11	92
Butler, Ga., U.S.	D1	116
Butler, In., U.S.	C1	114
Butler, Mo., U.S.	F3	120
Butler, Oh., U.S.	D3	114
Butler, Pa., U.S.	D6	114
Butner, N.C., U.S.	H7	114
Buto, hist., Egypt	G1	58
Buton, Pulau, i., Indon.	F7	44
Butrint, sci., Alb.	E14	24
Butru, Austl.	C3	76
Butte, Mt., U.S.	D14	136
Butte, Ne., U.S.	E14	126
Butte Creek, stm., Ca., U.S.	D4	134
Butte Falls, Or., U.S.	H4	136
Butternut, Wi., U.S.	E8	118
Butterworth, Malay.	J5	48
Butterworth, S. Afr.	H9	70
Buttle Lake, l., B.C., Can.	G5	138
Button Islands, is., Nu., Can.	C17	106
Buttonwillow, Ca., U.S.	H6	134
Butuan, Phil.	F5	52
Buturlino, Russia	I21	8
Butwal, Nepal	E9	54
Butzbach, Ger.	F4	16
Bützow, Ger.	C7	16
Buulobarde, Som.	D9	66
Buur Gaabo, Som.	E8	66
Buurgplaatz, mtn., Lux.	D15	14
Buxton, S. Afr.	E7	70
Buxton, Eng., U.K.	H11	12
Buxton, N.C., U.S.	A10	116
Buxton, Mount, mtn., B.C., Can.	C2	138
Buyant-Uhaa, Mong.	C7	36
Buyr nuur, l., Asia	B8	36
Büyükada, Tur.	C12	28
Büyükçekmece, Tur.	B11	28
Büyükkemikli Burnu, c., Tur.	C9	28
Büyükmenderes, stm., Tur.	F10	28
Büzäu, Rom.	D13	26
Büzäu, state, Rom.	D13	26
Büzäu, stm., Rom.	D13	26
Buzen, Japan	F4	40
Búzi, Moz.	A12	70
Buzias, Rom.	D8	26
Buzuluk, Russia	D8	32
Byādgi, India	D2	53
Byam Channel, strt., Nu., Can.	A19	140
Byam Martin Island, i., Nu., Can.	B19	140
Byčen', Bela.	H8	10
Byčki, Russia	F17	10
Byczyna, Pol.	E14	16
Bydgoszcz, Pol.	C13	16
Bydgoszcz, state, Pol.	C13	16
Byelorussia see Belarus, ctry., Eur.	E14	6
Byers, Tx., U.S.	G10	130
Byesville, Oh., U.S.	E4	114
Bygdin, l., Nor.	F3	8
Byhalia, Ms., U.S.	C9	122
Byhaŭ, Bela.	G13	10
Bykle, Nor.	G2	8
Bylnice, Czech Rep.	G14	16
Bylot Island, i., Nu., Can.	A15	106
Bynum, Mt., U.S.	C14	136
Bynum, N.C., U.S.	I6	114
Byrd, Lac, l., Qc., Can.	A13	112
Byrnedale, Pa., U.S.	C7	114
Byro, Austl.	E3	74
Byron, Ga., U.S.	D2	116
Byron, Il., U.S.	B8	120
Byron, Cape, c., Austl.	G9	76
Byron Bay, Austl.	G9	76
Byrranga, gory, mts., Russia	B8	34
Bystřice pod Hostýnem, Czech Rep.	G13	16
Bytantaj, stm., Russia	C15	34
Bytča, Slov.	G14	16
Bytom, Pol.	F14	16
Bytoš', Russia	G17	10
Bytów, Pol.	B13	16

C

Name	Map Ref.	Page
Ca, stm., Asia	C7	48
Caacupé, Para.	B9	92
Caaguazú, Para.	B9	92
Caaguazú, state, Para.	B10	92
Caála, Ang.	C2	68
Caapiranga, Braz.	I11	86
Caatinga, Braz.	I3	88
Caazapá, Braz.	C9	92
Caazapá, state, Para.	C9	92
Cabaiguán, Cuba	A8	102
Caballiana, Lago, l., Braz.	I11	86
Caballococha, Peru	D3	84
Caballo Reservoir, res., N.M., U.S.	K9	132
Cabanatuan, Phil.	C3	52
Cabano, Qc., Can.	C8	110
Cabarroquis, Phil.	B3	52
Cabedelo, Braz.	D8	88
Cabeza del Buey, Spain	F5	20
Cabezas, Bol.	C4	90
Cabildo, Arg.	I7	92
Cabimas, Ven.	B6	86
Cabinda, Ang.	B1	68
Cabinda, state, Ang.	B1	68
Cabinet Mountains, mts., U.S.	B10	136
Cable, Wi., U.S.	E7	118
Cabo, Braz.	E8	88
Cabo Blanco, Arg.	I3	90
Cabo Frio, Braz.	L4	88
Cabonga, Réservoir, res., Qc., Can.	F15	106
Cabool, Mo., U.S.	G5	120
Caboolture, Austl.	F9	76
Caborca, Mex.	F6	98
Cabo Rojo, P.R.	B1	104a
Cabot, Ar., U.S.	C7	122
Cabot Head, c., On., Can.	C8	112
Cabot Strait, strt., Can.	j21	107a
Cabourg, Fr.	E8	14
Cabra Corral, Embalse, res., Arg.	B5	92
Cabramurra, Austl.	J7	76
Cabrera, stm., Col.	F4	86
Cabrera, Illa de, i., Spain	E13	20
Cabri, Sk., Can.	D5	124
Cabriel, stm., Spain	E9	20
Cabrillo National Monument, p.o.i., Ca., U.S.	K8	134
Cabrobó, Braz.	E6	88
Cabruta, Ven.	D8	86
Čabulónes, Punta, c., P.R.	C2	104a
Cabusy, Phil.	H11	10
Cabuyaro, Col.	E5	86
Čačak, Serb.	F7	26
Caçapava, Braz.	L3	88
Caçapava do Sul, Braz.	E11	92
Cacapon, stm., W.V., U.S.	E7	114
Cacequi, Braz.	D10	92
Cáceres, Braz.	G6	84
Cáceres, Col.	D4	86
Cáceres, co., Spain	E4	20
Cáceres, Spain	E4	20
Čačèrsk, Bela.	H13	10
Cache, stm., Ar., U.S.	B7	122
Cache, stm., Il., U.S.	G8	120
Cache Creek, B.C., Can.	F9	138
Cache Creek, stm., Ca., U.S.	E4	134
Cache la Poudre, stm., Co., U.S.	G7	126
Cache Peak, mtn., Id., U.S.	A3	132
Cachi, Arg.	B4	92
Cachimbo, Braz.	E7	84
Cachimbo, Serra do, mts., Braz.	E6	84
Cachoeira Alta, Braz.	C6	90
Cachoeira de Manteiga, Braz.	I3	88
Cachoeira do Sul, Braz.	E11	92
Cachoeiro de Itapemirim, Braz.	K5	88
Cachos, Punta, c., Chile	C2	92
Cachuela Esperanza, Braz.	B3	90
Căciulați, Rom.	E13	26
Cacolo, Ang.	C2	68
Caconda, Ang.	C2	68
Cactus, Tx., U.S.	E6	128
Cactus Flat, pl., Nv., U.S.	F9	134
Caculé, Braz.	H4	88
Čadan, Russia	D16	32
Cadca, Slov.	G14	16
Caddo, Ok., U.S.	C2	122
Caddo, stm., Ar., U.S.	C5	122
Caddo Lake, res., U.S.	E4	122
Caddo Mills, Tx., U.S.	D2	122
Cadell, stm., Austl.	E12	122
Cadillac, Fr.	E5	18
Cadillac, Mi., U.S.	D4	112
Cádiz, Spain	H4	20
Cadiz, Ky., U.S.	H10	120
Cádiz, co., Spain	H5	20
Cádiz, Bahía de, b., Spain	H4	20
Cadiz Lake, l., Ca., U.S.	I1	134
Cadobec, stm., Russia	C17	32
Cadomin, Ab., Can.	C13	138
Cadore, reg., Italy	D9	22
Cadwell, Ga., U.S.	D2	116
Caek, Kyrg.	F12	32
Caen, Fr.	E8	14
Caengo (Kwenge), stm., Afr.	F3	66
Caernarfon, Wales, U.K.	H8	12
Caernarfon Bay, b., Wales, U.K.	H8	12
Caerphilly, Wales, U.K.	J9	12
Caesarea see Qesari, Horbat, sci., Isr.	F5	58
Caeté, Braz.	J4	88
Caetité, Braz.	H4	88
Cafayate, Arg.	C4	92
Cagayan, stm., Phil.	A3	52
Cagayan de Oro, Phil.	F5	52
Cagayan Islands, is., Phil.	F2	52
Cagayan Sulu Island, i., Phil.	G2	52
Čagda, Russia	E15	34
Çağış, Tur.	D10	28
Cagli, Italy	G9	22
Cagliari, Golfo di, b., Italy	E2	24
Cagliari, Stagno di, l., Italy	E2	24
Cagnes-sur-Mer, Fr.	F13	18
Čagoda, stm., Russia	A17	10
Cagodošča, stm., Russia	A18	10
Caguas, P.R.	B3	104a
Caguán, stm., Col.	G4	86
Cahaba, stm., Al., U.S.	E11	122
Cahama, Ang.	D1	68
Caher, Ire.	I4	12
Cahokia, Il., U.S.	F7	120
Cahora Bassa, Albufeira, res., Moz.	D5	68
Cahors, Fr.	E7	18
Cahto Peak, mtn., Ca., U.S.	D2	134
Cahuinari, stm., Col.	H6	86
Cahul, Mol.	D15	26
Cai, stm., Braz.	D12	92
Caiabis, Serra dos, mts., Braz.	G7	84
Caianda, Ang.	C3	68
Caiapó, stm., Braz.	C6	90
Caiapônia, Braz.	C6	90
Caibarién, Cuba	A8	102
Cai Bau, Dao, i., Viet.	B8	48
Caiçara, Braz.	D8	88
Caicara de Maturín, Ven.	C10	86
Caicara de Orinoco, Ven.	D8	86
Caicedonia, Col.	E4	86
Caicó, Braz.	D7	88
Caicos Islands, is., T./C. Is.	B11	102
Caicos Passage, strt., N.A.	B11	102
Caijiao, China	D2	42
Caima Bay, b., Phil.	D4	52
Caimanera, Cuba	C10	102
Caimanero, Laguna del, l., Mex.	D5	100
Cain Creek, stm., S.D., U.S.	C14	126
Cai Nuoc, Viet.	H7	48
Cairari, Braz.	B1	88
Caird Coast, cst., Ant.	C3	81
Cairns, Austl.	A5	76
Cairo see El-Qâhira, Egypt	H2	58
Cairo, Ga., U.S.	G1	116
Cairo, Il., U.S.	G8	120
Cairo, Ne., U.S.	F14	126
Cairo, W.V., U.S.	E4	114
Cairo Montenotte, Italy	F5	22
Cairu, Braz.	G6	88
Caisleán an Bharraigh see Castlebar, Ire.	H3	12
Caiundo, Ang.	D2	68
Caiwan, China	I4	42
Caizi Hu, l., China	F7	42
Caja de Muertos, Isla, i., P.R.	C2	104a
Cajamarca, Peru	E2	84
Cajapió, Braz.	B3	88
Cajazeiras, Braz.	D7	88
Cajon Summit, p., Ca., U.S.	I8	134
Cajuru, Braz.	K2	88
Caka, China	D4	36
Çakmak, Tur.	A5	58
Čakovec, Cro.	D13	22
Calabar, Nig.	H6	64
Calabozo, Ven.	C8	86
Calabozo, Ensenada de, b., Ven.	B6	86
Calabria, state, Italy	F10	24
Calafat, Rom.	F9	26
Calagua Islands, is., Phil.	C4	52
Calahorra, Spain	B8	20
Calais, Fr.	D10	14
Calais, Me., U.S.	E9	110
Calalaste, Sierra de, mts., Arg.	B4	92
Calama, Chile	D3	90
Calamar, Col.	B4	86
Calamar, Col.	F5	86
Calamian Group, is., Phil.	C2	52
Calamus, stm., Ne., U.S.	E13	126
Calañas, Spain	G3	20
Calang, Indon.	J2	48
Calapan, Phil.	D3	52
Călărași, Mol.	B15	26
Călărași, Rom.	E14	26
Călărași, state, Rom.	E14	26
Calasparra, Spain	F9	20
Calatafimi, Italy	G6	24
Calatayud, Spain	C9	20
Calau, Ger.	E9	16
Calavite, Cape, c., Phil.	D2	52
Calayan Island, i., Phil.	A3	52
Calbayog, Phil.	D5	52
Calbe, Ger.	E7	16
Calcasieu, stm., La., U.S.	G5	122
Calcasieu Lake, l., La., U.S.	G5	122
Calceta, Ec.	H1	86
Calchaqui, Arg.	D7	92
Calchaquí, stm., Arg.	B4	92
Calçoene, Braz.	C7	84
Calcutta see Kolkata, India	G12	54
Caldaro, Italy	D8	22
Caldas, Col.	D4	86
Caldas, state, Col.	E4	86
Caldas da Rainha, Port.	E1	20
Caldas de Reis, Spain	B2	20
Caldas Novas, Braz.	I1	88
Caldas de Reyes see Caldas de Reis, Spain	B2	20
Caldera, Chile	C2	92
Caldera, stm., Pan.	H6	102
Caldwell, Id., U.S.	G10	136
Caldwell, Ks., U.S.	D11	128
Caldwell, Oh., U.S.	E4	114
Caldwell, Tx., U.S.	G2	122
Caledon (Mohokare), stm., Afr.	F8	70
Caledonia, Belize	D3	102
Caledonia, N.S., Can.	F11	110
Caledonia, Mn., U.S.	H7	118
Caledonia, N.Y., U.S.	A8	114
Caledonia, Oh., U.S.	D3	114
Callão, Peru	F2	84
Callaquén, Volcán, vol., Chile	H2	92
Callaway, Ne., U.S.	F12	126
Calling Lake, l., Ab., Can.	A17	138
Callosa de Segura, Spain	F9	20
Calmar, Ab., Can.	C17	138
Calmar, Ia., U.S.	A6	120
Calm Lake, l., On., Can.	C6	118
Cal'mny-Varre, Russia	C17	8
Čalna, Russia	F15	8
Calp, Spain	F11	20
Calpe see Calp, Spain	F11	20
Caltagirone, Italy	G8	24
Caltanissetta, Italy	G8	24
Calulo, Ang.	B2	68
Calumet, Mn., U.S.	D5	118
Calumet City, Il., U.S.	G2	112
Calunda, Ang.	C3	68
Caluula, Som.	B10	66
Calvados, state, Fr.	E8	14
Calvert, Tx., U.S.	G2	122
Calvert Island, i., B.C., Can.	E2	138
Calvillo, Mex.	E7	100
Calvinia, S. Afr.	G4	70
Calw, Ger.	H4	16
Calwa, Ca., U.S.	G6	134
Calypso, N.C., U.S.	A7	116
Camabatela, Ang.	B2	68
Camaçari, Braz.	G6	88
Camacupa, Ang.	C2	68
Camaguán, Ven.	C8	86
Camaiore, Italy	G7	22
Camagüey, Cuba	B9	102
Camajuaní, Cuba	A8	102
Camana, Peru	G3	84
Camaná, stm., Peru	G3	84
Camanau, stm., Braz.	H11	86
Camanche Reservoir, res., Ca., U.S.	E4	134
Camapuã, Braz.	C6	90
Camaquã, Braz.	E12	92
Camaquã, stm., Braz.	E11	92
Camarajibe, Braz.	D8	88
Camararé, stm., Braz.	F6	84
Camarés, Fr.	F8	18
Camargo, Bol.	D3	90
Camargue, reg., Fr.	F10	18
Camariñas, Spain	A1	20
Camarillo, Ca., U.S.	I6	134
Camarón, Arroyo, stm., Mex.	G12	100
Camarón, Cabo, c., Hond.	D5	102
Camarones, Arg.	H3	90
Camarones, Bahía, b., Arg.	H3	90
Camas, Wa., U.S.	E4	136
Camas Creek, stm., Id., U.S.	F14	136
Camatagua, Embalse de, l., Ven.	C8	86
Ca Mau, Viet.	H7	48
Ca Mau, Mui, c., Viet.	H7	48
Camba, Indon.	F11	50
Cambodia, ctry., Asia	F7	48
Camboon, Austl.	E8	76
Camboriú, Braz.	C13	92
Camborne, Eng., U.K.	K7	12
Cambrai, Fr.	D12	14
Cambria, Ca., U.S.	H4	134
Cambrian Mountains, mts., Wales, U.K.	I9	12
Cambridge, On., Can.	E9	112
Cambridge, N.Z.	C6	80
Cambridge, Eng., U.K.	I12	12
Cambridge, Ia., U.S.	C4	120
Cambridge, Il., U.S.	C7	120
Cambridge, Ma., U.S.	B14	114
Cambridge, Md., U.S.	F9	114
Cambridge, Mn., U.S.	F5	118
Cambridge, Ne., U.S.	A8	128
Cambridge, N.Y., U.S.	G3	110
Cambridge, Oh., U.S.	D4	114
Cambridge Bay see Ikaluktutiak, Nu., Can.	B10	106
Cambridge Fiord, b., Nu., Can.	A15	106
Cambridge Springs, Pa., U.S.	C5	114
Cambuci, Braz.	K5	88
Cambulo, Ang.	B3	68
Cambundi-Catembo, Ang.	C2	68
Camden, Austl.	J8	76
Camden, Al., U.S.	F11	122
Camden, Ar., U.S.	D6	122
Camden, Me., U.S.	F7	110
Camden, N.J., U.S.	E10	114
Camden, N.Y., U.S.	E14	112
Camden, Oh., U.S.	E1	114
Camden, S.C., U.S.	B5	116
Camden, Tn., U.S.	H9	120
Camden Bay, b., Ak., U.S.	B11	140
Cameia, Parque Nacional, p.o.i., Ang.	C3	68
Cameli, Tur.	F11	28
Camenca, Mol.	A15	26
Camerino, Italy	G10	22
Cameron, La., U.S.	H5	122
Cameron, Mo., U.S.	E3	120
Cameron, Tx., U.S.	D10	130
Cameron, Wi., U.S.	F7	118
Cameron Hills, hills, Can.	D7	106
Cameroon, ctry., Afr.	C2	66
Cameroon Mountain, vol., Cam.	D1	66
Camerota, Italy	D9	24
Cametá, Braz.	D8	84
Camiguin Island, i., Phil.	A3	52
Camiguin Island, i., Phil.	F5	52
Camiling, Phil.	C3	52
Camilla, Ga., U.S.	E1	116
Camino, Ca., U.S.	E5	134
Camiranga, Braz.	A2	88
Camiri, Bol.	D4	90
Camissombo, Ang.	B3	68
Camlidere, Tur.	C15	28
Cam Lo, Viet.	D8	48
Camocim, Braz.	B5	88
Camooweal, Austl.	A2	76
Camorta Island, i., India	G7	46
Camotes Islands, is., Phil.	E5	52
Camotes Sea, s., Phil.	E5	52
Campagna di Roma, reg., Italy	C6	24
Campana, Arg.	G8	92
Campana, Isla, i., Chile	I1	90
Campania, state, Italy	D8	24
Campaspe, stm., Austl.	K5	76
Campbell, Mo., U.S.	H7	120
Campbell, Ne., U.S.	A10	128
Campbell, Cape, c., N.Z.	E6	80
Campbellford, On., Can.	D12	112
Campbell Hill, hill, Oh., U.S.	D2	114
Campbell Island, i., N.Z.	J7	72
Campbell Island, i., B.C., Can.	E2	138
Campbell Lake, l., B.C., Can.	C6	138
Campbell River, B.C., Can.	F5	138
Campbellsport, Wi., U.S.	E1	112
Campbellton, N.B., Can.	C10	110
Campbellton, P.E., Can.	D12	110
Campbellton, Fl., U.S.	G13	122
Campbelltown, Austl.	J8	76
Campbell Town, Austl.	n13	77a
Campbeltown, Scot., U.K.	F7	12
Campeche, Mex.	C2	102
Campeche, state, Mex.	C2	102
Campeche, Bahía de b., Mex.	D6	96
Campeche, Gulf of see Campeche, Bahía de, b., Mex.	E13	100
Campechuela, Cuba	B9	102
Câmpeni, Rom.	C10	26
Camperdown, Austl.	L4	76
Camperville, Mb., Can.	C13	124
Camp Hill, Al., U.S.	E13	122
Camp Hill, Pa., U.S.	H12	112
Campia Turzii, Rom.	C10	26
Campiglia Marittima, Italy	G7	22
Campillos, Spain	G6	20
Câmpina, Rom.	D12	26
Campina, reg., Spain	G5	20
Campina Grande, Braz.	D8	88
Campinas, Braz.	L2	88
Campina Verde, Braz.	J1	88
Campoalegre, Col.	F4	86
Campo Alegre de Goiás, Braz.	I2	88
Campobasso, Italy	C8	24
Campo Belo, Braz.	K3	88
Campo de Criptana, Spain	E7	20
Campo Erê, Braz.	C11	92
Campo Florido, Braz.	J1	88
Campo Formoso, Braz.	F5	88
Campo Gallo, Arg.	C6	92
Campo Grande, Braz.	D6	90
Campo Largo, Braz.	B13	92
Campo Maior, Braz.	C4	88
Campo Maior, Port.	F3	20
Campo Mourão, Braz.	A11	92
Campo Novo, Braz.	C11	92
Campos, Braz.	K5	88
Campos Altos, Braz.	J2	88
Campo Santo, Arg.	B5	92
Campos Belos, Braz.	G2	88
Campos do Jordão, Braz.	L3	88
Campos Gerais, Braz.	K2	88
Campos Novos, Braz.	C12	92
Campos Sales, Braz.	D5	88
Camp Point, Il., U.S.	D6	120
Campti, La., U.S.	F5	122
Campton, Ky., U.S.	G2	114
Câmpulung, Rom.	D11	26
Câmpulung Moldovenesc, Rom.	B12	26
Campuya, stm., Peru	H4	86
Camp Verde, Az., U.S.	I4	132
Cam Ranh, Viet.	G9	48
Cam Ranh Bay see Cam Ranh, Vinh b., Viet.	G9	48
Camrose, Ab., Can.	C18	138
Camsell, stm., N.T., Can.	B7	106
Camuy, P.R.	B2	104a
Can, Tur.	C10	28
Canaan, Vt., U.S.	E5	110
Cana-brava, stm., Braz.	G1	88
Cana-brava, stm., Braz.	G1	88
Canada, ctry., N.A.	D9	106
Canada Basin, unds.	A25	142
Cañada de Gómez, Arg.	F7	92
Cañada Honda, Arg.	F3	92
Canadian, Tx., U.S.	F8	128
Canadian, stm., U.S.	F13	128
Canadian, Deep Fork, stm., Ok., U.S.	F13	128
Canaguá, stm., Ven.	D7	86
Canaima, Parque Nacional, p.o.i., Ven.	E10	86
Canajoharie, N.Y., U.S.	B11	114
Çanakkale, Tur.	C9	28
Çanakkale, state, Tur.	D9	28
Çanakkale Boğazı (Dardanelles), strt., Tur.	C9	28
Canala, N. Cal.	m15	79d
Canal Fulton, Oh., U.S.	D4	114
Canal Point, Fl., U.S.	J5	116
Canals, Arg.	F6	92
Canal Winchester, Oh., U.S.	E3	114
Canandaigua, N.Y., U.S.	B8	114
Cananea, Mex.	F7	98
Canápolis, Braz.	J1	88
Cañar, Ec.	I2	86
Cañar, state, Ec.	I2	86
Canarias, Islas (Canary Islands), is., Spain	D1	64
Canarreos, Archipiélago de los, is., Cuba	B6	102
Canary Basin, unds.	F11	144
Canary Islands see Canarias, Islas, is., Spain	D1	64
Cañas, Cr.	G5	102
Canaseraga, N.Y., U.S.	B8	114
Canastota, N.Y., U.S.	E14	112
Canatlan, Mex.	C6	100
Canaveral, Cape, c., Fl., U.S.	H5	116
Canaveral National Seashore, p.o.i., Fl., U.S.	H5	116
Cañaveras, Spain	D8	20
Canavese, hist. reg., Italy	E4	22
Canavieiras, Braz.	H6	88
Canbelego, Austl.	H6	76
Canberra, Austl.	J7	76
Canby, Ca., U.S.	B5	134
Canby, Mn., U.S.	G2	118
Canby, Or., U.S.	E4	136
Cancon, Fr.	E6	18
Cancun, Mex.	B4	102
Çandarli Körfezi, b., Tur.	E9	28
Candé, Fr.	G7	14
Candeias, Braz.	G6	88
Candela, stm., Mex.	B8	100
Candelaria, Arg.	C10	92
Candelária, Braz.	D11	92
Cândido Aguilar, Mex.	C9	100
Cândido Mendes, Braz.	A3	88
Candlemas Islands, is., S. Geor.	K12	82
Candlestick, Ms., U.S.	E8	122
Cando, N.D., U.S.	F14	124
Candor, N.C., U.S.	A6	116
Canea see Chaniá, Grc.	H7	28
Canelas, Mex.	C5	100
Canelli, Italy	F5	22
Canelones, Ur.	G9	92
Caney, Ks., U.S.	G2	120
Caney Creek, stm., Tx., U.S.	F12	130
Canfranc, Spain	B10	20
Cangas de Narcea, Spain	A4	20
Cangas de Onís, Spain	A5	20
Cangkuang, Tanjung, c., Indon.	G4	50
Cangombe, Ang.	C3	68
Canguaretama, Braz.	D8	88
Canguçu, Braz.	E11	92
Cangumbe, Ang.	C2	68
Cangxi, China	F1	42
Cangzhou, China	B7	42
Caniapiscau, stm., Qc., Can.	D17	106
Caniapiscau, Lac, res., Qc., Can.	E17	106
Canicattì, Italy	G7	24

Canim Lake – Centralina I • 11

Name | Map Ref. | Page

Canim Lake, B.C., Can. E10 138
Canim Lake, l., B.C., Can. E9 138
Canindé, Braz. C6 88
Canindé, stm., Braz. D4 88
Canindeyú, state, Para. B10 92
Canisteo, N.Y., U.S. B8 114
Canistota, S.D., U.S. D15 126
Cañitas de Felipe Pescador, Mex. D7 100
Canjáyar, Spain G8 20
Çankırı, Tur. A3 56
Çankırı, state, Tur. C15 28
Canmore, Ab., Can. E15 138
Cannanore, India F2 53
Cannelton, In., U.S. G11 120
Cannes, Fr. F13 18
Canning, N.S., Can. E12 110
Cannington, On., Can. D10 112
Cannock, Eng., U.K. I10 12
Cannon, stm., Mn., U.S. G5 118
Cannonball, stm., N.D., U.S. A11 126
Cannon Beach, Or., U.S. E2 136
Cannon Falls, Mn., U.S. G6 118
Cannonvale, Austl. C7 76
Cann River, Austl. K7 76
Canoas, Braz. D12 92
Canoas, stm., Braz. C12 92
Canoe, B.C., Can. F11 138
Canoe, stm., B.C., Can. D12 138
Canoinhas, Braz. C12 92
Canon City, Co., U.S. C3 128
Cañon de Río Blanco, Parque Nacional, p.o.i., Mex. F10 100
Canonsburg, Pa., U.S. D5 114
Canoochee, stm., Ga., U.S. E4 116
Canora, Sk., Can. C11 124
Canosa di Púglia, Italy C10 24
Canossa, sci., Italy F7 22
Canouan, i., St. Vin. p11 105e
Canova, S.D., U.S. D15 126
Canova Beach, Fl., U.S. H5 116
Cañovanas, P.R. B4 104a
Canowindra, Austl. I7 76
Canso, N.S., Can. E16 110
Cantabria, state, Spain A6 20
Cantabrian Mountains see Cantábrica, Cordillera, mts., Spain A5 20
Cantábrica, Cordillera, mts., Spain A5 20
Cantagalo, Braz. K4 88
Cantal, state, Fr. D8 18
Cantalejo, Spain C7 20
Cantanhede, Braz. B3 88
Cantaura, Ven. C9 86
Canterbury, Eng., U.K. J14 12
Canterbury Bight, b., N.Z. G4 80
Canterbury Plains, pl., N.Z. G4 80
Can Tho, Viet. G7 48
Canton see Guangzhou, China J5 42
Canton, Il., U.S. D7 120
Canton, Ks., U.S. C11 128
Canton, Mn., U.S. H7 118
Canton, Mo., U.S. D6 120
Canton, Ms., U.S. E8 122
Canton, N.Y., U.S. D14 112
Canton, Oh., U.S. D4 114
Canton, Ok., U.S. E10 128
Canton, Pa., U.S. C9 114
Canton, S.D., U.S. H2 118
Canton, Tx., U.S. E3 122
Canton see Kanton, i., Kir. D9 72
Canton Lake, res., Ok., U.S. E10 128
Cantonment, Fl., U.S. G11 122
Cantù, Italy E6 22
Cantu, stm., Braz. B11 92
Cantwell, Ak., U.S. D10 140
Cañuelas, Arg. G8 92
Canumã, Braz. D6 84
Canutama, Braz. E5 84
Čany, Russia C13 32
Čany, ozero, l., Russia D13 32
Canyon, Tx., U.S. G7 128
Canyon City, Or., U.S. F8 136
Canyon Creek, Ab., Can. A15 138
Canyon de Chelly National Monument, p.o.i., Az., U.S. G7 132
Canyon Ferry Lake, res., Mt., U.S. D15 136
Canyon Lake, res., Tx., U.S. E9 130
Canyonlands National Park, p.o.i., Ut., U.S. E6 132
Canyonville, Or., U.S. H3 136
Cao, stm., China D5 38
Cao Bang, Viet. A7 48
Cao Lanh, Viet. G7 48
Caombo, Ang. B2 68
Caorle, Italy E9 22
Caoxian, China D6 42
Cap, Pointe du, c., St. Luc. I7 105c
Capac, Mi., U.S. E7 112
Capanaparo, stm., S.A. D8 86
Capanema, Braz. D8 84
Capão Bonito, Braz. L1 88
Capão Doce, Morro do, mtn., Braz. C12 92
Caparaó, Parque Nacional do, p.o.i., Braz. K4 88
Caparo Viejo, stm., Ven. D6 86
Capatárida, Ven. B6 86
Cap aux Meules, Île du, i., Qc., Can. C14 110
Cap-Chat, Qc., Can. A10 110
Cap-de-la-Madeleine, Qc., Can. D4 110
Cape, stm., Austl. C5 76
Cape Barren Island, i., Austl. n13 77a
Cape Basin, unds. L14 144
Cape Breton Highlands National Park, p.o.i., N.S., Can. D16 110
Cape Breton Island, i., N.S., Can. D16 110
Cape Charles, Va., U.S. G9 114
Cape Coast, Ghana H4 64
Cape Cod Bay, b., Ma., U.S. C15 114
Cape Cod National Seashore, p.o.i., Ma., U.S. B16 114
Cape Coral, Fl., U.S. J4 116
Cape Dorset see Kinngait, Nu., Can. C15 106
Cape Elizabeth, Me., U.S. G6 110
Cape Fear, stm., N.C., U.S. B8 116
Cape Girardeau, Mo., U.S. G8 120
Cape Hatteras National Seashore, p.o.i., N.C., U.S. A10 116
Capelinha, Braz. I4 88
Cape Lisburne, Ak., U.S. C6 140
Capel'ka, Russia B11 10
Capella, Austl. D7 76
Capelongo, Ang. C2 68
Cape Lookout National Seashore, p.o.i., N.C., U.S. B9 116
Cape May, N.J., U.S. F10 114
Cape May Court House, N.J., U.S. E11 114
Cape Porpoise, Me., U.S. G6 110
Capernaum see Kefar Naḥum, sci., Isr. F6 58
Cape Sable Island, i., N.S., Can. G11 110
Capesterre, Guad. i6 105c
Capesterre, Pointe de la, c., Guad. h5 105c
Capesterre-Belle-Eau, Guad. h5 105c
Cape Tormentine, N.B., Can. D12 110
Cape Town (Kaapstad), S. Afr. H4 70
Cape Verde, ctry., Afr. k9 65a
Cape Verde Basin, unds. G10 144
Cape Vincent, N.Y., U.S. D13 112
Cape York Peninsula, pen., Austl. B8 74
Cap-Haïtien, Haiti C11 102
Capilla del Monte, Arg. E5 92
Capim, stm., Braz. A2 88
Capinota, Bol. C3 90
Capira, Pan. H8 102
Capitan, N.M., U.S. H3 128
Capitán Arturo Prat, sci., Ant. B34 81
Capitán Bado, Para. D5 90
Capitán Bermúdez, Arg. F7 92
Capitán Meza, Para. C10 92
Capitão Enéas, Braz. I4 88
Capitola, Ca., U.S. G4 134
Capitol Peak, mtn., Nv., U.S. B8 134
Capitol Reef National Park, p.o.i., Ut., U.S. E5 132
Capivara, Represa de, res., Braz. D6 90
Capivari, Braz. L2 88
Capivari, stm., Braz. G6 88
Cap-Pelé, N.B., Can. D12 110
Cappella Islands, is., V.I.U.S. e7 104b
Capraia, Italy G6 22
Capraia, Isola di, i., Italy G6 22
Caprara, Punta, c., Italy C2 24
Caprarola, Italy B6 24
Capreol, On., Can. B9 112
Caprera, Isola, i., Italy C3 24
Capri, Italy D8 24
Capri, Isola di, i., Italy D8 24
Capricorn Channel, strt., Austl. D9 76
Capricorn Group, is., Austl. D9 76
Caprivi Strip, hist. reg., Nmb. D3 68
Capron, Il., U.S. B9 120
Captain Cook, Hi., U.S. d6 78a
Captain Cook Monument, hist., Norf. I. x25 78i
Captains Flat, Austl. J7 76
Capua, Italy C8 24
Capucapu, stm., Braz. H12 86
Capucin, c., Dom. i5 105c
Capulin Volcano National Monument, p.o.i., N.M., U.S. E5 128
Caquetá, state, Col. G4 86
Caquetá (Japurá), stm., S.A. H7 86
Čara, Russia E12 34
Čara, stm., Russia E12 34
Carabinani, stm., Braz. I10 86
Carabobo, state, Ven. B7 86
Caracal, Rom. E11 26
Caracaraí, Braz. G11 86
Caracas, Ven. B8 86
Caracol, Braz. E4 88
Caraguatatuba, Braz. L3 88
Caraguatay, Para. B9 92
Carajás, Braz. E7 84
Carajás, Serra dos, hills, Braz. E7 84
Carakol, sci., Belize D3 102
Caranavi, Bol. C3 90
Carandaí, Braz. K4 88
Carangola, Braz. K4 88
Caransebeş, Rom. D9 26
Carapá, stm., Para. B10 92
Carapajó, Braz. B1 88
Cara-Paraná, stm., Col. H5 86
Carapina, Braz. K5 88
Caraquet, N.B., Can. C11 110
Caraş-Severin, state, Rom. D8 26
Caratasca, Laguna de, b., Hond. E5 102
Caratinga, Braz. J4 88
Carauari, Braz. D4 84
Caraúbas, Braz. C7 88
Caravaca de la Cruz, Spain F8 20
Caravelas, Braz. I6 88
Caravelí, Peru G3 84
Caravelle, Presqu'île la, pen., Mart. k7 105c
Caraway, Ar., U.S. B8 122
Carayaó, Para. B9 92
Carazinho, Braz. D11 92
Carballiño, Spain B2 20
Carballo, Spain A2 20
Carberry, Mb., Can. E14 124
Carbon, Ab., Can. E17 138
Carbon, Tx., U.S. B9 130
Carbonara, Capo, c., Italy E3 24
Carbondale, Co., U.S. D9 132
Carbondale, Il., U.S. G8 120
Carbondale, Pa., U.S. C10 114
Carbonear, Nf., Can. j23 107a
Carboneras de Guadazaón, Spain E9 20
Carbon Hill, Al., U.S. D11 122
Carbonia, Italy E2 24
Carcagente see Carcaixent, Spain E10 20
Carcaixent, Spain E10 20
Carcajou, stm., N.T., Can. B5 106
Carcans, Lac de, b., Fr. D4 18
Carcarañá, Arg. F7 92
Carcarañá, stm., Arg. F7 92
Carcassonne, Fr. F8 18
Carchi, state, Ec. G3 86
Carcross, Yk., Can. C3 106
Çardak, Tur. F12 28
Cárdenas, Cuba A7 102
Cárdenas, Mex. F12 100
Cárdenas, Mex. D9 100
Cárdenas, Bahía de, b., Cuba A7 102
Cardiel, Lago, l., Arg. I2 90
Cardiff, Wales, U.K. J9 12
Cardigan, P.E., Can. D14 110
Cardigan, Wales, U.K. I8 12
Cardigan Bay, b., Wales, U.K. I8 12
Cardinal, On., Can. D14 112
Cardona, Ur. F9 92
Cardonal, Punta, c., Mex. A3 100
Cardoso, Ur. F9 92
Cardston, Ab., Can. G17 138
Cardwell, Austl. B5 76
Cardwell, Mo., U.S. H7 120
Cardwell Mountain, mtn., Tn., U.S. B13 122
Čardžev, Turkmen. B9 56
Carei, Rom. B9 26
Careiro, Braz. I12 86
Careiro, Ilha do, i., Braz. I12 86
Carèja, Bela. F12 10
Carencro, La., U.S. G6 122
Carey, Oh., U.S. D2 114
Carey, Lake, l., Austl. E4 74
Carey Downs, Austl. E3 74
Cargados Carajos Shoals, is., Mrts. K9 142
Carhaix-Plouguer, Fr. F5 14
Carhué, Arg. H6 92
Cariacica, Braz. K5 88
Cariaco, Golfo de, b., Ven. B9 86
Caribbean Sea, s. D7 82
Cariboo, stm., B.C., Can. D9 138
Cariboo Mountains, mts., B.C., Can. D10 138
Caribou, Me., U.S. D8 110
Caribou Lake, l., On., Can. A9 118
Caribou Mountain, mtn., Me., U.S. E6 110
Caribou Mountains, mts., Ab., Can. D7 106
Carichic, Mex. B5 100
Caridade, Braz. C6 88
Carigara, Phil. E5 52
Carignan, Fr. E14 14
Carinda, Austl. H6 76
Carinhanha, Braz. H4 88
Carinhanha, stm., Braz. H3 88
Carini, Italy F7 24
Carinthia see Kärnten, state, Aus. D10 22
Caripito, Ven. B10 86
Carira, Braz. F7 88
Cariré, Braz. C5 88
Cariús, Braz. D6 88
Carleton, Mi., U.S. B2 114
Carleton, Mount, mtn., N.B., Can. C10 110
Carleton Place, On., Can. C13 112
Carletonville, S. Afr. E8 70
Cârlibaba, Rom. B12 26
Carlin, Nv., U.S. C9 134
Carlingford Lough, b., Eur. H7 12
Carlinville, Il., U.S. E8 120
Carlisle, Eng., U.K. G9 12
Carlisle, Ia., U.S. C4 120
Carlisle, In., U.S. F10 120
Carlisle, Ky., U.S. F1 114
Carlisle, Pa., U.S. D8 114
Carl Junction, Mo., U.S. G3 120
Carlos, Isla, i., Chile J2 90
Carlos Casares, Arg. G7 92
Carlos Chagas, Braz. I5 88
Carlos Pellegrini, Arg. E6 92
Carlow, Ire. I5 12
Carlow, state, Ire. I6 12
Carloway, Scot., U.K. C6 12
Carlsbad see Karlovy Vary, Czech Rep. F8 16
Carlsbad, Ca., U.S. J8 134
Carlsbad, N.M., U.S. B3 130
Carlsbad, Tx., U.S. C7 130
Carlsbad Caverns National Park, p.o.i., N.M., U.S. B3 130
Carlsberg Ridge, unds. I9 142
Carlton, Or., U.S. E3 136
Carlton, Tx., U.S. C9 130
Carlyle, Sk., Can. E11 124
Carlyle Lake, res., Il., U.S. F8 120
Carmacks, Yk., Can. C3 106
Carmagnola, Italy F4 22
Carman, Mb., Can. E16 124
Carmangay, Ab., Can. F17 138
Carmarthen, Wales, U.K. J8 12
Carmarthen Bay, b., Wales, U.K. J8 12
Carmel, Ca., U.S. G3 134
Carmel, In., U.S. I3 112
Carmel, N.Y., U.S. G16 112
Carmel Head, c., Wales, U.K. H8 12
Carmelo, Ur. F8 92
Carmel Valley, Ca., U.S. G4 134
Carmen see Ciudad del Carmen, Mex. F12 100
Carmen, stm., Chile D2 92
Carmen, Isla, i., Mex. C3 100
Carmen, Isla del, i., Mex. F13 100
Carmen de Areco, Arg. G8 92
Carmen de Patagones, Arg. H4 90
Carmi, Il., U.S. F9 120
Carmila, Austl. C7 76
Carmine, Tx., U.S. D11 130
Carmo do Paranaíba, Braz. J2 88
Carmona, Spain G5 20
Carmópolis de Minas, Braz. K3 88
Carnarvon, Austl. D2 74
Carnarvon, S. Afr. G5 70
Carnarvon National Park, p.o.i., Austl. E6 76
Čarnaučycy, Bela. H6 10
Carnduff, Sk., Can. E12 124
Carnegie, Austl. E4 74
Carnegie, Lake, l., Austl. E4 74
Carney Island, i., Ant. C29 81
Carnia, reg., Italy D9 22
Carnic Alps, mts., Eur. D9 22
Car Nicobar Island, i., India G7 46
Carnot, C.A.R. D3 66
Carnoustie, Scot., U.K. E10 12
Carnsore Point, c., Ire. I6 12
Carnwath, stm., N.T., Can. B5 106
Caro, Mi., U.S. E6 112
Carol City, Fl., U.S. K5 116
Carolina, Braz. D2 88
Carolina, P.R. B4 104a
Carolina, S. Afr. E10 70
Carolina Beach, N.C., U.S. B8 116
Caroline, at., Kir. D12 72
Caroline Islands, is., Oc. C5 72
Caron, Sk., Can. D8 124
Caroní, stm., Ven. C10 86
Carora, Ven. B6 86
Carpathian Mountains, mts., Eur. B13 26
Carpaţii Meridionali (Transylvanian Alps), mts., Rom. D11 26
Carpentaria, Gulf of, b., Austl. B7 74
Carpenter, Wy., U.S. F8 126
Carpenter Lake, res., B.C., Can. F8 138
Carpentersville, Il., U.S. B9 120
Carpentras, Fr. E11 18
Carpi, Italy F7 22
Carpina, Braz. D8 88
Cărpineni, Mol. C15 26
Carpinteria, Ca., U.S. I6 134
Carpio, N.D., U.S. F12 124
Carp Lake, l., B.C., Can. B7 138
Carpolac, Austl. K3 76
Carrabelle, Fl., U.S. H14 122
Carranza, Cabo, c., Chile G1 92
Carrara, Italy F7 22
Carrathool, Austl. J5 76
Carrauntoohil, mtn., Ire. I3 12
Carreta, Punta, c., Peru F2 84
Carriacou, i., Gren. q11 105e
Carrick on Shannon, Ire. H4 12
Carrick-on-suir, Ire. I5 12
Carrie, Mount, mtn., Wa., U.S. C3 136
Carriers Mills, Il., U.S. G9 120
Carrieton, Austl. I2 76
Carrillo, Mex. B6 100
Carrington, N.D., U.S. G14 124
Carrión, stm., Spain B6 20
Carrión de los Condes, Spain B6 20
Carrizal Bajo, Chile D2 92
Carrizo Creek, stm., U.S. E5 128
Carrizo Mountain, mtn., N.M., U.S. H3 128
Carrizo Springs, Tx., U.S. F7 130
Carroll, Ia., U.S. B3 120
Carroll, Ne., U.S. E15 126
Carrollton, Al., U.S. D10 122
Carrollton, Ga., U.S. D13 122
Carrollton, Mi., U.S. E5 112
Carrollton, Mo., U.S. E4 120
Carrollton, Ms., U.S. D8 122
Carrollton, Oh., U.S. D4 114
Carrollton, Tx., U.S. A10 130
Carrolltown, Pa., U.S. D7 114
Carron, stm., Austl. A3 76
Carrot, stm., Can. E10 106
Carrot River, Sk., Can. A10 124
Carry Falls Reservoir, res., N.Y., U.S. F2 110
Carseland, Ab., Can. F17 138
Carson, N.D., U.S. A11 126
Carson, Wa., U.S. E5 136
Carson, East Fork, stm., U.S. E6 134
Carson City, Nv., U.S. D6 134
Carson Lake, res., Nv., U.S. D7 134
Carson Range, mts., U.S. D6 134
Carson Sink, l., Nv., U.S. D7 134
Carstairs, Ab., Can. E16 138
Cartagena, Chile F2 92
Cartagena, Col. B4 86
Cartagena, Spain G9 20
Cartago, Col. E3 86
Cartago, C.R. H6 102
Cartaxo, Port. E2 20
Cartaya, Spain G3 20
Carter, Ok., U.S. F9 128
Carter Lake, Ia., U.S. C2 120
Cartersville, Ga., U.S. C14 122
Carthage, Tun. H4 24
Carthage, Ar., U.S. C6 122
Carthage, Mo., U.S. G3 120
Carthage, Ms., U.S. E9 122
Carthage, N.C., U.S. A6 116
Carthage, S.D., U.S. C15 126
Carthage, Tn., U.S. H11 120
Carthage, Tx., U.S. E4 122
Carthage, sci., Tun. H4 24
Cartier Islands, is., Austl. B4 74
Cartwright, Mb., Can. E14 124
Caruaru, Braz. E8 88
Carúpano, Ven. B10 86
Carutapera, Braz. D8 84
Caruthersville, Mo., U.S. H8 120
Carutu, stm., Ven. E10 86
Carvoeiro, Braz. H10 86
Carvoeiro, Cabo, c., Port. E1 20
Cary, Ms., U.S. E8 122
Cary, N.C., U.S. I7 114
Čaryškoe, Russia D14 32
Caryville, Fl., U.S. G13 122
Casablanca (Dar-el-Beida), Mor. C3 64
Casa Branca, Braz. K2 88
Casa de Piedra, Embalse, res., Arg. I4 92
Casa Grande, Az., U.S. K5 132
Casa Grande Ruins National Monument, p.o.i., Az., U.S. K5 132
Casale Monferrato, Italy E5 22
Casanare, state, Col. E6 86
Casanare, stm., Col. D6 86
Casa Nova, Braz. E5 88
Casar, N.C., U.S. A4 116
Casarano, Italy D12 24
Casar de Cáceres, Spain E4 20
Casas Adobes, Az., U.S. K6 132
Casas Grandes, stm., Mex. F9 98
Casavieja, Spain D6 20
Casca, Braz. D12 92
Cascadas Basaseachic, Parque Nacional, p.o.i., Mex. A4 100
Cascade, B.C., Can. G12 138
Cascade, Norf. I. y25 78i
Cascade, Ia., U.S. B6 120
Cascade, Mt., U.S. C15 136
Cascade, Wi., U.S. E1 112
Cascade Bay, b., Norf. I. y25 78i
Cascade Mountains see Cascade Range, mts., N.A. C3 108
Cascade Range, mts., N.A. C3 108
Cascade Reservoir, res., Id., U.S. F10 136
Cascade-Siskiyou National Monument, p.o.i., Or., U.S. H4 136
Cascais, Port. F1 20
Cascapédia, stm., Qc., Can. B10 110
Cascavel, Braz. B11 92
Cascavel, Braz. C6 88
Cascina, Italy G7 22
Case-Pilote, Mart. k6 105c
Caserta, Italy C8 24
Caseville, Mi., U.S. E6 112
Casey, Il., U.S. E9 120
Casey, sci., Ant. B16 81
Casey, Mount, mtn., Id., U.S. B10 136
Cashel, Ire. I5 12
Cashiers, N.C., U.S. A2 116
Cashmere, Wa., U.S. C6 136
Cashton, Wi., U.S. H8 118
Casigua, Ven. C5 86
Casilda, Arg. F7 92
Casino, Austl. G9 76
Casiquiare, stm., Ven. F8 86
Čáslav, Czech Rep. G11 16
Casma, Peru E2 84
Čašniki, Bela. F12 10
Casoli, Italy H11 22
Caspe, Spain C10 20
Casper, Wy., U.S. E6 126
Caspian Depression (Prikaspijskaja nizmennost'), pl. E7 32
Caspian Sea, s. F7 32
Cass, stm., Mi., U.S. E6 112
Cassano allo Ionio, Italy E10 24
Cass City, Mi., U.S. E6 112
Casselman, On., Can. E1 110
Cássia, Braz. K2 88
Cassiar, B.C., Can. D5 106
Cassiar Mountains, mts., Can. D5 106
Cassilândia, Braz. C6 90
Cassinga, Ang. D2 68
Cassino, Italy C7 24
Cass Lake, Mn., U.S. D4 118
Cass Lake, res., Mn., U.S. D4 118
Cassongue, Ang. C1 68
Cassopolis, Mi., U.S. G3 112
Cassumba, Ilha, i., Braz. I6 88
Cassville, Mo., U.S. H4 120
Cassville, Wi., U.S. B7 120
Castagniccia, reg., Fr. G15 18
Castaños, Mex. H6 130
Castelbuono, Italy G8 24
Castelfranco Veneto, Italy E8 22
Castellammare, Golfo di, b., Italy F6 24
Castellammare del Golfo, Italy F6 24
Castellammare di Stabia, Italy D8 24
Castellana Grotte, Italy D11 24
Castellane, Fr. F12 18
Castellaneta, Italy D10 24
Castelli, Arg. B7 92
Castelli, Arg. H9 92
Castelló, co., Spain D10 20
Castelló de la Plana, Spain E11 20
Castellón de la Plana see Castelló de la Plana, Spain E11 20
Castellón de la Plana see Castelló, co., Spain D10 20
Castelnaudary, Fr. F7 18
Castelnau-Montratier, Fr. E7 18
Castelo, Braz. K5 88
Castelo Branco, Port. E3 20
Castelo Branco, state, Port. E3 20
Castelo de Paiva, Port. C2 20
Castel San Giovanni, Italy E6 22
Castelsarrasin, Fr. E6 18
Casteltermini, Italy G7 24
Castelvetrano, Italy G6 24
Casterton, Austl. K3 76
Castets, Fr. F4 18
Castiglione del Lago, Italy G8 22
Castile, N.Y., U.S. B7 114
Castilla, Peru E1 84
Castilla, Playa de, cst., Spain G4 20
Castilla-La Mancha, state, Spain E9 20
Castilla la Nueva, hist. reg., Spain E7 20
Castilla la Vieja (Old Castille), hist. reg., Spain C7 20
Castilla y León, state, Spain C6 20
Castillo de San Marcos National Monument, p.o.i., Fl., U.S. F5 116
Castillo Incaico de Ingapirca, sci., Ec. I2 86
Castillon-la-Bataille, Fr. E5 18
Castillos, Ur. G11 92
Castillos, Laguna de, l., Ur. G11 92
Castine, Me., U.S. F8 110
Castlebar, Ire. H3 12
Castle Bruce, Dom. j6 105c
Castle Dome Peak, mtn., Az., U.S. J2 132
Castlegar, B.C., Can. G13 138
Castle Hills, Tx., U.S. E9 130
Castleisland, Ire. I3 12
Castlemaine, Austl. K5 76
Castle Mountain, mtn., Yk., Can. C3 106
Castle Peak, mtn., Co., U.S. D9 132
Castlerea, Ire. H4 12
Castlereagh, stm., Austl. H7 76
Castle Rock, Co., U.S. B3 128
Castle Rock, Wa., U.S. D3 136
Castle Rock, mtn., Or., U.S. F8 136
Castle Rock Butte, mtn., S.D., U.S. B9 126
Castle Rock Lake, res., Wi., U.S. H8 118
Castletown, I. of Man G8 12
Castlewood, S.D., U.S. G1 118
Castor, Ab., Can. D19 138
Castor, stm., Mo., U.S. G7 120
Castres, Fr. F8 18
Castries, St. Luc. I6 105c
Castro, Braz. B13 92
Castro, Chile H2 90
Castro Barros, Arg. E5 92
Castro Daire, Port. D3 20
Castro del Río, Spain G6 20
Castronuño, Spain C5 20
Castro Verde, Port. G2 20
Castrovillari, Italy E10 24
Castroville, Ca., U.S. G4 134
Catacamas, Hond. E5 102
Catacaos, Peru E1 84
Catacocha, Ec. D2 84
Cataguazes, Braz. K4 88
Catahoula Lake, l., La., U.S. F6 122
Çatalan, Tur. A6 58
Catalão, Braz. J2 88
Çatalca, Tur. B11 28
Catalina, Chile B3 92
Catalina see Santa Catalina Island, i., Ca., U.S. J7 134
Catalina, Punta, c., Chile J3 90
Catalonia see Catalunya, state, Spain C12 20
Cataluña see Catalunya, state, Spain C12 20
Catalunya, state, Spain C12 20
Catamarca, state, Arg. C4 92
Catamayo, Ec. D2 84
Catanauan, Phil. D4 52
Catanduanes Island, i., Phil. D5 52
Catanduva, Braz. K1 88
Catania, Italy G9 24
Catania, Golfo di, b., Italy G9 24
Cataño, P.R. B3 104a
Catanzaro, Italy F10 24
Cataract Canyon, p., Az., U.S. H4 132
Catarina, Braz. D6 88
Catarino Rodríguez, Mex. C8 100
Catarman, Phil. F5 52
Catarman, Phil. D5 52
Catarroja, Spain E10 20
Catatumbo, stm., Ven. C5 86
Catawba, stm., U.S. B5 116
Catawissa, Pa., U.S. D9 114
Cat Ba, Dao, i., Viet. B8 48
Catbalogan, Phil. E5 52
Catedral, Cerro, hill, Ur. G10 92
Catete, Ang. B1 68
Cathcart, S. Afr. H8 70
Cathedral City, Ca., U.S. J9 134
Catherine, Mount see Katherîna, Gebel, mtn., Egypt J4 58
Catherines Peak, mtn., Jam. i14 104d
Cat Island, i., Bah. C9 96
Cat Lake, l., On., Can. E12 106
Catlettsburg, Ky., U.S. F3 114
Catlin, Il., U.S. H2 112
Catoche, Cabo, c., Mex. B4 102
Catolé do Rocha, Braz. D7 88
Catoosa, Ok., U.S. H2 120
Catriló, Arg. H6 92
Catrimani, stm., Braz. G11 86
Catskill, N.Y., U.S. B12 114
Catskill Mountains, mts., N.Y., U.S. B11 114
Catt, Mount, mtn., B.C., Can. B2 138
Cattaraugus, N.Y., U.S. B7 114
Cattolica, Italy G9 22
Catu, Braz. G6 88
Catuane, Moz. E11 70
Catur, Moz. C6 68
Çatwick, Îles, is., Viet. G9 48
Čatyrtaš, Kyrg. F13 32
Cau, stm., Viet. A7 48
Cauaburi, stm., Braz. G8 86
Caubvick, Mount, mtn., Can. F13 141
Cauca, state, Col. F3 86
Cauca, stm., Col. D4 86
Caucaia, Braz. B6 88
Caucasia, Col. D4 86
Caucasus, mts. F6 32
Caucete, Arg. E3 92
Cauchari, Salar de, pl., Arg. D3 90
Caudry, Fr. D12 14
Çaungula, Ang. B2 68
Čaunskaja guba, b., Russia C22 34
Cauquenes, Chile G1 92
Caura, stm., Ven. D9 86
Caurés, stm., Braz. H10 86
Căuşani, Mol. C16 26
Causapscal, Qc., Can. B9 110
Caussade, Fr. E7 18
Cauto, stm., Cuba B9 102
Caux, Pays de, reg., Fr. E9 14
Cávado, stm., Port. C3 20
Cavaillon, Fr. F11 18
Cavalcante, Braz. G2 88
Cavalese, Italy D8 22
Cavalier, N.D., U.S. F16 124
Cavalla (Cavally), stm., Afr. H3 64
Cavalleria, Cap de, c., Spain D15 20
Cavally (Cavalla), stm., Afr. H3 64
Cavan, Ire. G5 12
Cavan, state, Ire. H5 12
Cavarzere, Italy E9 22
Çavdır, Tur. F12 28
Cave City, Ky., U.S. G11 120
Cave In Rock, Il., U.S. G9 120
Caveiras, stm., Braz. C12 92
Cavendish, Austl. K4 76
Cave Run Lake, res., Ky., U.S. F2 114
Cave Spring, Ga., U.S. C13 122
Caviana de Fora, Ilha, i., Braz. C8 84
Cavite, Phil. C3 52
Cavour, Canale, can., Italy E5 22
Çavuş, Tur. A2 58
Čavusy, Bela. G14 10
Cawood, Ky., U.S. H2 114
Cawston, B.C., Can. G11 138
Caxambu, Braz. K3 88
Caxias, Braz. C4 88
Caxias do Sul, Braz. D12 92
Caxito, Ang. B1 68
Çay, Tur. E13 28
Cayambe, Ec. G2 86
Cayambe, vol., Ec. G3 86
Cayce, S.C., U.S. C4 116
Çaycuma, Tur. B15 28
Cay Duong, Vinh, b., Viet. G7 48
Cayenne, Fr. Gu. C7 84
Cayey, P.R. B3 104a
Caylus, Fr. E7 18
Cayman Brac, i., Cay. Is. C8 102
Cayman Islands, dep., N.A. C7 102
Caynaba, Som. C9 66
Cayon, St. K./N. C2 105a
Cayuga, In., U.S. I2 112
Cayuga, Tx., U.S. F3 122
Cayuga Heights, N.Y., U.S. B9 114
Cayuga Lake, res., N.Y., U.S. B9 114
Cazalla de la Sierra, Spain G5 20
Cazaux et de Sanguinet, Étang de, l., Fr. E4 18
Cazères, Fr. F6 18
Cazombo, Ang. C3 68
Cazorla, Spain G7 20
Cea, stm., Spain B5 20
Ceanannas see Kells, Ire. H6 12
Ceará, state, Braz. C6 88
Ceará-Mirim, Braz. C8 88
Ceará-Mirim, stm., Braz. C8 88
Ceatharlach see Carlow, Ire. I5 12
Cebaco, Isla de, i., Pan. I7 102
Ceballos, Mex. B6 100
Čeboksary, Russia C7 32
Cebollar, Arg. D4 92
Cebollas, Mex. D6 100
Cebollatí, Ur. F11 92
Cebollatí, stm., Ur. F10 92
Céboruco, Volcán, vol., Mex. E6 100
Cebu, Phil. E4 52
Cebu, i., Phil. E4 52
Cebu Strait, strt., Phil. F4 52
Ceceda, Mex. H4 130
Čechtice, Czech Rep. G11 16
Čechy, hist. reg., Czech Rep. G10 16
Cecilia, Ky., U.S. G12 120
Cecil Plains, Austl. F8 76
Cecina, Italy G7 22
Čečnja, state, Russia F7 32
Cedar, stm., Ne., U.S. F14 126
Cedar, stm., U.S. J7 118
Cedar Bluffs, Ne., U.S. J2 118
Cedar Breaks National Monument, p.o.i., Ut., U.S. F3 132
Cedarburg, Wi., U.S. E1 112
Cedar City, Ut., U.S. F3 132
Cedar Creek, stm., Ia., U.S. C5 120
Cedar Creek, stm., Id., U.S. B2 132
Cedar Creek, stm., N.D., U.S. A11 126
Cedar Falls, Ia., U.S. B5 120
Cedar Grove, Wi., U.S. E2 112
Cedar Hill, Tn., U.S. H10 120
Cedar Key, Fl., U.S. G2 116
Cedar Lake, In., U.S. J11 118
Cedar Lake, l., On., Can. B11 112
Cedar Lake, res., Mb., Can. E10 106
Cedar Mountain, mtn., Ca., U.S. B5 134
Cedar Rapids, Ia., U.S. C6 120
Cedars of Lebanon see Arz Lubnān, for., Leb. D7 58
Cedar Springs, Mi., U.S. E4 112
Cedartown, Ga., U.S. C13 122
Cedar Tree Point, c., Antig. e4 105b
Cedarvale, B.C., Can. A2 138
Cedar Vale, Ks., U.S. D12 128
Cedarville, Ca., U.S. B5 134
Cedarville, Mi., U.S. B5 112
Cedeira, Spain A2 20
Cedillo, Embalse de, res., Eur. E3 20
Cedro, Braz. D6 88
Cedros, Mex. C8 100
Cedros, Isla, i., Mex. A1 100
Ceduna, Austl. F6 74
Ceelbuur, Som. D9 66
Ceepeecee, B.C., Can. G4 138
Ceerigaabo, Som. B9 66
Cefalonia see Kefalloniá, i., Grc. E3 28
Cefalù, Italy F8 24
Cega, stm., Spain C6 20
Čegdomyn, Russia F15 34
Cegléd, Hung. B6 26
Ceglie Messapico, Italy D11 24
Cehegín, Spain F9 20
Čehov, Russia E20 10
Čehov, Russia G17 34
Čekalin, Russia F19 10
Čekuevo, Russia E18 8
Čelákovice, Czech Rep. F10 16
Celano, Italy H10 22
Celaya, Mex. E8 100
Celebes see Sulawesi, i., Indon. F7 44
Celebes Basin, unds. I15 142
Celebes Sea, s., Asia E7 44
Čeleken, Turkmen. B7 56
Celeste, Tx., U.S. D2 122
Celestún, Mex. B2 102
Celina, Tn., U.S. H12 120
Celina, Tx., U.S. D2 122
Čeljabinsk, Russia C10 32
Celjahany, Bela. H8 10
Celje, Slvn. D12 22
Čeljuskin, mys, c., Russia A9 34
Celle, Ger. D6 16
Čelmozero, Russia D14 8
Celtic Sea, s., Eur. J6 12
Çeltikçi, Tur. A1 58
Čemal, Russia D15 32
Cement, Ok., U.S. G10 128
Cenajo, Embalse del, res., Spain F9 20
Cenderawasih, Teluk, b., Indon. F10 44
Cenovo, Blg. F12 26
Centenario, Arg. I3 92
Center, Co., U.S. D2 128
Center, Mo., U.S. E6 120
Center, N.D., U.S. G12 124
Center, Tx., U.S. F4 122
Centerburg, Oh., U.S. D3 114
Center Hill, Fl., U.S. H3 116
Center Hill Lake, res., Tn., U.S. H12 120
Center Moriches, N.Y., U.S. D13 114
Center Point, Al., U.S. D12 122
Center Point, Ia., U.S. B6 120
Centerville, Ia., U.S. D5 120
Centerville, Mo., U.S. G7 120
Centerville, Pa., U.S. D5 114
Centerville, Tn., U.S. B11 122
Centerville, Tx., U.S. F2 122
Centerville, Ut., U.S. C4 132
Central, Braz. F4 88
Central, Phil. D3 52
Central, Az., U.S. K7 132
Central, N.M., U.S. K8 132
Central, state, Bots. C8 70
Central, state, Para. B9 92
Central, state, Sol. Is. e8 79b
Central, Cordillera, mts., Col. E4 86
Central, Cordillera, mts., Peru E2 84
Central, Cordillera, mts., Phil. B3 52
Central, Cordillera, mts., P.R. B2 104a
Central, Massif, mts., Fr. D8 18
Central, Sistema, mts., Spain D6 20
Central African Republic, ctry., Afr. C4 66
Central Aguirre, P.R. C3 104a
Central Arizona Project Aqueduct, aq., U.S. J3 132
Central Bohemia see Středočeský, state, Czech Rep. G10 16
Central Borneo see Kalimantan Tengah, state, Indon. D8 50
Central Brāhui Range, mts., Pak. D10 56
Central Celebes see Sulawesi Tengah, state, Indon. D12 50
Central City, Ia., U.S. B6 120
Central City, Il., U.S. F8 120
Central City, Ky., U.S. G10 120
Central City, Pa., U.S. D7 114
Central Division, state, Fiji q19 79e
Centralia, Il., U.S. F8 120
Centralia, Ks., U.S. E1 120
Centralia, Mo., U.S. E5 120
Centralia, Wa., U.S. D4 136
Centralina, Braz. J1 88

Name	Map Ref.	Page
Central Java see Jawa Tengah, state, Indon.	G7	50
Central Kalahari Game Reserve, Bots.	C6	70
Central Lake, Mi., U.S.	C4	112
Central Makrān Range, mts., Pak.	D9	56
Central'nyj, Russia	C15	32
Central Pacific Basin, unds.	I21	142
Central Point, Or., U.S.	A2	134
Central Range, mts., Pap. N. Gui.	a3	79a
Central Russian Upland see Srednerusskaja vozvyšennost', plat., Russia	H20	10
Central Siberian Plateau see Srednesibirskoe ploskogor'e, plat., Russia	C10	34
Central Siberian Uplands see Srednesibirskoe ploskogor'e, plat., Russia	C10	34
Central Slovakia see Stredoslovenský Kraj, state, Slov.	H15	16
Central Utah Canal, can., Ut., U.S.	D4	132
Central Valley, Ca., U.S.	C3	134
Central Valley see Longitudinal, Valle, Chile.	H1	92
Centre, Canal du, can., Fr.	C10	18
Centreville, Al., U.S.	E11	122
Centreville, Md., U.S.	E9	114
Centreville, Ms., U.S.	F7	122
Centro Puntas, P.R.	B1	104a
Century, Fl., U.S.	G11	122
Ceos see Kéa, i., Grc.	F7	28
Cepelare, Blg.	H11	26
Cephalonia see Kefalloniá, i., Grc.	E3	28
Cepu, Indon.	G7	50
Ceram see Seram, i., Indon.	F8	44
Ceram Sea see Seram, Laut, s., Indon.	F8	44
Čerčany, Czech Rep.	G10	16
Cerdas, Bol.	D3	90
Cereal, Ab., Can.	C3	124
Čereha, stm., Russia	C11	10
Čeremhovo, Russia	D18	32
Čeremšany, Russia	B11	38
Čerepanovo, Russia	D14	32
Čerepet', Russia	F19	10
Čerepovec, Russia	A20	10
Ceres, Arg.	D7	92
Ceres, Braz.	G8	84
Ceres, S. Afr.	H4	70
Ceresio see Lugano, Lago di, l., Eur.	D14	18
Cereté, Col.	C4	86
Čerevkovo, Russia	F21	8
Cerignola, Italy	C9	24
Cérilly, Fr.	H11	14
Čerkessk, Russia	F6	32
Čerkezköy, Tur.	B10	28
Čerlak, Russia	D12	32
Čermei, Rom.	C9	26
Čermoz, Russia	C8	32
Cerna, Rom.	D15	26
Černá hora, mtn., Czech Rep.	G9	16
Cernavodă, Rom.	E15	26
Černay, Fr.	G16	14
Černigovka, Russia	B10	38
Černjahovsk, Russia	F4	10
Černogorsk, Russia	D16	32
Černovskij, Russia	C9	32
Černyševa, Russia	F12	34
Černyševskij, Russia	D11	34
Cerralvo, Isla, i., Mex.	C4	100
Čerrik, Alb.	C14	24
Čérriku see Čërrik, Alb.	C14	24
Cerrillos, Arg.	B5	92
Cerrillos, N.M., U.S.	F2	128
Cerritos, Mex.	D8	100
Cerro Azul, Braz.	B13	92
Cerro Azul, Mex.	E9	100
Cerro Azul, Peru	F2	84
Cerro Chato, Ur.	F10	92
Cerro de las Mesas, sci., Mex.	F2	100
Cerro Gordo, Il., U.S.	E9	120
Cerro Largo, Braz.	D10	92
Cerro Moreno, Chile	A2	92
Cerrón, Cerro, mtn., Ven.	B6	86
Cerrón Grande, Embalse, res., El Sal.	K10	134
Cerros Colorados, Embalse, res., Arg.	I3	92
Cerro Tololo, Observatorio Astronómico, sci., Chile	E2	92
Čerskij, Russia	C21	34
Čerskogo, hrebet (Cherskiy Mountains), mts., Russia	D16	34
Čertolino, Russia	C17	34
Červen', Bela.	G10	10
Červen Brjag, Blg.	F11	26
Cervera, Spain	C12	20
Cervera de Pisuerga, Spain	B6	20
Cervia, Italy	F9	22
Cervialto, Monte, mtn., Italy	D9	24
Cervino see Matterhorn, mtn., Eur.	D13	18
Cervione, Fr.	G15	18
Cervo, Spain	A3	20
Cesar, state, Col.	C5	86
Cesar, stm., Col.	B5	86
Cesena, Italy	F9	22
Cesenatico, Italy	F9	22
Cēsis, Lat.	C8	10
Česká Kamenice, Czech Rep.	F10	16
Česká Lípa, Czech Rep.	F10	16
Česká Třebová, Czech Rep.	G12	16
České Budějovice, Czech Rep.	H10	16
Český Brod, Czech Rep.	F10	16
Çeşme, Tur.	E9	28
Česskaja guba (Chesha Bay), b., Russia.	C21	8
Cessnock, Austl.	I8	76
Cesvaine, Lat.	D9	10
Cetina, stm., Cro.	G13	22
Cetinje, Serb.	G5	26
Ceuta, Sp. N. Afr.	B3	64
Cévennes, reg., Fr.	E9	18
Cévennes, Parc National des, p.o.i., Fr.	E9	18
Cevizli, Tur.	F14	28
Ceyhan, Tur.	A6	58
Ceyhan, stm., Tur.	B6	58
Ceylon, Mn., U.S.	H4	118
Ceylon see Sri Lanka, ctry., Asia	G5	53
Cèze, stm., Fr.	E10	18
Cha-am, Thai.	F5	48
Chabanais, Fr.	D6	18
Chabás, Arg.	F7	92
Chabjuwardoo Bay, b., Austl.	D2	74
Chablais, reg., Fr.	C12	18
Chacabuco, Arg.	G7	92
Chachani, Nevado, vol., Peru	G3	84
Chachapoyas, Peru	E2	84
Cháchora, India	F6	54
Cháchro, Pak.	F3	54
Chaco, state, Arg.	C7	92
Chaco, stm., N.M., U.S.	G8	132
Chaco, Parque Nacional, p.o.i., Arg.	C8	92
Chaco Austral, reg., Arg.	C7	92
Chaco Boreal, reg., Para.	D4	90
Chaco Central, reg., Arg.	D4	90
Chaco Mesa, mtn., N.M., U.S.	H9	132
Chad, ctry., Afr.	E3	62
Chad, Lake, l., Afr.	G7	64
Chadbourn, N.C., U.S.	B7	116
Chadron, Ne., U.S.	E10	126
Chadwick, Il., U.S.	I9	118
Chaem, stm., Thai.	C4	48
Chāgai Hills, hills, Asia	D9	56
Chagos Archipelago, is., B.I.O.T.	J10	142
Chagos-Lacadive Plateau, unds.	J10	142
Chaguanas, Trin.	s12	105f
Chaguaramas, Ven.	C8	86
Chahal, Guat.	E3	102
Chahanwusu see Dulan, China.	D4	36
Chahe, China	E4	36
Chāībāsa, India	G10	54
Chaihe, China	B8	38
Chai Nat, Thai.	E4	48
Chaiya, Thai.	H4	48
Chaiyaphum, Thai.	E6	48
Chajarí, Arg.	E8	92
Chākdaha, India	H14	54
Chake Chake, Tan.	F7	66
Chākia, India	E10	54
Chakkarat, Thai.	E6	48
Chakradharpur, India	G10	54
Chaksu, India	E5	54
Chakwāl, Pak.	B4	54
Chala, Peru	G3	84
Chalais, Fr.	D6	18
Chalatenango, El Sal.	E3	102
Chalaxung, China.	E4	36
Chalbi Desert, des., Kenya	D7	66
Chalcidice see Chalkidikí, hist. reg., Grc.	C6	28
Chalcis see Chalkída, Grc.	E6	28
Chaleur Bay, b., Can.	C11	110
Chalia, stm., Arg.	I2	90
Chālisgaon, India	H5	54
Chalke see Chálki, i., Grc.	G10	28
Chálki, i., Grc.	G10	28
Chalkída, Grc.	E6	28
Chalkidikí, hist. reg., Grc.	C6	28
Chalk River, On., Can.	B12	112
Chalkére, India	D3	53
Challapata, Bol.	C3	90
Challenger Deep, unds.	H17	142
Chalmette, La., U.S.	H9	122
Châlons-sur-Marne, Fr.	F13	14
Chalon-sur-Saône, Fr.	H13	14
Chaltel, Cerro (Fitz Roy, Monte), mtn., S.A.	I2	90
Chaluhe, China	C6	38
Cham, Ger.	G8	16
Chama, N.M., U.S.	G10	132
Chama, stm., Ven.	C6	86
Chamaicó, Arg.	H5	92
Chaman, Pak.	C10	56
Chamba, India	B6	54
Chambal, stm., India	E6	54
Chamberlain, Sk., Can.	D8	124
Chamberlain, S.D., U.S.	D13	126
Chamberlain, stm., Austl.	C5	74
Chamberlain Lake, l., Me., U.S.	D7	110
Chambers, Ne., U.S.	E14	126
Chambersburg, Pa., U.S.	E8	114
Chambers Island, i., Wi., U.S.	C2	112
Chambéry, Fr.	D11	18
Chambi, Jebel, mtn., Tun.	B6	64
Chambord, Qc., Can.	B4	110
Chamdo see Qamdo, China.	E4	36
Chamical, Arg.	E4	92
Chamo, Lake see Ch'amo Hāyk', l., Eth.	F7	62
Ch'amo Hāyk', l., Eth.	F7	62
Chamoli, India	C7	54
Chamonix-Mont-Blanc, Fr.	D12	18
Chāmpa, India	G9	54
Champagne, hist. reg., Fr.	F13	14
Champagne Castle, mtn., S. Afr.	F9	70
Champagnole, Fr.	H14	14
Champaign, Il., U.S.	D9	120
Champaquí, Cerro, mtn., Arg.	F5	92
Champasak, Laos	E7	48
Champdoré, Lac, l., Can.	D17	106
Champion, Ab., Can.	F17	138
Champion, Mi., U.S.	B1	112
Champion, Oh., U.S.	C4	114
Champlain, Lake, l., N.A.	D16	112
Champlitte-et-le-Prélot, Fr.	G14	14
Champotón, Mex.	C2	102
Chāmrājnagar Rāmasamudram, India	F3	53
Chañar, Arg.	E4	92
Chañaral, Chile	C2	92
Chañaral, Isla, i., Chile	D2	92
Chancay, Peru	F2	84
Chanchiang see Zhanjiang, China	K4	42
Chanco, Chile	G1	92
Chandalar, Ak., U.S.	C10	140
Chandalar, stm., Ak., U.S.	C10	140
Chandannagar, India	G11	54
Chandausi, India	D7	54
Chāndbāli, India	H11	54
Chandeleur Islands, is., La., U.S.	H10	122
Chandeleur Sound, strt., La., U.S.	H9	122
Chandigarh, India	C6	54
Chandler, Qc., Can.	B12	110
Chandler, Az., U.S.	J5	132
Chandler, In., U.S.	F10	120
Chandler, Tx., U.S.	E3	122
Chandlerville, Il., U.S.	D7	120
Chāndpur, Bngl.	G13	54
Chāndpur, India	D7	54
Chandrapur, India	H7	54
Chandvad, India	H5	54
Chang (Yangtze), stm., China.	F8	36
Chang, stm., China	G1	42
Chang, Ko, i., Thai.	F6	48
Changanācheri, India	G3	53
Changane, stm., Moz.	D11	70
Changcheng (Great Wall), misc. cult., China	A7	54
Changchiakow see Zhangjiakou, China	A6	42
Ch'angch'ŏn see Changzhi, China.	C5	42
Changchou see Changzhou, China.	F8	42
Changchow see Zhangzhou, China.	I7	42
Changchow see Changzhou, China.	F8	42
Changchow see Zhangzhou, China.	I7	42
Changchun, China	C6	38
Changde, China	G4	42
Changhua, Tai.	I9	42
Changhŭng, Kor., S.	G7	38
Changji, China	C2	36
Changjiang, China	L3	42
Changkiakow see Zhangjiakou, China	A6	42
Changli, China	B8	42
Changling, China	B5	38
Changlun, Malay.	I5	48
Changmar, China	A7	54
Changning, China	H5	42
Changning, China	H5	42
Ch'angnyŏng, Kor., S.	D1	40
Changping, China	A7	42
Changsan-got, c., Kor., N.	E6	38
Changsha, China	G5	42
Changshan Qundao, is., China	B10	42
Changshou, China	G2	42
Changshu, China	F9	42
Ch'angte see Changde, China	G4	42
Changteh see Anyang, China	C6	42
Changtien see Zibo, China	C8	42
Changting, China	I7	42
Changting, China	B8	38
Changwŏn, Kor., S.	D1	40
Changwu, China	D2	42
Changxing, China	F8	42
Changxing Dao, i., China	B9	42
Changyi, China	C8	42
Changyŏn-ŭp, Kor., N.	E6	38
Changzhi, China	C5	42
Changzhou, China	F8	42
Chaniá, Grc.	H7	28
Chanión, Kólpos, b., Grc.	H6	28
Chankiang see Zhanjiang, China	K4	42
Channagiri, India	D2	53
Channapatna, India	E3	53
Channel Country, reg., Austl.	E3	76
Channel Islands, is., Eur.	L10	12
Channel Islands, is., Ca., U.S.	J6	134
Channel Islands National Park, p.o.i., Ca., U.S.	J6	134
Channel-Port aux Basques, Nf., Can.	j22	107a
Channelview, Tx., U.S.	H3	122
Channing, Mi., U.S.	B1	112
Channing, Tx., U.S.	F6	128
Chan-si see Shanxi, state, China	B5	42
Chantada, Spain	B3	20
Chanthaburi, Thai.	F6	48
Chantilly, Fr.	E11	14
Chantrey Inlet, b., Nu., Can.	B11	106
Chanute, Ks., U.S.	G2	120
Chao, stm., China	A7	42
Chao'an, China	J7	42
Ch'aochou see Chao'an, China	J7	42
Chaochow see Chao'an, China	J7	42
Chao Hu, l., China	F7	42
Chao Phraya, stm., Thai.	F5	48
Chaor, stm., China	B9	36
Chaoxian, China	F7	42
Chaoyang, China	J7	42
Chaoyang, China	B7	38
Chaoyang, China	D8	38
Chaoyangshan, China	C6	38
Chapada dos Veadeiros, Parque Nacional da, p.o.i., Braz.	H2	88
Chapadinha, Braz.	B4	88
Chapaevo, Kaz.	E8	32
Chapala, Mex.	E7	100
Chapala, Laguna de, l., Mex.	E7	100
Chāparmukh, India	E14	54
Chaparral, Col.	F4	86
Chapecó, Braz.	C11	92
Chapel Hill, N.C., U.S.	I6	114
Chapelton, Jam.	i13	104d
Chapéu, Morro do, mtn., Braz.	H4	88
Chapicuy, Ur.	E9	92
Chapin, Il., U.S.	E7	120
Chapleau, Sk., Can.	D7	124
Chaplin, Sk., Can.	D7	124
Chaplin Lake, l., Sk., Can.	D7	124
Chapman, Ne., U.S.	F14	126
Chapman, Cape, c., Nu., Can.	B13	106
Chapmanville, W.V., U.S.	G3	114
Chapo, Mex.	C8	100
Chappal, Waddi, mtn., Afr.	H7	64
Chappell Hill, Tx., U.S.	G2	122
Chāpra, India	F10	54
Chapultepec, Mex.	L9	134
Chaquiago, Arg.	C4	92
Charadai, Arg.	C8	92
Charalá, Col.	D5	86
Charata, Arg.	C7	92
Chār Borjak, Afg.	C9	56
Charcas, Mex.	D8	100
Charco Hondo, P.R.	B2	104a
Charcos de Risa, Mex.	B7	100
Charcot Island, i., Ant.	B33	81
Chard, Eng., U.K.	K10	12
Charente, state, Fr.	D6	18
Charente, stm., Fr.	C6	18
Charente-Maritime, state, Fr.	C5	18
Chari, stm., Afr.	E3	62
Chārikār, Afg.	B10	56
Chariton, U.S.	C4	120
Chariton, stm., U.S.	E5	120
Chariton, Mussel Fork, stm., Mo., U.S.	E5	120
Charity, Guy.	B6	86
Charkhāri, India	F7	54
Charkhlik see Ruoqiang, China.	D2	36
Charleroi, Bel.	D13	14
Charles, Cape, c., Va., U.S.	G10	114
Charles, Peak, mtn., Austl.	F4	74
Charles City, Ia., U.S.	A5	120
Charles City, Va., U.S.	G8	114
Charles Island, i., Nu., Can.	C16	106
Charles Mound, hill, Il., U.S.	B7	120
Charles Point, c., Austl.	B6	74
Charleston, Ar., U.S.	B4	122
Charleston, Il., U.S.	E9	120
Charleston, Mo., U.S.	H8	120
Charleston, Ms., U.S.	D8	122
Charleston, S.C., U.S.	D6	116
Charleston, W.V., U.S.	F4	114
Charleston Peak, mtn., Nv., U.S.	G10	134
Charlestown, St. K./N.	C2	105a
Charlestown, In., U.S.	F12	120
Charlestown, N.H., U.S.	G4	110
Charleville, Austl.	F5	76
Charleville-Mézières, Fr.	E13	14
Charlevoix, Mi., U.S.	C5	112
Charlieu, Fr.	C10	18
Charlotte, Mi., U.S.	B1	114
Charlotte, N.C., U.S.	A5	116
Charlotte, Tx., U.S.	F9	130
Charlotte Amalie, V.I.U.S.	e7	104b
Charlotte Harbor, b., Fl., U.S.	J3	116
Charlotte Lake, l., B.C., Can.	D5	138
Charlottesville, Va., U.S.	F7	114
Charlottetown, P.E., Can.	D13	110
Charlotteville, Trin.	r13	105f
Charlton Island, i., Nu., Can.	E14	106
Charouine, Alg.	D4	64
Charron Lake, l., Mb., Can.	B18	124
Charroux, Fr.	C6	18
Chārsadda, Pak.	A3	54
Charter Oak, Ia., U.S.	I3	118
Charters Towers, Austl.	C6	76
Chartres, Fr.	F10	14
Chascomús, Arg.	G8	92
Chase, B.C., Can.	F11	138
Chase, Mount, mtn., Me., U.S.	D8	110
Chase City, Va., U.S.	H7	114
Chaska, Mn., U.S.	G5	118
Chasŏng, Kor., N.	o11	105e
Château-Chinon, Fr.	G13	14
Châteaubriant, Fr.	G7	14
Château-du-Loir, Fr.	G9	14
Châteaudun, Fr.	F10	14
Chateauguay (Châteauguay), stm., N.A.	D15	112
Châteaulin, Fr.	F4	14
Châteauneuf-sur-Charente, Fr.	D5	18
Château-Renault, Fr.	G9	14
Château-Richer, Qc., Can.	C5	110
Châteauroux, Fr.	H10	14
Château-Thierry, Fr.	E12	14
Châtellerault, Fr.	H9	14
Chatfield, Mn., U.S.	H6	118
Chatham, N.B., Can.	C11	110
Chatham, On., Can.	F7	112
Chatham, Eng., U.K.	J13	12
Chatham, Il., U.S.	E8	120
Chatham, La., U.S.	E6	122
Chatham, Ma., U.S.	C15	114
Chatham, N.Y., U.S.	B12	114
Chatham, Isla, i., Chile	J2	90
Chatham, Islands, is., N.Z.	H9	72
Chatham Rise, unds.	N20	142
Chatham Strait, strt., Ak., U.S.	E13	140
Châtillon-en-Bazois, Fr.	G12	14
Châtillon-sur-Seine, Fr.	G13	14
Chatkal Range, mts., Asia	F12	32
Chatom, Al., U.S.	F10	122
Chatra, India	F10	54
Chatsworth, Austl.	E3	76
Chatsworth, Ga., U.S.	C14	122
Chatsworth, Il., U.S.	D9	120
Chattahoochee, Fl., U.S.	G14	122
Chattahoochee, stm., U.S.	G14	122
Chattanooga, Tn., U.S.	B13	122
Chattaroy, W.V., U.S.	G3	114
Chaturat, Thai.	E5	48
Chaubourg, Mount, hill, St. Luc.	I7	105c
Chaudière, stm., Qc., Can.	D5	110
Chau Doc, Viet.	G7	48
Chauk, Mya.	B2	48
Chaumont, Fr.	F13	14
Chaungwabyin, Mya.	F4	48
Chaupāran, India	F10	54
Chauvin, La., U.S.	H8	122
Chavakkad, India	F2	53
Chavarría, Arg.	D8	92
Chaves, Port.	C3	20
Chaviva, Col.	E5	86
Chawa'nanake, China	C12	54
Chay, stm., Viet.	A7	48
Chayuan, China	G9	42
Chazy, N.Y., U.S.	F3	110
Chbar, stm., Camb.	F8	48
Cheaha Mountain, mtn., Al., U.S.	D13	122
Cheat, stm., W.V., U.S.	E6	114
Cheat, Shavers Fork, stm., W.V., U.S.	E6	114
Cheb, Czech Rep.	F8	16
Chebanse, Il., U.S.	G2	112
Cheboygan, Mi., U.S.	C5	112
Chech, 'Erg, des., Afr.	E4	64
Chechnya see Čečnja, state, Russia	F7	32
Chech'ŏn, Kor., S.	B1	40
Chęciny, Pol.	F16	16
Checleset Bay, b., B.C., Can.	F3	138
Checotah, Ok., U.S.	B3	122
Chedabucto Bay, b., N.S., Can.	E15	110
Cheduba Island, i., Mya.	C1	48
Cheduba Strait, strt., Mya.	C1	48
Cheektowaga, N.Y., U.S.	B7	114
Cheepie, Austl.	F5	76
Chef-Boutonne, Fr.	C5	18
Chefoo see Yantai, China	C9	42
Chehalis, Wa., U.S.	D3	136
Chehalis, stm., Wa., U.S.	D3	136
Cheju, Kor., S.	H7	38
Cheju-do (Quelpart Island), i., Kor., S.	H7	38
Chekiang see Zhejiang, state, China	G8	42
Chela, Serra da, mts., Ang.	D1	68
Chelan, Lake, res., Wa., U.S.	B6	136
Chelif, Oued, stm., Alg.	B5	64
Chełm, Pol.	E19	16
Chełm, state, Pol.	E19	16
Chełmno, Pol.	C14	16
Chelmsford, Eng., U.K.	J13	12
Chełmża, Pol.	C14	16
Chelsea, Ia., U.S.	C5	120
Chelsea, Mi., U.S.	B1	114
Chelsea, Vt., U.S.	F4	110
Cheltenham, Eng., U.K.	J10	12
Chelva see Xelva, Spain	E9	20
Chelyuskin, Cape see Čeljuskin, mys, c., Russia	A9	34
Chemainus, B.C., Can.	H7	138
Chemba, Moz.	D5	68
Chemnitz, Ger.	F8	16
Chemult, Or., U.S.	H5	136
Chenāb, stm., Asia	D3	54
Chenachane, Alg.	D4	64
Chenderoh, Tasik, l., Malay.	J5	48
Chénéville, Qc., Can.	E1	110
Cheney, Wa., U.S.	C9	136
Cheney Reservoir, res., Ks., U.S.	D10	128
Cheneyville, La., U.S.	F6	122
Chengbu, China	H4	42
Chengchou see Zhengzhou, China.	D5	42
Chengde, China	A7	42
Chengdu, China	E5	36
Chenghai, China	J7	42
Chengjiang, China	E5	36
Chengmai, China	L3	42
Chengshan Jiao, c., China	C10	42
Chengteh see Chengde, China.	A7	42
Chengtu see Chengdu, China.	E5	36
Chengxian, China	E1	42
Chengyang, China	C9	42
Chengzitan, China	B10	42
Chenjiang see Zhenjiang, China.	E8	42
Chennai (Madras), India	E5	53
Chenxi, China	G4	42
Chenzhou, China	I5	42
Chentang, China	J4	42
Chenxiangtun, China	D5	38
Chenyang see Shenyang, China	D5	38
Chenzhou, China	I5	42
Cheonan see Ch'ŏnan, Kor., S.	F7	38
Cheongju see Ch'ŏngju, Kor., S.	F7	38
Chepén, Peru	E2	84
Chepes, Arg.	E4	92
Chepkotet, mtn., Kenya	D7	66
Chepo, Pan.	H8	102
Cher, state, Fr.	B8	18
Cher, stm., Fr.	B7	18
Cherán, Mex.	F7	100
Cheraw, S.C., U.S.	A6	116
Cherbourg, Fr.	E7	14
Cherchell, Alg.	H13	20
Chergui, Chott ech, l., Alg.	C5	64
Cheriton, Va., U.S.	G10	114
Cheriyam Island, i., India	F1	53
Cherkassy see Cherkasy, Ukr.	E4	32
Cherkasy, Ukr.	E4	32
Cherkessia see Karačaevo-Čerkesija, state, Russia	F6	32
Cherkessk see Čerkessk, Russia	F6	32
Chernihiv, Ukr.	D4	32
Chernivtsi, Ukr.	A12	26
Chernivtsi, co., Ukr.	A13	26
Chernobyl see Chornobyl', Ukr.	D4	32
Cherokee, Ia., U.S.	B2	120
Cherokee, Ks., U.S.	G3	120
Cherokee, Ok., U.S.	E10	128
Cherokee, Tx., U.S.	C9	130
Cherokee Lake, res., Tn., U.S.	H2	114
Cherokee Point, c., Bah.	D12	140
Cherokees, Lake O' The, res., Ok., U.S.	H2	120
Cherokee Sound, Bah.	J8	116
Cherrapunji, India	F13	54
Cherry Creek, stm., S.D., U.S.	C11	126
Cherry Hill, N.J., U.S.	E10	114
Cherryvale, Ks., U.S.	G2	120
Cherry Valley, Ar., U.S.	B8	122
Cherryville, N.C., U.S.	A4	116
Cherskiy Mountains see Čerskogo, hrebet, mts., Russia	C17	34
Chesapeake, Va., U.S.	H9	114
Chesapeake Bay, b., U.S.	F9	114
Chesapeake Bay Bridge-Tunnel, Va., U.S.	G9	114
Chesapeake Beach, Md., U.S.	F9	114
Chesha Bay see Česskaja guba, b., Russia	C21	8
Cheshire, Ma., U.S.	B12	114
Cheslatta Lake, l., B.C., Can.	C5	138
Chesnee, S.C., U.S.	A4	116
Chest Creek, stm., Pa., U.S.	D7	114
Chester, Eng., U.K.	H10	12
Chester, Ca., U.S.	C4	134
Chester, Il., U.S.	F8	120
Chester, Mt., U.S.	B15	136
Chester, Ne., U.S.	A11	128
Chester, Ok., U.S.	E10	128
Chester, Pa., U.S.	E10	114
Chester, S.C., U.S.	B5	116
Chester, Va., U.S.	G8	114
Chester Basin, N.S., Can.	F12	110
Chesterfield, Eng., U.K.	H11	12
Chesterfield, S.C., U.S.	B5	116
Chesterfield, Îles, is., N. Cal.	E6	72
Chesterfield Inlet see Igluligaarjuk, Nu., Can.	C12	106
Chesterfield Inlet, b., Nu., Can.	C12	106
Chesterhill, Oh., U.S.	E4	114
Chester-le-Street, Eng., U.K.	G11	12
Chestertown, Md., U.S.	E9	114
Chesterville, On., Can.	C14	112
Chesuncook Lake, l., Me., U.S.	E7	110
Cheviot, Oh., U.S.	E13	120
Cheviot Hills, hills, U.K.	F10	12
Ch'ew Bahir see Stefanie, Lake, l., Afr.	G7	62
Chewelah, Wa., U.S.	B9	136
Cheyenne, Ok., U.S.	F9	128
Cheyenne, Wy., U.S.	F8	126
Cheyenne, stm., U.S.	C11	126
Cheyenne Wells, Co., U.S.	C6	128
Cheyne Bay, b., Austl.	F3	74
Chhabra, India	F6	54
Chhapra, India	F10	54
Chhatak, Bngl.	F13	54
Chhatarpur, India	F7	54
Chhatrapur, India	I10	54
Chhattisgarh, state, India	D5	46
Chha Arëng, stm., Camb.	G6	48
Chhindwāra, India	H7	54
Chhlong, stm., Camb.	F8	48
Chhota-Chhindwāra, India	A7	54
Chhota Udepur Mhow, India	D3	46
Chi, stm., Thai.	E7	48
Chi, stm., Thai.	E7	48
Chiahsing see Jiaxing, China	F9	42
Chiai, Tai.	J9	42
Chiamussu see Jiamusi, China	B11	36
Chian see Ji'an, China	H6	42
Chiang Dao, Thai.	C4	48
Chiange, Ang.	D1	68
Chiang Kham, Thai.	C5	48
Chiang Khan, Thai.	D5	48
Chiang Mai, Thai.	C4	48
Chiang Rai, Thai.	C4	48
Chiang Saen, Thai.	B4	48
Chiangtu see Yangzhou, China	E8	42
Chiangyin see Jiangyin, China	F9	42
Chiaohsien see Jiaoxian, China.	C8	42
Chiaotso see Jiaozuo, China.	D5	42
Chiapas, state, Mex.	D6	96
Chiari, Italy	E6	22
Chiavari, Italy	F6	22
Chiavenna, Italy	D6	22
Chiba, Japan	D13	40
Chibabava, Moz.	B11	70
Chibemba, Ang.	D1	68
Chibia, Ang.	D1	68
Chibougamau, Qc., Can.	F15	106
Chibuto, Moz.	D11	70
Chibuzhangchu Hu, l., China	B13	54
Chicago, Il., U.S.	B2	120
Chicago Heights, Il., U.S.	C10	120
Chicapa, stm., Afr.	B3	68
Chichagof Island, i., Ak., U.S.	E12	140
Chichāwatni, Pak.	C4	54
Chichén Itzá, sci., Mex.	B3	102
Chichester, Eng., U.K.	K12	12
Chichibu, Japan	D12	40
Chichíhriviche, Ven.	B7	86
Chickamauga, Ga., U.S.	C13	122
Chickamauga Lake, res., Tn., U.S.	B14	122
Chickasaw, Al., U.S.	G10	122
Chickasawhay, stm., Ms., U.S.	F10	122
Chickasaw National Recreation Area, p.o.i., Ok., U.S.	G12	128
Chickasha, Ok., U.S.	F11	128
Chicken, Ak., U.S.	D11	140
Chiclana de la Frontera, Spain	H4	20
Chiclayo, Peru	E2	84
Chico, Ca., U.S.	D4	134
Chico, Tx., U.S.	H11	128
Chico, stm., Arg.	I2	90
Chico, stm., Arg.	I3	90
Chico, stm., Phil.	B3	52
Chicomba, Ang.	C2	68
Chicopee, Ga., U.S.	B2	116
Chicopee, Ma., U.S.	B13	114
Chicoutimi, Qc., Can.	B5	110
Chicualacuala, Moz.	D11	70
Chidambaram, India	F4	53
Chidenguele, Moz.	D12	70
Chiefland, Fl., U.S.	G3	116
Chiehyang see Jieyang, China	J7	42
Chiemsee, l., Ger.	I8	16
Chieo Lan Reservoir, res., Thai.	H4	48
Chieri, Italy	E4	22
Chiese, stm., Italy	E7	22
Chieti, Italy	H11	22
Chifeng, China	C3	38
Chigasaki, Japan	D12	40
Chignahuapan, Mex.	F9	100
Chignecto Bay, b., Can.	E12	110
Chignik, Ak., U.S.	E8	140
Chigoubiche, Lac, l., Qc., Can.	A3	110
Chigubo, Moz.	C11	70
Chigu Co, l., China	D13	54
Ch'ihfeng see Chifeng, China	C3	38
Chihli, Gulf of see Bo Hai, b., China	B8	42
Chihsi see Jixi, China	B9	38
Chihuahua, Mex.	A5	100
Chihuahua, state, Mex.	B3	96
Chihuahua, Desierto de, des., N.A.	F6	108
Chihuahuan Desert see Chihuahua, Desierto de, des., N.A.	F6	108
Chii-san, mtn., Kor., S.	G7	38
Chikaskia, stm., U.S.	E11	128
Chik Ballāpur, India	E3	53
Chikhli, India	H6	54
Chikmagalūr, India	E2	53
Chiknāyakanhalli, India	E3	53
Chikodi, India	C2	53
Chikrēng, stm., Camb.	F7	48
Chikuma, stm., Japan	C11	40
Chi-kyaw, Mya.	B1	48
Chilakalūrupet, India	C4	53
Chilako, stm., B.C., Can.	C7	138
Chilanko Forks, B.C., Can.	D6	138
Chilapa de Álvarez, Mex.	G9	100
Chilas, Pak.	B11	56
Chilcotin, stm., B.C., Can.	E8	138
Chilca, Peru	F2	84
Chile, ctry., S.A.	F2	90
Chile Chico, Chile	I2	90
Chilecito, Arg.	D4	92
Chile Rise, unds.	M5	144
Chilhowie, Va., U.S.	H4	114
Chilia, Bratul, stm., Eur.	D16	26
Chilika Lake, l., India	I10	54
Chililabombwe, Zam.	C4	68
Chilin see Jilin, China	C7	38
Chilko, stm., B.C., Can.	D7	138
Chilko Lake, l., B.C., Can.	E7	138
Chillagoe, Austl.	C8	76
Chillán, Chile	H1	92
Chillicothe, Mo., U.S.	E4	120
Chillicothe, Oh., U.S.	E3	114
Chilliwack, B.C., Can.	G9	138
Chiloé, Isla Grande de, i., Chile	H2	90
Chilón, Mex.	G12	100
Chiloquin, Or., U.S.	H5	136
Chilpancingo de los Bravo, Mex.	G9	100
Chiluage, Ang.	B3	68
Chilumba, Mwi.	C5	68
Chilung, Tai.	I9	42
Chilwa, Lake, l., Afr.	D6	68
Chimaltenango, Guat.	E2	102
Chimán, Pan.	H8	102
Chimayo, N.M., U.S.	G2	128
Chimbarongo, Chile	G2	92
Chimbas, Arg.	E3	92
Chimborazo, state, Ec.	H2	86
Chimborazo, vol., Ec.	H2	86
Chimbote, Peru	E2	84
Chimoio, Moz.	D5	68
Chimpay, Arg.	G3	90
Chin, state, Mya.	B1	48
China, Mex.	C9	100
China, ctry., Asia	B8	46
Chinan see Jinan, China	C7	42
Chinandega, Nic.	F4	102
Chinati Peak, mtn., Tx., U.S.	E3	130
Chincha Alta, Peru	F2	84
Chinchaga, stm., Can.	D7	106
Chinchilla, Austl.	F8	76
Chinchilla de Monte-Aragón, Spain	F9	20
Chinchiná, Col.	E4	86
Chinchón see Jinzhou, China	A9	42
Chincoteague, Va., U.S.	G10	114
Chinde, Moz.	D6	68
Chin-do, i., Kor., S.	G7	38
Chindo, Kor., S.	G7	38
Chindwin, stm., Mya.	D7	46
Ch'ingchiang see Qingjiang, China	E8	42
Chinghai see Qinghai, state, China	D4	36
Chingleput, India	E5	53
Chingola, Zam.	C4	68
Chingshih see Jinshi, China	G4	42
Ch'ingtao see Qingdao, China	C9	42
Chingtechen see Jingdezhen, China	G7	42
Chinguetti, Maur.	E2	64
Chinhae, Kor., S.	D1	40
Chin Hills, hills, Mya.	D7	46
Chinhoyi, Zim.	D5	68
Chinhsien see Jinzhou, China	B9	42
Chinhua see Jinhua, China	G8	42
Ch'inhuangtao, China	B8	42
Chining see Jining, China	A5	42
Chini see Jining, China	D7	42
Chiniot, Pak.	C4	54
Chinĭt, stm., Camb.	F7	48

Name	Map Ref.	Page
Chinjan, Pak.	C1	54
Chinju, Kor., S.	G7	38
Chinkiang see Zhenjiang, China.		
Chinko, stm., C.A.R.	C4	66
Chinle, Az., U.S.	G7	132
Chinle Wash, stm., Az., U.S.	G7	132
Chinmen Tao (Quemoy), i., Tai.	I8	42
Chino, Ca., U.S.	J8	134
Chinon, Fr.	G9	14
Chinook, Ab., Can.	G2	124
Chinook Cove, B.C., Can.	E10	138
Chino Valley, Az., U.S.	I4	132
Chinquapin, N.C., U.S.	B8	116
Chinsali, Zam.	C5	68
Chintâmani, India	E4	53
Chinú, Col.	C4	86
Chinwangtao see Qinhuangdao, China.	B8	42
Chioco, Moz.	D5	68
Chioggia, Italy	E9	22
Chíos, Grc.	E8	28
Chíos, i., Grc.	E8	28
Chíos see Chíos, i., Grc.	E8	28
Chipata, Zam.	C5	68
Chip Lake, l., Ab., Can.	C15	138
Chiplún, India	C1	53
Chipman, N.B., Can.	D11	110
Chipola, stm., Fl., U.S.	G13	122
Chippenham, Eng., U.K.	J10	12
Chippewa, stm., Mn., U.S.	F3	118
Chippewa, stm., Wi., U.S.	G6	118
Chippewa, East Fork, stm., Wi., U.S.	F8	118
Chippewa Falls, Wi., U.S.	G7	118
Chiquimula, Guat.	E3	102
Chiquinquirá, Col.	E4	86
Chîrāla, India	D5	53
Chirāwa, India	D5	54
Chiredzi, Zimb.	B10	70
Chireno, Tx., U.S.	F4	122
Chirfa, Niger	E7	64
Chirgaon, India	F7	54
Chiribiquete, Parque Nacional, p.o.i., Col.	G5	86
Chiricahua Mountains, mts., Az., U.S.	L7	132
Chiricahua National Monument, p.o.i., Az., U.S.	L7	132
Chiricahua Peak, mtn., Az., U.S.	L7	132
Chiriguaná, Col.	C5	86
Chirikof Island, i., Ak., U.S.	E8	140
Chiriquí, Golfo de, b., Pan.	H6	102
Chiriquí, Laguna de, b., Pan.	H6	102
Chiromo, Mwi.	D5	68
Chirpan see Čirpan, Blg.	G12	26
Chirripó, Cerro, mtn., C.R.	H6	102
Chirripó, Parque Nacional, p.o.i., C.R.	H6	102
Chisago City, Mn., U.S.	F5	118
Chisamba, Zam.	C4	68
Chisasibi, Qc., Can.	E15	106
Chisep'o, Kor., S.	E1	40
Ch'ishan, Tai.	J9	42
Chisholm, Ab., Can.	B16	138
Chisholm, Me., U.S.	F6	110
Chisholm, Mn., U.S.	D5	118
Chishtiān Mandi, Pak.	D4	54
Chishui, China	G1	42
Chishui, stm., China	F6	36
Chisimaiu see Kismaayo, Som.	E8	66
Chişinău, Mol.	B15	26
Chişineu-Criş, Rom.	C8	26
Chita, Col.	D5	86
Chitado, Ang.	D1	68
Chitagá, Col.	D5	86
Chita-hantō, pen., Japan		
Chitato, Ang.	B3	68
Chitek Lake, l., Mb., Can.	B14	124
Chitembo, Ang.	C2	68
Chitina, Ak., U.S.	D11	140
Chitina, stm., Ak., U.S.	D11	140
Chitipa, Mwi.	B5	68
Chitokoloki, Zam.	C3	68
Chitose, Japan	C14	38
Chitradurga, India	D3	53
Chitrakūt Dham, India	F8	54
Chitrāl, Pak.	B11	56
Chitrāvati, stm., India	D3	53
Chitré, Pan.	H7	102
Chittagong, Bngl.	G13	54
Chittagong, state, Bngl.	G13	54
Chittaurgarh, India	F5	54
Chittoor, India	E4	53
Chittūr, India	F3	53
Chitungwiza, Zimb.	D5	68
Chiuchiang see Jiujiang, China.	G6	42
Chiumbe (Tshumbe), stm., Afr.	B3	68
Chiume, Ang.	D3	68
Chiusi, Italy	G8	22
Chiva see Xiva, Spain	E10	20
Chivacoa, Ven.	B7	86
Chivasso, Italy	E4	22
Chivi, Zimb.	B10	70
Chivilcoy, Arg.	G7	92
Chivirira Falls, wtfl., Zimb.	B11	70
Chizu, Japan	D7	40
Chloride, Az., U.S.	H2	132
Chmielnik, Pol.	F16	16
Chôâm Khsant, Camb.	E7	48
Choapa, stm., Chile	E2	92
Choceň, Czech Rep.	F12	16
Chochís, Cerro, mtn., Bol.	C5	90
Chŏch'iwŏn, Kor., S.	F7	38
Chociwel, Pol.	C11	16
Chocó, state, Col.	E3	86
Chocolate Mountains, mts., U.S.	J1	132
Chocontá, Col.	E5	86
Chocope, Peru	E2	84
Choctawhatchee, West Fork, stm., Al., U.S.	G13	122
Choctawhatchee Bay, b., Fl., U.S.	G12	122
Chodziez, Pol.	D12	16
Choele Choel, Arg.	G3	90
Choiseul, St. Luc.	m6	105c
Choiseul, state, Sol. Is.	d7	79b
Choiseul, i., Sol. Is.	d7	79b
Chojna, Pol.	D10	16
Chojnice, Pol.	C13	16
Chojnów, Pol.	E11	16
Ch'ok'ē, mts., Eth.	E7	62
Choke Canyon Reservoir, res., Tx., U.S.	F9	130
Chokio, Mn., U.S.	F2	118
Chôkwe, Moz.	D11	70
Cholet, Fr.	G8	14
Choluteca, Hond.	F4	102
Choluteca, stm., Hond.	F4	102
Choma, Zam.	D4	68
Chomo Lhári, mtn., Asia	E12	54
Chomutov, Czech Rep.	F9	16
Chon Buri, Thai.	F5	48
Ch'ŏnan, Kor., S.	F7	38
Chon Daen, Thai.	D5	48
Chone, Ec.	H1	86
Chong'an, China	H8	42
Ch'ŏngdo, Kor., S.	D1	40
Ch'ŏngjin, Kor., N.	D8	38
Chŏngju, Kor., S.	F7	38
Chŏng Kal, Camb.	E6	48
Chongming, China	I4	38
Chongming Dao, i., China	F9	42
Chongoroi, Ang.	C1	68
Chongqing (Chungking), China.	G2	42
Chongqing, state, China	F6	36
Chŏngsŏn, Kor., S.	B1	40
Chŏngŭp, Kor., S.	G7	38
Chongxin, China	D2	42
Chongxin, China		
Chongzuo, China	A8	48
Chŏnju, Kor., S.	G7	38
Chonos, Archipiélago de los, is., Chile	I1	90
Chontaleña, Cordillera, mts., Nic.	G5	102
Cho Oyu see Qowowuyag, mtn., Asia	D11	54
Chop, Ukr.	A9	26
Chopda, India	H5	54
Chopim, stm., Braz.	C11	92
Chopinzinho, Braz.	B11	92
Chopu (Qowowuyag), mtn., Asia	D11	54
Chorna, Ukr.	B16	26
Chornobyl', Ukr.	D4	32
Choros, Isla, i., Chile	D2	92
Ch'ŏrwŏn, Kor., S.	E7	38
Chosen, Fl., U.S.	J5	116
Chōshi, Japan	D13	40
Chosica, Peru	F2	84
Chos Malal, Arg.	H2	92
Choszczno, Pol.	C11	16
Choteau, Mt., U.S.	C14	136
Chotila, India	H5	54
Chouchiak'ou see Shangshui, China	E6	42
Chouk'ou see Shangshui, China	E6	42
Choushan Islands see Zhoushan Qundao, is., China	F10	42
Chowchilla, Ca., U.S.	F5	134
Chown, Mount, mtn., Ab., Can.	C11	138
Choybalsan, Mong.	B7	36
Choyr, Mong.	B6	36
Chrisman, Il., U.S.	I2	112
Christanshåb (Qasigiannguit), Grnld.	D15	141
Christchurch, N.Z.	F5	80
Christian, Cape, c., Nu., Can.	A17	106
Christian, Point, c., Pit.	c28	78k
Christiana, Jam.	i13	104d
Christiana, S. Afr.	E7	70
Christian Island, i., On., Can.	D9	112
Christiansburg, Va., U.S.	G5	114
Christian Sound, strt., Ak., U.S.	E12	140
Christiansted, V.I.U.S.	h11	104c
Christmas Island, dep., Oc.	K13	142
Christmas Island, i., Christ. I.	E1	72
Christmas Island see Kiritimati, at., Kir.	C11	72
Christmas Ridge, unds.	I22	142
Christoval, Tx., U.S.	C7	130
Chrudim, Czech Rep.	G11	16
Chrzanów, Pol.	F15	16
Chu (Xam), stm., Asia.	B7	48
Chuādanga, Bngl.	G12	54
Chuanchou see Quanzhou, China	I8	42
Chubbuck, Id., U.S.	H14	136
Chūbu-Sangaku-kokuritsu-kōen, p.o.i., Japan.	C10	40
Chubut, state, Arg.	H3	90
Chubut, stm., Arg.	H3	90
Ch'uchiang see Shaoguan, China	I5	42
Chuchi Lake, l., B.C., Can.	A6	138
Chuchow see Zhuzhou, China.	H5	42
Chu Chua, B.C., Can.	E10	138
Chucunaque, stm., Pan.	H9	102
Chugach Mountains, mts., Ak., U.S.	D10	140
Chuginadak Island, i., Ak., U.S.	g25	140a
Chūgoku-sanchi, mts., Japan	D6	40
Chugwater Creek, stm., Wy., U.S.	F8	126
Chuhuichupa, Mex.	G8	98
Chui, Braz.	F11	92
Chukchi Sea, s.	C5	94
Chuke Hu, l., China	C11	54
Chukotsk Peninsula see Čukotskij poluostrov, pen., Russia	C26	34
Chula Vista, Ca., U.S.	K8	134
Chulucanas, Peru	E1	84
Chumbicha, Arg.	D4	92
Chum Phae, Thai.	D6	48
Chumphon, Thai.	G4	48
Chumphon Buri, Thai.	E6	48
Chum Saeng, Thai.	E5	48
Chumunjin, Kor., S.	B1	40
Chun'an, China	G8	42
Chunan, Tai.	I9	42
Chuncheon see Ch'unch'ŏn, Kor., S.	F7	38
Chunchi, Ec.	I2	86
Ch'unch'ŏn, Kor., S.	F7	38
Chunchula, Al., U.S.	G10	122
Ch'ungch'ŏng-bukto, state, Kor., S.	B1	40
Ch'ungju, Kor., S.	F7	38
Chungking see Chongqing, China	G2	42
Ch'ungmu, Kor., S.	E1	40
Chungshan see Zhongshan, China	J5	42
Chungyang Shanmo, mts., Tai.	J9	42
Chunhua, China	D3	42
Chunhuhux, Mex.	C3	102
Chuquibamba, Peru	G3	84
Chuquicamata, Chile	B3	90
Chur (Coire), Switz.	D6	22
Church Hill, Tn., U.S.	H3	114
Churchill, Mb., Can.	D12	106
Churchill, stm., Nf., Can.	E18	106
Churchill, stm., Can.	D11	106
Churchill, Mount, mtn., B.C., Can.	D7	138
Churchill Falls, wtfl., Nf., Can.	E17	106
Churchill Lake, l., Sk., Can.	D9	106
Church Point, La., U.S.	G6	122
Church Rock, N.M., U.S.	H8	132
Chūru, India	D5	54
Churubusco, In., U.S.	G4	112
Churuguara, Ven.	B7	86
Chushul, India	B7	54
Chute-Saint-Philippe, Qc., Can.	D1	110
Chutung, Tai.	I9	42
Chuuk, i., Micron.	C6	72
Chuvashia see Čuvašija, state, Russia.	C7	32
Chuxian, China	E8	42
Chuxiong, China	F5	36
Ci, stm., China	E6	42
Ciamis, Indon.	G6	50
Cianjur, Indon.	G5	50
Cianorte, Braz.	A11	92
Ciatura, Geor.	F6	32
Ciawi, Indon.	G5	50
Cibaliung, Indon.	G4	50
Cibatu, Indon.	G6	50
Cibinong, Indon.	G5	50
Cibolo Creek, stm., Tx., U.S.	E3	130
Cibola Creek, stm., Tx., U.S.	E10	130
Cicero, Il., U.S.	G2	112
Cicero, In., U.S.	H3	112
Cicero Dantas, Braz.	F6	88
Cicurug, Indon.	G5	50
Cidra, P.R.	B3	104a
Ciechanów, Pol.	D16	16
Ciechanów, state, Pol.	C16	16
Ciechanowiec, Pol.	D18	16
Ciego de Avila, Cuba	B8	102
Ciempozuelos, Spain	D7	20
Ciénaga, Col.	B4	86
Ciénega de Flores, Mex.	H7	130
Cienfuegos, Cuba	A7	102
Cíes, Illas, is., Spain	B1	20
Cíes, Islas see Cíes, Illas, is., Spain	B1	20
Cieszanów, Pol.	F19	16
Cieszyn, Pol.	G14	16
Cieza, Spain	F9	20
Cifteler, Tur.	D13	28
Cifuentes, Spain	D8	20
Cigüela, stm., Spain	E7	20
Cihanbeyli, Tur.	E15	28
Cijara, Embalse de, res., Spain	E6	20
Cijulang, Indon.	G6	50
Cikampek, Indon.	G5	50
Cikobia, i., Fiji	o20	79e
Cikoj, Russia	F10	34
Cilacap, Indon.	G6	50
Cilamaya, Indon.	G5	50
Cilento, reg., Italy	D9	24
Cili, China	F4	42
Cilician Gates see Gülek Boğazı, p., Tur.	A5	58
Çilik see Shelek, Kaz.	F13	32
Cill Chainnigh see Kilkenny, Ire.	I5	12
Cilleruelo de Bezana, Spain	B7	20
Cil'na, stm., Russia	D24	8
Cimarron, N.M., U.S.	E4	128
Cimarron, stm., U.S.	F12	128
Cimarron, North Fork, stm., U.S.	D7	128
Čimbaj, Uzb.	F9	32
Çimişlia, Mol.	C15	26
Cimljanskoe vodohranilišče, res., Russia.	E6	32
Cimone, Monte, mtn., Italy.	F7	22
Cimpu, Indon.	E12	50
Cina, Tanjung, c., Indon.	G4	50
Cinaruco, stm., Ven.	D7	86
Cinaruco-Capanaparo, Santo Luzardo, Parque Nacional, p.o.i., Ven.	D8	86
Cinca, stm., Spain	C11	20
Cincinnati, Ia., U.S.	D4	120
Cincinnati, Oh., U.S.	E1	114
Cinco, Canal Numero, can., Arg.	H9	92
Cinco de Mayo, Mex.	I3	130
Cinco Saltos, Arg.	F10	28
Ciney, Bel.	D14	14
Cinfães, Port.	C2	20
Ciniṣeuţi, Mol.	B15	26
Cintalapa, Mex.	G12	100
Cinto, Monte, mtn., Fr.	G14	18
Cintra, Golfe de, b., W. Sah.	E1	64
Ciociaria, reg., Italy	I10	22
Cipó, Braz.	F11	34
Cipó, stm., Braz.	J4	88
Cipolletti, Arg.	G3	90
Circeo, Parco Nazionale del, p.o.i., Italy	C6	24
Čirčik, Uzb.	F11	32
Circle, Ak., U.S.	C11	140
Circle, Mt., U.S.	G8	124
Circleville, Oh., U.S.	E3	114
Circleville, Ut., U.S.	E4	132
Circleville Mountain, mtn., Ut., U.S.	E4	132
Cirebon, Indon.	G5	50
Ciremay, Gunung, vol., Indon.	G6	50
Cirencester, Eng., U.K.	J11	12
Çırgalandy, Russia	D17	32
Ciriè, Italy	E4	22
Cirò Marina, Italy	E11	24
Čirpan, Blg.	G12	26
Ciskei, hist. reg., S. Afr.	H8	70
Cisnădie, Rom.	D11	26
Cisne, Il., U.S.	F9	120
Cisne, Islas del see Santanilla, Islas, is., Hond.	D6	102
Cisneros, Col.	D4	86
Cisolok, Indon.	G5	50
Cissna Park, Il., U.S.	H2	112
Čistoozërnoe, Russia	D13	32
Čistopol', Russia	C8	32
Cita, Russia	F11	34
Citlaltépetl, Volcán see Pico de Orizaba, Volcán, vol., Mex.	F10	100
Citra, Fl., U.S.	G3	116
Citrus Heights, Ca., U.S.	E4	134
Città di Castello, Italy	G9	22
Cittanova, Italy	F10	24
City of Sunrise see Sunrise, Fl., U.S.	J5	116
City Point, Fl., U.S.	H5	116
Ciudad Acuña, Mex.	A8	100
Ciudad Altamirano, Mex.	F8	100
Ciudad Anáhuac, Mex.	B8	100
Ciudad Bolívar, Ven.	C10	86
Ciudad Bolivia, Ven.	C6	86
Ciudad Camargo, Mex.	B6	100
Ciudad Camargo, Mex.	B9	100
Ciudad Constitución, Mex.	C3	100
Ciudad Cortés, C.R.	H6	102
Ciudad Darío, Nic.	F4	102
Ciudad de Libertador General San Martín, Arg.	A5	92
Ciudad de México (Mexico City), Mex.	F9	100
Ciudad de Nutrias, Ven.	C7	86
Ciudad Guayana, Ven.	C10	86
Ciudad Hidalgo, Mex.	F8	100
Ciudad Jiménez see Jiménez, Mex.	B6	100
Ciudad Juárez, Mex.	C1	130
Ciudad Lerdo see Lerdo, Mex.	C7	100
Ciudad Madero, Mex.	D9	100
Ciudad Mante, Mex.	D9	100
Ciudad Morelos, Mex.	E5	98
Ciudad Netzahualcóyotl, Mex.	F9	100
Ciudad Obregón, Mex.	B4	100
Ciudad Ojeda, Ven.	B6	86
Ciudad Piar, Ven.	A2	92
Ciudad Real, Spain	F6	20
Ciudad Real, co., Spain	F6	20
Ciudad Rodrigo, Spain	D4	20
Ciudad Valles, Mex.	E9	100
Ciudad Victoria, Mex.	D9	100
Ciudadela de Menorca, Spain	D14	20
Civa Castellana, Italy	H9	22
Civitanova Marche, Italy	G10	22
Civitavecchia, Italy	H8	22
Çivril, Tur.	E12	28
Cixi, China	F9	42
Ciža, Russia	C21	8
Cjalusa, Bela.	G12	10
Cakousk, Russia	H20	8
Clackamas, stm., Or., U.S.	E4	136
Clacton-on-Sea, Eng., U.K.	J14	12
Claflin, Ks., U.S.	C10	128
Claiborne, Al., U.S.	F11	122
Clain, stm., Fr.	C6	18
Claire, Lake, l., Ab., Can.	D8	106
Clair Engle Lake, res., Ca., U.S.	C3	134
Clallam Bay, Wa., U.S.	B2	136
Clanton, Al., U.S.	E12	122
Clanwilliam, S. Afr.	H4	70
Clapperton Island, i., On., Can.	B7	112
Clara, Ms., U.S.	F10	122
Clara, stm., Austl.	B4	76
Clara, Punta, c., Arg.	H4	90
Clare, Austl.	I4	76
Clare, Mi., U.S.	E5	112
Clare Island, i., Ire.	H2	12
Clare, state, Ire.	I3	12
Claremont, N.H., U.S.	G4	110
Claremont, S.D., U.S.	B15	126
Claremont, mtn., Ca., U.S.	H2	120
Claremore, Ok., U.S.	H2	120
Clarence, Mo., U.S.	E5	120
Clarence, stm., Austl.	G9	76
Clarence, stm., N.Z.	F5	80
Clarence, Cape, c., Nu., Can.	A13	106
Clarence, Isla, i., Chile	J2	90
Clarence Strait, strt., Austl.	B6	74
Clarence Strait, strt., Ak., U.S.	E13	140
Clarence Town, Bah.	C9	96
Clarendon, Ar., U.S.	C7	122
Clarendon, Tx., U.S.	G8	128
Claresholm, Ab., Can.	F17	138
Clarinda, Ia., U.S.	D2	120
Clarines, Ven.	C9	86
Clarion, Ia., U.S.	B4	120
Clarion, Pa., U.S.	C6	114
Clarion, stm., Pa., U.S.	C6	114
Clarion Fracture Zone, unds.	H25	142
Clarissa, Mn., U.S.	E3	118
Clark, Mount, mtn., N.T., Can.	C6	106
Clark, stm., Austl.	B5	76
Clarke Island, i., Austl.	n14	77a
Clarkesville, Ga., U.S.	B2	116
Clark Fork, Id., U.S.	B10	136
Clark Fork, stm., U.S.	C11	136
Clarks, La., U.S.	E6	122
Clarksburg, W.V., U.S.	E5	114
Clarksdale, Ms., U.S.	C8	122
Clarkson, Ky., U.S.	G11	120
Clarks Summit, Pa., U.S.	C10	114
Clarkston, Wa., U.S.	D9	136
Clarks Town, Jam.	i13	104d
Clarksville, Ar., U.S.	B5	122
Clarksville, Ia., U.S.	B5	120
Clarksville, Tn., U.S.	H10	120
Clarksville, Tx., U.S.	D4	122
Clarkton, Mo., U.S.	H7	120
Clarkton, N.C., U.S.	B7	116
Claro, stm., Braz.	G7	84
Claude, Tx., U.S.	G8	128
Clausthal-Zellerfeld, Ger.	E5	16
Claveria, Phil.	B7	44
Clavering Ø, i., Grnld.	C22	141
Clavet, Sk., Can.	B7	124
Claxton, Ga., U.S.	D3	116
Clay, Ky., U.S.	G10	120
Clay, W.V., U.S.	F4	114
Clay Center, Ne., U.S.	G14	126
Clay City, Il., U.S.	F9	120
Clay City, In., U.S.	E10	120
Clay City, Ky., U.S.	G1	114
Claymont, De., U.S.	E10	114
Claypool, Az., U.S.	J6	132
Claysburg, Pa., U.S.	D7	114
Clayton, Al., U.S.	F13	122
Clayton, Ga., U.S.	B2	116
Clayton, Il., U.S.	D7	120
Clayton, La., U.S.	F7	122
Clayton, Mo., U.S.	F7	120
Clayton, N.M., U.S.	E5	128
Clayton, N.Y., U.S.	D13	112
Clayton, Ok., U.S.	C3	122
Clayton, Wa., U.S.	B9	136
Clear, Cape, c., Ire.	J3	12
Clear Boggy Creek, stm., Ok., U.S.	C2	122
Clearbrook, Mn., U.S.	D3	118
Clear Creek, stm., Wy., U.S.	C6	126
Clearfield, Pa., U.S.	D7	114
Clearfield, Ut., U.S.	B4	132
Clearlake, Ca., U.S.	E3	134
Clear Lake, Ia., U.S.	A4	120
Clear Lake, S.D., U.S.	G2	118
Clear Lake, Wi., U.S.	F6	118
Clear Lake, l., Mb., Can.	D14	124
Clear Lake, l., Ca., U.S.	D3	134
Clear Lake, res., La., U.S.	F5	122
Clear Lake Reservoir, res., Ca., U.S.	B4	134
Clearmont, Wy., U.S.	C6	126
Clearwater, Mb., Can.	E14	124
Clearwater, Fl., U.S.	I3	116
Clearwater, Ne., U.S.	E14	126
Clearwater, stm., U.S.	D15	138
Clearwater, stm., B.C., Can.	D10	138
Clearwater, stm., Id., U.S.	D8	136
Clearwater, stm., Id., U.S.	D10	136
Clearwater, stm., Mn., U.S.	D3	118
Clearwater, Middle Fork, stm., Id., U.S.	D11	136
Clearwater, North Fork, stm., Id., U.S.	D11	136
Clearwater Lake, l., B.C., Can.	D10	138
Clearwater Mountains, mts., Id., U.S.	D11	136
Clebit, Ok., U.S.	C4	122
Cleburne, Tx., U.S.	B10	130
Cle Elum, Wa., U.S.	C5	136
Cle Elum, stm., Wa., U.S.	C5	136
Cle Elum Lake, res., Wa., U.S.	C5	136
Cleethorpes, Eng., U.K.	H12	12
Clementsport, N.S., Can.	F11	110
Clemson, S.C., U.S.	B3	116
Clermont, Austl.	D6	76
Clermont, Fl., U.S.	H4	116
Clermont-en-Argonne, Fr.	E14	14
Clermont-Ferrand, Fr.	D9	18
Clermont-l'Hérault, Fr.	F9	18
Clevedon, Eng., U.K.	J10	12
Cleveland, Al., U.S.	D12	122
Cleveland, Ms., U.S.	D8	122
Cleveland, N.C., U.S.	A5	116
Cleveland, Oh., U.S.	C4	114
Cleveland, Ok., U.S.	A2	122
Cleveland, Tn., U.S.	B14	122
Cleveland, Tx., U.S.	G3	122
Cleveland, Wi., U.S.	E2	112
Cleveland, Cape, c., Austl.	B6	76
Cleveland, Mount, mtn., Mt., U.S.	B13	136
Clevelândia, Braz.	C11	92
Clew Bay, b., Ire.	H3	12
Clewiston, Fl., U.S.	J4	116
Clifden, Ire.	H2	12
Clifton, St. Vin.	p11	105e
Clifton, Az., U.S.	J7	132
Clifton, Tn., U.S.	B11	122
Clifton, Tx., U.S.	C10	130
Clifton Forge, Va., U.S.	G6	114
Clifton Hills, Austl.	G3	76
Climax, Sk., Can.	E5	124
Climax, Co., U.S.	B2	128
Clinch, stm., U.S.	I13	120
Clinchco, Va., U.S.	G4	114
Clingmans Dome, mtn., U.S.	I2	114
Clinton, B.C., Can.	E9	138
Clinton, On., Can.	E8	112
Clinton, Ar., U.S.	B6	122
Clinton, Ct., U.S.	C13	114
Clinton, Ia., U.S.	C7	120
Clinton, Il., U.S.	I2	112
Clinton, In., U.S.	I2	112
Clinton, Ky., U.S.	H9	120
Clinton, La., U.S.	G7	122
Clinton, Mi., U.S.	B2	114
Clinton, Ms., U.S.	E8	122
Clinton, Mo., U.S.	F4	120
Clinton, N.C., U.S.	A7	116
Clinton, Ok., U.S.	F9	128
Clinton, S.C., U.S.	B4	116
Clinton, Wi., U.S.	B9	120
Clinton, Cape, c., Austl.	D8	76
Clinton-Colden Lake, l., N.T., Can.	C9	106
Clinton Lake, res., Ks., U.S.	F1	120
Clintonville, Wi., U.S.	G10	118
Clintwood, Va., U.S.	G3	114
Clio, Mi., U.S.	E6	112
Clio, S.C., U.S.	B6	116
Clipperton, Île, at., Oc.	H28	142
Clipperton Fracture Zone, unds.	I25	142
Clipperton Island see Clipperton, Île, at., Oc.	H28	142
Clisson, Fr.	G7	14
Clodomira, Arg.	C5	92
Cloete, Mex.	G6	130
Cloncurry, Austl.	C3	76
Cloncurry, stm., Austl.	C3	76
Clonmel, Ire.	I5	12
Clo-oose, B.C., Can.	H6	138
Cloppenburg, Ger.	D3	16
Cloquet, Mn., U.S.	E6	118
Clorinda, Arg.	B9	92
Cloud Peak, mtn., Wy., U.S.	C5	126
Clova, Qc., Can.	A1	110
Clover, S.C., U.S.	A4	116
Cloverdale, Ca., U.S.	E2	134
Cloverdale, In., U.S.	E11	120
Cloverport, Ky., U.S.	G11	120
Clovis, Ca., U.S.	G6	134
Clovis, N.M., U.S.	G5	128
Cluain Meala see Clonmel, Ire.	I5	12
Cluj, hist. reg., Rom.	C10	26
Cluj-Napoca, Rom.	C10	26
Clunes, Austl.	K4	76
Cluny, Austl.	E2	76
Cluny, Fr.	C10	18
Clusone, Italy	E7	22
Clute, Tx., U.S.	E12	130
Clutha, stm., N.Z.	H3	80
Clyde, Ab., Can.	B15	138
Clyde, N.C., U.S.	A3	116
Clyde, Oh., U.S.	C3	114
Clyde, Tx., U.S.	B8	130
Clyde, stm., Scot., U.K.	F9	12
Clyde, Firth of, b., Scot., U.K.	F7	12
Clyde Inlet, b., Nu., Can.	A17	106
Clyde Park, Mt., U.S.	D15	136
Clyde River see Kangiqtugaapik, Nu., Can.	A16	106
Clymer, Pa., U.S.	D6	114
Čmielów, Pol.	F17	16
Cna, stm., Russia	C17	10
Cna, stm., Russia	D6	32
Cnossus see Knosós, sci., Grc.	H8	28
Coa, stm., Port.	D3	20
Coachella, Ca., U.S.	J9	134
Coachella Canal, can., Ca., U.S.	K1	132
Coahoma, Tx., U.S.	B6	130
Coahuila, state, Mex.	B7	100
Coal, stm., B.C., Can.	D5	106
Coal City, Il., U.S.	C9	120
Coalcomán de Matamoros, Mex.	F7	100
Coaldale, Ab., Can.	G18	138
Coaldale, Ok., U.S.	C2	122
Coal Grove, Oh., U.S.	F3	114
Coal Hill, Ar., U.S.	B5	122
Coalinga, Ca., U.S.	G5	134
Coalmont, B.C., Can.	G10	138
Coalport, Pa., U.S.	D7	114
Coal River, B.C., Can.	D5	106
Coal Valley, val., Nv., U.S.	F1	132
Coalville, Eng., U.K.	I11	12
Coalville, Ut., U.S.	C5	132
Coamo, P.R.	B3	104a
Coari, Braz.	D5	84
Coari, stm., Braz.	D5	84
Coast Mountains, mts., N.A.	D4	106
Coast Ranges, mts., U.S.	C2	134
Coatbridge, Scot., U.K.	F9	12
Coatesville, Pa., U.S.	E10	114
Coaticook, Qc., Can.	E5	110
Coats Island, i., Nu., Can.	C14	106
Coats Land, reg., Ant.	C2	81
Coatzacoalcos, Mex.	F11	100
Cobá, sci., Mex.	B4	102
Cobán, Guat.	E2	102
Cobar, Austl.	H6	76
Cobberas, Mount, mtn., Austl.	K6	76
Cobden, On., Can.	C13	112
Cobequid Bay, b., N.S., Can.	E13	110
Cobh, Ire.	J4	12
Cobham, stm., Can.	B18	124
Cobija, Bol.	B3	90
Cobleskill, N.Y., U.S.	B11	114
Cobourg, On., Can.	E11	112
Cobourg Peninsula, pen., Austl.	B6	74
Coca, stm., Ec.	H3	86
Cocal, Braz.	B4	88
Cocentaina, Spain	F10	20
Côch, stm., Asia		
Cochabamba, Bol.	C3	90
Cochem, Ger.	F3	16
Cochin, Isla, i., Mex.	B3	100
Cochin see Kochi, India	G3	53
Cochin China see Nam Phan, hist. reg., Viet.	G8	48
Cochinos, Bahía de (Pigs, Bay of), b., Cuba	B7	102
Cochise Head, mtn., Az., U.S.	K7	132
Cochran, Ga., U.S.	D2	116
Cochrane, Ab., Can.	E16	138
Cochrane, On., Can.	F14	106
Cochrane, Wi., U.S.	G7	118
Cochrane, Lago (Pueyrredón, Lago), l., S.A.	I2	90
Cochranton, Pa., U.S.	C5	114
Cockburn, Austl.	I3	76
Cockburn, Mount, mtn., Austl.	E5	74
Cockburn Island, i., On., Can.	C6	112
Cockermouth, Eng., U.K.	G9	12
Cockpit Country, reg., Jam.	i13	104d
Coco, stm., Braz.	F1	88
Coco, stm., N.A.	F5	102
Coco, Cayo, i., Cuba	A8	102
Coco, Isla del, i., C.R.	F7	96
Cocoa, Fl., U.S.	H5	116
Cocoa Beach, Fl., U.S.	H5	116
Coco Channel, strt., Asia	F7	46
Coco Islands, is., Mya.	F7	46
Coconino Plateau, plat., Az., U.S.	H4	132
Cocos, Braz.	H3	88
Cocos Islands, dep., Oc.	K12	142
Cocos Lagoon, b., Guam	k9	78c
Cocos Ridge, unds.	H5	144
Cocula, Mex.	E7	100
Cod, Cape, pen., Ma., U.S.	C15	114
Codajás, Braz.	D5	84
Codera, Cabo, c., Ven.	B8	86
Coderre, Sk., Can.	D7	124
Codigoro, Italy	F9	22
Codlea, Rom.	D12	26
Codó, Braz.	C3	88
Codogno, Italy	E6	22
Codózinho, Braz.	C3	88
Codroy, Nf., Can.	C17	110
Cody, Ne., U.S.	E11	126
Cody, Wy., U.S.	C3	126
Coelho Neto, Braz.	C4	88
Coen, Austl.	B8	74
Coetivy, i., Sey.	k13	69b
Coeur d'Alene, Id., U.S.	C10	136
Coeur d'Alene, stm., Id., U.S.	C10	136
Coeur d'Alene Lake, res., Id., U.S.	C10	136
Coffeville, Ms., U.S.	D9	122
Coffeyville, Ks., U.S.	G2	120
Coffs Harbour, Austl.	H9	76
Cofre de Perote, Cerro, mtn., Mex.	F10	100
Cofre de Perote, Parque Nacional, p.o.i., Mex.	F10	100
Cofrents see Cofrentes, Spain	E9	20
Cofrentes, Spain	E9	20
Cogălnic (Kohyl'nyk), stm., Eur.	C15	26
Coggon, Ia., U.S.	B6	120
Cognac, Fr.	D5	18
Cogolludo, Spain	D7	20
Cogoon, stm., Austl.	F7	76
Cohasset, Ma., U.S.	B15	114
Cohocton, stm., N.Y., U.S.	B12	114
Cohoes, N.Y., U.S.	B12	114
Cohuna, Austl.	J5	76
Coiba, Isla de, i., Pan.	I6	102
Coig, stm., Arg.	J3	90
Coihaique, Chile	I2	90
Coimbatore (Koyambattur), India	F3	53
Coimbra, Braz.	K4	88
Coimbra, Port.	D2	20
Coimbra, state, Port.	D2	20
Coin, Spain	H6	20
Coipasa, Lago, l., Bol.	C3	90
Coipasa, Salar de, pl., S.A.	C3	90
Coire see Chur, Switz.	D6	22
Cojedes, state, Ven.	C7	86
Cojudo Blanco, Cerro, mtn., Arg.	I3	90
Cojutepeque, El Sal.	F3	102
Cokato, Mn., U.S.	F4	118
Cokeville, Wy., U.S.	A6	132
Čokurdah, Russia	B18	34
Colac, Austl.	L4	76
Colatina, Braz.	J5	88
Colbeck, Cape, c., Ant.	C21	81
Colbert, Ok., U.S.	C2	122
Colbinabbin, Austl.	K5	76
Colborne, On., Can.	E12	112
Colby, Ks., U.S.	B7	128
Colby, Wi., U.S.	G8	118
Colchester, Eng., U.K.	J13	12
Colchester, Il., U.S.	D7	120
Cold Bay, Ak., U.S.	E7	140
Cold Lake, Ab., Can.	E8	106
Cold Spring, Mn., U.S.	F4	118
Coldwater, Ks., U.S.	D9	128
Coldwater, Mi., U.S.	G5	112
Coldwater, Oh., U.S.	D1	114
Coldwater, stm., Ms., U.S.	C8	122
Coldwater Creek, stm., U.S.	E7	128
Coleambally, Austl.	J5	76
Colebrook, N.H., U.S.	F5	110
Cole Camp, Mo., U.S.	F4	120
Coleman, Ab., Can.	G16	138
Coleman, Mi., U.S.	E5	112
Coleman, Tx., U.S.	C8	130
Coleman, Wi., U.S.	C1	112
Coleman, stm., Austl.	B8	74
Colenso, S. Afr.	F9	70
Coleraine, Austl.	K3	76
Coleraine, N. Ire., U.K.	E6	12
Coleridge, Ne., U.S.	E15	126
Colesberg, S. Afr.	G7	70
Coleville, Sk., Can.	C4	124
Colfax, Ca., U.S.	D5	134
Colfax, In., U.S.	H3	112
Colfax, La., U.S.	F6	122
Colfax, Wa., U.S.	D9	136
Colfax, Wi., U.S.	F7	118
Colgong, India	F11	54
Colhué Huapi, Lago, l., Arg.	I3	90
Colibris, Pointe des, c., Guad.	h6	105c
Colico, Italy	D6	22
Coligny, S. Afr.	E8	70
Colihaut, Dom.	j5	105c
Colima, Mex.	F7	100
Colima, Nevado de, vol., Mex.	F7	100
Colinas, Braz.	D3	88
Colinas, Braz.	H1	88
Colinton, Ab., Can.	B17	138
Coll, i., Scot., U.K.	E6	12
Collarenebri, Austl.	G7	76
College, Ak., U.S.	D10	140
Collegedale, Tn., U.S.	B13	122
College Park, Ga., U.S.	D14	122
College Park, Md., U.S.	E8	114
College Place, Wa., U.S.	D8	136
College Station, Ar., U.S.	C6	122
College Station, Tx., U.S.	G2	122
Collerina, Austl.	G6	76
Collie, Austl.	F3	74
Collier Bay, b., Austl.	C4	74
Collingwood, On., Can.	D9	112
Collins, Ms., U.S.	F9	122
Collins Head, c., Norf.	y25	78i
Collinston, La., U.S.	E7	122
Collinsville, Austl.	C6	76
Collinsville, Al., U.S.	C13	122
Collinsville, Il., U.S.	F8	120
Collinsville, Tx., U.S.	D2	122
Collinwood, Tn., U.S.	B11	122
Collipulli, Chile	H2	92
Colmar, Fr.	F16	14
Colmenar, Spain	H6	20
Colmenar Viejo, Spain	D7	20
Colmeneros, Mex.	F8	100
Colmesneil, Tx., U.S.	G4	122
Colnett, Punta, c., Mex.	F4	98

Name	Map Ref.	Page
Cologne see Köln, Ger.	F2	16
Cologne, Mn., U.S.	G5	118
Coloma, Mi., U.S.	F3	112
Coloma, Wi., U.S.	G9	118
Colomb-Béchar see Béchar, Alg.	C4	64
Colombia, Col.	F4	86
Colombia, ctry., S.A.	C3	84
Colombie-Britannique see British Columbia, state, Can.	E5	106
Colombo, Braz.	B13	92
Colombo, Sri L.	H4	53
Colome, S.D., U.S.	D13	126
Colomiers, Fr.	F7	18
Colón, Arg.	F8	92
Colón, Arg.	F7	92
Colón, Cuba	A7	102
Colón, Pan.	H7	102
Colón, Ur.	F10	92
Colón, Mi., U.S.	G4	112
Colón, Archipiélago de (Galapagos Islands), is., Ec.	h12	84a
Colonia, Austl.	E8	74
Coloneiganj, India	E6	54
Colônia, stm., Braz.	H6	88
Colonia Alvear Norte see General Alvear, Arg.	G3	92
Colonia del Sacramento, Ur.	G9	92
Colonia Dora, Arg.	D6	92
Colonia Elisa, Arg.	C8	92
Colonia Lavalleja, Ur.	E9	92
Colonial Heights, Va., U.S.	G8	114
Colonia Providencia, P.R.	C4	104a
Colonia Suiza, Ur.	G9	92
Colonias Unidas, Arg.	C8	92
Colonne, Capo, c., Italy	E11	24
Colonsay, Sk., Can.	B8	124
Colonsay, i., Scot., U.K.	E6	12
Colony, Ks., U.S.	F2	120
Colorado Grande, Salina, pl., Arg.	I5	92
Coloradas, Lomas, hills, Arg.	H3	90
Colorado, Hond.	E4	102
Colorado, state, U.S.	D6	108
Colorado, stm., Arg.	G4	90
Colorado, stm., N.A.	E5	98
Colorado, stm., Tx., U.S.	F11	130
Colorado, Cerro, mtn., Arg.	H3	90
Colorado City, Co., U.S.	C4	128
Colorado City, Tx., U.S.	B7	130
Colorado Kolonie see Lago Kolonie, Aruba	p20	104g
Colorado National Monument, p.o.i., Co., U.S.	D8	132
Colorado Plateau, plat., U.S.	E7	132
Colorado River Aqueduct, aq., Ca., U.S.	E5	98
Colorado Springs, Co., U.S.	C4	128
Colotlán, Mex.	D7	100
Colquechaca, Bol.	C3	90
Colstrip, Mt., U.S.	B6	126
Colt, Ar., U.S.	B8	122
Coltauco, Chile	G2	92
Colton, Ca., U.S.	I8	134
Colton, S.D., U.S.	H2	118
Columbia, Ca., U.S.	E5	134
Columbia, Il., U.S.	F7	120
Columbia, Ky., U.S.	G12	120
Columbia, La., U.S.	E6	122
Columbia, Md., U.S.	E9	114
Columbia, Mo., U.S.	F5	120
Columbia, N.C., U.S.	I9	114
Columbia, Tn., U.S.	B11	122
Columbia, stm., N.A.	D3	136
Columbia, Cape, c., Nu.	A11	141
Columbia, Mount, mtn., Ab., Can.	D13	138
Columbia Basin, bas., Wa., U.S.	C8	136
Columbia City, In., U.S.	G4	112
Columbia Falls, Me., U.S.	F9	110
Columbia Icefield, ice, Can.	D13	138
Columbia Mountains, mts., N.A.	G13	138
Columbiana, Al., U.S.	D12	122
Columbiana, Oh., U.S.	D5	114
Columbine, Cape, c., S. Afr.	H3	70
Columbrets, Illes, is., Spain	E11	20
Columbus, Ga., U.S.	E14	122
Columbus, In., U.S.	E12	120
Columbus, Ks., U.S.	G3	120
Columbus, Ms., U.S.	D10	122
Columbus, N.C., U.S.	A3	116
Columbus, N.D., U.S.	F11	124
Columbus, Ne., U.S.	F15	126
Columbus, N.M., U.S.	L9	132
Columbus, Oh., U.S.	E2	114
Columbus, Tx., U.S.	H2	122
Columbus, Wi., U.S.	H9	118
Columbus Point, c., Trin.	r13	105f
Columbus Salt Marsh, pl., Nv., U.S.	E8	134
Colusa, Ca., U.S.	D3	134
Colville, Wa., U.S.	B8	136
Colville, stm., Ak., U.S.	C9	140
Colville Lake, l., N.T., Can.	B5	106
Colwyn Bay, Wales, U.K.	H9	12
Comacchio, Italy	F9	22
Comacchio, Valli di, l., Italy	F9	22
Comala, Mex.	F7	100
Comalcalco, Mex.	F12	100
Comales, Mex.	H9	130
Coman, Mount, mtn., Ant.	C34	81
Comana, Rom.	F15	26
Comanche, Ok., U.S.	G10	128
Comandante Ferraz, sci., Ant.	B35	81
Comandante Fontana, Arg.	B7	92
Comandante Leal, Arg.	E5	92
Comandante Luis Piedra Buena, Arg.	I3	90
Comănești, Rom.	C13	26
Comayagua, Hond.	E4	102
Combarbalá, Chile	E2	92
Combermere Bay, b., Mya.	C1	48
Combourg, Fr.	F7	14
Comboyne, Austl.	H9	76
Comendador, Dom. Rep.	C12	102
Comer, Ga., U.S.	B2	116
Comercinho, Braz.	I5	88
Comet, Austl.	E7	76
Cometela, Moz.	B12	70
Comfort, N.C., U.S.	B8	116
Comfort, Tx., U.S.	E8	130
Comfort, Cape, c., Nu., Can.	B14	106
Comfrey, Mn., U.S.	G4	118
Comilla, Bngl.	G13	54
Comino see Kemmuna, i., Malta	H8	24
Comiso, Italy	H8	24
Comitán de Domínguez, Mex.	G12	100
Commerce, Ga., U.S.	B2	116
Commerce, Ok., U.S.	H2	120
Commerce, Tx., U.S.	D3	122
Commercy, Fr.	F14	14
Commingés, reg., Fr.	F6	18
Committee Bay, b., Nu., Can.	B13	106
Communism Peak see Ismail Samani, pik, mtn., Taj.	B11	56
Como, Italy	E6	22
Como, Tx., U.S.	D3	122
Como, Lago di, l., Italy	D6	22
Comodoro Rivadavia, Arg.	I3	90
Comores, Archipel des, is., Afr.	C7	68
Comorin, Cape, c., India	G3	53
Comoros, ctry., Afr.	C7	68
Comox, B.C., Can.	G6	138
Compiègne, Fr.	E11	14
Compostela, Mex.	E6	100
Compton, Ca., U.S.	J7	134
Comrat, Mol.	C15	26
Comstock, Mi., U.S.	F13	126
Comstock, Tx., U.S.	E6	130
Comstock Park, Mi., U.S.	E4	112
Con, stm., Viet.	C7	48
Cona, stm., Russia	B19	32
Co Nag, l., China	B13	54
Conakry, Gui.	H2	64
Conambo, stm., Ec.	H3	86
Cona Niyeo, Arg.	H3	90
Conasauga, stm., U.S.	C14	122
Concarán, Arg.	F5	92
Concarneau, Fr.	G5	14
Conceição, Braz.	D6	88
Conceição da Barra, Braz.	J6	88
Conceição das Alagoas, Braz.	J1	88
Conceição do Araguaia, Braz.	E1	88
Conceição do Canindé, Braz.	D5	88
Conceição do Coité, Braz.	F6	88
Conceição do Mato Dentro, Braz.	J4	88
Conceição do Norte, Braz.	G2	88
Concepción, Arg.	C5	92
Concepción, Bol.	C4	90
Concepción, Chile	H1	92
Concepción, Col.	D5	86
Concepción, Para.	D5	90
Concepción, Bahía, b., Mex.	B2	100
Concepción, Canal, strt., Chile	J2	90
Concepción, Laguna, l., Bol.	C4	90
Concepción, Volcán, vol., Nic.	G5	102
Concepción de la Sierra, Arg.	D10	92
Concepción del Oro, Mex.	C8	100
Concepción del Uruguay, Arg.	F8	92
Conception, Point, c., Ca., U.S.	I5	134
Conception Bay, b., Nf., Can.	j23	107a
Conception Bay, b., Nmb.	C2	70
Conchas Dam, N.M., U.S.	F4	128
Conchas Lake, res., N.M., U.S.	F4	128
Concho, Az., U.S.	I7	132
Concho, stm., Tx., U.S.	C8	130
Conchos, stm., Mex.	A6	100
Conchos, stm., Mex.	C10	100
Conconully, Wa., U.S.	B7	136
Concord, Ca., U.S.	E4	134
Concord, Ga., U.S.	D14	122
Concord, N.C., U.S.	A5	116
Concord, N.H., U.S.	G5	110
Concordia, Arg.	E8	92
Concórdia, Braz.	C11	92
Concordia, Mex.	D5	100
Concordia, Mo., U.S.	F4	120
Concrete, Wa., U.S.	B5	136
Con Cuong, Viet.	C7	48
Conda, Ang.	C1	68
Condamine, Austl.	F7	76
Condamine, stm., Austl.	F8	76
Condat, Fr.	D8	18
Conde, S.D., U.S.	B14	126
Condeúba, Braz.	H5	88
Condobolin, Austl.	I6	76
Condom, Fr.	F6	18
Condon, Or., U.S.	E6	136
Condoto, Col.	E3	86
Condroz, hist. reg., Bel.	D14	14
Cone, Tx., U.S.	H7	128
Conecuh, stm., U.S.	F12	122
Conegliano, Italy	E9	22
Conejos, Co., U.S.	D2	128
Conejos, stm., Co., U.S.	D3	128
Confuso, stm., Para.	B8	92
Congaree Swamp National Monument, p.o.i., S.C., U.S.	C5	116
Congaz, Mol.	C15	26
Conghua, China	J5	42
Congjiang, China	I3	42
Congo, ctry., Afr.	E3	66
Congo (Zaire), stm., Afr.	F2	66
Congo, Democratic Republic of the (Zaire), ctry., Afr.	E4	66
Congo Basin, bas., Afr.	E4	66
Congonhinhas, Braz.	A12	92
Congress, Sk., Can.	E8	124
Conitaca, Mex.	C5	100
Conn, Lough, l., Ire.	G3	12
Connaught see Connacht, hist. reg., Ire.	H3	12
Connacht, hist. reg., Ire.	H3	12
Conneaut, Oh., U.S.	C5	114
Conneautville, Pa., U.S.	C5	114
Connecticut, state, U.S.	C13	114
Connecticut, stm., U.S.	A14	110
Connellsville, Pa., U.S.	D6	114
Connemara, reg., Ire.	H3	12
Connersville, In., U.S.	E12	120
Conn Lake, l., Nu., Can.	A15	106
Connors Range, mts., Austl.	C7	76
Conoco, stm., Ec.	H3	86
Conorochro, stm., Ven.	F8	86
Conover, N.C., U.S.	I4	114
Conquest, Sk., Can.	C6	124
Conquista, Braz.	J2	88
Conrad, Ia., U.S.	B5	120
Conroe, Tx., U.S.	G3	122
Conroe, Lake, res., Tx., U.S.	G3	122
Consecon, On., Can.	D12	112
Conselheiro Lafaiete, Braz.	K4	88
Conselheiro Pena, Braz.	J5	88
Conselice, Italy	F8	22
Consett, Eng., U.K.	G10	12
Consolación del Sur, Cuba	A6	102
Con Son, i., Viet.	H8	48
Consort, Ab., Can.	B3	124
Constance, Lake (Bodensee), l., Eur.	I5	16
Constance, Ger.	I4	16
Constância, Port.	E2	20
Constanța, Rom.	E15	26
Constanța, state, Rom.	E15	26
Constantina, Spain	G5	20
Constantine see Qacentina, Alg.	B6	64
Constantine, Mi., U.S.	G4	112
Constantine, Cape, c., Ak., U.S.	E8	140
Constantinople see İstanbul, Tur.	B12	28
Constitución, Chile	G1	92
Constitución, Ur.	E9	92
Constitución de 1857, Parque Nacional, p.o.i., Mex.	K10	134
Consuegra, Spain	E7	20
Contai, India	H11	54
Contas, stm., Braz.	H6	88
Contentea Creek, stm., N.C., U.S.	A8	116
Continental Peak, mtn., Wy., U.S.	E4	126
Contratación, Col.	D5	86
Contreras, Embalse de, res., Spain	E9	20
Contreras, Isla, i., Chile	J1	90
Contursi, Italy	D9	24
Contwoyto Lake, l., Can.	B8	106
Convent, La., U.S.	G8	122
Conversano, Italy	D10	24
Converse, In., U.S.	H4	112
Conway, Ar., U.S.	B6	122
Conway, Mo., U.S.	G5	120
Conway, N.C., U.S.	H8	114
Conway, N.H., U.S.	F5	110
Conway, S.C., U.S.	C6	116
Conway, Wales, U.K.	H9	12
Conway Lake, res., Ar., U.S.	C6	122
Conway National Park, p.o.i., Austl.	C7	76
Conway Springs, Ks., U.S.	D11	128
Coober Pedy, Austl.	F6	74
Cook, Austl.	F6	74
Cook, Mn., U.S.	D6	118
Cook, Ne., U.S.	D1	120
Cook, Cape, c., B.C., Can.	F2	138
Cook, Mount see Aoraki, mtn., N.Z.	F4	80
Cook, Mount Procópio, Braz.	D6	90
Cook, Récif de, rf., N. Cal.	I14	79d
Cookeville, Tn., U.S.	H12	120
Cooking Lake, l., Ab., Can.	C17	138
Cook Inlet, b., Ak., U.S.	D9	140
Cook Islands, dep., Oc.	E10	72
Cook Strait, strt., N.Z.	E6	80
Cooktown, Austl.	C9	74
Coolabah, Austl.	H6	76
Cooladdi, Austl.	F5	76
Coolamon, Austl.	J6	76
Coolangatta, Austl.	G9	76
Cooleemee, N.C., U.S.	I5	114
Coolgardie, Austl.	F4	74
Coolidge, Ga., U.S.	E2	116
Coolidge, Tx., U.S.	F2	122
Coolidge, Mount, mtn., S.D., U.S.	D9	126
Coolidge Dam, dam, Az., U.S.	J6	132
Coolin, Id., U.S.	B10	136
Cooloola National Park, p.o.i., Austl.	F9	76
Cooma, Austl.	K7	76
Coonabarabran, Austl.	H7	76
Coonalpyn, Austl.	J2	76
Coonamble, Austl.	H7	76
Coondapoor, India	F3	53
Coon Rapids, Mn., U.S.	F5	118
Coon Valley, Wi., U.S.	H8	118
Cooper, Tx., U.S.	D3	122
Cooper Creek, stm., Austl.	G2	76
Cooper Road, La., U.S.	E5	122
Coopers, Al., U.S.	E12	122
Cooperstown, N.Y., U.S.	B11	114
Coopersville, Mi., U.S.	E4	112
Coopracambra National Park, p.o.i., Austl.	K7	76
Coorow, Austl.	E3	74
Cooroy, Austl.	F9	76
Coosa, stm., U.S.	E12	122
Coos Bay, Or., U.S.	G2	136
Cootamundra, Austl.	J7	76
Cootehill, Ire.	G5	12
Copacabana, Arg.	D4	92
Copacabana, Col.	D4	86
Copainalá, Mex.	G12	100
Copán, sci., Hond.	E3	102
Copatana, Braz.	I8	86
Copeland, Fl., U.S.	K4	116
Copenhagen see København, Den.	I4	8
Copenhagen, N.Y., U.S.	E14	112
Copertino, Italy	D11	24
Copiapó, Chile	C2	92
Copiapó, stm., Chile	C2	92
Copley, Oh., U.S.	H2	76
Copparo, Italy	F8	22
Copper, stm., Ak., U.S.	D11	140
Copperas Cove, Tx., U.S.	C9	130
Copper Butte, mtn., Wa., U.S.	B8	136
Copper Canyon see Cobre, Barranca del, misc. cult., Mex.	B5	100
Copper Center, Ak., U.S.	D10	140
Copper Harbor, Mi., U.S.	D10	118
Coppermine see Kugluktuk, Nu., Can.	B8	106
Coppermine, stm., Nu., Can.	B7	106
Copper Mine Point, c., Br. Vir. Is.	e9	104b
Copper Mountain, B.C., Can.	G10	138
Coqui, P.R.	C3	104a
Coquilhatville see Mbandaka, D.R.C.	D3	66
Coquimbo, Chile	E2	92
Coquimbo, state, Chile	E2	92
Corabia, Rom.	F11	26
Coração de Jesus, Braz.	I3	88
Coradi, Isole see Cheradi, Isole, i., Italy	D11	24
Coral Gables, Fl., U.S.	K5	116
Coral Harbour, Bah.	n18	104f
Coral Harbour see Salliq, Nu., Can.	C14	106
Coral Sea, Oc.	C6	72
Coral Sea Basin, unds.	K18	142
Coral Sea Islands Territory, dep., Oc.	B9	76
Coralville, Ia., U.S.	C6	120
Coram, Mt., U.S.	B12	136
Coramba, Austl.	H9	76
Corangamite, Lake, l., Austl.	K4	76
Corato, Italy	C10	24
Corbeil-Essonnes, Fr.	F11	14
Corbett National Park, p.o.i., India	D7	54
Corbigny, Fr.	G12	14
Corbin, Ky., U.S.	H1	114
Corbones, stm., Spain	G5	20
Corby, Eng., U.K.	I12	12
Corcaigh see Cork, Ire.	J4	12
Corcega, P.R.	B1	104a
Corcoran, Ca., U.S.	G6	134
Corcovado, Golfo, b., Chile	H2	90
Corcovado, Parque Nacional, p.o.i., C.R.	H6	102
Corcovado, Volcán, vol., Chile	H2	90
Corcubión, Spain	B1	20
Cordeiro, Braz.	L4	88
Cordele, Ga., U.S.	E2	116
Cordell, Ok., U.S.	F9	128
Cordenons, Italy	G8	22
Cordes, Fr.	E8	18
Cordillera, state, Para.	B9	92
Cordillo Downs, Austl.	E3	76
Córdoba, Arg.	E5	92
Córdoba, Mex.	F10	100
Córdoba, state, Arg.	E5	92
Córdoba (Cordova), Spain	G6	20
Córdoba, state, Col.	C4	86
Córdoba, co., Spain	F6	20
Córdoba, Peru	F2	84
Cordova see Córdoba, Spain	G6	20
Cordova, Al., U.S.	D11	122
Cordova, Il., U.S.	C7	120
Cordova Peak, mtn., Ak., U.S.	D10	140
Coreaú, Braz.	B5	88
Corella, Spain	B9	20
Corentyne (Courantyne), stm., S.A.	C6	84
Corfield, Austl.	C4	76
Corfu see Kérkyra, Grc.	D2	28
Corfu see Kérkyra, i., Grc.	D2	28
Coria, Spain	D4	20
Coria del Río, Spain	G4	20
Coribe, Braz.	G3	88
Coricudgy, Mount, mtn., Austl.	I8	76
Corigliano Calabro, Italy	E10	24
Corinne, Ut., U.S.	B4	132
Corinne, W.V., U.S.	G4	114
Corinth see Kórinthos, Grc.	F5	28
Corinth, Ms., U.S.	C10	122
Corinth, N.Y., U.S.	G3	110
Corinth, Gulf of see Korinthiakós Kólpos, b., Grc.	E5	28
Corinto, Braz.	J3	88
Corinto, Nic.	G4	102
Corisco, Isla de, i., Eq. Gui.	I6	64
Coriţeni, Mol.	A14	26
Cork, Ire.	J4	12
Cork, state, Ire.	I4	12
Corleone, Italy	G7	24
Çorlu, Tur.	B10	28
Cornelia, Ga., U.S.	B2	116
Cornelius, N.C., U.S.	A5	116
Cornelius Grinnell Bay, b., Nu., Can.	E13	141
Cornell, Wi., U.S.	F7	118
Corner Brook, Nf., Can.	j22	107a
Corneşti, Mol.	B14	26
Corneta, Punta, c., Mex.	H10	100
Corning, Ar., U.S.	H7	120
Corning, Ca., U.S.	D3	134
Corning, Ia., U.S.	D3	120
Corning, Ks., U.S.	B12	128
Corning, N.Y., U.S.	B8	114
Cornish, Me., U.S.	G6	110
Cornoe more see Black Sea, s.	G15	6
Corno Grande, mtn., Italy	H10	22
Cornwall, On., Can.	E2	110
Cornwallis Island, i., Nu., Can.	B7	141
Cornwall Island, i., Nu., Can.	B6	141
Coro, Ven.	B7	86
Coro, Golfete de, b., Ven.	B6	86
Coroaci, Braz.	J4	88
Coroatá, Braz.	C3	88
Corocoro, Bol.	C3	90
Corocoro, Isla, i., S.A.	C11	86
Coroico, Bol.	C3	90
Coromandel, Braz.	J2	88
Coromandel Coast, cst., India	E5	53
Coromandel Peninsula, pen., N.Z.	C6	80
Corona, Ca., U.S.	J8	134
Corona, N.M., U.S.	G3	128
Coronado, Ca., U.S.	K8	134
Coronado, Bahía de, b., C.R.	H6	102
Coronado, Islas, is., Mex.	K8	134
Coronation, Ab., Can.	D19	138
Coronation Gulf, b., Can.	B8	106
Coronation Island, i., Ant.	B36	81
Coronda, Arg.	E7	92
Coronel, Chile	H1	92
Coronel Bogado, Para.	C9	92
Coronel Dorrego, Arg.	I7	92
Coronel Fabriciano, Braz.	J4	88
Coronel Moldes, Arg.	B5	92
Coronel Moldes, Arg.	F5	92
Coronel Oviedo, Para.	B9	92
Coronel Pringles, Arg.	H7	92
Coronel Suárez, Arg.	H6	92
Coronel Vidal, Arg.	H9	92
Coronel Vivida, Braz.	C11	92
Corongo, Peru	E2	84
Coropuna, Nevado, vol., Peru	G3	84
Corossol, Guad.	B2	105a
Çorovodë, Alb.	D14	24
Corowa, Austl.	J6	76
Corozal, Belize	D3	102
Corozal, Col.	C4	86
Corozal, P.R.	B3	104a
Corpus Christi, Tx., U.S.	G10	130
Corpus Christi Bay, b., Tx., U.S.	G10	130
Corral, Chile	H2	90
Corral de Almaguer, Spain	E7	20
Corral de Bustos, Arg.	F6	92
Corrales, Cerro, mtn., Mex.	F4	102
Corralito, Arg.	B5	92
Correctionville, Ia., U.S.	B2	120
Corregidor Island, i., Phil.	C3	52
Corrente, Braz.	F3	88
Corrente, stm., Braz.	G3	88
Corrente, stm., Braz.	G2	88
Correntes, Cabo das, c., Moz.	D12	70
Correntina, Braz.	G3	88
Corrèze, state, Fr.	D7	18
Corrib, Lough, l., Ire.	H3	12
Corrientes, Arg.	D8	92
Corrientes, state, Arg.	D9	92
Corrientes, stm., S.A.	D2	84
Corrientes, Cabo, c., Arg.	I9	92
Corrientes, Cabo, c., Col.	E3	86
Corrientes, Cabo, c., Mex.	E6	100
Corrigan, Tx., U.S.	G3	122
Corrigin, Austl.	F3	74
Corry, Pa., U.S.	C6	114
Corryong, Austl.	K6	76
Corse (Corsica), i., Fr.	G15	18
Corse, Cap, c., Fr.	F15	18
Corse-du-Sud, state, Fr.	H15	18
Corsica see Corse, i., Fr.	G15	18
Corsicana, Tx., U.S.	E2	122
Cort Adelaer, Kap, c., Grnld.	E17	141
Cortazar, Mex.	E8	100
Corte, Fr.	G15	18
Cortegana, Spain	G3	20
Cortemilia, Italy	F5	22
Cortes, Mar de see California, Golfo de, b., Mex.	B2	96
Cortez, Co., U.S.	F8	132
Cortez, Sea of see California, Golfo de, b., Mex.	B2	96
Cortina d'Ampezzo, Italy	D8	22
Cortland, N.Y., U.S.	B9	114
Cortland, Oh., U.S.	C5	114
Cortona, Italy	G8	22
Corubal, stm., Afr.	G2	64
Coruche, Port.	F2	20
Çorum, Tur.	A4	56
Corumbá, Braz.	C5	90
Corumbá, stm., Braz.	I1	88
Corumbaíba, Braz.	J1	88
Corumbataí, stm., Braz.	B11	92
Corumbau, Ponta, c., Braz.	D11	86
Coruña see A Coruña, Spain	A2	20
Corunna, Mi., U.S.	F5	112
Coruripe, Braz.	F7	88
Corvallis, Mt., U.S.	D12	136
Corvallis, Or., U.S.	F3	136
Corwith, Ia., U.S.	A4	120
Corydon, In., U.S.	F11	120
Corydon, Ia., U.S.	D4	120
Corydon, Ky., U.S.	G10	120
Corzu, Rom.	E10	26
Cosalá, Mex.	C5	100
Cosamaloapan de Carpio, Mex.	F10	100
Coscomate, Mex.	I2	130
Cosenza, Italy	E10	24
Coshocton, Oh., U.S.	D4	114
Cosigüina, Punta, c., Nic.	F4	102
Cosigüina, Volcán, vol., Nic.	F4	102
Cosmoledo, Atoll de, i., Sey.	k11	69b
Cosmos, Mn., U.S.	G4	118
Cosne-sur-Loire, Fr.	G11	14
Cosquín, Arg.	E5	92
Cossato, Italy	E5	22
Cossatot, stm., Ar., U.S.	C4	122
Costa Mesa, Ca., U.S.	J8	134
Costa Rica, Mex.	C5	100
Costa Rica, ctry., N.A.	H5	102
Coswig, Ger.	E9	16
Coswig, Ger.	E8	16
Cotabato, Phil.	G4	52
Cotahuasi, Peru	G3	84
Cotati, Ca., U.S.	E3	134
Coteaux, Haiti	C10	102
Cote d'Ivoire, ctry., Afr.	H3	64
Côte-d'Or, state, Fr.	G13	14
Cotegipe, Braz.	F3	88
Cotentin, pen., Fr.	E7	14
Côtes-d'Armor, state, Fr.	F6	14
Cotinga, stm., Braz.	B15	26
Cotonou, Benin	H5	64
Cotopaxi, state, Ec.	H2	86
Cotopaxi, vol., Ec.	H2	86
Cotopaxi, Parque Nacional, p.o.i., Ec.	H2	86
Cotswold Hills, hills, Eng., U.K.	J10	12
Cottage Grove, Or., U.S.	G3	136
Cottbus, Ger.	E10	16
Cotter, Ar., U.S.	H5	120
Cottian Alps, mts., Eur.	E12	18
Cottondale, Fl., U.S.	G13	122
Cotton Plant, Ar., U.S.	C7	122
Cottonport, La., U.S.	G6	122
Cotton Valley, La., U.S.	E5	122
Cottonwood, Az., U.S.	I5	132
Cottonwood, Ca., U.S.	C3	134
Cottonwood, Mn., U.S.	G3	118
Cottonwood, stm., Ks., U.S.	C12	128
Cottonwood, stm., Mn., U.S.	G3	118
Cottonwood Creek, stm., Mt., U.S.	F5	124
Cottonwood Falls, Ks., U.S.	C12	128
Coubre, Pointe de la, c., Fr.	D4	18
Couchiching, Lake, l., On., Can.	D10	112
Coudersport, Pa., U.S.	C8	114
Coudres, Île aux, i., Qc., Can.	C6	110
Coulee City, Wa., U.S.	C7	136
Coulee Dam, Wa., U.S.	B8	136
Coulommiers, Fr.	F12	14
Coulonge, stm., Qc., Can.	C13	112
Counce, Tn., U.S.	B10	122
Council, Id., U.S.	F10	136
Council Bluffs, Ia., U.S.	C2	120
Council Grove, Ks., U.S.	C12	128
Coupeville, Wa., U.S.	B4	136
Courantyne see Corentyne, stm., S.A.	C6	84
Courland (Kurzeme), hist. reg., Lat.	C5	10
Courland Lagoon, b., Eur.	E3	10
Courmayeur, Italy	E3	22
Courtenay, B.C., Can.	G5	138
Courtland, Al., U.S.	C11	122
Courtland, Va., U.S.	H8	114
Courtrai see Kortrijk, Bel.	D12	14
Coutras, Fr.	D5	18
Coutts, Ab., Can.	E18	138
Couture, Lac, l., Qc., Can.	C16	106
Covasna, state, Rom.	C12	26
Cove, Or., U.S.	E9	136
Cove Island, i., On., Can.	C8	112
Covelo, Ca., U.S.	D2	134
Coventry, Eng., U.K.	I11	12
Covert, Mi., U.S.	F3	112
Covilhã, Port.	D3	20
Covington, Ga., U.S.	C2	116
Covington, In., U.S.	H2	112
Covington, Ky., U.S.	E1	114
Covington, La., U.S.	G8	122
Covington, Oh., U.S.	E11	120
Covington, Tn., U.S.	B9	122
Covington, Va., U.S.	G5	114
Cowal, pen., Scot., U.K.	E7	12
Cowal, Lake, l., Austl.	I6	76
Cowan, Tn., U.S.	B13	122
Cowan, Lake, l., Austl.	F4	74
Cowansville, Qc., Can.	E4	110
Cowarie, Austl.	E2	76
Cow Creek, stm., Ks., U.S.	C10	128
Cow Creek, stm., Mt., U.S.	H3	136
Cowdenbeath, Scot., U.K.	E9	12
Cowell, Austl.	F7	74
Cowen, W.V., U.S.	F5	114
Coweta, Ok., U.S.	I2	120
Cowhouse Creek, stm., Tx., U.S.	C10	130
Cowichan Bay, B.C., Can.	H7	138
Cowichan Lake, l., B.C., Can.	H6	138
Cowley, Wy., U.S.	C5	126
Cowlic, Az., U.S.	L4	132
Cowlitz, stm., Wa., U.S.	D4	136
Cowpasture, stm., Va., U.S.	F6	114
Cowpens, S.C., U.S.	A4	116
Cowra, Austl.	I7	76
Coxá, stm., Braz.	H3	88
Coxim, Braz.	C6	90
Cox's Bāzār, Bngl.	H13	54
Coyaguaima, Cerro, mtn., Arg.	D3	90
Coyame, Mex.	A6	100
Coyle see Coig, stm., Arg.	J3	90
Coyote, stm., Mex.	A6	100
Coyote Wash, stm., N.M., U.S.	G8	132
Coyuca de Benítez, Mex.	G8	100
Coyuca de Catalán, Mex.	F8	100
Cozad, Ne., U.S.	G13	126
Cozumel, Mex.	B4	102
Cozumel, Isla, i., Mex.	B4	102
Crab Orchard, Tn., U.S.	I13	120
Crab Orchard Lake, res., Il., U.S.	G9	120
Cradle Mountain-Lake Saint Clair National Park, p.o.i., Austl.	n12	77a
Cradock, S. Afr.	H7	70
Craig, Co., U.S.	C9	132
Craig, Ne., U.S.	J2	118
Craigellachie, B.C., Can.	F11	138
Craigmont, Id., U.S.	D10	136
Craik, Sk., Can.	C8	124
Crailsheim, Ger.	G6	16
Craiova, Rom.	E10	26
Cranberry Lake, l., N.Y., U.S.	F1	110
Cranbrook, Austl.	F3	74
Cranbrook, B.C., Can.	G15	138
Crandon, Wi., U.S.	F9	118
Crane, Az., U.S.	K2	132
Crane, Mo., U.S.	G4	120
Crane, Or., U.S.	G8	136
Crane, Tx., U.S.	C5	130
Crane Lake, l., Sk., Can.	D4	124
Crane Mountain, mtn., Or., U.S.	A5	134
Crângeni, Rom.	E11	26
Cranston, R.I., U.S.	C14	114
Crasna, Rom.	C10	26
Crasna, stm., Eur.	I18	16
Crasnoe, Mol.	C16	26
Crater Lake, l., Or., U.S.	H4	136
Crater Lake National Park, p.o.i., Or., U.S.	H5	136
Craters of the Moon National Monument, p.o.i., Id., U.S.	G13	136
Crateús, Braz.	C5	88
Crato, Braz.	D6	88
Crawford, Cape, c., Nu., Can.	A14	106
Cravo Norte, Col.	D6	86
Cravo Norte, stm., Col.	D6	86
Cravo Sur, stm., Col.	E6	86
Crawford, Co., U.S.	E9	132
Crawford, Tx., U.S.	C10	130
Crawford, Ms., U.S.	D10	122
Crawford, Tx., U.S.	C10	130
Crawford Bay, B.C., Can.	G14	138
Crawfordsville, Ar., U.S.	B8	122
Crawfordsville, In., U.S.	H2	112
Crawfordville, Ga., U.S.	C3	116
Crawley, Eng., U.K.	J12	12
Crazy Woman Creek, stm., Wy., U.S.	C6	126
Creal Springs, Il., U.S.	G9	120
Cree, stm., Sk., Can.	D9	106
Creede, Co., U.S.	F10	132
Creedmoor, N.C., U.S.	H7	114
Cree Lake, l., Sk., Can.	D9	106
Creemore, On., Can.	D9	112
Creighton, Ne., U.S.	E15	126
Creighton Mine, On., Can.	B8	112
Creil, Fr.	E11	14
Crema, Italy	E6	22
Cremona, Italy	E7	22
Crenshaw, Ms., U.S.	C8	122
Crepori, stm., Braz.	E6	84
Crépy-en-Valois, Fr.	E11	14
Cres, Cro.	F11	22
Cres, Otok, i., Cro.	F11	22
Cresaptown, Md., U.S.	E7	114
Crescent, Or., U.S.	G5	136
Crescent City, Ca., U.S.	B1	134
Crescent Spur, B.C., Can.	C10	138
Cresco, Ia., U.S.	H6	118
Crespo, Arg.	F7	92
Cresson, Tx., U.S.	B10	130
Cressy, Austl.	K4	76
Crested Butte, Co., U.S.	E9	132
Crestline, Ca., U.S.	I8	134
Creston, B.C., Can.	G14	138
Creston, Ia., U.S.	C3	120
Crestone Peak, mtn., Co., U.S.	D3	128
Crestview, Fl., U.S.	G12	122
Crestwood Hills, Tn., U.S.	I1	114
Creswell, Or., U.S.	G3	136
Creswell Bay, b., Nu., Can.	A12	106
Crete, Il., U.S.	G2	112
Crete, Ne., U.S.	G16	126
Crete see Kriti, i., Grc.	H7	28
Crete, Sea of see Kritikón Pélagos, s., Grc.	H8	28
Créteil, Fr.	F11	14
Cretin, Cape, c., Pap. N. Gui.	b4	79a
Creus, Cap de, c., Spain	B14	20
Creuse, state, Fr.	C8	18
Creuse, stm., Fr.	C7	18
Creussen, Ger.	G7	16
Creve Coeur, Il., U.S.	K9	118
Crevillent, Spain	F10	20
Crevillente see Crevillent, Spain	F10	20
Crewe, Eng., U.K.	H10	12
Crewe, Va., U.S.	G7	114
Cricaré, stm., Braz.	J5	88
Criciúma, Braz.	D13	92
Crikvenica, Cro.	E11	22
Crimea see Kryms'kyi pivostriv, pen., Ukr.	E4	32
Crimean Peninsula see Kryms'kyi pivostriv, pen., Ukr.	E4	32
Crimmitschau, Ger.	F8	16
Cripple Creek, Co., U.S.	C3	128
Crisfield, Md., U.S.	F10	114
Criss Creek, B.C., Can.	E10	138
Crissiumal, Braz.	C10	92
Cristal, Monts de, mts., Afr.	I7	64
Cristalândia, Braz.	F1	88
Cristalina, Braz.	I2	88
Cristinápolis, Braz.	F7	88
Cristino Castro, Braz.	E3	88
Cristóbal Colón, Pico, mtn., Col.	B5	86
Crişul Alb, stm., Eur.	C8	26
Crişul Negru, stm., Eur.	C8	26
Crişul Repede (Sebes Körös), stm., Eur.	B8	26
Crivitz, Wi., U.S.	C1	112
Crna, stm., Mac.	B4	28
Crna Gora (Montenegro), state, Serb.	G6	26
Crni Drim (Drinit të Zi), stm., Eur.	C14	24
Crnomelj, Slvn.	E12	22
Croajingolong National Park, p.o.i., Austl.	K7	76
Croatia, ctry., Eur.	E13	22
Croche, stm., Qc., Can.	C4	110
Crocker, Mo., U.S.	G5	120
Crocker, Banjaran, mts., Malay.	H1	52
Crockett, Tx., U.S.	F3	122
Crocodilopolis, hist. Egypt	I1	58
Crocus Hill, hill, Anguilla	A1	105a
Crofton, Ky., U.S.	G10	120
Croghan, N.Y., U.S.	E14	112
Croix, Lac la, l., N.A.	C6	118
Croker, Cape, c., Austl.	B6	74
Croker Island, i., Austl.	B6	74
Cromer, Eng., U.K.	I14	12
Crominia, Braz.	I1	88
Crompton Point, c., Dom.	i6	105c
Cromwell, N.Z.	G3	80
Cromwell, Al., U.S.	E10	122
Crooked, stm., Or., U.S.	F5	136
Crooked Creek, Ak., U.S.	D8	140
Crooked Creek, stm., U.S.	D8	128
Crooked Island, i., Bah.	A10	102
Crooked Island Passage, strt., Bah.	A10	102
Crooked River, Sk., Can.	B10	124
Crookston, Mn., U.S.	D2	118
Crooksville, Oh., U.S.	E3	114
Crosby, Mn., U.S.	E5	118
Crosby, N.D., U.S.	F10	124
Crosby, Mount, mtn., Wy., U.S.	D3	126
Crosbyton, Tx., U.S.	H7	128
Cross, stm., Afr.	H6	64
Cross City, Fl., U.S.	D7	122
Cross Lake, res., Mb., Can.	E11	106
Crossman Peak, mtn., Az., U.S.	I2	132
Cross Plains, Tn., U.S.	H11	120
Cross Plains, Wi., U.S.	H9	118
Cross Sound, strt., Ak., U.S.	E12	140
Crossville, Il., U.S.	F9	120
Crossville, Tn., U.S.	I12	120
Croswell, Mi., U.S.	E7	112
Crotone, Italy	E11	24
Crow, stm., Mn., U.S.	F4	118
Crow, North Fork, stm., Mn., U.S.	F4	118
Crow, South Fork, stm., Mn., U.S.	G4	118
Crow Agency, Mt., U.S.	B5	126
Crow Creek, stm., U.S.	G8	126
Crowder, Ms., U.S.	C8	122
Crowduck Lake, l., Mb., Can.	A3	118
Crowdy Head, c., Austl.	H9	76

Name	Map Ref.	Page
Crowell, Tx., U.S.	H9	128
Crow Lake, On., Can.	B5	118
Crowley, La., U.S.	G6	122
Crowleys Ridge, mts., U.S.	B8	122
Crown Mountain, mtn., V.I.U.S.	e7	104b
Crown Point, In., U.S.	G2	112
Crownpoint, N.M., U.S.	H8	132
Crown Point, N.Y., U.S.	G3	110
Crown Prince Frederik Island, i., Nu., Can.	A13	106
Crowsnest Pass, Ab., Can.	G16	138
Crowsnest Pass, p., Can.	G16	138
Crows Nest Peak, mtn., S.D., U.S.	C8	126
Crow Wing, stm., Mn., U.S.	E4	118
Croydon, Austl.	B4	76
Croydon Station, B.C., Can.	C11	138
Crozet, Va., U.S.	F7	114
Crozet, Îles, is., Afr.	J16	4
Crozet Basin, unds.	M9	142
Crucea, Rom.	E15	26
Cruces, Cuba	A7	102
Cruger, Ms., U.S.	D8	122
Crump Lake, l., Or., U.S.	A6	134
Cruz, Cabo, c., Cuba	C9	102
Cruz Alta, Arg.	F6	92
Cruz Alta, Braz.	D11	92
Cruz Bay, V.I.U.S.	e7	104b
Cruz del Eje, Arg.	E5	92
Cruzeiro, Braz.	L3	88
Cruzeiro do Oeste, Braz.	A11	92
Cruzeiro do Sul, Braz.	E3	84
Cruzeta, Braz.	D7	88
Cruz Grande, Chile	D2	92
Crysler, On., Can.	C14	112
Crystal, Mn., U.S.	F5	118
Crystal, N.D., U.S.	F16	124
Crystal Brook, Austl.	I2	76
Crystal City, Mb., Can.	E15	124
Crystal City, Mo., U.S.	F7	120
Crystal City, Tx., U.S.	F8	130
Crystal Falls, Mi., U.S.	B11	112
Crystal Lake, l., Mi., U.S.	D3	112
Crystal Springs, Ms., U.S.	E8	122
Csongrád, Hung.	C7	26
Csongrád, state, Hung.	C7	26
Csorna, Hung.	B4	26
Cu Swe Shū, stm., Asia	F12	32
Cúa, Ven.	B8	86
Cuajinicuilapa, Mex.	G9	100
Cuamba, Moz.	C6	68
Cuando (Kwando), stm., Afr.	D3	68
Cuangar, Ang.	D2	68
Cuango, Ang.	B2	68
Cuango see Kwango, stm., Afr.	F3	66
Cuanza, stm., Ang.	C2	68
Cuao, stm., Ven.	E9	86
Cuareim (Quaraí), stm., S.A.	E9	92
Cuaró, Ur.	E9	92
Cuarto, stm., Arg.	F6	92
Cuatrociénegas, Mex.	B7	100
Cuauhtémoc, Mex.	A5	100
Cuautitlán, Mex.	F6	100
Cuba, Port.	F3	20
Cuba, Al., U.S.	E10	122
Cuba, Il., U.S.	D7	120
Cuba, Mo., U.S.	F6	120
Cuba, N.M., U.S.	G10	132
Cuba, ctry., N.A.	C9	96
Cubagua, Isla, i., Ven.	B9	86
Cubal, Ang.	C1	68
Cubango (Okavango), stm., Afr.	D2	68
Cubati, Braz.	D7	88
Cublas, Russia	D21	8
Çubuk, Tur.	C15	28
Cuchi, stm., Ang.	C2	68
Cuchillo Co, Arg.	I5	92
Cuchivero, stm., Ven.	D9	86
Cucuí, Braz.	G8	86
Cúcuta, Col.	C5	86
Cucuy, Piedra de, hill, Ven.	G8	86
Cudahy, Wi., U.S.	F2	112
Cudalore, India	F4	53
Cuddapah, India	D4	53
Čudovo, Russia	A14	10
Cudworth, Sk., Can.	B8	124
Çudzin, Bela.	H9	10
Cue, Austl.	E3	74
Cuemba, Ang.	C2	68
Cuenca, Ec.	I2	86
Cuenca, Spain	D8	20
Cuenca, co., Spain	E9	20
Cuencamé de Ceniceros, Mex.	C7	100
Cuernavaca, Mex.	F9	100
Cuero, Tx., U.S.	E10	130
Cuers, Fr.	F12	18
Cuervo, Laguna del, l., Mex.	A6	100
Cuesta Pass, p., Ca., U.S.	H5	134
Cueto, Cuba	B9	102
Cugir, Rom.	D10	26
Čuguyevka, Russia	B10	38
Čulhornoye, ozero, l., Russia	G19	8
Cuiabá, Braz.	G6	84
Cuiabá, stm., Braz.	G6	84
Cuiari, Braz.	G7	86
Cuicatlán, Mex.	G10	100
Cuilapa, Guat.	E2	102
Cuilco see Grijalva, stm., N.A.	G12	100
Cuilo (Kwilu), stm., Afr.	F3	66
Cuité, Braz.	D7	88
Cuíto, stm., Braz.	D2	68
Cuito Cuanavale, Ang.	D2	68
Cuitzeo, Lago de, l., Mex.	F8	100
Cuiuni, stm., Braz.	H10	86
Cukai, Malay.	J6	48
Cukas, Indon.	D4	50
Čukotskij, mys, c., Russia	D26	34
Čukotskij poluostrov (Chukotsk Peninsula), pen., Russia	C26	34
Culbertson, Mt., U.S.	F9	124
Cul de Sac, Guad.	A1	105a
Cul de Sac, Neth. Ant.	A1	105a
Culebra, P.R.	B5	104a
Culebra, Isla de, i., P.R.	B5	104a
Culebra Peak, mtn., Co., U.S.	D3	128
Culfa, Azer.	B6	56
Culgoa, stm., Austl.	G6	76
Culiacán, Mex.	C5	100
Culiacán, Mex.	C5	100
Culion Island, i., Phil.	E2	52
Cúllar, Spain	G8	20
Cullen, La., U.S.	E5	122
Culleoka, Tn., U.S.	B12	122
Cullera, Spain	E10	20
Cullman, Al., U.S.	C12	122
Cullom, Il., U.S.	D9	120
Čul'man, Russia	E13	34
Culpeper, Va., U.S.	F7	114
Culpina, Bol.	D4	90
Culuene, stm., Braz.	F7	84
Culver, In., U.S.	G3	112
Culver, Or., U.S.	F5	136
Culverden, N.Z.	F4	80
Čulym, Russia	C14	32
Čulym, stm., Russia	C14	32
Cum, Russia	C1	34
Cumaná, Ven.	B9	86
Cumare, Cerro, hill, Col.	G5	86
Cumari, Braz.	J1	88
Cumbal, Nevado, vol., Col.	G2	86
Cumbe, Braz.	F7	88
Cumberland, B.C., Can.	G5	138
Cumberland, Ky., U.S.	G2	114
Cumberland, Md., U.S.	E7	114
Cumberland, Va., U.S.	G7	114
Cumberland, Wi., U.S.	F6	118
Cumberland, Lake, res., Ky., U.S.	H13	120
Cumberland, South Fork, stm., U.S.	H13	120
Cumberland Gap, p., U.S.	H2	114
Cumberland Island National Seashore, p.o.i., Ga., U.S.	F4	116
Cumberland Islands, is., Austl.	C7	76
Cumberland Lake, l., Sk., Can.	E10	106
Cumberland Peninsula, pen., Nu., Can.	B17	106
Cumberland Plateau, plat., U.S.	G14	120
Cumberland Sound, strt., Nu., Can.	B17	106
Cumbernauld, Scot., U.K.	F9	12
Cumbrian Mountains, mts., Eng., U.K.	G9	12
Cumby, Tx., U.S.	D3	122
Čumikan, Russia	F16	34
Cumming, Ga., U.S.	B1	116
Cummins, Austl.	F7	74
Cummings, Mex.	F8	98
Cumra, Tur.	F15	28
Čumyš, stm., Russia	D15	32
Čuna, stm., Russia	C17	32
Cunani, Braz.	C7	84
Cunaviche, Ven.	D8	86
Cunco, Chile	G2	90
Cundinamarca, state, Col.	E4	86
Cunene (Kunene), stm., Afr.	D1	68
Cuneo (Coni), Italy	F4	22
Cunha Porã, Braz.	C11	92
Cunja, stm., Russia	B17	32
Cunnamulla, Austl.	G5	76
Cunningham, Ks., U.S.	D10	128
Cunucunuma, stm., Ven.	F9	86
Cuny, Russia	G17	8
Cuorgnè, Italy	E4	22
Cupar, Sk., Can.	D9	124
Cupar, Scot., U.K.	E9	12
Cúpica, Golfo de, b., Col.	D3	86
Čuprovo, Russia	D22	8
Čuquenes, stm., Ven.	E11	86
Curaçá, Braz.	E6	88
Curaçao, i., Neth. Ant.	p21	104g
Curacautín, Chile	I2	92
Curanilahue, Chile	H1	92
Curanipe, Chile	G1	92
Čurapča, Russia	D15	34
Curaray, stm., S.A.	H4	86
Curepipe, Mrts.	I10	69a
Curepto, Chile	G1	92
Curicó, Chile	G2	92
Curicuriari, stm., Braz.	H8	86
Curimatá, Braz.	E3	88
Curitiba, Braz.	B13	92
Curitibanos, Braz.	C12	92
Curiuaú, stm., Braz.	H11	86
Curlew, Wa., U.S.	B8	136
Curnamona, Austl.	H2	76
Čuroviči, Russia	H15	10
Currais Novos, Braz.	D7	88
Curralinho, Braz.	D8	84
Currant Mountain, mtn., Nv., U.S.	E1	132
Current, stm., U.S.	H7	120
Currie, Austl.	m12	77a
Currituck, N.C., U.S.	H9	114
Currituck Sound, strt., N.C., U.S.	H10	114
Curtea de Argeş, Rom.	D11	26
Curtina, Ur.	F9	92
Curtis, Ar., U.S.	D5	122
Curtis, Ne., U.S.	G12	126
Curtis, Port, b., Austl.	D8	76
Curtis Channel, strt., Austl.	D8	76
Curtis Island, i., Austl.	D8	76
Curtis Island, i., N.Z.	G9	72
Curuá, stm., Braz.	B6	88
Curuá, stm., Braz.	D7	84
Curuá, Ilha do, i., Braz.	C7	84
Curuá-Una, stm., Braz.	D7	84
Curuçá, Braz.	D8	84
Curumu, Braz.	D7	84
Curup, Indon.	E3	50
Curupá, Braz.	E2	88
Cururupu, Braz.	A3	88
Curuzú Cuatiá, Arg.	D8	92
Curvelo, Braz.	J3	88
Cusco, Peru	F3	84
Cushing, Ok., U.S.	B2	122
Cushing, Tx., U.S.	F4	122
Cushman, Ar., U.S.	I6	120
Cusiana, stm., Col.	E5	86
Čusovaja, stm., Russia	C9	32
Čusovoj, Russia	C9	32
Cusset, Fr.	C9	18
Cusseta, Ga., U.S.	E14	122
Čust, Uzb.	F12	32
Custer, Mt., U.S.	A5	126
Custer, Mt., U.S.	G9	138
Custódia, Braz.	E7	88
Cut, Nuhu, i., Indon.	G9	44
Cut Bank, Mt., U.S.	B14	136
Cutbank, stm., Ab., Can.	A13	138
Cut Bank Creek, stm., Mt., U.S.	B14	136
Cut Bank Creek, stm., U.S.	F12	124
Cutervo, Peru	E2	84
Cuthbert, Ga., U.S.	F14	122
Cutler, Ca., U.S.	G6	134
Cutler, Me., U.S.	F9	110
Cutlerville, Mi., U.S.	F4	112
Cutral-Có, Arg.	G3	90
Cutro, Italy	E10	24
Cuttack, India	H10	54
Čutzamala, stm., Mex.	F8	100
Čuvašija, state, Russia	C7	32
Cuvier, Cape, c., Austl.	E2	74
Cuxhaven, Ger.	C4	16
Cuyahoga Falls, Oh., U.S.	C4	114
Cuyahoga Valley National Park, p.o.i., Oh., U.S.	C4	114
Cuyama, stm., Ca., U.S.	I6	134
Cuyamaca Peak, mtn., Ca., U.S.	J9	134
Cuyo, Phil.	E3	52
Cuyo East Pass, strt., Phil.	E3	52
Cuyo Islands, is., Phil.	E3	52
Cuyo West Pass, strt., Phil.	E3	52
Cuyubini, stm., S.A.	D11	86
Cuyuni, stm., S.A.	B6	84
Cuyuni-Mazaruni, state, Guy.	D11	86
Cwmbran, Wales, U.K.	J10	12
Cyclades see Kikládes, is.	F7	28
Cypress, Ca., U.S.	J8	134
Cypress, Tx., U.S.	F5	122
Cypress Hills, hills, Can.	E4	124
Cypress River, Mb., Can.	E15	124
Cypress Springs, Lake, res., Tx., U.S.	D3	122
Cyprus, i., Asia	D15	4
Cyprus, ctry., Asia	C4	58
Cyprus, North, ctry., Asia	C4	58
Cyrenaica see Barqah, hist. reg., Libya	A4	62
Cyril, Ok., U.S.	G10	128
Cyril E. King Airport, V.I.U.S.	e7	104b
Cyrus Field Bay, b., Nu., Can.	E13	141
Çyrvonae, vozero, l., Bela.	H10	10
Cythera see Kýthira, i., Grc.	G5	28
Czaplinek, Pol.	C12	16
Czarna Woda, Pol.	C16	16
Czarnków, Pol.	D12	16
Czechoslovakia see Czech Republic, ctry., Eur.	G11	16
Czechowice-Dziedzice, Pol.	G15	16
Czech Republic, ctry., Eur.	G11	16
Czerniejewo, Pol.	D13	16
Czerwieńsk, Pol.	D11	16
Częstochowa, Pol.	F15	16
Częstochowa, state, Pol.	F15	16
Człuchów, Pol.	C13	16

D

Name	Map Ref.	Page
Da, stm., China	G8	42
Da, Song see Black, stm., Asia.	D9	46
Da'an, China	J4	42
Dabajuro, Ven.	B6	86
Daba Ling, mtn., China	I5	42
Daba Shan, mts., China	E3	42
Dabat, Eth.	E7	62
Dabeiba, Col.	D3	86
Dabhoi, India	G4	54
Dabie, Pol.	D14	16
Dabie Shan, mts., China.	F6	42
Dabrou, Niger	G5	64
Dabola, Gui.	H2	64
Dabou, C. Iv.	H4	64
Daboya, Ghana	H4	64
Dabra, India	F7	54
Dąbrowa Białostocka, Pol.	C19	16
Dabu, China	J7	42
Dacca see Dhaka, Bngl.	G13	54
Dac Glei, Viet.	E8	48
Dachau, Ger.	H7	16
Dačice, Czech Rep.	G11	16
Dacoma, Ok., U.S.	E10	128
Dadanawa, Guy.	F12	86
Dade City, Fl., U.S.	H3	116
Dadeldhurā, Nepal	D8	54
Dadeville, Al., U.S.	E13	122
Dādra and Nagar Haveli, state, India	I4	54
Dādu, Pak.	D10	56
Daejeon see Taejŏn, Kor., S.	F7	38
Daerhanwangfu, China	C4	52
Daet, Phil.	D4	52
Dafang, China	F6	36
Dafeng, China	E9	42
Dafla, Grc.	F5	28
Dafoe, Sk., Can.	C9	124
Dafu, stm., China	D2	48
Dagã, stm., Mya.	D2	48
Daga Post, Sudan	F6	62
Dagana, Sen.	F1	64
Daga Post, Sudan	F6	62
Dagda, Lat.	D10	10
Dagda, stm., Tur.	D12	28
Dagestan, state, Russia	F7	32
Daglung, China	D13	54
Dagu, China	B7	42
Dagua, Pap. N. Gui.	a3	79a
Daguan, China	F5	36
Daguan Hu, l., China	F7	42
Dagua, P.R.	B4	104a
Dagujia, China	C6	38
Dagupan, Phil.	B3	52
Dagzê Co, l., China	B11	54
Dahei, India	H4	54
Daheiding Shan, mts., China	B10	36
Da Hinggan Ling (Greater Khingan Range), mts., China	B9	36
Dahlak Archipelago, is., Erit.	D8	62
Dahlonega, Ga., U.S.	B1	116
Dahlonega Plateau, plat., U.S.	C14	122
Dahmani, Tun.	I2	24
Dahme, Ger.	E9	16
Dāhod, India	G5	54
Dahomey see Benin, ctry., Afr.	G5	64
Dahra, Libya	B3	62
Dahra, mts., Alg.	H11	20
Dahshur, Pyramides de (Dashur, Pyramids of), hist., Egypt	I1	58
Dai, i., Sol. Is.	d9	79b
Daia, Rom.	E12	26
Dai Hai, l., China	A5	42
Daik-u, Mya.	D3	48
Đả'il, Syria	F7	58
Daimiel, Spain	E7	20
Daingean, Ire.	H5	12
Daingerfield, Tx., U.S.	D4	122
Dainkog, China	F4	36
Daireaux, Arg.	H7	92
Dairen see Dalian, China	B9	42
Dairût, Egypt	K1	58
Dai-sen, vol., Japan	D6	40
Daisetta, Tx., U.S.	G4	122
Daixian, China	B5	42
Daiyun Shan, mts., China	I8	42
Dajarra, Austl.	C2	76
Dajian Shan, mtn., China	F5	36
Dakar, Sen.	G1	64
Dakeng, China	I8	42
Dakhin Shāhbāzpur Island, i., Bngl.	G13	54
Dakhla, W. Sah.	E1	64
Dākoānk, India	G7	46
Dakoro, Niger	G6	64
Dakota City, Ia., U.S.	B3	120
Dakota City, Ne., U.S.	B1	120
Đakovica, Serb.	G7	26
Đakovo, Cro.	E15	22
Dala, Gui.	H3	64
Dalaba, Gui.	G2	64
Dalad Qi, China	A4	42
Dalälven, stm., Swe.	F7	8
Dalaman, Tur.	G11	28
Dalāmi, Sudan	E6	62
Dalandzadgad, Mong.	C5	36
Dalarna, state, Swe.	F6	8
Da Lat, Viet.	F9	48
Dalbandin, Pak.	D9	56
Dalbosjön, b., Swe.	G5	8
Dalby, Austl.	F8	76
Dale, Nor.	F1	8
Dale City, Va., U.S.	F8	114
Dale Hollow Lake, res., U.S.	H12	120
Daleville, In., U.S.	H4	112
Dalga, Egypt	K1	58
Dalhart, Tx., U.S.	E6	128
Dalhousie, N.B., Can.	B10	110
Dalhousie, India	B5	54
Dalhousie, Cape, c., N.T., Can.	B14	140
Dali, China	F5	36
Dalian (Dairen), China	B9	42
Daliang Shan, mts., China	F5	36
Daling, stm., China	A9	42
Dalizi, China	C7	38
Dalkola, India	F11	54
Dallas, Ga., U.S.	D14	122
Dallas, Or., U.S.	F3	136
Dallas, Pa., U.S.	C9	114
Dallas, Tx., U.S.	B11	130
Dallas, Wi., U.S.	F7	118
Dallas Center, Ia., U.S.	C4	118
Dallas City, Il., U.S.	D6	120
Dalli Rājhara, India	H8	54
Dall Island, i., Ak., U.S.	E13	140
Dall Lake, l., Ak., U.S.	D7	140
Dalmacija (Dalmatia), hist. reg., Eur.	G12	22
Dalmatia, hist. reg., Eur.	G12	22
Dalmau, India	E8	54
Dal'negorsk, Russia	B11	38
Dal'nerečensk, Russia	B11	36
Dal'nyk, Ukr.	C17	26
Daloa, C. Iv.	H3	64
Dalqū, Sudan	C6	62
Dalroy, Ab., Can.	E17	138
Dalrymple, Mount, mtn., Austl.	C7	76
Dalsing Sarai, India	F10	54
Dāltenganj, India	F10	54
Dalton, Ga., U.S.	C13	122
Dalton, Ma., U.S.	B12	114
Dalton, Oh., U.S.	D4	114
Dalton, Ne., U.S.	F10	126
Daludalu, Indon.	C2	50
Dalupiri Island, i., Phil.	A3	52
Dalwallinu, Austl.	F3	74
Daly, stm., Austl.	B6	74
Daly City, Ca., U.S.	F3	134
Daly Lake, l., Sk., Can.	D9	106
Daly Waters, Austl.	C6	74
Dam, stm., China	B14	54
Dāmān, India	H4	54
Damān and Diu, state, India	H4	54
Damanhûr, Egypt	G1	58
Damanzhuang, China	B7	42
Damão, Pulau, i., Indon.	G8	44
Damaraland, hist. reg., Nmb.	B3	70
Damascus see Dimashq, Syria	E7	58
Damascus, Ar., U.S.	B5	122
Damascus, Ga., U.S.	F14	122
Damascus, Md., U.S.	E8	114
Damaturu, Nig.	G7	64
Damâvand, Qolleh-ye, vol., Iran	B7	56
Damba, Ang.	B2	68
Dambarta, Nig.	G6	64
Damboa, Nig.	G7	64
Dâmbovița, state, Rom.	E12	26
Dâmbovița, stm., Rom.	D12	26
Dam Doi, Viet.	H7	48
Dāmghān, Iran	B7	56
Damiao, China	C1	42
Damietta see Dumyât, Egypt	G2	58
Damietta Mouth see Dumyât, Masabb, mth., Egypt	G3	58
Daming, China	C6	42
Dāmodar, stm., India	G11	54
Damoh, India	G7	54
Damongo, Ghana	H4	64
Dampier, Austl.	D3	74
Dampier, Selat, strt., Indon.	F9	44
Dampier Land, pen., Austl.	C4	74
Dampier Strait, strt., Pap. N. Gui.	b4	79a
Dâmrei, Chuŏr Phnum, mts., Camb.	G7	48
Damxung, China	C13	54
Dan, stm., U.S.	H6	114
Dan, In., U.S.	I2	112
Dana, Indon.	C3	50
Danakil, reg., Afr.	E8	62
Danané, C. Iv.	H3	64
Da Nang, Viet.	D9	48
Danao, Phil.	E5	52
Dānāpur, India	F10	54
Danba, China	E5	36
Danbury, Ct., U.S.	C12	114
Danbury, Ne., U.S.	A8	128
Danby Lake, l., Ca., U.S.	I1	132
Dandeli, India	D2	53
Dandenong, Austl.	K5	76
Dandong, China	D5	38
Dandridge, Tn., U.S.	H2	114
Danfeng, China	E4	42
Danforth, Me., U.S.	E9	110
Dangan Liedao, is., China	J6	42
Dangara, Taj.	B10	56
Dangchang, China	E5	36
Danger Point, c., S. Afr.	I4	70
Danggali Conservation Park, p.o.i., Austl.	I3	76
Dangila, Eth.	E7	62
Dangriga, Belize	D3	102
Dangshan, China	D7	42
Dani, Indon.	F5	44
Dangtu, China	F8	42
Dan-Gulbi, Nig.	G6	64
Dangyang, China	F4	42
Daniel, Wy., U.S.	H16	136
Daniel-Johnson, Barrage, dam, Qc., Can.	E17	106
Daniëlskuil, S. Afr.	F6	70
Danielson, Ct., U.S.	C13	114
Daniels Pass, p., Ut., U.S.	C5	132
Danielsville, Ga., U.S.	B2	116
Danilov, Russia	G18	8
Danilovka, Kaz.	D12	32
Daning, China	I4	42
Danjiangkou Shuiku, res., China	E4	42
Danjo-guntō, is., Japan	G1	40
Danli, Hond.	E4	102
Danmark Fjord, b., Grnld.	A22	141
Dannebrog, Ne., U.S.	F14	126
Dannenberg, Ger.	C6	16
Dannevirke, N.Z.	E7	80
Danshui, China	J6	42
Dansville, N.Y., U.S.	B8	114
Dante, Va., U.S.	H3	114
Dantewāra, India	B5	53
Danube, stm., Eur.	F11	6
Danube, Mouths of the, mth., Eur.	D15	26
Danubyu, Mya.	D2	48
Danvers, Il., U.S.	D8	120
Danville, Ar., U.S.	B5	122
Danville, Ca., U.S.	F4	134
Danville, Ga., U.S.	D2	116
Danville, Il., U.S.	H2	112
Danville, In., U.S.	I3	112
Danville, Ky., U.S.	G13	120
Danville, Oh., U.S.	D3	114
Danville, Pa., U.S.	D9	114
Danville, Va., U.S.	H6	114
Danville, Wa., U.S.	B8	136
Danyang, China	F8	42
Danzhai, China	H2	42
Danzig see Gdańsk, Pol.	B14	16
Danzig, Gulf of see Gdansk, Gulf of, b., Eur.	B15	16
Daocheng, China	F5	36
Daodi, China	B8	42
Daojiang, China	H5	42
Daoukro, C. Iv.	H4	64
Daoxian, China	H4	42
Dapaong, Togo	G5	64
Daphabum, mtn., India	C8	46
Daphnae, hist., Egypt	H3	58
Dapoli, India	C1	53
Da Qaidam, China	D4	36
Daqing, China	B10	36
Dara, Sen.	F1	64
Dar'ā, state, Syria	F7	58
Dārāb, Iran	D7	56
Dārāban, Pak.	C3	54
Darabani, Rom.	A13	26
Darasun, Russia	F11	34
Đaravica, mtn., Serb.	G7	26
Darb al-Hajj, Jabal, mtn., Jord.	H6	58
Darbhanga, India	E10	54
Darby, Mt., U.S.	D12	136
Dardanelle, Ar., U.S.	B5	122
Dardanelle Lake, res., Ar., U.S.	B5	122
Dardanelles see Çanakkale Boğazi, strt., Tur.	C9	28
Dar-el-Beida see Casablanca, Mor.	C3	64
Darfo, Italy	E7	22
Dargai, Pak.	A3	54
Dargan-Ata, Turkmen.	A9	56
Dargaville, N.Z.	B5	80
Dargol, Niger	G5	64
Darica, Tur.	C12	28
Darién, Col.	F3	86
Darién, Ga., U.S.	E4	116
Darien, Parque Nacional, p.o.i., Pan.	D2	86
Darién, Serranía del, mts.	C2	86
Darjiling, India	E12	54
Dark Head, c., St. Vin.	o11	105e
Darlag, China	F4	36
Darling, S. Afr.	H4	70
Darling, stm., Austl.	C8	122
Darling, stm., Austl.	I4	76
Darling Downs, reg., Austl.	F8	76
Darling Range, mts., Austl.	F3	74
Darlington, Eng., U.K.	G11	12
Darlington, Wi., U.S.	B7	120
Darlington Dam, res., S. Afr.	H7	70
Darlot, Lake, l., Austl.	E4	74
Darłowo, Pol.	B12	16
Darmstadt, Ger.	G4	16
Darnah, Libya	A4	62
Darnall, S. Afr.	F10	70
Darney, Fr.	F15	14
Darnley, Cape, c., Ant.	B11	81
Darnley Bay, b., N.T., Can.	B6	106
Darr, stm., Austl.	D4	76
Darregueira, Arg.	H6	92
Darreh Gaz, Iran	B8	56
Darrington, Wa., U.S.	B5	136
Darrouzett, Tx., U.S.	E8	128
Dart, Cape, c., Ant.	C27	81
Dartmoor, for., Eng., U.K.	K9	12
Dartmoor National Park, p.o.i., Eng., U.K.	K9	12
Dartmouth, N.S., Can.	F13	110
Dartmouth, Eng., U.K.	K9	12
Dartmouth, Lake, l., Austl.	E5	76
Dartmouth Reservoir, res., Austl.	K6	76
Daru, Pap. N. Gui.	b3	79a
Daruvar, Cro.	E14	22
Darvaza, Turkmen.	A8	56
Darwha, India	H6	54
Darwin, Austl.	B6	74
Darwin, Bahía, b., Chile	I2	90
Darya Khān, Pak.	C3	54
Dashbalbar, Mong.	B7	36
Dashitou, China	C8	38
Dašhovuz, Turkmen.	A8	56
Dasht, stm., Pak.	D9	56
Dashur, Pyramides de, hist., Egypt	I1	58
Dashutang, China	A6	48
Dasol Bay, b., Phil.	C2	52
Dastgardān, Iran	C8	56
Datang, China	I3	42
Datia, India	F7	54
Datian, China	I7	42
Datian Ding, mtn., China	J4	42
Datong, China	B5	42
Datong, stm., China	D5	36
Datong Shan, mts., China	D4	36
Datu, stm., Asia	E4	44
Datu Piang, Phil.	G5	52
Daua (Dawa), stm., Afr.	F8	62
Daudnagar, India	F10	54
Daugai, Lith.	F7	10
Daugavpils, Lat.	E9	10
Dauin, Phil.	F4	52
Daule, stm., Ec.	H1	86
Daund, India	B2	53
Daung Kyun, i., Mya.	F3	48
Dauphin, Mb., Can.	C13	124
Dauphin, stm., Mb., Can.	C15	124
Dauphiné, hist. reg., Fr.	E11	18
Dauphin Island, Al., U.S.	G10	122
Dauphin Island, i., Al., U.S.	G10	122
Dauphin Lake, l., Mb., Can.	C13	124
Daura, Nig.	G6	64
Dāvangere, India	D2	53
Davao, Phil.	G5	52
Davao, Gulf of, b., Phil.	G5	52
Davenport, Ia., U.S.	C7	120
Davenport, Ok., U.S.	B2	122
Davenport, Wa., U.S.	C8	136
Davenport Downs, Austl.	D3	76
Davey, Port, b., Austl.	o12	77a
David, Pan.	H6	102
David City, Ne., U.S.	F15	126
Davidson, Sk., Can.	C7	124
Davidson Mountains, mts., Ak., U.S.	C11	140
Davie, Fl., U.S.	J5	116
Davis, Ca., U.S.	E4	134
Davis, Ok., U.S.	G11	128
Davis, W.V., U.S.	E6	114
Davis, sci., Ant.	B12	81
Davis, Mount, mtn., Pa., U.S.	E6	114
Davisboro, Ga., U.S.	C3	116
Davis Dam, dam, U.S.	I2	132
Davis Inlet, Nf., Can.	D18	106
Davis Sea, s., Ant.	B11	81
Davis Strait, strt., N.A.	D17	141
Davos, Switz.	D6	22
Davy, W.V., U.S.	G4	114
Davyd-Haradok, Bela.	H9	10
Dawa (Daua), stm., Afr.	F8	62
Dawei (Tavoy), Mya.	E4	48
Dawna Range, mts., Mya.	D4	48
Dawson, Yk., Can.	C3	106
Dawson, Ga., U.S.	F14	122
Dawson, Mn., U.S.	G2	118
Dawson, Ne., U.S.	D1	120
Dawson, stm., Austl.	E7	76
Dawson, Isla, i., Chile	J2	90
Dawson, Mount, mtn., B.C., Can.	E13	138
Dawson Bay, b., Mb., Can.	B13	124
Dawson Creek, B.C., Can.	D7	106
Dawson Inlet, Nu., Can.	C12	106
Dawson Range, mts., Yk., Can.	C3	106
Dawsonville, Ga., U.S.	B1	116
Dax, Fr.	F4	18
Daxian, China	F2	42
Daxing, China	B7	42
Daxu, China	I4	42
Daxue Shan, mts., China	F5	36
Dayang, stm., China	D5	38
Dayangshu, China	B9	36
Dayao, China	F5	36
Daye, China	F6	42
Daylesford, Austl.	K5	76
Daymán, stm., Ur.	E9	92
Dayong, China	G4	42
Dayr az-Zawr, Syria	B4	56
Dayr Ḥāfir, Syria	B8	58
Daysland, Ab., Can.	D18	138
Dayton, Oh., U.S.	E1	114
Dayton, Or., U.S.	E3	136
Dayton, Tn., U.S.	B13	122
Dayton, Tx., U.S.	G4	122
Dayton, Wa., U.S.	D9	136
Dayton, Wy., U.S.	C5	126
Daytona Beach, Fl., U.S.	G5	116
Dayu, China	I6	42
Da Yunhe (Grand Canal), can., China	E8	42
Dazhu, China	F2	42
Dazkiri, Tur.	F12	28
De Aar, S. Afr.	G7	70
Deadhorse, Ak., U.S.	B10	140
Deadman's Cay, Bah.	A10	102
Deadwood, S.D., U.S.	C9	126
Deakin, Austl.	F5	74
Deal, Eng., U.K.	J14	12
Dealesville, S. Afr.	F7	70
Deal Island, Md., U.S.	F10	114
De'an, China	G6	42
Deán Funes, Arg.	E5	92
Deans Dundas Bay, b., N.T., Can.	B16	140
Dearborn, Mi., U.S.	B2	114
Dearg, Beinn, mtn., Scot., U.K.	D8	12
Dease, stm., B.C., Can.	D5	106
Dease Arm, b., N.T., Can.	B6	106
Dease Strait, strt., Nu., Can.	B9	106
Death Valley, Ca., U.S.	G9	134
Death Valley, val., Ca., U.S.	G9	134
Death Valley National Park, p.o.i., U.S.	G8	134
Deatsville, Al., U.S.	E12	122
Deauville, Fr.	E8	14
Debar, Mac.	B3	28
De Bary, Fl., U.S.	H4	116
Debe, Trin.	s12	105f
De Berry, Tx., U.S.	E4	122
Dębica, Pol.	F17	16
Dębno, Pol.	E17	16
Débo, Lac, l., Mali	F4	64
Deborah West, Lac, l., Austl.	F3	74
Deboyne Islands, is., Pap. N. Gui.	B10	74
Debre Birhan, Eth.	F7	62
Debrecen, Hung.	B8	26
Debre Mark'os, Eth.	E7	62
Debre Tabor, Eth.	E7	62
Debre Zeyit, Eth.	F7	62
Debrzno, Pol.	C13	16
Decatur, Ga., U.S.	C1	116
Decatur, Il., U.S.	E9	120
Decatur, In., U.S.	H4	112
Decatur, Mi., U.S.	F3	112
Decatur, Ms., U.S.	E9	122
Decatur, Ne., U.S.	B1	120
Decatur, Tn., U.S.	B14	122
Decaturville, Tn., U.S.	B10	122
Decazeville, Fr.	E8	18
Deccan, plat., India	B4	53
Decelles, Réservoir, res., Qc., Can.	F15	106
Deception, stm., Bots.	B6	70
Deception, Mount, mtn., Wa., U.S.	C3	136
Decherd, Tn., U.S.	B12	122
Dechhu, India	E4	54
Děčín, Czech Rep.	F10	16
Decize, Fr.	H12	14
Decker Lake, B.C., Can.	B5	138
Decorah, Ia., U.S.	H7	118
Dedaye, Mya.	D2	48
Dededo, Guam	i10	78c
Dedegöl Tepesi, mtn., Tur.	F14	28
De Doorns, S. Afr.	H4	70
Dédougou, Burkina	G4	64
Dedovichi, Russia	E20	10
Dedovsk, Russia	E20	10
Dee, stm., Scot., U.K.	D10	12
Dee, stm., U.K.	I9	12
Deenwood, Ga., U.S.	E3	116
Deep Creek Mts., U.S.	D4	132
Deep Creek, stm., Ms., U.S.	D8	122
Deep River, On., Can.	B12	112
Deep River, Ia., U.S.	C5	120
Deepwater, Mo., U.S.	F4	120
Deep Well, Austl.	D6	74
Deering, Ak., U.S.	C7	140
Deer Island, i., N.B., Can.	F10	110
Deer Isle, Me., U.S.	F8	110
Deer Lake, Nf., Can.	j22	107a
Deer Lodge, Mt., U.S.	D14	136
Deer Park, Al., U.S.	F10	122
Deer Park, Wa., U.S.	C9	136
Deer Trail, Co., U.S.	B4	128
Deerpass Bay, b., N.T., Can.	B6	106
Deer River, Mn., U.S.	D5	118
Defiance, Oh., U.S.	C1	114
Defiance, Mount, mtn., Or., U.S.	E5	136
De Funiak Springs, Fl., U.S.	G12	122
Dêgê, China	E4	36
Degeh Bur, Eth.	F8	62
Dégelis, Qc., Can.	C8	110
Degerfors, Swe.	G6	8
Deggendorf, Ger.	H8	16
Değirmendere, Tur.	E10	28
De Gray Lake, res., Ar., U.S.	C5	122
De Grey, stm., Austl.	D3	74
Dehalak' Desêt, i., Erit.	D8	62
Dehalwala-Mount Lavinia, Sri L.	H4	53
Dehlorān, Iran	C6	56
Dehra Dūn, India	C7	54
Dehra Dūn Cantonment, India	C6	54
Dehri, India	F10	54
Dei Mawās, Egypt	K1	58
Dej, Rom.	B10	26
Deje, Swe.	G5	8
De Kalb, Il., U.S.	C9	120
De Kalb, Ms., U.S.	E10	122
De Kalb, Tx., U.S.	D4	122
Dekese, D.R.C.	E4	66
Deke Sokehs, i., Micron.	m11	78d
Dékoa, C.A.R.	C3	66
Delamere, Austl.	B6	74
De Land, Fl., U.S.	H5	116
Delano, Mn., U.S.	F5	118

Name	Map Ref.	Page

Delaport Point, c., Bah. — m18 104f
Delapu, China — C13 54
Delarof Islands, is., Ak., U.S. — g23 140a
Delaware, Oh., U.S. — D1 112
Delaware, Ok., U.S. — H2 120
Delaware, state, U.S. — F10 114
Delaware, stm., Ks., U.S. — E2 120
Delaware, stm., U.S. — D10 114
Delaware, East Branch, stm., U.S. — B10 114
Delaware, West Branch, stm., U.S. — B11 114
Delaware Bay, b., U.S. — E10 114
Delaware City, De., U.S. — E10 114
Delburne, Ab., Can. — D17 138
Del Campillo, Arg. — G5 92
Del City, Ok., U.S. — F11 128
Delegate, Austl. — K7 76
Delémont, Switz. — C4 22
De Leon, Tx., U.S. — B9 130
Delfinópolis, Braz. — K2 88
Délfoi, sci., Grc. — E5 28
Delft, Neth. — B13 14
Delft Island, i., Sri L. — G4 53
Deltzijl, Neth. — A15 14
Delgado, Cabo, c., Moz. — C7 68
Delger, stm., Mong. — G8 34
Delgerhet, Mong. — B7 36
Delhi, On., Can. — F9 112
Delhi, India — D6 54
Delhi, Ia., U.S. — B6 120
Delhi, La., U.S. — E7 122
Delhi, N.Y., U.S. — B11 114
Delhi, state, India — D6 54
Delia, Ab., Can. — E18 138
Deliblato, Serb. — E8 26
Delicias, Mex. — A6 100
Delight, Ar., U.S. — C5 122
Delijān, Iran — C7 56
Deline, N.T., Can. — B6 106
Delingde, Russia — B11 34
Delingha, China — D4 36
Dēlinkānis, hill, Lat. — C9 10
Delisle, Sk., Can. — C6 124
Delitzsch, Ger. — E8 16
Dell City, Tx., U.S. — C2 130
Delle, Fr. — G16 14
Dellys, Alg. — H14 20
Del Mar, Ca., U.S. — K8 134
Delmar, Ia., U.S. — B6 120
Delmar, Md., U.S. — F10 114
Delmarva Peninsula, pen., U.S. — F10 114
Delmas, Sk., Can. — B5 124
Delmenhorst, Ger. — C4 16
Delmiro Gouveia, Braz. — E7 88
Delnice, Cro. — E11 22
Del Norte, Co., U.S. — D2 128
De-Longa, ostrova, is., Russia — A19 34
De Long Mountains, mts., Ak., U.S. — C7 140
Deloraine, Mb., Can. — E13 124
Delorme, Lac, l., Qc., Can. — E16 106
Delos see Dílos, sci., Grc. — F8 28
Delphi, In., U.S. — H3 112
Delphi see Délfoi, sci., Grc. — E5 28
Delphos, Ks., U.S. — B11 128
Delportshoop, S. Afr. — F7 70
Delray Beach, Fl., U.S. — J5 116
Del Río, Tx., U.S. — E7 130
Delta, Co., U.S. — E8 132
Delta, Mo., U.S. — G7 120
Delta, Ut., U.S. — D4 132
Delta Amacuro, state, Ven. — C11 86
Delta Beach, Mb., Can. — D15 124
Delta City, Ms., U.S. — D8 122
Delta Downs, Austl. — C8 74
Delta Junction, Ak., U.S. — D10 140
Delta Peak, mtn., B.C., Can. — D4 106
Del Valle, Tx., U.S. — D10 130
Del Verme Falls, wtfl., Eth. — F8 62
Delvinë, Alb. — E14 24
Demak, Indon. — G7 50
Demarcation Point, c., Ak., U.S. — C11 140
Demavend, Mount see Damāvand, Qolleh-ye, vol., Iran — B7 56
Demba, D.R.C. — F4 66
Dembī, Eth. — F7 62
Dembia, C.A.R. — C4 66
Dembī Dolo, Eth. — F6 62
Demidov, Russia — E14 10
Deming, N.M., U.S. — K9 132
Demini, stm., Braz. — H10 86
Demirci, Tur. — D11 28
Demirköprü Baraji, res., Tur. — E11 28
Demirköy, Tur. — B10 28
Demjanka, stm., Russia — C12 32
Demjanovo, Russia — F22 8
Demjanskoe, Russia — C11 32
Demmin, Ger. — C8 16
Demmitt, Ab., Can. — A11 138
Demopolis, Al., U.S. — E11 122
Demorest, Ga., U.S. — B2 116
Dempo, Gunung, vol., Indon. — F3 50
Demta, Indon. — F11 44
Demin, Fr. — D12 14
Denali, Ak., U.S. — D10 140
Denali National Park, Ak., U.S. — D10 140
Denan, Eth. — F8 62
Denau, Uzb. — G11 32
Den Burg, Neth. — A13 14
Denbigh, Indon. — E5 50
Dendermonde (Termonde), Bel. — C12 14
Deng Deng, Cam. — C2 66
Dengkou, China — A2 42
Dênggên, China — E4 36
Dengxian, China — E5 42
Denham, Austl. — E2 74
Denham, Mount, mtn., Jam. — i13 104d
Denham Range, mts., Austl. — C6 76
Denham Springs, La., U.S. — G8 122
Den Helder (Helder), Neth. — B13 14
Dénia, Spain — F11 20
Deniliquin, Austl. — J5 76
Deniskoviči, Russia — H14 10
Denison, Tx., U.S. — D2 122
Denison, Mount, vol., Ak., U.S. — E9 140
Denizli, Tur. — F12 28
Denizli, state, Tur. — F12 28
Denkanikota, India — E3 53
Denmark, Austl. — F3 74
Denmark, S.C., U.S. — C4 116
Denmark, Wi., U.S. — D2 112
Denmark, ctry., Eur. — D10 6
Denmark Strait, strt. — m7 105c
Dennery, St. Luc. — m7 105c
Denpasar, Indon. — H9 50
Denton, Md., U.S. — F10 114
Denton, Mt., U.S. — C17 136
Denton, N.C., U.S. — A5 116
Denton, Tx., U.S. — H11 128
Denton Creek, stm., Tx., U.S. — H11 128
D'Entrecasteaux, Point, c., Austl. — F3 74
D'Entrecasteaux Islands, is., Pap. N. Gui. — D6 72
Denver, Co., U.S. — B3 128
Denver, Pa., U.S. — D9 114
Denver City, Tx., U.S. — A5 130
Deoband, India — D6 54
Deogarh, India — F7 54
Deogarh, India — H4 54
Deogarh, India — G9 54
Deogarh Hills, hills, India — G9 54
Deoghar, India — F11 54
Deori, India — G7 54
Deoria, India — E9 54

De Pere, Wi., U.S. — D1 112
Depew, N.Y., U.S. — B2 122
Depoe Bay, Or., U.S. — F2 136
Depok, Indon. — G5 50
Deposit, N.Y., U.S. — B10 114
Depue, Il., U.S. — C8 120
Dêqên, China — F4 36
Deqing, China — J4 42
Dhanbād, India — G11 54
De Queen, Ar., U.S. — C4 122
De Quincy, La., U.S. — G5 122
Dera, Lach, stm., Afr. — D8 66
Dera Bugti, Pak. — C3 54
Dera Ghāzi Khān, Pak. — C4 54
Dera Ismāīl Khān, Pak. — C3 54
Derawar Fort, Pak. — D3 54
Derbent, Russia — F7 32
Derby, Austl. — C4 74
Derby, Eng., U.K. — I11 12
Derby, Ks., U.S. — D11 128
Derby, N.Y., U.S. — B6 114
Dereköy, Tur. — B10 28
De Ridder, La., U.S. — G5 122
Dermott, Ar., U.S. — D7 122
Dernieres, Isles, is., La., U.S. — H8 122
Dêrong, China — F4 36
Derry see Londonderry, N. Ire., U.K. — F6 12
Derry, N.H., U.S. — B14 114
Derudeb, Sudan — D7 62
Derventa, Bos. — E4 26
Derwent, Ab., Can. — C19 138
Derwent, stm., Austl. — o13 77a
Derwent, stm., Eng., U.K. — G12 12
Derwent Water, l., Eng., U.K. — G9 12
Derzhavinsk, Kaz. — D11 32
Desaguadero, stm., Arg. — F4 92
Desaguadero, stm., S.A. — G4 84
Désappointement, Îles du, is., Fr. Poly. — E12 72
Des Arc, Ar., U.S. — C7 122
Descabezado Grande, Volcán, vol., Chile — G2 92
Descanso, Braz. — C11 92
Descanso, Punta, c., Mex. — K9 134
Descartes, Fr. — C9 14
Deschambault Lake, l., Sk., Can. — E10 106
Deschutes, stm., Or., U.S. — E6 136
Desdunes, Haiti — C11 102
Desê, Eth. — F8 62
Desengaño, Punta, c., Arg. — I3 90
Deseret Peak, mtn., Ut., U.S. — C4 132
Deseronto, On., Can. — D12 112
Désert, stm., Qc., Can. — B13 112
Désert, Lac, l., Qc., Can. — B13 112
Desert Hot Springs, Ca., U.S. — J9 134
Desert Lake, l., Nv., U.S. — F8 134
Desert Peak, mtn., Ut., U.S. — B3 132
Desert Valley, val., Nv., U.S. — B7 134
Desha, Ar., U.S. — B7 122
Deshaies, Guad. — h5 105c
Deshler, Oh., U.S. — C1 114
Deshnok, India — E4 54
Desiderio Tello, Arg. — E4 92
Deskáti, Grc. — D4 28
Desloge, Mo., U.S. — G7 120
Des Moines, Ia., U.S. — C4 120
Des Moines, N.M., U.S. — E5 128
Des Moines, stm., U.S. — K7 118
Des Moines, East Fork, stm., U.S. — H4 118
Desna, stm., Eur. — D4 32
Desolación, Isla, i., Chile — J2 90
De Soto, Il., U.S. — G8 120
De Soto, Mo., U.S. — F7 120
Despatch, S. Afr. — H7 70
Despeñaperros, Desfiladero de, p., Spain — F7 20
Des Plaines, Il., U.S. — F1 112
Des Plaines, stm., U.S. — C9 120
Desroches, i., Sey. — m7 105c
Desruisseaux, St. Luc. — m7 105c
Dessau, Ger. — E8 16
Destruction Bay, Yk., Can. — C3 106
Desvres, Fr. — D10 14
Detčino, Russia — F19 10
Dete, Zimb. — D4 68
Detmold, Ger. — E4 16
Detour, Point, c., Mi., U.S. — C3 112
De Tour Village, Mi., U.S. — C5 112
Detrital Wash, stm., Az., U.S. — H2 132
Detroit, Mi., U.S. — B2 114
Detroit, Or., U.S. — F4 136
Detroit, Tx., U.S. — D3 122
Detroit Beach, Mi., U.S. — C2 114
Dettifoss, wtfl., Ice. — k31 8a
Det Udom, Thai. — E7 48
Detva, Slov. — H15 16
Deua National Park, p.o.i., Austl. — J7 76
Deülgaon Rāja, India — H5 54
Deutsche Bucht, b., Ger. — C4 16
Deutschlandsberg, Aus. — D12 22
Deux-Sèvres, state, Fr. — C5 18
Deva, Rom. — D9 26
Devakottai, India — G4 53
Dévaványa, Hung. — B7 26
Deventer, Neth. — B15 14
Deveron, stm., Scot., U.K. — D10 12
De Vaih Bárivā, India — G4 54
De View, Bayou, stm., Ar., U.S. — B8 122
Devikot, India — E3 54
Devils, stm., Tx., U.S. — E6 130
Devils Island see Diable, Île du, i., Fr. Gu. — B7 84
Devils Lake, l., N.D., U.S. — F15 124
Devils Lake, N.D., U.S. — F14 124
Devils Postpile National Monument, p.o.i., Ca., U.S. — F6 134
Devils Tower National Monument, p.o.i., Wy., U.S. — C8 126
Devine, B.C., Can. — F8 138
Devine, Tx., U.S. — E9 130
Deviatiny, Russia — F17 8
Devli, India — F5 54
Devoll, stm., Alb. — D14 24
Devon, Ab., Can. — C17 138
Devon Island, i., Nu., Can. — B8 141
Devonport, Austl. — n13 77a
Devoto, Arg. — E6 92
Devrek, Tur. — B14 28
Dewangan-lompo, Pulau, i., Indon. — F11 50
Dewar, Ok., U.S. — B3 122
Dewey, Ok., U.S. — H1 120
Deweyville, Tx., U.S. — G5 122
De Witt, Ar., U.S. — C7 122
De Witt, Ia., U.S. — C7 120
De Witt, N.Y., U.S. — A9 114
Dexing, China — G7 42
Dexter, Me., U.S. — E7 110
Dexter, Mi., U.S. — B2 114
Dexter, N.M., U.S. — H4 128
Dexter, N.Y., U.S. — D13 112
Dexterity Fiord, b., Nu., Can. — A16 106
Deyang, China — E5 36
Dey-Dey, Lake, l., Austl. — E6 74
Dezfūl, Iran — C6 56
Dezhou, China — C7 42
Deževa, mys, c., Russia — C27 34
Dezong, China — B13 54

Dhahran see Az̧-Z̧ahrān, Sau. Ar. — D6 56
Dhaka (Dacca), Bngl. — G13 54
Dhaka, state, Bngl. — F13 54
Dhamār, Yemen — G5 56
Dhāmpur, India — D7 54
Dhamtari, India — H8 54
Dhanbād, India — G11 54
Dhandhuka, India — G3 54
Dhangadhī, Nepal — D8 54
D'Hanis, Tx., U.S. — E8 130
Dhankuta, Nepal — E11 54
Dhār, India — G5 54
Dharān, Nepal — E11 54
Dhārāpuram, India — F3 53
Dharmābād, India — B3 53
Dharmapuri, India — E4 53
Dharmavaram, India — D3 53
Dharmjaygarh, India — G9 54
Dharmshāla, India — B6 54
Dhaulpur, India — E6 54
Dhawalāgiri, mtn., Nepal — D9 54
Dhenkānāl, India — H10 54
Dherinia, Cyp. — C4 58
Dhofar see Z̧ufar, reg., Yemen — F7 56
Dholka, India — G4 54
Dhone, India — D3 53
Dhoomadheere, Som. — D8 66
Dhorāji, India — H3 54
Dhrāngadhra, India — G3 54
Dhrol, India — G3 54
Dhubri, India — E13 54
Dhule, India — H5 54
Dhulian, India — F12 54
Dhupgāri, India — E12 54
Dhuusamarreeb, Som. — C9 66
Diable, Île du (Devils Island), i., Fr. Gu. — B7 84
Diable, Pointe du, c., Mart. — k7 105c
Diables, Morne aux, vol., Dom. — i5 105c
Diablo, Canyon, p., Az., U.S. — H5 132
Diablo, Mount, mtn., Ca., U.S. — F4 134
Diablo, Pico del, mtn., Mex. — F4 98
Diablo Range, mts., Ca., U.S. — G4 134
Diablotins, Morne, vol., Dom. — j6 105c
Diaca, Moz. — C6 68
Diakon, Mali — G2 64
Diakovce, Sen. — G2 64
Diamante, Arg. — F7 92
Diamante, stm., Arg. — G4 92
Diamantina, Braz. — J4 88
Diamantina, stm., Austl. — E2 76
Diamantina Lakes, Austl. — D3 76
Diamantino, Braz. — F6 84
Diamond, Mo., U.S. — G3 120
Diamond Harbour, India — G12 54
Diamond Islets, is., Austl. — A8 76
Diamond Peak, mtn., Id., U.S. — F13 136
Diamond Peak, mtn., Wa., U.S. — D9 136
Diana Bay, b., Can. — B16 106
Dianbai, China — K4 42
Dian Chi, l., China — G5 36
Dianjiang, China — F2 42
Dianópolis, Braz. — F2 88
Diapaga, Burkina — G5 64
Diaz, Ar., U.S. — B7 122
Diaz Point, c., Nmb. — E2 70
Dibai, India — D7 54
Dibaya, D.R.C. — F4 66
Dibeng, S. Afr. — E6 70
D'Iberville, Ms., U.S. — G9 122
Dibete, Bots. — C8 70
Dibrugarh, India — C7 46
Dickens, Tx., U.S. — H8 128
Dickinson, N.D., U.S. — A10 126
Dickinson, Tx., U.S. — H3 122
Dickson, Tn., U.S. — H10 120
Didao, China — B9 38
Didcot, Eng., U.K. — J11 12
Didwāna, India — E5 54
Didymóteicho, Grc. — B9 28
Diebling, Ger. — G4 16
Dieciocho de Julio, Ur. — F11 92
Diefenbaker, Lake, res., Sk., Can. — C7 124
Diego de Almagro, Chile — C2 92
Diego de Almagro, Isla, i., Chile — J1 90
Diego de Ocampo, Pico, mtn., Dom. Rep. — C12 102
Diego-Suarez see Antsiranana, Madag. — C8 68
Diemuchuoke, China — B7 54
Dien Bien, Viet. — B6 48
Dien Bien Phu see Dien Bien, Viet. — B6 48
Diepholz, Ger. — D4 16
Dieppe, N.B., Can. — D12 110
Dieppe, Fr. — E9 14
Dieppe Bay Town, St. K/N. — C2 105a
Dierks, Ar., U.S. — C4 122
Diest, Bel. — D14 14
Dieulefit, Fr. — E10 18
Dieveniškės, Lith. — F8 10
Diez de Octubre, Mex. — C6 100
Dif, Kenya — D8 66
Diffa, Niger — G7 64
Differdange, Lux. — E14 14
Dig, India — E6 54
Digba, D.R.C. — D5 66
Digboi, India — C8 46
Digby, N.S., Can. — F11 110
Digby Neck, pen., N.S., Can. — F10 110
Digges Islands, is., Nu., Can. — C15 106
Dighton, Ks., U.S. — C8 128
Diglūr, India — B3 53
Digne-les-Bains, Fr. — E12 18
Digoin, Fr. — C9 18
Digos, Phil. — G5 52
Digras, India — H6 54
Digul, stm., Indon. — G10 44
Dihok, Iraq — B5 56
Dijlah (Tigris), stm., Asia — C5 56
Dijon, Fr. — G14 14
Dikaja, Russia — A22 10
Dike, Ia., U.S. — B5 120
Dikhil, Dji. — E8 62
Dikili, Tur. — D9 28
Dikirnis, Egypt — G2 58
Dikodougou, C. Iv. — H3 64
Diksmuide, Bel. — C11 14
Dikson, Russia — B5 34
Dikwa, Nig. — G7 64
Dīla, Eth. — F7 62
Dilek Yarımdası Milli Parkı, p.o.i., Tur. — F10 28
Dili, E. Timor — G8 44
Dilenburg, Ger. — F4 16
Diller, Ne., U.S. — A12 128
Dilley, Tx., U.S. — F8 130
Dilling, Sudan — E5 62
Dillingen an der Donau, Ger. — H6 16
Dillingham, Ak., U.S. — E8 140
Dillon, Mt., U.S. — E14 136
Dillon, S.C., U.S. — B6 116
Dillon Mountain, mtn., N.M., U.S. — J8 132
Dilwyn, Va., U.S. — G7 114
Dilolo, D.R.C. — G4 66
Dilos, sci., Grc. — F8 28
Dilworth, Mn., U.S. — H17 124
Dīmāpur, India — C7 46
Dimashq (Damascus), Syria — E7 58
Dimashq, state, Syria — E7 58
Dimbelenge, D.R.C. — F4 66
Dimboola, Austl. — A5 76
Dimitrovgrad, Blg. — G12 26

Dimitrovgrad, Russia — D8 32
Dimitsána, Grc. — F4 28
Dimki, India — H7 54
Dimlang, mtn., Nig. — H7 64
Dimmitt, Tx., U.S. — G6 128
Dimona, Isr. — G6 58
Dinagat, Phil. — E5 52
Dinagat Island, i., Phil. — E5 52
Dinājpur, Bngl. — F12 54
Dinan, Fr. — F6 14
Dinant, Bel. — D13 14
Dinar, Tur. — E13 28
Dinard, Fr. — F6 14
Dinaric Alps (Dinara), mts., Eur. — G13 22
Dindi, stm., India — C4 53
Dindigul, India — F4 53
Dindori, India — G8 54
Dingalan Bay, b., Phil. — C3 52
Ding'an, China — I6 42
Dingan, China — D7 76
Dingolfing, Ger. — H8 16
Dingshuzhen, China — F8 42
Dingtao, China — D6 42
Dinguiraye, Gui. — G2 64
Dingwall, N.S., Can. — D16 110
Dingxian, China — B6 42
Dingxiang, China — B5 42
Dingyuan, China — E7 42
Dinh'Àta, India — E12 54
Dinh Hoa, Viet. — B7 48
Dinh Lap, Viet. — B8 48
Dinkelsbühl, Ger. — G6 16
Dinnebito Wash, stm., Az., U.S. — H5 132
Dinorwic, On., Can. — B6 118
Dinorwic Lake, l., On., Can. — B6 118
Dinosaur National Monument, p.o.i., U.S. — C8 132
Dinsmore, Sk., Can. — C6 124
Dinuba, Ca., U.S. — G6 134
Dinwiddie, Va., U.S. — G8 114
Dionísio Cerqueira, Braz. — C11 92
Dioulouolou, Sen. — G1 64
Diourbel, Sen. — G1 64
Dīpālpur, Pak. — C4 54
Diplo, Pak. — F2 54
Dipolog, Phil. — F4 52
Dippoldiswalde, Ger. — F9 16
Dir, Pak. — B11 56
Diré, Mali — F4 64
Diré Dawa, Eth. — F8 62
Dirico, Ang. — D3 68
Dirj, Libya — A2 62
Dirk Hartog Island, i., Austl. — E2 74
Dirkou, Niger — F7 64
Dirranbandi, Austl. — G7 76
Disa, India — F4 54
Disappointment, Cape, c., S. Geor. — J9 90
Disappointment, Cape, c., Wa., U.S. — D2 136
Disappointment, Lake, l., Austl. — D4 74
Disaster Bay, b., Austl. — K8 76
Discovery Bay, b., Austl. — L3 76
Dishman, Wa., U.S. — C9 136
Disko see Qeqertarsuaq, i., Grnld. — D15 141
Disko Bugt, b., Grnld. — D15 141
Dismal, stm., Ne., U.S. — F12 126
Dispur, India — E13 54
Disraëli, Qc., Can. — E4 110
Distrito Capital, state, Col. — E4 86
Distrito Federal, state, Braz. — H2 88
Distrito Federal, state, Mex. — F9 100
Distrito Federal, state, Ven. — B8 86
Dis Ūq, Egypt — G1 58
Dithmarschen, reg., Ger. — B5 16
Diu, India — H3 54
Dive, can., Fr. — B5 18
Divenskaja, Russia — A12 10
Diveria, stm., Italy — D5 22
Divernon, Il., U.S. — E8 120
Divi Point, c., India — D5 53
Divin, Bela. — H14 10
Divinópolis, Braz. — K3 88
Divisor, Serra do, plat., S.A. — E3 84
Divnoe, Russia — E6 32
Divnogorsk, Russia — C16 32
Divo, C. Iv. — H3 64
Diwāl Qol, Afg. — A1 54
Dix, Ne., U.S. — F9 126
Dixie Valley, val., Nv., U.S. — D8 134
Dixon, Ca., U.S. — E4 134
Dixon, Il., U.S. — C8 120
Dixon, Ky., U.S. — G10 120
Dixon, Mo., U.S. — G5 120
Dixon, N.M., U.S. — E3 128
Dixon Entrance, strt., N.A. — E4 106
Diyarbakır, Tur. — B4 56
Dizhou, China — J2 42
Djado, Niger — E7 64
Djado, Plateau du, plat., Niger — E7 64
Djakarta see Jakarta, Indon. — G5 50
Djamâa, Alg. — C6 64
Djanet, Alg. — E6 64
Djaret, Oued, stm., Alg. — D5 64
Djat'kovo, Russia — G17 10
Djédi, Oued, stm., Alg. — C5 64
Djéma, C.A.R. — C5 66
Djenné, Mali — G4 64
Djenoun, Garet el, mtn., Alg. — D6 64
Djibo, Burkina — G4 64
Djibouti, Dji. — E8 62
Djibouti, ctry., Afr. — E8 62
Djoku-Punda, D.R.C. — F4 66
Djolu, D.R.C. — D4 66
Djougou, Benin — H5 64
Djourab, Erg du, sand, Chad — D3 62
Djugu, D.R.C. — D6 66
Djūrās, Swe. — F6 8
Djurtjuli, Russia — C8 32
Dmítrija Lapteva, proliv, strt., Russia — B16 34
Dmitrov, Russia — D20 10
Dneprovskoe, Russia — E16 10
Dnieper, stm., Eur. — F15 6
Dniester (Dnister), stm., Eur. — G19 16
Dnipro, stm., Ukr. — E5 32
Dnipropetrovs'k, Ukr. — E5 32
Dnistrovs'kyi lyman, l., Ukr. — C17 26
Dnjaprouska Buhski, kanal, can., Bela. — I8 10
Do, Lac, l., Mali — F4 64
Dôa, Moz. — D5 68
Doaktown, N.B., Can. — D10 110
Doangdoangan-Besar, Pulau, i., Indon. — F10 50
Doba, Chad — F3 62
Dobczyce, Pol. — G16 16
Döbeln, Ger. — E8 16
Doberai, Jazirah (Doberai Peninsula), pen., Indon. — F9 44
Doberai Peninsula see Doberai, Jazirah, pen., Indon. — F9 44
Dobo, Indon. — G9 44
Doboj, Bos. — E4 26
Dobre Miasto, Pol. — C16 16
Dobrič, Blg. — F14 26

Dobříš, Czech Rep. — G10 16
Dobrjanka, Russia — C9 32
Dobroe, Russia — C15 10
Dobroteasa, Rom. — E11 26
Dobruš, Bela. — H14 10
Dobruška, Czech Rep. — F12 16
Dobrzyń nad Wisła, Pol. — D15 16
Dobzha, China — D12 54
Doce, stm., Braz. — J6 88
Dock Junction, Ga., U.S. — E4 116
Doctor Cecilio Báez, Para. — B9 92
Doctor Coss, Mex. — I8 130
Doctor González, Mex. — I8 130
Doddridge, Ar., U.S. — D4 122
Dodecanese see Dodekánisos, is., Grc. — G10 28
Dodekanisoy (Dodecanese), is., Grc. — G10 28
Dodge Center, Mn., U.S. — G5 118
Dodge City, Ks., U.S. — D9 128
Dodgeville, Wi., U.S. — B7 120
Dodoma, Tan. — F7 66
Dodori, sci., Grc. — D3 28
Dodsland, Sk., Can. — C5 124
Dodson, Mt., U.S. — F5 124
Dodson, Tx., U.S. — G8 128
Doerun, Ga., U.S. — E1 116
Doetinchem, Neth. — C15 14
Dogai Coring, l., China — A12 54
Doğanbey, Tur. — E9 28
Doğanhisar, Tur. — E14 28
Dog Island, i., Fl., U.S. — H14 122
Dog Islands, is., Br. Vir. Is. — e9 104b
Dog Lake, l., Mb., Can. — C15 124
Dog Lake, l., On., Can. — C9 118
Dogliani, Italy — F4 22
Dōgo, i., Japan — C6 40
Do Gonbadān, Iran — C7 56
Dogondoutchi, Niger — G5 64
Dogu Karadeniz Dağları, mts., Tur. — A5 56
Doha see Ad-Dawhah, Qatar — D7 56
Dohrighāt, India — E9 54
Doiran, Lake, l., Eur. — B5 28
Doi Suthep-Pui National Park, p.o.i., Thai. — C4 48
Doka, Indon. — G9 44
Dokkum, Neth. — A14 14
Doksy, Czech Rep. — F10 16
Doland, S.D., U.S. — C14 126
Dolbeau, Qc., Can. — B4 110
Dol-de-Bretagne, Fr. — F7 14
Dole, Fr. — G14 14
Dolega, Pan. — H6 102
Dolgellau, Wales, U.K. — I9 12
Dolgij Most, Russia — C17 32
Dolgoščele, Russia — C20 8
Dolinsk, Russia — G17 34
Dolj, state, Rom. — E10 26
Dolní Dábnik, Blg. — F11 26
Dolný Kubín, Slov. — G15 16
Dolomites see Dolomiti, mts., Italy — D8 22
Dolomiti, mts., Italy — D8 22
Dolores, Arg. — H9 92
Dolores, Col. — F4 86
Dolores, Guat. — D3 102
Dolores, Mex. — H6 130
Dolores, Ur. — F8 92
Dolores, stm., U.S. — E7 132
Dolores Hidalgo, Mex. — E8 100
Dolphin, Cape, c., Falk. Is. — J5 90
Dolphin and Union Strait, strt., Nu., Can. — B7 106
Dolphin Head, mtn., Jam. — i12 104d
Dolyna, Ukr. — D13 16
Dolžicy, Russia — C12 10
Domažlice, Czech Rep. — G8 16
Dombás, Nor. — E3 8
Dombes, reg., Fr. — D11 18
Dombóvár, Hung. — C4 26
Dom Cavati, Braz. — J4 88
Dôme, Puy de, mtn., Fr. — D8 18
Dome Creek, B.C., Can. — C9 138
Domeyko, Chile — D2 92
Domeyko, Cordillera, mts., Chile — D3 90
Domfront, Fr. — F8 14
Domiciano Ribeiro, Braz. — D3 62
Domingo M. Irala, Para. — B10 92
Domingos Martins, Braz. — K5 88
Dominica, ctry., N.A. — l6 105c
Dominica Channel see Martinique Passage, strt., N.A. — k6 105c
Dominica, República see Dominican Republic, ctry., N.A. — D10 96
Dominican Republic, ctry., N.A. — D10 96
Dominica Passage, strt., N.A. — l6 105c
Dominion, Cape, c., Nu., Can. — B15 106
Dominion City, Mb., Can. — E16 124
Dom Joaquim, Braz. — J4 88
Domo, Eth. — F9 62
Domodedovo, Russia — E20 10
Domodossola, Italy — D5 22
Dom Pedrito, Braz. — E10 92
Dom Pedro, Braz. — C3 88
Dompu, Indon. — H11 50
Domremy, Sk., Can. — B8 124
Dom Yai, stm., Thai. — E7 48
Dom'yas'tir, Russia — H2 92
Don, stm., India — C2 53
Don, stm., Laos — E6 48
Don, stm., Scot., U.K. — D10 12
Donaduz, Arg. — C6 92
Donaghadee, N. Ire., U.K. — G7 12
Donald, Austl. — K4 76
Donaldson, Ar., U.S. — C6 122
Donaldsonville, La., U.S. — G7 122
Doñana, Parque Nacional de, p.o.i., Spain — H4 20
Donau, stm., Eur. — F11 6
Donaueschingen, Ger. — I4 16
Donauwörth, Ger. — H6 16
Don Benito, Spain — F5 20
Doncaster, Eng., U.K. — H11 12
Dondaicha, India — H5 54
Dondo, Ang. — B1 68
Dondo, Moz. — D5 68
Dondra Head, c., Sri L. — I5 53
Dondușeni, Mol. — A14 26
Donegal, Ire. — G4 12
Donegal, state, Ire. — G4 12
Donegal Bay, b., Ire. — G4 12
Donets'k, Ukr. — E5 32
Donetsk, Russia — E6 32

Dongjingcheng, China — B8 38
Dongxi, China — I2 42
Dongliao, stm., China — C5 38
Dong Nai, stm., Viet. — G8 48
Dongning, China — B9 38
Dongo, D.R.C. — D3 66
Dongou, Congo — D3 66
Dongping, China — D7 42
Dongping, China — K5 42
Dong San Shen (Manchuria), hist. reg., China — L4 42
Dongshan, China — I7 42
Dongshan Dao, i., China — J7 42
Dongtai, China — E9 42
Dongtai Hu, l., China — G5 42
Dongxi, China — G2 42
Dongxiang, China — G9 42
Dongyang, China — G9 42
Dongzhi, China — F7 42
Donie, Tx., U.S. — F2 122
Doniphan, Ne., U.S. — G14 126
Donja Stubica, Cro. — E12 22
Donjek, stm., Yk., Can. — C3 106
Don Martin, Mex. — G7 130
Donna, Tx., U.S. — H9 130
Donnacona, Qc., Can. — D5 110
Donnelly, Id., U.S. — F10 136
Donner, La., U.S. — H7 122
Donner Pass, p., Ca., U.S. — D5 134
Donner und Blitzen, stm., Or., U.S. — G8 136
Donnybrook, Austl. — F3 74
Donora, Pa., U.S. — D6 114
Donostia see Donostia-San Sebastián, Spain — A9 20
Donostia-San Sebastián, Spain — A9 20
Don Pedro Reservoir, res., Ca., U.S. — F5 134
Don Peninsula, pen., B.C., Can. — D2 138
Donskoj, Russia — G21 10
Doolow, Som. — D8 66
Doonerak, Mount, mtn., Ak., U.S. — C9 140
Doornik see Tournai, Bel. — D11 14
Door Peninsula, pen., Wi., U.S. — D2 112
Dor, Isr. — F5 58
Dora, Al., U.S. — D11 122
Dora, Lake, l., Austl. — D4 74
Dora Baltea, stm., Italy — E4 22
Dorado, P.R. — B3 104a
Doraville, Ga., U.S. — D14 122
Dorchester, On., Can. — E8 112
Dorchester, Eng., U.K. — K10 12
Dorchester, Ne., U.S. — G15 126
Dorchester, Cape, c., Nu., Can. — B15 106
Dordabis, Nmb. — C3 70
Dordogne, state, Fr. — D6 18
Dordogne, stm., Fr. — D8 18
Dordrecht, S. Afr. — G8 70
Dordrecht, Neth. — C13 14
Dore Lake, l., Sk., Can. — E9 106
Dore Lake, Sk., Can. — E9 106
Dorena, Or., U.S. — G4 136
Dorfen, Ger. — H8 16
Dorgali, Italy — D3 24
Dörgön nuur, l., Mong. — B3 36
Dori, Burkina — G4 64
Doring, stm., S. Afr. — G4 70
Dornbirn, Aus. — C6 22
Dornoch, Scot., U.K. — D9 12
Dorog, Hung. — B5 26
Dorogobuž, Russia — F16 10
Dorohoi, Rom. — A13 26
Dorokempo, Indon. — H11 50
Dorre Island, i., Austl. — E2 74
Dorrigo, Austl. — H9 76
Dorris, Ca., U.S. — B4 134
Dorsale, mts., Tun. — I3 24
Dort see Dordrecht, Neth. — C13 14
Dortmund, Ger. — E3 16
Dorton, Ky., U.S. — G3 114
Dörtyol, Tur. — B7 58
Dos, Canal Numero, can., Arg. — H9 92
Dosatuj, Russia — A8 36
Dos Bahías, Cabo, c., Arg. — H3 90
Dos Bocas, P.R. — B2 104a
Dôşemealtı, Tur. — F13 28
Dos Hermanas, Spain — G4 20
Dos Pos, Neth. Ant. — p23 104g
Dos Quebradas, Col. — E4 86
Dosso, Niger — G5 64
Dossor, Kaz. — E8 32
Dostyq, Kaz. — E14 32
Dothan, Al., U.S. — F13 122
Dotnuva, Lith. — E6 10
Dou, stm., China — B8 42
Douai, Fr. — D11 14
Douala, Cam. — D1 66
Douarnenez, Fr. — F4 14
Doublé, Pointe, c., Guad. — h7 105c
Double Island Point, c., Austl. — E9 76
Double Springs, Al., U.S. — C11 122
Doubletop Peak, mtn., Wy., U.S. — G16 136
Doubs, state, Fr. — G15 14
Doubs, stm., Eur. — H14 14
Doubtful Sound, strt., N.Z. — G2 80
Doubtless Bay, b., N.Z. — B5 80
Douentza, Mali — F4 64
Douga, stm., Iran — H3 24
Douglas, Mb., Can. — E14 124
Douglas, I. of Man — G8 12
Douglas, S. Afr. — F6 70
Douglas, Ak., U.S. — E13 140
Douglas, Az., U.S. — L7 132
Douglas, Ga., U.S. — E3 116
Douglas, Wy., U.S. — E7 126
Douglas Channel, strt., B.C., Can. — C1 138
Douglas Lake, B.C., Can. — F10 138
Douglas Lake, res., Tn., U.S. — I3 114
Douglasville, Ga., U.S. — D14 122
Doullens, Fr. — D11 14
Dourada, Serra, plat., Braz. — G1 88
Dourados, Braz. — D6 90
Dourbali, Chad — E3 62
Douro (Duero), stm., Eur. — G13 10
Dousk, Bela. — G13 10
Douz, Tun. — C6 64
Dove Creek, Co., U.S. — F7 132
Dover, Austl. — o13 77a
Dover, Eng., U.K. — J14 12
Dover, De., U.S. — E10 114
Dover, N.H., U.S. — G6 110
Dover, N.J., U.S. — D11 114
Dover, Oh., U.S. — D4 114
Dover, Ok., U.S. — E11 128
Dover, Tn., U.S. — H10 120
Dover, Strait of, strt., Eur. — K14 12
Dover-Foxcroft, Me., U.S. — E7 110
Doverfjell Nasjonalpark, p.o.i., Nor. — E3 8
Dow City, Ia., U.S. — C2 120
Dowlatābād, Iran — D8 56
Downey, Id., U.S. — H14 136
Downieville, Ca., U.S. — D5 134
Downing, Mo., U.S. — D5 120
Downingtown, Pa., U.S. — D10 114

Downpatrick – Elektrostal' I • 17

Name — Map Ref. — Page

Downpatrick, N. Ire., U.K. G7 12
Downs, Ks., U.S. B10 128
Downton, Mount, mtn., B.C., Can. D6 138
Dows, Ia., U.S. B4 120
Dowshī, Afg. B10 56
Doyle, Ca., U.S. C5 134
Doyles, Nf., Can. C17 110
Doylestown, Pa., U.S. D10 114
Doyline, La., U.S. E5 122
Dōzen, is., Japan C5 40
Dozier, Al., U.S. F12 122
Dra, Cap, c., Mor. D2 64
Dra'a, Hamada du, des., Alg. D3 64
Drâa, Oued, stm., Afr. D2 64
Drac, stm., Fr. E2 22
Dracena, Braz. D6 90
Drachten, Neth. A15 14
Dracut, Ma., U.S. B14 114
Dragalina, Rom. E14 26
Drăgănești-Vlașca, Rom. E12 26
Drăgășani, Rom. E11 26
Dragonera, Sa, i., Spain E13 20
Dragons Mouths, strt. s12 105f
Dragoon, Az., U.S. K6 132
Draguignan, Fr. F12 18
Drahičyn, Bela. H8 10
Drake, N.D., U.S. G13 124
Drakensberg, mts., Afr. F9 70
Drake Passage, strt. K8 82
Drakesboro, Ky., U.S. G10 120
Drakes Branch, Va., U.S. H7 114
Dráma, Grc. B7 28
Drammen, Nor. G3 8
Drang, stm., Asia F8 48
Drangajökull, ice, Ice. j28 8a
Dranov, Ostrovul, i., Rom. E16 26
Drau (Dráva), stm., Eur. D11 22
Dráva (Drau), stm., Eur. D14 22
Dravograd, Slvn. D12 22
Drawsko Pomorskie, Pol. C11 16
Drayton, N.D., U.S. C1 118
Drayton, S.C., U.S. B4 116
Drayton Valley, Ab., Can. C15 138
Dresden, On., Can. F7 112
Dresden, Ger. E9 16
Dresden, Oh., U.S. D3 114
Drètun', Bela. E12 10
Dreux, Fr. F10 14
Drew, Ms., U.S. D8 122
Drienov, Slov. H17 16
Driftwood, B.C., Can. D5 106
Driftwood, stm., In., U.S. E12 120
Driggs, Id., U.S. G15 136
Drin, stm., Alb. C13 24
Drina, stm., Eur. F16 22
Drinit, Gjiri i, b., Alb. C13 24
Drinit të Zi (Crni Drim), stm., Eur. C14 24
Driskill Mountain, hill, La., U.S. E6 122
Drissa (Drysa), stm., Eur. E11 10
Drniš, Cro. G13 22
Drobeta-Turnu Severin, Rom. E9 26
Drochia, Mol. A14 26
Drogheda, Ire. H6 12
Droichead Átha *see* Drogheda, Ire. H6 12
Droichead Nua, Ire. H6 12
Drôme, state, Fr. E11 18
Dronero, Italy F4 22
Dronne, stm., Fr. D6 18
Dronning Louise Land, reg., Grnld. B20 141
Druc', stm., Bela. G12 10
Druif, Aruba o19 104g
Druja, Bela. E10 10
Drūkšiai, l., Eur. E9 10
Drumheller, Ab., Can. E18 138
Drummond, Mt., U.S. D13 136
Drummond, Wi., U.S. E7 118
Drummond Island, i., Mi., U.S. C6 112
Drummondville, Qc., Can. E4 110
Druskininkai, Lith. F7 10
Družba *see* Dostyq, Kaz. E14 32
Druzhba *see* Dostyq, Kaz. E14 32
Družina, Russia C18 34
Drvar, Bos. E3 26
Dry Arm, b., Mt., U.S. G7 124
Dry Bay, b., Ak., U.S. E12 140
Dryberry Lake, l., On., Can. B4 118
Dry Cimarron, stm., U.S. B2 122
Dry Creek Mountain, mtn., Nv., U.S. B9 134
Dryden, On., Can. B6 118
Dry Devils, stm., Tx., U.S. D7 130
Dry Prong, La., U.S. F6 122
Dry Ridge, Ky., U.S. F1 114
Drysdale, stm., Austl. C5 74
Dry Tortugas, is., Fl., U.S. G11 108
Dry Tortugas National Park, p.o.i., Fl., U.S. L3 116
Drzewica, Pol. E16 16
Dschang, Cam. C1 66
Du, stm., China E4 42
Du'an, China I3 42
Duaringa, Austl. D7 76
Duarte, Pico, mtn., Dom. Rep. C12 102
Duartina, Braz. L1 88
Ḍubā, Sau. Ar. K6 58
Dubach, La., U.S. E6 122
Dubai *see* Dubayy, U.A.E. D8 56
Dubăsari, Mol. B16 26
Dubăsari, Lacul, res., Mol. B15 26
Dubawnt, stm., Can. C10 106
Dubawnt Lake, l., Can. C10 106
Dubayy (Dubai), U.A.E. D8 56
Dubbo, Austl. I7 76
Dubh Artach, r., Scot., U.K. E6 12
Dublin (Baile Átha Cliath), Ire. H6 12
Dublin, Ga., U.S. D3 116
Dublin, Tx., U.S. B9 130
Dublin, Va., U.S. G5 114
Dublin, state, Ire. H6 12
Dubna, Russia D20 10
Dubna, Russia F19 10
Dubna, stm., Russia D21 10
Dubnica nad Váhom, Slov. H14 16
Dubois, In., U.S. F11 120
Du Bois, Ne., U.S. D1 120
Du Bois, Pa., U.S. C7 114
Dubois, Wy., U.S. D3 126
Dubossary Reservoir see Dubăsari, Lacul, res., Mol. B15 26
Dubovka, Russia E6 32
Dubrājpur, India G11 54
Dubréka, Gui. H2 64
Dubrouna, Bela. F13 10
Dubrovka, Russia G16 10
Dubrovnik, Cro. H15 22
Dubrovnoe, Russia C11 32
Dubuque, Ia., U.S. B7 120
Dubysa, stm., Lith. E6 10
Duchang, China G7 42
Duchesne, Ut., U.S. C6 132
Duchesne, stm., Ut., U.S. C7 132
Duchess, Austl. C2 76
Duck, stm., Tn., U.S. B11 122
Duck Creek, stm., Nv., U.S. D2 132
Duck Hill, Ms., U.S. D9 122
Duck Lake, Sk., Can. B7 124
Ducktown, Tn., U.S. B14 122
Duda, stm., Col. F4 86
Dudačkino, Russia A15 10
Duderstadt, Ger. E6 16
Dudinka, Russia C6 34
Dudley, Eng., U.K. I10 12
Dudleyville, Az., U.S. K6 132
Dudna, stm., India B2 53
Dudorovskij, Russia G18 10
Dudwa National Park, p.o.i., India D8 54
Dueré, stm., Braz. F1 88
Duero (Douro), stm., Eur. C2 20
Due West, S.C., U.S. B3 116
Dufourspitze, mtn., Eur. D13 18
Dufur, Or., U.S. E5 136
Duga-Zapadnaja, mys, c., Russia E18 34
Dugdemona, stm., La., U.S. F6 122
Dugi Otok, i., Cro. F11 22
Dugna, Russia F19 10
Du Gué, stm., Qc., Can. D16 106
Duhovščina, Russia E15 10
Duida, Cerro, mtn., Ven. F9 86
Duisburg, Ger. E2 16
Duitama, Col. E5 86
Duiwelskloof, S. Afr. C10 70
Dujuuma, Som. D8 66
Duke, Ok., U.S. G9 128
Duke of York Bay, b., Nu., Can. B13 106
Duk Fadiat, Sudan F6 62
Dukhān, Qatar D7 56
Duki, Pak. C2 54
Dukla Pass, p., Eur. G17 16
Dukou, China F5 36
Dūkštas, Lith. E9 10
Dulan, China D4 36
Dulce, N.M., U.S. G9 132
Dulce, stm., Arg. D6 92
Dulce, Golfo, b., C.R. H6 102
Dul'durga, Russia F11 34
Dulgalah, stm., Russia C15 34
Dullstroom, S. Afr. D10 70
Dulovka, Russia C11 10
Dulq Maghār, Syria B9 58
Duluth, Ga., U.S. C14 122
Duluth, Mn., U.S. E6 118
Dūmā, Syria E7 58
Dumaguete, Phil. F4 52
Dumai, Indon. C2 50
Dumalag, Phil. E4 52
Dumali Point, c., Phil. D3 52
Dumaran Island, i., Phil. E2 52
Dumaresq, stm., Austl. G8 76
Dumaring, Indon. C11 50
Dumas, Tx., U.S. F7 128
Dumbarton, Scot., U.K. F8 12
Dumbrăveni, Rom. C11 26
Dume, Point, c., Ca., U.S. J7 134
Dumfries, Scot., U.K. F9 12
Dumka, India F11 54
Dumlupınar, Tur. E12 28
Dummar, Syria E7 58
Dumoine, Lac, l., Qc., Can. B12 112
Dumont, Ia., U.S. B4 120
Dumont d'Urville, sci., Ant. B18 81
Dumpu, Pap. N. Gui. b4 79a
Dumraon, India F10 54
Dumyâṭ, Masabb (Damietta Mouth), mth., Egypt G3 58
Duna see Danube, stm., Eur. F11 6
Dunaharaszti, Hung. B6 26
Dunaj see Danube, stm., Eur. F11 6
Dunajec, stm., Eur. F16 16
Dunajská Streda, Slov. H13 16
Dunakeszi, Hung. B6 26
Dunărea Veche, Bratul, stm., Rom. E15 26
Dunaújváros, Hung. C5 26
Dunavățu de Sus, Rom. E16 26
Duna-völgyi-főcsatorna, can., Hung. C6 26
Dunav-Tisa-Dunav, Kanal, can., Serb. D6 26
Dunbar, Scot., U.K. E10 12
Dunblane, Sk., Can. C6 124
Duncan, B.C., Can. H7 138
Duncan, Az., U.S. K7 132
Duncan, Ok., U.S. G11 128
Duncan, stm., B.C., Can. F13 138
Duncan Lake, res., B.C., Can. F14 138
Duncannon, Pa., U.S. D8 114
Duncan Passage, strt., India F7 46
Duncans, Jam. i13 104d
Duncansby Head, c., Scot., U.K. C9 12
Dundaga, Lat. C5 10
Dundalk, On., Can. D9 112
Dundalk (Dún Dealgan), Ire. G6 12
Dundalk, Md., U.S. E9 114
Dundalk Bay, b., Ire. H6 12
Dundas, On., Can. E9 112
Dundas, Lake, l., Austl. F4 74
Dundas Peninsula, pen., Can. B17 140
Dundas Strait, strt., Austl. B6 74
Dún Dealgan *see* Dundalk, Ire. G6 12
Dundee, S. Afr. F10 70
Dundee, Scot., U.K. E10 12
Dundee, Fl., U.S. H4 116
Dundee, Mi., U.S. C2 114
Dundurn, Sk., Can. C7 124
Dund-Us, Mong. B3 36
Dunedin, N.Z. G4 80
Dunedin, Fl., U.S. H3 116
Dunedoo, Austl. I7 76
Dunfermline, Scot., U.K. E9 12
Dungannon, N. Ire., U.K. G6 12
Dūngarpur, India G4 54
Dungarvan, Ire. I5 12
Dungeness, c., Eng., U.K. K13 12
Dungog, Austl. I8 76
Dungu, D.R.C. D5 66
Dungun, Malay. J6 48
Dunhua, China C8 38
Dunhuang, China C3 36
Dunilovo, Russia C21 10
Dunkerque (Dunkirk), Fr. C11 14
Dunkirk *see* Dunkerque, Fr. C11 14
Dunkirk, In., U.S. H4 112
Dunkirk, N.Y., U.S. B6 114
Dunkirk, Oh., U.S. D2 114
Dunkwa, Ghana H4 64
Dún Laoghaire, Ire. H6 12
Dunlap, Tn., U.S. B13 122
Dunmore, Pa., U.S. C10 114
Dunmore Town, Bah. K9 116
Dunn, N.C., U.S. A7 116
Dunnellon, Fl., U.S. G3 116
Dunnet Head, c., Scot., U.K. C9 12
Dunning, Ne., U.S. F12 126
Dunnville, On., Can. F10 112
Dunoon, Scot., U.K. F8 12
Dunqulah, Sudan D5 62
Dunqunāb, Sudan C7 62
Duns, Scot., U.K. F10 12
Dunseith, N.D., U.S. F13 124
Dunsmuir, Ca., U.S. B3 134
Dunstable, Eng., U.K. J12 12
Dunster, B.C., Can. C11 138
Dunyāpur, Pak. D3 54
Duolun, China C2 38
Duolundabohuer, China B14 54
Duomula, China A9 54
Duozhu, China J6 42
Dupang Ling, mts., China I4 42
Dupnica, Blg. G10 26
Dupnitsa *see* Dupnica, Blg. G10 26
Dupuyer, Mt., U.S. B14 136
Duque Bacelar, Braz. C4 88
Duque de Caxias, Braz. L4 88
Duque de York, Isla, i., Chile J1 90
Duran, N.M., U.S. G3 128
Durance, stm., Fr. F11 18
Durand, Il., U.S. B8 120
Durand, Wi., U.S. G7 118
Durand, Récif, rf., N. Cal. n17 79d
Durand Reef see Durand, Récif, rf., N. Cal. n17 79d
Durango, Mex. C6 100
Durango, Spain A8 20
Durango, Co., U.S. F9 132
Durango, state, Mex. C6 100
Durant, Ia., U.S. C6 120
Durant, Ms., U.S. D9 122
Durant, Ok., U.S. D2 122
Duras, Fr. E6 18
Durazno, Ur. F9 92
Durban, S. Afr. F10 70
Đurđevac, Cro. D14 22
Düren, Ger. F2 16
Durg, India H8 54
Durgāpur, India G11 54
Durham, On., Can. D9 112
Durham, Eng., U.K. G11 12
Durham, Ca., U.S. D4 134
Durham, N.C., U.S. H6 114
Durham, N.H., U.S. G5 110
Durham Downs, Austl. F3 76
Durham Heights, mtn., N.T., Can. A6 106
Durlas éile *see* Thurles, Ire. I5 12
Durlești, Mol. B15 26
Durmitor, mtn., Serb. F5 26
Durmitor Nacionalni Park, p.o.i., Serb. F6 26
Dürnkrut, Aus. B13 22
Durrës, Alb. C13 24
Durrësi *see* Durrës, Alb. C13 24
Durrie, Austl. E3 76
Dursunbey, Tur. D11 28
Duru Gölü, l., Tur. B11 28
Durūz, Jabal ad-, mtn., Syria F7 58
D'Urville, Tanjung, c., Indon. F10 44
D'Urville Island, i., N.Z. E5 80
Dušak, Turkmen. B9 56
Dusa Marreb *see* Dhuusamarreeb, Som. C9 66
Dušanbe, Taj. B10 56
Dušekan, Russia B19 32
Dusetos, Lith. E8 10
Dushan, China I2 42
Du Shan, mtn., China A8 42
Dushanzi, China C1 36
Duson, La., U.S. G6 122
Düsseldorf, Ger. E2 16
Dustin, Ok., U.S. B2 122
Dutch John, Ut., U.S. C7 132
Dutton, Mt., U.S. C15 136
Dutton, stm., Austl. C4 76
Duvno, Bos. F4 26
Duxun, China J7 42
Duyfken Point, c., Austl. B8 74
Duyun, China H2 42
Düzce, Tur. C14 28
Dve Mogili, Blg. F12 26
Dvine, ozero, l., Russia D14 10
Dvinskaja guba, b., Russia D17 8
Dvuh Cirkov, gora, mtn., Russia C22 34
Dvůr Králové nad Labem, Czech Rep. F11 16
Dwārka, India G2 54
Dwight, Il., U.S. C9 120
Dworshak Reservoir, res., Id., U.S. D11 136
Dwyka, stm., S. Afr. H5 70
Dyer, Tn., U.S. H8 120
Dyer, Cape, c., Nu., Can. D13 141
Dyer Bay, b., On., Can. C8 112
Dyersburg, Tn., U.S. H8 120
Dyje (Thaya), stm., Eur. H12 16
Dyment, On., Can. B6 118
Dynów, Pol. G18 16
Dysart, Sk., Can. D9 124
Dysart, Ia., U.S. B5 120
Dysna (Dzisna), stm., Eur. E9 10
Dytikí Elláda, state, Grc. E4 28
Dytikí Makedonía, state, Grc. C4 28
Džagdy, hrebet, mts., Russia F15 34
Džalal-Abad, Kyrg. F12 32
Džalinda, Russia F13 34
Dzaoudzi, May. C8 68
Džardžan, Russia C13 34
Dzavhan, stm., Mong. B3 36
Dzeržinsk, Russia H20 8
Dzeržinskoe, Russia C16 32
Džetygara *see* Zhetiqara, Kaz. D10 32
Dzhankoi, Ukr. E4 32
Dzhugdzhur Mountains see Džugdžur, hrebet, mts., Russia E16 34
Dzhungarian Alatau Mountains, mts., Asia E14 32
Działoszyce, Pol. F16 16
Dzibilchaltún, sci., Mex. B3 102
Dzierżoniów, Pol. F12 16
Dzilam González, Mex. B3 102
Dzisna, Bela. E11 10
Dzisna (Dysna), stm., Eur. E9 10
Dzitbalché, Mex. B2 102
Dziwnów, Pol. B10 16
Džizak, Uzb. F11 32
Dzjarèčyn, Bela. G7 10
Dzjaršynskaja, hara, hill, Bela. G9 10
Dzjaržynsk, Bela. G9 10
Dzjatlavičy, Bela. H9 10
Dzöölön, Mong. F8 34
Džugdžur, hrebet, mts., Russia E16 34
Dzūkijos nacionalinis parkas, p.o.i., Lith. F7 10
Dzungarian Basin see Junggar Pendi, bas., China B2 36
Dzungarian Gate, p., Asia E14 32
Dzüünharaa, Mong. B6 36
Dzuunmod, Mong. B6 36
Dzyhivka, Ukr. A15 26

E

Eads, Co., U.S. C6 128
Eagle, Ak., U.S. D11 140
Eagle, Co., U.S. D10 132
Eagle, stm., Co., U.S. B2 128
Eagle Bay, B.C., Can. F11 138
Eagle Butte, S.D., U.S. C11 126
Eagle Creek, stm., Sk., Can. B6 124
Eagle Grove, Ia., U.S. B4 120
Eaglehawk, Austl. K4 76
Eagle Lake, Tx., U.S. H2 122
Eagle Lake, l., On., Can. B5 118
Eagle Lake, l., Ca., U.S. C5 134
Eagle Lake, l., Me., U.S. D7 110
Eagle Mountain, Ca., U.S. J1 132
Eagle Mountain, mtn., Id., U.S. D11 136
Eagle Mountain, mtn., Mn., U.S. D8 118
Eagle Mountain Lake, res., Tx., U.S. A10 130
Eagle Pass, Tx., U.S. F7 130
Eagle Peak, mtn., Ca., U.S. B5 134
Eagle River, Mi., U.S. D10 118
Eagle River, Wi., U.S. F9 118
Eagletown, Ok., U.S. C4 122
Ear Falls, On., Can. A5 118
Earle, Ar., U.S. B8 122
Earl Grey, Sk., Can. D9 124
Earlham, Ia., U.S. C3 120
Earlimart, Ca., U.S. H6 134
Earlville, Il., U.S. C8 120
Early, Ia., U.S. B2 120
Early, Tx., U.S. C9 130
Eas, Vanuatu k17 79d
Easley, S.C., U.S. B3 116
East Alton, Il., U.S. F7 120
East Angus, Qc., Can. E5 110
East Antarctica, reg., Ant. C8 81
East Aurora, N.Y., U.S. B7 114
East Bay, b., Tx., U.S. H4 122
East Bend, N.C., U.S. H5 114
East Bernard, Tx., U.S. H2 122
East Bernstadt, Ky., U.S. G1 114
East Borneo see Kalimantan Timur, state, Indon. C10 50
Eastbourne, Eng., U.K. K13 12
East Brady, Pa., U.S. D6 114
East Brewton, Al., U.S. F11 122
East Cache Creek, stm., Ok., U.S. G10 128
East Caicos, i., T./C. Is. B12 102
East Cape, c., N.Z. C8 80
East Cape, c., Fl., U.S. K4 116
East Carbon, Ut., U.S. D6 132
East Caroline Basin, unds. I17 142
East Chicago, In., U.S. G2 112
East China Sea, s., Asia F9 36
East Cote Blanche Bay, b., La., U.S. H7 122
East Coulee, Ab., Can. E18 138
East Dereham, Eng., U.K. I13 12
East Dismal Swamp, sw., N.C., U.S. A9 116
East Dubuque, Il., U.S. B7 120
East Ely, Nv., U.S. D2 132
East End, V.I.U.S. e8 104b
Easter Island see Pascua, Isla de, i., Chile f30 78l
Eastern Cape, state, S. Afr. G8 70
Eastern Channel see Tsushima-kaikyō, strt., Japan F2 40
Eastern Creek, stm., Austl. C3 76
Eastern Desert see Arabian Desert, des., Egypt B6 62
Eastern Division, state, Fiji q20 79e
Eastern Ghāts, mts., India E4 53
Eastern Point, c., Guad. A1 105a
Eastern Sayans see Vostočnyj Sajan, mts., Russia D17 32
East Falkland, i., Falk. Is. J5 90
East Fayetteville, N.C., U.S. A7 116
East Frisian Islands see Ostfriesische Inseln, is., Ger. C3 16
East Gaffney, S.C., U.S. A4 116
East Germany see Germany, ctry., Eur. E6 16
East Glacier Park, Mt., U.S. B13 136
East Grand Forks, Mn., U.S. D2 118
East Grand Rapids, Mi., U.S. F4 112
East Grinstead, Eng., U.K. J12 12
Easthampton, Ma., U.S. B13 114
East Java see Jawa Timur, state, Indon. G8 50
East Jordan, Mi., U.S. C4 112
East Kelowna, B.C., Can. G11 138
East Kilbride, Scot., U.K. F8 12
Eastlake, Mi., U.S. D3 112
Eastlake, Oh., U.S. C4 114
Eastland, Tx., U.S. B9 130
East Lansing, Mi., U.S. B1 114
East Laurinburg, N.C., U.S. B6 116
Eastleigh, Eng., U.K. K11 12
East Liverpool, Oh., U.S. D5 114
East London (Oos-Londen), S. Afr. H9 70
Eastmain, Qc., Can. E15 106
Eastmain, stm., Qc., Can. E15 106
Eastmain-Opinaca, Réservoir, res., Qc., Can. E15 106
Eastman, Ga., U.S. D2 116
East Mariana Basin, unds. H18 142
East Matagorda Bay, b., Tx., U.S. F11 130
East Missoula, Mt., U.S. D13 136
East Moline, Il., U.S. C7 120
East Naples, Fl., U.S. J4 116
East Nishnabotna, stm., Ia., U.S. C2 120
East Nusa Tenggara see Nusa Tenggara Timur, state, Indon. H12 50
East Olympia, Wa., U.S. D3 136
Easton, Md., U.S. F9 114
Easton, Pa., U.S. D10 114
East Pacific Rise, unds. N27 142
East Palatka, Fl., U.S. G4 116
East Pecos, N.M., U.S. F3 128
East Peoria, Il., U.S. D8 120
Eastpoint, Fl., U.S. H14 122
East Point, Ga., U.S. D14 122
East Point, c., P.E., Can. D15 110
East Point, c., V.I.U.S. g11 104c
Eastport, Id., U.S. B10 136
Eastport, Me., U.S. F9 110
East Prairie, Mo., U.S. H8 120
East Prairie, stm., Ab., Can. A14 138
East Pryor Mountain, mtn., Mt., U.S. B4 126
East Retford, Eng., U.K. H12 12
East Saint Louis, Il., U.S. F7 120
East Sea (Japan, Sea of), s., Asia D11 38
East Shoal Lake, l., Mb., Can. D16 124
East Siberian Sea see Vostočno-Sibirskoe more, s., Russia B20 34
East Sister Island, i., Austl. L6 76
East Slovakia see Východoslovenský Kraj, state, Slov. H17 16
East Stroudsburg, Pa., U.S. D11 114
East Timor, ctry., Asia G8 44
East Troy, Wi., U.S. B9 120
Eastville, Va., U.S. G10 114
East Wenatchee, Wa., U.S. C6 136
East Wilmington, N.C., U.S. B8 116
Eaton, In., U.S. H4 112
Eaton, Oh., U.S. E1 114
Eaton Rapids, Mi., U.S. B1 114
Eatonton, Ga., U.S. C2 116
Eatonville, Wa., U.S. D4 136
Eau Claire, Wi., U.S. G7 118
Eau Claire, Lac à l', l., Qc., Can. D16 106
Eauripik, at., Micron. C5 72
Eauripik Rise, unds. I17 142
Eauze, Fr. F6 18
Ebano, Mex. D9 100
Ebb and Flow Lake, l., Mb., Can. D14 124
Ebbw Vale, Wales, U.K. J9 12
Ebebiyín, Eq. Gui. I7 64
Eben Junction, Mi., U.S. B2 112
Ebensee, Aus. C10 22
Eberbach, Ger. G4 16
Eber Gölü, l., Tur. E14 28
Ebern, Ger. F6 16
Ebersbach, Ger. E10 16
Eberswalde-Finow, Ger. D9 16
Ebetsu, Japan C14 38
Ebino, Japan G3 40
Ebinur Hu, l., China F14 32
Eboli, Italy D9 24
Ebolowa, Cam. D2 66
Ebon, at., Marsh. Is. C7 72
Ebre see Ebro, stm., Spain C11 20
Ebre, Delta de l', Spain D11 20
Ebro (Ebre), stm., Spain C11 20
Ebro, Delta del see Ebre, Delta de l', Spain D11 20
Ebro, Embalse del, res., Spain B7 20
Eceabat, Tur. C9 28
Ech Cheliff, Alg. B5 64
Echeng, China E7 36
Echínos, Grc. B7 28
Echt, Neth. E1 16
Echuca, Austl. K5 76
Écija, Spain G5 20
Eckernförde, Ger. B5 16
Eckerö, i., Fin. F8 8
Eckville, Ab., Can. D16 138
Eclectic, Al., U.S. E12 122
Eclipse Sound, strt., Nu., Can. A14 106
Ecoporanga, Braz. J5 88
Écorce, Lac de l', res., Qc., Can. B13 112
Écrins, Barre des, mtn., Fr. E12 18
Écrins, Massif des, plat., Fr. E12 18
Ecru, Ms., U.S. C9 122
Ecuador, ctry., S.A. D2 84
Ed, Swe. G4 8
Edam, Sk., Can. A5 124
Eddrachillis Bay, b., Scot., U.K. C7 12
Eddystone Rocks, r., Eng., U.K. K8 12
Eddyville, Ia., U.S. C5 120
Eddyville, Ky., U.S. G9 120
Ede, Neth. B14 14
Ede, Nig. H5 64
Edéa, Cam. D2 66
Edehon Lake, l., Nu., Can. C11 106
Edelény, Hung. A7 26
Eden, Austl. K7 76
Eden, Ms., U.S. D8 122
Eden, N.C., U.S. H6 114
Eden, Wy., U.S. A7 132
Eden, stm., Eng., U.K. G10 12
Edendale, S. Afr. F10 70
Eden Valley, Mn., U.S. F4 118
Edenville, S. Afr. E8 70
Eder, stm., Ger. E4 16
Édessa, Grc. C4 28
Edfu, Egypt C6 62
Edgar, Ne., U.S. G14 126
Edgar, Wi., U.S. G8 118
Edgard, La., U.S. H8 122
Edgartown, Ma., U.S. C15 114
Edgeley, N.D., U.S. A14 126
Edgell Island, i., Grnld. E13 141
Edgemont, S.D., U.S. D9 126
Edgeøya, i., Nor. B30 141
Edgeroi, Austl. H7 76
Edgerton, Ab., Can. B3 124
Edgerton, Mn., U.S. H2 118
Edgerton, Oh., U.S. C1 114
Edgerton, Wi., U.S. B8 120
Edgewater, Fl., U.S. H5 116
Edgewood, Ia., U.S. B6 120
Edgewood, Il., U.S. F9 120
Edgewood, Md., U.S. E9 114
Edgewood, Tx., U.S. E3 122
Edina, Mn., U.S. G5 118
Edina, Mo., U.S. D5 120
Edinburg, Il., U.S. E8 120
Edinburg, In., U.S. E11 120
Edinburg, Ms., U.S. E9 122
Edinburg, Tx., U.S. H9 130
Edinburg, Va., U.S. F7 114
Edinburgh, Scot., U.K. F9 12
Edincik, Tur. C10 28
Edineț, Mol. A14 26
Edirne, Tur. B9 28
Edirne, state, Tur. B9 28
Edison, Ga., U.S. F14 122
Edisto, stm., S.C., U.S. D5 116
Edisto, North Fork, stm., S.C., U.S. C4 116
Edisto Island, i., S.C., U.S. D5 116
Edith, Mount, mtn., Mt., U.S. D15 136
Edith Cavell, Mount, mtn., Ab., Can. D12 138
Edjeleh, Alg. D6 64
Edmond, Ok., U.S. F11 128
Edmonds, Wa., U.S. C4 136
Edmonton, Austl. A5 76
Edmonton, Ab., Can. C17 138
Edmonton, Ky., U.S. G12 120
Edmore, N.D., U.S. F15 124
Edmundston, N.B., Can. C8 110
Edna, Ks., U.S. G2 120
Edna, Tx., U.S. E11 130
Edremit, Tur. D10 28
Edremit Körfezi, b., Tur. D9 28
Edrovo, Russia C16 10
Edson, Ab., Can. C14 138
Eduardo Castex, Arg. G5 92
Eduni, Mount, mtn., N.T., Can. C5 106
Edward, stm., Austl. J5 76
Edward, Lake, l., Afr. E5 66
Edward Island, i., On., Can. C10 118
Edwards, Ms., U.S. E8 122
Edwards Air Force Base, Ca., U.S. I8 134
Edwards Plateau, plat., Tx., U.S. D7 130
Edwardsville, Il., U.S. F8 120
Edward VII Peninsula, pen., Ant. C25 81
Eek, Ak., U.S. D7 140
Eeklo, Bel. C12 14
Eel, stm., Ca., U.S. D2 134
Eel, stm., In., U.S. E10 120
Eel, stm., In., U.S. G4 112
Eems (Ems), stm., Eur. A16 14
Éfaté, state, Vanuatu k17 79d
Éfaté, i., Vanuatu k17 79d
Eferding, Aus. B10 22
Efes (Ephesus), sci., Tur. F10 28
Effigy Mounds National Monument, p.o.i., Ia., U.S. A6 120
Effingham, Il., U.S. E9 120
Effingham, Ks., U.S. E2 120
Eflâni, Tur. B15 28
Eforie Nord, Rom. E15 26
Eforie Sud, Rom. F15 26
Efremov, Russia G20 10
Eg, stm., Mong. F9 34
Egadi, Isole, is., Italy G5 24
Egaña, Arg. H8 92
Egan Range, mts., Nv., U.S. D2 132
Egedesminde (Aasiaat), Grnld. D15 141
Egegik, Ak., U.S. E8 140
Eger, Hung. B7 26
Egersund, Nor. G1 8
Eggenfelden, Ger. H8 16
Egg Harbor City, N.J., U.S. E11 114
Égletons, Fr. D7 18
Egmont, Cape, c., N.Z. D5 80
Egmont, Mount see Taranaki, Mount, vol., N.Z. D6 80
Egmont Bay, b., P.E., Can. D12 110
Egmont National Park, p.o.i., N.Z. D5 80
Egorevsk, Russia E22 10
Egremont, Ab., Can. B17 138
Eğridir, Tur. F13 28
Eğridir Gölü, l., Tur. E13 28
Éguas, stm., Braz. G3 88
Egvekinot, Russia C25 34
Egypt, ctry., Afr. B5 62
Eha-Amufu, Nig. H6 64
Ehime, state, Japan F5 40
Ehingen, Ger. H5 16
Ehrhardt, S.C., U.S. C4 116
Eibar, Spain A8 20
Eibiswald, Aus. D12 22
Eichstätt, Ger. H7 16
Eidsvold, Austl. E8 76
Eifel, mts., Ger. F2 16
Eigg, i., Scot., U.K. E6 12
Eight Degree Channel, strt., Asia h12 46a
Eights Coast, cst., Ant. C31 81
Eighty Mile Beach, cst., Austl. C4 74
Eildon, Austl. K5 76
Eildon, Lake, res., Austl. K5 76
Eilenburg, Ger. E8 16
Eiler Rasmussen, Kap, c., Grnld. A21 141
Einasleigh, Austl. B5 76
Einasleigh, stm., Austl. A4 76
Einbeck, Ger. E5 16
Eindhoven, Neth. C14 14
Einme, Mya. D2 48
Eirunepé, Braz. E4 84
Eiseb, stm., Afr. B4 70
Eisenach, Ger. E6 16
Eisenberg, Ger. F7 16
Eisenerz, Aus. C11 22
Eisenhüttenstadt, Ger. D10 16
Eisenstadt, Aus. C13 22
Eisfeld, Ger. F6 16
Eišiškės, Lith. F7 10
Eislingen, Ger. H5 16
Eitorf, Ger. F3 16
Eivissa (Iviza), Spain F12 20
Eivissa (Ibiza), i., Spain F12 20
Ejea de los Caballeros, Spain B9 20
Ejeda, Madag. E7 68
Ejido Jaboncillos, Mex. A7 100
Ejin Horo Qi, China B3 42
Ejin Qi, China C5 36
Ejsk, Russia E5 32
Ejura, Ghana H4 64
Ejutla de Crespo, Mex. G10 100
Ekaterinburg, Russia C10 32
Ekaterinino, Russia E16 10
Ekateriny, proliv, strt., Russia B17 38
Ekenäs *see* Tammisaari, Fin. G10 8
Ekibastuz, Kaz. D13 32
Ekimčan, Russia F15 34
Ekonda, Russia C10 34
Ekwan, stm., On., Can. E14 106
Ela, Mya. C3 48
El Aaiún (Laayoune), W. Sah. D2 64
El 'Açâba, plat., Maur. F2 64
El Affroun, Alg. H13 20
El Agreb, Alg. C6 64
El Ahijadero, Cerro, mtn., Mex. E1 130
Elaine, Ar., U.S. C8 122
El-'Aiyât, Egypt I2 58
El-Alamein, Egypt A5 62
El Álamo, Mex. G7 130
El Álamo, Mex. L9 134
El Álamo, Mex. H8 130
El Alto, Arg. D5 92
Elan', Russia D6 32
Elancy, Russia F10 34
El Ángel, Ec. G2 86
El-Arish, Egypt G4 58
Elat, Isr. I5 58
Elat, Gulf of see Aqaba, Gulf of, b. J5 58
El Ávila, Parque Nacional, p.o.i., Ven. B8 86
Elazığ, Tur. B4 56
Elba, Isola d', i., Italy H7 22
El-Badâri, Egypt K2 58
El-Bahnasa, Egypt J1 58
El-Balyana, Egypt B6 62
El'ban, Russia F16 34
El Banco, Col. C4 86
El Barco de Ávila, Spain D5 20
Elbasan, Alb. C13 24
Elbasani *see* Elbasan, Alb. C13 24
El Baúl, Ven. C7 86
El Baúl, Cerro, mtn., Mex. G11 100
Elbe (Labe), stm., Eur. C5 16
Elbe-Havel-Kanal, can., Ger. D8 16
Elbert, Co., U.S. B4 128
Elbert, Mount, mtn., Co., U.S. D10 132
Elberta, Mi., U.S. D3 112
Elberton, Ga., U.S. B3 116
Elbeuf, Fr. E10 14
Elbeyli, Tur. B8 58
El Beyyadh, Alg. C5 64
Elbląg, Pol. B15 16
Elbląg, state, Pol. B15 16
El Bluff, Nic. G6 102
El Bonillo, Spain F8 20
El Boulaïda, Alg. B5 64
Elbow, stm., Ab., Can. E16 138
Elbow Lake, Mn., U.S. E3 118
El'brus, gora, mtn., Russia F6 32
Elbrus, Mount see El'brus, gora, mtn., Russia F6 32
El-Burg, Egypt G1 58
El-Burgâya, Egypt J1 58
Elburs see Alborz, Reshteh-ye Kūhhā-ye, mts., Iran B7 56
Elburz Mountains see Alborz, Reshteh-ye Kūhhā-ye, mts., Iran B7 56
El Cadilla, Embalse, res., Arg. C5 92
El Cajon, Ca., U.S. K9 134
El Calafate, Arg. J2 90
El Callao, Ven. D11 86
El Calvario, Ven. C8 86
El Campamento, P.R. B3 104a
El Campo, Tx., U.S. H2 122
El Capitan, mtn., Mt., U.S. D12 136
El Carmen, Arg. B5 92
El Carmen, Col. C5 86
El Carmen, stm., Mex. F9 98
El Carmen de Bolívar, Col. C4 86
El Carricito, Mex. A7 100
El Carril, Arg. B5 92
El Centinela, Mex. K10 134
El Centro, Ca., U.S. K10 134
El Cerrito, Col. F3 86
El Cerro Del Aripo, mtn., Trin. s12 105f
Elche *see* Elx, Spain F10 20
El Chile, Montaña, mtn., Nic. E4 102
Elcho, Wi., U.S. F9 118
Elcho Island, i., Austl. B7 74
El Cocuy, Col. D5 86
El Colorado, Arg. C8 92
El Cóndor, Cerro, vol., Arg. C3 92
El Corazón, Ec. H2 86
El Corpus, Hond. F4 102
El Coto, P.R. B2 104a
El'cy, Russia D16 10
Elda, Spain F10 20
El Desemboque, Mex. G6 98
El Desemboque, Mex. F6 98
El'dikan, Russia D16 34
El-Dilingât, Egypt H1 58
El Diviso, Col. G2 86
El Djazaïr (Algiers), Alg. B5 64
El Djelfa, Alg. C5 64
Eldon, Ia., U.S. D5 120
Eldora, Ia., U.S. B4 120
Eldorado, Arg. C10 92
Eldorado, Braz. B13 92
El Dorado, Ar., U.S. D6 122
Eldorado, Il., U.S. G9 120
El Dorado, Ks., U.S. D12 128
Eldorado, Ok., U.S. G9 128
El Dorado, Ven. D11 86
El Dorado Springs, Mo., U.S. G3 120
Eldoret, Kenya D7 66
Eldred, Pa., U.S. C7 114
Eldridge, Ia., U.S. C7 120
Eleanor, W.V., U.S. F3 114
Elec, Russia H21 10
Electric City, Wa., U.S. C7 136
Elefantes (Olifants), stm., Afr. D10 70
Elefsína, Grc. E6 28
Eleftheroúpoli, Grc. C7 28
Elektrostal', Russia E21 10

Name	Map Ref.	Page
Elena, Blg.	G12	26
El Encanto, Col.	H5	86
Elephant Butte Reservoir, res., N.M., U.S.	J9	132
Elephant Mountain, mtn., Me., U.S.	F6	110
Elesbão Veloso, Braz.	D4	88
El Estor, Guat.	E3	102
Eleuthera, i., Bah.	B9	96
Eleva, Wi., U.S.	G7	118
Eleven Point, stm., U.S.	H6	120
El Fahs, Tun.	H3	24
El Faro, P.R.	C2	104a
El-Fashn, Egypt	J1	58
El-Fayoum, Egypt	I1	58
El Ferrol del Caudillo see Ferrol, Spain	A2	20
El-Figriya, Egypt	K1	58
Elfrida, Az., U.S.	L7	132
El Fuerte, Mex.	B4	100
El Galpón, Arg.	B5	92
Elgin, Scot., U.K.	D9	12
Elgin, Il., U.S.	B6	120
Elgin, N.D., U.S.	B9	120
Elgin, Mn., U.S.	G6	118
Elgin, N.D., U.S.	A11	126
Elgin, Ne., U.S.	F14	126
Elgin, Ok., U.S.	G10	128
Elgin, Or., U.S.	E8	136
El-Gindiya, Egypt	J1	58
El-Giza (Giza), Egypt	H1	58
Elgon, Mount, mtn., Afr.	D6	66
El Grara, Alg.	C5	64
El Grove see O Grove, Spain	B2	20
El Guaje, Mex.	A7	100
El Guamo, Col.	B4	86
El Guapo, Ven.	B9	86
El Hachero, Cerro, mtn., Mex.	H2	130
El Hammāmi, reg., Maur.	E2	64
El-Hamûl, Egypt	H1	58
El Hank, clf., Afr.	E3	64
El-Hawâmdîya, Egypt	I2	58
Elhovo, Blg.	G13	26
El Huisache, Mex.	D8	100
Eliase, Indon.	G9	44
Elida, N.M., U.S.	H5	128
Elila, stm., D.R.C.	E5	66
Elim, Ak., U.S.	D7	140
Elisenvaara, Russia	F13	8
Eliseu Martins, Braz.	E4	88
El-Iskandarîya (Alexandria), Egypt	A6	62
Elista, Russia	E6	32
Elizabeth, Austl.	J2	76
Elizabeth, Co., U.S.	B4	128
Elizabeth, Il., U.S.	B7	120
Elizabeth, N.J., U.S.	D11	114
Elizabeth, W.V., U.S.	E4	114
Elizabeth City, N.C., U.S.	H9	114
Elizabethton, Tn., U.S.	H3	114
Elizabethtown, Il., U.S.	G9	120
Elizabethtown, Ky., U.S.	G11	120
Elizabethtown, N.Y., U.S.	F3	110
Elizabethtown, Pa., U.S.	D9	114
Elizavety, mys, Russia	F17	34
Elizovo, Russia	F20	34
El-Jadida, Mor.	C3	64
El Jaralito, Mex.	B6	100
El Jebel, Co., U.S.	D9	132
Elk, Pol.	C18	16
Elk, stm., B.C., Can.	F16	138
Elk, stm., Ks., U.S.	D12	128
Elk, stm., W.V., U.S.	F4	114
Elk, stm., U.S.	C12	122
Elkader, Ia., U.S.	B6	120
Elk City, Ok., U.S.	F9	128
Elk Creek, Ca., U.S.	D3	134
Elk Creek, stm., S.D., U.S.	C10	126
El Kef, Tun.	H2	24
El-Kelaa-Srarhna, Mor.	C3	64
El Keré, Eth.	F8	62
Elk Grove, Ca., U.S.	E4	134
El-Khânka, Egypt	H2	58
El-Khârga, Egypt	B6	62
Elkhart, In., U.S.	G4	112
Elkhart, Ks., U.S.	D7	128
Elkhart, Tx., U.S.	F3	122
El Khnâchîch, clf., Mali	E4	64
Elkhorn, Mb., Can.	D12	124
Elk Horn, Ia., U.S.	C2	120
Elkhorn, Wi., U.S.	B9	120
Elkhorn, stm., Ne., U.S.	F16	126
Elkhorn City, Ky., U.S.	G3	114
Elkhorn Mountains, mtn., B.C., Can.	G4	138
Elkhovo see Elhovo, Blg.	G13	26
Elkins, W.V., U.S.	F6	114
Elk Island, i., Mb., Can.	D17	124
Elk Island National Park, p.o.i., Ab., Can.	C18	138
Elkland, Pa., U.S.	C8	114
Elk Mountain, mtn., Wy., U.S.	B10	132
Elko, B.C., Can.	G15	138
Elko, Nv., U.S.	C1	132
Elk Point, Ab., Can.	C19	138
Elk Point, S.D., U.S.	B1	120
Elk Rapids, Mi., U.S.	D4	112
Elk River, Mn., U.S.	F5	118
Elkton, Md., U.S.	E10	114
Elkton, Mi., U.S.	E6	112
Elkton, S.D., U.S.	G2	118
Elkton, Va., U.S.	F7	114
Ellaville, Ga., U.S.	D1	116
Ellef Ringnes Island, i., Nu., Can.	B5	141
Ellen, Mount, mtn., Ut., U.S.	E6	132
Ellendale, Mn., U.S.	H5	118
Ellendale, N.D., U.S.	A14	126
Ellensburg, Wa., U.S.	C6	136
Ellenton, Fl., U.S.	E2	116
Ellesmere, N.Z.	F5	80
Ellesmere Island, i., Nu., Can.	B9	141
Ellettsville, In., U.S.	E11	120
Ellice, stm., Nu., Can.	B10	106
Ellice Islands see Tuvalu, ctry., Oc.	D8	72
Ellicottville, N.Y., U.S.	B7	114
Ellijay, Ga., U.S.	B1	116
Ellinwood, Ks., U.S.	C10	128
Elliot, S. Afr.	G8	70
Elliot, Mount, mtn., Austl.	B6	76
Elliot Lake, On., Can.	B7	112
Elliot Lake, i., Mb., Can.	B18	124
Elliott, Ia., U.S.	C2	120
Elliott, Ms., U.S.	D9	122
Ellisras, S. Afr.	C8	70
Elliston, Austl.	F6	74
Elliston, Mt., U.S.	D14	136
Ellisville, Ms., U.S.	F9	122
Ellon, Scot., U.K.	D10	12
Ellora, India	H5	54
Ellora Caves, hist., India	A2	53
Elloree, Ks., U.S.	C10	128
Ellsworth, Ks., U.S.	C10	128
Ellsworth, Me., U.S.	F8	110
Ellsworth, Mi., U.S.	C4	112
Ellsworth, Wi., U.S.	G6	118
Ellsworth Land, reg., Ant.	C32	81
Ellsworth Mountains, mts., Ant.	C32	81
El Lucero, Mex.	I4	130
Ellwangen, Ger.	H5	16
Ellwood City, Pa., U.S.	D5	114
Elma, Wa., U.S.	D3	136
El-Mahalla el-Kubra, Egypt	H2	58
El-Maimûn, Egypt	I2	58
Elmalı, Tur.	G12	28
El Maneadero, Mex.	L9	134
El-Mansûra, Egypt	G2	58
El Manteco, Ven.	D10	86
El-Manzala, Egypt	G2	58
El-Matariya, Egypt	G3	58
Elm Creek, Mb., Can.	E16	124
Elm Creek, Ne., U.S.	G13	126
El Médano, Mex.	C3	100
El Menia, Alg.	C5	64
Elmer, N.J., U.S.	E10	114
Elmhurst, Il., U.S.	B9	120
El-Minya (Minya), Egypt	J1	58
Elmira, On., Can.	E9	112
Elmira, P.E., Can.	D14	110
Elmira, N.Y., U.S.	B9	114
El Moral, Mex.	F7	130
Elmore, Austl.	K5	76
Elmore, Mn., U.S.	H5	118
Elmore, Oh., U.S.	C2	114
Elmore City, Ok., U.S.	G11	128
El Morro, hist., P.R.	B3	104a
El Morro National Monument, p.o.i., N.M., U.S.	H8	132
El Mreyyé, reg., Maur.	F3	64
Elmshorn, Ger.	C5	16
Elm Springs, Ar., U.S.	H3	120
El Mulato, Mex.	E3	130
El-Mutî'a, Egypt	K2	58
Elmvale, On., Can.	D10	112
Elmwood, Il., U.S.	K8	118
Elmwood, Ne., U.S.	K2	118
El Negrito, Hond.	E4	102
Elnora, Ab., Can.	D17	138
Elnora, In., U.S.	F10	120
Eloguj, stm., Russia	B15	32
Eloise, Fl., U.S.	H4	116
Elora, On., Can.	E9	112
Elorza, Ven.	D7	86
El Otate, Cerro, mtn., Mex.	F1	130
Éloten, Turkmen.	B9	56
Eloy, Az., U.S.	K5	132
Eloy Alfaro, Ec.	I2	86
El Palmar, Ven.	D10	86
El Palmar de los Sepúlveda, Mex.	C5	100
El Palmito, Mex.	I8	130
El Palqui, Chile	E2	92
El Pao, Ven.	C7	86
El Paso, Il., U.S.	D8	120
El Paso, Tx., U.S.	L10	132
El Paso de Robles see Paso Robles, Ca., U.S.	H5	134
El Paso Peaks, mtn., Ca., U.S.	H8	134
El Perú, Peru	D11	86
El Piñón, Col.	B4	86
El Pintado, Arg.	B7	92
El Pital, Cerro, mtn., N.A.	E3	102
El Planchón, Volcán (Planchón, Cerro del), vol., S.A.	G2	92
El Polvorín, P.R.	B3	104a
El Portal, Ca., U.S.	F6	134
El Porvenir, Mex.	G3	130
El Porvenir, Mex.	K9	134
El Porvenir, Pan.	H8	102
El Potrero, Mex.	H7	130
El Potro, Cerro (Potro, Cerro del), mtn., S.A.	D3	92
El Prat de Llobregat, Spain	C12	20
El Progreso, Hond.	E4	102
El Puerto de Santa María, Spain	H4	20
El Puesto, Arg.	C3	92
El-Qâhira (Cairo), Egypt	H2	58
El-Qantara el-Sharqîya, Egypt	H3	58
El-Qasr, Egypt	B5	62
El Quebrachal, Arg.	B5	92
El Quelite, Mex.	D5	100
Elqui, stm., Chile	E2	92
El Real de Santa María, Pan.	H9	102
El Remolino, Mex.	F6	130
El Reno, Ok., U.S.	F10	128
El Rio, Ca., U.S.	I6	134
El Roble, Mesa, mtn., Mex.	L10	134
Elroy, Wi., U.S.	H8	118
El Rosario, Mex.	C3	100
Elsa, Tx., U.S.	H9	130
Elsa, stm., Italy	G8	22
El-Saff, Egypt	I1	58
El-Sa'îd (Upper Egypt), hist. reg., Egypt	J2	58
El Salado, Chile	C2	92
El Salado, Parque Nacional, p.o.i., Ec.	I1	86
El Salto, Mex.	D6	100
El Salvador, Chile	B3	92
El Salvador, ctry., N.A.	F3	102
Elsberry, Mo., U.S.	E7	120
El Seibo, Dom. Rep.	C13	102
Elsen Nur, l., China	D5	36
El-Simbillawein, Egypt	G2	58
Elsinore see Helsingør, Den.	H5	8
Elsinore, Ut., U.S.	E4	132
El Sombrero, Ven.	C8	86
Elsterwerda, Ger.	E9	16
El Sueco, Mex.	E1	130
El-Suweis (Suez), Egypt	I3	58
El Tajín, sci., Mex.	E10	100
El Tala, Arg.	C5	92
El Tanque, Mex.	H8	130
El Tecuán, Mex.	C5	100
El-Thamad, Egypt	I5	58
El Tigre, Ven.	C9	86
Eltmann, Ger.	G6	16
El Toco, Chile	D3	90
El Tocuyo, Ven.	C7	86
Elton, La., U.S.	G6	122
El Tránsito, Chile	D2	92
El Trébol, Arg.	F7	92
El Tule, Mex.	G1	130
El Tuparro, Parque Nacional, p.o.i., Col.	E7	86
El-Tûr, Egypt	J4	58
El Turbio, Arg.	J2	90
El-Uqsor (Luxor), Egypt	B6	62
Elûru, India	C5	53
El Valle, Pan.	H7	102
Elvas, Port.	F3	20
El Vendrell, Spain	C12	20
Elverum, Nor.	F4	8
El Viejo, Nic.	F4	102
El Vigía, Ven.	C6	86
El Vínculo, Ven.	p20	104g
Elvira, Arg.	G8	92
El Volcán, Chile	F2	92
El Wad, Alg.	C6	64
El-Wâsta, Egypt	I1	58
Elwell, Lake, res., Mt., U.S.	B15	136
Elwood, In., U.S.	H4	112
Elwood, Ne., U.S.	G13	126
Elx, Spain	F10	20
Ely, Eng., U.K.	I13	12
Ely, Mn., U.S.	D7	118
Ely, Nv., U.S.	D2	132
El Yagual, Ven.	D7	86
Elyria, Oh., U.S.	C4	114
El Yunque, mtn., P.R.	B4	104a
El-Zarqa, Egypt	G2	58
Emãé, i., Vanuatu	k17	79d
Emajõgi, stm., Est.	B9	10
Emâmrûd, Iran	B8	56
Emba see Embi, stm., Kaz.	E9	32
Emba, stm., Kaz.	E9	32
Embarcación, Arg.	B5	92
Embarras, stm., Il., U.S.	F10	120
Embarras, Wi., U.S.	G10	118
Embi, Kaz.	E9	32
Embi, stm., Kaz.	E9	32
Emborcação, Represa da, res., Braz.	J2	88
Embreeville, Tn., U.S.	H3	114
Embrun, Fr.	E12	18
Embu, Kenya	E7	66
Emca, stm., Russia	E19	8
Emden, Ger.	C3	16
Emden, Il., U.S.	K9	118
Emelle, Al., U.S.	E10	122
Emerado, N.D., U.S.	G16	124
Emerald, Austl.	D6	76
Emerson, Mb., Can.	E16	124
Emerson, Ar., U.S.	D5	122
Emerson, Ia., U.S.	C2	120
Emery, S.D., U.S.	D15	126
Emery, Ut., U.S.	E5	132
Emet, Tur.	D12	28
Emiliano Zapata, Mex.	G13	100
Emilia-Romagna, state, Italy	F8	22
Emin, China	B1	36
Emine, nos, c., Blg.	G14	26
Eminence, Mo., U.S.	G6	120
Emirdağ, Tur.	D14	28
Emir Dağları, mts., Tur.	E14	28
Emita, Austl.	m13	77a
Emlembe, mtn., Afr.	D10	70
Emlenton, Pa., U.S.	C6	114
Emmaste, Est.	B5	10
Emmaus, Pa., U.S.	D10	114
Emmaville, Austl.	G8	76
Emmen, Neth.	B15	14
Emmendingen, Ger.	H3	16
Emmerich, Ger.	E2	16
Emmet, Ar., U.S.	D5	122
Emmetsburg, Ia., U.S.	A3	120
Emmiganūru, India	D3	53
Emmitsburg, Md., U.S.	E8	114
Emmonak, Ak., U.S.	D7	140
Emo, On., Can.	C4	118
Emory Peak, mtn., Tx., U.S.	E4	130
Empalme, Mex.	A3	100
Empangeni, S. Afr.	F10	70
Empedrado, Arg.	C8	92
Emperor Seamounts, unds.	E19	142
Empire, La., U.S.	H9	122
Empire, Nv., U.S.	C6	134
Empoli, Italy	G7	22
Emporia, Ks., U.S.	F1	120
Emporia, Va., U.S.	H8	114
Emporium, Pa., U.S.	C7	114
Empty Quarter see Ar-Rub' al-Khālī, des., Asia	E6	56
Ems, stm., Eur.	C3	16
Emsdetten, Ger.	D3	16
Emu, China	C8	38
Emu Park, Austl.	D8	76
Enarotali, Indon.	F10	44
Enašimskij Polkan, gora, mtn., Russia	C16	32
Encampment, Wy., U.S.	B10	132
Encantado, Braz.	D11	92
Encarnación, Para.	C9	92
Enchi, Ghana	H4	64
Encinal, Tx., U.S.	F8	130
Encinitas, Ca., U.S.	J8	134
Encino, N.M., U.S.	G3	128
Encontrados, Ven.	C5	86
Encounter Bay, b., Austl.	J2	76
Encruzilhada, Braz.	H5	88
Encruzilhada do Sul, Braz.	E11	92
Encs, Hung.	A8	26
Endako, B.C., Can.	B5	138
Ende, Indon.	G7	44
Endeavour, Wi., U.S.	H9	118
Endeavour Strait, strt., Austl.	B8	74
Enderby, B.C., Can.	F11	138
Enderby Land, reg., Ant.	B10	81
Enderlin, N.D., U.S.	A15	126
Endicott, N.Y., U.S.	B9	114
Endicott, Wa., U.S.	D9	136
Endicott Mountains, mts., Ak., U.S.	C9	140
Ene, stm., Peru	F3	84
Enewetak, at., Marsh. Is.	B7	72
Enez, Tur.	C9	28
Enfield, N.C., U.S.	H8	114
Engaño, Cabo, c., Dom. Rep.	C13	102
Engcobo, S. Afr.	G9	70
Engelhard, N.C., U.S.	A10	116
Engel's, Russia	D7	32
Engen, B.C., Can.	B6	138
Engenheiro Navarro, Braz.	I3	88
Enggano, Pulau, i., Indon.	F2	50
England, state, U.K.	I112	12
Englefield, Cape, c., Nu., Can.	B13	106
Englehart, On., Can.	F15	106
Englewood, B.C., Can.	F3	138
Englewood, Co., U.S.	B4	128
Englewood, Fl., U.S.	J3	116
Englewood, Ks., U.S.	D8	128
Englewood, Tn., U.S.	A1	116
English, In., U.S.	A4	118
English Channel, strt., Eur.	D7	14
English Coast, cst., Ant.	C33	81
English Grand Lac, l., Lat.	C6	10
Engures ezers, l., Lat.	C6	10
Enid, Ok., U.S.	E11	128
Enid Lake, res., Ms., U.S.	C9	122
Enisej, stm., Russia	C6	34
Enisejsk, Russia	C16	32
Enisejskij krjaž, mts., Russia	C16	32
Enisejskij zaliv, b., Russia	B5	34
Eniwetok see Enewetak, at., Marsh. Is.	B7	72
Enka, N.C., U.S.	A3	116
Enkhuizen, Neth.	B14	14
Enköping, Swe.	G7	8
Enmedio, Mex.	E4	130
Enmedio, Cerro de, mtn., Mex.	F8	100
Enna, Italy	G8	24
Ennadai Lake, l., Nu., Can.	C10	106
Ennedi, plat., Chad	D4	62
Ennis, Ire.	I3	12
Ennis, Mt., U.S.	E15	136
Ennis, Tx., U.S.	E2	122
Enniscorthy, Ire.	I6	12
Enniskillen, N. Ire., U.K.	G5	12
Enns, Aus.	B11	22
Enns, stm., Aus.	B11	22
Enontekiö, Fin.	B10	8
Enoree, stm., S.C., U.S.	B3	116
Enosburg Falls, Vt., U.S.	F4	110
Enping, China	J5	42
Enrekang, Indon.	E11	50
Enrique Urien, Arg.	C7	92
Enriquillo, Dom. Rep.	D12	102
Enriquillo, Lago, l., Dom. Rep.	C12	102
Enschede, Neth.	B15	14
Ensenada, Arg.	G9	92
Enshi, China	F3	42
Enshū-nada, s., Japan	E10	40
Entebbe, Ug.	D6	66
Enterprise, N.T., Can.	C7	106
Enterprise, Or., U.S.	E9	136
Enterprise, Ms., U.S.	E10	122
Enterprise, Ut., U.S.	F3	132
Entrepeñas, Embalse de, res., Spain	D8	20
Entre Rios, Bol.	D4	90
Entre Ríos, Braz.	G7	88
Entre Ríos, state, Arg.	F8	92
Entrevaux, Fr.	F12	18
Entroncamento, Port.	E2	20
Entwistle, Ab., Can.	C16	138
Enugu, Nig.	H6	64
Enurmino, Russia	C26	34
Envalira, Port d', p., And.	B12	20
Envigado, Col.	D4	86
Envira, stm., Braz.	E3	84
Enyamba, D.R.C.	E5	66
Enyellé, Congo	D3	66
Eola, Mo., U.S.	E6	120
Epanomi, Grc.	C5	28
Épernay, Fr.	E12	14
Epes, Al., U.S.	E10	122
Ephesus see Efes, sci., Tur.	F10	28
Ephraim, Ut., U.S.	D5	132
Ephrata, Pa., U.S.	D9	114
Ephrata, Wa., U.S.	C7	136
Épi, state, Vanuatu	k17	79d
Épila, Spain	C9	20
Epinal, Fr.	F15	14
Epirus see Ípeiros, hist. reg., Grc.	D3	28
Epsom, Eng., U.K.	J12	12
Epukiro, Nmb.	B4	70
Epukiro, stm., Nmb.	B4	70
Éqlīd, Iran	C7	56
Equatorial Guinea, ctry., Afr.	I6	64
Erap, Pap. N. Gui.	b4	79a
Erath, La., U.S.	H6	122
Erave, Pap. N. Gui.	b3	79a
Erawan National Park, p.o.i., Thai.	E4	48
Erbach, Ger.	G5	16
Erbogačën, Russia	B19	32
Ercevo, Russia	F18	8
Ercolano, Italy	D8	24
Érd, Hung.	B5	26
Erdao, stm., China	C8	38
Erdaohezi, China	B8	38
Erdek, Tur.	C10	28
Erdemli, Tur.	B5	58
Erding, Ger.	H7	16
Erebato, stm., Ven.	E9	86
Erebus, Mount, mtn., Ant.	C21	81
Erechim, Braz.	C11	92
Ereğli, Tur.	B14	28
Ereğli, Tur.	A4	58
Erenhot, China	C7	36
Erepecuru, Lago do, l., Braz.	D6	84
Ereymentaū, Kaz.	D12	32
Erft, stm., Ger.	E2	16
Erfurt, Ger.	F7	16
Ergene, stm., Tur.	B10	28
Ergeni, hills, Russia	E6	32
Érgli, Lat.	D8	10
Ergun Youqi, China	A9	36
Ergun Zuoqi, China	F13	34
Er Hai, l., China	F5	36
Erice, Italy	F6	24
Ericeira, Port.	F1	20
Erichsen Lake, l., Nu., Can.	A14	106
Erick, Ok., U.S.	F9	128
Erickson, Mb., Can.	D14	124
Ericson, Ne., U.S.	F14	126
Erie, Co., U.S.	A3	128
Erie, Il., U.S.	C7	120
Erie, Pa., U.S.	B5	114
Erie, Lake, l., N.A.	B4	114
Erie Canal see New York State Barge Canal, can., N.Y., U.S.	E12	112
Eriksdale, Mb., Can.	D15	124
Erimo-misaki, c., Japan	D15	38
Erin, On., Can.	E9	112
Erin, Tn., U.S.	H10	120
Eriskay, i., Scot., U.K.	D5	12
Eritrea, ctry., Afr.	D7	62
Erivan see Yerevan, Arm.	A5	56
Erkelenz, Ger.	E2	16
Erkner, Ger.	D9	16
Erlangen, Ger.	G7	16
Erlian see Erenhot, China	C7	36
Erldunda, Austl.	D6	74
Ermelo, Neth.	B14	14
Ermelo, S. Afr.	E10	70
Ermenek, Tur.	B3	58
Ermenek, stm., Tur.	B3	58
Ermica, Russia	C25	8
Ermolaevo, Russia	D9	32
Ermolino, Russia	E19	10
Ermoúpoli, Grc.	F7	28
Erne, Lower Lough, l., N. Ire., U.K.	G4	12
Erne, Upper Lough, l., Eur.	G5	12
Erode, India	F3	53
Eromanga, Austl.	F4	76
Erongo, state, Nmb.	B2	70
Erongo, mtn., Nmb.	B2	70
Eropol, Russia	C22	34
Erota, Erit.	D7	62
Er-Rachidia, Mor.	C4	64
Errego, Moz.	D6	68
Erregol Mountain, mtn., Ire.	H2	12
Errinundra National Park, p.o.i., Austl.	K7	76
Erris Head, c., Ire.	G2	12
Errol Heights, Or., U.S.	E4	136
Erromango, i., Vanuatu	k17	79d
Eršiči, Russia	F17	10
Eršov, Russia	D7	32
Erstein, Fr.	F16	14
Ertai, China	B3	36
Ertil', Russia	D5	32
Ertis, Kaz.	D12	32
Ertis see Irtysh, stm., Asia	D13	32
Ertix see Irtysh, stm., Asia	E15	32
Ertoma, Russia	E22	8
Erval, Braz.	F11	92
Erval Grande, Braz.	C11	92
Erwin, N.C., U.S.	A7	116
Erwin, Tn., U.S.	H3	114
Erwood, Sk., Can.	B11	124
Erymanthos, mtn., Grc.	F4	28
Eryuan, China	A5	48
Erzgebirge (Krušné hory), mts., Eur.	F8	16
Erzhan, China	B8	38
Erzin, Russia	D17	32
Erzincan, Tur.	B4	56
Erzurum, Tur.	B5	56
Esa'ala, Pap. N. Gui.	b5	79a
Esashi, Japan	D13	38
Esbjerg, Den.	I3	8
Esbo see Espoo, Fin.	F11	8
Escada, Braz.	E8	88
Escalada, Ven.	D8	86
Escalante, stm., Ut., U.S.	F6	132
Escalón, Mex.	B6	100
Escalon, Ca., U.S.	F5	134
Escambia, stm., Fl., U.S.	G11	122
Escanaba, Mi., U.S.	C2	112
Escárcega, Mex.	C2	102
Escondido, stm., Mex.	F7	130
Escondido, Ca., U.S.	J8	134
Escondido, stm., Nic.	F6	102
Escondón, Puerto, p., Spain	D10	20
Escocesa, Bahía, b., Dom. Rep.	C13	102
Escudo de Veraguas, Isla, i., Pan.	H6	102
Escuinapa de Hidalgo, Mex.	D5	100
Escuintla, Guat.	E2	102
Escuintla, Mex.	H12	100
Eséka, Cam.	D2	66
Eşen, Tur.	G12	28
Eşen, stm., Tur.	G12	28
Eşfahān, Iran	C7	56
Esgueva, stm., Spain	C7	20
Eshkāshem, Afg.	B11	56
Eshowe, S. Afr.	F10	70
Esil, Kaz.	D11	32
Esil see Ishim, stm., Asia	D11	32
Esil', stm., Kaz.	D11	32
Eškar-Ola, Russia	C7	32
Eskdale, W.V., U.S.	F4	114
Es'ki, Russia	C19	10
Eskilstrup, Den.	B7	16
Eskilstuna, Swe.	G7	8
Eskimo Lakes, l., N.T., Can.	B4	106
Eskimo Point see Arviat, Nu., Can.	C12	106
Eskişehir, Tur.	D13	28
Eskişehir, state, Tur.	D13	28
Eskridge, Ks., U.S.	F1	120
Esla, stm., Spain	C5	20
Eslāmābād, Iran	C6	56
Eşme, Tur.	E11	28
Esmeralda, Cuba	B8	102
Esmeralda, Isla, i., Chile	I1	90
Esmeraldas, Ec.	G2	86
Esmeraldas, state, Ec.	G2	86
Esnagami Lake, l., On., Can.	A11	118
Espada, Punta, c., Col.	A6	86
Espalion, Fr.	E8	18
Espanola, On., Can.	B8	112
Espanola, N.M., U.S.	F2	128
Espejo, Spain	G6	20
Espelkamp, Ger.	D4	16
Espera Feliz, Braz.	K5	88
Esperança, Braz.	D7	88
Esperance, Austl.	F4	74
Esperantina, Braz.	B4	88
Esperanza, Arg.	E7	92
Esperanza, Mex.	G8	100
Esperanza, P.R.	B5	104a
Esperanza, sci., Ant.	B35	81
Espichel, Cabo, c., Port.	F1	20
Espinal, Col.	E4	86
Espinazo, Mex.	H6	130
Espinhaço, Serra do, mts., Braz.	I4	88
Espinho, Port.	D2	20
Espinilho, Arg.	B8	92
Espino, Ven.	C9	86
Espinosa, Braz.	H4	88
Espírito Santo, state, Braz.	J5	88
Espíritu Santo, i., Vanuatu	j16	79d
Espíritu Santo, Isla del, i., Mex.	C3	100
Espita, Mex.	B3	102
Esplanada, Braz.	F7	88
Espoo, Fin.	F11	8
Espungabera, Moz.	B11	70
Esquel, Arg.	H2	90
Esquimalt, B.C., Can.	H7	138
Esquina, Arg.	D8	92
Esquiú, Arg.	D5	92
Essaouira, Mor.	C3	64
Essej, Russia	C9	34
Essen, Ger.	E3	16
Essendon, Mount, mtn., Austl.	D4	74
Essequibo, stm., Guy.	C6	84
Es Sers, Tun.	H2	24
Essex, On., Can.	F7	112
Essex, Md., U.S.	E9	114
Essex, Co., U.S.	B13	136
Essex Junction, Vt., U.S.	F3	110
Essexville, Mi., U.S.	E6	112
Esslingen am Neckar, Ger.	H5	16
Est, Pointe de l', c., Can.	A15	110
Estacada, Or., U.S.	E4	136
Estaca de Bares, Punta da, c., Spain	A3	20
Estaca de Bares, Punta da see Estaca de Bares, Punta da, c., Spain	A3	20
Estación Adolfo Rodríguez Sáa see Santa Rosa del Conlara, Arg.	F5	92
Estación Colonia Alvear Norte see General Alvear, Arg.	G3	92
Estación Foguista J. F. Juárez see El Galpón, Arg.	B5	92
Estación Gobernador Vera see Vera, Arg.	D7	92
Estación J. J. Castelli see Castelli, Arg.	B7	92
Estación Justino Solari see Mariano I. Loza, Arg.	D8	92
Estación Manuel F. Mantilla see Pedro R. Fernández, Arg.	D8	92
Estación Vela see María Ignacia, Arg.	H8	92
Estados, Isla de los, i., Arg.	J4	90
Eṣṭahbān, Iran	D7	56
Estância, Braz.	F7	88
Estanislao del Campo, Arg.	B7	92
Estareja, Port.	D2	20
Estats, Pic d' (Estats, Pique d'), mtn., Eur.	G7	18
Estats, Pico de see Estats, Pic d', mtn., Eur.	G7	18
Estats, Pique d' (Estats, Pic d'), mtn., Eur.	G7	18
Estcourt, S. Afr.	F9	70
Este, Italy	E8	22
Esteio, Braz.	D12	92
Esteli, Nic.	F4	102
Estella, Spain	B8	20
Estelline, S.D., U.S.	G2	118
Estelline, Tx., U.S.	G8	128
Estepona, Spain	H5	20
Estes Park, Co., U.S.	F7	126
Este Sudeste, Cayos del, is., Col.	F7	102
Estevan, Sk., Can.	E10	124
Estevan Point, B.C., Can.	G4	138
Estherville, Ia., U.S.	H4	118
Estill, S.C., U.S.	D4	116
Estiva, stm., Braz.	G3	88
Eston, Sk., Can.	C5	124
Estonia, ctry., Eur.	G11	8
Estrela, Braz.	D11	92
Estrela, mtn., Port.	D3	20
Estrela do Sul, Braz.	J2	88
Estremadura, hist. reg., Port.	E1	20
Estremoz, Port.	F3	20
Estrondo, Serra do, plat., Braz.	E1	88
Esztergom, Hung.	B5	26
Etadunna, Austl.	G2	76
Etah, Grnld.	B11	141
Etah, India	E7	54
Étampes, Fr.	F11	14
Etamunbarie, Lake, l., Austl.	F2	76
Étaples, Fr.	D10	14
Ētāwah, India	E7	54
Etchojoa, Mex.	B4	100
Etelä-Suomi, state, Fin.	F12	8
Ethan, S.D., U.S.	D14	126
Ethel, W.V., U.S.	G4	114
Ethelbert, Mb., Can.	C13	124
Ethete, Wy., U.S.	E4	126
Ethiopia, ctry., Afr.	F7	62
Ethiopian Plateau, plat., Eth.	F7	62
Etive, Loch, b., Scot., U.K.	E7	12
Etna, Ca., U.S.	B3	134
Etna, Monte, vol., Italy	G8	24
Etobicoke, ngh., On., Can.	E10	112
Etolin Island, i., Ak., U.S.	E13	140
Etolin Strait, strt., Ak., U.S.	D6	140
Etomami, stm., Sk., Can.	B11	124
Eton, U.S.	C7	76
Etorofu-tō (Iturup, ostrov), i., Russia	B17	38
Etosha Pan, pl., Nmb.	D2	68
Etoumbi, Congo	D2	66
Etowah, Tn., U.S.	B14	122
Etowah, stm., Ga., U.S.	C14	122
Étretat, Fr.	E9	14
Etsch see Adige, stm., Italy	E8	22
Et Tidra, i., Maur.	F1	64
Ettlingen, Ger.	H4	16
Etzikom Coulee, stm., Ab., Can.	G2	124
Etzná, sci., Mex.	C2	102
Eu, Fr.	D10	14
Eua, i., Tonga	F9	72
Eua Iki, i., Tonga	n15	78e
Euboea see Évvoia, i., Grc.	E6	28
Euboea, Gulf of see Vóreios Evvoïkós, b., Grc.	E5	28
Eucla, Austl.	F5	74
Euclid, Oh., U.S.	C4	114
Euclides da Cunha, Braz.	F6	88
Eucumbene, Lake, res., Austl.	K7	76
Eudora, Ar., U.S.	D7	122
Eudora, Ks., U.S.	F2	120
Eufaula, Al., U.S.	F13	122
Eufaula, Ok., U.S.	B3	122
Eufaula Lake, res., Ok., U.S.	B3	122
Eugene, Or., U.S.	F3	136
Eugenia, Punta, c., Mex.	B1	100
Eugenio Bustos, Arg.	F3	92
Eugowra, Austl.	I7	76
Eumungerie, Austl.	H7	76
Eunápolis, Braz.	I6	88
Eungella National Park, p.o.i., Austl.	C7	76
Eunice, La., U.S.	G6	122
Eunice, N.M., U.S.	B4	130
Euphrates (Al-Furāt), stm., Asia	C6	56
Eupora, Ms., U.S.	D9	122
Eure, state, Fr.	E9	14
Eure, stm., Fr.	E10	14
Eure-et-Loir, state, Fr.	F10	14
Eureka, Ca., U.S.	C1	134
Eureka, Il., U.S.	K9	118
Eureka, Ks., U.S.	D12	128
Eureka, Mt., U.S.	B11	136
Eureka, Nv., U.S.	D10	134
Eureka, S.C., U.S.	B4	116
Eureka Springs, Ar., U.S.	H4	120
Eurinilla Creek, stm., Austl.	H3	76
Euroa, Austl.	K5	76
Europa, Île, i., Reu.	E7	68
Europa, Picos de, mts., Spain	A6	20
Europa Island see Europa, Île, i., Reu.	E7	68
Europa Point, c., Gib.	H5	20
Europe, cont.	C13	4
Euskal Herriko, state, Spain	A8	20
Euskirchen, Ger.	F2	16
Eustace, Tx., U.S.	E2	122
Eustis, Fl., U.S.	H4	116
Eustis, Lake, l., Fl., U.S.	H4	116
Eutaw, Al., U.S.	E11	122
Eutin, Ger.	B6	16
Eutsuk Lake, l., B.C., Can.	C4	138
Eva, Al., U.S.	C12	122
Evadale, Tx., U.S.	G4	122
Evandale, Austl.	n13	77a
Evans, Lac, l., Qc., Can.	E15	106
Evans, Mount, mtn., Co., U.S.	B3	128
Evansburg, Ab., Can.	C15	138
Evans City, Pa., U.S.	D5	114
Evansdale, Ia., U.S.	B5	120
Evanston, Il., U.S.	F2	112
Evanston, Wy., U.S.	B6	132
Evansville, In., U.S.	F10	120
Evansville, Mn., U.S.	E3	118
Evansville, Wi., U.S.	B8	120
Evansville, Wy., U.S.	E6	126
Evart, Mi., U.S.	E4	112
Eveleth, Mn., U.S.	D6	118
Evening Shade, Ar., U.S.	H6	120
Evensk, Russia	D20	34
Everard, Lake, l., Austl.	F6	74
Everest, Mount (Qomolangma Feng), mtn., Asia	D11	54
Everett, Pa., U.S.	F7	114
Everett, Wa., U.S.	C4	136
Everett, Mount, mtn., Ma., U.S.	B12	114
Everglades, The, sw., Fl., U.S.	K4	116
Everglades City, Fl., U.S.	K4	116
Everglades National Park, p.o.i., Fl., U.S.	K5	116
Evergreen, Al., U.S.	F12	122
Evergreen, Mt., U.S.	B12	136
Evermann, Cerro, vol., Mex.	F3	100
Evesham, Eng., U.K.	I11	12
Évian-les-Bains, Fr.	C12	18
Evje, Nor.	G2	8
Évora, Port.	F3	20
Évora, state, Port.	F3	20
Evoron, ozero, l., Russia	F16	34
Évreux, Fr.	E10	14
Évry, Fr.	F11	14
E. V. Spence Reservoir, res., Tx., U.S.	C7	130
Évvoia, i., Grc.	E6	28
'Ewa, Hi., U.S.	b3	78a
Ewing, Ne., U.S.	E14	126
Ewing, Va., U.S.	H2	114
Ewo, Congo	D2	66
Exaltación, Bol.	B3	90
Excelsior Mountain, mtn., Ca., U.S.	E6	134
Excelsior Springs, Mo., U.S.	E3	120
Exeter, On., Can.	E8	112
Exeter, Eng., U.K.	K9	12
Exeter, Ca., U.S.	G6	134
Exeter, N.H., U.S.	G6	110
Exeter Sound, strt., Nu., Can.	D13	141
Exira, Ia., U.S.	C3	120
Exmoor National Park, p.o.i., Eng., U.K.	J9	12
Exmore, Va., U.S.	G10	114
Exmouth, Austl.	D2	74
Exmouth, Eng., U.K.	K9	12
Exmouth Gulf, b., Austl.	D2	74
Exmouth Plateau, unds.	K15	138
Exshaw, Ab., Can.	E15	138
Extremadura, state, Spain	E4	20
Exuma Cays, is., Bah.	C9	96
Exuma Sound, strt., Bah.	C9	96
Eyasi, Lake, l., Tan.	E6	66
Eyebrow, Sk., Can.	D7	124
Eyemouth, Scot., U.K.	F10	12
Eye Peninsula, pen., Scot., U.K.	C6	12
Eyjafjörður, b., Ice.	j30	8a
Eyl, Som.	C9	66
Eyl, val., Som.	C9	66
Eylar Mountain, mtn., Ca., U.S.	F4	134
Eyota, Mn., U.S.	H6	118
Eyrarbakki, Ice.	I29	8a
Eyre, Austl.	F5	74

Name	Map Ref.	Page
Eyre Creek, stm., Austl.	F2	76
Eyre North, Lake, l., Austl.	E7	74
Eyre Peninsula, pen., Austl.	F7	74
Eyre South, Lake, l., Austl.	E7	74
Ezequiel Ramos Mexía, Embalse, res., Arg.	G3	90
Ežerėlis, Lith.	F6	10
Ezine, Tur.	D9	28

F

Name	Map Ref.	Page
Faaone, Fr. Poly.	v22	78h
Faber Lake, l., N.T., Can.	C7	106
Fabriano, Italy.	G9	22
Facatativá, Col.	E4	86
Fachi, Niger.	F7	64
Facpi Point, c., Guam.	j9	78c
Factoryville, Pa., U.S.	C10	114
Fada, Chad.	D4	62
Fada-Ngourma, Burkina.	G5	64
Faddeevskij, ostrov, i., Russia.	A18	34
Faddeja, zaliv, b., Russia.	A10	34
Fadiffolu Atoll, at., Mald.	h12	46a
Faenza, Italy.	F8	22
Fafe, Port.	C2	20
Făgăraș, Rom.	D11	26
Fagernes, Nor.	F3	8
Fagersta, Swe.	F6	8
Faguibine, Lac, l., Mali.	F4	64
Fagurhólsmýri, Ice.	I31	8a
Fairbank, Ia., U.S.	B5	120
Fairbanks, Ak., U.S.	D10	140
Fairbanks, La., U.S.	E6	122
Fair Bluff, N.C., U.S.	B6	116
Fairborn, Oh., U.S.	E1	114
Fairbury, Il., U.S.	K10	118
Fairbury, Ne., U.S.	A11	128
Fairchance, Pa., U.S.	E6	114
Fairchild, Wi., U.S.	G8	118
Fairfax, Mn., U.S.	G4	118
Fairfax, Mo., U.S.	D2	120
Fairfax, S.C., U.S.	D4	116
Fairfax, S.D., U.S.	D14	126
Fairfax, Va., U.S.	B8	114
Fairfax, Vt., U.S.	F3	110
Fairfield, Al., U.S.	D11	122
Fairfield, Ca., U.S.	E3	134
Fairfield, Id., U.S.	G12	136
Fairfield, Il., U.S.	F9	120
Fairfield, Me., U.S.	F7	110
Fairfield, Oh., U.S.	E1	114
Fairfield, Tx., U.S.	F2	122
Fairgrove, Mi., U.S.	E6	112
Fairhaven, Ma., U.S.	C15	114
Fair Haven, N.Y., U.S.	E13	112
Fair Head, c., N. Ire., U.K.	F6	12
Fairhope, Al., U.S.	G11	122
Fair Isle, i., Scot., U.K.	B11	12
Fairland, In., U.S.	E12	120
Fairlie, N.Z.	G4	80
Fairmont, Mn., U.S.	H4	118
Fairmont, N.C., U.S.	B6	116
Fairmont, Ne., U.S.	G15	126
Fairmont, W.V., U.S.	E5	114
Fairmont Hot Springs, B.C., Can.	F14	138
Fairmount, Il., U.S.	H2	112
Fairmount, In., U.S.	H4	112
Fairmount, N.D., U.S.	E2	118
Fair Ness, c., Nu., Can.	C16	106
Fair Oaks, Ca., U.S.	E4	134
Fair Plain, Mi., U.S.	F3	112
Fairplay, Co., U.S.	B3	128
Fairview, Ga., U.S.	C13	122
Fairview, Il., U.S.	D7	120
Fairview, Mi., U.S.	D5	112
Fairview, Mt., U.S.	G9	124
Fairview, Tn., U.S.	I10	120
Fairview, Ut., U.S.	D5	132
Fairview, Ut., U.S.	I2	112
Fairview Peak, mtn., Nv., U.S.	D7	134
Fairweather Mountain, mtn., N.A.	D3	106
Faisalabad (Lyallpur), Pak.	C4	54
Faison, N.C., U.S.	A7	116
Faistós, sci., Grc.	H7	28
Faith, S.D., U.S.	B10	126
Faizābād, India.	E9	54
Fajardo, P.R.	B4	104a
Fajou, Îlet à, i., Guad.	h5	105c
Fajr, Bi'r, well, Sau. Ar.	J8	58
Fajr, Wādī, stm., Sau. Ar.	H9	58
Fajr, Wādī, stm., Sau. Ar.	J8	58
Faku, China.	A8	16
Falaba, S.L.	H2	64
Falaise, Fr.	F8	14
Fālākāta, India.	E12	54
Falam, Mya.	A1	48
Falcón, state, Ven.	B7	86
Falcón, Presa (Falcon Reservoir), res., N.A.	H8	130
Falconara Marittima, Italy	G10	22
Falcon Reservoir (Falcón, Presa), res., N.A.	H8	130
Falelatai, Samoa	g11	79c
Falémé, stm., Afr.	G2	64
Faleşti, Mol.	B14	26
Falfurrias, Tx., U.S.	G9	130
Falkenberg, Ger.	E9	16
Falkenberg, Swe.	H5	8
Falkensee, Ger.	D9	16
Falkenstein, Ger.	F8	16
Falkirk, Scot., U.K.	E9	12
Falkland, B.C., Can.	F11	138
Falkland Islands, dep., S.A.	J4	90
Falkland Sound, strt., Falk. Is.	J5	90
Falköping, Swe.	G5	8
Falkville, Al., U.S.	C11	122
Fall, Ks., U.S.	D13	128
Fallbrook, Ca., U.S.	J8	134
Fallon, Nv., U.S.	D7	134
Fall River, Ma., U.S.	C15	114
Fall River, Wi., U.S.	H9	118
Fall River Lake, l., Ks., U.S.	G1	120
Fall River Mills, Ca., U.S.	C4	134
Falls City, Ne., U.S.	D2	120
Falls City, Tx., U.S.	E10	130
Falls Creek, Pa., U.S.	C7	114
Falls Lake, res., N.C., U.S.	I7	114
Falmouth, Jam.	i13	104d
Falmouth, Eng., U.K.	K7	12
Falmouth, Ky., U.S.	F1	114
Falmouth, Ma., U.S.	C15	114
Falmouth, Me., U.S.	G6	110
False Bay, b., S. Afr.	I4	70
False Divi Point, c., India.	D5	53
False Pass, Ak., U.S.	F7	140
Falset, Spain	C11	20
Falso, Cabo, c., Dom. Rep.	D12	102
Fălticeni, Rom.	B13	26
Falun, Swe.	F6	8
Famagusta see Gazimağusa, N. Cyp.	C4	58
Famaillá, Arg.	C5	92
Famatina, Sierra de, mts., Arg.	D4	92
Famenne, reg., Bel.	D14	14
Family Lake, l., Mb., Can.	B18	124
Fanchang, China.	F8	42
Fanch'eng see Xiangfan, China.	F4	42
Fanchon, Pointe, c., Haiti.	C10	102
Fancy, St. Vin.	o11	105e
Fang, Thai.	C4	48
Fangak, Sudan.	F6	62
Fangcheng, China.	E5	42
Fangxian, China.	E4	42
Fangzheng, China.	B10	36
Fanipal', Bela.	G10	10
Fanjiatun, China.	C6	38
Fanny Bay, B.C., Can.	G6	138
Fano, Italy.	G10	22
Fan Si Pan, mtn., Viet.	A6	48
Faradje, D.R.C.	D5	66
Farafangana, Madag.	E8	68
Farāh, Afg.	C9	56
Farāh, stm., Afg.	C9	56
Farallon de Pajaros, i., N. Mar. Is.	A5	72
Farallon Islands, is., Ca., U.S.	F2	134
Faranah, Gui.	G2	64
Farāsān, Jazā'ir, is., Sau. Ar.	F5	56
Fareham, Eng., U.K.	K11	12
Farewell, Ak., U.S.	D9	140
Farewell, Cape, c., N.Z.	E5	80
Fargo, N.D., U.S.	E2	118
Faribault, Mn., U.S.	G5	118
Faribault, Lac, l., Qc., Can.	D16	106
Faridābād, India.	D6	54
Faridkot, India.	C5	54
Faridpur, Bngl.	G12	54
Farīdpur, India.	D7	54
Farilhões, is., Port.	E1	20
Farīm, Gui.-B.	G2	64
Farina, Il., U.S.	F9	120
Farīskūr, Egypt.	G2	58
Fārīt, Amba, mtn., Eth.	E7	62
Fārjestaden, Swe.	H7	8
Farley, Ia., U.S.	B7	120
Farmer City, Il., U.S.	D9	120
Farmersville, Il., U.S.	E8	120
Farmersville, Tx., U.S.	D2	122
Farmersville, La., U.S.	E6	122
Farmington, Il., U.S.	D7	120
Farmington, Me., U.S.	F6	110
Farmington, Mn., U.S.	G5	118
Farmington, Mo., U.S.	G7	120
Farmington, Mt., U.S.	C14	136
Farmington, N.H., U.S.	G5	110
Farmington, N.M., U.S.	G8	132
Farmington, Ut., U.S.	C5	132
Far Mountain, mtn., B.C., Can.	D5	138
Farmville, N.C., U.S.	A8	116
Farmville, Va., U.S.	G7	114
Farnborough, Eng., U.K.	J12	12
Farne Islands, is., Eng., U.K.	F11	12
Farnham, Qc., Can.	E3	110
Faro, Braz.	D6	84
Faro, Yk., Can.	C3	106
Faro, Port.	H3	20
Faro, state, Port.	G3	20
Faroe Islands, dep., Eur.	n34	8b
Fårön, i., Swe.	H8	8
Farquhar, Atoll de, i., Sey.	I12	69b
Farquhar, Cape, c., Austl.	D2	74
Farragut, In., U.S.	D2	120
Farrars Creek, stm., Austl.	D3	76
Farrell, Pa., U.S.	D5	114
Farrukhābād, India.	E7	54
Fārsala, Grc.	D5	28
Fartak, Ra's, c., Yemen.	F7	56
Farvel, Kap, c., Grnld.	F17	141
Farwell, Mi., U.S.	E5	112
Fasā, Iran.	D7	56
Fasano, Italy.	D11	24
Fatehābād, India.	D5	54
Fatehjang, Pak.	B4	54
Fatehpur, India.	F8	54
Fatehpur, India.	E5	54
Fatehpur Sīkri, India.	E6	54
Fathom Five National Marine Park, p.o.i., On., Can.	C8	112
Fatick, Sen.	G1	64
Fátima, Port.	E2	20
Fatshan see Foshan, China.	J5	42
Fatu Hiva, i., Fr. Poly.	E13	72
Fatumu, Tonga.	n14	78e
Fatwā, India.	F10	54
Fauabu, Sol. Is.	e9	79b
Faucilles, Monts, mts., Fr.	F15	14
Faulkton, S.D., U.S.	B13	126
Fauquier, B.C., Can.	G12	138
Făurei, Rom.	D14	26
Fauresmith, S. Afr.	F7	70
Fauro Island, i., Sol. Is.	d6	79b
Fauske, Nor.	C6	8
Faust, Ab., Can.	A15	138
Favara, Italy.	G7	24
Fawcett Lake, l., Ab., Can.	A17	138
Fawn, stm., On., Can.	E13	106
Fawnie Nose, mtn., B.C., Can.	C5	138
Faxaflói, b., Ice.	k28	8a
Faxinal do Soturno, Braz.	D11	92
Faya-Largeau, Chad.	D3	62
Fayette, Al., U.S.	D11	122
Fayette, Ia., U.S.	B6	120
Fayette, Mo., U.S.	E5	120
Fayette, Ms., U.S.	F7	122
Fayette, Lake, res., Tx., U.S.	E2	122
Fayetteville, Ar., U.S.	H3	120
Fayetteville, Ga., U.S.	D14	122
Fayetteville, N.C., U.S.	A7	116
Fayetteville, Tn., U.S.	B12	122
Fayetteville, W.V., U.S.	F5	114
Fāyid, Egypt.	H3	58
Fāzilka, India.	C5	54
Fāzilpur, Pak.	D3	54
Fazzān, hist. reg., Libya.	B2	62
Fdérik, Maur.	E2	64
Fear, Cape, c., N.C., U.S.	C8	116
Feather, stm., Ca., U.S.	D4	134
Feather, Middle Fork, stm., Ca., U.S.	D5	134
Feather, North Fork, East Branch, stm., Ca., U.S.	C5	134
Fécamp, Fr.	E9	14
Federación, Arg.	E8	92
Federal, Arg.	E8	92
Federally Administered Tribal Areas, state, Pak.	B2	54
Federal Republic of Germany see Germany, ctry., Eur.	E6	16
Federalsburg, Md., U.S.	F10	114
Federated States of Micronesia see Micronesia, Federated States of, ctry., Oc.	C6	72
Fehérgyarmat, Hung.	A9	26
Fehmarn, i., Ger.	B7	16
Fehrbellin, Ger.	C8	16
Fei Huang, stm., China.	D8	42
Feijó, Braz.	E3	84
Feiketu, China.	B7	38
Feira de Santana, Braz.	F6	88
Feixi, China.	F7	42
Feixian, China.	D7	42
Felanitx, Spain.	E14	20
Feldbach, Aus.	D12	16
Feldberg, mtn., Ger.	B7	16
Feldkirch, Aus.	C6	22
Feliciano, Arroyo, stm., Arg.	E8	92
Felipe Carrillo Puerto, Mex.	C4	102
Felix, Cape, c., Nu., Can.	B11	106
Felixlândia, Braz.	J3	88
Felixstowe, Eng., U.K.	I14	12
Felletin, Fr.	D8	18
Fellsmere, Fl., U.S.	I5	116
Feltre, Italy.	D8	22
Femunden, l., Nor.	E4	8
Femundsmarka Nasjonalpark, p.o.i., Nor.	E4	8
Fen, stm., China.	D4	42
Fenelon Falls, On., Can.	D11	112
Fengcheng, China.	G6	42
Fengcheng, China.	D6	38
Fengdu, China.	G2	42
Fengfeng, China.	C6	42
Fenggang, China.	G2	42
Fenghua, China.	H3	42
Fengjiabao, China.	C1	42
Fengjie, China.	F3	42
Fengning, China.	A7	42
Fengqing, China.	G4	36
Fengqiu, China.	D6	42
Fengtai, China.	B7	42
Fengtien see Shenyang, China.	D5	38
Fengxian, China.	D7	42
Fengxiang, China.	D2	42
Fengyang, China.	E7	42
Fengyüan, Tai.	I9	42
Fengzhen, China.	A5	42
Feni, Bngl.	G13	54
Fenoarivo Atsinanana, Madag.	D8	68
Fenton, Mi., U.S.	B2	114
Fentress, Tx., U.S.	E10	130
Fenwick, W.V., U.S.	F5	114
Fenyang, China.	C4	42
Fenyi, China.	H6	42
Feodosia, Ukr.	F5	32
Fer, Cap de, c., Alg.	B6	64
Ferdinand, In., U.S.	F10	120
Ferdows, Iran.	C8	56
Ferentino, Italy.	I10	22
Fergana, Uzb.	F12	32
Fergana Mountains see Ferganskij hrebet, mts., Kyrg.	F12	32
Ferganskij hrebet, mts., Kyrg.	F12	32
Fergus, On., Can.	E9	112
Fergus Falls, Mn., U.S.	E2	118
Ferguson, B.C., Can.	F13	138
Ferguson, Ky., U.S.	G13	120
Ferguson, Mo., U.S.	F7	120
Fergusson Island, i., Pap. N. Gui.	b5	79a
Ferkéssédougou, C. Iv.	H4	64
Ferlo, reg., Sen.	F2	64
Ferme-Neuve, Qc., Can.	B14	112
Fermo, Italy.	G10	22
Fermont, Qc., Can.	E17	106
Fermoselle, Spain.	C4	20
Fernández, Arg.	C6	92
Fernandina, Isla, i., Ec.	I11	84a
Fernandina Beach, Fl., U.S.	F4	116
Fernando de la Mora, Para.	B9	92
Fernando de Noronha, Ilha, i., Braz.	F11	82
Fernandópolis, Braz.	D6	90
Fernando Póo see Bioko, i., Eq. Gui.	I6	64
Fernán-Núñez, Spain.	G6	20
Ferndale, Ca., U.S.	C1	134
Ferndale, B.C., Can.	G15	138
Fernley, Nv., U.S.	D6	134
Fern Park, Fl., U.S.	H4	116
Fern Ridge Lake, res., Or., U.S.	F3	136
Fernwood, Id., U.S.	C10	136
Ferokh, India.	F2	53
Ferrandina, Italy.	D10	24
Ferrara, Italy.	F8	22
Ferrato, Capo, c., Italy	E3	24
Ferreira Gomes, Braz.	C7	84
Ferreñafe, Peru.	E2	84
Ferret, Cap, c., Fr.	E4	18
Ferrières, Fr.	F11	14
Ferris, Tx., U.S.	E2	122
Ferrol, Spain.	A2	20
Ferron, Ut., U.S.	D5	132
Ferrysburg, Mi., U.S.	E3	112
Fertö-tavi Nemzeti Park, p.o.i., Hung.	B3	26
Feshi, D.R.C.	F3	66
Fessenden, N.D., U.S.	G14	124
Festus, Mo., U.S.	F7	120
Fetești, Rom.	E14	26
Fethiye, Tur.	G12	28
Fetisovo, Kaz.	F8	32
Fetlar, i., Scot., U.K.	n19	12a
Feucht, Ger.	G7	16
Feuchtwangen, Ger.	G6	16
Feuilles, stm., Qc., Can.	D16	106
Feuilles, Baie aux, b., Qc., Can.	D16	106
Feurs, Fr.	D10	18
Feyzābād, Afg.	B11	56
Fez see Fès, Mor.	C3	64
Fezzan see Fazzān, hist. reg., Libya.	B2	62
Ffestiniog, Wales, U.K.	I9	12
Fianarantsoa, Madag.	E8	68
Fianga, Chad.	F3	62
Fichē, Eth.	F7	62
Fichtelgebirge, mts., Eur.	F7	16
Ficksburg, S. Afr.	F8	70
Fidalgo, stm., Braz.	F5	88
Fidenza, Italy.	F7	22
Field, B.C., Can.	E14	138
Fier, Alb.	D13	24
Fieri see Fier, Alb.	D13	24
Fiery Creek, stm., Austl.	B2	76
Fierzës, Liqeni i, res., Alb.	B14	24
Fife Lake, Sk., Can.	E8	124
Fife Lake, Mi., U.S.	D4	112
Fife Lake, l., Sk., Can.	E8	124
Fife Ness, c., Scot., U.K.	E10	12
Fifield, Wi., U.S.	F8	118
Fifth Cataract see Khämis, Ash-Shallāl al-, wtfl., Sudan.	D6	62
Figeac, Fr.	E8	18
Figtree, Zimb.	B9	70
Figueira da Foz, Port.	D1	20
Figueras see Figueres, Spain.	B13	20
Figueres, Spain.	B13	20
Figuig, Mor.	C4	64
Fiji, ctry., Oc.	E8	72
Filabusi, Zimb.	B9	70
Filadelfia, Italy.	F10	24
Filchner Ice Shelf, ice, Ant.	C1	81
Filey, Eng., U.K.	G12	12
Filiași, Rom.	E10	26
Filingué, Niger.	G5	64
Filippoi, sci., Grc.	C7	28
Fillmore, Ca., U.S.	I7	134
Fillmore, Sk., Can.	E10	124
Fillmore, Ut., U.S.	E4	132
Filtu, Eth.	F8	62
Fimi, stm., D.R.C.	E3	66
Finale Emilia, Italy	F8	22
Finale Ligure, Italy	F5	22
Finca El Rey, Parque Nacional, p.o.i., Arg.	B5	92
Finke, Austl.	E6	74
Finke, stm., Austl.	D6	74
Finland, ctry., Eur.	C12	8
Finland, Gulf of, b., Eur.	G11	8
Finlay, stm., B.C., Can.	D5	106
Finley, Austl.	J5	76
Finley, N.D., U.S.	G16	124
Finmoore, B.C., Can.	C7	138
Finnegan, Ab., Can.	E18	138
Finnis, Cape, c., Austl.	F6	74
Finnmark, state, Nor.	B11	8
Finnsnes, Nor.	B8	8
Finschhafen, Pap. N. Gui.	b4	79a
Finse, Nor.	F2	8
Finspång, Swe.	G6	8
Finsterwalde, Ger.	E9	16
Fiordland National Park, p.o.i., N.Z.	G2	80
Fiorenzuola d'Arda, Italy.	F6	22
Fire Island National Seashore, p.o.i., N.Y., U.S.	D12	114
Firenze (Florence), Italy	G8	22
Firmat, Arg.	F7	92
Firminy, Fr.	D10	18
Firovo, Russia	C16	10
Firozābād, India	E7	54
Firozpur, India	C5	54
Firozpur Jhirka, India	E6	54
First Cataract, wtfl., Egypt.	C6	62
Firth, Ne., U.S.	K2	118
Firth, stm., N.A.	C11	140
Firūzābād, Iran	D7	56
Fisher, Ar., U.S.	B7	122
Fisher, La., U.S.	F5	122
Fisher Bay, b., Mb., Can.	C17	124
Fisher Branch, Mb., Can.	C16	124
Fisher Peak, mtn., Va., U.S.	H4	114
Fishers Island, i., N.Y., U.S.	C14	114
Fisher Strait, strt., Nu., Can.	C14	106
Fishing Creek, Md., U.S.	F9	114
Fishing Lake, l., Mb., Can.	B18	124
Fisk, Mo., U.S.	H7	120
Fiskárdo, Grc.	E3	28
Fisterra, Cabo de, c., Spain.	B1	20
Fitchburg, Ma., U.S.	B14	114
Fito, Mount, vol., Samoa	g12	79c
Fitri, Lac, l., Chad	E3	62
Fitz Roy, Arg.	I3	90
Fitzroy, stm., Austl.	D8	76
Fitz Roy, Monte (Chaltel, Cerro), mtn., S.A.	I2	90
Fitzroy Crossing, Austl.	C5	74
Fitzwilliam Island, i., On., Can.	C8	112
Fiuggi, Italy.	I10	22
Fiume see Rijeka, Cro.	E11	22
Fiumicino, Italy.	I9	22
Five Islands, N.S., Can.	E12	110
Five Islands Harbour, b., Antig.	f4	105b
Fivemile Creek, stm., Wy., U.S.	D4	126
Five Points, N.M., U.S.	H10	132
Fivizzano, Italy.	F7	22
Fizi, D.R.C.	E5	66
Fjällåsen, Swe.	C8	8
Flagler, Co., U.S.	B5	128
Flagler Beach, Fl., U.S.	G4	116
Flagstaff, Az., U.S.	H5	132
Flagstaff Lake, res., Me., U.S.	E6	110
Flamands, Anse des, Guad.	B2	105a
Flambeau, stm., Wi., U.S.	F8	118
Flamborough, On., Can.	E9	112
Flamborough Head, c., Eng., U.K.	G12	12
Fläming, reg., Ger.	E8	16
Flaming Gorge National Recreation Area, p.o.i., U.S.	B7	132
Flaming Gorge Reservoir, res., U.S.	B7	132
Flanagan, Il., U.S.	D9	120
Flanders, On., Can.	C6	118
Flasher, N.D., U.S.	A11	126
Flåsjön, l., Swe.	D6	8
Flat, Ak., U.S.	D8	140
Flat, stm., Mi., U.S.	E4	112
Flat, stm., N.C., U.S.	H8	114
Flateyri, Ice.	j28	8a
Flathead (Flathead, North Fork), stm., N.A.	H16	138
Flathead, Middle Fork, stm., Mt., U.S.	C12	136
Flathead, North Fork (Flathead), stm., N.A.	H16	138
Flathead, South Fork, stm., Mt., U.S.	C13	136
Flathead Lake, l., Mt., U.S.	C12	136
Flat Lake, l., Ab., Can.	B17	138
Flatonia, Tx., U.S.	E10	130
Flat River, P.E., Can.	D13	110
Flat River, Mo., U.S.	G7	120
Flat Rock, Al., U.S.	C13	122
Flattery, Cape, c., Wa., U.S.	B2	136
Flatts, Ber.	k15	104e
Flatwillow Creek, stm., Mt., U.S.	C17	136
Flatwoods, Ky., U.S.	F3	114
Flaxville, Mt., U.S.	F8	124
Fleetwood, Eng., U.K.	H10	12
Fleetwood, Pa., U.S.	D10	114
Flekkefjord, Nor.	G2	8
Fleming-Neon, Ky., U.S.	G3	114
Flemingsburg, Ky., U.S.	F2	114
Flen, Swe.	G7	8
Flensburg, Ger.	B5	16
Fletcher, N.C., U.S.	A3	116
Fletcher Pond, l., Mi., U.S.	D5	112
Fleurance, Fr.	F6	18
Flinders, stm., Austl.	A3	76
Flinders, Cape, c., Austl.	B8	74
Flinders Island, i., Austl.	m14	77a
Flinders Ranges National Park, p.o.i., Austl.	H2	76
Flinders Reefs, rf., Austl.	A7	76
Flin Flon, Mb., Can.	E10	106
Flint, Wales, U.K.	H9	12
Flint, Mi., U.S.	E6	112
Flint, i., Kir.	D12	72
Flint, stm., Ga., U.S.	G14	122
Flint, stm., Mi., U.S.	E6	112
Flint Lake, l., Nu., Can.	B16	106
Flippin, Ar., U.S.	H5	120
Floodwood, Mn., U.S.	E6	118
Flora, Il., U.S.	F9	120
Flora, In., U.S.	H3	112
Florac, Fr.	E9	18
Floral City, Fl., U.S.	H3	116
Flora Vista, N.M., U.S.	G8	132
Florence see Firenze, Italy	G8	22
Florence, Al., U.S.	C11	122
Florence, Az., U.S.	J5	132
Florence, Co., U.S.	C3	128
Florence, Ks., U.S.	C12	128
Florence, Or., U.S.	G2	136
Florence, S.C., U.S.	B6	116
Florence, Tx., U.S.	D10	130
Florence, Wi., U.S.	C1	112
Florencia, Col.	G4	86
Florentino Ameghino, Embalse, res., Arg.	H3	90
Flores, Braz.	D7	88
Flores, i., Laut (Flores Sea), s., Indon.	G7	50
Flores, Selat, strt., Indon.	G7	50
Flores, Laut (Flores Sea), s., Indon.	G11	50
Flores de Goiás, Braz.	G2	88
Flores Island, i., B.C., Can.	G4	138
Flores Sea see Flores, Laut, s., Indon.	G11	50
Floresta, Braz.	E6	88
Florești, Mol.	B15	26
Floresville, Tx., U.S.	E9	130
Floriano, Braz.	D4	88
Floriano Peixoto, Braz.	E4	84
Florianópolis, Braz.	C13	92
Florida, Col.	F3	86
Florida, Cuba	B8	102
Florida, P.R.	B4	104a
Florida, Ur.	G9	92
Florida, state, U.S.	F11	108
Florida, Straits of, strt., N.A.	G11	108
Florida Bay, b., Fl., U.S.	K5	116
Floridablanca, Col.	D5	86
Florida City, Fl., U.S.	K5	116
Florida Islands, is., Sol. Is.	e9	79b
Florida Keys, is., Fl., U.S.	L4	116
Floridia, Italy.	G9	24
Florido, stm., Mex.	B5	100
Florien, La., U.S.	F5	122
Flórina, Grc.	C4	28
Florissant, Mo., U.S.	F7	120
Florissant Fossil Beds National Monument, p.o.i., U.S.	B3	128
Florø, Nor.	F1	8
Flotte, Cap de, c., N. Cal.	m16	79d
Floyd, N.M., U.S.	G5	128
Floyd, Va., U.S.	H5	114
Floyd, stm., Ia., U.S.	I2	118
Floydada, Tx., U.S.	G7	128
Flumendosa, stm., Italy.	E3	24
Fluminimaggiore, Italy.	E2	24
Flushing see Vlissingen, Neth.	C12	14
Fluvanna, Tx., U.S.	B6	130
Fly, stm., Pap. N. Gui.	b3	79a
Foam Lake, Sk., Can.	C10	124
Foča, Bos.	F5	26
Foça, Tur.	E9	28
Focșani, Rom.	D14	26
Fogang, China.	J5	42
Foggaret ez Zoua, Alg.	D5	64
Foggia, Italy.	I12	22
Fogo, i., C.V.	k10	65a
Fogo, i., Nf., Can.	j23	107a
Fogo Island, i., Nf., Can.	j23	107a
Foguista J. F. Juárez see El Galpón, Arg.	B5	92
Föhr, i., Ger.	B4	16
Fóia, mtn., Port.	G2	20
Foix, Fr.	G7	18
Foix, hist. reg., Fr.	F7	18
Fojnica, Bos.	E4	26
Fokino, Russia	G17	10
Folādī, Koh-e, mtn., Afg.	C10	56
Folda, b., Nor.	C6	8
Foleyet, On., Can.	F14	106
Foley Island, i., Nu., Can.	B15	106
Folgefonni, ice, Nor.	G2	8
Foligno, Italy.	H9	22
Folkestone, Eng., U.K.	J14	12
Folkston, Ga., U.S.	F3	116
Follett, Tx., U.S.	E8	128
Föllinge, Swe.	E6	8
Follonica, Italy	H7	22
Folsom, Ca., U.S.	E4	134
Folsom Lake, res., Ca., U.S.	E4	134
Fomboni, Com.	C7	68
Fominiči, Russia	F17	10
Fominskoe, Russia	A22	10
Fonda, N.Y., U.S.	B11	114
Fond-du-Lac, Sk., Can.	D9	106
Fond du Lac, Wi., U.S.	H10	118
Fond du Lac, stm., Sk., Can.	D9	106
Fondi, Italy.	C7	24
Fonni, Italy.	D3	24
Fonseca, Col.	B5	86
Fonseca, Golfo de, b., N.A.	F4	102
Fontainebleau, Fr.	F11	14
Fontana, Arg.	C8	92
Fontana Lake, res., N.C.	A2	116
Fontas, stm., Can.	D6	106
Fonte Boa, Braz.	I8	86
Fontenay-le-Comte, Fr.	C5	18
Fontenelle Reservoir, res., Wy., U.S.	A6	132
Fontur, c., Ice.	j32	8a
Fonyód, Hung.	C4	26
Foochow see Fuzhou, China.	H8	42
Foothills, Ab., Can.	C14	138
Forari, Vanuatu	k17	79d
Forbach, Ger.	H5	16
Forbach, Fr.	E15	14
Forbes, Austl.	I7	76
Forbes, Mount, mtn., Ab., Can.	E14	138
Forchheim, Ger.	G7	16
Ford, Ks., U.S.	D9	128
Ford, stm., Mi., U.S.	B2	112
Ford City, Ca., U.S.	H6	134
Ford City, Pa., U.S.	D6	114
Førde, Nor.	F1	8
Ford Ranges, mts., Ant.	C26	81
Fords Bridge, Austl.	G5	76
Fordville, N.D., U.S.	F16	124
Fordyce, Ar., U.S.	D6	122
Forécariah, Gui.	H2	64
Forel, Mont, mtn., Grnld.	D18	141
Foreman, Ar., U.S.	D4	122
Forest, On., Can.	E8	112
Forest, Ms., U.S.	E9	122
Forest Acres, S.C., U.S.	B4	116
Forestburg, Ab., Can.	D18	138
Forest City, N.C., U.S.	A4	116
Forest City, Pa., U.S.	C10	114
Forest Grove, B.C., Can.	E9	138
Foresthill, Ca., U.S.	D5	134
Forestier Peninsula, pen., Austl.	o14	77a
Forest Park, Ga., U.S.	D1	116
Forestville, Qc., Can.	B7	110
Forestville, Mi., U.S.	E7	112
Forfar, Scot., U.K.	E10	12
Forges-les-Eaux, Fr.	E10	14
Forillon, Parc national de, p.o.i., Qc., Can.	B12	110
Forked Deer, stm., Tn., U.S.	I8	120
Forks, Wa., U.S.	C2	136
Forlì, Italy	F9	22
Formby Point, c., Eng., U.K.	H9	12
Formentera, i., Spain	F12	20
Formentor, Cap de, c., Spain.	E14	20
Formia, Italy.	C7	24
Formiga, Braz.	K3	88
Formosa see Taiwan, ctry., Asia	I9	42
Formosa, state, Arg.	B8	92
Formosa Strait see Taiwan Strait, strt., Asia	I8	42
Formosa, stm., Braz.	G8	84
Formoso, stm., Braz.	F3	88
Fornosovo, Russia	A13	10
Forres, Scot., U.K.	D9	12
Forrest, Austl.	F5	74
Forrest, Il., U.S.	D9	120
Forrest City, Ar., U.S.	B8	122
Forreston, Il., U.S.	B8	120
Forsayth, Austl.	B4	76
Forssa, Fin.	F10	8
Forst, Ger.	E10	16
Forsyth, Ga., U.S.	D2	116
Forsyth, Mo., U.S.	H4	120
Forsyth, Mt., U.S.	A6	126
Fort Abbās, Pak.	D4	54
Fort Albany, On., Can.	E14	106
Fortaleza, Braz.	B6	88
Fortaleza do Ituxi, Braz.	E4	84
Fort Assiniboine, Ab., Can.	B15	138
Fort Atkinson, Wi., U.S.	B9	120
Fort Bayard see Zhanjiang, China.	K4	42
Fort Beaufort, S. Afr.	H8	70
Fort Belknap Agency, Mt., U.S.	F5	124
Fort Benton, Mt., U.S.	C16	136
Fort Bragg, Ca., U.S.	D2	134
Fort Branch, In., U.S.	F10	120
Fort Calhoun, Ne., U.S.	C1	120
Fort Chipewyan, Ab., Can.	D8	106
Fort Collins, Co., U.S.	A3	128
Fort Coulonge, Qc., Can.	C13	112
Fort Covington, N.Y., U.S.	E2	110
Fort Davis, Al., U.S.	E13	122
Fort Davis, Tx., U.S.	D4	130
Fort-de-France, Mart.	k6	105c
Fort-de-France-Lamentin, Aérodrome de, Mart.	k7	105c
Fort Deposit, Al., U.S.	F12	122
Fort Dodge, Ia., U.S.	B3	120
Fort Duchesne, Ut., U.S.	C7	132
Forte dei Marmi, Italy	G7	22
Fort Edward, N.Y., U.S.	G3	110
Fort Erie, On., Can.	F10	112
Fortescue, stm., Austl.	D3	74
Fortezza, Italy.	D8	22
Fort Frances, On., Can.	C5	118
Fort Fraser, B.C., Can.	B6	138
Fort Frederica National Monument, p.o.i., Ga., U.S.	E4	116
Fort Gaines, Ga., U.S.	F13	122
Fort Garland, Co., U.S.	D3	128
Fort Gibson, Ok., U.S.	I2	120
Fort Good Hope, N.T., Can.	B5	106
Forth, Firth of, b., Scot., U.K.	E10	12
Fort Hall, Id., U.S.	G14	136
Fortín, Mt., U.S.	B12	136
Fortín Uno, Arg.	I5	92
Fort Jones, Ca., U.S.	B3	134
Fort Klamath, Or., U.S.	H4	136
Fort Knox, Ky., U.S.	G12	120
Fort-Lamy see N'Djamena, Chad	E3	62
Fort Laramie, Wy., U.S.	E8	126
Fort Lauderdale, Fl., U.S.	J5	116
Fort Liard, N.T., Can.	C6	106
Fort Loramie, Oh., U.S.	D1	114
Fort Loudoun Lake, res., Tn., U.S.	B15	122
Fort Lyon Canal, can., Co., U.S.	C5	128
Fort MacKay, Ab., Can.	D8	106
Fort Macleod, Ab., Can.	G17	138
Fort Madison, Ia., U.S.	D6	120
Fort Matanzas National Monument, p.o.i., Fl., U.S.	G4	116
Fort McMurray, Ab., Can.	D8	106
Fort McPherson, N.T., Can.	B4	106
Fort Meade, Fl., U.S.	I4	116
Fort Mill, S.C., U.S.	A5	116
Fort Morgan, Co., U.S.	A5	128
Fort Myers, Fl., U.S.	J3	116
Fort Myers Beach, Fl., U.S.	J3	116
Fort Nelson, B.C., Can.	D6	106
Fort Nelson, stm., B.C., Can.	D6	106
Fort Ogden, Fl., U.S.	I4	116
Fort Payne, Al., U.S.	C13	122
Fort Peck, Mt., U.S.	F7	124
Fort Peck Dam, dam, Mt., U.S.	G7	124
Fort Peck Lake, res., Mt., U.S.	G7	124
Fort Pierce, Fl., U.S.	I5	116
Fort Plain, N.Y., U.S.	B11	114
Fort Portal, Ug.	D6	66
Fort Providence, N.T., Can.	C7	106
Fort Pulaski National Monument, p.o.i., Ga., U.S.	E5	116
Fort Qu'Appelle, Sk., Can.	D10	124
Fort Randall Dam, dam, S.D., U.S.	D14	126
Fort Recovery, Oh., U.S.	D1	114
Fort Resolution, N.T., Can.	C8	106
Fort Rixon, Zimb.	B9	70
Fort Saint James, B.C., Can.	B6	138
Fort Saint John, B.C., Can.	D7	106
Fort Sakatchewan, Ab., Can.	C17	138
Fort Scott, Ks., U.S.	G3	120
Fort Severn, On., Can.	D13	106
Fort-Shevchenko, Kaz.	E7	32
Fort Simpson, N.T., Can.	C6	106
Fort Smith, N.T., Can.	C8	106
Fort Smith, Ar., U.S.	B4	122
Fort Stockton, Tx., U.S.	C5	130
Fort Sumner, N.M., U.S.	G4	128
Fort Sumter National Monument, p.o.i., S.C., U.S.	D6	116
Fort Supply, Ok., U.S.	E9	128
Fort Thomas, Az., U.S.	J7	132
Fort Totten, N.D., U.S.	G14	124
Fort Towson, Ok., U.S.	D3	122
Fortuna, Ca., U.S.	C1	134
Fortuna, C.R.	G5	102
Fortuna, Mo., U.S.	F5	120
Fortuna, N.D., U.S.	F9	124
Fortune Bay, b., Nf., Can.	j22	107a
Fortuneswell, Eng., U.K.	K10	12
Fort Union National Monument, p.o.i., N.M., U.S.	F3	128
Fort Valley, Ga., U.S.	D2	116
Fort Vermilion, Ab., Can.	D7	106
Fort Victoria, sci., Ber.	k16	104e
Fort Walton Beach, Fl., U.S.	G12	122
Fort Wayne, In., U.S.	G4	112
Fort White, Fl., U.S.	F3	116
Fort William, Scot., U.K.	E7	12
Fort Worth, Tx., U.S.	B10	130
Fort Yates, N.D., U.S.	A12	126
Fort Yukon, Ak., U.S.	C10	140
Foshan, China.	J5	42
Fosheim Peninsula, pen., Nu., Can.	B9	141
Foso, Ghana.	H4	64
Fossano, Italy.	F4	22
Fossil Butte National Monument, p.o.i., Wy., U.S.	B6	132
Fossil Lake, l., Or., U.S.	G7	136
Fossombrone, Italy.	G9	22
Foster, Austl.	L6	76
Foster Bugt, strt., Grnld.	C21	141
Fostoria, Oh., U.S.	C2	114
Fou-kien see Fujian, state, China.	I7	42
Fouling see Fuling, China.	G2	42
Foulwind, Cape, c., N.Z.	E4	80
Foum el-Hassan, Mor.	D3	64
Foumban, Cam.	C2	66
Foundiougne, Sen.	G1	64
Fountain, Co., U.S.	C4	128
Fountain, Fl., U.S.	G13	122
Fountain City, Wi., U.S.	G7	118
Fountain Green, Ut., U.S.	D5	132
Fountain Peak, mtn., Ca., U.S.	I1	132

Name	Map Ref.	Page
Fountain Place, La., U.S.	G7	122
Fourche LaFave, stm., Ar., U.S.	C6	122
Fourchu, N.S., Can.	E16	110
Four Corners, Or., U.S.	F4	136
Fourmies, Fr.	D13	14
Four Mountains, Islands of, is., Ak., U.S.	g24	140a
Four Oaks, N.C., U.S.	A7	116
Fourth Cataract see Rābī, Ash-Shallāl ar-, wtfl., Sudan	D6	62
Fous, Pointe des, c., Dom.	j6	105c
Fouta Djalon, reg., Gui.	G2	64
Foux, Cap à, c., Haiti	C11	102
Fouyang see Fuyang, China	E6	42
Foveaux Strait, strt., N.Z.	H3	80
Fowler, Co., U.S.	C4	128
Fowler, In., U.S.	H2	112
Fowler, Mi., U.S.	E5	112
Fowlers Bay, Austl.	F6	74
Fowlerville, Mi., U.S.	B1	114
Fox, stm., Wi., U.S.	H10	118
Fox, stm., U.S.	D5	120
Fox, stm., U.S.	C9	120
Fox Creek, Ab., Can.	B14	138
Foxe Basin, b., Nu., Can.	B15	106
Foxe Channel, strt., Nu., Can.	C15	106
Foxe Peninsula, pen., Nu., Can.	C15	106
Foxford, Ire.	H3	12
Fox Islands, is., Ak., U.S.	g25	140a
Fox Lake, Il., U.S.	B9	120
Foxpark, Wy., U.S.	B10	132
Fox Valley, Sk., Can.	D4	124
Foxworth, Ms., U.S.	F9	122
Foyle, Lough, b., Eur.	F5	12
Foz do Areia, Represa de, res., Braz.	B12	92
Foz do Cunene, Ang.	D1	68
Foz do Iguaçu, Braz.	B10	92
Foz do Jordão, Braz.	E3	84
Foz Giraldo, Port.	E3	20
Fraga, Spain	C11	20
Fraile Muerto, Ur.	F10	92
Framingham, Ma., U.S.	B14	114
Franca, Braz.	K2	88
França, Braz.	F5	88
Franca-Iosifa, Zemlja, is., Russia	B9	30
Francavilla al Mare, Italy	H11	22
Francavilla Fontana, Italy	D11	24
France, ctry., Eur.	C8	18
Frances, stm., Yk., Can.	C5	106
Frances Lake, l., Yk., Can.	C4	106
Francés Viejo, Cabo, c., Dom. Rep.	C13	102
Franceville, Gabon	E2	66
Franche-Comté, hist. reg., Fr.	B12	18
Francis Case, Lake, res., S.D., U.S.	D13	126
Francisco Beltrão, Braz.	B11	92
Francisco I. Madero, Mex.	I4	130
Francisco I. Madero, Mex.	C6	100
Francisco Murguía, Mex.	C7	100
Francistown, Bots.	B8	70
Francofonte, Italy	G8	24
François Lake, B.C., Can.	B5	138
François Lake, l., B.C., Can.	C5	138
Francs Peak, mtn., Wy., U.S.	C3	132
Frankel City, Tx., U.S.	B5	130
Franken, hist. reg., Ger.	G6	16
Frankenberg, Ger.	F9	16
Frankenberg, Ger.	E4	16
Frankenmuth, Mi., U.S.	E6	112
Frankford, On., Can.	D12	112
Frankfort, Mo., U.S.	E6	120
Frankfort, S. Afr.	E9	70
Frankfort, In., U.S.	H3	112
Frankfort, Ks., U.S.	B12	128
Frankfort, Ky., U.S.	F13	120
Frankfort, Oh., U.S.	E2	114
Frankfort, S.D., U.S.	C14	126
Frankfurt, Ger.	D10	16
Frankfurt am Main, Ger.	F4	16
Franklin, Az., U.S.	K7	132
Franklin, Ga., U.S.	D13	122
Franklin, Id., U.S.	A5	132
Franklin, Il., U.S.	E7	120
Franklin, In., U.S.	E11	120
Franklin, Ma., U.S.	B14	114
Franklin, N.C., U.S.	A2	116
Franklin, N.H., U.S.	G5	110
Franklin, N.J., U.S.	C11	114
Franklin, Oh., U.S.	E1	114
Franklin, Pa., U.S.	C6	114
Franklin, Tn., U.S.	I11	120
Franklin, Tx., U.S.	F2	122
Franklin, Va., U.S.	H9	114
Franklin, Wi., U.S.	F2	112
Franklin Bay, b., N.T., Can.	B5	106
Franklin D. Roosevelt Lake, res., Wa., U.S.	B4	108
Franklin Gordon Wild Rivers National Park, p.o.i., Austl.	o12	77a
Franklin Grove, Il., U.S.	C8	120
Franklin Lake, l., Nu., Can.	B12	106
Franklin Mountains, mts., N.T., Can.	B5	106
Franklin Strait, strt., Nu., Can.	A11	106
Franklinton, La., U.S.	G8	122
Franklinville, N.Y., U.S.	B7	114
Frankston, Tx., U.S.	E3	122
Frankton, In., U.S.	H4	112
Fransfontein, Nmb.	B2	70
Franzensfeste see Fortezza, Italy	D8	22
Franz Josef Land see Franca-Iosifa, Zemlja, is., Russia	B9	30
Frascati, Italy	I9	22
Fraser, B.C., Can.	G13	138
Fraser, Co., U.S.	B3	128
Fraser, stm., B.C., Can.	G9	138
Fraser, Mount, mtn., Austl.	E3	74
Fraserburgh, Scot., U.K.	D11	12
Fraser Island, i., Austl.	E9	76
Fraser Lake, l., B.C., Can.	B6	138
Fraser Plateau, plat., B.C., Can.	E8	138
Fraser Range, Austl.	F4	74
Frauenfeld, Switz.	C5	22
Fray Bentos, Ur.	F8	92
Fray Jorge, Parque Nacional, p.o.i., Chile	E2	92
Fray Marcos, Ur.	G10	92
Frazer, Mt., U.S.	F7	124
Frederic, Wi., U.S.	F6	118
Fredericia, Den.	I3	8
Frederick, Md., U.S.	E8	114
Frederick, S.D., U.S.	B14	126
Frederick Hills, hills, Austl.	B7	74
Frederick Reef, rf., Austl.	C10	76
Fredericksburg, Ia., U.S.	B5	120
Fredericksburg, Tx., U.S.	D9	130
Fredericksburg, Va., U.S.	F8	114
Fredericktown, Oh., U.S.	D3	114
Frederick Westphalen, Braz.	C11	92
Fredericton, N.B., Can.	E10	110
Fredericton Junction, N.B., Can.	E10	110
Frederiksborg, state, Den.	H5	8
Frederikskål, Grnld.	E17	141
Frederikshåb (Paamiut), Grnld.	E15	141
Frederikshavn, Den.	H4	8
Frederiksted, V.I.U.S.	h10	104c
Fredonia, Ks., U.S.	G2	120
Fredonia, N.Y., U.S.	B6	114
Fredrika, Swe.	D8	8
Fredrikstad, Nor.	G4	8
Freeburg, Il., U.S.	F8	120
Freeland, Mi., U.S.	E5	112
Freeland, Pa., U.S.	C9	114
Freel Peak, mtn., Ca., U.S.	E5	134
Freels, Cape, c., Nf., Can.	j23	107a
Freeman, S.D., U.S.	D15	126
Freeport, Bah.	B9	96
Freeport, N.S., Can.	F10	110
Freeport, Fl., U.S.	G12	122
Freeport, Il., U.S.	B8	120
Freeport, N.Y., U.S.	H16	112
Freeport, Tx., U.S.	F12	130
Freetown, Antig.	f4	105b
Freetown, S.L.	H2	64
Fregenal de la Sierra, Spain	F4	20
Freiberg, Ger.	F9	16
Freiburg see Fribourg, Switz.	D4	22
Freiburg im Breisgau, Ger.	I3	16
Freirina, Chile	D2	92
Freising, Ger.	H7	16
Freistadt, Aus.	B11	22
Freital, Ger.	F9	16
Fréjus, Fr.	F12	18
Fremantle, Austl.	F3	74
Fremont, Ca., U.S.	F4	134
Fremont, Ia., U.S.	C5	120
Fremont, In., U.S.	G1	112
Fremont, Mi., U.S.	E4	112
Fremont, Ne., U.S.	C1	120
Fremont, Oh., U.S.	C2	114
Fremont, Wi., U.S.	G10	118
Fremont, stm., Ut., U.S.	E6	132
French, stm., On., Can.	B9	112
French Broad, stm., U.S.	H2	114
French Cap Cay, i., V.I.U.S.	f7	104b
French Creek, stm., N.A.	E5	124
Frenchman (Frenchman Creek), stm., N.A.	E5	124
Frenchman, stm., N.A.	E5	124
Frenchman Creek, stm., U.S.	G11	126
Frenchmans Cap, mtn., Austl.	o12	77a
French Polynesia, dep., Oc.	K24	142
French Somaliland see Djibouti, ctry., Afr.	E8	62
Fresco, C. Iv.	H3	64
Fresco, stm., Braz.	E7	84
Fresnillo, Mex.	D7	100
Fresno, Ca., U.S.	G6	134
Fresno, stm., Ca., U.S.	F6	134
Fresno Reservoir, res., Mt., U.S.	B16	136
Freu, Cap des, c., Spain	E14	20
Freudenstadt, Ger.	H4	16
Frewena, Austl.	C7	74
Frewsburg, N.Y., U.S.	B6	114
Freycinet National Park, p.o.i., Austl.	o14	77a
Freycinet Peninsula, pen., Austl.	o14	77a
Freyre, Arg.	E6	92
Fria, Gui.	G2	64
Fria, Cape, c., Nmb.	D1	68
Friant, Ca., U.S.	G6	134
Friars Point, Ms., U.S.	C8	122
Frias, Arg.	D5	92
Fribourg (Freiburg), Switz.	D4	22
Fridtjof Nansen, Mount, mtn., Ant.	D25	81
Friedberg, Ger.	C12	22
Friedberg, Ger.	H7	16
Friedberg, Ger.	F4	16
Friedland, Ger.	C9	16
Friedrichshafen, Ger.	I5	16
Friend, Ne., U.S.	G15	126
Friendship, N.Y., U.S.	B7	114
Friendship, Tn., U.S.	I8	120
Fries, Va., U.S.	H4	114
Friesach, Aus.	D11	22
Frio, stm., Tx., U.S.	F9	130
Frio, Cabo, c., Braz.	L5	88
Frio Draw, stm., U.S.	G6	128
Friona, Tx., U.S.	G6	128
Frisco, Tx., U.S.	D2	122
Frisian Islands, is., Eur.	A14	14
Fritch, Tx., U.S.	F7	128
Fritzlar, Ger.	E5	16
Friuli, hist. reg., Italy	D9	22
Friuli-Venezia Giulia, state, Italy	D9	22
Frjazino, Russia	E21	10
Frobisher, Sk., Can.	E11	124
Frobisher Bay, b., Nu., Can.	C17	106
Frobisher Lake, l., Sk., Can.	D9	106
Froid, Mt., U.S.	F9	124
Frolovo, Russia	E6	32
Frome, Eng., U.K.	J10	12
Frome, stm., Austl.	G2	76
Frome, Lake, l., Austl.	H2	76
Fronteiras, Braz.	D5	88
Frontenac, Ks., U.S.	G3	120
Frontera, Mex.	F12	100
Frontera, Mex.	B8	100
Frontier, Wy., U.S.	B6	132
Frontino, Col.	D3	86
Frontino, Páramo, mtn., Col.	D3	86
Front Range, mts., Co., U.S.	H7	126
Front Royal, Va., U.S.	F7	114
Frosinone, Italy	I9	22
Frostburg, Md., U.S.	E6	114
Frostproof, Fl., U.S.	I4	116
Frøya, i., Nor.	E3	8
Fruges, Fr.	D11	14
Fruita, Co., U.S.	D8	132
Fruitdale, Or., U.S.	H3	136
Fruithurst, Al., U.S.	D13	122
Fruitland, Id., U.S.	F10	136
Fruitvale, B.C., Can.	G13	138
Frunzivka, Ukr.	B16	26
Frutal, Braz.	J1	88
Frutigen, Switz.	D4	22
Frýdek-Místek, Czech Rep.	G14	16
Fryeburg, Me., U.S.	G5	110
Fu, stm., China	G7	42
Fu, stm., China	G7	42
Fu, stm., China	G6	42
Fua'amotu International Airport, Tonga	n14	78e
Fu'an, China	H8	42
Fuchou see Fuzhou, China	H8	42
Fuchū, Japan	E6	40
Fuchun, stm., China	G8	42
Fuding, China	H9	42
Fuego, Volcán de, vol., Guat.	E2	102
Fuencaliente, Spain	F6	20
Fuengirola, Spain	H6	20
Fuensalida, Spain	D6	20
Fuente, Mex.	F7	130
Fuente de Cantos, Spain	F4	20
Fuente de Oro, Col.	F5	86
Fuentes de Ebro, Spain	C10	20
Fuerte, stm., Mex.	B4	100
Fuerte Olimpo, Para.	D5	90
Fugou, China	D6	42
Fuhai, China	B2	36
Fuhsien see Wafangdian, China	B9	42
Fuji, Japan	D11	40
Fuji, Mount see Fuji-san, vol., Japan	D11	40
Fujian, state, China	I7	42
Fujieda, Japan	E11	40
Fujin, China	B11	36
Fujinomiya, Japan	D11	40
Fuji-san (Fuji, Mount), vol., Japan	D11	40
Fujisawa, Japan	D12	40
Fujiyama see Fuji-san, vol., Japan	D11	40
Fuji-yoshida, Japan	D11	40
Fukagawa, Japan	C14	38
Fukue, Japan	G1	40
Fukue-jima, i., Japan	G1	40
Fukui, Japan	C9	40
Fukui, state, Japan	C9	40
Fukuoka, Japan	F3	40
Fukuoka, state, Japan	F3	40
Fukuroi, Japan	E10	40
Fukushima, Japan	B13	40
Fukushima, state, Japan	B12	40
Fukuyama, Japan	E6	40
Fulaga Passage, strt., Fiji	q20	79e
Fulda, Ger.	F5	16
Fulda, Mn., U.S.	H3	118
Fulda, stm., Ger.	E5	16
Fuling, China	G2	42
Fullarton, stm., Austl.	C3	76
Fullerton, Ca., U.S.	J8	134
Fullerton, Ne., U.S.	F15	126
Fullerton Point, c., Antig.	f4	105b
Fulton, Al., U.S.	F11	122
Fulton, Ar., U.S.	D5	122
Fulton, Il., U.S.	C7	120
Fulton, Ks., U.S.	F3	120
Fulton, Ky., U.S.	H9	120
Fulton, Mo., U.S.	F5	120
Fulton, N.Y., U.S.	E13	112
Fulton, Tx., U.S.	F10	130
Fumay, Fr.	D13	14
Funabashi, Japan	D12	40
Funafuti, i., Tuvalu	D8	72
Funan, China	E6	42
Funchal, Port.	C1	64
Fundación, Col.	B4	86
Fundão, Port.	D3	20
Fundy, Bay of, b., Can.	F10	110
Fundy National Park, p.o.i., N.B., Can.	E11	110
Funhalouro, Moz.	C12	70
Funing, China	E8	42
Funing, China	E5	42
Funiu Shan, mts., China	E5	42
Funsi, Ghana	G4	64
Funtua, Nig.	G6	64
Fuping, China	D3	42
Fuping, China	I8	42
Fuquay-Varina, N.C., U.S.	A7	116
Furculeşti, Rom.	F12	26
Furmanov, Russia	H19	8
Furnas, Represa de, res., Braz.	K2	88
Furneaux Group, is., Austl.	m13	77a
Furnes see Veurne, Bel.	C11	14
Fürstenberg / Havel, Ger.	C9	16
Fürstenfeld, Aus.	C12	22
Fürstenfeldbruck, Ger.	H7	16
Fürstenwalde, Ger.	D9	16
Fürth, Ger.	G6	16
Furth im Wald, Ger.	G8	16
Furukawa, Japan	C10	40
Furukawa, Japan	A13	40
Fury and Hecla Strait, strt., Nu., Can.	B14	106
Fusagasugá, Col.	E4	86
Fusan see Pusan, Kor., S.	D2	40
Fushan, China	C9	42
Fushan, China	D4	42
Fushun see Yan'an, China	C3	42
Fushun, China	D5	42
Fushun, China	G1	42
Fusilier, Sk., Can.	C4	124
Fusong, China	C7	38
Füssen, Ger.	I6	16
Fuste, Picacho del, mtn., Mex.	G5	130
Fusui, China	J2	42
Futun, stm., China	H7	42
Futuna, Île, i., Wal.IF.	E9	72
Futuyu, China	B6	42
Fuwa, Egypt	G1	58
Fuxian Hu, l., China	G5	36
Fuxin, China	C4	38
Fuyang, China	E6	42
Fuyang, China	F8	42
Fuyang, stm., China	B6	42
Fuyu, China	B9	36
Fuyu, China	B5	38
Fuyuan, China	H5	36
Fuyuan see Tongjiang, China	B11	36
Fuyun, China	B2	36
Fuzhou, China	H7	42
Fuzhou, China	H8	42
Fyli, sci., Grc.	E6	28
Fyn, i., Den.	I4	8
Fyn, state, Den.	I4	8
Fyne, Loch, b., Scot., U.K.	F7	12
Fyresvatnet, l., Nor.	G2	8

G

Name	Map Ref.	Page
Gaalkacyo, Som.	C9	66
Gabare, Blg.	F10	26
Gabarus, N.S., Can.	E16	110
Gabela, Ang.	C1	68
Gaberones see Gaborone, Bots.	D7	70
Gabès, Tun.	C7	64
Gabiarra, Braz.	I6	88
Gabon, ctry., Afr.	E2	66
Gaborone, Bots.	D7	70
Gabras, Sudan	E5	62
Gabriel Strait, strt., Nu., Can.	C17	106
Gabriel y Galán, Embalse de, res., Spain	D4	20
Gabrovo, Blg.	G12	26
Gacé, Fr.	F9	14
Gackle, N.D., U.S.	A13	126
Gadag, India	D2	53
Gādarwāra, India	G7	54
Gado Bravo, Ilha do, i., Braz.	F4	88
Gádor, Spain	H8	20
Gadsden, Al., U.S.	C12	122
Gadsden, Az., U.S.	K2	132
Gadwāl, India	C4	53
Gael Hamke Bugt, b., Grnld.	C22	141
Găeşti, Rom.	E12	26
Gaeta, Italy	C7	24
Gaeta, Golfo di, b., Italy	C7	24
Gaferut, i., Micron.	C5	72
Gaffney, S.C., U.S.	A4	116
Gafour, Tun.	H3	24
Gafsa, Tun.	C6	64
Gag, Pulau, i., Indon.	F8	44
Gagarin, Russia	E17	10
Gage, Ok., U.S.	E9	128
Gaggenau, Ger.	H4	16
Gagliano del Capo, Italy	E12	24
Gagnoa, C. Iv.	H3	64
Gagra, Geor.	F5	32
Gail, Tx., U.S.	B6	130
Gaillac, Fr.	F7	18
Gaillimh see Galway, Ire.	H3	12
Gaimán, Arg.	H3	90
Gainesboro, Tn., U.S.	H12	120
Gainesville, Fl., U.S.	G3	116
Gainesville, Ga., U.S.	B2	116
Gainesville, Mo., U.S.	H5	120
Gainesville, Tx., U.S.	H11	128
Gainsborough, Eng., U.K.	H12	12
Gainsborough Creek, stm., Can.	E12	124
Gairdner, Lake, l., Austl.	F7	74
Gaithersburg, Md., U.S.	E8	114
Gaixian, China	A10	42
Gaizina Kalns, hill, Lat.	D8	10
Gajendragarh, India	B2	53
Gajny, Russia	B8	32
Gajuapara, stm., Braz.	C2	88
Gajutino, Russia	B21	10
Gakarosa, mtn., S. Afr.	E7	70
Gakona, Ak., U.S.	D10	140
Galahad, Ab., Can.	D19	138
Galâla el Bahrîya, Gebel el-, mts., Egypt	I3	58
Galâla el-Qiblîya, Gebel el-, mts., Egypt	J3	58
Galán, Cerro, mtn., Arg.	C4	92
Galana, stm., Kenya	E7	66
Galanta, Slov.	H13	16
Galapagos Islands see Colón, Archipiélago de, is., Ec.	h12	84a
Galashiels, Scot., U.K.	F9	12
Galați, Rom.	D14	26
Galați, state, Rom.	D14	26
Galatina, Italy	D12	24
Galax, Va., U.S.	H4	114
Galaxídi, Grc.	E5	28
Galdhøpiggen, mtn., Nor.	F2	8
Galeana, Mex.	C8	100
Gao'an, China	G6	42
Galela, Indon.	E8	44
Galena, Ak., U.S.	D8	140
Galena, Il., U.S.	B7	120
Galena, Mo., U.S.	H4	120
Galena Park, Tx., U.S.	E12	130
Galeota Point, c., Trin.	s13	105f
Galera, Punta, c., Chile	G2	90
Galera, Punta, c., Ec.	G1	86
Galera Point, c., Trin.	s13	105f
Galesburg, Il., U.S.	D7	120
Galesville, Wi., U.S.	G7	118
Galeton, Pa., U.S.	C8	114
Galiano Island, i., B.C., Can.	H7	138
Galič, Russia	G20	8
Galicia, state, Spain	B2	20
Galicia, hist. reg., Eur.	G18	16
Galičica Nacionalni Park, p.o.i., Mac.	C3	28
Galičskaja vozvyšennost', hills, Russia	G20	8
Galičskoe, ozero, l., Russia	G20	8
Galilee, Lake, l., Austl.	D5	76
Galilee, Sea of see Kinneret, Yam, l., Isr.	F6	58
Galiléia, Braz.	J5	88
Galion, Oh., U.S.	D3	114
Gallarate, Italy	E5	22
Gallatin, Tn., U.S.	H11	120
Gallatin, stm., U.S.	E15	136
Galle, Sri L.	H5	53
Gállego, stm., Spain	B10	20
Gallegos, stm., Arg.	J3	90
Galliano, La., U.S.	H8	122
Gallinas, stm., N.M., U.S.	F4	128
Gallinas, Punta, c., Col.	A6	86
Gallipoli, Italy	D11	24
Gallipoli see Gelibolu, Tur.	C9	28
Gallipoli Peninsula see Gelibolu Yarımadası, pen., Tur.	C9	28
Gallipolis, Oh., U.S.	F3	114
Gällivare, Swe.	C9	8
Gallo, Capo, c., Italy	F7	24
Gallo Arroyo, stm., N.M., U.S.	G3	128
Galloo Island, i., N.Y., U.S.	E13	112
Galloway, hist. reg., Scot., U.K.	G8	12
Galloway, Mull of, c., Scot., U.K.	H8	12
Gallup, N.M., U.S.	H7	132
Gallura, reg., Italy	C3	24
Gallura Harbour, b., Fiji	q19	79e
Galt, Ca., U.S.	E4	134
Galt, Mo., U.S.	D4	120
Galtat Zemmour, W. Sah.	D2	64
Galty Mountains, mts., Ire.	I4	12
Galva, Il., U.S.	C7	120
Galveston, In., U.S.	H3	112
Galveston, Tx., U.S.	H4	122
Galveston Bay, b., Tx., U.S.	H4	122
Galveston Island, i., Tx., U.S.	E13	130
Gálvez, Arg.	F7	92
Galway (Gaillimh), Ire.	H3	12
Galway, state, Ire.	H4	12
Galway Bay, b., Ire.	H3	12
Gam (Jin), stm., Asia	A7	48
Gama, Isla, i., Arg.	H4	90
Gamagōri, Japan	E10	40
Gamarra, Col.	C5	86
Gamay, Phil.	D5	52
Gamba, China	D12	54
Gambaga, Ghana	G4	64
Gambela, Eth.	F6	62
Gambell, Ak., U.S.	D5	140
Gambia, The, ctry., Afr.	G1	64
Gambia (Gambie), stm., Afr.	G1	64
Gambier, Îles, is., Fr. Poly.	F13	72
Gamboa, Pan.	H8	102
Gamboma, Congo	E3	66
Gamboula, C.A.R.	D2	66
Gamka, stm., S. Afr.	H5	70
Gamlakarleby see Kokkola, Fin.	E10	8
Gamleby, Swe.	H7	8
Gammon Ranges National Park, p.o.i., Austl.	H2	76
Ga-Mogara, stm., S. Afr.	E7	70
Gan, stm., China	B10	36
Gan, stm., China	G6	42
Ganado, Az., U.S.	H7	132
Ganado, Tx., U.S.	E11	130
Gananoque, On., Can.	D13	112
Gāncā, Azer.	A6	56
Gand see Gent, Bel.	C12	14
Ganda, Ang.	C1	68
Gandadiwata, Bukit, mtn., Indon.	E11	50
Gandajika, D.R.C.	F4	66
Gandak (Nārāyaṇī), stm., Asia	E10	54
Gāndara, Spain	B2	20
Gander, Nf., Can.	j23	107a
Ganderkesee, Ger.	C4	16
Gandesa, Spain	C11	20
Gandevi, India	H4	54
Gāndhīnagar, India	G4	54
Gandhi Reservoir see Gāndhī Sāgar, res., India	F5	54
Gāndhī Sāgar, res., India	F5	54
Gandia, Spain	F10	20
Ganga see Ganges, stm., Asia	F11	54
Gan Gan, Arg.	H3	90
Gangānagar, India	D4	54
Gangāpur, India	E6	54
Gangāpur, India	F5	54
Gangārāmpur, India	F12	54
Gangaw, Mya.	A2	48
Gangāwati, India	D3	53
Gangdhār, India	F5	54
Gangdisê Shan, mts., China	C9	54
Ganges, B.C., Can.	H7	138
Ganges (Ganga) (Padma), stm., Asia	G13	54
Ganges, Mouths of the, mth., Asia	H12	54
Ganghu, China	B11	54
Gangmar Co, l., China	B10	54
Gangneung see Kangnung, Kor., S.	B1	40
Gangoa, China	D5	36
Gangotri, India	C7	54
Gangotri, India	C7	54
Gangoumen, China	D2	38
Gangtok, India	E12	54
Gangu, China	D1	42
Gangwon see Kangwŏn-do, state, Kor., S.	B1	40
Gannan, China	B9	36
Gannett Peak, mtn., Wy., U.S.	D3	126
Gannvalley, S.D., U.S.	C14	126
Ganquan, China	C3	42
Gansbaai, S. Afr.	I4	70
Gansu, state, China	D5	36
Gantang, China	H8	42
Gantt, Al., U.S.	F12	122
Gantung, Indon.	E6	50
Ganyanchi, China	C1	42
Ganyesa, S. Afr.	E7	70
Ganzê, China	E4	36
Ganzhou, China	I6	42
Gao, Mali	F4	64
Gaochun, China	F8	42
Gaohebu, China	C1	42
Gaojian, China	F9	36
Gaolong, China	H5	42
Gaoping, China	D5	42
Gaotai, China	D4	36
Gaotang, China	C7	42
Gaoua, Burkina	G4	64
Gaoual, Gui.	G2	64
Gaoxian, China	F5	36
Gaoyi, China	C6	42
Gaoyou, China	E8	42
Gaoyou Hu, l., China	E8	42
Gaozhou, China	K4	42
Gap, Fr.	E12	18
Gar, stm., China	C8	54
Gara, Lough, l., Ire.	H4	12
Garagumskij kanal (Kara-Kum Canal), can., Turkmen.	B9	56
Garagumy (Kara-Kum), des., Turkmen.	A8	56
Garaina, Pap. N. Gui.	b4	79a
Garanhuns, Braz.	E7	88
Garapan, N. Mar. Is.	B5	72
Garara, Pap. N. Gui.	b4	79a
Garber, Ok., U.S.	E11	128
Garbsen, Ger.	D5	16
Garça, Braz.	L1	88
García, Mex.	C8	100
García de Sola, Embalse de, res., Spain	E5	20
Gard, state, Fr.	F10	18
Gardelegen, Ger.	D7	16
Garden City, Ga., U.S.	D4	116
Garden City, Ks., U.S.	C8	128
Garden City, Mo., U.S.	F3	120
Garden City, Tx., U.S.	C6	130
Gardendale, Al., U.S.	D12	122
Garden Grove, Ca., U.S.	J7	134
Garden Grove, Ia., U.S.	D4	120
Garden Island, i., Mi., U.S.	C4	112
Garden Peninsula, pen., Mi., U.S.	C3	112
Garden Reach, India	H11	54
Gardenton, Mb., Can.	E17	124
Gardeyz, Afg.	C10	56
Gardiner, Mt., U.S.	E16	136
Gardiner, Or., U.S.	G2	136
Gardiner Dam, dam, Sk., Can.	C7	124
Gardner, Ks., U.S.	F2	120
Gardner Canal, b., B.C., Can.	C2	138
Gardnerville, Nv., U.S.	E6	134
Garessio, Italy	F5	22
Garet, Mont, vol., Vanuatu	j16	79d
Garfield, N.M., U.S.	K9	132
Garfield Mountain, mtn., Mt., U.S.	F14	136
Gargano, Promontorio del, mts., Italy	I13	22
Gargždai, Lith.	E4	10
Garhākota, India	G7	54
Garibaldi, Braz.	D12	92
Garibaldi, B.C., Can.	G7	138
Garibaldi, Mount, vol., B.C., Can.	G8	138
Gariep Dam, res., S. Afr.	G7	70
Garies, S. Afr.	G4	70
Garigliano, stm., Italy	C7	24
Garissa, Kenya	E7	66
Garland, Tx., U.S.	E2	122
Garland, Ut., U.S.	B4	132
Garlasco, Italy	E5	22
Garlin, Fr.	F5	18
Garm, Taj.	B11	56
Garmisch-Partenkirchen, Ger.	I7	16
Garnavillo, Ia., U.S.	A6	120
Garner, Ia., U.S.	A4	120
Garnett, Ks., U.S.	F2	120
Garona (Garonne), stm., Eur.	E5	18
Garonne (Garona), stm., Eur.	E5	18
Garoowe, Som.	C9	66
Garoua Boulaï, Cam.	C2	66
Garrel, Ger.	C4	16
Garretson, S.D., U.S.	H2	118
Garrett, In., U.S.	C1	112
Garrett, Ks., U.S.	F2	120
Garrison, N.D., U.S.	G12	124
Garrison Dam, dam, N.D., U.S.	G13	124
Garry, stm., Scot., U.K.	E9	12
Garry Bay, b., Nu., Can.	B13	106
Garry Lake, l., Nu., Can.	B10	106
Garsen, Kenya	E7	66
Garson, On., Can.	B9	112
Garut, Indon.	G5	50
Garwolin, Pol.	E17	16
Garwood, Tx., U.S.	H2	122
Gary, In., U.S.	G2	112
Gary, Tx., U.S.	E4	122
Gary, W.V., U.S.	G4	114
Garyarsa, China	C8	54
Garza, Arg.	D6	92
Garza Ayala, Mex.	H7	130
Garza García, Mex.	I7	130
Garzón, Col.	F4	86
Garzón, Ur.	G10	92
Gasan-Kuli, Turkmen.	B7	56
Gas City, In., U.S.	H4	112
Gascogne (Gascony), hist. reg., Fr.	F6	18
Gasconade, stm., Mo., U.S.	G6	120
Gasconade, Osage Fork, stm., Mo., U.S.	G5	120
Gascony see Gascogne, hist. reg., Fr.	F6	18
Gascoyne, stm., Austl.	D2	74
Gashaka, Nig.	H7	64
Gashua, Nig.	G7	64
Gaspar, Braz.	C13	92
Gasparilla Island, i., Fl., U.S.	J3	116
Gaspé, Qc., Can.	B12	110
Gaspé, Baie de, b., Qc., Can.	B12	110
Gaspé, Cap, c., Qc., Can.	B12	110
Gaspé Peninsula see Gaspésie, Péninsule de la, pen., Qc., Can.	B11	110
Gaspésie, Péninsule de la (Gaspé Peninsula), pen., Qc., Can.	B11	110
Gassaway, W.V., U.S.	F5	114
Gasteiz (Vitoria), Spain	B8	20
Gaston, Lake, res., U.S.	H7	114
Gastonia, N.C., U.S.	A4	116
Gastre, Arg.	H3	90
Gata, Cabo de, c., Spain	H8	20
Gata, Sierra de, mts., Spain	D4	20
Gătaia, Rom.	D8	26
Gata, Akrotírion, c., Cyp.	D4	58
Gatčina, Russia	A12	10
Gate City, Va., U.S.	H3	114
Gateshead, Eng., U.K.	G11	12
Gateshead Island, i., Nu.	A11	106
Gatesville, N.C., U.S.	H9	114
Gatesville, Tx., U.S.	C10	130
Gateway, Co., U.S.	E8	132
Gatineau, Qc., Can.	C14	112
Gatineau, stm., Qc., Can.	C14	112
Gatineau, Parc de la, p.o.i., Qc., Can.	C13	112
Gatlinburg, Tn., U.S.	I2	114
Gattinara, Italy	E5	22
Gatun, Lago, res., Pan.	H7	102
Gauer Lake, l., Mb., Can.	D11	106
Gauja (Koiva), stm., Eur.	C7	10
Gaula, stm., Nor.	E4	8
Gauley, stm., W.V., U.S.	F4	114
Gauley Bridge, W.V., U.S.	F4	114
Gaurela, India	G8	54
Gauribidanūr, India	E3	53
Gause, Tx., U.S.	G2	122
Gaustatoppen, mtn., Nor.	G3	8
Gauteng, state, S. Afr.	D9	70
Gavà, Spain	C12	20
Gávdos, i., Grc.	I7	28
Gāvião, stm., Braz.	H5	88
Gavins Point Dam, dam, U.S.	E15	126
Gävle, Swe.	F7	8
Gävleborg, state, Swe.	F7	8
Gavorrano, Italy	H7	22
Gavrilov-Jam, Russia	H18	8
Gawachab, Nmb.	E3	70
Gāwān, India	F10	54
Gawler, Austl.	J2	76
Gawler Ranges, mts., Austl.	F6	74
Gaya, India	F10	54
Gaya, Nig.	G6	64
Gaya, Niger	G5	64
Gaylord, Mi., U.S.	D5	112
Gayndah, Austl.	E8	76
Gays Mills, Wi., U.S.	H8	118
Gaza, state, Moz.	C11	70
Gaza see Ghazzah, Gaza	G5	58
Gazandzhyk see Gazandžyk, Turkmen.	B8	56
Gazandžyk, Turkmen.	B8	56
Gazaoua, Niger	G6	64
Gaza Strip, dep., Asia	G5	58
Gazelle Peninsula, pen., Pap. N. Gui.	a5	79a
Gaziantep, Tur.	A8	58
Gaziantep, state, Tur.	B8	58
Gazimağusa (Famagusta), N. Cyp.	C4	58
Gazimağusa Körfezi, b., N. Cyp.	C4	58
Gazipaşa, Tur.	G15	28
Gazivodo Jezero, res., Serb.	G8	26
Gbanga, Lib.	H3	64
Gboko, Nig.	H6	64
Gdańsk (Danzig), Pol.	B14	16
Gdańsk, state, Pol.	B14	16
Gdańsk, Gulf of, b., Eur.	B15	16
Gdov, Russia	B10	10
Gdynia, Pol.	B14	16
Geary, N.B., Can.	E10	110
Geary, Ok., U.S.	F10	128
Gebe, Pulau, i., Indon.	E8	44
Gebze, Tur.	C12	28
Geçitkale, N. Cyp.	C4	58
Gediz, Tur.	D12	28
Gediz (Hermus), stm., Tur.	E10	28
Gedser, Den.	B7	16
Geel, Bel.	C14	14
Geelong, Austl.	L5	76
Geelvink Channel, strt., Austl.	E2	74
Geesthacht, Ger.	C6	16
Geevestown, Austl.	o13	77a
Ge Hu, l., China	F8	42
Geiger, Al., U.S.	E10	122
Geikie, stm., Sk., Can.	D9	106
Geisenfeld, Ger.	H7	16
Geislingen an der Steige, Ger.	H5	16
Geistown, Pa., U.S.	D7	114
Geita, Tan.	E6	66
Geji, China	B12	54
Gejiu, China	G5	36
Gela, Italy	G8	24
Gela, Golfo di, b., Italy	G8	24
Gelādī, Eth.	F9	62
Geleen, Neth.	D14	14
Gelang, Tanjong, c., Malay.	K6	48
Gelasa, Selat, strt., Indon.	E5	50
Geldern, Ger.	E2	16
Gelendžik, Russia	F5	32
Gelgaudiškis, Lith.	F6	10
Gelibolu, Tur.	C9	28
Gelibolu Yarımadası (Gallipoli Peninsula), pen., Tur.	C9	28
Gellibrand, Austl.	L4	76
Gelsenkirchen, Ger.	E3	16
Gemas, Malay.	K6	48
Gemena, D.R.C.	D3	66
Gemert, Neth.	C14	14
Gemlik, Tur.	C12	28
Gemlik Körfezi, b., Tur.	C11	28
Gemona del Friuli, Italy	D10	22
Gemsa, Egypt	K4	58
Gemsbok National Park, p.o.i., Bots.	D5	70

Name	Map Ref.	Page

Gemünden, Ger. F5 16
Gen, stm., China. A9 36
Genalē (Jubba), stm., Afr.. . . . C8 66
Gending, Indon. G8 50
General Acha, Arg. H5 92
General Alvear, Arg. G3 92
General Alvear, Arg. H8 92
General Belgrano, Arg. G8 92
General Bernardo
  O'Higgins, sci., Ant. B35 81
General Bravo, Arg. C9 100
General Cabrera, Arg. F6 92
General Campos, Arg. E8 92
General Carrera, Lago, l.,
  S.A.. . . . . I2 90
General Conesa, Arg. H4 90
General Conesa, Arg. H9 92
General Daniel Cerri, Arg.. . I6 92
General Elizardo Aquino,
  Para. C9 92
General Enrique
  Martínez, Arg. F10 92
General Escobedo, Mex.. . . . I7 130
General Eugenio A.
  Garay, Para. D4 90
General Galarza, Arg. F8 92
General Güemes, Arg. B5 92
General Guido, Arg. H8 92
General José de San
  Martín, Arg. C8 92
General Juan José Ríos,
  Mex. C4 100
General Juan Madariaga,
  Arg. H9 92
General La Madrid, Arg. . . . H7 92
General Lavalle, Arg. H9 92
General Levalle, Arg.. . . . . G5 92
General Manuel Belgrano,
  Cerro, mtn., Arg. D4 92
General Pico, Arg. G6 92
General Pinedo, Arg. C7 92
General Pizarro, Arg. B6 92
General Ramírez, Arg. F7 92
General Roca, Arg. G3 90
General San Martín, Arg. . . . G8 92
General Santos, Phil. G5 52
General Terán, Mex. C9 100
General Toševo, Blg. F14 26
General Toševo see
  General Toševo, Blg. F14 26
General Treviño, Mex. H8 130
General Trias, Mex. F1 130
General Viamonte, Arg. . . . G7 92
General Villegas, Arg. G6 92
Genesee, Id., U.S. D9 136
Genesee, stm., U.S.. . . . . . F12 112
Geneseo, Il., U.S. C7 120
Geneseo, Ks., U.S. C10 128
Geneseo, N.Y., U.S. B8 114
Geneva see Genève, Switz.. . . D3 22
Geneva, Il., U.S. J10 118
Geneva, In., U.S. H5 112
Geneva, N.Y., U.S. G15 126
Geneva, Oh., U.S. C4 114
Geneva, Lake, l., Eur. C12 18
Genève (Geneva), Switz. . . . D3 22
Genève, Lac de see
  Geneva, Lake, l., Eur. . . . C12 18
Genf see Genève, Switz. D3 22
Gengma, China. G4 36
Genil, stm., Spain G5 20
Genk, Bel. C14 14
Genkai-nada, s., Japan F2 40
Genoa, Austl. K7 76
Genoa see Genova, Italy . . . F5 22
Genoa, Oh., U.S. C2 114
Genoa, Wi., U.S. H7 118
Genova (Genoa), Italy F5 22
Genova, Golfo di, b., Italy . . G5 22
Genrietty, ostrov, i., Russia . . A20 34
Gens de Terre, stm.,
  Qc., Can. B13 112
Genshiryoku-kenkyūsho,
  sci., Japan C13 40
Gent (Ghent), Bel. C12 14
Genteng, Gili, i., Indon.. . . . G8 50
Genthin, Ger. D8 16
Gentio do Ouro, Braz. F4 88
Genzano di Roma, Italy I9 22
Geographe Bay, b., Austl. . . . F3 74
Geographical Society
  Ø, i., Grnld. C21 141
Geok-Tepe, Turkmen. B8 56
George, S. Afr. H6 70
George, Ia., U.S. H2 118
George, stm., Qc., Can.. . . . D17 106
George, Lake, l., Austl. J7 76
George, Lake, l., Austl. D4 74
George, Lake, l., Fl., U.S. . . . G4 116
George, Lake, res., N.Y., U.S. . G3 110
George Town, Austl. n13 77a
Georgetown, Austl. B4 76
Georgetown, On., Can. E9 112
Georgetown, P.E., Can. D14 110
George Town, Cay. Is. C7 102
Georgetown, Gam. G2 64
Georgetown, Guy. B6 84
George Town (Penang),
  Malay. J4 48
Georgetown, St. Vin. o11 105e
Georgetown, Co., U.S.. . . . . B3 128
Georgetown, De., U.S. F10 114
Georgetown, Fl., U.S. G4 116
Georgetown, Id., U.S. H15 136
Georgetown, Ky., U.S. F1 114
Georgetown, Ms., U.S. F8 122
Georgetown, Oh., U.S. F2 114
Georgetown, S.C., U.S. C6 116
Georgetown, Tx., U.S. D10 130
George V Coast, cst., Ant. . . . B19 81
George Washington
  Birthplace National
  Monument, p.o.i.,
  Va., U.S. F9 114
George Washington Carver
  National Monument,
  p.o.i., Mo., U.S. H3 120
George West, Tx., U.S. F9 130
Georgia, ctry., Afr. F6 32
Georgia, state, U.S. E11 108
Georgia, Strait of, strt., N.A. . G7 138
Georgian Bay, b., On., Can. . . C8 112
Georgian Bay Islands
  National Park, p.o.i.,
  On., Can. D9 112
Georgievka, Kaz. E14 32
Georgina, stm., Austl. D2 76
Georg von Neumayer,
  sci., Ant. B3 81
Gera, Ger. F7 16
Geral, Serra, mts., Braz.. . . . C12 92
Geral, Serra, clf., Braz. F2 88
Gerald, Mo., U.S. F6 120
Geral de Goiás,
  Serra, clf., Braz. G2 88
Geraldine, Mt., U.S. C16 136
Geraldton, Austl. E2 74
Geraldton, On., Can. F15 14
Gerber, Ca., U.S. C3 134
Gerdine, Mount, mtn.,
  Ak., U.S. D9 140
Gerede, Tur. C15 28
Gereshk, Afg. C9 56
Gérgal, Spain G8 20
Gerik, Malay. J5 48
Gerlachovský
  štít, mtn., Slov. G16 16
German Democratic
  Republic see Germany,
  ctry., Eur. E6 16
Germania Land, reg., Grnld. . B21 141

Germantown, Il., U.S.. . . . . F8 120
Germantown, Tn., U.S.. . . . . B9 122
Germantown, Wi., U.S. E1 112
Germany, ctry., Eur. E6 16
Germany, Federal Republic
  of see Germany, ctry., Eur.. . E6 16
Germencik, Tur. F10 28
Germfask, Mi., U.S. B4 112
Germiston, S. Afr. E9 70
Gernika, Spain. A8 20
Gero, Japan. D10 40
Gerolimēnas, Grc. G5 28
Gerona see Girona, Spain . . B13 20
Geronimo, Ok., U.S. G10 128
Gers, state, Fr. F6 18
Gers, stm., Fr. F6 18
Gêrzê, China B10 54
Geseke, Ger. E4 16
Geser, Indon. F9 44
Getafe, Spain. D7 20
Gettysburg, Pa., U.S.. . . . . . E8 114
Getúlio Vargas, Braz.. . . . . C11 92
Geumpang, Indon. J2 48
Gevgelija, Mac. B5 28
Geyikli, Tur. D9 28
Geyser, Mt., U.S. C16 136
Geyserville, Ca., U.S. E3 134
Geyve, Tur. C13 28
Ghaapplato, plat., S. Afr. . . . E7 70
Ghadāmis, Libya B1 62
Ghaghar, stm., India D5 54
Ghāghara (Kauriālā), stm.,
  Asia E9 54
Ghāghra see
  Ghāghara, stm., Asia E9 54
Ghakhar, Pak. B4 54
Ghana, ctry., Afr. H4 64
Ghanzi, Bots. B5 70
Ghanzi, state, Bots. C6 70
Gharandal, sci., Jord. H6 58
Gharaunda, India D6 54
Ghardaïa, Alg. C5 64
Ghardimaou, Tun. H2 24
Gharyān, Libya A2 62
Ghāt, Libya C2 62
Ghatere, Mount, mtn.,
  Sol. Is. d8 79b
Ghātprabha, stm., India . . . C2 53
Ghatsila, India. G11 54
Ghawdex (Gozo), i., Malta . . H8 24
Ghazāl, Bahr al-, stm.,
  Sudan F6 62
Ghāziābād, India D6 54
Ghāzipur, India F9 54
Ghazlūna, Pak. C1 54
Ghazni, Afg. C10 56
Ghazni, state, Afg. B1 54
Ghazni, stm., Afg. B2 54
Ghazzah (Gaza), Gaza G5 58
Ghazzah, Leb. E6 58
Ghent see Gent, Bel. C12 14
Gheorgheni, Rom. C12 26
Gherla, Rom. C10 26
Ghinah, Wādī al-, stm.,
  Sau. Ar.. . . . . H9 58
Ghisonaccia, Fr. H15 18
Ghizo see Gizo Island,
  i., Sol. Is. e7 79b
Ghizunabeana Islands,
  is., Sol. Is. d8 79b
Ghorīān, Afg. C9 56
Ghotki, Pak. E2 54
Ghubaysh, Sudan E5 62
Gianh, stm., Viet. C7 48
Giannitsá, Grc. C5 28
Giant Mountain, mtn.,
  N.Y., U.S. F3 110
Giant's Castle see
  Giant's Castle, mtn., S. Afr. . F9 70
Giant's Castle Game
  Reserve, S. Afr. F9 70
Gia Rai, Viet. H7 48
Giarre, Italy G9 24
Gibara, Cuba B9 102
Gibbon, Mn., U.S. G4 118
Gibbons, Ab., Can. C17 138
Gibbonsville, Id., U.S. E13 136
Gibb River, Austl. C5 74
Gibeon, Nmb. D3 70
Gibraleón, Spain G3 20
Gibraltar, Gib. H5 20
Gibraltar, dep., Eur. H5 20
Gibraltar, Strait of, strt. B3 64
Gibraltar Point, c.,
  Eng., U.K. H13 12
Gibsland, La., U.S. E5 122
Gibson City, Il., U.S. D9 120
Gibson Desert, des., Austl.. . . D4 74
Gibsons, B.C., Can. G7 138
Gibsonville, N.C., U.S.. . . . . H6 114
Giddalūr, India D4 53
Giddings, Tx., U.S. D11 130
Gidgi, Lake, l., Austl. E5 74
Giedraičiai, Lith. E8 10
Gien, Fr. G11 14
Giessen, Ger. F4 16
Gifatīn, Gezīra, is., Egypt . . . K4 58
Gifford, Fl., U.S. I5 116
Gifford, stm., Nu., Can. A14 106
Gifford Creek, Austl. D3 74
Gifgafa, Bîr, well, Egypt . . . H4 58
Gifhorn, Ger. D6 16
Gifu, Japan. D9 40
Gifu, state, Japan D10 40
Giganta, Sierra de la,
  mts., Mex. C3 100
Gigena see Alcira, Arg. F5 92
Gigha Island, i., Scot., U.K. . . F7 12
Giglio, Isola del, i., Italy H7 22
Gihu see Gifu, Japan D9 40
Gijón, Spain A5 20
Gila, stm., U.S. K2 132
Gila Bend, Az., U.S. K4 132
Gila Cliff Dwellings
  National Monument,
  p.o.i., N.M., U.S.. . . . . . . J8 132
Gilbert, La., U.S. E7 122
Gilbert, stm., Austl. C8 74
Gilbert Islands see
  Kiribati, ctry., Oc. D9 72
Gilbert Islands, is., Kir. D8 72
Gilbert Peak, mtn., Wa., U.S. . D5 136
Gilbert Plains, Mb., Can. . . . C13 124
Gilbués, Braz. E3 88
Gildford, Mt., U.S.. . . . . . . B16 136
Gilford Island, i., B.C., Can. . . F4 138
Gilgandra, Austl. H7 76
Gilgil, Kenya E7 66
Gil Gil Creek, stm., Austl. . . . G8 76
Gilgit, Pak. B11 56
Gilirang, Indon. E12 50
Gil Island, i., B.C., Can. C1 138
Giljuj, stm., Russia. F14 34
Gillam, Mb., Can. D12 106
Gillen, Lake, l., Austl. E5 74
Gillespie, Il., U.S. E8 120
Gillett, Ar., U.S. C7 122
Gillette, Wy., U.S.. . . . . . . C7 126
Gillian, Lake, l., Nu., Can. . . B16 106
Gillingham, Eng., U.K. J13 12
Gills Rock, Wi., U.S. C3 112
Gilman, Il., U.S. D10 120
Gilman, Wi., U.S. F8 118
Gilmer, Tx., U.S. E4 122
Gilmore City, Ia., U.S. B3 120
Gilroy, Ca., U.S. F4 134
Giluwe, Mount, mtn.,
  Pap. N. Gui. b3 79a
Gimbī, Eth.. . . . . F7 62
Gimcheon see Kimch'ŏn,
  Kor., S. F8 38
Gimie, Mount, vol., St. Luc. . . m6 105c

Gimli, Mb., Can.. . . . . D16 124
Gimpu, Indon. D12 50
Gineina, Râs el-,
  mtn., Egypt. I4 58
Gin Gin, Austl.. . . . . E8 76
Gingoog, Phil. F5 52
Ginir, Eth. F8 62
Ginosa, Italy. D10 24
Gioia, Golfo di, b., Italy F9 24
Gioia del Colle, Italy D10 24
Gioia Tauro, Italy. F9 24
Giong Rieng, Viet. H7 48
Gipuzkoako, co., Spain A8 20
Girafi, Wadi (Paran, Nahal),
  stm. I5 58
Giralia, Austl. D2 74
Girard, Il., U.S. E8 120
Girard, Ks., U.S. G3 120
Girard, Oh., U.S. C5 114
Girard, Pa., U.S. C5 114
Girardot, Col. E4 86
Giraud, Pointe, c., Dom. . . . j6 105c
Girgarre, Austl. K5 76
Giridih, India F11 54
Girna, stm., India. H5 54
Gir National Park,
  p.o.i., India H3 54
Girne (Kyrenia), N. Cyp. . . . C4 58
Girón, Ec. D2 84
Girona, Spain B13 20
Girona, co., Spain B13 20
Gironde, state, Fr. E5 18
Gironde, est., Fr. D5 18
Gir Range, mts., India. H3 54
Giru, Austl.. . . . . B6 76
Giruá, Braz. D10 92
Girvan, Scot., U.K. F8 12
Gisborne, N.Z. D8 80
Giscome, B.C., Can. B8 138
Gislaved, Swe. H5 8
Gisors, Fr. E10 14
Gitarama, Rw. E5 66
Gitega, Bdi. E5 66
Giuliánova, Italy H10 22
Giurgiu, Rom. F12 26
Giurgiu, state, Rom. E13 26
Giuvala, Pasul, p., Rom.. . . . D12 26
Givet, Fr. D13 14
Givors, Fr. D10 18
Giyon, Eth. F7 62
Giza see El-Gîza, Egypt H1 58
Gizhduvan, Uzb.. . . . . F11 32
Gizhiga, Russia. D21 34
Gizhiginskaja guba,
  b., Russia. D20 34
Gizo Island, i., Sol. Is. e7 79b
Giżycko, Pol. B17 16
Gjirokastër, Alb. D14 24
Gjirokastër see
  Gjirokastër, Alb. D14 24
Gjoa Haven see
  Oqsuqtooq, Nu., Can. . . . B11 106
Gjøvik, Nor. F4 8
Gjuhëzës, Kepi i, c., Alb. . . . D13 24
Gjumri, Arm. A5 56
Glace Bay, N.S., Can. D17 110
Glacier, B.C., Can. E13 138
Glacier Bay, b., Ak., U.S. . . . E12 140
Glacier National Park,
  p.o.i., B.C., Can. E13 138
Glacier National Park,
  p.o.i., Mt., U.S. B12 136
Glacier Peak, vol., Wa., U.S. . B5 136
Glacier Strait, strt.,
  Nu., Can. B10 141
Glad', Russia. A15 10
Gladbrook, Ia., U.S. B5 120
Gladewater, Tx., U.S. E4 122
Gladstone, Austl. D8 76
Gladstone, Mb., Can. D14 124
Gladstone, Mi., U.S. C2 112
Gladstone, Mo., U.S. E3 120
Gláma, stm., Nor. F4 8
Glan, Phil. H5 52
Glaris see Glarus, Switz. . . . C5 22
Glarner Alpen, mts., Switz. . . D6 22
Glarus, Switz. C5 22
Glarus Alps see Glarner
  Alpen, mts., Switz. D6 22
Glasco, Ks., U.S. B11 128
Glasgow, Scot., U.K. F8 12
Glasgow, Ky., U.S. G12 120
Glasgow, Mo., U.S. E5 120
Glasgow, Mt., U.S. F7 124
Glasgow, Va., U.S. G6 114
Glassboro, N.J., U.S. E10 114
Glastonbury, Eng., U.K. J10 12
Glauchau, Ger. F8 16
Glazov, Russia C8 32
Glazunovka, Russia. H19 10
Gleichen, Ab., Can.. . . . . . F17 138
Glen Alpine, N.C., U.S. A4 116
Glenavon, Sk., Can. D11 124
Glenboro, Mb., Can. E14 124
Glenburn, N.D., U.S. F12 124
Glen Burnie, Md., U.S. E9 114
Glen Canyon, p., U.S. F6 132
Glen Canyon Dam, dam,
  Az., U.S. G5 132
Glen Canyon National
  Recreation Area,
  p.o.i., U.S. F6 132
Glencoe, On., Can. F8 112
Glencoe, S. Afr. F10 70
Glencoe, Mn., U.S.. . . . . . . G4 118
Glen Cove, N.Y., U.S. D12 114
Glendale, Ca., U.S. J4 132
Glendale, Ca., U.S. I7 134
Glendale, Ms., U.S. F9 122
Glendale, Ut., U.S. F4 132
Glendale, Wi., U.S. A10 120
Glendive, Mt., U.S. G9 124
Glendo, Wy., U.S. E7 126
Glendo Reservoir, res.,
  Wy., U.S. E8 126
Glen Elder, Ks., U.S. B10 128
Glenelg, stm., Austl. K3 76
Glengarriff, Ire. J3 12
Glengyle, Austl. E2 76
Glen Innes, Austl. G8 76
Glenmora, La., U.S. G6 122
Glennallen, Ak., U.S. D11 140
Glenns Ferry, Id., U.S. H11 136
Glenoma, Wa., U.S. D4 136
Glenormiston, Austl. D7 74
Glenreagh, Austl. G9 76
Glen Robertson, On., Can. . . E2 110
Glen Rock, Pa., U.S. E9 114
Glen Rose, Tx., U.S. B10 130
Glenrothes, Scot., U.K. E9 12
Glens Falls, N.Y., U.S. G3 110
Glenville, W.V., U.S. H5 118
Glenwood, Ab., Can.. . . . . . G17 138
Glenwood, Ar., U.S.. . . . . . C5 122
Glenwood, Ga., U.S.. . . . . . D3 116
Glenwood, Mn., U.S. F3 118
Glenwood, Va., U.S. H6 114
Glenwood City, Wi., U.S. . . . F6 118
Glenwood Springs, Co., U.S. . D9 132
Glidden, Wi., U.S. E8 118
Glide, Or., U.S. G3 136
Glina, Cro.. . . . . E13 22
Glittertind see
  Glittertinden, mtn., Nor. . . F3 8
Glittertinden, mtn., Nor. . . . F3 8
Gliwice, Pol. F14 16
Globe, Az., U.S. J6 132
Głogów, Pol. E11 16

Głogów Małopolski, Pol.. . . . F17 16
Glomma see Gláma,
  stm., Nor. F4 8
Glommersträsk, Swe. D8 8
Glorieta, N.M., U.S. F3 128
Glorieuses, Îles, is., Reu. . . . C8 68
Glorioso Islands see
  Glorieuses, Îles, is., Reu. . . C8 68
Gloucester, Eng., U.K. J10 12
Gloucester, Ma., U.S. B15 114
Gloucester, Va., U.S. G9 114
Gloucester Island, i., Austl. . . B7 76
Glouster, Oh., U.S. E3 114
Gloversville, N.Y., U.S. A11 114
Głowno, Pol. E15 16
Głubczyce, Pol. F13 16
Głubokoe, Kaz. D14 32
Głubokoje see
  Glûbokoe, Kaz. D14 32
Głucholazy, Pol. F13 16
Glücksburg, Ger. B5 16
Glückstadt, Ger. C5 16
Glucomanka, gora, mtn.,
  Russia B11 38
Glyndon, Mn., U.S. E2 118
Gmünd, Aus. B12 22
Gmünd, Aus. D10 22
Gmunden, Aus. C10 22
Gnalta, Austl. H4 76
Gnezdovo, Russia F14 10
Gniew, Pol. C14 16
Gniezno, Pol. D13 16
Gnilec, Russia H19 10
Gnjilane, Serb. G8 26
Gnowangerup, Austl. F3 74
Gô, stm., Japan E5 40
Goa, state, India D2 53
Goālpāra, India E13 54
Goaso, Ghana. H4 64
Goat Island, i., Antig. e4 105b
Goat Point, c., Antig. e4 105b
Goba, Eth. F8 62
Gobabis, Nmb. C4 70
Göbel, Tur. D11 28
Gobernador Gregores, Arg. . I2 90
Gobernador Ingeniero
  Valentín Virasoro, Arg.. . . D9 92
Gobernador Juan E.
  Martínez, Arg.. . . . . D8 92
Gobernador Vera see
  Vera, Arg.. . . . . D7 92
Gobi Desert, des., Asia C5 36
Gobô, Japan. E8 40
Goce Delčev, Blg. H10 26
Godafoss, wtfl., Ice. k31 8a
Godávari, stm., India C5 53
Godávari, Mouths of
  the, mth., India. C5 53
Godbout, Qc., Can.. . . . . . . A9 110
Goderich, On., Can. E8 112
Godfrey, Il., U.S. F7 120
Godhavn (Qeqertarsuaq),
  Grnld. D15 141
Godhra, India. G4 54
Godoy Cruz, Arg. F3 92
Gods, stm., Mb., Can. D12 106
Gods Lake, l., Mb., Can. . . . E12 106
Gods Mercy, Bay of, b.,
  Nu., Can. C13 106
Godthåb (Nuuk), Grnld. . . . E15 141
Godwin Austen see K2,
  mtn., Asia B12 56
Goeie Hoop, Kaap die see
  Good Hope, Cape of,
  c., S. Afr. I4 70
Goéland, Lac au, l.,
  Qc., Can. E15 106
Goes, Neth. C12 14
Goffstown, N.H., U.S. G5 110
Gogebic, Lake, res.,
  Mi., U.S. E9 118
Gogoi, Moz. B11 70
Gogrial, Sudan F5 62
Gohad, India. E7 54
Gohpur, India E14 54
Goiana, Braz. D8 88
Goianésia, Braz.. . . . . H1 88
Goiânia, Braz. I1 88
Goiás, Braz. G7 84
Goiás, state, Braz. C7 90
Goiatuba, Braz. J1 88
Goio-Erê, Braz.. . . . . B11 92
Góio-Erê, stm., Braz. B11 92
Góis, Port. D2 20
Gojô, Japan. E8 40
Gojra, Pak.. . . . . C4 54
Gokak, India. C2 53
Gökçeada, i., Tur.. . . . . C8 28
Gökova Körfezi
  (Kerme, Gulf of), b., Tur. . . G10 28
Göksu, stm., Tur.. . . . . B4 58
Göksu, stm., Tur.. . . . . A6 58
Göktepe, Tur. F11 28
Gökwe, Zimb. D4 68
Gólağhāt, India E14 54
Gola Gokarannāth, India . . . D8 54
Golan, stm., Russia. D13 16
Gölbaşı, Tur. D15 28
Gölbaşı, Tur. A8 58
Gölcük, Tur.. . . . . H3 80
Golconda, sci., India C4 53
Golconda, Il., U.S. G9 120
Golconda, Nv., U.S. H6 126
Gölcük, Tur.. . . . . C12 28
Goldap, Pol. B18 16
Gold Bridge, B.C., Can. F8 138
Gold Coast see
  Southport, Austl. F9 76
Gold Coast, cst., Ghana I4 64
Golden, B.C., Can. E13 138
Golden, Co., U.S. B3 128
Golden, Il., U.S. D7 120
Golden Bay, b., N.Z. E5 80
Golden City, Mo., U.S. G3 120
Goldendale, Wa., U.S. E6 136
Golden Gate Highlands
  National Park, p.o.i.,
  S. Afr. F9 70
Golden Hinde, mtn.,
  B.C., Can. G5 138
Golden Lake, l., On., Can. . . C12 112
Golden Meadow, La., U.S. . . H8 122
Goldfield, Ia., U.S. B3 120
Goldfield, Nv., U.S. F8 134
Gold Mountain, mtn.,
  Nv., U.S. F8 134
Goldonna, La., U.S. E6 122
Gold River, B.C., Can. G5 138
Gold Rock, On., Can. B6 118
Goldsboro, N.C., U.S. A7 116
Goldsmith, Tx., U.S. A6 130
Goldsworthy, Austl. D3 74
Goldthwaite, Tx., U.S. C9 130
Goleniów, Pol. C10 16
Goleta, Ca., U.S. I6 134
Golfito, C.R. H6 102
Golfo de Santa Clara, Mex. . . F5 98
Gölhisar, Tur. F12 28
Goliad, Tx., U.S. F10 130
Golicyno, Russia E19 10
Golina, Pol. D13 16
Golin Baixing, China. B4 38
Gölmarmara, Tur. E10 28
Golmud, China. D3 36
Golmud, stm., China. D3 36
Golongösa, stm., Moz. A7 46
Gölpazari, Tur. C13 28
Gölpāzari's, Iran C7 56
Golub-Dobrzyń, Pol. C14 16

Golva, N.D., U.S. A8 126
Golyšmanovo, Russia C11 32
Goma, D.R.C. E5 66
Gomang Co, l., China C12 54
Gomati, stm., India E8 54
Gombe, Nig. G7 64
Gombi, Nig. G7 64
Gómez Farías, Mex.. . . . . . . A5 100
Gómez Palacio, Mex. C7 100
Gómez Plata, Col.. . . . . D4 86
Gomo Co, l., China B10 54
Gomogomo, Indon. b1 79a
Gomoh, Indon. G10 54
Gonābād, Iran C8 56
Gonaïves, Haiti. C11 102
Gonam, Russia E15 34
Gonam, stm., Russia E14 34
Gonarezhou National
  Park, p.o.i., Zimb. B10 70
Gonâve, Golfe de la,
  b., Haiti C11 102
Gonâve, Île de la, i., Haiti . . . C11 102
Gonbad-e Qābūs, Iran B8 56
Gonda, India E8 54
Gondal, India H3 54
Gondar see Gonder, Eth. . . . E7 62
Gondarbal, India A5 54
Gonder, Eth. E7 62
Gondia, India H8 54
Gönen, Tur. C10 28
Gong, stm., China I6 42
Gong'an, China F4 42
Gonge, China I4 42
Gongchengiao, China. F8 42
Gonggar, China D13 54
Gongga Shan, mtn., China . . F5 36
Gonghe, China. D5 36
Gongliu, China F14 32
Gongola, stm., Nig. G7 64
Gongshiya, China. C10 54
Gongxi, China H6 42
Gongxian, China. D5 42
Gongzhuling, China C6 38
Goñi, Ur. F9 92
Goniądz, Pol. C18 16
Gônoura, Japan. F2 40
Góbel, Tur. D11 28
Gonzales, Ca., U.S. G4 134
Gonzales, La., U.S. G7 122
Gonzales, Tx., U.S. E10 130
González, Mex.. . . . . D9 100
González Moreno, Arg. G6 92
Goochland, Va., U.S. G8 114
Goodenough Island, i.,
  Pap. N. Gui. b5 79a
Gooderham, On., Can. D11 112
Goodeve, Sk., Can.. . . . . . . C10 124
Good Hope, Cape of
  (Goeie Hoop, Kaap die),
  c., S. Afr. I4 70
Good Hope Mountain,
  mtn., B.C., Can. E6 138
Goodhue, Mn., U.S. G6 118
Goodland, Fl., U.S. K4 116
Goodland, In., U.S. H2 112
Goodland, Ks., U.S. B7 128
Goodman, Mo., U.S. H3 120
Goodman, Wi., U.S. C1 112
Goodnews Bay, Ak., U.S. . . . E7 140
Goodnight, Tx., U.S. G7 128
Goodooga, Austl. G6 76
Goodrich, N.D., U.S. G13 124
Good Spirit Lake, l.,
  Sk., Can. C11 124
Goodwater, Al., U.S. D12 122
Goodwin, Az., U.S. J4 132
Goodyear, Az., U.S. J4 132
Goole, Eng., U.K. H12 12
Goolgowi, Austl. I5 76
Goolwa, Austl. J2 76
Goomalling, Austl. F3 74
Goombalie, Austl. G5 76
Goomeri, Austl. F9 76
Goondiwindi, Austl. G8 76
Goongarrie, Austl.. . . . . . . F4 74
Goose, stm., N.D., U.S. G17 124
Goose Creek, S.C., U.S. C6 116
Goose Island, i., B.C., Can. . . E2 138
Goose Lake, l., Sk., Can. . . . C6 124
Goose Lake, l., U.S. B5 134
Gooty, India D3 53
Gopālganj, Bngl. G12 54
Gopālganj, India E10 54
Gopichettipālaiyam, India . . F3 53
Göppingen, Ger.. . . . . H5 16
Goqên, China F4 36
Go Quao, Viet. H7 48
Góra Kalwaria, Pol. E17 16
Gorakhpur, India E9 54
Goražde, Bos. F5 26
Gorda, Punta, c., Cuba A6 102
Gorda, Punta, c., Nic. H6 102
Gordeevka, Russia. H14 10
Gordil, C.A.R. C4 66
Gordion, sci., Tur. D15 28
Gordo, Al., U.S. D11 122
Gordon, Ga., U.S. D2 116
Gordon, Lake, res., Austl.. . . o13 77a
Gordon Creek, stm., Ne.,
  U.S. E11 126
Gordon Downs, Austl. C5 74
Gordon Horne Peak, mtn.,
  B.C., Can. E12 138
Gordonsville, Va., U.S. F7 114
Gordonvale, Austl. A6 76
Gore, N.S., Can. E13 110
Gore, Chad F3 62
Gore, Eth. F7 62
Gore, N.Z.. . . . . H3 80
Goreda, Indon. F9 44
Goree, Tx., U.S. H10 128
Gore Range, mts., Co., U.S. . . D10 132
Goreville, Il., U.S. G9 120
Gorgān, Iran. B7 56
Gorgona, Isla, i., Col. F2 86
Gorgota, Rom. E13 26
Gorham, Me., U.S.. . . . . . . G6 110
Gori, Geor. F6 32
Gorica see Gorizia, Italy . . . E10 22
Goricy, Russia C19 10
Gorinchem, Neth. C14 14
Gorizia (Gorica), Italy E10 22
Gorj, state, Rom. E10 26
Gorkhā, Nepal E10 54
Gorki see Nižnij
  Novgorod, Russia H21 8
Gorlice, Pol. G17 16
Görlitz, Ger. E10 16
Gorman, Tx., U.S. B9 130
Gorna Orjahovica, Blg. F12 26
Gornjak, Russia D14 32
Gornji Vakuf, Bos. F4 26
Gorno-Altajsk, Russia D15 32
Gornozavodsk, Russia B13 36
Gornye Ključi, Russia B11 38
Gornyak, Russia E4 42
Gorodec, Russia H20 8
Gorodec, Russia D14 10
Gorodok, Russia E12 10
Gorontalo, Indon. E7 44
Gorovo Ilaveckie, Pol. B16 16
Gorškovo, Russia. F20 10
Görükle, Tur. C11 28
Gorutuba, stm., Braz.. . . . . H4 88
Gorzów Śląski, Pol. E14 16
Gorzów Wielkopolski
  (Landsberg), Pol. D11 16

Goschen Strait, strt.,
  Pap. N. Gui.. . . . . c5 79a
Gosen, Japan. B12 40
Gosford, Austl.. . . . . I8 76
Goshen, N.S., Can. E15 110
Goshen, Ca., U.S. G6 134
Goshen, In., U.S. G4 112
Goshen, N.Y., U.S. C11 114
Goshute Lake, l., Nv., U.S. . . C2 132
Goshute Valley, val., Nv., U.S. . C2 132
Goslar, Ger. E6 16
Gosnells, Austl. F3 74
Gossinga, Sudan F5 62
Gostivar, Mac. B3 28
Gostynin, Pol. D15 16
Gota, stm., Swe. G5 8
Gotebo, Ok., U.S.. . . . . F10 128
Göteborg (Gothenburg),
  Swe.. . . . . H4 8
Gotemba, Japan. D11 40
Goteşti, Mol. C15 26
Gotha, Ger. F6 16
Gothenburg see
  Göteborg, Swe. H4 8
Gothenburg, Ne., U.S. G12 126
Gothèye, Niger G5 64
Gotland, state, Swe. G8 8
Gotland, i., Swe. H8 8
Gotō-rettō, is., Japan. F1 40
Gotska Sandön, i., Swe.. . . . G8 8
Götsu, Japan. D5 40
Göttingen, Ger. E5 16
Goubangzi, China D4 38
Gouda, Neth. B13 14
Goudge, Arg.. . . . . G3 92
Goudiri, Sen. G2 64
Gough Island, i., St. Hel. . . . K5 60
Gough Lake, l., Ab., Can. . . . D18 138
Gouin, Réservoir, res.,
  Qc., Can. B1 110
Goulais, stm., On., Can. B6 112
Goulburn, Austl. J7 76
Goulburn Islands, is., Austl. . B6 74
Goulburn River National
  Park, p.o.i., Austl. I7 76
Gould, Ar., U.S. D7 122
Goulds, Fl., U.S. K5 116
Goumbou, Mali G3 64
Goundam, Mali G4 64
Goundi, Chad F3 62
Gourbeyre, Guad. h5 105c
Gourdon, Fr. E7 18
Gouré, Niger G7 64
Gourma-Rharous, Mali F4 64
Gournay-en-Bray, Fr. E10 14
Gouro, Chad D3 62
Gouverneur, N.Y., U.S. D14 112
Govan, Sk., Can. C9 124
Gove, Ks., U.S. C8 128
Govena, mys, c., Russia E22 34
Govenlock, Sk., Can. E4 124
Governador Valadares,
  Braz.. . . . . J5 88
Govind Ballabh Pant
  Reservoir see Govind
  Ballabh Pant Sāgar,
  res., India F9 54
Govind Ballabh Pant
  Sāgar, res., India F9 54
Govind Reservoir see
  Govind Sāgar, res., India . . C6 54
Govind Sāgar, res., India . . . C6 54
Gowanda, N.Y., U.S. B7 114
Gower, Mo., U.S. E3 120
Gowmal, Afg. B2 54
Gowmal (Gumal), stm., Asia . B2 54
Gowrie, Ia., U.S. B3 120
Goya, Arg. D8 92
Goyaves, Îlets à, is., Guad. . . h5 105c
Goz Beïda, Chad E4 62
Gozdnica, Pol. E11 16
Gozha Co, l., China A5 46
Gozo see Ghawdex,
  i., Malta H8 24
Graaff-Reinet, S. Afr. H7 70
Grabo, C. Iv.. . . . . I3 64
Grabow, Ger. C7 16
Grabów nad Prosną, Pol. . . . E13 16
Gračac, Cro. F12 22
Gračanica, Bos.. . . . . E5 26
Grace, Id., U.S. H15 136
Graceville, Fl., U.S. G13 122
Gracias a Dios, Cabo, c., N.A. . E6 102
Grado, Italy E10 22
Grado, Spain A4 20
Grad Sofija, state, Blg. G10 26
Grady, Ar., U.S. C7 122
Grady, N.M., U.S. G5 128
Graettinger, Ia., U.S.. . . . . . H4 118
Grafenhainichen, Ger. E8 16
Grafing bei München, Ger. . . H7 16
Grafton, Austl. G9 76
Grafton, Il., U.S. F7 120
Grafton, N.D., U.S. F16 124
Grafton, Oh., U.S.. . . . . . . C3 114
Grafton, W.V., U.S. E5 114
Grafton, Cape, c., Austl. . . . A5 76
Grafton, Mount, mtn.,
  Nv., U.S. E2 132
Graham Island, i., B.C., Can. . E4 106
Graham Island, i., Nu., Can. . B7 141
Graham Lake, res., Me., U.S. . F8 110
Graham Land, reg., Ant. . . . B34 81
Graham Moore, Cape, c.,
  Nu., Can. A15 106
Grahamstad
  Grahamstown, S. Afr. H8 70
Grahamstown, S. Afr. H8 70
Graian Alps, mts., Eur.. . . . . E3 22
Grain Coast, cst., Lib. I3 64
Grinchem, Neth. C14 14
Grajaú, Braz. D2 88
Grajaú, stm., Braz. B3 88
Grajewo, Pol. C18 16
Gramada, Blg. F9 26
Grambling, La., U.S. E6 122
Gramilla, Arg. C5 92
Grammichele, Italy. G8 24
Grampian Mountains,
  mts., Scot., U.K. E9 12
Grampians National Park,
  p.o.i., Austl. K3 76
Gramsh, Alb. D14 24
Granada, Col. F5 86
Granada, Nic. G5 102
Granada, Spain G7 20
Granada, co., Spain G7 20
Granadella, Spain C11 20
Granby, Qc., Can. E4 110
Granby, Mo., U.S. H3 120
Granby, stm., B.C., Can. G12 138
Granby, Lake, res., Co.,
  U.S. B10 130
Gran Chaco, reg., S.A. D5 90
Grand, stm., Mi., U.S. E4 112
Grand, stm., Mo., U.S. E4 120
Grand, stm., S.D., U.S. B12 126
Grand, East Fork, stm.,
  U.S. D3 120
Grand, Lac, l., Qc., Can. A12 112
Grand, North Fork, stm.,
  S.D., U.S. B10 126
Grand, South Fork, stm.,
  S.D., U.S. B9 126

Name	Map Ref.	Page
Grandas, Spain	A4	20
Grand Bahama, i., Bah.	B9	96
Grand Ballon, mtn., Fr.	G16	14
Grand Bank, Nf., Can.	j22	107a
Grand-Bassam, C. Iv.	H4	64
Grand Bay, Al., U.S.	G10	122
Grand Beach, Mb., Can.	D17	124
Grand Bend, On., Can.	E8	112
Grand-Bourg, Guad.	i6	105c
Grand Caille Point, c., St. Luc.	m6	105c
Grand Calumet, Île du, i., Qc., Can.	C13	112
Grand Canal see Da Yunhe, can., China	E8	42
Grand Canal, can., Ire.	H6	12
Grand Cane, La., U.S.	E5	122
Grand Canyon, Az., U.S.	G4	132
Grand Canyon, p., Az., U.S.	G4	132
Grand Canyon National Park, p.o.i., Az., U.S.	G4	132
Grand Canyon-Parashant National Monument, p.o.i., Az., U.S.	G3	132
Grand Case, Guad.	A1	105a
Grand Cayman, i., Cay. Is.	C7	102
Grand Cess, Lib.	I3	64
Grand Chenier, La., U.S.	H6	122
Grand Coulee Dam, dam, Wa., U.S.	C8	136
Grand Cul de Sac, Guad.	B2	105a
Grande, Arg.	A5	92
Grande, Arg.	H3	92
Grande, stm., Bol.	C4	90
Grande, stm., Braz.	C4	90
Grande, stm., Braz.	C7	90
Grande, stm., S.A.	J3	90
Grande, stm., Ven.	C11	86
Grande, Arroyo, stm., Ur.	F9	92
Grande, Bahía, b., Arg.	J3	90
Grande, Boca, mth., Ven.	C11	86
Grande, Cerro, mtn., Mex.	G2	130
Grande, Cerro, mtn., Mex.	E7	100
Grande, Cayemite, i., Haiti	C11	102
Grande de Manacapuru, Lago, l., Braz.	I11	86
Grande de Matagalpa, stm., Nic.	F6	102
Grande de Santiago, stm., Mex.	E6	100
Grande do Gurupá, Ilha, i., Braz.	D7	84
Grande-Entrée, Qc., Can.	C15	110
Grande Prairie, Ab., Can.	A12	138
Grand Erg de Bilma, des., Niger	F7	64
Grand Erg Occidental, des., Alg.	C5	64
Grand Erg Oriental, des., Alg.	C6	64
Grande-Rivière, Qc., Can.	B12	110
Grande-Rivière, La, stm., Qc., Can.	E15	106
Grande Ronde, stm., U.S.	E9	136
Grandes, Salinas, pl., Arg.	A4	92
Grandes, Salinas, pl., Arg.	D5	92
Grand-Étang, N.S., Can.	D15	110
Grande-Terre, i., Guad.	h6	105c
Grande Vigie, Pointe de la, c., Guad.	g6	105c
Grand Falls, N.B., Can.	C9	110
Grandfather Mountain, mtn., N.C., U.S.	H4	114
Grandfield, Ok., U.S.	G10	128
Grand Forks, B.C., Can.	G12	138
Grand Forks, N.D., U.S.	D1	118
Grand Haven, Mi., U.S.	E3	112
Grandin, La., N.T., Can.	C7	106
Grand Island, Ne., U.S.	G14	126
Grand Island, i., Mi., U.S.	B3	112
Grand Isle, La., U.S.	H9	122
Grand Junction, Co., U.S.	D8	132
Grand Junction, Ia., U.S.	B3	120
Grand Lake, Co., U.S.	A3	128
Grand Lake, l., N.B., Can.	D11	110
Grand Lake, l., Nf., Can.	E9	110
Grand Lake, l., La., U.S.	H6	122
Grand Lake, l., Mi., U.S.	C6	112
Grand Lake, res., Oh., U.S.	D1	114
Grand Ledge, Mi., U.S.	B1	114
Grand Manan, N.B., Can.	F10	110
Grand Manan Island, i., N.B., Can.	F10	110
Grand Marais, Mi., U.S.	B4	112
Grand Meadow, Mn., U.S.	H6	118
Grand-Mère, Qc., Can.	D4	110
Grand Morin, stm., Fr.	F12	14
Grand Portage, Mn., U.S.	D9	118
Grand Portage National Monument, p.o.i., Mn., U.S.	C9	118
Grand Prairie, Tx., U.S.	B11	130
Grand Rapids, Mb., Can.	A14	124
Grand Rapids, Mi., U.S.	F4	112
Grand Rapids, Mn., U.S.	D5	118
Grand Rhône, stm., Fr.	F10	18
Grand Saline, Tx., U.S.	E3	122
Grand Staircase-Escalante National Monument, p.o.i., Ut., U.S.	F5	132
Grand Teton, mtn., Wy., U.S.	G16	136
Grand Teton National Park, p.o.i., Wy., U.S.	F16	136
Grand Tower, Il., U.S.	G8	120
Grand Traverse Bay, b., Mi., U.S.	C4	112
Grand Turk, T./C. Is.	B12	102
Grandview, Mb., Can.	C13	124
Grandview, Mo., U.S.	F3	120
Grandview, Tx., U.S.	B10	130
Grandview, Wa., U.S.	D6	136
Grand View, Wi., U.S.	E7	118
Grand Wash Cliffs, clf., Az., U.S.	H3	132
Grañén, Spain	C10	20
Graneros, Chile	G2	92
Granger, Wy., U.S.	D6	136
Granger, Wy., U.S.	B6	132
Granger Draw, stm., Tx., U.S.	D7	130
Granges see Grenchen, Switz.		
Grangeville, Id., U.S.	E10	136
Granite City, Il., U.S.	F7	120
Granite Falls, Mn., U.S.	G3	118
Granite Falls, N.C., U.S.	I4	114
Granite Falls, Wa., U.S.	B5	136
Granite Pass, Wy., U.S.	C5	126
Granite Peak, Austl.	E4	74
Granite Peak, mtn., Mt., U.S.	E17	136
Granite Peak, mtn., Mt., U.S.	E14	136
Granite Peak, mtn., Nv., U.S.	C6	134
Graniteville, S.C., U.S.	C4	116
Granitola, Capo, c., Italy	G6	24
Granja, Braz.	B5	88
Gran Laguna Salada, l., Arg.	H3	90
Gränna, Swe.	G6	8
Granollers, Spain	C13	20
Gran Paradiso, mtn., Italy	E4	22
Gran Paradiso, Parco Nazionale del, p.o.i., Italy.	E4	22
Gran Río, stm., Sur.	C6	84
Gran Sasso d'Italia, mts., Italy	H10	22

Name	Map Ref.	Page
Gransee, Ger.	C9	16
Grant, Fl., U.S.	I5	116
Grant, Mi., U.S.	E4	112
Grant City, Mo., U.S.	D3	120
Grantham, Eng., U.K.	I12	12
Grantley Adams International Airport, Barb.	n9	105d
Grant Park, Il., U.S.	C10	120
Grant Point, c., Nu., Can.	B11	106
Grants, N.M., U.S.	H9	132
Grantsburg, Wi., U.S.	F6	118
Grants Pass, Or., U.S.	A2	134
Grantsville, W.V., U.S.	F4	114
Grantville, Ga., U.S.	D14	122
Granum, Ab., Can.	G17	138
Granville, Fr.	F7	14
Granville, Il., U.S.	J9	118
Granville, N.D., U.S.	F13	124
Granville, W.V., U.S.	E5	114
Granville Lake, l., Mb., Can.	D10	106
Granvin, Nor.	F2	8
Grão Mogol, Braz.	I4	88
Grapeland, Tx., U.S.	F3	122
Grapevine Lake, res., Tx., U.S.	B10	130
Grapevine Peak, mtn., Nv., U.S.	G8	134
Gras, Lac de, l., N.T., Can.	C8	106
Gräsö, i., Swe.	F8	8
Grasonville, Md., U.S.	F9	114
Grass, stm., N.Y., U.S.	F3	110
Grass Creek, Wy., U.S.	D4	126
Grasse, Fr.	F12	18
Grassflat, Pa., U.S.	D7	114
Grasslands National Park, p.o.i., Sk., Can.	E6	124
Grass Valley, Ca., U.S.	D4	134
Grass Valley, Or., U.S.	E6	136
Grassy, Austl.	n12	77a
Grassy Plains, B.C., Can.	C4	138
Graulhet, Fr.	F7	18
Gravelbourg, Sk., Can.	E7	124
Gravelines, Fr.	D11	14
Gravelotte, S. Afr.	C10	70
Gravenhage, 's- see 's-Gravenhage, Neth.	B12	14
Gravenhurst, On., Can.	D10	112
Gravesend, Eng., U.K.	J13	12
Gravette, Ar., U.S.	H3	120
Gravina in Puglia, Italy	D10	24
Gray, Fr.	G14	14
Gray, Ga., U.S.	D2	116
Grayback Mountain, mtn., Or., U.S.	A2	134
Grayling, Mi., U.S.	D5	112
Grays, Eng., U.K.	J13	12
Grays Harbor, b., Wa., U.S.	D2	136
Grays Lake, sw., Id., U.S.	G15	136
Grayson, Sk., Can.	D11	124
Grayson, Al., U.S.	C11	122
Grayson, La., U.S.	E6	122
Grays Peak, mtn., Co., U.S.	B3	128
Graysville, Tn., U.S.	B13	122
Grayville, Il., U.S.	F9	120
Graz, Aus.	C12	22
Grdelica, Serb.	G9	26
Great Artesian Basin, bas., Austl.	E3	76
Great Australian Bight, b., Austl.	F5	74
Great Barrier Island, i., N.Z.	C6	80
Great Barrier Reef, rf., Austl.	C9	74
Great Basin, bas., U.S.	C4	108
Great Basin National Park, p.o.i., Nv., U.S.	E2	132
Great Bear, stm., N.T., Can.	B6	106
Great Bear Lake, l., N.T., Can.	B6	106
Great Beaver Lake, l., B.C., Can.	B7	138
Great Belt see Storebælt, strt., Den.	I4	8
Great Bend, Ks., U.S.	C10	128
Great Bitter Lake see Murrat el-Kubra, Buheirat, l., Egypt	H3	58
Great Britain see United Kingdom, ctry., Eur.	D8	6
Great Camanoe, i., Br. Vir. Is.	e8	104b
Great Central, B.C., Can.	G6	138
Great Channel, strt., Asia	G7	46
Great Dismal Swamp, sw., U.S.	H9	114
Great Divide Basin, bas., Wy., U.S.	F4	126
Great Dividing Range, mts., Austl.	C8	74
Great Driffield, Eng., U.K.	G12	12
Greater Antilles, is., N.A.	H15	94
Greater Khingan Range see Da Hinggan Ling, mts., China	B9	36
Greater Sunda Islands, is., Asia	F4	44
Great Exuma, i., Bah.	C9	96
Great Falls, Mb., Can.	D18	124
Great Falls, Mt., U.S.	C15	136
Great Falls, S.C., U.S.	B4	116
Great Himalayan National Park, p.o.i., India	C6	54
Great Inagua, i., Bah.	B11	102
Great Indian Desert (Thar Desert), des., Asia	D3	54
Great Karroo (Groot Karroo), plat., S. Afr.	H6	70
Great La Cloche Island, i., On., Can.	B8	112
Great Lake, res., Austl.	n13	77a
Great Limpopo Transfrontier Park, p.o.i., Afr.	C10	70
Great Malvern, Eng., U.K.	I10	12
Great Miami, stm., U.S.	E13	120
Great Namaqualand (Groot Namaland), hist. reg., Nmb.	D3	70
Great Nicobar, i., India	G7	46
Great Ouse, stm., Eng., U.K.	I13	12
Great Palm Island, i., Austl.	B6	76
Great Pee Dee, stm., S.C., U.S.	C6	116
Great Plain of the Koukdjuak, pl., Nu., Can.	B16	106
Great Plains, pl., N.A.	C4	108
Great Point, c., Ma., U.S.	C15	114
Great Ruaha, stm., Tan.	F7	66
Great Sacandaga Lake, res., N.Y., U.S.	G2	110
Great Sale Cay, i., Bah.	I7	116
Great Salt Lake, l., Ut., U.S.	C4	132
Great Salt Lake Desert, des., Ut., U.S.	C3	132
Great Salt Plains Lake, res., Ok., U.S.	E10	128
Great Sand Dunes National Monument, p.o.i., Co., U.S.	D3	128
Great Sand Hills, hills, Sk., Can.	D4	124
Great Sandy Desert, des., Austl.	D4	74
Great Sandy National Park, p.o.i., Austl.	E9	76
Great Scarcies, stm., Afr.	H2	64
Great Sea Reef, rf., Fiji	p19	79e
Great Slave Lake, l., N.T., Can.	C8	106
Great Smoky Mountains, mts., U.S.	A2	116

Name	Map Ref.	Page
Great Smoky Mountains National Park, p.o.i., U.S.	A2	116
Great Tenasserim, stm., Mya.	F4	48
Great Thatch Island, i., Br. Vir. Is.	e7	104b
Great Tobago, i., Br. Vir. Is.	e7	104b
Great Victoria Desert, des., Austl.	E5	74
Great Wall see Chang Cheng, misc. cult., China	D6	36
Great Yarmouth, Eng., U.K.	I14	12
Gréboun, mtn., Niger	F6	64
Grecco, Ur.	F9	92
Gredos, Sierra de, mts., Spain	D5	20
Greece, N.Y., U.S.	E12	112
Greece, ctry., Eur.	H13	6
Greeley, Co., U.S.	G8	126
Greeley, Ks., U.S.	F2	120
Greeleyville, S.C., U.S.	C6	116
Greely Fiord, b., Nu., Can.	A9	141
Green, stm., Il., U.S.	C8	120
Green, stm., Ky., U.S.	G10	120
Green, stm., N.D., U.S.	G17	136
Green, stm., Wa., U.S.	C5	136
Green, stm., U.S.	E7	132
Green Bay, Wi., U.S.	D1	112
Green Bay, b., U.S.	D2	112
Greenbrier, Ar., U.S.	B6	122
Greenbrier, stm., W.V., U.S.	F5	114
Greenburg, La., U.S.	G7	122
Greenbush, Mn., U.S.	C2	118
Greencastle, In., U.S.	E10	120
Greencastle, Pa., U.S.	E8	114
Green Cove Springs, Fl., U.S.	G4	116
Greendale, In., U.S.	E13	120
Greene, Ia., U.S.	B5	120
Greeneville, Tn., U.S.	H3	114
Greenfield, Ca., U.S.	G4	134
Greenfield, Ia., U.S.	C3	120
Greenfield, Il., U.S.	E7	120
Greenfield, Ma., U.S.	H4	110
Greenfield, Mo., U.S.	G4	120
Greenfield, Oh., U.S.	E2	114
Greenfield, Ok., U.S.	F10	128
Green Forest, Ar., U.S.	H4	120
Green Island Bay, b., Phil.	E2	52
Green Islands, is., Pap. N. Gui.	D7	72
Green Lake, Wi., U.S.	H10	118
Green Lake, l., B.C., Can.	E9	138
Green Lake, l., Wi., U.S.	H9	118
Greenland, Ar., U.S.	I3	120
Greenland, dep., N.A.	B19	94
Greenland Basin, unds.	A14	144
Greenland Sea, s.	D5	8
Greenleaf, Ks., U.S.	B11	128
Greenock, Scot., U.K.	F8	12
Greenore Point, c., Ire.	I6	12
Greenough, stm., Austl.	E3	74
Greenport, N.Y., U.S.	C13	114
Greenvale, Austl.	B5	76
Green Valley, Az., U.S.	L6	132
Greenwater Lake, l., On., Can.	C8	118
Greenwich, Ct., U.S.	C12	114
Greenwich, Oh., U.S.	C3	114
Greenwood, B.C., Can.	G12	138
Greenwood, Ar., U.S.	B4	122
Greenwood, In., U.S.	E11	120
Greenwood, Ms., U.S.	D8	122
Greenwood, S.C., U.S.	B3	116
Greenwood, Wi., U.S.	G8	118
Greenwood Lake, res., S.C., U.S.	B4	116
Greer, S.C., U.S.	B3	116
Greers Ferry Lake, res., Ar., U.S.	B6	122
Greeson, Lake, res., Ar., U.S.	C5	122
Gregório, stm., Braz.	E3	84
Gregory, Fl., U.S.	D10	24
Gregory, S.D., U.S.	D13	126
Gregory, Tx., U.S.	G10	130
Gregory, stm., Austl.	C7	74
Gregory, Lake, l., Austl.	E3	74
Gregory, Lake, l., Austl.	G2	76
Gregory, Lake, l., Austl.	D5	74
Gregory Range, mts., Austl.	B4	76
Greifswald, Ger.	B9	16
Greifswalder Bodden, b., Ger.	B9	16
Greiz, Ger.	F8	16
Gremiha, Russia	B18	8
Grenaa, Den.	H4	8
Grenada, Ms., U.S.	D9	122
Grenada Lake, res., Ms., U.S.	D9	122
Grenada, ctry., N.A.	q11	105e
Grenadines, is., N.A.	p11	105e
Grenen, c., Den.	H4	8
Grenfell, Austl.	I7	76
Grenoble, Fr.	D11	18
Grenola, Ks., U.S.	D12	128
Grenville, N.D., U.S.	F10	124
Gresham, Or., U.S.	E4	136
Gresik, Indon.	G8	50
Gresik, Indon.	E9	50
Gressåmoen Nasjonalpark, p.o.i., Nor.	D5	8
Gretna, Mb., Can.	E16	124
Gretna, La., U.S.	H8	122
Gretna, Va., U.S.	H6	114
Gretna Green, Scot., U.K.	F9	12
Greven, Ger.	D3	16
Grevená, Grc.	C4	28
Grevenbroich, Ger.	E2	16
Grevesmühlen, Ger.	C7	16
Greybull, Wy., U.S.	C4	126
Grey Eagle, Mn., U.S.	F4	118
Greylock, Mount, mtn., Ma., U.S.	B12	114
Greymouth, N.Z.	F4	80

Name	Map Ref.	Page
Grey Range, mts., Austl.	F4	76
Greytown, S. Afr.	F10	70
Gribbel Island, i., B.C., Can.	C1	138
Gribingui, stm., C.A.R.	C3	66
Gridley, Ca., U.S.	D4	134
Gridley, Il., U.S.	D9	120
Griesheim, Ger.	G4	16
Griffin, Ga., U.S.	E10	124
Griffin, Sk., Can.	D1	116
Griffith, Lake, l., Fl., U.S.	H4	116
Griffith, Austl.	J5	76
Griggsville, Il., U.S.	E7	120
Grignols, Fr.	E5	18
Grigorioipol, Mol.	B16	26
Grijalva (Cuilco), stm., N.A.	G12	100
Grim, Cape, c., Austl.	n12	77a
Grimari, C.A.R.	C3	66
Grimma, Ger.	E8	16
Grimmen, Ger.	B9	16
Grimsby, On., Can.	E10	112
Grimsby, Eng., U.K.	H12	12
Grimsel Pass, p., Switz.	D5	22
Grímsey, i., Ice.	j30	8a
Grimshaw, Ab., Can.	D7	106
Grimstad, Nor.	G3	8
Grindavík, Ice.	k28	8a
Grindelwald, Switz.	D5	22
Grinnell, Ia., U.S.	C5	120
Grinnell Peninsula, pen., Nu., Can.	B7	141
Grintavec, mtn., Slvn.	D11	22
Griqualand East, hist. reg., S. Afr.	G9	70
Griqualand West, hist. reg., S. Afr.	F6	70
Grise Fiord see Ausuittuq, Nu., Can.	B9	141
Gris-Nez, Cap, c., Fr.	D10	14
Griswold, Mb., Can.	E13	124
Griswold, Ia., U.S.	C2	120
Grizzly Bear Mountain, mtn., N.T., Can.	B6	106
Grizzly Mountain, mtn., Id., U.S.	C10	136
Grjadcy, Russia	D14	10
Grjazovec, Russia	G18	8
Groairas, Braz.	B5	88
Groblersdal, S. Afr.	D9	70
Grodków, Pol.	F13	16
Grodzisk Mazowiecki, Pol.	D16	16
Grodzisk Wielkopolski, Pol.	D12	16
Groesbeck, Tx., U.S.	F2	122
Grofa, hora, mtn., Ukr.	A10	26
Groix, Fr.	G5	14
Groix, Île de, i., Fr.	G5	14
Grójec, Pol.	E16	16
Grombalia, Tun.	H4	24
Gronau, Ger.	D3	16
Grong, Nor.	D5	8
Groningen, Neth.	A15	14
Groningen, Sur.	B6	84
Groom, Tx., U.S.	F7	128
Groot, stm., S. Afr.	H7	70
Groot, stm., S. Afr.	H4	70
Groot-Berg, stm., S. Afr.	H4	70
Groot-Brakrivier, S. Afr.	I6	70
Grootdraaidam, res., S. Afr.	E9	70
Groote Eylandt, i., Austl.	B7	74
Grootfontein, Nmb.	D2	68
Grootgeluk, S. Afr.	C8	70
Groot Karasberge, mts., Nmb.	E4	70
Groot Karroo see Great Karroo, plat., S. Afr.	H6	70
Groot-Kei, stm., S. Afr.	H9	70
Groot Laagte, stm., Afr.	B5	70
Groot Namaland see Great Namaqualand, hist. reg., Nmb.	D3	70
Groot-Swartberge, mts., S. Afr.	H6	70
Groot-Vis, stm., S. Afr.	H8	70
Grootvloer, pl., S. Afr.	F5	70
Gros Islet, St. Luc.	l7	105c
Gros-Morne, Mart.	k6	105c
Gros Morne, mtn., Nf., Can.	j22	107a
Gros Piton, vol., St. Luc.	m6	105c
Grossenhain, Ger.	E9	16
Grosse Pointe, Mi., U.S.	B11	114
Grosse Pointe, c., Guad.	h6	105c
Grosser Beerberg, mtn., Ger.	F6	16
Grosseto, Italy	H7	22
Gross-Gerau, Ger.	G4	16
Grossglockner, mtn., Aus.	C9	16
Grossos, Braz.	C7	88
Grossvenediger, mtn., Aus.	C9	22
Groton, N.Y., U.S.	F13	112
Groton, S.D., U.S.	B14	126
Grottaglie, Italy	D11	24
Grottammare, Italy	H11	22
Grottoes, Va., U.S.	F7	114
Grouard Mission, Ab., Can.	D7	106
Groundhog, stm., On., Can.	F14	106
Grove City, Mn., U.S.	F4	118
Grove City, Oh., U.S.	E2	114
Grove City, Pa., U.S.	C5	114
Grove Hill, Al., U.S.	F11	122
Grove Mountains, mts., Ant.	C12	81
Grover City, Ca., U.S.	H5	134
Groves, Tx., U.S.	H5	122
Groveton, N.H., U.S.	F5	110
Groveton, Tx., U.S.	F3	122
Growa Point, c., Lib.	I3	64
Growler Peak, mtn., Az., U.S.	K3	132
Groznyj, Russia	F7	32
Grubišno Polje, Cro.	E14	22
Grudziądz, Pol.	C14	16
Grulla, Tx., U.S.	H9	130
Grumo Appula, Italy	D10	24
Grundy, Va., U.S.	G3	114
Grundy Center, Ia., U.S.	B5	120
Grušino, Russia	G21	8
Gruver, Tx., U.S.	E7	128
Gruznovka, Russia	E10	34
Gryfice, Pol.	C11	16
Gryfino, Pol.	C10	16
Grytviken, S. Geor.	J9	90

Name	Map Ref.	Page
Guadarrama, Puerto de, p., Spain	D6	20
Guadarrama, Sierra de, mts., Spain	D6	20
Guadeloupe, dep., N.A.	h15	96a
Guadeloupe Passage, strt., N.A.	g5	105c
Guadiana, stm., Eur.	G3	20
Guadiana Menor, stm., Spain	G7	20
Guadiaro, stm., Spain	F5	20
Guadiela, stm., Spain	D8	20
Guadix, Spain	G7	20
Guafo, Isla, i., Chile	H1	90
Guaíba, Braz.	E12	92
Guaíba, est., Braz.	E12	92
Guaimaca, Hond.	E4	102
Guaitecas, Islas, is., Chile	H2	90
Guajaba, Cayo, i., Cuba	B9	102
Guajará-Açu, Braz.	A1	88
Guajará-Mirim, Braz.	F4	84
Guaje, Laguna del, l., Mex.	B7	100
Gualaca, Pan.	H6	102
Gualaceo, Ec.	I2	86
Gualala, Ca., U.S.	E2	134
Gualdo Tadino, Italy	G9	22
Gualeguay, Arg.	F8	92
Gualeguay, stm., Arg.	F8	92
Gualeguaychú, Arg.	F8	92
Gualicho, Salina del, pl., Arg.	j10	78c
Guam, dep., Oc.	A1	88
Güere, stm., Ven.	C9	86
Guamá, stm., Braz.	F5	86
Guamini, Arg.	H6	92
Guam International Airport, Guam	i10	78c
Guamote, Ec.	H2	86
Guamúchil, Mex.	C4	100
Guamués, stm., Col.	G3	86
Gua Musang, Malay.	J5	48
Guanacaste, Cordillera de, mts., C.R.	G5	102
Guanacevi, Mex.	C6	100
Guanahacabibes, Golfo de, b., Cuba	A5	102
Guana Island, i., Br. Vir. Is.	e8	104b
Guanaja, Isla de, i., Hond.	D5	102
Guanajay, Cuba	A6	102
Guanajuato, Mex.	E8	100
Guanajuato, state, Mex.	E8	100
Guanambi, Braz.	H4	88
Guanare, Ven.	C7	86
Guanare, stm., Ven.	C7	86
Guandacol, Arg.	D3	92
Guandu, China	I5	42
Guane, Cuba	A5	102
Guang'an, China	F2	42
Guangchang, China	H7	42
Guangde, China	F8	42
Guangdong, state, China	J6	42
Guangfeng, China	G8	42
Guangji, China	F6	42
Guangling, China	B6	42
Guangming Ding, mtn., China	F7	42
Guangnan, China	G5	36
Guangshui, China	E5	42
Guangxi Zhuangzu Zizhiqu see Guangxi, state, China	G6	36
Guangze, China	H7	42
Guangzhou (Canton), China	J5	42
Guanhães, Braz.	J4	88
Guánica, P.R.	C2	104a
Guaniguanico, stm., Ven.	C10	86
Guanta, Ven.	B9	86
Guantánamo, Cuba	B10	102
Guantao, China	C6	42
Guanting Shuiku, res., China	A6	42
Guanxian, China	E5	36
Guanxian, China	D4	36
Guanyun, China	D8	42
Guapi, Col.	F3	86
Guapiara, Braz.	B13	92
Guápiles, C.R.	D11	92
Guaporé, Braz.	D11	92
Guaporé (Iténez), stm., S.A.	F5	84
Guaqui, Bol.	C3	90
Guará, stm., Braz.	D8	88
Guarabira, Braz.	D8	88
Guaraciaba do Norte, Braz.	C5	88
Guaraciama, Braz.	I4	88
Guaranda, Ec.	H2	86
Guaraniaçu, Braz.	B11	92
Guarapari, Braz.	K5	88
Guarapuava, Braz.	B12	92
Guaraqueçaba, Braz.	B13	92
Guaratinguetá, Braz.	L3	88
Guaratuba, Braz.	B13	92
Guarda, Port.	D3	20
Guarda, state, Port.	D3	20
Guardafui, Cape see Gwardafuy, Gees, c., Som.	B10	66
Guardia Escolta, Arg.	D6	92
Guardiagrele, Italy	H11	22
Guardia Mitre, Arg.	H4	90
Guardo, Spain	B6	20
Guareña, Ven.	F4	20
Guarenas, Ven.	B8	86
Guárico, stm., Ven.	C8	86
Guárico, Embalse del, l., Ven.	C8	86
Guarujá, Braz.	L2	88
Guarulhos, Braz.	L2	88
Guasave, Mex.	C4	100
Guasdualito, Ven.	D6	86
Guatemala, Guat.	E2	102
Guatemala, ctry., N.A.	E2	102
Guatemala Basin, unds.	H29	142
Guateque, Col.	E5	86
Guatimozin, Arg.	F6	92
Guatopo, Parque Nacional, p.o.i., Ven.	B8	86
Guatraché, Arg.	H6	92
Guaviare, stm., Col.	F7	86
Guaxupé, Braz.	K2	88
Guayabal, Cuba	B9	102
Guayabal, Ven.	C8	86
Guayabero, stm., Col.	F5	86
Guayacán, Chile	D2	92
Guayama, P.R.	C3	104a
Guayana see Guyana, ctry., S.A.	C6	84
Guayaneco, Archipiélago, is., Chile	I1	90

Name	Map Ref.	Page
Guayape, stm., Hond.	E4	102
Guayapo, stm., Ven.	E8	86
Guayaquil, Ec.	I1	86
Guayaquil, Golfo de, b., S.A.	D1	84
Guayas, state, Ec.	H1	86
Guayas, stm., Ec.	I2	86
Guaymallén, Arg.	F3	92
Guaymas, Mex.	B3	100
Guaynabo, P.R.	B3	104a
Guayquiraró, stm., Arg.	E8	92
Guazapares, Mex.	B4	100
Guazárachi, Mex.	B5	100
Guba, D.R.C.	G5	66
Guba, Russia	C9	32
Gubai, Madiq (Jubal, Strait of), strt., Egypt	K4	58
Gubavica, vtfl., Cro.	G13	22
Gubbi, India	E3	53
Gubbio, Italy	G9	22
Guben, Ger.	E10	16
Gubin, Pol.	E10	16
Gucheng, China	E4	42
Güdalür, India	G3	53
Gúdar, Sierra de, mts., Spain	D10	20
Gudauta, Geor.	F6	32
Gudermes, Russia	F7	32
Gudivāda, India	C5	53
Gudiyāttam, India	E4	53
Güdül, Tur.	C15	28
Gudūr, India	D4	53
Guebwiller, Fr.	G16	14
Güejar, stm., Col.	F5	86
Guékédou, Gui.	H2	64
Guélengdeng, Chad	E3	62
Guelma, Alg.	B6	64
Guelmime, Mor.	D2	64
Guelph, On., Can.	E9	112
Guérande, Fr.	G6	14
Guercif, Mor.	C4	64
Guerdjoumane, Djebel, mtn., Alg.	H13	20
Güere, stm., Ven.	C9	86
Guéréda, Chad	E4	62
Guéret, Fr.	C7	18
Guerla Mandata Shan, mtn., China	C8	54
Guernesey see Guernsey, dep., Eur.	L10	12
Guernica see Gernika, Spain	A8	20
Guernica y Luno see Gernika, Spain	A8	20
Guernsey, dep., Eur.	E6	14
Guernsey, i., Guern.	A5	100
Guerrero, Mex.	F7	130
Guerrero, Mex.	F3	100
Guerrero, state, Mex.	G8	100
Guerrero Negro, Mex.	B1	100
Gueydan, La., U.S.	G6	122
Guga, Russia	F16	34
Gugê, mtn., Eth.	F7	62
Guguan, i., N. Mar. Is.	B5	72
Gui, stm., China	I4	42
Guiana Basin, unds.	G9	144
Guiana Highlands (Guayana, Macizo de), mts., S.A.	E10	86
Güicán, Col.	D5	86
Guichi, China	F7	42
Guide, China	D5	36
Guidimouni, Niger	G6	64
Guiding, China	H2	42
Guier, Lac de, l., Sen.	F1	64
Guijuelo, Spain	D5	20
Guilarte, Monte, mtn., P.R.	B2	104a
Guildford, Eng., U.K.	J12	12
Guildhall, Vt., U.S.	F5	110
Guilford, Me., U.S.	E7	110
Guilin, China	I4	42
Guillaume-Delisle, Lac, l., Qc., Can.	D15	106
Guillestre, Fr.	E12	18
Guimarães, Braz.	B3	88
Guimaras Island, i., Phil.	E4	52
Guimba, Phil.	C3	52
Guin, Al., U.S.	D11	122
Guinan, China	D5	36
Guinda, Ca., U.S.	E3	134
Guindulman, Phil.	F5	52
Guinea, ctry., Afr.	G2	64
Guinea, Gulf of, b., Afr.	I6	64
Guinea Basin, unds.	H13	144
Guinea-Bissau, ctry., Afr.	G1	64
Güines, Cuba	A7	102
Guingamp, Fr.	F5	14
Güinope, Hond.	F4	102
Guiping, China	J4	42
Guipúzcoa see Gipuzkoako, co., Spain	A8	20
Guiratinga, Braz.	G7	84
Güiria, Ven.	H3	64
Guitry, C. Iv.	B2	52
Guiuan, Phil.	E5	52
Guixian, China	J3	42
Guiyang, China	H2	42
Guiyang, China	I5	42
Güiza, stm., Col.	G2	86
Guizhou, state, China	F6	36
Gujarāt, state, India	G13	22
Gujar Khān, Pak.	B4	54
Gujrānwāla, Pak.	B5	54
Gujrāt, Pak.	B5	54
Gukovo, Russia	H5	42
Gulargambone, Austl.	H7	76
Gulbarga, India	C3	53
Gulbene, Lat.	C9	10
Güldüzü, Tur.	B8	58
Guledagudda, India	C2	53
Gülek Boğazı, p., Tur.	A5	58
Gulf Islands National Seashore, p.o.i., U.S.	G10	122
Gulfport, Ms., U.S.	G9	122
Gulf Shores, Al., U.S.	G11	122
Gulgong, Austl.	I7	76
Gulian, China	F13	34
Gulistan, Uzb.	F11	32
Gulkana, Ak., U.S.	D10	140
Gull Lake, Sk., Can.	D5	124
Gullfoss, vtfl., Ice.	k29	8a
Gull Lake, l., Ab., Can.	D17	138
Gull Lake, l., Mn., U.S.	E4	118
Güllük, Tur.	F10	28
Güllük Körfezi, b., Tur.	F10	28
Gülpınar, Tur.	D9	28
Gulu, Ug.	D6	66
Gulugonggba, China	A10	54
Gumaca, Phil.	D4	52
Gumal (Gowmal), stm., Asia	C10	56
Gumbalie, Austl.	G5	76
Gumdag, Turkmen.	B7	56
Gumel, Nig.	G6	64
Gumia, India	G10	54
Gumma, state, Japan	C11	40
Gummersbach, Ger.	E3	16
Gumpang, stm., Indon.	K3	48
Gumti, stm., India	G6	54
Guna, India	G6	54
Gundagai, Austl.	J7	76
Gundji, D.R.C.	D4	66
Gundlupet, India	F3	53
Güney, Tur.	E12	28
Gungu, D.R.C.	F3	66
Gunisao, stm., Mb., Can.	B17	124
Gunma see Gumma, state, Japan	C11	40
Gunnar, Sk., Can.	D9	106
Gunnarn, Swe.	D7	8
Gunnbjørn Fjeld, mtn., Grnld.	D19	141
Gunnedah, Austl.	H7	76
Gunnison, Co., U.S.	E9	132
Gunnison, Ut., U.S.	D5	132
Gunnison, stm., Co., U.S.	E8	132

Name	Map Ref.	Page
Gunong Mulu National Park, p.o.i., Malay.	A9	50
Gun Point, c., Gren.	p11	105e
Gunpowder Creek, stm., Austl.	B2	76
Gunsan see Kunsan, Kor., S.	F7	38
Guntakal, India	D3	53
Guntersville, Al., U.S.	C12	122
Guntersville Dam, dam, Al., U.S.	C12	122
Guntersville Lake, res., Al., U.S.	C12	122
Guntūr, India	C5	53
Gunungkencana, Indon.	G4	50
Gunungsahilan, Indon.	C2	50
Gunungsitoli, Indon.	L3	48
Gunupur, India	B6	53
Günzburg, Ger.	H6	16
Gunzenhausen, Ger.	G6	16
Guo, stm., China	E7	42
Guoyang, China	E7	42
Guoyangzhen, China.	B5	42
Gupis, Pak.	B11	56
Gurabo, P.R.	B4	104a
Gura Humorului, Rom.	B12	26
Gurais, India	A5	54
Gurdāspur, India	B5	54
Gurdon, Ar., U.S.	D5	122
Güre, Tur.	E12	28
Gurevsk, Russia	D15	32
Gurgueia, stm., Braz.	D4	88
Gurha, India	F3	54
Guri, Embalse de, res., Ven.	D10	86
Gurskøe, Russia	F16	34
Gurskøya, i., Nor.	E1	8
Gürsu, Tur.	C12	28
Gurupá, Braz.	D7	84
Gurupi, Braz.	F1	88
Gurupi, stm., Braz.	D8	84
Guru Sikhar, mtn., India	F4	54
Gurvan Sayhan uul, mts., Mong.	C5	36
Gusau, Nig.	G6	64
Gusev, Russia	F5	10
Gušgy, Turkmen.	B9	56
Gushan, China	B10	42
Gushi, China	E6	42
Gus'-Hrustal'nyj, Russia	I19	8
Gusino, Russia	F14	10
Gusinoozersk, Russia	F10	34
Gus'-Khrustal'nyy see Gus'-Hrustal'nyj, Russia	I19	8
Guspini, Italy	E2	24
Güssing, Aus.	C13	22
Gustav Holm, Kap, c., Grnld.	D19	141
Gustavus, Ak., U.S.	E12	140
Gustine, Ca., U.S.	F5	134
Gustine, Tx., U.S.	C9	130
Güstrow, Ger.	C8	16
Gütersloh, Ger.	E4	16
Guthrie, Ok., U.S.	F11	128
Guthrie, Tx., U.S.	H8	128
Guthrie Center, Ia., U.S.	C3	120
Gutian, China	H8	42
Gutiérrez Zamora, Mex.	E10	100
Guttenberg, Ia., U.S.	B6	120
Guwāhāti, India	E13	54
Guxian, China	E5	42
Guyana, ctry., S.A.	C6	84
Guyang, China	A4	42
Guye, China	B8	42
Guy Fawkes River National Park, p.o.i., Austl.	H9	76
Guymon, Ok., U.S.	E7	128
Guyot, Mount, mtn., U.S.	I2	114
Guyra, Austl.	H8	76
Guyton, Ga., U.S.	D4	116
Guyuan, China	D4	36
Guzar, Uzb.	G11	32
Güzelyurt, N. Cyp.	C3	58
Güzelyurt Körfezi, b., N. Cyp.	C3	58
Guzhen, China	E7	42
Guzmán, Mex.	F7	100
Guzmán, Mex.	F9	98
Gvardejsk, Russia	F4	10
Gwa, Mya.	D2	48
Gwaai, Zimb.	D4	68
Gwädar, Pak.	D9	56
Gwalia, Austl.	E4	74
Gwalior (Lashkar), India	E7	54
Gwanda, Zimb.	B9	70
Gwane, D.R.C.	D5	66
Gwangju see Kwangju, Kor., S.	G7	38
Gwardafuy, Gees, c., Som.	B10	66
Gwätar Bay, b., Asia.	E9	56
Gwayi, stm., Zimb.	D4	68
Gwda, stm., Pol.	C12	16
Gweedore, Ire.	F4	12
Gweru, Zimb.	D4	68
Gwinn, Mi., U.S.	B2	112
Gwydir, stm., Austl.	H7	76
Gyangtse see Gyangzê, China	D12	54
Gyangzê, China	D12	54
Gyaring Co, l., China	C12	54
Gyaring Hu, l., China	E4	36
Gyda, Russia	B4	34
Gydanskaja guba, b., Russia	B4	34
Gydanskij poluostrov, pen., Russia	B4	34
Gyeongju see Kyŏngju, Kor., S.	D2	40
Gyirong, China	D10	54
Gyldenløves Fjord, b., Grnld.	E17	141
Gym Peak, mtn., N.M., U.S.	K9	132
Gympie, Austl.	F9	76
Gyobingauk, Mya.	C2	48
Gyoma, Hung.	C7	26
Gyöngyös, Hung.	B6	26
Győr (Raab), Hung.	B4	26
Győr-Moson-Sopron, state, Hung.	B4	26
Gypsum, Co., U.S.	D10	132
Gypsum, Ks., U.S.	C11	128
Gypsumville, Mb., Can.	C15	124
Gyula, Hung.	C8	26
Gyulafehérvár see Alba Iulia, Rom.	C10	26
Gyzylarbat, Turkmen.	B8	56

H

Name	Map Ref.	Page
Haag in Oberbayern, Ger.	H8	16
Haaksbergen, Neth.	D2	16
Haapiti, Fr. Poly.	v20	78h
Haapsalu, Est.	G10	8
Haar, Ger.	H7	16
Ha'Arava ('Arabah, Wādī al-), Asia	H6	58
Ha'Arava (Jayb, Wādī al-), stm., Asia	H6	58
Haarlem, Neth.	B13	14
Habahe, China	C6	36
Habary, Russia	D13	32
Habashiyah, Jabal, mts., Yemen	F7	56
Habbān, Yemen	G6	56
Habiganj, Bngl.	F13	54
Habomai Islands see Malaja Kuril'skaja Grjada, is., Russia	C17	38
Hachijō-jima, i., Japan.	F12	40
Hachiman, Japan	D9	40
Hachinohe, Japan	D14	38
Hachiōji, Japan	D12	40
Hackberry, La., U.S.	H5	122
Hackberry Creek, stm., Ks., U.S.	C8	128
Hackett, Ar., U.S.	B4	122
Hackettstown, N.J., U.S.	D11	114
Hadāli, Pak.	B4	54
HaDarom, state, Isr.	H5	58
Hadd, Ra's al-, c., Oman	E8	56
Haddam, Ks., U.S.	B11	128
Haddington, Scot., U.K.	F10	12
Haddock, Ga., U.S.	C2	116
Haddon Downs, Austl.	F3	76
Hadejia, Nig.	G7	64
Hadejia, stm., Nig.	G6	64
Haden, Austl.	F8	76
Hadera, Isr.	F5	58
Hadersley, Den.	I3	8
Hadibu, Iraq	C5	56
Hadleigh, Swe.	G7	56
Hadlock, Wa., U.S.	B4	136
Ha Dong, Viet.	B7	48
Hadramawt, reg., Yemen	F7	56
Hadrian's Wall, misc. cult., Eng., U.K.	G10	12
Hadzilavičy, Bela.	G13	10
Haeju, Kor., N.	E6	38
Haenam, Kor., S.	G7	38
Haerhpin see Harbin, China.	B7	38
Haffner Bjerg, mtn., Grnld.	B13	141
Hafford, Sk., Can.	B6	124
Haffouz, Tun.	I3	24
Hāfizābād, Pak.	B4	54
Hāflong, India	F14	54
Hafnarfjörður, Ice.	k28	8a
Haft Gel, Iran	C6	56
Hagan, Ga., U.S.	D3	116
Hagari, stm., India	D3	53
Hagåtña (Agana), Guam	j10	78c
Hagemeister Island, i., Ak., U.S.	E7	140
Hagen, Ger.	E3	16
Hagenow, Ger.	C7	16
Hagensborg, B.C., Can.	D4	138
Hagerman, N.M., U.S.	A3	130
Hagerstown, In., U.S.	I4	112
Hagerstown, Md., U.S.	E8	114
Hagersville, On., Can.	F9	112
Hagfors, Swe.	F5	8
Haggin, Mount, mtn., Mt., U.S.	D13	136
Hagi, Japan	E4	40
Ha Giang, Viet.	A7	48
Hagondange, Fr.	E15	14
Hags Head, c., Ire.	I3	12
Hague, Sk., Can.	B7	124
Hague, Cap de la, c., Fr.	E7	14
Haguenau, Fr.	F16	14
Hagues Peak, mtn., Co., U.S.	G7	126
Hahira, Ga., U.S.	F2	116
Hai'an, China.	B9	42
Haibei, China.	B10	36
Haichow Bay see Haizhou Wan, b., China	D8	42
Haidargarh, India	E8	54
Hai Duong, Viet.	B8	48
Haifa see Hefa, Isr.	F5	58
Haifeng, China	J6	42
Haig, Austl.	F5	74
Haigler, Ne., U.S.	A7	128
Haikang, China	K3	42
Haikou, China.	K4	42
Haikou, China	G9	42
Hā'il, Sau. Ar.	D5	56
Hailākāndi, India	F14	54
Hailar, China	B8	36
Hailar, stm., China	B8	36
Haileyville, Ok., U.S.	C3	122
Hailin, China	B8	38
Hailun, China	B10	36
Hailuoto, i., Fin.	D11	8
Haimen, China	J7	42
Haimen, China	G9	42
Haimen, China	L3	42
Hainan Dao (Hainan Island), i., China	L4	42
Hainan Island see Hainan Dao, i., China	L4	42
Hainan Strait see Qiongzhou Haixia, strt., China	K4	42
Haines, Ak., U.S.	E12	140
Haines, Or., U.S.	F8	136
Haines City, Fl., U.S.	H4	116
Haines Junction, Yk., Can.	C3	106
Haining, China	F9	42
Hai Ninh, Viet.	B8	48
Hai Phong, Viet.	B8	48
Haiphong see Hai Phong, Viet.	B8	48
Haiti, ctry., N.A.	C11	102
Haitun, China	D4	36
Haivoron, Ukr.	A16	26
Haiyuan, China	C1	42
Haizhou, China	D8	42
Haizhou Wan, b., China	D8	42
Hajdú-Bihar, state, Hung.	B8	26
Hajdúböszörmény, Hung.	B8	26
Hajdúnánás, Hung.	B8	26
Hajdúszoboszló, Hung.	B8	26
Hājīpur, India	F10	54
Hajnówka, Pol.	D19	16
Hakaša, state, Russia	D16	32
Hakha, Mya.	A1	48
Hakkâri, Tur.	B6	56
Hakodate, Japan.	D14	38
Haku-san, vol., Japan	C9	40
Haku-san-kokuritsu-kōen, p.o.i., Japan	C9	40
Hal see Halle, Bel.	D13	14
Halab (Aleppo), Syria	B8	58
Halab, state, Syria	B8	58
Halachó, Mex.	B2	102
Halahai, China	B6	38
Halā'ib, Sudan	C7	62
Halawa, Cape, c., Hi., U.S.	b5	78a
Halberstadt, Ger.	E7	16
Halbrite, Sk., Can.	E9	124
Halcon, Mount, mtn., Phil.	D3	52
Halden, Nor.	G4	8
Haldensleben, Ger.	D7	16
Haldimand, On., Can.	F10	112
Haldwāni, India	D7	54
Hale, Mo., U.S.	E4	120
Haleakalā Crater, crat., Hi., U.S.	c5	78a
Haleakalā National Park, p.o.i., Hi., U.S.	c5	78a
Hale Center, Tx., U.S.	G7	128
Halenkov, Czech Rep.	G14	16
Halfmoon Bay, B.C., Can.	G7	138
Halfway, Md., U.S.	E8	114
Halfway, Or., U.S.	F9	136
Halicarnassus, sci., Tur.	F10	28
Halifax, Austl.	B6	76
Halifax, Eng., U.K.	H11	12
Halifax, N.S., Can.	F13	110
Halifax, Va., U.S.	H8	114
Halifax, stm., Fl., U.S.	H4	116
Halifax Bay, b., Austl.	B6	76
Haliyal, India	D2	53
Haljala, Est.	A9	10
Halkapınar, Tur.	A5	58
Halland, state, Swe.	H5	8
Hallandale, Fl., U.S.	K5	116
Hallāniyah, Juzur al- (Kuria Muria Islands), is., Oman	F8	56
Hallasan, mtn., Kor., S.	H7	38
Hall Basin, stm., N.A.	A13	141
Halle, Bel.	D13	14
Halle, Ger.	E7	16
Hällefors, Swe.	G6	8
Hallein, Aus.	C10	22
Hallettsville, Tx., U.S.	E11	130
Halley, sci., Ant.	C2	81
Halligen, is., Ger.	B4	16
Hall in Tirol, Aus.	C8	22
Hall Islands, is., Micron.	C6	72
Hall Lake, l., Nu., Can.	B14	106
Hall Mountain, mtn., Wa., U.S.	B9	136
Hallock, Mn., U.S.	C2	118
Hallowell, Me., U.S.	F7	110
Hall Peninsula, pen., Nu., Can.	C17	106
Halls, Tn., U.S.	I8	120
Hallsberg, Swe.	G6	8
Halls Creek, Austl.	C5	74
Hallstahammar, Swe.	G7	8
Hallstavik, Swe.	F8	8
Hallstead, Pa., U.S.	C10	114
Hallsville, Mo., U.S.	E5	120
Halmahera, i., Indon.	E8	44
Halmahera, Laut (Halmahera Sea), s., Indon.	F8	44
Halmahera Sea see Halmahera, Laut, s., Indon.	F8	44
Hal'mer-Ju, Russia	A10	32
Halmstad, Swe.	H5	8
Haloučyn, Bela.	F12	10
Hal'šany, Bela.	F8	10
Halsey, Or., U.S.	F3	136
Halstead, Ks., U.S.	D11	128
Haltiatunturi, mtn., Eur.	B9	8
Haltom City, Tx., U.S.	B10	130
Halton Hills see Georgetown, On., Can.	E9	112
Halvorson, Mount, mtn., B.C., Can.	C10	138
Ham, stm., Nmb.	F4	70
Hamada, Japan	E4	40
Hamadān, Iran	C6	56
Hamāh, Syria	C7	58
Hamāh, state, Syria	C7	58
Hamamatsu, Japan.	E10	40
Hamar, Nor.	F4	8
Hamana-ko, l., Japan	E10	40
Hamar-Daban, hrebet, mts., Russia	F9	34
Hamāta, Gebel, mtn., Egypt	C6	62
Hamburg, Ger.	C6	16
Hamburg, Ar., U.S.	D7	122
Hamburg, Ia., U.S.	D2	120
Hamburg, N.J., U.S.	C11	114
Hamburg, N.Y., U.S.	B7	114
Hamburg, state, Ger.	C6	16
Hamden, Ct., U.S.	C13	114
Hamden, Oh., U.S.	E3	114
Hämeenlinna (Tavastehus), Fin.	F10	8
Hamelin, Ger.	D5	16
Hameln, Ger.	D5	16
HaMerkaz, state, Isr.	F5	58
Hamersley Range, mts., Austl.	D3	74
Hamgyŏng-sanjulgi, mts., Kor., N.	D8	38
Hamhŭng, Kor., N.	E7	38
Hami, China.	C2	36
Hamilton, Austl.	K4	76
Hamilton, Ber.	k15	104e
Hamilton, On., Can.	E10	112
Hamilton, N.Z.	C6	80
Hamilton, Scot., U.K.	F8	12
Hamilton, Al., U.S.	C11	122
Hamilton, Ga., U.S.	E14	122
Hamilton, Il., U.S.	D6	120
Hamilton, Mi., U.S.	F4	112
Hamilton, Mo., U.S.	E3	120
Hamilton, Mt., U.S.	D12	136
Hamilton, N.Y., U.S.	B10	114
Hamilton, Oh., U.S.	E1	114
Hamilton, stm., Austl.	D3	76
Hamilton, Lake, res., Ar., U.S.	C5	122
Hamilton, Mount, mtn., Ca., U.S.	F4	134
Hamilton City, Ca., U.S.	D3	134
Hamilton Dome, Wy., U.S.	D4	126
Hamilton Hotel, Austl.	D3	76
Hamilton Mountain, mtn., N.Y., U.S.	G2	110
Hamina, Fin.	F12	8
Hamiota, Mb., Can.	D13	124
Hamīrpur, India	F7	54
Hamlin, Tx., U.S.	B7	130
Hamlin, W.V., U.S.	F3	114
Hamlin Valley Wash, stm., U.S.	E3	132
Hamm, Ger.	E3	16
Hammamet, Tun.	H4	24
Hammamet, Golfe de, b., Tun.	H4	24
Hammon, Ok., U.S.	F9	128
Hammonasset, stm., Ct., U.S.	C13	114
Hammond, La., U.S.	G8	122
Hammondsport, N.Y., U.S.	F12	112
Hampden, Me., U.S.	F8	110
Hampden, N.D., U.S.	F15	124
Hampi, India	D3	53
Hampshire, Il., U.S.	I10	118
Hampstead, N.C., U.S.	B8	116
Hampton, N.B., Can.	E11	110
Hampton, Ar., U.S.	D6	122
Hampton, Fl., U.S.	G3	116
Hampton, Ga., U.S.	C1	116
Hampton, Ia., U.S.	B4	120
Hampton, N.H., U.S.	H6	110
Hampton, S.C., U.S.	D4	116
Hampton, Tn., U.S.	H3	114
Hampton, Va., U.S.	G9	114
Hampton Butte, mtn., Or., U.S.	G6	136
Hampton Tableland, plat., Austl.	F5	74
Hamra, Swe.	F6	8
Ḥamrā', Al-Ḥamādah al-, des., Libya	B2	62
Hamra as Saquia al, stm., W. Sah.	D2	64
Hamsara, stm., Russia	D16	32
Ham Tan, Viet.	G9	48
Hāmūn, Daryācheh-ye, l., Iran	C9	56
Han, stm., China	F6	42
Han, stm., China	I7	42
Han, Nong, l., Thai.	D6	48
Hāna, Hi., U.S.	c6	78a
Hanahan, S.C., U.S.	D5	116
Hanak, Sau. Ar.	D4	56
Hanamaki, Japan	E14	38
Hananui see Anglem, Mount, mtn., N.Z.	H2	80
Hanapepe, Hi., U.S.	b2	78a
Hanateio, Fr. Poly.	s18	78g
Hanatetena, Fr. Poly.	s18	78g
Hanau am Main, Ger.	F4	16
Hanbury, stm., N.T., Can.	C9	106
Hancavičy, Bela.	H9	10
Hâncesti, Mol.	C15	26
Hanceville, Al., U.S.	C12	122
Hanceville, B.C., Can.	D7	138
Hancheng, China	D4	42
Hanchung see Hanzhong, China	E2	42
Hancock, Md., U.S.	E7	114
Hancock, Mi., U.S.	D10	118
Hancock, Mn., U.S.	F3	118
Hancock, N.Y., U.S.	C10	114
Handa, Japan	E9	40
Handan, China	C6	42
Handlová, Slov.	H14	16
Handsworth, Sk., Can.	E11	124
Hāndwāra, India	A5	54
HaNegev (Negev Desert), reg., Isr.	H5	58
Hanford, Ca., U.S.	G6	134
Hanga Roa, Chile.	e29	78l
Hangayn nuruu, mts., Mong.	B4	36
Hangchou see Hangzhou, China	F9	42
Hangchow see Hangzhou, China	F9	42
Hangchow Bay see Hangzhou Wan, b., China	F9	42
Hanggin Houqi, China	A2	42
Hanggin Qi, China	B3	42
Hangö see Hanko, Fin.	G10	8
Hangokurt, Russia	B10	32
Hangu, China	B7	42
Hangu, Pak.	B3	54
Hanguang, China	I5	42
Hangzhou, China	F9	42
Hangzhou Wan, b., China	F9	42
Hanino, Russia	F19	10
Hanish, is., Yemen	G5	56
Hanish Islands see Hanish, is., Yemen	G5	56
Hanjiang, China	I8	42
Hankinson, N.D., U.S.	E2	118
Hanko, Fin.	G10	8
Hankow see Wuhan, China	F6	42
Hänle, India	B7	54
Hanley, Sk., Can.	C7	124
Hanna, Ab., Can.	E19	138
Hanna, Ok., U.S.	B3	122
Hanna, Wy., U.S.	B10	132
Hanna City, Il., U.S.	D8	120
Hannah, N.D., U.S.	F15	124
Hannah Bay, b., On., Can.	E14	106
Hannibal, Mo., U.S.	E6	120
Hannover, Ger.	D5	16
Hanoi see Ha Noi, Viet.	B7	48
Ha Noi (Hanoi), Viet.	B7	48
Hanover, On., Can.	D8	112
Hanover see Hannover, Ger.	D5	16
Hanover, S. Afr.	G7	70
Hanover, Il., U.S.	B7	120
Hanover, N.H., U.S.	G4	110
Hanover, N.M., U.S.	K8	132
Hanover, Pa., U.S.	E9	114
Hanover, Va., U.S.	G8	114
Hanover, Isla, i., Chile	J2	90
Hanshou, China	H4	42
Hänsi, India	D5	54
Hanska, Mn., U.S.	G4	118
Hantajskoe, ozero, l., Russia	C6	34
Hantan see Handan, China	C6	42
Hantsport, N.S., Can.	E12	110
Hanty-Mansijsk, Russia	B11	32
Hantzsch, stm., Nu., Can.	B16	106
Hanumangarh, India	C4	54
Hanumannagar, India	D4	54
Hanuy, stm., Mong.	B5	36
Hanyin, China	E2	42
Hanzhong, China	E2	42
Hanzhuang, China	F5	42
Haojiadian, China	F5	42
Haoli see Hegang, China	B11	36
Hāora, India	G12	54
Haparanda, Swe.	D10	8
Hapčeranga, Russia	G11	34
Happy, Tx., U.S.	G7	128
Happy Jack, Az., U.S.	I5	132
Happy Valley-Goose Bay, Nf., Can.	E18	106
Hāpur, India	D6	54
Haql, Sau. Ar.	I5	58
Har-Us nuur, l., Mong.	B3	36
Harad, Sau. Ar.	E6	56
Haradok, Bela.	E13	10
Haradzec, Bela.	H7	10
Haradzišče, Bela.	G13	10
Haramachi, Japan	B13	40
Haranor, Russia	A8	36
Harar see Härer, Eth.	F8	62
Harare, Zimb.	D5	68
Harazé Mangueigne, Chad.	E4	62
Harbala, Russia	D13	34
Harbavičy, Bela.	G13	10
Harbin, China	B7	38
Harbiye, Tur.	B7	58
Harbor, Or., U.S.	A1	134
Harbor Beach, Mi., U.S.	E7	112
Harbour Breton, Nf., Can.	j22	107a
Harbourville, N.S., Can.	E12	110
Harbour Grace, Nf., Can.	j23	107a
Hardangerfjorden, b., Nor.	F2	8
Hardangervidda Nasjonalpark, p.o.i., Nor.	F2	8
Hardap, state, Nmb.	D3	70
Hardeeville, S.C., U.S.	D4	116
Hardenberg, Neth.	B14	14
Harderwijk, Neth.	B14	14
Hardin, Il., U.S.	E7	120
Hardin, Mt., U.S.	B5	126
Harding, S. Afr.	G9	70
Harding, Lake, res., U.S.	E13	122
Hardinsburg, Ky., U.S.	G11	120
Hardisty Lake, l., N.T., Can.	C7	106
Hardoī, India	E7	54
Hardtner, Ks., U.S.	D10	128
Hardwar, India	D7	54
Hardwick, Ga., U.S.	D2	116
Hardwick, Vt., U.S.	F4	110
Hardy, Ar., U.S.	H6	120
Hardy, Ne., U.S.	A11	128
Hare Bay, b., Nf., Can.	i22	107a
Hare Indian, stm., N.T., Can.	B5	106
Härer, Eth.	F8	62
Harhorin, Mong.	B5	36
Hari, stm., Indon.	D2	50
Haridwar see Hardwar, India	D7	54
Harihar, India	D2	53
Harīpur, Pak.	B4	54
Harīrūd (Tedžen), stm., Asia.	C9	56
Harischandra Range, mts., India	B1	53
Haritonovo, Russia	F22	8
Harkers Island, N.C., U.S.	B9	116
Harlan, Ia., U.S.	C2	120
Harlan, Ky., U.S.	H2	114
Harlem, Fl., U.S.	J5	116
Harlem, Mt., U.S.	F7	124
Harleton, Tx., U.S.	E4	122
Harlingen, Neth.	A14	14
Harlingen, Tx., U.S.	H10	130
Harlow, Eng., U.K.	J13	12
Harlowton, Mt., U.S.	D17	136
Harman, W.V., U.S.	F6	114
Harmancık, Tur.	D12	28
Harmanli, Blg.	H12	26
Harmony, In., U.S.	E10	120
Harnai, India	C1	53
Harney Basin, bas., Or., U.S.	G8	136
Harney Lake, l., Or., U.S.	G7	136
Harney Peak, mtn., S.D., U.S.	D9	126
Härnösand, Swe.	E8	8
Har nuur, l., Mong.	B3	36
Haro, Spain	B8	20
Haro, Cabo, c., Mex.	B3	100
Harohalli, India	D3	53
Harpanahalli, India	D3	53
Harper, Lib.	I3	64
Harper, Ks., U.S.	D10	128
Harper, Tx., U.S.	D8	130
Harper, Mount, mtn., Ak., U.S.	D11	140
Harqin Qi, China	D3	38
Harrah, Ok., U.S.	G7	128
Harricana, stm., Can.	E15	106
Harriman, Tn., U.S.	I13	120
Harrington, De., U.S.	F10	114
Harrington, Me., U.S.	F9	110
Harris, Sk., Can.	C6	124
Harris, Mont.	D3	105a
Harris, reg., Scot., U.K.	D7	120
Harris, Lake, l., Fl., U.S.	H4	116
Harrisburg, Ar., U.S.	B8	122
Harrisburg, Ne., U.S.	F9	126
Harrisburg, Or., U.S.	F3	136
Harrisburg, Pa., U.S.	D8	114
Harrismith, S. Afr.	F9	70
Harrison, Ar., U.S.	H4	120
Harrison, Mi., U.S.	D5	112
Harrison, Ne., U.S.	E9	126
Harrison Bay, b., Ak., U.S.	B9	140
Harrisonburg, La., U.S.	F7	122
Harrisonburg, Va., U.S.	F6	114
Harrison Islands, is., Nu., Can.	B13	106
Harriston, On., Can.	E9	112
Harriston, Ms., U.S.	F7	122
Harrisville, N.Y., U.S.	D14	112
Harrisville, W.V., U.S.	E4	114
Harrodsburg, Ky., U.S.	G13	120
Harrogate, Eng., U.K.	H11	12
Harrowsmith, On., Can.	D13	112
Harry S. Truman Reservoir, res., Mo., U.S.	F4	120
Har Sai Shan, mtn., China	D4	36
Harsin, Iran	C6	56
Hârşova, Rom.	E14	26
Harstad, Nor.	B7	8
Harsūd, India	G6	54
Hart, Mi., U.S.	E3	112
Hart, Tx., U.S.	G6	128
Hart, stm., Yk., Can.	B3	106
Hartbees, stm., S. Afr.	F5	70
Hartberg, Aus.	C12	22
Hartford, Ar., U.S.	C4	122
Hartford, Ct., U.S.	C13	114
Hartford, Ky., U.S.	F2	120
Hartford, Mi., U.S.	F3	112
Hartford, S.D., U.S.	H2	118
Hartford, Wi., U.S.	H10	118
Hartford City, In., U.S.	H4	112
Hartland, N.B., Can.	D9	110
Hartland, Me., U.S.	F7	110
Hartlepool, Eng., U.K.	G11	12
Hartley, Ia., U.S.	H3	118
Hartley Bay, B.C., Can.	C1	138
Hart Mountain, mtn., Mb., Can.	B12	124
Hartney, Mb., Can.	E13	124
Harts, stm., S. Afr.	E7	70
Hartselle, Al., U.S.	C11	122
Hartshorne, Ok., U.S.	C3	122
Hartsville, S.C., U.S.	B5	116
Hartville, Mo., U.S.	G5	120
Hartwell, Ga., U.S.	B3	116
Hartwell Lake, res., U.S.	B2	116
Hartz Mountains National Park, p.o.i., Austl.	o13	77a
Harūniye, Tur.	A7	58
Harvard, Ne., U.S.	G15	126
Harvard, Mount, mtn., Co., U.S.	C10	132
Harvey, N.B., Can.	E12	110
Harvey, Il., U.S.	G2	112
Harvey, N.D., U.S.	G14	124
Harwich, Eng., U.K.	J14	12
Haryāna, state, India	D6	54
Haryn', stm., Eur.	H10	10
Harz, mts., Ger.	E6	16
Hasavjurt, Russia	F7	32
Hase, stm., Ger.	D3	16
Hasenkamp, Arg.	E8	92
Hashima, Japan	D9	40
Hashimoto, Japan	E8	40
Hāshīpur, Pak.	D4	54
Haskell, Ok., U.S.	I2	112
Haskell, Tx., U.S.	A8	130
Haskovo, Blg.	H12	26
Haslemere, Eng., U.K.	J12	12
Hasparren, Fr.	F4	18
Hasperos Canyon, p., N.M., U.S.	H3	128
Hassa, Tur.	B7	58
Hassan, India	E3	53
Hassayampa, stm., Az., U.S.	J4	132
Hasselt, Bel.	D14	14
Hasselt, Neth.	B14	14
Hassfurt, Ger.	F6	16
Hassi Messaoud, Alg.	C6	64
Hässleholm, Swe.	H5	8
Hastings, N.Z.	D7	80
Hastings, Barb.	p11	105e
Hastings, On., Can.	D11	112
Hastings, Eng., U.K.	K13	12
Hastings, Mi., U.S.	F4	112
Hastings, Mn., U.S.	G6	118
Hastings, Ne., U.S.	G14	126
Haswell, Co., U.S.	C6	128
Hatanga, Russia	B9	34
Hatangskij zaliv, b., Russia	B10	34
Hatay (Antioch), Tur.	B7	58
Hatay, state, Tur.	B7	58
Hatch, N.M., U.S.	K10	132
Hatch, Ut., U.S.	F4	132
Hat Chao Mai National Park, p.o.i., Thai.	I4	48
Hatfield, Austl.	I4	76
Hatfield, Ma., U.S.	B13	114
Hatgal, Mong.	F9	34
Hāthras, India	E7	54
Ha Tien, Viet.	G7	48
Hatillo, P.R.	A2	104a
Ha Tinh, Viet.	C7	48
Hato, Bocht van, b., Neth. Ant.	p21	104g
Hato Mayor del Rey, Dom. Rep.	C13	102
Hatta, India	G7	54
Hattah, Austl.	J4	76
Hatteras, Cape, c., N.C., U.S.	A10	116
Hatteras Island, i., N.C., U.S.	A10	116
Hattiesburg, Ms., U.S.	F9	122
Hatton, Al., U.S.	C11	122
Hatton, N.D., U.S.	G16	124
Hatunsaray, Tur.	A3	58
Hatvan, Hung.	B6	26
Hat Yai, Thai.	I5	48
Hatyrka, Russia	D24	34
Haugesund, Nor.	G1	8
Haukeligrend, Nor.	G2	8
Haukivesi, l., Fin.	E12	8
Hauraki Gulf, b., N.Z.	C6	80
Hausach, Ger.	H4	16
Haut, Isle au, i., Me., U.S.	F8	110
Haut Atlas, mts., Mor.	C3	64
Haute-Corse, state, Fr.	G15	18
Haute-Garonne, state, Fr.	F7	18
Haute-Loire, state, Fr.	D9	18
Haute-Marne, state, Fr.	F14	14
Hautes-Alpes, state, Fr.	E12	18
Haute-Saône, state, Fr.	G14	14
Haute-Savoie, state, Fr.	C12	18
Hautes-Pyrénées, state, Fr.	F6	18
Haute-Vienne, state, Fr.	D7	18
Haut-Rhin, state, Fr.	G16	14
Hauts Plateaux, reg., Afr.	C11	110
Hau'ula, Hi., U.S.	b4	78a
Hauwāret el-Maqta', Egypt.	I1	58
Havana see La Habana, Cuba	A6	102
Havana, Fl., U.S.	G14	122
Havana, Il., U.S.	D7	120
Havana, N.D., U.S.	B15	126
Havannah, Canal de la, strt., N. Cal.	n16	79d
Havant, Eng., U.K.	K12	12
Havast, Uzb.	F11	32
Havasu, Lake, res., U.S.	I2	132
Havasu Creek, stm., Az., U.S.	H4	132
Havel, stm., Ger.	D8	16
Havelberg, Ger.	D8	16
Haveli, Pak.	C4	54
Havelland, reg., Ger.	D8	16
Havelock, On., Can.	D12	112
Havelock, N.C., U.S.	B8	116
Haverfordwest, Wales, U.K.	J7	12
Haverhill, Eng., U.K.	I13	12
Haverhill, Ma., U.S.	B14	114
Häveri, India	D2	53
Haviland, Ks., U.S.	D9	128
Havířov, Czech Rep.	G14	16
Havre see Le Havre, Fr.	E8	14
Havre, Mt., U.S.	B17	136
Havre-Aubert, Qc., Can.	C15	110
Havre-Aubert, Île (Amherst Island), i., Qc., Can.	C14	110
Havre de Grace, Md., U.S.	E9	114
Havre North, Mt., U.S.	B17	136
Havsa, Tur.	B9	28
Haw, stm., N.C., U.S.	A7	116
Hawaii, state, U.S.	b5	78a
Hawaii, i., Hi., U.S.	c4	78a
Hawaiian Islands, is., Oc.	c4	78a
Hawaiian Ridge, unds.	G21	142
Hawai'i Volcanoes National Park, p.o.i., Hi., U.S.	d6	78a
Hawarden, Sk., Can.	c7	124
Hawea, Lake, l., N.Z.	G3	80
Hawera, N.Z.	D6	80
Hawesville, Ky., U.S.	G11	120
Hawi, Hi., U.S.	c6	78a
Hawick, Scot., U.K.	F10	12
Hawke, Cape, c., Austl.	I9	76
Hawke Bay, b., N.Z.	D7	80
Hawkes, Mount, mtn., Ant.	D36	81
Hawkesbury, On., Can.	E2	110
Hawkesbury Island, i., B.C., Can.	C1	138
Hawkeye, Ia., U.S.	B6	120
Hawkins, Tx., U.S.	E3	122
Hawkins, Wi., U.S.	F8	118
Haw Knob, mtn., U.S.	A1	116
Hawksbill Creek, b., Bah.	J7	116
Hawkwood, Austl.	E8	76
Hawley, Mn., U.S.	E2	118
Hawley, Pa., U.S.	C10	114
Hawthorne, Fl., U.S.	G3	116
Hawthorne, Nv., U.S.	E7	134
Hawwāret 'Adlan, Egypt.	I1	58
Hay, Austl.	J5	76
Hay, stm., Can.	D7	106
Hay, stm., Austl.	D7	74
Hayang, Kor., S.	D1	40
Hayange, Fr.	E14	14
Haybān, Jabal, mtn., Sudan.	E6	62
Haydarlı, Tur.	E13	28
Hayden, Co., U.S.	C9	132
Hayden, Id., U.S.	C10	136
Hayes, La., U.S.	G6	122
Hayes, stm., Mb., Can.	D12	106
Hayes, stm., Nu., Can.	B11	106
Hayes, Mount, mtn., Ak., U.S.	D10	140
Hayes Center, Ne., U.S.	G11	126
Hayesville, N.C., U.S.	A2	116
Hayfield, Mn., U.S.	H6	118
Hayford Peak, mtn., Nv., U.S.	G1	132
Hay Lakes, Ab., Can.	C17	138
Hayneville, Al., U.S.	E12	122
Haynesville, La., U.S.	E5	122
Hayrabolu, Tur.	B10	28
Hay River, N.T., Can.	C7	106
Hays, Ab., Can.	E3	124
Hays, Ks., U.S.	C9	128
Hays, Mt., U.S.	B7	124
Hay Springs, Ne., U.S.	E10	126
Haystack Mountain, mtn., Nv., U.S.	B1	132
Hayti, Mo., U.S.	H8	120
Hayti, S.D., U.S.	C15	126
Hayward, Ca., U.S.	F3	134
Hayward, Wi., U.S.	E7	118
Haywards Heath, Eng., U.K.	J13	12
Hazafon, state, Isr.	F6	58
Hazard, Ky., U.S.	G2	114
Hazāribāg, India	G10	54
Hazawzā', Sabkhat, l., Sau. Ar.	H9	58
Hazebrouck, Fr.	D11	14
Hazel Green, Wi., U.S.	I8	118
Hazelton, B.C., Can.	A3	138
Hazelton, N.D., U.S.	A12	126
Hazen Mountains, mts., B.C., Can.	B3	138
Hazen, Ar., U.S.	C7	122
Hazen, N.D., U.S.	G12	124
Hazen, Lake, l., Nu., Can.	A11	141
Hazlehurst, Ga., U.S.	E3	116
Hazlehurst, Ms., U.S.	F8	122
Hazlet, Sk., Can.	D5	124
Hazleton, Ia., U.S.	B6	120
Hazlett, Lake, l., Austl.	D5	74
Hazro, Tur.	B5	56
He, stm., China	I4	42
Healdsburg, Ca., U.S.	E2	134
Healdton, Ok., U.S.	G11	128
Healesville, Austl.	K5	76
Healy, Ks., U.S.	C8	128
Heard Island, i., Austl.	O10	142
Hearne, Tx., U.S.	F14	122
Heart, stm., N.D., U.S.	H12	124
Heart Lake, l., Ab., Can.	A19	138
Heart's Content, Nf., Can.	j23	107a
Heath, Pointe, c., Qc., Can.	A15	110
Heathcote, Austl.	K5	76
Heath Springs, S.C., U.S.	B5	116
Heavener, Ok., U.S.	C4	122
Hebbronville, Tx., U.S.	G9	130
Hebei, state, China	B6	42
Hebel, Austl.	G6	76
Heber, Az., U.S.	I6	132
Heber City, Ut., U.S.	C5	132
Heber Springs, Ar., U.S.	B6	122

Name	Map Ref.	Page
Hebgen Lake, res., Mt., U.S.	F15	136
Hebi, China	D6	42
Hebrides, is., Scot., U.K.	D5	12
Hebrides, Sea of the, s., Scot., U.K.	D6	12
Hebron, Mt., Can.	F13	141
Hebron, Il., U.S.	B9	120
Hebron, N.D., U.S.	H11	124
Hebron, Ne., U.S.	A11	128
Hebron see Al-Khalīl, W.B.		
Hecate Strait, strt., B.C., Can.	E4	106
Hecelchakán, Mex.	B2	102
Hechi, China	I3	42
Hechiceros, Mex.	F4	130
Hechingen, Ger.	H4	16
Hechuan, China	G2	42
Hecla, Mb., Can.	C17	124
Hecla, Cape, c., Nu., Can.	A13	141
Hecla Island, i., Mb., Can.	C17	124
Hectanooga, N.S., Can.	F10	110
Hector, Mn., U.S.	G4	118
Hede, Swe.	E5	8
Hedemora, Swe.	F6	8
He Devil, mtn., Id., U.S.	E10	136
Hedley, Tx., U.S.	G8	128
Hedmark, state, Nor.	F3	8
Hedrick, Ia., U.S.	C5	120
Heerenveen, Neth.	B14	14
Heerlen, Neth.	D15	14
Hefa (Haifa), Isr.	F5	58
Hefa, state, Isr.	F5	58
Hefei, China	F7	42
Heflin, Al., U.S.	D13	122
Hegang, China	B11	36
Heho, Mya.	B3	48
Hei, stm., China	A7	42
Heide, Ger.	B5	16
Heidelberg, Ger.	G4	16
Heidelberg, S. Afr.	E9	70
Heidelberg, Ms., U.S.	F10	122
Heidenheim, Ger.	G6	16
Heihe, China	A10	36
Heilbad Heiligenstadt, Ger.	E6	16
Heilbron, S. Afr.	E8	70
Heilbronn, Ger.	G5	16
Heiligenhafen, Ger.	B6	16
Heilong (Amur), stm., Asia	F14	34
Heilongguan, China	C4	42
Heilongjiang, state, China	B10	36
Heilongkiang see Heilongjiang, state, China	B8	38
Heimaey, I., Ice.	I29	8a
Heinola, Fin.	F12	8
Heishan, China	D4	38
Heishuisi, China	C3	42
Hejaz see Al-Ḥijāz, reg., Sau. Ar.	D4	56
Hejian, China	B7	42
Hejiang, China	G1	42
Hejing, China	C2	36
Hekla, vol., Ice.	k30	8a
Hekou, China	A6	48
Hekou, China	G4	42
Helagsfjället, mtn., Swe.	E5	8
Helan Mountains see Helan Shan, mts., China	B1	42
Helan Shan, mts., China	B1	42
Helbra, Ger.	E7	16
Helder see Den Helder, Neth.	B13	14
Helder, Den see Den Helder, Neth.	B13	14
Helen, Mount, hill, Austl.	C8	122
Helena, Ar., U.S.	C8	122
Helena, Mt., U.S.	D14	136
Helena, Ok., U.S.	E10	128
Helensburgh, Scot., U.K.	E8	12
Helenwood, Tn., U.S.	H13	120
Helgoland, i., Ger.	B4	16
Helgoländer Bucht, b., Ger.	C4	16
Heli, China	B11	36
Heliopolis, sci., Egypt	H2	58
Helixi, China	F8	42
Hellesylt, Nor.	E2	8
Hellín, Spain	F9	20
Hells Canyon, p., U.S.	E10	136
Hells Canyon National Recreation Area, p.o.i., Or., U.S.	E10	136
Hells Gate, p., B.C., Can.	G9	138
Helmand, stm., Asia	C9	56
Helmcken Falls, wtfl., B.C., Can.	E10	138
Helmond, Neth.	C14	14
Helmstedt, Ger.	D6	16
Helong, China	C8	38
Helper, Ut., U.S.	D6	132
Helsingborg, Swe.	H5	8
Helsingfors see Helsinki, Fin.	F11	8
Helsingør, Den.	H5	8
Helsinki (Helsingfors), Fin.	F11	8
Helska, Mierzeja, pen., Pol.	B14	16
Helston, Eng., U.K.	K7	12
Helvecia, Arg.	E7	92
Helwan, Egypt	I2	58
Helwan Observatory, sci., Egypt	I2	58
Hemau, Ger.	G7	16
Hemāvati, stm., India	E2	53
Hemel Hempstead, Eng., U.K.	J12	12
Hemet, Ca., U.S.	J9	134
Hemingford, Ne., U.S.	E9	126
Hemingway, S.C., U.S.	C6	116
Hemphill, Tx., U.S.	F5	122
Hemsön, i., Swe.	E8	8
Henan, state, China	E5	42
Henares, stm., Spain	D7	20
Henbury, Austl.	D6	74
Hendek, Tur.	C13	28
Henderson, Ky., U.S.	G10	120
Henderson, Mn., U.S.	G5	118
Henderson, N.C., U.S.	H7	114
Henderson, Ne., U.S.	G15	126
Henderson, Nv., U.S.	G1	132
Henderson, Tn., U.S.	B10	122
Henderson, Tx., U.S.	E4	122
Hendersonville, Tn., U.S.	H11	120
Hendricks, Mn., U.S.	G2	118
Hendricks, W.V., U.S.	E6	114
Henefer, Ut., U.S.	B5	132
Henganofi, Pap. N. Gui.	b4	79a
Hengchow see Hengyang, China	H5	42
Hengdaozi, China	C7	38
Hengelo, Neth.	B15	14
Hengfeng, China	G7	42
Henglu, China	D7	38
Hengshan, China	C3	42
Hengshan, China	H5	42
Heng Shan, mts., China	B5	42
Hengshui, China	C6	42
Hengyang, China	H5	42
Hénin-Beaumont, Fr.	D11	14
Henlopen, Cape, c., De., U.S.	F10	114
Hennebont, Fr.	G5	14
Hennef, Ger.	F3	16
Hennessey, Ok., U.S.	E11	128
Henniker, N.H., U.S.	G5	110
Henning, Mn., U.S.	E3	118
Henrietta, N.Y., U.S.	A8	114
Henrietta, Tx., U.S.	H10	128
Henrietta Island see Genrietty, ostrov, i., Russia	A20	34
Henrietta Maria, Cape, c., On., Can.	D14	106
Henri Pittier, Parque Nacional, p.o.i., Ven.	B8	86
Henry, Il., U.S.	C8	120
Henry, Cape, c., Va., U.S.	H10	114
Henry, Mount, mtn., Mt., U.S.	B11	136
Henryetta, Ok., U.S.	B2	122
Henry Kater, Cape, c., Nu., Can.	B17	106
Henrys Fork, stm., Id., U.S.	F15	136
Hensall, On., Can.	E8	112
Hensley, Ar., U.S.	C6	122
Henslow, Cape, c., Sol. Is.	e9	79b
Hentiesbaai, Nmb.	C2	70
Hentiyn nuruu, mts., Mong.	G10	34
Henzada, Mya.	D2	48
Hephzibah, Ga., U.S.	C3	116
Heping, China	H7	42
Heppenheim, Ger.	G4	16
Heppner, Or., U.S.	E7	136
Hequ, China	B4	42
Héradsflói, b., Ice.	k32	8a
Herāt, Afg.	C9	56
Hérault, state, Fr.	F9	18
Hérault, stm., Fr.	F9	18
Herbert, Sk., Can.	D6	124
Herberton, Austl.	A5	76
Herbertsdale, S. Afr.	H5	70
Herborn, Ger.	F4	16
Herceg-Novi, Serb.	G5	26
Hércules, Mex.	A7	100
Herðubreið, vol., Ice.	k31	8a
Heredia, C.R.	G5	102
Hereford, Eng., U.K.	I10	12
Hereford, Az., U.S.	L6	132
Hereford, Tx., U.S.	G6	128
Hereke, Tur.	C12	28
Herencia, Spain	E7	20
Herford, Ger.	D4	16
Herington, Ks., U.S.	C11	128
Herisau, Switz.	C6	22
Herkimer, N.Y., U.S.	E15	112
Hermagor, Aus.	D10	22
Herman, Mn., U.S.	F2	118
Herman, Ne., U.S.	C1	120
Hermanas, Mex.	G6	130
Hermanns-Denkmal, hist., Ger.	E4	16
Hermansverk, Nor.	F2	8
Hermanville, Mi., U.S.	C2	112
Hermanus, S. Afr.	I4	70
Hermanville, Ms., U.S.	F8	122
Hermiston, Or., U.S.	E7	136
Hermitage, Ar., U.S.	D6	122
Hermit Islands, is., Pap. N. Gui.	a4	79a
Hermleigh, Tx., U.S.	B7	130
Hermon, Mount (Shaykh, Jabal ash-), mtn., Asia	E6	58
Hermosillo, Mex.	A3	100
Hermyingyi, Mya.	E4	48
Hernád (Hornad), stm., Eur.	H17	16
Hernandarias, Arg.	E8	92
Hernandarias, Para.	B10	92
Hernando, Arg.	F6	92
Hernando, Fl., U.S.	H3	116
Hernando, Ms., U.S.	B9	122
Herndon, Pa., U.S.	D9	114
Herne Bay, Eng., U.K.	J14	12
Herning, Den.	H3	8
Heroica Zitácuaro, Mex.	F8	100
Heron Island, i., Austl.	D8	76
Heron Lake, Mn., U.S.	H3	118
Hérouville-Saint-Clair, Fr.	E8	14
Herradura, Arg.	C8	92
Herreid, S.D., U.S.	B12	126
Herrera de Pisuerga, Spain	B6	20
Herrick, Austl.	n13	77a
Herrin, Il., U.S.	G8	120
Hersbruck, Ger.	G7	16
Herschel, S. Afr.	G8	70
Herschel Island, i., Yk., Can.	C12	140
Herscher, Il., U.S.	C9	120
Hershey, Ne., U.S.	F11	126
Hershey, Pa., U.S.	D9	114
Herstal, Bel.	D14	14
Hertford, Eng., U.K.	J12	12
Hertogenbosch, 's- see 's-Hertogenbosch, Neth.	C14	14
Herval d'Oeste, Braz.	C12	92
Hervás, Spain	D5	20
Hervey Bay, b., Austl.	E9	76
Hervey-Jonction, Qc., Can.	D4	110
Herzberg, Ger.	E9	16
Herzberg am Harz, Ger.	E6	16
Heshan, China	J3	42
Heshui, China	D3	42
Heshun, China	C5	42
Hesperange, Lux.	E15	14
Hesperia, Mi., U.S.	E3	112
Hesperus Mountain, mtn., Co., U.S.	F8	132
Hess, stm., Yk., Can.	C4	106
Hessen, state, Ger.	F5	16
Hesston, Ks., U.S.	C11	128
Het, stm., Laos	B6	48
Heta, stm., Russia	B8	34
Hetang, China	H8	42
Hetaundā, Nepal	E10	54
Hetch Hetchy Aqueduct, aq., Ca., U.S.	F4	134
Hetgeli, I., Swe.	D6	8
Hettstedt, Ger.	E7	16
Heuvelton, N.Y., U.S.	D14	112
Heves, Hung.	B7	26
Heves, state, Hung.	A7	26
Hewanorra International Airport, St. Luc.	m6	105c
Hewu, China	H5	42
Hexham, Eng., U.K.	F11	12
Hexian, China	I4	42
Heyang, China	D3	42
Heyburn, Id., U.S.	H13	136
Heysham, Eng., U.K.	G10	12
Heyuan, China	J6	42
Heywood, Austl.	L3	76
Heze, China	D6	42
Hezheng, China	D5	36
Hialeah, Fl., U.S.	K5	116
Hiawatha, Ks., U.S.	E2	120
Hiawatha, Ut., U.S.	D6	132
Hibbard, Qc., Can.	E15	106
Hibbing, Mn., U.S.	D5	118
Hickman, Ne., U.S.	H8	120
Hickory, Ms., U.S.	E9	122
Hickory, N.C., U.S.	I4	114
Hickory Flat, Ms., U.S.	C9	122
Hicks, Point, c., Austl.	K7	76
Hico, Tx., U.S.	C9	130
Hida see Hita, Japan	F3	40
Hidaka, Mex.	C9	100
Hidalgo, Mex.	B8	100
Hidalgo, Mex.	B9	100
Hidalgo, state, Mex.	E9	100
Hidalgo del Parral, Mex.	B6	100
Hida-sammyaku, mts., Japan	C10	40
Hidrolândia, Braz.	I1	88
Hieflau, Aus.	C11	22
Hienghène, N. Cal.	m15	79d
Hierápolis see Pamukkale, sci., Tur.	F12	28
Higashihiroshima, Japan	E5	40
Higashiichiki, Japan	H3	40
Higashine, Japan	A13	40
Higashiōsaka, Japan	E8	40
Higgins, Tx., U.S.	E8	128
Higginsville, Mo., U.S.	F4	120
Highbury, Austl.	C8	74
Highland, Il., U.S.	F8	120
Highland, In., U.S.	G2	112
Highland, Ks., U.S.	E2	120
Highland Park, Il., U.S.	F2	112
Highlands, N.C., U.S.	A2	116
Highlands, N.J., U.S.	D12	114
Highlands, Tx., U.S.	H3	122
High Level, Ab., Can.	D7	106
High Point, N.C., U.S.	I5	114
High Point, mtn., N.J., U.S.	C11	114
High Point, mtn., Wy., U.S.	B9	132
High Prairie, Ab., Can.	D10	106
Highrock Lake, l., Mb., Can.	D10	106
Highrock Lake, l., Sk., Can.	D9	106
High Rock Lake, res., N.C., U.S.	A5	116
High Springs, Fl., U.S.	G3	116
Hightstown, N.J., U.S.	D11	114
High Willhays, mtn., Eng., U.K.	K9	12
Highwood, Mt., U.S.	C16	136
Highwood, stm., Ab., Can.	F17	138
Highwood Baldy, mtn., Mt., U.S.	C16	136
High Wycombe, Eng., U.K.	J11	12
Higuera de Abuya, Mex.	C5	100
Higueras, Mex.	I8	130
Higüero, Punta, c., P.R.	B1	104a
Higüey, Dom. Rep.	C13	102
Hiiumaa, i., Est.	G10	8
Hikari, Japan	F4	40
Hikone, Japan	D9	40
Hilbert, Wi., U.S.	D1	112
Hilda, Ab., Can.	D3	124
Hildburghausen, Ger.	F6	16
Hildesheim, Ger.	D5	16
Hildotaluwa, Indon.	L3	48
Hillaby, Mount, mtn., Barb.	n8	105d
Hill Bank, Belize	D3	102
Hill City, Ks., U.S.	B9	128
Hill City, S.D., U.S.	D9	126
Hillcrest Mines, Ab., Can.	G16	138
Hillerød, Den.	I4	8
Hilliard, Fl., U.S.	F4	116
Hill Island Lake, l., N.T., Can.	C9	106
Hillister, Tx., U.S.	G4	122
Hills, Mn., U.S.	H2	118
Hillsboro, Il., U.S.	E8	120
Hillsboro, Mo., U.S.	F7	120
Hillsboro, N.D., U.S.	D1	118
Hillsboro, Oh., U.S.	E2	114
Hillsboro, Or., U.S.	E3	136
Hillsboro, Wi., U.S.	H8	118
Hillsboro Canal, can., Fl., U.S.	J5	116
Hillsborough, Gren.	q10	105e
Hillsborough, N.C., U.S.	H6	114
Hillsborough, stm., Fl., U.S.	I3	116
Hillsborough, Cape, c., Austl.	C7	76
Hillsborough Bay, b., P.E., Can.	D13	110
Hillsdale, Mi., U.S.	G5	112
Hillston, Austl.	I5	76
Hillsville, Va., U.S.	H5	114
Hillswick, Scot., U.K.	n18	12a
Hilo, Hi., U.S.	d6	78a
Hilok, Russia	F10	34
Hilok, stm., Russia	F10	34
Hilton, N.Y., U.S.	E12	112
Hilton Head Island, i., S.C., U.S.	D5	116
Hilvan, Tur.	A9	58
Hilversum, Neth.	B14	14
Himachal Pradesh, state, India	B6	54
Himalayas, mts., Asia	F10	142
Himarë, Alb.	D13	24
Himatnagar, India	G4	54
Himeji, Japan	E7	40
Himi, Japan	C9	40
Himki, Russia	E20	10
Himis (Homs), Syria	D7	58
Hims, state, Syria	D8	58
Hinchinbrook Island, i., Austl.	B6	76
Hinchinbrook Island, i., Ak., U.S.	D10	140
Hinchinbrook Island National Park, p.o.i., Austl.	B6	76
Hinckley, Il., U.S.	C9	120
Hinckley, Mn., U.S.	E5	118
Hinckley, Ut., U.S.	D4	132
Hindang, Phil.	E5	52
Hindaun, India	E6	54
Hindmarsh, Lake, l., Austl.	J3	76
Hindu Kush, mts., Asia	B10	56
Hindupur, India	E3	53
Hines, Or., U.S.	G7	136
Hinesville, Ga., U.S.	E4	116
Hinganghāt, India	H7	54
Hingham, Ma., U.S.	B15	114
Hingol, stm., Pak.	D10	56
Hingoli, India	B3	53
Hinnøya, i., Nor.	B6	8
Hinojosa del Duque, Spain	F5	20
Hinokage, Japan	G4	40
Hinsdale, Mt., U.S.	F6	124
Hinterrhein, stm., Switz.	D6	22
Hinton, Ab., Can.	C13	138
Hinton, Ok., U.S.	F10	128
Hinton, W.V., U.S.	G5	114
Hipólito, Mex.	C8	100
Hipólito Yrigoyen, Arg.	F4	92
Hirado, Japan	F2	40
Hirado-shima, i., Japan	F2	40
Hirakud, India	H9	54
Hirākud Reservoir, res., India	H10	54
Hirara, Japan	G10	36
Hirata, Japan	D5	40
Hiratsuka, Japan	D12	40
Hiriyūr, India	E3	53
Hirosaki, Japan	D14	38
Hiroshima, Japan	E5	40
Hiroshima, state, Japan	E5	40
Hirosima see Hiroshima, Japan	E5	40
Hirovo, Russia	B16	10
Hirson, Fr.	E13	14
Hisār, India	D5	54
Hisarönü, Tur.	B14	28
Hispaniola, i., N.A.	D10	96
Hisua, India	F10	54
Hisyah, Syria	D7	58
Hita, Japan	F3	40
Hitachi, Japan	C13	40
Hitachi-ōta, Japan	C13	40
Hitchcock, Tx., U.S.	H3	122
Hitchins, Ky., U.S.	F3	114
Hitiaa, Fr. Poly.	v22	78h
Hitoyoshi, Japan	G3	40
Hitra, i., Nor.	E3	8
Hitra-gake, vol., Japan	C12	40
Híuchi-nada, s., Japan	E6	40
Hiva, Uzb.	F10	32
Hiva Oa, i., Fr. Poly.	s19	78g
Hiwannee, Ms., U.S.	F10	122
Hiwasa, Japan	F7	40
Hiwassee Lake, res., N.C., U.S.	A1	116
Hixon, Tn., U.S.	B1	116
Hjälmaren, l., Swe.	G6	8
Hjo, Swe.	G6	8
Hjørring, Den.	H3	8
Hkakabo Razi, mtn., Mya.	C8	46
Hkok (Kok), stm., Asia	B4	48
Hlaingbwe, Mya.	D3	48
Hlathikhulu, Swaz.	E10	70
Hlinsko, Czech Rep.	G11	16
Hlohovec, Slov.	H13	16
Hlotse, Leso.	F9	70
Hluhluwe, S. Afr.	F11	70
Hluhluwe Game Reserve, S. Afr.	F10	70
Hlúša, Bela.	G11	10
Hlyboka, Ukr.	A12	26
Hlybokae, Bela.	E10	10
Hmelita, Russia	E16	10
Ho, Ghana	H5	64
Hoa Binh, Viet.	B7	48
Hoare Bay, b., Nu., Can.	D13	141
Hobart, Austl.	o13	77a
Hobart, Ok., U.S.	F9	128
Hobbs, N.M., U.S.	B4	130
Hobbs Coast, cst., Ant.	C28	81
Hobe Sound, Fl., U.S.	I5	116
Hobgood, N.C., U.S.	H8	114
Hobq Shamo, des., China	A2	42
Hobson Lake, l., B.C., Can.	D10	138
Hobyo, Som.	C9	66
Hochalmspitze, mtn., Aus.	C10	22
Hochfeld, Nmb.	B3	70
Ho Chi Minh City see Thanh Pho Ho Chi Minh, Viet.	G8	48
Hochkönig, mtn., Aus.	C10	22
Höchstadt an der Aisch, Ger.	G6	16
Hochstetter Forland, pen.	B21	141
Hoch'uan see Hechuan, China	G2	42
Hocimsk, Bela.	G15	10
Hockenheim, Ger.	G4	16
Hocking, stm., Oh., U.S.	E15	120
Hodal, India	E6	54
Hodeida see Al-Hudaydah, Yemen	G5	56
Hodge, La., U.S.	E6	122
Hodgenville, Ky., U.S.	G12	120
Hodgeville, Sk., Can.	D7	124
Hodmezővásárhely, Hung.	C7	26
Hodna, Chott el, l., Alg.	B6	64
Hodonín, Czech Rep.	H12	16
Hodžanur'jah, gora, mtn., Uzb.	G11	32
Hodžejli, Uzb.	F9	32
Hædic, Île de, i., Fr.	G6	14
Hoei see Huy, Bel.	D14	14
Hoek van Holland, Neth.	C12	14
Hoeryŏng-ŭp, Kor., N.	C8	38
Hoeyang-ŭp, Kor., N.	E7	38
Hof, Ger.	F7	16
Hof, Ice.	k32	8a
Hofei see Hefei, China	F7	42
Hoffman, Mn., U.S.	F3	118
Hofgeismar, Ger.	E5	16
Hofheim am Taunus, Ger.	F4	16
Hofheim in Unterfranken, Ger.	F6	16
Hofors, Swe.	F7	8
Hofsjökull, ice, Ice.	k30	8a
Höfu, Japan	E4	40
Hofuf see Al-Hufūf, Sau. Ar.	D6	56
Hoganville, Ga., U.S.	D14	122
Hogback Mountain, mtn., Ne., U.S.	F9	126
Hogback Mountain, mtn., S.C., U.S.	A3	116
Högsby, Swe.	H6	8
Hohenwald, Tn., U.S.	B11	122
Hoher Dachstein, mtn., Aus.	C10	22
Hohe Tauern, mts., Aus.	C9	22
Hohhot, China	A4	42
Hohoe, Ghana	H5	64
Höhoku, Japan	E3	40
Hoh Xil Hu, l., China	D3	36
Hoh Xil Shan, mts., China	D2	36
Hoihong see Haikang, China	K3	42
Hoihow see Haikou, China	K4	42
Hoima, Ug.	D6	66
Hoisington, Ks., U.S.	C10	128
Hōjai, India	E14	54
Hŏjŏ, Japan	F5	40
Hōjō, Japan	E13	40
Hokah, Mn., U.S.	H7	118
Hokang see Hegang, China	B11	36
Hokitika, N.Z.	F4	80
Hokkaidō, i., Japan	C15	38
Holalkere, India	D3	53
Holberg, B.C., Can.	F2	138
Holbrook, Austl.	J6	76
Holbrook, Az., U.S.	I6	132
Holbrook, Ne., U.S.	A8	128
Holden, Ab., Can.	C18	138
Holden, Mo., U.S.	F4	120
Holden, W.V., U.S.	G3	114
Holden Village, Wa., U.S.	B6	136
Holdfast, Sk., Can.	D8	124
Holdingford, Mn., U.S.	F4	118
Holdrege, Ne., U.S.	A8	128
Holguín, Cuba	B9	102
Holíč, Slov.	H13	16
Holladay, Ut., U.S.	C5	132
Holland see Netherlands, ctry., Eur.	B15	14
Holland, Mi., U.S.	F3	112
Holland, Tx., U.S.	D10	130
Holland, hist. reg., Neth.	B13	14
Hollandale, Ms., U.S.	D8	122
Hollandia see Jayapura, Indon.	F11	44
Hollandsbird Island, i., Nmb.	D2	70
Holley, N.Y., U.S.	E11	112
Holliday, Tx., U.S.	H10	128
Hollins, Va., U.S.	H5	114
Hollister, Ca., U.S.	G4	134
Hollow Rock, Tn., U.S.	H9	120
Holly, Co., U.S.	C6	128
Holly Grove, Ar., U.S.	C7	122
Holly Hill, Fl., U.S.	G4	116
Holly Mills, N.C., U.S.	B7	116
Hollywood, Fl., U.S.	J5	116
Hollywood, Ms., U.S.	C9	122
Holm, stm., Russia	E17	6
Holm, Ut., U.S.	C14	10
Holman, N.T., Can.	A7	106
Hólmavík, Ice.	k28	8a
Holmen, Wi., U.S.	H7	118
Holmes, Mount, mtn., Wy., U.S.	F16	136
Holm Land, pen., Grnld.	A22	141
Holm Ø, i., Grnld.	C14	141
Holmogorskaja, Russia	E19	8
Holms, Russia	G17	34
Holmsund, Swe.	D9	8
Holon, Isr.	F5	58
Holoog, Nmb.	E4	70
Holovanivs'k, Ukr.	A17	26
Holstebro, Den.	H3	8
Holstein, Ia., U.S.	B2	120
Holsteinsborg (Sisimiut), Grnld.	D15	141
Holston, stm., Tn., U.S.	H2	114
Holston, North Fork, stm., Tn., U.S.	H3	114
Holsworthy, Eng., U.K.	K8	12
Holt, Fl., U.S.	G12	122
Holt, Mi., U.S.	B1	114
Holton, Ks., U.S.	E2	120
Holts Summit, Mo., U.S.	F5	120
Holy Cross, Ak., U.S.	D8	140
Holy Cross Mountain, mtn., B.C., Can.	C10	138
Holyhead, Wales, U.K.	H8	12
Holy Island, i., Eng., U.K.	F11	12
Holyoke, Co., U.S.	G10	126
Holyoke, Ma., U.S.	B13	114
Holyrood, Nf., Can.	C10	128
Holzkirchen, Ger.	I7	16
Hom, stm., Nmb.	F4	70
Homa Bay, Kenya	E6	66
Homalin, Mya.	D7	46
Homathko, stm., B.C., Can.	G6	138
Homathko Icefield, ice, B.C., Can.	E6	138
Homberg, Ger.	E5	16
Hombori Tondo, mtn., Mali	F4	64
Hombre Muerto, Salar del, pl., Arg.	B4	92
Homburg, Ger.	G3	16
Home Bay, b., Nu., Can.	B17	106
Home Hill, Austl.	B6	76
Homel', Bela.	H13	10
Homeland Park, S.C., U.S.	B3	116
Homer, Ak., U.S.	E9	140
Homer, Ga., U.S.	B2	116
Homer, La., U.S.	E5	122
Homer, Ne., U.S.	B1	120
Homer City, Pa., U.S.	D6	114
Homerville, Ga., U.S.	E3	116
Homestead, Fl., U.S.	K5	116
Homestead National Monument of America, p.o.i., Ne., U.S.	A11	128
Homewood, Al., U.S.	D12	122
Hommura, Japan	E12	40
Homnābād, India	C3	53
Homochitto, stm., Ms., U.S.	F7	122
Homoine, Moz.	C12	70
Homosassa, Fl., U.S.	H3	116
Homs see Al-Khums, Libya	A2	62
Homs see Hims, Syria	D7	58
Honaker, Va., U.S.	H4	114
Honan see Luoyang, China	D5	42
Honan see Henan, state, China	E5	42
Honāvar, India	D2	53
Hon Chong, Viet.	G7	48
Honda, Col.	E4	86
Honda, Bahía, b., Col.	A5	86
Honda Bay, b., Phil.	F2	52
Hondeklipbaai, S. Afr.	G3	70
Hon Dien, Nui, mtn., Viet.	G9	48
Hondo, Ab., Can.	A16	138
Hondo, N.M., U.S.	H3	128
Hondo, stm., N.A.	C3	102
Hondo Creek, stm., Tx., U.S.	E8	130
Honduras, ctry., N.A.	E4	102
Honduras, Cabo de, c., Hond.	D5	102
Honduras, Gulf of, b., N.A.	D4	102
Honea Path, S.C., U.S.	B3	116
Honefoss, Nor.	F4	8
Honesdale, Pa., U.S.	C10	114
Honey Grove, Tx., U.S.	D3	122
Honey Lake, l., Ca., U.S.	C5	134
Honeyville, Ut., U.S.	B4	132
Honfleur, Fr.	E9	14
Hong, stm., China	E6	42
Hong, Song see Red, stm., China	D9	46
Hon Gai, Viet.	B8	48
Hong Hu, l., China	F5	42
Hongjiang, China	H4	42
Hong Kong see Xianggang, China	J6	42
Hongliuyuan, China	F17	32
Hong Ngu, Viet.	G7	48
Hongqi, China	B7	38
Hongshui, stm., China	J3	42
Hongtong, China	C4	42
Honguedo, Détroit d', strt., Qc., Can.	A12	110
Hongze Hu, l., China	E8	42
Honiara, Sol. Is.	e8	79b
Honjō, Japan	E13	38
Honningsvåg, Nor.	A11	8
Honoka'a, Hi., U.S.	c6	78a
Honolulu, Hi., U.S.	b4	78a
Honomu, Hi., U.S.	d6	78a
Hon Quan, Viet.	G8	48
Honshū, i., Japan	G12	38
Honuu, Russia	C17	34
Hood, stm., Nu., Can.	B9	106
Hood, Mount, vol., Or., U.S.	E5	136
Hood Canal, b., Wa., U.S.	C4	136
Hoodoo Peak, mtn., Wa., U.S.	B6	136
Hood Point, c., Austl.	F3	74
Hoodsport, Wa., U.S.	C3	136
Hoogeveen, Neth.	B15	14
Hoogeveense Vaart, can., Neth.	B15	14
Hooker, Ok., U.S.	E7	128
Hook Head, c., Ire.	I6	12
Hookina, Austl.	H2	76
Hook Island, i., Austl.	C7	76
Hook Point, c., Austl.	E9	76
Hooks, Tx., U.S.	D4	122
Hooper, Ne., U.S.	C1	120
Hooper Bay, Ak., U.S.	D6	140
Hooper, N.D., U.S.	F16	124
Hoopeston, Il., U.S.	H2	112
Hoorn, Neth.	B14	14
Hoosick Falls, N.Y., U.S.	G3	110
Hoover Dam, dam, U.S.	G2	132
Hooversville, Pa., U.S.	H11	112
Hopatcong, N.J., U.S.	D11	114
Hope, B.C., Can.	D5	122
Hope, Ar., U.S.	G9	138
Hope, Ben, mtn., Scot., U.K.	C8	12
Hope, Point, c., Ak., U.S.	C6	140
Hopedale, La., U.S.	H9	122
Hopeh see Hebei, state, China	D8	36
Hopei see Hebei, state, China	D8	36
Hopelchén, Mex.	C3	102
Hope Mills, N.C., U.S.	B7	116
Hopes Advance, Cap, Qc., Can.	C17	106
Hopetoun, Austl.	F4	74
Hopetoun, Austl.	J4	76
Hopetown, S. Afr.	F6	70
Hope Valley, R.I., U.S.	C14	114
Hopewell, Va., U.S.	G8	114
Hopewell Culture National Historical Park, p.o.i., Oh., U.S.	E2	114
Hopewell Islands, is., Nu., Can.	D14	106
Hopi see Hebi, China	D6	42
Hopkins, Mo., U.S.	D3	120
Hopkins, stm., Austl.	L4	76
Hopkinsville, Ky., U.S.	H10	120
Hopkinton, Ia., U.S.	B6	120
Hoplite Bouchard, Arg.	G6	92
Hoppo see Hepu, China	K3	42
Hopwood, Mount, hill, Austl.	C5	76
Hoquiam, Wa., U.S.	C3	136
Hor, Russia	G16	34
Hor, stm., Russia	G16	34
Hor, stm., Russia	B12	36
Horatio, Ar., U.S.	D4	122
Hordaland, state, Nor.	F2	8
Horezu, Rom.	D10	26
Horicon, Wi., U.S.	H10	118
Horinger, China	A4	42
Horinsk, Russia	F10	34
Horizontina, Braz.	C10	92
Horlick Mountains, mts., Ant.	D29	81
Horlivka, Ukr.	E5	32
Horlovo, Russia	E21	10
Hormiguero, P.R.	B1	104a
Hormuz, Strait of, strt., Asia	D8	56
Horn, Aus.	B12	22
Horn, c., Ice.	j28	8a
Horn, stm., N.T., Can.	C7	106
Horn, Cape see Hornos, Cabo de, c., Chile	K3	90
Hornad (Hernád), stm., Eur.	H17	16
Hornaday, stm., Can.	B6	106
Hornafjördur, b., Ice.	k32	8a
Hornavan, l., Swe.	C7	8
Hornbeck, La., U.S.	F5	122
Hornbrook, Ca., U.S.	B3	134
Hornby Bay, b., N.T., Can.	B7	106
Hornell, N.Y., U.S.	B8	114
Hornepayne, On., Can.	F13	106
Horn Island, i., Ms., U.S.	G10	122
Horn Lake, Ms., U.S.	C8	122
Hornos, Cabo de (Horn, Cape), c., Chile	K3	90
Horn Plateau, plat., N.T., Can.	C6	106
Hornsea, Eng., U.K.	H12	12
Horodivka, Ukr.	A15	26
Horodok, Ukr.	G19	16
Horog, Taj.	B11	56
Horol', Russia	B10	38
Horqin Youyi Zhongqi, China	B4	38
Horqin Zuoyi Houqi, China	C4	38
Horqin Zuoyi Zhongqi, China	B5	38
Horqueta, Para.	D5	90
Horse Cave, Ky., U.S.	G12	120
Horse Creek, stm., Co., U.S.	C5	128
Horse Creek, stm., U.S.	F8	126
Horsefly, B.C., Can.	D9	138
Horsefly Lake, l., B.C., Can.	D10	138
Horseheads, N.Y., U.S.	B9	114
Horse Islands, is., Nf., Can.	i22	107a
Horsens, Den.	I3	8
Horseshoe Bend, Id., U.S.	G10	136
Horsham, Austl.	K4	76
Horsham, Eng., U.K.	J12	12
Horšovský Týn, Czech Rep.	G8	16
Horten, Nor.	G4	8
Hortobágy, reg., Hung.	B8	26
Hortobágyi Nemzeti Park, p.o.i., Hung.	B8	26
Horton, Ks., U.S.	E2	120
Horton, stm., N.T., Can.	B6	106
Horton Lake, l., N.T., Can.	B6	106
Hortonville, Wi., U.S.	G10	118
Hory, Bela.	F14	10
Hosa'ina, Eth.	F7	62
Hösbach, Ger.	F5	16
Hosedahard, Russia	A9	32
Hosford, Fl., U.S.	G14	122
Hoshāb, Pak.	D9	56
Hoshangābād, India	G6	54
Hoshiārpur, India	C5	54
Hosh Īsa, Egypt	H1	58
Hosmer, B.C., Can.	G15	138
Hospers, Ia., U.S.	A2	120
Hospet, India	D3	53
Hospitalet see l'Hospitalet de Llobregat, Spain	C13	20
Hossegor, Fr.	F4	18
Hosston, La., U.S.	E5	122
Hosta Butte, mtn., N.M., U.S.	H8	132
Hoste, Isla, i., Chile	K3	90
Hosūr, India	E3	53
Hotagen, l., Swe.	E5	8
Hotaka-dake, mtn., Japan	C10	40
Hotamış, Tur.	A4	58
Hotan, China	A5	46
Hotazel, S. Afr.	E6	70
Hotevilla, Az., U.S.	H6	132
Hotilovo, Russia	C17	10
Hot'kovo, Russia	D21	10
Hot Springs, Ar., U.S.	C6	122
Hot Springs, N.C., U.S.	I3	114
Hot Springs, S.D., U.S.	D9	126
Hot Springs, Va., U.S.	F6	114
Hot Springs National Park see Hot Springs, Ar., U.S.	C5	122
Hot Springs Peak, mtn., Nv., U.S.	B8	134
Hot Sulphur Springs, Co., U.S.	A2	128
Hottah Lake, l., N.T., Can.	B7	106
Hottentotsbaai, b., Nmb.	E2	70
Hotynec, Russia	F19	10
Houaïlou, N. Cal.	m15	79d
Houat, Île de, i., Fr.	G6	14
Houdan, Fr.	F10	14
Houghton, Mi., U.S.	D10	118
Houghton, N.Y., U.S.	B7	114
Houghton Lake, l., Mi., U.S.	D4	112
Houlka, Ms., U.S.	C10	122
Houlton, Me., U.S.	D9	110
Houma, China	D4	42
Houma, Tonga	n13	78e
Houma, La., U.S.	H8	122
Hou-pei see Hubei, state, China	F5	42
Hourtin, Étang d', l., Fr.	D4	18
Housatonic, stm., U.S.	B12	114
House, N.M., U.S.	G5	128
Houston, B.C., Can.	B4	138
Houston, Mn., U.S.	H7	118
Houston, Mo., U.S.	G6	120
Houston, Tx., U.S.	H3	122
Houston, Lake, res., Tx., U.S.	H3	122
Houtman Abrolhos, is., Austl.	E2	74
Houtou, S. Afr.		
Hovd, Mong.	C5	36
Hovd, stm., Mong.	E16	32
Hove, Eng., U.K.	K12	12
Hoven, S.D., U.S.	B13	126
Hovenweep National Monument, p.o.i., U.S.	F7	132
Hoverla, hora, mtn., Ukr.	A11	26
Hovgaard Ø, i., Grnld.	A22	141
Hövsgöl nuur, l., Mong.	F16	32
Hovu-Aksy, Russia	D16	32
Howar, Wādī, val., Afr.	D5	62
Howard, Austl.	E9	76
Howard, Ks., U.S.	D12	128
Howard, Pa., U.S.	C8	114
Howard, S.D., U.S.	C15	126
Howard City, Mi., U.S.	E4	112
Howard Draw, stm., Tx., U.S.	D6	130
Howard Lake, Mn., U.S.	F4	118
Howe, In., U.S.	G4	112
Howe, Cape, c., Austl.	K7	76
Howe Island, i., On., Can.	D13	112
Howell, Mi., U.S.	B2	114
Howell, Ut., U.S.	B4	132
Howells, Ne., U.S.	F15	126
Howick, S. Afr.	F10	70
Howitt, Mount, mtn., Austl.	K6	76
Howland Island, i., Oc.	C9	72
Howser, B.C., Can.	F13	138
Howson Peak, mtn., B.C., Can.	B3	138
Hoxie, Ar., U.S.	H6	120
Hoxie, Ks., U.S.	B8	128

Höxter – Inverness I • 25

Name	Map Ref.	Page
Höxter, Ger.	E5	16
Hoxtolgay, China	B2	36
Hoy, i., Scot., U.K.	C9	12
Hoyerswerda, Ger.	E10	16
Hoyos, Spain	D4	20
Höytiäinen, l., Fin.	E13	8
Hoyt Lakes, Mn., U.S.	D6	118
Hradec Králové, Czech Rep.	F11	16
Hradzjanka, Bela.	G11	10
Hranice, Czech Rep.	G13	16
Hrèsk, Bela.	G10	10
Hristoforovo, Russia	F22	8
Hrodna, Bela.	G6	10
Hrodna, state, Bela.	G7	10
Hroma, stm., Russia	B17	34
Hron, stm., Slov.	H14	16
Hronov, Czech Rep.	F12	16
Hrubieszów, Pol.	F19	16
Hrustal'nyj, Russia	B11	38
Hsiakuan *see* Dali, China	F5	36
Hsiamen *see* Xiamen, China	I7	42
Hsian *see* Xi'an, China	D3	42
Hsiangt'an *see* Xiangtan, China	H5	42
Hsiangyang *see* Xiangfan, China	F4	42
Hsienyang *see* Xianyang, China	D3	42
Hsi-hseng, Mya.	B3	48
Hsilo, Tai.	J9	42
Hsim, stm., Mya.	B4	48
Hsinchu, Tai.	I9	42
Hsinghua *see* Xinghua, China	E8	42
Hsingt'ai *see* Xingtai, China	C6	42
Hsinhailien *see* Lianyungang, China	D8	42
Hsinhsiang *see* Xinxiang, China	D5	42
Hsining *see* Xining, China	D5	36
Hsinking *see* Changchun, China	C6	38
Hsinp'u *see* Lianyungang, China	D8	42
Hsintien, Tai.	I9	42
Hsinyang *see* Xinyang, China	E6	42
Hsipaw, Mya.	A3	48
Hsüanhua *see* Xuanhua, China	A6	42
Hsüch'ang *see* Xuchang, China	D5	42
Hsüchou *see* Xuzhou, China	D7	42
Hua'an, China	I7	42
Huab, stm., Nmb.	B2	70
Huacaraje, Bol.	B4	90
Huacho, Peru	F2	84
Huachuca City, Az., U.S.	L6	132
Huadian, China	C7	38
Huading Shan, mtn., China	G9	42
Hua Hin, Thai.	F4	48
Huai, stm., China	E8	42
Huai, stm., China	C6	42
Huai'an, China	E8	42
Huai'an, China	A6	42
Huaibin, China	E6	42
Huaicheng *see* Huai'an, China	E8	42
Huaidezhen, China	C6	38
Huaiji, China	I5	42
Huailai, China	A6	42
Huainan, China	E7	42
Huairou, China	A7	42
Huaite *see* Gongzhuling, China	C6	38
Huaiyang, China	E6	42
Huai Yot, Thai.	I4	48
Huaiyuan, China	E7	42
Huajuapan de León, Mex.	G10	100
Hualahuises, Mex.	C9	100
Hualālai, vol., Hi., U.S.	d6	78a
Hualañé, Chile	G2	92
Hualfín, Arg.	C4	92
Hualien, Tai.	J9	42
Huallaga, stm., Peru	E2	84
Huallanca, Peru	E2	84
Hualong, China	D5	36
Huambo, Ang.	C2	68
Huamei Shan, mtn., China	I5	42
Huan, stm., China	F6	42
Huanan, China	B11	36
Huancabamba, Peru	E2	84
Huancané, Peru	G4	84
Huancavelica, Peru	F2	84
Huancayo, Peru	F2	84
Huang (Yellow), stm., China	D8	36
Huangchuan, China	E6	42
Huanggai Hu, l., China	G5	42
Huanggang, China	F6	42
Huanggangliang, mtn., China	C2	38
Huanghua, China	B7	42
Huangjinbu, China	G7	42
Huangling, China	D3	42
Huanglong, China	D3	42
Huangnihe, China	C7	38
Huangpi, China	F6	42
Huangqi, China	H8	42
Huangshahe, China	H4	42
Huangshan, China	G8	42
Huangshan see Guangming Ding, mtn., China	F7	42
Huangshi, China	G4	42
Huangshi, China	F6	42
Huangtang Hu, l., China	G6	42
Huangtuliangzi, China	A8	42
Huanguelén, Arg.	H6	92
Huangxian, China	C9	42
Huangyan, China	G9	42
Huangyuan, China	D5	36
Huangzhong, China	D5	36
Huangzhu, China	L4	42
Huanjiang, China	I3	42
Huanren, China	D6	38
Huánuco, Peru	E2	84
Huanuni, Bol.	C3	90
Huanxian, China	C2	42
Huara, Chile	C3	90
Huaral, Peru	F2	84
Huaraz, Peru	E2	84
Huariaca, Peru	F2	84
Huarmey, Peru	F2	84
Huarong, China	G5	42
Huasaga, stm., S.A.	I3	86
Hua Sai, Thai.	H5	48
Huascarán, Nevado, mtn., Peru	E2	84
Huasco, Chile	D2	92
Huasco, stm., Chile	D2	92
Huatabampo, Mex.	B4	100
Huating, China	D2	42
Huatong, China	A9	42
Huauchinango, Mex.	E9	100
Huaxian, China	J5	42
Huaxian, China	D6	42
Huaxian, China	D3	42
Huaynamota, stm., Mex.	D6	100
Huazamota, Mex.	D6	100
Huazhou, China	K4	42
Hubbard, Ia., U.S.	B4	120
Hubbard Creek Reservoir, l., Tx., U.S.	B8	130
Hubbard Lake, l., Mi., U.S.	D6	112
Hubbards, N.S., Can.	F12	110
Hubbell, Mi., U.S.	D10	118
Hubei, state, China	F5	42
Huberdeau, Qc., Can.	E2	110
Hubli-Dhārwār, India	D2	53
Hubuleng, China	A4	42
Huchow *see* Huzhou, China	F9	42
Huckleberry Mountain, mtn., Or., U.S.	G4	136
Hucknall, Eng., U.K.	H11	12
Huddersfield, Eng., U.K.	H11	12
Huddinge, Swe.	G8	8
Huder, China	A9	36
Hudiksvall, Swe.	F7	8
Hudson, Fl., U.S.	H3	116
Hudson, Ia., U.S.	B5	120
Hudson, N.C., U.S.	I4	114
Hudson, N.Y., U.S.	H3	110
Hudson, Oh., U.S.	C4	114
Hudson, S.D., U.S.	H2	118
Hudson, Wy., U.S.	E4	126
Hudson, stm., U.S.	G16	112
Hudson, Baie d' see Hudson Bay, b., Can.	C13	106
Hudson Bay, Sk., Can.	B11	124
Hudson Bay, b., Can.	C13	106
Hudson Falls, N.Y., U.S.	G3	110
Hudson's Hope, B.C., Can.	D6	106
Hudson Strait, strt., Can.	C16	106
Hudžand, Taj.	A10	56
Hue, Viet.	D8	48
Huebra, stm., Spain	D4	20
Huehuetenango, Guat.	E2	102
Huejutla de Reyes, Mex.	E9	100
Huelgoat, Fr.	F5	14
Huelva, Spain	G3	20
Huelva, co., Spain	G4	20
Huentelauquén, Chile	E2	92
Huércal-Overa, Spain	G8	20
Huerfano, stm., Co., U.S.	C4	128
Huerlumada, China	B13	54
Huerva, stm., Spain	C9	20
Huesca, Spain	B10	20
Huesca, co., Spain	B10	20
Huéscar, Spain	G8	20
Huetamo de Núñez, Mex.	F8	100
Hueytown, Al., U.S.	D11	122
Ḥufrat an-Naḥās, Sudan	F4	62
Hughenden, Austl.	C4	76
Hughes, Ak., U.S.	C9	140
Hughes, Ar., U.S.	C8	122
Hughes Springs, Tx., U.S.	E4	122
Hugh Keenleyside Dam, dam, B.C., Can.	G12	138
Hughson, Ca., U.S.	F5	134
Hugh Town, Eng., U.K.	L6	12
Hugli, stm., India	G12	54
Hugo, Co., U.S.	B5	128
Hugo, Ok., U.S.	C3	122
Hugoton, Ks., U.S.	D7	128
Huhar, stm., China	B4	38
Huhehaote *see* Hohhot, China	A4	42
Huhehot *see* Hohhot, China	A4	42
Huichang, China	I6	42
Huicheng *see* Huilai, China	J7	42
Hŭich'ŏn, Kor., N.	D7	38
Huichou *see* Huizhou, China	J6	42
Huila, state, Col.	F4	86
Huila, Nevado del, vol., Col.	F3	86
Huilai, China	J7	42
Huili, China	F5	36
Huillapima, Arg.	D4	92
Huimin, China	C7	42
Huinan, China	C7	38
Huisachal, Mex.	H6	130
Huishui, China	H2	42
Huisne, stm., Fr.	F9	14
Huitong, China	H3	42
Huitzo, Mex.	G10	100
Huitzuco de los Figueroa, Mex.	F9	100
Huixian, China	E2	42
Huixian, China	D5	42
Huixtla, Mex.	H12	100
Huize, China	F5	36
Huizhou, China	J6	42
Hŭksan-chedo, is., Kor., S.	G6	38
Hukuntsi, Bots.	D5	70
Hulan, China	B7	38
Hulan Ergi, China	B9	36
Hulbert, Mi., U.S.	B4	112
Hulett, Wy., U.S.	C8	126
Hulga, stm., Russia	B10	32
Hulin, China	B11	36
Hulin, stm., China	B4	38
Huliu, stm., China	A6	42
Hull, Ia., U.S.	H2	118
Hull, Il., U.S.	E6	120
Hull, ngh., Qc., Can.	C14	112
Hullo, Est.	A6	10
Hulun *see* Hailar, China	B8	36
Hulun Nur, l., China	B8	36
Huma, China	F14	34
Huma, Tonga	o15	78e
Humacao, P.R.	B4	104a
Humahuaca, Arg.	D3	90
Humaitá, Braz.	E5	84
Humaitá, Para.	C8	92
Humansdorp, S. Afr.	I7	70
Humansville, Mo., U.S.	G4	120
Humara, Jabal al-, hill, Sudan	D6	62
Humbe, Ang.	D1	68
Humber, stm., Eng., U.K.	H12	12
Humbird, Wi., U.S.	G8	118
Humboldt, Sk., Can.	B8	124
Humboldt, Az., U.S.	I4	132
Humboldt, Ia., U.S.	B3	120
Humboldt, Il., U.S.	E9	120
Humboldt, Ne., U.S.	D2	120
Humboldt, S.D., U.S.	D15	126
Humboldt, stm., Nv., U.S.	C7	134
Humboldt, North Fork, stm., Nv., U.S.	B1	132
Humboldt, South Fork, stm., Nv., U.S.	C1	132
Humboldt Gletscher, ice, Grnld.	B13	141
Humboldt Lake, l., Nv., U.S.	D7	134
Hume, Ca., U.S.	G7	134
Hume, Lake, res., Austl.	J6	76
Humeburn, Austl.	F5	76
Humenné, Slov.	H17	16
Humeston, Ia., U.S.	D4	120
Hummi, ozero, l., Russia	F16	34
Humphrey, Ne., U.S.	F15	126
Humphreys, Mount, mtn., Ca., U.S.	F7	134
Humphreys Peak, mtn., Az., U.S.	H5	132
Humpolec, Czech Rep.	G11	16
Humpty Doo, Austl.	B6	74
Hūn, Libya	B3	62
Hun, stm., China	D5	38
Hun, stm., China	D6	38
Húnaflói, b., Ice.	j29	8a
Hunan, state, China	H4	42
Hunchun, China	C9	38
Hundred, W.V., U.S.	E5	114
Hunedoara, Rom.	D9	26
Hunedoara, state, Rom.	C9	26
Hünfeld, Ger.	F5	16
Hungary, ctry., Eur.	B6	26
Hungchiang *see* Hongjiang, China	H4	42
Hŭngdŏki-dong, Kor., N.	E7	38
Hungerford, Austl.	G5	76
Hungerford, Tx., U.S.	H2	122
Hungry Horse Dam, dam, Mt., U.S.	B13	136
Hungry Horse Reservoir, res., Mt., U.S.	B12	136
Hung Yen, Viet.	B8	48
Hunjiang, China	C7	38
Hunlen Falls, wtfl., B.C., Can.	D5	138
Hunsberge, mts., Nmb.	E3	70
Hunsrück, mts., Ger.	G3	16
Hunsūr, India	E3	53
Hunte, stm., Ger.	D4	16
Hunter, N.D., U.S.	D1	118
Hunter, stm., Austl.	I8	76
Hunter Island, i., Austl.	n12	77a
Hunter Island, i., B.C., Can.	E2	138
Hunter Mountain, mtn., N.Y., U.S.	B11	114
Hunter River, P.E., Can.	D13	110
Hunters, Wa., U.S.	B8	136
Hunters Bay, b., Mya.	C1	48
Huntingdon, Qc., Can.	E2	110
Huntingdon, Eng., U.K.	I12	12
Huntingdon, Pa., U.S.	D7	114
Huntingdon, Tn., U.S.	I9	120
Huntington, In., U.S.	H4	112
Huntington, Tx., U.S.	F4	122
Huntington, Ut., U.S.	D5	132
Huntington, W.V., U.S.	F3	114
Huntington Beach, Ca., U.S.	J7	134
Huntland, Tn., U.S.	B12	122
Huntley, Mt., U.S.	B4	126
Huntly, N.Z.	C6	80
Huntly, Scot., U.K.	D10	12
Huntsville, On., Can.	C10	112
Huntsville, Al., U.S.	C12	122
Huntsville, Mo., U.S.	E5	120
Huntsville, Tn., U.S.	H13	120
Huntsville, Tx., U.S.	G3	122
Huntsville, Ut., U.S.	B5	132
Hunyuan, China	B5	42
Huong Hoa, Viet.	D8	48
Huon Gulf, b., Pap. N. Gui.	b4	79a
Huon Peninsula, pen., Pap. N. Gui.	b4	79a
Huonville, Austl.	o13	77a
Huoqiu, China	E7	42
Huoshan, China	F7	42
Huoxian, China	C4	42
Hurd, Cape, c., On., Can.	C8	112
Hüren Tovon uul, mtn., Mong.	C4	36
Hure Qi, China	C4	38
Hurghada, Egypt	K4	58
Hurley, N.M., U.S.	K8	132
Hurley, S.D., U.S.	D15	126
Hurley, Wi., U.S.	E8	118
Huron, Ca., U.S.	G5	134
Huron, Oh., U.S.	C3	114
Huron, S.D., U.S.	C14	126
Huron, stm., Mi., U.S.	B2	114
Huron, Lake, l., N.A.	D7	112
Huron Mountains, hills, Mi., U.S.	B2	112
Hurricane, Ut., U.S.	F3	132
Hurstbridge, Austl.	K5	76
Hurtado, stm., Chile	E2	92
Hurtsboro, Al., U.S.	E13	122
Hurunui, stm., N.Z.	F5	80
Husainīwāla, India	C5	54
Húsavik, Far. Is.	n34	8b
Húsavík, Ice.	j31	8a
Hushitai, China	C5	38
Huși, Rom.	C15	26
Huslia, Ak., U.S.	C8	140
Hussar, Ab., Can.	E18	138
Husum, Ger.	B4	16
Hutag, Mong.	B5	36
Hutanopan, Indon.	C1	50
Hutchinson, S. Afr.	G6	70
Hutchinson, Ks., U.S.	C11	128
Hutchinson, Mn., U.S.	G4	118
Hutch Mountain, mtn., Az., U.S.	I5	132
Hutsonville, Il., U.S.	E10	120
Huttig, Ar., U.S.	D6	122
Hutto, Tx., U.S.	D10	130
Hutuo, stm., China	B5	42
Huwei, Tai.	J9	42
Huxi, China	H6	42
Huxian, China	D3	42
Huxley, Ab., Can.	E17	138
Huy, Bel.	D14	14
Huzhen, China	G9	42
Huzhou, China	F9	42
Hvannadalshnúkur, mtn., Ice.	k31	8a
Hvar, Cro.	G13	22
Hvar, Otok, i., Cro.	G13	22
Hveragerđi, Ice.	k29	8a
Hvolsvöllur, Ice.	l29	8a
Hwainan *see* Huainan, China	E7	42
Hwange, Zimb.	D4	68
Hwang Ho see Huang, stm., China	D8	36
Hwangju-ŭp, Kor., N.	E6	38
Hwangshih *see* Huangshi, China	F6	42
Hyannis, Ma., U.S.	C15	114
Hyannis, Ne., U.S.	F11	126
Hyargas nuur, l., Mong.	B3	36
Hyattville, Wy., U.S.	C5	126
Hyden, Austl.	F3	74
Hyden, Ky., U.S.	G2	114
Hyde Park, Guy.	B6	84
Hyde Park, N.Y., U.S.	C12	114
Hyde Park, Vt., U.S.	F4	110
Hyderābād, India	C4	53
Hyderābād, Pak.	F2	54
Hydra see Ýdra, i., Grc.	F6	28
Hydraulic, B.C., Can.	D9	138
Hydro, Ok., U.S.	F10	128
Hydrographers Passage, strt., Austl.	C8	76
Hyères, Fr.	F12	18
Hyères, Îles d', is., Fr.	G12	18
Hyesan, Kor., N.	D8	38
Hyland, stm., Can.	C5	106
Hyndman, Pa., U.S.	E7	114
Hyndman Peak, mtn., Id., U.S.	G12	136
Hyōgo, state, Japan	D7	40
Hyrum, Ut., U.S.	B5	132
Hysham, Mt., U.S.	A5	126
Hythe, Eng., U.K.	J13	12
Hyūga, Japan	G4	40
Hyūga-nada, s., Japan	G4	40
Hyvinge *see* Hyvinkää, Fin.	F11	8
Hyvinkää, Fin.	F11	8

I

Name	Map Ref.	Page
Iaciara, Braz.	H2	88
Iaco (Yaco), stm., S.A.	F4	84
Iaçu, Braz.	G5	88
Iaeger, W.V., U.S.	G4	114
Ialomița, state, Rom.	E14	26
Ialomița, stm., Rom.	E13	26
Ialomiței, Balta, sw., Rom.	E14	26
Iamonia, Lake, l., Fl., U.S.	F1	116
Iapu, Braz.	J4	88
Iargara, Mol.	C15	26
Iași, Rom.	B14	26
Iași, state, Rom.	B14	26
Iatt, Lake, res., La., U.S.	F6	122
Ib, stm., India	G10	54
Iba, Phil.	C2	52
Ibadan, Nig.	H5	64
Ibagué, Col.	E4	86
Ibaiti, Braz.	A12	92
Ibănești, Rom.	A13	26
Ibapah Peak, mtn., Ut., U.S.	D3	132
Ibar, stm., Serb.	F7	26
Ibaraki, state, Japan	C13	40
Ibarra, Ec.	G2	86
Ibarreta, Arg.	B8	92
Ibb, Yemen	G5	56
Ibbenbüren, Ger.	D3	16
Ibembo, D.R.C.	D4	66
Iberá, Esteros del, sw., Arg.	D8	92
Iberia, Mo., U.S.	F5	120
Iberian Mountains see Ibérico, Sistema, mts., Spain	D8	20
Iberian Peninsula, pen., Eur.	D12	4
Ibérico, Sistema (Iberian Mountains), mts., Spain	D8	20
Ibiá, Braz.	J2	88
Ibiapina, Braz.	B5	88
Ibicaraí, Braz.	H6	88
Ibicuí, Braz.	H5	88
Ibicuí, stm., Braz.	D9	92
Ibiquera, Braz.	G5	88
Ibiraçu, Braz.	J5	88
Ibirapuã, Braz.	I5	88
Ibirapuitã, stm., Braz.	D10	92
Ibirataia, Braz.	H6	88
Ibirubá, Braz.	D11	92
Ibitiara, Braz.	G4	88
Ibitinga, Braz.	K1	88
Ibiza *see* Eivissa, Spain	F12	20
Ibiza see Eivissa, i., Spain	F12	20
Ibotirama, Braz.	G4	88
İbriktepe, Tur.	B9	28
Ibshawâi, Egypt	I1	58
Ibusuki, Japan	H3	40
Ica, Peru	F2	84
Içá (Putumayo), stm., S.A.	D4	84
Icabarú, stm., Ven.	E10	86
Icacos Point, c., Trin.	s11	105f
Icamaquã, stm., Braz.	D10	92
Icamole, Mex.	I7	130
Içana, Braz.	G8	86
Içana (Isana), stm., S.A.	G7	86
Icaño, Arg.	D5	92
Icatu, Braz.	B3	88
Iceberg Pass, p., Co., U.S.	G7	126
İçel (Mersin), Tur.	B5	58
İçel, state, Tur.	B4	58
Iceland, ctry., Eur.	k30	8a
Iceland Basin, unds.	C11	144
Ice Mountain, mtn., B.C., Can.	B9	138
Ichaikaronji, India	C2	53
Ichchāpuram, India	B7	53
Ichikawa, Japan	D12	40
Ichinomiya, Japan	D9	40
Ichkeul, Lac, l., Tun.	G3	24
Ichnia, Ukr.	D4	32
Ich'un *see* Yichun, China	B10	36
Ičinskaja Sopka, vulkan, vol., Russia	E20	34
Icó, Braz.	D6	88
Icy Cape, c., Ak., U.S.	B7	140
Ida, Mount see Ídi Óros, mtn., Grc.	H7	28
Idabel, Ok., U.S.	D4	122
Ida Grove, Ia., U.S.	B2	120
Idah, Nig.	H6	64
Idaho, state, U.S.	G12	136
Idaho City, Id., U.S.	G11	136
Idaho Falls, Id., U.S.	G14	136
Idaho National Engineering Laboratory, sci., Id., U.S.	G14	136
Idalou, Tx., U.S.	H7	128
Idanha-a-Nova, Port.	E3	20
Idāppādi, India	F3	53
Idar, India	G4	54
Idar-Oberstein, Ger.	G3	16
Idelès, Alg.	E6	64
Idi, Indon.	J3	48
Idiofa, D.R.C.	F3	66
Ídi Óros, mtn., Grc.	H7	28
Idku, Bahra el-, l., Egypt	G1	58
Idlib, Syria	C7	58
Idlib, state, Syria	C7	58
Ídolo, Isla del, i., Mex.	E10	100
Idoûkâl-en-Taghès, mtn., Niger	F6	64
Idre, Swe.	F5	8
Idrija, Slvn.	D11	22
Idutywa, S. Afr.	H9	70
Iecava, stm., Lat.	D7	10
Ieper, Bel.	D11	14
Ierápetra, Grc.	H8	28
Ierzu, Italy	E3	24
Iesolo, Italy	E9	22
Ifakara, Tan.	F7	66
Ife, Nig.	H5	64
Iferouâne, Niger	F6	64
Iferten *see* Yverdon-les-Bains, Switz.	D3	22
Ifôghas, Adrar des, mts., Afr.	F5	64
Igan, Malay.	B7	50
Igan, stm., Malay.	B7	50
Iganga, Ug.	D6	66
Igaporã, Braz.	G4	88
Igara, Braz.	F5	88
Igara Paraná, stm., Col.	H5	86
Igarapé-Açu, Braz.	D8	84
Igarapé-Miri, Braz.	B1	88
Igarka, Russia	A15	32
Igatpuri, India	B1	53
Igboho, Nig.	H5	64
Igharghar, Oued, stm., Alg.	D6	64
Igiugig, Ak., U.S.	E8	140
Iglesias, Italy	E2	24
Iglesias, Cerro las, mtn., Mex.	B5	100
Iglesiente, reg., Italy	E2	24
Igluligaarjuk (Chesterfield Inlet), Nu., Can.	C12	106
Iglulik, Nu., Can.	B14	106
'Igma, Gebel el-, mts., Egypt	I4	58
Ignacio, Co., U.S.	F9	132
Ignalina, Lith.	E9	10
Ignaței, Mol.	B15	26
Igoumenítsa, Grc.	D3	28
Igra, Russia	C8	32
Iguaçu (Iguazú), stm., S.A.	B10	92
Iguaçu, Parque Nacional do, p.o.i., Braz.	B11	92
Iguaí, Braz.	H5	88
Iguala, Mex.	F9	100
Igualada, Spain	C12	20
Iguana, stm., Ven.	D9	86
Iguape, Braz.	B14	92
Iguape, stm., Braz.	B13	92
Iguassu Falls, wtfl., S.A.	B10	92
Iguatemi, stm., Braz.	A10	92
Iguatu, Braz.	D6	88
Iguazú (Iguaçu), stm., S.A.	B10	92
Iguazú, Parque Nacional, p.o.i., S.A.	B10	92
Iguéla, Gabon	E1	66
Iguéla, Lagune, b., Gabon	E1	66
Iguîdi, 'Erg, sand, Afr.	D3	64
Igžej, Russia	D18	32
Iharaña, Madag.	C9	68
Iheya-shima, i., Japan	I18	39a
Ihnâsiya el-Madina, Egypt	I1	58
Ihosy, Madag.	E8	68
Ihtiman, Blg.	G10	26
Iida, Japan	D10	40
Iisalmi, Fin.	E12	8
Iiyama, Japan	C11	40
Iizuka, Japan	F3	40
Ijâfene, des., Maur.	E3	64
Ijebu-Ode, Nig.	H5	64
IJmuiden, Neth.	B13	14
IJssel, stm., Neth.	B15	14
IJsselmeer, l., Neth.	B14	14
Ijuí, Braz.	D11	92
Ijuí, stm., Braz.	D10	92
Ika, Russia	C19	32
Ikali, D.R.C.	E4	66
Ikaluktutiak (Cambridge Bay), Nu., Can.	B10	106
Ikaría, i., Grc.	F9	28
Ikatskij hrebet, mts., Russia	F11	34
Ikeda, Japan	E6	40
Ikej, Russia	D17	32
Ikeja, Nig.	H5	64
Ikela, D.R.C.	E4	66
Ikerre, Nig.	H6	64
İkizce, Tur.	D15	28
Ikom, Nig.	H6	64
Ikot-Ekpene, Nig.	H6	64
Ikuno, Japan	D7	40
Ikurangi, hill, Cook Is.	a26	78j
Ila, Nig.	H6	64
Ilagan, Phil.	B3	52
Ilaiyānkudi, India	G4	53
Īlām, Iran	C6	56
Ilām, Nepal	E11	54
Ilan, Tai.	I9	42
Ilanskij, Russia	C17	32
Ilaro, Nig.	H5	64
Iława, Pol.	C15	16
Ilbenge, Russia	D13	34
Île-à-la-Crosse, Sk., Can.	D9	106
Ilebo, D.R.C.	E4	66
Île-de-France, hist. reg., Fr.	E11	14
Île de France, i., Grnld.	B22	141
Île-du-Prince-Édouard see Prince Edward Island, state, Can.	D13	110
Ilek, stm., Asia	D8	32
Ilesha, Nig.	H5	64
Îles Loyauté, state, N. Cal.	m16	79d
Île Tintamarre, i., Anguilla	A2	105a
Ilevskij Pogost, Russia	F20	8
Ileza, Russia	F20	8
Ilfracombe, Austl.	D5	76
Ilfracombe, Eng., U.K.	J8	12
Ilhabela, Braz.	L3	88
Ilha Grande, Baía da, b., Braz.	L3	88
Ilha Solteira, Represa de, res., Braz.	D6	90
Ilhea Point, c., Nmb.	C2	70
Ilhéus, Braz.	H6	88
Ilia, Rom.	D9	26
Iliamna, Ak., U.S.	E8	140
Iliamna Lake, l., Ak., U.S.	D9	140
Ilicinea, Braz.	K3	88
Iliff, Co., U.S.	G9	126
Iligan, Phil.	F5	52
Iligan Bay, b., Phil.	F4	52
Iliniza, vol., Ec.	H2	86
Ilion, N.Y., U.S.	A10	114
Ilir, Russia	C18	32
Ilizi, Alg.	D6	64
Il'ja, Bela.	F10	10
Iljino, Russia	E14	10
Iljinskij, Russia	G17	34
Iljinskoe, Russia	D19	10
Iljinsko-Podomskoe, Russia	F23	8
Iljiny gory, hills, Russia	D17	10
Ilkal, India	D2	53
Ilkley, Eng., U.K.	H11	12
Illampu, Nevado, mtn., Bol.	C3	90
Illana Bay, b., Phil.	G4	52
Illapel, Chile	E2	92
Ille-et-Vilaine, state, Fr.	F7	14
Illéla, Niger	G6	64
Iller, stm., Ger.	I6	16
Illertissen, Ger.	H6	16
Illescas, Mex.	D7	100
Illichivs'k, Ukr.	C17	26
Illimani, Nevado, mtn., Bol.	C3	90
Illinois, state, U.S.	D8	120
Illinois, stm., Il., U.S.	E7	120
Illinois, stm., Or., U.S.	H3	136
Illinois, stm., U.S.	B3	122
Il'men', ozero, l., Russia	B14	10
Ilo, Peru	G3	84
Iloilo, Phil.	E4	52
Ilomantsi, Fin.	E14	8
Ilorin, Nig.	H5	64
Il'pyrskij, Russia	D21	34
Ilūkste, Lat.	E9	10
Ilulissat *see* Jakobshavn, Grnld.	D15	141
Ilwaki, Indon.	G8	44
Ilwŏl-san, mtn., Kor., S.	C1	40
Īlyīch, Kaz.	F11	32
Imabari, Japan	E5	40
Imaichi, Japan	C12	40
Imandra, ozero, l., Russia	C14	8
Imari, Japan	F2	40
Imaruí, Braz.	D13	92
Imaruí, Lagoa do, l., Braz.	D13	92
Imatra, Fin.	F13	8
Imavere, Est.	B8	10
Imbabura, state, Ec.	G2	86
Imbituba, Braz.	D13	92
Imeni Cjurupy, Russia	E21	10
Imeni Kirova, Russia	E14	34
Imeni Poliny Osipenko, Russia	F16	34
Imeni Stepana Razina, Russia	I21	8
Imeni Željabova, Russia	A19	10
Īmī, Eth.	F8	62
Imías, Cuba	B10	102
Imilac, Chile	B3	92
Imlay, Nv., U.S.	C7	134
Imlay City, Mi., U.S.	E6	112
Immenstadt, Ger.	I6	16
Immokalee, Fl., U.S.	J4	116
Imnaha, stm., Or., U.S.	E10	136
Imola, Italy	F8	22
Imonda, Pap. N. Gui.	a3	79a
Impasugong, Phil.	F5	52
Imperatriz, Braz.	C2	88
Imperia, Italy	G5	22
Imperial, Sk., Can.	C8	124
Imperial, Ca., U.S.	K10	134
Imperial, Tx., U.S.	C5	130
Imperial Beach, Ca., U.S.	K8	134
Imperial Dam, dam, U.S.	K2	132
Imperial de Aragón, Canal, can., Spain	C9	20
Imperial Valley, val., Ca., U.S.	E5	98
Impfondo, Congo	D3	66
Imphāl, India	D7	46
Imroz, Tur.	C8	28
Imst, Aus.	C7	22
Imuris, Mex.	F7	98
Ina, Japan	D10	40
Ina, Il., U.S.	F9	120
Inajá, Braz.	E7	88
I-n-Amenas, Alg.	D6	64
Iñapari, Peru	F4	84
Inarajan, Guam	j10	78c
Inari, Fin.	B12	8
Inarigda, Russia	B19	32
Inarijärvi, l., Fin.	B12	8
Inawashiro-ko, l., Japan	B12	40
Inca, Spain	E13	20
Inca de Oro, Chile	C3	92
Incahuasi, Cerro de, mtn., S.A.	C3	92
İnce Burun, c., Tur.	C10	28
İncekum Burnu, c., Tur.	B4	58
Inchelium, Wa., U.S.	B8	136
Inch'ŏn, Kor., S.	F7	38
İncirliova, Tur.	F10	28
Incomati (Komati), stm., Afr.	E10	70
Incudine, Monte, mtn., Fr.	H15	18
Incy, Russia	D19	8
Indaiá, stm., Braz.	J3	88
Indalsälven, stm., Swe.	E6	8
Indé, Mex.	I2	130
Independence, Ca., U.S.	G7	134
Independence, Ia., U.S.	B6	120
Independence, Ks., U.S.	G2	120
Independence, Ky., U.S.	F13	120
Independence, La., U.S.	G8	122
Independence, Mo., U.S.	E3	120
Independence, Va., U.S.	H4	114
Independence, Wi., U.S.	G7	118
Independence Fjord, b., Grnld.	A20	141
Independencia, Bol.	C3	90
Independência, Braz.	C5	88
Inderbor, Kaz.	E8	32
Indi, India	C2	53
India, ctry., Asia	D4	46
Indialantic, Fl., U.S.	H5	116
Indiana, Pa., U.S.	D6	114
Indiana, state, U.S.	D11	120
Indiana Dunes National Lakeshore, p.o.i., In., U.S.	G2	112
Indianapolis, In., U.S.	I3	112
Indian Bayou, stm., Ar., U.S.	C7	122
Indian Church, Belize	D3	102
Indian Head, Sk., Can.	D10	124
Indian Lake, N.Y., U.S.	G2	110
Indian Lake, l., On., Can.	A7	112
Indian Lake, l., Mi., U.S.	B3	112
Indian Ocean	K11	142
Indianola, Ia., U.S.	C4	120
Indianola, Ms., U.S.	D8	122
Indianola, Ne., U.S.	A8	128
Indian Peak, mtn., Ut., U.S.	E3	132
Indian River, Mi., U.S.	C5	112
Indian Rock, mtn., Wa., U.S.	E6	136
Indiantown, Fl., U.S.	I5	116
Indiera Alta, P.R.	B2	104a
Indiga, Russia	C23	8
Indigirka, stm., Russia	C18	34
Indin, Mya.	H14	54
Indio, Ca., U.S.	J9	134
Indira Gandhi Canal, can., India	E4	54
Indispensable Strait, strt., Sol. Is.	e9	79b
Indochina, reg., Asia	D7	48
Indonesia, ctry., Asia	J16	30
Indore, India	G5	54
Indragiri, stm., Indon.	D2	50
Indramayu, Indon.	G6	50
Indrāvati, stm., India	B5	53
Indravati Tiger Reserve, p.o.i., India	B5	53
Indre, state, Fr.	C7	18
Indre, stm., Fr.	G10	14
Indre-et-Loire, state, Fr.	G9	14
Indus, stm., Asia	D2	46
Industry, Tx., U.S.	H2	122
İnece, Tur.	B10	28
In Ecker, Alg.	E6	64
İnegöl, Tur.	C12	28
Ineu, Rom.	C8	26
Inez, Ky., U.S.	G3	114
Inez, Tx., U.S.	F11	130
Inferior, Laguna, b., Mex.	G11	100
Infiernillo, Canal del, strt., Mex.	G6	98
Infiernillo, Presa del, res., Mex.	F7	100
Ing, stm., Thai.	C5	48
Ingá, Braz.	D8	88
Ingabu, Mya.	D2	48
Ingal, Niger	F6	64
Ingall Point, c., On., Can.	B10	118
Ingelheim, Ger.	G4	16
Ingende, D.R.C.	E3	66
Ingeniero Jacobacci, Arg.	H3	90
Ingeniero Luiggi, Arg.	G5	92
Ingham, Austl.	B6	76
Inglefield Land, reg., Grnld.	B12	141
Ingleside, Tx., U.S.	G10	130
Inglewood, Austl.	G8	76
Inglewood, Austl.	K4	76
Inglewood, Ca., U.S.	J7	134
Inglis, Mb., Can.	D12	124
Ingolf Fjord, b., Grnld.	A22	141
Ingolstadt, Ger.	H7	16
Ingonish, N.S., Can.	D16	110
Ingrāj Bāzār, India	F12	54
Ingrid Christensen Coast, cst., Ant.	B12	81
In Guezzam, Alg.	F6	64
Ingušetija, state, Russia	F6	32
Ingushetia see Ingušetija, state, Russia	F6	32
Inhaca, Ilha da, i., Moz.	E11	70
Inhambane, Moz.	C12	70
Inhambane, state, Moz.	C12	70
Inhambane, Baía de, b., Moz.	C12	70
Inhambupe, Braz.	F6	88
Inhaminga, Moz.	D5	68
Inhapim, Braz.	J4	88
Inharrime, Moz.	D12	70
Inhassoro, Moz.	B12	70
Inhuma, Braz.	D5	88
Inhumas, Braz.	I1	88
Inimutaba, Braz.	J3	88
Ining *see* Yining, China	F14	32
Inírida, stm., Col.	F7	86
Inis *see* Ennis, Ire.	I3	12
Inis Córthaidh *see* Enniscorthy, Ire.	I6	12
Inishbofin, i., Ire.	H2	12
Inishmore, i., Ire.	H3	12
Inishowen, pen., Ire.	F5	12
Inishturk, i., Ire.	H2	12
Inja, Russia	E17	34
Inja, stm., Russia	D18	34
Injune, Austl.	E7	76
Inkom, Id., U.S.	H14	136
Inkster, N.D., U.S.	F16	124
Inland Lake, l., Mb., Can.	B14	124
Inland Sea see Seto-naikai, s., Japan	E5	40
Inle Lake, l., Mya.	B3	48
Inman, Ks., U.S.	C11	128
Inman Mills, S.C., U.S.	A3	116
Inn, stm., Eur.	B10	22
Innamincka, Austl.	F3	76
Inner Channel, strt., Belize	D3	102
Inner Hebrides, is., Scot., U.K.	E6	12
Inner Mongolia see Nei Monggol, state, China	C7	36
Inner Sister Island, i., Austl.	m13	77a
Innisfail, Austl.	A6	76
Innisfail, Ab., Can.	D17	138
Innisfree, Ab., Can.	C19	138
Innokentevka, Russia	G16	34
Innoko, stm., Ak., U.S.	D8	140
Innoshima, Japan	E6	40
Innsbruck, Aus.	C8	22
Innviertel, reg., Aus.	B10	22
Inola, Ok., U.S.	H2	120
Inongo, D.R.C.	E3	66
İnönü, Tur.	D13	28
Inowrocław, Pol.	D14	16
In Salah, Alg.	D5	64
Instow, Sk., Can.	E5	124
Inta, Russia	A10	32
Intendente Alvear, Arg.	G6	92
İntepe, Tur.	D9	28
Interlaken, Switz.	D4	22
Interlândia, Braz.	I1	88
International Falls, Mn., U.S.	C5	118
Inthanon, Doi, mtn., Thai.	C4	48
Intiyaco, Arg.	D7	92
Intracoastal Waterway, strt., U.S.	H10	130
Intracoastal Waterway, strt., U.S.	L5	116
Intu, Indon.	D9	50
Inubō-saki, c., Japan	D13	40
Inukjuak, Qc., Can.	D15	106
Inuvik, N.T., Can.	B4	106
Inverbervie, Scot., U.K.	E10	12
Invercargill, N.Z.	H3	80
Inverell, Austl.	G8	76
Inverloch, Austl.	L5	76
Invermay, Sk., Can.	C10	124
Invermere, B.C., Can.	F14	138
Inverness, N.S., Can.	D15	110
Inverness, Scot., U.K.	D8	12
Inverness, Ca., U.S.	E3	134
Inverness, Fl., U.S.	H3	116

Name	Map Ref.	Page
Inverurie, Scot., U.K.	D10	12
Inverway, Austl.	C5	74
Investigator Strait, strt., Austl.	G7	74
Inwood, Mb., Can.	D16	124
Inyangani, mtn., Zimb.	D5	68
Inyathi, Zimb.	D4	68
Inyo, Mount, mtn., Ca., U.S.	G8	134
Inyokern, Ca., U.S.	H8	134
Inyo Mountains, mts., Ca., U.S.	G7	134
Inzana Lake, l., B.C., Can.	B6	138
Ioánnina, Grc.	D3	28
Iokanga, stm., Russia	C18	8
Iola, Ks., U.S.	G2	120
Iola, Pap. N. Gui.	b4	79a
Iona, Ang.	D1	68
Iona, N.S., Can.	D16	110
Iona, Id., U.S.	G15	136
Iona, i., Scot., U.K.	E6	12
Ione, Ca., U.S.	E5	134
Ione, Wa., U.S.	B9	136
Ionia, Mi., U.S.	E4	112
Ionian Islands see Iónioi Nísoi, is., Grc.	E3	28
Ionian Sea, s., Eur.	F11	24
Iónioi Nísoi, state, Grc.	E3	28
Iónioi Nísoi (Ionian Islands), is., Grc.	E3	28
Iony, ostrov, i., Russia	E17	34
Ios, i., Grc.	G8	28
Iosegun Lake see Fox Creek, Ab., Can.	B14	138
Iowa, La., U.S.	G5	122
Iowa, state, U.S.	I5	118
Iowa, stm., Ia., U.S.	C6	120
Iowa City, Ia., U.S.	C6	120
Iowa Falls, Ia., U.S.	B4	120
Iowa Park, Tx., U.S.	H10	128
Ipameri, Braz.	I1	88
Ipanema, stm., Braz.	E7	88
Ipanguaçu, Braz.	C7	88
Ipatinga, Braz.	J4	88
Ipatovo, Russia	E6	32
Ipaumirim, Braz.	D6	88
Ipeiros, state, Grc.	D3	28
Ipeiros, hist. reg., Grc.	D3	28
Ipel' (Ipoly), stm., Eur.	I14	16
Ipiales, Col.	G3	86
Ipiaú, Braz.	H5	88
Ipin see Yibin, China	F5	36
Ipirá, Braz.	G6	88
Ipixuna, Braz.	C3	88
Ipoh, Malay.	J5	48
Ipojuca, stm., Braz.	E7	88
Ipoly (Ipel'), stm., Eur.	I14	16
Iporá, Braz.	G7	84
Iporã, Braz.	A11	92
Ipota, Vanuatu	I17	79d
Ipsala, Tur.	C9	28
Ipswich, Austl.	F9	76
Ipswich, Eng., U.K.	I14	12
Ipswich, Ma., U.S.	B15	114
Ipswich, S.D., U.S.	B13	126
Ipu, Braz.	C5	88
Ipubi, Braz.	D6	88
Ipuç (Iput'), stm., Eur.	H14	10
Ipueiras, Braz.	C5	88
Iput' (Ipuç), stm., Eur.	H14	10
Iqaluit, Nu., Can.	C17	106
Iqfahs, Egypt	J1	58
Iquique, Chile	D2	90
Iquitos, Peru	D3	84
Ira, Tx., U.S.	B7	130
Iracema, Braz.	C6	88
Irákleia, i., Grc.	G8	28
Iráklio, Grc.	H8	28
Iran, ctry., Asia	C7	56
Iran Mountains, mts., Asia	C9	50
Irānshahr, Iran	D9	56
Irapa, Ven.	B10	86
Irapuato, Mex.	E8	100
Iraq, ctry., Asia	C5	56
Irará, Braz.	F6	88
Irati, Braz.	B12	92
Irazú, Volcán, vol., C.R.	G6	102
Irbejskoe, Russia	C17	32
Irbid, Jord.	F6	58
Irbid, state, Jord.	F6	58
Irbit, Russia	C10	32
Irdning, Aus.	C11	22
Irebu, D.R.C.	E3	66
Irecê, Braz.	F5	88
Ireland, ctry., Eur.	H4	12
Ireland Island North, i., Ber.	k15	104e
Irene, S.D., U.S.	D15	126
Irenç (Maú), stm., S.A.	F12	86
Ireton, Ia., U.S.	B1	120
Iri, Kor., S.	G7	38
Iriba, Chad	E4	62
Iriga, Phil.	D4	52
Irígui, reg., Afr.	F3	64
Iringa, Tan.	F7	66
Irinjälakuda, India	H3	53
Iriomote-jima, i., Japan	G9	36
Iriri, stm., Braz.	D7	84
Irish, Mount, mtn., Nv., U.S.	F1	132
Irish Sea, s., Eur.	H7	12
Irituia, Braz.	A2	88
Irkutsk, Russia	D18	32
Irma, Ab., Can.	D19	138
Irminger Basin, unds.	B10	144
Irnijärvi, l., Fin.	D13	8
Iroise, b., Fr.	F4	14
Iron Bottom Sound, strt., Sol. Is.	e8	79b
Iron Bridge, On., Can.	B6	112
Iron City, Tn., U.S.	B11	122
Irondale, Al., U.S.	D12	122
Irondale, Mo., U.S.	G7	120
Irondequoit, N.Y., U.S.	E12	112
Iron Gate, p., Eur.	E9	26
Iron Knob, Austl.	F7	74
Iron Mountain, Mi., U.S.	C1	112
Iron Range, Austl.	B8	74
Iron River, Mi., U.S.	E10	118
Ironton, Mn., U.S.	E4	118
Ironton, Mo., U.S.	G7	120
Ironton, Oh., U.S.	F3	114
Ironwood, Mi., U.S.	E8	118
Ironwood Forest National Monument, p.o.i., Az., U.S.	K5	132
Iroquois, On., Can.	D14	112
Iroquois, stm., U.S.	H2	112
Iroquois Falls, On., Can.	F14	106
Iro-zaki, c., Japan	E11	40
Irrawaddy see Ayeyarwady, stm., Mya.	E8	46
Irricana, Ab., Can.	E17	138
Irrigon, Or., U.S.	E7	136
Irsina, Italy	D10	24
Irtysh see Irtyš, stm., Asia	C11	32
Irtyš (Irtyš) (Ertis) (Ertix), stm., Asia	C11	32
Irún, Spain	A9	20
Iruña see Pamplona, Spain	B9	20
Irurzun, Spain	B9	20
Irú Tepuy, mtn., Ven.	E11	86
Isa, Nig.	G6	64
Isaac, stm., Austl.	D7	76
Isaac Lake, l., B.C., Can.	C10	138
Isabel, state, Sol. Is.	d8	79b
Isabela, Phil.	G3	52
Isabela, P.R.	A1	104a
Isabela, Cabo, c., Dom. Rep.	C12	102
Isabela, Isla, i., Ec.	i11	84a
Isabelia, Cordillera, mts., Nic.	F5	102
Isaccea, Rom.	D15	26
Isachsen, Cape, c., Nu., Can.	B4	141
Ísafjarðardjúp, b., Ice.	j28	8a
Ísafjörður, Ice.	j28	8a
Isahaya, Japan	G3	40
Isak, India	J3	48
Isaka, Tan.	E6	66
Isa Khel, Pak.	B3	54
Işalnița, Rom.	E10	26
Isana (Içana), stm., S.A.	G7	86
Isangel, Vanuatu	I17	79d
Isanti, Mn., U.S.	F5	118
Isar, stm., Eur.	H8	16
Isarog, Mount, vol., Phil.	D4	52
Iscehisar, Tur.	E13	28
Ischia, Italy	D7	24
Ischia, Isola d', i., Italy	D7	24
Ise, Japan	E9	40
Iseo, Lago d', l., Italy	E6	22
Isère, state, Fr.	D11	18
Isère, stm., Fr.	D11	18
Iserlohn, Ger.	E3	16
Isernia, Italy	C8	24
Isesaki, Japan	C12	40
Ise-shima-kokuritsu-kōen, p.o.i., Japan	E9	40
Ise-wan, b., Japan	E9	40
Iseyin, Nig.	H5	64
Isezaki see Isesaki, Japan	C12	40
Isfahan see Eşfahān, Iran	C7	56
Isfara, Taj.	A11	56
Isherton, Guy.	F12	86
Ishigaki, Japan	G9	36
Ishikari, Japan	C14	38
Ishikari-wan, b., Japan	C14	38
Ishikawa, state, Japan	C9	40
Ishim (Esil) (Išim), stm., Asia	C12	32
Ishinomaki, Japan	A14	40
Ishioka, Japan	C13	40
Ishizuchi-san, mtn., Japan	F5	40
Ishpeming, Mi., U.S.	B2	112
Ishurdi, Bngl.	F12	54
Isigny-sur-Mer, Fr.	E7	14
Işıklı, Tur.	E12	28
Isil'kul', Russia	C12	32
Išim, Russia	C11	32
Išimskaja ravnina, pl., Asia	C11	32
Isiolo, Kenya	D7	66
Isipíngo, ngh., S. Afr.	G10	70
Isiro, D.R.C.	D5	66
Isis, Austl.	E9	76
Iskăr, stm., Blg.	F11	26
Iskăr, Jazovir, res., Blg.	G10	26
İskenderun (Alexandretta), Tur.	B6	58
İskenderun Körfezi, b., Tur.	B6	58
Iskitim, Russia	D14	32
Iskut, stm., B.C., Can.	D4	106
Isla, Mex.	G11	100
Isla, Salar de la, pl., Chile	B3	92
Islâhiye, Tur.	A7	58
Islâmâbâd, Pak.	B4	54
Islâmkot, Pak.	F3	54
Islâmpur, India	F10	54
Islâmpur, India	E12	54
Islâmpur, India	C2	53
Island, Ky., U.S.	G10	120
Island Falls, Me., U.S.	E8	110
Island Harbour, Anguilla	A1	105a
Island Lake, l., Mb., Can.	E12	106
Island Park, Id., U.S.	F15	136
Island Pond, Vt., U.S.	F5	110
Islands, Bay of, b., Nf., Can.	j22	107a
Isla Patrulla, Ur.	F10	92
Isla Vista, Ca., U.S.	I5	134
Islay, i., Scot., U.K.	F6	12
Isle, Mn., U.S.	E5	118
Isle, stm., Fr.	D5	18
Isle of Man, dep., Eur.	G8	12
Isle of Wight, U.K.	H9	114
Isle Royale National Park, p.o.i., Mi., U.S.	C10	118
Islesboro Island, i., Me., U.S.	F8	110
Isleta, N.M., U.S.	I10	132
Isleton, Ca., U.S.	E4	134
Islon, Chile	D2	92
Ismailia (Al-Ismā'īlīyah), Egypt	H3	58
Ismail Samani, pik, mtn., Taj.	B11	56
Isna, Egypt	B6	62
Isny, Ger.	I5	16
Isoka, Zam.	C5	68
Isola dei Liri, Italy	C7	24
Isola di Capo Rizzuto, Italy	F11	24
Isonzo, stm., Eur.	E10	22
Isparta, Tur.	F13	28
Isparta, state, Tur.	F13	28
Ispica, Italy	H8	24
Israel, ctry., Asia	G5	58
Israʾil see Israel, ctry., Asia	G5	58
Issa, stm., Braz.	D11	10
Isser, Oued, stm., Alg.	H14	20
Issia, C. Iv.	H3	64
Issoire, Fr.	D9	18
Issoudun, Fr.	H10	14
Issyk-Kul', Kyrg.	F13	32
Issyk-Kul, Lake see Issyk-Kul', ozero, l., Kyrg.	F13	32
Issyk-Kul', ozero, l., Kyrg.	F13	32
Ivan'kovskoe vodohranilišče, res., Russia	D19	10
İstanbul, Tur.	B12	28
İstanbul, state, Tur.	B11	28
İstanbul Boğazı (Bosporus), strt., Tur.	B12	28
Istiaía, Grc.	E6	28
Istmina, Col.	E3	86
Isto, Mount, mtn., Ak., U.S.	C11	140
Istra, Russia	E19	10
Istria, pen., Eur.	E10	22
Ita, Para.	B9	92
Itabaiana, Braz.	D8	88
Itabaiana, Braz.	F7	88
Itabaianinha, Braz.	F7	88
Itabapoana, Braz.	K5	88
Itaberaba, Braz.	G5	88
Itaberaí, Braz.	G8	84
Itaberaí, Braz.	I1	88
Itabira, Braz.	J4	88
Itabuna, Braz.	H6	88
Itacajá, Braz.	E2	88
Itacambiruçu, Braz.	I4	88
Itacoatiara, Braz.	D6	84
Itacurubí del Rosario, Para.	B9	92
Itaeté, Braz.	G5	88
Itaguajé, Braz.	D6	90
Itaguaru, Braz.	D1	88
Itaguí, Col.	D4	86
Itaí, Braz.	L1	88
Itaiçaba, Braz.	C7	88
Itaim, stm., Braz.	D5	88
Itaipu, Braz.	L3	88
Itaipú, Represa de, res., Braz.	B10	92
Itainópolis, Braz.	D5	88
Itaipu Reservoir see Itaipu, Represa de, res., Braz.	B10	92
Itaisen Suonenlahden kansallispuisto, p.o.i., Fin.	F12	8
Itaituba, Braz.	D6	84
Itajai, Braz.	C13	92
Itajubá, Braz.	L3	88
Itaju do Colônia, Braz.	H6	88
Itajuípe, Braz.	H6	88
Itala Game Reserve, S. Afr.	E10	70
Itálica, sci., Spain	G4	20
Italy, Tx., U.S.	B11	130
Italy, ctry., Eur.	G11	6
Itamaraju, Braz.	I6	88
Itamarandiba, Braz.	I4	88
Itamarandiba, stm., Braz.	I4	88
Itambacuri, Braz.	I5	88
Itambé, Braz.	H5	88
Itami, Japan	E8	40
Itampolo, Madag.	E7	68
Itânagar, India	E14	54
Itanhaém, Braz.	B14	92
Itanhém, Braz.	I5	88
Itaobim, Braz.	I5	88
Itaparica, Ilha de, i., Braz.	G6	88
Itaparica, Represa de, res., Braz.	E6	88
Itapebi, Braz.	H6	88
Itapecerica, Braz.	K3	88
Itapecuru-Mirim, Braz.	B3	88
Itaperuna, Braz.	K5	88
Itapetim, Braz.	D7	88
Itapetinga, Braz.	H5	88
Itapetininga, Braz.	L1	88
Itapetininga, stm., Braz.	A14	92
Itapeva, Braz.	L1	88
Itapicuru, Braz.	F6	88
Itapicuru, stm., Braz.	F6	88
Itapicuru, stm., Braz.	B3	88
Itapipoca, Braz.	B6	88
Itapiranga, Braz.	D6	84
Itapirapuã, Braz.	G7	84
Itapiúna, Braz.	C6	88
Itápolis, Braz.	K1	88
Itaporã de Goiás, Braz.	G8	84
Itaporanga, Braz.	D6	88
Itaporanga d'Ajuda, Braz.	F7	88
Itapúa, state, Para.	C10	92
Itaquara, Braz.	G6	88
Itaquari, Braz.	K5	88
Itaqui, Braz.	D9	92
Itarantim, Braz.	H5	88
Itararé, Braz.	B13	92
Itararé, stm., Braz.	A13	92
Itârsi, India	G6	54
Itarumã, Braz.	C6	90
Itasca, Tx., U.S.	B10	130
Itasca, Lake, l., Mn., U.S.	D3	118
Itä-Suomi, state, Fin.	E12	8
Itata, stm., Chile	H1	92
Itatira, Braz.	L1	88
Itatupã, Braz.	D7	84
Itaueira, Braz.	D4	88
Itaueira, stm., Braz.	D4	88
Itaúna, Braz.	K3	88
Itbayat Island, i., Phil.	K9	42
Itéa (Guaporé), stm., S.A.	F5	84
Ithaca, Mi., U.S.	E5	112
Ithaca, N.Y., U.S.	B9	114
Ithaca see Itháki, i., Grc.	E3	28
Itháki, i., Grc.	E3	28
Itimbiri, stm., D.R.C.	D4	66
Itinga, Braz.	I5	88
Itiquira, stm., Braz.	G6	84
Itiruçu, Braz.	G5	88
Itiúba, Braz.	F5	88
Itla el-Bâsha, hill, Egypt	K3	58
Itô, Japan	E12	40
Itoigawa, Japan	B10	40
Iton, stm., Fr.	F9	14
Itororó, Braz.	H5	88
Itsuki, Japan	G3	40
Ittiri, Italy	D2	24
Ittoqqortoormiit see Scoresbysund, Grnld.	C21	141
Itu, stm., Braz.	L2	88
Itu, Braz.	D10	92
Ituaçu, Braz.	G5	88
Ituango, Col.	D4	86
Itubera, Braz.	G6	88
Itueta, Braz.	J5	88
Ituí, stm., Braz.	E3	84
Ituiutaba, Braz.	J1	88
Itumbiara, Braz.	J1	88
Ituna, Sk., Can.	C10	124
Itupiranga, Braz.	E8	84
Ituporanga, Braz.	C13	92
Iturama, Braz.	C6	90
Iturbide, Mex.	C3	102
Iturup, ostrov (Etorofu-tō), i., Russia	B17	38
Ituverava, Braz.	K2	88
Ituxi, stm., Braz.	E4	84
Ituzaingó, Arg.	C9	92
Itzehoe, Ger.	C5	16
Iuka, Ms., U.S.	C10	122
Iul'tin, Russia	C25	34
Iúna, Braz.	K5	88
Ivacevičy, Bela.	H8	10
Ivačovo, Russia	F17	8
Ivaí, stm., Braz.	D6	90
Ivaiporã, Braz.	B12	92
Ivakoany, massif, Madag.	E8	68
Ivalo, Fin.	B12	8
Ivalojoki, stm., Fin.	B12	8
Ivanava, Bela.	H8	10
Ivančice, Czech Rep.	G12	16
Ivangorod, Russia	A11	10
Ivangrad, Serb.	G6	26
Ivanhoe, Austl.	I5	76
Ivanhoe, Ca., U.S.	G6	134
Ivanhoe, Mn., U.S.	G2	118
Ivanhoe, Va., U.S.	H4	114
Ivanišči, Russia	D18	10
Ivanjica, Serb.	F7	26
Ivano-Frankivs'k, Ukr.	F13	6
Ivano-Frankivs'k, co., Ukr.	A11	26
Ivanovka, Russia	F14	34
Ivanovo, Russia	H19	8
Ivanovskaja oblast', co., Russia	A11	10
Ivanovskoe, Russia	A11	10
Ivatsevichi see Ivacevičy, Bela.	H8	10
Ivdel', Russia	B9	32
Ivigtut, Grnld.	E16	141
Ivindo, stm., Gabon	D2	66
Ivinheima, stm., Braz.	D6	90
Iviza see Eivissa, Spain	F12	20
Ivjanec, Bela.	G9	10
Ivohibe, Madag.	E8	68
Ivory Coast see Cote d'Ivoire, ctry., Afr.	H3	64
Ivory Coast, cst, C. Iv.	I3	64
Ivrea, Italy	E4	22
Ivujivik, Qc., Can.	C15	106
Ivybridge, Eng., U.K.	K9	12
Iwaki, Japan	B13	40
Iwaki-san, vol., Japan	D14	38
Iwakuni, Japan	E5	40
Iwami, Japan	D7	40
Iwamizawa, Japan	C14	38
Iwanuma, Japan	A13	40
Iwata, Japan	E10	40
Iwate, state, Japan	A14	40
'Iweibid, Gebel, mtn., Egypt	H3	58
Iwo, Nig.	H5	64
Iximiquilpan, Mex.	E9	100
Ixopo, S. Afr.	G10	70
Ixtapa, Mex.	G8	100
Ixtepec, Mex.	G11	100
Ixtlán del Río, Mex.	E6	100
Iyang see Yiyang, China	G5	42
Iyo, Japan	F5	40
Iyo-mishima, Japan	F6	40
Iyo-nada, s., Japan	F4	40
Izabal, Lago de, l., Guat.	E3	102
Izamal, Mex.	B3	102
Izapa, sci., Mex.	H12	100
Izberbaš, Russia	F7	32
Izbica, Pol.	F19	16
Izegem, Bel.	D12	14
İževsk, Russia	C8	32
Izium, Ukr.	E5	32
Izmail, Ukr.	D15	26
Izmalkovo, Russia	H21	10
İzmir (Smyrna), Tur.	E10	28
İzmir, state, Tur.	E10	28
İzmir Körfezi, b., Tur.	E9	28
İzmit (Kocaeli), Tur.	C12	28
İzmit Körfezi, b., Tur.	C12	28
İznik, Tur.	C12	28
İznik Gölü, l., Tur.	C12	28
Iznoski, Russia	E18	10
Izozog, Bañados del, sw., Bol.	C4	90
Izra', Syria	F7	58
Iztaccíhuatl, Volcán, vol., Mex.	F9	100
Iztaccíhuatl y Popocatéptl, Parques Nacionales, p.o.i., Mex.	F9	100
Izúcar de Matamoros, Mex.	F9	100
Izu-hantō, pen., Japan	E11	40
Izuhara, Japan	E2	40
Izu Islands see Izu-shotō, is., Japan	E12	40
Izumi, Japan	G3	40
Izumi, Japan	A13	40
Izumi, Japan	E8	40
Izumo, Japan	D5	40
Izu-shotō (Izu Islands), is., Japan	E12	40
Izu Trench, unds.	G17	142
Izvestij CIK, ostrova, is., Russia	A5	34
Izvorul Muntelui, Lacul, l., Rom.	C12	26

J

Name	Map Ref.	Page
Jabal, Bahr al- see Mountain Nile, stm., Afr.	F6	62
Jabal al-Awlīyā', Sudan	D6	62
Jabal Lubnān, state, Leb.	D6	58
Jabalón, stm., Spain	F7	20
Jabalpur, India	G7	54
Jabālyah, Gaza	G5	58
Jabbūl, Sabkhat al-, l., Syria	B8	58
Jabiru, Austl.	B6	74
Jablah, Syria	C6	58
Jablanica, Bos.	F4	26
Jablaničko jezero, res., Bos.	F4	26
Jablonec nad Nisou, Czech Rep.	F11	16
Jabłonka, Pol.	G15	16
Jablonovyj hrebet, mts., Russia	F11	34
Jablunkov, Czech Rep.	G14	16
Jaboticabal, Braz.	K1	88
Jaca, Spain	B10	20
Jacala, Mex.	E9	100
Jacaré, stm., Braz.	F5	88
Jacarei, Braz.	L3	88
Jacarezinho, Braz.	D7	90
Jáchal, stm., Arg.	E4	92
Jaciara, Braz.	G6	84
Jacinto, Braz.	I5	88
Jacinto Aráuz, Arg.	I6	92
Jacinto City, N.C., U.S.	A8	116
Jackfish Lake, l., Sk., Can.	A5	124
Jackhead Harbour, Mb., Can.	C16	124
Jack Mountain, mtn., Mt., U.S.	D14	136
Jackpot, Nv., U.S.	B2	132
Jacksboro, Tn., U.S.	H1	114
Jacksboro, Tx., U.S.	H10	128
Jackson, Ca., U.S.	E5	134
Jackson, Ky., U.S.	G2	114
Jackson, La., U.S.	G7	122
Jackson, Mi., U.S.	B1	114
Jackson, Mn., U.S.	H4	118
Jackson, Ms., U.S.	E8	122
Jackson, N.C., U.S.	H8	114
Jackson, Oh., U.S.	E3	114
Jackson, S.C., U.S.	C4	116
Jackson, Tn., U.S.	B10	122
Jackson, Wy., U.S.	G16	136
Jackson, stm., Va., U.S.	G6	114
Jackson, Mount, mtn., Ant.	C34	81
Jackson, Mount, mtn., Austl.	F3	74
Jackson Creek, stm., Can.	E12	124
Jackson Lake, l., Wy., U.S.	G16	136
Jacksonville, Al., U.S.	D13	122
Jacksonville, Ar., U.S.	C6	122
Jacksonville, Fl., U.S.	F4	116
Jacksonville, Il., U.S.	E7	120
Jacksonville, N.C., U.S.	B8	116
Jacksonville, Or., U.S.	A2	134
Jacksonville, Tx., U.S.	F3	122
Jacksonville Beach, Fl., U.S.	F4	116
Jacmel, Haiti	C11	102
Jaco, Mex.	B6	100
Jacobābād, Pak.	D2	54
Jacobina, Braz.	F5	88
Jacob Lake, Az., U.S.	G4	132
Jacques-Cartier, Mont, mtn., Qc., Can.	A11	110
Jacu, stm., Braz.	D8	88
Jacuí, stm., Braz.	D11	92
Jacuipe, stm., Braz.	F5	88
Jacumba, Ca., U.S.	K9	134
Jacundá, Braz.	D8	84
Jacupiranga, Braz.	B13	92
Jacurici, stm., Braz.	F6	88
Jadebusen, b., Ger.	C4	16
J.A.D. Jensens Nunatakker, mtn., Grnld.	E16	141
Jadraque, Spain	D8	20
Jādū, Libya	A2	62
Jaén, Peru	E2	84
Jaén, co., Spain	G7	20
Jaén, Spain	G7	20
Jaffa, Cape, c., Austl.	K2	76
Jaffna, Sri L.	G4	53
Jaffna Lagoon, b., Sri L.	G4	53
Jaffrey, N.H., U.S.	B13	114
Jafr, Qāʻ al-, depr., Jord.	H7	58
Jagalūr, India	D3	53
Jagatsinghpur, India	H11	54
Jagdalpur, India	B6	53
Jagdaqi, China	B9	36
Jaggayyapeta, India	C5	53
Jagodina, Serb.	F8	26
Jagraon, India	C5	54
Jagtial, India	B4	53
Jaguapita, Braz.	D6	90
Jaguaquara, Braz.	G5	88
Jaguarão (Yaguarón), stm., S.A.	F11	92
Jaguarari, Braz.	F5	88
Jaguaretama, Braz.	C7	88
Jaguari, Braz.	D10	92
Jaguariaíva, Braz.	B13	92
Jaguaribara, Braz.	C6	88
Jaguaribe, Braz.	C6	88
Jaguaribe, stm., Braz.	C7	88
Jaguaruana, Braz.	C7	88
Jaguaruna, Braz.	D13	92
Jaguê, stm., Arg.	D3	92
Jagüey Grande, Cuba	A7	102
Jahānābād, India	F10	54
Jahmah, Iran	D7	56
Jahromā, Russia	D20	10
Jahrom, Iran	D7	56
Jaicós, Braz.	D5	88
Jailolo, Indon.	E8	44
Jaintiāpur, Bngl.	F14	54
Jaipur, India	E5	54
Jaisalmer, India	E3	54
Jaito, India	C5	54
Jajarm, Iran	B8	56
Jajce, Bos.	E4	26
Jakarta, Indon.	G5	50
Jakarta, Teluk, b., Indon.	F5	50
Jakobselv, Bela.	F13	10
Jakobshavn (Ilulissat), Grnld.	D15	141
Jakobstad see Pietarsaari, Fin.	E10	8
Jakovlevka, Russia	B10	38
Jakša, Russia	B9	32
Jakutsk, state, Russia	C14	34
Jakutsk, Russia	D14	34
Jal, N.M., U.S.	B4	130
Jalaid Qi, China	B9	36
Jalālābād, Afg.	C11	56
Jalālpur, India	E9	54
Jalandhar, India	C5	54
Jalapa, Guat.	E3	102
Jalapa see Xalapa, Mex.	F10	100
Jalāun, India	E7	54
Jales, Braz.	D6	90
Jalesar, India	E7	54
Jaleshwar, India	H11	54
Jālgaon, India	H5	54
Jālgaon, India	H6	54
Jalingo, Nig.	H7	64
Jalisco, state, Mex.	E6	100
Jalna, India	B2	53
Jalón, stm., Spain	C9	20
Jalor, India	F4	54
Jalostotitlán, Mex.	E7	100
Jalpa, Mex.	E7	100
Jalpaiguri, India	E12	54
Jaluit, at., Marsh. Is.	C7	72
Jalutorovsk, Russia	C11	32
Jamaame, Som.	E8	66
Jamaica, ctry., N.A.	D9	102
Jamaica Channel, strt., N.A.	D9	102
Jamālpur, Bngl.	F12	54
Jamālpur, India	F11	54
Jamanota, hill, Aruba	o20	104g
Jamantau, gora, mtn., Russia	D9	32
Jamanxim, stm., Braz.	E6	84
Jamari, stm., Braz.	E5	84
Jamarovka, Russia	F11	34
Jambeli, Canal de, strt., Ec.	I2	86
Jambi, Indon.	D3	50
Jambi, state, Indon.	D3	50
Jamboaye, stm., Indon.	J3	48
Jambol, Blg.	G13	26
Jambongan, Pulau, i., Malay.	G1	52
Jambuair, Tanjung, c., Indon.	J3	48
James, stm., Va., U.S.	G8	114
James, stm., U.S.	C8	108
James, Isla, i., Chile	H2	90
James Bay, b., Can.	E14	106
James City, N.C., U.S.	A8	116
James Craik, Arg.	F6	92
James Island, S.C., U.S.	D5	116
James Point, c., Bah.	K9	116
Jamesport, Mo., U.S.	E4	120
James Ross, Cape, c., N.T., Can.	B17	140
James Ross Island, i., Ant.	B35	81
James Ross Strait, strt., Nu., Can.	A11	106
Jamestown, Austl.	I2	76
Jamestown, S. Afr.	G8	70
Jamestown, Ky., U.S.	G12	120
Jamestown, N.C., U.S.	I6	114
Jamestown, N.D., U.S.	H15	124
Jamestown, N.Y., U.S.	B6	114
Jamestown, Tn., U.S.	H13	120
Jamestown, misc. cult., Va., U.S.	G9	114
Jämijärvi, Fin.	F10	8
Jāmkhandi, India	C2	53
Jamm, Russia	B10	10
Jammerbugten, b., Den.	H3	8
Jammu, India	B5	54
Jammu and Kashmir see Kashmir, hist. reg., Asia	B4	46
Jamnagar (Navanagar), India	G3	54
Jampang-kulon, Indon.	G5	50
Jāmpur, Pak.	D3	54
Jāmsā, Fin.	F11	8
Jamshedpur, India	G10	54
Jamsk, Russia	E19	34
Jämtland, state, Swe.	E6	8
Jamūī, India	F11	54
Jamuna, stm., Bngl.	F12	54
Jana, stm., Russia	C16	34
Janaúba, Braz.	H4	88
Janaucu, Ilha, i., Braz.	C7	84
Jand, Pak.	B4	54
Jandaia, Braz.	C6	90
Jandiāla, India	C5	54
Jandowae, Austl.	F8	76
Jándula, stm., Spain	F6	20
Janeiro, stm., Braz.	G3	88
Janesville, Ca., U.S.	C5	134
Janesville, Mn., U.S.	G5	118
Janesville, Wi., U.S.	B9	120
Jangamo, Moz.	D12	70
Jangaon, India	B4	53
Jangijul', Uzb.	F11	32
Janīn, W.B.	F6	58
Janisjärvi, ozero, l., Russia	E14	8
Janiuay, Phil.	E4	52
Janj, hrebet, mts., Russia	E12	34
Jan Kempdorp, S. Afr.	E7	70
Janlohong, Indon.	B10	50
Jan Mayen, i., Nor.	B22	94
Janos, Mex.	F8	98
Jánoshza, Hung.	C4	26
Janowiec Wielkopolski, Pol.	D13	16
Janskij, Russia	C15	34
Janskij zaliv, b., Russia	B16	34
Jantra, stm., Blg.	F12	26
Januária, Braz.	H3	88
Januário Cicco, Braz.	C8	88
Jaora, India	G5	54
Jaraíz de la Vera, Spain	D5	20
Jarales, N.M., U.S.	I10	132
Jarama, stm., Spain	D7	20
Jaramānah, Syria	F7	58
Jaransk, Russia	C7	32
Jarānwāla, Pak.	C4	54
Jarash, Jord.	F6	58
Jarash, sci., Jord.	F6	58
Jarcevo, Russia	E15	10
Jardim, Braz.	D6	88
Jardim, Braz.	D5	90
Jardim de Piranhas, Braz.	D7	88
Jardim América, Arg.	C10	92
Jardines de la Reina, Archipiélago de los, is., Cuba	B8	102
Jardinópolis, Braz.	K1	88
Jarej-Uliga-Delap, Marsh. Is.	C8	72
Jarenga, Russia	E23	8
Jarensk, Russia	E23	8
Jargalant, Mong.	B4	36
Jari, stm., Braz.	C7	84
Jaridih, India	G11	54
Jarkand see Shache, China	B12	56
Jarkino, Russia	C17	32
Jarocin, Pol.	D13	16
Jarohta, Russia	C17	32
Jaroměř, Czech Rep.	F11	16
Jaroslavl', Russia	H19	8
Jaroslavskaja oblast', co., Russia	H18	8
Jarosław, Pol.	F18	16
Jarratt, Va., U.S.	H8	114
Jar-Sale, Russia	A12	32
Jartai Yanchi, l., China	B1	42
Jarud Qi, China	B4	38
Järvakandi, Est.	G11	8
Järvenpää, Fin.	F11	8
Jarvie, Ab., Can.	B17	138
Jarvis, On., Can.	F9	112
Jarvisburg, N.C., U.S.	H10	114
Jarvis Island, i., Oc.	D10	72
Jasdan, India	G3	54
Jasel'da, stm., Bela.	H8	10
Jashpurnagar, India	D5	46
Jasień, Pol.	E11	16
Jāsk, Iran	D8	56
Jaškul', Russia	E7	32
Jasło, Pol.	G17	16
Jasnogorsk, Russia	F20	10
Jasnyj, Russia	D9	32
Jason Islands, is., Falk. Is.	J4	90
Jasper, Ab., Can.	D12	138
Jasper, Al., U.S.	D11	122
Jasper, Ar., U.S.	I4	120
Jasper, Fl., U.S.	F3	116
Jasper, Ga., U.S.	B1	116
Jasper, In., U.S.	F10	120
Jasper, Mn., U.S.	H2	118
Jasper, Mo., U.S.	G3	120
Jasper, Tn., U.S.	B13	122
Jasper, Tx., U.S.	G5	122
Jasper Lake, l., Ab., Can.	C13	138
Jasper National Park, p.o.i., Ab., Can.	D13	138
Jastarnia, Pol.	B14	16
Jászapáti, Hung.	B7	26
Jászberény, Hung.	B6	26
Jász-Nagykun-Szolnok, state, Hung.	B7	26
Jataí, Braz.	G7	84
Jatapu, stm., Braz.	D6	84
Jataté, stm., Mex.	G13	100
Játi, Braz.	D6	88
Jāti, Pak.	F2	54
Játiva see Xàtiva, Spain	F10	20
Jatni, India	H10	54
Jaú, Braz.	L1	88
Jaú, Parque Nacional do, p.o.i., Braz.	I10	86
Jauaperi, stm., Braz.	H11	86
Jauá Sarisariñama, Parque Nacional, p.o.i., Ven.	E9	86
Jauja, Peru	F2	84
Jaunjelgava, Lat.	D7	10
Jaunpiebalga, Lat.	C9	10
Jaunpur, India	F9	54
Java see Jawa, i., Indon.	H6	50
Javalambre, mtn., Spain	D9	20
Java Sea see Jawa, Laut, s., Indon.	F6	50
Java Trench, unds.	J13	142
Jávea see Xàbia, Spain	F11	20
Javorník, Czech Rep.	F13	16
Javorová skála, mtn., Czech Rep.	G10	16
Jawa (Java), i., Indon.	H6	50
Jawa, Laut (Java Sea), s., Indon.	F6	50
Jawa Barat, state, Indon.	G5	50
Jawa Tengah, state, Indon.	G7	50
Jawa Timur, state, Indon.	G8	50
Jawhar, Som.	D9	66
Jawi, Indon.	D6	50
Jawor, Pol.	E12	16
Jaworzno, Pol.	F15	16
Jay, Fl., U.S.	G11	122
Jay, Ok., U.S.	H3	120
Jaya, Puncak (Jaya Peak), mtn., Indon.	F10	44
Jaya Peak see Jaya, Puncak (Jaya Peak), mtn., Indon.	F10	44
Jayapura, Indon.	F11	44
Jayb, Wādī al- (Ha 'Arava), stm., Asia	H6	58
Jaynes, Az., U.S.	K5	132
Jaypur, India	B6	53
Jayuya, P.R.	B2	104a
Jaželbicy, Russia	B15	10
Jeanerette, La., U.S.	H7	122
Jeannette Island see Žannetty, ostrov, i., Russia	A20	34
Jebba, Nig.	H5	64
Jebel, Rom.	D8	26
Jedburgh, Scot., U.K.	F10	12
Jeddah see Jiddah, Sau. Ar.	E4	56
Jędrzejów, Pol.	F16	16
Jeffers, Mn., U.S.	G3	118
Jefferson, Ga., U.S.	B2	116
Jefferson, Oh., U.S.	C5	114
Jefferson, S.C., U.S.	B5	116
Jefferson, Tx., U.S.	E4	122
Jefferson, Wi., U.S.	A9	120
Jefferson, Mount, mtn., Nv., U.S.	E8	134
Jefferson, Mount, mtn., U.S.	F15	136
Jefferson, Mount, vol., Or., U.S.	F5	136
Jefferson City, Mo., U.S.	F5	120
Jefferson City, Tn., U.S.	H2	114
Jeffersonville, In., U.S.	F12	120
Jeffrey City, Wy., U.S.	E5	136
Jega, Nig.	G5	64
Jehol see Chengde, China	A7	42
Jeju see Cheju, Kor., S.	H7	38
Jejsk see Ejsk, Russia	E5	32
Jēkabpils, Lat.	D8	10
Jekyll Island, i., Ga., U.S.	E4	116
Jelcz-Laskowice, Pol.	E13	16
Jelenia Góra, Pol.	F11	16
Jelenia Góra, state, Pol.	E11	16
Jelgava, Lat.	D6	10
Jelgavkrasti, Lat.	C7	10
Jellicoe, On., Can.	B13	118

Name / Map Ref. / Page

Jelm Mountain, mtn., Wy., U.S. F7 126
Jemaja, Pulau, i., Indon. B4 50
Jember, Indon. H8 50
Jemez Canyon Reservoir, res., N.M., U.S. H9 132
Jemez Springs, N.M., U.S. H10 132
Jemnice, Czech Rep. H11 16
Jempang, Kenohan, l., Indon. D9 50
Jena, Ger. F7 16
Jena, La., U.S. F6 122
Jendouba, Tun. H2 24
Jeneponto, Indon. F11 50
Jenks, Ok., U.S. H2 120
Jennings, Fl., U.S. F2 116
Jennings, La., U.S. G6 122
Jensen, Ut., U.S. C7 132
Jens Munk Island, i., Nu., Can. B14 106
Jens Munks Ø, i., Grnld. E17 141
Jenu, Indon. D6 50
Jeonju see Chŏnju, Kor., S. G7 38
Jepara, Indon. G7 50
Jeparit, Austl. K4 76
Jeptha Knob, hill, Ky., U.S. F12 120
Jequié, Braz. G5 88
Jequitinhonha, Braz. I5 88
Jequitinhonha, stm., Braz. H5 88
Jerada, Mor. C4 64
Jerba, Île de, i., Tun. C7 64
Jerécuaro, Mex. E8 100
Jérémie, Haiti C10 102
Jeremoabo, Braz. F6 88
Jerevan see Yerevan, Arm. A5 56
Jerez de García Salinas, Mex. D7 100
Jerez de la Frontera, Spain H4 20
Jerez de los Caballeros, Spain F4 20
Jericho, Austl. D5 76
Jericho see Arīḥā, Gaza G6 58
Jericó, Braz. D7 88
Jerid, Chott, l., Tun. C6 64
Jerimoth Hill, hill, R.I., U.S. C14 114
Jeroaquara, Braz. G7 84
Jerome, Az., U.S. I4 132
Jerome, Id., U.S. H12 136
Jersey, dep., Eur. E6 14
Jersey, i., Jersey E6 14
Jersey City, N.J., U.S. D11 114
Jerseyville, Il., U.S. E7 120
Jerumenha, Braz. D4 88
Jerusalem see Yerushalayim, Isr. G6 58
Jervis, Cape, c., Austl. J1 76
Jervis Bay, b., Austl. J8 76
Jervis Bay Territory, co., Austl. J8 76
Jervis Inlet, b., B.C., Can. F7 138
Jesenice, Czech Rep. F9 16
Jeseník, Czech Rep. F13 16
Jesi (Iesi), Italy G10 22
Jessen, Ger. E9 16
Jessore, Bngl. G12 54
Jesup, Ga., U.S. E4 116
Jesup, Ia., U.S. B5 120
Jesús Carranza, Mex. G11 100
Jesús María, Arg. E5 92
Jesús Menéndez, Cuba B9 102
Jet, Ok., U.S. E10 128
Jetmore, Ks., U.S. C9 128
Jetpur, India H3 54
Jeune Landing, B.C., Can. F3 138
Jever, Ger. C3 16
Jewel Cave National Monument, p.o.i., S.D., U.S. D8 126
Jewell, Ks., U.S. B10 128
Jewell Ridge, Va., U.S. G4 114
Jewett, Il., U.S. E9 120
Jewett City, Ct., U.S. C13 114
Jezercës, maja e, mtn., Alb. B13 24
Jeziorany, Pol. B16 16
Jhābua, India G5 54
Jha Jha, India F11 54
Jhālakāti, Bngl. G13 54
Jhālāwār, India F6 54
Jhang Sadar, Pak. C4 54
Jhānsi, India F7 54
Jhārgrām, India G11 54
Jharia, India G11 54
Jharkhand, state, India G10 54
Jhārsuguda, India H10 54
Jhelum, Pak. B4 54
Jhelum, stm., Asia C4 54
Jhinkpāni, India G10 54
Jhok Rind, Pak. C3 54
Jhunjhunūn, India D5 54
Jiaban, China I2 42
Jiading, China F9 42
Jiāganj, India F12 54
Jiahe, China I5 42
Jiali, China C14 54
Jialing, stm., China G2 42
Jialu, stm., China E5 42
Jiamusi, China B11 36
Ji'an, China D7 38
Ji'an, China H6 42
Jian, stm., China H8 42
Jianchang, China A8 42
Jianchang, China B10 42
Jianchuan, China F4 36
Jiande, China G8 42
Jiang'an, China G1 42
Jiangcheng, China A5 48
Jiangdu, China E8 42
Jiange, China E1 42
Jianghua, China I4 42
Jiangjin, China G2 42
Jiangkou, China J4 42
Jiangkou, China H3 42
Jiangkou, China F4 42
Jiangle, China H7 42
Jiangling, China F4 42
Jiangmen, China J5 42
Jiangmifeng, China B7 38
Jiangshan, China G8 42
Jiangsu, state, China E8 42
Jiangtun, China J5 42
Jiangxi, state, China H6 42
Jiangya, China G4 42
Jiangyin, China F9 42
Jiangyou, China F1 42
Jiangzhong, China D14 54
Jianli, China G5 42
Jianning, China H7 42
Jian'ou, China H8 42
Jianping, China D3 38
Jianshi, China F3 42
Jianshui, China G5 36
Jianyang, China E5 36
Jianyang, China H8 42
Jiaocheng, China C4 42
Jiaohe, China C7 38
Jiaolai, stm., China C4 38
Jiaonan, China D8 42
Jiaoxian, China C8 42
Jiaozhou Wan, b., China C9 42
Jiaozuo, China D5 42
Jiashan, China E7 42
Jiashi, China B12 56
Jiashun Hu, l., China A10 54
Jiawang, China D7 42
Jiaxian, China D5 42
Jiaxian, China B4 42
Jiaxing, China F9 42
Jiazi, China J6 42
Jibuti see Djibouti, Dji. E8 62
Jicarón, Isla, i., Pan. I7 102
Jičín, Czech Rep. F11 16
Jiddah (Jeddah), Sau. Ar. E4 56
Jidingxilin, China B14 54
Jieshi Wan, b., China J6 42
Jieshou, China E6 42
Jiexi, China J6 42
Jiexiu, China C4 42
Jieyang, China J7 42
Jieznas, Lith. F7 10
Jiguaní, Cuba B9 102
Jigüey, Bahía de, strt., Cuba A8 102
Jigzhi, China E5 36
Jihlava, Czech Rep. G11 16
Jihlava, stm., Czech Rep. G12 16
Jihočeský kraj, state, Czech Rep. G10 16
Jihomoravský kraj, state, Czech Rep. G12 16
Jijia, stm., Rom. B14 26
Jijiga, Eth. F8 62
Jilantai, China B1 42
Jilib, Som. D8 66
Jili Hu, l., China B2 36
Jilin, China C7 38
Jilin, state, China C10 36
Jill, Kediet ej, mtn., Maur. E2 64
Jiloca, stm., Spain C9 20
Jīma, Eth. F7 62
Jimbolia, Rom. D7 26
Jimena de la Frontera, Spain H5 20
Jiménez, Mex. B6 100
Jiménez, Mex. A8 100
Jiménez del Téul, Mex. D7 100
Jimeta, Nig. H7 64
Jim Ned Creek, stm., Tx., U.S. C8 130
Jimo, China C9 42
Jimsar, China C2 36
Jim Thorpe, Pa., U.S. D10 114
Jin (Gam), stm., Asia A7 48
Jin, stm., China H7 42
Jinan (Tsinan), China C7 42
Jincang, China C9 38
Jincheng, China D5 42
Jīnd, India D6 54
Jindabyne, Austl. K7 76
Jindřichův Hradec, Czech Rep. G11 16
Jing, stm., China D3 42
Jing'an, China G6 42
Jingbian, China C3 42
Jingbohu, res., China C8 38
Jingde, China F8 42
Jingdezhen, China G7 42
Jinggangshan, China H6 42
Jinghai, China B7 42
Jinghe, China F14 32
Jinghong, China B5 48
Jingle, China B4 42
Jingmen, China F5 42
Jingning, China D1 42
Jingxi, China J2 42
Jingxian, China F8 42
Jingxian, China C7 42
Jingxian, China H3 42
Jingxin, China I6 42
Jingyu, China C7 38
Jingzhi, China C8 42
Jinhae see Chinhae, Kor., S. D1 40
Jinhua, China G8 42
Jining, China D7 42
Jining, China A5 42
Jinja, Ug. D6 66
Jinjiazhen, China C5 38
Jinju see Chinju, Kor., S. G7 38
Jinmu Jiao, c., China L3 42
Jinning, China G5 36
Jinotega, Nic. F5 102
Jinotepe, Nic. G4 102
Jinping, China H3 42
Jinqian, stm., China E3 42
Jinsha, China H1 42
Jinsha (Yangtze), stm., China F5 36
Jinshi, China G4 42
Jintian, China H6 42
Jintotolo Channel, strt., Phil. E4 52
Jinxi, China A9 42
Jinxi, China H7 42
Jinxian, China G7 42
Jinxian, China B6 42
Jinzhou, China B9 42
Jinzhou, China A9 42
Ji-Paraná, Braz. F5 84
Jipijapa, Ec. H1 86
Jiquiriçá, stm., Braz. G6 88
Jiri, stm., India F14 54
Jirkov, Czech Rep. F9 16
Jishou, China G3 42
Jisr ash-Shughūr, Syria C7 58
Jitaúna, Braz. G6 88
Jiu, stm., Rom. F10 26
Jiudaoliang, China F4 42
Jiufeng, China I7 42
Jiujiang, China G6 42
Jiulian Shan, mts., China I6 42
Jiuliguan, China F6 42
Jiuling Shan, mts., China G6 42
Jiulong, China J5 42
Jiulong, stm., China I7 42
Jiuquan, China D4 36
Jiutai, China B6 38
Jiuyuanqu, China D4 42
Jiuzhan, China C7 38
Jiuzhen, China I7 42
Jiwen, China A9 36
Jixi, China B9 38
Jixi, China F8 42
Jixian, China A7 42
Jixian, China D6 42
Jiyi, China D4 42
Jiyuan, China D5 42
Jiyun, stm., China B7 42
Jīzān, Sau. Ar. F5 56
Jizl, Wādī al-, stm., Sau. Ar. K8 58
J. J. Castelli see Castelli, Arg. B7 92
J.M. Lencinas see Las Catitas, Arg. F3 92
Joaçaba, Braz. C12 92
Joana Coeli, Braz. A1 88
Joanes, Braz. D8 84
João Câmara, Braz. C8 88
João Monlevade, Braz. J4 88
João Pessoa, Braz. D8 88
João Pinheiro, Braz. I2 88
Joaquim Távora, Braz. A12 92
Joaquin, Tx., U.S. F4 122
Joaquín V. González, Arg. B5 92
Jobos, P.R. C3 104a
Job Peak, mtn., Nv., U.S. D7 134
Jocolí, Arg. F3 92
Jódar, Spain G7 20
Jodhpur, India E4 54
Jodiya, India G3 54
Joensuu, Fin. E13 8
Joetsu, Japan B11 40
Jõgeva, Est. G12 8
Jog Falls, wtfl., India D2 53
Joggins, N.S., Can. E12 110
Jogjakarta see Yogyakarta, Indon. G7 50
Jōhana, Japan C9 40
Johannesburg, S. Afr. E8 70
John Day, Or., U.S. F8 136
John Day, stm., Or., U.S. E6 136
John Day, Middle Fork, stm., Or., U.S. F8 136
John Day, North Fork, stm., Or., U.S. F8 136
John Day Fossil Beds National Monument, p.o.i., Or., U.S. F7 136
John F. Kennedy Space Center, sci., Fl., U.S. H5 116
John H. Kerr Reservoir, res., U.S. H7 114
John Martin Reservoir, res., Co., U.S. C6 128
John o' Groats, Scot., U.K. C9 12
John Redmond Reservoir, res., Ks., U.S. F1 120
Johns Island, i., S.C., U.S. D5 116
Johnson, Ar., U.S. H3 120
Johnson, Ks., U.S. D7 128
Johnsonburg, Pa., U.S. C7 114
Johnson City, N.Y., U.S. B10 114
Johnson City, Tn., U.S. H3 114
Johnson City, Tx., U.S. D9 130
Johnsondale, Ca., U.S. H7 134
Johnson Draw, stm., Tx., U.S. D6 130
Johnson Point, c., St. Vin. o11 105e
Johnsonville, S.C., U.S. C6 116
Johnston, Ia., U.S. C4 120
Johnston, S.C., U.S. C4 116
Johnston, Lake, l., Austl. F4 74
Johnston Atoll, at., Oc. B10 72
Johnstown, Co., U.S. G8 126
Johnstown, N.Y., U.S. G2 110
Johnstown, Oh., U.S. D3 114
Johnstown, Pa., U.S. D7 114
Johor, state, Malay. L6 48
Johor Bahru, Malay. L6 48
Joigny, Fr. G12 14
Joiner, Ar., U.S. B8 122
Joinville, Braz. C13 92
Joinville Island, i., Ant. B35 81
Jojogan, Indon. G7 50
Jokkmokk, Swe. C8 8
Jökulsá á Brú, stm., Ice. k32 8a
Jökulsárgljúfur Nasjonalpark, p.o.i., Ice. k32 8a
Joliet, Il., U.S. C9 120
Joliette, Qc., Can. D3 110
Jolo, Phil. G3 52
Jolo Group, is., Phil. G3 52
Jolo Island, i., Phil. H3 52
Jombang, Indon. G8 50
Jomda, China E4 36
Jonava, Lith. E7 10
Jones, Ok., U.S. F11 128
Jonesboro, Ar., U.S. I7 120
Jonesboro, Ga., U.S. C1 116
Jonesboro, Il., U.S. G8 120
Jonesboro, La., U.S. E6 122
Jonesborough, Tn., U.S. H3 114
Jones Mill, Ar., U.S. C6 122
Jonesport, Me., U.S. F9 110
Jones Sound, strt., Nu., Can. B8 141
Jonestown, Ms., U.S. C8 122
Jonesville, La., U.S. F7 122
Jonesville, Mi., U.S. B1 114
Jonglei Canal, can., Sudan F6 62
Joniškėlis, Lith. D6 10
Joniškis, Lith. D6 10
Jönköping, Swe. H6 8
Jönköping, state, Swe. H6 8
Jonquière, Qc., Can. B5 110
Jonuta, Mex. F12 100
Jonzac, Fr. D5 18
Joplin, Mo., U.S. G3 120
Joplin, Mt., U.S. B16 136
Joppa, Il., U.S. G9 120
Jora, India E6 54
Jordan, Mn., U.S. G5 118
Jordan, Mt., U.S. G6 124
Jordan, ctry., Asia H7 58
Jordan (Al-Urdunn) (HaYarden), stm., Asia F6 58
Jordan, stm., Ut., U.S. C5 132
Jordan Creek, stm., U.S. H10 136
Jordânia, Braz. H5 88
Jordan Valley, Or., U.S. G10 136
Jordão, stm., Braz. B12 92
Jorge Montt, Isla, i., Chile J2 90
Jorhāt, India C7 46
Jornado del Muerto, des., N.M., U.S. J10 132
Joroinen, Fin. E12 8
Jos, Nig. G6 64
Jose Abad Santos, Phil. H5 52
José Batlle y Ordóñez, Ur. F10 92
José Bonifácio, Braz. K1 88
José de Freitas, Braz. C4 88
José de San Martín, Arg. H2 90
José Pedro Varela, Ur. F10 92
Joseph, Or., U.S. E9 136
Joseph, Lac, l., Nf., Can. E17 106
Joseph Bonaparte Gulf, b., Austl. B5 74
Joshīmath, India C7 54
Jōshin-Etsu-kōgen-kokuritsu-kōen, p.o.i., Japan C11 40
Joshua, Tx., U.S. B10 130
Joshua Tree, Ca., U.S. I9 134
Joshua Tree National Park, p.o.i., Ca., U.S. J10 134
Jostedalsbreen, ice, Nor. F2 8
Jostedalsbreen Nasjonalpark, p.o.i., Nor. F2 8
Jotunheimen Nasjonalpark, p.o.i., Nor. F2 8
Joubertina, S. Afr. H6 70
Jourdanton, Tx., U.S. F9 130
Joutsijärvi, Fin. C13 8
Joviânia, Braz. I1 88
Jowai, India F14 54
Joya, Mex. H6 130
Joyce, La., U.S. F6 122
Joyuda, P.R. B1 104a
J. Percy Priest Lake, res., Tn., U.S. H11 120
J. Strom Thurmond Reservoir, res., U.S. C3 116
Juami, stm., Braz. I7 86
Juana Díaz, P.R. B2 104a
Juan Aldama, Mex. C7 100
Juan Bautista Alberdi, Arg. C5 92
Juan de Fuca, Strait of, strt., N.A. B2 136
Juan de Garay, Arg. I5 92
Juan de Nova, Île, i., Reu. D7 68
Juan E. Barra, Arg. H7 92
Juan Fernández, Archipiélago, is., Chile I6 82
Juanjuí, Peru E2 84
Juan N. Fernández, Arg. I8 92
Juan Viñas, C.R. H6 102
Juárez see Benito Juárez, Arg. H8 92
Juárez, Mex. B8 100
Juárez, Mex. F8 98
Juatinga, Ponta de, c., Braz. L3 88
Juazeirinho, Braz. D7 88
Juazeiro, Braz. E5 88
Juazeiro do Norte, Braz. D6 88
Juba, Sudan G6 62
Juba see Jubba, stm., Afr. D8 66
Juba see Genalē, stm., Afr. C8 66
Jubal, Strait of see Gûbâi, Madîq, strt., Egypt. K4 58
Jubayl, Leb. D6 58
Jubba (Genalē), stm., Afr. D8 66
Juby, Cap, c., Mor. D2 64
Júcar (Xúquer), stm., Spain E10 20
Juchipila, Mex. E7 100
Juchitán de Zaragoza, Mex. G11 100
Jucurucu, stm., Braz. I5 88
Jucurutu, Braz. C7 88
Judenburg, Aus. C11 22
Judino, Russia B22 10
Judique, N.S., Can. E15 110
Judith, stm., Mt., U.S. C17 136
Judith Gap, Mt., U.S. D17 136
Judith Peak, mtn., Mt., U.S. C17 136
Judoma, stm., Russia E16 34
Jufari, stm., Braz. H10 86
Jug, stm., Russia G21 8
Jugorskij poluostrov, pen., Russia A10 32
Juhnov, Russia F18 10
Juidongshan, China J7 42
Juigalpa, Nic. F5 102
Juist, i., Ger. C2 16
Juiz de Fora, Braz. K4 88
Jujuy, state, Arg. D3 90
Jukagirskoe ploskogor'e, plat., Russia C19 34
Jukta, Russia B19 32
Jula, stm., Russia E21 8
Julesburg, Co., U.S. G10 126
Juliaca, Peru G3 84
Julia Creek, Austl. C3 76
Julia Creek, stm., Austl. C3 76
Julianadorp, Neth. Ant. p22 104g
Julian Alps, mts., Eur. D10 22
Juliana Top, mtn., Sur. C6 84
Julianehåb (Qaqortoq), Grnld. E16 141
Jülich, Ger. F2 16
Juliette, Lake, res., Ga., U.S. D2 116
Julimes, Mex. A6 100
Júlio de Castilhos, Braz. D11 92
Juma, Russia D15 8
Juma, stm., China B6 42
Jumba, Som. E8 66
Jumilla, Spain F9 20
Jumlā, Nepal D9 54
Jūnāgadh, India H3 54
Juncos, P.R. B4 104a
Junction, Tx., U.S. D8 130
Junction City, Ar., U.S. E6 122
Junction City, Ks., U.S. B12 128
Junction City, Ky., U.S. G13 120
Jundah, Austl. E4 76
Jundiaí, Braz. L2 88
Juneau, Ak., U.S. E13 140
Juneau, Wi., U.S. H10 118
Junee, Austl. J6 76
June Lake, Ca., U.S. F6 134
Jungar Qi, China B4 42
Jungfrau, mtn., Switz. D4 22
Junggar Pendi, bas., China B2 36
Juniata, Ne., U.S. G14 126
Juniata, stm., Pa., U.S. D8 114
Junín, Arg. G7 92
Junín, Ec. H1 86
Junín de los Andes, Arg. G2 90
Juniper, N.B., Can. D9 110
Junipero Serra Peak, mtn., Ca., U.S. G4 134
Jūniyah, Leb. E6 58
Junlian, China F5 36
Junnar, India B1 53
Junqueiro, Braz. E7 88
Junxian, China E4 42
Juodkrantė, Lith. E3 10
Juozapinės kalnas, hill, Lith. F8 10
Juparanã, Lagoa, l., Braz. J5 88
Jupiter, Fl., U.S. J5 116
Juquiá, Braz. B14 92
Juquiá, Ponta do, c., Braz. B14 92
Jur, Russia E16 34
Jur, stm., Sudan F5 62
Jura, Mol. B16 26
Jura, state, Fr. C11 18
Jura, mts., Eur. B12 18
Jura, i., Scot., U.K. F7 12
Jūra, stm., Lith. E5 10
Jurbarkas, Lith. E5 10
Jurenino, Russia G20 8
Jurevec, Russia H20 8
Jurga, Russia C15 32
Juriti, Braz. D6 84
Jūrmala, Lat. C6 10
Jurong, China F8 42
Juruá, stm., S.A. D4 84
Juruena, stm., Braz. E6 84
Jurumirim, Represa de, res., Braz. L1 88
Jusepín, Ven. C10 86
Juškovo, Russia G21 8
Justiniano Posse, Arg. F6 92
Justino Solari see Mariano I. Loza, Arg. D8 92
Justo Daract, Arg. F5 92
Jutaí, stm., Braz. D4 84
Jüterbog, Ger. D9 16
Jutiapa, Guat. E3 102
Juticalpa, Hond. E4 102
Jutland see Jylland, reg., Den. H3 8
Jutrosin, Pol. E13 16
Juventud, Isla de la (Pines, Isle of), i., Cuba B6 102
Juxian, China D8 42
Juye, China D6 42
Juža, Russia H20 8
Južna Morava, stm., Serb. F8 26
Južno-Enisejskij, Russia C17 32
Južno-Sahalinsk, Russia G17 34
Južno-Ural'sk, Russia D10 32
Južnyj, mys, c., Russia E20 34
Južnyj Ural, mts., Russia D9 32
Jwayyā, Leb. E6 58
Jyekundo see Yushu, China E4 36
Jylland (Jutland), reg., Den. H3 8
Jyväskylä, Fin. E11 8

K

K2, mtn., Asia B12 56
Kaabong, Ug. D6 66
Kaahka, Turkmen. B8 56
Ka'ala, mtn., Hi., U.S. b3 78a
Kaala-Gomen, N. Cal. m15 79d
Kaapstad see Cape Town, S. Afr. H4 70
Kaarli, Est. A9 10
Kaatoan, Mount, mtn., Phil. F5 52
Kabacan, Phil. G5 52
Kabaena, Pulau, i., Indon. G7 44
Kabah, sci., Mex. B3 102
Kabala, S.L. H2 64
Kabale, Ug. E5 66
Kabalega Falls, wtfl., Ug. D6 66
Kabalo, D.R.C. F5 66
Kabambare, D.R.C. E5 66
Kabanjahe, Indon. K4 48
Kabankalan, Phil. F4 52
Kabardin-Balkaria see Kabardino-Balkarija, state, Russia F6 32
Kabardino-Balkarija, state, Russia F6 32
Kabba, Nig. H6 64
Kabbani, stm., India F3 53
Kåbdalis, Swe. C8 8
Kabetogama Lake, l., Mn., U.S. C5 118
Kab-hegy, mtn., Hung. B4 26
Kabinda, D.R.C. F4 66
Kabinu, Indon. A9 50
Kabīr Kūh, mts., Iran C6 56
Kabna, Sudan D6 62
Kābol, Afg. C10 56
Kābol, state, Afg. A2 54
Kabompo, Zam. C3 68
Kabompo, stm., Zam. C3 68
Kabongo, D.R.C. F5 66
Kābul see Kābol, Afg. C10 56
Kabul (Kābol), stm., Asia A4 54
Kabwe, Zam. C4 68
Kabylie, reg., Alg. H14 20
Kačanik, Serb. G8 26
Kačerginė, Lith. F6 10
Kachchh, Gulf of, b., India G2 54
Kachīry, Kaz. D13 32
Kačkanar, Russia C10 32
Kačug, Russia D19 32
Kadaiyanallūr, India G3 53
Kadaň, Czech Rep. F9 16
Kadan Kyun, i., Mya. F4 48
Kadapongan, Pulau, i., Indon. F9 50
Kaddam, res., India B4 53
Kade, Ghana H4 64
Kadéï, stm., Afr. G2 62
Kadi, India G4 54
Kadina, Austl. F7 74
Kading, stm., Laos C7 48
Kadınhanı, Tur. E15 28
Kadiolo, Mali G3 64
Kādīpur, India E9 54
Kadiri, India D4 53
Kadirli, Tur. A7 58
Kadoka, S.D., U.S. D11 126
Kadoma, Zimb. D4 68
Kaduj, Russia A20 10
Kaduna, Nig. G6 64
Kaduna, stm., Nig. G6 64
Kāduqlī, Sudan E5 62
Kadūr, India E3 53
Kaduvu, i., Fiji q19 79e
Kaduvu Passage, strt., Fiji q18 79e
Kadyj, Russia H20 8
Kadžerom, Russia B9 32
Kaédi, Maur. F2 64
Kaélé, Cam. B2 66
Ka'ena Point, c., Hi., U.S. b3 78a
Kaesŏng, Kor., N. F7 38
Kafanchan, Nig. H6 64
Kaffrine, Sen. G1 64
Kafia Kingi, Sudan F4 62
Kafr el-Dauwar, Egypt G1 58
Kafr el-Sheikh, Egypt G1 58
Kafr el-Zaiyât, Egypt H1 58
Kafr Sa'd, Egypt G2 58
Kafue, Zam. D4 68
Kafue, stm., Zam. D4 68
Kaga, Japan C9 40
Kaga Bandoro, C.A.R. C3 66
Kāgān, Pak. A4 54
Kagan, Uzb. G10 32
Kagawa, state, Japan E6 40
Kagawong, Lake, l., On., Can. C7 112
Kagaznagar, India B4 53
Kagera, stm., Afr. E6 66
Kagmar, Sudan E6 62
Kagoshima, Japan H3 40
Kagoshima, state, Japan H3 40
Kagoshima-wan, b., Japan H3 40
Kahama, Tan. E6 66
Kahayan, stm., Indon. D8 50
Ka-Hem see Malyj Enisej, stm., Russia F8 34
Kahemba, D.R.C. F3 66
Kahiu Point, c., Hi., U.S. b5 78a
Kahoka, Mo., U.S. D6 120
Kaho'olawe, i., Hi., U.S. c5 78a
Kahouanne, Îlet à, i., Guad. h5 105c
Kahramanmaraş (Maraş), Tur. A7 58
Kahraman Maraş, state, Tur. A7 58
Kahuku Point, c., Hi., U.S. b4 78a
Kahului, Hi., U.S. c5 78a
Kai, Kepulauan (Kai Islands), is., Indon. G9 44
Kaiapoi, N.Z. F5 80
Kaibab Plateau, plat., Az., U.S. G4 132
Kaidu, stm., China F15 32
Kaieteur Fall, wtfl., Guy. E12 86
Kaieteur National Park, p.o.i., Guy. E12 86
Kaifeng, China D6 42
Kaihua, China G8 42
Kai Islands see Kai, Kepulauan, is., Indon. G9 44
Kaijian, China J4 42
Kaijiang, China F2 42
Kai Kecil, i., Indon. G9 44
Kaikoura, N.Z. F5 80
Kailahun, S.L. H2 64
Kailas see Kangrinboqê Feng, mtn., China C8 54
Kailāshahar, India F14 54
Kailas Range see Gangdisê Shan, mts., China C9 54
Kaili, China H2 42
Kailu, China C4 38
Kailua, Hi., U.S. b4 78a
Kailua Kona, Hi., U.S. d6 78a
Kaïmaktsalán (Kajmakčalan), mtn., Eur. C15 24
Kaimana, Indon. F9 44
Kaimon-dake, vol., Japan H3 40
Kainabrivier, stm., Nmb. E4 70
Kainan, Japan E8 40
Kainantu, Pap. N. Gui. b4 79a
Kainji Reservoir, res., Nig. G5 64
Kaipara Harbour, b., N.Z. C5 80
Kaiparowits Plateau, plat., Ut., U.S. F5 132
Kaiping, China J5 42
Kairouan, Tun. I3 24
Kairuku, Pap. N. Gui. b4 79a
Kaiserslautern, Ger. G3 16
Kaišiadorys, Lith. F7 10
Kait, Tanjung, c., Indon. E5 50
Kaitangata, N.Z. H3 80
Kaithal, India D6 54
Kaituma, stm., Guy. D12 86
Kaiwi Channel, strt., Hi., U.S. b4 78a
Kaixian, China F3 42
Kaiyang, China H2 42
Kaiyuan, China G5 36
Kaiyuan, China C6 38
Kaiyuancheng, China C6 38
Kaiyuh Mountains, mts., Ak., U.S. D8 140
Kajaani, Fin. D12 8
Kajabbi, Austl. B2 76
Kajakī, Band-e, res., Afg. C10 56
Kajang, Malay. K5 48
Kajmysovy, Russia C13 32
Kajo Kaji, Sudan G6 62
Kaka, Sudan E6 62
Kakabeka Falls, wtfl., On., Can. C9 118
Kakagi Lake, l., On., Can. B5 118
Kakamas, S. Afr. F5 70
Kakamega, Kenya D6 66
Kakamigahara, Japan D9 40
Kakata, Lib. H2 64
Kākdwīp, India H12 54
Kakegawa, Japan E10 40
Kakhonak, Ak., U.S. E9 140
Kakhovka Reservoir see Kakhovs'ke vodoskhovyshche, res., Ukr. E4 32
Kakhovs'ke vodoskhovyshche, res., Ukr. E4 32
Kākināda (Cocanada), India C6 53
Kakisa Lake, l., N.T., Can. C7 106
Kakizaki, Japan B11 40
Kakogawa, Japan E7 40
Kakšaal-Too, hrebet, mts., Asia F13 32
Kaktovik, Ak., U.S. B11 140
Kakuda, Japan B13 40
Kakus, stm., Malay. B8 50
Kakwa, stm., Ab., Can. B12 138
Kala, stm., Sri L. G4 53
Kalaa Kebira, Tun. I4 24
Kalabahi, Indon. G7 44
Kalabakan, Malay. A10 50
Kalabo, Zam. D3 68
Kalač, Russia D6 32
Kalačinsk, Russia D12 32
Kalač-na-Donu, Russia E6 32
Kaladan, stm., Asia G14 54
Kalae, c., Hi., U.S. e6 78a
Kalahari Desert, des., Afr. C5 70
Kalahari Gemsbok National Park, p.o.i., S. Afr. D5 70
Kalajoki, Fin. D10 8
Kalakan, Russia E12 34
Kalām, Pak. B11 56
Kalama, Wa., U.S. D4 136
Kalamalka Lake, l., B.C., Can. F11 138
Kalamáta, Grc. F5 28
Kalamazoo, Mi., U.S. F4 112
Kalamazoo, stm., Mi., U.S. F4 112
Kalamb, India B1 53
Kalampising, Indon. B10 50
Kalao, Pulau, i., Indon. G12 50
Kalaotoa, Pulau, i., Indon. G7 44
Kalar, stm., Russia E12 34
Kalasin, Thai. D6 48
Kalašnikovo, Russia C18 10
Kalāt, Pak. D10 56
Kalávryta, Grc. E5 28
Kalaw, Mya. B3 48
Kalbarri, Austl. E2 74
Kale, Tur. G12 28
Kale, Tur. F11 28
Kaleden, B.C., Can. G11 138
Kalegauk Island, i., Mya. E3 48
Kalehe, D.R.C. E5 66
Kalemie, D.R.C. F5 66
Kalemyo, Mya. D7 46
Kaletwa, Mya. H14 54
Kalevala, Russia D14 8
Kalewa, Mya. D7 46
Kálfafell, Ice. k31 8a
Kalgan see Zhangjiakou, China A6 42
Kalgoorlie-Boulder, Austl. F4 74
Kaliakra, nos, c., Blg. F15 26
Kalianda, Indon. F4 50
Kalibo, Phil. E4 52
Kalima, D.R.C. E5 66
Kalimantan (Borneo), i., Asia F5 44
Kalimantan Barat, state, Indon. D7 50
Kalimantan Selatan, state, Indon. E9 50
Kalimantan Tengah, state, Indon. D8 50
Kalimantan Timur, state, Indon. C10 50
Kālimpang, India E12 54
Kālīnadi, stm., India D2 53
Kalinin see Tver', Russia D18 10
Kaliningrad (Königsberg), Russia F3 10
Kaliningradskaja oblast', co., Russia F4 10
Kalinkavičy, Bela. H12 10
Kaliro, Ug. D6 66
Kalisat, Indon. H8 50
Kāli Sindh, stm., India F6 54
Kalispell, Mt., U.S. B12 136
Kalisz, Pol. E14 16
Kalisz, state, Pol. E13 16
Kalisz Pomorski, Pol. C11 16
Kaliua, Tan. E6 66
Kaliveli Tank, l., India E4 53
Kalixälven, stm., Swe. C9 8
Kaljazin, Russia C20 10
Kālka, India C6 54
Kalkaska, Mi., U.S. D4 112
Kalkfonteindam, res., S. Afr. F7 70
Kalkım, Tur. D10 28
Kalkrand, Nmb. D3 70
Kallar Kahār, Pak. B4 54
Kallavesi, l., Fin. E12 8
Kallsjön, l., Swe. E5 8
Kalmar, Swe. H6 8
Kalmar, state, Swe. H7 8
Kalmarsund, strt., Swe. H7 8
Kalmykia see Kalmykija, state, Russia E7 32
Kalmykija, state, Russia E7 32
Kālna, India G12 54
Kalocsa, Hung. C5 26
Kalofer, Blg. G12 26
Kalohi Channel, strt., Hi., U.S. b4 78a
Kalol, India G4 54
Kālol, India G4 54
Kalomo, Zam. D4 68
Kalona, Ia., U.S. J7 118
Kalone Peak, mtn., B.C., Can. D4 138
Kalpeni Island, i., India F1 53
Kālpi, India E7 54
Kalpin, China A12 56
Kalsūbai, mtn., India B1 53
Kaltag, Ak., U.S. D8 140
Kaluga, Russia F19 10
Kalukalukuang, Pulau, i., Indon. F10 50
Kalumburu, Austl. B5 74
Kałuszyn, Pol. D17 16
Kalutara, Sri L. H4 53
Kalužskaja oblast', co., Russia F18 10
Kalyān, India B1 53
Kalyāndurg, India D3 53
Kálymnos, Grc. G9 28
Kálymnos, i., Grc. F9 28
Kama, stm., Russia C8 32
Kamae, Japan G4 40
Kamaishi, Japan E14 38
Kamakou, mtn., Hi., U.S. b5 78a
Kamakura, Japan D12 40
Kamālia, Pak. C4 54
Kamamaung, Mya. D3 48
Kaman, stm., Laos E8 48
Kamanjab, Nmb. D1 68
Kamarān, i., Yemen F5 56
Kāmāreddi, India B4 53
Kama Reservoir see Kamskoe vodohranilišče, res., Russia C9 32
Kamas, Ut., U.S. C5 132
Kamay, Tx., U.S. H10 128
Kambalda, Austl. F4 74
Kambam, India G3 53
Kambarka, Russia C8 32
Kambja, Est. B9 10
Kambove, D.R.C. G5 66
Kamčatka, stm., Russia E21 34
Kamčatka, poluostrov, pen., Russia E19 34
Kamčatskij poluostrov, pen., Russia E21 34
Kamčatskij zaliv, b., Russia E21 34
Kamchatka Peninsula see Kamčatka, poluostrov, pen., Russia E20 34
Kameda, Japan B12 40
Kámeiros, sci., Grc. G10 28
Kamen', gora, mtn., Russia C8 34
Kameng, stm., India E14 54
Kamenjak, Rt, c., Cro. F10 22
Kamenka, Kaz. D11 32
Kamenka, Russia D6 32
Kamenka, Russia D21 8
Kamen'-na-Obi, Russia D14 32
Kameno, Blg. G14 26
Kamen-Rybolov, Russia B9 38
Kamenskoe, Russia D22 34
Kamensk-Ural'skij, Russia C10 32
Kamenz, Ger. E10 16
Kāmet, mtn., Asia C7 54
Kam'ians'ke, Ukr. D16 26
Kamień Krajeński, Pol. C13 16
Kamienna Góra, Pol. F12 16
Kamieńsk, Pol. E15 16

Name　Map Ref.　Page

Kamieskroon, S. Afr. — G3 70
Kamiiso, Japan — D14 38
Kamilukuak Lake, l., Can. — C10 106
Kamina, D.R.C. — F4 66
Kaminak Lake, l., Nu., Can. — C12 106
Kaminoyama, Japan — A13 40
Kaminuriak Lake, l., Nu., Can. — C12 106
Kamioka, Japan — C10 40
Kamjanec, Bela. — H6 10
Kamkhat Muhaywir, hill, Jord. — G7 58
Kamloops, B.C., Can. — F10 138
Kamnik, Slvn. — D11 22
Kamo, Japan — B12 40
Kamoa Mountains, mts., Guy. — C6 84
Kamojima, Japan — F2 40
Kāmoke, Pak. — B5 54
Kampala, Ug. — D6 66
Kampar, Malay. — J5 48
Kampar, stm., Indon. — C3 50
Kamparkalns, hill, Lat. — C5 10
Kampar Kanan, stm., Indon. — C2 50
Kampen, Neth. — B14 14
Kamphaeng Phet, Thai. — D4 48
Kampinoski Park Narodowy, p.o.i., Pol. — D16 16
Kâmpóng Cham, Camb. — F7 48
Kâmpóng Chhnǎng, Camb. — F7 48
Kâmpóng Kântuŏt, Camb. — F7 48
Kâmpóng Saôm, Camb. — G6 48
Kâmpóng Saôm, Chhâk, b., Camb. — G6 48
Kâmpóng Thum, Camb. — F7 48
Kampong Ulu, Mya. — G4 48
Kâmpôt, Camb. — G7 48
Kampsville, Il., U.S. — E7 120
Kampti, Burkina. — G4 64
Kampuchea see Cambodia, ctry., Asia — C3 48
Kampungbaru, Indon. — D3 50
Kampung Litang, Malay. — A11 50
Kamrau, Teluk, b., Indon. — F9 44
Kamsack, Sk., Can. — C12 124
Kamskoe vodohranilišče, res., Russia — C9 32
Kāmthi, India — H7 54
Kamuela, Hi., U.S. — d6 78a
Kamuk, Cerro, mtn., C.R. — H6 102
Kamundan, stm., Indon. — F9 44
Kamyšin, Russia — D7 32
Kamyšlov, Russia — C10 32
Kan, stm., Russia — C17 32
Kanaaupscow, stm., Qc., Can. — E15 106
Kanab, Ut., U.S. — F4 132
Kanab Creek, stm., U.S. — G4 132
Kanaga Island, i., Ak., U.S. — g23 140a
Kanagawa, state, Japan. — D12 40
Kanakapura, India — E3 53
Kananga (Luluabourg), D.R.C. — F4 66
Kananggar, Indon. — I12 50
Kananga-Boyd National Park, p.o.i., Austl. — I7 76
Kanaš, Russia — C7 32
Kanawha, Ia., U.S. — B4 120
Kanawha, stm., W.V., U.S. — F4 114
Kanazawa, Japan — C9 40
Kanbauk, Mya. — E3 48
Kanchanaburi, Thai. — F4 48
Kānchanjaṅgā (Kānchenjunga), mtn., Asia — E11 54
Kānchenjunga (Kānchanjaṅgā), mtn., Asia — E11 54
Kānchipuram, India — E4 53
Kanchow see Ganzhou, China — I6 42
Kańczuga, Pol. — F18 16
Kanda, Japan — F3 40
Kandahār, Afg. — C10 56
Kandahār, Sk., Can. — C9 124
Kandalaksa, Russia — C15 8
Kandalakskaja guba, b., Russia — C15 8
Kandangan, Indon. — K3 48
Kandangan, Indon. — E9 50
Kandanghaur, Indon. — G6 50
Kandé, Togo — H5 64
Kandhkot, Pak. — D2 54
Kandi, India — G12 54
Kandi, Tanjung, c., Indon. — D7 50
Kandira, Tur. — B13 28
Kandla, India — G3 54
Kandos, Austl. — I7 76
Kandreho, Madag. — D8 68
Kandy, Sri L. — H5 53
Kane, Pa., U.S. — C7 114
Kane Basin, b., N.A. — B12 141
Kanem, state, Chad. — E3 62
Kane'ohe, Hi., U.S. — b4 78a
Kanevka, Russia — C18 8
Kang, Bots. — C6 70
Kangaba, Mali — G3 64
Kangalassy, Russia — D15 34
Kangāmiut, Grnld. — D15 141
Kāngān, Iran — D7 56
Kāngar, Malay. — I5 48
Kangaroo Island, i., Austl. — G7 74
Kangāvar, Iran — C6 56
Kangbao, China — C7 36
Kangding, China — C9 46
Kangean, Kepulauan (Kangean Islands), is., Indon. — G9 50
Kangean, Pulau, i., Indon. — G9 50
Kangean Islands see Kangean, Kepulauan, is., Indon. — G9 50
Kangeeak Point, c., Nu., Can. — B18 106
Kangerlussuaq, b., Grnld. — D19 141
Kangerlussuaq see Prøven, Grnld. — C14 141
Kanger Valley National Park, p.o.i., India — B6 53
Kanggye, Kor., N. — D7 38
Kanghwa-do, i., Kor., S. — F7 38
Kangiqsliniq (Rankin Inlet), Nu., Can. — C12 106
Kangiqsualujjuaq, Qc., Can. — D17 106
Kangiqsujuaq, Qc., Can. — C16 106
Kangiqtugaapik (Clyde River), Nu., Can. — A16 106
Kangirsuk, Qc., Can. — C17 106
Kangmar, China — D12 54
Kangnŭng, Kor., S. — B1 40
Kango, Gabon — D2 66
Kangpu, China — C5 38
Kangpu, China — F4 36
Kangrinboqê Feng, mtn., China — C8 54
Kangshan, Tai. — J9 42
Kangsŏ, Kor., N. — E6 38
Kangto, mtn., Asia — D14 54
Kangwŏn-do, state, Kor., S. — B1 40
Kanha National Park, p.o.i., India — G8 54
Kanhar, stm., India — F9 54
Kanhsien see Ganzhou, China — I6 42
Kani, Mya. — A2 48
Kaniama, D.R.C. — F4 66
Kanibadam, Taj. — A11 56
Kaniet Islands, is., Pap. N. Gui. — a4 79a
Kanigiri, India — D4 53
Kanin, poluostrov, pen., Russia — C21 8
Kanin-Kamen', mts., Russia — B21 8

Kanin Nos, Russia — B20 8
Kanin Nos, mys, c., Russia — B20 8
Kaniva, Austl. — K3 76
Kanjiža, Serb. — C7 26
Kankaanpää, Fin. — F10 8
Kankakee, Il., U.S. — G2 112
Kankan, Gui. — G3 64
Känker, India — H8 54
Kankunskij, Russia — E14 34
Kannack, Viet. — E9 48
Kannapura Kyun, i., Mya. — G4 48
Kannad, India — H5 54
Kannapolis, N.C., U.S. — A5 116
Kannauj, India — E7 54
Kanniyākumari, India — G3 53
Kannod, India — G6 54
Kannur see Cannanore, India — F2 53
Kannus, Fin. — E10 8
Kano, Nig. — G6 64
Kanonji, Japan — E6 40
Kanopolis, Ks., U.S. — C10 128
Kanorado, Ks., U.S. — B6 128
Kanosh, Ut., U.S. — E4 132
Kanoya, Japan — H3 40
Kanpetlet, Mya. — B1 48
Kānpur (Cawnpore), India — E7 54
Kansas, state, U.S. — C10 128
Kansas, stm., Ks., U.S. — B13 128
Kansas City, Ks., U.S. — E3 120
Kansas City, Mo., U.S. — E3 120
Kansk, Russia — C17 32
Kansŏng, Kor., S. — A1 40
Kan-sou see Gansu, state, China — D5 36
Kansu see Gansu, state, China — D5 36
Kantang, Thai. — I4 48
Kantchari, Burkina. — G5 64
Kānth, India — D7 54
Kantishna, stm., Ak., U.S. — D9 140
Kantō-heiya, pl., Japan — D12 40
Kanton, i., Kir. — D9 72
Kantō-sanchi, mts., Japan — D11 40
Kantu-long, Mya. — C3 48
Kantunilkin, Mex. — B4 102
Kanuku Mountains, mts., Guy. — F12 86
Kanuma, Japan — C12 40
Kanye, Bots. — D7 70
Kanyutkwin, Mya. — C3 48
Kaohiung see Kaohsiung, Tai. — J8 42
Kaohsiung, Tai. — J8 42
Kaohsiunghsien, Tai. — J9 42
Kaoka Bay, b., Sol. Is. — e9 79b
Kaoko Veld, plat., Nmb. — D1 68
Kaolack, Sen. — G1 64
Kaolinovo, Blg. — F14 26
Kaoma, Zam. — C3 68
Kaouar, reg., Niger — F7 64
Kapaa, Hi., U.S. — a2 78a
Kapadvanj, India — G4 54
Kapanga, D.R.C. — F4 66
Kapaonik, mts., Serb. — G8 26
Kapatkevičy, Bela. — H11 10
Kapčagajskoe vodohranilišče see Kapshahay bögeni, res., Kaz. — F13 32
Kapchagay Reservoir see Kapshagay bögeni, res., Kaz. — F13 32
Kapfenberg, Aus. — C12 22
Kapidağ Yarımadası, pen., Tur. — C10 28
Kapikotongwa, stm., On., Can. — A11 118
Kapingamarangi, at., Micron. — C6 72
Kapiri Mposhi, Zam. — C4 68
Kapisigdlit, Grnld. — E16 141
Kapiskau, stm., On., Can. — E14 106
Kapit, Malay. — C8 50
Kaplan, La., U.S. — G6 122
Kaplice, Czech Rep. — H10 16
Kapoeta, Sudan — G6 62
Kapona, D.R.C. — F5 66
Kapos, stm., Hung. — C5 26
Kaposvár, Hung. — C4 26
Kaposvar Creek, stm., Sk., Can. — D11 124
Kappeln, Ger. — B5 16
Kapshagay bögeni, res., Kaz. — F13 32
Kaptai, Bngl. — G14 54
Kaptai Lake see Karnaphuli Reservoir, res., Bngl. — G14 54
Kapuas, stm., Indon. — D6 50
Kapuas, stm., Indon. — E9 50
Kapunda, Austl. — J2 76
Kapūrthala, India — C5 54
Kapuskasing, On., Can. — F14 106
Kapuvár, Hung. — B4 26
Kapyl', Bela. — G10 10
Kara, stm., Russia — C1 34
Kara-Balta, Kyrg. — F12 32
Karabanovo, Russia — D21 10
Karabaš, Russia — C9 32
Kara-Bogaz-Gol, zaliv, b., Turkmen. — A7 56
Kara-Bogaz-Gol Gulf see Kara-Bogaz-Gol, zaliv, b., Turkmen. — A7 56
Karabük, Tur. — B15 28
Karabula, Russia — C17 32
Karaburun, Tur. — E9 28
Karacabey, Tur. — C11 28
Karačaevo-Čerkesija, state, Russia — F6 32
Karacasu, Tur. — F11 28
Karačev, Russia — G17 10
Karachay see Karačaevo-Čerkesija, state, Russia. — F6 32
Karachay-Cherkessia see Karačaevo-Čerkesija, state, Russia. — F6 32
Karachi, Pak. — E10 56
Karād, India — C2 53
Karaftit, Russia — F11 34
Karaganda see Karagandy, Kaz. — E12 32
Karagandy (Karaganda), Kaz. — E12 32
Karagayly see Qarqaraly, Kaz. — E13 32
Karaginskij, ostrov, i., Russia — E21 34
Karaginskij zaliv, b., Russia. — E21 34
Karagoš, gora, mtn., Russia — D15 32
Karahallı, India — E12 28
Kāraikkudi, India — F4 53
Karaisalı, Tur. — A6 58
Karaj, Iran — B7 56
Kara-Kala, Turkmen. — B8 56
Karakalong, Pulau, is., Indon. — E7 44
Karakax, stm., China — A7 54
Karakol, Kyrg. — F13 32
Karakoram Pass, p., Asia — A6 54
Karakoram Range, mts., Asia — A4 46
Karakul', Uzb. — G10 32
Kara-Kum Canal see Garagumskij kanal, can., Turkmen. — B9 56
Karama, stm., Indon. — E11 50
Karamay see Karamay, China. — B1 36
Karaman, Tur. — A4 58
Karaman, state, Tur. — A4 58
Karamanlı, Tur. — F12 28
Karamay, China — B1 36
Karamea Bight, b., N.Z. — E4 80

Karamyševo, Russia — C18 32
Karanzino, Russia — D17 10
Karangasem, Indon. — H9 50
Karangnunggal, Indon. — G6 50
Kāranja, India — H6 54
Karanja, India — H10 54
Karapınar, Tur. — A4 58
Karaqoyyn köli, l., Kaz. — E11 32
Karas, state, Nmb. — E3 70
Karasjok, Nor. — B11 8
Karasu, Tur. — T13 28
Karasu, stm., Tur. — B4 56
Karasuk, Russia — D13 32
Karatal, Kaz. — E15 32
Karataş Burun, c., Tur. — B6 58
Karataş hriebet see Qarataū zhotasy, mts., Kaz. — F11 32
Karatöbe, Kaz. — E8 32
Karatsu, Japan — F2 40
Karaul, Russia — B5 34
Karauli, India — E6 54
Karawang, Indon. — G5 50
Karawang, Tanjung, c., Indon. — F5 50
Karawanken, mts., Eur. — D11 22
Karazal see Qarazhal, Kaz. — E12 32
Karbalā', Iraq — C5 56
Kârböle, Swe. — E6 8
Karcag, Hung. — B7 26
Kardámaina, Grc. — G9 28
Kardeljevo, Cro. — G14 22
Kardítsa, Grc. — D4 28
Kärdla, Est. — G10 8
Kârdžali, Blg. — H12 26
Karelia see Karelija, state, Russia — D15 8
Karelia, hist. reg., Eur. — E14 8
Karelija, state, Russia — D15 8
Karelija see Karelija, hist. reg., Eur. — E14 8
Karel'skij Gorodok, Russia — B19 10
Karema, Tan. — F6 66
Karen, India — F7 46
Kåresuando, Swe. — B9 8
Kärevere, Est. — B9 10
Kargasok, Russia — C14 32
Kargat, Russia — C14 32
Kargil, India — A5 54
Kargopol', Russia — F18 8
Kariba, Zimb. — D4 68
Kariba Lake, res., Afr. — D4 68
Karibib, Nmb. — B2 70
Kariega, stm., S. Afr. — H6 70
Karimata, Kepulauan, is., Indon. — D6 50
Karimata, Selat, strt., Indon. — E6 50
Karīmganj, India — F14 54
Karīmnagar, India — B4 53
Karimunjawa, Kepulauan, is., Indon. — F7 50
Karimunjawa, Pulau, i., Indon. — F7 50
Karisimbi, vol., Afr. — E5 66
Karistos, Grc. — E7 28
Kariya, Japan — D10 40
Kārkal, India — E2 53
Karkaralinsk see Qarqaraly, Kaz. — E13 32
Karkar Island, i., Pap. N. Gui. — a4 79a
Karkonoski Park Narodowy, p.o.i., Pol. — F11 16
Karkük, Iraq — B5 56
Karleby see Kokkola, Fin. — E10 8
Karlino, Pol. — B11 16
Karl-Marx-Stadt see Chemnitz, Ger. — F8 16
Karlovac, Cro. — E12 22
Karlovo, Blg. — G11 26
Karlovy Vary, Czech Rep. — F8 16
Karlsborg, Swe. — D10 8
Karlsburg see Alba Iulia, Rom. — C10 26
Karlshamn, Swe. — H6 8
Karlskoga, Swe. — G6 8
Karlskrona, Swe. — H6 8
Karlsruhe, Ger. — G4 16
Karlstad, Swe. — G5 8
Karlstadt, Ger. — G5 16
Karluk, Ak., U.S. — E9 140
Karma, Bela. — H14 10
Karma, Niger — G5 64
Karmah an Nuzul, Sudan — D6 62
Karmāla, India — B2 53
Karmøy, i., Nor. — G1 8
Karnack, Tx., U.S. — E4 122
Karnāl, Il., U.S. — G9 120
Karnāl, India — D6 54
Karnāli, stm., Asia — D8 54
Karnāli, stm., Nepal — D8 54
Karnaphuli Reservoir, res., Bngl. — G14 54
Karnātaka, state, India — D2 53
Karnobat, Blg. — G13 26
Kärnten, state, Aus. — D10 22
Karoli, India — G7 54
Karonga, Mwi. — B5 68
Karoo National Park, p.o.i., S. Afr. — H6 70
Karoonda, Austl. — J2 76
Kárpathos, Grc. — D3 54
Kárpathos, i., Grc. — H10 28
Kárpathos, i., Grc. — H10 28
Karpats'ky Pryrodnyi Natsional'nyi Park, p.o.i., Ukr. — A11 26
Karpenísi, Grc. — E5 28
Karpogory, Russia — D21 8
Karpuzlu, Tur. — F10 28
Karratha, Austl. — D3 74
Karrats Fjord, b., Grnld. — C14 141
Kars, Tur. — A5 56
Karsantı, Tur. — A6 58
Karši, Uzb. — G11 32
Karsin, Pol. — C13 16
Karskoe more (Kara Sea), s., Russia — B10 30
Kartala, vol., Com. — C7 68
Kartaly, Russia — D10 32
Kartārpur, India — C5 54
Karthaus, Pa., U.S. — C7 114
Kartuzy, Pol. — B14 16
Karumba, Austl. — A3 76
Karungi, Swe. — C10 8
Karunjie, Austl. — C5 74
Karūr, India — F4 53
Karvār, India — D1 53
Karyés, Grc. — C6 28
Karymskoe, Russia — F11 34
Kasai (Cassai), stm., Afr. — G4 66
Kasama, D.R.C. — C5 66
Kasama, Japan — C13 40
Kasama, Zam. — C5 68
Kasane, Bots. — D3 68
Kasanga, Tan. — F6 66
Kasangulu, D.R.C. — E3 66
Kasaoka, Japan — E6 40
Kāsāragod, India — E2 53
Kasba, India — F11 54
Kasba Lake, l., Can. — C10 106
Kascjukoŭka, Bela. — H13 10
Kascjukovičy, Bela. — G14 10

Kaseda, Japan — H3 40
Kasempa, Zam. — C4 68
Kasenga, D.R.C. — G5 66
Kasenye, D.R.C. — D6 66
Kasese, D.R.C. — E5 66
Kasese, Ug. — D6 66
Kaset Sombun, Thai. — D5 48
Kāshān, Iran — C7 56
Kashgar see Kashi, China — B12 56
Kashi, China — B12 56
Kashihara, Japan — E8 40
Kashima, Japan — F3 40
Kashima-nada, s., Japan — C13 40
Kashing see Jiaxing, China — F9 42
Kāshīpur, India — D7 54
Kashiwazaki, Japan — B11 40
Kāshmar, Iran — B8 56
Kashmir, hist. reg., Asia — A3 46
Kasia, India — E9 54
Kasimbar, Indon. — D12 50
Kasimov, Russia — I19 8
Kašin, Russia — C20 10
Kāsipur, India — G11 54
Kasira, Russia — F21 10
Kasiruta, Pulau, i., Indon. — F8 44
Kasiskaia, stm., Il., U.S. — E9 120
Kaskinen, Fin. — E9 8
Kaslo, B.C., Can. — G13 138
Kasnja, Russia — E17 10
Kasongo, D.R.C. — E5 66
Kasongo-Lunda, D.R.C. — F3 66
Kásos, i., Grc. — H9 28
Kasota, Mn., U.S. — G5 118
Kaspijsk, Russia — F7 32
Kaspijskij, Russia — E7 32
Kaspijskoe more see Caspian Sea, s. — F7 32
Kasplja, stm., Eur. — E13 10
Kasr, Ra's, c., Afr. — D7 62
Kassab, Syria — C6 58
Kassala, Sudan — D7 62
Kassándra, Gulf of see Kassándras, Kólpos, b., Grc. — C6 28
Kassándra, Kólpos, b., Grc. — C6 28
Kassándras, Kólpos, b., Grc. — C6 28
Kassel, Ger. — E5 16
Kasserine, Tun. — B6 64
Kastamonu, Tur. — A3 56
Kastamonu, state, Tur. — A3 56
Kastélli, Grc. — H6 28
Kastoria, Grc. — C4 28
Kastoriás, Limni, l., Grc. — C4 28
Kastrákiou, Technití Limni, res., Grc. — C4 28
Kasugai, Japan — D9 40
Kasulu, Tan. — E6 66
Kasumiga-ura, l., Japan — C13 40
Kasungan, Indon. — E8 50
Kasūr, Pak. — C5 54
Kaszuby, hist. reg., Pol. — B13 16
Kataba, Zam. — D4 68
Katahdin, Mount, mtn., Me., U.S. — E7 110
Katako-Kombe, D.R.C. — E4 66
Katanga, hist. reg., D.R.C. — F4 66
Katanga, stm., Russia — C18 32
Katangi, India — G7 54
Katangli, Russia — F17 34
Katanning, Austl. — F3 74
Katchall Island, i., India — G7 46
Katepwa Beach, Sk., Can. — D10 124
Katerini, Grc. — C5 28
Kates Needle, mtn., N.A. — D4 106
Katete, Zam. — C5 68
Katha, Mya. — D8 46
Katherīna, Gebel, mtn., Egypt — J4 58
Katheríne, Austl. — B6 74
Katherine, stm., Austl. — B6 74
Katherine Creek, stm., Austl. — D4 76
Kāthiāwār Peninsula, pen., India — H3 54
Kathla, India — C6 54
Kāthmāṇḍau (Kathmandu), Nepal — E10 54
Kathmandu see Kāthmāṇḍau, Nepal — E10 54
Kathor, India — H4 54
Kathua, India — B5 54
Kati, Mali — G3 64
Katibas, stm., Malay. — C8 50
Katihār, India — F11 54
Katikati, N.Z. — C6 80
Katimik Lake, l., Mb., Can. — B14 124
Katiola, C.I. — H4 64
Katipunan, Phil. — F4 52
Kia Tiriti o Moana see Southern Alps, mts., N.Z. — F4 80
Katmai, Mount, vol., Ak., U.S. — E8 140
Káto Achaía, Grc. — E4 28
Kātol, India — H7 54
Katonah, Austl. — I8 76
Katowice, Pol. — F15 16
Katowice, state, Pol. — F15 16
Katrineholm, Swe. — G7 8
Katsina, Nig. — G6 64
Katsina Ala, stm., Afr. — H6 64
Katsuta, Japan — C13 40
Katsuura, Japan — D13 40
Katsuyama, Japan — C9 40
Katsuyama, Japan — D6 40
Kattakurgan, Uzb. — G11 32
Kattegat, strt., Eur. — H4 8
Katul, Jabal, mtn., Sudan — E5 62
Katun', stm., Russia — D15 32
Katunino, Russia — G21 8
Katwa, India — G11 54
Katwijk aan Zee, Neth. — B13 14
Katyn, Russia — F14 10
Katzenbuckel, mtn., Ger. — G5 16
Kaua'i, i., Hi., U.S. — b2 78a
Kauai Channel, strt., Hi., U.S. — b3 78a
Kaufbeuren, Ger. — I6 16
Kaukauna, Wi., U.S. — D1 112
Kaukauna, Wi., U.S. — D1 112
Kaukauveld, plat., Afr. — D3 68
Kaukonen, Fin. — C11 8
Kaulakahi Channel, strt., Hi., U.S. — b2 78a
Kaunakakai, Hi., U.S. — c4 78a
Kaunas, Lith. — F6 10
Kaura-Namoda, Nig. — G6 64
Kauti (Ghāghara), stm., Asia — D8 54
Kautokeino, Nor. — B10 8
Kau-ye Kyun, i., Mya. — G4 48
Kavača, Russia — D23 34
Kavadarci, Mac. — B5 28
Kavajë, Alb. — C13 24
Kavak, Tur. — D13 28
Kavaklidere, Tur. — F11 28
Kavali, India — D5 53
Kavalerovo, Russia — B11 38
Kavali, India — D4 53
Kavaratti, India — F3 46
Kavaratti Island, i., India — F3 46
Kāveri (Cauvery), stm., India — F3 53
Kāveri Falls, wtfl., India — E3 53
Kavieng, Pap. N. Gui. — a5 79a
Kavir, Dasht-e, des., Iran — C8 56
Kaw, C.I. — E12 128
Kawa, Mya. — D3 48
Kawagama Lake, l., On., Can. — C10 112
Kawagoe, Japan — D12 40
Kawaguchi, Japan — D12 40
Kawaihae, Hi., U.S. — b1 78a
Kawaikini, mtn., Hi., U.S. — a2 78a
Kawambwa, Zam. — B4 68
Kawanoe, Japan — E6 40

Kawardha, India — H8 54
Kawasaki, Japan — D12 40
Kawatana, Japan — F2 40
Kawde, Mya. — E3 48
Kaweenakumik Lake, l., Mb., Can. — B14 124
Kawhia Harbour, b., N.Z. — D6 80
Kawich Peak, mtn., Nv., U.S. — F9 134
Kawkareik, Mya. — D4 48
Kaw Lake, res., Ok., U.S. — E12 128
Kawlin, Mya. — D8 46
Kawnipi Lake, l., On., Can. — C7 118
Kawthaung, Mya. — H4 48
Kaxgar, stm., China — B12 56
Kaya, Burkina — G4 64
Kayah, state, Mya. — C3 48
Kayak Island, i., Ak., U.S. — E11 140
Kāyalpattinam, India — G4 53
Kayan, stm., Indon. — B10 50
Kāyankulam, India — G3 53
Kaycee, Wy., U.S. — D6 126
Kayenta, Az., U.S. — G6 132
Kayes, Mali — G2 64
Kayin, state, Mya. — D3 48
Kaymaz, Tur. — D14 28
Kayseri, Tur. — B3 56
Kaysville, Ut., U.S. — B4 132
Kayuadi, Pulau, i., Indon. — G12 50
Kayuagung, Indon. — E4 50
Kayumas, Indon. — G9 50
Kazačě, Russia — B16 34
Kazačinskoe, Russia — E7 34
Kazačinskoe, Russia — C19 32
Kazahskij melkosopočnik see Qazaqtyng usaqshoyghyghy, hills, Kaz. — D12 32
Kazakh Hills see Qazaqtyng usaqshoyghyghy, hills, Kaz. — E12 32
Kazakhstan, ctry., Asia — E10 32
Kazaki, Russia — H21 10
Kazan', Russia — C11 106
Kazan, stm., Can. — C7 32
Kazanlák, Blg. — G12 26
Kazanlı, Tur. — B5 58
Kazan-rettō, is., Japan — G18 30
Kazanskoe, Russia — C11 32
Kāzerūn, Iran — D7 56
Kazimbarka, Russia — B11 32
Kazimierza Wielka, Pol. — F16 16
Kazincbarcika, Hung. — A7 26
Kaziranga National Park, p.o.i., India — E14 54
Kazlų Rūda, Lith. — F6 10
Kaztalovka, Kaz. — E7 32
Kazula, Moz. — D5 68
Kazym, Russia — B11 32
Kazym, stm., Russia — B11 32
Kazy, stm., Russia — D16 32
Kbal Dâmrei, Camb. — E7 48
Kdyně, Czech Rep. — G9 16
Kéa, Grc. — F7 28
Kéa, i., Grc. — F7 28
Keahole Point, c., Hi., U.S. — d5 78a
Kealaikahiki Channel, strt., Hi., U.S. — c5 78a
Kealapana Point, c., Hi., U.S. — c4 78a
Kearns Canyon, Az., U.S. — H6 132
Kearney, Mo., U.S. — E3 120
Kearney, Ne., U.S. — G13 126
Kearns, Ut., U.S. — C4 132
Kearny, Az., U.S. — J6 132
Keban Baraji, res., Tur. — B4 56
Keban Reservoir see Keban Barajı, res., Tur. — B4 56
Kebbi, stm., Afr. — G7 64
Kebnekaise, mtn., Swe. — B8 8
K'ebrī Dehar, Eth. — F8 62
Kech, stm., Pak. — D9 56
Kechika, stm., B.C., Can. — D5 106
Keçiborlu, Tur. — F13 28
Kecskemét, Hung. — C6 26
Kedah, state, Malay. — J5 48
Kédainiai, Lith. — E6 10
Kediri, Indon. — G8 50
Kedon, Russia — D20 34
Kédougou, Sen. — G2 64
Keele, stm., N.T., Can. — C5 106
Keele Peak, mtn., Yk., Can. — C4 106
Keeler, Ca., U.S. — G8 134
Keeling Islands see Cocos Islands, dep., Oc. — K12 142
Keelung see Chilung, Tai. — I9 42
Keene, Ky., U.S. — G13 120
Keene, N.H., U.S. — B13 114
Keene, Tx., U.S. — B10 130
Keeney Knob, mtn., W.V., U.S. — G5 114
Keetmanshoop, Nmb. — E4 70
Keetwatin, On., Can. — B4 118
Keewatin, Mn., U.S. — D5 118
Kefallonía, i., Grc. — E3 28
Kefamenanu, Indon. — G7 44
Kefar Naḥum (Capernaum), sci., Isr. — F6 58
Kefar Sava, Isr. — F5 58
Keffi, Nig. — H6 64
Keflavík, Ice. — k28 8a
Ke Ga, Mui, c., Viet. — F9 48
Kegalla, Sri L. — H5 53
Keg River, Ab., Can. — D7 106
Kegums, Lat. — D7 10
Ke-hsi Mānsām, Mya. — B3 48
Keighley, Eng., U.K. — H10 12
Keila, Est. — G11 8
Keimoes, S. Afr. — F5 70
Keith, Scot., U.K. — D9 12
Keith, Arm b., N.T., Can. — B6 106
Keithley Creek, B.C., Can. — D9 138
Keithsburg, Il., U.S. — J8 118
Keiyasi, Fiji — p18 79e
Keizer, Or., U.S. — F3 136
Kejimkujik National Park, p.o.i., N.S., Can. — F11 110
Keka, Mya., mts. — E2 122
Kekaha, Hi., U.S. — C17 8
Kékes, mtn., Hung. — B7 26
Kekri, India — E5 54
K'elafo, Eth. — F8 62
Kelai, stm., Indon. — C10 50
Kelang, Malay. — K5 48
Kelani-Namoda, Nig. — G6 64
Kelantan, state, Malay. — J6 48
Kelantan, stm., Malay. — J6 48
Kelapa, Indon. — D4 50
Kelberg, Ger. — F2 16
Kélé, Congo — E2 66
Kelheim, Ger. — H7 16
Kelibia, Tun. — H5 24
Kéllé, Congo — E2 66
Kellerberrin, Austl. — F3 74
Kellett, Cape, c., N.T., Can. — B14 140
Kellett, Cape, c., N.T., Can. — B14 140
Kelloselkä, Fin. — C13 8
Kellogg, Id., U.S. — C10 136
Kellogg, Mn., U.S. — G6 118
Kelokedalan, Indon. — D12 50
Kelowna, B.C., Can. — G11 138
Kelsey Bay, B.C., Can. — F4 138
Kelso, Scot., U.K. — F10 12
Kelso, Wa., U.S. — D4 136
Keluang, Malay. — K6 48
Kelvington, Sk., Can. — B10 124
Kelvin Island, i., On., Can. — B10 118
Kem', Russia — D16 8

Kem', stm., Russia — D15 8
Kemano, B.C., Can. — C2 138
Kemena, stm., Malay. — B8 50
Kemer, Tur. — F13 28
Kemer Baraji, res., Tur. — F11 28
Kemerhisar, Tur. — A5 58
Kemerovo, Russia — C15 32
Kemi, Fin. — D11 8
Kemijärvi, Fin. — C12 8
Kemijärvi, l., Fin. — C12 8
Kemijoki, stm., Fin. — C12 8
Kemmerer, Wy., U.S. — B6 132
Kemmuna (Comino), i., Malta — H8 24
Kemnath, Ger. — G7 16
Kemp, Tx., U.S. — E2 122
Kemp, Lake, res., Tx., U.S. — H9 128
Kempner, Tx., U.S. — C9 130
Kempsey, Austl. — H9 76
Kempt, Lac, l., Qc., Can. — F16 106
Kempten, Ger. — I6 16
Kemptville, On., Can. — C14 112
Kemujan, Pulau, i., Indon. — F7 50
Ken, stm., India — F8 54
Kenai, Ak., U.S. — D9 140
Kenai Mountains, mts., Ak., U.S. — E9 140
Kenai Peninsula, pen., Ak., U.S. — E9 140
Kenansville, Fl., U.S. — I5 116
Kenansville, N.C., U.S. — B7 116
Kenbridge, Va., U.S. — H7 114
Kendal, Sk., Can. — D10 124
Kendal, Indon. — G7 50
Kendal, Eng., U.K. — G10 12
Kendall, Austl. — H9 76
Kendall, Fl., U.S. — K5 116
Kendall, Wi., U.S. — H8 118
Kendall, Cape, c., Nu., Can. — C13 106
Kendari, Indon. — F7 44
Kendawangan, Indon. — E7 50
Kendrāparha, India — H11 54
Kendrick, Fl., U.S. — H3 116
Kendrick, Id., U.S. — D10 136
Kendujhargarh, India — H10 54
Kenedy, Tx., U.S. — F10 130
Kenema, S.L. — H2 64
Kenga, Russia — C14 32
Kenge, D.R.C. — E3 66
Keng Tung, Mya. — B4 48
Kenhardt, S. Afr. — F5 70
Kenilworth, Ut., U.S. — D6 132
Kénitra, Mor. — C3 64
Kenly, N.C., U.S. — A7 116
Kenmare, Ire. — J3 12
Kenmare, N.D., U.S. — F11 124
Kenmore, N.Y., U.S. — F8 112
Kennebec, S.D., U.S. — D13 126
Kennebecasis Bay, b., N.B., Can. — E11 110
Kennebunk, Me., U.S. — G6 110
Kennedy, Cape see Canaveral, Cape, c., Fl., U.S. — H5 116
Kennedy, Mount, mtn., B.C., Can. — F5 138
Kennedy, Mount, mtn., Yk., Can. — C3 106
Kennedy Lake, l., B.C., Can. — G5 138
Kenner, La., U.S. — G8 122
Kennetcook, N.S., Can. — E13 110
Kennett, Mo., U.S. — H7 120
Kennewick, Wa., U.S. — D7 136
Kenney Dam, dam, B.C., Can. — C6 138
Kennydale, N.A. — E11 110
Kenmen, China — N.B., Can. — E11 110
Kenogami, stm., On., Can. — E13 106
Kénogami, Lac, l., Qc., Can. — B5 110
Keno Hill, Yk., Can. — C3 106
Kenora, On., Can. — B4 118
Kenosha, Wi., U.S. — F2 112
Kenozero, ozero, l., Russia — E18 8
Kensal, N.D., U.S. — G15 124
Kensett, Ar., U.S. — B7 122
Kensington, Ks., U.S. — B9 128
Kensington Park, Fl., U.S. — I3 116
Kent, Oh., U.S. — C4 114
Kent, Wa., U.S. — C4 136
Kentaū, Kaz. — F11 32
Kentland, In., U.S. — H2 112
Kenton, Mi., U.S. — E10 118
Kenton, Tn., U.S. — H8 120
Kent Peninsula, pen., Nu., Can. — B9 106
Kentriki Makedonía, state, Grc. — C6 28
Kentucky, state, U.S. — G12 120
Kentucky, stm., Ky., U.S. — F13 120
Kentucky, Middle Fork, stm., Ky., U.S. — G2 114
Kentucky, North Fork, stm., Ky., U.S. — H9 120
Kentucky Lake, res., U.S. — H9 120
Kentwood, La., U.S. — G8 122
Kenya, ctry., Afr. — D7 66
Kenya, Mount see Kirinyaga, mtn., Kenya — E7 66
Kenyon, Mn., U.S. — G6 118
Keokuk, Ia., U.S. — D6 120
Keoladeo National Park, p.o.i., India — E6 54
Keokuk, Ia., U.S. — D6 120
Keosauqua, Ia., U.S. — D5 120
Keota, Ia., U.S. — C6 120
Keota, Ok., U.S. — B4 122
Keowee, Lake, res., S.C., U.S. — B2 116
Kepi, Indon. — G10 44
Keppel Bay, b., Austl. — D8 76
Kepno, Pol. — E13 16
Kepsut, Tur. — D11 28
Kerala, state, India — F3 53
Keramadoo, mtn., Palau — f8 78b
Keramian, Pulau, i., Indon. — F9 50
Kerang, Austl. — J4 76
Keravat, Pap. N. Gui. — a5 79a
Kerch, Ukr. — E5 32
Kerc, mys, c., Russia — D18 34
Kerema, Pap. N. Gui. — b4 79a
Keremeos, B.C., Can. — G11 138
Keren, Erit. — D7 62
Kerens, Tx., U.S. — E2 122
Kerenyi, ozero, l., Russia — C15 8
Kerewan, Gam. — G1 64
Kerguélen, Îles, is., Ind. Oc. — J17 4
Kerguelen Plateau, unds. — O10 142
Kerí, Grc. — F3 28
Kericho, Kenya — E7 66
Kerinci, Gunung, vol., Indon. — D2 50
Keriya, Îles, is., Tur. — F2 50
Kerki, Turkmen. — B10 56
Kerkrade, Neth. — F2 16
Kérkyra (Corfu), Grc. — D2 28
Kérkyra (Corfu), i., Grc. — D2 28
Kermadec Islands, is., N.Z. — F9 72
Kermadec Ridge, unds. — L19 142
Kermadec Trench, unds. — M21 142
Kermān, Iran — C8 56
Kermānshāh (Bākhtarān), Iran — C6 56
Kerme, Gulf of see Gökova Körfezi, b., Tur. — G10 28
Kermit, Tx., U.S. — C4 130
Kern, stm., Ca., U.S. — H7 134

Kern – Komsomol'sk I • 29

Name — Map Ref. — Page

Kern, South Fork, stm., Ca., U.S. H7 134
Kernersville, N.C., U.S. H5 114
Kernville, Ca., U.S. H7 134
Kérouané, Gui. H3 64
Kerrobert, Sk., Can. C4 124
Kerrville, Tx., U.S. D8 130
Kerry, state, Ire. I2 12
Kerry Head, c., Ire. I2 12
Kershaw, S.C., U.S. B5 116
Kersley, B.C., Can. D8 138
Kertamulia, Indon. D6 50
Kerulen, stm., Asia B7 36
Kesagami Lake, l., On., Can. E14 106
Keşan, Tur. C9 28
Kesennuma, Japan E14 38
Keshan, China B10 36
Keshod, India H3 54
Kes'ma, Russia B20 10
Kesova Gora, Russia C20 10
Kestell, S. Afr. F9 70
Keswick, Eng., U.K. G9 12
Keszthely, Hung. C4 26
Ket', stm., Russia C14 32
Keta, Ghana H5 64
Keta, ozero, l., Russia C6 34
Ketapang, Indon. D6 50
Ketapang, Indon. F4 50
Ketchikan, Ak., U.S. E13 140
Ketchum, Id., U.S. G12 136
Kete-Krachi, Ghana H4 64
Ketoj, ostrov, i., Russia G19 34
Kętrzyn, Pol. B17 16
Kettering, Eng., U.K. I12 12
Kettering, Oh., U.S. E1 114
Kettle, stm., N.A. H12 138
Kettle Falls, Wa., U.S. B8 136
Kęty, Pol. G15 16
Keudeteunom, Indon. J2 48
Keuka Lake, l., N.Y., U.S. B8 114
Keukenhof, misc. cult., Neth. B13 14
Keul', Russia C18 32
Kevelaer, Ger. E2 16
Kevin, Mt., U.S. B14 136
Kew, T/C. Is. A12 102
Kewanee, Il., U.S. C7 120
Kewaunee, Wi., U.S. D2 112
Keweenaw Bay, b., Mi., U.S. E10 118
Keweenaw Peninsula, pen., Mi., U.S. D11 118
Keweenaw Point, c., Mi., U.S. D11 118
Key, Lough, l., Ire. G4 12
Keya Paha, stm., U.S. E13 126
Keyes, Ok., U.S. E6 128
Keyhole Reservoir, res., Wy., U.S. C8 126
Key Largo, Fl., U.S. K5 116
Key Largo, i., Fl., U.S. K5 116
Keyser, W.V., U.S. E7 114
Keystone, S.D., U.S. D9 126
Keystone, W.V., U.S. G4 114
Keystone Lake, res., Ok., U.S. A2 122
Keystone Peak, mtn., Az., U.S. L5 132
Keysville, Va., U.S. G7 114
Keytesville, Mo., U.S. E5 120
Key West, Fl., U.S. L4 116
Kezi, Zimb. B9 70
Kežma, Russia C18 32
Kežmarok, Slov. G16 16
Kgalagadi, state, Bots. D5 70
Kgatleng, state, Bots. D8 70
Khadki, India B1 53
Khadzhybeis'kyi lyman, l., Ukr. C17 26
Khagaria, India F11 54
Khairāgarh, India H8 54
Khairpur, Pak. E2 54
Khairpur, Pak. D4 54
Khajrāho, India F8 54
Khakassia see Hakasija, state, Russia D16 32
Kha Khaeng, stm., Thai. E4 48
Khakhea, Bots. D6 70
Khalatse, India A6 54
Khālidī, Khirbat al-, sci., Jord. I6 58
Khalîya, Gebel, mtn., Egypt I3 58
Khalūf, Oman E8 56
Khambhāliya, India G2 54
Khambhāt, India G4 54
Khambhāt, Gulf of, b., India H3 54
Khāmgaon, India H6 54
Khāmis, Ash-Shallāl al- (Fifth Cataract), wtfl., Sudan D6 62
Khamīs Mushayṭ, Sau. Ar. F5 56
Khammam, India C5 53
Khan, stm., Laos C6 48
Khan, stm., Nmb. C2 70
Khānābād, Afg. B10 56
Khān Abū Shāmāt, Syria E7 58
Khancoban, Austl. K7 76
Khandela, India E5 54
Khandwa, India H6 54
Khānewāl, Pak. C3 54
Khāngarh, Pak. D3 54
Khangchendzonga National Park, p.o.i., India E12 54
Khangkhai, Laos C6 48
Khania, Gulf of see Chanión, Kólpos, b., Grc. H6 28
Khanka, Lake, l., Asia B10 38
Khanna, India C6 54
Khānpur, Pak. D3 54
Khansiir, Raas, c., Som. B9 66
Khantaū, Kaz. F12 32
Khān Yūnus, Gaza G5 58
Khao Laem Reservoir, res., Thai. E4 48
Khao Sok National Park, p.o.i., Thai. H4 48
Khao Yoi, Thai. F4 48
Kharagpur, India G11 54
Khārān, Pak. D10 56
Kharāyij, Sabkhat al-, l., Syria C8 58
Kharg Island see Khārk, Jazīreh-ye, i., Iran D7 56
Khargon, India H5 54
Khāriān Cantonment, Pak. B4 54
Khārk, Jazīreh-ye, i., Iran D7 56
Kharkiv, Ukr. D5 32
Kharmanli *see* Harmanli, Blg. H12 26
Khartoum *see* Al-Kharṭūm, Sudan D6 62
Khartoum North *see* Al-Kharṭām Baḥrī, Sudan D6 62
Khasebake, Bots. B7 70
Khāsh, Afg. C9 56
Khāsh, Iran D9 56
Khashm al-Qirbah, Sudan D7 62
Khaskovo *see* Haskovo, Blg. H12 26
Khatanga *see* Hatanga, Russia B9 34
Khatanga see Hatanga, stm., Russia B9 34
Khatauli, India D6 54
Khatt, Oued al, stm., W. Sah. D2 64
Khavast *see* Havast, Uzb. F11 32
Khawsa, Mya. E3 48
Khayung, stm., Thai. E7 48
Khed, India C1 53
Kheil, Katîb el-, sand, Egypt H3 58
Khemis el Khechna, Alg. H14 20
Khemis Melyana, Alg. H13 20
Khemmarat, Thai. D7 48
Khenchla, Alg. B6 64
Khenifra, Mor. C3 64
Kherson, Ukr. F15 6
Kheta see Heta, stm., Russia B8 34
Khetia, India H5 54
Khimki *see* Himki, Russia E20 10
Khipro, Pak. F2 54
Khisfīn, Golan F6 58
Khiva *see* Hiva, Uzb. F10 32
Khlong Thom, Thai. I4 48
Khlung, Thai. F6 48
Khok Kloi, Thai. H4 48
Khok Samrong, Thai. E5 48
Kholm, Afg. B10 56
Khomas, state, Nmb. C3 70
Khomeynīshahr, Iran C7 56
Khondmāl Hills, hills, India H10 54
Khong see Mekong, stm., Asia E10 46
Khon Kaen, Thai. D6 48
Khordha, India H10 54
Khorixas, Nmb. B2 70
Khorog *see* Horog, Taj. B11 56
Khorramābād, Iran C6 56
Khorramshahr, Iran C6 56
Khotyn, Ukr. A13 26
Khouribga, Mor. C3 64
Khowai, India F13 54
Khowst, Afg. C10 56
Khrisokhoús, Kólpos, b., Cyp. C3 58
Khuis, Bots. E5 70
Khuīyāla, India E3 54
Khulna, Bngl. G12 54
Khulna, state, Bngl. G12 54
Khun Tan, Doi, mtn., Thai. C4 48
Khunti, India G10 54
Khurai, India F7 54
Khurja, India D6 54
Khushāb, Pak. B4 54
Khust, Ukr. A10 26
Khuzdār, Pak. D10 56
Khvoy, Iran B6 56
Khwae Noi, stm., Thai. E4 48
Khyber Pass, p., Asia A3 54
Khyriv, Ukr. G18 16
Kiama, Austl. J8 76
Kiama, D.R.C. F3 66
Kiamba, Phil. H5 52
Kiambi, D.R.C. F5 66
Kiamichi, stm., Ok., U.S. C3 122
Kiamusze *see* Jiamusi, China B11 36
Kian *see* Ji'an, China H6 42
Kiangarow, Mount, mtn., Austl. F8 76
Kiang-si see Jiangxi, state, China H6 42
Kiangsi see Jiangxi, state, China H6 42
Kiang-sou see Jiangsu, state, China E8 42
Kiangsu see Jiangsu, state, China E8 42
Kiaohsien *see* Jiaoxian, China C8 42
Kibangou, Congo E2 66
Kibombo, D.R.C. E5 66
Kibondo, Tan. E6 66
Kibre Mengist, Eth. F7 62
Kıbrıs see Cyprus, ctry., Asia C4 58
Kıbrısçık, Tur. C14 28
Kibuye, Rw. E5 66
Kičevo, Mac. B3 28
Kickapoo, stm., Wi., U.S. H8 118
Kicking Horse Pass, p., Can. E14 138
Kidal, Mali F5 64
Kidapawan, Phil. G5 52
Kidatu, Tan. F7 66
Kidderminster, Eng., U.K. I10 12
Kidira, Sen. G2 64
Kidnappers, Cape, c., N.Z. D7 80
Kidston, Austl. B5 76
Kiefersfelden, Ger. I8 16
Kiel, Ger. B6 16
Kiel, Wi., U.S. H10 118
Kiel Bay see Kieler Bucht, b., Ger. B6 16
Kiel Canal see Nord-Ostsee-Kanal, can., Ger. B5 16
Kielce, Pol. F16 16
Kielce, state, Pol. F16 16
Kieler Bucht, b., Ger. B6 16
Kiester, Mn., U.S. H5 118
Kiev *see* Kyïv, Ukr. D4 32
Kīevka, Kaz. D12 32
Kiev Reservoir see Kyïvs'ke vodoskhovyshche, res., Ukr. D4 32
Kiffa, Maur. F2 64
Kifisiá, Grc. E6 28
Kigali, Rw. E6 66
Kigoma, Tan. E5 66
Kihčik, Russia F20 34
Kīhei, Hi., U.S. c5 78a
Kihniö, Fin. E10 8
Kihnu, i., Est. G10 8
Kii-hantō, pen., Japan F8 40
Kīik, Kaz. E12 32
Kii-suidō, strt., Japan F7 40
Kikerino, Russia A12 10
Kikinda, Serb. D7 26
Kikládes (Cyclades), is., Grc. F7 28
Kikori, Pap. N. Gui. b3 79a
Kikori, stm., Pap. N. Gui. b3 79a
Kikuchi, Japan G3 40
Kikwit, D.R.C. F3 66
Kīlakkarai, India G4 53
Kilauea, Hi., U.S. a2 78a
Kīlauea Crater, crat., Hi., U.S. d6 78a
Kılbasan, Tur. A4 58
Kilbuck Mountains, mts., Ak., U.S. D8 140
Kilchu-ŭp, Kor., N. D8 38
Kilcoy, Austl. F9 76
Kildare, state, Ire. H6 12
Kildare, Cape, c., P.E., Can. D13 110
Kildurk, Austl. C5 74
Kilembe, D.R.C. F3 66
Kilgore, Tx., U.S. E4 122
Kilian Island, i., Nu., Can. B18 140
Kılıç, Tur. C12 28
Kiliia, Ukr. D16 26
Kilikollūr, India G3 53
Kilimanjaro, mtn., Tan. E7 66
Kilimli, Tur. B14 28
Kilindoni, Tan. F7 66
Kilis, Tur. B8 58
Kilkee, Ire. I3 12
Kilkenny, Ire. I5 12
Kilkenny, state, Ire. I5 12
Kilkís, Grc. C5 28
Killaloe, Ire. I4 12
Killaloe Station, On., Can. C12 112
Killam, Ab., Can. D19 138
Killarney, Austl. G9 76
Killarney, Mb., Can. E14 124
Killarney, On., Can. C8 112
Killarney, Ire. I3 12
Killdeer, N.D., U.S. G11 124
Killeen, Tx., U.S. C10 130
Killen, Al., U.S. C11 122
Killington Peak, mtn., Vt., U.S. G4 110
Killiniq Island, i., Can. E13 141
Killybegs, Ire. G4 12
Kilmarnock, Scot., U.K. F8 12
Kilmarnock, Va., U.S. G9 114
Kilmore, Austl. K5 76
Kilo, Indon. H11 50
Kilombero, stm., Tan. F7 66
Kilomines, D.R.C. D5 66
Kilosa, Tan. F7 66
Kilrush, Ire. I3 12
Kilttān Island, i., India F3 46
Kilwa, D.R.C. F5 66
Kilwa Kivinje, Tan. F7 66
Kim, Co., U.S. D5 128
Kimba, Austl. F7 74
Kimball, Ne., U.S. F9 126
Kimball, S.D., U.S. D13 126
Kimbe Bay, b., Pap. N. Gui. b5 79a
Kimberley, B.C., Can. G15 138
Kimberley, S. Afr. F7 70
Kimberley Downs, Austl. C4 74
Kimberley Plateau, plat., Austl. C5 74
Kimberling City, Mo., U.S. H4 120
Kimberly, Id., U.S. H12 136
Kimberly, Wi., U.S. G10 118
Kimch'aek, Kor., N. D8 38
Kimch'ŏn, Kor., S. F8 38
Kimhae, Kor., S. D1 40
Kimito, Fin. F10 8
Kim-me-ni-oli Wash, stm., N.M., U.S. H8 132
Kimmirut, Nu., Can. C17 106
Kímolos, i., Grc. G7 28
Kimovsk, Russia F21 10
Kimpō-zan, mtn., Japan D11 40
Kimry, Russia D20 10
Kinabalu, Gunong (Kinabalu, Mount), mtn., Malay. G1 52
Kinabalu National Park, p.o.i., Malay. H1 52
Kinabatangan, stm., Malay. H2 52
Kinbasket Lake, res., B.C., Can. D12 138
Kincaid, Sk., Can. E6 124
Kincardine, On., Can. D8 112
Kinchafoonee Creek, stm., Ga., U.S. F14 122
Kinchega National Park, p.o.i., Austl. I4 76
Kinda, D.R.C. F4 66
Kinde, Mi., U.S. E7 112
Kinder, La., U.S. G6 122
Kindersley, Sk., Can. C4 124
Kindia, Gui. G2 64
Kindu, D.R.C. E5 66
Kinešma, Russia H19 8
King, N.C., U.S. H5 114
King and Queen Court House, Va., U.S. G9 114
Kingaok (Bathurst Inlet), Nu., Can. B9 106
Kingaroy, Austl. F8 76
King City, On., Can. E10 112
King City, Ca., U.S. G4 134
Kingfield, Me., U.S. F6 110
Kingfisher, Ok., U.S. F10 128
King George, Va., U.S. F8 114
King George, Mount, mtn., B.C., Can. F15 138
King George Islands, is., Nu., Can. D14 106
King George Sound, strt., Austl. G3 74
King Hill, Id., U.S. G11 136
Kingisepp, Russia A11 10
King Island, i., Austl. m12 77a
King Island, i., B.C., Can. D3 138
King Leopold Ranges, mts., Austl. C4 74
Kingman, Az., U.S. H2 132
Kingman, Ks., U.S. D10 128
Kingman Reef, rf., Oc. C10 72
King Mountain, mtn., Or., U.S. H3 136
Kingombe, D.R.C. E5 66
Kingoonya, Austl. F7 74
King Peak, mtn., Ca., U.S. C1 134
Kings, stm., Ca., U.S. G6 134
Kings Beach, Ca., U.S. D5 134
Kingsbridge, Eng., U.K. K9 12
Kingsburg, Ca., U.S. G6 134
Kings Canyon National Park, p.o.i., Ca., U.S. G7 134
Kingsford, Mi., U.S. C1 112
Kingshill, V.I.U.S. h10 104c
Kingsland, Ar., U.S. D6 122
Kingsland, Ga., U.S. F4 116
Kingsley, S. Afr. E10 70
Kingsley, Ia., U.S. B2 120
Kingsley, Mi., U.S. D4 112
Kingsley Dam, dam, Ne., U.S. F11 126
King's Lynn, Eng., U.K. I13 12
Kings Mountain, N.C., U.S. A4 116
King Solomon's Mines see Mikhrot Timna', hist., Isr. I5 58
King Sound, strt., Austl. C4 74
Kings Peak, mtn., Ut., U.S. C6 132
Kingsport, Tn., U.S. H3 114
Kingston, N.S., Can. E11 110
Kingston, On., Can. D13 112
Kingston, Jam. i14 104d
Kingston, Norf. I. y25 78i
Kingston, N.Z. G3 80
Kingston, Ga., U.S. C14 122
Kingston, Mo., U.S. E3 120
Kingston, N.Y., U.S. C11 114
Kingston, Ok., U.S. C2 122
Kingston, Pa., U.S. C9 114
Kingston, Tn., U.S. I13 120
Kingston Southeast, Austl. K2 76
Kingston upon Hull, Eng., U.K. H12 12
Kingston upon Thames, Eng., U.K. J12 12
Kingstown, St. Vin. o11 105e
Kingstree, S.C., U.S. C6 116
Kingsville, On., Can. G7 112
Kingsville, Tx., U.S. G10 130
Kingtechen *see* Jingdezhen, China G7 42
King William Island, i., Nu., Can. B11 106
King William's Town, S. Afr. H8 70
Kinhwa *see* Jinhua, China G8 42
Kınık, Tur. D10 28
Kinira, stm., S. Afr. G9 70
Kinistino, Sk., Can. B9 124
Kinkala, Congo E2 66
Kinlochleven, Scot., U.K. E8 12
Kinnaird Head, c., Scot., U.K. D10 12
Kinneret, Yam (Galilee, Sea of), l., Isr. F6 58
Kinngait (Cape Dorset), Nu., Can. C15 106
Kinosaki, Japan D7 40
Kinpoku-san, mtn., Japan A11 40
Kinross, Scot., U.K. E9 12
Kinsale, Monts. D3 105a
Kinsale, Old Head of, c., Ire. J4 12
Kinsarvik, Nor. F2 8
Kinshasa (Léopoldville), D.R.C. E3 66
Kinsley, Ks., U.S. D9 128
Kinsman, Oh., U.S. C5 114
Kinston, N.C., U.S. A8 116
Kintampo, Ghana H4 64
Kintyre, pen., Scot., U.K. F7 12
Kintyre, Mull of, c., Scot., U.K. F7 12
Kinuseo Falls, wtfl., B.C., Can. B9 138
Kinuso, Ab., Can. A15 138
Kinyangiri, Tan. E6 66
Kinyeti, mtn., Sudan G6 62
Kinzia, D.R.C. E3 66
Kinzua, Or., U.S. E7 136
Kinzua Dam, dam, Pa., U.S. C6 114
Kiowa, Co., U.S. B4 128
Kiowa, Ok., U.S. C3 122
Kiowa Creek, stm., Co., U.S. A4 128
Kipawa, stm., Qc., Can. B11 112
Kipawa, Lac, res., Qc., Can. A10 112
Kipembawe, Tan. F6 66
Kipengere Range, mts., Tan. F6 66
Kipili, Tan. F6 66
Kipini, Kenya E8 66
Kipling, Sk., Can. D11 124
Kipnuk, Ak., U.S. E7 140
Kipushi, D.R.C. G5 66
Kirakira, Sol. Is. f9 79b
Kirandul, India B5 53
Kirau̱sk, Bela. G12 10
Kirazlı, Tur. C9 28
Kirbla, Est. B6 10
Kirchberg, Ger. G5 16
Kirchmöser, Ger. D8 16
Kireevsk, Russia G20 10
Kirejkovo, Russia G18 10
Kirenga, stm., Russia C19 32
Kirensk, Russia C19 32
Kirghizia see Kyrgyzstan, ctry., Asia F12 32
Kirgiz Range, mts., Asia F12 32
Kirgiz Soviet Socialist Republic see Kyrgyzstan, ctry., Asia F12 32
Kiri, D.R.C. E3 66
Kiribati, ctry., Oc. D9 72
Kırıkhan, Tur. B7 58
Kırıkkale, Tur. B3 56
Kirillovo, Russia H21 8
Kirin *see* Jilin, China C7 38
Kirin see Jilin, state, China C10 36
Kirinyaga (Kenya, Mount), mtn., Kenya E7 66
Kirishima-Yaku-kokuritsu-kōen, p.o.i., Japan H3 40
Kirishima-yama, vol., Japan H3 40
Kiriši, Russia A15 10
Kiritimati (Christmas Island), at., Kir. C11 72
Kiriwina Islands (Trobriand Islands), is., Pap. N. Gui. b5 79a
Kırka, Tur. D13 28
Kırkağaç, Tur. D10 28
Kirkcaldy, Scot., U.K. E9 12
Kirkcudbright, Scot., U.K. G8 12
Kirkenes, Nor. B14 8
Kirkland, Il., U.S. B9 120
Kirkland, Tx., U.S. G8 128
Kirkland, Wa., U.S. C4 136
Kirkland Lake, On., Can. F14 106
Kırklareli, Tur. B10 28
Kırklareli, state, Tur. B10 28
Kirklin, In., U.S. H3 112
Kirkpatrick, Mount, mtn., Ant. D21 81
Kirksville, Mo., U.S. D5 120
Kirkwall, Scot., U.K. B9 12
Kirkwood, S. Afr. H7 70
Kirkwood, Mo., U.S. F7 120
Kirmir, stm., Tur. C15 28
Kirn, Ger. G3 16
Kirov, Russia F17 10
Kirov, Russia C7 32
Kirovakan *see* Vanadzor, Arm. A5 56
Kirovohrad, Ukr. E4 32
Kirovohrad, co., Ukr. A17 26
Kirovsk, Russia C15 8
Kirovsk, Turkmen. B9 56
Kirovskaja oblast', co., Russia F22 8
Kirovskij, Russia F20 34
Kirovskij, Russia B10 38
Kīrovskīy, Kaz. F13 32
Kirriemuir, Scot., U.K. E9 12
Kirs, Russia C8 32
Kirsanov, Russia D6 32
Kırşehir, Tur. B3 56
Kīrthar Range, mts., Pak. D10 56
Kirtland, N.M., U.S. G8 132
Kiruna, Swe. C8 8
Kirundu, D.R.C. E5 66
Kirwin, Ks., U.S. B9 128
Kiryū, Japan C12 40
Kiržač, Russia D21 10
Kisa, Swe. G6 8
Kisangani (Stanleyville), D.R.C. D5 66
Kisar, Pulau, i., Indon. G8 44
Kisaran, Indon. B1 50
Kisarazu, Japan D12 40
Kisbey, Sk., Can. E11 124
Kiselëvsk, Russia D15 32
Kīsh, Jazīreh-ye, i., Iran D7 56
Kishanganj, India E11 54
Kishangarh, India E3 54
Kishangarh Bās, India E5 54
Kishi, Nig. H5 64
Kishinev *see* Chișinău, Mol. B15 26
Kishiwada, Japan E8 40
Kishorganj, Bngl. F13 54
Kisii, Kenya E6 66
Kisiju, Tan. F7 66
Kisiwada *see* Kishiwada, Japan E8 40
Kiska Island, i., Ak., U.S. g22 140a
Kiskatinaw, stm., B.C., Can. A10 138
Kiska Volcano, vol., Ak., U.S. g22 140a
Kiskörei-viztároló, res., Hung. B7 26
Kiskőrös, Hung. C6 26
Kiskunfélegyháza, Hung. C6 26
Kiskunhalas, Hung. C6 26
Kiskunmajsa, Hung. C6 26
Kiskunsági Nemzeti Park, p.o.i., Hung. C6 26
Kislovodsk, Russia F6 32
Kismaayo, Som. E8 66
Kiso, stm., Japan D9 40
Kiso-sammyaku, mts., Japan D10 40
Kissidougou, Gui. H2 64
Kissimmee, Fl., U.S. H4 116
Kissimmee, stm., Fl., U.S. I4 116
Kissimmee, Lake, l., Fl., U.S. I4 116
Kississing Lake, l., Mb., Can. D10 106
Kisújszállás, Hung. B7 26
Kisuki, Japan D5 40
Kisumu, Kenya E6 66
Kisvárda, Hung. A9 26
Kita, Mali G3 64
Kitaa see Vestgrønland, state, Grnld. D16 141
Kitaibaraki, Japan C13 40
Kitakami, stm., Japan E14 38
Kitakata, Japan B12 40
Kitakyūshū, Japan F3 40
Kitale, Kenya D7 66
Kitami, Japan C15 38
Kitangiri, Lake, l., Tan. E6 66
Kitchener, On., Can. E9 112
Kithārah, Khirbat, sci., Jord. I6 58
Kitimat, B.C., Can. B2 138
Kitimat Ranges, mts., B.C., Can. C2 138
Kitinen, stm., Fin. C12 8
Kitíou, Akrotírion, c., Cyp. D4 58
Kitridge Point, c., Barb. n9 105d
Kitsuki, Japan F4 40
Kittanning, Pa., U.S. D6 114
Kittitas, Wa., U.S. D6 136
Kitt Peak National Observatory, sci., Az., U.S. K5 132
Kitui, Kenya E7 66
Kitunda, Tan. F6 66
Kitwanga, B.C., Can. A2 138
Kitwe, Zam. C4 68
Kityang *see* Jieyang, China J7 42
Kitzbühel, Aus. C9 22
Kitzingen, Ger. G6 16
Kiukiang *see* Jiujiang, China G6 42
Kiunga, Pap. N. Gui. b3 79a
Kiuruvesi, Fin. E12 8
Kivalina, Ak., U.S. C7 140
Kivijärvi, l., Fin. E11 8
Kiviõli, Est. G12 8
Kivu, Lake, l., Afr. E5 66
Kıyıköy, Tur. B11 28
Kiyiu Lake, l., Sk., Can. C5 124
Kızıl Adalar, is., Tur. C11 28
Kızılcabölük, Tur. F11 28
Kızılcahamam, Tur. C15 28
Kızıldağ Milli Parkı, p.o.i., Tur. F14 28
Kızılırmak, stm., Tur. A4 56
Kızılören, Tur. F15 28
Kizimkazi, Tan. F7 66
Kızkalesi, sci., Tur. B4 58
Kizljar, Russia F7 32
Kizyl-Atrek, Turkmen. B7 56
Kizyl-Su, Turkmen. B7 56
Kjahta, Russia F10 34
Kjungej-Ala-Too, hrebet, mts., Asia F13 32
Kjusjur, Russia B14 34
Kjustendil, Blg. G9 26
Klabat, Gunung, vol., Indon. E8 44
Kladno, Czech Rep. F10 16
Kladovo, Serb. E9 26
Klagan, Malay. G1 52
Klagenfurt, Aus. D11 22
Klaipėda (Memel), Lith. E3 10
Klakah, Indon. G8 50
Klamath, stm., U.S. B2 134
Klamath Falls, Or., U.S. A3 134
Klamath Marsh, sw., Or., U.S. H5 136
Klamath Mountains, mts., U.S. B2 134
Klamono, Indon. F9 44
Klang, Malay. K5 48
Klangenan, Indon. G6 50
Klangenang, Indon. G6 50
Klangpi, Mya. G14 54
Klatovy, Czech Rep. G9 16
Klawer, S. Afr. G4 70
Kleck, Bela. G9 10
Kleczew, Pol. D14 16
Kleena Kleene, B.C., Can. E5 138
Klein Curaçao, i., Neth. Ant. q22 104g
Klein Karroo see Little Karroo, plat., S. Afr. H5 70
Klein Namaland see Little Namaqualand, hist. reg., S. Afr. F3 70
Klekovača, mtn., Bos. E3 26
Klemme, Ia., U.S. A4 120
Klemtu, B.C., Can. D2 138
Klerksdorp, S. Afr. E8 70
Kletnja, Russia G16 10
Kleve, Ger. E2 16
Klickitat, stm., Wa., U.S. E5 136
Klimavičy, Bela. G14 10
Klimino, Russia C17 32
Klimovo, Russia H15 10
Klimovsk, Russia E20 10
Klimpfjäll, Swe. D6 8
Klin, Russia D19 10
Klinaklini, stm., B.C., Can. E5 138
Klincy, Russia H15 10
Klingenthal, Ger. F8 16
Klínovec, mtn., Czech Rep. F8 16
Klintehamn, Swe. H8 8
Klip, stm., S. Afr. E9 70
Klipdale, S. Afr. I4 70
Klipplaat, S. Afr. H7 70
Klisura, Blg. G11 26
Kljazma, stm., Russia E21 10
Ključ, Bos. E3 26
Ključevskaja Sopka, vulkan, vol., Russia E21 34
Ključi, Russia E21 34
Kljukvenka, Russia C15 32
Kłobuck, Pol. F14 16
Kłodawa, Pol. D14 16
Kłodzko, Pol. F12 16
Klondike, hist. reg., Yk., Can. C3 106
Klooga, Est. A7 10
Klosterneuburg, Aus. B13 22
Kloten, Switz. C5 22
Klotz, Lac, l., Qc., Can. C16 106
Klötze, Ger. D7 16
Kluane Lake, l., Yk., Can. C3 106
Kluczbork, Pol. F14 16
Klungkung, Indon. H9 50
Knaddah, Syria C7 58
Knapp, Wi., U.S. G6 118
Kneehills Creek, stm., Ab., Can. E17 138
Knee Lake, l., Mb., Can. D12 106
Kneža, Blg. F11 26
Knić, Serb. F7 26
Knickerbocker, Tx., U.S. C7 130
Knife, stm., N.D., U.S. G12 124
Knight Inlet, b., B.C., Can. F4 138
Knights Landing, Ca., U.S. E4 134
Knin, Cro. F13 22
Knippa, Tx., U.S. E8 130
Knittelfeld, Aus. C11 22
Knjaževac, Serb. F9 26
Knob Noster, Mo., U.S. F4 120
Knokke-Heist, Bel. C12 14
Knosós, sci., Grc. H8 28
Knox, Pa., U.S. C6 114
Knox, Cape, c., B.C., Can. E4 106
Knox City, Tx., U.S. H9 128
Knox Coast, cst., Ant. B15 81
Knoxville, Ga., U.S. D2 116
Knoxville, Il., U.S. D7 120
Knoxville, Tn., U.S. I2 114
Knuckles, mtn., Sri L. H5 53
Knud Rasmussen Land, reg., Grnld. A14 141
Knysna, S. Afr. I6 70
Knyszyn, Pol. C18 16
Kob', Russia C18 32
Kobar Sink, depr., Eth. E8 62
Kobayashi, Japan H3 40
Kōbe, Japan E8 40
København (Copenhagen), Den. I4 8
København, state, Den. I5 8
Kobjaj, Russia D14 34
Koblenz, Ger. F3 16
K'obo, Eth. E7 62
Koboža, Russia B18 10
Koboža, stm., Russia A18 10
Kobroor, Pulau, i., Indon. G10 44
Kobryn, Bela. H7 10
Kobuk, Ak., U.S. C8 140
Kobuk, stm., Ak., U.S. C8 140
Kobuleti, Geor. F6 32
Kobylin, Pol. E13 16
Kocaali, Tur. B13 28
Kocaavşar, stm., Tur. D10 28
Kocaeli, state, Tur. C12 28
Kočani, Mac. B5 28
Koçarlı, Tur. F10 28
Kočečum, stm., Russia C8 34
Kočevje, Slvn. E11 22
Kočevo, Russia C8 32
Kŏch'ang, Kor., S. G7 38
Koch Bihār, India E12 54
Kocher, stm., Ger. G5 16
Kochi (Cochin), India G3 53
Kōchi, Japan F6 40
Kōchi, state, Japan F6 40
Koch Island, i., Nu., Can. B15 106
Kochiu *see* Gejiu, China G5 36
Kochnay Darvīshān, Afg. C9 56
Kodaikānal, India F3 53
Kodar, hrebet, mts., Russia E12 34
Kodāri, Nepal E10 54
Kodarma, India F10 54
Kodiak, Ak., U.S. E9 140
Kodiak Island, i., Ak., U.S. E9 140
Kodinār, India H3 54
Kodok, Sudan F6 62
Kodyma, Ukr. A16 26
Kodyma, stm., Ukr. B17 26
Koës, Nmb. D4 70
Köflach, Aus. C11 22
Koforidua, Ghana H4 64
Kōfu, Japan D11 40
Koga, Japan C12 40
Kogaluc, stm., Qc., Can. D15 106
Kogaluc, Baie, b., Qc., Can. D15 106
Kogan, Austl. F8 76
Køge, Den. I5 8
Kogon, stm., Gui. G2 64
Koh̲anava, Bela. F12 10
Kohāt, Pak. B3 54
Kohīma, India C7 46
Kohler, Wi., U.S. E2 112
Kohtla-Järve, Est. G12 8
Kohyl'nyk (Cogâlnic), stm., Eur. C15 26
Koide, Japan B11 40
Koigi, Est. B8 10
Koindu, S.L. H2 64
Koiva (Gauja), stm., Eur. C7 10
Kojda, Russia C20 8
Kŏje-do, i., Kor., S. E1 40
Kojgorodok, Russia B8 32
Kojonup, Austl. F3 74
Kok (Hkok), stm., Asia B4 48
Kokand, Uzb. F12 32
Kokas, Indon. F9 44
Kokemäki, Fin. F9 8
Kokenau, Indon. F10 44
Kokhav HaYarden, sci., Isr. F6 58
Kokiu *see* Gejiu, China G5 36
Kokkilai Lagoon, b., Sri L. G5 53
Kokkola, Fin. E10 8
Kokoda, Pap. N. Gui. b4 79a
Kokomo, In., U.S. H3 112
Kokomo, Ms., U.S. F8 122
Kokong, Bots. D6 70
Kokopo, Pap. N. Gui. a5 79a
Kokorevka, Russia H17 10
Koksan-ŭp, Kor., N. E7 38
Kökshetaū, Kaz. D12 32
Kökshetaū *see* Kokčetav, Kaz. D12 32
Koksoak, stm., Qc., Can. D17 106
Kokstad, S. Afr. G9 70
Kokubu, Japan H3 40
Kola, Russia B15 8
Kolachel, India G3 53
Kolaka, Indon. F7 44
Kolangār, Afg. A2 54
Kola Peninsula see Kol'skij poluostrov, pen., Russia C17 8
Kolār, India E3 53
Kolāras, India F6 54
Kolār Gold Fields, India E4 53
Kolárovo, Slov. I13 16
Kolašin, Serb. G6 26
Kolbio, Kenya E8 66
Kolbuszowa, Pol. F17 16
Kol'čugino, Russia D22 10
Kolda, Sen. G2 64
Kolding, Den. I3 8
Kole, D.R.C. E4 66
Kolea, Alg. H13 20
Kolguev, ostrov, i., Russia B18 6
Kolhāpur, India C4 53
Kolhāpur, India C1 53
Koli, Russia A17 10
Kolín, Czech Rep. F11 16
Koljubakino, Russia E19 10
Kolkata (Calcutta), India G12 54
Kollam *see* Quilon, India G3 53
Kollegāl, India E3 53
Kolleru Lake, l., India C5 53
Kolmogorovo, Russia C16 32
Köln (Cologne), Ger. E2 16
Kolno, Pol. C17 16
Koło, Pol. D14 16
Koloa, Hi., U.S. b2 78a
Kołobrzeg, Pol. B11 16
Kolodnja, Russia F15 10
Kolokani, Mali G3 64
Kolombangara Island, i., Sol. Is. d7 79b
Kolomna, Russia E21 10
Kolomyia, Ukr. A12 26
Kolonga, Tonga n14 78e
Kolonia, Micron. m11 78d
Kolonodale, Indon. F7 44
Kolosib, India F14 54
Kolosovka, Russia C12 32
Kolovai, Tonga n13 78e
Kolozsvár *see* Cluj-Napoca, Rom. C10 26
Kolp', stm., Russia A19 10
Kolpaševo, Russia C14 32
Kolpino, Russia A13 10
Kolpny, Russia H19 10
Kol'skij poluostrov (Kola Peninsula), pen., Russia C17 8
Kolwezi, D.R.C. G5 66
Kolyma, stm., Russia C20 34
Kolyma Plain see Kolymskaja nizmennost', pl., Russia C19 34
Kolymskaja, Russia C20 34
Kolymskaja nizmennost' (Kolyma Plain), pl., Russia C19 34
Kom, mtn., Blg. F10 26
Koma, Mya. E4 48
Komadugu Gana, stm., Nig. G7 64
Komagane, Japan D10 40
Komandorskie ostrova, is., Russia D20 30
Komandorski Islands see Komandorskie ostrova, is., Russia D20 30
Komárno, Slov. I13 16
Komarnyky, Ukr. G19 16
Komárom, Hung. B5 26
Komárom-Esztergom, state, Hung. B5 26
Komati (Incomati), stm., Afr. E10 70
Komatipoort, S. Afr. D10 70
Komatsu, Japan C9 40
Komatsushima, Japan E7 40
Kome Island, i., Ug. E6 66
Komering, stm., Indon. E4 50
Komfane, Indon. G9 44
Komi, state, Russia B8 32
Komissarovo, Russia B9 38
Komló, Hung. C5 26
Kommunizma, pik see Ismail Samani, pik, mtn., Taj. B11 56
Komodo, Pulau, i., Indon. H11 50
Komodo National Park, p.o.i., Indon. H11 50
Komoé, stm., Afr. H4 64
Kom Ombo, Egypt C6 62
Komoran, Pulau, i., Indon. G10 44
Komoro, Japan C11 40
Komotiní, Grc. B8 28
Kompasberg, mtn., S. Afr. G7 70
Komsomolets, Kaz. D10 32
Komsomolets shyghanaghy, b., Kaz. E8 32
Komsomol'sk, Russia H18 8
Komsomol'sk, Russia C15 32

Name	Map Ref.	Page
Komsomol'sk-na-Amure, Russia	F16	34
Komsomol'skoj Pravdy, ostrova, is., Russia	A10	34
Konakovo, Russia	D19	10
Konakpinar, Tur.	D10	28
Konar, stm., Asia	A3	54
Konārak, India	I11	54
Konawa, Ok., U.S.	C2	122
Konch, India	F7	54
Konda, stm., Russia	B10	32
Kondagaon, India	B5	53
Kondega, Russia	F15	8
Kondinin, Austl.	F3	74
Kondoa, Tan.	E7	66
Kondopoga, Russia	E16	8
Kondoz, Afg.	B10	56
Kondukūr, India	D4	53
Koné, N. Cal.	m15	79d
Kong, stm., Asia	F8	48
Kông, Kaôh, i., Camb.	G6	48
Kongcheng, China.	F7	42
Kong Christian IX Land, reg., Grnld.	D18	141
Kong Christian X Land, reg., Grnld.	C19	141
Kong Frederik VIII Land, reg., Grnld.	B19	141
Kong Frederik VI Kyst, cst., Grnld.	E17	141
Kongjiawopeng, China	B5	38
Kongju, Kor., S.	F7	38
Kongmoon see Jiangmen, China	J5	42
Kongolo, D.R.C.	F5	66
Kongor, Sudan	F6	62
Kong Oscar Fjord, strt., Grnld.	C21	141
Kongsvinger, Nor.	F5	8
Kongur Shan, mtn., China..	G13	32
Kong Wilhelms Land, reg., Grnld.	B21	141
Konice, Czech Rep.	G12	16
Königsberg see Kaliningrad, Russia	F3	10
Königswinter, Ger.	F3	16
Konin, Pol.	D14	16
Konin, state, Pol.	D14	16
Konispol, Alb.	E14	24
Konitsa, Grc.	C3	28
Konjic, Bos.	F4	26
Konkiep, stm., Nmb.	E3	70
Konkouré, stm., Gui.	G2	64
Konna, Mali	G4	64
Konnevesi, l., Fin.	E12	8
Konnur, India	C2	53
Konosha, Russia	F18	8
Kōnosu, Japan	C12	40
Konotop, Ukr.	E15	6
Końskie, Pol.	E16	16
Konstantinovskij, Russia..	C22	10
Konstanz, Ger.	I4	16
Kontagora, Nig.	G5	64
Kontcha, Cam.	C2	66
Kontha, Mya.	A3	48
Kontseba, Russia	A16	26
Kon Tum, Viet.	E8	48
Konya, Tur.	F15	28
Konya, state, Tur.	E15	28
Konz, Ger.	G2	16
Konza, Kenya	E7	66
Konžakovskij Kamen', gora, mtn., Russia	C9	32
Koocanusa, Lake, res., N.A.	B11	136
Kookynie, Austl.	E4	74
Koolatah, Austl.	C8	74
Kooloonong, Austl.	J4	76
Koontz Lake, In., U.S.	G3	112
Koorawatha, Austl.	J7	76
Koosa, Est.	B9	10
Kooskia, Id., U.S.	D11	136
Kootenai (Kootenay), stm., N.A.	G13	138
Kootenay (Kootenai), stm., N.A.	G13	138
Kootenay Lake, l., B.C., Can.	G14	138
Kootenay National Park, p.o.i., B.C., Can.	F14	138
Kopāganj, India	E9	54
Kopargaon, India	B2	53
Kópavogur, Ice.	k29	8a
Kopejsk, Russia	C10	32
Koper, Slvn.	E10	22
Kopervik, Nor.	G1	8
Kopet Mountains, mts., Asia	B8	56
Köping, Swe.	G6	8
Koplik, Alb.	B13	24
Koppal, India	D3	53
Koppang, Nor.	F4	8
Koppies, S. Afr.	E8	70
Koprivnica, Cro.	D13	22
Köprü, stm., Tur.	F14	28
Köprülü Kanyon Milli Parkı, p.o.i., Tur.	F14	28
Kopylovo, Russia	F21	8
Korab (Korabit, Maja e), mtn., Eur.	C14	24
Korabit, Maja e (Korab), mtn., Eur.	C14	24
Koraput, India	B6	53
Korarou, Lac, l., Mali	F4	64
Koratla, India	B4	53
Korba, India	G9	54
Korba, Tun.	H4	24
Korbach, Ger.	E4	16
Korça see Korçë, Alb.	D14	24
Korčula, Cro.	H14	22
Korčula, Otok, i., Cro.	H13	22
Korea, North, ctry., Asia	D7	38
Korea, South, ctry., Asia	G8	38
Korea Bay, b., Asia	E5	38
Korea Strait, strt., Asia	E2	40
Korelakša, Russia	D15	8
Korenovsk, Russia	E5	32
Korf, Russia	D22	34
Korhogo, C. Iv.	H3	64
Korientzé, Mali	F4	64
Korim, Indon.	F10	44
Korinthiakós Kólpos (Corinth, Gulf of), b., Grc..	E5	28
Kórinthos, Grc.	F5	28
Kōriyama, Japan	B13	40
Korjakskaja Sopka, vulkan, vol., Russia	F20	34
Korjakskoe nagor'e, mts., Russia	D22	34
Korjažma, Russia	F22	8
Korkino, Russia	D10	32
Korkuteli, Tur.	F13	28
Korla, China	C2	36
Körlki, Russia	B14	32
Körmend, Hung.	C3	26
Kornat, Otok, i., Cro.	G12	22
Kornati, Nacionalni Park, p.o.i., Cro.	G12	22
Korner, Mt.,	A14	136
Korneuburg, Aus.	B13	22
Koro, i., Fiji	p19	79e
Köroğlu Tepesi, mtn., Tur.	C14	28
Korogwe, Tan.	F7	66
Koroleve, Ukr.	H19	16
Koromere see East Cape, c., N.Z.	C8	80
Koronadal, Phil.	G5	52
Koróni, Grc.	G4	28
Korónia, Límni, l., Grc.	C6	28
Korópi, Grc.	E7	28
Koror, Palau	g8	78b
Körös, stm., Hung.	C7	26
Koro Sea, s., Fiji	p20	79e
Korosten', Ukr.	E14	6
Koro Toro, Chad.	D3	62
Korotyš, Russia	H20	10
Korovin Volcano, vol.,	g24	140a
Korovou, Fiji	p19	79e
Koroyanitu, mtn., Fiji	p18	79e
Korsakov, Japan	G17	34
Korsakovo, Russia	G20	10
Korsør, Den.	I4	8
Koršunovo, Russia	C20	32
Kortrijk, Bel.	D12	14
Korucam, Cape see Korucam Burnu, c., N. Cyp.	C3	58
Korucam Burnu, c., N. Cyp.	C3	58
Korucu, Tur.	D10	28
Korumburra, Austl.	L5	76
Koryak Mountains see Korjakskoe nagor'e, mts., Russia	D22	34
Koryŏng, Kor., S.	D1	40
Kos (Cos), i., Grc.	G10	28
Kosa, Russia	C8	32
Kosa, Russia	F10	34
Kosai, Japan	E10	40
Kosaja Gora, Russia	F20	10
Kosčagyl, Kaz.	E8	32
Kościerzyna, Pol.	B14	16
Kosciusko, Ms., U.S.	D9	122
Kosciuszko, Mount, mtn., Austl.	K6	76
Kosciuszko National Park, p.o.i., Austl.	K6	76
Kose, Est.	A8	10
Koshikijima-rettō, is., Japan.	H2	40
Koshkonong, Lake, l., Wi., U.S.	B9	120
Kōshoku, Japan	C11	40
Košice, Slov.	H17	16
Kosi Kalan, India	E6	54
Kosimeer, l., S. Afr.	E11	70
Kosiv, Ukr.	A12	26
Kösk, Tur.	F11	28
Koslan, Russia	E23	8
Kosŏng, Kor., S.	E1	40
Kosŏng-ŭp, Kor., N.	E8	38
Kosovo-Metohija, co., Serb.	G7	26
Kosovska Mitrovica, Serb.	C7	72
Kosrae, i., Micron.	C7	72
Kośreli, Tur.	A6	58
Kosse, Tx., U.S.	F2	122
Kossou, Lac de, res., C. Iv.	H3	64
Kostanaj, Kaz.	D10	32
Koster, S. Afr.	D8	70
Kostomukša, Russia	D14	8
Kostonjärvi, l., Fin.	D12	8
Kostroma, Russia	H19	8
Kostroma, stm., Russia	G19	8
Kostromskaja oblast', co., Russia	G20	8
Kostrzyn, Pol.	D10	16
Kosum Phisai, Thai.	D6	48
Koszalin, Pol.	B12	16
Koszalin, state, Pol.	C12	16
Kőszeg, Hung.	B3	26
Kota, India	E5	54
Kota, India.	F5	54
Kotaagung, Indon.	F4	50
Kotabaru, Indon.	D10	50
Kota Belud, Malay.	G1	52
Kota Bharu, Malay.	I6	48
Kotabumi, Indon.	D4	50
Kotabumi, Indon.	F4	50
Kotadabok, Indon.	C5	54
Kot Addu, Pak.	C3	54
Kota Kinabalu, Malay.	G1	52
Kotamobagu, Indon.	E7	44
Kotapinang, Indon.	C1	50
Kota Tinggi, Malay.	L6	48
Kotawaringin, Indon.	E7	50
Kotcho Lake, l., B.C., Can.	D6	106
Kot Chutta, Pak.	D3	54
Kotel'nič, Russia	C7	32
Kotel'nikovo, Russia	E6	32
Kotel'nyj, ostrov, i., Russia	A16	34
Kotelnyj, ostrov, i., Russia..	B3	34
Köthen, Ger.	E7	16
Kotikovo, Russia	G17	34
Kotka, Fin.	F12	8
Kot Kapūra, India	C5	54
Kotlas, Russia	F22	8
Kotli, Pak.	B4	54
Kotlik, Ak., U.S.	D7	140
Kōtōmo, Île, i., N. Cal.	n16	79d
Kotor, Serb.	G5	26
Kotoriba, Cro.	D13	22
Kotovs'k, Ukr.	B16	26
Kot Putli, India	E6	54
Kotri, Pak.	F2	54
Kottagūdem, India	C5	53
Kottayam, India	G3	53
Kotto, stm., C.A.R.	C4	66
Kōttūru, India.	D3	53
Kotuj, stm., Russia	B9	34
Kotzebue, Ak., U.S.	C7	140
Kotzebue Sound, strt., Ak., U.S.	C7	140
Kötzting, Ger.	G8	16
Kouang-si see Guangxi, state, China.	J6	42
Kouang-tong see Guangdong, state, China..	J6	42
Kouaoua, N. Cal.	m15	79d
Kouchibouguac National Park, p.o.i., N.B., Can.	D11	110
Koudougou, Burkina	G4	64
Kouei-tcheou see Guizhou, state, China	H2	42
Kouga, stm., S. Afr.	H7	70
Kougaberge, mts., S. Afr.	H6	70
Koukdjuak, stm., Nu., Can.	B16	106
Kouki, C.A.R.	C3	66
Koúklia, Cyp.	D3	58
Koulamoutou, Gabon	E2	66
Koulikoro, Mali	G3	64
Koumala, Austl.	C7	76
Koumbia, Gui.	G2	64
Koumpentoum, Sen.	G2	64
Koumra, Chad	F3	62
Koundâra, Gui.	G2	64
Koundian, Gui.	G2	64
Koungou, Fr. Gu.	B7	84
Kourou, Fr. Gu.	B7	84
Kouroussa, Gui.	G3	64
Kousséri, Cam.	B2	66
Koutiala, Mali	G3	64
Kouts, In., U.S.	G2	112
Kouvola, Fin.	F12	8
Kova, Russia	C18	32
Kovada Milli Parkı, p.o.i., Tur.	F13	28
Kovarskas, Lith.	E7	10
Kovdor, Russia	C14	8
Kovožozero, ozero, l., Russia	C14	8
Kovilpatti, India	G3	53
Kovrov, Russia	H19	8
Kovūr, India	D5	53
Kovža, Russia	F18	8
Kowalewo Pomorskie, Pol.	C14	16
Kowloon see Jiulong, China.	J5	42
Kowŏn-ŭp, Kor., N.	E7	38
Kowt-e 'Ashrow, Afg.	C10	56
Koxtag, China	A4	46
Kōyama Reservoir, res., India	C1	53
Koyuk, Ak., U.S.	D7	140
Koyukuk, Ak., U.S.	D8	140
Koyukuk, stm., Ak., U.S.	C8	140
Ko-zaki, c., Japan	E1	40
Kozan, Tur.	A6	58
Kozáni, Grc.	C4	28
Kožany, Russia	H14	10
Kozel'sk, Russia	F18	10
Koževnikovo, Russia	C14	32
Kozhikode (Calicut), India	F2	53
Kozienice, Pol.	E17	16
Kozlov Bereg, Russia	B10	10
Kozlovo, Russia	D19	10
Kozlu, Tur.	B14	28
Koz'mino, Russia	F22	8
Kozŏshima, i., Japan	E12	40
Kozposёlok, Russia	E17	8
Kōzu-shima, i., Japan	E12	40
Kpalimé, Togo	H5	64
Kpandu, Ghana	H5	64
Kra, Isthmus of, isth., Asia	H4	48
Kraai, stm., S. Afr.	G8	70
Krabi, Thai.	H4	48
Krâchéh, Camb.	F8	48
Kraeva, Russia	B9	38
Kragan, Indon.	G7	50
Kragujevac, Serb.	F7	26
Krajenka, Pol.	C13	16
Krakatoa see Rakata, Pulau, i., Indon.	G4	50
Krakovets', Ukr.	G19	16
Kraków, Pol.	F15	16
Kraków, state, Pol.	G15	16
Kralendijk, Neth. Ant.	p23	104g
Kraljevo, Serb.	F7	26
Kralovice, Czech Rep.	G9	16
Kralupy nad Vltavou, Czech Rep.	F10	16
Kramators'k, Ukr.	E5	32
Kramfors, Swe.	E7	8
Kraníidi, Grc.	F6	28
Kranj (Krainburg), Slvn.	D11	22
Kranskop, S. Afr.	F10	70
Kranzberg, Nmb.	G18	10
Krasavino, Russia	F22	8
Krasieo, stm., Thai.	E4	48
Krasivaja Meča, stm., Russia..	G20	10
Kráslava, Lat.	E10	10
Krasnae, Bela.	F10	10
Krasnaja Gorbatka, Russia	I19	8
Krasnaja Slabada, Bela.	H9	10
Krasnaluki, Bela.	F11	10
Krasneno, Russia	D23	34
Krasnik, Pol.	F18	16
Kraśnik Fabryczny, Pol.	F18	16
Krasni Okny, Ukr.	B16	26
Krasnoarmejsk, Russia	D21	10
Krasnoarmejskij, Russia	C23	34
Krasnobrod, Pol.	F19	16
Krasnodar, Russia	E5	32
Krasnoe, ozero, l., Russia	D23	34
Krasnoe Selo, Russia	A12	10
Krasnoe Znamja, Russia	C18	10
Krasnogorodskoe, Russia	D11	10
Krasnogorsk, Russia	E20	10
Krasnogorsk, Russia	G17	34
Krasnojarovo, Russia	F14	34
Krasnojarsk, Russia	C16	32
Krasnojarskoe vodohranilišče, res., Russia	D16	32
Krasnokamsk, Russia	C8	32
Krasnomajskij, Russia	C17	10
Krasnoščele, Russia	C17	8
Krasnosel'kup, Russia	A14	32
Krasnoturjinsk, Russia	C10	32
Krasnoufimsk, Russia	C9	32
Krasnoural'sk, Russia	C10	32
Krasnovišersk, Russia	B9	32
Krasnovodskij poluostrov, pen., Turkmen.	A7	56
Krasnozavodsk, Russia	D20	10
Krasnoznamensk, Russia	D14	32
Krasnoznamenskoe, Kaz.	D11	32
Krasnye Gory, Russia	B12	10
Krasnyj Čikoj, Russia	F10	34
Krasnyj Gorodok, Russia	C16	10
Krasnyj Jar, Russia	C12	32
Krasnyj Oktjabr', Russia	D21	10
Krasnyj Tkač, Russia	E22	10
Krasnystaw, Pol.	E19	16
Kratovo, Mac.	A5	28
Krávanh, Chuŏr Phnum, mts., Camb.	F6	48
Krbava, reg., Cro.	F12	22
Krečetovo, Russia	F18	8
Krefeld, Ger.	E2	16
Kremenchug Reservoir see Kremenchuts'ke vodoskhovyshche, res., Ukr.	E4	32
Kremenchuk, Ukr.	E4	32
Kremenchuts'ke vodoskhovyshche, res., Ukr.	E4	32
Kremenskoe, Russia	E18	10
Kremmling, Co., U.S.	C10	132
Krems an der Donau, Aus.	B12	22
Kress, Tx., U.S.	G7	128
Kresta, zaliv, b., Russia..	F4	40
Krestcy, Russia	B15	10
Krestcy, Russia	B22	10
Krest-Maёr, Russia	C17	34
Kretinga, Lith.	E4	10
Kribi, Cam.	D1	66
Křimice, Czech Rep.	G9	16
Krishna, India	C5	53
Krishna, Mouths of the, mth., India	D5	53
Krishnagiri, India	E4	53
Krishnanagar, India	G12	54
Krishnarāja Sāgara, res., India	E3	53
Krishnarājpet, India	E3	53
Kristiansand, Nor.	G3	8
Kristiansand, Swe.	I6	8
Kristiansund, Nor.	E2	8
Kristiinankaupunki (Kristinestad), Fin.	E9	8
Kristinehamn, Swe.	G6	8
Kristinestad see Kristiinankaupunki, Fin.	E9	8
Kriti, state, Grc.	H7	28
Kríti (Crete), i., Grc.	H7	28
Kritikón Pélagos (Crete, Sea of), s., Grc.	H8	28
Kriva Palanka, Mac.	A5	28
Krivodol, Blg.	F10	26
Križevci, Cro.	D13	22
Krjukovo, Russia	E20	10
Krk, Otok, i., Cro.	E11	22
Krnov, Czech Rep.	F13	16
Krobia, Pol.	E13	16
Krøderen, l., Nor.	F3	8
Krokodil, stm., S. Afr.	G4	70
Krom, stm., S. Afr.	H7	70
Kromy, Russia	H18	10
Kroměříž, Czech Rep.	G13	16
Kronach, Ger.	F7	16
Kröng Kêb, Camb.	G7	48
Kronoberg, state, Swe.	H6	8
Kronocka Sopka, vulkan, vol., Russia	F21	34
Kronocki, Russia	F21	34
Kronprins Christian Land, reg., Grnld.	A22	141
Kronshtadt, Russia	A12	10
Kroonstad, S. Afr.	E8	70
Kropotkin, Russia	E6	32
Kropotkin, Russia	E11	34
Krosno, Pol.	G17	16
Krośniewice, Pol.	D15	16
Krotoszyn, Pol.	E13	16
Krotz Springs, La., U.S.	G7	122
Kroya, Indon.	G6	50
Krško, Slvn.	E12	22
Kruger National Park, p.o.i., S. Afr.	C10	70
Krugersdorp, S. Afr.	E8	70
Kruhlae, Bela.	F12	10
Krui, Indon.	F3	50
Kruisfontein, S. Afr.	H7	70
Kruja see Krujë, Alb.	C13	24
Krujë, Alb.	C13	24
Krumbach, Ger.	H6	16
Krung Thep (Bangkok), Thai.	F5	48
Kruševac, Serb.	F8	26
Krušinovka, Bela.	G12	10
Krutcy, Russia	C12	10
Krutoe, Russia	H20	10
Kruzenšterna, proliv, strt., Russia	G19	34
Kruzof Island, i., Ak., U.S.	E12	140
Kryčaŭ, Bela.	G14	10
Kryms'kyi pivostriv (Crimean Peninsula), pen., Ukr.	E4	32
Krynica, Pol.	G16	16
Krynychne, Ukr.	D15	26
Kryve Ozero, Ukr.	B17	26
Kryvošyn, Bela.	H8	10
Kryvyj Rih, Ukr.	E4	32
Kryzhopil', Ukr.	A15	26
Krzeszowice, Pol.	F15	16
Krzyż, Pol.	D11	16
Ksenevka, Russia	F12	34
Kstovo, Russia	H20	8
Kuah, Malay.	I4	48
Kuai, stm., China	E7	42
Kualacenako, Indon.	D3	50
Kuala Kangsar, Malay.	J5	48
Kualakapuas, Indon.	E9	50
Kuala Krai, Malay.	J6	48
Kuala Kubu Baharu, Malay.	K5	48
Kualakurun, Indon.	D8	50
Kualalangsa, Indon.	J4	48
Kuala Lipis, Malay.	J6	48
Kuala Lumpur, Malay.	K5	48
Kuala Nerang, Malay.	I5	48
Kuala Pembuang, Indon.	E6	50
Kuala Pilah, Malay.	K6	48
Kuala Rompin, Malay.	K6	48
Kuala Sepetang, Malay.	J5	48
Kualasimpang, Indon.	J4	48
Kuala Terengganu, Malay.	J6	48
Kualu, stm., Indon.	B1	50
Kuamut, stm., Malay.	A10	50
Kuancheng, China	A8	42
Kuandian, China	D6	38
Kuan Shan, mtn., Tai.	J9	42
Kuantan, Malay.	K6	48
Kuanyin see Guanyun, China	D8	42
Kuban', stm., Russia	E6	32
Kubenskoe, ozero, l., Russia	G18	8
Kubokawa, Japan	F6	40
Kubrat, Blg.	F13	26
Kučema, Russia	D20	8
Kuchaibari, India	G11	54
Kuchāman, India	E5	54
Kuching, Malay.	C7	50
Kuchurhan, stm., Eur.	B16	26
Kuçova see Kuçovë, Alb.	D13	24
Kuçovë, Alb.	D13	24
Kudamatsu, Japan	F4	40
Kudat, Malay.	G1	52
Kudever', Russia	D12	10
Kudirkos Naumiestis, Lith.	F5	10
Kudus, Indon.	G7	50
Kudymkar, Russia	C8	32
Kü'é'é Ruins, sci., Hi., U.S.	d6	78a
Kueisui see Hohhot, China	A4	42
Kueiyang see Guiyang, China	H2	42
Kufstein, Aus.	C9	22
K'uerhlo see Korla, China...	C2	36
Kugaaruk, Nu., Can.	B8	106
Kugmallit Bay, b., N.T., Can.	C13	140
Kugluktuk (Coppermine), Nu., Can.	B8	106
Kuhmoinen, Fin.	F11	8
Kuhn Ø, i., Grnld.	C22	141
Kuial'nyts'kyi lyman, l., Ukr.	C17	26
Kuiseb, stm., Nmb.	C2	70
Kuitan, China.	J7	42
Kuito, Ang.	C2	68
Kuiu Island, i., Ak., U.S.	E13	140
Kuivastu, Est.	G10	8
Kuja, Russia	D18	8
Kujang-ŭp, Kor., N.	E7	38
Kujawy, reg., Pol.	D14	16
Kujbyšev, Russia	C13	32
Kujbyševskoe vodohranilišče, res., Russia	C7	32
Kujū-san, vol., Japan	F4	40
Kuju, stm., Nic.	F6	102
Kukawa, Nig.	G7	64
Kukës, Alb.	B14	24
Kukoboj, Russia	B22	10
Kūkong see Shaoguan, China	I5	42
Kukshi, India	G5	54
Kukuj, Russia	A15	10
Kukukus Lake, l., On., Can.	B7	118
Kukurtli, Turkmen.	B9	56
Kula, Tur.	E11	28
Kula, Serb.	D6	26
Kulagi, Russia	H15	10
Kula Gulf, strt., Sol. Is.	e7	79b
Kula Kangri, mtn., Bhu.	E13	54
Kular, Russia	B15	34
Kulaura, Bngl.	F13	54
Kuldīga, Lat.	D5	10
Kuldja see Yining, China	F14	32
Kule, Bots.	C5	70
Kulebaki, Russia	I20	8
Kulen Vakuf, Bos.	F4	26
Kulim, Malay.	J5	48
Kuljab, Taj.	B10	56
Kulkyne Creek, stm., Austl.	H5	76
Kullu, India	B6	54
Kulm, N.D., U.S.	A13	126
Kulmbach, Ger.	F7	16
Kuloj, Russia	C20	8
Kuloj, stm., Russia	D20	8
Kulp, Tur.	B5	56
Kulpahar, India	F7	54
Kulpmont, Pa., U.S.	D9	114
Kulti, India	G11	54
Kulu, Tur.	D16	28
Kulunda, Russia	D13	32
Kulundinskaja ravnina, pl., Asia	D13	32
Kulwin, Austl.	J4	76
Kulyab see Kuljab, Taj.	B10	56
Kuma, stm., Russia	F7	32
Kumagaya, Japan	C12	40
Kumai, Teluk, b., Indon.	E7	50
Kumajri see Gjumri, Arm.	A5	56
Kumamoto, Japan	G3	40
Kumamoto, state, Japan	G3	40
Kumano, Japan	F9	40
Kumano-nada, s., Japan	F9	40
Kumanovo, Mac.	A4	28
Kumara, Russia	F14	34
Kumārghat, India	F14	54
Kumasi, Ghana	H4	64
Kumba, Cam.	D1	66
Kumbakonam, India	F4	53
Kumbarilla, Austl.	F8	76
Kume-jima, i., Japan	I18	39a
Kŭm-gang, stm., Kor., S.	F7	38
Kumla, Swe.	G6	8
Kumluca, Tur.	G13	28
Kumluca, Tur.	B15	28
Kumo, Nig.	H7	64
Kumon Range, mts., Mya.	C8	46
Kumora, Russia	E11	34
Kumta, India	D2	53
Kumu, D.R.C.	D5	66
Kumukahi, Cape, c., Hi., U.S.	d6	135a
Kumūx, China	C2	36
Kŭmya-ŭp, Kor., N.	E7	38
Kuna, Id., U.S.	G10	136
Kunašir, ostrov (Kunashiri-tŏ), i., Russia	C16	38
Kunda, Est.	G12	8
Kunda Hills, hills, India	F3	53
Kundapura, India	E2	53
Kundar, stm., Asia	C2	54
Kunderu, stm., India	D4	53
Kundiān, Pak.	B3	54
Kundiawa, Pap. N. Gui.	b3	79a
Kundla, India	H3	54
Kundur, Pulau, i., Indon.	C3	50
Kunene, Pol.	G16	16
Kŭnene (Cunene), stm., Afr.	D1	68
Kunes, Nor.	A12	8
Kungchuling see Gongzhuling, China	C6	38
Kunggyū Yumco, l., China...	C9	54
Kunghit Island, i., B.C., Can.	E4	106
Kungrad, Uzb.	F9	32
Kungsbacka, Swe.	H4	8
Kungsör, Swe.	G7	8
Kuningan, Indon.	G6	50
Kunisaki, Japan	F4	40
Kunisaki-hantō, pen., Japan..	F4	40
Kunja, Russia	D13	10
Kunja, stm., Russia	D13	10
Kunlong, Mya.	D8	46
Kunlun Mountains see Kunlun Shan, mts., China..	A5	46
Kunlun Shan, mts., China	A5	46
Kunming, China	F5	36
Kunnamkulam, India	F2	53
Kunsan, Kor., S.	F7	38
Kunshan, China	F9	42
Kunting, China	C5	42
Kununurra, Austl.	C5	74
Kunya, Nig.	G6	64
Künzelsau, Ger.	G5	16
Kuopio, Fin.	E12	8
Kupa, stm., Eur.	E12	22
Kupang, Indon.	H7	44
Kupanskoe, Russia	D21	10
Kup'jans'k, Ukr.	E5	32
Kupino, Russia	D13	32
Kupiškis, Lith.	E7	10
Kupreanof Island, i., Ak., U.S.	E13	140
Kuqa, China	F14	32
Kuqa, China	F14	32
Kuragino, Russia	D16	32
Kuraymah, Sudan	D6	62
Kurayoshi, Japan	D6	40
Kurchatov, Kaz.	D13	32
Kurdistan, hist. reg., Asia	B5	56
Kurdistān see Kurdistan, hist. reg., Asia	B5	56
Kurdufān, state, Sudan	E6	62
Kurduvādi, India	B2	53
Kure, Japan	E5	40
Kurejka, stm., Russia	C7	34
Kuresaare, Est.	G10	8
Kurgan, Russia	C11	32
Kurgan-Tjube, Taj.	B10	56
Kuria, i., Kir.	C8	72
Kuria Muria Islands see Hallāniyah, Juzur al-, is., Oman	F8	56
Kuridala, Austl.	C3	76
Kurikka, Fin.	E10	8
Kuril Islands see Kuril'skie ostrova, is., Russia	E19	30
Kuril'sk, Russia	B14	36
Kuril'skie ostrova (Kuril Islands), is., Russia	E19	30
Kuril Strait see Pervyj Kuril'skij proliv, strt., Russia	F20	34
Kuril Trench, unds.	E18	142
Kurinjippadi, India	F4	53
Kurinwás, stm., Nic.	F5	102
Kurjanovskaja, Russia	F19	8
Kurkliai, Lith.	E8	10
Kurmuk, Sudan	E6	62
Kurnool, India	D3	53
Kurobe, Japan	C10	40
Kurort Schmalkalden, Ger.	F6	16
Kurovskoe, Russia	E21	10
Kurow, N.Z.	G4	80
Kuršėnai, Lith.	D6	10
Kurseong, India	E12	54
Kurskaja kosa (Kuršiu nerija), spit, Eur.	E3	10
Kursk, Russia	D5	32
Kurskaja oblast', co., Russia	H19	10
Kuršumlija, Serb.	F8	26
Kurt, Sudan	D6	62
Kurti, Sudan	D6	62
Kurtistown, Hi., U.S.	d6	78a
Kurtoğlu Burnu, c., Tur.	G11	28
Kuruktag, mts., China	C3	36
Kuruman, stm., S. Afr.	E5	70
Kurume, Japan	F3	40
Kurumkan, Russia	F11	34
Kurunegala, Sri L.	H5	53
Kuruqi, China	B9	36
Kuryongp'o, Kor., S.	C2	40
Kuşadası Körfezi, b., Tur.	F9	28
Kuşadası, Tur.	F9	28
Kuşa, Kaz.	D12	32
Kusawa Lake, l., Yk., Can.	D12	140
Kuş Gölü, l., Tur.	C10	28
Kuş Gölü Milli Parkı, p.o.i., Tur.	C10	28
Kushālgarh, India	G5	54
Kushikino, Japan	H3	40
Kushima, Japan	H4	40
Kushiro, Japan	C16	38
Kusiyara, stm., Bngl.	F13	54
Kuskokwim, stm., Ak., U.S.	D7	140
Kuskokwim Bay, b., Ak., U.S.	D7	140
Kuskokwim Mountains, mts., Ak., U.S.	D8	140
Kúsmá, Nepal	D9	54
Kusmuryn, Kaz.	D10	32
Küsti, Sudan	E6	62
Kusu, Japan	F4	40
Kut, Ko, i., Thai.	G6	48
Kutabaru, Indon.	D3	50
Kutacane, Indon.	K3	48
Kūtahya, Tur.	D13	28
Kūtahya, state, Tur.	D12	28
Kutaisi, Geor.	F6	32
Kutch, Rann of (Kachchh, Rann of), reg., Asia	D2	46
Kutima, Russia	C19	32
Kutina, Cro.	E13	22
Kutiyāna, India	H3	54
Kutná Hora, Czech Rep.	G11	16
Kutno, Pol.	D15	16
Kutse Game Reserve, Bots.	C7	70
Kutu, D.R.C.	E3	66
Kutubdia Island, i., Bngl.	H13	54
Kutum, Sudan	E4	62
Kúty, Slov.	H13	16
Kuujjuaq, Qc., Can.	D17	106
Kuuli-Majak, Turkmen.	A7	56
Kuusamo, Fin.	D13	8
Kuusankoski, Fin.	F12	8
Kuvango, Ang.	C2	68
Kuvšinovo, Russia	C16	10
Kuwait see Al-Kuwayt, Kuw.	D6	56
Kuwait, ctry., Asia	D6	56
Kuwana, Japan	D9	40
Kuybyshev Reservoir see Kujbyševskoe vodohranilišče, res., Russia	D7	32
Kuye, stm., China	B4	42
Kuytun, Mount, mtn., Asia..	E15	32
Kuženkino, Russia	C16	10
Kuz'minič, Russia	F16	10
Kuz'movka, Russia	B16	32
Kuzneck, Russia	D7	32
Kuznecovka, Russia	D15	32
Kuznecovka, Russia	D11	10
Kuznetsk see Kuzneck, Russia	D7	32
Kuzomen', Russia	C17	8
Kvænangen, b., Nor.	A9	8
Kvaløya, i., Nor.	B8	8
Kvaløya, i., Nor.	A5	8
Kvam, Nor.	F3	8
Kvarnbergsvattnet, l., Swe.	D5	8
Kvarner, b., Cro.	F11	22
Kvarnerić, b., Cro.	F11	22
Kverkfjöll, vol., Ice.	k31	8a
Kvichak Bay, b., Ak., U.S.	E8	140
Kwa, stm., D.R.C.	E3	66
Kwa see Khwae Noi, stm., Thai.	E4	48
Kwajalein, at., Marsh. Is.	C7	72
Kwakoegron, Sur.	B6	84
Kwamisa, mtn., Ghana	H4	64
Kwamouth, D.R.C.	E3	66
Kwando (Cuando), stm., Afr.	D3	68
Kwangchow see Guangzhou, China.	J5	42
Kwangju, Kor., S.	G7	38
Kwango (Cuango), stm., Afr.	E3	66
Kwangsi Chuang see Guangxi, state, China	J6	42
Kwangtung see Guangdong, state, China	J6	42
KwaZulu-Natal, state, S. Afr.	F10	70
Kweichow see Guizhou, state, China	H2	42
Kweihwa see Hohhot, China	A4	42
Kweilin see Guilin, China	I4	42
Kweisui see Hohhot, China	A4	42
Kweiyang see Guiyang, China	H2	42
Kwekwe, Zimb.	D4	68
Kweneng, state, Bots.	C7	70
Kwethluk, Ak., U.S.	D7	140
Kwidzyn, Pol.	C14	16
Kwigillingok, Ak., U.S.	E7	140
Kwilu (Cuilo), stm., Afr.	F3	66
Kyabra, Austl.	F4	76
Kyabra Creek, stm., Austl.	E4	76
Kyabram, Austl.	K5	76
Kyaikkami, Mya.	D3	48
Kyaiklat, Mya.	D2	48
Kyaikto, Mya.	D3	48
Kya-in, Mya.	D4	48
Kyalite, Austl.	J4	76
Kyancutta, Austl.	F7	74
Ky Anh, Viet.	C8	48
Kyaukhnyat, Mya.	D3	48
Kyaukme, Mya.	A3	48
Kyaukpadaung, Mya.	B2	48
Kyaukse, Mya.	B3	48
Kyauktaw, Mya.	D7	46
Kyaunggon, Mya.	D2	48
Kybartai, Lith.	F5	10
Kyebang-san, mtn., Kor., S.	B1	40
Kyeikdon, Mya.	E4	48
Kyidaunggan, Mya.	B3	48
Kyiv (Kiev), Ukr.	D4	32
Kyiv's'ke vodoskhovyshche, res., Ukr.	D4	32
Kyjov, Czech Rep.	G13	16
Kykotsmovi Village, Az., U.S.	H6	132
Kyle, Tx., U.S.	D10	130
Kyle, S.D., U.S.	D10	126
Kyle, Lake, res., Zimb.	B10	70
Kyllíni, Grc.	F4	28
Kyneton, Austl.	K5	76
Kynšperk nad Ohří, Czech Rep.	F8	16
Kyoga, Lake, l., Ug.	D6	66
Kyogle, Austl.	G9	76
Kyŏngju, Kor., S.	D2	40
Kyŏngsang-bukto, state, Kor., S.	C1	40
Kyŏngsang-namdo, state, Kor., S.	D1	40
Kyŏngsŏng-ŭp, Kor., N.	D8	38
Kyŏnp'o, Kor., S.	B1	40
Kyōto, Japan	D8	40
Kyōto, state, Japan	D8	40
Kyparissía, Grc.	F4	28
Kyparissiakós Kólpos, b., Grc.	F4	28
Kyra, Russia	G11	34
Kyren, Russia	D18	32
Kyrgyzstan, ctry., Asia	F12	32
Kyritz, Ger.	D8	16
Kyrönjoki, stm., Fin.	E10	8
Kyrta, Russia	B9	32
Kyštym, Russia	C10	32
Kýthira, Grc.	G5	28
Kýthira, i., Grc.	G5	28
Kýthnos, i., Grc.	F7	28
Kyūshū, i., Japan	G2	40
Kyushu-Palau Ridge, unds.	H16	142
Kyūshū-sanchi, mts., Japan	G3	40
Kywong, Austl.	J6	76
Kyyjärvi, Fin.	E11	8
Kyyvesi, l., Fin.	E12	8
Kyzyl, Russia	D16	32
Kyzylbair, Turkmen.	B8	56
Kyzyl-Kyja, Kyrg.	F12	32
Kyzylkum, des., Asia	F10	32
Kyzyl-Orda see Qyzylorda, Kaz.	F11	32

L

Name	Map Ref.	Page
La Aguja, Cabo de, c., Col.	B4	86
La Albuera, Spain	F4	20
La Alcarria, reg., Spain	D8	20
La Algaba, Spain	G4	20

Name / Map Ref. / Page

La Almunia de Doña Godina, Spain — C9 20
La Antigua, salina, pl., Arg. — D4 92
La Araucanía, state, Chile — I1 92
Laascaanood, Som. — C9 66
La Ascensión, hill, Mex. — C8 100
La Asunción, Ven. — B10 86
Laau Point, c., Hi., U.S. — b4 78a
Laayoune see El Aaiún, W. Sah. — D2 64
La Azufrosa, Mex. — F7 130
La Babia, Mex. — A7 100
Labadieville, La., U.S. — H8 122
La Baie, Qc., Can. — B6 110
La Banda, Arg. — C5 92
La Bandera, Cerro, mtn., Mex. — C6 100
La Bañeza, Spain — B4 20
La Barca, Mex. — E7 100
La Barge, Wy., U.S. — H16 136
Labasa, Fiji — p19 79e
La Baule-Escoublac, Fr. — G6 14
Labé, Gui. — G2 64
Labe (Elbe), stm., Eur. — C5 16
Labelle, Qc., Can. — D2 110
La Belle, Mo., U.S. — D5 120
Laberge, Lake, l., Yk., Can. — C4 106
Labi, Bru. — A9 50
Labian, Tanjong, c., Malay. — A11 50
La Biche, stm., Ab., Can. — B18 138
Labis, Malay. — K6 48
La Bisbal d'Empordà, Spain — C13 20
Łabiszyn, Pol. — D13 16
La Blanca Grande, Laguna, l., Arg. — I5 92
Labná, sci., Mex. — B3 102
Laboe, Ger. — B6 16
Laborde, Arg. — F6 92
Laborie, St. Luc. — m7 105c
La Bostonnais, Qc., Can. — C4 110
Laboulaye, Arg. — G6 92
Labrador, reg., Nf., Can. — E18 106
Labrador Basin, unds. — C9 144
Labrador City, Nf., Can. — E17 106
Labrador Sea, s., N.A. — D17 94
Lábrea, Braz. — E5 84
La Brea, Trin. — s12 105f
Labuan, Malay. — A9 50
Labuan, state, Malay. — A9 50
Labuan, Pulau, i., Malay. — A9 50
Labuchonggyan, mts., China — C10 54
La Bufadora, Mex. — L9 134
Labuhan, Indon. — G4 50
Labuhanbajo, Indon. — H11 50
Labuhanbilik, Indon. — B2 50
Labuhanpandan, Indon. — H10 50
Labuhanruku, Indon. — B1 50
Labuk, stm., Malay. — H1 52
Labu Kananga, Indon. — H10 50
Labutta, Mya. — D2 48
Labytnangi, Russia — A11 32
Laç, Alb. — C13 24
Laca, och, i., Russia — F18 8
Lac-à-Beauce, Qc., Can. — C4 110
La Cadena, Mex. — I3 130
La Calera, Chile — F2 92
La Campana, Arg. — G5 20
La Canada Flintridge, Ca., U.S. — I7 134
La Candelaria, Arg. — C5 92
La Candelaria, Mex. — C1 130
Lacantum, stm., Mex. — D2 102
La Capelle-en-Thiérache, Fr. — D12 14
La Carlota, Arg. — F6 92
La Carlota, Phil. — E4 52
La Carolina, Spain — F7 20
Lacaune, Fr. — F8 18
Laccadive Islands see Lakshadweep, is., India — F3 46
Lac-Édouard, Qc., Can. — C4 110
La Ceiba, Hond. — E4 102
Lacepede Bay, b., Austl. — K2 76
Lac-Etchemin, Qc., Can. — D6 110
Lacey, Wa., U.S. — C4 136
Lac-Frontière, Qc., Can. — D6 110
La Chapelle-d'Angillon, Fr. — G11 14
La Châtaigneraie, Fr. — C5 18
La Chaux-de-Fonds, Switz. — C3 22
Lachhmangarh Sīkar, India — E5 54
Lachine, ngh., Qc., Can. — E13 110
Lachlan, stm., Austl. — J5 76
La Chorrera, Col. — H5 86
La Chorrera, Pan. — H8 102
Lachute, Qc., Can. — E2 110
Laçi see Laç, Alb. — C13 24
La Ciénaga, Arg. — C4 92
La Ciotat, Fr. — F11 18
La Citadelle, hist., Haiti — C11 102
La Ciudad, Mex. — D6 100
Lackawanna, N.Y., U.S. — B6 114
Lac La Biche, Ab., Can. — B18 138
Lac la Hache, B.C., Can. — E9 138
Laclede, Id., U.S. — B10 136
Laclede, Mo., U.S. — E4 120
La Clotilde, Arg. — C7 92
La-Mégantic, Qc., Can. — E5 110
La Colorada, Mex. — A3 100
La Coma, Mex. — C9 100
Lacombe, Ab., Can. — D17 138
Lacombe, La., U.S. — G9 122
Lacona, Ia., U.S. — C4 120
La Concepción, Pan. — H6 102
La Concepción, Ven. — B5 86
Laconi, Italy — E2 24
Laconia, N.H., U.S. — G5 110
Laconia, Gulf of see Lakonikós Kólpos, b., Grc. — G5 28
La Consulta, Arg. — F3 92
Lacoochee, Fl., U.S. — H3 116
La Coruña see A Coruña, Spain — A2 20
La Coruña see A Coruña, co., Spain — A2 20
La Coste, Tx., U.S. — E9 130
La Courtine, Fr. — D8 18
La Crescent, Mn., U.S. — H7 118
La Crosse, Ks., U.S. — C9 128
La Crosse, Va., U.S. — H7 114
Lacrosse, Wa., U.S. — D9 136
La Crosse, Wi., U.S. — H7 118
La Cruz, Arg. — D9 92
La Cruz, Col. — G3 86
La Cruz, Mex. — G2 130
La Cruz de Rio Grande, Nic. — F5 102
Lac Seul, On., Can. — A6 118
La Cuesta, P.R. — B2 104a
La Cumbre, Arg. — E5 92
La Cygne, Ks., U.S. — F3 120
Ladákh, hist. reg., Pak. — A6 54
Ladākh Range, mts., Asia — A6 54
Ladder Creek, stm., Ks., U.S. — C7 128
Laddonia, Mo., U.S. — E6 120
La Désirade, i., Guad. — h6 105c
La Digue, i., Sey. — j13 69b
Ladismith, S. Afr. — H5 70
Ladispoli, Italy — I8 22
Lädiz, Iran — D9 56
Ladner, B.C., Can. — G9 138
Lādnūn, India — E5 54
Ladoga, In., U.S. — I3 112
Ladoga, Lake see Ladozhskoe ozero, l., Russia — F14 8
La Dorada, Col. — E4 86
La Dormida, Arg. — F4 92
Ladozhskoe ozero (Ladoga, Lake), l., Russia — F14 8
Ladushkin, Russia — F3 10
Ladva-Vetka, Russia — F15 8
Lady Ann Strait, strt., Nu., Can. — B10 141
Lady Barron, Austl. — n14 77a
Ladybrand, S. Afr. — F8 70
Lady Elliot Island, i., Austl. — E9 76

Ladysmith, B.C., Can. — H7 138
Ladysmith, S. Afr. — F9 70
Ladysmith, Wi., U.S. — F7 118
Lae, Pap. N. Gui. — b4 79a
La Encantada, Mex. — C8 100
La Escondida, Mex. — H8 130
La Esmeralda, Mex. — B7 100
Laesø, i., Den. — H4 8
La Esperanza, Cuba — A5 102
La Esperanza, Hond. — E3 102
La Esperanza, Mex. — H4 130
La Estrada see A Estrada, Spain — B2 20
Lafa, China — C7 38
La Falda, Arg. — E5 92
La Farge, Wi., U.S. — H8 118
Lafayette, Al., U.S. — E13 122
Lafayette, Ca., U.S. — F3 134
Lafayette, Co., U.S. — A3 128
Lafayette, Ga., U.S. — C13 122
Lafayette, In., U.S. — H3 112
Lafayette, La., U.S. — G6 122
Lafayette, Tn., U.S. — H11 120
Lafayette, Mount, mtn., N.H., U.S. — F5 110
La Feria, Tx., U.S. — H10 130
La Ferté-Bernard, Fr. — F9 14
La Ferté-Saint-Aubin, Fr. — G10 14
Lafia, Nig. — H6 64
Lafiagi, Nig. — H6 64
Laflèche, Sk., Can. — E7 124
La Flèche, Fr. — G8 14
La Florida, Guat. — D2 102
La Foa, N. Cal. — m15 79d
La Follette, Tn., U.S. — H1 114
Lafourche, Bayou, stm., La., U.S. — H8 122
La Fragua, Arg. — C5 92
La Fría, Ven. — C5 86
La Fuente de San Esteban, Spain — D4 20
La Galite, i., Tun. — G2 24
La Gallareta, Arg. — D7 92
Lagarto, Braz. — F7 88
Lagawe, Phil. — B3 52
Lage, China — D10 54
Lågen, stm., Nor. — F4 8
Lages, Braz. — C12 92
Laghmān, state, Afg. — A3 54
Laghouat, Alg. — C5 64
Lagkadás, Grc. — C5 28
Lagoa da Prata, Braz. — K3 88
Lagoa Vermelha, Braz. — D12 92
Lago da Pedra, Braz. — C3 88
Lago Kolonie, Aruba — p20 104g
Lagolândia, Braz. — H1 88
Lagonegro, Italy — D9 24
Lagonoy Gulf, b., Phil. — D4 52
Lago Posadas, Arg. — I2 90
Lagos, Nig. — H5 64
Lagos, Port. — G2 20
Lagos de Moreno, Mex. — E7 100
La Gouèra, W. Sah. — E1 64
La Goulette, Tun. — H4 24
Lago Verde, Braz. — I2 90
La Granadella, Spain — C11 20
La Grande, Or., U.S. — E8 136
La Grande Deux, Réservoir, res., Qc., Can. — E15 106
La Grande Quatre, Réservoir, res., Qc., Can. — E16 106
LaGrange, Austl. — C4 74
La Grange, Ga., U.S. — D13 122
La Grange, Ky., U.S. — F12 120
La Grange, Mo., U.S. — D6 120
La Grange, Tx., U.S. — E11 130
Lagrange, Wy., U.S. — F8 126
Lagrange Bay, b., Austl. — C4 74
La Gran Sabana, pl., Ven. — E10 86
La Guadeloupe, Qc., Can. — E6 110
La Guajira, state, Col. — G11 102
La Guajira, Península de, pen., S.A. — A6 86
La Guardia, Arg. — D5 92
La Guardia, Bol. — C4 90
La Guardia see A Guardia, Spain — C1 20
La Guerche-sur-l'Aubois, Fr. — G11 14
Laguiole, Fr. — E8 18
Laguna, Braz. — D13 92
Laguna, N.M., U.S. — H9 132
Laguna, Ilha da, i., Braz. — D7 84
Laguna Beach, Ca., U.S. — J8 134
Laguna de Jaco, Mex. — K2 132
Laguna Larga, Arg. — E6 92
Laguna Paiva, Arg. — E7 92
Lagunas, Peru — E2 84
Lagunas de Chacagua, Parque Nacional, p.o.i., Mex. — H9 100
Lagunillas, Bol. — C4 90
Laha, China — B9 36
La Habana (Havana), Cuba — A6 102
Lahad Datu, Malay. — A11 50
Lahad Datu, Telukan, b., Malay. — A11 50
La Harpe, Il., U.S. — K7 118
La Harpe, Ks., U.S. — G2 120
Lahat, Indon. — E3 50
Lahdenpohja, Russia — F14 8
Lahemaa rahvus, p.o.i., Est. — G11 8
Lahewa, Indon. — L3 48
Lāhījān, Bir, well, Egypt — G4 58
Lahij, Yemen — G5 56
Lahijan, Iran — B7 56
Lahnstein, Ger. — F3 16
Laholm, Swe. — H5 8
Lahontan Reservoir, res., Nv., U.S. — D6 134
Lahore, Pak. — C5 54
La Horqueta, Col. — F5 86
Lahr, Ger. — H3 16
Lahti, Fin. — F11 8
La Huerta, N.M., U.S. — B3 130
Lahva, Bela. — H10 10
Laï, Chad — F3 62
Laiagam, Pap. N. Gui. — b3 79a
Laibin, China — J3 42
Laichow Bay see Laizhou Wan, b., China — C8 42
Laifeng, China — G3 42
L'Aigle, Fr. — F9 14
Laimbélé, Mont, mtn., Vanuatu — k16 79d
Laingsburg, S. Afr. — H5 70
Laingsburg, Mi., U.S. — B1 114
Lainioälven, stm., Swe. — C10 8
Lainsitz see Lužnice, stm.
Laird Hill, Tx., U.S. — E3 122
Lais, Indon. — E3 50
Lais, Indon. — C12 50
Laitila, Fin. — F9 8
Laiwu, China — C7 42
Laixi, China — C9 42
Laiyang, China — C9 42
Laizhou, China — C7 42
Laizhou Bay see Laizhou Wan, b., China — C8 42
Laizhou Wan (Laizhou Bay), b., China — C8 42
Laja, stm., Chile — H2 92
Laja, Salto del, wtfl, Chile — H2 92
La Jara, Co., U.S. — D2 128
La Jara, reg., Spain — E5 20
La Jara Canyon, p., N.M., U.S. — G9 132
La Jarita, Mex. — H4 130
Lajas, P.R. — B1 104a

Laje, Braz. — G6 88
Lajeado, Braz. — D11 92
Lajedo, Braz. — E7 88
Lajes, Braz. — C7 88
Lajinha, Braz. — K5 88
Laji Shan, mts., China — D5 36
Lajosmizse, Hung. — B6 26
Lajta (Leitha), stm., Eur. — H12 16
La Junta, Co., U.S. — D5 128
Lakar Kūh, mtn., Iran — D8 56
Lakatoro, Vanuatu — k16 79d
Lake, Ms., U.S. — E9 122
Lake Alfred, Fl., U.S. — H4 116
Lake Andes, S.D., U.S. — D14 126
Lake Arthur, La., U.S. — G6 122
Lake Benton, Mn., U.S. — G2 118
Lake Brownwood, Tx., U.S. — C8 130
Lake Cargelligo, Austl. — I6 76
Lake Charles, La., U.S. — G5 122
Lake Chelan National Recreation Area, p.o.i., Wa., U.S. — B6 136
Lake City, Ar., U.S. — B8 122
Lake City, Co., U.S. — E9 132
Lake City, Fl., U.S. — F3 116
Lake City, Mi., U.S. — D4 112
Lake City, Pa., U.S. — B5 114
Lake City, S.C., U.S. — C6 116
Lake City, Tn., U.S. — H1 114
Lake Cowichan, B.C., Can. — H6 138
Lake Crystal, Mn., U.S. — G4 118
Lake Dallas, Tx., U.S. — A10 130
Lake Delton, Wi., U.S. — H9 118
Lake District National Park, p.o.i., Eng., U.K. — G9 12
Lake Elsinore, Ca., U.S. — J8 134
Lakefield, On., Can. — D11 112
Lakefield, Mn., U.S. — H3 118
Lake Forest, Il., U.S. — F2 112
Lake Fork Reservoir, res., Tx., U.S. — D3 122
Lake Geneva, Wi., U.S. — B9 120
Lake George, N.Y., U.S. — G3 110
Lake Harbor, Fl., U.S. — J5 116
Lake Havasu City, Az., U.S. — I2 132
Lake Helen, Fl., U.S. — H4 116
Lake Jackson, Tx., U.S. — E12 130
Lake King, Austl. — F3 74
Lakeland, Fl., U.S. — H3 116
Lakeland, Ga., U.S. — E2 116
Lake Linden, Mi., U.S. — D10 118
Lake Louise, Ab., Can. — E14 138
Lake Mead National Recreation Area, p.o.i., U.S. — G2 132
Lake Mills, Wi., U.S. — A8 120
Lake Minchumina, Ak., U.S. — D9 140
Lake Mohawk see Sparta, N.J., U.S. — C11 114
Lake Nash, Austl. — D7 74
Lake Norden, S.D., U.S. — C15 126
Lake Oswego, Or., U.S. — E4 136
Lake Ozark, Mo., U.S. — F5 120
Lake Park, Fl., U.S. — J5 116
Lake Park, Ia., U.S. — H3 118
Lake Placid, Fl., U.S. — I4 116
Lake Placid, N.Y., U.S. — F3 110
Lake Pleasant, N.Y., U.S. — G2 110
Lakeport, Ca., U.S. — D3 134
Lakeport, Mi., U.S. — E7 112
Lake Preston, S.D., U.S. — C15 126
Lakes Entrance, Austl. — K7 76
Lakeshore, Ms., U.S. — G9 122
Lakeside, Ca., U.S. — K8 134
Lakeside, Mt., U.S. — B12 136
Lake Stevens, Wa., U.S. — B4 136
Laketown, Ut., U.S. — B5 132
Lake View, Ar., U.S. — C8 122
Lake View, Ia., U.S. — B3 120
Lakeview, Mi., U.S. — E4 112
Lakeview, Oh., U.S. — D2 114
Lakeview, Or., U.S. — A5 134
Lakeview, Tx., U.S. — G8 128
Lake Village, Ar., U.S. — D7 122
Lake Wales, Fl., U.S. — I4 116
Lakewood, Co., U.S. — B3 128
Lakewood, N.J., U.S. — D11 114
Lakewood, Oh., U.S. — C4 114
Lakewood, Wa., U.S. — C4 136
Lakewood, Wi., U.S. — C1 112
Lakewood Park, N.D., U.S. — F15 124
Lake Worth, Fl., U.S. — J5 116
Lakhdaria, Alg. — H14 20
Lakheri, India — F6 54
Lakhimpur, India — D8 54
Lakhnādon, India — G7 54
Lakhpat, India — H18 8
Lāla Mūsa, Pak. — B4 54
Lālapasa, Tur. — B9 28
L'Albufera, l., Spain — E10 20
Lalganj, India — F10 54
Lālgola, India — F12 54
Lalibela, Eth. — E7 62
La Libertad, Guat. — D2 102
La Ligua, Chile — F2 92
La Lima, Hond. — E4 102
Lalin, stm., China — B7 38
Lalin, China — B7 38
Lalindi, Indon. — I12 50
La Línea de la Concepción, Spain — H5 20
Lalitpur, India — F7 54
Lalitpur, Nepal — E10 54
Lalla Khedidja, Tamgout de, mtn., Alg. — H14 20
Lālmanir Hāt, Bngl. — F12 54
La Loche, Sk., Can. — D9 106
La Lora, plat., Spain — B7 20
La Louvière, Bel. — D13 14
L'Alpe-d'Huez, Fr. — D12 18
Lālpur, India — G2 54
Lālsot, India — E6 54
Lama, ozero, l., Russia — C6 34
La Macarena, Parque Nacional, p.o.i., Col. — F5 86
La Macarena, Serranía de, mts., Col. — F5 86
La Maddalena, Italy — C3 24
La Madrid, Arg. — C5 92
Lamadrid, Mex. — B8 100
La Magdalena, Mex. — H1 130
Lama-Kara, Togo — H5 64
La Malbaie, Qc., Can. — C6 110
La Mancha, reg., Spain — E8 20
Lamandau, stm., Indon. — E7 50
Lamap, Vanuatu — k16 79d
Lamar, Co., U.S. — C6 128
Lamar, Mo., U.S. — G3 120
Lamarche, Fr. — F14 14
La Marmora, Punta, mtn., Italy — D3 24
La Maroma, Mex. — F7 130
La Marque, Tx., U.S. — H4 122
La Marsa, Tun. — H4 24
La Martre, Qc., Can. — A10 110
Lamas, Peru — E2 84

Lamballe, Fr. — F6 14
Lambaréné, Gabon — E1 66
Lambari, stm., Braz. — J3 88
Lambayeque, Peru — E2 84
Lambay Island, i., Ire. — H7 12
Lambert, Ms., U.S. — C8 122
Lambert, Mt., U.S. — G9 124
Lambert, Cape, c., Pap. N. Gui. — a5 79a
Lambert Glacier, ice, Ant. — C11 81
Lambert Land, reg., Grnld. — B21 141
Lamberton, Mn., U.S. — G3 118
Lambertsbaai see Lambert's Bay, S. Afr. — H3 70
Lambert's Bay, S. Afr. — H3 70
Lambton, Cape, c., N.T., Can. — A6 106
Lame Deer, Mt., U.S. — B6 126
La Media Luna, Arrecifes de, rf., Hond. — E6 102
Lamego, Port. — C3 20
Lameque, N.B., Can. — C12 110
Lamèque, Île, i., N.B., Can. — C12 110
La Merced, Arg. — B5 92
La Merced, Arg. — D5 92
Lameroo, Austl. — J3 76
La Mesa, Ca., U.S. — K8 134
Lamesa, Tx., U.S. — B6 130
Lamia, Grc. — E5 28
Lamine, stm., Mo., U.S. — F5 120
La Misión, Mex. — K9 134
Lamitan, Phil. — G4 52
Lamlam, Mount, hill, Guam — j9 78c
Lamneuo, Indon. — J3 48
La Moille, Il., U.S. — C8 120
Lamoille, Nv., U.S. — C1 132
Lamoille, stm., Vt., U.S. — F4 110
Lamon Bay, b., Phil. — C4 52
Lamone, stm., Italy — F9 22
Lamongan, Indon. — G8 50
Lamoni, Ia., U.S. — D3 120
Lamont, Ca., U.S. — H6 134
Lamont, Ia., U.S. — I7 118
Lamont, Ok., U.S. — E11 128
La Monte, Mo., U.S. — F4 120
La Mothe, Lac, l., Qc., Can. — B5 110
La Mothe-Achard, Fr. — H7 14
Lamotrek, at., Micron. — C5 72
Lamotte-Beuvron, Fr. — G10 14
Lampang, Thai. — C4 48
Lampasas, Tx., U.S. — C9 130
Lampasas, stm., Tx., U.S. — C9 130
Lampazos de Naranjo, Mex. — B8 100
Lampedusa, Isola di, i., Italy — I6 24
Lampertheim, Ger. — G4 16
Lamphun, Thai. — C4 48
Lampman, Sk., Can. — E11 124
Lampung, state, Indon. — F4 50
Lamskoe, Russia — H21 10
Lamu, Kenya — E8 66
La Mure, Fr. — E11 18
Lan', stm., Bela. — H10 10
Lana, Italy — D8 22
Lanai, i., Hi., U.S. — c4 78a
Lanai City, Hi., U.S. — c4 78a
Lanaihale, mtn., Hi., U.S. — c5 78a
Lanalhue, Lago, l., Chile. — I1 92
Lanark, On., Can. — C13 112
Lanark, Scot., U.K. — F9 12
Lanbi Kyun, i., Mya. — G4 48
Lancang see Mekong, stm., Asia — D9 46
Lancaster, Eng., U.K. — G10 12
Lancaster, Ca., U.S. — I7 134
Lancaster, Mn., U.S. — C2 118
Lancaster, Mo., U.S. — D5 120
Lancaster, N.H., U.S. — F5 110
Lancaster, Oh., U.S. — E3 114
Lancaster, Pa., U.S. — D9 114
Lancaster, S.C., U.S. — B5 116
Lancaster, Tx., U.S. — E2 122
Lancaster, Va., U.S. — G9 114
Lancaster, Wi., U.S. — B7 120
Lancaster Sound, strt., Nu., Can. — C8 141
Lance Creek, Wy., U.S. — D8 126
Lancelin, Austl. — F2 74
Lanchou see Lanzhou, China — D5 36
Lanchow see Lanzhou, China — D5 36
Lanciano, Italy — H11 22
Lancun, China — C9 42
Łańcut, Pol. — F18 16
Ländana, Ang. — B1 68
Landau an der Isar, Ger. — H8 16
Landau in der Pfalz, Ger. — G4 16
Landeck, Aus. — C7 22
Lander, Wy., U.S. — E4 126
Landerneau, Fr. — F4 14
Landes, state, Fr. — F5 18
Landes, reg., Fr. — E4 18
Landete, Spain — E9 20
Land O'Lakes, Wi., U.S. — E9 118
Landsborough Creek, stm., Austl. — D5 76
Land's End, c., Eng., U.K. — K7 12
Landshut, Ger. — H7 16
Landskrona, Swe. — I5 8
Lane, mth., Fr. — G9 14
Lanett, Al., U.S. — E13 122
Lanezi Lake, l., B.C., Can. — C10 138
La'nga Co, l., China — C8 54
Langa-Langa, D.R.C. — E3 66
Langbank, Sk., Can. — D11 124
Langdale, Al., U.S. — E13 122
Langdon, N.D., U.S. — F15 124
Langeberg, mts., S. Afr. — H5 70
Langeland, i., Den. — I4 8
Langenhagen, Ger. — D5 16
Langenthal, Switz. — C4 22
Langfang, China — B7 42
Langford, S.D., U.S. — B15 126
Langgam, Indon. — C2 50
Langham, Sk., Can. — B6 124
Langhe, hist. reg., Italy — F5 22
Langholm, Scot., U.K. — F9 12
Langjökull, ice, Ice. — k29 8a
Langkawi, Pulau, i., Malay. — I4 48
Langley, B.C., Can. — G8 138
Langlois, Or., U.S. — A1 134
Langnau im Emmental, Switz. — C4 22
Lang Suan, Thai. — H4 48
Langsa, Indon. — K3 48
Langsa, Teluk, b., Indon. — K3 48
Langshan, China — A2 42
Langtang, China — B7 42
Langtry, Tx., U.S. — E7 130
Langruth, Mb., Can. — D15 124

Länkipohja, Fin. — F11 8
Lannemezan, Fr. — F6 18
Lannion, Fr. — F5 14
Lanping, China — F4 36
Lansdowne, India — D7 54
Lansdowne House, On., Can. — E13 106
L'Anse, Mi., U.S. — B1 112
Lansing, Ia., U.S. — H7 118
Lansing, Mi., U.S. — B1 114
Länsi-Suomi, state, Fin. — E10 8
Lantana, Fl., U.S. — J5 116
Lantau Island, i., China — J6 42
Lanta Yai, Ko, i., Thai. — I4 48
Lantian, China — D3 42
Lanusei, Italy — E3 24
Lanxi, China — G8 42
Lan Yü, i., Tai. — J9 42
Lanzhou, China — D5 36
Lanzo Torinese, Italy — E4 22
Lao, stm., Thai. — C4 48
Laoag, Phil. — A3 52
Laoang, Phil. — D5 52
Lao Cai, Viet. — A6 48
Laodao, stm., China — G5 42
Laofu, China — C3 38
Laoha, stm., China — C3 38
Laohekou, China — E4 42
Laohokow see Laohekou, China — E4 42
Laois, state, Ire. — I5 12
Lao Ling, mtn., China — C9 38
Laon, Fr. — E12 14
Laona, Wi., U.S. — F10 118
La Orchila, Isla, i., Ven. — B8 86
La Oroya, Peru — F2 84
Laos, ctry., Asia — C6 48
Laoshan Wan, b., China — C9 42
Lapa, Braz. — B13 92
Lapai, Nig. — H6 64
Lapalisse, Fr. — C9 18
La Palma, Col. — E4 86
La Palma, Pan. — H8 102
La Palma, Pan. — I7 102
La Palma del Condado, Spain — G4 20
La Paloma, Ur. — G10 92
La Pampa, state, Arg. — G3 90
La Paragua, Ven. — D10 86
La Pasión, stm., Guat. — D2 102
La Paya, Parque Nacional, p.o.i., Col. — G4 86
La Paz, Arg. — D5 92
La Paz, Arg. — F4 92
La Paz, Bol. — C3 90
La Paz, Col. — B5 86
La Paz, Hond. — E4 102
La Paz, Mex. — C3 100
La Paz, Mex. — D9 92
La Paz, Bahía de, b., Mex. — C3 100
La Perla, Mex. — A6 100
La Perouse, Bahía, b., Chile. — e30 78l
La Perouse Strait, strt., Asia — B13 36
La Pesca, Mex. — D10 100
La Piedad de Cabadas, Mex. — E7 100
La Pine, Or., U.S. — G5 136
La Place, La., U.S. — G8 122
Lap Lae, Thai. — D4 48
Lapland, hist. reg., Eur. — C11 8
La Plata, Arg. — G8 92
La Plata, Col. — F3 86
La Plata, Md., U.S. — F9 114
La Plata, Mo., U.S. — D5 120
La Plata Peak, mtn., Co., U.S. — D10 132
La Pobla de Segur, Spain — B11 20
La Pocatière, Qc., Can. — C6 110
Lapominka, Russia — D19 8
Laporte, Co., U.S. — G7 126
Laporte, In., U.S. — G3 112
La Porte, Tx., U.S. — H4 122
La Porte City, Ia., U.S. — B5 120
La Potherie, Lac, l., Qc., Can. — D16 106
Lappajärvi, l., Fin. — E10 8
Lappeenranta, Fin. — F12 8
Lappi, state, Fin. — C12 8
Laprida, Arg. — D5 76
Laprida, Arg. — H7 92
La Pryor, Tx., U.S. — F8 130
Lapta, N. Cyp. — C4 58
Laptev Sea see Laptevyh, more, s., Russia — B4 32
Laptevyh, more, s., Russia — B4 32
La Puebla de Montalbán, Spain — E6 20
La Puerta, Arg. — D5 92
La Puerta de Cabrera, Mex. — H2 130
La Purísima, Mex. — B2 100
Lāpus, Rom. — B11 26
Lapwai, Id., U.S. — D10 136
La Quiaca, Arg. — D3 90
L'Aquila, Italy — H10 22
Lār, Iran — D7 56
Lara, state, Ven. — B7 86
Laracha, Spain — A2 20
Larache, Mor. — B3 64
Laramie, Wy., U.S. — F7 126
Laramie, stm., U.S. — F7 126
Laramie Mountains, mts., Wy., U.S. — E7 126
Laramie Peak, mtn., Wy., U.S. — E7 126
Laranjal, Braz. — K4 88
Laranjeiras, Braz. — F7 88
Laranjeiras do Sul, Braz. — B11 92
Larantuka, Indon. — G7 44
Larap, Phil. — C4 52
Larat, Indon. — G9 44
Larat, Pulau, i., Indon. — G9 44
Larche, Col de, p., Eur. — E12 18
Larchwood, Ia., U.S. — H2 118
Laredo, Spain — A7 20
Laredo, Tx., U.S. — F8 130
La Reforma, Mex. — B2 100
Lares, P.R. — B2 104a
Larga, Mol. — A13 26
Larga, Laguna, l., Tx., U.S. — G10 130
Largo, Fl., U.S. — I3 116
Largo, Cañon, p., N.M., U.S. — G9 132
Largo, Cayo, i., Cuba — B7 102
Largs, Scot., U.K. — F8 12
Lārī, Iran — B7 56
Larimore, N.D., U.S. — G16 124
Larino, Italy — I11 22
Lárisa, Grc. — D5 28
Larjak, Russia — B14 32
Larkana, Pak. — D10 56
La Robla, Spain — B5 20
La Rochelle, Fr. — C4 18
La Rochefoucauld, Fr. — D6 18
La Roche-sur-Yon, Fr. — H7 14
La Roda, Spain — E8 20
La Romana, Dom. Rep. — C13 102
La Ronge, Sk., Can. — D10 106
Larose, La., U.S. — H8 122

Larrys River, N.S., Can. — E15 110
Larsen Ice Shelf, ice, Ant. — B34 81
La Rubia, Arg. — E7 92
La Rue, Oh., U.S. — D2 114
Larvik, Nor. — G3 8
Larzac, Causse du, plat., Fr. — F9 18
La Sabanilla, Mex. — C8 100
La Sal, Ut., U.S. — E7 132
La Salle, Co., U.S. — G8 126
La Salle, Il., U.S. — C8 120
La Salle, stm., Mb., Can. — E16 124
Lasan, Indon. — C9 50
Las Animas, Co., U.S. — C5 128
Las Arenas, P.R. — B1 104a
La Sarre, Qc., Can. — F15 106
Las Ballenas, Canal de, strt., Mex. — G6 98
Las Breñas, Arg. — C7 92
Las Cabezas de San Juan, Spain — G5 20
Lascano, Ur. — F10 92
Las Casitas, mtn., Mex. — D4 100
Las Catitas, Arg. — F3 92
Las Choapas, Mex. — G11 100
Las Chorreras, Mex. — A6 100
Las Cruces, N.M., U.S. — K10 132
Las Cuatas, Mex. — D1 130
Las Cuevas, Mex. — A8 100
Las Cumaraguas, Ven. — p20 104g
La Selle, Morne, mtn., Haiti — C11 102
La Serena, Chile — D2 92
La Serena, reg., Spain — F5 20
La Seu d'Urgell, Spain — B12 20
La Seyne, Fr. — F11 18
Las Flores, Arg. — G8 92
Las Flores, P.R. — B3 104a
Las Flores, Arroyo, stm., Arg. — H7 92
Las Garcitas, Arg. — C7 92
Las Guayabas, Mex. — C10 100
Lashburn, Sk., Can. — A4 124
Las Heras, Arg. — F3 92
Las Heras, Arg. — I3 90
Lashio, Mya. — A3 48
Lashkar Gāh, Afg. — C9 56
Las Hormigas, Mex. — C3 100
Lasia, Pulau, i., Indon. — K3 48
Łasin, Pol. — C15 16
La Sirena, Ven. — p20 104g
Laskarzew, Pol. — E17 16
Las Lajas, Arg. — I2 92
Las Lajas, Pan. — H7 102
Las Lomitas, Arg. — B7 92
Las Malvinas, Arg. — G3 92
Las Mareas, P.R. — C3 104a
Las Margaritas, Mex. — G13 100
Las Marianas, Arg. — B1 92
Las Marías, P.R. — B1 104a
Las Minas, Cerro, mtn., Hond. — E3 102
Las Nopaleras, Cerro, mtn., Mex. — C7 100
La Solana, Spain — F7 20
Las Ovejas, Arg. — H2 92
Las Palmas, Arg. — C8 92
Las Palmas, P.R. — C3 104a
Las Palomas, Mex. — F9 98
La Spezia, Italy — F6 22
Las Piedras, P.R. — B4 104a
Las Piedras, Ur. — G9 92
Las Piedras, stm., Peru — F3 84
Las Plumas, Arg. — H3 90
Lasqueti Island, i., B.C., Can. — G7 138
Las Rosas, Arg. — F7 92
Las Rosas, Mex. — G12 100
Lassance, Braz. — I3 88
Lassen Peak, vol., Ca., U.S. — C4 134
Lassen Volcanic National Park, p.o.i., Ca., U.S. — C4 134
L'Assomption, stm., Qc., Can. — D3 110
Las Tablas, Pan. — I7 102
Las Tinajas, Mex. — C6 92
Last Mountain Lake, l., Sk., Can. — C8 124
Las Tórtolas, Cerro (Tórtolas, Cerro de las), mtn., S.A. — D2 92
Lastoursville, Gabon — E2 66
Las Tunas, Cuba — B9 102
Las Tunas Grandes, Laguna, l., Arg. — H6 92
Las Varas, Mex. — E6 100
Las Varas, Mex. — D6 100
Las Varillas, Arg. — E6 92
Las Vegas, P.R. — B1 104a
Las Vegas, N.M., U.S. — F3 128
Las Vegas, Nv., U.S. — G1 132
Las Vegas, Ven. — C7 86
Latacunga, Ec. — H2 86
La Tagua, Col. — H4 86
Latakia see Al-Lādhiqīyah, Syria — C6 58
Lata Mountain, vol., Am. Sam. — h13 79c
Latehar, India — G10 54
La Teste-de-Buch, Fr. — E4 18
Lāthi, India — H3 54
Lathrop, Mo., U.S. — E3 120
Latimer, Ia., U.S. — I5 118
Latisana, Italy — E10 22
Latium see Lazio, state, Italy — H9 22
Latjuga, Russia — D23 8
La Torrecilla, mtn., P.R. — B3 104a
La Tortuga, Isla, i., Ven. — B9 86
Latouche Treville, Cape, c., Austl. — C4 74
La Tour-d'Auvergne, Fr. — D8 18
La Trimouille, Fr. — C7 18
La Trinidad, Nic. — F4 102
La Trinidad de Orichuna, Ven. — D7 86
La Trinité, Mart. — k6 105c
Latrobe, Austl. — n13 77a
Latrobe, Pa., U.S. — D6 114
Latta, S.C., U.S. — B6 116
Lattes, Fr. — F10 18
Lātūr, India — B3 53
Latvia, ctry., Eur. — D7 10
Lau, Nig. — H7 64
Lauchhammer, Ger. — E9 16
Lauf an der Pegnitz, Ger. — G7 16
Lauge Koch Kyst, cst., Grnld. — B13 141
Laughlin, Nv., U.S. — H2 132
Laughlin Peak, mtn., N.M., U.S. — E4 128
Lau Group, is., Fiji — p20 79e
Lauis see Lugano, Switz. — D5 22
Laun, Thai. — E5 48
Launceston, Austl. — n13 77a
Launceston, Eng., U.K. — K8 12
La Unión, Chile — H2 90
La Unión, El Sal. — F4 102
La Unión, Mex. — G8 100
La Unión, Spain — G10 20
La Unión, Ven. — C8 86
La Unión, N.M., U.S. — L10 132
Laupāhoehoe, Hi., U.S. — c6 78a
Laupheim, Ger. — H5 16
La Urbana, Ven. — D8 86
Laura, Austl. — B5 76
Laureana di Borrello, Italy — F9 24
Laurel, De., U.S. — F10 114
Laurel, Fl., U.S. — I3 116
Laurel, Md., U.S. — E9 114
Laurel, Ms., U.S. — F9 122
Laurel, Mt., U.S. — B4 126
Laurel, Ne., U.S. — E15 126
Laurel Bay, S.C., U.S. — D5 116

Name	Map Ref.	Page
Laureldale, Pa., U.S.	D10	114
Laureles, Ur.	E9	92
Laurel River Lake, res., Ky., U.S.	G1	114
Laurelville, Oh., U.S.	E15	120
Laurencekirk, Scot., U.K.	E10	12
Laurens, S.C., U.S.	B3	116
Laurentides, Les, plat., Qc., Can.	F16	106
Lau Ridge, unds.	L21	142
Laurier, Mb., Can.	D14	124
Laurier-Station, Qc., Can.	D5	110
Laurinburg, N.C., U.S.	B6	116
Laurium, Mi., U.S.	D10	118
Lausanne, Switz.	D3	22
Lausitzer Neisse (Nysa Łużycka), stm., Eur.	F10	16
Laut, Pulau, i., Indon.	A5	50
Laut, Pulau, i., Indon.	E10	50
Laut, Selat, strt., Indon.	E9	50
Lauta, Ger.	E9	16
Lautaro, Chile	I1	92
Lauterbach, Ger.	F5	16
Lauter Sachsen, Ger.	F8	16
Laut Kecil, Kepulauan, is., Indon.	F9	50
Lautoka, Fiji	p18	79e
Lauzerte, Fr.	E7	18
Lava (Łyna), stm., Eur.	B16	16
Lava Beds National Monument, p.o.i., Ca., U.S.	B4	134
Lavaca, stm., Tx., U.S.	E11	130
Laval, Qc., Can.	E3	110
Laval, Fr.	F8	14
La Vall d'Uixó, Spain	E10	20
Lavalle, Arg.	D5	92
Lavalle, Arg.	D8	92
Lavapié, Punta, c., Chile	H1	92
Lavassaare, Est.	B7	10
La Vega, Dom. Rep.	C12	102
La Vela de Coro, Ven.	B7	86
Lavelanet, Fr.	G7	18
Lavello, Italy	C9	24
La Venada, Mex.	I10	130
La Venta, sci., Mex.	F11	100
La Ventura, Mex.	C8	100
La Vera, reg., Spain	D5	20
La Vergne, Tn., U.S.	H11	120
Laverne, Ok., U.S.	E9	128
Laverton, Austl.	E4	74
La Veta, Co., U.S.	D4	128
Lavieille, Lake, l., On., Can.	C11	112
La Vila Joiosa, Spain	F10	20
Lavillette, N.B., Can.	C11	110
La Viña, Arg.	A4	92
Lavina, Mt., U.S.	A4	126
La Vista, Ne., U.S.	C1	120
La Voulte-sur-Rhône, Fr.	E10	18
Lavras, Braz.	K3	88
Lávrio, Grc.	F7	28
Lavumisa, Swaz.	E10	70
Lawang, Indon.	G8	50
Lawas, Malay.	A9	50
Lawdar, Yemen	G6	56
Lawers, Ben, mtn., Scot., U.K.	E8	12
Lawgi, Austl.	E8	76
Lawksawk, Mya.	B3	48
Lawler, Ia., U.S.	A5	120
Lawn, Tx., U.S.	B8	130
Lawndale, N.C., U.S.	A4	116
Lawn Hill Creek, stm., Austl.	C7	74
Lawrence, In., U.S.	I3	112
Lawrence, Ks., U.S.	F2	120
Lawrence, Ma., U.S.	B14	114
Lawrenceburg, In., U.S.	E12	120
Lawrenceburg, Ky., U.S.	F12	120
Lawrenceburg, Tn., U.S.	B11	122
Lawrenceville, Il., U.S.	F10	120
Lawrenceville, N.J., U.S.	D11	114
Lawson, Mo., U.S.	E3	120
Lawtey, Fl., U.S.	F3	116
Lawton, N.D., U.S.	F15	124
Lawton, Ok., U.S.	G10	128
Lawu, Gunung, vol., Indon.	G7	50
Lawz, Jabal al-, mtn., Sau. Ar.	J6	58
Laxå, Swe.	G6	8
Laxe, Spain	A1	20
Lay Lake, res., Al., U.S.	D12	122
Layou, St. Vin.	o11	105e
Layton, Ut., U.S.	B4	132
Laytonville, Ca., U.S.	D2	134
La Zarca, Mex.	C6	100
Lazarev, Russia	F17	34
Lázaro Cárdenas, Mex.	G7	100
Lázaro Cárdenas, Presa, res., Mex.	C6	100
Lazdijai, Lith.	F6	10
Lazio, state, Italy	B6	24
Léach, Camb.	F6	48
Leachville, Ar., U.S.	I7	120
Leadbetter Point, c., Wa., U.S.	D2	136
Leader, Sk., Can.	D4	124
Lead Hill, hill, Mo., U.S.	H4	120
Leadore, Id., U.S.	F13	136
Leadville, Co., U.S.	D10	132
Leaf, stm., Ms., U.S.	F10	122
Leaf Lake, l., Sk., Can.	A11	124
Leaghur, Lake, l., Austl.	I4	76
League City, Tx., U.S.	H3	122
Leakey, Tx., U.S.	E8	130
Leaksville, N.C., U.S.	H5	114
Lealman, Fl., U.S.	I3	116
Leamington, On., Can.	F7	112
Le'an, China	H6	42
Leandro, Braz.	C3	88
Leandro N. Alem, Arg.	C10	92
Leary, Ga., U.S.	F14	122
Leatherman Peak, mtn., Id., U.S.	F13	136
Leavenworth, Ks., U.S.	E2	120
Leavenworth, Wa., U.S.	C6	136
Leawood, Ks., U.S.	F3	120
Lebak, Phil.	G5	52
Lebam, Wa., U.S.	D3	136
Lebanon, In., U.S.	H3	112
Lebanon, Ks., U.S.	B10	128
Lebanon, Ky., U.S.	G12	120
Lebanon, Mo., U.S.	G4	120
Lebanon, N.H., U.S.	G4	110
Lebanon, Oh., U.S.	E1	114
Lebanon, Or., U.S.	F3	136
Lebanon, Pa., U.S.	D9	114
Lebanon, Tn., U.S.	H11	120
Lebanon, Va., U.S.	H3	114
Lebanon, ctry., Asia	C6	58
Lebec, Ca., U.S.	I7	134
Lebesby, Nor.	A12	8
Le Bic, Qc., Can.	B8	110
Le Blanc, Fr.	H10	14
Lebo, D.R.C.	D4	66
Lebo, Ks., U.S.	F2	120
Łebork, Pol.	B13	16
Lebrija, Spain	H4	20
Łebsko, Jezioro, l., Pol.	B13	16
Lebu, Chile	H1	92
Lebyazh'e, Kaz.	D13	32
Le Carbet, Mart.	k6	105c
Lecce, Italy	D12	24
Lecco, Italy	E6	22
Le Center, Mn., U.S.	G5	118
Lech, stm., Eur.	H6	16
Lechainá, Grc.	F4	28
Lechang, China	I5	42
Le Chesne, Fr.	E13	14
Lechiguanas, Islas de las, is., Arg.	F8	92
Lechuguilla, Cerro, mtn., Mex.	D6	100
Lecompte, La., U.S.	F6	122
Le Creusot, Fr.	H13	14
Le Croisic, Fr.	G6	14
Łęczyca, Pol.	D15	16
Ledesma, Spain	C4	20
Le Diamant, Mart.	I6	105c
Ledjanaja, gora, mtn., Russia	D23	34
Ledo, India	C8	46
Ledong, Indon.	C6	50
Ledong, China	L3	42
Le Dorat, Fr.	C7	18
Ledu, China	D5	36
Leduc, Ab., Can.	C17	138
Leechburg, Pa., U.S.	D6	114
Leech Lake, l., Mn., U.S.	D4	118
Leedey, Ok., U.S.	F9	128
Leeds, Eng., U.K.	H11	12
Leeds, Al., U.S.	D12	122
Leeds, N.D., U.S.	F14	124
Leek, Eng., U.K.	H10	12
Leelanau, Lake, l., Mi., U.S.	D4	112
Leelanau Peninsula, pen., Mi., U.S.	C4	112
Leer, Ger.	A4	16
Leesburg, Fl., U.S.	H4	116
Leesburg, Ga., U.S.	E1	116
Leesburg, Va., U.S.	E8	114
Lee Summit, Mo., U.S.	F3	120
Leesville, La., U.S.	F5	122
Leesville, Tx., U.S.	E10	130
Leeton, Austl.	J6	76
Leeu-Gamka, S. Afr.	H6	70
Leeuwarden, Neth.	A14	14
Leeuwin, Cape, c., Austl.	F2	74
Lee Vining, Ca., U.S.	F6	134
Leeward Islands, is., N.A.	h15	96a
Lefkáda, Grc.	E3	28
Lefkáda, i., Grc.	E3	28
Lefke, N. Cyp.	C3	58
Lefkosia see Nicosia, Cyp.	C4	58
Lefors, Tx., U.S.	F8	128
Le François, Mart.	k7	105c
Lefroy, Lake, l., Austl.	F4	74
Legal, Ab., Can.	C17	138
Leganés, Spain	D7	20
Legaspi, Phil.	D4	52
Leggett, Ca., U.S.	D2	134
Leghorn see Livorno, Italy	G7	22
Legion, Zimb.	B9	70
Legionowo, Pol.	D16	16
Legnago, Italy	E8	22
Legnano, Italy	E5	22
Legnica, Pol.	E12	16
Legnica, state, Pol.	E12	16
Le Gosier, Guad.	h6	105c
Le Grand, Ca., U.S.	F5	134
La Guelta, Alg.	H11	20
Legume, Austl.	G9	76
Leh, India	A6	54
Le Havre, Fr.	E8	14
Lehčevo, Blg.	F10	26
Lehigh, Ia., U.S.	B3	120
Lehigh, Ok., U.S.	C2	122
Lehigh Acres, Fl., U.S.	J4	116
Lehighton, Pa., U.S.	D10	114
Lehrte, Ger.	D5	16
Lehtse, Est.	A11	10
Lehua, i., Hi., U.S.	a1	78a
Lehututu, Bots.	C5	70
Lei, stm., China	H5	42
Leiah, Pak.	C3	54
Leibnitz, Aus.	D12	22
Leicester, Eng., U.K.	I11	12
Leichhardt, stm., Austl.	A2	76
Leichhardt Falls, wtfl., Austl.	B2	76
Leiden (Leyden), Neth.	B13	14
Leighton, Al., U.S.	C11	122
Leighton Buzzard, Eng., U.K.	J12	12
Leinan, Sk., Can.	D6	124
Leine, stm., Ger.	D5	16
Leinster, hist. reg., Ire.	I6	12
Leinster, Mount, mtn., Ire.	I6	12
Leipalingis, Lith.	F6	10
Leipsic, Oh., U.S.	C2	114
Leipsoí, i., Grc.	F9	28
Leipzig, Ger.	E8	16
Leiria, Port.	E2	20
Leiria, state, Port.	E2	20
Leisler, Mount, mtn., Austl.	D6	74
Leitariegos, Puerto de, p., Spain	A4	20
Leitha (Lajta), stm., Eur.	H12	16
Leitrim, Ire.	H4	12
Leitrim, state, Ire.	H5	12
Leivádia, Grc.	E5	28
Leiyang, China	H5	42
Leizhou Bandao, pen., China	K3	42
Lejasciems, Lat.	C9	10
Lekeitio, Spain	A8	20
Leksozero, ozero, l., Russia	E14	8
Le Lamentin, Mart.	k6	105c
Leland, Il., U.S.	C9	120
Leland, Mi., U.S.	C4	112
Leland, Ms., U.S.	D8	122
Lelystad, Neth.	B14	14
Le Maire, Estrecho de, strt., Arg.	J4	90
Le Mans, Fr.	G9	14
Le Marin, Mart.	I7	105c
Le Mars, Ia., U.S.	B1	120
Lema Shilindi, Eth.	G8	62
Lemay, Mo., U.S.	F7	120
Lembak, Indon.	C10	50
Lemdiyya, Alg.	H13	20
Leme, Braz.	L2	88
Lemesós (Limassol), Cyp.	D4	58
Lemhi, stm., Id., U.S.	F13	136
Lemhi Pass, p., U.S.	F13	136
Lemhi Range, mts., Id., U.S.	F13	136
Lemieux Islands, is., Nu., Can.	E13	141
Leming, Tx., U.S.	E9	130
Lemitar, N.M., U.S.	I10	132
Lemmatsi, Est.	B9	10
Lemmenjoki kansallispuisto, p.o.i., Fin.	B11	8
Lemmon, S.D., U.S.	B10	126
Lemmon, Mount, mtn., Az., U.S.	K6	132
Lemnos see Límnos, i., Grc.	D8	28
Lemoncove, Ca., U.S.	G7	134
Le Mont-Dore, N. Cal.	n16	79d
Le Moule, Guad.	h6	105c
Lempa, stm., N.A.	F3	102
Lempe, Indon.	D12	50
Lemro, stm., Mya.	B1	48
Le Murge, hills, Italy	D10	24
Le Muy, Fr.	F12	18
Lemyethna, Mya.	D2	48
Lena, Wi., U.S.	D1	112
Lena, Il., U.S.	B8	120
Lena, stm., Russia	B14	34
Lenart, Slvn.	D12	22
Lençóis, Braz.	G5	88
Lençóis Maranhenses, Parque Nacional dos, p.o.i., Braz.	B4	88
Léndery, Russia	E14	8
Lendinara, Italy	E8	22
Lengby, Mn., U.S.	F12	124
Lengguru, stm., Malay.	K6	48
Lenggor, stm., Malay.	D4	42
Lenghu, China	H4	42
Lengshuitan, China	H4	42
Lenhovda, Swe.	H6	8
Leningrad see Sankt-Peterburg, Russia	A13	10
Leningradskaja oblast', co., Russia	G15	8
Leninogor see Leninogorsk, Kaz.	D14	32
Leninogorsk, Kaz.	D14	32
Lenin Peak, mtn., Asia	B11	56
Leninsk, Kaz.	E10	32
Leninsk, Uzb.	F12	32
Leninskij, Russia	F20	10
Leninsk-Kuzneckij, Russia	D15	32
Leninskoe, Russia	G15	34
Lennonville, Austl.	E3	74
Lennox, S.D., U.S.	H2	118
Lennox, Isla, i., Chile	K3	90
Lennoxville, Qc., Can.	E5	110
Lenoir, N.C., U.S.	I4	114
Lenora, Ne., U.S.	D3	70
Lenox, Ga., U.S.	E2	116
Lenox, Ia., U.S.	D3	120
Lenox, Tn., U.S.	D11	14
Lenski, Russia	B20	32
Lensk, Russia	D11	34
Lenti, Hung.	C3	26
Lentini, Italy	G9	24
Lentua, l., Fin.	D13	8
Lentvaris, Lith.	F8	10
Lenya, stm., Mya.	G4	48
Léo, Burkina	G4	64
Leoben, Aus.	C12	22
Léogâne, Haiti	C11	102
Leola, Ar., U.S.	C6	122
Leola, S.D., U.S.	B14	126
Leominster, Eng., U.K.	I10	12
Leominster, Ma., U.S.	B14	114
Léon, Fr.	F4	18
León, Mex.	E8	100
León, Nic.	F4	102
León, Spain	B5	20
Leon, Ks., U.S.	D12	128
León, co., Spain	B5	20
Leon, stm., Tx., U.S.	C10	130
León, Montes de, mts., Spain	B4	20
Leona, stm., Tx., U.S.	F8	130
Leonard, Tx., U.S.	D2	122
Leonardtown, Md., U.S.	F9	114
Leonardville, Ks., U.S.	B11	128
Leonberg, Ger.	H4	16
Leones, Arg.	F6	92
Leonforte, Italy	G8	24
Leongatha, Austl.	L5	76
Leoniha, Russia	G18	8
Leonora, Austl.	E4	74
Leopold and Astrid Coast, cst., Ant.	B13	81
Leopoldina, Braz.	K4	88
Leopoldo de Bulhões, Braz.	I1	88
Léopoldville see Kinshasa, D.R.C.	E3	66
Leoti, Ks., U.S.	C7	128
Leova, Mol.	C15	26
Lepanto see Nafpaktos, Grc.	E4	28
Lepanto, Ar., U.S.	B8	122
Lepar, Pulau, i., Indon.	E5	50
Lepe, Spain	G3	20
Lepel', Bela.	F11	10
Leping, China	G7	42
L'Épiphanie, Qc., Can.	E3	110
Lepontine Alps, mts., Eur.	C14	18
Lepreau, Point, c., N.B., Can.	E10	110
Le Prêcheur, Mart.	k6	105c
Lepsi, Kaz.	E13	32
Lepsy see Lepsi, Kaz.	E13	32
Le Puy, Fr.	D9	18
Lequeitio see Lekeitio, Spain	A8	20
Lercara Friddi, Italy	G7	24
Lerdo, Mex.	C7	100
Lerici, Italy	F7	22
Lérida, Col.	G6	86
Lérida see Lleida, Spain	C11	20
Lerma, stm., Mex.	E8	100
Le Roy, Il., U.S.	D9	120
Le Roy, Ks., U.S.	F2	120
Le Roy, N.Y., U.S.	B7	114
Lerum, Swe.	H5	8
Lerwick, Scot., U.K.	n18	12a
Les Abymes, Guad.	h5	105c
Le Saint-Esprit, Mart.	k7	105c
Les Andelys, Fr.	E10	14
Les Anses-d'Arlets, Mart.	l6	105c
Les Borges Blanques, Spain	C11	20
Les Cayes, Haiti	C11	102
Leshan, China	F5	36
Les Herbiers, Fr.	H7	14
Lesina, Lago di, b., Italy	I12	22
Lesko, Pol.	G18	16
Leskovac, Serb.	F8	26
Leskov Island, i., S. Geor.	K12	82
Les Laurentides see Laurentides, Les, plat., Qc., Can.	F16	106
Leslie, Ar., U.S.	I5	120
Leslie, Mi., U.S.	B1	114
Leslie, W.V., U.S.	F5	114
Lesneven, Fr.	F4	14
Lesnoe, Russia	B18	10
Lesogorsk, Russia	G17	34
Lesosibirsk, Russia	C16	32
Lesotho, ctry., Afr.	F9	70
Lesozavodsk, Russia	B10	38
Lesozavodskij, Russia	C15	8
Les Sables-d'Olonne, Fr.	H7	14
Les Saintes, is., Guad.	i5	105c
Lesser Antilles, is.	D8	82
Lesser Khingan Range see Xiao Hinggan Ling, mts., China	B10	36
Lesser Slave, stm., Ab., Can.	A16	138
Lesser Slave Lake, l., Ab., Can.	D8	106
Lesser Sunda Islands see Tenggara, Nusa, is., Indon.	G5	44
L'Esterre, Gren.	q10	105e
Lestock, Sk., Can.	C9	124
Le Sueur, Mn., U.S.	G4	118
Le Sueur, stm., Mn., U.S.	G4	118
Lešukonskoe, Russia	D21	8
Lésvos (Lesbos), i., Grc.	D9	28
Leszno, Pol.	E12	16
Leszno, state, Pol.	E12	16
Letaba, stm., S. Afr.	C10	70
Letcher, S.D., U.S.	D14	126
Letea, Ostrovul, i., Rom.	D16	26
Letenye, Hung.	C3	26
Lethbridge, Ab., Can.	G18	138
Lethem, Guy.	F12	86
Le Thillot, Fr.	B12	18
Leti, Kepulauan, is., Indon.	G8	44
Leticia, Col.	D4	84
Letlhakane, Bots.	B7	70
Letlhakeng, Bots.	D7	70
Letpadan, Mya.	D2	48
Le Tréport, Fr.	D10	14
Letsôk-aw Kyun, i., Mya.	G3	48
Letung, Indon.	B4	50
Leucas see Lefkáda, i., Grc.	E3	28
Leucate, Étang de, l., Fr.	G9	18
Leuk, Switz.	D4	22
Leuser, Gunung, mtn., Indon.	K3	48
Leutkirch, Ger.	I6	16
Leuven, Bel.	D13	14
Levack, On., Can.	B8	112
Levan, Ut., U.S.	D5	132
Levanger, Nor.	E4	8
Levante, Riviera di, cst., Italy	F6	22
Levanzo, Isola di, i., Italy	F6	24
Le Vauclin, Mart.	k7	105c
Leveland, Tx., U.S.	H6	128
Leveque, Cape, c., Austl.	C4	74
Leverkusen, Ger.	E3	16
Levice, Slov.	H14	16
Levin, N.Z.	E6	80
Lévis, Qc., Can.	D5	110
Levisa Fork, stm., U.S.	G3	114a
Levittown, N.Y., U.S.	D12	114
Levittown, Pa., U.S.	D11	114
Levkosia see Nicosia, Cyp.	C4	58
Levoča, Slov.	H16	16
Levski, Blg.	F12	26
Levuka, Fiji	p19	79e
Lévuo, stm., Lith.	E7	10
Lewe, Mya.	C3	48
Lewellen, Ne., U.S.	F10	126
Lewes, Eng., U.K.	K13	12
Lewes, De., U.S.	F10	114
Lewin Brzeski, Pol.	F13	16
Lewis, Ia., U.S.	C2	120
Lewis, Butt of, c., Scot., U.K.	C6	12
Lewis, Isle of, i., Scot., U.K.	C6	12
Lewis, Mount, mtn., Nv., U.S.	C8	134
Lewis and Clark Lake, res., U.S.	E15	126
Lewis Range, mts., N.A.	B13	136
Lewis Run, Pa., U.S.	C7	114
Lewis Smith Lake, res., Al., U.S.	C11	122
Lewisburg, Ky., U.S.	H10	120
Lewisburg, Pa., U.S.	D8	114
Lewisburg, Tn., U.S.	B12	122
Lewisburg, W.V., U.S.	G5	114
Lewisport, Ky., U.S.	C7	114
Lewisville, Ar., U.S.	D5	122
Lewisville, Tx., U.S.	A10	130
Lewisville Lake, res., Tx., U.S.	H12	128
Lexington, Ga., U.S.	C2	116
Lexington, Il., U.S.	D9	120
Lexington, Ky., U.S.	F1	114
Lexington, Ma., U.S.	B14	114
Lexington, Ms., U.S.	D8	122
Lexington, Mo., U.S.	E4	120
Lexington, Ne., U.S.	G13	126
Lexington, N.C., U.S.	I5	114
Lexington, Ok., U.S.	F11	128
Lexington, Or., U.S.	E7	136
Lexington, S.C., U.S.	C4	116
Lexington, Tn., U.S.	B10	122
Lexington, Tx., U.S.	D10	130
Lexington, Va., U.S.	G6	114
Lexington Park, Md., U.S.	F9	114
Leyden see Leiden, Neth.	B13	14
Leye, China	I2	42
Leyte, i., Phil.	E5	52
Leyte Gulf, b., Phil.	E5	52
Lezhë, Alb.	C13	24
Lezhi, China	F1	42
Lëzna, Bela.	E13	10
L'gov, Russia	D5	32
Lhasa, China	D13	54
Lhasa, stm., China	D13	54
Lhazê, China	D11	54
Lhoknga, Indon.	J2	48
Lhokseumawe, Indon.	J3	48
Lhoksukon, Indon.	J3	48
Lhorong, China	E4	36
L'Hospitalet de Llobregat, Spain	C13	20
Lhuntsi Dzong, Bhu.	E13	54
Li, Thai.	D4	48
Li, stm., China	G4	42
Li, stm., Thai.	D4	48
Liamuiga, Mount, vol., St. K./N.	c2	105a
Lian, stm., China	I5	42
Liancheng, China	I7	42
Lianga, Phil.	F6	52
Liangbua, Indon.	C10	50
Liangdang, China	E1	42
Lianghekou, China	G3	42
Liangmentou, China	G9	42
Liangping, China	F2	42
Liangzi Hu, l., China	F4	42
Lianhuapao, China	B8	38
Lianhua Shan, mts., China	J6	42
Lianjiang, China	K4	42
Liannan, China	I5	42
Lianshui, China	E8	42
Lianxian, China	I5	42
Lianyuan, China	H4	42
Lianyungang, China	D8	42
Liao, stm., China	C7	42
Liaocheng, China	C7	42
Liaodong Bandao (Liaotung Peninsula), pen., China	D5	38
Liaodong Wan (Liaotung, Gulf of), b., China	A9	42
Liaoning, state, China	D5	38
Liaotung, Gulf of see Liaodong Wan, b., China	A9	42
Liaotung Peninsula see Liaodong Bandao, pen., China	E5	38
Liaoyang, China	D5	38
Liaozhong, China	D5	38
Liard, stm., Can.	C6	106
Liard River, B.C., Can.	D5	106
Libagon, Phil.	E5	52
Libano, Col.	E4	86
Libby, Mt., U.S.	B11	136
Libby Dam, dam, Mt., U.S.	B11	136
Libenge, D.R.C.	D3	66
Liberal, Ks., U.S.	D7	128
Liberec, Czech Rep.	F11	16
Liberia, C.R.	G5	102
Liberia, ctry., Afr.	H3	64
Libertad, Antig.	f4	105b
Libertad, Ven.	C7	86
Libertador General Bernardo O'Higgins, state, Chile	G2	92
Liberty, Mo., U.S.	E3	120
Liberty, Ms., U.S.	F8	122
Liberty, N.Y., U.S.	C11	114
Liberty, N.C., U.S.	I6	114
Liberty, S.C., U.S.	B3	116
Liberty, Tx., U.S.	G4	122
Liberty Center, Oh., U.S.	C1	114
Libertyville, Il., U.S.	F2	112
Libo, China	I2	42
Libobo, Tanjung, c., Indon.	F8	44
Libode, S. Afr.	G9	70
Libourne, Fr.	E5	18
Librazhd, Alb.	C14	24
Libres, Mex.	F10	100
Libreville, Gabon	D1	66
Libya, ctry., Afr.	B3	62
Libyan Desert, des., Afr.	C5	62
Libyan Plateau, plat., Afr.	A4	62
Licancábur, Volcán, vol., S.A.	D3	90
Licantén, Chile	G1	92
Licata, Italy	G7	24
Lich, Ger.	F4	16
Licheng see Liyang, China	F8	42
Licheng, China	C5	42
Lichfield, Eng., U.K.	I11	12
Lichinga, Moz.	C6	68
Lichtenau, Ger.	E5	16
Lichtenburg, S. Afr.	E7	70
Lichtenfels, Ger.	F7	16
Lichuan, China	H7	42
Lichuan, China	F3	42
Licking, Mo., U.S.	G6	120
Licking, stm., Ky., U.S.	F1	114
Ličko Polje, val., Cro.	F12	22
Lida, Bela.	G8	10
Lidgerwood, N.D., U.S.	E1	118
Lidköping, Swe.	G5	8
Lido di Ostia, Italy	I9	22
Lidzbark, Pol.	C15	16
Lidzbark Warmiński, Pol.	B16	16
Liebenbergsvlei, stm., S. Afr.	E8	70
Liebig, Mount, mtn., Austl.	D6	74
Liechtenstein, ctry., Eur.	C6	22
Liège (Luik), Bel.	D14	14
Lienchou see Hepu, China	K3	42
Lienz, Aus.	D9	22
Liepāja, Lat.	D3	10
Liepājas ezers, l., Lat.	D4	10
Lier, Bel.	C13	14
Lierre see Lier, Bel.	C13	14
Liestal, Switz.	C4	22
Liešti, Rom.	D14	26
Liévin, Fr.	D11	14
Lièvre, stm., Qc., Can.	C14	112
Liezen, Aus.	C11	22
Liffey, stm., Ire.	H6	12
Lifford, Ire.	G5	12
Lifou, i., N. Cal.	m16	79d
Ligatne, Lat.	C7	10
Lighthouse Point, Fl., U.S.	J5	116
Lighthouse Point, c., Fl., U.S.	H14	122
Lighthouse Point, c., Mi., U.S.	C4	112
Lightning Creek, stm., Wy., U.S.	D7	126
Lightning Ridge, Austl.	G6	76
Lignite, N.D., U.S.	F11	124
Ligny-en-Barrois, Fr.	F14	14
Ligonha, stm., Moz.	D6	68
Ligonier, In., U.S.	G4	112
Ligonier, Pa., U.S.	H10	112
Liguria, state, Italy	F5	22
Ligurian Sea, s., Eur.	F6	22
Lihir Island, i., Pap. N. Gui.	a5	79a
Lihou Reefs and Cays, rf., Austl.	A8	76
Lihue, Hi., U.S.	b2	78a
Lihuel Calel, Parque Nacional, p.o.i., Arg.	H5	92
Lihula, Est.	B6	10
Lijiang, China	F5	36
Lik, stm., Laos	C5	48
Likasi (Jadotville), D.R.C.	G5	66
Likati, D.R.C.	D4	66
Likely, B.C., Can.	D9	138
Liki, Indon.	D2	50
Likino-Dulevo, Russia	E21	10
Lilbourn, Mo., U.S.	H8	120
Lilibeo, Capo see Boeo, Capo, c., Italy	G6	24
Lilienfeld, Aus.	B12	22
Liling, China	H5	42
Lille, Fr.	D12	14
Lillebælt, strt., Den.	I3	8
Lillebonne, Fr.	E9	14
Lillehammer, Nor.	F3	8
Lillers, Fr.	D11	14
Lillestrøm, Nor.	F4	8
Lillhärdal, Swe.	F6	8
Lillington, N.C., U.S.	A7	116
Lillooet, B.C., Can.	F9	138
Lillooet, stm., B.C., Can.	G8	138
Lillooet Lake, l., B.C., Can.	F8	138
Liloy, Phil.	F4	52
Lilydale, Austl.	n13	77a
Lim, stm., Eur.	F5	26
Lima, Para.	A9	92
Lima, Peru	F2	84
Lima, Mt., U.S.	F14	136
Lima, N.Y., U.S.	B8	114
Lima, Oh., U.S.	D1	114
Lima (Limia), stm., Eur.	C2	20
Limay, stm., Arg.	H4	92
Limay Mahuida, Arg.	H4	92
Limbang, Malay.	A9	50
Limbang, stm., Malay.	A9	50
Limbdi, India	G4	54
Limbé, Haiti	C11	102
Limburg an der Lahn, Ger.	F4	16
Limeira, Braz.	L2	88
Limerick (Luimneach), Ire.	I4	12
Limerick, state, Ire.	I4	12
Limestone, Me., U.S.	D9	110
Limestone, Lake, res., Tx., U.S.	F2	122
Limfjorden, l., Den.	H3	8
Limia (Lima), stm., Eur.	C2	20
Limingen, l., Nor.	D5	8
Limmared, Swe.	H5	8
Limmen Bight, b., Austl.	B7	74
Límnos, i., Grc.	D8	28
Limoeiro, Braz.	D8	88
Limoeiro do Norte, Braz.	C6	88
Limoges, Fr.	D7	18
Limón, Hond.	E5	102
Limone Piemonte, Italy	F4	22
Limoux, Fr.	F8	18
Limpopo, Parque Nacional de, Moz.	D10	70
Limpopo, stm., Afr.	C10	70
Lin'an, China	F8	42
Linakhamari, Russia	B14	8
Linapacan Island, i., Phil.	E2	52
Linares, Chile	G2	92
Linares, Mex.	C9	100
Linares, Spain	F7	20
Linch, Wy., U.S.	C6	126
Linch'ing see Linqing, China	C6	42
Lincoln, Arg.	G7	92
Lincoln, Eng., U.K.	H12	12
Lincoln, Ar., U.S.	B3	122
Lincoln, Ca., U.S.	E4	134
Lincoln, Il., U.S.	D8	120
Lincoln, Me., U.S.	E8	110
Lincoln, Mi., U.S.	D6	112
Lincoln, Ne., U.S.	K2	118
Lincoln, N.H., U.S.	F5	110
Lincoln, Mount, mtn., Co., U.S.	B2	128
Lincoln City, Or., U.S.	F2	136
Lincoln Creek, stm., Ne., U.S.	F15	126
Lincoln Park, Co., U.S.	C2	128
Lincoln Park, Mi., U.S.	B2	114
Lincoln Sea, s., Arctic	A13	141
Lincolnton, Ga., U.S.	C3	116
Lincolnton, N.C., U.S.	A4	116
Lincoln Village, Ca., U.S.	F4	134
Lindale, Ga., U.S.	C13	122
Lindale, Tx., U.S.	E3	122
Lindau, Ger.	I5	16
Linde, stm., Russia	C13	34
Linden, Guy.	B6	84
Linden, Al., U.S.	E11	122
Linden, In., U.S.	H3	112
Linden, Tn., U.S.	B11	122
Lindesnes, c., Nor.	H2	8
Lindi, Tan.	F7	66
Lindi, stm., D.R.C.	D5	66
Líndos, sci., Grc.	G10	28
Lind Point, c., V.I.U.S.	e7	104b
Lindsay, On., Can.	D11	112
Lindsay, Ca., U.S.	G6	134
Lindsay, Ok., U.S.	F11	128
Line Islands, is., Oc.	D11	72
Linesville, Pa., U.S.	C5	114
Lineville, Al., U.S.	D13	122
Lineville, Ia., U.S.	D4	120
Linfen, China	C4	42
Linganamakki Reservoir, res., India	D2	53
Lingao, China	L3	42
Lingayen, Phil.	B3	52
Lingayen Gulf, b., Phil.	B3	52
Lingbao, China	D4	42
Lingbi, China	E7	42
Lingbo, Swe.	F7	8
Lingchuan, China	I3	42
Lingen, Ger.	D3	16
Lingfengwei, China	I6	42
Lingga, Kepulauan, is., Indon.	C4	50
Lingga, Pulau, i., Indon.	D4	50
Lingomo II, D.R.C.	D4	66
Lingqiu, China	B6	42
Lingshan, China	J3	42
Lingshi, China	L4	42
Lingshui, China	L4	42
Linguère, Sen.	F2	64
Lingtai, China	D2	42
Lingwu, China	B2	42
Lingxian, China	H5	42
Lingyuan, China	A8	42
Linh, Ngoc, mtn., Viet.	E9	48
Linhai, China	E9	42
Linhares, Braz.	J5	88
Linhe, China	A2	42
Linhsia see Linxia, China	D5	36
Lini see Linyi, China	D8	42
Linjiang, China	D7	38
Linkou, China	B8	38
Linköping, Swe.	G7	8
Linksmakalnis, Lith.	F6	10
Linkuva, Lith.	D6	10
Linn, Ks., U.S.	B11	128
Linn, Mo., U.S.	F5	120
Linnansaaren kansallispuisto, p.o.i., Fin.	E13	8
Linnhe, Loch, b., Scot., U.K.	E7	12
Linqi, China	D5	42
Linqing, China	C6	42
Linqu, China	C8	42
Linquan, China	E6	42
Linru, China	D5	42
Lins, Braz.	K1	88
Linstead, Jam.	i13	104d
Lintan, China	E5	36
Lintao, China	D5	36
Linton, In., U.S.	E10	120
Linton, N.D., U.S.	A12	126
Linwood, On., Can.	E9	112
Linwu, China	I5	42
Linxi, China	C3	36
Linxi, China	C8	38
Linxia, China	D5	36
Linxian, China	B4	42
Linxiang, China	G5	42
Linyi, China	B12	42
Linyi, China	C5	42
Linyi, China	C7	42
Linyü see Shanhaiguan, China	A8	42
Linz, Aus.	B11	22
Lio Matoh, Malay.	B9	50
Lion, Golfe du, b., Fr.	G10	18
Lion, Gulf of see Lion, Golfe du, b., Fr.	G10	18
Lionel Town, Jam.	j13	104d
Liouesso, Congo	D3	66
Lipa, Phil.	D3	52
Lipan, Tx., U.S.	B9	130
Lipari, Italy	F9	24
Lipari, Isola, i., Italy	F9	24
Lipari, Isole see Eolie, Isole, is., Italy	F8	24
Lipcani, Mol.	A13	26
Lipeck, Russia	D6	32
Lípez, Cerro, mtn., Bol.	D3	90
Liping, China	H3	42
Lipki, Russia	G20	10
Lipník nad Bečvou, Czech Rep.	G13	16
Lipno, Pol.	D15	16
Lipno, údolní nádrž, res., Czech Rep.	H10	16
Lipova, Rom.	C8	26
Lipovcy, Russia	B9	38
Lippe, stm., Ger.	E2	16
Lippstadt, Ger.	E4	16
Lipscomb, Tx., U.S.	E8	128
Liptovská Teplička, Slov.	G15	16
Liptovský Mikuláš, Slov.	G15	16
Liptrap, Cape, c., Austl.	L5	76
Lipu, China	I4	42
Lira, Ug.	D6	66
Liri, stm., Italy	C7	24
Liria see Llíria, Spain	E10	20
Liro, Vanuatu	k17	79d
Lisala, D.R.C.	D4	66
Lisboa (Lisbon), Port.	F1	20
Lisboa, state, Port.	F1	20
Lisbon see Lisboa, Port.	F1	20
Lisbon, Me., U.S.	F6	110
Lisbon, N.D., U.S.	A15	126
Lisbon, N.H., U.S.	F5	110
Lisbon, Oh., U.S.	D5	114
Lisbon Falls, Me., U.S.	G6	112
Lisburne, Cape, c., Ak., U.S.	C6	140
Lishi, China	C4	42
Lishu, China	C6	38
Lishui, China	G8	42
Lishuzhen, China	B9	38
Lisičansk see Lysychansk, Ukr.	E5	32
Lisieux, Fr.	E9	14
Liski, Russia	D5	32
L'Isle-Jourdain, Fr.	C6	18
Lisman, Al., U.S.	E10	122
Lismore, Austl.	G9	76
Lismore, Ire.	I5	12
Lišov, Czech Rep.	G10	16
Listowel, On., Can.	E9	112
Listowel, Ire.	I3	12
Litang, China	E5	36
Litang, China	J3	42
Litang, stm., China	F5	36
Litchfield, Il., U.S.	E8	120
Litchfield, Mi., U.S.	B1	114
Litchfield, Mn., U.S.	F4	118
Litchfield, Ne., U.S.	F13	126
Litchville, N.D., U.S.	A14	126
Lithgow, Austl.	I8	76
Lithinó, Akra, c., Grc.	H8	28
Lithonia, Ga., U.S.	C1	116
Lithuania, ctry., Eur.	E7	10
Litija, Slvn.	D11	22
Lititz, Pa., U.S.	D9	114
Litoměřice, Czech Rep.	F10	16
Litomyšl, Czech Rep.	G12	16
Litovko, Russia	G16	34
Little, stm., Ga., U.S.	C3	116
Little, stm., N.C., U.S.	A6	116
Little, stm., Ok., U.S.	F11	128
Little, stm., U.S.	D11	130
Little, stm., U.S.	B8	122

Name	Map Ref.	Page

Little, stm., U.S. — D5 122
Little, Mountain Fork, stm., U.S. — C4 122
Little Abaco, i., Bah. — B9 96
Little Andaman, i., India. — F7 46
Little Arkansas, stm., U.S. — C11 128
Little Beaver Creek, stm., U.S. — B7 128
Little Beaver Creek, stm., U.S. — A8 126
Little Belt see Lillebaelt, strt., Den. — I3 8
Little Belt Mountains, mts., Mt., U.S. — D16 136
Little Bighorn, stm., U.S. — B5 126
Little Bighorn Battlefield National Monument, p.o.i., Mt., U.S. — B5 126
Little Blue, stm., U.S. — G15 126
Little Buffalo, stm., U.S. — C8 106
Little Carpathians see Malé Karpaty, mts., Slov. — H13 16
Little Cayman, i., Cay. Is. — C7 102
Little Chute, Wi., U.S. — D1 112
Little Colorado, stm., Az., U.S. — H5 132
Little Current, On., Can. — C8 112
Little Current, On., stm., Can. — A12 118
Little Deep Creek, stm., N.D., U.S. — F12 124
Little Deschutes, stm., Or., U.S. — G5 136
Little Desert, des., Austl. — K3 76
Little Desert National Park, p.o.i., Austl. — K3 76
Little Dry Creek, stm., Mt., U.S. — G7 124
Little Falls, Mn., U.S. — E4 118
Little Falls, N.Y., U.S. — E15 112
Littlefork, Mn., U.S. — C5 118
Little Fork, stm., Mn., U.S. — C5 118
Little Hurricane Creek, stm., Ga., U.S. — E3 116
Little Inagua, i., Bah. — B11 102
Little Kanawha, stm., W.V., U.S. — E4 114
Little Karroo (Klein Karroo), plat., S. Afr. — H5 70
Little Lake, l., La., U.S. — H8 122
Little London, Jam. — i12 104d
Little Lost, stm., Id., U.S. — F13 136
Little Mexico, Tx., U.S. — D4 130
Little Missouri, stm., Ar., U.S. — D5 122
Little Missouri, stm., U.S. — B7 108
Little Namaqualand (Klein Namaland), hist. reg., S. Afr. — F3 70
Little Nicobar, i., India — G7 46
Little Osage, stm., U.S. — G3 120
Little Pee Dee, stm., S.C., U.S. — B6 116
Little Pic, stm., On., Can. — C12 118
Little Powder, stm., U.S. — B3 126
Little Quill Lake, l., Sk., Can. — C10 124
Little Rann of Kachchh, reg., India — G3 54
Little Red, stm., Ar., U.S. — B7 122
Little Red, Middle Fork, stm., Ar., U.S. — B6 122
Little Red Deer, stm., Ab., Can. — E16 138
Little River, stm., U.S. — C10 128
Little Rock, Ar., U.S. — C6 122
Little Rock, stm., U.S. — H2 118
Little Sable Point, c., Mi., U.S. — E3 112
Little Saint Bernard Pass, p., Eur. — D12 18
Little Sandy Creek, stm., Wy., U.S. — E3 126
Little Sioux, stm., U.S. — J3 118
Little Sioux, West Fork, stm., Ia., U.S. — B2 120
Little Smoky, stm., Ab., Can. — A14 138
Little Snake, stm., U.S. — C8 132
Littlestown, Pa., U.S. — E8 114
Little Tallapoosa, stm., U.S. — D13 122
Little Tennessee, stm., U.S. — A1 116
Little Tobago, i., Trin. — r13 105f
Littleton, Co., U.S. — B3 128
Littleton, N.H., U.S. — F5 110
Littleton, W.V., U.S. — E5 114
Little Valley, N.Y., U.S. — B7 114
Little Wabash, stm., Il., U.S. — F9 120
Little White, stm., S.D., U.S. — D12 126
Little Wood, stm., Id., U.S. — G12 136
Litvinov, Czech Rep. — F9 16
Liu, stm., China — J3 42
Liu, stm., China — C5 38
Liu, stm., China — I3 42
Liuaniua see Ontong Java, at., Sol. Is. — D7 72
Liuba, China — E2 42
Liuboml', Ukr. — E20 16
Liuchen, China — J4 42
Liucheng, China — I3 42
Liuchow see Liuzhou, China — I3 42
Liucura, Chile — I2 92
Liufang, China — H7 42
Liuhe, China — C6 38
Liuheng Dao, i., China — G10 42
Liujiazi, China — A9 42
Liupan Shan, mts., China — D2 42
Liushuquan, China — F16 32
Liuxi, China — J5 42
Liuyang, China — G5 42
Liuyang, stm., China — G5 42
Liuzhou, China — I3 42
Livada, Rom. — B10 26
Livadija, Russia — C10 38
Livani, Lat. — D9 10
Livanjsko Polje, val., Bos. — E3 26
Lively, On., Can. — B8 112
Lively Island, i., Falk. Is. — J5 90
Live Oak, Ca., U.S. — D4 134
Live Oak, Fl., U.S. — F2 116
Liveringa, Austl. — C4 74
Livermore, Ia., U.S. — B3 120
Livermore, Ky., U.S. — G10 120
Livermore, Mount, mtn., Tx., U.S. — D3 130
Livermore Falls, Me., U.S. — F6 110
Liverpool, N.S., Can. — F12 110
Liverpool, Eng., U.K. — H10 12
Liverpool, Cape, c., N...., Can. — C10 141
Liverpool Bay, b., N.T., Can. — A5 106
Liverpool Bay, b., Eng., U.K. — H9 12
Livingston, Guat. — E3 102
Livingston, Al., U.S. — E10 122
Livingston, Ca., U.S. — F5 134
Livingston, Il., U.S. — F8 120
Livingston, La., U.S. — G8 122
Livingston, Mt., U.S. — E16 136
Livingston, Tn., U.S. — H12 120
Livingston, Tx., U.S. — G4 122
Livingston, Wi., U.S. — B7 120
Livingston, Lake, res., Tx., U.S. — G3 122
Livingstone, Zam. — D4 68
Livingstone Falls, wtfl., Afr. — A1 68
Livingston Manor, N.Y., U.S. — C11 114
Livno, Bos. — E3 26
Livny, Russia — H20 10
Livonia, La., U.S. — G7 122
Livonia, Mi., U.S. — B2 114
Livonia, N.Y., U.S. — B8 114
Livorno (Leghorn), Italy — G7 22
Livramento do Brumado, Braz. — G5 88
Liwale, Tan. — F7 66
Lixi, China — G6 42
Lixian, China — G4 42

Lixian, China — D1 42
Lixian see Black, stm., Asia — D9 56
Lixin, China — E7 42
Lixoúri, Grc. — E3 28
Liyang, China — F8 42
Lizarda, Braz. — E2 88
Lizard Point, c., Eng., U.K. — L7 12
Lizarra see Estella, Spain — B8 20
Ljady, Bela. — F14 10
Ljahavičy, Bela. — G9 10
Ljahovskie ostrova, is., Russia — B17 34
Ljamca, Russia — D17 8
Ljaskavičy, Bela. — H11 10
Ljasnaja, Bela. — G8 10
Ljuban', Bela. — H10 10
Ljuban', Russia — A14 10
Ljubercy, Russia — E20 10
Ljubimec, Blg. — H12 26
Ljubljana, Slvn. — D11 22
Ljubnica, Russia — C15 10
Ljubohna, Russia — G17 10
Ljubuški, Bos. — F4 26
Ljudinovo, Russia — G17 10
Ljudkovo, Russia — F17 10
Ljungan, stm., Swe. — E5 8
Ljungby, Swe. — H5 8
Ljusdal, Swe. — F7 8
Ljusina, Bela. — H9 10
Ljusnan, stm., Swe. — F6 8
Llancanelo, Laguna, l., Arg. — G3 92
Llandeilo, Wales, U.K. — J8 12
Llandrindod Wells, Wales, U.K. — I9 12
Llandudno, Wales, U.K. — H9 12
Llanelli, Wales, U.K. — J8 12
Llangefni, Wales, U.K. — H8 12
Llanidloes, Wales, U.K. — I9 12
Llano, stm., Tx., U.S. — D8 130
Llano Colorado, Mex. — L9 134
Llanos, pl., S.A. — E7 86
Llanquihue, Lago, l., Chile — H2 90
Lleida, Spain — C11 20
Lleida, co., Spain — B12 20
Llera de Canales, Mex. — D9 100
Llerena, Spain — F4 20
Lleulleu, Lago, l., Chile — I1 92
Llíco, Chile — G1 92
Llíria, Spain — E10 20
Llivia, Spain — B12 20
Llobregat, stm., Spain — C12 20
Lloydminster, Sk., Can. — E9 106
Llucena, Spain — D10 20
Lluchmayor see Llucmajor, Spain — E13 20
Llucmajor, Spain — E13 20
Llullaillaco, Volcán, vol., S.A. — B3 92
Lo (Panlong), stm., Asia — A7 48
Loa, Ut., U.S. — E5 132
Loa, stm., Chile — D3 90
Loanda, Braz. — D6 90
Loange (Luangue), stm., Afr. — F3 66
Lobamba, Swaz. — E10 70
Lobanovo, Russia — G21 10
Lobatse, Bots. — D7 70
Löbau, Ger. — E10 16
Lobaye, stm., C.A.R. — D3 66
Lobelville, Tn., U.S. — B11 122
Lobería, Arg. — I8 92
Lobnja, Russia — D20 10
Lobos, Arg. — G8 92
Lobos, Cay, i., Bah. — A9 102
Lobos, Isla, i., Mex. — B3 100
Lobositz see Lovosice, Czech Rep. — F10 16
Łobżenica, Pol. — C13 16
Locarno, Switz. — D5 22
Loches, Fr. — G10 14
Loch Garman see Wexford, Ire. — I6 12
Lochinver, Scot., U.K. — C7 12
Lochsa, stm., Id., U.S. — D12 136
Lock, Austl. — F7 74
Lockeport, N.S., Can. — G11 110
Lockerbie, Scot., U.K. — F9 12
Lockesburg, Ar., U.S. — D4 122
Lockhart, Austl. — J6 76
Lock Haven, Pa., U.S. — C8 114
Lockney, Tx., U.S. — G7 128
Lockport, Il., U.S. — C9 120
Lockport, La., U.S. — H8 122
Lockport, N.Y., U.S. — E11 112
Lockwood, Mo., U.S. — G4 120
Locminé, Fr. — G6 14
Loc Ninh, Viet. — G8 48
Locust Creek, stm., U.S. — D4 120
Locust Fork, stm., Al., U.S. — D11 122
Locust Grove, Ok., U.S. — H2 120
Lod (Lydda), Isr. — G5 58
Lodalskåpa, mtn., Nor. — F2 8
Loddon, stm., Austl. — K4 76
Lodejnoe Pole, Russia — F15 8
Lodève, Fr. — F9 18
Lodge Creek, stm., N.A. — F4 124
Lodge Grass, Mt., U.S. — B5 126
Lodgepole, Ab., Can. — C15 138
Lodgepole, Ne., U.S. — F10 126
Lodgepole Creek, stm., U.S. — F10 126
Lodhran, Pak. — D3 54
Lodi, Italy — E6 22
Lodi, Ca., U.S. — E4 134
Lodi, Wi., U.S. — H9 118
Lodja, D.R.C. — E4 66
Lodwar, Kenya — D7 66
Łódź, Pol. — E15 16
Łódź, state, Pol. — E15 16
Loei, Thai. — D5 48
Loei, stm., Thai. — D5 48
Loeriesfontein, S. Afr. — G4 70
Lofer, Aus. — C9 22
Lofoten, is., Nor. — B5 8
Lofoten Basin, unds. — A14 144
Loga, Niger — G5 64
Logan, Ia., U.S. — C2 120
Logan, Ks., U.S. — B9 128
Logan, Oh., U.S. — E3 114
Logan, Ut., U.S. — B5 132
Logan, W.V., U.S. — G4 114
Logan, Mount, mtn., Yk., Can. — C2 106
Logan, stm., Ne., U.S. — E15 126
Logan Island, i., On., Can. — A10 118
Logan Martin Lake, res., Al., U.S. — D12 122
Logan Mountains, mts., Yk., Can. — C5 106
Logan Pass, p., Mt., U.S. — B13 136
Logansport, In., U.S. — H3 112
Logansport, La., U.S. — F5 122
Loganville, Ga., U.S. — C2 116
Logone, stm., Afr. — F3 62
Logroño, Spain — B8 20
Løgstør, Den. — H3 8
Logudoro, reg., Italy — D2 24
Lohiniva, Fin. — C11 8
Lohne, Ger. — E6 42
Lohne see Luohe, China — E6 42
Lohrville, Ia., U.S. — B3 120
Loi (Nanlei), stm., Asia — B4 48
Loi, Phou, mtn., Laos — B6 48
Loi-kaw, Mya. — C3 48
Loi Mwe, Mya. — B4 48
Loing, stm., Fr. — F11 14
Loir, stm., Fr. — G10 14
Loir, Canal du, can., Fr. — F7 14
Loire, stm., Fr. — D10 18
Loire, state, Fr. — D10 18
Loire, Canal latéral à la, can., Fr. — C9 18
Loire-Atlantique, state, Fr. — G7 14
Loiret, state, Fr. — F11 14
Loir-et-Cher, state, Fr. — G10 14
Loja, Ec. — D2 84
Loja, Spain — G6 20
Loja, co., Spain — G6 20
Lokandu, D.R.C. — E5 66

Lokan Reservoir see Lokan tekojärvi, res., Fin. — C12 8
Lokan tekojärvi, res., Fin. — C12 8
Lokeren, Bel. — C13 14
Loket, Czech Rep. — F8 16
Lokichar, Kenya — D7 66
Lokichokio, Kenya — D6 66
Loknja, Russia — D13 10
Lokoja, Nig. — H6 64
Lokolama, D.R.C. — E3 66
Lokot', Russia — H17 10
Loksa, Est. — A8 10
Loks Land, i., Nu., Can. — E13 141
Lola, Gui. — H3 64
Loleta, Ca., U.S. — C1 134
Loliondo, Tan. — E7 66
Lolita, Tx., U.S. — F11 130
Lolland, i., Den. — I4 8
Lolo, Mt., U.S. — D12 136
Lolodorf, Cam. — D2 66
Loío Pass, p., U.S. — D12 136
Lolowai, Vanuatu — j16 79d
Loltong, Vanuatu — j16 79d
Lolvavana, Passage, strt., Vanuatu — j16 79d
Lom, China — A5 46
Lom, Nor. — F3 8
Lom, stm., Viet. — F8 48
Lomami, stm., D.R.C. — D4 66
Lomas de Zamora, Arg. — G8 92
Lomax, Il., U.S. — D6 120
Łomazy, Pol. — E19 16
Lombardia, state, Italy — E6 22
Lombardy see Lombardia, state, Italy — E6 22
Lomblen, Pulau, i., Indon. — G7 44
Lombok, Indon. — H10 50
Lombok, i., Indon. — H10 50
Lombok, Selat, strt., Indon. — H9 50
Lomé, Togo — H5 64
Lomela, D.R.C. — E4 66
Lomela, stm., D.R.C. — E4 66
Lometa, Tx., U.S. — D2 66
Lomié, Cam. — D2 66
Lomira, Wi., U.S. — H10 118
Lomond, Loch, l., Scot., U.K. — E8 12
Lomonosov, Russia — A12 10
Lomonosova, Kaz. — D11 32
Lomovoe, Russia — D19 8
Lompobatang, Gunung, mtn., Indon. — F11 50
Lompoc, Ca., U.S. — I5 134
Lom Sak, Thai. — D5 48
Łomża, Pol. — C18 16
Łomża, state, Pol. — C18 16
Lonaconing, Md., U.S. — E7 114
Lonàvale, India — B1 53
Loncoche, Chile — H2 90
Loncopué, Arg. — I2 92
London, On., Can. — F8 112
London, Eng., U.K. — J12 12
London, Ar., U.S. — B5 122
London, Ky., U.S. — G1 114
London, Oh., U.S. — E2 114
London, stm., U.S. — D8 130
Londonderry, N.S., Can. — E13 110
Londonderry (Derry), N. Ire., U.K. — F6 12
Londonderry, Cape, c., Austl. — B5 74
Londonderry, Isla, i., Chile — K2 90
Londrina, Braz. — D6 90
Lone Grove, Ok., U.S. — G11 128
Lone Oak, Ky., U.S. — G9 120
Lone Pine, Ca., U.S. — G7 134
Lone Rock, Wi., U.S. — A7 120
Lone Tree, Ia., U.S. — C6 120
Lone Wolf, Ok., U.S. — G9 128
Long, stm., China — I3 42
Longa, Ang. — C2 68
Longá, stm., Braz. — B5 88
Longa, proliv, strt., Russia — B24 34
Long Akah, Malay. — B9 50
Longana, Vanuatu — j17 79d
Longarone, Italy — D9 22
Longaví, Chile — G2 92
Longbangun, Indon. — C9 50
Long Bay, b., U.S. — C7 116
Long Beach, Ca., U.S. — J7 134
Long Beach, Ms., U.S. — G9 122
Long Beach, N.Y., U.S. — D12 114
Long Beach, Wa., U.S. — D2 136
Long Beach, cst., N.J., U.S. — E11 114
Longboat Key, Fl., U.S. — I3 116
Long Branch, N.J., U.S. — D12 114
Long Cay, i., Bah. — m18 104f
Longchang, China — G1 42
Longchuan, China — I6 42
Long Creek, stm., N.A. — E10 124
Longde, China — D2 42
Long Eaton, Eng., U.K. — I11 12
Longford, Austl. — L6 76
Longford, Ire. — H5 12
Longford, state, Ire. — H5 12
Long Hu, i., China — A7 42
Longhua, China — A7 42
Longiram, Indon. — C9 50
Long Island, i., Antig. — f4 105b
Long Island, i., Austl. — D7 76
Long Island, i., Bah. — A10 102
Long Island, i., N.S., Can. — F10 110
Long Island, i., Nu., Can. — E14 106
Long Island, i., N.Y., U.S. — D12 114
Long Island Sound, strt., U.S. — D12 114
Longitudinal, Valle, val., Chile — H1 92
Longjiang, China — B9 36
Longjiang, stm., China — I3 42
Long Lake, N.Y., U.S. — G2 110
Long Lake, l., On., Can. — B11 118
Longleaf, La., U.S. — F6 122
Long Leaf Park, N.C., U.S. — B8 116
Longli, China — H2 42
Longling, China — G4 36
Longmeadow, Ma., U.S. — B13 114
Long Moc, Viet. — C7 48
Longmont, Co., U.S. — A3 128
Long Mountain, mtn., Mo., U.S. — H5 120
Longnan, China — I6 42
Longnawan, Indon. — C9 50
Long Pine, Ne., U.S. — E13 126
Long Point, c., Bah. — m18 104f
Long Point, c., N.S., Can. — D10 110
Long Point, pen., Mb., Can. — A15 124
Long Point, pen., On., Can. — F9 112
Long Point Bay, b., On., Can. — F9 112
Long Range Mountains, mts., Nf., Can. — j22 107a
Longreach, Austl. — D5 76
Longsegah, Indon. — B10 50
Longsheng, China — I3 42
Longs Peak, mtn., Co., U.S. — A3 128
Long Thanh, Viet. — G8 48
Longtown, Eng., U.K. — F10 12
Longué, Fr. — G8 14
Longuyon, Fr. — E14 14
Longview, Ab., Can. — F16 138
Longview, Tx., U.S. — E4 122
Longview, Wa., U.S. — D4 136
Longwai, Indon. — C10 50
Longwy, Fr. — E14 14
Longxi, China — D5 36
Longxian, China — D2 42
Long Xuyen, Viet. — G7 48
Longyan, China — I7 42

Longyou, China — G8 42
Longzhen, China — B10 36
Longzhou, China — J2 42
Lonsdale, Mn., U.S. — G5 118
Lons-le-Saunier, Fr. — H14 14
Lontra, stm., Braz. — D1 88
Loogootee, In., U.S. — F11 120
Lookout, Cape, c., N.C., U.S. — B9 116
Lookout Mountain, mts., U.S. — C13 122
Lookout Pass, p., U.S. — C11 136
Lookout Ridge, mts., Ak., U.S. — C8 140
Loolmalassin, vol., Tan. — E7 66
Loomis, Ne., U.S. — G13 126
Loomis, Wa., U.S. — B7 136
Loop, Tx., U.S. — B5 130
Loop Head, c., Ire. — I2 12
Lop, China — A5 46
Lopatka, mys, c., Russia — F17 34
Lopatovo, Russia — D10 10
Lopburi, Thai. — E5 48
Lopévi, i., Vanuatu — k17 79d
Lopez, Cap, c., Gabon — E1 66
Lop Nur, l., China — C3 36
Loptjuga, Russia — E22 8
Lora, Hāmūn-i-, l., Asia — D9 56
Lora del Rio, Spain — G5 20
Lorain, Oh., U.S. — C3 114
Loraine, Tx., U.S. — B7 130
Loralai, Pak. — C2 54
Lorca, Spain — G9 20
Lord Howe Island, i., Austl. — L19 142
Lord Howe Rise, unds. — L19 142
Lord Mayor Bay, b., Nu., Can. — B12 106
Lordsburg, N.M., U.S. — K8 132
Loreauville, La., U.S. — G7 122
Lorena, Braz. — L3 88
Lorengau, Pap. N. Gui. — a4 79a
Lorenzo, Tx., U.S. — H7 128
Lorenzo Geyres, Ur. — F9 92
Loreto, Arg. — C9 92
Loreto, Mex. — D8 100
Loreto, Mex. — B3 100
Loreto, Peru — H4 86
Loreto, Ky., U.S. — G12 120
Loretto, Tn., U.S. — B11 122
Lorient, Fr. — G5 14
Lorimor, Ia., U.S. — C3 120
Loriol-sur-Drôme, Fr. — E10 18
Loris, S.C., U.S. — B7 116
Lorman, Ms., U.S. — F7 122
Lorne, Austl. — L5 76
Lorne, N.B., Can. — C10 110
Lörrach, Ger. — I3 16
Lorraine, hist. reg., Fr. — F14 14
Los, Îles de, is., Gui. — H2 64
Losada, stm., Col. — F4 86
Los Alamos, N.M., U.S. — F2 128
Los Aldamas, Mex. — B9 100
Los Andes, Chile — F2 92
Los Angeles, Chile — H1 92
Los Angeles, Ca., U.S. — I7 134
Los Angeles Aqueduct, aq., Ca., U.S. — H7 134
Los Antiguos, Arg. — I2 90
Los Banos, Ca., U.S. — F5 134
Los Blancos, Arg. — D4 90
Los Bolones, Cerro, mtn., Mex. — G12 100
Los Cerrillos, Arg. — C3 92
Los Conquistadores, Arg. — E8 92
Los Fresnos, Tx., U.S. — H10 130
Los Garza, Mex. — H8 130
Los Gatos, Ca., U.S. — F4 134
Loshan see Leshan, China — F5 36
Los Hermanos, Islas, is., Ven. — B9 86
Łosice, Pol. — D18 16
Los Idolos, Parque Arqueológico de, hist., Col. — F4 86
Lošinj, Otok, i., Cro. — F11 22
Los Juries, Arg. — D6 92
Los Lagos, Chile — G2 90
Los Llanos, P.R. — B3 104a
Los Lopez, Mex. — H8 130
Los Lunas, N.M., U.S. — H10 132
Los Mochis, Mex. — C4 100
Los Nogales, Mex. — H8 130
Losolava, Vanuatu — j16 79d
Los Padillas, N.M., U.S. — I10 132
Los Palacios, Arg. — D3 92
Los Palacios, Cuba — A6 102
Los Palacios y Villafranca, Spain — G4 20
Los Picachos, Parque Nacional, p.o.i., Col. — F4 86
Los Rábanos, P.R. — B2 104a
Los Ríos, state, Ec. — H2 86
Los Roques, Islas, is., Ven. — B8 86
Los Sauces, Chile — G1 92
Lossiemouth, Scot., U.K. — D9 12
Lost, stm., U.S. — A4 134
Los Taques, Ven. — B6 86
Los Teques, Ven. — B8 86
Los Testigos, Islas, is., Ven. — B10 86
Lost Hills, Ca., U.S. — H6 134
Lost Nation, Ia., U.S. — C7 120
Lost River Range, mts., Id., U.S. — F13 136
Lost Trail Pass, p., U.S. — E13 136
Losuia, Pap. N. Gui. — b5 79a
Los Vidrios, Mex. — F6 98
Los Vilos, Chile — E2 92
Los Yébenes, Spain — E6 20
Lot, state, Fr. — E7 18
Lot, stm., Fr. — E7 18
Lota, Chile — H1 92
Lot-et-Garonne, state, Fr. — E6 18
Lothair, S. Afr. — E10 70
Lotoşino, Russia — D18 10
Lotsane, stm., Bots. — C8 70
Lotta, stm., Eur. — B15 8
Lotuke, Jabal, mtn., Sudan — G6 62
Lotung, Tai. — I9 42
Louang Namtha, Laos — B5 48
Louangphrabang, Laos — C6 48
Loudéac, Fr. — F6 14
Loudi, China — H4 42
Loudon, Tn., U.S. — A1 116
Loudonville, Oh., U.S. — D3 114
Loudun, Fr. — H9 14
Loué, Fr. — G8 14
Louga, Sen. — F1 64
Loughborough, Eng., U.K. — I11 12
Loughrea, Ire. — H4 12
Louhi, Russia — C15 8
Louin, Ms., U.S. — E9 122
Louisa, Ky., U.S. — F3 114
Louisburg, N.S., Can. — E16 110
Louisburg, N.C., U.S. — H7 114
Louisburgh, Ire. — H3 12
Louisdale, N.S., Can. — E15 110
Louise, Ms., U.S. — D8 122
Louise, Tx., U.S. — H2 122
Louisiade Archipelago, is., Pap. N. Gui. — B10 74
Louisiana, Mo., U.S. — E6 120
Louisiana, state, U.S. — G6 122
Louis Trichardt, S. Afr. — C9 70
Louisville, Al., U.S. — F13 122
Louisville, Ga., U.S. — C3 116

Louisville, Ky., U.S. — F12 120
Louisville, Ne., U.S. — D1 120
Louisville, Oh., U.S. — D4 114
Louisville Ridge, unds. — M22 142
Louis-XIV, Pointe, c., Qc., Can. — E14 106
Loulé, Port. — G2 20
Loum, Cam. — D1 66
Lount Lake, l., On., Can. — A4 118
Louny, Czech Rep. — F9 16
Loup, stm., Ne., U.S. — F14 126
Loup City, Ne., U.S. — F14 126
Loups Marins, Lacs des, l., Qc., Can. — D16 106
Lourdes, Fr. — F5 18
Lourenço Marques see Maputo, Moz. — D11 70
Lourinhã, Port. — E1 20
Lousã, Port. — D2 20
Louth, Austl. — H5 76
Louth, Eng., U.K. — H12 12
Louth, Ire. — H6 12
Louth, state, Ire. — H6 12
Loutrá Aidipsoú, Grc. — E6 28
Louvain see Leuven, Bel. — D13 14
Louviers, Fr. — E10 14
Louviers, Co., U.S. — B4 128
Lovat', stm., Russia — B14 10
Loveč, Blg. — F11 26
Loveč, state, Blg. — F11 26
Loveland, Co., U.S. — G7 126
Lovell, Wy., U.S. — C4 126
Lovell Village, St. Vin. — p11 105e
Lovelock, Nv., U.S. — C7 134
Lovely, Ky., U.S. — G13 114
Lovere, Italy — E7 22
Loves Park, Il., U.S. — B8 120
Loving, N.M., U.S. — B3 130
Loving, Tx., U.S. — H10 128
Lovington, Il., U.S. — E9 120
Lovington, N.M., U.S. — B4 130
Lovosice, Czech Rep. — F9 16
Lovozero, Russia — D13 8
Lovozero, ozero, l., Russia — C16 8
Lóvua, Ang. — B3 68
Low, Qc., Can. — C14 112
Low, Cape, c., Nu., Can. — C13 106
Lowa, D.R.C. — E5 66
Lowa, stm., D.R.C. — E5 66
Lowden, Ia., U.S. — C7 120
Lowell, In., U.S. — G2 112
Lowell, Ma., U.S. — B14 114
Lowell, Or., U.S. — G4 136
Lowell, Lake, res., Id., U.S. — G10 136
Löwen, stm., Nmb. — E3 70
Lower Arrow Lake, res., B.C., Can. — G12 138
Lower Austria see Niederösterreich, state, Aus. — B12 22
Lower California see Baja California, pen., Mex. — B2 96
Lower Egypt see Misr el-Bahri, hist. reg., Egypt — G2 58
Lower Glenelg National Park, p.o.i., Austl. — L3 76
Lower Hutt, N.Z. — E6 80
Lower Lake, l., U.S. — B5 134
Lower Manitou Lake, l., On., Can. — B6 118
Lower Post, B.C., Can. — D5 106
Lower Red Lake, l., Mn., U.S. — D3 118
Lower Saxony see Niedersachsen, state, Ger. — D4 16
Lower Trajan's Wall, misc. cult., Eur. — D15 26
Lower West End Point, c., Anguilla — A1 105a
Lower Woods Harbour, N.S., Can. — G10 110
Lowestoft, Eng., U.K. — I14 12
Lowgar, state, Afg. — A2 54
Łowicz, Pol. — D15 16
Lowmoor, Va., U.S. — G6 114
Lowry City, Mo., U.S. — F4 120
Lowville, N.Y., U.S. — E14 112
Loxton, Austl. — J3 76
Loyal, Wi., U.S. — G8 118
Loyalton, Ca., U.S. — D5 134
Loyalty Islands see Loyauté, Îles, is., N. Cal. — m16 79d
Loyang see Luoyang, China — D5 42
Loyauté, Îles (Loyalty Islands), is., N. Cal. — m16 79d
Loyoro, Ug. — D6 66
Lozère, state, Fr. — E9 18
Loznica, Serb. — E7 26
Lu'an, China — F7 42
Luan, stm., China — A7 42
Luancheng, China — J3 42
Luanda, Ang. — B1 68
Luando, stm., Ang. — C2 68
Luang, Khao (Maw Taung), mtn., Asia — G4 48
Luang, Thale, l., Thai. — I5 48
Luang Chiang Dao, Doi, mtn., Thai. — C4 48
Luanginga, stm., Afr. — D3 68
Luang Prabang see Louangphrabang, Laos — C6 48
Luangue (Loange), stm., Afr. — F3 66
Luanping, China — A7 42
Luanshya, Zam. — C4 68
Luan Toro, Arg. — H5 92
Luanxian, China — A8 42
Luapula, stm., Afr. — C5 68
Luar, Danau, l., Indon. — C8 50
Luarca, Spain — A4 20
Luba, Eq. Gui. — I6 64
Lubaantun, sci., Belize — D3 102
Lubań, Pol. — E11 16
Lubāns, l., Lat. — D9 10
Lubao, D.R.C. — F4 66
Lubartów, Pol. — E18 16
Lubawa, Pol. — C15 16
Lübben, Ger. — E9 16
Lübbenau, Ger. — E9 16
Lubbock, Tx., U.S. — H6 128
Lübeck, Ger. — C6 16
Lubefu, D.R.C. — E4 66
Lubefu, stm., D.R.C. — E4 66
Lubero, D.R.C. — D5 66
Lubilash, stm., D.R.C. — F4 66
Lubin, Pol. — E12 16
Lublin, Pol. — E18 16
Lublin, state, Pol. — E18 16
Lubliniec, Pol. — F14 16
Lubny, Ukr. — D4 32
Lubok Antu, Malay. — C7 50
Luboń, Pol. — D12 16
Lubsko, Pol. — E10 16
Lubuagan, Phil. — B3 52
Lubudi, D.R.C. — F5 66
Lubudi, stm., D.R.C. — F5 66
Lubukbatang, Indon. — E4 50
Lubuklinggau, Indon. — E3 50
Lubukpakam, Indon. — B1 50
Lubuksikaping, Indon. — C1 50
Lubumbashi (Élisabethville), D.R.C. — G5 66
Lubutu, D.R.C. — E5 66
Lübz, Ger. — C7 16
Lucala, stm., Ang. — B2 68
Lucan, On., Can. — E8 112
Lucania, hist. reg., Italy — D10 24
Lucania, Mount, mtn., Yk., Can. — C3 106

Lucas, Ia., U.S. — C4 120
Lucas, Ks., U.S. — B10 128
Lucban, Phil. — C3 52
Lucca, Italy — G7 22
Lucea, Jam. — i12 104d
Luce Bay, b., Scot., U.K. — G8 12
Lucedale, Ms., U.S. — G10 122
Lucélia, Braz. — D6 90
Lucena, Spain — G6 20
Lucena del Cid see Llucena, Spain — D10 20
Lučenec, Slov. — H15 16
Lucera, Italy — C9 24
Lucerne see Luzern, Switz. — C5 22
Lucerne, Lake of see Vierwaldstätter See, l., Switz. — D5 22
Lüchow, Ger. — C7 16
Luchuan, China — J4 42
Lucinda, Austl. — B6 76
Lucira, Ang. — C1 68
Luckau, Ger. — E9 16
Luckenwalde, Ger. — D9 16
Luckhoff, S. Afr. — F7 70
Luck Lake, l., Sk., Can. — C6 124
Lucknow, On., Can. — E8 112
Lucknow, India — E8 54
Lucky Lake, Sk., Can. — D6 124
Luçon, Fr. — C4 18
Luda Kamčija, stm., Blg. — G14 26
Lüdenscheid, Ger. — E3 16
Lüderitz, Nmb. — E2 70
Ludhiāna, India — C6 54
Ludian, China — F5 36
Ludington, Mi., U.S. — E3 112
Ludlow, Eng., U.K. — I10 12
Ludlow, Ma., U.S. — B13 114
Ludogorie, reg., Blg. — F13 26
Ludowici, Ga., U.S. — E4 116
Luduş, Rom. — C11 26
Ludvika, Swe. — F6 8
Ludwigsburg, Ger. — H4 16
Ludwigsfelde, Ger. — D9 16
Ludwigshafen am Rhein, Ger. — G4 16
Ludwigslust, Ger. — C7 16
Ludza, Lat. — D10 10
Luebo, D.R.C. — F4 66
Lueders, Tx., U.S. — B8 130
Luena, Ang. — C3 68
Luena, D.R.C. — F5 66
Luena, stm., Ang. — C3 68
Luepa, Ven. — E11 86
Lueyang, China — H1 42
Lufeng, China — J6 42
Lufico, Ang. — B1 68
Lufkin, Tx., U.S. — F4 122
Luga, Russia — B12 10
Luga, stm., Russia — A11 10
Lugano, Switz. — D5 22
Luganville, Vanuatu — j16 79d
Lugards Falls, wtfl., Kenya — E7 66
Lugenda, stm., Moz. — C6 68
Luggarus see Locarno, Switz. — D5 22
Lugnaquillia Mountain, mtn., Ire. — I6 12
Lugo, Italy — F8 22
Lugo, Spain — A3 20
Lugo, co., Spain — B3 20
Lugoj, Rom. — D8 26
Lugovoj, Russia — F12 32
Lugovskij, Russia — E11 34
Luhans'k, Ukr. — E5 32
Luhovicy, Russia — F21 10
Luhsien see Luzhou, China — G1 42
Luiana, Ang. — D3 68
Luido, Moz. — B12 70
Luik see Liège, Bel. — D14 14
Luimneach see Limerick, Ire. — I4 12
Luino, Italy — D5 22
Luishia, D.R.C. — G5 66
Luis I, León, Presa, res., Mex. — F2 130
Luis Muñoz Marín, Aeropuerto Internacional, P.R. — B3 104a
Luitpold Coast, cst., Ant. — C1 81
Luiza, D.R.C. — F4 66
Luján, Arg. — F3 92
Luján de Cuyo, Arg. — F3 92
Lukang, Tai. — I9 42
Lukenie, stm., D.R.C. — E3 66
Lukeville, Az., U.S. — L4 132
Lukojanov, Russia — I21 8
Lukolela, D.R.C. — E3 66
Lukovit, Blg. — F11 26
Łuków, Pol. — E18 16
Lukuga, stm., D.R.C. — F5 66
Lukula, D.R.C. — F2 66
Lukulu, Zam. — C3 68
Lule, stm., Swe. — D10 8
Luleälven, stm., Swe. — C9 8
Lüleburgaz, Tur. — B10 28
Lules, Arg. — C5 92
Luliang, China — G5 36
Lüliang Shan, mts., China — C4 42
Luling, Tx., U.S. — E10 130
Lulonga, stm., D.R.C. — D3 66
Lulu, stm., D.R.C. — F4 66

Lumajang, Indon. — H8 50
Lumajangdong Co, l., China — B8 54
Lumaku, Gunong, mtn., Malay. — A9 50
Lumana, D.R.C. — E5 66
Lumbala Kaquengue, Ang. — C3 68
Lumbala N'guimbo, Ang. — C3 68
Lumber, stm., U.S. — B6 116
Lumber City, Ga., U.S. — E3 116
Lumberport, W.V., U.S. — E5 114
Lumberton, N.C., U.S. — B7 116
Lumberton, Tx., U.S. — G4 122
Lumbrales, Spain — D4 20
Lumby, B.C., Can. — F12 138
Lumding, India — F14 54
Lumphat, Camb. — F8 48
Lumsden, Sk., Can. — D9 124
Lumut, Indon. — E4 50
Lumut, Malay. — J5 48
Lumut, Tanjung, c., Indon. — E4 50
Luna Pier, Mi., U.S. — C2 114
Lund, Swe. — I5 8
Lund, B.C., Can. — G6 138
Lund, Nv., U.S. — E2 132
Lundazi, Zam. — C5 68
Lundy, i., Eng., U.K. — C6 16
Lüneburg, Ger. — C6 16
Lüneburger Heide, reg., Ger. — C6 16
Lunel, Fr. — F10 18
Lünen, Ger. — E3 16
Lunenburg, N.S., Can. — F12 110
Lunenburg, Va., U.S. — H7 114
Lunéville, Fr. — F15 14
Lunga, stm., Zam. — C4 68
Lungch'i see Zhangzhou, China — I7 42
Lungki see Zhangzhou, China — I7 42
Lunglei, India — G14 54
Lungnan see Longnan, China — I6 42
Lungshen see Longsheng, China — I3 42
Lungué-Bungo (Lungwebungu), stm., Afr. — C3 68

Name	Map Ref.	Page
Lungwebungu (Lungué-Bungo), stm., Afr.	C3	68
Lúni, India	E4	54
Lúni, stm., India	F4	54
Luninec, Bela.	H9	10
Luninets see Luninec, Bela.	H9	10
Lünkaransar, India	D4	54
Luntai, China	F14	38
Luo, stm., China	D4	42
Luo, stm., China	D4	42
Luobei, China	B11	36
Luobu, China	I3	42
Luocheng, China	I3	42
Luoding, China	J4	42
Luofu, D.R.C.	E5	66
Luohe, China	E6	42
Luoji, China	E7	42
Luonan, China	D4	42
Luoning, China	D4	42
Luoqi, China	G2	42
Luotian, China	F6	42
Luowenba, China	F2	42
Luoxiao Shan, mts., China	D5	42
Luoyang, China	D5	42
Luoyuan, China	H8	42
Luqi, D.R.C.	F5	36
Lupanshui, China	F5	36
Lupar, stm., Malay.	C7	50
Łupawa, Pol.	B13	16
Lupeni, Rom.	D10	26
Lupin see Manzhouli, China	B8	36
Luputa, D.R.C.	F4	66
Luqiao, China	E7	42
Luqiao, China	G9	42
Luqiao, China	E5	36
Luqu, China	G2	42
Luque, Spain	G6	20
Luquillo, P.R.	B4	104a
Lure, Fr.	G15	14
Luremo, Ang.	B2	68
Lurgan, N. Ire., U.K.	G6	12
Luribay, Bol.	C3	90
Lurín, Peru	F2	84
Lúrio, Moz.	C7	68
Lúrio, stm., Moz.	C6	68
Lusaka, Zam.	D4	68
Lusambo, D.R.C.	E4	66
Lusanga, D.R.C.	E3	66
Lusangi, D.R.C.	E5	66
Luscar, Ab., Can.	C13	138
Luseland, Sk., Can.	B4	124
Lushan, China	E5	42
Lu Shan, mtn., China	G6	42
Lushnja see Lushnjë, Alb.	D13	24
Lushnjë, Alb.	D13	24
Lushoto, Tan.	E7	66
Lūshun (Port Arthur), China	E4	38
Lusk, Wy., U.S.	E8	126
Lussac-les-Châteaux, Fr.	C6	18
Lút, Dasht-e, des., Iran	C8	56
Lü-ta see Dalian, China	B9	42
Lü Tao, i., Tai.	J9	42
Lutembo, Ang.	C3	68
Lutesville, Mo., U.S.	G7	120
Luther, Mi., U.S.	D4	112
Luther, Ok., U.S.	F11	128
Lutherstadt Eisleben, Ger.	E7	16
Lutherstadt Wittenberg, Ger.	d7	79b
Luti, Sol. Is.	d7	79b
Luton, Eng., U.K.	J12	12
Lutong, Malay.	A8	50
Łutselk'e, N.T., Can.	C8	106
Lutz, Fl., U.S.	H3	116
Lützow, Ger.	C7	16
Lutzow-Holm Bay, b., Ant.	D8	81
Luuq, Som.	D8	66
Luverne, Al., U.S.	F12	122
Lu Verne, Ia., U.S.	I4	118
Luverne, Mn., U.S.	H2	118
Luvua, stm., D.R.C.	F5	66
Luvuvhu, stm., S. Afr.	C10	70
Luwegu, stm., Tan.	F7	66
Luwingu, Zam.	C4	68
Luwuk, Indon.	F7	44
Luxapallila Creek, stm., U.S.	D11	122
Luxembourg, Lux.	E14	14
Luxembourg, ctry., Eur.	E15	14
Luxembourg, Wi., U.S.	D2	112
Luxeuil-les-Bains, Fr.	G15	14
Luxi, China	A4	36
Luxor see El-Uqsor, Egypt	B6	62
Luz, Braz.	J3	88
Luza, Russia	F22	8
Luža, stm., Russia	A14	10
Luzern (Lucerne), Switz.	C5	22
Luzhai, China	I3	42
Luzhou, China	G1	42
Luziânia, Braz.	I2	88
Luzilândia, Braz.	B4	88
Lužki, Bela.	E10	10
Luzon, i., Phil.	B3	52
Luzon Strait, strt., Asia	G16	30
L'viv, Ukr.	F13	6
L'viv, co., Ukr.	G19	16
L'vovskij, Russia	E20	10
Lwówek, Pol.	D12	16
Lyallpur see Faisalabad, Pak.	C4	54
Lyčkovo, Russia	C15	10
Lycksele, Swe.	D8	8
Lydenburg, S. Afr.	D10	70
Lydia Mills, S.C., U.S.	B3	116
Lyell, Mount, mtn., Can.	E13	138
Lyerly, Ga., U.S.	C13	122
Lyford, Tx., U.S.	H10	130
Lykošino, Russia	B16	10
Lyle, Mn., U.S.	H6	118
Lyman, Ne., U.S.	F8	126
Lyman, S.C., U.S.	B3	116
Lymans'ke, Ukr.	C17	26
Lyme Bay, b., Eng., U.K.	K9	12
Łyna (Lava), stm., Eur.	B16	16
Lynch, Ne., U.S.	E14	126
Lynchburg, Oh., U.S.	E2	114
Lynchburg, S.C., U.S.	B5	116
Lynchburg, Tn., U.S.	B12	122
Lynchburg, Va., U.S.	G6	114
Lynd, stm., Austl.	B4	76
Lynden, Wa., U.S.	B4	136
Lyndhurst, Austl.	B5	76
Lyndon, Ks., U.S.	F2	120
Lyndon, Ky., U.S.	F12	120
Lyndon, stm., Austl.	D2	74
Lyndon B. Johnson, Lake, res., Tx., U.S.	D9	130
Lyndon B. Johnson Space Center, sci., Tx., U.S.	H3	122
Lyngen, b., Nor.	B9	8
Lyngseidet, Nor.	B8	8
Lynn, Al., U.S.	C11	122
Lynn, Ma., U.S.	B14	114
Lynndyl, Ut., U.S.	D4	132
Lynn Haven, Fl., U.S.	G13	122
Lynn Lake, Mb., Can.	D10	106
Lyntupy, Bela.	E9	10
Lynx Lake, l., N.T., Can.	C9	106
Lyon, Fr.	D10	18
Lyon Inlet, b., Nu., Can.	B14	106
Lyon Mountain, N.Y., U.S.	F2	110
Lyonnais, hist. reg., Fr.	D10	18
Lyons, In., U.S.	F10	120
Lyons, Co., U.S.	C10	128
Lyons, Mi., U.S.	F5	112
Lyons, Ne., U.S.	C1	120
Lyons, N.Y., U.S.	E13	112
Lyons, stm., Austl.	D3	74
Lysa Hora, Ukr.	A18	26
Łysica, mtn., Pol.	F16	16
Lyskovo, Russia	H21	8
Lys'va, Russia	C9	32
Lysychans'k, Ukr.	E5	32
Lytham Saint Anne's, Eng., U.K.	H9	12
Lytle, Tx., U.S.	E9	130

M

Name	Map Ref.	Page
Ma, stm., Asia	C7	48
Ma'ān, Jord.	H6	58
Ma'ān, state, Jord.	H7	58
Ma'anshan, China	F8	42
Maardu, Est.	G11	8
Maarianhamina see Mariehamn, Fin.	F9	8
Ma'arrat an-Nu'mān, Syria	C7	58
Maas (Meuse), stm., Eur.	D14	14
Maasin, Phil.	E5	52
Maastricht, Neth.	D14	14
Mabalane, Moz.	C11	70
Mabank, Tx., U.S.	E2	122
Mabaruma, Guy.	C12	86
Mabeleapodi, Bots.	B6	70
Mabel Lake, l., B.C., Can.	F12	138
Maben, Ms., U.S.	D9	122
Mablethorpe, Eng., U.K.	H13	12
Mableton, Ga., U.S.	D14	122
Mabton, Wa., U.S.	D6	136
Mabuasehube Game Reserve, Bots.	D6	70
Mača, Russia	E12	34
Maca, Cerro, vol., Chile	H2	90
Macachín, Arg.	H6	92
Macaé, Braz.	L5	88
Macaíba, Braz.	C8	88
Macajuba, Braz.	G5	88
Macalister, B.C., Can.	D8	138
Macalister, stm., Austl.	K6	76
Macalister, Mount, mtn., Austl.	J7	76
MacAlpine Lake, l., Nu., Can.	B10	106
Macan (Kepulauan, is., Indon.	G12	50
Macapá, Braz.	C7	84
Macará, Ec.	D2	84
Macareo, Caño, stm., Ven.	C11	86
MacArthur, Phil.	E5	52
Macas, Ec.	I2	86
Macau see Aomen, China	J5	42
Macaúbas, Braz.	G4	88
MacClenny, Fl., U.S.	F3	116
Macclesfield, Eng., U.K.	H10	12
Macdhui, Ben, mtn., ...	G9	70
Macdonald, Lake, l., Austl.	D5	74
MacDonald Pass, p., Mt., U.S.	D14	136
MacDonnell Ranges, mts., Austl.	D6	74
Macduí, Ben, mtn., Scot., U.K.	D9	12
Macedonia, ctry., Eur.	B4	28
Macedonia, hist. reg., Eur.	H10	26
Maceió, Braz.	E8	88
Macenta, Gui.	H3	64
Macerata, Italy	G10	22
MacFarlane, stm., Sk., Can.	D9	106
Macgillycuddy's Reeks, mts., Ire.	J3	12
MacGregor, Mb., Can.	D15	124
Machado, Braz.	K3	88
Machado, stm., Braz.	F5	84
Machagai, Arg.	C7	92
Machaíla, Moz.	C11	70
Machakos, Kenya	E7	66
Machala, Ec.	D2	84
Machali, Chile	G2	92
Machalilla, Parque Nacional, p.o.i., Ec.	H1	86
Machanga, Moz.	B12	70
Machaquila, stm., Guat.	D3	102
Machattie, Lake, l., Austl.	E2	76
Machaze, Moz.	B11	70
Mācherla, India	C4	53
Machias, Me., U.S.	F9	110
Machilipatnam (Bandar), India	C5	53
Machiques, Ven.	B5	86
Machkund, res., India	B6	53
Macho, Arroyo del, stm., N.M., U.S.	H4	128
Machu Picchu see Machupicchu, sci., Peru	F3	84
Machupicchu, sci., Peru	F3	84
Maciá, Arg.	F8	92
Macia, Moz.	D11	70
Măcin, Rom.	D15	26
Macintyre, stm., Austl.	G7	76
Mackay, Austl.	C7	76
Mackay, Id., U.S.	G13	136
Mackay, Lake, l., Austl.	D5	74
MacKay Lake, l., N.T., Can.	C8	106
Mackenzie, stm., Austl.	D7	76
Mackenzie, stm., N.T., Can.	B4	106
Mackenzie Bay, b., Can.	C12	140
Mackenzie King Island, i., Can.	B3	141
Mackenzie Mountains, mts., Can.	C4	106
Mackinac, Straits of, strt., Mi., U.S.	C5	112
Mackinac Bridge, br., Mi., U.S.	C5	112
Mackinac Island, Mi., U.S.	C5	112
Mackinaw, stm., Il., U.S.	D9	120
Mackinaw City, Mi., U.S.	C5	112
Mackinnon Road, Kenya	E7	66
Macklin, Sk., Can.	B4	124
Macksville, Austl.	H9	76
Macksville, Ks., U.S.	C9	128
Maclean, Austl.	G9	76
Maclear, S. Afr.	G9	70
Macleay, stm., Austl.	H9	76
Macleod, Lake, l., Austl.	D2	74
Macmillan, stm., Yk., Can.	C4	106
Macomb, Il., U.S.	D7	120
Macomer, Italy	D2	24
Mâcon, Fr.	C10	18
Macon, Ga., U.S.	D2	116
Macon, Il., U.S.	E9	120
Macon, Mo., U.S.	E5	120
Macon, Bayou, stm., U.S.	E7	122
Macondo, Ang.	C3	68
Macorís, Cabo, c., Dom. Rep.	C12	102
Macoupin Creek, stm., Il., U.S.	E8	120
Macovane, Moz.	B12	70
Macquarie, stm., Austl.	H6	76
Macquarie, stm., Austl.	n13	77a
Macquarie, Lake, l., Austl.	I8	76
Macquarie Harbour, b., Austl.	o12	77a
Macquarie Island, i., Austl.	A20	81
Macquarie Marshes, sw., Austl.	H6	76
Macquarie Ridge, unds.	O20	126
Mac. Robertson Land, reg., Ant.	B10	81
Macugnaga, Italy	E4	22
Macumba, stm., Austl.	E7	74
Macuro, Ven.	B10	86
Macusani, Peru	F3	84
Macuspana, Mex.	G12	100
Mad, stm., Ca., U.S.	C2	134
Mādabā, Jord.	G6	58
Madagascar, ctry., Afr.	D8	68
Madagascar Basin, unds.	M7	142
Madagascar Plateau, unds.	M7	142
Madan, Blg.	H11	26
Madanapalle, India	E4	53
Madang, Pap. N. Gui.	b4	79a
Mādārīpur, Bngl.	G13	54
Madaoua, Niger	G6	64
Madawaska, Me., U.S.	C8	110
Madawaska, stm., On., Can.	C13	112
Madawaska Highlands, plat., On., Can.	C12	112
Madaya, Mya.	A3	48
Maddalena, Isola, i., Italy	C3	24
Maddaloni, Italy	C8	24
Maddock, N.D., U.S.	G14	124
Madeira, i., Port.	C1	64
Madeira, stm., S.A.	E5	84
Madeira, Arquipélago da (Madeira Islands), is., Port.	C1	64
Madeira Islands see Madeira, Arquipélago da, is., Port.	C1	64
Madeleine, Îles de la, is., Qc., Can.	C15	110
Madeleine-Centre, Qc., Can.	A11	110
Madeline Island, i., Wi., U.S.	E8	118
Madera, Mex.	A4	100
Madera, Ca., U.S.	G5	134
Madera see Madeira, stm., S.A.	E5	84
Madgaon, India	D1	53
Madhepura, India	F11	54
Madhubani, India	E10	54
Madhugiri, India	E3	53
Madhupur, India	F11	54
Madhya Pradesh, state, India	D4	46
Madibogo, S. Afr.	E7	70
Madida, China	C9	38
Madill, Ok., U.S.	C2	122
Madimba, D.R.C.	E3	66
Madīnat ash-Sha'b, Yemen	G5	56
Madingo-Kayes, Congo	E2	66
Madingou, Congo	E2	66
Madirovalo, Madag.	D8	68
Madison, Al., U.S.	C12	122
Madison, Fl., U.S.	F2	116
Madison, Ga., U.S.	C2	116
Madison, In., U.S.	F12	120
Madison, Me., U.S.	F6	110
Madison, Mn., U.S.	F2	118
Madison, Mo., U.S.	E5	120
Madison, N.C., U.S.	H5	114
Madison, S.D., U.S.	C15	126
Madison, Wi., U.S.	A8	120
Madison, W.V., U.S.	F4	114
Madison, stm., U.S.	E15	136
Madison Heights, Va., U.S.	G6	114
Madison Range, mts., Mt., U.S.	E15	136
Madisonville, Ky., U.S.	G10	120
Madisonville, La., U.S.	G8	122
Madisonville, Tn., U.S.	A1	116
Madisonville, Tx., U.S.	G2	122
Madiun, Indon.	G7	50
Madiyi, China	G4	42
Mado Gashi, Kenya	D7	66
Madoi, China	E4	36
Madona, Lat.	D9	10
Madras see Chennai, India	F5	53
Madras, Or., U.S.	F5	136
Madre, Laguna, b., Mex.	C10	100
Madre, Laguna, b., Tx., U.S.	H10	130
Madre, Sierra, mts., Phil.	B3	52
Madre de Chiapas, Sierra, N.A.	G12	100
Madre de Dios, stm., S.A.	F4	84
Madre de Dios, Isla, i., Chile	J1	90
Madre del Sur, Sierra, mts., Mex.	G9	100
Madre Occidental, Sierra, mts., Mex.	B3	96
Madre Oriental, Sierra, mts., Mex.	C8	100
Madrid, Spain	D7	20
Madrid, Al., U.S.	F13	122
Madrid, Ne., U.S.	G11	126
Madrid, state, Spain	D7	20
Madridejos, Spain	E7	20
Madura, i., Indon.	G8	50
Madura, Selat, strt., Indon.	G8	50
Madurai, India	G4	53
Madurāntakam, India	E4	53
Maduru, stm., Sri L.	H5	53
Maebashi, Japan	C11	40
Mae Hong Son, Thai.	C3	48
Mae Klong, stm., Thai.	E4	48
Mae Ping Mae Hat Mae Kor National Park, p.o.i., Thai.	D4	48
Mae Ramat, Thai.	D4	48
Mae Sariang, Thai.	C3	48
Maesel, Ut., U.S.	C7	132
Mae Sot, Thai.	D4	48
Maestra, Sierra, mts., Cuba	B9	102
Maestu, Spain	B8	20
Mae Tha, Thai.	C4	48
Maevatanana, Madag.	D8	68
Maéwo, i., Vanuatu	j17	79d
Mafeking, Mb., Can.	B12	124
Mafeking see Mafikeng, S. Afr.	D7	70
Mafeteng, Leso.	F8	70
Maffra, Austl.	K6	76
Mafia Island, i., Tan.	F8	66
Mafikeng, S. Afr.	D7	70
Mafra, Braz.	C13	92
Magadan, Russia	E19	34
Magadi, Kenya	E7	66
Magaguadavic Lake, l., N.B., Can.	E9	110
Magalhães de Almeida, Braz.	B4	88
Magallanes, Phil.	D4	52
Magangué, Col.	C4	86
Magaria, Niger	G6	64
Magazine Mountain, mtn., Ar., U.S.	B5	122
Magdagači, Russia	F14	34
Magdalena, Arg.	G9	92
Magdalena, Bol.	B4	90
Magdalena, Mex.	E7	100
Magdalena, N.M., U.S.	I9	132
Magdalena, state, Col.	B4	86
Magdalena, stm., Col.	B4	86
Magdalena, Bahía, b., Mex.	C2	100
Magdalena, Isla, i., Chile	H2	90
Magdalena, Punta, c., Col.	C3	86
Magdalena de Kino, Mex.	F7	98
Magdeburg, Ger.	D7	16
Magelang, Indon.	G7	50
Magellan, Strait of, strt., S.A.	J2	90
Magenta, Italy	E5	22
Magetan, Indon.	G7	50
Maggiore, Lago, l., Eur.	D14	18
Maghama, Maur.	F2	64
Maghāghah, Egypt	J1	58
Magina, mtn., Spain	G7	20
Maglaj, Bos.	E5	26
Maglic, mtn., Bos.	F5	26
Maglie, Italy	D12	24
Magnetawan, stm., On., ...	C10	112
Magnetic Island, i., Austl.	B6	76
Magnitogorsk, Russia	D9	32
Magnolia, Ar., U.S.	D5	122
Magnolia, Ms., U.S.	F8	122
Magog, i., Fiji.	p20	79e
Magog, Qc., Can.	E4	110
Magozal, Mex.	E10	100
Magrath, Ab., Can.	G18	138
Maguarinho, Cabo, c., Braz.	A7	84
Maguari, Cabo, c., Braz.	D8	84
Magumeri, Nig.	G7	64
Magura, Bngl.	G12	54
Maguse Lake, l., Nu., Can.	C12	106
Magway, Mya.	B2	48
Magway, state, Mya.	B2	48
Mahābād, Iran	B6	56
Mahābaleshwar, India	C1	53
Mahabe, Madag.	D8	68
Mahābhārat Lek, mts., Nepal	E11	54
Mahābhārat Range see Mahābhārat Lek, mts., Nepal	E11	54
Mahabo, Madag.	E7	68
Mahačkala, Russia	F7	32
Mahād, India	B1	53
Mahādeo Range, mts., India	C5	53
Mahagi, D.R.C.	D6	66
Mahajamba, Madag.	D8	68
Mahajan, India	D4	54
Mahajanga, Madag.	D8	68
Mahākālī (Sārda), stm., Asia	D8	54
Mahakam, stm., Indon.	D9	50
Mahalapye, Bots.	C8	70
Maham, India	D6	54
Mahānadi, stm., India	H10	54
Mahanoro, Madag.	D8	68
Mahanoy City, Pa., U.S.	D9	114
Maharagama, Sri L.	H4	53
Mahārāganj, India	E10	54
Mahārājpur, India	F8	54
Mahārāshtra, state, India	E4	46
Mahāsamund, India	H9	54
Maha Sarakham, Thai.	D6	48
Mahatma, D.R.C.	E5	66
Mahavavy, stm., Sri L.	H5	53
Mahaxai, Laos	D7	48
Mahbūbābād, India	C5	53
Mahbūbnagar, India	C4	53
Mahd adh-Dhahab, Sau. Ar.	E5	56
Mahdia, Guy.	E12	86
Mahé, i., Sey.	k13	69a
Mahé, i., Sey.	j13	69b
Mahebourg, Mrts.	i10	69a
Mahendra Giri, mtn., India	B7	53
Mahendranagar, Nepal	D7	54
Mahenge, Tan.	F7	66
Mahesāna, India	G4	54
Maheshwar, India	G5	54
Mahi, stm., India	G4	54
Mahia Peninsula, pen., N.Z.	D7	80
Mahilëŭ, Bela.	G13	10
Mahilëŭ, state, Bela.	G13	10
Mahina, Fr. Poly.	u21	78h
Mahlabatini, S. Afr.	F10	70
Mahmūdābād, India	E8	54
Mahoba, India	F8	54
Mahogany Mountain, mtn., Or., U.S.	G9	136
Mahomet, Il., U.S.	D9	120
Mahón see Maó, Spain	E15	20
Mahone Bay, N.S., Can.	F12	110
Mahone Bay, b., N.S., Can.	F12	110
Mahood Lake, l., B.C., Can.	E10	138
Mahrāt, Jabal, plat., Yemen	F7	56
Mahrauni, India	F7	54
Mahuva, India	H3	54
Mai, stm., China	C4	38
Maicao, Col.	B5	86
Maichen, China	K3	42
Maiden, N.C., U.S.	A4	116
Maidenhead, Eng., U.K.	J12	12
Maidstone, Sk., Can.	A4	124
Maidstone, Eng., U.K.	J13	12
Maiduguri, Nig.	G7	64
Maihar, India	F8	54
Maijoma, Mex.	B3	130
Maikala Range, mts., India	G8	54
Maikoor, Pulau, i., Indon.	G9	44
Mailāni, India	D8	54
Main, stm., Ger.	F4	16
Mainaguri, India	E12	54
Mainburg, Ger.	H7	16
Main Channel, strt., On., Can.	C8	112
Mai-Ndombe, Lac, l., D.R.C.	E3	66
Main-Donau-Kanal, can., Ger.	G7	16
Maine, hist. reg., Fr.	F8	14
Maine, state, U.S.	E7	110
Maine, Gulf of, b., N.A.	G8	110
Maine-et-Loire, state, Fr.	G8	14
Maïné-Soroa, Niger	G7	64
Mainland, i., Scot., U.K.	n18	12a
Mainland, i., Scot., U.K.	B9	12
Mainpuri, India	F7	54
Maintirano, Madag.	D7	68
Mainz, Ger.	G4	16
Maipo, i., C.V.	k10	65a
Maipo, stm., Chile	F2	92
Maipo, Volcán, vol., S.A.	G3	92
Maipú, Arg.	H8	92
Maipú, Arg.	G2	92
Maiquetía, Ven.	B8	86
Maiqihamiao, China	C4	38
Maisí, Cuba	B11	102
Maišiagala, Lith.	F8	10
Maiskhal Island, i., Bngl.	H13	54
Maitland, Austl.	I8	76
Maitland, stm., On., Can.	E8	112
Maitri, sci., Ant.	C6	81
Maiz, Islas del, is., Nic.	F6	102
Maizuru, Japan	D8	40
Maja, stm., Russia	E15	34
Majagual, Col.	C4	86
Majene, Indon.	E11	50
Maji, Eth.	F7	62
Majiang, China	J4	42
Majiangzong, China	C12	54
Majia, Russia	D15	34
Majkain see Mayqayyng, Kaz.	D13	32
Majkop, Russia	F6	32
Major, Puig, mtn., Spain	E13	20
Majorca see Mallorca, i., Spain	E13	20
Majskij, Russia	F14	34
Majuro, at., Marsh. Is.	C8	72
Maka, Sen.	G2	64
Makabana, Congo	E2	66
Makale, Indon.	E11	50
Makālū, mtn., Asia	E11	54
Makapu'u Head, c., Hi., U.S.	b4	78a
Makarakomburu, Mount, mtn., Sol. Is.	e8	79b
Makarov, Russia	G17	34
Makasar see Makasar, Selat (Makassar Strait), strt., Indon.	D11	50
Makassar Strait see Makasar, Selat, strt., Indon.	D11	50
Makat, Kaz.	E8	32
Makatea, i., Fr. Poly.	E12	72
Makèni, S. Leo.	H2	64
Makgadikgadi, pl., Bots.	B7	70
Makgadikgadi Pans Game Reserve, Bots.	B7	70
Maki, Indon.	F9	44
Makindu, Kenya	E7	66
Makinsk, Kaz.	D11	32
Makira Harbour, b., Sol. Is.	f9	79b
Makkah (Mekka), Sau. Ar.	E4	56
Makkovik, Nf., Can.	D19	106
Makó, Hung.	C7	26
Makokou, Gabon	D2	66
Makongolosi, Tan.	F6	66
Makoua, Congo	D3	66
Maków Mazowiecki, Pol.	D16	16
Makrai, India	G6	54
Makrāna, India	E5	54
Makran Coast, cst., Asia	D9	56
Maksatiha, Russia	C18	10
Makšimkin Jar, Russia	C15	32
Maktar, Tun.	I3	24
Makumbi, D.R.C.	F4	66
Makung, Tai.	J8	42
Makurdi, Nig.	H6	64
Makushin Volcano, vol., Ak., U.S.	F6	140
Makušino, Russia	C11	32
Makwassie, S. Afr.	E8	70
Māl, India	E12	54
Mala see Mallow, Ire.	I4	12
Mala, Punta, c., Pan.	I8	102
Malabang, Phil.	G5	52
Malabar Coast, cst., India	F2	53
Malabo, Eq. Gui.	I6	64
Malacacheta, Braz.	I5	88
Malacca see Melaka, Malay.	K6	48
Malacca, Strait of, strt., Asia	B2	50
Malacky, Slov.	H13	16
Malad, stm., U.S.	H14	136
Malad City, Id., U.S.	A4	132
Maladzečna, Bela.	F9	10
Maladzečna, Bela.	G9	10
Málaga, Col.	D5	86
Málaga, Spain	H6	20
Málaga, co., Spain	H6	20
Malagarasi, Tan.	F6	66
Malagasy Republic see Madagascar, ctry., Afr.	D8	68
Malagón, Spain	E7	20
Malaimbandy, Madag.	E8	68
Malaita, state, Sol. Is.	e9	79b
Malaita, i., Sol. Is.	e9	79b
Malaja Kuril'skaja Grjada (Habomai-shotō), is., Russia	C17	38
Malaja Višera, Russia	B15	10
Malaka, Sempitan, strt., Indon.	J2	48
Malakal, Sudan	F6	62
Malakand, Pak.	A3	54
Malakoff, Tx., U.S.	E2	122
Malakula, state, Vanuatu	k16	79d
Malakula, i., Vanuatu	k16	79d
Malambo, Col.	B4	86
Malang, Indon.	H8	50
Malanggwa, Nepal	E10	54
Malanje, Ang.	B2	68
Malanville, Benin	G5	64
Malanzán, Arg.	E4	92
Mala Panew, stm., Pol.	F14	16
Mālaren, l., Swe.	G7	8
Malargüe, Arg.	G3	92
Malaspina, Arg.	H3	90
Malaspina Glacier, ice, Ak., U.S.	E11	140
Malatya, Tur.	B4	56
Malaut, India	C5	54
Malavalli, India	E3	53
Malawali, Pulau, i., Malay.	G1	52
Malawi, ctry., Afr.	C5	68
Malawi, Lake see Nyasa, Lake, l., Afr.	C5	68
Malaya see Semenanjung Malaysia, hist. reg., Malay.	K6	48
Malayagiri, mtn., India	H10	54
Malaybalay, Phil.	F5	52
Malāyer, Iran	C6	56
Malay Peninsula, pen., Asia	J5	48
Malay Reef, rf., Austl.	B7	76
Malayic, Sk., Can.	A9	124
Malbon, Austl.	C3	76
Malbork, Pol.	B15	16
Malchin, Ger.	C8	16
Malchow, Ger.	C8	16
Malcolm, Austl.	E4	74
Malcolm Island, i., B.C., Can.	F4	138
Malczyce, Pol.	E12	16
Malden, i., Kir.	D11	72
Mal di Ventre, Isola di, i., Italy	E2	24
Maldives, ctry., Asia	I11	30
Maldon, Austl.	K5	76
Maldonado, Ur.	G10	92
Male, Mya.	A2	48
Male', Mald.	i12	46a
Maléas, Akra, c., Grc.	G6	28
Mālegaon, India	H5	54
Malé Atoll, at., Mald.	i12	46a
Malé Karpaty (Little Carpathians), mts., Slov.	H13	16
Malema, Moz.	C6	68
Malente, Ger.	B6	16
Maler Kotla, India	C5	54
Malesherbes, Fr.	F11	14
Malgomaj, l., Swe.	D6	8
Malhanskij hrebet, mts., Russia	F10	34
Malheur, stm., Or., U.S.	G9	136
Malheur, South Fork, stm., Or., U.S.	G8	136
Malheur Lake, l., Or., U.S.	G8	136
Mali, Gui.	G2	64
Mali, ctry., Afr.	F4	64
Mali, stm., Mya.	C8	46
Malik, Sudan	D5	62
Mali Kyun, i., Mya.	F4	48
Malili, Indon.	E12	50
Malin, Or., U.S.	A4	134
Malin see Malyn, Ukr.	D14	6
Malindi, Kenya	E8	66
Malines see Mechelen, Bel.	C13	14
Malingping, Indon.	G4	50
Malino, Bukit, mtn., Indon.	C12	50
Malinovka, Russia	B7	38
Malitbog, Phil.	E5	52
Maljamar, N.M., U.S.	B4	130
Malka, Russia	F20	34
Malkāpur, India	H5	54
Malkara, Tur.	C9	28
Mallāh, Syria	F7	58
Mallan luonnonpuisto, p.o.i., Fin.	B9	8
Mallawī, Egypt	K1	58
Mallersdorf-Pfaffenberg, Ger.	H8	16
Mallery Lake, l., Nu., Can.	C11	106
Mallet, Braz.	B12	92
Malligasta, Arg.	D4	92
Mallorca (Majorca), i., Spain	E13	20
Mallow, Ire.	I4	12
Malm, Nor.	D4	8
Malmberget, Swe.	C9	8
Malmesbury, S. Afr.	H4	70
Malmok, c., Neth. Ant.	p23	104g
Malmö, Swe.	I5	8
Malmyž, Russia	C8	32
Maloca, Braz.	G11	86
Maloja, Russia	G19	10
Malojaroslavec, Russia	E19	10
Malolos, Phil.	C3	52
Malone, N.Y., U.S.	F2	110
Malonga, D.R.C.	C4	68
Małopolska, reg., Pol.	F17	16
Malošujka, Russia	E17	8
Malott, Wa., U.S.	B7	136
Małowice, Pol.	E11	16
Måløy, Nor.	E1	8
Malozemel'skaja Tundra, reg., Russia	C24	8
Malpas, Austl.	J3	76
Malpe, India	D2	53
Malpeque Bay, b., P.E., Can.	D13	110
Malprabha, stm., India	D2	53
Mālpura, India	E5	54
Malta, Braz.	D7	88
Malta, Mt., U.S.	F6	124
Malta, ctry., Eur.	I8	24
Malta, i., Malta	I8	24
Malta Channel, strt., Eur.	H8	24
Maltahöhe, Nmb.	D3	70
Maluku (Moluccas), is., Indon.	F8	44
Maluku, Laut (Molucca Sea), s., Indon.	E7	44
Malu Mare, Rom.	E10	26
Malunda, Indon.	E11	50
Mālvan, India	C1	53
Malvern, Ar., U.S.	C6	122
Malvern, Oh., U.S.	D4	114
Malvernia, Moz.	C10	70
Malvinas Sur, Arg.	D8	92
Malý Dunaj, stm., Slov.	H13	16
Malyja HaradzjaciČy, Bela.	H11	10
Malý Anjuj, stm., Russia	C21	34
Malyj Enisej, stm., Russia	G18	34
Malyj Tajmyr, ostrov, i., Russia	A10	34
Mama, Russia	E11	34
Mamaia, Rom.	E15	26
Mamanguape, Braz.	D8	88
Mamasa, Indon.	E11	50
Mamasa, stm., Indon.	E11	50
Mambajao, Phil.	F5	52
Mambasa, D.R.C.	D5	66
Mamberamo, stm., Indon.	F10	44
Mamburao, Phil.	D3	52
Mamehaktebo, Indon.	C9	50
Mameigwess Lake, l., On., Can.	B6	118
Mamfe, Cam.	C1	66
Mamlyutka, Kaz.	D11	32
Mammoth, Az., U.S.	K6	132
Mammoth Cave National Park, p.o.i., Ky., U.S.	G11	120
Mammoth Lakes, Ca., U.S.	F7	134
Mammoth Spring, Ar., U.S.	H6	120
Mamonovo, Russia	F2	10
Mamoré, stm., S.A.	E4	84
Mamou, Gui.	G2	64
Mamou, La., U.S.	G6	122
Mampikony, Madag.	D8	68
Mampong, Ghana	H4	64
Mamry, Jezioro, l., Pol.	B17	16
Mamuju, Indon.	E11	50
Mamuno, Bots.	C5	70
Man, W.V., U.S.	G4	114
Man, Isle of see Isle of Man, dep., Eur.	G8	12
Man, Isle of, dep., Eur.	G8	12
Man, C. Iv.	H3	64
Mana, Fr. Gu.	B7	84
Manabí, state, Ec.	a2	78a
Manacapuru, Braz.	I11	86
Manacor, Spain	E14	20
Manado (Menado), Indon.	E7	44
Managua, Nic.	F4	102
Managua, Lago de, l., Nic.	F4	102
Manakara, Madag.	E8	68
Manakau, mtn., N.Z.	B6	54
Manali, India	B6	54
Manama see Al-Manāmah, Bahr.	D7	56
Manam Island, i., Pap. N. Gui.	a4	79a
Mananara, Caño, stm., Ven.	C10	86
Mananara Avaratra, Madag.	D8	68
Mananjary, Madag.	E8	68
Manantenina, Madag.	E8	68
Manapire, stm., Ven.	D8	86
Manappārai, India	F4	53
Manār, stm., India	B3	53
Manāsa, India	G6	54
Manas Hu, l., China	C8	54
Manāslu, mtn., Nepal	D10	54
Manăstir, Rom.	D11	114
Manatí, Col.	B4	86
Manati, P.R.	B3	104a
Manatuto, E. Timor	G8	44
Manaung, Mya.	C1	48
Manaus, Braz.	D5	84
Manavgat, Tur.	G14	28
Manawa, Wi., U.S.	G10	118
Manawan, Pulau, i., Indon.	A9	44
Manban, China	A6	48
Manbij, Syria	B8	58
Mancelona, Mi., U.S.	D4	112
Mancha Real, Spain	G7	20
Manche, state, Fr.	E7	14
Manchester, Eng., U.K.	H10	12
Manchester, Ct., U.S.	C13	114
Manchester, Ga., U.S.	E14	122
Manchester, Ia., U.S.	B6	120
Manchester, Ky., U.S.	G2	114
Manchester, N.H., U.S.	H5	110
Manchester, Oh., U.S.	F2	114
Manchester, Tn., U.S.	B12	122
Manchester, Vt., U.S.	G3	110
Manchouli see Manzhouli, China	B8	36
Manchuria see Dong San Shen, hist. reg., China		
Manciano, Italy	H8	22
Mancos, Co., U.S.	F8	132
Mand, stm., Iran	D7	56
Manda, Tan.	G6	66
Manda, Jabal, mtn., Sudan	E4	62
Mandabe, Madag.	E7	68
Mandaguari, Braz.	A12	92
Manda Island, i., Kenya	E8	66
Mandal, Mong.	B6	36
Mandala, Puncak, mtn., Indon.	F10	44
Mandalay, Mya.	A2	48
Mandalay, state, Mya.	B2	48
Mandan, N.D., U.S.	A11	126
Mandar, Teluk, b., Indon.	E11	50
Mandara, Monts (Mandara Mountains), mts., Afr.	G7	64
Mandara, Monts (Mandara Monts), mts., Afr.	G7	64
Mandas, Italy	E3	24
Mandaue, Phil.	E4	52
Mandera, Kenya	D8	66
Manderson, Wy., U.S.	C5	126
Mandi, India	C6	54
Mandi Bahāuddin, Pak.	B4	54
Mandi Būrewāla, Pak.	C4	54
Mandi Dabwāli, India	C5	54
Mandimba, Moz.	C6	68
Mandioli, Pulau, i., Indon.	F8	44
Mandioré, Lagoa, l., S.A.	G6	84

Mandioré – Mawson I • 35

Name | Map Ref. | Page

Mandioré, Laguna see Mandioré, Lagoa, l., S.A. G6 84
Mandla, India G8 54
Mandlakazi, Moz. D11 70
Mandora, Austl. C4 74
Mandra, Pak. B4 54
Mandritsara, Madag. D8 68
Mandsaur, India F5 54
Mandun, China A4 48
Manduria, Italy D11 24
Māndvi, India H4 54
Māndvi, India G2 54
Mandya, India E3 53
Manendragarh, India G9 54
Manfalût, Egypt K1 58
Manfredonia, Italy I12 22
Manfredonia, Golfo di, b., Italy C10 24
Manga, Braz. H3 88
Manga, reg., Niger F7 64
Mangabeiras, Chapada das, hills, Braz. E2 88
Mangagoy, Phil. F6 52
Mangai, D.R.C. E3 66
Mangalagiri, India C5 53
Mangaldai, India E14 54
Mangalia, Rom. F15 26
Mangalore, India E2 53
Mangalvedha, India C2 53
Mangchang, China I2 42
Mange, China B9 54
Mangela, Mount see Nanggala Hill, mtn., Sol. Is. e7 79b
Manggar, Indon. E6 50
Mangham, La., U.S. E7 122
Mangin Range, mts., Mya. C8 46
Mangkalihat, Tanjung, c., Indon. C11 50
Manglares, Cabo, c., Col. G2 86
Mangla Reservoir, res., Pak. B4 54
Mangnai, China G16 32
Mangochi, Mwi. C6 68
Mangoky, stm., Madag. E7 68
Mangole, Pulau, i., Indon. F8 44
Mangrol, India H2 54
Mangrūl Pīr, India H6 54
Mangsang, Indon. E4 50
Mangshi see Luxi, China G4 36
Mangueira, Lagoa, b., Braz. F11 92
Mangueirinha, Braz. B11 92
Mangum, Ok., U.S. G9 128
Mangya, China D3 36
Manhattan, Ks., U.S. B12 128
Manhattan, Mt., U.S. E15 136
Manhiça, Moz. D11 70
Mān Hpāng, Mya. A4 48
Manhuaçu, Braz. K4 88
Manhuaçu, stm., Braz. J5 88
Manhumirim, Braz. K4 88
Maniago, Italy D9 22
Manica, Moz. D5 68
Manica, state, Moz. B11 70
Manicaland, state, Zimb. B11 70
Manic Deux, Réservoir, res., Qc., Can. A8 110
Manicoré, Braz. E5 84
Manicouagan, stm., Qc., Can. E17 106
Manicouagan, Réservoir, res., Qc., Can. E17 106
Maniganggo, China E4 36
Manigotagan, Mb., Can. C17 124
Manigotagan, stm., Can. C17 124
Manihiki, at., Cook Is. E10 72
Maniitsoq see Sukkertoppen, Grnld. D15 141
Mānikganj, Bngl. G13 54
Mānikpur, India F8 54
Manila, Phil. C3 52
Manila, Ar., U.S. I7 120
Manila, Ut., U.S. C7 132
Manila Bay, b., Phil. C3 52
Manilla, Austl. H8 76
Manily, Russia D22 34
Maningrida, Austl. B6 74
Maninjau, Danau, l., Indon. D1 50
Manipa, Selat, strt., Indon. F8 44
Manipur, state, India C7 46
Manipur, stm., Asia A1 48
Manisa, Tur. E10 28
Manisa, state, Tur. E11 28
Manistee, Mi., U.S. D3 112
Manistee, stm., Mi., U.S. D3 112
Manistique, Mi., U.S. C3 112
Manistique Lake, l., Mi., U.S. B4 112
Manito, Il., U.S. K9 118
Manitoba, state, Can. D11 106
Manitoba, Lake, l., Mb., Can. D15 124
Manitou, stm., On., Can. B5 118
Manitou, Lake, l., On., Can. C7 112
Manitou Beach, Sk., Can. C8 124
Manitou Lake, l., Sk., Can. B4 124
Manitoulin Island, i., On., Can. C7 112
Manitou Springs, Co., U.S. C3 128
Manitowaning, On., Can. C8 112
Manitowoc, Wi., U.S. D2 112
Maniwaki, Qc., Can. B13 112
Manizales, Col. E4 86
Manja, Madag. E7 68
Manjakandriana, Madag. D8 68
Manjeri, India F3 53
Mānjra, stm., India B3 53
Mankanza, D.R.C. D3 66
Mankato, Ks., U.S. B10 128
Mankato, Mn., U.S. G4 118
Mankera, Pak. C3 54
Mankota, Sk., Can. E6 124
Manley Hot Springs, Ak., U.S. D9 140
Manlleu, Spain B13 20
Manmād, India H5 54
Manna, Indon. F3 50
Mannahill, Austl. I3 76
Mannar, Sri L. G4 53
Mannar, Gulf of, b., Asia G4 53
Mannārgudi, India F4 53
Mannford, Ok., U.S. A2 122
Mannheim, Ger. G4 16
Manning, N.D., U.S. G11 124
Manning, S.C., U.S. C5 116
Manning Strait, strt., Sol. Is. d7 79b
Mannum, Austl. J2 76
Mannville, Ab., Can. C19 138
Manoharpur, India G10 54
Manokwari, Indon. F9 44
Manombo Atsimo, Madag. E7 68
Manono, D.R.C. F5 66
Manor, Sk., Can. E11 124
Manor, Tx., U.S. D10 130
Manosque, Fr. F11 18
Manouane, Lac, l., Qc., Can. C2 110
Manouane, Lac, res., Qc., Can. E16 106
Manp'o, Kor., N. D7 38
Mānpur, India H8 54
Manra, at., Kir. D9 72
Manresa, Spain C12 20
Mānsa, India C5 54
Mansa, Zam. C4 68
Mansafīs, Egypt J1 58
Mānsehra, Pak. A4 54
Mansel Island, i., Nu., Can. C14 106
Mansfield, Eng., U.K. H11 12
Mansfield, Ga., U.S. C2 116
Mansfield, Il., U.S. D9 120
Mansfield, La., U.S. E5 122
Mansfield, Mo., U.S. G5 120
Mansfield, Oh., U.S. D3 114
Mansfield, Pa., U.S. C8 114
Mansfield, Tx., U.S. B10 130
Mansfield, Mount, mtn., Vt., U.S. F4 110
Mansion, St. K./N. C2 105a
Mansôa, Gui.-B. G1 64
Manson, Ia., U.S. B3 120
Mansucum, Pan. H9 102
Mansura, La., U.S. F6 122
Manta, Ec. H1 86
Manta, Bahía de, b., Ec. H1 86
Mantagao, stm., Mb., Can. C16 124
Mantalingajan, Mount, mtn., Phil. F1 52
Mantanani Besar, Pulau, i., Malay. G1 52
Manteca, Ca., U.S. F4 134
Mantecal, Ven. D7 86
Mantena, Braz. J5 88
Manteo, N.C., U.S. I10 114
Mantes-la-Jolie, Fr. F10 14
Manti, Ut., U.S. D5 132
Mantiqueira, Serra da, mts., Braz. L3 88
Manton, Mi., U.S. D4 112
Mántova, Italy E7 22
Mantua, Cuba A5 102
Mantua see Mántova, Italy E7 22
Mantua, Oh., U.S. C4 114
Manturovo, Russia G21 8
Mäntyharju, Fin. F12 8
Manu, Peru F3 84
Manuae, at., Cook Is. E11 72
Manuae, at., Fr. Poly. E11 72
Manua Islands, is., Am. Sam. h13 79c
Manuel, Mex. D9 100
Manuel Alves, stm., Braz. F2 88
Manuel Alves Grande, stm., Braz. D2 88
Manuel Benavides, Mex. A6 100
Manuel F. Mantilla see Pedro R. Fernández, Arg. D8 92
Manuguru, India B5 53
Manui, Pulau, i., Indon. F7 44
Manukau, N.Z. C6 80
Manukau Harbour, b., N.Z. C6 80
Manus Island, i., Pap. N. Gui. a4 79a
Mānwat, India B3 53
Many, La., U.S. F5 122
Manyara, Lake, l., Tan. E7 66
Manyberries, Ab., Can. E3 124
Many Island Lake, l., Can. D3 124
Manyoni, Tan. F6 66
Many Peaks, Austl. E8 76
Manza, D.R.C. F5 66
Manzala, Bahra el-, l., Egypt G3 58
Manzanares, Spain E7 20
Manzanilla Point, c., Trin. s13 105f
Manzanillo, Cuba B9 102
Manzanillo, Mex. F6 100
Manzanillo Bay, b., N.A. C11 102
Manzano, N.M., U.S. G2 128
Manzano Peak, mtn., N.M., U.S. G2 128
Manzhouli, China B8 36
Manzini, Swaz. E10 70
Mao, Chad E3 62
Mao, Dom. Rep. C12 102
Maó, Spain E15 20
Maoba, China F3 42
Maoke, Pegunungan, mts., Indon. a2 79a
Maolin, China C5 38
Maoming, China K4 42
Mapaga, Indon. D11 50
Mapam Yumco, l., China C8 54
Mapane, Indon. D12 50
Mapari, stm., Braz. I8 86
Mapastepec, Mex. H12 100
Mapi, Indon. G10 44
Mapimí, Mex. C6 100
Mapimí, Bolsón de, des., Mex. B6 100
Mapire, Ven. D9 86
Mapiri, Bol. C3 90
Mapixari, Ilha, i., Braz. I9 86
Maple, stm., Ia., U.S. B2 120
Maple, stm., Mi., U.S. E5 112
Maple, stm., N.D., U.S. H16 124
Maple Creek, Sk., Can. E4 124
Maple Lake, Mn., U.S. F4 118
Maple Mount, Ky., U.S. G10 120
Maple Ridge, B.C., Can. G8 138
Mapleton, Ia., U.S. B2 120
Mapleton, Or., U.S. F3 136
Mapleton, Ut., U.S. C5 132
Mapuera, stm., Braz. C6 84
Maputo, Moz. D11 70
Maputo, state, Moz. D11 70
Maputo, stm., Afr. E11 70
Maqanshy, Kaz. E14 32
Maqat, Kaz. E8 32
Maqên Gangri, mtn., China E4 36
Maqna, Sau. Ar. J5 58
Maquan, stm., China D10 54
Maquela do Zombo, Ang. B2 68
Maquereau, Pointe au, c., Qc., Can. B12 110
Maquinchao, Arg. H3 90
Maquoketa, Ia., U.S. B7 120
Maquoketa, stm., Ia., U.S. B7 120
Maquoketa, North Fork, stm., Ia., U.S. B7 120
Mar, Serra do, mts., Braz. B13 92
Mara, stm., Afr. E7 66
Maraã, Braz. H9 86
Maraa, Fr. Poly. v21 78h
Marabá, Braz. C1 88
Marabahan, Indon. E9 50
Maraboon, Lake, res., Austl. D6 76
Maracá, Ilha de, i., Braz. F11 86
Maracá, Ilha de, i., Braz. C7 84
Maracaçumé, stm., Braz. A3 88
Maracaibo, Ven. B5 86
Maracaibo, Lago de, l., Ven. C6 86
Maracaju, Braz. D5 90
Maracanaú, Braz. B6 88
Maracás, Braz. G5 88
Maracay, Ven. B8 86
Marādah, Libya B3 62
Maradi, Niger G6 64
Marāghah, Sabkhat al-, l., Syria C8 58
Marāgheh, Iran B6 56
Maragogipe, Braz. G6 88
Maragoji, Braz. E8 88
Marahuaca, Cerro, mtn., Ven. F9 86
Maraial, Braz. E8 88
Marais des Cygnes, stm., U.S. F3 120
Marajó, Baía de, b., Braz. D8 84
Marajó, Ilha de, i., Braz. D8 84
Maralal, Kenya D7 66
Marali, C.A.R. C3 66
Maralinga, Austl. F6 74
Marambio, sci., Ant. B35 81
Marampa, S.L. H2 64
Maramsilli Reservoir, res., India H8 54
Maramureș, state, Rom. B10 26
Maran, Malay. K6 48
Marana, Az., U.S. K5 132
Marand, Iran B6 56
Marang, Malay. J6 48
Marangas, Phil. F1 52
Maranguape, Braz. B6 88
Maranhão, state, Braz. C3 88
Maranhão, stm., Braz. D9 84
Marano, Laguna di, b., Italy E10 22
Maranoa, stm., Austl. F7 76
Marañón, stm., Peru D2 84
Marasende, Pulau, i., Indon. F10 50
Mărășești, Rom. D14 26
Maratasã, stm., Braz. C4 88
Marathon, Austl. C4 76
Marathon, On., Can. C12 118
Marathon, Tx., U.S. D4 130
Marathon, Wi., U.S. G9 118
Marathónas, Grc. E6 28
Maratua, Pulau, i., Indon. B11 50
Marau, Braz. D11 92
Maraú, Braz. H6 88
Marauiá, stm., Braz. H9 86
Maravilha, Braz. C11 92
Maravillas, Mex. B6 100
Maravillas Creek, stm., Tx., U.S. E4 130
Marav Lake, l., Pak. D2 54
Maravovo, Sol. Is. e8 79b
Marawi, Phil. F5 52
Marawwaḩ, i., U.A.E. E7 56
Marayes, Arg. E4 92
Marbella, Spain H6 20
Marble, N.C., U.S. A2 116
Marble Bar, Austl. D3 74
Marble Canyon, p., Az., U.S. G5 132
Marble Falls, Tx., U.S. D9 130
Marble Hall, S. Afr. D9 70
Marble Hill, Mo., U.S. G8 120
Marblemount, Wa., U.S. B5 136
Marble Rock, Ia., U.S. I6 118
Marburg, Ger. F4 16
Marburg, S. Afr. G10 70
Marca, Ponta da, c., Ang. D1 68
Marcal, stm., Hung. B4 26
Marcelin, Sk., Can. B7 124
Marceline, Mo., U.S. E5 120
March, Eng., U.K. I12 12
March (Morava), stm., Eur. H12 16
Marche, state, Italy G10 22
Marche, hist. reg., Fr. C8 18
Marche-en-Famenne, Bel. D14 14
Marchena, Spain G5 20
Marches see Marche, state, Italy G10 22
Mar Chiquita, Laguna, b., Arg. H9 92
Mar Chiquita, Laguna, l., Arg. E6 92
Marcigny, Fr. C10 18
Marco, Braz. B5 88
Marcos Juárez, Arg. F6 92
Marcus, Ia., U.S. B2 120
Marcus Baker, Mount, mtn., Ak., U.S. D10 140
Marcus Island see Minami-Tori-shima, i., Japan G19 30
Marcy, Mount, mtn., N.Y., U.S. F2 110
Mardān, Pak. A4 54
Mardarivka, Ukr. B16 26
Mar del Plata, Arg. H9 92
Mardin, Tur. B5 56
Maré, i., N. Cal. m17 79d
Mare a Brăilei, Insula, i., Rom. D14 26
Marea de Portillo, Cuba C9 102
Marechal Cândido Rondon, Braz. B10 92
Marechal Deodoro, Braz. E8 88
Maree, Loch, l., Scot., U.K. D7 12
Mareeba, Austl. A5 76
Maremma, reg., Italy H8 22
Marengo, Ia., U.S. C5 120
Marengo, Il., U.S. B9 120
Marenisco, Mi., U.S. E9 118
Marennes, Fr. D4 18
Marettimo, Isola, i., Italy G5 24
Marfa, Tx., U.S. D3 130
Margai Caka, l., China A6 46
Margaree Harbour, N.S., Can. D15 110
Margaret, stm., Austl. C5 74
Margaret Bay, B.C., Can. E3 138
Margaret River, Austl. F2 74
Margaretville, N.Y., U.S. B11 114
Margarita, Isla de, i., Ven. B9 86
Margate, S. Afr. G10 70
Margate, Eng., U.K. J14 12
Margate, Fl., U.S. J5 116
Margecany, Slov. H16 16
Margelan see Margilan, Uzb. F12 32
Margherita di Savoia, Italy C10 24
Margherita Peak, mtn., Afr. D5 66
Margilan, Uzb. F12 32
Margonin, Pol. D13 16
Margosatubig, Phil. G4 52
Mārgow, Dasht-e, des., Afg. C9 56
Marha, Russia D13 34
Marha, stm., Russia C12 34
Maria, Îles, is., Fr. Poly. F11 72
María Cleofas, Isla, i., Mex. E5 100
María Elena, Chile D3 90
María Grande, Arg. E8 92
María Ignacia, Arg. H8 92
Maria Island, i., Austl. B7 74
Maria Island National Park, p.o.i., Austl. o14 77a
Mariakani, Kenya E7 66
María Madre, Isla, i., Mex. E5 100
María Magdalena, Isla, i., Mex. E5 100
Mariana, Braz. K4 88
Mariana Islands, is., Oc. B5 72
Mariana Ridge, unds. H17 142
Mariana Trench, unds. H17 142
Marian Lake, l., N.T., Can. C7 106
Marianna, Ar., U.S. C8 122
Marianna, Fl., U.S. G13 122
Mariano I. Loza, Arg. D8 92
Mariánské Lázně, Czech Rep. G8 16
Marias, stm., Mt., U.S. B16 136
Marias Pass, p., Mt., U.S. B13 136
María Teresa, Arg. G6 92
Mariato, Punta, c., Pan. I7 102
Maribo, Den. B7 16
Maribor, Slvn. D12 22
Maricao, P.R. B2 104a
Marico, stm., Afr. D8 70
Maricopa, Az., U.S. J4 132
Maricunga, Salar de, pl., Chile C3 92
Marié, stm., Braz. H8 86
Marie Byrd Land, reg., Ant. C29 81
Marie-Galante, i., Guad. i6 105c
Mariehamn, Fin. F9 8
Mariental, Nmb. D4 70
Marienville, Pa., U.S. C6 114
Mariestad, Swe. G5 8
Marieta, stm., Ven. E8 86
Marietta, Ga., U.S. D14 122
Marietta, Mn., U.S. G2 118
Marietta, Oh., U.S. E4 114
Marieville, Qc., Can. E3 110
Marignane, Fr. F11 18
Marigot, Dom. i6 105c
Marigot, Guad. A1 105a
Mariinsk, Russia C15 32
Mariinskoe, Russia F17 34
Marijampolė, Lith. F6 10
Marij El, state, Russia C7 32
Marília, Braz. D7 90
Marimba, Ang. B2 68
Marín, Mex. I7 130
Marín, Spain B2 20
Marina di Ravenna, Italy F9 22
Marina Fall, wtfl., Guy. E12 86
Mar"ina Horka, Bela. G11 10
Marinduque, i., Phil. D3 52
Marine City, Mi., U.S. B3 114
Marinette, Wi., U.S. C2 112
Maringá, Braz. D6 90
Marino, Vanuatu j16 79d
Marintu, Indon. C6 50
Marion, Al., U.S. E11 122
Marion, Ar., U.S. B8 122
Marion, Ia., U.S. B6 120
Marion, Il., U.S. G9 120
Marion, In., U.S. H4 112
Marion, Ks., U.S. C12 128
Marion, Ky., U.S. G9 120
Marion, La., U.S. E6 122
Marion, Ms., U.S. E10 122
Marion, N.C., U.S. I4 114
Marion, N.D., U.S. A14 126
Marion, Oh., U.S. D2 114
Marion, S.C., U.S. B6 116
Marion, Va., U.S. H4 114
Marion, Lake, res., S.C., U.S. C5 116
Marion Bay, b., Austl. o13 77a
Marion County Lake, res., Ks., U.S. C11 128
Marion Downs, Austl. D2 76
Marion Junction, Al., U.S. E11 122
Marion Reef, rf., Austl. B9 76
Marionville, Mo., U.S. G4 120
Maripa, Ven. D9 86
Mariposa, Ca., U.S. F5 134
Mariquita, Col. E4 86
Mariscal Estigarribia, Para. D4 90
Maritime Alps, mts., Eur. E12 18
Maritsa (Évros) (Marica) (Meriç), stm., Eur. C9 28
Mariupol', Ukr. E5 32
Mariusa, Caño, stm., Ven. C11 86
Mariveles, Phil. C3 52
Mariyampole see Marijampolė, Lith. F6 10
Marjanovka, Russia D12 32
Marka, Som. D8 66
Mārkāpur, India D4 53
Markaryd, Swe. H5 8
Markdale, On., Can. D9 112
Marked Tree, Ar., U.S. B8 122
Markesan, Wi., U.S. H10 118
Market Harborough, Eng., U.K. I12 12
Markham, On., Can. E10 112
Markham, Tx., U.S. F11 130
Markham Bay, b., Nu., Can. C16 106
Markit, China B12 56
Markle, In., U.S. H4 112
Markleeville, Ca., U.S. E6 134
Markovo, Russia D23 34
Marks, Russia D7 32
Marks, Ms., U.S. C8 122
Marktheidenfeld, Ger. G5 16
Marktoberdorf, Ger. I6 16
Marktredwitz, Ger. G8 16
Mark Twain Lake, res., Mo., U.S. E6 120
Marlboro, Ab., Can. C14 138
Marlboro, N.Y., U.S. C11 114
Marlborough, Austl. D7 76
Marlborough, Guy. B6 84
Marlborough, Ma., U.S. B14 114
Marlette, Mi., U.S. E6 112
Marlinton, W.V., U.S. F5 114
Marlow, Ok., U.S. G11 128
Marmaduke, Ar., U.S. H7 120
Marmande, Fr. E6 18
Marmara, Sea of see Marmara Denizi, s., Tur. C11 28
Marmara Adası, i., Tur. C10 28
Marmara Denizi (Marmara, Sea of), s., Tur. C11 28
Marmara Ereğlisi, Tur. C10 28
Marmara Gölü, l., Tur. E10 28
Marmaris, Tur. G11 28
Marmaton, stm., U.S. G3 120
Marmelos, stm., Braz. E5 84
Marmet, W.V., U.S. F4 114
Marmion Lake, l., On., Can. C7 118
Marmolada, mtn., Italy D8 22
Marmora, On., Can. D12 112
Marnay, Fr. G14 14
Marne, Ger. C4 16
Marne, Mi., U.S. E4 112
Marne, state, Fr. E13 14
Marne, stm., Fr. E11 14
Marne à la Saône, Canal de la, can., Fr. F14 14
Maroa, Ven. F8 86
Maroantsetra, Madag. D8 68
Maromandia, Madag. C8 68
Maromme, Fr. E10 14
Maromokotro, mtn., Madag. C8 68
Marondera, Zimb. D5 68
Maroni (Marowijne), stm., S.A. C7 84
Maros, Indon. F11 50
Maros (Mureș), stm., Eur. C7 26
Maroua, Cam. B2 66
Marovoay, Madag. D8 68
Marowijne (Maroni), stm., S.A. C7 84
Marqaköl köli, l., Kaz. E15 32
Marquand, Mo., U.S. G7 120
Marquard, S. Afr. F8 70
Marquesas Islands see Marquises, Îles, is., Fr. Poly. D12 72
Marquesas Keys, is., Fl., U.S. L3 116
Marquette, Ks., U.S. C11 128
Marquette, Mi., U.S. B2 112
Marquis, Gren. q10 105e
Marquises, Îles, is., Fr. Poly. D12 72
Marradi, Italy F8 22
Marrah, Jabal, hill, Sudan E4 62
Marrakech, Mor. C3 64
Marrakesh see Marrakech, Mor. C3 64
Marrawah, Austl. n12 77a
Marree, Austl. E7 74
Marrero, La., U.S. H8 122
Marromeu, Moz. D6 68
Marrupa, Moz. C6 68
Marsá al-Burayqah, Libya A3 62
Marsabit, Kenya D7 66
Marsala, Italy G6 24
Marsciano, Italy H9 22
Marseille, Fr. F11 18
Marseilles, Il., U.S. C9 120
Marsfjället, mtn., Swe. D6 8
Marshall, Lib. H2 64
Marshall, Ak., U.S. D7 140
Marshall, Ar., U.S. I5 120
Marshall, Mi., U.S. B1 114
Marshall, Mn., U.S. G3 118
Marshall, Mo., U.S. E4 120
Marshall, N.C., U.S. I3 114
Marshall, Tx., U.S. E4 122
Marshall, Va., U.S. F8 114
Marshall, stm., Austl. D7 74
Marshallberg, N.C., U.S. B9 116
Marshall Islands, ctry., Oc. H19 142
Marshall Islands, is., Marsh. Is. B7 72
Marshalltown, Ia., U.S. B5 120
Marshfield, Mo., U.S. G4 120
Marshfield, Wi., U.S. G8 118
Mars Hill, Me., U.S. D9 110
Mars Hill, N.C., U.S. I3 114
Marsh Island, i., La., U.S. H7 122
Marshville, N.C., U.S. A5 116
Marsing, Id., U.S. G10 136
Märsta, Swe. G7 8
Marstal, Den. B6 16
Martaban, Gulf of, b., Mya. D3 48
Martapura, Indon. E9 50
Martapura, Indon. F4 50
Marte R. Gómez, Presa, res., Mex. H9 130
Marthaguy Creek, stm., Austl. H6 76
Martha's Vineyard, i., Ma., U.S. C15 114
Martí, Cuba B9 102
Martigny, Switz. D4 22
Martigues, Fr. F11 18
Martin, Slov. G14 16
Martin, Ky., U.S. G3 114
Martin, Mi., U.S. F4 112
Martin, N.D., U.S. G13 124
Martin, Tn., U.S. H9 120
Martín, stm., Spain C10 20
Martina Franca, Italy D11 24
Martindale, Tx., U.S. E10 130
Mărtinești, Rom. D14 26
Martinez, Ca., U.S. E3 134
Martinez, Ga., U.S. C3 116
Martínez de la Torre, Mex. E10 100
Martinho Campos, Braz. J3 88
Martinique, dep., N.A. i15 96a
Martinique Passage, strt., N.A. k6 105c
Martin Lake, res., Al., U.S. E12 122
Martinópole, Braz. B5 88
Martinsberg, Aus. B12 22
Martinsburg, W.V., U.S. E7 114
Martins Ferry, Oh., U.S. D5 114
Martinsville, Il., U.S. E10 120
Martinsville, In., U.S. E11 120
Martinsville, Va., U.S. H5 114
Martin Vaz, Ilhas, is., Braz. H12 82
Martos, Spain G7 20
Martre, Lac la, l., N.T., Can. C7 106
Martti, Fin. C13 8
Marudi, Malay. A9 50
Marudu, Telukan, b., Malay. G1 52
Marugame, Japan E6 40
Maruim, Braz. F7 88
Maruoka, Japan C9 40
Marutea, at., Fr. Poly. E12 72
Marv Dasht, Iran D7 56
Marvine, Mount, mtn., Ut., U.S. E5 132
Mārwār, India F4 54
Mary, Turkmen. B9 56
Mary, stm., Austl. E9 76
Maryborough, Austl. E9 76
Maryborough, Austl. K4 76
Marydale, S. Afr. F5 70
Maryfield, Sk., Can. E12 124
Mary Kathleen, Austl. C2 76
Maryland, state, U.S. E8 114
Maryneal, Tx., U.S. B7 130
Maryport, Eng., U.K. G9 12
Marysvale, Ut., U.S. E4 132
Marysville, N.B., Can. D10 110
Marysville, Ca., U.S. D4 134
Marysville, Ks., U.S. L2 118
Marysville, Mi., U.S. B3 114
Marysville, Oh., U.S. D2 114
Marysville, Wa., U.S. B4 136
Maryville, Mo., U.S. D3 120
Maryville, Tn., U.S. I2 114
Marzagão, Braz. I1 88
Marzo, Punta, c., Col. D3 86
Masada see Mezada, Horvot, sci., Isr. G6 58
Masai Mara Game Reserve, Kenya E7 66
Masai Steppe, plat., Tan. E7 66
Masaka, Ug. E6 66
Masalembu Besar, Pulau, i., Indon. F9 50
Masamba, Indon. E12 50
Masan, Kor., S. D1 40
Masasi, Tan. G7 66
Masatepe, Nic. G4 102
Masaya, Nic. G4 102
Masbate, Phil. D4 52
Masbate, i., Phil. E4 52
Mascarene Basin, unds. K8 142
Mascarene Islands, is., Afr. i10 69a
Mascarene Plateau, unds. J8 142
Mascot, Tn., U.S. H2 114
Mascota, Mex. E6 100
Mascoutah, Il., U.S. F8 120
Maseru, Leso. F8 70
Mashan, China J3 42
Mashava, Zimb. D5 68
Mashhad, Iran B8 56
Mashi, China G6 42
Mashiko, Japan C13 40
Mashra'ar Raqq, Sudan F5 62
Masi-Manimba, D.R.C. E3 66
Masindi, Ug. D6 66
Masira, Gulf of see Maṣīrah, Khalīj, b., Oman F8 56
Maṣīrah, i., Oman E8 56
Maṣīrah, Khalīj, b., Oman F8 56
Masisea, Peru E3 84
Masjed-e Soleymān, Iran C6 56
Mask, Lough, l., Ire. H3 12
Maskanah, Syria B8 58
Masljanino, Russia D14 32
Mason, Mi., U.S. F5 112
Mason, Oh., U.S. E1 114
Mason, Tx., U.S. D8 130
Mason, W.V., U.S. E3 114
Mason City, Ia., U.S. A4 120
Mason City, Il., U.S. D8 120
Mason City, Ne., U.S. F13 126
Masqaṭ (Muscat), Oman E8 56
Massa, Italy F7 22
Massachusetts, state, U.S. B14 114
Massachusetts Bay, b., Ma., U.S. B15 114
Massafra, Italy D11 24
Massaguet, Chad E3 62
Massa Marittima, Italy G7 22
Massangena, Moz. B11 70
Massawa (Mitsiwa), Erit. D7 62
Massena, Ia., U.S. C3 120
Massena, N.Y., U.S. F2 110
Massenya, Chad E3 62
Massey, On., Can. B7 112
Massey Sound, strt., Nu., Can. B7 141
Massiac, Fr. D9 18
Massillon, Oh., U.S. D4 114
Massina, reg., Mali G4 64
Massinga, Moz. C12 70
Massingir, Moz. C11 70
Massive, Mount, mtn., Co., U.S. D10 132
Masson Island, i., Ant. B14 81
Mastābah, Sau. Ar. E4 56
Masterson, Tx., U.S. F6 128
Masterton, N.Z. E6 80
Mastic Point, Bah. K8 116
Mastung, Pak. D10 56
Masty, Bela. G7 10
Masuda, Japan E4 40
Masurai, Gunung, mtn., Indon. E2 50
Masuria see Mazury, reg., Pol. C16 16
Masvingo, Zimb. E5 68
Masvingo, state, Zimb. B10 70
Maṣyāf, Syria C7 58
Mata Amarilla, Arg. I2 90
Matabeleland North, state, Zimb. A9 70
Matabeleland South, state, Zimb. B9 70
Matabuena, Spain C7 20
Matacuni, stm., Ven. F9 86
Mata de São João, Braz. G6 88
Matadi, D.R.C. F2 66
Matagalpa, Nic. F5 102
Matagami, Qc., Can. F15 106
Matagorda, Tx., U.S. F12 130
Matagorda Island, i., Tx., U.S. F11 130
Matagorda Peninsula, pen., Tx., U.S. F11 130
Matahiae, Pointe, c., Fr. Poly. w22 78h
Matâi, Egypt J1 58
Mataiea, Fr. Poly. w22 78h
Mataiva, at., Fr. Poly. E12 72
Matak, Pulau, i., Indon. B5 50
Matakana, Austl. I5 76
Matale, Sri L. H5 53
Matam, Sen. F2 64
Matamoros, Mex. C10 100
Matamoros, Mex. C7 100
Matan, Indon. D7 50
Matandu, stm., Tan. F7 66
Matane, Qc., Can. B9 110
Matanni, Pak. B3 54
Matanzas, Cuba A7 102
Matanzas, Mex. E8 100
Matapan, Cape see Taínaro, Ákra, c., Grc. G5 28
Matape, stm., Mex. A3 100
Matapédia, Qc., Can. C9 110
Matapédia, Lac, l., Qc., Can. B9 110
Mataquito, stm., Chile G2 92
Matara, Sri L. I5 53
Mataram, Indon. H9 50
Mataranka, Austl. B6 74
Mataró, Spain C13 20
Matasiri, Pulau, i., Indon. F9 50
Matatiele, S. Afr. G9 70
Matatula, Cape, c., Am. Sam. h12 79c
Matâ'utu, Wal./F. E9 72
Matavera, Cook Is. a27 78j
Mataveri, Chile e29 78l
Mataveri, Aeropuerto, Chile f29 78l
Mataveri Airstrip see Mataveri, Aeropuerto, Chile f29 78l
Matehuala, Mex. D8 100
Mateke Hills, hills, Zimb. B10 70
Matera, Italy D10 24
Mateur, Tun. G3 24
Matha, Fr. D5 18
Mather, Mb., Can. E14 124
Mather, Pa., U.S. E5 114
Matheson, On., Can. F14 106
Mathews, Va., U.S. G9 114
Mathis, Tx., U.S. F10 130
Mathura (Muttra), India E6 54
Matias Barbosa, Braz. K4 88
Matías Romero, Mex. G11 100
Matícora, stm., Ven. B6 86
Matinha, Braz. B3 88
Matipó, Braz. K4 88
Matiyure, stm., Ven. D7 86
Mātli, Pak. F2 54
Mato, Cerro, mtn., Ven. D9 86
Mato Grosso, state, Braz. F6 84
Mato Grosso, Planalto do, plat., Braz. B5 90
Mato Grosso, Plateau of see Mato Grosso, Planalto do, plat., Braz. B5 90
Mato Grosso do Sul, state, Braz. C6 90
Matola Rio, Moz. D11 70
Matopos, Zimb. B9 70
Matosinhos, Port. C2 20
Matouying, China B8 42
Matozinhos, Braz. J3 88
Maṭraḩ, Oman E8 56
Matsudo, Japan D12 40
Matsue, Japan D6 40
Matsumoto, Japan C10 40
Matsusaka, Japan E9 40
Matsu Tao, i., Tai. H8 42
Matsutō, Japan C9 40
Matsuura, Japan F2 40
Matsuyama, Japan F5 40
Mattagami, stm., On., Can. F14 106
Mattamuskeet, Lake, l., N.C., U.S. A9 116
Mattaponi, stm., Va., U.S. G8 114
Mattawa, On., Can. B11 112
Mattawa, Wa., U.S. D7 136
Mattawamkeag, stm., Me., U.S. E8 110
Matterhorn, mtn., Eur. D13 18
Matterhorn, mtn., Nv., U.S. B1 132
Matthews Mountain, hill, Mo., U.S. G7 120
Matthew Town, Bah. C10 96
Mattighofen, Aus. B10 22
Mattoon, Il., U.S. E9 120
Mattoon, Wi., U.S. F9 118
Mattydale, N.Y., U.S. E13 112
Matua, Indon. E7 50
Matudo see Matsudo, Japan D12 40
Matue see Matsue, Japan D6 40
Matuku, i., Fiji q19 79e
Matumoto see Matsumoto, Japan C10 40
Maturín, Ven. C10 86
Matutina, Braz. J2 88
Matuzaka see Matsusaka, Japan E9 40
Maú (Ireng), stm., S.A. F12 86
Maúa, Moz. C6 68
Mau Aimma, India F8 54
Maubeuge, Fr. D12 14
Maud, Tx., U.S. D4 122
Maudaha, India F7 54
Maude, Austl. J5 76
Maués, Braz. D6 84
Maués, stm., Braz. D6 84
Mauganj, India F8 54
Maui, i., Hi., U.S. c5 78a
Mauk, Indon. F5 50
Mauldin, S.C., U.S. B3 116
Maule, state, Chile G2 92
Maule, stm., Chile G1 92
Maule, Laguna del, l., Chile G2 92
Mauléon-Licharre, Fr. F5 18
Maumee, Oh., U.S. G6 112
Maumee, stm., U.S. G6 112
Maumelle, Lake, res., Ar., U.S. C6 122
Maumere, Indon. G7 44
Maun, Bots. D3 68
Maunabo, P.R. B4 104a
Mauna Kea, vol., Hi., U.S. d6 78a
Maunaloa, Hi., U.S. b4 78a
Mauna Loa, vol., Hi., U.S. d6 78a
Maunath Bhanjan, India F9 54
Maungdaw, Mya. H14 54
Maungmagan, Mya. E3 48
Maunoir, Lac, l., N.T., Can. B6 106
Maupihaa, at., Fr. Poly. E11 72
Mau Rānīpur, India F7 54
Maurepas, Lake, l., La., U.S. G8 122
Maurice, Lake, l., Austl. E6 74
Mauricie, Parc national de la, p.o.i., Qc., Can. D3 110
Mauritania, ctry., Afr. F2 64
Mauritanie see Mauritania, ctry., Afr. F2 64
Mauritius, ctry., Afr. h10 69a
Mauron, Fr. F6 14
Mauston, Wi., U.S. H8 118
Mautau, c., Fr. Poly. r19 78g
Mauterndorf, Aus. C10 22
Mauthen, Aus. D9 22
Mauvais Coulee, stm., N.D., U.S. F14 124
Mava, Pap. N. Gui. b3 79a
Maverick, Az., U.S. J7 132
Mavinga, Ang. D3 68
Mavrovo Nacionalni Park, p.o.i., Mac. B3 28
Mavuradonha Mountains, mts., Zimb. D5 68
Mawchi, Mya. C3 48
Mawlaik, Mya. D7 46
Mawlamyine (Moulmein), Mya. D3 48
Mawson, sci., Ant. B11 81

Name	Map Ref.	Page
Maw Taung (Luang, Khao), mtn., Asia	G4	48
Max, N.D., U.S.	G12	124
Maxaranguape, Braz.	C8	88
Maxcanú, Mex.	B3	102
Maxixe, Moz.	C12	70
Maxville, On., Can.	E2	110
Maxwell, Ca., U.S.	D3	134
Maxwell, Ne., U.S.	F12	126
Maxwell, N.M., U.S.	E4	128
May, Tx., U.S.	B9	130
May, Cape, pen., N.J., U.S.	F11	114
May, Mount, mtn., Ab., Can.	B11	138
Maya, Pulau, i., Indon.	D6	50
Mayaguana, i., Bah.	A11	102
Mayaguana Passage, strt., Bah.	A11	102
Mayagüez, P.R.	B1	104a
Mayang, China	H3	42
Mayarí, Cuba	B10	102
Maybole, Scot., U.K.	F8	12
Maydena, Austl.	o13	77a
Maydh, Som.	B9	66
Mayen, Ger.	F3	16
Mayenne, Fr.	F8	14
Mayenne, state, Fr.	F8	14
Mayenne, stm., Fr.	F8	14
Mayer, Az., U.S.	I4	132
Mayerthorpe, Ab., Can.	C15	138
Mayfield, Ky., U.S.	H9	120
Mayfield, Ut., U.S.	D5	132
Mayflower, Ar., U.S.	C6	122
Māyir, Syria	B8	58
Maykain see Mayqayyng, Kaz.	D13	32
Maymyo, Mya.	A3	48
Maynard, Ia., U.S.	B6	120
Maynardville, Tn., U.S.	H2	114
Mayne, stm., Austl.	D3	76
Mayo, Yk., Can.	C3	106
Mayo, Fl., U.S.	F2	116
Mayo, state, Ire.	H3	12
Mayo, stm., Arg.	I3	90
Mayo, stm., Mex.	B4	100
Mayon Volcano, vol., Phil.	D4	52
Mayor Buratovich, Arg.	G4	90
Mayotte, dep., Afr.	C8	68
Mayoyoque, Col.	G4	86
May Pen, Jam.	j13	104d
Mayqayyng, Kaz.	D13	32
Mayreau, i., St. Vin.	p11	105e
Mayskoe, Kaz.	D13	32
Mays Landing, N.J., U.S.	E11	114
Maysville, Ky., U.S.	F2	114
Maysville, Mo., U.S.	E3	120
Maysville, N.C., U.S.	B8	116
Maysville, Ok., U.S.	G11	128
Mayumba, Gabon	E2	66
Māyūram, India	F4	53
Mayville, Mi., U.S.	E6	112
Mayville, N.D., U.S.	G16	124
Mayville, N.Y., U.S.	B6	114
Maywood, Ne., U.S.	G12	126
Maza, Arg.	H6	92
Mazabuka, Zam.	D4	68
Mazagão, Braz.	D7	84
Mazamet, Fr.	F8	18
Mazán, stm., Peru	I4	86
Mazara, Val di, reg., Italy	G7	24
Mazara del Vallo, Italy	G6	24
Mazār-e Sharīf, Afg.	B10	56
Mazarrón, Golfo de, b., Spain	G9	20
Mazaruni, stm., Guy.	D11	86
Mazatenango, Guat.	E2	102
Mazatlán, Mex.	D5	100
Mažeikiai, Lith.	D5	10
Mazenod, Sk., Can.	E7	124
Mazinga, mtn., Neth. Ant.	C5	105a
Mazirbe, Lat.	C5	10
Mazon, Il., U.S.	C9	120
Mazowe, stm., Afr.	D5	68
Mazury (Masuria), reg., Pol.	C16	16
Mazyr, Bela.	D3	32
Mbabane, Swaz.	E10	70
M'bahiakro, C. Iv.	H4	64
Mbaïki, C.A.R.	D3	66
Mbakė, Sen.	G1	64
Mbala, Zam.	B5	68
Mbalabala, Zimb.	B9	70
Mbale, Ug.	D6	66
Mbalmayo, Cam.	D2	66
Mbamba Bay, Tan.	G7	66
Mbandaka (Coquilhatville), D.R.C.	D3	66
Mbanga, Cam.	D1	66
Mbanika Island, i., Sol. Is.	e8	79b
M'banza Congo, Ang.	B1	68
Mbanza-Ngungu, D.R.C.	E6	66
Mbarara, Ug.	E6	66
Mbashe, stm., S. Afr.	H9	70
Mbava Island, i., Sol. Is.	d7	79b
Mbé, Cam.	B2	66
Mberengwa, Zimb.	B9	70
Mbeya, Tan.	F6	66
Mbigou, Gabon	E2	66
Mbinda, Congo	E2	66
Mbini, Eq. Gui.	I6	64
Mbini, stm., Afr.	I6	64
Mboi, D.R.C.	F4	66
Mboki, C.A.R.	C5	66
Mbola, Sol. Is.	e9	79b
Mboroluku, i., Sol. Is.	e9	79b
Mborong, Indon.	H12	50
Mbouda, Cam.	C2	66
Mbour, Sen.	G1	64
Mbout, Maur.	F2	64
Mbuji-Mayi (Bakwanga), D.R.C.	F4	66
Mbwemkuru, stm., Tan.	F7	66
McAdam, N.B., Can.	E9	110
McAdoo, Pa., U.S.	D9	114
McAlester, Ok., U.S.	C3	122
McAllen, Tx., U.S.	H9	130
McArthur, Oh., U.S.	E3	114
McArthur, stm., Austl.	C7	74
McArthur River, Austl.	C7	74
McBain, Mi., U.S.	D4	112
McBee, S.C., U.S.	B5	116
McBeth Fjord, b., Nu., Can.	B17	106
McBride, B.C., Can.	C10	138
McCall Creek, Ms., U.S.	F8	122
McCamey, Tx., U.S.	C5	130
McCammon, Id., U.S.	H14	136
McCauley Island, i., B.C., Can.	E4	106
McCleary, Wa., U.S.	C3	136
McClellan Creek, stm., Tx., U.S.	F8	128
McClellanville, S.C., U.S.	C6	116
McClintock, Mount, mtn., Ant.	D21	81
McCloud, Ca., U.S.	B3	134
McCloud, stm., Ca., U.S.	B3	134
McClure, Il., U.S.	G8	120
Mcclusky, N.D., U.S.	G13	124
McColl, S.C., U.S.	B6	116
McComb, Ms., U.S.	F8	122
McConaughy, Lake, res., Ne., U.S.	F11	126
McConnellsburg, Pa., U.S.	E7	114
McConnelsville, Oh., U.S.	E4	114
McCook, Ne., U.S.	A8	128
McCormick, S.C., U.S.	C3	116
McCreary, Mb., Can.	D14	124
McCullough Mountain, mtn., Nv., U.S.	H1	132
McCune, Ks., U.S.	G2	120
McCurtain, Ok., U.S.	B4	122
McDade, Tx., U.S.	D10	130
McDermitt, Nv., U.S.	B8	134
McDermott, Oh., U.S.	F2	114
McDonald, Ks., U.S.	B7	128
McDonald, Lake, l., Mt., U.S.	B12	136
McDowell Peak, mtn., Az., U.S.	J4	132
Mcensk, Russia	G19	10
McEwen, Tn., U.S.	H10	120
McFadden, Wy., U.S.	B10	132
McFarland, Ca., U.S.	H6	134
McGehee, Ar., U.S.	D7	122
McGill, Nv., U.S.	D2	132
McGrath, Ak., U.S.	D8	140
McGraw, N.Y., U.S.	B9	114
McGregor, Tx., U.S.	C10	130
McGregor, stm., B.C., Can.	B9	138
McGregor Lake, l., Ab., Can.	F18	138
McHenry, Il., U.S.	B9	120
McHenry, Ms., U.S.	G9	122
Mchinji, Mwi.	C5	68
McIntosh, Al., U.S.	F10	122
McIntosh, Mn., U.S.	D3	118
McIntyre Bay, b., On., Can.	B10	118
McKeand, stm., Nu., Can.	C17	106
McKee, Ky., U.S.	G2	114
McKeesport, Pa., U.S.	D6	114
McKenzie, Tn., U.S.	H9	120
McKenzie, stm., Or., U.S.	F4	136
McKenzie Bridge, Or., U.S.	F4	136
McKenzie Island, On., Can.	E12	106
McKinlay, Austl.	C3	76
McKinlay, stm., Austl.	C3	76
McKinley, Mount, mtn., Ak., U.S.	D9	140
McKinleyville, Ca., U.S.	C1	134
McKinney, Tx., U.S.	D2	122
McKittrick Summit, mtn., Ca., U.S.	H6	134
McLain, Ms., U.S.	F10	122
McLaurin, Ms., U.S.	F9	122
McLean, Il., U.S.	D8	120
McLean, Tx., U.S.	F8	128
McLeansboro, Il., U.S.	F9	120
McLennan, Ab., Can.	D7	106
McLeod, stm., Ab., Can.	C15	138
McLeod Bay, b., N.T., Can.	C8	106
McLeod Lake, B.C., Can.	B7	138
M'Clintock Channel, strt., Nu., Can.	A10	106
McLoughlin, Mount, mtn., Or., U.S.	A3	134
McLouth, Ks., U.S.	E2	120
M'Clure Strait, strt., N.T., Can.	B16	140
McMahon, Sk., Can.	D6	124
McMinnville, Or., U.S.	E3	136
McMinnville, Tn., U.S.	B13	122
McMurdo, sci., Ant.	C22	81
McMurdo Sound, strt., Ant.	C22	81
McNary, Az., U.S.	I7	132
McNeil, Ar., U.S.	D5	122
McPherson, Ks., U.S.	C11	128
McQueeney, Tx., U.S.	E9	130
McRae, Ar., U.S.	B7	122
McRae, Ga., U.S.	D3	116
McVeigh, Ky., U.S.	G3	114
McVille, N.D., U.S.	G15	124
MdWilliams, La., U.S.	F11	122
Mdantsane, S. Afr.	H8	70
M'drak, Viet.	F9	48
Mead, Ne., U.S.	C1	120
Mead, Lake, res., U.S.	G2	132
Meade, Ks., U.S.	D8	128
Meade Peak, mtn., Co., U.S.	C9	132
Meadow, Ia., U.S.	E4	120
Meadow Lake, Sk., Can.	E9	106
Meadow Valley Wash, stm., Nv., U.S.	F2	132
Meadowview, Va., U.S.	H3	114
Meadville, Ms., U.S.	F7	122
Meadville, Pa., U.S.	C5	114
Meaford, On., Can.	D9	112
Mealhada, Port.	D2	20
Meandarra, Austl.	F7	76
Meander River, Ab., Can.	D7	106
Mearim, stm., Braz.	B3	88
Meath, state, Ire.	H6	12
Meath, hist. reg., Ire.	H6	12
Meaux, Fr.	E11	14
Mecaya, stm., Col.	G4	86
Mecca see Makkah, Sau. Ar.	E4	56
Mechanicsburg, Pa., U.S.	D2	114
Mechanicsville, Ia., U.S.	C6	120
Mechanicsville, Va., U.S.	G8	114
Mechelen, N.Y., U.S.	B12	114
Mechelen (Malines), Bel.	C13	14
Mechelen, hist. reg., Ger.	C7	16
Mecklenburger Bucht, b., Ger.	B7	16
Mecklenburg-Vorpommern, state, Ger.	C8	16
Mecubúri, Moz.	C6	68
Mecula, Moz.	C6	68
Meda, Port.	D3	20
Medak, India	B4	53
Medan, Indon.	B1	50
Medanosa, Punta, c., Arg.	I3	90
Mede, Italy	E5	22
Medeiros Neto, Braz.	I5	88
Medellín, Col.	D4	86
Medenine, Tun.	C6	64
Mederdra, Maur.	F1	64
Medford, Ok., U.S.	E11	128
Medford, Or., U.S.	A2	134
Medford, Wi., U.S.	F8	118
Medgidia, Rom.	E15	26
Mediapolis, Ia., U.S.	C6	120
Mediaș, Rom.	C11	26
Medicine Bow, Wy., U.S.	B10	132
Medicine Bow, stm., Wy., U.S.	A10	132
Medicine Bow Mountains, mts., U.S.	F6	126
Medicine Creek, stm., Mo., U.S.	E4	120
Medicine Hat, Ab., Can.	D3	124
Medicine Lake, Mt., U.S.	F6	124
Medicine Lodge, Ks., U.S.	D10	128
Medicine Lodge, stm., U.S.	D5	128
Medina see Al-Madīnah, Sau. Ar.	E4	56
Medina, N.Y., U.S.	E11	112
Medina, Oh., U.S.	C4	114
Medina, Tn., U.S.	B8	130
Medina, stm., Tx., U.S.	E8	130
Medinaceli, Spain	C8	20
Medina del Campo, Spain	C6	20
Medina-Sidonia, Spain	H5	20
Medinīpur, India	G11	54
Medio, Punta, c., Chile	C2	92
Mediterranean Sea, s.	A4	62
Medje, D.R.C.	D5	66
Medjez el Bab, Tun.	H3	24
Medkovec, Blg.	F10	26
Médoc, reg., Fr.	D4	18
Médouneu, Gabon	D2	66
Meductic, N.B., Can.	E9	110
Medveđa, Serb.	G8	26
Medvedica, stm., Russia	C19	10
Medvedica, stm., Russia	D6	32
Medvégalis, hill, Lith.	E5	10
Medvežʹi ostrova, is., Russia	B21	34
Medynʹ, Russia	F18	10
Meekatharra, Austl.	E3	74
Meeker, Co., U.S.	D9	132
Meeks Bay, Ca., U.S.	D5	134
Meeladeen, Som.	B9	66
Meerane, Ger.	F8	16
Meersburg, Ger.	I5	16
Meerut, India	D6	54
Mēga, Eth.	G7	62
Mega, Pulau, i., Indon.	E2	50
Megalópoli, Grc.	F4	28
Mégantic, Lac, l., Qc., Can.	E5	110
Mégara, Grc.	E6	28
Megargel, Tx., U.S.	H9	128
Meghālaya, state, India	F13	54
Meghna, stm., Bngl.	G13	54
Mégisti, i., Grc.	G12	28
Megra, Russia	C19	8
Mehakit, Indon.	E9	50
Meharry, Mount, mtn., Austl.	D3	74
Mehedinti, state, Rom.	E10	26
Mehekar, India	H6	54
Meherrin, stm., U.S.	H7	114
Mehidpur, India	G5	54
Mehikoorma, Est.	B10	10
Mehndāwal, India	E9	54
Mehren'ga, Russia	F19	8
Mehrenga, stm., Russia	E19	8
Mehtar Lām, Afg.	C11	56
Mehun-sur-Yèvre, Fr.	G11	14
Mei, stm., China	I7	42
Mei, stm., China	I7	42
Meia Meia, Tan.	F7	66
Meia Ponte, stm., Braz.	I1	88
Meichuan, China	F6	42
Meiganga, Cam.	C2	66
Meighen Island, i., Nu., Can.	A5	141
Meigs, Ga., U.S.	E1	116
Meihekou, China	C6	38
Meihsien see Meizhou, China	I7	42
Meikeng, China	J6	42
Meiktila, Mya.	B2	48
Meiners Oaks, Ca., U.S.	I6	134
Meiningen, Ger.	F6	16
Meishan, China	F5	36
Meissen, Ger.	E9	16
Meitan, China	H2	42
Meizhou, China	I7	42
Mejillones, Chile	D2	90
Mejillones, Península, pen., Chile	A2	92
Mejnypilʹgyno, Russia	D24	34
Mékambo, Gabon	D2	66
Mek'elē, Eth.	E7	62
Mékhé, Sen.	F1	64
Mekhtar, Pak.	C2	54
Mekka see Makkah, Sau. Ar.	E4	56
Meknès, Mor.	C3	64
Mekong (Mékôngk) (Khong) (Lancang), stm., Asia	F9	46
Mekongga, Gunung, mtn., Indon.	F7	44
Mékôngk see Mekong, stm., Asia	F10	46
Melado, stm., Chile	H2	92
Melaka, Malay.	K6	48
Melaka, state, Malay.	K6	48
Melanesia, is., Oc.	D7	72
Melawi, stm., Indon.	D8	50
Melbourne, Austl.	K5	76
Melbourne, Ar., U.S.	H6	120
Melbourne, Fl., U.S.	H5	116
Melbourne Island, i., Nu., Can.	B10	106
Melcher, Ia., U.S.	C4	120
Melchor, Isla, i., Chile	I2	90
Melchor Múzquiz, Mex.	B8	100
Meldorf, Ger.	B5	16
Meldrum Bay, On., Can.	C6	112
Meldrum Creek, B.C., Can.	D8	138
Mélé, Baie, b., Vanuatu	k17	79d
Melekeok, Palau	g8	78b
Melenki, Russia	I19	8
Meleuz, Russia	D9	32
Mélèzes, stm., Qc., Can.	D16	106
Melfi, Chad	E3	62
Melfi, Italy	C9	24
Melfort, Sk., Can.	B9	124
Meligalás, Grc.	F4	28
Meliau, Indon.	D7	50
Melilla, Sp. N. Afr.	B4	64
Melimoyu, Cerro, vol., Chile	H2	90
Melincué, Arg.	F7	92
Melita, Mb., Can.	E12	124
Melitopolʹ, Ukr.	E5	32
Melk, Aus.	B12	22
Mellansel, Swe.	E8	8
Mellerud, Swe.	G5	8
Mellish Reef, at., Austl.	C11	74
Mellit, Sudan	E5	62
Mělník, Czech Rep.	F10	16
Melo, Ur.	F10	92
Melolo, Indon.	H12	50
Melos see Mílos, i., Grc.	G7	28
Melrhir, Chott, l., Alg.	C6	64
Melrose, Austl.	H3	76
Melrose, Mn., U.S.	F4	118
Melrose, N.M., U.S.	G5	128
Melrose, Wi., U.S.	G8	118
Melsungen, Ger.	E5	16
Meltaus, Fin.	C11	8
Melton Mowbray, Eng., U.K.	I12	12
Melūn, Fr.	F11	14
Melūr, India	F4	53
Melvern Lake, res., Ks., U.S.	F2	120
Melville, La., U.S.	G7	122
Melville, Sk., Can.	D11	124
Melville Bugt, b., Grnld.	B13	141
Melville Hall Airport, Dom.	i6	105c
Melville Hills, hills, Can.	B7	106
Melville Island, i., Austl.	B6	74
Melville Island, i., Can.	A17	140
Melville Peninsula, pen., Nu., Can.	B14	106
Melvin, Ky., U.S.	G3	114
Melvin, Tx., U.S.	C8	130
Melyana, Alg.	H13	20
Mélykút, Hung.	C6	26
Mêmar Co, l., China	A9	54
Memba, Moz.	C7	68
Membalong, Indon.	E5	50
Memboro, Indon.	H11	50
Memel see Klaipėda, Lith.	E3	10
Memel, S. Afr.	E9	70
Mêmêle (Nemunélis), stm., Eur.	D7	10
Memmingen, Ger.	I5	16
Mempawah, Indon.	D6	50
Memphis, Fl., U.S.	I3	116
Memphis, Mi., U.S.	B3	114
Memphis, Mo., U.S.	D6	120
Memphis, Tn., U.S.	B8	122
Memphis, Tx., U.S.	G8	128
Memphrémagog, Lac (Memphremagog, Lake), l., N.A.	E4	110
Memphremagog, Lake (Memphrémagog, Lac), l., N.A.	E4	110
Mena, Ar., U.S.	C4	122
Menaka, Mali	F5	64
Menan, Id., U.S.	G15	136
Menard, Tx., U.S.	D8	130
Menasha, Wi., U.S.	G10	118
Menate, Indon.	E8	50
Mendawai, Indon.	E8	50
Mendawai, stm., Indon.	E8	50
Mende, Fr.	E9	18
Mendebo, mts., Eth.	F7	62
Mendenhall, Ms., U.S.	F9	122
Mendī, Eth.	F7	62
Mendi, Pap. N. Gui.	b3	79a
Mendocino, Ca., U.S.	D2	134
Mendocino, Cape, c., Ca., U.S.	C1	134
Mendocino Fracture Zone, unds.	E24	142
Mendon, Il., U.S.	D6	120
Mendota, Ca., U.S.	G5	134
Mendoza, Arg.	F3	92
Mendoza, state, Arg.	F3	92
Mendoza, stm., Arg.	F3	92
Mene de Mauroa, Ven.	B6	86
Mene Grande, Ven.	C6	86
Menemen, Tur.	E9	28
Menen, Bel.	D12	14
Menfi, Italy	G6	24
Mengban, China	A5	48
Mengcheng, China	E7	42
Mengellang, Palau	f8	78b
Menggala, Indon.	F4	50
Menggudai, China	B2	42
Menghai, China	B5	48
Mengjiawan, China	B3	42
Mengla, China	B5	48
Menglian, China	A4	48
Mengmeng, China	A4	48
Mengyin, China	D7	42
Mengzi, China	A6	48
Menihek Lakes, l., Nf., Can.	E17	106
Menin see Menen, Bel.	D12	14
Menindee, Austl.	I4	76
Menlo Park, Ca., U.S.	F3	134
Menno, S.D., U.S.	D15	126
Menominee, Mi., U.S.	C2	112
Menominee, stm., U.S.	C1	112
Menomonee Falls, Wi., U.S.	A9	120
Menomonie, Wi., U.S.	G7	118
Menongue, Ang.	C2	68
Menor, Mar, b., Spain	G10	20
Menorca (Minorca), i., Spain	D15	20
Mentasta Lake, Ak., U.S.	D11	140
Mentawai, Kepulauan, is., Indon.	E1	50
Mentawai, Selat, strt., Indon.	D2	50
Menton, Fr.	F13	18
Mentor, Oh., U.S.	C4	114
Menyapa, Gunung, mtn., Indon.	C9	50
Menzel Bourguiba, Tun.	G3	24
Menzel Bou Zelfa, Tun.	H4	24
Menzelinsk, Russia	C8	32
Menzel Temime, Tun.	H5	24
Menzies, Austl.	E4	74
Menzies, Mount, mtn., Ant.	C10	81
Meobbaal, b., Nmb.	D2	70
Meoqui, Mex.	A6	100
Meota, Sk., Can.	A5	124
Meppel, Neth.	B15	14
Meppen, Ger.	D3	16
Meqerghane, Sebkha, pl., Alg.	D5	64
Mequinénza, Embalse de, res., Spain	C10	20
Mequon, Wi., U.S.	E2	112
Merah, Indon.	C10	50
Meramec, stm., Mo., U.S.	F7	120
Meran see Merano, Italy	D8	22
Merano (Meran), Italy	D8	22
Meratus, Pegunungan, mts., Indon.	E9	50
Merauke, Indon.	G11	44
Merbau, Indon.	C3	50
Merbein, Austl.	J4	76
Mercaderes, Col.	G3	86
Merced, Ca., U.S.	G5	134
Merced, stm., Ca., U.S.	F5	134
Mercedario, Cerro, mtn., Arg.	E2	92
Mercedes, Arg.	G8	92
Mercedes, Arg.	F7	92
Mercedes, Ur.	F8	92
Mercedes, Tx., U.S.	H10	130
Mercer, Mo., U.S.	D4	120
Mercer, Pa., U.S.	D5	114
Mercersburg, Pa., U.S.	E7	114
Merchants Bay, b., Nu., Can.	C13	106
Mercury, Nv., U.S.	G10	134
Mercury Islands, is., N.Z.	C6	80
Mercy, Cape, c., Nu., Can.	C13	141
Mercy Bay, b., N.T., Can.	B16	140
Meredith, Lake, res., Tx., U.S.	F7	128
Meredosia, Il., U.S.	E7	120
Mereeg, Som.	D9	66
Méré Lava, i., Vanuatu	j17	79d
Merefa, Ukr.	A19	10
Merevari, stm., Ven.	E9	86
Mergui, Mya.	F4	48
Mergui Archipelago, is., Mya.	G3	48
Meribah, Austl.	J3	76
Mérida, Mex.	B3	102
Mérida, Spain	F4	20
Mérida, Ven.	C6	86
Mérida, state, Ven.	C6	86
Mérida, Cordillera de, mts., Ven.	C6	86
Meriden, Ct., U.S.	C13	114
Meridian, Ms., U.S.	E10	122
Meridian, Tx., U.S.	C10	130
Meridianville, Al., U.S.	C12	122
Merikarvia, Fin.	F9	8
Merimbula, Austl.	K7	76
Merin, Laguna (Mirim, Lagoa), b., S.A.	F11	92
Merinda, Austl.	B6	76
Merino, Co., U.S.	G9	126
Merinos, Ur.	F9	92
Merizo, Guam	j9	78c
Merkinė, Lith.	F7	10
Merkys, stm., Lith.	F8	10
Merlin, On., Can.	F7	112
Merlin, Or., U.S.	H3	136
Merna, Ne., U.S.	F13	126
Merredin, Austl.	F3	74
Merrick, mtn., Scot., U.K.	F8	12
Merrill, Mi., U.S.	E5	112
Merrill, Or., U.S.	A4	134
Merrill, Wi., U.S.	F9	118
Merrillan, Wi., U.S.	G8	118
Merrillville, In., U.S.	G3	112
Merriman, Ne., U.S.	E11	126
Merritt, B.C., Can.	F10	138
Merritt Island, Fl., U.S.	H5	116
Merriwa, Austl.	I8	76
Mer Rouge, La., U.S.	E7	122
Merrygoen, Austl.	H7	76
Merryville, La., U.S.	G5	122
Mersa Matrûh, Egypt	A5	62
Mersea Island, i., Eng., U.K.	J13	12
Merseburg, Ger.	E7	16
Mersey, stm., Austl.	n13	77a
Mersey, stm., N.S., Can.	F12	110
Mersin, Tur.	B5	58
Mersing, Malay.	K6	48
Mērsrags, Lat.	C6	10
Merta, India	E5	54
Merthyr Tydfil, Wales, U.K.	J9	12
Mértola, Port.	G3	20
Mertz Glacier Tongue, ice, Ant.	B19	81
Méru, Fr.	E11	14
Meru, Kenya	D7	66
Meruoca, Braz.	B5	88
Merweville, S. Afr.	H5	70
Merzifon, Tur.	A4	56
Merzig, Ger.	G2	16
Mesa, Az., U.S.	J5	132
Mesabi Range, hills, Mn., U.S.	D6	118
Mesagne, Italy	D11	24
Mesáras, Órmos, b., Grc.	I7	28
Mesa Verde National Park, p.o.i., Co., U.S.	F8	132
Mescalero, N.M., U.S.	H3	128
Meschede, Ger.	E4	16
Meščura, Russia	E24	8
Mesgouez, Lac, l., Qc., Can.	E16	106
Mesick, Mi., U.S.	D4	112
Mesilla, N.M., U.S.	K10	132
Meškuičiai, Lith.	D6	10
Mesolóngi, Grc.	E4	28
Mesopotamia, hist. reg., Asia	C5	56
Mesquite, Tx., U.S.	E2	122
Messalo, stm., Moz.	C6	68
Messina, Italy	F9	24
Messina, S. Afr.	C9	70
Messina, Gulf of see Messiniakós Kólpos, b., Grc.	G5	28
Messina, Stretto di, strt., Italy	F9	24
Messíni, Grc.	F4	28
Messíni, sci., Grc.	F4	28
Messiniakós Kólpos, b., Grc.	G5	28
Messix Peak, mtn., Ut., U.S.	B4	132
Messkirch, Ger.	H5	16
Messoyakha, stm., Russia	C4	34
Mesta (Néstos), stm., Eur.	B6	28
Mestghanem, Alg.	B4	64
Mestre, Italy	E9	22
Mesuji, stm., Indon.	E4	50
Meta, state, Col.	F5	86
Meta, stm., S.A.	D7	86
Metabetchouan, Qc., Can.	B5	110
Métabetchouane, stm., Qc., Can.	B4	110
Meta Incognita Peninsula, pen., Nu., Can.	C17	106
Metairie, La., U.S.	H8	122
Metaline Falls, Wa., U.S.	B9	136
Metamora, Il., U.S.	D8	120
Metangula, Moz.	C5	68
Metapán, El Sal.	E3	102
Metaponto, sci., Italy	D10	24
Metapontum see Metaponto, sci., Italy	D10	24
Meteor Crater, crat., Az., U.S.	H6	132
Metharaw, Mya.	D4	48
Methow, stm., Wa., U.S.	B7	136
Methow, stm., Wa., U.S.	B6	136
Methven, N.Z.	F4	80
Metica, stm., Col.	E5	86
Metiskow, Ab., Can.	B3	124
Metlakatla, Ak., U.S.	E13	140
Metlika, Slvn.	E12	22
Meto, Bayou, stm., Ar., U.S.	C7	122
Metropolis, Il., U.S.	G9	120
Metropolitan, Mi., U.S.	C2	112
Metter, Ga., U.S.	D3	116
Mettuppalaiyam, India	F3	53
Mettūr, India	F3	53
Metz, Fr.	E15	14
Metzingen, Ger.	H5	16
Meu, stm., Fr.	F7	14
Meulaboh, Indon.	K3	48
Meureudu, Indon.	J3	48
Meurthe, stm., Fr.	F15	14
Meurthe-et-Moselle, state, Fr.	F15	14
Meuse (Maas), stm., Eur.	D14	14
Meuse, state, Fr.	E14	14
Meuselwitz, Ger.	E8	16
Mexiana, Ilha, i., Braz.	C8	84
Mexicali, Mex.	K10	134
Mexican Hat, Ut., U.S.	F7	132
México see Ciudad de México, Mex.	F9	100
Mexico, Me., U.S.	F6	110
Mexico, Mo., U.S.	E6	120
Mexico, N.Y., U.S.	E13	112
México, state, Mex.	F9	100
Mexico, Gulf of, b., N.A.	F6	96
Mexico Basin, unds.	F5	144
Mexico Bay, b., N.Y., U.S.	E13	112
Mexico City see Ciudad de México, Mex.	F9	100
Meycauayan, Phil.	C3	52
Meyenburg, Ger.	C8	16
Meymaneh, Afg.	B9	56
Meyersdale, Pa., U.S.	E6	114
Meyronne, Sk., Can.	E7	124
Meyungs, Palau	g7	78b
Mēža (Mʹoža), stm., Eur.	E14	10
Mezcala, stm., Mex.	G9	100
Mezcalapa, stm., Mex.	G12	100
Mezdra, Blg.	F10	26
Mezen', Russia	D21	8
Mezen', stm., Russia	D21	8
Mezenskaja guba, b., Russia	C20	8
Mežica, Slvn.	D11	22
Mezőberény, Hung.	C8	26
Mezőcsát, Hung.	B7	26
Mezőkövesd, Hung.	B7	26
Mezőtúr, Hung.	B7	26
Mezquital, stm., Mex.	D6	100
Mezquitic, Mex.	E7	100
Mfangano Island, i., Kenya	E6	66
M'Goun, Irhil, mtn., Mor.	C3	64
M'hai, B'nom, mtn., Viet.	G8	48
Mhasvād, India	C2	53
Mhow, India	G5	54
Mi, stm., China	H5	42
Mi, stm., China	H4	42
Miahuatlán de Porfirio Díaz, Mex.	G10	100
Miajadas, Spain	E5	20
Miami, Mb., Can.	E15	124
Miami, Az., U.S.	J6	132
Miami, Fl., U.S.	K5	116
Miami, Ok., U.S.	H2	120
Miami, Tx., U.S.	F8	128
Miami Beach, Fl., U.S.	K5	116
Miami Canal, can., Fl., U.S.	J5	116
Miamisburg, Oh., U.S.	E1	114
Miami Springs, Fl., U.S.	K5	116
Miän Channūn, Pak.	C4	54
Miandowāb, Iran	B6	56
Miandrivazo, Madag.	D8	68
Mīāneh, Iran	B6	56
Miang, Phu, mtn., Thai.	D5	48
Mianning, China	F5	36
Miānwāli, Pak.	B3	54
Mianyang, China	F1	42
Miaodao Qundao, is., China	C8	42
Miaoli, Tai.	I9	42
Miao Ling, mts., China	H2	42
Miass, Russia	C10	32
Miass, stm., Russia	C10	32
Miastko, Pol.	B12	16
Micang Shan, mts., China	E2	42
Michalovce, Slov.	H17	16
Michaud, Point, c., N.S., Can.	E16	110
Micheal Peak, mtn., B.C., Can.	C4	138
Michel, B.C., Can.	G16	138
Miches, Dom. Rep.	C13	102
Michigan, N.D., U.S.	F15	124
Michigan, state, U.S.	C10	108
Michigan, stm., Co., U.S.	G6	126
Michigan, Lake, l., U.S.	E2	112
Michigan City, In., U.S.	G3	112
Michinpicoten Island, i., On., Can.	F13	106
Michoacán, state, Mex.	F8	100
Micoud, St. Luc.	m7	105c
Micronesia, is., Oc.	B6	72
Micronesia, Federated States of, ctry., Oc.	C6	72
Mičurinsk, Russia	D6	32
Midai, Pulau, i., Indon.	B5	50
Midale, Sk., Can.	E10	124
Mid-Atlantic Ridge, unds.	F9	144
Middelburg, Neth.	C12	14
Middelburg, S. Afr.	G7	70
Middelburg, S. Afr.	D9	70
Middle, stm., B.C., Can.	B5	138
Middle Alkali Lake, l., Ca., U.S.	B5	134
Middle America Trench, unds.	H29	142
Middle Andaman, i., India	F7	46
Middleboro, Ma., U.S.	C15	114
Middlebourne, W.V., U.S.	E5	114
Middleburg, N.Y., U.S.	B11	114
Middleburg, Pa., U.S.	D8	114
Middlebury, Vt., U.S.	F3	110
Middle Caicos, i., T./C. Is.	B12	102
Middle Fabius, stm., Mo., U.S.	D5	120
Middlegate, Nv., U.S.	D7	134
Middle Island, Norf. I.	y25	78i
Middlemount, Austl.	D7	76
Middle Musquodoboit, N.S., Can.	E13	110
Middleport, Oh., U.S.	E3	114
Middle Raccoon, stm., Ia., U.S.	J4	118
Middlesboro, Ky., U.S.	H2	114
Middlesbrough, Eng., U.K.	G11	12
Middlesex, Belize	D3	102
Middle Stewiacke, N.S., Can.	E13	110
Middleton, N.S., Can.	F11	110
Middleton, Wi., U.S.	A8	120
Middleton Island, i., Ak., U.S.	E10	140
Middleton Reef, at., Austl.	E11	74
Middletown, Ca., U.S.	E3	134
Middletown, Ct., U.S.	C13	114
Middletown, De., U.S.	E10	114
Middletown, In., U.S.	H4	112
Middletown, Ky., U.S.	F12	120
Middletown, Md., U.S.	E8	114
Middletown, N.Y., U.S.	C11	114
Middletown, Oh., U.S.	E1	114
Middletown, Pa., U.S.	D9	114
Middletown, R.I., U.S.	C14	114
Middleville, Mi., U.S.	F4	112
Midgic, N.B., Can.	E12	110
Midi, Canal du, can., Fr.	F9	18
Midi de Bigorre, Pic du, mtn., Fr.	G5	18
Mid-Indian Basin, unds.	J10	142
Mid-Indian Ridge, unds.	K9	142
Midland, On., Can.	D9	112
Midland, Ca., U.S.	J2	132
Midland, Mi., U.S.	E5	112
Midland, S.D., U.S.	C11	126
Midland, Tx., U.S.	C5	130
Midlands, state, Zimb.	B10	70
Midleton, Ire.	J4	12
Midlothian, Tx., U.S.	B11	130
Midnapore, Ab., Can.	F16	138
Midongy Atsimo, Madag.	E8	68
Mid-Pacific Mountains, unds.	G19	142
Midsayap, Phil.	G5	52
Midville, Ga., U.S.	D3	116
Midway, B.C., Can.	G12	138
Midway, Al., U.S.	E13	122
Midway, Ky., U.S.	F13	120
Midway, Ut., U.S.	F5	132
Midway Islands, dep., Oc.	G22	30
Midway Park, N.C., U.S.	B8	116
Midwest City, Ok., U.S.	F11	128
Midyan, reg., Sau. Ar.	J6	58
Midžur (Midžor), mtn., Eur.	F9	26
Mie, Japan	E9	40
Mie, state, Japan	E8	40
Międzybórz, Pol.	E13	16
Międzylesie, Pol.	F12	16
Międzyrzec Podlaski, Pol.	D18	16
Międzyrzecz, Pol.	D11	16
Miélan, Fr.	F6	18
Mier, Mex.	B9	100
Miercurea-Ciuc, Rom.	C12	26
Mieres, Spain	A5	20
Mieroszów, Pol.	F12	16
Mier y Noriega, Mex.	D8	100
Miesbach, Ger.	I7	16
Mieszkowice, Pol.	D10	16
Mifflinburg, Pa., U.S.	D8	114
Mifflintown, Pa., U.S.	D8	114
Miguel Alemán, Presa, res., Mex.	F10	100
Miguel Alves, Braz.	C4	88
Miguel Auza, Mex.	C7	100
Miguel Calmon, Braz.	F5	88
Miguel Hidalgo, Presa, res., Mex.	B4	100
Miguel Riglos, Arg.	H6	92
Mihăeşti, Rom.	D12	26
Mihajlovka, Russia	D6	32
Mihajlovka, Russia	C10	38
Mihajlovka, Russia	D14	32
Mihajlovskij, Russia	F20	8
Mihara, Japan	E6	40
Mihara-yama, vol., Japan	E12	40
Mihninskaja, Russia	F15	8
Mikame, Japan	F5	40
Mikasa, Japan	C14	38
Mikaševičy, Bela.	H10	10
Mikhrot Timna' (King Solomon's Mines), hist., Isr.	I5	58
Mikindani, Tan.	G7	66
Mikkeli (Sankt Michel), Fin.	F12	8
Mikołajki, Pol.	C17	16
Mikołów, Pol.	F14	16
Mikrá Préspa, Límni, l., Eur.	D15	24
Mikšino, Russia	C18	10
Mikulino, Russia	E14	10
Mikulov, Czech Rep.	H12	16
Mikun', Russia	E23	8
Mikuni, Japan	C9	40
Miladummadulu Atoll, at., Mald.	h12	46a
Milagro, Arg.	E5	92
Milagro, Ec.	I2	86
Milan see Milano, Italy	E6	22
Milan, Ga., U.S.	D2	116
Milan, In., U.S.	E12	120

Milan – Moose Jaw I • 37

Name	Map Ref.	Page
Milan, Mi., U.S.	B2	114
Milan, Mn., U.S.	F3	118
Milan, Mo., U.S.	D4	120
Milan, N.M., U.S.	H8	132
Milang, Austl.	J2	76
Milange, Moz.	D6	68
Milano (Milan), Italy	E6	22
Milâs, Tur.	F10	28
Milavidy, Bela.	H8	10
Milazzo, Italy	F9	24
Milazzo, Golfo di, b., Italy	F9	24
Milbank, S.D., U.S.	F2	118
Milburn, Ok., U.S.	C2	122
Milden, Sk., Can.	C6	124
Mildmay, On., Can.	D8	112
Mildura, Austl.	J4	76
Mile, China	G5	36
Miles, Austl.	F8	76
Miles, Tx., U.S.	C7	130
Miles City, Mt., U.S.	A7	126
Milestone, Sk., Can.	E9	124
Milet, sci., Tur.	F10	28
Milford, De., U.S.	F10	114
Milford, Ia., U.S.	H3	118
Milford, Ma., U.S.	B14	114
Milford, Me., U.S.	F8	110
Milford, Mi., U.S.	B2	114
Milford, N.H., U.S.	B14	114
Milford, Pa., U.S.	C11	114
Milford, Ut., U.S.	E4	132
Milford Center, Oh., U.S.	D2	114
Milford Haven, Wales, U.K.	J7	12
Milford Lake, res., Ks., U.S.	B11	128
Milford Sound, strt., N.Z.	G2	80
Mili, at., Marsh. Is.	C8	72
Milian, stm., Malay.	A10	50
Milicz, Pol.	E13	16
Miljatino, Russia	F17	10
Milk, stm., N.A.	B6	108
Milk, North Fork (North Milk), stm., N.A.	B13	136
Mil'kovo, Russia	F20	34
Milk River, Ab., Can.	G18	138
Millard, Ne., U.S.	C1	120
Millau, Fr.	E9	18
Millboro, Va., U.S.	F6	114
Millbrook, N.Y., U.S.	C12	114
Mill City, Or., U.S.	F4	136
Millcreek, Pa., U.S.	B5	114
Millcreek, Ut., U.S.	C5	132
Mill Creek, W.V., U.S.	F5	114
Milledgeville, Ga., U.S.	C2	116
Milledgeville, Il., U.S.	C8	120
Mille Lacs, Lac des, l., On., Can.	C8	118
Mille Lacs Lake, l., Mn., U.S.	E5	118
Millen, Ga., U.S.	D4	116
Miller, Mo., U.S.	G4	120
Miller, S.D., U.S.	C14	126
Miller Mountain, mtn., Nv., U.S.	E7	134
Millerovo, Russia	E6	32
Millersburg, Ky., U.S.	F1	114
Millersburg, Mi., U.S.	C5	112
Millersburg, Oh., U.S.	D4	114
Millersport, Oh., U.S.	I7	112
Millerton, N.Y., U.S.	C12	114
Millet, Ab., Can.	C17	138
Millevaches, Plateau de, plat., Fr.	D7	18
Millicent, Austl.	K3	76
Milligan, Fl., U.S.	G12	122
Milligan, Ne., U.S.	G15	126
Millington, Mi., U.S.	E6	112
Millington, Tn., U.S.	B9	122
Millinocket, Me., U.S.	E8	110
Mill Island, i., Ant.	B15	81
Mill Island, i., Nu., Can.	C15	106
Millry, Al., U.S.	F10	122
Mills, Wy., U.S.	E6	126
Mills Creek, stm., Austl.	D4	76
Mills Lake, l., N.T., Can.	C7	106
Millstream, Austl.	D3	74
Milltown, Mt., U.S.	D13	136
Milltown, Wi., U.S.	F6	118
Milltown Malbay, Ire.	I3	12
Mill Valley, Ca., U.S.	F3	134
Millville, N.J., U.S.	E10	114
Millwood, Va., U.S.	E7	114
Millwood Lake, res., Ar., U.S.	D4	122
Milne Land, i., Grnld.	C20	141
Milnor, N.D., U.S.	A15	126
Milo, Ab., Can.	F18	138
Mílos, i., Grc.	G7	28
Miłosław, Pol.	D13	16
Milparinka, Austl.	G3	76
Milroy, In., U.S.	E12	120
Milroy, Pa., U.S.	D8	114
Miltenberg, Ger.	G5	16
Milton, On., Can.	E10	112
Milton, N.Z.	H4	80
Milton, Fl., U.S.	G11	122
Milton, Ia., U.S.	D5	120
Milton, Pa., U.S.	G13	112
Milton, Wi., U.S.	B9	120
Milton-Freewater, Or., U.S.	E8	136
Milton Keynes, Eng., U.K.	I12	12
Miltonvale, Ks., U.S.	B11	128
Miltou, Chad	E3	62
Miluo, stm., China	G5	42
Milwaukee, Wi., U.S.	E2	112
Milwaukee, stm., Wi., U.S.	H11	118
Milwaukie, Or., U.S.	E4	136
Mimbres, stm., N.M., U.S.	K9	132
Mimizan-les-Bains, Fr.	E4	18
Mimoň, Czech Rep.	F10	16
Mimoso do Sul, Braz.	K5	88
Mims, Fl., U.S.	H5	116
Min, stm., China	F5	36
Min, stm., China	I8	42
Mina, Mex.	H7	130
Mina, Nv., U.S.	E7	134
Mīnā' al-Aḥmadī, Kuw.	D6	56
Mīnāb, Iran	D8	56
Minahasa, pen., Indon.	E7	44
Minakuchi, Japan	E9	40
Minamata, Japan	G3	40
Minami-Alps-kokuritsu-kōen, p.o.i., Japan	D11	40
Minami-Tori-shima, i., Japan	G19	30
Minas, Cuba	B9	102
Minas, Indon.	C2	50
Minas, Ur.	G10	92
Minas Basin, b., N.S., Can.	E12	110
Minas de Barroterán, Mex.	B8	100
Minas de Corrales, Ur.	E10	92
Minas de Matahambre, Cuba	A5	102
Minas Gerais, state, Braz.	C8	90
Minas Novas, Braz.	I4	88
Minatare, Ne., U.S.	F9	126
Minatitlán, Mex.	F11	100
Minbu, Mya.	B2	48
Minbya, Mya.	B1	48
Minbyin, Mya.	C1	48
Mincio, stm., Italy	E7	22
Minco, Ok., U.S.	F10	128
Minčol, mtn., Slov.	G17	16
Mindanao, i., Phil.	G5	52
Mindanao, stm., Phil.	G5	52
Mindelheim, Ger.	H6	16
Mindelo, C.V.	k10	65a
Mindemoya, On., Can.	C7	112
Minden, On., Can.	D11	112
Minden, Ger.	D4	16
Minden, La., U.S.	E5	122
Minden, Ne., U.S.	G14	126
Minden, Nv., U.S.	E6	134
Minden City, Mi., U.S.	E7	112
Mindoro, i., Phil.	D3	52
Mindoro Strait, strt., Phil.	D3	52
Mine, Japan	E4	40
Mine Centre, On., Can.	C6	118
Minehead, Eng., U.K.	J9	12
Mineiros, Braz.	G7	84
Mineola, Tx., U.S.	E3	122
Mineral, Wa., U.S.	D4	136
Mineral Point, Wi., U.S.	B7	120
Mineral Springs, Ar., U.S.	D5	122
Mineral Wells, Tx., U.S.	B9	130
Minersville, Pa., U.S.	H13	112
Minerva, Oh., U.S.	D4	114
Minervino Murge, Italy	C9	24
Mineville, N.Y., U.S.	F3	110
Minfeng, China	A5	46
Minga, D.R.C.	G5	66
Mingäçevir, Azer.	A6	56
Mingāora, Pak.	C11	56
Mingary, Austl.	I3	76
Mingene, Austl.	E3	74
Mingin, Mya.	A2	48
Minglanilla, Spain	E9	20
Mingo Junction, Oh., U.S.	D5	114
Mingo Lake, l., Nu., Can.	C16	106
Mingshui, China	B10	36
Mingulay, i., Scot., U.K.	E5	12
Mingyuegou, China	C8	38
Minhang, China	F9	42
Minh Hai, Viet.	H7	48
Minhla, Mya.	B2	48
Minhla, Mya.	C2	48
Minho, hist. reg., Port.	C2	20
Minho (Miño), stm., Eur.	B2	20
Minićevo, Serb.	F9	26
Minicoy Island, i., India	G3	46
Minigwal, Lake, l., Austl.	E4	74
Minija, stm., Lith.	E4	10
Minilya, Austl.	D2	74
Minilya, stm., Austl.	D2	74
Miniota, Mb., Can.	D12	124
Minitonas, Mb., Can.	B12	124
Minle, China	D5	36
Minna, Nig.	H6	64
Minneapolis, Ks., U.S.	B11	128
Minneapolis, Mn., U.S.	G5	118
Minnedosa, Mb., Can.	D13	124
Minneola, Ks., U.S.	D8	128
Minneota, Mn., U.S.	G2	118
Minnesota, state, U.S.	E4	118
Minnesota, stm., Mn., U.S.	G5	118
Minnesota Lake, Mn., U.S.	H5	118
Minnewanka, Lake, res., Ab., Can.	E15	138
Minnitaki Lake, l., On., Can.	B6	118
Mino, Japan	D9	40
Miño (Minho), stm., Eur.	B2	20
Minocqua, Wi., U.S.	F9	118
Minong, Wi., U.S.	E7	118
Minonk, Il., U.S.	D8	120
Minorca see Menorca, i., Spain	D15	20
Minot, N.D., U.S.	F12	124
Minqing, China	H8	42
Minquan, China	D6	42
Minquiers, Plateau des, is., Jersey	E6	14
Min Shan, mts., China	E5	36
Minsk, Bela.	G10	10
Minsk, state, Bela.	G10	10
Minskae uzvyšša, plat., Bela.	G10	10
Mińsk Mazowiecki, Pol.	D17	16
Minta, Cam.	D2	66
Minto, Mb., Can.	E13	124
Minto, Yk., Can.	C3	106
Minto, N.D., U.S.	C1	118
Minto, Lac, l., Qc., Can.	D16	106
Minto, Mount, mtn., Ant.	C22	81
Minto Inlet, b., N.T., Can.	A7	106
Minton, Sk., Can.	E9	124
Minturn, Co., U.S.	D10	132
Minûf, Egypt	H1	58
Minusinsk, Russia	D16	32
Minvoul, Gabon	D2	66
Minxian, China	E5	36
Minya see El-Minya, Egypt	J1	58
Minya el-Qamh, Egypt	H2	58
Mio, Mi., U.S.	D5	112
Miquan, China	F15	32
Mir, Bela.	G9	10
Mira, stm., Col.	G2	86
Mīrābād, Afg.	C9	56
Mirabella, Gulf of see Mirampéllou, Kólpos, b., Grc.	H8	28
Miracema do Tocantins, Braz.	E1	88
Mirador, Braz.	D3	88
Miradouro, Braz.	K4	88
Miraflores, Col.	G5	86
Miraflores, Col.	E5	86
Miraj, India	C2	53
Miramar, Arg.	I9	92
Miramar, Moz.	C12	70
Miramas, Fr.	F10	18
Miramichi Bay, b., N.B., Can.	C11	110
Mirampéllou, Kólpos, b., Grc.	H8	28
Mīrān, Pak.	C3	54
Miranda, Braz.	D5	90
Miranda, Col.	F3	86
Miranda, state, Ven.	B8	86
Miranda, stm., Braz.	D5	90
Miranda de Ebro, Spain	B7	20
Mirande, Fr.	F6	18
Mirando City, Tx., U.S.	G8	130
Mirandola, Italy	F8	22
Mira Táglio, Italy	E9	22
Miravalles, Volcán, vol., C.R.	G5	102
Miravete, Puerto de, p., Spain	E5	20
Mirbāṭ, Oman	F7	56
Mirecourt, Fr.	F14	14
Miri, Malay.	A9	50
Miria, Niger	G6	64
Miriam Vale, Austl.	E8	76
Mirim, Lagoa (Merín, Laguna), b., S.A.	F11	92
Miriñay, stm., Arg.	D9	92
Miritiparaná, stm., Col.	H6	86
Miriyama, Pap. N. Gui.	a3	79a
Mirnoe Ozero, Russia	C13	32
Mirny, sci., Ant.	B14	81
Mirnyj, Russia	D11	34
Mirnyy, sci., Ant.	B14	81
Miroslav, Czech Rep.	H12	16
Mirow, Ger.	C8	16
Mīrpur, Bngl.	G13	54
Mīrpur, Pak.	B4	54
Mīrpur Batoro, Pak.	F2	54
Mīrpur Khās, Pak.	F2	54
Mirror, Ab., Can.	D17	138
Miryang, Kor., S.	D1	40
Mirzāpur, India	F9	54
Misantla, Mex.	F10	100
Misawa, Japan	D14	38
Miscou Centre, N.B., Can.	C12	110
Miscou Island, i., N.B., Can.	C12	110
Miscou Point, c., N.B., Can.	B12	110
Mishan, China	B9	38
Mishawaka, In., U.S.	G3	112
Mishicot, Wi., U.S.	D2	112
Misima Island, i., Pap. N. Gui.	B10	74
Misiones, state, Arg.	C10	92
Misiones, state, Para.	C9	92
Misión Santa Rosa, Para.	D4	90
Misión San Vicente, Mex.	F4	98
Miskitos, Cayos, is., Nic.	E6	102
Miskolc, Hung.	A7	26
Mišnëvo, Russia	G19	10
Misool, Pulau, i., Indon.	F9	44
Miṣrātah, Libya	A3	62
Misr el-Bahrî (Lower Egypt), hist. reg., Egypt	G2	58
Misrikh, India	E8	54
Missinaibi, stm., On., Can.	E14	106
Missinaibi Lake, l., On., Can.	F14	106
Mission, B.C., Can.	G8	138
Mission, S.D., U.S.	D12	126
Mission, Tx., U.S.	H9	130
Mission Mountain, hill, Ok., U.S.	H3	120
Mission Viejo, Ca., U.S.	J8	134
Mississagi, stm., On., Can.	B6	112
Mississauga, On., Can.	E10	112
Mississinewa, stm., U.S.	H4	112
Mississippi, state, U.S.	D9	122
Mississippi, stm., On., Can.	C13	112
Mississippi, stm., U.S.	E9	108
Mississippi Lake, l., On., Can.	C13	112
Mississippi River Delta, La., U.S.	H9	122
Mississippi Sound, strt., U.S.	G10	122
Mississippi State, Ms., U.S.	D10	122
Missoula, Mt., U.S.	D12	136
Missouri, state, U.S.	F5	120
Missouri, stm., U.S.	D9	108
Missouri City, Tx., U.S.	H3	122
Mistake Creek, stm., Austl.	D6	76
Mistassibi, stm., Qc., Can.	A4	110
Mistassini, Qc., Can.	E16	106
Mistassini, Qc., Can.	B4	110
Mistassini, stm., Qc., Can.	B4	110
Mistassini, Lac, l., Qc., Can.	E16	106
Mistatim, Sk., Can.	B10	124
Mistelbach an der Zaya, Aus.	B13	22
Misterbianco, Italy	G9	24
Misti, Volcán, vol., Peru	G3	84
Misumi, Japan	E4	40
Mišutino, Russia	A19	10
Mita, Punta de, c., Mex.	E6	100
Mitchell, Austl.	F6	76
Mitchell, On., Can.	E8	112
Mitchell, In., U.S.	F11	120
Mitchell, Or., U.S.	F6	136
Mitchell, S.D., U.S.	D14	126
Mitchell, stm., Austl.	K6	76
Mitchell, stm., Austl.	C8	74
Mitchell, Mount, mtn., N.C., U.S.	I3	114
Mitchinamecus, stm., Qc., Can.	C2	110
Mitchinamecus, Réservoir, res., Qc., Can.	C1	110
Mît Ghamr, Egypt	H2	58
Mithapur, India	G2	54
Mithi, Pak.	F2	54
Mitidja, Plaine de la, pl., Alg.	H14	20
Mitiškovo, Russia	F16	10
Mitla, sci., Mex.	G10	100
Mito, Japan	C13	40
Mitsio, Nosy, i., Madag.	C8	68
Mitsukaidō, Japan	C13	40
Mitsuke, Japan	B11	40
Mittellandkanal, can., Ger.	D5	16
Mittenwald, Ger.	I7	16
Mittersill, Aus.	C9	22
Mittimatalik (Pond Inlet), Nu., Can.	A15	106
Mittweida, Ger.	E9	16
Mitú, Col.	G6	86
Mitumba, Monts, mts., D.R.C.	F5	66
Mitwaba, D.R.C.	F5	66
Mitzic, Gabon	D2	66
Miura, Japan	D12	40
Miura-hantō, pen., Japan	D12	40
Mixian, China	D5	42
Miyagi, state, Japan	A13	40
Miyake-jima, i., Japan	E12	40
Miyako, Japan	E14	38
Miyako-jima, i., Japan	G10	36
Miyakonojō, Japan	H4	40
Miyama, Japan	E9	40
Miyanojō, Japan	H3	40
Miyazaki, Japan	H4	40
Miyazaki, state, Japan	G4	40
Miyazu, Japan	D8	40
Miyoshi, Japan	E5	40
Miyun, China	A7	42
Miyun Shuiku, res., China	A7	42
Mīzan Teferī, Eth.	F7	62
Mizdah, Libya	A2	62
Mize, Ms., U.S.	F9	122
Mizen Head, c., Ire.	J3	12
Mizen Head, c., Ire.	I6	12
Mizhhir'ia, Ukr.	A10	26
Mizhi, China	C4	42
Mizil, Rom.	E13	26
Mizoram, state, India	G14	54
Mizpah Creek, stm., Mt., U.S.	A7	126
Mizque, Bol.	C3	90
Mizukaidō see Mitsukaidō, Japan	C13	40
Mizusawa, Japan	E14	38
Mjadzel, Bela.	F9	10
Mjakit, Russia	D19	34
Mjaksa, Russia	B21	10
Mjölby, Swe.	G6	8
Mjøsa, l., Nor.	F4	8
Mkalama, Tan.	E6	66
Mkhondvo, stm., Afr.	E10	70
Mkokotoni, Tan.	F7	66
Mkomazi, stm., S. Afr.	G10	70
Mkulwe, Tan.	F6	66
Mkuze, S. Afr.	E10	70
Mkuze, stm., S. Afr.	E11	70
Mkuze Game Reserve, S. Afr.	E11	70
Mladá Boleslav, Czech Rep.	F11	16
Mladenovac, Serb.	E7	26
Mlava, stm., Serb.	E8	26
Mława, Pol.	C16	16
Mljet, Otok, i., Cro.	H14	22
Mljet Nacionalni Park, p.o.i., Cro.	H14	22
Mmabatho, S. Afr.	D7	70
Mmadinare, Bots.	B8	70
Moa, stm., Afr.	H2	64
Moab, Ut., U.S.	E7	132
Moala, i., Fiji	q18	79e
Moama, Austl.	K5	76
Moamba, Moz.	D11	70
Moanda, Gabon	E2	66
Moar Lake, l., Can.	C18	124
Moate, Ire.	H5	12
Moba, D.R.C.	F5	66
Mobara, Japan	D13	40
Mobaye, C.A.R.	D4	66
Mobeetie, Tx., U.S.	F8	128
Moberly, Mo., U.S.	E5	120
Mobile, Al., U.S.	G10	122
Mobile, Az., U.S.	J4	132
Mobile, stm., Al., U.S.	G11	122
Mobile Bay, b., Al., U.S.	G10	122
Mobridge, S.D., U.S.	B12	126
Moca, Dom. Rep.	C12	102
Mocajuba, Braz.	B1	88
Mo Cay, Viet.	G8	48
Mocha see Al-Mukhā, Yemen	G5	56
Mochudi, Bots.	D8	70
Mocksville, N.C., U.S.	I5	114
Moclips, Wa., U.S.	C2	136
Môco, Morro de, mtn., Ang.	C2	68
Mocoa, Col.	G3	86
Mococa, Braz.	K2	88
Mocodoene, Moz.	C12	70
Mocoretá, Arg.	E8	92
Moctezuma, Mex.	G8	98
Moctezuma, stm., Mex.	E9	100
Moctezuma, stm., Mex.	G8	98
Mocuba, Moz.	D6	68
Modane, Fr.	D12	18
Modāsa, India	G4	54
Modder, stm., S. Afr.	F7	70
Módena, Italy	F7	22
Modeste, Mount, mtn., B.C., Can.	H6	138
Modesto, Ca., U.S.	F4	134
Modica, Italy	H8	24
Mödling, Aus.	B13	22
Modowi, Indon.	F9	44
Modra, Slov.	H13	16
Moe, Austl.	L6	76
Moeda, Braz.	K3	88
Moei (Thaungyin), stm., Asia	D3	48
Moema, Braz.	J3	88
Moengo, Sur.	B7	84
Moen-jo-Daro, sci., Pak.	D10	56
Moenkopi, Az., U.S.	G5	132
Moenkopi Wash, stm., Az., U.S.	G6	132
Moeris, Lake see Qârûn, Birket, l., Egypt	I1	58
Moeskroen see Mouscron, Bel.	D12	14
Moffat, Scot., U.K.	F9	12
Moga, India	C5	54
Mogadiscio see Muqdisho, Som.	D9	66
Mogadishu see Muqdisho, Som.	D9	66
Mogalakwena, stm., S. Afr.	C9	70
Mogami, stm., Japan	A13	40
Mogaung, Mya.	C8	46
Mogdy, Russia	F15	34
Mogilno, Pol.	D13	16
Mogincual, Moz.	D7	68
Mogoča, Russia	F12	34
Mogočin, Russia	C14	32
Mogogh, Sudan	F6	62
Mogok, Mya.	A3	48
Mogollon Rim, clf., Az., U.S.	I6	132
Mogor, Afg.	B1	54
Mogotes, Col.	D5	86
Mogotón, mtn., N.A.	F4	102
Moguer, Spain	G4	20
Mogzon, Russia	F11	34
Mohács, Hung.	C5	26
Mohall, N.D., U.S.	F12	124
Mohammed, Râs, c., Egypt	K5	58
Mohammedia, Mor.	C3	64
Mohania, India	F9	54
Mohawk, Mi., U.S.	D10	118
Mohawk, stm., N.Y., U.S.	B11	114
Mohe, China	F13	34
Mohéli see Mwali, i., Com.	C7	68
Mohnyin, Mya.	D8	46
Mohokare (Caledon), stm., Afr.	F8	70
Mohyliv-Podil's'kyi, Ukr.	A14	26
Moi, Nor.	G2	8
Moinești, Rom.	C13	26
Moira, stm., On., Can.	D12	112
Moiraba, Braz.	B1	88
Mo i Rana, Nor.	C5	8
Moiseevka, Russia	C13	32
Moisés Ville, Arg.	E7	92
Moisie, Qc., Can.	E17	106
Moisie, stm., Qc., Can.	E17	106
Moitaco, Ven.	C9	86
Mojácar, Spain	G9	20
Mojave, Ca., U.S.	H7	134
Mojave, stm., Ca., U.S.	H9	134
Mojave Desert, des., Ca., U.S.	D4	98
Mojero, stm., Russia	C9	34
Mojiguaçu, stm., Braz.	K2	88
Mojikit Lake, res., On., Can.	A10	118
Moji-Mirim, Braz.	L2	88
Mojo, Eth.	F7	62
Moju, Braz.	A1	88
Moju, stm., Braz.	D8	84
Mōka, Japan	C12	40
Mokāma, India	F10	54
Mōkapu Peninsula, pen., Hi., U.S.	b4	78a
Mokau, stm., N.Z.	D6	80
Mokelumne, stm., Ca., U.S.	E5	134
Moknine, Tun.	B7	64
Mokochu, Khao, mtn., Thai.	E4	48
Mokokchūng, India	C7	46
Mokolo, Cam.	B2	66
Mokolo, stm., S. Afr.	C8	70
Mokpalin, Mya.	D3	48
Mokp'o, Kor., S.	G7	38
Mokša, stm., Russia	D6	32
Mokwa, Nig.	H5	64
Mol, Bel.	C14	14
Mola di Bari, Italy	C11	24
Molat, Otok, i., Cro.	F11	22
Moldau see Vltava, stm., Czech Rep.	F10	16
Moldavia, hist. reg., Rom.	C13	26
Molde, Nor.	E2	8
Moldova, ctry., Eur.	B15	26
Moldova, stm., Rom.	C13	26
Moldoveanu, Vârful, mtn., Rom.	D11	26
Môle, Cap du, c., Haiti	C11	102
Mole Creek, Austl.	n13	77a
Molega Lake, l., N.S., Can.	F12	110
Molène, Île de, i., Fr.	F3	14
Molepolole, Bots.	D7	70
Molėtai, Lith.	E8	10
Molfetta, Italy	C10	24
Molina, Chile	G2	92
Molina de Aragón, Spain	D9	20
Molina de Segura, Spain	F9	20
Moline, Il., U.S.	C7	120
Moline, Ks., U.S.	D12	128
Molino, Fl., U.S.	G11	122
Molino de Valdo de Piedras, Mex.	E3	130
Molinos, Arg.	B4	92
Molise, state, Italy	C8	24
Mollendo, Peru	G3	84
Mölln, Ger.	C6	16
Mölndal, Swe.	H4	8
Molodežjnaja, sci., Ant.	B9	81
Molodogvardeyskoe, Kaz.	D11	32
Mologa, stm., Russia	B19	10
Moloka'i, i., Hi., U.S.	b5	78a
Molokai Fracture Zone, unds.	G24	142
Molokovo, Russia	B19	10
Molong, Austl.	I7	76
Molopo, stm., Afr.	E5	70
Moloundou, Cam.	D3	66
Molson Lake, l., Mb., Can.	E11	106
Molu, Pulau, i., Indon.	G9	44
Moluccas see Maluku, is., Indon.	F8	44
Molucca Sea see Maluku, Laut, s., Indon.	F8	44
Molvoticy, Russia	C15	10
Moma, Moz.	D6	68
Moma, stm., Russia	C17	34
Mombaça, Braz.	C6	88
Mombasa, Kenya	E7	66
Mombetsu, Japan	B15	38
Momčilgrad, Blg.	H12	26
Momi, Fiji	p18	79e
Momotombo, Volcán, vol., Nic.	F4	102
Mompono, D.R.C.	D4	66
Mompós, Col.	C4	86
Momskij hrebet, mts., Russia	C18	34
Mon, state, Mya.	E3	48
Møn, i., Den.	I5	8
Mona, Ut., U.S.	D5	132
Mona, Isla de, i., P.R.	h14	96a
Mona, Punta, c., C.R.	H6	102
Monaca, Pa., U.S.	D5	114
Monach Islands, is., Scot., U.K.	D5	12
Monaco, Mon.	G4	22
Monaco, ctry., Eur.	F13	18
Monadnock Mountain, mtn., N.H., U.S.	B13	114
Monagas, state, Ven.	C10	86
Monaghan, Ire.	G6	12
Monaghan, state, Ire.	G6	12
Monahans, Tx., U.S.	C5	130
Monakino, Russia	C10	38
Mona Passage, strt., N.A.	C13	102
Monapo, Moz.	C7	68
Monarch, S.C., U.S.	B4	116
Monarch Mountain, mtn., B.C., Can.	E5	138
Monarch Pass, p., Co., U.S.	E10	132
Monashee Mountains, mts., B.C., Can.	F12	138
Monastir, Tun.	I4	24
Moncalieri, Italy	F4	22
Moncalvo, Italy	E5	22
Monção, Braz.	B3	88
Mončegorsk, Russia	B15	8
Mönchengladbach, Ger.	E2	16
Monchique, Port.	G2	20
Moncks Corner, S.C., U.S.	C5	116
Monclova, Mex.	B8	100
Moncton, N.B., Can.	D12	110
Monday, stm., Para.	B10	92
Mondego, stm., Port.	D3	20
Mondjamboli, D.R.C.	D4	66
Mondoubleau, Fr.	F9	14
Mondovi, Wi., U.S.	G7	118
Mondragone, Italy	C7	24
Monemvasía, Grc.	G6	28
Monessen, Pa., U.S.	D5	114
Monesterio, Spain	F4	20
Monett, Mo., U.S.	H4	120
Monette, Ar., U.S.	I7	120
Monfalcone, Italy	E10	22
Monferrato, hist. reg., Italy	F5	22
Monforte de Lemos, Spain	B3	20
Monga, D.R.C.	D4	66
Mongaguá, Braz.	B14	92
Mongalla, Sudan	F6	62
Mongers Lake, l., Austl.	E3	74
Monggon Qulu, China	B8	36
Möng Hai, Mya.	B4	48
Möng Hsat, Mya.	B4	48
Mongibello see Etna, Monte, vol., Italy	G8	24
Möng Küng, Mya.	B3	48
Möng Ma, Mya.	B4	48
Möng Nai, Mya.	B3	48
Mongo, Chad	E3	62
Mongol Altayn nuruu, mts., Asia	E16	32
Mongolia, ctry., Asia	E14	30
Mongonu, Nig.	G7	64
Möng Pai, Mya.	C3	48
Möng Pawn, Mya.	B3	48
Mongu, Zam.	D3	68
Möng Yai, Mya.	A4	48
Monico, Wi., U.S.	F9	118
Monida Pass, p., U.S.	F14	136
Monino, Russia	E21	10
Moniquirá, Col.	E5	86
Mõniste, Est.	H12	8
Monitor Valley, val., Nv., U.S.	E9	134
Mońki, Pol.	C18	16
Monkira, Austl.	E3	76
Monmouth, Wales, U.K.	J10	12
Monmouth, Or., U.S.	F3	136
Monmouth Mountain, mtn., B.C., Can.	E7	138
Mono, stm., Afr.	H5	64
Mono, Caño, stm., Col.	E7	86
Mono Island, i., Sol. Is.	d6	79b
Mono Lake, l., Ca., U.S.	E7	134
Monon, In., U.S.	H3	112
Monona, Ia., U.S.	H7	118
Monona, Wi., U.S.	A8	120
Monongahela, stm., U.S.	E6	114
Monopoli, Italy	D11	24
Monor, Hung.	B6	26
Monreal del Campo, Spain	D9	20
Monreale, Italy	F7	24
Monroe, La., U.S.	E6	122
Monroe, Mi., U.S.	C2	114
Monroe, N.C., U.S.	B5	116
Monroe, N.Y., U.S.	C11	114
Monroe, Or., U.S.	F3	136
Monroe, Ut., U.S.	E4	132
Monroe, Va., U.S.	G6	114
Monroe, Wa., U.S.	C4	136
Monroe, Wi., U.S.	B8	120
Monroe City, In., U.S.	F10	120
Monroe Lake, res., In., U.S.	E11	120
Monroeville, Al., U.S.	F11	122
Monroeville, In., U.S.	D1	114
Monroeville, Oh., U.S.	C3	114
Monroeville, Pa., U.S.	D6	114
Monrovia, Lib.	H2	64
Mons, Bel.	D12	14
Monsefú, Peru	E2	84
Monselice, Italy	E8	22
Monsenhor Hipólito, Braz.	D5	88
Monsenhor Tabosa, Braz.	C5	88
Mönsterås, Swe.	H7	8
Montabaur, Ger.	F3	16
Montagne, Neth. Ant.	p23	104g
Montagu, S. Afr.	H5	70
Montague, P.E., Can.	D14	110
Montague, Mi., U.S.	E3	112
Montague, Tx., U.S.	H11	128
Montague, Isla, i., Mex.	F5	98
Montague Island, i., Ak., U.S.	E10	140
Montagu Island, i., S. Geor.	K12	82
Montaigu, Fr.	H7	14
Montalbano Ionico, Italy	D10	24
Montalegre, Port.	C3	20
Montana, Blg.	F10	26
Montana, state, Blg.	F10	26
Montana, state, U.S.	B6	108
Montaña de Covadonga, Parque Nacional de la, p.o.i., Spain	A5	20
Montánchez, Spain	E4	20
Montanha, Braz.	J5	88
Montargis, Fr.	G11	14
Montauban, Fr.	E7	18
Montauk Point, c., N.Y., U.S.	C14	114
Montbard, Fr.	G13	14
Montbéliard, Fr.	G15	14
Mont Belvieu, Tx., U.S.	H3	122
Montblanc, Spain	C11	20
Montblanch see Montblanc, Spain	C11	20
Montbrison, Fr.	D9	18
Montbron, Fr.	D6	18
Montceau-les-Mines, Fr.	H13	14
Montclair, Ca., U.S.	I8	134
Mont-de-Marsan, Fr.	F5	18
Montdidier, Fr.	E11	14
Monte, Laguna del, l., Arg.	H6	92
Monteagudo, Bol.	C4	90
Monte Albán, sci., Mex.	G10	100
Monte Alegre, Braz.	D7	84
Monte Alegre de Goiás, Braz.	G2	88
Monte Alegre de Minas, Braz.	J1	88
Monte Alegre de Sergipe, Braz.	F7	88
Monte Azul, Braz.	H4	88
Montebello, Qc., Can.	C14	112
Montebello, P.R.	B2	104a
Montecarlo, Arg.	C10	92
Monte Carmelo, Braz.	J2	88
Monte Caseros, Arg.	E8	92
Montecassino, Abbazia di, rel., Italy	C7	24
Montecatini Terme, Italy	G7	22
Montecito, Ca., U.S.	I6	134
Monte Comán, Arg.	G4	92
Monte Creek, B.C., Can.	F11	138
Monte Cristi, Dom. Rep.	C12	102
Monte Cristo, Bol.	B4	90
Montecristo, Isola di, i., Italy	H7	22
Monte do Carmo, Braz.	F1	88
Monte Escobedo, Mex.	D7	100
Montefalco, Italy	H9	22
Montefiascone, Italy	H8	22
Montego Bay, Jam.	i12	104d
Monteiro, Braz.	D7	88
Montejicar, Spain	G7	20
Montejinni, Austl.	C6	74
Montelíbano, Col.	C4	86
Montélimar, Fr.	E10	18
Monte Lindo, stm., Para.	A9	92
Montellano, Spain	H5	20
Montello, Nv., U.S.	B2	132
Montello, Wi., U.S.	H9	118
Monte Maíz, Arg.	F6	92
Montemayor, Meseta de, plat., Arg.	H3	90
Montemorelos, Mex.	C9	100
Montemor-o-Velho, Port.	D2	20
Montemuro, mtn., Port.	C2	20
Montenegro, Braz.	D12	92
Montenegro see Crna Gora, state, Serb.	G6	26
Monte Pascoal, Parque Nacional de, p.o.i., Braz.	I5	88
Monte Patria, Chile	E2	92
Montepuez, Moz.	C6	68
Montepulciano, Italy	G8	22
Monte Quemado, Arg.	B6	92
Montereau-Faut-Yonne, Fr.	F11	14
Monterey, Ca., U.S.	G3	134
Monterey, Va., U.S.	F6	114
Monterey Bay, b., Ca., U.S.	G3	134
Montería, Col.	C3	86
Monteros, Arg.	C5	92
Monterotondo, Italy	H9	22
Monterrey, Mex.	C8	100
Montesano, Wa., U.S.	C3	136
Monte Sant'Angelo, Italy	I12	22
Monte Santu, Capo di, c., Italy	D3	24
Montes Claros, Braz.	I3	88
Montesilvano Marina, Italy	H11	22
Montevallo, Al., U.S.	D12	122
Montevarchi, Italy	G8	22
Montevideo, Ur.	G9	92
Montevideo, Mn., U.S.	G3	118
Monte Vista, Co., U.S.	D2	128
Montezuma, Ga., U.S.	D1	116
Montezuma, In., U.S.	I2	112
Montezuma, Ks., U.S.	D8	128
Montezuma Castle National Monument, p.o.i., Az., U.S.	I4	132
Montgenèvre, Col de, p., Fr.	E12	18
Montgomery, Al., U.S.	E12	122
Montgomery, La., U.S.	F6	122
Montgomery, Mn., U.S.	G5	118
Montgomery, Pa., U.S.	C8	114
Montgomery, Tx., U.S.	G3	122
Montgomery City, Mo., U.S.	E6	120
Montguyon, Fr.	D5	18
Monthey, Switz.	D3	22
Monticello, Ar., U.S.	D7	122
Monticello, Fl., U.S.	F2	116
Monticello, Il., U.S.	D9	120
Monticello, In., U.S.	H3	112
Monticello, Ky., U.S.	H13	120
Monticello, Mn., U.S.	F5	118
Monticello, Mo., U.S.	D6	120
Monticello, Ms., U.S.	F8	122
Monticello, N.Y., U.S.	C11	114
Monticello, Ut., U.S.	F7	132
Monticello, hist., Va., U.S.	G7	114
Montigny-le-Roi, Fr.	G14	14
Montigny-lès-Metz, Fr.	E15	14
Montijo, Pan.	I7	102
Montijo, Port.	F2	20
Montijo, Spain	F4	20
Montijo, Golfo de, b., Pan.	I7	102
Montilla, Spain	G6	20
Montivilliers, Fr.	E9	14
Mont-Joli, Qc., Can.	B8	110
Mont-Laurier, Qc., Can.	B14	112
Montluçon, Fr.	C8	18
Montmagny, Qc., Can.	D6	110
Montmédy, Fr.	E14	14
Montmorillon, Fr.	C6	18
Monto, Austl.	E8	76
Montoro, Spain	F6	20
Montour Falls, N.Y., U.S.	B9	114
Montpelier, Jam.	i13	104d
Montpelier, Id., U.S.	H15	136
Montpelier, In., U.S.	H4	112
Montpelier, Oh., U.S.	C1	114
Montpelier, Vt., U.S.	F4	110
Montpellier, Fr.	F9	18
Montréal, Qc., Can.	E3	110
Montreal, Wi., U.S.	E8	118
Montreal, stm., On., Can.	A10	112
Montreal Lake, l., Sk., Can.	E9	106
Montreuil-sur-Mer, Fr.	D10	14
Montreux, Switz.	D3	22
Montrose, Scot., U.K.	E10	12
Montrose, Co., U.S.	E9	132
Montrose, Mi., U.S.	E6	112
Montrose, Pa., U.S.	C9	114
Montrose, S.D., U.S.	D15	126
Montross, Va., U.S.	F9	114
Monts, Pointe des, c., Qc., Can.	A9	110
Mont-Saint-Michel, Qc., Can.	D1	110
Mont-Saint-Michel, Baie du, b., Fr.	F7	14
Mont-Saint-Michel, Le, rel., Fr.	F7	14
Montserrat, dep., N.A.	h15	96a
Mont-Tremblant, Parc de récréation du, p.o.i., Qc., Can.	D2	110
Monument, Or., U.S.	F7	136
Monument Draw, stm., U.S.	B5	130
Monument Peak, mtn., Co., U.S.	D9	132
Monument Valley, val., U.S.	F6	132
Monviso, mtn., Italy	F4	22
Monyo, Mya.	C2	48
Monywa, Mya.	A2	48
Monza, Italy	E6	22
Monze, Zam.	D4	68
Monzen, Japan	B9	40
Monzón, Spain	C11	20
Mooi, stm., S. Afr.	F10	70
Moolawatana, Austl.	G2	76
Moon, Mountains of the see Ruwenzori, mts., Afr.	D6	66
Moonie, Austl.	F8	76
Moonie, stm., Austl.	G7	76
Moora, Austl.	F3	74
Moorcroft, Wy., U.S.	C8	126
Moore, Id., U.S.	G13	136
Moore, Ok., U.S.	F11	128
Moore, Tx., U.S.	E8	130
Moore, Lake, l., Austl.	E3	74
Moorea, i., Fr. Poly.	v20	78h
Moorefield, W.V., U.S.	E7	114
Moore Haven, Fl., U.S.	J4	116
Mooreland, Ok., U.S.	E9	128
Mooresville, N.C., U.S.	A5	116
Moorhead, Mn., U.S.	E2	118
Moorhead, Ms., U.S.	D8	122
Mooringsport, La., U.S.	E5	122
Moornanyah Lake, l., Austl.	I4	76
Moorreesburg, S. Afr.	H4	70
Moosburg an der Isar, Ger.	H7	16
Moosehead Lake, l., Me., U.S.	E7	110
Moose Island, i., Mb., Can.	C16	124
Moose Jaw, Sk., Can.	D8	124

I·38 Moose Jaw – Mwenezi

Name	Map Ref.	Page
Moose Jaw, stm., Sk., Can.	D8	124
Moose Lake, Mn., U.S.	E6	118
Moose Lake, l., Ab., Can.	B19	138
Mooselookmeguntic Lake, l., Me., U.S.	F5	110
Moose Mountain, mtn., Sk., Can.	E11	124
Moose Mountain Creek, stm., Sk., Can.	E11	124
Moose Pass, Ak., U.S.	D10	140
Moosomin, Sk., Can.	D12	124
Moosonee, On., Can.	E14	106
Mootwingee National Park, p.o.i., Austl.	H4	76
Mopane, S. Afr.	C9	70
Mopipi, Bots.	B7	70
Moppo see Mokp'o, Kor., S.	G7	38
Mopti, Mali	G4	64
Moquegua, Peru	G3	84
Mór, Hung.	B5	26
Mòr, Glen, val., Scot., U.K.	D8	12
Mora, Cam.	B2	66
Mora, Port.	F2	20
Mora, Swe.	F6	8
Mora, Mn., U.S.	F5	118
Mora, stm., N.M., U.S.	F4	128
Morač, stm., Bela.	H10	10
Morādābād, India	D7	54
Morada Nova, Braz.	C6	88
Morada Nova de Minas, Braz.	J3	88
Morąg, Pol.	C15	16
Moral de Calatrava, Spain	F7	20
Moraleda, Canal, strt., Chile	H2	90
Morales, Laguna de, b., Mex.	D10	100
Moramanga, Madag.	D8	68
Moran, Ks., U.S.	G2	120
Moran, Mi., U.S.	B5	112
Moran, Tx., U.S.	B8	130
Morant Bay, Jam.	j14	104d
Morant Cays, is., Jam.	D10	102
Morant Point, c., Jam.	j14	104d
Morar, Loch, l., Scot., U.K.	E7	12
Moratalla, Spain	F9	20
Moratuwa, Sri L.	H4	53
Morava, hist. reg., Czech Rep.	G13	16
Morava (March), stm., Eur.	H12	16
Moravia, N.Y., U.S.	B9	114
Moravské Budějovice, Czech Rep.	G11	16
Morawa, Austl.	E3	74
Morawhanna, Guy.	C12	86
Moray Firth, b., Scot., U.K.	D9	12
Morbi, India	G3	54
Morbihan, state, Fr.	G6	14
Morcenx, Fr.	E5	18
Morden, Mb., Can.	E15	124
Mordovia see Mordovija, state, Russia	D6	32
Mordovija, state, Russia	D6	32
Mordves, Russia	F21	10
Mordvinia see Mordovija, state, Russia	D6	32
Mordy, Pol.	D18	16
More, Ben, mtn., Scot., U.K.	E7	12
Moreau, stm., S.D., U.S.	B12	126
Moreau, North Fork, stm., S.D., U.S.	B9	126
Moreau, South Fork, stm., S.D., U.S.	B9	126
Moreau Peak, mtn., S.D., U.S.	B9	126
Moreauville, La., U.S.	F7	122
Morecambe, Eng., U.K.	G9	12
Morecambe Bay, b., Eng., U.K.	H9	12
Moree, Austl.	G7	76
Morehead, Ky., U.S.	F2	114
Morehead City, N.C., U.S.	B9	116
Moreland, Ga., U.S.	D14	122
Moreland, Ky., U.S.	G13	120
Morelia, Mex.	F8	100
Morell, P.E., Can.	D14	110
Morella, Austl.	D4	76
Morelos, Mex.	I2	130
Morelos, Mex.	B5	100
Morelos, state, Mex.	F9	100
Morena, India	E6	54
Morena, Sierra, mts., Spain	F5	20
Morenci, Az., U.S.	J7	132
Moreni, Rom.	D12	26
Moreno, Bahía, b., Chile	A2	92
Møre og Romsdal, state, Nor.	E2	8
Moresby Island, i., B.C., Can.	E4	106
Moreton, Austl.	B8	74
Moreton Island, i., Austl.	F9	76
Moreuil, Fr.	E11	14
Morez, Fr.	H14	14
Morgan, Mn., U.S.	G3	118
Morgan, Mt., U.S.	F6	124
Morgan, Tx., U.S.	B10	130
Morgan, Ut., U.S.	B5	132
Morgan City, Al., U.S.	C12	122
Morgan City, La., U.S.	H7	122
Morganfield, Ky., U.S.	G10	120
Morgan Hill, Ca., U.S.	F4	134
Morganito, Ven.	E8	86
Morganton, N.C., U.S.	I4	114
Morgantown, In., U.S.	E11	120
Morgantown, Ms., U.S.	F8	122
Morgantown, Ms., U.S.	F7	122
Morgantown, W.V., U.S.	E6	114
Morgenzon, S. Afr.	E9	70
Morghāb (Murgab), stm., Asia	B9	56
Moriah, Mount, mtn., Nv., U.S.	D2	132
Moriarty, N.M., U.S.	G2	128
Morice, stm., B.C., Can.	B4	138
Morice Lake, l., B.C., Can.	B3	138
Morichal Largo, stm., Ven.	C10	86
Moricsala rezervāts, Lat.	C5	10
Moriki, Nig.	G6	64
Morino, Russia	C13	10
Morinville, Ab., Can.	C17	138
Morioka, Japan	E14	38
Morīri, Tso, l., India	B6	54
Morisset, Austl.	I8	76
Morjakovskij Zaton, Russia	C14	32
Morkoka, stm., Russia	D11	34
Morlaix, Fr.	F5	14
Morley, Mi., U.S.	E4	112
Mormal', Bela.	H12	10
Mormugao, India	D1	53
Morne-à-l'Eau, Guad.	h5	105c
Morne du Vitet, hill, Guad.	B2	105a
Morne Trois Pitons National Park, p.o.i., Dom.	j6	105c
Morney, Austl.	E3	76
Morning Sun, Ia., U.S.	C6	120
Mornington, Austl.	L5	76
Mornington, Isla, i., Chile	I1	90
Mornington Island, i., Austl.	C7	74
Morobe, Pap. N. Gui.	b4	79a
Morocco, In., U.S.	H2	112
Morocco, ctry., Afr.	C3	64
Moro Creek, stm., Ar., U.S.	D6	122
Morogoro, Tan.	F7	66
Moro Gulf, b., Phil.	G4	52
Moroleón, Mex.	E8	100
Morombe, Madag.	E7	68
Morón, Arg.	G8	92
Morón, Cuba	A8	102
Mörön, Mong.	B5	36
Morón, Ven.	B7	86
Morona, stm., S.A.	I3	86
Morona Santiago, state, Ec.	I3	86
Morondava, Madag.	E7	68
Morón de Almazán, Spain	C8	20
Morón de la Frontera, Spain	G5	20
Moroni, Com.	C7	68
Moroni, Ut., U.S.	D5	132
Moron Us, stm., China	E3	36
Morošečnoe, Russia	E20	34
Morotai, i., Indon.	E8	44
Moroto, Ug.	D6	66
Moroto, mtn., Ug.	D6	66
Morovis, P.R.	B3	104a
Morozovsk, Russia	E6	32
Morpeth, Eng., U.K.	F11	12
Morrilton, Ar., U.S.	B6	122
Morrin, Ab., Can.	E18	138
Morrinhos, Braz.	I1	88
Morrinhos, Braz.	B5	88
Morrinsville, N.Z.	C6	80
Morris, Mb., Can.	E16	124
Morris, Il., U.S.	C9	120
Morris, Mn., U.S.	F2	118
Morrisburg, On., Can.	D14	112
Morris Jesup, Kap, c., Grnld.	A19	141
Morrison, Arg.	F6	92
Morrison, Il., U.S.	C8	120
Morrisonville, Il., U.S.	E8	120
Morristown, Az., U.S.	J4	132
Morristown, In., U.S.	E12	120
Morristown, S.D., U.S.	B11	126
Morristown, Tn., U.S.	H2	114
Morrisville, Pa., U.S.	H15	112
Morro, Punta, c., Mex.	C2	102
Morro Bay, Ca., U.S.	H5	134
Morro do Chapéu, Braz.	F5	88
Morros, Braz.	B3	88
Morrosquillo, Golfo de, b., Col.	C3	86
Morrow, La., U.S.	G6	122
Morrumbala, Moz.	D6	68
Morrumbene, Moz.	C12	70
Morse, La., U.S.	G6	122
Morse, Tx., U.S.	E7	128
Morsi, India	H6	54
Mörskom see Myrskylä, Fin.	F11	8
Morson, On., Can.	B4	118
Mortagne-sur-Sèvre, Fr.	H8	14
Mortara, Italy	E5	22
Morteau, Fr.	G15	14
Morteros, Arg.	E6	92
Mortes, stm., Braz.	F7	84
Mortlach, Sk., Can.	D7	124
Mortlock Islands, is., Micron.	C6	72
Morton, Il., U.S.	D8	120
Morton, Mn., U.S.	G4	118
Morton, Tx., U.S.	H6	128
Morton, Wa., U.S.	D4	136
Morton National Park, p.o.i., Austl.	J7	76
Morua, Vanuatu	k17	79d
Moruya, Austl.	J7	76
Morvan, mts., Fr.	G13	14
Morvant, Trin.	s12	105f
Morven, Austl.	F6	76
Morven, Ga., U.S.	F2	116
Morven, N.C., U.S.	B5	116
Morwell, Austl.	L6	76
Moryń, Pol.	D10	16
Moržovec, ostrov, i., Russia	C20	8
Mosal'sk, Russia	F17	10
Mosbach, Ger.	G5	16
Moscos Islands, is., Mya.	E3	48
Moscow see Moskva, Russia	E20	10
Moscow, Id., U.S.	D10	136
Moscow see Moskva, stm., Russia	E21	10
Mosel (Moselle), stm., Eur.	G2	16
Moselebe, stm., Bots.	D7	70
Moselle, Ms., U.S.	F9	122
Moselle, state, Fr.	F15	14
Moselle (Mosel), stm., Eur.	G2	16
Moses Lake, Wa., U.S.	C7	136
Moses Point, Ak., U.S.	D7	140
Moshaweng, stm., S. Afr.	E6	70
Mosheim, Tn., U.S.	H3	114
Moshi, Tan.	E7	66
Mosinee, Wi., U.S.	G9	118
Mosjøen, Nor.	D5	8
Moskalvo, Russia	F17	34
Moskenesøya, i., Nor.	C5	8
Moskovskaja oblast', co., Russia	D19	10
Moskovskaja vozvyšennost', plat., Russia	E19	10
Moskva (Moscow), Russia	E20	10
Moskva, stm., Russia	E21	10
Moskvy, kanal imeni, can., Russia	D20	10
Mosomane, Bots.	C8	70
Mosonmagyaróvár, Hung.	B4	26
Mosopa, Bots.	D7	70
Mosqueiro, Braz.	D8	84
Mosquera, Col.	F2	86
Mosquito Coast see Mosquitos, Costa de, hist. reg., Nic.	F6	102
Mosquitos, Costa de, hist. reg., Nic.	F6	102
Mosquitos, Golfo de los, b., Pan.	H7	102
Moss, Nor.	G4	8
Mossaka, Congo	E3	66
Mossbank, Sk., Can.	E7	124
Mossburn, N.Z.	G2	80
Mosselbaai (Mossel Bay), S. Afr.	I6	70
Mossel Bay see Mosselbaai, S. Afr.	I6	70
Mossleigh, Ab., Can.	F17	138
Mossman, Austl.	C9	74
Moss Mountain, mtn., Ar., U.S.	C6	122
Mossoró, Braz.	C7	88
Moss Point, Ms., U.S.	G10	122
Moss Vale, Austl.	J8	76
Mossy, stm., Mb., Can.	C13	124
Most, Czech Rep.	F9	16
Mostar, Bos.	F4	26
Mostardas, Braz.	E12	92
Møsting, Kap, c., Grnld.	E17	141
Mostovaja, Russia	D16	10
Mostyn, Malay.	A11	50
Mosul see Al-Mawṣil, Iraq	B5	56
Møsvatnet, l., Nor.	G2	8
Mot'a, Eth.	E7	62
Mota del Cuervo, Spain	E8	20
Mota del Marqués, Spain	C5	20
Motagua, stm., N.A.	E3	102
Motal', Bela.	H8	10
Motala, Swe.	G6	8
Mota Lava, i., Vanuatu	i16	79d
Motaze, Moz.	D11	70
Moteve, Cap, c., Fr. Poly.	s18	78g
Motherwell, Scot., U.K.	F9	12
Motihāri, India	E10	54
Motloutse, stm., Bots.	B9	70
Motopu, Fr. Poly.	s18	78g
Motozintla de Mendoza, Mex.	H12	100
Motril, Spain	H7	20
Motru, Rom.	E10	26
Mott, N.D., U.S.	A10	126
Motu, stm., N.Z.	C7	80
Motueka, N.Z.	E5	80
Motul de Felipe Carrillo Puerto, Mex.	B3	102
Motutapu, i., Cook Is.	a27	78j
Motygino, Russia	C17	32
Motyklejka, Russia	E18	34
Mouaskar, Alg.	B5	64
Mouchoir Passage, strt., N.A.	B12	102
Moudjéria, Maur.	F2	64
Moúdros, Grc.	D8	28
Mouila, Gabon	E2	66
Mould Bay, N.T., Can.	A16	140
Moule à Chique, Cap, c., St. Luc.	m7	105c
Moulins, Fr.	H12	14
Moulmein see Mawlamyine, Mya.	D3	48
Moulmeingyun, Mya.	D2	48
Moulouya, Oued, stm., Mor.	C4	64
Moulton, Al., U.S.	C11	122
Moulton, Ia., U.S.	D5	120
Moulton, Tx., U.S.	E10	130
Moultrie, Ga., U.S.	E2	116
Moultrie, Lake, res., S.C., U.S.	C5	116
Mouly, N. Cal.	m16	79d
Mounana, Gabon	E2	66
Mound City, Ks., U.S.	F3	120
Mound City, Mo., U.S.	D2	120
Mound City, S.D., U.S.	B12	126
Moundou, Chad	F3	62
Moundridge, Ks., U.S.	C11	128
Mounds, Ok., U.S.	B2	122
Moundsville, W.V., U.S.	E5	114
Moundville, Al., U.S.	E11	122
Mounlapamôk, Laos	E7	48
Mountain, Wi., U.S.	C1	112
Mountain, stm., N.T., Can.	C5	106
Mountainair, N.M., U.S.	G2	128
Mountainaire, Az., U.S.	H5	132
Mountain Brook, Al., U.S.	D12	122
Mountain City, Ga., U.S.	B2	116
Mountain City, Nv., U.S.	B1	132
Mountain Creek, Al., U.S.	E12	122
Mountain Grove, Mo., U.S.	G5	120
Mountain Home, Ar., U.S.	H5	120
Mountain Home, Id., U.S.	G11	136
Mountain Iron, Mn., U.S.	D6	118
Mountain Lake, Mn., U.S.	H3	118
Mountain Nile, stm., Afr.	F6	62
Mountain Park, Ab., Can.	D13	138
Mountain Pine, Ar., U.S.	C5	122
Mountain View, Ar., U.S.	I5	120
Mountain View, Ca., U.S.	F3	134
Mountain View, Ok., U.S.	F10	128
Mountain View, Wy., U.S.	E6	126
Mountain Village, Ak., U.S.	D7	140
Mountain Zebra National Park, p.o.i., S. Afr.	H7	70
Mount Airy, N.C., U.S.	H5	114
Mount Alida, S. Afr.	F10	70
Mount Angel, Or., U.S.	E4	136
Mount Aspiring National Park, p.o.i., N.Z.	G3	80
Mount Athos see Ágio Óros, state, Grc.	C7	28
Mount Ayliff, S. Afr.	G9	70
Mount Ayr, Ia., U.S.	D3	120
Mount Barker, Austl.	F3	74
Mount Barker, Austl.	J2	76
Mount Berry, Ga., U.S.	C13	122
Mount Buffalo National Park, p.o.i., Austl.	K5	76
Mount Calm, Tx., U.S.	C11	130
Mount Carmel, Il., U.S.	F10	120
Mount Carmel, Pa., U.S.	D9	114
Mount Carroll, Il., U.S.	B7	120
Mount Clemens, Mi., U.S.	B3	114
Mount Cook National Park, p.o.i., N.Z.	F4	80
Mount Dora, Fl., U.S.	H4	116
Mount Enterprise, Tx., U.S.	F4	122
Mount Field National Park, p.o.i., Austl.	o13	77a
Mount Forest, On., Can.	D9	112
Mount Frere, S. Afr.	G9	70
Mount Gambier, Austl.	K3	76
Mount Garnet, Austl.	A5	76
Mount Gay, W.V., U.S.	G3	114
Mount Hagen, Pap. N. Gui.	b3	79a
Mount Holly, N.C., U.S.	A4	116
Mount Holly Springs, Pa., U.S.	H12	112
Mount Hope, Austl.	F7	74
Mount Hope, Ks., U.S.	D11	128
Mount Horeb, Wi., U.S.	B8	120
Mount Ida, Ar., U.S.	C5	122
Mount Isa, Austl.	C2	76
Mount Jackson, Va., U.S.	F7	114
Mount Juliet, Tn., U.S.	H11	120
Mount Kaputar National Park, p.o.i., Austl.	H8	76
Mount Lebanon, Pa., U.S.	D6	114
Mount Lofty Ranges, mts., Austl.	I2	76
Mount Magnet, Austl.	E3	74
Mount Manara, Austl.	I4	76
Mount Margaret, Austl.	F4	76
Mount Morgan, Austl.	D8	76
Mount Morris, Il., U.S.	I9	118
Mount Morris, Mi., U.S.	E6	112
Mount Olive, Il., U.S.	E8	120
Mount Olive, Ms., U.S.	F9	122
Mount Olive, N.C., U.S.	A7	116
Mount Orab, Oh., U.S.	E2	114
Mount Perry, Austl.	E8	76
Mount Pleasant, On., Can.	E9	112
Mount Pleasant, Ia., U.S.	D6	120
Mount Pleasant, Mi., U.S.	E5	112
Mount Pleasant, Pa., U.S.	D6	114
Mount Pleasant, S.C., U.S.	D6	116
Mount Pleasant, Tn., U.S.	B11	122
Mount Pleasant, Tx., U.S.	D4	122
Mount Pleasant, Ut., U.S.	D5	132
Mount Pulaski, Il., U.S.	D8	120
Mount Rainier National Park, p.o.i., Wa., U.S.	D5	136
Mount Revelstoke National Park, p.o.i., B.C., Can.	E12	138
Mount Riddock, Austl.	D6	74
Mount Saint Helens National Volcanic Monument, p.o.i., Wa., U.S.	D5	136
Mount Selinda, Zimb.	B11	70
Mount Somers, N.Z.	F4	80
Mount Sterling, Il., U.S.	E7	120
Mount Sterling, Ky., U.S.	F2	114
Mount Sterling, Oh., U.S.	E2	114
Mount Uniacke, N.S., Can.	F12	110
Mount Union, Pa., U.S.	D8	114
Mount Vernon, Austl.	D3	74
Mount Vernon, Al., U.S.	F10	122
Mount Vernon, Ga., U.S.	D3	116
Mount Vernon, Ia., U.S.	C6	120
Mount Vernon, Il., U.S.	F8	120
Mount Vernon, Ky., U.S.	G1	114
Mount Vernon, Mo., U.S.	G4	120
Mount Vernon, Oh., U.S.	D3	114
Mount Vernon, Or., U.S.	F7	136
Mount Vernon, S.D., U.S.	D14	126
Mount Vernon, Wa., U.S.	B4	136
Mount Vernon, hist., Va., U.S.	F8	114
Mount William National Park, p.o.i., Austl.	n13	77a
Mount Willoughby, Austl.	E6	74
Mount Wolf, Pa., U.S.	H13	112
Moura, Braz.	H11	86
Moura, Port.	F3	20
Mourdi, Dépression du, depr., Chad	D4	62
Mourdiah, Mali	G3	64
Mourne Mountains, mts., N. Ire., U.K.	G6	12
Mouscron, Bel.	D12	14
Moussa 'Ali, mtn., Afr.	B8	66
Moussoro, Chad	E3	62
Moutier, Switz.	C4	22
Moutong, Indon.	E7	44
Mouzáki, Grc.	D4	28
Movenda, D.R.C.	D4	66
Moweaqua, Il., U.S.	E8	120
Moxotó, stm., Braz.	E7	88
Moyahua, Mex.	E7	100
Moyale, Kenya	D7	66
Moyamba, S.L.	H2	64
Moyen Atlas, mts., Mor.	C4	64
Moyeuvre-Grande, Fr.	E14	14
Moyie, B.C., Can.	G15	138
Moyie, stm., N.A.	H14	138
Moyo, Pulau, i., Indon.	H10	50
Moyobamba, Peru	E2	84
Moyu, China	A4	46
M'oža (Mëža), stm., Eur.	E14	10
Možajsk, Russia	E18	10
Mozambique, ctry., Afr.	D5	68
Mozambique Channel, strt., Afr.	D7	68
Mozambique Plateau, unds.	M6	142
Mozdok, Russia	F6	32
Mozolevo, Russia	A16	10
Mpala, D.R.C.	F5	66
Mpanda, Tan.	F6	66
Mphoengs, Zimb.	B8	70
Mpika, Zam.	C5	68
Mporokoso, Zam.	B5	68
Mpui, Tan.	F6	66
Mpumalanga, state, S. Afr.	E9	70
Mpwapwa, Tan.	F7	66
Mqanduli, S. Afr.	G9	70
Mrągowo, Pol.	C17	16
Mrkonjić Grad, Bos.	E3	26
M'Saken, Tun.	I4	24
Mscislau, Bela.	F14	10
Msciž, Bela.	F11	10
Msta, Russia	C17	10
Msta, stm., Russia	B15	10
Mszczonów, Pol.	E16	16
Mtama, Tan.	G7	66
Mtamvuna, stm., S. Afr.	G9	70
Mtwara, Tan.	G8	66
Mu, N. Cal.	m16	79d
Mu, stm., Mya.	A2	48
Mu, Cerro, mtn., S.A.	C5	86
Mu'a, Tonga	n14	78e
Mualang, Indon.	C7	50
Muanda, D.R.C.	F2	66
Muang Hay, Laos	B5	48
Muang Hôngsa, Laos	C5	48
Muang Hounxianghoung, Laos	B6	48
Muang Khammouan, Laos	D7	48
Muang Khao, Laos	C6	48
Muang Không, Laos	E7	48
Muang Khôngxédôn, Laos	E7	48
Muang La, Laos	B6	48
Muang Long, Laos	B5	48
Muang Ngoy, Laos	B6	48
Muang Nong, Laos	D8	48
Muang Ou Tai, Laos	A5	48
Muang Pak-Lay, Laos	C5	48
Muang Paktha, Laos	B5	48
Muang Pakxan, Laos	C6	48
Muang Phalan, Laos	D7	48
Muang Phônthong, Laos	E7	48
Muang Sam Sip, Thai.	E7	48
Muang Sing, Laos	B5	48
Muang Souvannakhili, Laos	E7	48
Muang Sung, Laos	B6	48
Muang Thatèng, Laos	E8	48
Muang Va, Laos	B6	48
Muang Vangviang, Laos	C6	48
Muang Xaignabouri, Laos	C5	48
Muang Xamtong, Laos	C6	48
Muang Xépôn, Laos	D7	48
Muang Yo, Laos	B5	48
Muar, Malay.	L6	48
Muar, stm., Malay.	K6	48
Muara, Bru.	A9	50
Muaraancalung, Indon.	C10	50
Muarabenangin, Indon.	D9	50
Muarabungo, Indon.	D2	50
Muaradua, Indon.	F4	50
Muaraenim, Indon.	E3	50
Muarajuloi, Indon.	D8	50
Muarakelingi, Indon.	E3	50
Muaralabuh, Indon.	D2	50
Muaralakitan, Indon.	E3	50
Muaralembu, Indon.	D2	50
Muarapangean, Indon.	B10	50
Muarapayang, Indon.	D9	50
Muarasabak, Indon.	D3	50
Muarasiberut, Indon.	D1	50
Muaratebo, Indon.	D3	50
Muarateladang, Indon.	E4	50
Muaratembesi, Indon.	D3	50
Muaratewe, Indon.	D9	50
Muaratunan, Indon.	D10	50
Mubārakpur, India	E9	54
Mubende, Ug.	D6	66
Mubi, Nig.	G7	64
Mubur, Pulau, i., Indon.	B4	50
Mucaitá, stm., Braz.	D4	88
Mucajaí, stm., Braz.	F11	86
Muchinga Escarpment, clf., Zam.	C4	68
Muchinga Mountains, mts., Zam.	C5	68
Muckadilla, Austl.	F7	76
Mučkas, Russia	D23	8
Mucojo, Moz.	C7	68
Muconda, Ang.	C3	68
Mucujê, Braz.	G5	88
Muçum, Braz.	D11	92
Mucuri, Braz.	J6	88
Mucuri, stm., Braz.	J6	88
Muda, stm., Malay.	J5	48
Mudan, stm., China	B10	36
Mudanjiang, China	B8	38
Mudanya, Tur.	C11	28
Mud Creek, stm., Ne., U.S.	F13	126
Mud Creek, stm., Tx., U.S.	E3	122
Muddus Nationalpark, p.o.i., Swe.	C9	8
Muddy, stm., Nv., U.S.	G2	132
Muddy Boggy Creek, stm., Ok., U.S.	C3	122
Muddy Creek, stm., Ut., U.S.	E6	132
Mudgee, Austl.	I7	76
Mudhol, India	C2	53
Mudjuga, Russia	E18	8
Mud Lake, l., Nv., U.S.	F8	134
Mudon, Mya.	D3	48
Mudurnu, Tur.	C14	28
Muelle de los Bueyes, Nic.	G5	102
Muenster, Tx., U.S.	H11	128
Muerto, Mar, l., Mex.	G11	100
Mufulira, Zam.	C4	68
Mufu Shan, mtn., China	G5	42
Mufu Shan, mts., China	G6	42
Mughal Sarāi, India	F9	54
Mugi, Japan	F7	40
Mu Gia, Deo, p., Asia	D7	48
Muğla, Tur.	F11	28
Muğla, state, Tur.	F11	28
Muḥammad Qawl, Sudan	C7	62
Muhanovo, Russia	D21	10
Muhavec, stm., Bela.	H7	10
Muhino, Russia	F14	34
Mühlacker, Ger.	H4	16
Mühldorf am Inn, Ger.	H8	16
Mühlhausen, Ger.	E6	16
Muhlig-Hofmann Mountains, mts., Ant.	C5	81
Mühlviertel, reg., Aus.	B11	22
Muḥradah, Syria	C7	58
Muhu, i., Est.	G10	8
Muié, Ang.	C3	68
Mui Hopohoponga Point, c., Tonga	n14	78e
Muineachán see Monaghan, Ire.	G6	12
Muine Bheag, Ire.	I6	12
Muite, Moz.	C6	68
Muja, Russia	E12	34
Mujnak, Uzb.	F9	32
Mukah, Malay.	B8	50
Mukalla see Al-Mukallā, Yemen	G6	56
Mukatsjeve, Ukr.	A9	26
Mukāwir, sci., Jord.	G6	58
Mukdahan, Thai.	D7	48
Mukden see Shenyang, China	D5	38
Mukeriān, India	C5	54
Mukharram al-Fawqānī, Syria	D7	58
Mukilteo, Wa., U.S.	C4	136
Mukinbudin, Austl.	F3	74
Mukomuko, Indon.	E2	50
Mukry, Turkmen.	B10	56
Muktsar, India	C5	54
Mūl, India	A4	53
Mula, China	F5	36
Mula, Spain	F9	20
Mula, stm., India	B1	53
Mula, stm., India	B2	53
Mulaku Atoll, at., Mald.	i12	46a
Mulan, China	B10	36
Mulas, Punta de, c., Cuba	B10	102
Mulatos, Mex.	A4	100
Mulbāgal, India	E4	53
Mulberry, Ar., U.S.	B4	122
Mulberry, Fl., U.S.	I4	116
Mulberry Fork, stm., Al., U.S.	D12	122
Mulberry Mountain, mtn., Ar., U.S.	I5	120
Mulchatna, stm., Ak., U.S.	D8	140
Mulchén, Chile	H1	92
Mulde, stm., Ger.	E8	16
Muldoon, Tx., U.S.	E10	130
Muldraugh, Ky., U.S.	G12	120
Muldrow, Ok., U.S.	B4	122
Muleshoe, Tx., U.S.	G6	128
Mulgowie, Austl.	F9	76
Mulgrave, N.S., Can.	E15	110
Mulhacén, mtn., Spain	G7	20
Mulhall, Ok., U.S.	E11	128
Mulhouse, Fr.	G16	14
Muling, China	B9	38
Muling, China	B9	38
Muling, stm., China	B9	38
Mulinu'u, Cape, c., Samoa	g11	79c
Mūlki, India	E2	53
Mull, Island of, i., Scot., U.K.	E6	12
Mullengudgery, Austl.	H6	76
Muller, Pegunungan, mts., Indon.	C8	50
Mullet Peninsula, pen., Ire.	G2	12
Mullet Pond Bay, Neth. Ant.	A1	105a
Mullett Lake, l., Mi., U.S.	C5	112
Mullewa, Austl.	E3	74
Müllheim, Ger.	I3	16
Mullin, Tx., U.S.	C9	130
Mullingar, Ire.	H5	12
Mullins, S.C., U.S.	B6	116
Mulobezi, Zam.	D4	68
Mulongo, D.R.C.	F5	66
Mulshi Lake, res., India	B1	53
Multai, India	H7	54
Multān, Pak.	C3	54
Multé, Mex.	D2	102
Mulumbe, Monts, mts., D.R.C.	F5	66
Mulvane, Ks., U.S.	D11	128
Mumbai (Bombay), India	B1	53
Mumbwa, Zam.	D4	68
Mumen, China	E2	42
Mumeng, Pap. N. Gui.	b4	79a
Mumford, Tx., U.S.	G2	122
Mun, stm., Thai.	E7	48
Muna, stm., Russia	C13	34
Muna, Pulau, i., Indon.	F7	44
Muncar, Indon.	H9	50
Münchberg, Ger.	F7	16
München (Munich), Ger.	H7	16
Munchique, Cerro, mtn., Col.	F3	86
Munchique, Parque Nacional, p.o.i., Col.	F3	86
Muncie, In., U.S.	H4	112
Muncy, Pa., U.S.	C9	114
Mundare, Ab., Can.	C18	138
Munday, Tx., U.S.	H9	128
Mundelein, Il., U.S.	B9	120
Münden, Ger.	E5	16
Mundra, India	G2	54
Mundrabilla, Austl.	F5	74
Mundubbera, Austl.	E8	76
Munfordville, Ky., U.S.	G12	120
Mungallala Creek, stm., Austl.	F6	76
Mungana, Austl.	C8	74
Mungar Junction, Austl.	E9	76
Mungbere, D.R.C.	D5	66
Mungeli, India	G8	54
Munger, India	F11	54
Mungindi, Austl.	G7	76
Mungo, Ang.	C2	68
Mungo National Park, p.o.i., Austl.	I4	76
Munhango, Ang.	C2	68
Munich see München, Ger.	H7	16
Muniesa, Spain	C10	20
Munim, stm., Braz.	B3	88
Munising, Mi., U.S.	B3	112
Muniz Freire, Braz.	K5	88
Munku-Sardyk, gora, mtn., Asia	D17	32
Münsingen, Ger.	H5	16
Munson, Ab., Can.	E18	138
Münster, Ger.	D3	16
Munster, Ger.	C6	16
Munster, hist. reg., Ire.	I3	12
Munte, Indon.	C11	50
Muntok, Indon.	E4	50
Munuscong Lake, l., N.A.	B5	112
Muong Hinh, Viet.	C7	48
Muong Saiapoun, Laos	C5	48
Muonio, Fin.	C10	8
Muping, China	C9	42
Muqdisho (Mogadiscio), Som.	D9	66
Muqui, Braz.	K5	88
Mur (Mura), stm., Eur.	D12	22
Mura (Mur), stm., Eur.	D12	22
Murajá, Braz.	D8	84
Murakami, Japan	A12	40
Murana, Indon.	F9	44
Muraši, Russia	C7	32
Murat, Fr.	D8	18
Murat, stm., Tur.	H17	6
Murat Dağı, mtn., Tur.	E12	28
Muratlı, Tur.	B10	28
Muravera, Italy	E3	24
Murayama, Japan	A13	40
Murça, Port.	C3	20
Murchison, Tx., U.S.	E3	122
Murchison, stm., Austl.	E2	74
Murchison, Mount, mtn., N.Z.	F4	80
Murcia, Spain	G9	20
Murcia, state, Spain	G9	20
Mur-de-Barrez, Fr.	E8	18
Murdo, S.D., U.S.	D12	126
Mürefte, Tur.	C10	28
Mureș, state, Rom.	C11	26
Mureș (Maros), stm., Eur.	C8	26
Muret, Fr.	F7	18
Murewa, Zimb.	D5	68
Murfreesboro, Ar., U.S.	C5	122
Murfreesboro, Tn., U.S.	I11	120
Murgab, Taj.	B11	56
Murgab (Morghāb), stm., Asia	B9	56
Murgha Kibzai, Pak.	C2	54
Murgon, Austl.	F8	76
Muri, Cook Is.	a27	78j
Muriaé, Braz.	K4	88
Muriaé, stm., Braz.	K5	88
Muribeca dos Guararapes, Braz.	E8	88
Murici, Braz.	E8	88
Muricizal, stm., Braz.	D1	88
Murīdke, Pak.	C5	54
Muriege, Ang.	C3	68
Müritz, l., Ger.	C8	16
Murmansk, Russia	B15	8
Murmanskaja oblast', co., Russia	C16	8
Murnau, Ger.	I7	16
Muro Lucano, Italy	D9	24
Murom, Russia	I19	8
Muromcevo, Russia	C13	32
Muroran, Japan	C14	38
Muroto, Japan	F7	40
Muroto-zaki, c., Japan	F7	40
Murowana Goślina, Pol.	D13	16
Murphy, Id., U.S.	G10	136
Murphy, N.C., U.S.	A1	116
Murphys, Ca., U.S.	E5	134
Murra Murra, Austl.	G6	76
Murrat el-Kubra, Buheirat (Great Bitter Lake), l., Egypt	H3	58
Murray, Ia., U.S.	C3	120
Murray, Ky., U.S.	H9	120
Murray, Ut., U.S.	C5	132
Murray, stm., Austl.	J2	76
Murray, stm., B.C., Can.	B9	138
Murray, Lake, l., Pap. N. Gui.	b3	79a
Murray, Lake, res., S.C., U.S.	B4	116
Murray Bridge, Austl.	J2	76
Murray Fracture Zone, unds.	F24	142
Murray Harbour, P.E., Can.	E14	110
Murray Maxwell Bay, b., Nu., Can.	A14	106
Murray River, P.E., Can.	D14	110
Murraysburg, S. Afr.	G6	70
Murree, Pak.	B4	54
Murrhardt, Ger.	H5	16
Murrumbidgee, stm., Austl.	J4	76
Murrumburrah, Austl.	J7	76
Murrupula, Moz.	D6	68
Mursala, Pulau, i., Indon.	L4	48
Murshidābād, India	F12	54
Murska Sobota, Slvn.	D13	22
Murtajāpur, India	H6	54
Murtee, Austl.	H4	76
Murter, Otok, i., Cro.	G12	22
Murtle Lake, l., B.C., Can.	D11	138
Murtoa, Austl.	K4	76
Murtosa, Port.	D2	20
Muru, Capu di, c., Fr.	H14	18
Murud, India	B1	53
Murud, Gunong, mtn., Malay.	B9	50
Murukta, Russia	C9	34
Murung, stm., Indon.	C9	50
Mururoa, at., Fr. Poly.	F13	72
Murwāra (Katni), India	G8	54
Murwillumbah, Austl.	G9	76
Murzuq, Libya	B2	62
Murzūq, Idhān, des., Libya	C2	62
Mürzzuschlag, Aus.	C12	22
Muş, Tur.	B5	56
Mūša (Mūsa), stm., Eur.	D6	10
Mūsa (Mūša), stm., Eur.	D6	10
Mûsa, Gebel (Sinai, Mount), mtn., Egypt	J5	58
Musadi, D.R.C.	E4	66
Musā'id, Libya	A4	62
Musala, mtn., Blg.	G10	26
Musan-ŭp, Kor., N.	C8	38
Muscat see Masqaṭ, Oman	E8	56
Muscat and Oman see Oman, ctry., Asia	F8	56
Muscatine, Ia., U.S.	C6	120
Muscle Shoals, Al., U.S.	C11	122
Musclow, Mount, mtn., B.C., Can.	C3	138
Muscoda, Wi., U.S.	A7	120
Musgrave, Austl.	B8	74
Mus-Haja, gora, mtn., Russia	D17	34
Mushie, D.R.C.	E3	66
Mushin, Nig.	H5	64
Mūsi, stm., India	C4	53
Musi, stm., Indon.	E4	50
Musicians Seamounts, unds.	F22	142
Muskegon, Mi., U.S.	E3	112
Muskegon, stm., Mi., U.S.	E4	112
Muskingum, stm., Oh., U.S.	E4	114
Muskogee, Ok., U.S.	I2	120
Muskoka, Lake, l., On., Can.	D10	112
Musoma, Tan.	E6	66
Musquodoboit Harbour, N.S., Can.	F13	110
Mussau Island, i., Pap. N. Gui.	a4	79a
Musselshell, stm., Mt., U.S.	G6	124
Mussende, Ang.	C2	68
Mussidan, Fr.	D6	18
Mussomeli, Italy	G7	24
Mussuma, Ang.	C3	68
Mustafakemalpaşa, Tur.	C11	28
Mustafa Kemal Paşa, stm., Tur.	D11	28
Mustahīl, Eth.	F8	62
Mustāng, Nepal	D9	54
Mustang Draw, stm., Tx., U.S.	B5	130
Mustang Island, i., Tx., U.S.	G10	130
Musters, Lago, l., Arg.	I3	90
Mustla, Est.	B8	10
Mustvee, Est.	B9	10
Muswellbrook, Austl.	I8	76
Mût, Egypt	B5	62
Mut, Tur.	B4	58
Mutá, Ponta do, c., Braz.	G6	88
Mutanchiang see Mudanjiang, China	B8	38
Mutankiang see Mudanjiang, China	B8	38
Mutare, Zimb.	D5	68
Mutlu (Rezovska), stm., Eur.	G14	26
Mutoko, Zimb.	D5	68
Mutoraj, Russia	B17	32
Mutsamudu, Com.	C7	68
Mutshatsha, D.R.C.	G4	66
Mutsu, Japan	D14	38
Mutsu-wan, b., Japan	D14	38
Mutton Bay, Qc., Can.	i22	107a
Mutuípe, Braz.	G6	88
Mutum, Braz.	J5	88
Mu Us Shamo (Ordos Desert), des., China	B3	42
Mūvattupula, India	F3	53
Muxima, Ang.	B1	68
Muyinga, Bdi.	E6	66
Muyumba, D.R.C.	F5	66
Muzaffarābād, Pak.	A4	54
Muzaffargarh, Pak.	C3	54
Muzaffarnagar, India	D6	54
Muzaffarpur, India	E10	54
Muzat, stm., China	C2	36
Muži, Russia	A10	32
Muzillac, Fr.	G6	14
Muztag, mtn., China	A5	46
Muztag, mtn., China	D2	36
Mvolo, Sudan	F6	62
Mvoti, stm., S. Afr.	F10	70
Mvuma, Zimb.	D5	68
Mwadui, Tan.	E6	66
Mwali, i., Com.	C7	68
Mwanza, Tan.	E6	66
Mweelrea, mtn., Ire.	H3	12
Mweka, D.R.C.	E4	66
Mwene-Ditu, D.R.C.	F4	66
Mwenezi, Zimb.	B10	70

Mwenezi – Nevada I • 39

Name — Map Ref. — Page

Mwenezi, stm., Afr. B10 70
Mweru, Lake, l., Afr. B4 68
Mweru Wantipa, Lake, l., Zam. B4 68
Mwilitau Islands (Purdy Islands), is., Pap. N. Gui. a4 79a
Mwinilunga, Zam. C3 68
Myājlār, India E3 54
Myall Lakes National Park, p.o.i., Austl. I9 76
Myanaung, Mya. C2 48
Myanmar (Burma), ctry., Asia D8 46
Myaungmya, Mya. D2 48
Mycenae see Mykínes, sci., Grc. F5 28
Myebon, Mya. B1 48
Myingyan, Mya. B2 48
Myitkyinā, Mya. C8 46
Myitnge, stm., Mya. B3 48
Myitta, Mya. E4 48
Myittha, Mya. B2 48
Myittha, stm., Mya. B2 48
Myjava, Slov. H13 16
Mykines, i., Far. Is. m34 8b
Mykínes, sci., Grc. F5 28
Mykolaïv, Ukr. F15 6
Mykolaïv, co., Ukr. B17 26
Mykolaïvka, Ukr. C16 26
Mýkonos, i., Grc. F8 28
Myla, Russia D24 8
Mymensingh (Nasirābād), Bngl. F13 54
Mynaral, Kaz. E12 32
Mynfontein, S. Afr. G6 70
Myohaung, Mya. B1 48
Myohyang-san, mtn., Kor., N. D7 38
Myōkō-san, vol., Japan C11 40
Myra, sci., Tur. G12 28
Mýrdalsjökull, ice, Ice. I30 8a
Myrskylä, Fin. F11 8
Myrtle Beach, S.C., U.S. C7 116
Myrtle Creek, Or., U.S. G3 136
Myrtle Grove, Fl., U.S. G11 122
Myrtle Point, Or., U.S. G2 136
Myrtletowne, Ca., U.S. C1 134
Myrtóön Pélagos, s., Grc. G6 28
Myškino, Russia C21 10
Myślenice, Pol. G15 16
Myślibórz, Pol. D10 16
Mysłowice, Pol. F15 16
Mysore, India E3 53
Mysore see Karnātaka, state, India F4 46
Mystic, Ct., U.S. C14 114
Mystrás, sci., Grc. F5 28
Mys Vhodnoj, Russia B6 34
Myszków, Pol. F15 16
Myt, Russia H20 8
My Tho, Viet. G8 48
Mytilíni, Grc. D9 28
Mytišči, Russia E20 10
Myton, Ut., U.S. C6 132
Mývatn, l., Ice. k31 8a
Mzimba, Mwi. C5 68
Mzimvubu, stm., S. Afr. G9 70
Mzintlava, stm., S. Afr. G9 70
Mzuzu, Mwi. C5 68

N

Na (Tengtiao), stm., Asia A6 48
Naab, stm., Ger. G7 16
Nā'ālehu, Hi., U.S. d6 78a
Naas, Ire. H6 12
Nababeep, S. Afr. F3 70
Nabari, Japan E9 40
Nabberu, Lake, l., Austl. E4 74
Nabburg, Ger. G8 16
Naberežnye Čelny, Russia C8 32
Nabeul, Tun. H4 24
Nābha, India C6 54
Nabire, Indon. F10 44
Nabī Shu'ayb, Jabal an-, mtn., Yemen F5 56
Nabouwalu, Fiji p19 79e
Nabq, Egypt J5 58
Nabula, China C7 54
Nābulus, W.B. F6 58
Nacala-a-Velha, Moz. C7 68
Nachingwea, Tan. G7 66
Nāchna, India E3 54
Náchod, Czech Rep. F12 16
Nachvak Fiord, b., Nf., Can. F13 141
Nacimiento, Chile H1 92
Nacimiento, Lake, res., Ca., U.S. H5 134
Naco, Mex. F8 98
Naco, Az., U.S. L6 132
Nacogdoches, Tx., U.S. F4 122
Nácori Chico, Mex. G8 98
Nacozari de García, Mex. F8 98
Ñacunday, Para. B10 92
Nadarivatu, Fiji p18 79e
Nadela, Spain B3 20
Nadiād, India G4 54
Nadi Bay, b., Fiji p18 79e
Nădlac, Rom. C7 26
Naduri, Fiji p19 79e
Nadvoicy, Russia E16 8
Nadym, Russia A12 32
Nadym, stm., Russia A12 32
Naenwa, India F5 54
Nærbø, Nor. G1 8
Næstved, Den. I4 8
Nafada, Nig. G7 64
Nafī, Sau. Ar. D5 56
Náfpaktos, Grc. E4 28
Náfplio, Grc. F5 28
Nafūsah, Jabal, hills, Libya A2 62
Naga, Phil. D4 52
Nagahama, Japan D9 40
Nagahama, Japan F5 40
Naga Hills, mts., Asia C7 46
Nagai, Japan A12 40
Nagai Island, i., Ak., U.S. F7 140
Nāgāland, state, India C7 46
Nagano, Japan C11 40
Nagano, state, Japan C11 40
Nagaoka, Japan B11 40
Nagaon, India E14 54
Nāgappattinam, India F4 53
Nagara, stm., Japan D9 40
Nagarhole Tiger Reserve, India E2 53
Nāgārjuna Sāgar, res., India C4 53
Nagarote, Nic. F4 102
Nagasaki, Japan G2 40
Nagasaki, state, Japan G2 40
Nagato, Japan E4 40
Nāgaur, India E4 54
Nāgāvali, stm., India B6 53
Nagda, India G5 54
Nāgercoil, India G3 53
Nagīna, India D7 54
Nagłowice, Pol. F15 16
Nago, Japan I19 39a
Nagold, Ger. H4 16
Nagornyj, Russia E13 34
Nagoya, Japan D9 40
Nāgpur, India H7 54
Nagqu, China C14 54
Nagua, Dom. Rep. C12 102
Naguabo, P.R. B4 104a
Nagyatád, Hung. C4 26
Nagybánya *see* Baia Mare, Rom. B10 26
Nagyecsed, Hung. B9 26
Nagykanizsa, Hung. C4 26
Nagykáta, Hung. B6 26
Nagykőrös, Hung. B6 26
Naha, Japan I18 39a
Nahabuan, Indon. C9 50
Nāhan, India C6 54
Nahanni Butte, N.T., Can. C6 106
Nahariyya, Isr. E5 58
Nahāvand, Iran C6 56
Nahe, China B9 36
Nahe, stm., Ger. G3 16
Nahma, Mi., U.S. C3 112
Nahodka, Russia C10 38
Nahodka, Russia A13 32
Nahoe, Fr. Poly. r19 78g
Nahoï, Cap, c., Vanuatu j16 79d
Nahuel Huapi, Lago, l., Arg. H2 90
Nahuel Niyeu, Arg. H3 90
Naica, Mex. B6 100
Naicam, Sk., Can. B9 124
Naila, Ger. F7 16
Naiman Qi, China C4 38
Nā'īn, Iran C7 56
Naini Tāl, India D7 54
Nainpur, India G8 54
Nairai, i., Fiji p19 79e
Nairn, La., U.S. H9 122
Nairobi, Kenya E7 66
Naitauba, i., Fiji p20 79e
Naivasha, Kenya E7 66
Naizishan, China C7 38
Najac, Fr. E8 18
Najafābād, Iran C7 56
Najasa, stm., Cuba B9 102
Najd (Nejd), hist. reg., Sau. Ar. D5 56
Najībābād, India D7 54
Najin, Kor., N. C9 38
Naka, stm., Japan C13 40
Nakajō, Japan A12 40
Nakama, Japan F3 40
Nakaminato, Japan C13 40
Nakamura, Japan G5 40
Nakano, Japan C11 40
Nakano-shima, i., Japan k19 39a
Nakasongola, Ug. D6 66
Nakatsu, Japan F4 40
Nakatsugawa, Japan D10 40
Nakhl, Egypt I4 58
Nakhon Nayok, Thai. E5 48
Nakhon Pathom, Thai. F5 48
Nakhon Phanom, Thai. D7 48
Nakhon Ratchasima, Thai. E6 48
Nakhon Sawan, Thai. E4 48
Nakhon Si Thammarat, Thai. H5 48
Nakhon Thai, Thai. D5 48
Nakina, On., Can. A12 118
Nakło nad Notecią, Pol. C13 16
Nakodar, India C5 54
Nakonde, Zam. B5 68
Nakskov, Den. I4 8
Naktong-gang, stm., Kor., S. C1 40
Nakuru, Kenya E7 66
Nakusp, B.C., Can. F13 138
Nālanda, India F10 54
Nalayh, Mong. B6 36
Nalbāri, India E13 54
Nal'čik, Russia F6 32
Nałęczów, Pol. E18 16
Nalgonda, India C4 53
Nallamalla Hills, mts., India D4 53
Nallıhan, Tur. C14 28
Nalón, stm., Spain A5 20
Nalong, China J2 42
Nālūt, Libya A2 62
Nam (Nan'a), stm., Asia B4 48
Namaacha, Moz. D10 70
Namacurra, Moz. D6 68
Namadgi National Park, p.o.i., Austl. J7 76
Namak, Daryācheh-ye, l., Iran C7 56
Namakan Lake, l., N.A. C6 118
Nāmakkal, India F4 53
Namangan, Uzb. F12 32
Namanyere, Tan. F6 66
Namapa, Moz. C6 68
Namarrói, Moz. D6 68
Namatanai, Pap. N. Gui. a5 79a
Nambour, Austl. F9 76
Nam Co, l., China C13 54
Nam Dinh, Viet. B7 48
Nam Du, Quan Dao, is., Viet. H6 48
Nameh, Indon. B10 50
Namen *see* Namur, Bel. D13 14
Namerikawa, Japan C10 40
Nametil, Moz. D6 68
Nam-gang, stm., Kor., N. E7 38
Namhae-do, i., Kor., S. G8 38
Namhan-gang, stm., Kor., S. F7 38
Namhkam, Mya. D8 46
Namib Desert, des., Nmb. E1 68
Namibe, Ang. D1 68
Namibia, ctry., Afr. E2 68
Namib Naukluft Park, p.o.i., Nmb. D2 70
Namie, Japan B14 40
Namies, S. Afr. F4 70
Namji-ri, Kor., S. D1 40
Namlea, Indon. F8 44
Namling, China D12 54
Nam Nao National Park, p.o.i., Thai. D5 48
Nam Ngum Reservoir, res., Laos C6 48
Namnoi, Khao, mtn., Mya. G4 48
Namoi, stm., Austl. H7 76
Nampa, Id., U.S. G10 136
Nampala, Mali F3 64
Nam Pat, Thai. D5 48
Nampawng, Mya. A3 48
Nam Phan (Cochin China), hist. reg., Viet. G8 48
Namp'o, Kor., N. E6 38
Nampula, Moz. D6 68
Namsang, Mya. B3 48
Namsen, stm., Nor. D5 8
Namsos, Nor. D4 8
Nam Tok, Thai. E4 48
Nam Tok Mae Surin National Park, p.o.i., Thai. C4 48
Namtu, Mya. A3 48
Namu, B.C., Can. E3 138
Namuka-I-Lau, i., Fiji q20 79e
Namúli, Serra, mts., Moz. D6 68
Namur (Namen), Bel. D13 14
Namutoni, Nmb. D2 68
Namwala, Zam. D4 68
Namwŏn, Kor., S. G7 38
Namysłów, Pol. E13 16
Nan, Thai. C5 48
Nan, stm., Thai. D5 48
Nan'a (Nam), stm., Asia B4 48
Nanaimo, B.C., Can. G6 138
Nanam, Kor., N. D8 38
Nan'an, China I8 42
Nanango, Austl. F8 76
Nanao, Japan B9 40
Nanatsu-jima, is., Japan B9 40
Nanbu, China F1 42
Nancha, China B10 36
Nanchang, China G6 42
Nancheng, China H7 42
Nancheng *see* Hanzhong, China E2 42
Nanching *see* Nanjing, China E8 42
Nanchong, China F2 42
Nanchuan, China G2 42
Nanch'ung *see* Nanchong, China F2 42
Nancowry Island, i., India G7 46
Nancy, Fr. F15 14
Nanda Devi, mtn., India C8 54
Nandaime, Nic. G4 102
Nandan, Japan E7 40
Nānded, India B3 53
Nāndgaon, India H5 54
Nandi Drug, mtn., India E3 53
Nandikotkūr, India D4 53
Nandu, China F8 42
Nandu, stm., China L4 42
Nānḍūra, India H6 54
Nandurbār, India H4 54
Nandyāl, India D4 53
Nanfen, China D5 38
Nanfeng, China H7 42
Nanga-Eboko, Cam. D2 66
Nangakelawit, Indon. C8 50
Nangamau, Indon. D7 50
Nangaobat, Indon. C8 50
Nanga Parbat, mtn., Pak. B11 56
Nangapinoh, Indon. D7 50
Nangarhār, state, Afg. A3 54
Nangatayap, Indon. D7 50
Nanggala Hill, mtn., Sol. Is. e7 79b
Nangin, Mya. G4 48
Nangnim-ŭp, Kor., N. D7 38
Nangong, China C6 42
Nang Rong, Thai. E6 48
Nanguan, China C5 42
Nanhua, China F5 36
Nan Hulsan Hu, l., China D4 36
Nanika Lake, l., B.C., Can. C3 138
Nanjangūd, India E3 53
Nanjiang, China E2 42
Nanjing, China I7 42
Nanjing (Nanking), China E8 42
Nankang, China I6 42
Nanking *see* Nanjing, China E8 42
Nankoku, Japan F6 40
Nankye, Mya. E3 48
Nanle, China C6 42
Nanlei (Loi), stm., Asia A4 48
Nanling, China F8 42
Nan Ling, mts., China I5 42
Nanliu, stm., China J3 42
Nanlou Shan, mtn., China C7 38
Nannine, Austl. E3 74
Nanning, China J3 42
Na Noi, Thai. C5 48
Nanortalik, Grnld. E16 141
Nanpan, stm., China G5 36
Nānpāra, India E8 54
Nanpiao, China A9 42
Nanping, China H8 42
Nanping, China E5 36
Nansei, Japan E9 40
Nansei-shotō (Ryukyu Islands), is., Japan k19 39a
Nan Shan see Qilian Shan, mts., China D4 36
Nanshan Island, i., Asia C6 44
Nantais, Lac, l., Qc., Can. C16 106
Nantai-zan, vol., Japan C12 40
Nanterre, Fr. F11 14
Nantes, Fr. G7 14
Nantes à Brest, Canal de, can., Fr. F5 14
Nanticoke, Pa., U.S. C9 114
Nanto, Japan E9 40
Nanton, Ab., Can. F17 138
Nantong, China E9 42
Nant'ou, Tai. J9 42
Nantucket, Ma., U.S. C15 114
Nantucket Island, i., Ma., U.S. C15 114
Nantucket Sound, strt., Ma., U.S. C15 114
Nantulo, Moz. C6 68
Nantung *see* Nantong, China. E9 42
Nanty Glo, Pa., U.S. H11 112
Nanu, Pap. N. Gui. b3 79a
Nanuku Passage, strt., Fiji p20 79e
Nanumea, at., Tuvalu D8 72
Nanuque, Braz. I5 88
Nanusa, Kepulauan, is., Indon. E8 44
Nanxi, China G1 42
Nanxian, China G5 42
Nanxiang, China F9 42
Nanxiong, China I6 42
Nanyang, China E5 42
Nanyang Hu, l., China D7 42
Nanyi Hu, l., China F8 42
Nan-yō, Japan A13 40
Nanyuki, Kenya D7 66
Nanzamu, China C6 38
Nanzhao, China E5 42
Nao, Cabo de la see Nau, Cap de la, c., Spain F11 20
Naococane, Lac, l., Qc., Can. E16 106
Naogaon, Bngl. F12 54
Naokot, Pak. F2 54
Náousa, Grc. C5 28
Napa, Ca., U.S. E3 134
Napa, stm., Ca., U.S. E3 134
Napaku, Indon. B9 50
Napalkovo, Russia C3 34
Napanee, On., Can. D12 112
Napassoq, Grnld. D15 141
Naperville, Il., U.S. C9 120
Napido, Indon. F10 44
Napier, N.Z. D7 80
Napier, Mount, hill, Austl. C5 74
Napier Mountains, mts., Ant. B10 81
Naples *see* Napoli, Italy D8 24
Naples, Fl., U.S. J4 116
Naples, Id., U.S. B10 136
Naples, N.Y., U.S. B8 114
Naples, Tx., U.S. D4 122
Napo, state, Ec. H3 86
Napo, stm., S.A. D3 84
Napoleon, N.D., U.S. A13 126
Napoleonville, La., U.S. H7 122
Napoli (Naples), Italy D8 24
Napoli, Golfo di, b., Italy D8 24
Nappamerrie, Austl. F3 76
Nappanee, In., U.S. G4 112
Napu, Indon. H11 50
Nara, Japan E8 40
Nara, Mali F3 64
Nara, state, Japan E8 40
Nāra, stm., Pak. F2 54
Nara, stm., Russia E20 10
Narač, vozero, l., Bela. F9 10
Naracoorte, Austl. K3 76
Naradhan, Austl. I6 76
Naraini, India F8 54
Naramata, B.C., Can. G11 138
Naranjal, Ec. I2 86
Naranjito, P.R. B3 104a
Narasannapeta, India B7 53
Narasapur, India C5 53
Narasaraopet, India C4 53
Narasun, Russia A7 36
Narathiwat, Thai. I5 48
Narau (Narew), stm., Eur. D17 16
Nārāyanganj, Bngl. G13 54
Nārāyani (Gandak), stm., Asia E10 54
Nārāyanpet, India C3 53
Narbonne, Fr. F8 18
Nardò, Italy D11 24
Nares Strait, strt., N.A. B11 141
Narew (Narau), stm., Eur. D17 16
Nargund, India D2 53
Nariño, state, Col. G3 86
Narita, Japan D13 40
Nariva Swamp, sw., Trin. s12 105f
Nar'jan-Mar, Russia C25 8
Narkatiāganj, India E10 54
Narlı, Tur. A8 58
Narmada, stm., India H4 54
Nārnaul, India D6 54
Narodnaja, gora, mtn., Russia B10 32
Narodnaya, Mount see Narodnaja, gora, mtn., Russia B10 32
Naro-Fominsk, Russia E19 10
Narol, Pol. F19 16
Narooma, Austl. K8 76
Nārowāl, Pak. B5 54
Narrabri, Austl. H7 76
Narran, stm., Austl. G7 76
Narrandera, Austl. J6 76
Narraway, stm., Can. B11 138
Narrogin, Austl. F3 74
Narromine, Austl. I6 76
Narsaq *see* Narssaq, Grnld. E16 141
Narsimhapur, India G7 54
Narsinghgarh, India G6 54
Narsīpatnam, India C6 53
Narssaq, Grnld. E16 141
Naru, Japan G1 40
Naruto, Japan E7 40
Narva, Est. G13 8
Narva, Russia C16 32
Narva, stm., Eur. A11 10
Narvik, Nor. B7 8
Narvskij zaliv, b., Eur. A10 10
Narvskoe vodohranilišče, l., Eur. A10 10
Narwāna, India D6 54
Narwietooma, Austl. D6 74
Narym, Russia C14 32
Naryn, Kyrg. F13 32
Naryn, stm., Asia F13 32
Narynkol, Kaz. F13 32
Näsåker, Swe. E7 8
Na San, Thai. H4 48
Nasawa, Vanuatu j17 79d
Nasbinals, Fr. E9 18
Nasca, Peru F2 84
Nase *see* Naze, Japan k19 39a
Nash, Tx., U.S. D4 122
Nāshik, India H4 54
Nashua, Ia., U.S. B5 120
Nashua, N.H., U.S. B14 114
Nashville, Ar., U.S. D5 122
Nashville, Il., U.S. F8 120
Nashville, In., U.S. E11 120
Nashville, Mi., U.S. F4 112
Nashville, N.C., U.S. I8 114
Nashville, Tn., U.S. H11 120
Nashwaak, stm., N.B., Can. D10 110
Nashwauk, Mn., U.S. D5 118
Nasielsk, Pol. D16 16
Näsijärvi, l., Fin. F10 8
Nāṣir, Sudan F6 62
Nâsir, Buheirat see Nasser, Lake, res., Afr. C6 62
Nasīrābād, India E5 54
Nasr, Egypt H1 58
Nass, stm., B.C., Can. E5 106
Nassarawa, Nig. H6 64
Nassau, Bah. m18 104f
Nassau, N.Y., U.S. B12 114
Nassau International Airport, Bah. m18 104f
Nassau Island, i., Cook Is. E10 72
Nassawadox, Va., U.S. G10 114
Nasser, Lake (Nâsir, Buheirat), res., Afr. C6 62
Nässjö, Swe. H6 8
Nastapoka Islands, is., Nu., Can. D15 106
Nasu, Japan B13 40
Nasu-dake, vol., Japan B12 40
Nasukoin Mountain, mtn., Mt., U.S. B12 136
Nasva, Russia D13 10
Nata, Bots. E4 68
Nata, stm., Afr. B8 70
Natal, Braz. C8 88
Natal, B.C., Can. G16 138
Natal, Indon. C1 50
Natal see KwaZulu-Natal, state, S. Afr. F10 70
Natalia, Tx., U.S. E9 130
Natalkuz Lake, res., B.C., Can. C5 138
Natanes Plateau, plat., Az., U.S. J6 132
Natashquan, stm., Can. i21 107a
Natchez, Ms., U.S. F7 122
Natchez Trace Parkway, p.o.i., U.S. E9 122
Natchitoches, La., U.S. F5 122
Natewa Bay, b., Fiji p19 79e
Nāthdwāra, India F4 54
Natimuk, Austl. K3 76
Nation, stm., B.C., Can. A7 138
National City, Ca., U.S. K8 134
Natitingou, Benin G5 64
Native Bay, b., Nu., Can. C14 106
Natividade, Braz. F2 88
Natkyizin, Mya. E3 48
Natoma, Ks., U.S. B9 128
Nator, Bngl. F12 54
Natori, Japan A13 40
Natron, Lake, l., Afr. E7 66
Natrûn, Wadi el-, val., Egypt H1 58
Nattaung, mtn., Mya. C3 48
Natuna Besar, i., Indon. A6 50
Natuna Besar, Kepulauan, is., Indon. A5 50
Natuna Selatan, Kepulauan, is., Indon. B6 50
Natural Bridge, misc. cult., Va., U.S. G6 114
Natural Bridges National Monument, p.o.i., Ut., U.S. F6 132
Naturaliste, Cape, c., Austl. F2 74
Naturno, Italy D7 22
Nau, Cap de la, c., Spain F11 20
Naucelle, Fr. E8 18
Naucratis, hist., Egypt H1 58
Nauen, Ger. D8 16
Naugatuck, Ct., U.S. C12 114
Naughton, On., Can. B8 112
Naujaat (Repulse Bay), Nu., Can. B13 106
Naujamiestis, Lith. E6 10
Naujan, Lake, l., Phil. D3 52
Naujoji Akmenė, Lith. D5 10
Naumburg, Ger. E7 16
Naunglon, Mya. D3 48
Nā'ūr, Jord. G6 58
Nauru, state, Oc. p17 78f
Nauru International Airport, Nauru q17 78f
Nauški, Russia F10 34
Nausori, Fiji p19 79e
Nauta, Peru D3 84
Nautanwa, India E9 54
Nautla, Mex. E10 100
Nauvoo, Il., U.S. D6 120
Nava, Mex. A8 100
Navadwip, India G12 54
Navael'nja, Bela. G8 10
Navahrudak, Bela. G8 10
Navajo, N.M., U.S. H7 132
Navajo Mountain, mtn., Ut., U.S. F6 132
Navajo National Monument, p.o.i., Az., U.S. G6 132
Navajo Reservoir, res., U.S. G9 132
Naval, Phil. C7 44
Navalmoral de la Mata, Spain E5 20
Navan, Ire. H6 12
Navapolack, Bela. E11 10
Navāpur, India H4 54
Navarin, mys, c., Russia D24 34
Navarino, Isla, i., Chile K3 90
Navarra, state, Spain B9 20
Navarro Mills Lake, res., Tx., U.S. F2 122
Navasëlki, Bela. H7 10
Navasota, Tx., U.S. G2 122
Navasota, stm., Tx., U.S. D11 130
Navassa, N.C., U.S. B7 116
Navassa Island, i., N.A. C10 102
Navesnoe, Russia H20 10
Navia, Arg. G4 92
Navia, stm., Spain A4 20
Navidad, Chile F1 92
Navidad, stm., Tx., U.S. E11 130
Navio, Riacho do, stm., Braz. E6 88
Naviti, i., Fiji p18 79e
Navlja, Russia H17 10
Năvodari, Rom. E15 26
Navoi, Uzb. F11 32
Navojoa, Mex. B4 100
Navolato, Mex. C5 100
Navsāri, India H4 54
Nawa *see* Naha, Japan I18 39a
Nawābganj, Bngl. F12 54
Nawābganj, India E8 54
Nawābshāh, Pak. E2 54
Nawāda, India F10 54
Nāwah, Afg. B1 54
Nawalgarh, India E5 54
Nawāpāra, India H8 54
Naxçıvan, Azer. B6 56
Naxi, China G1 42
Náxos, i., Grc. F8 28
Nayāgarh, India H10 54
Nayarit, state, Mex. E6 100
Nāy Band, Kūh-e, mtn., Iran C8 56
Naylor, Mo., U.S. H7 120
Nayoro, Japan B15 38
Nazaré, Braz. D2 88
Nazaré, Port. E1 20
Nazaré da Mata, Braz. D8 88
Nazaré do Piauí, Braz. D4 88
Nazareth *see* Nazerat, Isr. F6 58
Nazarovo, Russia C16 32
Nazas, Mex. C6 100
Nazas, stm., Mex. C6 100
Nazca Ridge, unds. K5 144
Naze, Japan k19 39a
Naze, The see Lindesnes, c., Nor. H2 8
Nazerat (Nazareth), Isr. F6 58
Nazerat 'Illit, Isr. F6 58
Nazija, Russia A14 10
Nazilli, Tur. F11 28
Nazina, Russia B13 32
Nazko, stm., B.C., Can. D7 138
Nazlet el-'Amûdein, Egypt J1 58
Nazran', Russia F7 32
Nazrēt, Eth. F7 62
Nazwá, Oman E8 56
Nazyvaevsk, Russia C12 32
N'dalatando, Ang. B1 68
Ndali, Benin H5 64
Ndélé, C.A.R. C4 66
Ndendé, Gabon E2 66
N'Djamena (Fort-Lamy), Chad E3 62
Ndjolé, Gabon E2 66
Ndogo, Lagune, l., Gabon E2 66
Ndola, Zam. C4 68
Ndumu Game Reserve, S. Afr. E11 70
Neabul Creek, stm., Austl. F6 76
Neagh, Lough, l., N. Ire., U.K. G6 12
Neah Bay, Wa., U.S. B2 136
Neale, Lake, l., Austl. D6 74
Neamț, state, Rom. B13 26
Néa Páfos (Paphos), Cyp. D3 58
Neápoli, Grc. G6 28
Near Islands, is., Ak., U.S. g21 140a
Neath, Wales, U.K. J9 12
Nebine Creek, stm., Austl. G6 76
Nebitdag, Turkmen. B7 56
Neblina, Cerro de la see Neblina, Pico da, mtn., S.A. G9 86
Neblina, Pico da, mtn., S.A. G9 86
Nebo, Il., U.S. E7 120
Nebo, Mount, mtn., Ut., U.S. D5 132
Nebolči, Russia A16 10
Nebraska, state, U.S. C7 108
Nebraska City, Ne., U.S. D1 120
Necedah, Wi., U.S. G8 118
Nechako, stm., B.C., Can. C7 138
Nechako Reservoir, res., B.C., Can. C5 138
Neches, Tx., U.S. F3 122
Neches, stm., Tx., U.S. G4 122
Nechí, Col. C4 86
Nechí, stm., Col. D4 86
Nechranice, vodní nádrź, res., Czech Rep. F9 16
Neckarsulm, Ger. G5 16
Necker Island, i., Br. Vir. Is. d9 104b
Necochea, Arg. I8 92
Nederland, Tx., U.S. H4 122
Nêdong, China D13 54
Needhams Point, c., Barb. n8 105d
Needle Mountain, mtn., Wy., U.S. F17 136
Needles, Ca., U.S. I2 132
Needville, Tx., U.S. H3 122
Neegro, Qooriga, b., Som. C10 66
Ñeembucú, state, Para. C8 92
Neenah, Wi., U.S. G10 118
Neepawa, Mb., Can. D14 124
Nefëdovo, Russia C12 32
Nefta, Tun. C6 64
Neftçala, Azer. B6 56
Neftejugansk, Russia B12 32
Nefza, Tun. H3 24
Negage, Ang. B2 68
Negara, Indon. H9 50
Negara, stm., Indon. E9 50
Negaunee, Mi., U.S. B2 112
Negēlē, Eth. F7 62
Negeribatin, Indon. F4 50
Negeri Sembilan, state, Malay. K6 48
Negev Desert see HaNegev, reg., Isr. H5 58
Negombo, Sri L. H4 53
Negra, Laguna, l., Ur. G11 92
Negreira, Spain B2 20
Nègres, Pointe des, c., Mart. k6 105c
Negrești-Oaș, Rom. B10 26
Negritos, Peru D1 84
Negro, stm., Arg. H4 90
Negro, stm., Braz. C13 92
Negro, stm., Col. E4 86
Negro, stm., Para. B9 92
Negro, stm., S.A. I11 86
Negro, stm., S.A. F9 92
Negros, i., Phil. F4 52
Nehalem, stm., Or., U.S. E3 136
Neharèlae, Bela. G9 10
Nehawka, Ne., U.S. D1 120
Nehbandān, Iran C8 56
Nehe *see* Nahe, China B9 36
Néhoué, Baie de, b., N. Cal. m14 79d
Neiba, Dom. Rep. C12 102
Neichiang *see* Neijiang, China G1 42
Neidpath, Sk., Can. D6 124
Neiges, Piton des, mtn., Reu. i10 69a
Neijiang, China G1 42
Neikiang *see* Neijiang, China G1 42
Neilburg, Sk., Can. B4 124
Neillsville, Wi., U.S. G8 118
Nei Monggol, state, China C7 36
Nei Mongol see Nei Monggol, state, China C7 36
Neiqiu, China C6 42
Neira, Col. E4 86
Neisse see Lausitzer Neisse, stm., Eur. F10 16
Neisse see Nysa Łużycka, stm., Eur. E10 16
Neiva, Col. F4 86
Neixiang, China E4 42
Neja, Russia G20 8
Nejapa de Madero, Mex. G11 100
Nejd see Najd, hist. reg., Sau. Ar. D5 56
Nejdek, Czech Rep. F8 16
Nek'emtē, Eth. F7 62
Nelichu, mtn., Sudan F6 62
Nelidovo, Russia D15 10
Neligh, Ne., U.S. E14 126
Neljaty, Russia E12 34
Nel'kan, Russia E16 34
Nellikuppam, India F4 53
Nellore, India D4 53
Nel'ma, Russia G16 34
Nelson, B.C., Can. G13 138
Nelson, N.Z. E5 80
Nelson, Ne., U.S. A10 128
Nelson, stm., Mb., Can. D12 106
Nelson, Cape, c., Austl. L3 76
Nelson, Estrecho, strt., Chile J2 90
Nelson Lakes National Park, p.o.i., N.Z. E5 80
Nelson's Dockyard, hist., Antig. f4 105b
Nelsonville, Oh., U.S. E3 114
Nelspoort, S. Afr. H6 70
Nelspruit, S. Afr. D10 70
Néma, Maur. F3 64
Nemadji, stm., U.S. E6 118
Neman, Russia E4 10
Neman (Nemunas), stm., Eur. E4 10
Nembe, Nig. I6 64
Nemenčinė, Lith. F8 10
Nemeriči, Russia G16 10
Nemours, Fr. F11 14
Nemunas (Neman), stm., Eur. E4 10
Nemunėlis (Mēmele), stm., Eur. D7 10
Nemuro, Japan C16 38
Nemuro Strait, strt., Asia C16 38
Nen, stm., China B9 36
Nenagh, Ire. I4 12
Nenana, Ak., U.S. D10 140
Nenana, stm., Ak., U.S. D10 140
Nendo, i., Sol. Is. E7 72
Nene, stm., Eng., U.K. I13 12
Neneckij avtonomnyj okrug, Russia C23 8
Nenets see Neneckij avtonomnyj okrug, Russia C23 8
Nenetsia see Neneckij avtonomnyj okrug, Russia C23 8
Nenggiri, stm., Malay. J5 48
Neodesha, Ks., U.S. G2 120
Neoga, Il., U.S. E9 120
Néo Karlovási, Grc. F9 28
Neola, Ut., U.S. C6 132
Neopit, Wi., U.S. G10 118
Neosho, Mo., U.S. H3 120
Neosho, stm., U.S. H2 120
Nepa, stm., Russia C19 32
Nepal, ctry., Asia E9 54
Nepālgañj, Nepal D8 54
Nepa Nagar, India H6 54
Nepeña, Peru E2 84
Nephin, mtn., Ire. G3 12
Nepisiguit, stm., N.B., Can. C10 110
Nepisiguit Bay, b., N.B., Can. C11 110
Neptune, N.J., U.S. D11 114
Neptune Beach, Fl., U.S. F4 116
Nérac, Fr. E6 18
Nerča, stm., Russia F12 34
Nerčinsk, Russia F12 34
Nerčinskij Zavod, Russia F12 34
Nerehta, Russia H19 8
Neretva, stm., Eur. G15 22
Neriquinha, Ang. D3 68
Neris (Vilija), stm., Eur. F6 10
Nerja, Spain H7 20
Nerjungri, Russia E13 34
Nerl', Russia C20 10
Nerl', stm., Russia D22 10
Nerópolis, Braz. I1 88
Nerussa, stm., Russia H16 10
Nerva, Spain G4 20
Nes, Neth. C1 16
Nesbyen, Nor. F3 8
Neščarda, vozero, l., Bela. E12 10
Neskaupstaður, Ice. k32 8a
Nesna, Nor. C5 8
Nespelem, Wa., U.S. B7 136
Ness, Loch, l., Scot., U.K. D8 12
Ness City, Ks., U.S. C8 128
Nesselrode, Mount, mtn., N.A. D4 106
Nesterkovo, Russia A13 10
Nestoïta, Ukr. B16 26
Netanya, Isr. F5 58
Netherdale, Austl. C7 76
Netherlands, ctry., Eur. B14 14
Netherlands Antilles, dep., N.A. i14 96a
Netherlands Guiana see Surinam, ctry., S.A. C6 84
Netrakona, Bngl. F13 54
Nettilling Fiord, b., Nu., Can. B17 106
Nettilling Lake, l., Nu., Can. B17 106
Nett Lake, l., Mn., U.S. C5 118
Nettuno, Italy C6 24
Neubrandenburg, Ger. C9 16
Neuburg an der Donau, Ger. H7 16
Neuchâtel, Switz. D3 22
Neuchâtel, Lac de, l., Switz. D3 22
Neudorf, Sk., Can. D11 124
Neuenburg *see* Neuchâtel, Switz. D3 22
Neuenhagen, Ger. D9 16
Neuerburg, Ger. F2 16
Neufchâteau, Fr. F14 14
Neufchâtel-en-Bray, Fr. E10 14
Neu-Isenburg, Ger. F4 16
Neumarkt in der Oberpfalz, Ger. G7 16
Neumünster, Ger. B6 16
Neun, stm., Laos C6 48
Neunkirchen, Aus. C13 22
Neuquén, Arg. G3 90
Neuquén, state, Arg. G2 90
Neuquén, stm., Arg. G3 90
Neurara, Chile B3 92
Neuruppin, Ger. D8 16
Neuse, stm., N.C., U.S. A8 116
Neusiedl am See, Aus. C13 22
Neuss, Ger. E2 16
Neustadt, Ger. F7 16
Neustadt an der Aisch, Ger. G6 16
Neustadt an der Weinstrasse, Ger. G3 16
Neustadt bei Coburg, Ger. F6 16
Neustadt in Holstein, Ger. B6 16
Neustrelitz, Ger. C9 16
Neutral Hills, hills, Ab., Can. B3 124
Neu-Ulm, Ger. H6 16
Neuvic, Fr. D8 18
Neuwied, Ger. F3 16
Neva, stm., Russia A13 10
Nevada, Ia., U.S. B4 120
Nevada, Mo., U.S. G3 120
Nevada, state, U.S. D4 108

Name	Map Ref.	Page
Nevada, Sierra, mts., Spain	G7	20
Nevada, Sierra, mts., Ca., U.S.	F6	134
Nevada City, Ca., U.S.	D4	134
Nevado, Cerro, mtn., Arg.	G3	92
Nevado, Cerro, mtn., Col.	E4	86
Nevado de Colima, Parque Nacional del, p.o.i., Mex.	F7	100
Nevado de Toluca, Parque Nacional, p.o.i., Mex.	F8	100
Neve, Serra da, mts., Ang.	C1	68
Nevel', Russia	D12	10
Nevel'sk, Russia	G17	34
Nevel'skogo, proliv, strt., Russia	F17	34
Never, Russia	F13	34
Nevers, Fr.	G12	14
Nevesinje, Bos.	F5	26
Nevinnomyssk, Russia	F6	32
Nevis, i., St. K./N.	E7	105a
Nevis, Ben, mtn., Scot., U.K.	E7	12
Nevis Peak, vol., St. K./N.	C10	105a
Nevjansk, Russia	C10	32
Nevşehir, Tur.	B3	56
New, stm., Belize	D3	102
New, stm., Guy.	C6	84
New, stm., S.C., U.S.	D4	116
New, stm., U.S.	J2	66
Newala, Tan.	G7	66
New Albany, In., U.S.	F12	120
New Albany, Ms., U.S.	C9	122
New Amsterdam, Guy.	B6	84
New Angledool, Austl.	G6	76
Newark, De., U.S.	E10	114
Newark, N.J., U.S.	D11	114
Newark, N.Y., U.S.	A8	114
Newark, Oh., U.S.	D3	114
Newark Lake, l., Nv., U.S.	D1	132
Newark-on-Trent, Eng., U.K.	H12	12
Newark Valley, N.Y., U.S.	B9	114
New Athens, Il., U.S.	F8	120
New Augusta, Ms., U.S.	F9	122
New Baden, Il., U.S.	F8	120
New Bedford, Ma., U.S.	C15	114
Newberg, Or., U.S.	E4	136
New Berlin, Il., U.S.	E7	120
New Berlin, N.Y., U.S.	B10	114
New Berlin, Wi., U.S.	F1	112
Newbern, Al., U.S.	E11	122
New Bern, N.C., U.S.	A8	116
Newbern, Tn., U.S.	H8	120
Newberry, Fl., U.S.	G3	116
Newberry, S.C., U.S.	B4	116
Newberry National Volcanic Monument, p.o.i., Or., U.S.	G5	136
New Bethlehem, Pa., U.S.	D6	114
New Bloomfield, Pa., U.S.	H12	112
New Boston, Oh., U.S.	F3	114
New Boston, Tx., U.S.	D4	122
New Braunfels, Tx., U.S.	E9	130
New Britain, Ct., U.S.	C13	114
New Britain, i., Pap. N. Gui.	b5	79a
New Brockton, Al., U.S.	F12	122
Newbrook, Ab., Can.	B17	138
New Brunswick, N.J., U.S.	D11	114
New Brunswick, state, Can.	D11	110
Newburg, Mo., U.S.	G6	120
Newburgh, In., U.S.	G10	120
Newburgh, N.Y., U.S.	C11	114
Newbury, Eng., U.K.	J11	12
Newburyport, Ma., U.S.	B15	114
New Caledonia, dep., Oc.	F7	72
New Caledonia see Nouvelle-Calédonie, i., N. Cal.	m15	79d
New Caledonia Basin, unds.	L19	142
New Carlisle, Qc., Can.	B11	110
New Carlisle, Oh., U.S.	E2	114
New Castile see Castilla la Nueva, hist. reg., Spain	E7	20
Newcastle, Austl.	I8	76
Newcastle, N.B., Can.	C11	110
Newcastle, St. K./N.	C2	105a
Newcastle, N. Ire., U.K.	G7	12
New Castle, Co., U.S.	D9	132
New Castle, De., U.S.	E10	114
New Castle, In., U.S.	I4	112
Newcastle, Ne., U.S.	I2	118
Newcastle, Ok., U.S.	F11	128
New Castle, Pa., U.S.	D5	114
New Castle, Va., U.S.	A9	130
New Castle, Va., U.S.	G5	114
Newcastle, Wy., U.S.	D8	126
Newcastle Bay, b., Austl.	B8	74
Newcastle-under-Lyme, Eng., U.K.	I10	12
Newcastle upon Tyne, Eng., U.K.	G10	12
Newcastle Waters, Austl.	C6	74
Newcastle West, Ire.	I3	12
New City, N.Y., U.S.	C11	114
Newcomerstown, Oh., U.S.	D4	114
New Concord, Oh., U.S.	D5	114
New Cumberland, W.V., U.S.	D5	114
Newdegate, Austl.	F3	74
New Delhi, India	D6	54
New Denver, B.C., Can.	F13	138
New Edinburg, Ar., U.S.	D6	122
New Effington, S.D., U.S.	F1	118
Newell, Ia., U.S.	B2	120
Newell, S.D., U.S.	C9	126
Newell, Lake, l., Ab., Can.	F19	138
New Ellenton, S.C., U.S.	C4	116
Newellton, La., U.S.	E7	122
New England, N.D., U.S.	A10	126
New England National Park, p.o.i., Austl.	H9	76
Newfane, N.Y., U.S.	E11	112
Newfane, Vt., U.S.	A13	114
New Florence, Pa., U.S.	D6	114
Newfound Gap, p., U.S.	I3	114
Newfoundland, i., Nf., Can.	j22	107a
Newfoundland and Labrador, state, Can.	i23	107a
Newfoundland Basin, unds.	D9	144
New Franklin, Mo., U.S.	E5	120
New Freedom, Pa., U.S.	E9	114
New Galloway, Scot., U.K.	F8	12
Newgate, B.C., Can.	G15	138
New Georgia, i., Sol. Is.	e7	79b
New Georgia Group, is., Sol. Is.	d7	79b
New Georgia Sound, strt., Sol. Is.	e8	79b
New Germany, N.S., Can.	F12	110
New Glasgow, N.S., Can.	E14	110
New Guinea, i.	b3	79a
Newhalem, Wa., U.S.	B5	136
New Hamburg, On., Can.	E9	112
New Hampshire, state, U.S.	G5	110
New Hampton, Ia., U.S.	A5	120
New Hanover, S. Afr.	F10	70
New Hanover, i., Pap. N. Gui.	a4	79a
New Harmony, In., U.S.	F10	120
New Hartford, Ia., U.S.	I6	118
New Haven, Ct., U.S.	K13	12
New Haven, Eng., U.K.	—	—
New Haven, Il., U.S.	G9	120
New Haven, In., U.S.	G4	112
New Haven, Ky., U.S.	G12	120
New Haven, Mo., U.S.	F6	120
New Hazelton, B.C., Can.	A3	138
New Hebrides see Vanuatu, ctry., Oc.	k16	79d
New Hebrides, is., Vanuatu	k16	79d
New Hebrides Trench, unds.	L20	142
Newhebron, Ms., U.S.	F9	122
New Holland, Oh., U.S.	E2	114
New Holland, Pa., U.S.	D9	114
New Holstein, Wi., U.S.	E1	112
New Hope, Al., U.S.	C12	122

Name	Map Ref.	Page
New Iberia, La., U.S.	G7	122
New Ireland, i., Pap. N. Gui.	a5	79a
New Jersey, state, U.S.	D11	114
New Johnsonville, Tn., U.S.	H10	120
New Kensington, Pa., U.S.	D6	114
New Kent, Va., U.S.	G9	114
Newkirk, Ok., U.S.	E11	128
New Kowloon see Xinjiulong, China	J6	42
New Lexington, Oh., U.S.	C6	76
New Lexington, Oh., U.S.	E4	114
New Lisbon, Wi., U.S.	H8	118
New Liskeard, On., Can.	F14	106
New Llano, La., U.S.	F5	122
New London, Ct., U.S.	C13	114
New London, Mo., U.S.	E6	120
New London, N.H., U.S.	G5	110
New London, Tx., U.S.	E4	122
New London, Wi., U.S.	G10	118
New Madrid, Mo., U.S.	H8	120
Newman, Austl.	D3	74
Newman, Ca., U.S.	F4	134
Newman Grove, Ne., U.S.	F15	126
Newmarket, On., Can.	D10	112
Newmarket, Eng., U.K.	I13	12
New Market, Al., U.S.	C12	122
New Market, Ia., U.S.	D3	120
New Market, N.H., U.S.	G5	110
New Market, Va., U.S.	F7	114
New Martinsville, W.V., U.S.	E4	114
New Mexico, state, U.S.	D9	98
New Milford, Ct., U.S.	C12	114
New Milford, Pa., U.S.	C10	114
Newnan, Ga., U.S.	D14	122
New Norfolk, Austl.	o13	77a
New Norway, Ab., Can.	D18	138
New Orleans, La., U.S.	G8	122
New Paris, Oh., U.S.	I5	112
New Philadelphia, Oh., U.S.	D4	114
New Pine Creek, Or., U.S.	A5	134
New Plymouth, N.Z.	D5	80
New Plymouth, Id., U.S.	G10	136
Newport, Wales, U.K.	J10	12
Newport, Eng., U.K.	K11	12
Newport, Ar., U.S.	B7	122
Newport, Ky., U.S.	E1	114
Newport, Me., U.S.	F7	110
Newport, N.C., U.S.	B8	116
Newport, N.H., U.S.	G4	110
Newport, Or., U.S.	F2	136
Newport, Pa., U.S.	D8	114
Newport, R.I., U.S.	C14	114
Newport, Tn., U.S.	I2	114
Newport, Vt., U.S.	F4	110
Newport Beach, Ca., U.S.	J7	134
Newport News, Va., U.S.	G9	114
Newport Pagnell, Eng., U.K.	I12	12
Newport Richey, Fl., U.S.	H3	116
New Providence, i., Bah.	C9	96
Newquay, Eng., U.K.	K7	12
New Richland, Mn., U.S.	H5	118
New Richmond, Qc., Can.	B10	110
New Richmond, Wi., U.S.	F6	118
New River, St. K./N.	C2	105a
New Road, N.S., Can.	—	—
New Roads, La., U.S.	G7	122
New Rochelle, N.Y., U.S.	D12	114
New Ross, N.S., Can.	F12	110
New Ross, Ire.	I6	12
Newry, N. Ire., U.K.	G6	12
Newry, S.C., U.S.	B3	116
New Salem, N.D., U.S.	A11	126
New Schwabenland, reg.,	C5	81
New Sharon, Ia., U.S.	C5	120
New Siberian Islands see Novosibirskie ostrova, is., Russia	A18	34
New Smyrna Beach, Fl., U.S.	G5	116
New South Wales, state, Austl.	I6	76
New Tazewell, Tn., U.S.	H2	114
New Tecumseth, On., Can.	D9	112
Newton, Ga., U.S.	F14	122
Newton, Ia., U.S.	C4	120
Newton, Il., U.S.	F9	120
Newton, Ks., U.S.	C11	128
Newton, Ma., U.S.	B14	114
Newton, Ms., U.S.	E9	122
Newton, N.J., U.S.	C11	114
Newton, Tx., U.S.	G5	122
Newton Falls, N.Y., U.S.	D14	112
Newton Stewart, Scot., U.K.	G8	12
New Town, N.D., U.S.	F11	124
Newtownabbey, N. Ire., U.K.	G6	12
Newtownards, N. Ire., U.K.	G7	12
New Ulm, Mn., U.S.	G4	118
New Ulm, Tx., U.S.	H2	122
New Washington, Oh., U.S.	D3	114
New Waterford, N.S., Can.	D16	110
New Waverly, Tx., U.S.	G3	122
New Westminster, B.C., Can.	G8	138
New Whiteland, In., U.S.	E11	120
New York, N.Y., U.S.	D12	114
New York, state, U.S.	C12	108
New York Mills, Mn., U.S.	E3	118
New York State Barge Canal, can., N.Y., U.S.	E12	112
New Zealand, ctry., Oc.	D4	80
Neyrīz, Iran	D7	56
Neyshābūr, Iran	B8	56
Neyveli, India	F4	53
Neyyättinkara, India	G3	53
Nezahualcóyotl, Presa, res., Mex.	G12	100
Nezperce, Id., U.S.	D10	136
Ngabang, Indon.	C6	50
Ngabé, Congo	E3	66
Ngambè, Cam.	D2	66
Ngami, Lake, l., Bots.	B6	70
Ngamiland, state, Bots.	B6	70
Ngan-chouei see Anhui, state, China	F7	42
Ngangla Ringco, l., China	C9	54
Nganglong Kangri, mts., China	B9	54
Nganjuk see Nganjuk, Indon.	G7	50
Nganjuk, Indon.	G7	50
Ngao, Thai.	C5	48
Ngaoui, Mont, mtn., Afr.	C2	66
Ngaoundéré, Cam.	C2	66
Ngape, Mya.	B2	48
Ngaputaw, Mya.	D2	48
Ngara, Tan.	E6	66
Ngatangiia, Cook Is.	a27	78j
Ngatangiia Harbour, b., Cook Is.	a27	78j
Ngawi, Indon.	G7	50
Ngay Nua, Laos	B5	48
Ngcheangel, is., Palau	D9	44
Ngeaur, i., Palau	D9	44
Ngereklmadel, Palau	g7	78b
Ngerkeai, Palau	g8	78b
Ngeremlengui, Palau	g8	78b
Ngerukewid, i., Palau	h7	78b
Ngetbong, Palau	h7	78b
Nggatokae Island, i., Sol. Is.	e8	79b
Nggela Pile, i., Sol. Is.	e9	79b
Nghia Hanh, Viet.	E9	48
Ngiap, stm., Laos	C6	48
Ngiro, mtn., Kenya	D7	66
Ngira, Ewaso, stm., Kenya	D7	66
Ngo, Congo	E3	66
Ngoko, stm., Afr.	D3	66
Ngom, stm., China	B8	46
Ngomeni, Ras, c., Kenya	E8	66
Ngong, Kenya	E7	66
Ngoring Hu, l., China	E4	36
Ngounié, stm., Gabon	E2	66
Ngourti, Chad	F7	64
Nguigmi, Niger	G7	64

Name	Map Ref.	Page
Ngulu, at., Micron.	C4	72
Ngum, stm., Laos	C6	48
Nguna, Île, i., Vanuatu	k17	79d
Nguru, Nig.	G7	64
Nhacoongo, Moz.	D12	70
Nhamundá, stm., Braz.	D6	84
Nha Trang, Viet.	F9	48
Nhill, Austl.	K3	76
Nhoma, stm., Afr.	D2	68
Niafounké, Mali	F4	64
Niagara, stm., N.A.	F5	36
Ningpo see Ningbo, China	G9	42
Niagara Falls, On., Can.	E10	112
Niagara Falls, N.Y., U.S.	A6	114
Niagara Falls, wtfl., N.A.	E10	112
Niagara-on-the-Lake, On., Can.	E10	112
Niagassola, Gui.	G3	64
Niah, Malay.	B8	50
Niamey, Niger	G5	64
Niangara, D.R.C.	D5	66
Niangay, Lac, l., Mali	F4	64
Niangoloko, Burkina	G4	64
Niangua, stm., Mo., U.S.	G5	120
Nia-Nia, D.R.C.	D5	66
Niantic, Il., U.S.	E8	120
Nianyushan, China	G7	42
Nianzishan, China	B9	38
Niari, stm., Congo	E2	66
Nias, Pulau, i., Indon.	L3	48
Nicaragua, ctry., N.A.	F5	102
Nicaragua, Lago de, l., Nic.	G5	102
Nicaragua, Lake see Nicaragua, Lago de, l., Nic.	G5	102
Nicastro, Italy	F10	24
Nice, Fr.	F13	18
Niceville, Fl., U.S.	G12	122
Nichinan, Japan	H4	40
Nicholas Channel (San Nicolás, Canal de), strt., N.A.	G11	108
Nicholasville, Ky., U.S.	G13	120
Nicholls, Ga., U.S.	E3	116
Nicholl's Town, Bah.	B9	96
Nicholson, Pa., U.S.	C10	114
Nickel Centre, On., Can.	B8	112
Nickerson, Ks., U.S.	C10	128
Nicobar Islands, is., India	G7	46
Nicola, B.C., Can.	F10	138
Nicola, stm., B.C., Can.	F9	138
Nicolae Bălcescu, Rom.	B13	26
Nicolet, Qc., Can.	D4	110
Nicolet, Lake, l., Mi., U.S.	B5	112
Nicolet Sud-Ouest, stm., Qc., Can.	E5	110
Nicollet, Mn., U.S.	G4	118
Nicosia (Levkosia), Cyp.	C4	58
Nicosia, Italy	G8	24
Nicoya, Golfo de, b., C.R.	H5	102
Nicoya, Península de, pen., C.R.	H5	102
Nida, Lith.	E3	10
Nida, stm., Pol.	F16	16
Nidadavole, India	C5	53
Nidzica, Pol.	C16	16
Niebüll, Ger.	B4	16
Niedere Tauern, mts., Aus.	C10	22
Niedersachsen, state, Ger.	D4	16
Niederösterreich, state, Aus.	B12	22
Niefang, Eq. Gui.	I7	64
Niekerkshoop, S. Afr.	F6	70
Niemba, D.R.C.	F5	66
Niemodlin, Pol.	F13	16
Nienburg, Ger.	D5	16
Niers, stm., Eur.	C15	14
Niesky, Ger.	E10	16
Nieszawa, Pol.	D14	16
Nieu-Bethesda, S. Afr.	G7	70
Nieuport see Nieuwpoort, Bel.	C11	14
Nieuw Amsterdam, Sur.	B6	84
Nieuw Nickerie, Sur.	B6	84
Nieuwpoort, Bel.	C11	14
Nieuwpoort, Neth. Ant.	p22	104g
Nièvre, state, Fr.	G12	14
Nifisha, Egypt	H3	58
Niğde, Tur.	H15	6
Niğde, state, Tur.	A5	58
Nigel, S. Afr.	E9	70
Niger, ctry., Afr.	F6	64
Niger, stm., Afr.	H6	64
Niger Delta, Nig.	I6	64
Nigeria, ctry., Afr.	H6	64
Nightcaps, N.Z.	G3	80
Nighthawk, Wa., U.S.	B7	136
Nigríta, Grc.	C6	28
Niheidât el-Súd, Gebel el-, mtn., Egypt	J3	58
Niihama, Japan	F5	40
Ni'ihau, i., Hi., U.S.	b1	78a
Ni'ijima, i., Japan	E12	40
Niitsu, Japan	B12	40
Nijar, Spain	H8	20
Nijmegen, Neth.	C14	14
Nijvel see Nivelles, Bel.	D13	14
Nikel', Russia	B14	8
Nikki, Benin	G5	64
Nikkō, Japan	C12	40
Nikkō-kokuritsu-kōen, p.o.i., Japan	B12	40
Nikolaevo, Russia	B12	10
Nikolaevsk-na-Amure, Russia	F17	34
Nikol'sk, Russia	C6	32
Nikol'sk, Russia	G21	8
Nikolski, Ak., U.S.	F6	140
Nikol'skij, Russia	F15	8
Nikol'skoe, Russia	E22	34
Nikol'skoe, Russia	H19	10
Nikopol', Ukr.	E4	32
Nikshahr, Iran	D9	56
Nikšić, Serb.	G5	26
Nikumaroro, at., Kir.	D9	72
Nikunau, i., Kir.	D8	72
Nil, Bahr el- see Nile, stm., Afr.	B6	62
Nil, Nahr an- see Nile, stm., Afr.	D6	62
Nila, Pulau, i., Indon.	G9	44
Nilakka, l., Fin.	E12	8
Nile, stm., Afr.	D6	62
Nile Delta, Egypt	H1	58
Niles, Mi., U.S.	B10	120
Niles, Oh., U.S.	C5	114
Nilgiri, India	H11	54
Nilka, China	F14	32
Nilsiä, Fin.	E12	8
Nimach, India	F5	54
Nimba, Mount, mtn., Afr.	H3	64
Nimbàhera, India	F5	54
Nîmes, Fr.	F10	18
Nimpkish Lake, l., B.C., Can.	F3	138
Nimule, Sudan	G6	62
Ninda, Ang.	C3	68
Nindigully, Austl.	G7	76
Nine Degree Channel, strt., India	G3	46
Ninette, Mb., Can.	E14	124
Ninetyeast Ridge, unds.	K11	142
Ninety Mile Beach, cst.,	—	—
Ninety Six, S.C., U.S.	B3	116
Ninfas, Punta, c., Arg.	H4	90
Ninga, Mb., Can.	E14	124
Ningan, China	B8	38
Ningbo, China	G9	42
Ningcheng, China	D3	38
Ningde, China	H8	42

Name	Map Ref.	Page
Ningdu, China	H6	42
Ningguo, China	F8	42
Ninghai, China	G9	42
Ning-hia see Ningxia, state, China	D6	36
Ninghua, China	H7	42
Ningi, Nig.	G6	64
Ningjing Shan, mts., China	F4	36
Ningming, China	J2	42
Ningpo see Ningbo, China	F5	36
Ningqiang, China	E2	42
Ningsia see Yinchuan, China	E3	42
Ningsia Hui see Ningxia, state, China	B2	42
Ningsia Hui Autonomous Region see Ningxia, state, China	D6	36
Ningwu, China	B4	42
Ningxia, state, China	D6	36
Ningxiang, China	G5	42
Ningyuan, China	I4	42
Ninh Binh, Viet.	B7	48
Ninh Hoa, Viet.	F9	48
Ninhue, Chile	H1	92
Ninigo Group, is., Pap. N. Gui.	a3	79a
Ninnescah, North Fork, stm., Ks., U.S.	D10	128
Ninnescah, South Fork, stm., Ks., U.S.	D10	128
Ninohe, Japan	D14	38
Nioaque, Braz.	D5	90
Niobrara, stm., U.S.	E14	126
Nioghalvfjerdsfjorden, ice, Grnld.	B22	141
Nioki, D.R.C.	E3	66
Niono, Mali	G3	64
Nioro, Mali	F3	64
Niort, Fr.	C5	18
Niota, Tn., U.S.	B14	122
Nipāni, India	C2	53
Nipawin, Sk., Can.	E10	106
Nipe, Bahía de, b., Cuba	B10	102
Nipigon, On., Can.	B10	118
Nipigon, Lake, res., On., Can.	B10	118
Nipigon Bay, b., On., Can.	B10	118
Nipissing, Lake, l., On., Can.	B10	112
Nipomo, Ca., U.S.	H5	134
Niquelândia, Braz.	H1	88
Niquero, Cuba	B9	102
Niquivil, Arg.	E3	92
Nira, stm., India	B2	53
Nirasaki, Japan	D11	40
Nirgua, Ven.	B7	86
Nirmal, India	B4	53
Nirmāli, India	E11	54
Niš, Serb.	F8	26
Nişāb, Yemen	G6	56
Nišava, Eur.	F9	26
Niscemi, Italy	G8	24
Nishio, Japan	E10	40
Nishiwaki, Japan	E7	40
Nisporeni, Mol.	B15	26
Nisqually, stm., Wa., U.S.	D4	136
Nisswa, Mn., U.S.	E4	118
Nītaure, Lat.	C8	10
Niterói, Braz.	L4	88
Nith, stm., On., Can.	E9	112
Nitinat Lake, l., B.C., Can.	H6	138
Nitra, Slov.	H14	16
Nitra, stm., Slov.	H14	16
Nitro, W.V., U.S.	F4	114
Niue, dep., Oc.	E10	72
Niulakita, i., Tuvalu	E8	72
Niut, Gunung, mtn., Indon.	C6	50
Niutao, i., Tuvalu	D8	72
Niutoushan, China	B7	38
Niutou Shan, i., China	G9	42
Niuzhuang, China	A10	42
Nive, stm., Austl.	E6	76
Nivelles, Bel.	D13	14
Nivernais, hist. reg., Fr.	G12	14
Niverville, Mb., Can.	E16	124
Nixa, Mo., U.S.	G4	120
Nixon, Nv., U.S.	D6	134
Niža, Russia	C20	8
Nizāmābād, India	B4	53
Nizām Sāgar, res., India	C3	53
Nizhnegorodskaja oblast', co., Russia	H21	8
Nizip, Tur.	A8	58
Nízke Tatry, Narodny Park, p.o.i., Slov.	H15	16
Nizmennaja Kujto, ozero, l., Russia	D14	8
Nižneilimsk, Russia	C18	32
Nižnekamsk, Russia	C8	32
Nižnekamskoe vodohranilišče, res., Russia	C8	32
Nižneudinsk, Russia	D17	32
Nižnevartovsk, Russia	B13	32
Nižnij Časučej, Russia	F12	34
Nižnij Kuranah, Russia	E14	34
Nižnij Novgorod (Gorki), Russia	H21	8
Nižnij Pjandž, Taj.	B10	56
Nižnij Tagil, Russia	C10	32
Nižnjaja Peša, Russia	C22	8
Nižnjaja Pojma, Russia	C17	32
Nižnjaja Tavda, Russia	C11	32
Nižnjaja Tunguska, stm., Russia	B16	32
Nizza Monferrato, Italy	F5	22
Njandoma, Russia	F19	8
Njasviž, Bela.	G9	10
Njazidja, i., Com.	C7	68
Njombe, stm., Tan.	F7	66
Njuhča, Russia	E22	8
Njuja, Russia	D12	34
Njuja, stm., Russia	D12	34
Njuksenica, Russia	F21	8
Njurba, Russia	D12	34
Njuvčim, Russia	B8	32
Nkambe, Cam.	C2	66
Nkawkaw, Ghana	H4	64
Nkayi, Zimb.	D4	68
Nkhata Bay, Mwi.	C5	68
Nkhotakota, Mwi.	C5	68
Nkomi, Lagune, l., Gabon	E1	66
Nkongsamba, Cam.	D1	66
Nkwalini, S. Afr.	F10	70
Nmai, stm., Mya.	C8	46
Noakhali, Bngl.	G13	54
Noatak, Ak., U.S.	C7	140
Noatak, stm., Ak., U.S.	C8	140
Nobeoka, Japan	G4	40
Noble, Il., U.S.	F9	120
Noblesville, In., U.S.	H3	112
Nobres, Braz.	F6	84
Nocatee, Fl., U.S.	I4	116
Noce, stm., Italy	D8	22
Nocera Inferiore, Italy	D8	24
Nocona, Tx., U.S.	H11	128
Nocupétaro, Mex.	F8	100
Noetinger, Arg.	F6	92
Nogales, Mex.	F7	98
Nogales, Az., U.S.	L5	132
Nogata, Japan	F3	40
Nogent-le-Rotrou, Fr.	F9	14
Nogent-sur-Seine, Fr.	F12	14
Noginsk, Russia	E21	10
Nogliki, Russia	F17	34
Nogoa, stm., Austl.	E6	76
Nogoyá, Arg.	E8	92
Nógrád, state, Hung.	B6	26
Noguera Pallaresa, stm., Spain	B12	20

Name	Map Ref.	Page
Noguera Ribagorçana, stm., Spain	B11	20
Nohar, India	D5	54
Noia, Spain	B2	20
Noir, Causse, plat., Fr.	E9	18
Noir, Isla, i., Chile	J2	90
Noire, stm., Qc., Can.	B13	112
Noirmoutier, Île de, i., Fr.	H6	14
Noirmoutier-en-l'Île, Fr.	H6	14
Nojima-zaki, c., Japan	E12	40
Nokha Mandi, India	E4	54
Nokia, Fin.	F10	8
Nokomis, Sk., Can.	C8	124
Nokomis, Fl., U.S.	I3	116
Nokomis, Il., U.S.	E8	120
Nokou, Chad	E2	62
Nokuku, Vanuatu	j16	79d
Nola, C.A.R.	D3	66
Nola, Italy	D8	24
Nolichucky, stm., U.S.	H2	114
Nolin, stm., Ky., U.S.	G11	120
Nolin Lake, res., Ky., U.S.	G11	120
Nolinsk, Russia	C8	32
Nólsoy, i., Far. Is.	n34	8b
Nombre de Dios, Pan.	H8	102
Nome, Ak., U.S.	D6	140
Nomozaki, Japan	G2	40
Nomtsas, Nmb.	D3	70
Nonburg, Russia	D24	8
Nondalton, Ak., U.S.	D8	140
Nong'an, China	B6	38
Nong Han, Thai.	D6	48
Nong Khai, Thai.	D6	48
Nongoma, S. Afr.	E10	70
Nongpoh, India	F13	54
Nongstoin, India	F13	54
Nonoava, Mex.	B5	100
Nonogasta, Arg.	D4	92
Nonouti, at., Kir.	D8	72
Nonsuch Bay, b., Antig.	I4	105b
Nooksack, Wa., U.S.	B4	136
Noonkanbah, Austl.	C4	74
Noordoostpolder, reg., Neth.	B14	14
Noordpunt, c., Neth. Ant.	p21	104g
Noordwijk aan Zee, Neth.	B13	14
Noorvik, Ak., U.S.	C7	140
Nootka Island, i., B.C., Can.	G4	138
Nóqui, Ang.	B1	68
Norah, is., Erit.	D7	62
Nora Islands see Norah, is., Erit.	D7	62
Noralee, B.C., Can.	B4	138
Nora Springs, Ia., U.S.	A5	120
Norcatur, Ks., U.S.	B8	128
Norcross, Ga., U.S.	D14	122
Nord, Grnld.	A22	141
Nord, state, Fr.	D12	14
Nord, state, N. Cal.	m15	79d
Nord, Canal du, can., Fr.	E11	14
Nord, Canal du, can., Fr.	D12	14
Nordaustlandet, i., Nor.	B29	141
Nordborg, Den.	B4	16
Norddegg, Ab., Can.	D14	138
Nordegg, stm., Ab., Can.	D15	138
Norden, Ger.	C3	16
Nordenham, Ger.	C4	16
Norderney, i., Ger.	C3	16
Norderstedt, Ger.	C6	16
Nordfjord, b., Nor.	F1	8
Nordfold, Nor.	C6	8
Nordhausen, Ger.	E6	16
Nordhorn, Ger.	D2	16
Nordjylland, state, Den.	H4	8
Nordkapp (North Cape), c., Nor.	A11	8
Nordkinnhalvøya, pen., Nor.	A12	8
Nordland, state, Nor.	C6	8
Nördlingen, Ger.	H6	16
Nordmaling, Swe.	E8	8
Nordostrundingen, c., Grnld.	A23	141
Nord-Ostsee-Kanal (Kiel Canal), can., Ger.	B5	16
Nordrhein-Westfalen, state, Ger.	E3	16
Nordstrand, i., Ger.	B4	16
Nord-Trøndelag, state, Nor.	D5	8
Nordvik, Russia	B11	34
Norfolk, Ne., U.S.	E15	126
Norfolk, Va., U.S.	H9	114
Norfolk Island, dep., Norf. I.	x25	78i
Norfolk Island National Park, p.o.i., Norf. I.	y25	78i
Norfolk Ridge, unds.	L19	142
Norfork Lake, res., U.S.	H5	120
Norikura-dake, vol., Japan	C10	40
Noril'sk, Russia	C6	34
Norlina, N.C., U.S.	H7	114
Normal, Il., U.S.	D9	120
Norman, Ar., U.S.	C5	122
Norman, Ok., U.S.	F11	128
Norman, stm., Austl.	B3	76
Norman Island, i., Br. Vir. Is.	e8	104b
Normanton, Austl.	A3	76
Norman Wells, N.T., Can.	B5	106
Norogachi, Mex.	B5	100
Norquay, Sk., Can.	C11	124
Norquinco, Arg.	H2	90
Norra Storfjället, mtn., Swe.	D6	8
Norrbotten, state, Swe.	C9	8
Nørre Nebel, Den.	H3	8
Nørresundby, Den.	H3	8
Norridgewock, Me., U.S.	F7	110
Norris, S.C., U.S.	H1	114
Norris Lake, res., Tn., U.S.	H2	114
Norristown, Pa., U.S.	D10	114
Norrköping, Swe.	G7	8
Norrtälje, Swe.	G8	8
Norseman, Austl.	F4	74
Norsjö, Swe.	D8	8
Norsjø, l., Nor.	G3	8
Norske Øer, is., Grnld.	B22	141
Norsup, Vanuatu	k16	79d
Norte, Cabo, c., Braz.	C8	84
Norte, Serra do, plat., Braz.	F6	84
Norte de Santander, state, Col.	C5	86
Nortelândia, Braz.	F6	84
North, S.C., U.S.	C4	116
North, stm., N.S., Can.	D14	110
North, Cape, c., P.E., Can.	C16	110
North, Cape, c., Nf., Can.	A10	118
North, Plains, pl., N.M., U.S.	I8	132
North Adams, Mi., U.S.	C1	114
North Adams, Ma., U.S.	B12	114
North Albany, Or., U.S.	F3	136
North Andaman, i., India	F7	46
North Atlanta, Ga., U.S.	C1	116
North Augusta, S.C., U.S.	C4	116
North Aulatsivik Island, i., Nf., Can.	F13	141
North Australian Basin, unds.	K14	142
North Baltimore, Oh., U.S.	C2	114
North Battleford, Sk., Can.	B5	124
North Bay, On., Can.	B10	112
North Bend, B.C., Can.	G9	138
North Bend, Ne., U.S.	J2	118
North Bennington, Vt., U.S.	B12	114
North Berwick, Scot., U.K.	E10	12
North Berwick, Me., U.S.	G6	110
North Borneo see Sabah, state, Malay.	H1	52
North Bourke, Austl.	H5	76
North Branch, Mi., U.S.	E6	112
North Caicos, i., T./C. Is.	B11	102
North Canadian, stm., U.S.	F12	128
North Canton, Ga., U.S.	C14	122
North Canton, Oh., U.S.	D4	114
North Cape, c., P.E., Can.	C13	110
North Cape see Nordkapp, c., Nor.	A11	8
North Cape, c., N.Z.	B5	80
North Caribou Lake, l., On., Can.	E12	106
North Carolina, state, U.S.	D11	108
North Cascades National Park, p.o.i., Wa., U.S.	B5	136
North Channel, strt., On., Can.	B7	112
North Channel, strt., U.K.	F7	12
North Charleston, S.C., U.S.	D5	116
North Chicago, Il., U.S.	F2	112
North Chungcheong see Ch'ungch'ŏng-bukto, state, Kor., S.	B1	40
Northcliffe, Austl.	F3	74
North College Hill, Oh., U.S.	E13	120
North Collins, N.Y., U.S.	F11	112
North Concho, stm., Tx., U.S.	C7	130
North Conway, N.H., U.S.	F5	110
North Crossett, Ar., U.S.	D6	122
North Cyprus see Cyprus, North, ctry., Asia	C4	58
North Dakota, state, U.S.	G13	124
North Downs, hills, Eng., U.K.	J13	12
North East Butte, S.D., U.S.	B11	126
North East, Md., U.S.	E9	114
North-East, state, Bots.	B8	70
Northeast Cape, Ak., U.S.	D6	140
Northeast Cape Fear, stm., N.C., U.S.	B8	116
North East Point, c., Bah.	A11	102
Northeast Providence Channel, strt., Bah.	B9	96
Northeim, Ger.	E6	16
North English, Ia., U.S.	C5	120
Northern see Hazafon, state, Isr.	F6	58
Northern Cape, state, S. Afr.	F5	70
Northern Cook Islands, is., Cook Is.	E10	72
Northern Division, state, Fiji	p20	79e
Northern Donets, stm., Eur.	F16	6
Northern Dvina see Severnaja Dvina, stm., Russia	E19	8
Northern Indian Lake, l., Mb., Can.	G6	12
Northern Ireland, state, U.K.	G6	12
Northern Mariana Islands, dep., Oc.	B6	72
Northern Province, state, Zam.	C9	70
Northern Sporades see Vóreioi Sporades, is., Grc.	D6	28
Northern Territory, state, Austl.	D6	120
North Fabius, stm., U.S.	D6	120
Northfield, Ma., U.S.	B13	114
Northfield, Mn., U.S.	G5	118
Northfield, Vt., U.S.	F4	110
North Fiji Basin, unds.	K20	142
North Flinders Range, mts., Austl.	H2	76
North Fond du Lac, Wi., U.S.	H10	118
North Foreland, c., Eng., U.K.	J14	12
North Fork, Ca., U.S.	F6	134
North Fork, i., N.Z.	H5	120
North Fort Myers, Fl., U.S.	J4	116
North Frisian Islands, is., Eur.	B3	16
Northglenn, Co., U.S.	B4	128
North Gulfport, Ms., U.S.	G9	122
North Gyeongsang see Kyŏngsang-bukto, state, Kor., S.	C1	40
North Henik Lake, l., Nu., Can.	C11	106
North Hero, Vt., U.S.	F3	110
North Highlands, Ca., U.S.	E4	134
North Island, i., N.Z.	C5	80
North Judson, In., U.S.	G3	112
North Kent Island, i., Nu., Can.	B7	141
North Kingsville, Oh., U.S.	C5	114
North Knife Lake, l., Mb., Can.	D11	106
North Korea see Korea, North, ctry., Asia	D7	38
North Lakhimpur, India	E15	54
North Las Vegas, Nv., U.S.	G1	132
North La Veta Pass, p., Co., U.S.	D3	128
North Little Rock, Ar., U.S.	C6	122
North Llano, stm., Tx., U.S.	D8	130
North Loup, Ne., U.S.	F14	126
North Loup, stm., Ne., U.S.	F14	126
North Magnetic Pole, misc. cult.	A3	141
North Mamm Peak, mtn., Co., U.S.	D9	132
North Manchester, In., U.S.	H4	112
North Manitou Island, i., Mi., U.S.	C3	112
North Mankato, Mn., U.S.	G4	118
North Miami, Fl., U.S.	K5	116
North Miami Beach, Fl., U.S.	K5	116
North Milk (Milk, North Fork), stm., N.A.	B13	136
North Myrtle Beach, S.C., U.S.	C7	116
North New River Canal, Fl., U.S.	J5	116
North Newton, Ks., U.S.	C11	128
North Ogden, Ut., U.S.	B5	132
North Ossetia see Severnaja Osetija, state, Russia	F6	32
North Palisade, mtn., Ca., U.S.	F7	134
North Palm Beach, Fl., U.S.	J5	116
North Park, Il., U.S.	B9	120
North Cape, i., C16	110	—
North Peninsula, pen., On., Can.	A10	118
North Plains, pl., N.M., U.S.	I8	132
North Platte, Ne., U.S.	F12	126
North Platte, stm., U.S.	F11	126
North Point, c., Barb.	n8	105d
North Pole, misc. cult.	A4	94
Northport, Al., U.S.	D11	122

Name	Map Ref.	Page

Northport, Mi., U.S. — C4 112
Northport, Wa., U.S. — B9 136
North Portal, Sk., Can. — E11 124
North Raccoon, stm., Ia., U.S. — C3 120
North Rhine-Westphalia see Nordrhein-Westfalen, state, Ger. — E4 16
North Richland Hills, Tx., U.S. — B10 130
North Rim, Az., U.S. — G4 132
North Ronaldsay, i., Scot., U.K. — B10 12
North Rustico, P.E., Can. — D13 110
North Salt Lake, Ut., U.S. — C5 132
North Saskatchewan, stm., Can. — E9 106
North Sea, s., Eur. — D9 6
North Shoal Lake, l., Mb., Can. — D16 124
North Shore City, N.Z. — C6 80
North Shoshone Peak, mtn., Nv., U.S. — D8 134
North Siberian Lowland see Severo-Sibirskaja nizmennost', pl., Russia — B6 34
North Skunk, stm., Ia., U.S. — C5 120
North Solitary Island, i., Austl. — G9 76
North Solomons, state, Pap. N. Gui. — d7 79b
North Spicer Island, i., Nu., Can. — B15 106
North Stradbroke Island, i., Austl. — F9 76
North Sumatra see Sumatera Utara, state, Indon. — K4 48
North Sydney, N.S., Can. — D16 110
North Taranaki Bight, b., N.Z. — D5 80
North Terre Haute, In., U.S. — E10 120
North Thompson, stm., B.C., Can. — F10 138
North Troy, Vt., U.S. — F4 110
North Tunica, Ms., U.S. — C8 122
North Uist, i., Scot., U.K. — D5 12
Northumberland Isles, is., Austl. — C7 76
Northumberland National Park, p.o.i., Eng., U.K. — F10 12
Northumberland Strait, strt., Can. — D12 110
North Umpqua, stm., Or., U.S. — G4 136
North Vancouver, B.C., Can. — G7 138
North Vietnam see Vietnam, ctry., Asia. — E9 48
Northville, N.Y., U.S. — G2 110
North-West, state, S. Afr. — E7 70
North West Bluff, c., Monts. — D3 105a
North West Cape, c., Austl. — D2 74
North-West Frontier, state, Pak. — A4 54
Northwest Miramichi, stm., N.B., Can. — C10 110
Northwest Pacific Basin, unds. — F18 142
Northwest Providence Channel, strt., Bah. — m17 104f
Northwest Territories, state, Can. — C6 106
North Wichita, stm., Tx., U.S. — H9 128
North Wilkesboro, N.C., U.S. — H4 114
North Windham, Me., U.S. — G6 110
Northwood, Ia., U.S. — H5 118
Northwood, N.D., U.S. — G16 124
North York, ngh., On., Can. — E10 112
North York Moors National Park, p.o.i., Eng., U.K. — G12 12
North Zulch, Tx., U.S. — G2 122
Norton, Ks., U.S. — B9 128
Norton, Va., U.S. — H3 114
Norton Shores, Mi., U.S. — E3 112
Norton Sound, strt., Ak., U.S. — D6 140
Nortonville, Ks., U.S. — E2 120
Norvegia, Cape, c., Ant. — C3 81
Norwalk, Ct., U.S. — C12 114
Norwalk, Ia., U.S. — C4 120
Norwalk, Oh., U.S. — C3 114
Norway, Ia., U.S. — C6 120
Norway, Me., U.S. — F6 110
Norway, ctry., Eur. — E8 8
Norway Bay, b., Nu., Can. — A10 106
Norway House, Mb., Can. — E11 106
Norwegian Basin, unds. — B13 144
Norwegian Sea, s., Eur. — C3 30
Norwich, Eng., U.K. — E9 112
Norwich, Eng., U.K. — I14 12
Norwich, Ct., U.S. — C13 114
Norwich, N.Y., U.S. — B10 114
Norwood, On., Can. — D11 112
Norwood, Co., U.S. — E8 132
Norwood, La., U.S. — B14 114
Norwood, Mn., U.S. — G5 118
Norwood, N.C., U.S. — A5 116
Norwood, Oh., U.S. — E1 114
Noshiro, Japan — D13 38
Nosop (Nossob), stm., Afr. — D5 70
Nosovaja, Russia — B26 8
Nosovščina, Russia — E17 8
Nossa Senhora das Dores, Braz. — F7 88
Nossob (Nosop), stm., Afr. — D5 70
Nosy-Varika, Madag. — E8 68
Notasulga, Al., U.S. — E13 122
Notch Hill, B.C., Can. — F11 138
Noteć, stm., Pol. — D11 16
Notikewin, stm., Ab., Can. — D7 106
Notios Aigaíos, state, Grc. — G9 28
Noto, Italy — H9 24
Noto, Japan — B10 40
Noto, Golfo di, b., Italy — H9 24
Noto-hantō, pen., Japan — B10 40
Notozero, ozero, l., Russia — C14 8
Notre-Dame, N.B., Can. — D12 110
Notre-Dame, Monts, mts., Qc., Can. — B9 110
Notre Dame Bay, b., Nf., Can. — j22 107a
Notre-Dame-du-Laus, Qc., Can. — B14 112
Notrees, Tx., U.S. — C5 130
Nottawasaga, stm., On., Can. — D10 112
Nottawasaga Bay, b., On., Can. — D9 112
Nottaway, stm., Qc., Can. — E15 106
Nottingham, Eng., U.K. — I11 12
Nottingham Island, i., Nu., Can. — C15 106
Nottoway, stm., Va., U.S. — H8 114
Notukeu Creek, stm., Sk., Can. — E6 124
Notwane, stm., Afr. — D8 70
Nouâdhibou, Maur. — E1 64
Nouâdhibou, Râs, c., Afr. — E1 64
Nouakchott, Maur. — F1 64
Nouâmghâr, Maur. — F1 64
Nouméa, N. Cal. — n16 79d
Noupoort, S. Afr. — G7 70
Nouveau-Québec, Cratère du, crat., Qc., Can. — C16 106
Nouvelle, Qc., Can. — B10 110
Nouvelle-Calédonie (New Caledonia), i., N. Cal. — m15 79d
Nouvelle-Écosse see Nova Scotia, state, Can. — G18 106
Nouvelle-France, Cap de, c., Qc., Can. — C16 106
Nova Andradina, Braz. — D6 90
Nová Baňa, Slov. — H14 16

Nova Caipemba, Ang. — B1 68
Nova Friburgo, Braz. — L4 88
Nova Gorica, Slvn. — D10 22
Nova Gradiška, Cro. — E14 22
Nova Granada, Braz. — K1 88
Nova Iguaçu, Braz. — L4 88
Nova Ladoga, Russia — F14 8
Novaja Maluksa, Russia — A14 10
Novaja Sibir', ostrov, i., Russia — B19 34
Novaja Zemlja, is., Russia — B8 30
Nova Kakhovka, Ukr. — E4 32
Nova Lamego, Gui.-B. — G2 64
Nova Lima, Braz. — K4 88
Novalukoml', Bela. — F11 10
Nova Mambone, Moz. — B12 70
Nova Olinda, Braz. — D6 88
Nova Paka, Czech Rep. — F11 16
Nova Ponte, Braz. — J2 88
Nova Prata, Braz. — D12 92
Novara, Italy — E5 22
Nova Russas, Braz. — C5 88
Nova Scotia, state, Can. — G18 106
Nova Soure, Braz. — F6 88
Novato, Ca., U.S. — E3 134
Nova Venécia, Braz. — J5 88
Nova Vida, Braz. — F5 84
Novaya Kazanka, Kaz. — E7 32
Novaya Zemlya see Novaya Zemlja, is., Russia — B8 30
Nova Zagora, Blg. — G13 26
Nové Hrady, Czech Rep. — H10 16
Novelda, Spain — F10 20
Nové Město nad Váhom, Slov. — H13 16
Nové Zámky, Slov. — I14 16
Novgorod, Russia — B14 10
Novgorodskaja oblast', co., Russia — B15 10
Novi Bečej, Serb. — D7 26
Novi Beograd, Serb. — E7 26
Novice, Tx., U.S. — C8 130
Novigrad, Cro. — E10 22
Novikovo, Russia — G17 34
Novi Ligure, Italy — F5 22
Novinger, Mo., U.S. — D5 120
Novi Pazar, Blg. — F14 26
Novi Pazar, Serb. — F7 26
Novi Sad, Serb. — D6 26
Novo, Lago, l., Braz. — C7 84
Novo Airão, Braz. — H11 86
Novoaltajsk, Russia — D14 32
Novo Aripuanã, Braz. — E5 84
Novočerkassk, Russia — E6 32
Novodvinsk, Russia — D19 8
Novoe, Russia — C11 32
Novoeniseysk, Russia — C16 32
Novo Hamburgo, Braz. — D12 92
Novo Horizonte, Braz. — K1 88
Novoizborsk, Russia — C10 10
Novokačalinsk, Russia — B10 38
NovokašČirsk, Russia — F21 10
Novokazalinsk see Zhangaqazaly, Kaz. — E10 32
Novokujbyševsk, Russia — D7 32
Novokuzneck, Russia — D15 32
Novolazarevskaja, sci., Ant. — C6 81
Novo Mesto, Slvn. — E12 22
Novomoskovsk (Stalinogorsk), Russia — F21 10
Novo Oriente, Braz. — C5 88
Novopetrovskoe, Russia — E19 10
Novorossijsk, Russia — F5 32
Novorybnoe, Russia — B10 34
Novoržev, Russia — C12 10
Novošahtinsk, Russia — E6 32
Novoselytsia, Ukr. — A13 26
Novoselʺje, Russia — C14 10
Novosergievka, Russia — D8 32
Novosibirsk, Russia — D14 32
Novosibirskie ostrova, is., Russia — A18 34
Novosibirskoe vodohranilišče, res., Russia — D14 32
Novosilʹsʹke, Ukr. — D15 26
Novosokolʹniki, Russia — D12 10
Novotroick, Russia — D9 32
Novouzensk, Russia — D7 32
Novovjatsk, Russia — C7 32
Novozavidovskij, Russia — D19 10
Novozybkov, Russia — H14 10
Novska, Cro. — E13 22
Nový Bohumín, Czech Rep. — G14 16
Nový Bor, Czech Rep. — F10 16
Novja Valosavyči, Bela. — F11 10
Nový Jičín, Czech Rep. — G13 16
Nový Nekouz, Russia — C20 10
Novyj Port, Russia — A12 32
Novyj Uzenʹ see Zhangaözen, Kaz. — F8 32
Novyj Vasjugan, Russia — C13 32
Nowa Pahost, Bela. — E10 10
Nowa Ruda, Pol. — F12 16
Nowa Sól, Pol. — E11 16
Nowe, Pol. — C14 16
Nowe Miasto nad Pilicą, Pol. — E16 16
Nowendoc, Austl. — H8 76
Nowgong, India — F7 54
Nowitna, stm., Ak., U.S. — D9 140
Nowogard, Pol. — C11 16
Nowogrodziec, Pol. — E11 16
Nowood, stm., Wy., U.S. — C5 126
Nowra, Austl. — J8 76
Nowrangapur, India — B6 53
Nowshak, mtn., Asia — B11 56
Nowshera, Pak. — B4 54
Nowy Dwór Mazowiecki, Pol. — D16 16
Nowy Sącz, Pol. — G16 16
Nowy Sącz, state, Pol. — G16 16
Nowy Staw, Pol. — B15 16
Nowy Targ, Pol. — G15 16
Noxapater, Ms., U.S. — E9 122
Noxen, Pa., U.S. — C9 114
Noxubee, stm., U.S. — D10 122
Noy, stm., Laos — D7 48
Noya see Noia, Spain — B2 20
Noyant, Fr. — G9 14
Noyon, Fr. — E11 14
Nsanje, Mwi. — D6 68
Nsawam, Ghana — H4 64
Nsok, Eq. Gui. — I7 64
Nsukka, Nig. — H6 64
Nsuta, Ghana — H4 64
Ntwetwe Pan, pl., Bots. — B7 70
Nu see Salween, stm., Asia. — C8 46
Nūbah, Jibāl an-, mts., Sudan. — E6 62
Nubian Desert, des., Sudan — C6 62
Ñuble, stm., Chile — H2 92
Nudolʹ-Šarino, Russia — D19 10
Nueces, stm., Tx., U.S. — G10 130
Nueces Plains, pl., Tx., U.S. — F8 130
Nueltin Lake, l., Can. — C11 106
Nuestra Señora de Talavera, Arg. — B6 92
Nueva, Isla, i., Chile — K3 90
Nueva Antioquia, Col. — D7 86
Nueva Ciudad Guerrero, Mex. — B9 100
Nueva Esparta, state, Ven. — B9 86
Nueva Galia, Arg. — G5 92
Nueva Germania, Para. — A9 92
Nueva Gerona, Cuba — B6 102
Nueva Imperial, Chile — G2 90
Nueva Italia de Ruiz, Mex. — F7 100
Nueva Loja, Ec. — G3 86
Nueva Palmira, Ur. — F8 92
Nueva Rosita, Mex. — A8 100

Nueva San Salvador, El Sal. — F3 102
Nueva Toltén, Chile — G2 90
Nueve, Canal Numero, can., Arg. — H8 92
Nueve de Julio, Arg. — G7 92
Nuevitas, Cuba — B9 102
Nuevo, Bajo, unds., Col. — E8 102
Nuevo, Cayo, i., Mex. — E12 100
Nuevo, Golfo, b., Arg. — H4 90
Nuevo Camarón, Mex. — G8 130
Nuevo Casas Grandes, Mex. — F9 98
Nuevo Delicias, Mex. — B7 100
Nuevo Laredo, Mex. — B9 100
Nuevo León, state, Mex. — B8 100
Nuevo Primero de Mayo, Mex. — H9 130
Nuevo Progreso, Mex. — F12 100
Nuevo Rocafuerte, Ec. — H4 86
Nuevo San Lucas, Mex. — F2 130
Nûgssuaq, pen., Grnld. — C15 141
Nugu, res., India — F3 53
Nui, at., Tuvalu — D8 72
Nuku'alofa, Tonga — n14 78e
Nukuhu, Pap. N. Gui. — b4 79a
Nukus, Uzb. — F9 32
Nul, Vanuatu — k17 79d
Nulato, Ak., U.S. — D8 140
Nueva Casa de Juárez, Mex. — G10 100
Nullagine, Austl. — D4 74
Nullarbor, Austl. — F6 74
Nullarbor Plain, pl., Austl. — F5 74
Numan, Nig. — H7 64
Numancia (Numantia), sci., Spain. — C8 20
Numantia see Numancia, sci., Spain. — C8 20
Numata, Japan — C12 40
Numazu, Japan — D11 40
Numfoor, Pulau, i., Indon. — F10 44
Numto, Russia — B12 32
Nunavut, state, Can. — B12 106
Nunda, N.Y., U.S. — B7 114
Nuneaton, Eng., U.K. — I11 12
Nuñez, Cape, c., S. Geor. — J9 90
Nunivak Island, i., Ak., U.S. — D6 140
Nunjiang, China — B10 36
Nunkun, mtn., India — A6 54
Nunnelly, Tn., U.S. — I10 120
Nuomin, stm., China. — B10 36
Nuoro, Italy — D3 24
Nuqui, Col. — E3 86
Nura, Kaz. — E12 32
Nura, stm., Kaz. — E12 32
Nur Dağları, mts., Tur. — B7 58
Nuremberg see Nürnberg, Ger. — G6 16
Nuremberg see Nürnberg, Ger. — G6 16
Nuriootpa, Austl. — J2 76
Nürnberg (Nuremberg), Ger. — G6 16
Nürpur, India — B5 54
Nürtingen, Ger. — H5 16
Nusa Tenggara Barat, state, Indon. — G10 50
Nusa Tenggara Timur, state, Indon. — H12 50
Nusayrīyah, Jabal an-, mts., Syria — C7 58
Nu Shan, mts., China — F4 36
Nūshan Hu, l., China. — G15 34
Nushki, Pak. — D10 56
Nutrioso, Az., U.S. — J7 132
Nutter Fort, W.V., U.S. — E5 114
Nuuk see Godthåb, Grnld. — E15 141
Nuwerus, S. Afr. — G4 70
Nuweveldberge, mts., S. Afr. — H5 70
Núzvid, India — C5 53
Nyabéssan, Cam. — D2 66
Nyabing, Austl. — F3 74
Nyack, N.Y., U.S. — C12 114
Nyahanga, Tan. — E6 66
Nyainqêntanglha Feng, mtn., China — C13 54
Nyainqêntanglha Shan, mts., China. — C6 46
Nyainrong, China — E14 54
Nyakanazi, Tan. — E6 66
Nyala, Sudan — E5 62
Nyalam, China — D10 54
Nyamlell, Sudan — F5 62
Nyamtumbo, Tan. — G7 66
Nyang, stm., China — D14 54
Nyanga, stm., Afr. — J7 64
Nyasa, Lake, l., Afr. — C5 68
Nyaunglebin, Mya. — C3 48
Nyboe Land, reg., Grnld. — A14 141
Nyborg, Den. — I4 8
Nybro, Swe. — H6 8
Nyda, Russia — A12 32
Nyêmo, China — E13 54
Nyeri, Kenya — E7 66
Nyerol, Sudan — F6 62
Nyimba, Zam. — C5 68
Nyingchi, China — F3 36
Nyírbátor, Hung. — B9 26
Nyíregyháza, Hung. — B8 26
Nykøbing, Den. — I4 8
Nyköping, Swe. — G7 8
Nylstroom, S. Afr. — D9 70
Nymboida, stm., Austl. — G9 76
Nymburk, Czech Rep. — F11 16
Nynäshamn, Swe. — G7 8
Nyngan, Austl. — H6 76
Nyong, stm., Cam. — D2 66
Nyons, Fr. — E11 14
Nýrsko, Czech Rep. — G9 16
Nyrud, Nor. — B13 8
Nysa, Russia — F17 34
Nysa, Pol. — F13 16
Nysa Kłodzka, stm., Pol. — F12 16
Nysa Łużycka (Lausitzer Neisse), stm., Eur. — E10 16
Nyslott see Savonlinna, Fin. — F13 8
Nysted, Den. — B7 16
Nyunzu, D.R.C. — F5 66
Nyvrovo, Russia — F17 34
Nzébéla, Gui. — H3 64
Nzérékoré, Gui. — H3 64
N'zeto, Ang. — B1 68
Nzwani, i., Com. — C7 68

O

Oahe, Lake, res., U.S. — A12 126
Oahe Dam, dam, S.D., U.S. — C12 126
O'ahu, i., Hi., U.S. — a3 78a
Oakbank, Austl. — I3 76
Oak Bay, B.C., Can. — H7 138
Oak Bluffs, Ma., U.S. — C15 114
Oakburn, Mb., Can. — D13 124
Oak City, N.C., U.S. — I8 114
Oak City, Ut., U.S. — D4 132
Oakdale, Ca., U.S. — F5 134
Oakdale, La., U.S. — G6 122
Oakdale, Ne., U.S. — E14 126
Oakes, N.D., U.S. — A14 126
Oakesdale, Wa., U.S. — C9 136
Oakey, Austl. — F8 76
Oakfield, Wi., U.S. — H10 118
Oak Grove, La., U.S. — E7 122
Oak Harbor, Wa., U.S. — B4 136
Oak Hill, Fl., U.S. — H5 116
Oak Hill, Oh., U.S. — F3 114
Oak Hill, W.V., U.S. — G4 114
Oakhurst, Ca., U.S. — F6 134
Oak Knolls, Ca., U.S. — I5 134
Oak Lake, l., Mb., Can. — E13 124
Oak Lake, l., On., Can. — A5 118
Oakland, Ia., U.S. — C2 120
Oakland, Md., U.S. — E6 114
Oakland, Me., U.S. — F7 110
Oakland, Ms., U.S. — C9 122
Oakland, Ne., U.S. — C1 120
Oakland, Or., U.S. — G3 136
Oakland City, In., U.S. — F10 120
Oakland Park, Fl., U.S. — J5 116
Oak Lawn, Il., U.S. — G2 112
Oakley, Id., U.S. — H13 136
Oakley, Ks., U.S. — B8 128
Oakman, Al., U.S. — D11 122
Oakohay Creek, stm., Ms., U.S. — F9 122
Oakover, stm., Austl. — D4 74
Oak Park, Il., U.S. — G2 112
Oak Ridge, Tn., U.S. — H1 114
Oak Ridge National Laboratory, sci., Tn., U.S. — H1 114
Oakton, In., U.S. — F10 120
Oak View, Ca., U.S. — I6 134
Oakville, Mb., Can. — E15 124
Oakville, On., Can. — E10 112
Oakwood, Oh., U.S. — C1 114
Oamaru, N.Z. — G4 80
Oancea, Rom. — D14 26
Ōarai, Japan — C13 40
Oatman, Az., U.S. — H2 132
Oaxaca, state, Mex. — G10 100
Oaxaca de Juárez, Mex. — G10 100
Ob', stm., Russia. — A11 32
Obabika Lake, l., On., Can. — A9 112
Obaghan, stm., Kaz. — D10 32
Obal', stm., Bela. — E12 10
Obala, Cam. — D2 66
Obama, Japan — D8 40
Obama, Japan — G3 40
Oban, Austl. — C2 76
Oban, Scot., U.K. — E7 12
Obanazawa, Japan — A13 40
O Barco de Valdeorras, Spain. — B3 20
Ob Bay see Obskaja guba, b., Russia — A12 32
Obed, Ab., Can. — C13 138
Obeliai, Lith. — E8 10
Oberá, Arg. — C10 92
Oberhausen, Ger. — E2 16
Oberlin, La., U.S. — G6 122
Oberlin, Oh., U.S. — C3 114
Oberösterreich, state, Aus. — B10 22
Oberpullendorf, Aus. — C13 22
Oberursel, Ger. — F4 16
Oberviechtach, Ger. — G8 16
Ob Gulf see Obskaja guba, b., Russia — A12 32
Obi, Kepulauan, is., Indon. — F8 44
Obi, Pulau, i., Indon. — F8 44
Obi, Selat, strt., Indon. — F8 44
Óbidos, Braz. — D6 84
Obihiro, Japan — C15 38
Obi Islands see Obi, Kepulauan, is., Indon. — F8 44
Obion, Tn., U.S. — H8 120
Obion, stm., Tn., U.S. — H8 120
Obion, Middle Fork, stm., Tn., U.S. — H9 120
Oblačnaja, gora, mtn., Russia — C11 38
Oblong, Il., U.S. — F9 120
Obluče, Russia — G15 34
Obninsk, Russia — E19 10
Obo, C.A.R. — C4 66
Obock, Dji. — E8 62
Obokote, D.R.C. — E5 66
Obozërskij, Russia — E19 8
O'Brien, Or., U.S. — A2 134
Obrovac, Cro. — F12 22
Obša, stm., Russia — E16 10
Obuasi, Ghana — H4 64
Obudu, Nig. — H6 64
Ocala, Fl., U.S. — G3 116
Ocamo, stm., Ven. — F9 86
Ocampo, Mex. — A4 100
Ocaña, Col. — C5 86
Ocaña, Spain — E7 20
Occhito, Lago di, res., Italy — C8 24
Occidental, Cordillera, mts., Col. — E3 86
Oceana, W.V., U.S. — G4 114
Ocean Cape, c., Ak., U.S. — E12 140
Ocean City, Md., U.S. — F10 114
Ocean City, N.J., U.S. — E11 114
Ocean Falls, B.C., Can. — D3 138
Ocean Island see Banaba, i., Kir. — D7 72
Ocean Park, Wa., U.S. — D2 136
Oceanside, Ca., U.S. — J8 134
Ocean Springs, Ms., U.S. — G10 122
Ocheyedan, Ia., U.S. — H3 118
Ochi, Japan — E7 40
Ochlockonee, Ga., U.S. — F1 116
Ochlockonee, stm., U.S. — G14 122
Ocho Rios, Jam. — i13 104d
Ochsenfurt, Ger. — G5 16
Ocilla, Ga., U.S. — E2 116
Ockelbo, Swe. — F7 8
Ocmulgee National Monument, p.o.i., Ga., U.S. — D2 116
Ocniţa, Mol. — A14 26
Ocoa, Bahía de, b., Dom. Rep. — C12 102
Ocoee, Fl., U.S. — H4 116
Ocoña, Peru — G3 84
Oconee, stm., Ga., U.S. — D3 116
Oconee, Lake, res., Ga., U.S. — C2 116
Oconomowoc, Wi., U.S. — A9 120
Oconto, Wi., U.S. — D2 112
Oconto Falls, Wi., U.S. — D1 112
Ocosingo, Mex. — G12 100
Ocotal, Nic. — F4 102
Ocotes, Cerro, mtn., Mex. — B5 100
Ocotlán, Mex. — E7 100
Ocotlán de Morelos, Mex. — G10 100
Ococacuautla, Mex. — G12 100
Ocracoke Island, i., N.C., U.S. — A10 116
Ocumare del Tuy, Ven. — B8 86
Oda, Ghana — H4 64
Ōda, Japan — D5 40
Ōda, Jabal, mtn., Sudan. — C7 62
Odaka, Japan — B14 40
Ōdate, Japan — D14 38
Odawara, Japan — D12 40
Odebolt, Ia., U.S. — B2 120
Odei, stm., Mb., Can. — D12 106
Odell, Il., U.S. — C9 120
Odell, Tx., U.S. — G10 128
Odemira, Port. — G2 20
Ödemiş, Tur. — E10 28
Odendaalsrus, S. Afr. — E8 70
Odense, Den. — I3 8
Odenwald, mts., Ger. — G4 16
Oder (Odra), stm., Eur. — D10 16
Oderzo, Italy — E9 22
Odesa, Ukr. — C17 32
Odesa, co., Ukr. — C16 26
Odessa see Odesa, Ukr. — C17 32
Odessa, Tx., U.S. — C5 130
Odessa, Wa., U.S. — C8 136
Odesskoe, Russia — D12 32
Odiel, stm., Spain — G4 20
Odienné, C. Iv. — H3 64
Odin, Mount, mtn., B.C., Can. — F12 138
Odincovo, Russia — E20 10
Odobești, Rom. — D13 26
Odolanów, Pol. — E13 16
O'Donnell, Tx., U.S. — B6 130
Odorheiu Secuiesc, Rom. — C12 26
Odra (Oder), stm., Eur. — D10 16
Odrzywół, Pol. — E16 16

Odum, Ga., U.S. — E3 116
Odžaci, Serb. — D6 26
Oebisfelde, Ger. — D6 16
Oeiras, Braz. — D4 88
Oelsnitz, Ger. — F8 16
Oelwein, Ia., U.S. — B6 120
Oenpelli, Austl. — B6 74
Oetz, Aus. — C7 22
O'Fallon, Mo., U.S. — F7 120
Ofanto, stm., Italy — C9 24
Ofaqim, Isr. — G5 58
Offa, Nig. — H5 64
Offaly, state, Ire. — H5 12
Offenbach am Main, Ger. — F4 16
Offenburg, Ger. — H3 16
Oficina Alemania, Chile — B3 92
Ofu, i., Am. Sam. — h13 79c
Ogaden, reg., Afr. — F8 62
Ōgaki, Japan — D9 40
Ogallala, Ne., U.S. — F11 126
Ogan, stm., Indon. — E4 50
Ogasawara-guntō, is., Japan. — G18 30
Ogatsu, Japan — A14 40
Ogawa, Japan — G3 40
Ogbomosho, Nig. — H5 64
Ogden, Ks., U.S. — B12 128
Ogden, Ut., U.S. — B5 132
Ogdensburg, N.Y., U.S. — D14 112
Ogeechee, stm., Ga., U.S. — D4 116
Ogema, Sk., Can. — E8 124
Ogidaki Mountain, hill, On., Can. — A6 112
Ogilvie, Mn., U.S. — F5 118
Ogilvie Mountains, mts., Yk., Can. — C3 106
Oglesby, Il., U.S. — C9 120
Oglethorpe, Ga., U.S. — D1 116
Ogliastra, reg., Italy. — E3 24
Oglio, stm., Italy — E6 22
Ogmore, Austl. — D7 76
Ognon, stm., Fr. — G15 14
Ogoja, Nig. — H6 64
Ogoki, stm., On., Can. — E13 106
Ogooué, stm., Afr. — I7 64
Ogōri, Japan — E4 40
Ogosta, stm., Blg. — F10 26
Ogre, Lat. — D7 10
Ogre, stm., Lat. — D8 10
O Grove, Spain — B2 20
Ogulin, Cro. — E12 22
Ogunquit, Me., U.S. — G6 110
Ogurdžaly, ostrov, i., Turkmen. — A12 32
Oğuzeli, Tur. — B8 58
Oha, Russia — F17 34
Ohanet, Alg. — D6 64
Ohara, Japan — D13 40
O'Higgins, Cabo, c., Chile. — e30 78l
O'Higgins, Lago (San Martín, Lago), l., S.A. — I2 90
Ohio, state, U.S. — D3 114
Ohio, stm., U.S. — G9 120
Ohio Peak, mtn., Co., U.S. — E9 132
'Ohonua, Tonga — o15 78e
Ohoopee, stm., Ga., U.S. — D3 116
Ohota, stm., Russia — E17 34
Ohotsk, Russia — E17 34
Ohře, stm., Eur. — F9 16
Ohrid, Mac. — B3 28
Ohrid, Lake, l., Eur. — D14 24
Ohrigstad, S. Afr. — D10 70
Ohuira, Bahía de, b., Mex. — C4 100
Ōi, stm., Japan — E11 40
Oiapoque, Braz. — C7 84
Oiapoque (Oyapok), stm., S.A. — C7 84
Oies, Île aux, i., Qc., Can. — C6 110
Oil Center, N.M., U.S. — B4 130
Oil City, Pa., U.S. — C5 114
Oildale, Ca., U.S. — H7 134
Oilton, Ok., U.S. — A2 122
Oilton, Tx., U.S. — G9 130
Oil Trough, Ar., U.S. — B7 122
Oise, state, Fr. — E11 14
Oise, stm., Fr. — E11 14
Ōita, Japan — F4 40
Ōita, state, Japan — F4 40
Oituz, Pasul, p., Rom. — C13 26
Ojat', stm., Russia. — F16 8
Ōje, Swe. — F5 8
Ojinaga, Mex. — A6 100
Ojmjakon, Russia — D18 34
Ojmur, stm., i., Russia — F10 34
Ojocaliente, Mex. — D7 100
Ojo de la Casa, Mex. — C1 130
Ojo del Carrizo, Mex. — E2 130
Ojo de Liebre, Laguna, b., Mex. — B1 100
Ojos del Salado, Nevado, mtn., S.A. — C3 92
Ojos Negros, Mex. — L9 134
Oka, stm., Russia — D18 32
Oka, stm., Russia — D6 32
Okaba, Indon. — G10 44
Okahandja, Nmb. — B3 70
Okaihau, N.Z. — B5 80
Okak Islands, is., Nf., Can. — F13 141
Okanagan (Okanogan), stm., N.A. — G11 138
Okanagan Falls, B.C., Can. — G11 138
Okanagan Lake, l., B.C., Can. — G10 138
Okanagan Landing, B.C., Can. — F11 138
Okanogan, Wa., U.S. — B7 136
Okanogan (Okanagan), stm., N.A. — G11 138
Okanogan Range, mts., N.A. — A6 136
Ōkara, India — C4 54
Okaukuejo, Nmb. — D2 68
Okavango (Cubango), stm., Afr. — D2 68
Okavango Delta, Bots. — D3 68
Okawa, Japan — F3 40
Okawville, Il., U.S. — F8 120
Okaya, Japan — C11 40
Okayama, Japan — E6 40
Okayama, state, Japan — E6 40
Okazaki, Japan — E10 40
Okeechobee, Fl., U.S. — I5 116
Okeechobee, Lake, l., Fl., U.S. — J5 116
Okeene, Ok., U.S. — E10 128
Okefenokee Swamp, sw., U.S. — F3 116
Okemos, Mi., U.S. — B1 114
Okene, Nig. — H6 64
Okhaldunga, Nepal — E11 54
Okhotsk, Sea of, s., Asia. — E16 34
Okhotsk Basin, unds. — D17 142
Okhtyrka, Ukr. — D4 32
Okiep, S. Afr. — F3 70
Okinawa, Japan — l18 39a
Okinawa Island see Okinawa-jima, i., Japan. — l19 39a
Okinawa-jima, i., Japan. — l19 39a
Okinawa-shotō, is., Japan. — l19 39a
Okino-Erabu-shima, i., Japan — k19 39a
Oki-shotō, is., Japan. — C6 40
Okitipupa, Nig. — H5 64
Oklahoma, state, U.S. — F11 128
Oklahoma City, U.S. — F11 128
Oklawaha, Fl., U.S. — G12 122
Oklawaha, stm., Fl., U.S. — H4 116
Okmulgee, Ok., U.S. — B2 122
Okoja, Ug. — D6 66
Okollo, Ug. — D6 66
Okolona, Ar., U.S. — D5 122
Okolona, Ms., U.S. — D10 122

Okondja, Gabon. — E2 66
Okonek, Pol. — C12 16
Okotoks, Ab., Can. — F16 138
Okoyo, Congo. — E2 66
Oktjabr', Russia — C20 10
Oktjabr'skij, Russia — D8 32
Oktjabr'skij, Russia — F14 34
Oktjabr'skij, Russia — G21 8
Oktjabr'skij, Russia — F20 8
Oktjabr'skoe, Russia — B10 32
Oktyabr'skiy, Kaz. — G3 40
Oktyabr'skoe, Russia — D11 32
Ōkuchi, Japan — G3 40
Okulovka, Russia — B16 10
Okuněv Nos, Russia — C25 8
Okushiri-tō, i., Japan — C13 38
Okuta, Nig. — H5 64
Okwa, stm., Afr. — C6 70
Ola, Ar., U.S. — B5 122
Ólafsfjördur, Ice. — j30 8a
Olancha, Ca., U.S. — G8 134
Olancha Peak, mtn., Ca., U.S. — G7 134
Olanchito, Hond. — E4 102
Öland, i., Swe. — H7 8
Olanta, S.C., U.S. — C6 116
Olary, Austl. — I3 76
Olathe, Co., U.S. — E8 132
Olathe, Ks., U.S. — F3 120
Olavarría, Arg. — H7 92
Oława (Ohlau), Pol. — F13 16
Olbia, Italy — D3 24
Olcott, N.Y., U.S. — E11 112
Old Castille see Castilla la Vieja, hist. reg., Spain — C7 20
Old Cork, Austl. — D3 76
Old Crow, Yk., Can. — C12 140
Old Crow, stm., N.A. — C11 140
Olden, Tx., U.S. — B9 130
Oldenburg, Ger. — C4 16
Oldenburg in Holstein, Ger. — B6 16
Oldenzaal, Neth. — B15 14
Old Faithful Geyser, gysr., Wy., U.S. — F16 136
Old Forge, Pa., U.S. — C10 114
Old Fort Bay see Vieux-Fort, Qc., Can. — i22 107a
Oldham, Eng., U.K. — H10 12
Oldham, S.D., U.S. — C15 126
Old Harbor, Ak., U.S. — E9 140
Old Harbour, Jam. — j13 104d
Old Hickory Lake, res., Tn., U.S. — H11 120
Oldman, stm., Ab., Can. — G19 138
Old Mkushi, Zam. — C4 68
Old Norwood, Monts. — D3 105a
Old Road, Antig. — f4 105b
Old Road Bluff, c., Antig. — f4 105b
Old Road Town, St. K./N. — C2 105a
Olds, Ab., Can. — E16 138
Old Saybrook, Ct., U.S. — C13 114
Old Speck Mountain, mtn., Me., U.S. — F5 110
Old Tate, Bots. — B8 70
Old Town, Me., U.S. — F8 110
Olduvai Gorge, val., Tan. — E7 66
Old Wives Lake, l., Sk., Can. — D8 124
O'Lean, N.Y., U.S. — B7 114
O'Leary, P.E., Can. — D12 110
Olecko, Pol. — B18 16
Olëkma, stm., Russia — E13 34
Olëkminsk, Russia — D13 34
Olëkminskij Stanovik, mts., Russia. — F12 34
Olenegorsk, Russia — B15 8
Olenëk, stm., Russia — C11 34
Olenëk, stm., Russia — C12 34
Olenëkskij zaliv, b., Russia — B13 34
Olenino, Russia — D16 10
Oléron, Île d', i., Fr. — D4 18
Oleśnica, Pol. — E13 16
Olesno, Pol. — F14 16
Ol'ga, Russia — C11 38
Olgastretet, strt., Nor. — B30 141
Ölgiy, Mong. — E16 32
Olhão, Port. — G3 20
Olho d'Água das Flores, Braz. — E7 88
Ol'hon, ostrov, i., Russia — F10 34
Olib, Otok, i., Cro. — F11 22
Olifants (Elefantes), stm., S. Afr. — D10 70
Olifants, stm., S. Afr. — H6 70
Olifants, stm., S. Afr. — H4 70
Olifantshoek, S. Afr. — E6 70
Ólimbos (Olympus), mtn., Cyp. — C3 58
Olímpia, Braz. — K1 88
Olimpia, Ia., U.S. — B6 120
Olin, Ia., U.S. — B6 120
Olinda, Braz. — D8 88
Olinda, Austl. — C4 76
Olite, Spain — B9 20
Oliva, Arg. — F5 92
Oliva, Spain — F10 20
Oliva de la Frontera, Spain. — F3 20
Olivares, Cerro de, mtn., S.A. — E2 92
Olive Branch, Ms., U.S. — C9 122
Olivees Mountain, mtn., St. K./N. — C2 105a
Olive Hill, Ky., U.S. — F2 114
Olivehurst, Ca., U.S. — D4 134
Oliveira, Braz. — K3 88
Oliveira dos Brejinhos, Braz. — G4 88
Olivenza, Spain — F3 20
Oliver Springs, Tn., U.S. — H13 120
Olivet, Mi., U.S. — B1 114
Olji Moron, stm., China. — B4 38
Oljutorskij, myc, c., Russia — E23 34
Oljutorskij zaliv, b., Russia — D22 34
Olla, La., U.S. — F6 122
Ollagüe, Chile — D3 90
Ollagüe, Volcán, vol., S.A. — D3 90
Öllei, Palau — f8 78b
Olmedo, Spain — C6 20
Olney, Mt., U.S. — B12 136
Olney, Tx., U.S. — H10 128
Olomouc, Czech Rep. — G13 16
Olongapo, Phil. — C2 52
Oloron-Sainte-Marie, Fr. — F5 18
Olot, Spain — B13 20
Olovjannaja, Russia — F12 34
Olsztyn, Pol. — C16 16
Olsztyn, state, Pol. — C16 16
Olt, stm., Rom. — E11 26
Olt, stm., Rom. — D11 26
Olten, Switz. — C4 18
Olteni, Rom. — E12 26
Olteniţa, Rom. — E13 26
Olton, Tx., U.S. — G6 128
Oluan Pi, c., Tai. — K9 42
Olustee, Fl., U.S. — F3 116
Olutanga Island, i., Phil. — G4 52
Olvera, Spain — H5 20
Olympia, Wa., U.S. — C3 136
Olympia, sci., Grc. — F4 28
Olympia see Olympia, sci., Grc. — F4 28
Olympic Mountains, mts., Wa., U.S. — C3 136

I·42 Olympic National Park – Palamós

Name	Map Ref.	Page
Olympic National Park, p.o.i., Wa., U.S.	C3	136
Ólympos (Olympus, Mount), mtn., Grc.	C5	28
Olympus see Ólimbos, mtn., Cyp.	C3	58
Olympus, Mount see Ólympos, mtn., Grc.	C5	28
Olympus, Mount, mtn., Wa., U.S.	C3	136
Om', stm., Russia	D13	32
Ōmachi, Japan	C10	40
Omae-zaki, c., Japan	E11	40
Ōmagari, Japan	E14	38
Omagh, N. Ire., U.K.	G5	12
Omaha, Ne., U.S.	C2	120
Omaha, Tx., U.S.	D4	122
Omaheke, state, Nmb.	C4	70
Omak, Wa., U.S.	B7	136
Oman, ctry., Asia	F8	56
Oman, Gulf of, b., Asia	E8	56
Omaruru, Nmb.	B3	70
Omaruru, stm., Nmb.	B2	70
Omatako, mtn., Nmb.	B3	70
Omatako, stm., Nmb.	B3	70
Omate, Peru	G3	84
Omboué, Gabon	E1	66
Ombrone, stm., Italy	H8	22
Omčak, Russia	D18	34
Omdurman see Umm Durmān, Sudan	D6	62
Ōme, Japan	D12	40
Omega, Ga., U.S.	E2	116
Omegna, Italy	E5	22
Omemee, On., Can.	D11	112
Omeo, Austl.	K6	76
Ömerköy, Tur.	D10	28
Ömerli Barajı, res., Tur.	C12	28
Ometepe, Isla de, i., Nic.	G5	102
Ometepec, Mex.	G9	100
Ōmi-hachiman, Japan	D8	40
Omineca, stm., B.C., Can.	D6	106
Omineca Mountains, mts., B.C., Can.	D5	106
Ōmiya, Japan	D12	40
Ommaney, Cape, c., Ak., U.S.	E13	140
Ommanney Bay, b., Nu., Can.	A10	106
Omo, stm., Afr.	F7	62
Omoloj, stm., Russia	B15	34
Omolon, stm., Russia	C20	34
Omsk, Russia	C12	32
Omsukčan, Russia	D20	34
Omul, Vârful, mtn., Rom.	D12	26
Ōmura, Japan	G2	40
Omurtag, Blg.	F13	26
Ōmuta, Japan	F3	40
Omutinskij, Russia	C11	32
Omutninsk, Russia	C8	32
Onabas, Mex.	A4	100
Onaga, Ks., U.S.	E1	120
Onaman Lake, l., On., Can.	A11	118
Onamia, Mn., U.S.	E5	118
Onangué, Lac, l., Gabon	E1	66
Onaping Lake, l., On., Can.	A8	112
Onarga, Il., U.S.	D10	120
Onatchiway, Lac, res., Qc., Can.	A5	110
Onawa, Ia., U.S.	B1	120
Onaway, Mi., U.S.	C5	112
Oncativo, Arg.	E6	92
Once, Canal Numero, can., Arg.	H8	92
Oncócua, Ang.	D1	68
Onda, Spain	E10	20
Ondangwa, Nmb.	D2	68
Ondas, stm., Braz.	G3	88
Ondava, stm., Slov.	H17	16
Ondjiva, Ang.	D2	68
Ondo, Japan	E5	40
Ondo, Nig.	H5	64
Öndörhaan, Mong.	B7	36
Ondozero, ozero, l., Russia	E15	8
Oneco, Fl., U.S.	I3	116
Onega, Russia	E17	8
Onega, stm., Russia	E18	8
Onega, Lake see Onežskoe ozero, l., Russia	F16	8
Onega Bay see Onežskaja guba, b., Russia.	D17	8
One Hundred and Two, stm., Mo., U.S.	D3	120
One Hundred Fifty Mile House, B.C., Can.	D9	138
One Hundred Mile House, B.C., Can.	E9	138
Oneida, Il., U.S.	C7	120
Oneida, N.Y., U.S.	E14	112
Oneida, Tn., U.S.	H13	120
Oneida Lake, l., N.Y., U.S.	E14	112
O'Neill, Ne., U.S.	E14	126
Onekama, Mi., U.S.	D3	112
Onekotan, ostrov, i., Russia	G20	34
Oneonta, Al., U.S.	D12	122
Oneonta, N.Y., U.S.	B10	114
Onești, Rom.	C13	26
Onevai, i., Tonga	n14	78e
Onežskaja guba (Onega Bay), b., Russia	D17	8
Onežskij poluostrov, pen., Russia	D17	8
Onežskoe ozero (Onega, Lake), l., Russia	F16	8
Ongjin-ŭp, Kor., N.	F6	38
Ongniud Qi, China	C3	38
Ongole, India	D5	53
Onilahy, stm., Madag.	F7	68
Onion Creek, stm., Tx., U.S.	D10	130
Onitsha, Nig.	H6	64
Ōno, Japan	D9	40
Onoda, Japan	F4	40
Onomichi, Japan	E6	40
Onon, Mong.	B7	36
Onon Gol, stm., Asia	G11	34
Onoto, Ven.	C9	86
Onotoa, at., Kir.	D8	72
Onoway, Ab., Can.	C16	138
Ons, Illa de, i., Spain	B1	20
Onset, Ma., U.S.	C15	114
Onslow, Austl.	D3	74
Onslow Bay, b., N.C., U.S.	B8	116
On-take, vol., Japan	H3	40
Ontake-san, vol., Japan	D10	40
Ontario, Ca., U.S.	I8	134
Ontario, Or., U.S.	F10	136
Ontario, state, Can.	E13	106
Ontario, Lake, l., N.A.	E11	112
Ontinyent, Spain	F10	20
Ontojärvi, l., Fin.	D13	8
Ontonagon, Mi., U.S.	E9	118
Ontong Java, at., Sol. Is.	D7	72
Onverwacht, Sur.	B6	84
Oodnadatta, Austl.	E7	74
Ooldea, Austl.	F6	74
Oologah, Ok., U.S.	H2	120
Oologah Lake, res., Ok., U.S.	H2	120
Oorlogskloof, stm., S. Afr.	G4	70
Oos-Londen see East London, S. Afr.	H8	70
Oostburg, Wi., U.S.	E2	112
Oostelijk Flevoland, reg., Neth.	B14	14
Oostende, Bel.	C11	14
Oosterhout, Neth.	C13	14
Oosterschelde, est., Neth.	C12	14
Ootsa Lake, B.C., Can.	C4	138
Ootsa Lake, res., B.C., Can.	C4	138
Opaka, Blg.	F13	26
Opala, D.R.C.	E4	66
Oparino, Russia	G22	8
Opatija, Cro.	E11	22
Opava, Czech Rep.	G13	16
Opawica, stm., Qc., Can.	A2	110
Opečenskij Posad, Russia	B17	10
Opelika, Al., U.S.	E13	122
Opelousas, La., U.S.	G6	122
Opeongo, stm., On., Can.	C12	112
Opeongo Lake, l., On., Can.	C11	112
Ophir, Ak., U.S.	D8	140
Ophir, Or., U.S.	H2	136
Opihikao, Hi., U.S.	d7	78a
Opinaca, stm., Qc., Can.	E15	106
Opiscotéo, Lac, l., Qc., Can.	E17	106
Opobo, Nig.	I6	64
Opočka, Russia	D11	10
Opoczno, Pol.	E16	16
Opole, Pol.	F13	16
Opole, state, Pol.	F13	16
Opotiki, N.Z.	D7	80
Oppdal, Nor.	E3	8
Oppland, state, Nor.	F3	8
Opportunity, Mt., U.S.	D14	136
Opportunity, Wa., U.S.	C9	136
Optima Lake, res., Ok., U.S.	E7	128
Opua, N.Z.	B6	80
Opunake, N.Z.	D5	80
Opuwo, Nmb.	D1	68
Oqsuqtooq (Gjoa Haven), Nu., Can.	B11	106
Oquawka, Il., U.S.	K7	118
Or, Côte d', mts., Fr.	G13	14
Oracle, Az., U.S.	K6	132
Oradea, Rom.	B8	26
Öræfajökull, ice, Ice.	k31	8a
Orahovica, Cro.	E14	22
Orai, India	F7	54
Oraibi Wash, stm., Az., U.S.	H6	132
Oral, Kaz.	D8	32
Oran see Wahran, Alg.	B4	64
Orange, Austl.	I7	76
Orange, Fr.	E10	18
Orange, Ma., U.S.	B13	114
Orange, Tx., U.S.	G5	122
Orange, Va., U.S.	F7	114
Orange (Oranje) (Senqu), stm., Afr.	F3	70
Orange, Cabo, c., Braz.	C7	84
Orangeburg, S.C., U.S.	C4	116
Orange City, Ia., U.S.	A1	120
Orange Cove, Ca., U.S.	G6	134
Orange Free State see Free State, state, S. Afr.	F8	70
Orange Grove, Tx., U.S.	G9	130
Orange Lake, Fl., U.S.	G3	116
Orange Lake, l., Fl., U.S.	G3	116
Orangeville, On., Can.	E9	112
Orangeville, Ut., U.S.	D5	132
Orange Walk, Belize	C3	102
Orango, Ilha de, i., Gui.-B.	G1	64
Orani, Phil.	C3	52
Oranienburg, Ger.	D8	16
Oranje see Orange, stm., Afr.	F3	70
Oranje Gebergte, mts., Sur.	C6	84
Oranjemund, Nmb.	F3	70
Oranjestad, Aruba	o19	104g
Oranjestad, Neth. Ant.	C1	105a
Oranje Vrijstaat see Free State, state, S. Afr.	F8	70
Orăștie, Rom.	D10	26
Orba Co, l., China	A8	54
Orbetello, Italy	H8	22
Órbigo, stm., Spain	B5	20
Orbisonia, Pa., U.S.	D8	114
Orbost, Austl.	K7	76
Örbyhus, Swe.	F7	8
Orcadas, sci., Ant.	B36	81
Orchard City, Co., U.S.	E8	132
Orchard Homes, Mt., U.S.	D12	136
Orchard Mesa, Co., U.S.	E8	132
Orchard Park, N.Y., U.S.	B7	114
Ord, Ne., U.S.	F14	126
Ord, stm., Austl.	C5	74
Ord, Mount, mtn., Austl.	C5	74
Ordenes see Ordes, Spain	A2	20
Orderville, Ut., U.S.	F4	132
Ordes, Spain	A2	20
Ordesa y Monte Perdido, Parque Nacional de, p.o.i., Spain	B10	20
Ord Mountain, mtn., Ca., U.S.	I9	134
Ordos Desert see Mu Us Shamo, des., China	B3	42
Ord River, Austl.	C5	74
Ordu, Tur.	A4	56
Ordway, Co., U.S.	C5	128
Ordžonikidzeabad, Taj.	B10	56
Örebro, Swe.	G6	8
Örebro, state, Swe.	G6	8
Oredež, Russia	B13	10
Oredež, stm., Russia	B13	10
Oregon, Il., U.S.	B8	120
Oregon, Mo., U.S.	D2	120
Oregon, Oh., U.S.	C2	114
Oregon, state, U.S.	G6	136
Oregon Caves National Monument, p.o.i., Or., U.S.	A2	134
Oregon City, Or., U.S.	E4	136
Oregon Dunes National Recreation Area, p.o.i., Or., U.S.	G2	136
Orehovo-Zuevo, Russia	E21	10
Orel, Russia	G18	10
Orel', ozero, l., Russia	F16	34
Orellana, Peru	E2	84
Orellana, state, Ec.	H3	86
Orellana, Embalse de, res., Spain	E5	20
Orem, Ut., U.S.	C5	132
Ore Mountains, mts., Eur.	F8	16
Orenburg, Russia	D8	32
Örencik, Tur.	D12	28
Orense, Arg.	I8	92
Orense see Ourense, Spain	B3	20
Orense see Ourense, co., Spain	B3	20
Oreor, i., Palau	g8	78b
Orestes Pereyra, Mex.	B6	100
Orestiáda, Grc.	B9	28
Orford Ness, c., Eng., U.K.	I14	12
Organ Pipe Cactus National Monument, p.o.i., Az., U.S.	K4	132
Orgelet, Fr.	H14	14
Orgosolo, Italy	D3	24
Orgun, Afg.	C10	56
Orhangazi, Tur.	C12	28
Orhei, Mol.	B15	26
Orhon, stm., Mong.	B5	36
Orichuna, stm., Ven.	D7	86
Orick, Ca., U.S.	B1	134
Orient, Ia., U.S.	C3	120
Orient, Wa., U.S.	B8	136
Oriental, Cordillera, mts., Col.	E5	86
Oriental, Cordillera, mts., Peru	F3	84
Orientos, Austl.	G3	76
Orihuela see Oriola, Spain	F10	20
Orillia, On., Can.	D10	112
Orimattila, Fin.	F11	8
Orinduik, Guy.	E11	86
Orinoco, stm., S.A.	C10	86
Orinoco, Delta del, Ven.	C11	86
Oriola, Spain	F10	20
Orion, Il., U.S.	C7	120
Oriskany, N.Y., U.S.	E14	112
Orissa, state, India	D5	46
Orissaare, Est.	B5	10
Oristano, Italy	E2	24
Oristano, Golfo di, b., Italy	E2	24
Orituco, stm., Ven.	C8	86
Orivesi, l., Fin.	E13	8
Oriximiná, Braz.	D6	84
Orizaba, Mex.	F10	100
Orjahovo, Blg.	F10	26
Orjen, mtn., Serb.	G5	26
Orkney, Sk., Can.	E5	124
Orkney, S. Afr.	E8	70
Orkney Islands, is., Scot., U.K.	C10	12
Orlândia, Braz.	K1	88
Orlando, Fl., U.S.	H4	116
Orléanais, hist. reg., Fr.	F11	14
Orleans, On., Can.	C14	112
Orléans, Fr.	G10	14
Orleans, Ca., U.S.	B2	134
Orleans, Ma., U.S.	C15	114
Orleans, Ne., U.S.	A9	128
Orleans, Vt., U.S.	F4	110
Orléans, Canal d', can., Fr.	G11	14
Orléans, Île d', i., Qc., Can.	D6	110
Orlik, Russia	D18	32
Orlovskaja oblast', co., Russia	H19	10
Orly, Fr.	F11	14
Ormāra, Pak.	D9	56
Ormiston, Sk., Can.	E8	124
Ormoc, Phil.	E5	52
Ormond Beach, Fl., U.S.	G4	116
Ornain, stm., Fr.	F14	14
Ornans, Fr.	G15	14
Orne, state, Fr.	F8	14
Orne, stm., Fr.	F8	14
Orne, stm., Fr.	E14	14
Ornö, i., Swe.	G8	8
Örnsköldsvik, Swe.	E8	8
Oročen, Russia	E14	34
Orocovis, P.R.	B3	104a
Orocué, Col.	E6	86
Orofino, Id., U.S.	D10	136
Orog nuur, l., Mong.	B5	36
Orohena, Mont, mtn., Fr. Poly.	v22	78h
Oroluk, at., Micron.	C6	72
Oromocto, N.B., Can.	E10	110
Oromocto Lake, l., N.B., Can.	E10	110
Oron, Nig.	I6	64
Orona, at., Kir.	D9	72
Orono, On., Can.	D11	112
Orono, Me., U.S.	F8	110
Orontes (Asi), stm., Asia	B7	58
Oroquieta, Phil.	F4	52
Orós, Braz.	D6	88
Orós, Açude, res., Braz.	D6	88
Orosei, Italy	D3	24
Orosei, Golfo di, b., Italy	D3	24
Orosháza, Hung.	C7	26
Oroszlány, Hung.	B5	26
Orote Peninsula, pen., Guam	j9	78c
Oroville, Ca., U.S.	D4	134
Oroville, Lake, res., Ca., U.S.	D4	134
Orpheus Island, i., Austl.	B6	76
Orrick, Mo., U.S.	E3	120
Orrin, N.D., U.S.	F13	124
Orroroo, Austl.	I2	76
Orrs Island, Me., U.S.	G7	110
Orša, Bela.	F13	10
Orsk, Russia	D9	32
Orșova, Rom.	E9	26
Ortaca, Tur.	G11	28
Ortakent, Tur.	F10	28
Ortaklar, Tur.	F10	28
Orta Nova, Italy	C9	24
Ortega, Col.	F4	86
Ortegal, Cabo, c., Spain	A2	20
Orteguaza, stm., Col.	G4	86
Orthon, stm., Bol.	B3	90
Ortigueira, Spain	A3	20
Orting, Wa., U.S.	C4	136
Ortiz, Mex.	A3	100
Ortiz, Ven.	C8	86
Ortona, Italy	H11	22
Ortonville, Mn., U.S.	F2	118
Orūmīyeh, Iran	B6	56
Orūmīyeh, Daryācheh-ye (Urmia, Lake), l., Iran	B6	56
Orust, i., Swe.	G4	8
Orvieto, Italy	H9	22
Orwell, Oh., U.S.	C5	114
Orxon, stm., China	B8	36
Orzinuovi, Italy	E6	22
Orzyc, stm., Pol.	D17	16
Oš, Kyrg.	F12	32
Os, Nor.	E4	8
Osa, Península de, pen., C.R.	H6	102
Osage, Ia., U.S.	H6	118
Osage, Wy., U.S.	D8	126
Osage, stm., Mo., U.S.	F5	120
Osage Beach, Mo., U.S.	F5	120
Osage City, Ks., U.S.	F2	120
Ōsaka, Japan	E8	40
Ōsaka, state, Japan	E8	40
Osakarovka, Kaz.	D12	32
Ōsaka-wan, b., Japan	E8	40
Osăm, stm., Blg.	F11	26
Osawatomie, Ks., U.S.	F3	120
Osborne, Ks., U.S.	B10	128
Osburn, Id., U.S.	C11	136
Osceola, Ar., U.S.	B8	122
Osceola, Ia., U.S.	C4	120
Osceola, Mo., U.S.	F4	120
Osceola, Wi., U.S.	F6	118
Osceola Mills, Pa., U.S.	D7	114
Oschatz, Ger.	E8	16
Oschersleben, Ger.	D7	16
Osečina, Serb.	E6	26
Osëtr, stm., Russia	F21	10
Osetrovo, Russia	E10	34
Osgood, In., U.S.	E12	120
Oshawa, On., Can.	E11	112
Oshika, Japan	A14	40
Oshika-hantō, pen., Japan	A14	40
Ō-shima, i., Japan	E12	40
Oshima-hantō, pen., Japan	C14	38
Oshkosh, Ne., U.S.	F10	126
Oshkosh, Wi., U.S.	G10	118
Oshogbo, Nig.	H5	64
Oshwe, D.R.C.	E3	66
Osica de Jos, Rom.	E11	26
Osijek, Cro.	E15	22
Osilo, Italy	D2	24
Osimo, Italy	G10	22
Osinniki, Russia	D15	32
Osipovo Selo, Russia	D13	10
Osire Süd, Nmb.	B3	70
Oskaloosa, Ia., U.S.	C5	120
Oskaloosa, Ks., U.S.	E2	120
Oskarshamn, Swe.	H7	8
Öskemen, Kaz.	E14	32
Oskolkovo, Russia	B26	8
Oslo, Nor.	G4	8
Oslo, state, Nor.	F4	8
Oslofjorden, b., Nor.	G4	8
Osmānābād, India	B3	53
Osmaneli, Tur.	C12	28
Osmaniye, Tur.	A7	58
Os'mino, Russia	A11	10
Osmussaar, i., Est.	A6	10
Osnabrück, Ger.	D4	16
Osorno, Chile	H2	90
Osorno, Spain	B6	20
Osoyoos, B.C., Can.	G11	138
Oss, Neth.	C14	14
Ossa, Mount, mtn., Austl.	n13	77a
Ossabaw Island, i., Ga., U.S.	E4	116
Osseo, Wi., U.S.	G7	118
Ossian, Ia., U.S.	A6	120
Ossining, N.Y., U.S.	C12	114
Ossipee, N.H., U.S.	G5	110
Ossjøen, l., Nor.	F4	8
Ossora, Russia	E21	34
Ostaškov, Russia	C16	10
Ostašovo, Russia	E18	10
Ostende see Oostende, Bel.	C11	14
Ostër (Ascör), stm., Eur.	G15	10
Osterburg, Ger.	D7	16
Östergötland, state, Swe.	G7	8
Osterholz-Scharmbeck, Ger.	C4	16
Osterode am Harz, Ger.	E6	16
Osterøyni, i., Nor.	F1	8
Östersund, Swe.	E6	8
Osterwieck, Ger.	E6	16
Østfold, state, Nor.	G4	8
Ostfriesische Inseln (East Frisian Islands), is., Ger.	C3	16
Ostfriesland, hist. reg., Ger.	C3	16
Østgrønland (Tunu), state, Grnld.	C18	141
Östhammar, Swe.	F8	8
Ostpreussen, hist. reg., Eur.	F4	10
Ostrava, Czech Rep.	G14	16
Ostróda, Pol.	C15	16
Ostrogožsk, Russia	D5	32
Ostrołęka, Pol.	C17	16
Ostrołęka, state, Pol.	D17	16
Ostroróg, Pol.	D12	16
Ostrov, Czech Rep.	F8	16
Ostrov, Russia	C11	10
Ostrov, i., Slov.	I13	16
Ostrov-Zalit, Russia	B11	10
Ostrowiec Świętokrzyski, Pol.	F17	16
Ostrów Mazowiecka, Pol.	D17	16
Ostrów Wielkopolski, Pol.	E13	16
Ostrzeszów, Pol.	E13	16
Ostuni, Italy	D11	24
O'Sullivan Lake, l., On., Can.	A11	118
Osum, stm., Alb.	D14	24
Ōsumi-hantō, pen., Japan	H3	40
Osumi Islands see Ōsumi-shotō, is., Japan	I9	38
Ōsumi-kaikyō, strt., Japan	I9	38
Ōsumi-shotō, is., Japan	I9	38
Osuna, Spain	G5	20
Oswego, Il., U.S.	C9	120
Oswego, Ks., U.S.	G2	120
Oswego, N.Y., U.S.	E13	112
Oswestry, Eng., U.K.	I9	12
Oświęcim (Auschwitz), Pol.	F15	16
Osyka, Ms., U.S.	F8	122
Ōta, Japan	C12	40
Otaci, Mol.	A14	26
Ōtake, Japan	E5	40
Otaki, N.Z.	E6	80
Otaru, Japan	C14	38
Otautau, N.Z.	H2	80
Otava, Fin.	F12	8
Otava, stm., Czech Rep.	G9	16
Otavalo, Ec.	G2	86
Otavi, Nmb.	D2	68
Ōtawara, Japan	C12	40
Otego Creek, stm., N.Y., U.S.	G3	110
Oteotea, Sol. Is.	e9	79b
Oteros, stm., Mex.	B4	100
Otinapa, Mex.	C6	100
Otis, Co., U.S.	A6	128
Otis, Ks., U.S.	C9	128
Otish, Monts, mts., Qc., Can.	E16	106
Otjimbingwe, Nmb.	C2	70
Otjinene, Nmb.	B4	70
Otjiwarongo, Nmb.	B3	70
Otjozondjou, stm., Nmb.	B5	70
Otjozondjupa, state, Nmb.	B3	70
Otočac, Cro.	F12	22
Otoskwin, stm., On., Can.	E13	106
Otra, stm., Nor.	G2	8
Otradnyj, Russia	D8	32
Ótranto, Italy	D12	24
Otranto, Strait of, strt., Eur.	D12	24
Otrokovice, Czech Rep.	G13	16
Otrøya, i., Nor.	E2	8
Ötscher, mtn., Aus.	C12	22
Ōtsu, Japan	D8	40
Otta, Nor.	F3	8
Ottawa, On., Can.	C14	112
Ottawa, Il., U.S.	C9	120
Ottawa, Ks., U.S.	F2	120
Ottawa, Oh., U.S.	C1	114
Ottawa (Outaouais), stm., Can.	C15	112
Ottawa Islands, is., Nu., Can.	D14	106
Otterburne, Mb., Can.	E16	124
Otter Creek, Fl., U.S.	G3	116
Otter Creek, stm., Vt., U.S.	F3	110
Otter Lake, Mi., U.S.	E6	112
Otterøya see Otrøya, i., Nor.	E2	8
Otter Tail, stm., Mn., U.S.	E2	118
Otter Tail Lake, l., Mn., U.S.	E2	118
Otterville, Mo., U.S.	F5	120
Ottosdal, S. Afr.	E7	70
Ottoshoop, S. Afr.	D8	70
Ottoville, Oh., U.S.	D1	114
Ottumwa, Ia., U.S.	C5	120
Ottweiler, Ger.	G3	16
Otway, Cape, c., Austl.	L4	76
Otwock, Pol.	D17	16
Ötztaler Alpen (Venoste, Alpi), mts., Eur.	D7	22
Ou, stm., China	I5	42
Ou, stm., China	G9	42
Ou, stm., Laos	B6	48
Ouacha, Niger	G6	64
Ouachita, stm., U.S.	F7	122
Ouachita, Lake, res., Ar., U.S.	C5	122
Ouachita Mountains, mts., U.S.	C4	122
Ouaco, N. Cal.	m15	79d
Ouadda, C.A.R.	C4	66
Ouagadougou, Burkina	G4	64
Ouahigouya, Burkina	G4	64
Ouahran see Wahran, Alg.	B4	64
Ouaka, stm., C.A.R.	C4	66
Oualâta, Maur.	F3	64
Ouallene, Alg.	E5	64
Ouanary, Fr. Gu.	C7	84
Ouanda Djallé, C.A.R.	C4	66
Ouango, C.A.R.	D4	66
Ouangolodougou, C. Iv.	H3	64
Ouarâne, reg., Maur.	E2	64
Ouarkziz, Jbel, mts., Afr.	D3	64
Ouarzazate, Mor.	C3	64
Ouasiemsca, stm., Qc., Can.	A4	110
Oubangui (Ubangi), stm., Afr.	E3	66
Oudenaarde, Bel.	D12	14
Oudtshoorn, S. Afr.	H6	70
Oued Fodda, Alg.	H12	20
Oued-Zem, Mor.	C3	64
Ouémé, stm., Benin	H5	64
Ouen, Île, i., N. Cal.	n16	79d
Ouessant, Île d' (Ushant), i., Fr.	F3	14
Ouesso, Congo	D3	66
Ouezzane, Mor.	C3	64
Ouham, stm., Afr.	F3	62
Ouidah, Benin	H5	64
Ouimet Canyon, misc. cult., On., Can.	C10	118
Ouistreham, Fr.	E8	14
Oujda, Mor.	C4	64
Oulangan kansallispuisto, p.o.i., Fin.	C13	8
Oulu (Uleåborg), Fin.	D11	8
Oulu, state, Fin.	D12	8
Oulujärvi, l., Fin.	D12	8
Oum-Chalouba, Chad	D4	62
Oumé, C. Iv.	H3	64
Oum-Hadjer, Chad	E3	62
Oumiao, China	F5	42
Ounasjoki, stm., Fin.	C11	8
Ounianga Kébir, Chad	D3	62
Ourém, Braz.	A2	88
Ourense, Spain	B3	20
Ourense, co., Spain	B3	20
Ouricuri, Braz.	D5	88
Ourinhos, Braz.	D7	90
Ouro Branco, Braz.	D7	88
Ouro Fino, Braz.	L2	88
Ouro Preto, Braz.	K4	88
Ours, Grande chute à l', wtfl., Qc., Can.	B4	110
Ourthe, stm., Bel.	D14	14
Ōu-sammyaku, mts., Japan	E14	38
Oust, can., Fr.	F6	14
Outaouais (Ottawa), stm., Can.	C15	112
Outardes, stm., Qc., Can.	E17	106
Outer Hebrides, is., Scot., U.K.	D5	12
Outer Island, i., Wi., U.S.	D8	118
Outer Santa Barbara Passage, strt., Ca., U.S.	J7	134
Outjo, Nmb.	B3	70
Outlook, Sk., Can.	C6	124
Outlook, Mt., U.S.	F9	124
Out Skerries, is., Scot., U.K.	n19	12a
Ouvéa, i., N. Cal.	m16	79d
Ouyen, Austl.	J4	76
Ovacık, Tur.	B15	28
Ovada, Italy	F5	22
Ovalle, Chile	E2	92
Ovana, Cerro, mtn., Ven.	E8	86
Ovar, Port.	D2	20
Ovejas, Col.	C4	86
Overbrook, Ks., U.S.	F2	120
Overflowing, stm., Can.	A12	124
Overland Park, Ks., U.S.	F3	120
Overton, Ne., U.S.	G13	126
Overton, Tx., U.S.	E4	122
Overton Arm, b., Nv., U.S.	G2	132
Övertorneå, Swe.	C10	8
Ovett, Ms., U.S.	F9	122
Ovid, N.Y., U.S.	B9	114
Ovidiopol', Ukr.	C17	26
Oviedo, Spain	A5	20
Ovinišče, Russia	B20	10
Ovīši, Lat.	C4	10
Ovoot, Mong.	B7	36
Øvre Anárjohka Nasjonalpark, p.o.i., Nor.	B13	8
Øvre Dividal Nasjonalpark, p.o.i., Nor.	B8	8
Ovstug, Russia	G16	10
Owando, Congo	E3	66
Owase, Japan	E9	40
Owasso, Ok., U.S.	H2	120
Owatonna, Mn., U.S.	G5	118
Owbī, Afg.	C9	56
Owego, N.Y., U.S.	B9	114
Owen, Wi., U.S.	G8	118
Owendo, Gabon	D1	66
Owens, stm., Ca., U.S.	F7	134
Owensboro, Ky., U.S.	G10	120
Owens Lake, l., Ca., U.S.	G8	134
Owen Sound, On., Can.	D8	112
Owen Sound, b., On., Can.	D9	112
Owen Stanley Range, mts., Pap. N. Gui.	b4	79a
Owensville, In., U.S.	F10	120
Owensville, Mo., U.S.	F6	120
Owerri, Nig.	H6	64
Owikeno Lake, l., B.C., Can.	E3	138
Owingsville, Ky., U.S.	F2	114
Owl, stm., Ab., Can.	A19	138
Owl, stm., Mb., Can.	D12	106
Owo, Nig.	H6	64
Owosso, Mi., U.S.	E5	112
Owyhee, Nv., U.S.	B9	134
Owyhee, stm., U.S.	G9	136
Owyhee, Lake, res., Or., U.S.	G9	136
Owyhee, South Fork, stm., U.S.	H10	136
Öxarfjörður, b., Ice.	j31	8a
Oxbow, Sk., Can.	E11	124
Oxelösund, Swe.	G7	8
Oxford, N.S., Can.	E13	110
Oxford, N.Z.	F5	80
Oxford, Eng., U.K.	J11	12
Oxford, Al., U.S.	D13	122
Oxford, In., U.S.	H2	112
Oxford, Ks., U.S.	D11	128
Oxford, Md., U.S.	F9	114
Oxford, Me., U.S.	F6	110
Oxford, Ms., U.S.	C9	122
Oxford, N.C., U.S.	H7	114
Oxford, N.Y., U.S.	B10	114
Oxford, Oh., U.S.	E13	120
Oxford, Pa., U.S.	I14	112
Oxford, Wi., U.S.	H9	118
Oxford Junction, Ia., U.S.	J8	118
Oxford Lake, l., Mb., Can.	E11	106
Oxford Peak, mtn., Id., U.S.	H14	136
Oxkutzcab, Mex.	B3	102
Oxley Downs, Austl.	J4	76
Oxley Wild Rivers National Park, p.o.i., Austl.	H8	76
Oxnard, Ca., U.S.	I6	134
Oxus see Amu Darya, stm., Asia	F10	32
Oya, stm., Malay.	B8	50
Oyabe, Japan	C9	40
Oyama, Japan	C12	40
Ōyano, Japan	G3	40
Oyapok (Oiapoque), stm., S.A.	C7	84
Oyem, Gabon	D2	66
Oyen, Ab., Can.	C3	124
Oyo, Nig.	H5	64
Oyonnax, Fr.	C11	18
Oyster Creek, mth., Tx., U.S.	E12	130
Oyyl, Kaz.	E8	32
Ozamis, Phil.	F4	52
Ozark, Al., U.S.	F13	122
Ozark, Ar., U.S.	B5	122
Ozark, Mo., U.S.	G4	120
Ozark Plateau, plat., U.S.	H4	120
Ozarks, Lake of the, res., Mo., U.S.	F5	120
Ózd, Hung.	A7	26
Ožerele, Russia	F21	10
Ozernovskij, Russia	F20	34
Ozërnyj, Russia	D10	32
Ozery, Russia	F21	10
Ozette Lake, l., Wa., U.S.	B2	136
Ozieri, Italy	D2	24
Ozimek, Pol.	F14	16
Ozinki, Russia	D7	32
Ozorków, Pol.	E15	16
Ōzu, Japan	F5	40
Ozuluama, Mex.	E9	100
Ozurgeti, Geor.	F6	32

P

Name	Map Ref.	Page
Paagoumène, N. Cal.	m14	79d
Paama, state, Vanuatu	k17	79d
Paama, i., Vanuatu	k17	79d
Paamiut see Frederikshåb, Grnld.	E15	141
Paarl, S. Afr.	H4	70
Pa'auilo, Hi., U.S.	c6	78a
Pabbay, i., Scot., U.K.	D5	12
Pabbiring, Kepulauan, is., Indon.	F11	50
Pabean, Indon.	G9	50
Pabellón, Ensenada del, b., Mex.	C4	100
Pabianice, Pol.	E15	16
Pablo, Mt., U.S.	C12	136
Pābna, Bngl.	G12	54
Pabradė, Lith.	F8	10
Pacaás Novos, Serra dos, mts., Braz.	F5	84
Pacajus, Braz.	C6	88
Pacasmayo, Peru	E2	84
Pacatuba, Braz.	C6	88
Pachino, Italy	H9	24
Pachitea, stm., Peru	E3	84
Pachmarhi, India	G7	54
Pāchora, India	H5	54
Pachuca de Soto, Mex.	E9	100
Pacific, B.C., Can.	B2	138
Pacific, Mo., U.S.	F7	120
Pacifica, Ca., U.S.	F3	134
Pacific-Antarctic Ridge, unds.	P22	142
Pacific Grove, Ca., U.S.	G3	134
Pacific Ocean	F20	142
Pacific Ranges, mts., B.C., Can.	E5	138
Pacific Rim National Park, p.o.i., B.C., Can.	H5	138
Paciran, Indon.	G8	50
Pacitan, Indon.	H7	50
Pacora, Pan.	C2	86
Pacov, Czech Rep.	G11	16
Pacuí, stm., Braz.	I3	88
Padada, Phil.	G5	52
Padamo, stm., Ven.	F9	86
Padampur, India	H9	54
Padang, Indon.	D2	50
Padang, Indon.	G12	50
Padang, Indon.	D6	50
Padang, Pulau, i., Indon.	C3	50
Padang Endau, Malay.	K6	48
Padangpanjang, Indon.	D2	50
Padangsidempuan, Indon.	C1	50
Padany, Russia	E15	8
Padas, stm., Malay.	A9	50
Padauari, stm., Braz.	G9	86
Paddle, stm., Ab., Can.	B16	138
Paddle Prairie, Ab., Can.	D7	106
Paderborn, Ger.	E4	16
Padjelanta Nationalpark, p.o.i., Swe.	C7	8
Padloping Island, i., Nu., Can.	D13	141
Padma see Ganges, stm., Asia	G13	54
Pádova (Padua), Italy	E8	22
Pādra, India	G4	54
Padrauna, India	E9	54
Padre Bernardo, Braz.	H1	88
Padre Island, i., Tx., U.S.	G10	130
Padre Island National Seashore, p.o.i., Tx., U.S.	G10	130
Padre Paraíso, Braz.	I5	88
Padstow, Eng., U.K.	K8	12
Padua see Pádova, Italy	E8	22
Paducah, Ky., U.S.	G9	120
Paducah, Tx., U.S.	G8	128
Paea, Fr. Poly.	v21	78h
Paedun, Kor., S.	D1	40
Paektu-san, mtn., Asia	C10	36
Paestum, sci., Italy	D8	24
Páez, stm., Col.	F4	86
Pafúri, Moz.	C10	70
Pag, Otok, i., Cro.	F11	22
Pagadenbaru, Indon.	G5	50
Pagadian, Phil.	G4	52
Pagai Selatan, Pulau, i., Indon.	E2	50
Pagai Utara, Pulau, i., Indon.	E2	50
Pagan, Mya.	B2	48
Pagan, i., N. Mar. Is.	B5	72
Pagaralam, Indon.	E3	50
Pagasitikós Kólpos, b., Grc.	D5	28
Page, Az., U.S.	G5	132
Page, N.D., U.S.	G16	124
Pagėgiai, Lith.	E4	10
Pagerdewa, Indon.	E4	50
Paget, Mount, mtn., S. Geor.	J9	90
Pagoda Peak, mtn., Co., U.S.	C9	132
Pagoda Point, c., Mya.	E2	48
Pagon, Bukit, mtn., Asia	A9	50
Pago Pago, Am. Sam.	h12	79c
Pagosa Springs, Co., U.S.	F9	132
Paguate, N.M., U.S.	H9	132
Pagudpud, Phil.	A3	52
Pahača, Russia	D22	34
Pāhala, Hi., U.S.	d6	78a
Pahang, state, Malay.	K6	48
Pahang, stm., Malay.	K6	48
Pahokee, Fl., U.S.	J5	116
Pahost, Bela.	G12	10
Pahrump, Nv., U.S.	G10	134
Pai, Thai.	C4	48
Pai, stm., Asia	C3	48
Paico, Peru	F3	84
Paide, Est.	B8	10
Paige, Tx., U.S.	D10	130
Paignton, Eng., U.K.	K9	12
Paiguano, Chile	E2	92
Päijänne, l., Fin.	F11	8
Paikü Co, l., China	D10	54
Pailolo Channel, strt., Hi., U.S.	b5	78a
Paimpol, Fr.	F5	14
Painan, Indon.	D2	50
Painesdale, Mi., U.S.	D10	118
Painesville, Oh., U.S.	C4	114
Paint, stm., Mi., U.S.	E10	118
Paint Creek, stm., Oh., U.S.	E14	120
Painted Desert, des., Az., U.S.	H5	132
Painted Rock Reservoir, res., Az., U.S.	K3	132
Paintsville, Ky., U.S.	G3	114
Paisley, Scot., U.K.	F8	12
Paisley, Or., U.S.	H6	136
Païta, N. Cal.	n16	79d
Paita, Peru	E1	84
Paitan, Telukan, b., Malay.	G1	52
Paiton, Indon.	G8	50
Pajala, Swe.	C10	8
Paján, Ec.	H1	86
Pajares, Puerto de, p., Spain	B5	20
Pajaros Point, c., Br. Vir. Is.	d9	104b
Pajęczno, Pol.	E14	16
Pajer, gora, mtn., Russia	C1	34
Pajeú, stm., Braz.	E6	88
Paj-Hoj, hills, Russia	A10	32
Paka, Malay.	J6	48
Pākāla, India	E4	53
Pakaraima Mountains, mts., S.A.	E11	86
Pakashkan Lake, l., On., Can.	B8	118
Pākaur, India	F11	54
Pak Chong, Thai.	E5	48
Pākhāl, l., India	C5	53
Pákhna, Cyp.	D3	58
Pakhoi see Beihai, China	K3	42
Pakistan, ctry., Asia	C2	46
Paklenica Nacionalni Park, p.o.i., Cro.	F12	22
Pakokku, Mya.	B2	48
Pakowki Lake, l., Ab., Can.	E2	124
Pākpattan, Pak.	C4	54
Pak Phanang, Thai.	H5	48
Pak Phayun, Thai.	I5	48
Pak Phraek, Thai.	H5	48
Pakrac, Cro.	E14	22
Pakruojis, Lith.	E6	10
Paks, Hung.	C5	26
Paktīā, state, Afg.	B2	54
Paktīkā, state, Afg.	B2	54
Pakwash Lake, l., On., Can.	A5	118
Pakxé, Laos	E7	48
Pala, Chad	F2	62
Pala, Mya.	F4	48
Palacios, Tx., U.S.	F11	130
Palagruža, Otoci, is., Cro.	H13	22
Palai, India	G3	53
Palaiochóra, Grc.	H6	28
Pālakodu, India	C5	53
Palamós, Spain	C14	20

Pālampur – Pembuang I • 43

Name | Map Ref. | Page

Pālampur, India B6 54
Palamu National Park, p.o.i., India G10 54
Palamut, Tur. D10 28
Palana, Russia E20 34
Palanan Bay, b., Phil. B4 52
Palanga, Lith. E3 10
Palangkaraya, Indon. E8 50
Palani, India F3 53
Pālanpur, India F4 54
Palaoa Point, c., Hi., U.S. c4 78a
Palapye, Bots. C8 70
Pālār, stm., India E4 53
Palas de Rei, Spain B3 20
Palatka, Russia D19 34
Palatka, Fl., U.S. G4 116
Palau, Italy C3 24
Palau, ctry., Oc. g8 78b
Palau Islands, is., Palau D10 44
Palauk, Mya. F4 48
Palaw, Mya. F4 48
Palawan, i., Phil. F2 52
Palawan Passage, strt., Phil. F1 52
Palayan, Phil. C3 52
Pālayankottai, India G3 53
Palembang, Indon. E4 50
Palena, Italy I11 22
Palena, stm., S.A. H2 90
Palencia, Spain B6 20
Palencia, co., Spain B6 20
Palen Lake, l., Ca., U.S. J1 132
Palenque, Mex. G13 100
Palenque, sci., Mex. G12 100
Palermo, Col. F4 86
Palermo, Italy F7 24
Palermo, Ur. F10 92
Palestina, Mex. E6 130
Palestine, Ar., U.S. B7 122
Palestine, Il., U.S. E10 120
Palestine, Tx., U.S. F3 122
Palestine, hist. reg., Asia G6 58
Palestine, Lake, res., Tx., U.S. E3 122
Palestrina, Italy I9 22
Paletwa, Mya. D7 46
Pālghāt, India F3 53
Palgrave Point, c., Nmb. E1 68
Palhano, stm., Braz. C6 88
Pāli, India F4 54
Palikir, Micron. m11 78d
Palima, Indon. F12 50
Palinuro, Capo, c., Italy D9 24
Palisade, Ne., U.S. A7 128
Palisades, Id., U.S. G15 136
Palisades Reservoir, res., U.S. G15 136
Pālitāna, India H3 54
Palivere, Est. A6 10
Palizada, Mex. F12 100
Palk Bay, b., Asia G4 53
Palkino, Russia G20 8
Pālkonda, India B6 53
Pālkonda Range, mts., India D4 53
Palk Strait, strt., Asia G4 53
Pallastunturi, mtn., Fin. B11 8
Palliser, Cape, c., N.Z. E6 80
Palma, Braz. K4 88
Palma, Moz. C7 68
Palma, stm., Braz. G2 88
Palma, Badia de, b., Spain E13 20
Palmácia, Braz. C6 88
Palma del Río, Spain G5 20
Palma de Mallorca, Spain E13 20
Palma di Montechiaro, Italy G7 24
Palmar, stm., Ven. B6 86
Palmar, Lago Artificial del, res., Ur. F9 92
Palmar Camp, Belize D3 102
Palmarejo, P.R. B1 104a
Palmares, Braz. E8 88
Palmarito, Ven. D6 86
Palmarola, Isola, i., Italy D6 24
Palmas, Braz. F1 88
Palmas, Braz. C12 92
Palmas Bellas, Pan. H7 102
Palmas de Monte Alto, Braz. H4 88
Palma Soriano, Cuba B9 102
Palm Bay, Fl., U.S. H5 116
Palm Beach, Fl., U.S. J5 116
Palmdale, Ca., U.S. I7 134
Palm Desert, Ca., U.S. J9 134
Palmeira, Braz. B13 92
Palmeira das Missões, Braz. C11 92
Palmeira dos Índios, Braz. E7 88
Palmeiras, stm., Braz. F2 88
Palmeirinhas, Ponta das, c., Ang. B1 68
Palmelo, Braz. I1 88
Palmer, P.R. B4 104a
Palmer, Ak., U.S. D10 140
Palmer, Ma., U.S. B13 114
Palmer, Ne., U.S. F14 126
Palmer, Tn., U.S. B13 122
Palmer, sci., Ant. B34 81
Palmer Lake, Co., U.S. B3 128
Palmer Land, reg., Ant. C34 81
Palmerston, N.Z. G4 80
Palmerston, at., Cook Is. E10 72
Palmerston, Cape, c., Austl. C7 76
Palmerston North, N.Z. E6 80
Palmerton, Pa., U.S. D10 114
Palmetto, Ga., U.S. D14 122
Palmetto, La., U.S. G6 122
Palmetto Point, c., Antig. e4 105b
Palmi, Italy F9 24
Palmira, Col. F3 86
Palmira, Cuba A7 102
Palmira, Ec. I2 86
Palmitas, Ur. F9 92
Palm Springs, Ca., U.S. J9 134
Palmyra see Tudmur, Syria D9 58
Palmyra, Il., U.S. E7 120
Palmyra, Mo., U.S. E6 120
Palmyra, N.Y., U.S. A8 114
Palmyra, Va., U.S. G7 114
Palmyra, sci., Syria D9 58
Palmyra Atoll, at., Oc. C10 72
Palo Alto, Mex. H8 130
Palo Alto, Ca., U.S. F3 134
Palo Blanco, P.R. B2 104a
Palo Flechado Pass, p., N.M., U.S. E3 128
Paloh, Malay. B7 50
Paloich, Sudan E6 62
Palojoensuu, Fin. B10 8
Palomar Mountain, mtn., Ca., U.S. J9 134
Palomas, Mex. F4 130
Palo Pinto, Tx., U.S. B9 130
Palopo, Indon. E12 50
Palos, Cabo de, c., Spain G10 20
Palo Santo, Arg. B8 92
Palos Verdes Point, c., Ca., U.S. J7 134
Palouse, stm., U.S. D8 136
Palo Verde, Ca., U.S. J2 132
Palpa, Peru F2 84
Palpalá, Arg. B5 92
Palu, Indon. D11 50
Palu, Teluk, b., Indon. D11 50
Paluga, Russia D21 8
Palwal, India D6 54
Pama, Burkina G5 64
Pamanukan, Indon. G5 50
Pāmban Channel, strt., India G4 53
Pāmban Island, i., India G4 53
Pamekasan, Indon. G8 50
Pamenang, Indon. E3 50
Pameungpeuk, Indon. G5 50
Pamiers, Fr. F7 18
Pamir, mts., Asia B11 56

Pamlico Sound, strt., N.C., U.S. A10 116
Pampa, Tx., U.S. F8 128
Pampã, stm., Braz. I5 88
Pampa (Pampas), reg., Arg. G4 90
Pampa Almirón, Arg. C8 92
Pampa del Chañar, Arg. E3 92
Pampa del Indio, Arg. B7 92
Pampanga, stm., Phil. C3 52
Pampanua, Indon. F12 50
Pampas, Peru F3 84
Pampas, stm., Peru F3 84
Pampas see Pampa, reg., Arg. F4 90
Pamplico, S.C., U.S. B6 116
Pamplona, Col. D5 86
Pamplona, Spain B9 20
Pamukkale (Hierapolis), sci., Tur. F12 28
Pamukova, Tur. C13 28
Pana, Il., U.S. E8 120
Panabá, Mex. B3 102
Panabo, Phil. G5 52
Panacea, Fl., U.S. G14 122
Panadura, Sri L. H4 53
Panagjurište, Blg. G11 26
Panaitan, Pulau, i., Indon. G4 50
Panaji, India D1 53
Panamá, Pan. H8 102
Panama, Ok., U.S. B4 122
Panama, ctry., N.A. F9 96
Panamá, Bahía de, b., Pan. H8 102
Panamá, Canal de (Panama Canal), can., Pan. H8 102
Panamá, Golfo de, b., Pan. D2 86
Panama, Gulf of see Panamá, Golfo de, b., Pan. D2 86
Panama, Isthmus of see Panamá, Istmo de, isth., Pan. H8 102
Panamá, Istmo de (Panama, Isthmus of), isth., Pan. H8 102
Panama Basin, unds. H5 144
Panama Canal see Panamá, Canal de, can., Pan. H8 102
Panama City, Fl., U.S. G13 122
Panambi, Braz. D11 92
Panamint Range, mts., Ca., U.S. G8 134
Panamint Valley, val., Ca., U.S. G8 134
Panao, Peru E2 84
Panarea, Isola, i., Italy F9 24
Panaro, stm., Italy F8 22
Panay, i., Phil. E4 52
Panay Gulf, b., Phil. E4 52
Pančevo, Serb. E7 26
Panciu, Rom. D14 26
Panda, Moz. D12 70
Pandaria, India G8 54
Pan de Azúcar, Ur. G10 92
Pandėlys, Lith. D8 10
Pāndharkawada, India A4 53
Pandharpur, India C2 53
Pāndhurna, India H7 54
Pando, Ur. G10 92
Panevėžys, Lith. E7 10
Pang, stm., Mya. B4 48
Panga, D.R.C. D5 66
Pangala, Congo E2 66
Pangandaran, Indon. G6 50
Pangani, Tan. F7 66
Pangani, stm., Tan. E7 66
Pangburn, Ar., U.S. B7 122
Pangfou see Bengbu, China E7 42
Panghkam, Mya. D8 46
Pangi, D.R.C. E5 66
Pangkajene, Indon. F11 50
Pangkalanbrandan, Indon. J4 48
Pangkalanbuun, Indon. E7 50
Pangkalpinang, Indon. E5 50
Pango Aluquem, Ang. B1 68
Pangōjin, Kor., S. D2 40
Pangong Tso, l., Asia B7 54
Pangsau Pass, p., Asia C8 46
Panguipulli, Chile G2 90
Panguitch, Ut., U.S. F4 132
Pangutaran, Phil. G3 52
Pangutaran Group, is., Phil. G3 52
Panhandle, Tx., U.S. F7 128
Pāni'au, mtn., Hi., U.S. b1 78a
Panié, Mont, mtn., N. Cal. m15 79d
Pānīpat, India D6 54
Panitan, Phil. E4 52
Panj (Pjandž), stm., Asia B11 56
Panjang, Indon. F4 50
Panjang, Selat, strt., Indon. C3 50
Pankshin, Nig. H6 64
Panlong (Lo), stm., Asia A7 48
P'anmunjŏm-ni, Kor., N. E7 38
Panna, India F8 54
Panna National Park, p.o.i., India F7 54
Pannawonica, Austl. D3 74
Pannirtuuq, Nu., Can. B17 106
Panola, Al., U.S. E10 122
Pano Lévkara, Cyp. D4 58
Panopah, Indon. D7 50
Panorama, Braz. D6 90
Panovo, Russia C18 32
Panruti, India F4 53
Panshan, China D4 38
Pantanal, reg., S.A. C5 90
Pantanaw, Mya. D2 48
Pantar, Pulau, i., Indon. G7 44
Pantelleria, Isola di, i., Italy H6 24
Pantonlabu, Indon. J3 48
Pánuco, Mex. E10 100
Pánuco, stm., Mex. E9 100
Panxian, China F5 36
Panyam, Nig. H6 64
Panzós, Guat. E3 102
Pao, stm., Thai. D6 48
Pao, stm., Ven. C9 86
Pao, stm., Ven. C8 86
Paochi see Baoji, China D2 42
Paoki see Baoji, China D2 42
Paola, Italy E9 24
Paola, Ks., U.S. F3 120
Paoli, In., U.S. F11 120
Paopao, Fr. Poly. v20 78h
Paoting see Baoding, China B6 42
Paotou see Baotou, China A4 42
Paotow see Baotou, China A4 42
Pápa, Hung. B4 26
Papagaio, stm., Braz. I10 86
Papagaios, Braz. D3 88
Papagayo, Golfo de, b., C.R. G4 102
Pāpa'ikou, Hi., U.S. d6 78a
Papantla de Olarte, Mex. E10 100
Papara, Fr. Poly. v22 78h
Papa Stour, i., Scot., U.K. n18 12a
Papeari, Fr. Poly. w22 78h
Papeete, Fr. Poly. v21 78h
Papenburg, Ger. C3 16
Papetoai, Fr. Poly. v20 78h
Paphos see Néa Páfos, Cyp. D3 58
Papigochic, stm., Mex. G8 98
Papillion, Ne., U.S. C1 120
Paposo, Chile B2 92
Papua, Gulf of, b., Pap. N. Gui. D5 72
Papua New Guinea, ctry., Oc. D5 72
Papulovo, Russia F23 8
Papun, Mya. C3 48
Papunáua, stm., Col. G6 86
Papurí (Papurí), stm., S.A. G6 86
Papurí (Papurí), stm., S.A. G6 86
Pará, state, Braz. D7 84
Pará, stm., Braz. A1 88
Pará, stm., Braz. J3 88

Parabel', Russia C14 32
Paraburdoo, Austl. D3 74
Paracatu, Braz. I2 88
Paracatu, stm., Braz. I3 88
Paracel Islands see Xisha Qundao, is., China B5 50
Pārachinār, Pak. B3 54
Paracho de Verduzco, Mex. F7 100
Parachute, Co., U.S. D8 132
Paraćin, Serb. F8 26
Paracuru, Braz. B6 88
Parada, Punta, c., Peru G2 84
Paradise, Ca., U.S. D4 134
Paradise, Mt., U.S. C12 136
Paradise, Nv., U.S. G1 132
Paradise Island, i., Bah. m18 104f
Paradise Valley, Az., U.S. J5 132
Paradise Valley, Nv., U.S. B8 134
Pāradwīp, India H11 54
Paragonah, Ut., U.S. F4 132
Paragould, Ar., U.S. H7 120
Paraguá, stm., Bol. B4 90
Paragua, stm., Ven. D10 86
Paraguaçu, stm., Braz. G6 88
Paraguai (Paraguay), stm., S.A. D5 90
Paraguaipoa, Ven. B6 86
Paraguaná, Península de, pen., Ven. A6 86
Paraguarí, Para. B9 92
Paraguarí, state, Para. C9 92
Paraguay, ctry., S.A. D5 90
Paraguay (Paraguai), stm., S.A. E5 90
Paraíba, state, Braz. D7 88
Paraíba do Sul, stm., Braz. K5 88
Paraibano, Braz. D3 88
Parainen, Fin. F9 8
Paraíso, Mex. F12 100
Paraíso, Pan. H8 102
Parakou, Benin H5 64
Paramakkudi, India G4 53
Paramaribo, Sur. B6 84
Parambu, Braz. D5 88
Paramillo, Parque Nacional, p.o.i., Col. D3 86
Paramirim, Braz. G4 88
Paramirim, stm., Braz. F4 88
Páramo de Masa, Puerto de, p., Spain B7 20
Paramušir, ostrov, i., Russia F20 34
Paramythiá, Grc. D3 28
Paran, Naḥal (Girafi, Wadi), stm. I5 58
Paraná, Arg. E7 92
Paranã, Braz. G1 88
Paraná, state, Braz. D6 90
Paranã, stm., Braz. G1 88
Paraná, stm., S.A. F5 90
Paranaguá, Braz. B13 92
Paranaguá, Baía de, b., Braz. B13 92
Paranaíba, Braz. C6 90
Paranaíba, stm., Braz. C6 90
Paranaidji, Braz. D2 88
Paranapanema, stm., Braz. D6 90
Paranapiacaba, Serra do, mts., Braz. B13 92
Paranavaí, Braz. D6 90
Parang, Phil. G5 52
Parang, Pulau, i., Indon. F7 50
Parângu Mare, Vârful, mtn., Rom. D10 26
Paranhos, Braz. A10 92
Paranoá, Lago do, res., Braz. H2 88
Parapeba, Braz. J3 88
Parapetí, stm., Bol. C4 90
Parara, Indon. E12 50
Paratinga, Braz. G4 88
Paratoo, Austl. I2 76
Paray-le-Monial, Fr. C9 18
Pārbati, stm., India F6 54
Pārbatipur, Bngl. F12 54
Parbhani, India B3 53
Parchim, Ger. C7 16
Pardeeville, Wi., U.S. H9 118
Pārdi, India H4 54
Parding, China B12 54
Pardo, stm., Braz. D6 90
Pardo, stm., Braz. H6 88
Pardo, stm., Braz. L1 88
Pardo, stm., Braz. D11 92
Pardo, stm., Braz. K1 88
Pardubice, Czech Rep. F11 16
Paredón, Mex. C8 100
Parelhas, Braz. D7 88
Paren', Russia D21 34
Paren', stm., Russia D21 34
Parent, Qc., Can. C2 110
Parentis-en-Born, Fr. E4 18
Parepare, Indon. E11 50
Parera, Arg. G5 92
Parfenevo, Russia F20 8
Párga, Grc. D3 28
Parham, Antig. f4 105b
Paria, Gulf of, b. B10 86
Paria, Península de, pen., Ven. B10 86
Pariaguán, Ven. C9 86
Pariaman, Indon. D1 50
Paricutín, vol., Mex. F7 100
Parigi, Indon. D12 50
Parika, Guy. B6 84
Parikkala, Fin. F13 8
Parima, stm., Braz. F10 86
Parima, Serra (Parima, Sierra), mts., S.A. F9 86
Parima, Sierra (Parima, Serra), mts., S.A. F9 86
Parima Tapirapecó, Parque Nacional, p.o.i., Ven. F9 86
Parintins, Braz. D6 84
Paris, On., Can. E9 112
Paris, Fr. F11 14
Paris, Ar., U.S. B5 122
Paris, Il., U.S. I2 112
Paris, Ky., U.S. F1 114
Paris, Mo., U.S. E5 120
Paris, Tn., U.S. H9 120
Paris, Tx., U.S. D3 122
Parisienne, Île, i., On., Can. B5 112
Parita, Bahía de, b., Pan. H7 102
Parit Buntar, Malay. J5 48
Parkano, Fin. E10 8
Park City, Mt., U.S. B3 126
Park City, Ut., U.S. C5 132
Parkdale, Or., U.S. E5 136
Parker, Az., U.S. I2 132
Parker, Co., U.S. B4 128
Parker, Fl., U.S. G13 122
Parker, Cape, c., Nu., Can. B10 141
Parker City, In., U.S. H4 112
Parker Dam, Ca., U.S. I2 132
Parker Dam, dam, U.S. I2 132
Parkersburg, Ia., U.S. B5 120
Parkersburg, Il., U.S. F9 120
Parkersburg, W.V., U.S. E4 114
Parkes, Austl. I7 76
Park Falls, Wi., U.S. F8 118
Park Forest, Il., U.S. G2 112
Parkhill, On., Can. E8 112
Parkland, Wa., U.S. C4 136
Park Range, mts., Co., U.S. C10 132
Park Rapids, Mn., U.S. E3 118
Parkrose, Or., U.S. E4 136
Park Rynie, S. Afr. G10 70
Parksley, Va., U.S. G10 114
Parkston, S.D., U.S. D14 126
Parksville, B.C., Can. G6 138
Parkville, Md., U.S. E9 114
Parkville, Mo., U.S. E3 120
Parla, Spain D7 20

Parlākimidi, India B7 53
Parli, India B3 53
Parma, Italy F7 22
Parma, Mo., U.S. H8 120
Parma, Oh., U.S. C4 114
Parnaguá, Braz. F3 88
Parnaíba, Braz. B5 88
Parnaíba, stm., Braz. B5 88
Parnaibinha, stm., Braz. E2 88
Parnamirim, Braz. E6 88
Parnassós, mtn., Grc. E5 28
Párnitha, mtn., Grc. E6 28
Pärnu, Est. G11 8
Pärnu laht, b., Est. G11 8
Paro, Bhu. E12 54
Pārola, India H5 54
Paromaj, Russia F17 34
Paroo, stm., Austl. G5 76
Páros, i., Grc. F8 28
Parowan, Ut., U.S. F4 132
Parque Nacional da Chapada da Diamantina, p.o.i., Braz. G4 88
Parral, Chile H2 92
Parral, stm., Mex. B6 100
Parramatta, Austl. I8 76
Parras de la Fuente, Mex. C7 100
Parrish, Fl., U.S. I3 116
Parrsboro, N.S., Can. E12 110
Parry, Cape, c., N.T., Can. A6 106
Parry Bay, b., Nu., Can. B14 106
Parry Island, i., On., Can. C9 112
Parry Peninsula, pen., N.T., Can. B6 106
Parry Sound, On., Can. C9 112
Parsberg, Ger. G7 16
Parseta, stm., Pol. B11 16
Parshall, N.D., U.S. G11 124
Paršino, Russia C20 32
Parsnip, stm., B.C., Can. A8 138
Parsons, Ks., U.S. G2 120
Parsons, Tn., U.S. B10 122
Pārsti, Est. B8 10
Partanna, Italy G6 24
Parthenay, Fr. H8 14
Partinico, Italy F7 24
Partizansk, Russia C10 38
Partizánske, Slov. H14 16
Paru, stm., Braz. D7 84
Parú, stm., Ven. E9 86
Paru de Oeste, stm., Braz. C6 84
Parūr, India F3 53
Pārvatīpuram, India B6 53
Paryang, China. C9 54
Parys, S. Afr. E8 70
Pasadena, Ca., U.S. I7 134
Pasadena, Tx., U.S. H3 122
Pasaje, Ec. D2 84
Pa Sak, stm., Thai. E5 48
Paşaköy, N. Cyp. C4 58
Pasarbantal, Indon. E2 50
Pasawng, Mya. C3 48
Pascagoula, Ms., U.S. G10 122
Pascagoula, stm., Ms., U.S. G10 122
Paşcani, Rom. B13 26
Pasco, Wa., U.S. D7 136
Pascoag, R.I., U.S. C14 114
Pascua, Isla de (Easter Island) (Rapa Nui), i., Chile f30 78l
Pas-de-Calais, state, Fr. D11 14
Pasewalk, Ger. C10 16
Pasir Mas, Malay. J6 48
Pasirpengarayan, Indon. C2 50
Pasir Puteh, Malay. J6 48
Paškovo, Russia G15 34
Pasłęka, stm., Pol. C16 16
Pasley Bay, b., Nu., Can. A11 106
Pašman, Otok, i., Cro. G12 22
Pasmore, stm., Austl. H2 76
Pasni, Pak. D9 56
Paso de Indios, Arg. H3 90
Paso del Cerro, Ur. E9 92
Paso de los Libres, Arg. D9 92
Paso de los Toros, Ur. F9 92
Paso de Patria, Para. C8 92
Paso de San Antonio, Mex. E3 130
Paso Hondo, Mex. H13 100
Paso Robles, Ca., U.S. H5 134
Pasozero, Russia F16 8
Pasquia Hills, hills, Sk., Can. A11 124
Pasrūr, Pak. B5 54
Passadumkeag, Me., U.S. E8 110
Passadumkeag Mountain, hill, Me., U.S. E8 110
Passage Point, c., N.T., Can. B16 140
Passaic, N.J., U.S. H15 112
Passamaquoddy Bay, b., N.A. E10 110
Passau, Ger. H9 16
Passero, Capo, c., Italy H9 24
Passo Fundo, Braz. D11 92
Passo Real, Represa do, res., Braz. D11 92
Passos, Braz. K2 88
Pastavy, Bela. E9 10
Pastaza, state, Ec. H3 86
Pastaza, stm., S.A. D2 84
Pastillo, P.R. B3 104a
Pasto, Col. G3 86
Pastos Bons, Braz. D3 88
Pasuruan, Indon. G8 50
Pasvalys, Lith. D7 10
Pásztó, Hung. B6 26
Patacamaya, Bol. C3 90
Patadkal, sci., India C3 53
Patagonia, Az., U.S. L6 132
Patagonia, reg., Arg. I2 90
Pātan, India G3 54
Patchogue, N.Y., U.S. D13 114
Patea, N.Z. D6 80
Pategi, Nig. H6 64
Pate Island, i., Kenya E8 66
Patensie, S. Afr. H7 70
Paterna, Spain E10 20
Paternion, Aus. D10 22
Paternò, Italy G8 24
Paterson, N.J., U.S. D11 114
Pathānkot, India B5 54
Pathein, Mya. D2 48
Pathfinder Reservoir, res., Wy., U.S. E5 126
Pathiu, Thai. G4 48
Pathum Thani, Thai. E5 48
Pati, Indon. G7 50
Patía, Col. F3 86
Patía, stm., Col. F2 86
Patiāla, India C6 54
Patillas, P.R. B3 104a
Pati Point, c., Guam i10 78c
Pativilca, Peru F2 84
Pātkai Range, mts., Asia F4 36
Pat Mayse Lake, res., Tx., U.S. D3 122
Pátmos, i., Grc. F9 28
Patna, India F10 54
Patna, India H11 54
Patnāgarh, India H9 54
Patnanongan Island, i., Phil. C4 52
Pato Branco, Braz. C11 92
Patoka, Il., U.S. F8 120
Patoka, stm., In., U.S. F10 120
Patoka Lake, res., In., U.S. F11 120
Patomskoe nagor'e, plat., Russia E12 34
Patonga, Ug. D6 66
Patos, Braz. D7 88
Patos, Alb. D13 24
Patos, stm., Arg. E3 92
Patos, Lagoa dos, b., Braz. E12 92
Patos de Minas, Braz. J2 88
Patquía, Arg. D4 92
Pátra, Grc. E4 28
Patrai, Gulf of see Patraïkós Kólpos, b., Grc. E4 28
Patraïkós Kólpos, b., Grc. E4 28

Patricio Lynch, Isla, i., Chile I1 90
Patrocínio, Braz. J2 88
Pattani, Thai. I5 48
Pattaya, Thai. F5 48
Patten, Me., U.S. D8 110
Patterson, Ca., U.S. F4 134
Patterson, La., U.S. E3 116
Patterson, Mount, mtn., Yk., Can. C4 106
Patti, Golfo di, b., Italy F9 24
Pattison, Ms., U.S. F8 122
Pattoki, Pak. C4 54
Pattonsburg, Mo., U.S. D3 120
Pattukkottai, India F4 53
Pattullo, Mount, mtn., B.C., Can. D5 106
Patuākhāli, Bngl. G13 54
Patuca, stm., Hond. E5 102
Pātūr, India H6 54
Patusi, Pap. N. Gui. a4 79a
Patuxent, stm., Md., U.S. F9 114
Pátzcuaro, Mex. F8 100
Pau, Fr. F5 18
Pau, Gave de, stm., Fr. F5 18
Pau Brasil, Braz. H6 88
Pau dos Ferros, Braz. D6 88
Pauh, Indon. E3 50
Pauini, stm., Braz. E4 84
Pauini, stm., Braz. H10 86
Pauk, Mya. B2 48
Pauksa Taung, mtn., Mya. C2 48
Paul, Id., U.S. H13 136
Paulding, Ms., U.S. E9 122
Paulicéia, Braz. D6 90
Paulina Peak, mtn., Or., U.S. G5 136
Pauline, Mount, mtn., Can. C11 138
Paulino Neves, Braz. B4 88
Paulistana, Braz. E5 88
Paulistas, Braz. J4 88
Paullina, Ia., U.S. B2 120
Paulo Afonso, Braz. E6 88
Paulo Afonso, Cachoeira de, wtfl., Braz. E6 88
Paulpietersburg, S. Afr. E10 70
Pauls Valley, Ok., U.S. G11 128
Paung, Mya. D3 48
Paungde, Mya. C2 48
Pauri, India C7 54
Paute, Ec. I2 86
Paute, stm., Ec. I2 86
Pauto, stm., Col. E6 86
Pavia, Italy E6 22
Pavilion, B.C., Can. F9 138
Pāvilosta, Lat. D4 10
Pavlikeni, Blg. F12 26
Pavlodar, Kaz. D13 32
Pavlof Volcano, vol., Ak., U.S. E7 140
Pavlovo, Russia I20 8
Pavlovsk, Russia A13 10
Pavlovsk, Russia D14 32
Pavlovskij Posad, Russia E21 10
Pavo, Ga., U.S. F2 116
Pavullo nel Frignano, Italy F7 22
Pavuvu Island, i., Sol. Is. e8 79b
Pawan, stm., Indon. D7 50
Pawhuska, Ok., U.S. E12 128
Pawn, stm., Mya. C3 48
Pawnee, Il., U.S. E8 120
Pawnee, Ok., U.S. A2 122
Pawnee, stm., Ks., U.S. C9 128
Pawnee Rock, Ks., U.S. C9 128
Pawni, India H7 54
Pawota, Mya. D3 48
Paw Paw, Il., U.S. C8 120
Paw Paw, Mi., U.S. F4 112
Pawtucket, R.I., U.S. C14 114
Paxoí, i., Grc. D3 28
Paxson, Ak., U.S. D10 140
Paxton, Ne., U.S. F11 126
Paya, Hond. E5 102
Payakumbuh, Indon. D2 50
Payamlı, Tur. A9 58
Payerne, Switz. D3 22
Payeti, Indon. H12 50
Payette, Id., U.S. F10 136
Payette, stm., Id., U.S. G10 136
Payette, North Fork, stm., Id., U.S. F11 136
Payette, South Fork, stm., Id., U.S. F11 136
Payne, Oh., U.S. C1 114
Payne, Lac, l., Can. D16 106
Paynes Find, Austl. E3 74
Paynton, Sk., Can. A5 124
Paysandú, Ur. F8 92
Payson, Az., U.S. I5 132
Payson, Il., U.S. E6 120
Payson, Ut., U.S. C5 132
Payún, Cerro, mtn., Arg. H3 92
Pazarbaşı Burnu, c., Tur. B13 28
Pazarcık, Tur. A8 58
Pazardžik, Blg. G11 26
Pazaryeri, Tur. D12 28
Paz de Ariporo, Col. E6 86
Pazin, Cro. A15 10
Pe, Mya. F4 48
Pea, stm., U.S. F12 122
Peabody, Ks., U.S. C11 128
Peabody, Ma., U.S. B14 114
Peace, stm., Can. D8 106
Peace, stm., Fl., U.S. I4 116
Peace River, Ab., Can. D7 106
Peachland, B.C., Can. G11 138
Peach Orchard, Ga., U.S. C3 116
Peach Springs, Az., U.S. H3 132
Peak District National Park, p.o.i., Eng., U.K. H11 12
Peak Downs, Austl. D7 76
Peak Hill, Austl. E3 74
Peak Hill, Austl. I7 76
Peäldoajvi, mtn., Fin. B12 8
Peale, Mount, mtn., Ut., U.S. E7 132
Pearisburg, Va., U.S. G5 114
Pearl, Il., U.S. E7 120
Pearl, Ms., U.S. E8 122
Pearl, stm., U.S. G9 122
Pearland, Tx., U.S. H3 122
Pearl Harbor, b., Hi., U.S. b3 78a
Pearl Peak, mtn., Nv., U.S. C1 132
Pearl River, La., U.S. G9 122
Pearson, Ga., U.S. E3 116
Peary Land, reg., Grnld. A18 141
Pease, stm., Tx., U.S. G9 128
Pebane, Moz. D6 68
Pebas, Peru D3 84
Pebble Island, i., Falk. Is. J4 90
Peć, Serb. G7 26
Pecan Gap, Tx., U.S. D3 122
Peçanha, Braz. J4 88
Peças, Ilha das, i., Braz. B13 92
Pecatonica, Il., U.S. B8 120
Pecatonica, stm., U.S. B8 120
Pečenga, Russia B14 8
Pechenizhyn, Ukr. A11 26
Pechora see Pečora, stm., Russia C25 8
Pechora Bay see Pečorskaja guba, b., Russia A8 32
Pečora, Russia A9 32
Pečora (Pechora), stm., Russia A8 32
Pecoraro, Monte, mtn., Italy F10 24
Pečorskaja guba, b., Russia A8 32
Pečorskoe more, s., Russia A8 32
Pečory, Russia C10 10
Pecos, N.M., U.S. F3 128
Pecos, Tx., U.S. C4 130
Pecos, stm., U.S. F12 98
Pecos National Monument, p.o.i., N.M., U.S. F3 128

Pécs, Hung. C5 26
Pedana, India C5 53
Pedasí, Pan. I7 102
Pedder, Lake, res., Austl. o12 77a
Peddie, S. Afr. H8 70
Pededze, stm., Eur. C10 10
Pedernales, Dom. Rep. C12 102
Pedernales, Ven. C10 86
Pedernales, stm., Tx., U.S. D9 130
Pedernales, Salar de, pl., Chile C3 92
Pedra Azul, Braz. I5 88
Pedra Branca, Braz. C6 88
Pedra Lume, C.V. k10 65a
Pedras de Fogo, Braz. D8 88
Pedras Salgadas, Port. C3 20
Pedraza, Col. B4 86
Pedregal, Ven. B6 86
Pedreiras, Braz. C3 88
Pedriceña, Mex. C6 100
Pedro, Point, c., Sri L. G5 53
Pedro Afonso, Braz. E1 88
Pedro Avelino, Braz. C7 88
Pedro Cays, is., Jam. D9 102
Pedro Gomes, Braz. G7 84
Pedro II, Braz. C5 88
Pedro II, Ilha, i., S.A. G8 86
Pedro Juan Caballero, Para. D5 90
Pedro Leopoldo, Braz. J3 88
Pedro Osório, Braz. E11 92
Pedro R. Fernández, Arg. D8 92
Pedro Velho, Braz. D8 88
Peebles, Scot., U.K. F9 12
Peebles, Oh., U.S. F2 114
Pee Dee, stm., U.S. A6 116
Peekskill, N.Y., U.S. C12 114
Peel, I. of Man G8 12
Peel, stm., Can. B4 106
Peel Point, c., N.T., Can. B17 140
Peel Sound, strt., Nu., Can. A11 106
Peene, stm., Ger. C9 16
Peerless, Mt., U.S. F8 124
Peesane, Sk., Can. B10 124
Peetz, Co., U.S. G9 126
Pegasus Bay, b., N.Z. F5 80
Pegnitz, Ger. G7 16
Pegu, stm., Mya. D3 48
Pegu Yoma, mts., Mya. C2 48
Pegyš, Russia E24 8
Pehlivanköy, Tur. B9 28
Pehuajó, Arg. G7 92
Peian see Bei'an, China B10 36
Peiching see Beijing, China B7 42
Peihai see Beihai, China K3 42
Peikang, Tai. J9 42
Peine, Ger. D6 16
Peine, Pointe à, c., Dom. j6 105c
Peipa, see ...
Peip'ing see Beijing, China B7 42
Peipus, Lake, l., Eur. B10 10
Peiraiás (Piraeus), Grc. F6 28
Peissenberg, Ger. I7 16
Peixe, Braz. G1 88
Peixe, stm., Braz. D6 90
Peixian, China D7 42
Peixoto, Represa de, res., Braz. K2 88
Pekalongan, Indon. G6 50
Pekan, Malay. K6 48
Pekanbaru, Indon. C2 50
Pekin, Il., U.S. D8 120
Pekin, In., U.S. F11 120
Peking see Beijing, China B7 42
Pekino, Russia G16 10
Pekul'nej, hrebet, mts., Russia C24 34
Pelabohan Klang, Malay. K5 48
Pelabuhanratu, Indon. G5 50
Pelagie, Isole, is., Italy I6 24
Pelaihari, Indon. E9 50
Pelat, Mont, mtn., Fr. E12 18
Pełczyce, Pol. C11 16
Peleduj, Russia C20 32
Pelée, Montagne, vol., Mart. k6 105c
Pelee, Point, c., On., Can. G7 112
Pelee Island, i., On., Can. G7 112
Pelega, Vârful, mtn., Rom. D9 26
Pelelu see Beliliou, i., Palau D9 44
Peleng, Pulau, i., Indon. F7 44
Pelham, Al., U.S. D12 122
Pelham, Ga., U.S. E1 116
Pelhřimov, Czech Rep. G11 16
Pelican, Ak., U.S. E12 140
Pelican Bay, b., Mb., Can. B13 124
Pelican Lake, Wi., U.S. F9 118
Pelican Lake, l., Mb., Can. B13 124
Pelican Lake, l., Mn., Can. E14 124
Pelican Lake, l., Mn., U.S. C5 118
Pelican Rapids, Mb., Can. B13 124
Pelican Rapids, Mn., U.S. E2 118
Pelister Nacionalni Park, p.o.i., Mac. B4 28
Peljekaise Nationalpark see Pieljekaise Nationalpark, p.o.i., Swe. C6 8
Pelješac, Poluotok, pen., Cro. H14 22
Peljušnja, Russia B15 10
Pella, Ia., U.S. C5 120
Pélla, sci., Grc. C5 28
Pell City, Al., U.S. D12 122
Pellegrini, Arg. H6 92
Pellegrini, Lago, l., Arg. I4 92
Pello, Fin. C11 8
Pellworm, i., Ger. B4 16
Pelly, Sk., Can. C12 124
Pelly, stm., Yk., Can. C4 106
Pelly Bay, b., Nu., Can. B12 106
Pelly Crossing, Yk., Can. C3 106
Pelly Lake, l., Nu., Can. B10 106
Pelly Mountains, mts., Yk., Can. C4 106
Pelón de Ñado, mtn., Mex. E9 100
Peloponnesus see Pelopónnisos, pen., Grc. F5 28
Pelopónnisos, state, Grc. F5 28
Pelopónnisos (Peloponnesus), pen., Grc. F5 28
Pelotas, Braz. E11 92
Pelotas, stm., Braz. C12 92
Pelusium Bay see Tīna, Khalîg el-, b., Egypt G3 58
Pemadumcook Lake, l., Me., U.S. E7 110
Pemalang, Indon. G6 50
Pemangkat, Indon. C6 50
Pematangsiantar, Indon. B1 50
Pemba, Moz. C7 68
Pemba, Zam. D4 68
Pemba, i., Tan. F7 66
Pemberton, Austl. F3 74
Pemberton, B.C., Can. F8 138
Pembina, N.D., U.S. C1 118
Pembina, stm., Ab., Can. B16 138
Pembina, stm., N.A. F16 124
Pembina Hills, hills, N.A. E15 124
Pembroke, On., Can. C12 112
Pembroke, Wales, U.K. J7 12
Pembroke, Ga., U.S. D4 116
Pembroke, Ky., U.S. H10 120
Pembroke, Me., U.S. F9 110
Pembroke, N.C., U.S. B6 116
Pembroke, Cape, c., Nu., Can. C14 106
Pembroke Pines, Fl., U.S. K5 116
Pembrokeshire Coast National Park, p.o.i., Wales, U.K. J7 12
Pembuang, Indon. E7 50
Pembuang, stm., Indon. D8 50

Name	Map Ref.	Page
Pemigewasset, stm., N.H., U.S.	G5	110
Pemuco, Chile	H1	92
Penafiel, Port.	C2	20
Peñalara, Pico de, mtn., Spain	D6	20
Penalva, Braz.	B3	88
Penang see George Town, Malay.	J4	48
Peñaranda de Bracamonte, Spain	D5	20
Pen Argyl, Pa., U.S.	D10	114
Peñarroya-Pueblonuevo, Spain.	F5	20
Peñas, Cabo de, c., Spain	A5	20
Penas, Golfo de b., Chile.	I2	90
Penasco, N.M., U.S.	E3	128
Pench National Park, p.o.i., India	H7	54
Pendembu, S.L.	H2	64
Pendembu, S.L.	H2	64
Pendências, Braz.	C7	88
Pendleton, In., U.S.	H4	112
Pendleton, Or., U.S.	E8	136
Pendleton, S.C., U.S.	B3	116
Pendolo, Indon.	E12	50
Pend Oreille, stm., N.A.	B9	136
Pend Oreille, Lake, l., Id., U.S.	B10	136
Pendžikent, Taj.	B10	56
Penebel, Indon.	H9	50
Penedo, Braz.	F7	88
Penetanguishene, On., Can.	D9	112
Peneus see Pineiós, stm., Grc.	D5	28
Penfield, Pa., U.S.	C7	114
Penganga, stm., India	H6	54
Penghu, China	I8	42
P'enghu Ch'üntao (Pescadores), is., Tai.	J8	42
P'enghu Shuitao, strt., Tai.	J8	42
Pengkou, China	I7	42
Penglai, China	C9	42
Pengshui, China	E7	42
Pengshui, China	G2	42
Pengwaluate Shan, mtn., China	B11	54
Pengxi, China	F1	42
Pengxian, China	E5	36
Pengze, China	G7	42
Penha, Braz.	C13	92
Penhsi see Benxi, China	D5	38
Penibética, Cordillera, mts., Spain	G8	20
Peniche, Port.	E1	20
Penicuik, Scot., U.K.	F9	12
Penida, Nusa, i., Indon.	H9	50
Peninsular Malaysia see Semenanjung Malaysia, hist. reg., Malay.	K6	48
Peniscola, Spain	D11	20
Penki see Benxi, China	D5	38
Pennant Station, Sk., Can.	D5	124
Penne, Italy	H10	22
Penneru, stm., India	D4	53
Penn Hills, Pa., U.S.	H10	112
Pennine Alps, mts., Eur.	C13	18
Pennines, mts., Eng., U.K.	G10	12
Pennington Gap, Va., U.S.	H2	114
Pennsboro, W.V., U.S.	E5	114
Pennsylvania, state, U.S.	C8	114
Penn Yan, N.Y., U.S.	B8	114
Penny Ice Cap, ice, Nu., Can.	B17	106
Penny Strait, strt., Nu., Can.	B6	141
Peno, Russia	D15	10
Penobscot, stm., Me., U.S.	F8	110
Penobscot, East Branch, stm., Me.	D8	110
Penobscot, West Branch, stm., Me.	D7	110
Penobscot Bay, b., Me., U.S.	F7	110
Penola, Austl.	K3	76
Peñón de Ifac see Penyal d'Ifac, misc. cult., Spain.	F11	20
Penong, Austl.	F6	74
Penonomé, Pan.	H7	102
Penrhyn, at., Cook Is.	D11	72
Penrith, Austl.	I8	76
Penrith, Eng., U.K.	G10	12
Pensacola, Fl., U.S.	G11	122
Pensacola Bay, b., Fl., U.S.	G11	122
Pensacola Mountains, mts., Ant.	D36	81
Pense, Sk., Can.	D9	124
Pensilvania, Col.	E4	86
Pentagon Mountain, mtn., Mt., U.S.	C13	136
Pentecostes, Braz.	B6	88
Pentecost Island see Pentecôte, i., Vanuatu	j17	79d
Pentecôte, i., Vanuatu	j17	79d
Pentecôte (Pentecost Island), i., Vanuatu	j17	79d
Penticton, B.C., Can.	G11	138
Pentland, Austl.	C5	76
Pentland Firth, strt., Scot., U.K.	C9	12
Pentwater, Mi., U.S.	E3	112
Penuba, Indon.	D4	50
Peñuelas, P.R.	B2	104a
Penuguan, Indon.	E4	50
Penukonda, India	D3	53
Penyal d'Ifac, misc. cult., Spain.	F11	20
Penza, Russia	D7	32
Penzance, Eng., U.K.	K7	12
Penzberg, Ger.	I7	16
Penžina, stm., Russia	D22	34
Penžinskaja guba, b., Russia	D21	34
Penžinskij hrebet, mts., Russia	D22	34
Peoples Creek, stm., Mt., U.S.	F5	124
People's Democratic Republic of Korea see Korea, North, ctry., Asia	D7	38
Peoria, Az., U.S.	J4	132
Peoria, Il., U.S.	D8	120
Peoria Heights, Il., U.S.	K9	118
Peotone, Il., U.S.	C9	120
Pepel, S.L.	H2	64
Pepin, Wi., U.S.	G6	118
Pepin, Lake, l., U.S.	G7	118
Peqin, Alb.	C13	24
Perabumulih, Indon.	E4	50
Perak, state, Malay.	J5	48
Perak, stm., Malay.	J5	48
Perak, Kuala, b., Malay.	J5	48
Perales de Alfambra, Spain	D9	20
Peralillo, Chile	G2	92
Peralta, N.M., U.S.	I10	132
Perambalur, India	F4	53
Percé, Qc., Can.	B12	110
Perchas, P.R.	B2	104a
Perche, Collines du, hills, Fr.	F9	14
Percival Lakes, l., Austl.	D4	74
Percy Isles, is., Austl.	C8	76
Perdida, stm., Braz.	E2	88
Perdido, stm., U.S.	G11	122
Perdido, Monte, mtn., Spain.	B10	20
Perdizes, Braz.	J2	88
Perdue, Sk., Can.	B6	124
Perechyn, Ukr.	H18	16
Pereira, Col.	E4	86
Perelazy, Russia	G14	10
Peremyšl', Russia	F18	10
Pereña, stm., Braz.	G22	8
Pereslavl'-Zalesskij, Russia	D21	10
Pérez, Arg.	F7	92
Pergamino, Arg.	F7	92
Pergamum, sci., Tur.	D10	28
Pergine Valsugana, Italy	D8	22
Perham, Mn., U.S.	E3	118
Péribonka, Qc., Can.	B4	110
Péribonka, stm., Qc., Can.	B5	110
Péribonka, Lac, l., Qc., Can.	E16	106
Perico, Arg.	B5	92
Pericumã, stm., Braz.	B3	88
Peridot, Az., U.S.	J6	132
Perigiraja, Indon.	D3	50
Périgord, hist. reg., Fr.	D6	18
Périgueux, Fr.	D6	18
Perijá, Serranía de, mts., S.A.	C5	86
Perim see Barīm, i., Yemen	G5	56
Peri-Mirim, Braz.	B3	88
Perito Moreno, Arg.	I2	90
Peritoró, Braz.	C3	88
Periyār, stm., India	F3	53
Periyar Tiger Reserve, India	G3	53
Perkasie, Pa., U.S.	D10	114
Perkins, Ok., U.S.	A2	122
Perlas, Archipiélago de las, is., Pan.	H8	102
Perlas, Laguna de b., Nic.	F6	102
Perleberg, Ger.	C7	16
Perlez, Serb.	D7	26
Perlis, state, Malay.	I5	48
Perm', Russia	C9	32
Përmet, Alb.	D14	24
Pernambuco, state, Braz.	E6	88
Pernik, Blg.	G10	26
Péronne, Fr.	E11	14
Perote, Mex.	F10	100
Perow, B.C., Can.	B4	138
Perpignan, Fr.	G8	18
Perrault Falls, On., Can.	A5	118
Perrine, Fl., U.S.	A9	130
Perrine, Fl., U.S.	K5	116
Perris, Ca., U.S.	J8	134
Perro, Laguna del, l., N.M., U.S.	G3	128
Perro, Punta del, c., Spain	H4	20
Perros, Bahía de, strt., Cuba	A8	102
Perros-Guirec, Fr.	F5	14
Perry, Fl., U.S.	F2	116
Perry, Ia., U.S.	C3	120
Perry, Ks., U.S.	E2	120
Perry, Mi., U.S.	B1	114
Perry, Mo., U.S.	E6	120
Perry, N.Y., U.S.	B7	114
Perry, Kap, c., Grnld.	B11	141
Perry Lake, res., Ks., U.S.	E2	120
Perrysburg, Oh., U.S.	C2	114
Perry's Victory and International Peace Memorial, hist., Oh., U.S.	C2	114
Perrysville, Oh., U.S.	D3	114
Perryton, Tx., U.S.	E8	128
Perryville, Ak., U.S.	E8	140
Perryville, Ky., U.S.	G12	120
Perseverancia, Bol.	B4	90
Persia, Ia., U.S.	C2	120
Persia see Iran, ctry., Asia	C7	56
Persian Gulf, b., Asia	D7	56
Perth, Austl.	F3	74
Perth, On., Can.	D13	112
Perth, Scot., U.K.	E9	12
Perth Amboy, N.J., U.S.	D11	114
Perth Basin, unds.	L13	142
Pertominsk, Russia	D18	8
Peru, Il., U.S.	C8	120
Peru, In., U.S.	H3	112
Peru, Ne., U.S.	D2	120
Peru, N.Y., U.S.	F3	110
Peru, ctry., S.A.	E2	84
Peru Basin, unds.	J5	144
Perućac, Jezero, res., Eur.	G16	22
Peru-Chile Trench, unds.	K6	144
Perugia, Italy	H9	22
Perugorría, Arg.	D8	92
Peruíbe, Braz.	B14	92
Perušić, Cro.	F12	22
Pervomais'k, Ukr.	A17	26
Pervomajsk, Russia	I20	8
Pervomajskij, Russia	F15	10
Pervoural'sk, Russia	C9	32
Pervyj Kuril'skij proliv, strt., Russia.	F20	34
Pes', Russia	B17	10
Pesaro, Italy	G9	22
Pescadores see P'enghu Ch'üntao, is., Tai.	J8	42
Pescadores Channel see P'enghu Shuitao, strt., Tai.	J8	42
Pescara, Italy	H11	22
Pescara, stm., Italy	H11	22
Pescasseroli, Italy	C7	24
Pescia, Italy	G7	22
Pesé, Pan.	D1	86
Peshāwar, Pak.	B3	54
Peshkopi, Alb.	C14	24
Peshkopija see Peshkopi, Alb.	C14	24
Peshtigo, Wi., U.S.	C2	112
Peshtigo, stm., Wi., U.S.	F10	118
Peski, Bela.	G7	10
Pesočnoe, Russia	B22	10
Peso da Régua, Port.	C3	20
Pesqueira, Braz.	E7	88
Pessac, Fr.	E5	18
Pest, state, Hung.	B6	26
Peštera, Blg.	G11	26
Pestovo, Russia	B18	10
Peštraja Dresva, Russia	D20	34
Petacalco, Bahía, b., Mex.	G7	100
Petah Tiqwa, Isr.	F5	58
Petal, Ms., U.S.	F9	122
Petalcingo, Mex.	G12	100
Petalión, Kólpos, b., Grc.	F7	28
Petaluma, Ca., U.S.	E3	134
Petare, Ven.	B8	86
Petatlán, Mex.	G8	100
Petawawa, On., Can.	C12	112
Petén Itzá, Lago, l., Guat.	D2	102
Petenwell Lake, res., Wi., U.S.	G8	118
Peterborough, Austl.	I2	76
Peterborough, On., Can.	D11	112
Peterborough, Eng., U.K.	I12	12
Peterhead, Scot., U.K.	D11	12
Peter Island, i., Br. Vir. Is.	e8	104b
Peter I Øy, i., Ant.	B31	81
Peter Lake, l., Nu., Can.	C12	106
Peterlee, Eng., U.K.	G11	12
Peter Pond Lake, l., Sk., Can.	D9	106
Petersburg, Ak., U.S.	E13	140
Petersburg, Il., U.S.	K9	118
Petersburg, In., U.S.	F10	120
Petersburg, Tx., U.S.	B12	122
Petersburg, Tx., U.S.	H7	128
Petersburg, Va., U.S.	G8	114
Petersburg, W.V., U.S.	F6	114
Petersfield, Eng., U.K.	J12	12
Peterson, Ia., U.S.	B2	120
Peter the Great Bay see Petra Velikogo, zaliv, b., Russia	C9	38
Petilia Policastro, Italy	E10	24
Petion-Ville, Haiti	C11	102
Petit-Bourg, Guad.	h5	105c
Petitcodiac, N.B., Can.	E11	110
Petite Rivière Noire, Piton de la, mtn., Mrts.	i10	69a
Petites-Anses, Guad.	i5	105c
Petit-Goâve, Haiti	C11	102
Petit Jean, stm., Ar., U.S.	B5	122
Petit Jean, stm., Ar., U.S.	D6	106
Petit Piton, vol., St. Luc.	m6	105c
Petitsikapau Lake, l., Nf., Can.	E17	106
Petlād, India	G4	54
Peto, Mex.	B3	102
Petoskey, Mi., U.S.	C5	112
Petra see Al-Batrā', sci., Jord.	H6	58
Petra Velikogo, zaliv (Peter the Great Bay), b., Russia	C9	38
Petre, Point, c., On., Can.	E12	112
Petrič, Blg.	H10	26
Petrified Forest National Park, p.o.i., Az., U.S.	I7	132
Petrila, Rom.	D10	26
Petrinja, Cro.	E13	22
Petriševo, Russia	E19	10
Petrodvorec, Russia	A12	10
Petrolândia, Braz.	E6	88
Petrolea, Col.	C5	86
Petrolia, Tx., U.S.	G10	128
Petrolina, Braz.	E5	88
Petrolina de Goiás, Braz.	I1	88
Petrona, Punta, c., P.R.	C3	104a
Petrópolis, Braz.	L4	88
Petropavl see Petropavlovsk, Kaz.	D11	32
Petropavlovka, Russia	F10	34
Petropavlovsk, Kaz.	D11	32
Petropavlovsk-Kamčatskij, Russia	F20	34
Petrópolis, Braz.	L4	88
Petros, Tur.	H13	120
Petroşani, Rom.	D10	26
Petrovac, Serb.	E8	26
Petrovsk, Russia	D6	32
Petrovskij, Russia	H18	8
Petrovsk-Zabajkal'skij, Russia	F10	34
Petrozavodsk, Russia	F15	8
Petrusburg, S. Afr.	F7	70
Petrusville, S. Afr.	G7	70
Petrykau, Bela.	H11	10
Pettus, Tx., U.S.	F10	130
Petuhovo, Russia	C11	32
Peuetsagoe, Gunung, vol., Indon.	J3	48
Peureulak, Indon.	J3	48
Peusangan, stm., Indon.	J3	48
Pevek, Russia	C23	34
Peza, stm., Russia	D23	8
Pezawa Taung, mtn., Mya.	C2	48
Pézenas, Fr.	F9	18
Pezinok, Slov.	H13	16
Pfarrkirchen, Ger.	H8	16
Pforzheim, Ger.	H4	16
Pfronten, Ger.	I6	16
Pfunds, Aus.	D7	22
Pfungstadt, Ger.	G4	16
Pha-an, Mya.	D3	48
Phagwara, India	C5	54
Phalaborwa, S. Afr.	C10	70
Phalodi, India	E4	54
Phaltan, India	C2	53
Phan, Thai.	C4	48
Phanat Nikhom, Thai.	F5	48
Phangan, Ko, i., Thai.	H5	48
Phangnga, Thai.	H4	48
Phaniang, stm., Thai.	D6	48
Pharom Dongrak Range (Dângrêk, Chuŏr Phnum), mts., Asia	C3	44
Phan Rang, Viet.	G9	48
Phan Thiet, Viet.	G9	48
Phan Thong, Thai.	F5	48
Pharenda, India	E9	54
Pharr, Tx., U.S.	H9	130
Phat Diem, Viet.	B8	48
Phatthalung, Thai.	I5	48
Phayao, Thai.	C4	48
Phelps, N.Y., U.S.	B8	114
Phelps, Wi., U.S.	E9	118
Phelps Lake, l., N.C., U.S.	I9	114
Phenix City, Al., U.S.	E13	122
Phepane, stm., S. Afr.	E6	70
Phet Buri, stm., Thai.	F4	48
Phetchabun, Thai.	D5	48
Phetchabun, Thiu Khao, mts., Thai.	D4	48
Phetchaburi, Thai.	F4	48
Phibun Mangsahan, Thai.	E7	48
Phichai, Thai.	D5	48
Phichit, Thai.	D5	48
Philadelphia, Ms., U.S.	E9	122
Philadelphia, N.Y., U.S.	D14	112
Philadelphia, Pa., U.S.	E10	114
Phil Campbell, Al., U.S.	C11	122
Philip, S.D., U.S.	C11	126
Philippeville see Skikda, Alg.	B6	64
Philippeville, Bel.	D13	14
Philippi, W.V., U.S.	E5	114
Philippi see Filippoi, sci., Grc.	B7	28
Philippi, Lake, l., Austl.	E2	76
Philippine Basin, unds.	H15	142
Philippines, ctry., Asia	C4	52
Philippine Sea, s.	H15	142
Philippine Trench, unds.	H15	142
Philippolis, S. Afr.	F7	70
Philipsburg, Mt., U.S.	D13	136
Philipsburg, Pa., U.S.	D7	114
Philip Smith Mountains, mts., Ak., U.S.	C10	140
Philipstown, S. Afr.	G7	70
Phillaur, India	C5	54
Phillip Island, i., Austl.	L5	76
Phillips, Tx., U.S.	F6	110
Phillips, Tx., U.S.	C5	114
Phillips, Wi., U.S.	F8	118
Phillipsburg, Ga., U.S.	E2	116
Phillipsburg, N.J., U.S.	D10	114
Philo, Il., U.S.	E9	120
Philo, Oh., U.S.	E4	114
Philpots Island, i., Nu., Can.	C10	141
Phimai, Thai.	E6	48
Phitsanulok, Thai.	D5	48
Phnom Penh see Phnum Pénh, Camb.	G7	48
Phnum Pénh (Phnom Penh), Camb.	G7	48
Phoenix, Mi., U.S.	D9	112
Phoenix, Az., U.S.	J4	132
Phoenix, N.Y., U.S.	E13	112
Phoenix, Or., U.S.	A3	134
Phoenix Islands, is., Kir.	D9	72
Phoenixville, Pa., U.S.	D10	114
Phofung (Sources, Mont-aux-), mtn., Afr.	F9	70
Phon, Thai.	E6	48
Phong, stm., Thai.	D6	48
Phon Phisai, Thai.	D6	48
Phra Chedi Sam Ong, p., Asia	E4	48
Phrae, Thai.	C5	48
Phra Nakhon Si Ayutthaya, Thai.	E5	48
Phran Kratai, Thai.	D4	48
Phrom Phiram, Thai.	D5	48
Phu Cat, Viet.	E9	48
Phuket, Thai.	I4	48
Phuket, Ko, i., Thai.	I4	48
Phu Ly, Viet.	B7	48
Phum Duang, stm., Thai.	H4	48
Phumĭ Bǎ Khăm, Camb.	F8	48
Phumĭ Bĕng, Camb.	F7	48
Phumĭ Chámbák, Camb.	G7	48
Phumĭ Chhuk, Camb.	G7	48
Phumĭ Chruŏy Slĕng, Camb.	F8	48
Phumĭ Kâmpóng Srâlau, Camb.	E7	48
Phumĭ Kaôh Kŏng, Camb.	G6	48
Phumĭ Kaôh Kêrt, Camb.	F7	48
Phumĭ Khpôb, Camb.	G7	48
Phumĭ Lvéa Kraôm, Camb.	F6	48
Phumĭ Narŭng, Camb.	F7	48
Phumĭ Prêk Kák, Camb.	F7	48
Phumĭ Puŏk Chás, Camb.	F7	48
Phumĭ Sâmraông, Camb.	E6	48
Phumĭ Srê Kôkir, Camb.	F8	48
Phumĭ Tbĕng, Camb.	F7	48
Phumĭ Thmâ Pôk, Camb.	F6	48
Phumĭ Tœk Choŭ, Camb.	F6	48
Phu My, Viet.	E9	48
Phuoc Long, Viet.	G8	48
Phuoc Long, Viet.	H7	48
Phu Pan National Park, p.o.i., Thai.	D6	48
Phu Quoc, Dao, i., Viet.	G6	48
Phu Tho, Viet.	B7	48
Phu Vang, Viet.	D8	48
Pi, stm., China	F7	42
Piaçabuçu, Braz.	F7	88
Piacenza, Italy	E6	22
Pialba, Austl.	E9	76
Piancó, Braz.	D7	88
Pianosa, Isola, i., Italy	H6	22
Piapot, Sk., Can.	E4	124
Piaseczno, Russia	D16	16
Piaski, Pol.	E18	16
Piatra-Neamţ, Rom.	B13	26
Piauí, state, Braz.	D4	88
Piauí, stm., Braz.	D4	88
Piauí, Morro do, mtn., Braz.	H2	88
Piave, stm., Italy	E9	22
Piaxtla, stm., Mex.	D5	100
Piazza Armerina, Italy	G8	24
Pibor Post, Sudan	F6	62
Pic, stm., On., Can.	B12	118
Picacho, Az., U.S.	K5	132
Picardie, hist. reg., Fr.	E11	14
Picardy see Picardie, hist. reg., Fr.	E11	14
Picayune, Ms., U.S.	G9	122
Pichanal, Arg.	D4	90
Picher, Ok., U.S.	H3	120
Pichilemu, Chile	G1	92
Pichimá, Col.	E3	86
Pichi Mahuida, Arg.	I5	92
Pichincha, state, Ec.	H2	86
Pichucalco, Mex.	G12	100
Pickardville, Ab., Can.	B16	138
Pickens, Ms., U.S.	E9	122
Pickens, S.C., U.S.	B3	116
Pickerel Lake, l., Mb., Can.	B14	124
Pickering, Eng., U.K.	G12	12
Pickle Lake, On., Can.	E12	106
Pickstown, S.D., U.S.	D14	126
Pickton, Tx., U.S.	D3	122
Pickwick Lake, res., U.S.	B10	122
Pico, mtn., C.V.	I10	65a
Pico, i., Port.	C3	60
Pico da Neblina, Parque Nacional, p.o.i., Braz.	G9	86
Pico de Orizaba, Parque Nacional, p.o.i., Mex.	F10	100
Pico de Orizaba, Volcán (Citlaltépetl, Volcán), vol., Mex.	F10	100
Picos, Braz.	D5	88
Picquigny, Fr.	E11	14
Picton, On., Can.	D12	112
Picton, N.Z.	E6	80
Picton, Isla, i., Chile	K3	90
Pictou, N.S., Can.	E14	110
Pictou Island, i., N.S., Can.	E14	110
Picture Butte, Ab., Can.	G18	138
Pictured Rocks National Lakeshore, p.o.i., Mi., U.S.	B3	112
Picuí, Braz.	D7	88
Picún Leufú, Arg.	G3	90
Pidálion, Akrotírion, c., Cyp.	D5	58
Pidhorodna, Ukr.	A17	26
Pidurutalagala, mtn., Sri L.	H5	53
Piedecuesta, Col.	D5	86
Piedimonte Matese, Italy	C8	24
Piedmont, Al., U.S.	D13	122
Piedmont, Mo., U.S.	G7	120
Piedmont see Piemonte, state, Italy	F5	22
Piedra, stm., Co., U.S.	F9	132
Piedra, Cerro, mtn., Chile	H1	92
Piedra del Águila, Arg.	H3	90
Piedrafita, Puerto, p., Spain	D5	20
Piedrahíta, Spain	D5	20
Piedras, Punta, c., Arg.	G9	92
Piedras, Punta, c., Ven.	B11	86
Piedras Blancas, Arg.	E8	92
Piedras Negras, Guat.	D2	102
Piedras Negras, Mex.	A8	100
Pieksämäki, Fin.	E12	8
Pielinen, l., Fin.	E13	8
Pieljekaise Nationalpark, p.o.i., Swe.	C6	8
Piemonte, state, Italy	F5	22
Pienaarsrivier, S. Afr.	D8	70
Pienaars, stm., S. Afr.	D8	70
Pieniński Park Narodowy, p.o.i., Pol.	G16	16
Pienza, Italy	G8	22
Pierce, Co., U.S.	G8	126
Pierpont, S.D., U.S.	B15	126
Pierce, S.D., U.S.	C12	126
Pierre, Bayou, stm., La., U.S.	F5	122
Pierre, Bayou, stm., Ms., U.S.	F8	122
Pierre Part, La., U.S.	G7	122
Pierreville, Trin.	s13	105f
Pierz, Mn., U.S.	F4	118
Pietarsaari, Fin.	E10	8
Pietermaritzburg, S. Afr.	F10	70
Pietersburg, S. Afr.	C9	70
Pietrasanta, Italy	F7	22
Piet Retief, S. Afr.	E10	70
Pietrosu, Vârful, mtn., Rom.	B12	26
Pigeon, Mi., U.S.	E7	112
Pigeon Forge, Tn., U.S.	I2	114
Pigeon Lake, l., Mb., Can.	B17	124
Pigeon Lake, l., Ab., Can.	C18	138
Pigg's Peak, Swaz.	E10	70
Pigs, Bay of see Cochinos, Bahía de, b., Cuba	B7	102
Pigüé, Arg.	H6	92
Pihāri, India	B8	54
Pihlajavesi, l., Fin.	F13	8
Pihtipudas, Fin.	E11	8
Pikalëvo, Russia	A17	10
Pikes Peak, mtn., Co., U.S.	C3	128
Pikeville, Md., U.S.	E9	114
Piketberg, S. Afr.	H4	70
Piketon, Oh., U.S.	E2	114
Pikou, China	B13	122
Pikounda, Congo	D3	66
Piła, Pol.	C12	16
Piła, state, Pol.	C12	16
Pilanesberg Game Reserve, p.o.i., S. Afr.	D8	70
Pilão Arcado, Braz.	E4	88
Pilar, Arg.	E5	92
Pilar, Braz.	E7	88
Pilar, Para.	C8	90
Pilar de Goiás, Braz.	H1	88
Pilares, Mex.	A3	130
Pilas Group, is., Phil.	G3	52
Pilawa, Pol.	D17	16
Pilcomayo, stm., S.A.	D4	90
Pilcomayo, Brazo Norte, stm., Para.	B8	92
Pilcomayo, Brazo Sur del, stm., S.A.	B8	92
Pilcomayo, Parque Nacional, p.o.i., Arg.	B8	92
Pilger, Ne., U.S.	E15	126
Pilgrim's Rest, S. Afr.	D10	70
Pili, Phil.	D4	52
Pilibhit, India	D7	54
Pilica, stm., Pol.	E16	16
Pilliga, Austl.	H7	76
Pilot, The, mtn., Austl.	K7	76
Pilot Butte, Sk., Can.	D9	124
Pilot Knob, Mo., U.S.	G7	120
Pilot Knob, mtn., Id., U.S.	E11	136
Pilot Mound, Mb., Can.	E15	124
Pilot Mountain, N.C., U.S.	H5	114
Pilot Peak, mtn., Nv., U.S.	C2	134
Pilot Peak, mtn., Wy., U.S.	F16	136
Pilot Rock, Or., U.S.	E8	136
Pilottown, La., U.S.	H9	122
Pilsen see Plzeň, Czech Rep.	G9	16
Pilu, stm., Mya.	B3	48
Pilzno, Pol.	G17	16
Pima, Az., U.S.	K7	132
Pimenta, Braz.	J2	88
Pimental, Braz.	B3	88
Pimenteira, Vereda, stm., Braz.	F4	88
Pimentel, Braz.	B3	88
Pimentel, Peru	E2	84
Pinang, Pulau, i., Malay.	J4	48
Pınarbaşı, Tur.	B16	28
Pinar del Río, Cuba	A5	102
Pinarello, Fr.	H15	18
Pinarhisar, Tur.	B10	28
Pinas, Arg.	E5	92
Pinatubo, Mount, vol., Phil.	C3	52
Pincher Creek, Ab., Can.	G17	138
Pinchi Lake, l., B.C., Can.	B6	138
Pinckneyville, Il., U.S.	F8	120
Pinconning, Mi., U.S.	E5	112
Pindale, Mya.	A3	48
Pindamonhangaba, Braz.	L3	88
Pindaré, stm., Braz.	B3	88
Pindaré-Mirim, Braz.	B3	88
Pindi Gheb, Pak.	B4	54
Pindobaçu, Braz.	F5	88
Pindos Óros (Pindus Mountains), mts., Grc.	D4	28
Pindus Mountains see Pindos Óros, mts., Grc.	D4	28
Pindwara, India	F4	54
Pine, stm., Mi., U.S.	E5	112
Pine Apple, Al., U.S.	F11	122
Pine Castle, Fl., U.S.	H4	116
Pine City, Mn., U.S.	F6	118
Pine Creek, Austl.	B6	74
Pine Creek, stm., Nv., U.S.	C9	134
Pine Creek, stm., Pa., U.S.	C8	114
Pine Falls, Mb., Can.	D17	124
Pine Grove, W.V., U.S.	E5	114
Pine Hill, Austl.	D6	76
Pine Hill, Al., U.S.	F11	122
Pine Hills, Fl., U.S.	H4	116
Pinehouse Lake, l., Sk., Can.	D9	106
Pinehurst, Ga., U.S.	D2	116
Pinehurst, Id., U.S.	E10	136
Pinehurst, N.C., U.S.	A6	116
Pineiós (Peneus), stm., Grc.	D5	28
Pine Island, Mn., U.S.	G6	118
Pine Island, i., Fl., U.S.	J3	116
Pine Island Bay, b., Ant.	C30	81
Pinellas Park, Fl., U.S.	I3	116
Pine Mountain, mtn., Ca., U.S.	H4	134
Pine Pass, p., B.C., Can.	A8	138
Pine Point, N.T., Can.	C8	106
Pine Ridge, S.D., U.S.	D10	126
Pine River, Mn., U.S.	E4	118
Pine River, stm., Mi., U.S.	C13	124
Pinerolo, Italy	F4	22
Piñeros, Isla, i., P.R.	B4	104a
Pines, Isle of see Juventud, Isla de la, i., Cuba	B6	102
Pines, Lake O' The, res., Tx., U.S.	E4	122
Pine Swamp Knob, mtn., W.V., U.S.	F5	114
Pinetop-Lakeside, Az., U.S.	I6	132
Pinetops, N.C., U.S.	A8	116
Pinetown, S. Afr.	F10	70
Pineville, Ky., U.S.	H2	114
Pineville, La., U.S.	F6	122
Pineville, Mo., U.S.	H3	120
Pineville, W.V., U.S.	G4	114
Pinewood, S.C., U.S.	C5	116
Ping, stm., Thai.	E5	48
Pingaring, Austl.	F3	74
Pingba, China	F2	42
Pingchang, China	F2	42
Pingding, China	C5	42
Pingdingshan, China	E5	42
Pingdu, China	C8	42
Pingelly, Austl.	F3	74
Pinghe, China	I7	42
Pingjiang, China	G5	42
Pinglu, China	C4	42
Pingli, China	E3	42
Pingliang, China	D2	42
Pingluo, China	B2	42
Pingnan, China	J4	42
Pingnan, China	H8	42
Pingquan, China	A8	42
Pingshan, China	B7	42
Pingtang, China	I2	42
Pingtan Dao, i., China	I8	42
Pingtung, Tai.	J9	42
Pingwu, China	E5	36
Pingxiang, China	J4	42
Pingxiang, China	H5	42
Pingyang, China	G9	42
Pingyao, China	C5	42
Pingyi, China	D7	42
Pingyin, China	C7	42
Pinhal, Braz.	L2	88
Pinhão, Braz.	B12	92
Pinheiro, Braz.	B3	88
Pinheiros, Braz.	J5	88
Piní, Pulau, i., Indon.	L2	48
Pinsk, Bela.	H9	10
Pinsk Marshes see Pripet Marshes, reg., Eur.	H12	10
Pinta, Al., U.S.	D12	122
Pinta, Isla, i., Ec.	h11	84a
Pintada Arroyo, stm., N.M., U.S.	G3	128
Pintados, Chile	D3	90
Pintasan, Malay.	A10	50
Pinto Butte, mtn., Sk., Can.	E6	124
Pintoyacu, stm., Ec.	H3	86
Pin Valley National Park, p.o.i., India	C6	54
Pioche, Nv., U.S.	F2	132
Piombino, Italy	H7	22
Pioneer Mine, B.C., Can.	F8	138
Pionerskij, Russia	F3	10
Pionki, Pol.	E17	16
Piorini, stm., Braz.	D5	84
Piorini, Lago, l., Braz.	D5	84
Piotrków, state, Pol.	E15	16
Piotrków Trybunalski, Pol.	E15	16
Pio V. Corpuz, Phil.	E5	52
Piove di Sacco, Italy	E8	22
Pio XII, Braz.	B3	88
Pipanaco, Salar de, pl., Arg.	D4	92
Pīpār, India	E4	54
Pipariya, India	G7	54
Pipar Road, India	E4	54
Pipe Spring National Monument, p.o.i., Az., U.S.	G4	132
Pipestem Creek, stm., N.D., U.S.	G14	124
Pipestone, Mn., U.S.	H2	118
Pipestone, stm., On., Can.	E12	106
Pipestone Creek, stm., Can.	E12	124
Pipestone National Monument, p.o.i., Mn., U.S.	G2	118
Pipinas, Arg.	G9	92
Piplān, Pak.	B3	54
Pipmuacan, Réservoir, res., Qc., Can.	A6	110
Piqua, Oh., U.S.	D1	114
Piquet Carneiro, Braz.	C6	88
Piquiri, stm., Braz.	B11	92
Piracanjuba, Braz.	I1	88
Piracanjuba, stm., Braz.	I1	88
Piracicaba, Braz.	L2	88
Piracicaba, stm., Braz.	L1	88
Piracuruca, Braz.	B5	88
Pirae, Fr. Poly.	v21	78h
Piraeus see Peiraiás, Grc.	F6	28
Piraí do Sul, Braz.	B12	92
Piraju, Braz.	L1	88
Pirajuí, Braz.	L1	88
Piran, Slvn.	E10	22
Pirané, Arg.	B8	92
Piranga, Braz.	K4	88
Piranhas, Braz.	G7	84
Piranhas, stm., Braz.	C7	88
Piranhas, stm., Braz.	C7	88
Piranji, stm., Braz.	C6	88
Pirapemas, Braz.	B3	88
Pirapora, Braz.	I3	88
Piraquara, Braz.	B13	92
Pirassununga, Braz.	K2	88
Pirata, Monte, hill, P.R.	B4	104a
Piratinga, Braz.	H2	88
Piratini, Braz.	E11	92
Piratini, stm., Braz.	D10	92
Piratuba, Braz.	C11	92
Pires do Rio, Braz.	I1	88
Piriápolis, Ur.	G10	92
Pirin, Parki Narodowe, p.o.i., Blg.	H10	26
Piripiri, Braz.	C5	88
Piritu, Ven.	C7	86
Pirmasens, Ger.	G3	16
Pirna, Ger.	F9	16
Pirojpur, Bngl.	G12	54
Pirot, Serb.	F9	26
Pirovskoe, Russia	C16	32
Pir Panjal Range, mts., Asia.	B5	54
Pirtleville, Az., U.S.	L7	132
Pirttikylä, Fin.	E9	8
Piru, Indon.	F8	44
Pisa, Italy	G7	22
Pisagua, Chile	D2	90
Pisco, Peru	F2	84
Piscolt, Rom.	B9	26
Písek, Czech Rep.	G10	16
Pishan, China	A4	46
Pishchanka, Ukr.	A15	26
Pisinemo, Az., U.S.	K4	132
Pismo Beach, Ca., U.S.	H5	134
Pisticci, Italy	D10	24
Pistoia, Italy	G7	22
Pisuerga, stm., Spain	C6	20
Pit, stm., Ca., U.S.	C4	134
Pit, North Fork, stm., Ca., U.S.	B5	134
Pita, Gui.	G2	64
Pitalito, Col.	G4	86
Pitanga, Braz.	B12	92
Pitangui, Braz.	J3	88
Pitcairn, dep., Pit.	c28	78k
Piteå, Swe.	D9	8
Piteälven, stm., Swe.	D8	8
Piteşti, Rom.	E11	26
Pithapuram, India	C6	53
Pithiviers, Fr.	F11	14
Pithom, hist., Egypt	H2	58
Pithorāgarh, India	C9	54
Pitinga, stm., Braz.	H12	86
Pitiquito, Mex.	F6	98
Pitkäranta, Russia	F14	8
Pitljar, Russia	C2	34
Pitman, N.J., U.S.	E10	114
Pitoa, Cam.	C2	66
Pitomača, Cro.	D14	22
Pitrufquén, Chile	G2	90
Pitt Island, i., B.C., Can.	D1	138
Pitt Lake, l., B.C., Can.	G8	138
Pittsboro, N.C., U.S.	I6	114
Pittsburg, Ca., U.S.	E4	134
Pittsburg, Ks., U.S.	G3	120
Pittsburg, Tx., U.S.	E4	122
Pittsburgh, Pa., U.S.	D6	114
Pittsfield, Il., U.S.	E7	120
Pittsfield, Me., U.S.	F7	110
Pittsfield, Ma., U.S.	B12	114
Pittsfield, N.H., U.S.	G5	110
Pittston, Pa., U.S.	C10	114
Pittsview, Al., U.S.	E13	122
Pittsworth, Austl.	F8	76
Pituil, Braz.	D4	92
Pium, Braz.	F1	88
Piura, Peru	E1	84
Piute Peak, mtn., Ca., U.S.	H7	134
Pivan', Russia	F16	34
Pivdennyy Buh, stm., Ukr.	A17	26
Pizarro, Col.	E3	86
Pizzo, Italy	F10	24
Pjakupur, stm., Russia	B13	32
Pjalica, Russia	C19	8
Pjandž (Panj), stm., Asia	B10	56
Pjaozero, ozero, l., Russia	C14	8
Pjasina, stm., Russia	B6	34
Pjasino, ozero, l., Russia	C6	34
Pjatigorsk, Russia	F6	32
Pjatovskij, Russia	F19	10
Placentia Bay, b., Nf., Can.	j23	107a
Placerville, Ca., U.S.	E5	134
Placetas, Cuba	A8	102
Plácido Rosas, Ur.	F11	92
Plain City, Ut., U.S.	B4	132
Plain Dealing, La., U.S.	E5	122
Plainfield, Ct., U.S.	C13	114
Plainfield, In., U.S.	I3	112
Plainfield, N.J., U.S.	D11	114

Name	Map Ref.	Page
Plains, Ga., U.S.	E14	122
Plains, Ks., U.S.	D8	128
Plains, Mt., U.S.	C12	136
Plainview, Mn., U.S.	G6	118
Plainview, Ne., U.S.	E15	126
Plainview, Tx., U.S.	G7	128
Plainville, In., U.S.	F10	120
Plainwell, Mi., U.S.	F4	112
Plakhtiivka, Ukr.	C16	26
Plamondon, Ab., Can.	B18	138
Plampang, Indon.	H10	50
Planá, Czech Rep.	G8	16
Plana, L'Illa, i., Spain	F10	20
Planada, Ca., U.S.	F5	134
Planalto, Braz.	C11	92
Planchón, Cerro del (El Planchón, Volcán), vol., S.A.	G2	92
Planeta Rica, Col.	C4	86
Plano, Il., U.S.	C9	120
Plano, Tx., U.S.	D2	122
Plantagenet, On., Can.	E2	110
Plantation, Fl., U.S.	J5	116
Plant City, Fl., U.S.	I3	116
Plantersville, Ms., U.S.	C10	122
Plantsite, Az., U.S.	J7	132
Plaquemine, La., U.S.	G7	122
Plasencia, Spain	D4	20
Plaster Rock, N.B., Can.	D9	110
Plasy, Czech Rep.	G9	16
Plata, Isla de la, i., Ec.	H1	86
Plata, Río de la, est., S.A.	G9	92
Plato, Col.	C4	86
Platte, stm., U.S.	C7	108
Platte, stm., U.S.	E3	120
Platte, Île, i., Sey.	k13	69b
Platte Center, Ne., U.S.	F15	126
Platte City, Mo., U.S.	E3	120
Platteville, Co., U.S.	A4	128
Platteville, Wi., U.S.	B7	120
Plattsburgh, N.Y., U.S.	F3	110
Plattsmouth, Ne., U.S.	D2	120
Plau, Ger.	C8	16
Plauen, Ger.	F8	16
Plav, Serb.	G6	26
Plavsk, Russia	G20	10
Playa Azul, Mex.	G7	100
Playa de Fajardo, P.R.	B2	104a
Playa de Guayanilla, P.R.	B2	104a
Playa de Naguabo, P.R.	B4	104a
Playa de Ponce, P.R.	C2	104a
Playa Noriega, Laguna, l., Mex.	A3	100
Playa Vicente, Mex.	G11	100
Playgreen Lake, l., Mb., Can.	E11	106
Play Ku, Viet.	F8	48
Plaza, N.D., U.S.	F12	124
Pleasant, Mount, hill, N.B., Can.	E9	110
Pleasant Bay, N.S., Can.	D16	110
Pleasantdale, Sk., Can.	B9	124
Pleasant Grove, Ut., U.S.	C5	132
Pleasant Hill, Il., U.S.	E7	120
Pleasant Hill, La., U.S.	F5	122
Pleasant Hill, Mo., U.S.	F3	120
Pleasanton, Ks., U.S.	F3	120
Pleasanton, Tx., U.S.	F9	130
Pleasantville, N.J., U.S.	E11	114
Pleasantville, Pa., U.S.	C6	114
Pleaux, Fr.	D8	18
Plehanovo, Russia	F20	10
Plenty, Sk., Can.	C5	124
Plenty, Bay of, b., N.Z.	C7	80
Plentywood, Mt., U.S.	F9	124
Pleščeevo, ozero, l., Russia	D21	10
Pleseck, Russia	E19	8
Plessisville, Qc., Can.	D5	110
Pleszew, Pol.	E13	16
Plétipi, Lac, l., Qc., Can.	E16	106
Plettenbergbaai, S. Afr.	I6	70
Pleven, Blg.	F11	26
Plevna, Mt., U.S.	A8	126
Plitvička Jezera Nacionalni Park, p.o.i., Cro.	F12	22
Pljevlja, Serb.	F6	26
Pljuskovo, Russia	H16	10
Pljussa, stm., Russia	A11	10
Płock, Pol.	D15	16
Płock, state, Pol.	D15	16
Ploërmel, Fr.	G6	14
Ploiești, Rom.	E12	26
Plomb du Cantal, mtn., Fr.	D8	18
Plomer, Point, c., Austl.	H9	76
Plön, Ger.	B6	16
Płońsk, Pol.	D16	16
Ploskoe, Russia	H21	10
Plotnica, Bela.	H9	10
Ploudalmézeau, Fr.	F4	14
Plovdiv, Blg.	G11	26
Plovdiv, state, Blg.	G11	26
Plumerville, Ar., U.S.	B6	122
Plummer, Id., U.S.	C9	136
Plumridge Lakes, l., Austl.	E5	74
Plumtree, Zimb.	B8	70
Plungė, Lith.	E4	10
Plutarco Elías Calles, Presa, res., Mex.	G8	98
Plymouth, Monts.	D3	105a
Plymouth, Eng., U.K.	K8	12
Plymouth, Ca., U.S.	E5	134
Plymouth, In., U.S.	G3	112
Plymouth, Il., U.S.	D6	120
Plymouth, Ma., U.S.	C15	114
Plymouth, N.C., U.S.	I9	114
Plymouth, Ne., U.S.	A11	128
Plymouth, N.H., U.S.	G5	110
Plymouth, Oh., U.S.	C3	114
Plymouth, Pa., U.S.	C10	114
Plzeň, Czech Rep.	G9	16
Pô, Burkina	G4	64
Po, stm., Italy	F8	22
Po, Foci del, mth., Italy	F9	22
Po, Mouths of the see Po, Foci del, mth., Italy	F9	22
Poarta Orientală, Pasul, p., Rom.	D9	26
Pobè, Benin	H5	64
Pobeda, gora, mtn., Russia	C18	34
Pobedino, Russia	G17	34
Pobedy, pik, mtn., Asia	F14	32
Poblado Cerro Gordo, P.R.	A3	104a
Poblado Jacaguas, P.R.	B2	104a
Poblado Mediania Alta, P.R.	B4	104a
Poblado Santana, P.R.	B2	104a
Pobra de Trives, Spain	B3	20
Pocahontas, Ar., U.S.	H7	120
Pocahontas, Ia., U.S.	B3	120
Poção, Braz.	E7	88
Pocatello, Id., U.S.	H14	136
Počep, Russia	H16	10
Pocinok, Russia	D4	32
Pocitos, Salar, pl., Arg.	B4	92
Poço da Cruz, Açude, res., Braz.	E7	88
Poções, Braz.	H5	88
Pocola, Ok., U.S.	B4	122
Pocomoke City, Md., U.S.	F10	114
Poconé, Braz.	G6	84
Pocono Mountains, hills, Pa., U.S.	C10	114
Pocono Summit, Pa., U.S.	C10	114
Poço Redondo, Braz.	F7	88
Poços de Caldas, Braz.	K2	88
Pocrane, Braz.	J5	88
Podbereze, Russia	D13	10
Podborove, Russia	A18	10
Poddębice, Russia	E14	16
Poddore, Russia	C13	10
Poděbrady, Czech Rep.	F11	16
Podgorica (Titograd), Serb.	G6	26
Podjuga, Russia	F19	8
Podkamennaja Tunguska, Russia	B16	32
Podkamennaja Tunguska, stm., Russia	B16	32
Podlasie, reg., Pol.	D19	16
Podol'sk, Russia	E20	10
Podor, Sen.	F2	64
Podporože, Russia	F16	8
Podravina, reg., Cro.	C15	22
Podtěsovo, Russia	C16	32
Podujevo, Serb.	G8	26
Poel, i., Ger.	B7	16
Poelela, Lagoa, l., Moz.	D12	70
Pofadder, S. Afr.	F4	70
Pogar, Russia	H16	10
Poggibonsi, Italy	G8	22
Pogoanele, Rom.	E13	26
Pogoreloe Gorodišče, Russia	D17	10
Pogradec, Alb.	D14	24
Pogradeci see Pogradec, Alb.	D14	24
Pograničnyj, Russia	B9	38
P'ohang, Kor., S.	C2	40
Pohjanmaa, reg., Fin.	D11	8
Pohnpei, i., Micron.	I11	78d
Pohri, India	F6	54
Pohvistnevo, Russia	D8	32
Põide, Est.	B6	10
Poinsett, Cape, c., Ant.	B16	81
Poinsett, Lake, l., S.D., U.S.	C15	126
Point, Tx., U.S.	E3	122
Point Arena, Ca., U.S.	E2	134
Point Au Fer Island, i., La., U.S.	H7	122
Point Baker, Ak., U.S.	E13	140
Pointe-à-la-Garde, Qc., Can.	B10	110
Pointe a la Hache, La., U.S.	H9	122
Pointe-à-Pitre, Guad.	h5	105c
Pointe-à-Pitre-le Raizet, Aéroport de, Guad.	h5	105c
Pointe du Canonnier, c., Guad.	A1	105a
Pointe-Noire, Congo	E2	66
Pointe-Noire, Guad.	h5	105c
Point Fortin, Trin.	s12	105f
Point Hope, Ak., U.S.	C6	140
Point Jupiter, c., St. Vin.	p11	105e
Point Lake, l., N.T., Can.	B8	106
Point Marion, Pa., U.S.	E5	114
Point Pelee National Park, p.o.i., On., Can.	G7	112
Point Pleasant, N.J., U.S.	D11	114
Point Reyes National Seashore, p.o.i., Ca., U.S.	E2	134
Point Roberts, Wa., U.S.	B3	136
Point Salines International Airport, Green.	q10	105e
Point Sapin, N.B., Can.	D12	110
Poisson Blanc, Lac du, res., Qc., Can.	B14	112
Poissy, Fr.	F10	14
Poitiers, Fr.	H9	14
Poitou, hist. reg., Fr.	C5	18
Poivre Atoll, i., Sey.	k12	69b
Pojarkovo, Russia	G14	34
Pojoaque Valley, N.M., U.S.	F2	128
Pojuca, Braz.	G6	88
Pojuca, stm., Braz.	G6	88
Pokaran, India	E3	54
Pokataroo, Austl.	G7	76
Pokhara, Nepal	D10	54
Poko, D.R.C.	D5	66
Pokrovsk, Russia	D14	34
Pokrovskoe, Russia	H19	10
Pola, stm., Russia	C14	10
Polacca Wash, stm., Az., U.S.	H6	132
Polack, Bela.	E11	10
Pola de Lena, Spain	A5	20
Pola de Siero, Spain	A5	20
Polán, Spain	D6	20
Poland, ctry., Eur.	D15	6
Polanów, Pol.	B12	16
Polatlı, Tur.	D15	28
Polcura, Chile	H2	92
Poldnevica, stm., Russia	G22	8
Polebridge, Mt., U.S.	B12	136
Pol-e Khomrī, Afg.	B10	56
Polese see Pripet Marshes, reg., Eur.	H12	10
Polesine, reg., Italy	E8	22
Polewali, Indon.	E11	50
Polgár, Hung.	B8	26
Poli, Cam.	C2	66
Poli, China	D8	42
Policastro, Golfo di, b., Italy	E9	24
Police (Pölitz), Pol.	C10	16
Polička, Czech Rep.	G11	16
Polillo Island, i., Phil.	C3	52
Polillo Islands, is., Phil.	C4	52
Pólis, Cyp.	C3	58
Polist', stm., Russia	C14	10
Polistena, Italy	F10	24
Poljarnyj, Russia	C24	34
Poljarnyj, Russia	B15	8
Poljarnyj Ural, mts., Russia	A10	32
Polk, Ne., U.S.	F15	126
Polk, Pa., U.S.	C6	114
Pol'kino, Russia	B8	34
Pollāchi, India	F3	53
Põllau, Aus.	C12	22
Pollino, Monte, mtn., Italy	E10	24
Pollock, La., U.S.	F6	122
Pollock, S.D., U.S.	B12	126
Polnovo-Seliger, Russia	C15	10
Polo, Il., U.S.	B8	120
Polomet', stm., Russia	C15	10
Polonnaruwa, Sri L.	H5	53
Polonnaruwa, sci., Sri L.	H5	53
Polotnjanyj, Russia	F19	10
Polotsk see Polack, Bela.	E11	10
Polski Trămbeš, Blg.	F12	26
Polson, Mt., U.S.	C12	136
Poltava, Ukr.	E4	32
Poltimore, Qc., Can.	C14	112
Põltsamaa, Est.	B8	10
Poluj, stm., Russia	A11	32
Polunočnoe, Russia	B10	32
Polur, India	E4	53
Polvijärvi, Fin.	E13	8
Polyaigos, i., Grc.	G7	28
Polynésie, is. see Polynesia, is.	J22	142
Polýsajevo, Russia	F6	34
Pomarkku, Fin.	F9	8
Pombal, Braz.	D7	88
Pomeranian Bay, b., Eur.	C11	16
Pomeranian Bay, b., Eur.	B6	16
Pomerene, Az., U.S.	K6	132
Pomeroy, Ia., U.S.	C13	92
Pomeroy, Oh., U.S.	E3	114
Pomeroy, Wa., U.S.	D9	136
Pomfret, S. Afr.	D6	70
Pomi, Rom.	B10	26
Pomme de Terre, stm., Mn., U.S.	F3	118
Pomme de Terre, stm., Mo., U.S.	G4	120
Pomme de Terre Lake, res., Mo., U.S.	G4	120
Pomona, Ca., U.S.	I8	134
Pomona, Ks., U.S.	F2	120
Pomona Lake, res., Ks., U.S.	F2	120
Pomorskij proliv, strt., Russia	B24	8
Pomozdino, Russia	B8	32
Pompano Beach, Fl., U.S.	J5	116
Pompei, sci., Italy	D8	24
Pompeyevka, Russia	G15	34
Pompéu, Braz.	J3	88
Pomquet, N.S., Can.	E15	110
Ponask Lake, l., Sk., Can.	B9	124
Ponazyrevo, Russia	G22	8
Ponca, Ne., U.S.	B1	120
Ponca City, Ok., U.S.	E11	128
Ponce, P.R.	B2	104a
Ponce, Aeropuerto, P.R.	B2	104a
Ponce de Leon, Fl., U.S.	G12	122
Poncha Pass, p., Co., U.S.	C2	128
Pond Creek, Ok., U.S.	E11	128
Ponderay, Id., U.S.	B10	136
Pondicherry (Puducherri), India	F4	53
Pondicherry, state, India	E5	53
Pond Inlet see Mittimatalik, Nu., Can.	A15	106
Pond Inlet, b., Nu., Can.	A15	106
Pondosa, Ca., U.S.	B4	134
Ponente, Riviera di, cst., Italy	F5	22
Ponérihouen, N. Cal.	m15	79d
Ponferrada, Spain	B4	20
Pongola, stm., S. Afr.	E10	70
Poniatowa, Pol.	E17	16
Ponizove, Russia	E14	10
Ponnaiyār, stm., India	E4	53
Ponnāni, India	F2	53
Ponnūru Nidubrolu, India	C5	53
Ponoj, Russia	C18	8
Ponoj, stm., Russia	C18	8
Ponoka, Ab., Can.	D17	138
Ponorogo, Indon.	G7	50
Pons, Fr.	D5	18
Ponta Delgada, Port.	C3	60
Ponta Grossa, Braz.	B12	92
Pontalina, Braz.	I1	88
Ponta Porã, Braz.	D5	90
Pontarlier, Fr.	H15	14
Pontas de Pedra, Braz.	D8	88
Pontassieve, Italy	G8	22
Pontchartrain, Lake, l., La., U.S.	G8	122
Pontchâteau, Fr.	G6	14
Pont-de-Vaux, Fr.	C10	18
Ponte Alta do Bom Jesus, Braz.	G2	88
Ponte-Caldelas, Spain	B2	20
Ponte de Lima, Port.	C2	20
Pontederas, Italy	G7	22
Pontedeume, Spain	A2	20
Ponte do Púngoè, Moz.	A12	70
Ponteix, Sk., Can.	E6	124
Ponte Nova, Braz.	K4	88
Ponte Serrada, Braz.	C12	92
Pontevedra, Spain	B2	20
Pontevedra, co., Spain	B2	20
Pontiac, Il., U.S.	D9	120
Pontiac, Mi., U.S.	B2	114
Pontianak, Indon.	C6	50
Pontine Islands see Ponziane, Isole, is., Italy	D6	24
Pontivy, Fr.	F5	14
Pontoise, Fr.	E11	14
Pontotoc, Ms., U.S.	C9	122
Pontotoc, Tx., U.S.	D9	130
Pontremoli, Italy	F6	22
Pontresina, Switz.	D6	22
Pont-Rouge, Qc., Can.	D5	110
Ponts, Spain	C12	20
Pont-sur-Yonne, Fr.	F12	14
Pontus Mountains see Doğu Karadeniz Dağları, mts., Tur.	A5	56
Pontypridd, Wales, U.K.	J9	12
Ponyri, Russia	H19	10
Ponziane, Isole (Pontine Islands), is., Italy	D6	24
Poole, Eng., U.K.	K11	12
Pooley Island, i., B.C., Can.	D2	138
Poolville, Tx., U.S.	B10	130
Pooncarie, Austl.	I4	76
Poopó, Bol.	C3	90
Poopó, Lago, l., Bol.	C3	90
Popayán, Col.	F3	86
Pope, Ms., U.S.	C8	122
Popeşti-Leordeni, Rom.	E13	26
Popham Bay, b., Nu., Can.	C17	106
Popigaj, Russia	B10	34
Popigaj, stm., Russia	B10	34
Popиljah Lake, l., Austl.	I3	76
Poplar, Mt., U.S.	F8	124
Poplar, stm., Can.	B16	124
Poplar, stm., Can.	N4	124
Poplar, West Fork (West Poplar), stm., N.A.	F8	124
Poplar Bluff, Mo., U.S.	H7	120
Poplar Hill, On., Can.	E12	106
Poplar Point, Mb., Can.	D16	124
Poplarville, Ms., U.S.	G9	122
Popocatépetl, Volcán, vol., Mex.	F9	100
Popoh, Indon.	H7	50
Popokabaka, D.R.C.	F3	66
Popoli, Italy	H11	22
Popondetta, Pap. N. Gui.	b4	79a
Popovo, Blg.	F13	26
Poprad, Slvk.	G16	16
Poprad, stm., Eur.	G16	16
Popricani, Rom.	B14	26
Porangaba, Braz.	L2	88
Poquoson, Va., U.S.	G9	114
Porangatu, Braz.	G1	88
Porbandar, India	H2	54
Porce, stm., Col.	D4	86
Porcher Island, i., B.C., Can.	E4	106
Porco, Bol.	C3	90
Porcos, stm., Braz.	G3	88
Porcuna, Spain	G6	20
Porcupine, stm., N.A.	C10	140
Pordenone, Italy	D9	22
Pordim, Blg.	F11	26
Poreče, Russia	E18	10
Poreče-Rybnoe, Russia	C22	10
Porhov, Russia	C12	10
Pori (Björneborg), Fin.	F9	8
Porjaguba, Russia	C15	8
Porlamar, Ven.	B10	86
Pornic, Fr.	G6	14
Poronaysk, Russia	G17	34
Poroshkovo, Russia	H18	16
Porpoise Bay, b., Ant.	B17	81
Porrentruy, Switz.	C3	22
Porretta Terme, Italy	F7	22
Porsangen, b., Nor.	A11	8
Porsangerhalvøya, pen., Nor.	A11	8
Porsgrunn, Nor.	G3	8
Porsuk, stm., Tur.	D13	28
Portachuelo, Bol.	C4	90
Port Adelaide, Austl.	J2	76
Portadown, N. Ire., U.K.	G6	12
Portage, Mi., U.S.	F4	112
Portage, Ut., U.S.	F5	22
Portage, Wi., U.S.	H9	118
Portage Bay, b., Mb., Can.	C15	124
Portage Lake, l., Mi., U.S.	D10	118
Portage la Prairie, Mb., Can.	E15	124
Portageville, Mo., U.S.	H8	120
Portal, Ga., U.S.	D4	116
Portal, N.D., U.S.	F11	124
Portalegre, Port.	E3	20
Portalegre, state, Port.	E3	20
Portales, N.M., U.S.	G5	128
Port Alfred, S. Afr.	H8	70
Port Alice, B.C., Can.	F3	138
Port Allen, La., U.S.	G7	122
Port Angeles, Wa., U.S.	B3	136
Port Antonio, Jam.	i14	104d
Port Aransas, Tx., U.S.	G10	130
Port Arthur see Lüshun, China	E4	38
Port Arthur, Tx., U.S.	H4	122
Port Askaig, Scot., U.K.	F6	12
Port Augusta, Austl.	F7	74
Port au Port Peninsula, pen., Nf., Can.	B17	110
Port-au-Prince, Haiti	C11	102
Port-au-Prince, Baie de, b., Haiti	C11	102
Port Austin, Mi., U.S.	D6	112
Port Blair, India	F7	46
Port Borden, P.E., Can.	D13	110
Port Byron, Il., U.S.	J8	118
Port Canning, India	G12	54
Port-Cartier, Qc., Can.	E17	106
Port Chalmers, N.Z.	G4	80
Port Charlotte, Fl., U.S.	J3	116
Port Clinton, Oh., U.S.	C3	114
Port Clyde, Me., U.S.	G7	110
Port Colborne, On., Can.	F10	112
Port Coquitlam, B.C., Can.	G8	138
Port-de-Paix, Haiti	C11	102
Port Dickson, Malay.	K5	48
Port Edward see Weihai, China	C10	42
Port Edward, S. Afr.	G10	70
Port Edwards, Wi., U.S.	G9	118
Porteirinha, Braz.	H4	88
Portel, Braz.	D7	84
Port Elgin, N.B., Can.	D12	110
Port Elgin, On., Can.	D8	112
Port Elizabeth, S. Afr.	H7	70
Port-en-Bessin, Fr.	E8	14
Porter, Tx., U.S.	G3	122
Port Erin, I. of Man	G8	12
Porter Point, c., St. Vin.	o11	105e
Porterville, S. Afr.	H4	70
Porterville, Ca., U.S.	G7	134
Porterville, Ms., U.S.	E10	122
Portete, Bahía de, b., Col.	A6	86
Port Fairy, Austl.	L4	76
Port Gamble, Wa., U.S.	C4	136
Port-Gentil, Gabon	E1	66
Port Gibson, Ms., U.S.	F8	122
Port Graham, Ak., U.S.	E9	140
Port-Harcourt, Nig.	I6	64
Port Hardy, B.C., Can.	F3	138
Port Hawkesbury, N.S., Can.	E15	110
Port Hedland, Austl.	D3	74
Port Heiden, Ak., U.S.	E8	140
Port Hill, P.E., Can.	D13	110
Port Hood, N.S., Can.	D15	110
Port Hope, On., Can.	E11	112
Port Hope, Mi., U.S.	E7	112
Port Huron, Mi., U.S.	B3	114
Portimão, Port.	G2	20
Port Isabel, Tx., U.S.	H10	130
Port Jervis, N.Y., U.S.	C11	114
Port Kembla, Austl.	J8	76
Port Laoise see Portlaoise, Ire.	H5	12
Portland, Austl.	K3	76
Portland, Ar., U.S.	D7	122
Portland, In., U.S.	H5	112
Portland, Me., U.S.	G6	110
Portland, N.D., U.S.	G16	124
Portland, Or., U.S.	E4	136
Portland, Tn., U.S.	H11	120
Portland, Tx., U.S.	G10	130
Portland, Bill of, c., Eng., U.K.	K10	12
Portland, Cape, c., Austl.	n13	77a
Portland, Isle of, i., Eng., U.K.	K10	12
Portland Bay, b., Austl.	L3	76
Portland Bight, b., Jam.	j13	104d
Portland Point, c., Jam.	j13	104d
Portlaoise, Ire.	H5	12
Port Lavaca, Tx., U.S.	E11	130
Port Leyden, N.Y., U.S.	E14	112
Port Lincoln, Austl.	F7	74
Port Loko, S.L.	H2	64
Port-Louis, Guad.	h5	105c
Port Louis, Mrts.	h10	69a
Port-Lyautey see Kénitra, Mor.	C3	64
Port MacDonnell, Austl.	L3	76
Port Macquarie, Austl.	H9	76
Port Maria, Jam.	i14	104d
Port McNeill, B.C., Can.	F3	138
Port McNicol, On., Can.	D10	112
Port Moller, Ak., U.S.	E7	140
Port Morant, Jam.	j14	104d
Portmore, Jam.	j13	104d
Port Moresby, Pap. N. Gui.	b4	79a
Port Morien, N.S., Can.	D17	110
Port Neches, Tx., U.S.	H4	122
Port Nelson, Mb., Can.	D12	106
Portneuf, stm., Qc., Can.	B7	110
Portneuf, stm., Id., U.S.	H14	136
Port Neville, B.C., Can.	F4	138
Port Nolloth, S. Afr.	F3	70
Port Norris, N.J., U.S.	E10	114
Porto, Port.	C2	20
Porto, state, Port.	C2	20
Pôrto Acre, Braz.	E4	84
Porto Alegre, Braz.	E12	92
Porto Alegre, S. Tom./P.	J6	64
Porto Amboim, Ang.	C1	68
Portobelo, Pan.	H8	102
Porto Calvo, Braz.	E8	88
Porto de Moz, Braz.	D7	84
Porto de Pedras, Braz.	E8	88
Porto dos Gaúchos, Braz.	F6	84
Porto Empédocle, Italy	G7	24
Porto Esperança, Braz.	G6	84
Porto Esperidião, Braz.	G6	84
Porto Feliz, Braz.	L2	88
Portoferraio, Italy	H7	22
Porto Ferreira, Braz.	K2	88
Port of Ness, Scot., U.K.	C6	12
Porto Franco, Braz.	D2	88
Portogruaro, Italy	E9	22
Portomaggiore, Italy	F8	22
Porto Mendes, Braz.	B10	92
Porto Murtinho, Braz.	D5	90
Porto Nacional, Braz.	F1	88
Porto-Novo, Benin	H5	64
Porto Novo, India	F4	53
Port Orange, Fl., U.S.	G5	116
Port Orchard, Wa., U.S.	C4	136
Port Orford, Or., U.S.	H2	136
Porto San Giorgio, Italy	G10	22
Porto Santana, Braz.	D7	84
Porto Santo, i., Port.	C1	64
Porto Santo Stefano, Italy	H7	22
Porto Seguro, Braz.	I6	88
Porto Tolle, Italy	F9	22
Porto Torres, Italy	D2	24
Porto União, Braz.	C12	92
Pôrto Válter, Braz.	E3	84
Porto-Vecchio, Fr.	H15	18
Porto Velho, Braz.	E5	84
Pôrto Velho, Ec.	H1	86
Port Patrick, Vanuatu	m17	79d
Port Perry, On., Can.	D11	112
Port Phillip Bay, b., Austl.	L5	76
Port Pirie, Austl.	F7	74
Port Renfrew, B.C., Can.	H6	138
Port Rowan, On., Can.	F9	112
Port Royal, Jam.	j14	104d
Port Royal, Pa., U.S.	D8	114
Port Royal Sound, strt., S.C., U.S.	D5	116
Port Said see Būr Sa'īd, Egypt	G3	58
Port Saint Joe, Fl., U.S.	H13	122
Port Saint Johns, S. Afr.	I5	116
Port Saint Lucie, Fl., U.S.	I5	116
Port Sanilac, Mi., U.S.	E7	112
Port Saunders, Nf., Can.	i22	107a
Port Shepstone, S. Afr.	G10	70
Port Simpson, B.C., Can.	E4	106
Portsmouth, Dom.	i6	105c
Portsmouth, Eng., U.K.	K11	12
Portsmouth, N.H., U.S.	G6	110
Portsmouth, Oh., U.S.	F2	114
Portsmouth, Va., U.S.	H9	114
Portsoy, Scot., U.K.	D10	12
Port Stanley, On., Can.	F8	112
Port Sudan see Būr Sūdān, Sudan	D7	62
Port Sulphur, La., U.S.	H9	122
Port Talbot, Wales, U.K.	J9	12
Porttipahdan tekojärvi, l., Fin.	B12	8
Port Townsend, Wa., U.S.	B4	136
Portugal, ctry., Eur.	E2	20
Portugalete, Spain	A7	20
Portuguesa, state, Ven.	C7	86
Portuguesa, stm., Ven.	C8	86
Portuguese Guinea see Guinea-Bissau, ctry., Afr.	G1	64
Port Vila, Vanuatu	k17	79d
Portville, N.Y., U.S.	B7	114
Port-Vladimir, Russia	B15	8
Port Wentworth, Ga., U.S.	D4	116
Port Wing, Wi., U.S.	E7	118
Porus, Jam.	i13	104d
Porvenir, Chile	J2	90
Porvoo, Fin.	F11	8
Porzuna, Spain	E6	20
Posadas, Arg.	C10	92
Posadas, Spain	G5	20
Poschiavo, Switz.	D10	22
Posen, N.Y., U.S.	C6	112
Poshan see Boshan, China	C7	42
Posio, Fin.	C12	8
Poso, Indon.	D12	50
Poso, Danau, l., Indon.	D12	50
Poso, Teluk, b., Indon.	D12	50
Pospeliha, Russia	D14	32
Posse, Braz.	H2	88
Possession Island, i., Nmb.	E2	70
Pössneck, Ger.	F7	16
Possum Kingdom Lake, res., Tx., U.S.	B9	130
Post, Tx., U.S.	A6	130
Posta de Jihuites, Mex.	I2	130
Postelle, Tn., U.S.	A1	116
Postmasburg, S. Afr.	F6	70
Postojna, Slvn.	E11	22
Postrevalle, Bol.	C4	90
Postville, La., U.S.	A6	120
Potaro, stm., Guy.	E12	86
Potaro-Siparuni, state, Guy.	E12	86
Potchefstroom, S. Afr.	E8	70
Poté, Braz.	I5	88
Poteau, Ok., U.S.	B4	122
Poteet, Tx., U.S.	E9	130
Potenza, Italy	D9	24
Potgietersrus, S. Afr.	D9	70
Poth, Tx., U.S.	E9	130
Potholes Reservoir, res., Wa., U.S.	D7	136
Poti, Geor.	F6	32
Poti, stm., Braz.	C4	88
Potiraguá, Braz.	H6	88
Potiskum, Nig.	G7	64
Potomac, Il., U.S.	H2	112
Potomac, stm., U.S.	F9	114
Potomac, North Fork South Branch, stm., U.S.	F6	114
Potomac, South Branch, stm., U.S.	E7	114
Potomac Heights, Md., U.S.	F8	114
Potosí, Bol.	C3	90
Potosí, Mo., U.S.	G7	120
Potosí, Cerro, mtn., Mex.	C8	100
Potrero, Cerro del (El Potro, Cerro), mtn., S.A.	D3	92
Potsdam, Ger.	D9	16
Potsdam, N.Y., U.S.	F2	110
Pott, Île, i., N. Cal.	l14	79d
Potter, Ne., U.S.	F9	126
Potterville, Mi., U.S.	B1	114
Potts Camp, Ms., U.S.	C9	122
Pottstown, Pa., U.S.	D10	114
Pottsville, Pa., U.S.	D9	114
Pouancé, Fr.	G7	14
Poughkeepsie, N.Y., U.S.	C11	114
Poulan, Ga., U.S.	E2	116
Poulsbo, Wa., U.S.	C4	136
Poultney, Vt., U.S.	G3	110
Poum, N. Cal.	m14	79d
Pouso Alegre, Braz.	L3	88
Poŭthĭsăt, Camb.	F6	48
Poŭthĭsăt, stm., Camb.	F6	48
Poutini see Westland National Park, p.o.i., N.Z.	F3	80
Poutrincourt, Lac, l., Qc., Can.	A2	110
Povážská Bystrica, Slov.	G14	16
Povenec, Russia	E16	8
Póvoa de Varzim, Port.	C2	20
Povorino, Russia	D6	32
Povorotnyj, mys, c., Russia	C10	38
Povungnituk, Qc., Can.	C15	106
Povungnituk, stm., Qc., Can.	C15	106
Powassan, On., Can.	B10	112
Poway, Ca., U.S.	K9	134
Powder, stm., U.S.	A7	126
Powder, South Fork, stm., Wy., U.S.	D6	126
Powderly, Tx., U.S.	D3	122
Powder River Pass, p., Wy., U.S.	C5	126
Powell, Wy., U.S.	C4	126
Powell, Lake, res., U.S.	F5	132
Powell, Mount, mtn., Austl.	C6	76
Powell Creek, stm., Austl.	C7	74
Powell River, B.C., Can.	G6	138
Powers, Or., U.S.	H2	136
Powers Lake, N.D., U.S.	F11	124
Powhatan, Va., U.S.	G7	114
Powhatan Point, Oh., U.S.	E4	114
Poxoréu, Braz.	G7	84
Poya, N. Cal.	m15	79d
Poyang, Hu's, l., China	G7	42
Poyen, Ar., U.S.	C6	122
Poygan, Lake, l., Wi., U.S.	G9	118
Požarevac, Serb.	E8	26
Poza Rica de Hidalgo, Mex.	E10	100
Požega, Cro.	E14	22
Požega, Serb.	F7	26
Poznań, Pol.	D12	16
Poznań, state, Pol.	D12	16
Pozoblanco, Spain	F6	20
Pozo-Cañada, Spain	F9	20
Pozo del Molle, Arg.	F6	92
Pozo del Tigre, Arg.	B7	92
Pozos, Punta, c., Arg.	I3	90
Pozo Verde, Ec.	H1	86
Pozuzo, Peru	F2	84
Pozzallo, Italy	H8	24
Pozzuoli, Italy	D7	24
Prachatice, Czech Rep.	G10	16
Prachin Buri, Thai.	F5	48
Prachuap Khiri Khan, Thai.	G4	48
Pradera, Col.	F3	86
Prado, Braz.	I6	88
Prados, Braz.	K3	88
Praești, Den.	I5	8
Prague see Praha, Czech Rep.	F10	16
Prague, Ne., U.S.	F16	126
Prague, Ok., U.S.	B2	122
Praha (Prague), Czech Rep.	F10	16
Praha, state, Czech Rep.	F10	16
Prahova, state, Rom.	D13	26
Praia, C.V.	l10	65a
Praia Grande, Braz.	D13	92
Prainha Nova, Braz.	E5	84
Prairie, Austl.	C5	76
Prairie, stm., Mi., U.S.	G4	112
Prairie City, Ia., U.S.	C4	120
Prairie City, Il., U.S.	D7	120
Prairie Creek, stm., Ne., U.S.	F15	126
Prairie Dog Creek, stm., Ks., U.S.	B8	128
Prairie du Chien, Wi., U.S.	A6	120
Prairie du Sac, Wi., U.S.	H9	118
Prairie River, Sk., Can.	B11	124
Prairies, Coteau des, hills, U.S.	C16	126
Prairies, Lake of the, res., Can.	C12	124
Prairie View, Tx., U.S.	G3	122
Prairie Village, Ks., U.S.	B14	128
Pran Buri, Thai.	F4	48
Pran Buri, stm., Thai.	F4	48
Prânhita, stm., India	B5	53
Praslin, i., Sey.	j13	69b
Prasonísi, Ákra, c., Grc.	H10	28
Praszka, Pol.	E14	16
Prata, Braz.	J1	88
Prata, stm., Braz.	J1	88
Prata, stm., Braz.	I2	88
Pratāpgarh, India	F5	54
Pratápolis, Braz.	K2	88
Pratas Island see Tungsha Tao, i., Tai.	K7	42
Prat de Llobregat see El Prat de Llobregat, Spain	C12	20
Prato, Italy	G8	22
Pratt, Ks., U.S.	D10	128
Prattville, Al., U.S.	E12	122
Pratudão, stm., Braz.	H3	88
Pravdinskij, Russia	D20	10
Pravia, Spain	A4	20
Praya, Indon.	H10	50
Preajba, Rom.	E12	26
Prečistoe, Russia	G19	8
Predeal, Rom.	D12	26
Preeceville, Sk., Can.	C11	124
Preetz, Ger.	B6	16
Pregolja, stm., Russia	F3	10
Pregonero, Ven.	D6	86
Preguiças, stm., Braz.	B4	88
Preila, Lith.	E4	10
Prêk Poŭthĭ, Camb.	G7	48
Prelate, Sk., Can.	D4	124
Prémontré, Fr.	G5	120
Premont, Tx., U.S.	G9	130
Premuda, Otok, i., Cro.	F11	22
Prenjasi see Prrenjas, Alb.	C14	24
Prentiss, Ms., U.S.	F9	122
Prenzlau, Ger.	C9	16
Preobraženie, Russia	C10	38
Preparis Island, i., Mya.	F7	46
Preparis North Channel, strt., Mya.	E7	46
Preparis South Channel, strt., Mya.	F7	46
Přerov, Czech Rep.	G13	16
Prescott, On., Can.	D14	112
Prescott, Ar., U.S.	D5	122
Prescott, Wi., U.S.	G6	118
Prescott Island, i., Nu., Can.	A11	106
Presidencia de la Plaza, Arg.	C7	92
Presidencia Roca, Arg.	C8	92
Presidencia Roque Sáenz Peña, Arg.	C7	92
Presidente Dutra, Braz.	C3	88
Presidente Epitácio, Braz.	D6	90
Presidente Hayes, state, Para.	B8	92
Presidente Prudente, Braz.	D6	90
Presidio, Tx., U.S.	E3	130
Presidio, stm., Mex.	D6	100
Presnogor'kovka, Kaz.	D11	32
Prešov, Slvk.	H17	16
Prespa, Lake, l., Eur.	D14	24
Presque Isle, Me., U.S.	D8	110
Presque Isle, pen., Pa., U.S.	B5	114
Prestea, Ghana	H4	64
Preston, Eng., U.K.	H10	12
Preston, Id., U.S.	A5	132
Preston, Ks., U.S.	D10	128
Preston, Mn., U.S.	H6	118
Prestonsburg, Ky., U.S.	G3	114
Prestwick, Scot., U.K.	F8	12
Preto, stm., Braz.	G1	88
Preto, stm., Braz.	B4	88
Preto, stm., Braz.	G1	88
Pretoria, S. Afr.	D9	70
Pretty Prairie, Ks., U.S.	D10	128
Préveza, Grc.	E3	28
Prey Lvêa, Camb.	G7	48
Prey Vêng, Camb.	G8	48
Pribilof Islands, is., Ak., U.S.	E5	140
Priboj, Serb.	F6	26
Příbram, Czech Rep.	G10	16
Price, Ut., U.S.	D6	132
Price, stm., Ut., U.S.	D6	132
Price Island, i., B.C., Can.	D2	138
Prichard, Al., U.S.	G10	122
Prickly Pear Cays, is., Anguilla	A1	105a
Priddy, Tx., U.S.	C9	130
Priego de Córdoba, Spain	G6	20
Priekule, Lith.	E4	10
Priekule, Lat.	D4	10
Priekulė, Lith.	E4	70
Priest, stm., Id., U.S.	B10	136
Priest Lake, res., Id., U.S.	B9	136
Priest River, Id., U.S.	B10	136
Prieta, Peña, mtn., Spain	A6	20
Prieto Díaz, Phil.	D5	52
Prievidza, Slov.	H14	16
Prijedor, Bos.	E2	26
Prilep, Mac.	A22	10
Prilep, Mac.	B4	24
Primeira Cruz, Braz.	B4	88
Primera, Tx., U.S.	H10	130
Primero, stm., Arg.	E6	92
Primghar, Ia., U.S.	A2	120
Primone, Russia	C9	38
Primorskij hrebet, mts., Russia	F10	34
Primorsko, Blg.	G14	26
Primo Tapia, Mex.	K8	134
Primrose Lake, l., Can.	A8	124
Prince Albert, Sk., Can.	A8	124
Prince Albert, S. Afr.	H6	70
Prince Albert Sound, strt., N.T., Can.	A7	106
Prince Alfred, Cape, c., N.T., Can.	B15	140
Prince Charles Island, i., Nu., Can.	B15	106
Prince Charles Mountains, mts., Ant.	C11	81
Prince Edward Island, state, Can.	D13	110
Prince Edward Island National Park, p.o.i., P.E., Can.	D13	110
Prince Frederick, Md., U.S.	F9	114
Prince George, B.C., Can.	C8	138
Prince George, Va., U.S.	G8	114
Prince Gustaf Adolf Sea, s., Nu., Can.	B4	141
Prince of Wales Island, i., Austl.	B8	74
Prince of Wales Island, i., Nu., Can.	A11	106

I·46 Prince of Wales Island – Rājbāri

Name	Map Ref.	Page
Prince of Wales Island, i., Ak., U.S.	E13	140
Prince of Wales Strait, strt., N.T., Can.	B15	140
Prince Olav Coast, cst., Ant.	B9	81
Prince Patrick Island, i., N.T., Can.	A16	140
Prince Regent Inlet, b., Nu., Can.	A12	106
Prince Rupert, B.C., Can.	E4	106
Prince Rupert Bluff Point, c., Dom.	i5	105c
Princes Islands see Kızıl Adalar, is., Tur.	C11	28
Princess Anne, Md., U.S.	F10	114
Princess Astrid Coast, cst., Ant.	C6	81
Princess Charlotte Bay, b., Austl.	B8	74
Princess Martha Coast, cst., Ant.	C4	81
Princess Ragnhild Coast, cst., Ant.	C7	81
Princess Royal Island, i., B.C., Can.	C1	138
Princes Town, Trin.	s12	105f
Princeton, B.C., Can.	G10	138
Princeton, Ca., U.S.	D3	134
Princeton, In., U.S.	F10	120
Princeton, Ky., U.S.	G9	120
Princeton, Me., U.S.	E9	110
Princeton, Mi., U.S.	B2	112
Princeton, N.C., U.S.	A7	116
Princeton, N.J., U.S.	D11	114
Princeton, Wi., U.S.	H9	118
Princeton, W.V., U.S.	G4	114
Princeville, Qc., Can.	D4	110
Princeville, Il., U.S.	D8	120
Prince William Sound, strt., Ak., U.S.	D10	140
Príncipe, i., S. Tom./P.	I6	64
Príncipe da Beira, Braz.	F5	84
Prineville, Or., U.S.	F6	136
Pringsewu, Indon.	F4	50
Prinses Margrietkanaal, can., Neth.	A14	14
Prins Karls Forland, i., Nor.	B27	141
Prinzapolka, stm., Nic.	F5	102
Priozersk, Russia	F14	8
Pripet (Prypjac'), stm., Eur.	H10	10
Pripet Marshes, reg., Eur.	H12	10
Pripoljarnyj Ural, mts., Russia	A9	32
Priština, Serb.	G8	26
Pritchett, Co., U.S.	D6	128
Pritzwalk, Ger.	C8	16
Privas, Fr.	E10	18
Priverno, Italy	C7	24
Privodino, Russia	F22	8
Prizren, Serb.	G7	26
Prjaža, Russia	F15	8
Probolinggo, Indon.	G8	50
Probstzella, Ger.	F7	16
Procida, Isola di, i., Italy	D7	24
Procter, B.C., Can.	G13	138
Proctor, Mn., U.S.	E6	118
Proctor Lake, res., Tx., U.S.	C9	130
Proddatūr, India	D4	53
Proença-a-Nova, Port.	E2	20
Progreso, Mex.	B3	102
Progreso, Mex.	B8	100
Progreso, Mex.	K10	134
Progreso, Ur.	G9	92
Prohladnyj, Russia	F6	32
Project City, Ca., U.S.	C3	134
Prokopevsk, Russia	D15	32
Prokuplje, Serb.	F8	26
Prokuševo, Russia	G16	8
Proletarskij, Russia	E20	10
Prome (Pyè), Mya.	C2	48
Pronja, stm., Bela.	G14	10
Pronja, stm., Russia	F21	10
Prony, Baie de, b., N. Cal.	n16	79d
Prophet, stm., B.C., Can.	D6	106
Prophetstown, Il., U.S.	C8	120
Propriá, Braz.	F7	88
Propriano, Fr.	H14	18
Proserpine, Austl.	C7	76
Prosna, stm., Pol.	E14	16
Prospect, Oh., U.S.	D2	114
Prosperidad, Phil.	F5	52
Prosser, Wa., U.S.	D7	136
Prostějov, Czech Rep.	G12	16
Prostki, Pol.	C18	16
Proston, Austl.	F8	76
Proszowice, Pol.	F16	16
Protection, Ks., U.S.	D9	128
Protem, S. Afr.	I5	70
Protva, stm., Russia	F20	10
Provadija, Blg.	F14	26
Prøven (Kangersuatsiaq), Grnld.	C14	141
Provence, hist. reg., Fr.	F12	18
Providence, Ky., U.S.	G10	120
Providence, R.I., U.S.	C14	114
Providence, Ut., U.S.	B5	132
Providence, Atoll de, i., Sey.	k12	69b
Providence, Cape, c., N.Z.	H2	80
Providencia, Mex.	G4	130
Providencia, Isla de, i., Col.	F7	102
Providenciales, i., T./C. Is.	B11	102
Providenija, Russia	D26	34
Provincetown, Ma., U.S.	B15	114
Provins, Fr.	F12	14
Provo, Ut., U.S.	C5	132
Provo, stm., Ut., U.S.	C5	132
Provost, Ab., Can.	B3	124
Prrenjas, Alb.	C14	24
Prudentópolis, Braz.	B12	92
Prudhoe Bay, Ak., U.S.	B10	140
Prudhoe Island, i., Austl.	C7	76
Prudnik, Pol.	F13	16
Pruszków, Pol.	D16	16
Prut, stm., Eur.	D15	26
Pružany, Bela.	H7	10
Prydz Bay, b., Ant.	B12	81
Pryluky, Ukr.	D4	32
Pryor, Ok., U.S.	H2	120
Przasnysz, Pol.	D16	16
Przedbórz, Pol.	E15	16
Przemyśl, Pol.	G18	16
Przemyśl, state, Pol.	F18	16
Przeworsk, Pol.	F18	16
Psachná, Grc.	E6	28
Pskov, Russia	C11	10
Pskov, Lake, l., Eur.	B11	10
Pskovskaja oblast', co., Russia	C11	10
Pszczyna, Pol.	G14	16
Ptarmigan, Cape, c., N.T., Can.	A7	106
Ptolemaís, Grc.	C4	28
Ptuj, Slvn.	D12	22
Puakatike, Volcán, vol., Chile	e30	78l
Puán, Arg.	H6	92
Pucallpa, Peru	E3	84
Pucará, Bol.	C4	90
Pučeveem, stm., Russia	C23	34
Pučež, Russia	H20	8
Pucheng, China	H8	42
Pucheng, China	D3	42
Púchov, Slov.	G14	16
Pučišća, Cro.	G13	22
Pudasjärvi, Fin.	D12	8
Pudož, Russia	F17	8
Puduari, stm., Braz.	I11	86
Puduchcheri *see* Pondicherry, India	F4	53
Pudukkottai, India	F4	53
Puebla, state, Mex.	F10	100
Puebla de Don Fadrique, Spain	G8	20
Puebla de Sanabria, Spain	B4	20
Puebla de Zaragoza, Mex.	F9	100
Pueblito, Mex.	E2	130
Pueblito de Ponce, P.R.	B1	104a
Pueblo, Co., U.S.	C4	128
Pueblonuevo, Col.	C4	86
Pueblo Nuevo, P.R.	B2	104a
Pueblo Nuevo, Ven.	B7	86
Pueblo Viejo, Laguna, l., Mex.	D10	100
Pueblo Yaqui, Mex.	B4	100
Puente-Caldelas *see* Ponte-Caldelas, Spain	B2	20
Puente del Arzobispo, Spain	E5	20
Puentedeume *see* Pontedeume, Spain	A2	20
Puente Genil, Spain	G6	20
Puerca, Punta, c., P.R.	B4	104a
Puerco, stm., N.M., U.S.	I10	132
Puerco, stm., U.S.	I7	132
Puerto Acosta, Bol.	C3	90
Puerto Adela, Para.	B10	92
Puerto Aisén, Chile	I2	90
Puerto Alegre, Bol.	B4	90
Puerto Ángel, Mex.	H10	100
Puerto Arista, Mex.	H11	100
Puerto Armuelles, Pan.	H6	102
Puerto Asís, Col.	G3	86
Puerto Ayacucho, Ven.	E8	86
Puerto Baquerizo Moreno, Ec.	i12	84a
Puerto Barrios, Guat.	E3	102
Puerto Bermúdez, Peru	F3	84
Puerto Berrío, Col.	D4	86
Puerto Bolívar, Col.	A5	86
Puerto Boyacá, Col.	E4	86
Puerto Cabello, Ven.	B7	86
Puerto Cabezas, Nic.	F6	102
Puerto Carreño, Col.	D8	86
Puerto Chicama, Peru	E2	84
Puerto Colombia, Col.	B4	86
Puerto Cortés, Hond.	E3	102
Puerto Cumarebo, Ven.	B7	86
Puerto Deseado, Arg.	I3	90
Puerto Escondido, Mex.	H10	100
Puerto Escondido, c., Ven.	p20	104g
Puerto Esperanza, Arg.	B10	92
Puerto Fonciere, Para.	D5	90
Puerto Francisco de Orellana, Ec.	H3	86
Puerto Heath, Bol.	B3	90
Puerto Iguazú, Arg.	B10	92
Puerto Ingeniero Ibáñez, Chile	I2	90
Puerto Inírida, Col.	F7	86
Puerto Juárez, Mex.	B4	102
Puerto la Cruz, Ven.	B9	86
Puerto Leguízamo, Col.	H4	86
Puerto Libertad, Mex.	G6	98
Puerto Limón, Col.	F5	86
Puerto Limón, C.R.	G6	102
Puertollano, Spain	F6	20
Puerto Lobos, Arg.	H4	90
Puerto López, Col.	E5	86
Puerto Madero, Mex.	H12	100
Puerto Madryn, Arg.	H3	90
Puerto Maldonado, Peru	F4	84
Puerto Montt, Chile	H2	90
Puerto Morelos, Mex.	B4	102
Puerto Natales, Chile	J2	90
Puerto Padre, Cuba	B9	102
Puerto Páez, Ven.	D8	86
Puerto Palmer, Pico, mtn., Mex.	G6	130
Puerto Peñasco, Mex.	F6	98
Puerto Pinasco, Para.	D5	90
Puerto Pirámides, Arg.	H4	90
Puerto Piray, Arg.	C10	92
Puerto Píritu, Ven.	B9	86
Puerto Plata, Dom. Rep.	C12	102
Puerto Princesa, Phil.	F2	52
Puerto Real, P.R.	B1	104a
Puerto Real, Spain	H4	20
Puerto Rico, Arg.	C10	92
Puerto Rico, Bol.	B3	90
Puerto Rico, Col.	G4	86
Puerto Rico, dep., N.A.	b3	104a
Puerto Rico Trench, unds.	G7	144
Puerto Rondón, Col.	D6	86
Puerto San José, Guat.	F2	102
Puerto San Julián, Arg.	I3	90
Puerto Santa Cruz, Arg.	J3	90
Puerto Sastre, Para.	D5	90
Puerto Suárez, Bol.	C5	90
Puerto Tejada, Col.	F3	86
Puerto Tolosa, Col.	H4	86
Puerto Umbría, Col.	G3	86
Puerto Vallarta, Mex.	E6	100
Puerto Varas, Chile	H2	90
Puerto Victoria, Arg.	C10	92
Puerto Viejo, C.R.	G5	102
Puerto Villamil, Ec.	i11	84a
Puerto Villamizar, Col.	C5	86
Puerto Wilches, Col.	D5	86
Puerto Ybapobó, Para.	D5	90
Pueyrredón, Lago (Cochrane, Lago), l., S.A.	I2	90
Pugačov, Russia	D7	32
Puget Sound, strt., Wa., U.S.	C4	136
Puglia, state, Italy	C10	24
Pugŏ-ri, Kor., N.	D9	38
Puhi-waero see South West Cape, c., N.Z.	H2	80
Puhja, Est.	B9	10
Puiești, Rom.	C14	26
Puigcerdà, Spain	B12	20
Puigmal d' Err (Puigmal), mtn., Eur.	G8	18
Pujiang, China	G8	42
Pujilí, Ec.	H2	86
Puka *see* Pukë, Alb.	B13	24
Pukaki, Lake, l., N.Z.	F3	80
Pukch'ŏng-ŭp, Kor., N.	D8	38
Pukë, Alb.	B13	24
Pukekohe, N.Z.	C6	80
Pukhrāyān, India	E7	54
Pukou, China	H8	42
Puksoozero, Russia	E19	8
Pula, Cro.	F10	22
Pula, Italy	F3	24
Pulacayo, Bol.	D3	90
Pulantien *see* Xinjin, China	B9	42
Pulap, at., Micron.	C5	72
Púlar, Cerro, vol., Chile	B3	92
Pulaski, N.Y., U.S.	E13	112
Pulaski, Tn., U.S.	B11	122
Pulaski, Va., U.S.	G5	114
Pulau, stm., Indon.	G10	44
Pulaukida, Indon.	E3	50
Pulau Pinang, state, Malay.	J5	48
Puławy, Pol.	E18	16
Pulgaon, India	H7	54
Puli, Tai.	J9	42
Pulicat, India	E5	53
Pulicat Lake, l., India	E4	53
Puliyangudi, India	G3	53
Pullman, Wa., U.S.	D9	136
Pulog, Mount, mtn., Phil.	B3	52
Pulon'ga, Russia	C18	8
Pułtusk, Pol.	D16	16
Puma Yumco, l., China	D13	54
Pumei, China	A7	48
Pumpkin Buttes, mtn., Wy., U.S.	D7	126
Pumpkin Creek, stm., Mt., U.S.	B7	126
Pumpkin Creek, stm., Ne., U.S.	F10	126
Puná, Isla, i., Ec.	I1	86
Punaauia, Fr. Poly.	v21	78h
Punakha, Bhu.	E12	54
Punan, Indon.	B10	50
Punata, Bol.	C3	90
Pūnch, India	B5	54
Punchaw, B.C., Can.	C7	138
Pune (Poona), India	B1	53
Punganūru, India	E4	53
P'ungsan-ŭp, Kor., N.	D7	38
Pungué, stm., Afr.	A12	70
Punia, D.R.C.	E5	66
Punilla, Sierra de la, mts., Arg.	D3	92
Punitaqui, Chile	E2	92
Punjab, state, India	C5	54
Punjab, state, Pak.	C4	54
Punnichy, Sk., Can.	C9	124
Puno, Peru	G3	84
Punta, Cerro de, mtn., P.R.	B2	104a
Punta Alta, Arg.	I6	92
Punta Arenas, Chile	J2	90
Punta Banda, Cabo, c., Mex.	L9	134
Punta Cardón, Ven.	B6	86
Punta Colnett, Mex.	F4	98
Punta de Agua Creek (Tramperos Creek), stm., U.S.	E5	128
Punta de Díaz, Chile	C2	92
Punta del Cobre, Chile	C2	92
Punta del Este, Ur.	G10	92
Punta Delgada, Arg.	H4	90
Punta de los Llanos, Arg.	E4	92
Punta de Piedras, Ven.	B9	86
Punta Gorda, Nic.	G6	102
Punta Gorda, Fl., U.S.	J3	116
Punta Gorda, Bahía de, b., Nic.	G6	102
Punta Negra, Salar de, pl., Chile	B3	92
Punta Prieta, Mex.	A1	100
Puntarenas, C.R.	G5	102
Punta Santiago, P.R.	B4	104a
Punto Fijo, Ven.	B6	86
Punung, Indon.	H7	50
Puper, Indon.	F9	44
Puppy's Point, c., Norf. I.	y24	78i
Puqi, China	G5	42
Puqian, China	L4	42
Puquio, Peru	F3	84
Pur, stm., Russia	A13	32
Puracé, Volcán, vol., Col.	F3	86
Pūranpur, India	D7	54
Purcell, Ok., U.S.	F11	128
Purcell Mountains, mts., N.A.	F14	138
Purcellville, Va., U.S.	E8	114
Purdy, Mo., U.S.	H3	120
Puré (Puruí), stm., S.A.	I6	86
Purgatoire, stm., Co., U.S.	D5	128
Puri, India	I10	54
Purificación, Col.	F4	86
Purificación, stm., Mex.	C9	100
Purísima, Mex.	E7	130
Purmerend, Neth.	B13	14
Pūrna, stm., India	H5	54
Pūrna, stm., India	H6	54
Pūrnia, India	F11	54
Puronga, Russia	F19	8
Puruí (Puré), stm., S.A.	I6	86
Puruliya, India	G11	54
Puruni, stm., Guy.	D12	86
Purús, stm., S.A.	E4	84
Puruvesi, l., Fin.	F13	8
Purvis, Ms., U.S.	F9	122
Purwakarta, Indon.	G5	50
Purwodadi, Indon.	G6	50
Purwodadi, Indon.	G7	50
Purwokerto, Indon.	G6	50
Purworejo, Indon.	G6	50
Pusa, Malay.	C7	50
Pusad, India	B3	53
Pusan (Fusan), Kor., S.	D2	40
Pusan-jikhalsi, state, Kor., S.	D2	40
Pusat Gayo, Pegunungan, mts., Indon.	J3	48
Pushkar, India	E5	54
Puškin, Russia	A13	10
Puškino, Russia	D20	10
Püspökladány, Hung.	B8	26
Püssi, Est.	A10	10
Pustozersk, Russia	C25	8
Putaendo, Chile	F2	92
Putao, Mya.	C8	46
Putian, China	I8	42
Putian, China	G6	42
Putignano, Italy	D10	24
Puting, Tanjung, c., Indon.	E7	50
Putnam, Ct., U.S.	C14	114
Putney, Ga., U.S.	E1	116
Putney, Vt., U.S.	B13	114
Putorana, plato, plat., Russia	C7	34
Puttalam, Sri L.	G4	53
Puttalam Lagoon, b., Sri L.	G4	53
Puttūr, India	E4	53
Putú, Chile	G1	92
Putumayo, state, Col.	G4	86
Putumayo (Içá), stm., S.A.	D3	84
Putuo, China	F10	42
Putussibau, Indon.	C8	50
Putyla, Ukr.	B12	26
Puula, l., Fin.	F12	8
Puurmani, Est.	B9	10
Puyallup, Wa., U.S.	C4	136
Puyang, China	D6	42
Puy-de-Dôme, state, Fr.	D9	18
Puymorens, Col de, p., Fr.	G7	18
Puyo, Ec.	H3	86
Pweto, D.R.C.	F5	66
Pwinbyu, Mya.	B2	48
Pyalo, Mya.	C2	48
Pyapon, Mya.	D2	48
Pyawbwe, Mya.	B3	48
Pyhäjärvi, l., Fin.	E11	8
Pyhäjärvi, l., Fin.	F9	8
Pyhäjoki, Fin.	D10	8
Pyhäjoki, stm., Fin.	D11	8
Pyhäselkä, l., Fin.	E13	8
Pyhätunturi, mtn., Fin.	C12	8
Pyinbongyi, Mya.	D3	48
Pyinmana, Mya.	C3	48
Pyin Oo Lwin *see* Maymyo, Mya.	A3	48
Pýlos, Grc.	G4	28
Pymatuning Reservoir, res., U.S.	C5	114
Pyŏktong-ŭp, Kor., N.	D6	38
P'yŏngch'ang, Kor., S.	B1	40
P'yonghae, Kor., S.	C2	40
P'yŏngt'aek, Kor., S.	F7	38
P'yŏngyang, Kor., N.	E6	38
Pyote, Tx., U.S.	C4	130
Pyramid Lake, l., Nv., U.S.	D6	134
Pyramid Peak, mtn., Wy., U.S.	G16	136
Pyrenees, mts., Eur.	G6	18
Pyrénées-Atlantiques, state, Fr.	F5	18
Pyrénées Occident, Parc National des, p.o.i., Fr.	G5	18
Pyrénées-Orientales, state, Fr.	G8	18
Pýrgos, Grc.	F4	28
Pytalovo, Russia	C10	10
Pyu, Mya.	C3	48
Pyūṭhān, Nepal	D9	54

Q

Name	Map Ref.	Page
Qaanaaq *see* Thule, Grnld.	B12	141
Qabbāsīn, Syria	B8	58
Qacentina (Constantine), Alg.	B6	64
Qā'en, Iran	C8	56
Qagan Moron, stm., China	C3	38
Qagan Nur, l., China	C7	36
Qahar Youyi Zhongqi, China	A5	42
Qaidam, stm., China	D4	36
Qaidam Pendi, bas., China	D3	36
Qalāt, Afg.	C10	56
Qal'at ash-Shaqīf (Beaufort Castle), sci., Leb.	E6	58
Qal'at Bīshah, Sau. Ar.	E5	56
Qal'at Ṣāliḥ, Iraq	C6	56
Qal'eh-ye Now, Afg.	C9	56
Qallābāt, Sudan	E7	62
Qalyûb, Egypt	H2	58
Qamani'tuaq (Baker Lake), Nu., Can.	C11	106
Qamar, Ghubbat al-, b., Yemen	F7	56
Qamdo, China	E4	36
Qamea, i., Fiji	p20	79e
Qamīnis, Libya	A3	62
Qānā, Leb.	E6	58
Qandahār *see* Kandahār, Afg.	C10	56
Qandala, Som.	B9	66
Qapshaghay, Kaz.	F13	32
Qaqortoq *see* Julianehåb, Grnld.	E16	141
Qarabutaq, Kaz.	D10	32
Qārah, Syria	D7	58
Qaratal, stm., Kaz.	E13	32
Qarataū, Kaz.	F11	32
Qarataū zhotasy, mts., Kaz.	F11	32
Qaraton, Kaz.	E8	32
Qaraūyl, Kaz.	E13	32
Qarazhal, Kaz.	E12	32
Qardho, Som.	C9	66
Qarqan, stm., China	G15	32
Qarqaraly, Kaz.	E13	32
Qarsaqbay, Kaz.	E11	32
Qârûn, Birket (Moeris, Lake), l., Egypt	I1	58
Qarwāw, Ra's, c., Oman	F8	56
Qasigiannguit *see* Christanshåb, Grnld.	D15	141
Qaṣr al-Azraq, sci., Jord.	G7	58
Qaṣr al-Kharānah, sci., Jord.	G7	58
Qaṣr al-Mushattá, sci., Jord.	G7	58
Qaṣr aṭ-Ṭūbah, sci., Jord.	G7	58
Qaṣr Ḍab'ah, sci., Jord.	G7	58
Qaṣr-e Shīrīn, Iran	C6	56
Qasr Farâfra, Egypt	B5	62
Qaṭanā, Syria	E6	58
Qatar, ctry., Asia	D7	56
Qatrani, Gebel, hill, Egypt	I1	58
Qattâra, Munkhafad el- (Qattara Depression), depr., Egypt	B5	62
Qattara Depression see Qattâra, Munkhafad el-, depr., Egypt	B5	62
Qaṭṭīnah, Buḥayrat, res., Syria	D7	58
Qausuittuq (Resolute), Nu., Can.	C7	141
Qayghy, Kaz.	D10	32
Qazaly, Kaz.	E10	32
Qazaqtyng usaqshoqylyghy (Kazakh Hills), hills, Kaz.	D12	32
Qāzigund, India	B5	54
Qazımämmäd, Azer.	B6	56
Qazvīn, Iran	B6	56
Qena, Egypt	B6	62
Qena, Wadi (Qinā, Wādī), stm., Egypt	K3	58
Qeqertarsuaq *see* Godhavn, Grnld.	D15	141
Qesari, Horbat (Caesarea), sci., Isr.	F5	58
Qeshm, Jazīreh-ye, i., Iran	D8	56
Qetura, Isr.	I5	58
Qezel Owzan, stm., Iran	B6	56
Qian, stm., China	J3	42
Qian'an, China	B6	38
Qian Gorlos, China	B6	38
Qianning, China	E5	36
Qianshan, China	F7	42
Qianwei, China	F5	36
Qianxi, China	H1	42
Qianyang, China	H3	42
Qiaolima, China	A8	54
Qiaowan, China	C4	36
Qidong, China	H5	42
Qiemo, China	G15	32
Qigong, China	F5	36
Qijiang, China	G2	42
Qila Saifullāh, Pak.	C2	54
Qilian Shan, mtn., China	D4	36
Qilian Shan, mts., China	D4	36
Qimen, China	G7	42
Qin, stm., China	D5	42
Qing, stm., China	F4	42
Qingcheng, China	C7	42
Qingchengzi, China	D5	38
Qingdao (Tsingtao), China	C9	42
Qingfeng, China	D6	42
Qinggang, China	B10	36
Qinghai, state, China	D4	36
Qinghai Hu, l., China	D5	36
Qingjiang, China	G6	42
Qingjiang, China	E8	42
Qinglong, China	F6	36
Qinglonggang, China	F9	42
Qingshen, China	F5	36
Qingshui, China	D2	42
Qingshui, China	D4	36
Qingshui, stm., China	C2	42
Qingshui, stm., China	H3	42
Qingtang, China	I5	42
Qingyang, China	F7	42
Qingyang, China	B8	38
Qingyang, China	C2	42
Qingyuan, China	J5	42
Qingyuan, China	H8	42
Qingyuan, China	I3	42
Qingyuan, China	C6	38
Qing Zang Gaoyuan (Tibet, Plateau of), plat., China	B6	46
Qingzhen, China	H2	42
Qinhuangdao, China	B8	42
Qin Ling, mts., China	E3	42
Qinshihuang Mausoleum (Terra Cotta Army), sci., China	D3	42
Qinshui, China	D5	42
Qinxian, China	C5	42
Qinyang, China	D5	42
Qinyuan, China	C5	42
Qinzhou, China	J3	42
Qionghai, China	L4	42
Qionglai, China	E5	36
Qionglaishan, mts., China	E5	36
Qiongzhong, China	L3	42
Qiongzhou Haixia, strt., China	K4	42
Qiqian, China	F13	34
Qiqihar, China	B9	36
Qira, China	A5	46
Qiryat Ata, Isr.	F6	58
Qiryat Gat, Isr.	G5	58
Qiryat Shemona, Isr.	E6	58
Qishn, Yemen	F7	56
Qitai, China	C2	36
Qitaihe, China	B11	36
Qitamu, China	B7	38
Qixia, China	C9	42
Qixian, China	D6	42
Qiyang, China	H4	42
Qizhou, China	F6	42
Qizil Jilga, China	A7	54
Qom, Iran	C7	56
Qomsheh, Iran	C7	56
Qonggyai, China	D13	54
Qongyrat, Kaz.	E12	32
Qorghalzhyn, Kaz.	D12	32
Qôrnoq, Grnld.	E15	141
Qosshaghyl, Kaz.	E8	32
Qostanay, Kaz.	D10	32
Qowowuyag (Chopu), mtn., Asia	D11	54
Qu, stm., China	F2	42
Qu, stm., China	G8	42
Quabbin Reservoir, res., Ma., U.S.	B13	114
Quadra Island, i., B.C., Can.	F5	138
Quadros, Lagoa dos, l., Braz.	D12	92
Quakenbrück, Ger.	D3	16
Qualicum Beach, B.C., Can.	G6	138
Quambatook, Austl.	J4	76
Quang Ngai, Viet.	E9	48
Quang Trach, Viet.	D8	48
Quantico, Va., U.S.	F8	114
Quanyang, China	C7	38
Quanzhou, China	I8	42
Qu'Appelle, Sk., Can.	D10	124
Qu'Appelle, stm., Can.	D12	124
Qu'Appelle Dam, dam, Sk., Can.	D7	124
Quaraí, Braz.	E9	92
Quaraí (Cuareim), stm., S.A.	E9	92
Quarles, Pegunungan, mts., Indon.	E11	50
Quarryville, Pa., U.S.	E9	114
Quartier d'Orléans, Guad.	A1	105a
Quartu Sant'Elena, Italy	E3	24
Quartz Lake, l., Nu., Can.	A14	106
Quartz Mountain, mtn., Or., U.S.	G4	136
Quartzsite, Az., U.S.	J2	132
Quba, Azer.	A6	56
Qūchān, Iran	B8	56
Quchijie, China	G4	42
Queanbeyan, Austl.	J7	76
Québec, Qc., Can.	D5	110
Québec, state, Can.	E16	106
Quebeck, Tn., U.S.	I12	120
Quebra-Anzol, stm., Braz.	J2	88
Quebracho, Ur.	E9	92
Quebrada Seca, P.R.	B4	104a
Quedal, Cabo, c., Chile	H2	90
Quedlinburg, Ger.	E7	16
Queen Charlotte Islands, is., B.C., Can.	E4	106
Queen Charlotte Sound, strt., B.C., Can.	E2	138
Queen Charlotte Strait, strt., B.C., Can.	F3	138
Queen City, Mo., U.S.	D5	120
Queen City, Tx., U.S.	D4	122
Queen Elizabeth Islands, is., Can.	B13	94
Queen Mary Coast, cst., Ant.	B14	81
Queen Maud Gulf, b., Nu., Can.	B10	106
Queen Maud Land, reg., Ant.	C4	81
Queen Maud Mountains, mts., Ant.	D23	81
Queenscliff, Austl.	L5	76
Queensland, state, Austl.	D8	74
Queensport, N.S., Can.	E15	110
Queenstown, Austl.	o12	77a
Queenstown, N.Z.	G3	80
Queenstown, S. Afr.	G8	70
Queguay Grande, stm., Ur.	F9	92
Queimada Nova, Braz.	E5	88
Queimadas, Braz.	F6	88
Queimados, Braz.	L4	88
Quela, Ang.	B2	68
Quelelevu, i., Fiji	p20	79e
Quelimane, Moz.	D6	68
Quelpart Island see Cheju-do, i., Kor., S.	H7	38
Quemado, Tx., U.S.	F7	130
Quemado, Punta de, c., Cuba	B10	102
Quemoy see Chinmen Tao, i., Tai.	I8	42
Quemú Quemú, Arg.	H6	92
Quequén, Arg.	I8	92
Querary, stm., Col.	G6	86
Quercy, hist. reg., Fr.	E7	18
Querétaro, Mex.	E8	100
Querétaro, state, Mex.	E8	100
Querobabi, Mex.	F7	98
Quesada, Spain	G7	20
Queshan, China	E5	42
Quesnel, B.C., Can.	C8	138
Quesnel, stm., B.C., Can.	D8	138
Quesnel Lake, l., B.C., Can.	D9	138
Que Son, Viet.	E9	48
Questa, N.M., U.S.	E3	128
Quetico Lake, l., On., Can.	C7	118
Quetta, Pak.	C10	56
Quetzaltenango, Guat.	E2	102
Quevedo, Ec.	H2	86
Quezon City, Phil.	C3	52
Qufu, China	D7	42
Quibala, Ang.	C2	68
Quibdó, Col.	E3	86
Quiberon, Fr.	G5	14
Quíbor, Ven.	C7	86
Quiculungo, Ang.	B2	68
Quila, Mex.	C5	100
Quilengues, Ang.	C1	68
Quilimarí, Chile	F2	92
Quillabamba, Peru	F3	84
Quillacollo, Bol.	C3	90
Quill Lake, Sk., Can.	B9	124
Quillota, Chile	F2	92
Quilon, India	G3	53
Quilpie, Austl.	F5	76
Quilpué, Chile	F2	92
Quimarí, Alto de, mtn., Col.	C3	86
Quimaria, Ang.	B1	68
Quimby, Ia., U.S.	B2	120
Quimilí, Arg.	C6	92
Quimper (Kemper), Fr.	F5	14
Quimperlé, Fr.	G5	14
Quinault, stm., Wa., U.S.	C3	136
Quince Mil, Peru	F3	84
Quincy, Ca., U.S.	D4	134
Quincy, Fl., U.S.	G14	122
Quincy, Il., U.S.	E6	120
Quincy, Ma., U.S.	B14	114
Quincy, Wa., U.S.	C7	136
Quindío, state, Col.	E4	86
Quines, Arg.	F5	92
Quinhagak, Ak., U.S.	E7	140
Quinlan, Tx., U.S.	E2	122
Quinn, stm., Nv., U.S.	B7	134
Quintanar de la Orden, Spain	E7	20
Quintana Roo, state, Mex.	C3	102
Quinte, Bay of, b., On., Can.	D12	112
Quinto, Spain	C10	20
Quinto, stm., Arg.	G5	92
Quinton, Ok., U.S.	B3	122
Quipapá, Braz.	E7	88
Quirauk Mountain, mtn., Md., U.S.	E8	114
Quiriguá, sci., Guat.	E3	102
Quirihue, Chile	H1	92
Quirindi, Austl.	H8	76
Quirinópolis, Braz.	C6	90
Quiriquire, Ven.	C10	86
Quiroga, Mex.	F8	100
Quiros, Cap, c., Vanuatu	j16	79d
Quissanga, Moz.	C7	68
Quissico, Moz.	D12	70
Quitaque, Tx., U.S.	G7	128
Quitasueño, unds., Col.	E7	102
Quitasueño, Banco see Quitasueño, unds., Col.	E7	102
Quita Sueno Bank see Quitasueño, unds., Col.	E7	102
Quiterajo, Moz.	C7	68
Quitilipi, Arg.	C7	92
Quitman, Ga., U.S.	F2	116
Quitman, Tx., U.S.	E3	122
Quito, Ec.	H2	86
Quixadá, Braz.	C6	88
Quixeramobim, Braz.	C6	88
Qujiadian, China	C5	38
Qujing, China	F5	36
Qujiu, China	J2	42
Qulin, Mo., U.S.	H7	120
Qumarlêb, China	E4	36
Qumrān, Khirbat, hist., W.B.	G6	58
Quoich, stm., Nu., Can.	C12	106
Quorn, Austl.	F7	74
Quoxo, stm., Bots.	C7	70
Qurdūd, Sudan	E5	62
Qus, Egypt	B6	62
Quseir, Egypt	B6	62
Qutdligssat, Grnld.	C15	141
Quthing, Leso.	G8	70
Quweisna, Egypt	H2	58
Quxian, China	F2	42
Qūxū, China	D13	54
Quyang, China	B6	42
Quyghan, Kaz.	E12	32
Quy Nhon, Viet.	F9	48
Quyon, Qc., Can.	C13	112
Quyquyó, Para.	C9	92
Quzhou, China	G8	42
Quzhou, China	C6	42
Qyzylorda, Kaz.	F11	32
Qyzyltū, Kaz.	D12	32

R

Name	Map Ref.	Page
Raab (Rába), stm., Eur.	D12	22
Raalte, Neth.	B15	14
Ra'anana, Isr.	F5	58
Raas, Pulau, i., Indon.	G9	50
Raasay, i., Scot., U.K.	D6	12
Raasiku, Est.	A8	10
Rab, Otok, i., Cro.	F11	22
Raba, Indon.	H11	50
Rába (Raab), stm., Eur.	D12	22
Rábade, Spain	A3	20
Rabak, Sudan	E6	62
Rabat, Malta	I8	24
Rabat, Malta	H8	24
Rabat, Mor.	C3	64
Rabaul, Pap. N. Gui.	a5	79a
Rabbit Creek, stm., S.D., U.S.	B10	126
Rabbit Ears Pass, p., Co., U.S.	C10	132
Rabi, i., Fiji	p20	79e
Rābi', Ash-Shallāl ar- (Fourth Cataract), wtfl., Sudan	D6	62
Rābigh, Sau. Ar.	E4	56
Rabka, Pol.	G15	16
Rabkavi Banhatti, India	C2	53
Râbnița, Mol.	B16	26
Rabočeostrovsk, Russia	D16	8
Rabwāh, Pak.	C4	54
Rabyānah, Ramlat, des., Libya	C4	62
Raccoon, stm., Ia., U.S.	C4	120
Raccoon Creek, stm., Oh., U.S.	E15	120
Race, Cape, c., Nf., Can.	j23	107a
Race Point, c., Ma., U.S.	B15	114
Rach Gia, Viet.	G7	48
Rach Gia, Vinh, b., Viet.	H7	48
Raciąż, Pol.	D16	16
Racibórz, Pol.	F14	16
Racine, Wi., U.S.	F2	112
Radaškovičy, Bela.	F10	10
Rădăuți, Rom.	B12	26
Radcliff, Ky., U.S.	G12	120
Radeberg, Ger.	E9	16
Radebeul, Ger.	E9	16
Radford, Va., U.S.	G5	114
Rādhanpur, India	G3	54
Rădinești, Rom.	E10	26
Radisson, Sk., Can.	B6	124
Radium Hot Springs, B.C., Can.	F14	138
Radnice, Czech Rep.	G9	16
Radofinnikovo, Russia	A13	10
Radom, Pol.	E17	16
Radom, state, Pol.	E16	16
Radomsko, Pol.	E15	16
Radomyśl Wielki, Pol.	F17	16
Radoviš, Mac.	B5	28
Radstadt, Aus.	C10	22
Radutino, Russia	H17	10
Radviliškis, Lith.	E6	10
Radville, Sk., Can.	E9	124
Radymno, Pol.	G18	16
Radzyń Chełmiński, Pol.	C14	16
Rae, N.T., Can.	C7	106
Rae, stm., Nu., Can.	B7	106
Rāe Bareli, India	E8	54
Raeford, N.C., U.S.	B6	116
Rae Isthmus, isth., Nu., Can.	B13	106
Rae Strait, strt., Nu., Can.	B12	106
Rafaela, Arg.	E7	92
Rafael Freyre, Cuba	B10	102
Rafaḥ, Gaza	G5	58
Rafḥā', Sau. Ar.	D5	56
Rafsanjān, Iran	C8	56
Raft, stm., U.S.	H13	136
Raga, Sudan	F5	62
Ragay Gulf, b., Phil.	D4	52
Ragged Island, i., Bah.	A10	102
Ragged Island Range, is., Bah.	A10	102
Ragged Top Mountain, mtn., Wy., U.S.	F7	126
Ragland, Al., U.S.	D12	122
Raguva, Lith.	E7	10
Rahačou, Bela.	G12	10
Rahad al-Bardī, Sudan	E4	62
Rāhatgarh, India	G7	54
Rahimatpur, India	C1	53
Rahīm Ki Bāzār, Pak.	F2	54
Rahīmyār Khān, Pak.	D3	54
Rāichūr, India	C3	53
Raiganj, India	F12	54
Raigarh, India	H9	54
Rāikot, India	C5	54
Railroad Valley, val., Nv., U.S.	E10	134
Railton, Austl.	n13	77a
Rainbow Bridge National Monument, p.o.i., Ut., U.S.	F6	132
Rainbow Falls, wtfl., B.C., Can.	D11	138
Rainelle, W.V., U.S.	G5	114
Rainier, Mount, vol., Wa., U.S.	D5	136
Rainy, stm., N.A.	C4	118
Rainy Lake, l., N.A.	C5	118
Rainy River, On., Can.	C4	118
Raipur, India	H8	54
Raipur Uplands, plat., India	H9	54
Raisen, India	G6	54
Raisin, stm., Mi., U.S.	G6	112
Raivavae, i., Fr. Poly.	F12	72
Rajabasa, Indon.	F4	50
Rājahmundry, India	C5	53
Rājaldesar, India	E5	54
Rājampet, India	D4	53
Rajang, stm., Malay.	B7	50
Rājapālaiyam, India	G3	53
Rājāpur, India	C1	53
Rājasthān, state, India	E4	54
Rājbāri, Bngl.	G12	54

Rajčihinsk – River Cess I • 47

Name	Map Ref.	Page
Rajčihinsk, Russia	G14	34
Rāj Gangpur, India	G10	54
Rājgarh, India	E6	54
Rājgarh, India	G6	54
Rājgarh, India	D5	54
Rajik, Indon.	E4	50
Rājkot, India	G3	54
Rāj Nāndgaon, India	H8	54
Rājpipla, India	H4	54
Rājpur, India	G5	54
Rājpura, India	C6	54
Rājshāhi, Bngl.	F12	54
Rājshāhi, state, Bngl.	F12	54
Rājula, India	H3	54
Raka, stm., China	D11	54
Rakamaz, Hung.	A8	26
Rakaposhi, mtn., Pak.	B11	56
Rakata, Pulau (Krakatoa), i., Indon.	G4	50
Rakhine, state, Mya.	C1	48
Rakhiv, Ukr.	A11	26
Rakitnoe, Russia	B11	36
Rakiura see Stewart Island, i., N.Z.	H3	80
Rakoniewice, Pol.	D12	16
Rakops, Bots.	B7	70
Rakovník, Czech Rep.	F9	16
Råkvåg see Råkvågen, Nor.	E4	8
Råkvågen, Nor.	E4	8
Rakvere, Est.	G12	8
Raleigh, Ms., U.S.	E9	122
Raleigh, N.C., U.S.	I7	114
Ralik Chain, is., Marsh. Is.	C7	72
Ralls, Tx., U.S.	H7	128
Ralston, Pa., U.S.	C9	114
Ramah, N.M., U.S.	H8	132
Rām Allāh, W.B.	G6	58
Rāmanagaram, India	E3	53
Rāmanāthapuram, India	G4	53
Rāmānuj Ganj, India	G9	54
Ramat Gan, Isr.	F5	58
Ramat HaSharon, Isr.	F5	58
Ramatlabama, Bots.	D7	70
Rambervillers, Fr.	F15	14
Rambouillet, Fr.	F10	14
Rambutyo Island, i., Pap. N. Gui.	a4	79a
Rām Dās, India	B5	54
Rāmdurg, India	C2	53
Ramea, Nf., Can.	j22	107a
Ramene, Russia	F20	8
Ramenskoe, Russia	E21	10
Rāmeswaram, India	G4	53
Rāmgarh, Bngl.	G13	54
Rāmgarh, India	E5	54
Rāmgarh, India	G10	54
Ram Head, c., V.I.U.S.	e8	104b
Rāmhormoz, Iran	C6	56
Ramírez, Mex.	I10	130
Ramírez, Mex.	G7	130
Ramla, Isr.	G5	58
Ramlu, mtn., Afr.	E8	62
Ramm, Jabal, mtn., Jord.	I6	58
Rāmnagar, India	F9	54
Rāmnagar, India	D7	54
Râmnicu Sărat, Rom.	D14	26
Râmnicu Vâlcea, Rom.	D11	26
Ramona, Ca., U.S.	J9	134
Ramona, S.D., U.S.	C15	126
Ramos, Mex.	D8	100
Ramos, stm., Mex.	C6	100
Ramotswa, Bots.	D7	70
Rampart, Ak., U.S.	C9	140
Ramparts, stm., N.T., Can.	B4	106
Rāmpur, India	D7	54
Rāmpur, India	C6	54
Rāmpura, India	F5	54
Rāmpur Hāt, India	F11	54
Ramree Island, i., Mya.	C1	48
Ramseur, N.C., U.S.	I6	114
Ramsey, I. of Man	G8	12
Ramsey Lake, l., On., Can.	A7	112
Ramsgate, Eng., U.K.	J14	12
Ramshorn Peak, mtn., Mt., U.S.	E15	136
Rāmtek, India	H7	54
Rāmu, Bngl.	H14	54
Ramu, stm., Pap. N. Gui.	a3	79a
Ramville, Îlet, i., Mart.	k7	105c
Ramygala, Lith.	E7	10
Rānāghāt, India	G12	54
Rana Kao, Volcán, vol., Chile	f29	78l
Rāna Pratāp Sāgar, res., India	F5	54
Ranau, Malay.	H1	52
Ranau, Danau, l., Indon.	F3	50
Ranburne, Al., U.S.	D13	122
Rancagua, Chile	G2	92
Rancah, Indon.	G6	50
Rancevo, Russia	D16	10
Rancharia, Braz.	D6	90
Ranchería, stm., Col.	B5	86
Ranchester, Wy., U.S.	C5	126
Rānchi, India	G10	54
Ranchillos, Arg.	C5	92
Ranch Lake, l., Sk., Can.	B9	124
Rancho Cordova, Ca., U.S.	E4	134
Rancho Nuevo, Mex.	H7	130
Ranchos, Arg.	G8	92
Ranco, Lago, l., Chile	H2	90
Rancul, Arg.	G5	92
Randazzo, Italy	G8	24
Randers, Den.	H4	8
Randleman, N.C., U.S.	I6	114
Randlett, Ok., U.S.	G10	128
Randolph, Az., U.S.	K5	132
Randolph, Me., U.S.	F7	110
Randolph, Ne., U.S.	E15	126
Randolph, N.Y., U.S.	B7	114
Randolph, Ut., U.S.	B5	132
Random Lake, Wi., U.S.	E2	112
Randsfjorden, l., Nor.	F3	8
Ranfurly, N.Z.	G4	80
Rāngāmāti, Bngl.	G13	54
Rangantemiang, Indon.	D8	50
Rangas, Tanjung, c., Indon.	E11	50
Rangasa, Tanjung, c., Indon.	E11	50
Rangaunu Bay, b., N.Z.	B5	80
Rangeley, Me., U.S.	E6	110
Ranger, Tx., U.S.	B9	130
Rangia, India	E13	54
Rangitaiki, stm., N.Z.	D7	80
Rangitata, stm., N.Z.	F4	80
Rangitikei, stm., N.Z.	D7	80
Rangkasbitung, Indon.	G4	50
Rangoon see Yangon, Mya.	D2	48
Rangoon, stm., Mya.	D3	48
Rangpur, Bngl.	F12	54
Rangpur, Pak.	C3	54
Rangsang, Pulau, i., Indon.	C3	50
Rānībennur, India	D2	53
Rānīganj, India	G11	54
Rānikhet, India	D7	54
Rankamhaeng National Park, p.o.i., Thai.	D4	48
Ranken, stm., Austl.	D7	74
Ranken Store, Austl.	C7	74
Rankin, Il., U.S.	H2	112
Rankin, Tx., U.S.	C6	130
Rankin Inlet see Kangiqsliniq, Nu., Can.	C12	106
Rankins Springs, Austl.	I6	76
Rann of Kutch see Kutch, Rann of, reg., Asia	D2	46
Ranong, Thai.	H4	48
Ranongga Island, i., Sol. Is.	e7	79b
Ranot, Thai.	I5	48
Ransiki, Indon.	F9	44
Ransom, Ks., U.S.	C8	128
Ranson, W.V., U.S.	E8	114
Rantabe, Madag.	D8	68
Rantaukampar, Indon.	C2	50
Rantaupanjang, Indon.	D2	50
Rantauprapat, Indon.	B1	50
Rantekombola, Bulu, mtn., Indon.	E12	50
Rantepao, Indon.	E11	50
Rantoul, Il., U.S.	D9	120
Raohe, China	B11	36
Raoping, China	J7	42
Raoul, Ga., U.S.	B2	116
Raoul-Blanchard, Mont, mtn., Qc., Can.	C6	110
Raoul Island, i., N.Z.	F9	72
Rapa, i., Fr. Poly.	F12	72
Rapallo, Italy	F6	22
Rapang, Indon.	E11	50
Rapa Nui see Pascua, Isla de, i., Chile	f30	78l
Rāpar, India	G3	54
Rapel, stm., Chile	F2	92
Rapel, Embalse, res., Chile	G2	92
Rapelli, Arg.	C5	92
Raper, Cape, c., Nu., Can.	B17	106
Rapidan, stm., Va., U.S.	F7	114
Rapid City, Mb., Can.	D13	124
Rapid City, S.D., U.S.	C9	126
Rapid Creek, stm., S.D., U.S.	D9	126
Rapide-Blanc, Qc., Can.	C4	110
Rapid River, Mi., U.S.	C2	112
Räpina, Est.	G12	8
Rappahannock, stm., Va., U.S.	G9	114
Rāpti, stm., Asia	E9	54
Rapu Rapu Island, i., Phil.	D5	52
Raraka, at., Fr. Poly.	E12	72
Rarotonga, i., Cook Is.	a26	78j
Rarotonga International Airport, Cook Is.	a26	78j
Rasa, Punta, c., Arg.	H9	92
Ra's al-Khaymah, U.A.E.	D8	56
Ra's Ba'labakk, Leb.	D7	58
Râșcani, Mol.	B14	26
Rașcov, Mol.	B15	26
Ras Dashen Terara, mtn., Eth.	E7	62
Ras Dejen see Ras Dashen Terara, mtn., Eth.	E7	62
Ras Djebel, Tun.	G4	24
Raseiniai, Lith.	E5	10
Râs el-Barr, Egypt	G2	58
Rashād, Sudan	E6	62
Rashid (Rosetta), Egypt	G1	58
Rashid, Masabb (Rosetta Mouth), mth., Egypt	G1	58
Rasht, Iran	B6	56
Raška, Serb.	F7	26
Rās Koh, mtn., Pak.	D10	56
Rasm al-Arwām, Sabkhat, l., Syria	C8	58
Râșnov, Rom.	D12	26
Rasra, India	F9	54
Rasšua, ostrov, i., Russia	G19	34
Rast, Rom.	F10	26
Rastatt, Ger.	H4	16
Rastede, Ger.	C4	16
Rastenburg see Kętrzyn, Pol.	B17	16
Rásttigáisá, mtn., Nor.	A12	8
Ratak Chain, is., Marsh. Is.	C8	72
Ratamka, Bela.	G10	10
Ratangarh, India	D5	54
Rat Buri, Thai.	F4	48
Rāth, India	F7	54
Rathbun Lake, res., Ia., U.S.	D4	120
Rathdrum, Id., U.S.	C9	136
Rathenow, Ger.	D8	16
Rathkeale, Ire.	I3	12
Ráth Luirc, Ire.	I4	12
Rathwell, Mb., Can.	E15	124
Rat Island, i., Ak., U.S.	g22	140a
Rat Islands, is., Ak., U.S.	g22	140a
Ratlām, India	G5	54
Ratmanova, ostrov, i., Russia	C27	34
Ratnāgiri, India	C1	53
Ratnapura, Sri L.	H5	53
Raton, N.M., U.S.	E4	128
Raton Pass, p., N.M., U.S.	E4	128
Rats, stm., Qc., Can.	A4	110
Rattanaburi, Thai.	E6	48
Rattaphum, Thai.	I5	48
Rattlesnake, Mt., U.S.	D13	136
Rattlesnake Creek, stm., Ks., U.S.	D10	128
Ratz, Mount, mtn., B.C., Can.	D4	106
Ratzeburg, Ger.	C6	16
Rau, Indon.	C2	50
Raub, Malay.	K5	48
Rauch, Arg.	H8	92
Raul Soares, Braz.	K4	88
Rauma, Fin.	F9	8
Rauma, stm., Nor.	E2	8
Rauna, Lat.	C8	10
Raung, Gunung, vol., Indon.	H9	50
Raurkela, India	G10	54
Răut, stm., Mol.	B14	26
Ravalgaon, India	H5	54
Ravanusa, Italy	G7	24
Ravena, N.Y., U.S.	B12	114
Ravenna, Italy	F9	22
Ravenna, Ky., U.S.	G2	114
Ravenna, Ne., U.S.	F13	126
Ravenna, Oh., U.S.	G8	112
Ravensburg, Ger.	I5	16
Ravenscrag, Sk., Can.	E4	124
Ravenshoe, Austl.	A5	76
Ravensthorpe, Austl.	F4	74
Ravenswood, W.V., U.S.	F4	114
Rāvi, stm., Asia	C4	54
Ravnina, Turkmen.	B9	56
Rāwah, Iraq	C5	56
Rawaki, at., Kir.	D9	72
Rāwalpindi, Pak.	B4	54
Rawas, stm., Indon.	E3	50
Rawdon, Qc., Can.	D3	110
Rawicz, Pol.	E12	16
Rawlinna, Austl.	F4	74
Rawlins, Wy., U.S.	B9	132
Rawson, Arg.	H4	90
Rawson, Arg.	G7	92
Raxāul, India	E10	54
Ray, Cape, c., Nf., Can.	C17	110
Raya, Indon.	C11	50
Raya, Bukit, mtn., Indon.	D8	50
Rāyachoti, India	D4	53
Rāyadurg, India	D3	53
Rāyagarha, India	B6	53
Ray Hubbard, Lake, res., Tx., U.S.	E2	122
Raymond, Ab., Can.	G18	138
Raymond, Il., U.S.	E8	120
Raymond, Mn., U.S.	F3	118
Raymond, Wa., U.S.	D3	136
Raymond Terrace, Austl.	I8	76
Raymondville, Tx., U.S.	H10	130
Raymore, Sk., Can.	C9	124
Rayne, La., U.S.	G6	122
Rayones, Mex.	C8	100
Rayong, Thai.	F5	48
Rayside-Balfour, On., Can.	B8	112
Raytown, Mo., U.S.	E3	120
Rayville, La., U.S.	E7	122
Raz, Pointe du, c., Fr.	F4	14
Războieni, Rom.	B13	26
Razdolinsk, Russia	C16	32
Răzeni, Mol.	C15	26
Razgrad, Blg.	F13	26
Razim, Lacul, l., Rom.	E15	26
Rāznas ezers, l., Lat.	D10	10
Razorback Mountain, mtn., B.C., Can.	E6	138
Răzvani, Rom.	E13	26
Ré, Île de, i., Fr.	C4	18
Reading, Eng., U.K.	J11	12
Reading, Mi., U.S.	C1	114
Reading, Oh., U.S.	E1	114
Reading, Pa., U.S.	D9	114
Readlyn, Ia., U.S.	B5	120
Readstown, Wi., U.S.	H8	118
Real, stm., Braz.	F6	88
Real, Cordillera, mts., S.A.	G4	84
Real del Castillo, Mex.	L9	134
Real del Padre, Arg.	G4	92
Realicó, Arg.	G5	92
Reardan, Wa., U.S.	C8	136
Reata, Mex.	B8	100
Reay, Scot., U.K.	C9	12
Rebecca, Lake, l., Austl.	F4	74
Rebiana Sand Sea see Rabyānah, Ramlat, des., Libya	C4	62
Reboly, Russia	E14	8
Rebouças, Braz.	B12	92
Rebun-tō, i., Japan	B14	38
Recanati, Italy	G10	22
Recherche, Archipelago of the, is., Austl.	F4	74
Recife, Braz.	E8	88
Recinto, Chile	H2	92
Recklinghausen, Ger.	E2	16
Reconquista, Arg.	D8	92
Recreio, Braz.	K4	88
Recreo, Arg.	D5	92
Rector, Ar., U.S.	H7	120
Rèčyča, Bela.	H13	10
Recz, Pol.	C11	16
Red (Hong, Song) (Yuan), stm., Asia	D9	46
Red, stm., N.A.	A2	118
Red, stm., U.S.	H10	120
Red, stm., U.S.	E9	108
Red, Elm Fork, stm., U.S.	F8	128
Red, North Fork, stm., U.S.	G9	128
Red, Prairie Dog Town Fork, stm., U.S.	H7	122
Red, Salt Fork, stm., U.S.	G9	128
Redang, Pulau, i., Malay.	J6	48
Red Bank, N.J., U.S.	D11	114
Red Bank, Tn., U.S.	B13	122
Red Bay, Nf., Can.	i22	107a
Red Bay, Al., U.S.	C10	122
Redbay, Fl., U.S.	G12	122
Redberry Lake, l., Sk., Can.	B6	124
Red Bluff, Ca., U.S.	C3	134
Red Bluff Reservoir, res., U.S.	C4	130
Red Boiling Springs, Tn., U.S.	H12	120
Red Canyon, p., S.D., U.S.	D9	126
Redcar, Eng., U.K.	G11	12
Red Cedar, stm., Mi., U.S.	F5	112
Red Cedar Lake, l., On., Can.	B9	112
Redcliff, Ab., Can.	D3	124
Red Cliff, Co., U.S.	D10	132
Redcliff see Red Cliff, Co., U.S.	D10	132
Redcliffe, Austl.	F9	76
Redcliffe, Mount, mtn., Austl.	E4	74
Red Cliffs, Austl.	J3	76
Red Cloud, Ne., U.S.	A10	128
Red Creek, stm., Ms., U.S.	G10	122
Red Deer, Ab., Can.	D17	138
Red Deer, stm., Can.	F19	138
Red Deer, stm., Can.	B12	124
Red Deer Lake, l., Mb., Can.	B12	124
Reddersburg, S. Afr.	F8	70
Red Devil, Ak., U.S.	D8	140
Redding, Ca., U.S.	C3	134
Redditch, Eng., U.K.	I10	12
Redenção, Braz.	C6	88
Redfield, S.D., U.S.	C14	126
Redford, Tx., U.S.	E3	130
Redhead, Trin.	s13	105f
Redja, stm., Russia	C14	10
Redkey, In., U.S.	H4	112
Redkino, Russia	D19	10
Red Lake, On., Can.	E12	106
Red Lake, l., On., Can.	E12	106
Red Lake, l., Az., U.S.	H2	132
Red Lake, stm., Mn., U.S.	D2	118
Red Lake Falls, Mn., U.S.	D2	118
Red Lake Road, On., Can.	B5	118
Redlands, Ca., U.S.	I8	134
Redlands, Co., U.S.	D8	132
Red Level, Al., U.S.	F12	122
Red Lion, Pa., U.S.	E9	114
Red Lodge, Mt., U.S.	B3	126
Redmond, Or., U.S.	F5	136
Redmond, Ut., U.S.	D5	132
Redmond, Wa., U.S.	C4	136
Red Mountain, mtn., Mt., U.S.	C14	136
Red Mountain Pass, p., Co., U.S.	F9	132
Red Oak, Ia., U.S.	D2	120
Redon, Fr.	G6	14
Redonda, Isla, i., Ven.	t12	105f
Redonda Islands, is., B.C., Can.	F6	138
Redondela, Spain	B2	20
Redondo, Port.	F3	20
Redondo Beach, Ca., U.S.	J7	134
Redoubt Volcano, vol., Ak., U.S.	D9	140
Red Pass, B.C., Can.	D11	138
Red Rock, B.C., Can.	C8	138
Red Rock, On., Can.	C10	118
Red Rock, stm., Mt., U.S.	F14	136
Red Rock, Lake, res., Ia., U.S.	C4	120
Redruth, Eng., U.K.	K7	12
Red Sea, s.	C7	62
Redvers, Sk., Can.	E12	124
Redwater, Ab., Can.	C17	138
Redwater, stm., Mt., U.S.	G8	124
Redwillow, stm., Can.	A11	138
Red Willow Creek, stm., Ne., U.S.	G12	126
Red Wing, Mn., U.S.	G6	118
Redwood, stm., Mn., U.S.	G3	118
Redwood Falls, Mn., U.S.	G3	118
Redwood National Park, p.o.i., Ca., U.S.	B1	134
Ree, Lough, l., Ire.	H5	12
Reed City, Mi., U.S.	E4	112
Reeder, N.D., U.S.	A10	126
Reed Lake, l., Sk., Can.	D6	124
Reedley, Ca., U.S.	G6	134
Reedsburg, Wi., U.S.	H8	118
Reedsville, Wi., U.S.	D2	112
Reefton, N.Z.	F4	80
Reelfoot Lake, l., Tn., U.S.	H8	120
Rees, Ger.	E2	16
Reese, Mi., U.S.	E6	112
Reese, stm., Nv., U.S.	C9	134
Reeseville, Wi., U.S.	H10	118
Refuge Cove, B.C., Can.	F6	138
Refugio, Tx., U.S.	F10	130
Rega, stm., Pol.	C11	16
Regência, Braz.	J6	88
Regeneração, Braz.	D4	88
Regensburg, Ger.	H8	16
Regent, N.D., U.S.	A10	126
Reggâne, Alg.	D5	64
Reggio di Calabria, Italy	F9	24
Reggio nell'Emilia, Italy	F7	22
Reghin, Rom.	C11	26
Regina, Sk., Can.	D9	124
Región Metropolitana, state, Chile	F2	92
Registan see Rīgestān, reg., Afg.	C9	56
Registro, Braz.	B14	92
Regozero, Russia	D14	8
Rehau, Ger.	F7	16
Rehoboth, Nmb.	C3	70
Rehoboth Beach, De., U.S.	F10	114
Reḥovot, Isr.	G5	58
Reichenbach, Ger.	F8	16
Reidsville, Ga., U.S.	D3	116
Reidsville, N.C., U.S.	H6	114
Reigate, Eng., U.K.	J12	12
Reihoku, Japan	G2	40
Reims (Rheims), Fr.	E12	14
Rein Anteriur (Vorderrhein), stm., Switz.	D6	22
Reinbeck, Ia., U.S.	B5	120
Reindeer Lake, l., Can.	D10	106
Reinga, Cape, c., N.Z.	B5	80
Reinosa, Spain	A6	20
Reisa Nasjonalpark, p.o.i., Nor.	B10	8
Reisterstown, Md., U.S.	E9	114
Reitz, S. Afr.	E9	70
Reliance, N.T., Can.	C9	106
Remada, Tun.	C7	64
Remagen, Ger.	F3	16
Remanso, Braz.	E4	88
Rembang, Indon.	G7	50
Remedios, Col.	D4	86
Remedios, Pan.	H7	102
Remedios, Punta, c., El Sal.	F2	102
Remer, Mn., U.S.	D5	118
Remington, Va., U.S.	F8	114
Rémiré, Fr. Gu.	C7	84
Remiremont, Fr.	G15	14
Remoulins, Fr.	F10	18
Rempang, Pulau, i., Indon.	C3	50
Remscheid, Ger.	E3	16
Remsen, Ia., U.S.	B1	120
Remus, Mi., U.S.	E4	112
Renaix see Ronse, Bel.	D12	14
Renata, B.C., Can.	G12	138
Rencēni, Lat.	C8	10
Rende, Italy	E10	24
Rend Lake, res., Il., U.S.	F8	120
Rendova Island, i., Sol. Is.	e7	79b
Rendsburg, Ger.	B5	16
Renfrew, On., Can.	C13	112
Rengat, Indon.	D3	50
Rengel, Indon.	G8	50
Rengo, Chile	G2	92
Reng Tlāng, mtn., Asia	H14	54
Renheji, China	F6	42
Renhuai, China	H2	42
Reni, Ukr.	D15	26
Renland, reg., Grnld.	C20	141
Renmark, Austl.	J3	76
Rennell, i., Sol. Is.	E7	72
Rennell, Islas, is., Chile	J2	90
Rennell and Bellona, state, Sol. Is.	f9	79b
Rennes, Fr.	F7	14
Rennie, Mb., Can.	E18	124
Reno, Nv., U.S.	D6	134
Reno, stm., Italy	F8	22
Reno Hill, mtn., Wy., U.S.	E6	126
Renoster, stm., S. Afr.	G5	70
Renous, N.B., Can.	D11	110
Renovo, Pa., U.S.	C8	114
Rensjön, Swe.	B8	8
Rensselaer, In., U.S.	H2	112
Rensselaer, N.Y., U.S.	B12	114
Rentería, Spain	A9	20
Renton, Wa., U.S.	C4	136
Renville, Mn., U.S.	G3	118
Renwick, Ia., U.S.	B4	120
Reo, Indon.	H12	50
Repetek, Turkmen.	B9	56
Repton, Al., U.S.	F11	122
Republic, Mi., U.S.	B1	112
Republic, Mo., U.S.	G4	120
Republic, Wa., U.S.	B8	136
Republican, stm., U.S.	B11	128
Republican, North Fork, stm., U.S.	A6	128
Republican, South Fork, stm., U.S.	B7	128
Republic of Korea see Korea, South, ctry., Asia	G8	38
Repulse Bay see Naujaat, Nu., Can.	B13	106
Repulse Bay, b., Austl.	C7	76
Repvåg, Nor.	A11	8
Requena, Spain	E9	20
Reriutaba, Braz.	C5	88
Reşadiye Yarımadası, pen., Tur.	G10	28
Reschenpass (Resia, Passo di), p., Eur.	C16	18
Reschenscheideck see Reschenpass, p., Eur.	C16	18
Reschenscheideck see Resia, Passo di, p., Eur.	C16	18
Resen, Mac.	B4	28
Reserva, Braz.	B12	92
Reserve, La., U.S.	G8	122
Reserve, N.M., U.S.	J8	132
Resia, Passo di (Reschenpass), p., Eur.	C16	18
Resistencia, Arg.	C8	92
Reșița, Rom.	D8	26
Resko, Pol.	C11	16
Resolute see Qausuittuq, Nu., Can.	C7	141
Resolution Island, i., Nu., Can.	E12	141
Resolution Island, i., N.Z.	G2	80
Resplendor, Braz.	J5	88
Restigouche, stm., Can.	C9	110
Restinga Seca, Braz.	D11	92
Reston, Mb., Can.	E12	124
Retalhuleu, Guat.	E2	102
Retamosa, Ur.	F10	92
Retezat, Parcul Național, p.o.i., Rom.	D9	26
Rethel, Fr.	E13	14
Réthymno, Grc.	H7	28
Rettihovka, Russia	B10	38
Reunion, dep., Afr.	I11	60
Reus, Spain	C12	20
Reuss, stm., Switz.	C5	22
Reuterstadt Stavenhagen, Ger.	C8	16
Reutlingen, Ger.	H5	16
Revda, Russia	C16	8
Revelstoke, B.C., Can.	F12	138
Revelstoke, Lake, res., B.C., Can.	E12	138
Reventazón, Peru	E1	84
Revilla del Campo, Spain	B7	20
Revillagigedo, Islas, is., Mex.	F2	100
Revillagigedo Island, i., Ak., U.S.	E13	140
Revillagigedo Islands see Revillagigedo, Islas, is., Mex.	F2	100
Revin, Fr.	E13	14
Revolución, Mex.	H2	130
Rewa, India	F8	54
Rewāri, India	D6	54
Rexburg, Id., U.S.	G15	136
Rexford, Ks., U.S.	B8	128
Rexford, Mt., U.S.	B11	136
Rey, Isla del, i., Pan.	H8	102
Rey, Laguna del, l., Mex.	B7	100
Reyes, Bol.	B3	90
Reyes, Point, c., Ca., U.S.	F2	134
Reyhanlı, Tur.	B7	58
Reykjanes Ridge, unds.	C10	144
Reykjavík, Ice.	k28	8a
Reyno, Ar., U.S.	H7	120
Reynolds, Ga., U.S.	D1	116
Reynolds, N.D., U.S.	G16	124
Reynosa, Mex.	B9	100
Rezé, Fr.	G7	14
Rēzekne, Lat.	D10	10
Rezina, Mol.	B15	26
Rezovo, Blg.	G15	26
Rezovska (Mutlu), stm., Eur.	G14	26
Rhaetian Alps, mts., Eur.	C15	18
Rhame, N.D., U.S.	A9	126
Rheda-Wiedenbrück, Ger.	E4	16
Rheims see Reims, Fr.	E12	14
Rhein, Sk., Can.	C11	124
Rhein see Rhine, stm., Eur.	C15	14
Rheine, Ger.	D3	16
Rheinland-Pfalz, state, Ger.	G3	16
Rhine, Ga., U.S.	E2	116
Rhine (Rhein) (Rhin), stm., Eur.	C15	14
Rhinelander, Wi., U.S.	F9	118
Rhineland-Palatinate see Rheinland-Pfalz, state, Ger.	G3	16
Rhinns Point, c., Scot., U.K.	F6	12
Rhir, Cap, c., Mor.	C2	64
Rho, Italy	E5	22
Rhode Island, state, U.S.	C14	114
Rhode Island Sound, strt., U.S.	C14	114
Rhodes see Ródos, Grc.	G11	28
Rhodes see Ródos, i., Grc.	G10	28
Rhodesia see Zimbabwe, ctry., Afr.	D4	68
Rhodes Matopos National Park, p.o.i., Zimb.	B8	70
Rhodes' Tomb, hist., Zimb.	B9	70
Rhodope Mountains, mts., Eur.	H11	26
Rhön, mts., Ger.	F5	16
Rhondda, Wales, U.K.	J9	12
Rhône, state, Fr.	D10	18
Rhône, stm., Eur.	F10	18
Rhyl, Wales, U.K.	H9	12
Riachão, Braz.	D2	88
Riachão do Jacuípe, Braz.	F6	88
Riacho de Santana, Braz.	G4	88
Riachos, Islas de los, is., Arg.	H4	90
Riamkanan, Waduk, res., Indon.	E9	50
Riaño, Spain	A6	20
Riau, state, Indon.	D2	50
Riau, Kepulauan, is., Indon.	C4	50
Riaza, Spain	C7	20
Ribadeo, Spain	A3	20
Ribas do Rio Pardo, Braz.	D6	90
Ribáuè, Moz.	C6	68
Ribe, Den.	I3	8
Ribe, state, Den.	I3	8
Ribeira, Braz.	B13	92
Ribeira do Pombal, Braz.	F6	88
Ribeirão, Braz.	E8	88
Ribeirão Preto, Braz.	K2	88
Ribeirão Vermelho, Braz.	K3	88
Ribeiro Gonçalves, Braz.	D3	88
Ribera, Italy	G7	24
Riberalta, Bol.	B3	90
Rib Lake, Wi., U.S.	F8	118
Ribnica, Slvn.	E11	22
Ribnitz-Damgarten, Ger.	B8	16
Ribstone Creek, stm., Ab., Can.	D19	138
Ricardo Flores Magón, Mex.	F9	98
Riccione, Italy	F9	22
Rice, Tx., U.S.	E2	122
Rice Lake, l., On., Can.	D11	112
Riceville, Ia., U.S.	H6	118
Riceville, Tn., U.S.	B14	122
Richan, On., Can.	B6	118
Richard B. Russell Lake, res., U.S.	B3	116
Richard Collinson Inlet, b., N.T., Can.	B17	140
Richards, Tx., U.S.	G3	122
Richards Bay, S. Afr.	F11	70
Richards Bay, b., S. Afr.	F11	70
Richards Island, i., N.T., Can.	C13	140
Richardson, Tx., U.S.	E2	122
Richardson, Wa., U.S.	B4	136
Richardson Mountains, mts., Can.	B3	106
Richard Toll, Sen.	F1	64
Riche, Pointe, c., Nf., Can.	i22	107a
Richelieu, Fr.	G9	14
Richelieu, stm., Qc., Can.	E3	110
Richer, Mb., Can.	E17	124
Richey, Mt., U.S.	G8	124
Richfield, Mn., U.S.	G5	118
Richfield, Pa., U.S.	D8	114
Richfield, Ut., U.S.	E4	132
Richfield Springs, N.Y., U.S.	B11	114
Richford, Vt., U.S.	F4	110
Rich Hill, Mo., U.S.	F3	120
Richibucto, N.B., Can.	D12	110
Richland, Ga., U.S.	E14	122
Richland, Mi., U.S.	F4	112
Richland, Mt., U.S.	F7	124
Richland, Wa., U.S.	D7	136
Richland Center, Wi., U.S.	H8	118
Richland Creek, stm., Tx., U.S.	C11	130
Richlands, Va., U.S.	G4	114
Richland Springs, Tx., U.S.	C9	130
Richmond, Austl.	C4	76
Richmond, Austl.	I8	76
Richmond, B.C., Can.	G7	138
Richmond, On., Can.	C14	112
Richmond, Qc., Can.	E4	110
Richmond, N.Z.	E5	80
Richmond, S. Afr.	G6	70
Richmond, S. Afr.	F10	70
Richmond, Eng., U.K.	G11	12
Richmond, Ca., U.S.	F3	134
Richmond, In., U.S.	I5	112
Richmond, Ky., U.S.	G1	114
Richmond, Me., U.S.	F7	110
Richmond, Mi., U.S.	B3	114
Richmond, Mn., U.S.	F4	118
Richmond, Mo., U.S.	E4	120
Richmond, Tx., U.S.	H3	122
Richmond, Ut., U.S.	B5	132
Richmond, Va., U.S.	G8	114
Richmond Heights, Fl., U.S.	K5	116
Richmond Highlands, Wa., U.S.	C4	136
Richmond Hill, On., Can.	E10	112
Richmond Hill, Ga., U.S.	E4	116
Richmond Peak, mtn., St. Vin.	o11	105e
Richton, Ms., U.S.	F9	122
Richwood, Oh., U.S.	D2	114
Richwood, W.V., U.S.	F5	114
Ricobayo, Embalse de, res., Spain	C4	20
Riddle, Or., U.S.	H3	136
Rideau, stm., On., Can.	C14	112
Ridgecrest, Ca., U.S.	H8	134
Ridgedale, Sk., Can.	A9	124
Ridgeland, Ms., U.S.	E8	122
Ridgeland, S.C., U.S.	D4	116
Ridgetown, On., Can.	F8	112
Ridgeville, Mb., Can.	E16	124
Ridgeville, S.C., U.S.	C5	116
Ridgeway, Mo., U.S.	D4	120
Ridgway, Co., U.S.	E9	132
Ridgway, Il., U.S.	G9	120
Ridgway, Pa., U.S.	C7	114
Riding Mountain National Park, p.o.i., Mb., Can.	D13	124
Riegelwood, N.C., U.S.	B7	116
Riesa, Ger.	E9	16
Riesco, Isla, i., Chile	J2	90
Riesi, Italy	G8	24
Riet, stm., S. Afr.	F7	70
Riet, stm., S. Afr.	H5	70
Rietavas, Lith.	E4	10
Rietfontein (Buitsivango), stm., Afr.	B4	70
Rieti, Italy	H9	22
Rif, mts., Mor.	C4	64
Riffe Lake, res., Wa., U.S.	D4	136
Rifle, Co., U.S.	D9	132
Rifstangi, c., Ice.	j31	8a
Rift Valley, val., Afr.	F7	62
Rīga, Lat.	D7	10
Riga, Gulf of, b., Eur.	C6	10
Rigaih, Indon.	J2	48
Rigby, Id., U.S.	G14	136
Rīgestān, reg., Afg.	C9	56
Riggins, Id., U.S.	E10	136
Rigi, mtn., Switz.	C5	22
Rigo, Pap. N. Gui.	b4	79a
Rig-Rig, Chad	E2	62
Riihimäki, Fin.	F11	8
Riiser-Larsen Peninsula, pen., Ant.	B8	81
Riječki Zaljev, b., Cro.	E11	22
Rijeka (Fiume), Cro.	E11	22
Rijssen, Neth.	D2	16
Rillito, Az., U.S.	K5	132
Rimatara, i., Fr. Poly.	F11	72
Rimavská Sobota, Slov.	H15	16
Rimbey, Ab., Can.	D16	138
Rimersburg, Pa., U.S.	C6	114
Rimini, Italy	F9	22
Rimouski, Qc., Can.	B8	110
Rimouski, stm., Qc., Can.	B8	110
Rinbung, China	C7	46
Rinca, Pulau, i., Indon.	H11	50
Rincon, Ga., U.S.	D4	116
Rincon, N.M., U.S.	K9	132
Rinconada, Arg.	D3	90
Rincón del Bonete, Lago Artificial de, res., Ur.	F9	92
Rincón de Romos, Mex.	D7	100
Rīngas, India	E5	54
Ringdove, Vanuatu	k16	79d
Ringebu, Nor.	F4	8
Ringgold, Ga., U.S.	C13	122
Ringim, Nig.	G6	64
Ringkøbing, Den.	H2	8
Ringkøbing, state, Den.	H3	8
Ringkøbing Fjord, b., Den.	H2	8
Ringling, Ok., U.S.	G11	128
Ringsted, Ia., U.S.	H4	118
Ringvassøya, i., Nor.	A8	8
Rinjani, Gunung, vol., Indon.	H10	50
Rinteln, Ger.	D5	16
Rio, Wi., U.S.	H9	118
Riobamba, Ec.	H2	86
Río Blanco, Chile	F2	92
Rio Branco, Braz.	E4	84
Río Branco, Ur.	F11	92
Río Bravo, Mex.	C9	100
Río Bravo, Parque Internacional del, p.o.i., Mex.	F5	130
Rio Brilhante, Braz.	D6	90
Río Bueno, Chile	H2	90
Rio Casca, Braz.	K4	88
Río Ceballos, Arg.	E5	92
Río Chico, Ven.	B9	86
Rio Claro, Braz.	L2	88
Rio Claro, Trin.	s12	105f
Río Colorado, Arg.	I5	92
Río Cuarto, Arg.	F5	92
Rio das Pedras, Moz.	C12	70
Rio de Janeiro, Braz.	L4	88
Rio de Janeiro, state, Braz.	L4	88
Rio Dell, Ca., U.S.	C1	134
Río de Oro, Col.	C5	86
Rio do Sul, Braz.	C13	92
Rio Espera, Braz.	K4	88
Rio Felix, stm., N.M., U.S.	H3	128
Río Gallegos, Arg.	J3	90
Río Grande, Arg.	J3	90
Rio Grande, Braz.	F11	92
Río Grande, Mex.	D7	100
Río Grande, Nic.	F4	102
Río Grande, P.R.	B4	104a
Rio Grande (Bravo), stm., N.A.	H13	98
Rio Grande do Norte, state, Braz.	C7	88
Rio Grande do Sul, state, Braz.	D11	92
Ríohacha, Col.	B5	86
Río Hato, Pan.	H7	102
Rio Hondo, Tx., U.S.	H10	130
Rio Hondo, stm., N.M., U.S.	H3	128
Rio Hondo, Embalse, res., Arg.	C5	92
Río Jueyes, P.R.	B3	104a
Riolândia, Braz.	D6	90
Rio Largo, Braz.	E8	88
Riom, Fr.	D9	18
Río Mayo, Arg.	I2	90
Río Mulatos, Bol.	C3	90
Riondel, B.C., Can.	G14	138
Rio Negro, Braz.	C13	92
Ríonegro, Col.	D5	86
Río Negro, state, Arg.	G3	90
Rio Negro, Pantanal do, sw., Braz.	C5	90
Rionero in Vulture, Italy	D9	24
Riópar, Spain	F8	20
Rio Pardo, Braz.	E11	92
Rio Pardo de Minas, Braz.	H4	88
Río Piedras, P.R.	B3	104a
Rio Piracicaba, Braz.	J4	88
Rio Pomba, Braz.	K4	88
Rio Preto, Braz.	L3	88
Rio Rancho, N.M., U.S.	H10	132
Rio Real, Braz.	F6	88
Río Segundo, Arg.	E5	92
Ríosucio, Col.	E4	86
Río Tercero, Arg.	F5	92
Rio Tinto, Braz.	D8	88
Rio Verde, Braz.	G7	84
Ríoverde, Mex.	E8	100
Rio Verde de Mato Grosso, Braz.	C6	90
Rio Vista, Ca., U.S.	E4	134
Riozinho, stm., Braz.	E3	88
Riozinho, stm., Braz.	D4	84
Ripley, N.Y., U.S.	B6	114
Ripley, Oh., U.S.	F2	114
Ripley, Tn., U.S.	B9	122
Ripoll, Spain	B13	20
Ripon, Qc., Can.	E1	110
Ripon, Eng., U.K.	G11	12
Ripon, Ca., U.S.	F4	134
Ripon, Wi., U.S.	H10	118
Riposto, Italy	G9	24
Risaralda, state, Col.	E3	86
Risbäck, Swe.	D6	8
Rishīkesh, India	C7	54
Rishiri-suidō, strt., Japan	B14	38
Rishiri-tō, i., Japan	B14	38
Rishon LeẔiyyon, Isr.	G5	58
Rising Star, Tx., U.S.	B9	130
Rising Sun, In., U.S.	F12	120
Rising Sun, Md., U.S.	E9	114
Risle, stm., Fr.	E9	14
Risnjak, mtn., Cro.	E11	22
Risti, Est.	A7	10
Ristna, Est.	G9	8
Rita Blanca Creek, stm., Tx., U.S.	F6	128
Ritchie, S. Afr.	F7	70
Ritidian Point, c., Guam	i10	78c
Ritter, Mount, mtn., Ca., U.S.	F6	134
Rittman, Oh., U.S.	D4	114
Ritzville, Wa., U.S.	C8	136
Rivadavia, Arg.	E3	92
Rivadavia, Arg.	G6	92
Rivadavia, Chile	D2	92
Riva del Garda, Italy	E7	22
Rivas, Nic.	G5	102
Rive-de-Gier, Fr.	D10	18
Rivera, Arg.	H6	92
Rivera, Ur.	E10	92
River Cess, Lib.	H3	64

Name	Map Ref.	Page
Riverdale, Ca., U.S.	G6	134
Riverdale, N.D., U.S.	G12	124
River Falls, Al., U.S.	F12	122
River Falls, Wi., U.S.	G6	118
Riverhead, N.Y., U.S.	D13	114
Riverhurst, Sk., Can.	D7	124
Riverina, reg., Austl.	J5	76
River John, N.S., Can.	E13	110
River Jordan, B.C., Can.	H6	138
River Road, Or., U.S.	F3	136
Rivers, Mb., Can.	D13	124
Riversdale, S. Afr.	I5	70
Riverside, Ca., U.S.	J8	134
Riverside, Ia., U.S.	C6	120
Riverside, Tx., U.S.	G3	122
Riverside, Wa., U.S.	B7	136
Rivers Inlet, B.C., Can.	E3	138
Riversleigh, Austl.	C7	74
Riverton, N.Z.	H2	80
Riverton, Il., U.S.	E8	120
Riverton, Ne., U.S.	A10	128
Riverton, Ut., U.S.	C4	132
Riverton, Va., U.S.	F7	114
Riverton, Wy., U.S.	D4	126
Riverton Heights, Wa., U.S.	C4	136
River View, Al., U.S.	E13	122
Rives, Tn., U.S.	H8	120
Rivesville, W.V., U.S.	E5	114
Riviera Beach, Fl., U.S.	J5	116
Rivière-à-Pierre, Qc., Can.	C5	110
Rivière-Bleue, Qc., Can.	C7	110
Rivière-de-la-Chaloupe, Qc., Can.	A14	110
Rivière-du-Loup, Qc., Can.	C7	110
Rivière-Matawin, Qc., Can.	D3	110
Rivière-Pilote, Mart.	I7	105c
Rivière-Salée, Mart.	k7	105c
Rivne, Ukr.	E14	6
Rivoli, Italy	E4	22
Rivoli Bay, b., Austl.	K2	76
Riyadh see Ar-Riyāḍ, Sau. Ar.	E6	56
Riyāq, Leb.	E7	58
Rize, Tur.	A5	56
Rizzuto, Capo, c., Italy	F11	24
Rjad, Russia	C18	10
Rjazan', Russia	D5	32
Rjazancevo, Russia	D22	10
Rjazanskaja oblast', co., Russia	I19	8
Rjažsk, Russia	D6	32
Rjukan, Nor.	G3	8
Ro, N. Cal.	m16	79d
Roachdale, In., U.S.	I3	112
Road Town, Br. Vir. Is.	e8	104b
Roan Mountain, Tn., U.S.	H3	114
Roanne, Fr.	C9	18
Roanoke, Al., U.S.	D13	122
Roanoke, In., U.S.	D8	120
Roanoke, Va., U.S.	G6	114
Roanoke, stm., U.S.	H8	114
Roanoke Island, i., N.C., U.S.	I10	114
Roanoke Rapids, N.C., U.S.	H8	114
Roanoke Rapids Lake Dam, dam, N.C., U.S.	H8	114
Roaring Spring, Pa., U.S.	D7	114
Roaring Springs, Tx., U.S.	H7	128
Roatán, Isla de, i., Hond.	D4	102
Robbins, N.C., U.S.	A6	116
Robbins, Tn., U.S.	H13	120
Robbins Island, i., Austl.	n12	77a
Robbinsville, N.C., U.S.	A2	116
Robe, Austl.	K2	76
Robe, Mount, hill, Austl.	H3	76
Röbel, Ger.	C8	16
Robersonville, N.C., U.S.	I8	114
Roberta, Ga., U.S.	D1	116
Robert Lee, Tx., U.S.	C7	130
Robert Louis Stevenson's Tomb, hist., Samoa	g12	79c
Roberts, Id., U.S.	G14	136
Roberts, Mt., U.S.	B3	126
Robertsdale, Al., U.S.	G11	122
Robertsfors, Swe.	D9	8
Robert S. Kerr Lake, res., Ok., U.S.	B3	122
Robertson, S. Afr.	H4	70
Roberts Peak, mtn., B.C., Can.	D10	138
Roberts Port, Lib.	H2	64
Roberval, Qc., Can.	B4	110
Robinson, Il., U.S.	E10	120
Robinson, Tx., U.S.	C10	130
Robinson Crusoe, Isla, i., Chile	I7	82
Robinvale, Austl.	J4	76
Robledo, Spain	F8	20
Roblin, Mb., Can.	C12	124
Roboré, Bol.	C5	90
Rob Roy Island, i., Sol. Is.	d7	79b
Robson, Mount, mtn., B.C., Can.	C11	138
Robstown, Tx., U.S.	G10	130
Roby, Tx., U.S.	B7	130
Roca, Cabo da, c., Port.	F1	20
Roçado, Braz.	D3	88
Rocafuerte, Ec.	H1	86
Roca Partida, Isla, i., Mex.	F2	100
Rocas, Atol das, i., Braz.	F11	82
Rocciamelone, mtn., Italy	E4	22
Rocha, Ur.	G10	92
Rochdale, Eng., U.K.	H10	12
Rochechouart, Fr.	D6	18
Rochefort, Fr.	D5	18
Rochelle, Ga., U.S.	E2	116
Rochelle, Il., U.S.	C8	120
Roche-Percée, Sk., Can.	E10	124
Rochester, Eng., U.K.	J13	12
Rochester, In., U.S.	G3	112
Rochester, Mi., U.S.	B2	114
Rochester, Mn., U.S.	G6	118
Rochester, N.H., U.S.	G5	110
Rochester, N.Y., U.S.	E12	112
Rochester, Tx., U.S.	H9	128
Rochlitz, Ger.	E8	16
Rock, stm., U.S.	J8	118
Rock, i., Palau	D6	44
Rockall, i., Scot., U.K.	D6	6
Rockall Rise, unds.	C12	144
Rock Bay, B.C., Can.	F5	138
Rock Creek, B.C., Can.	G11	138
Rock Creek, stm., N.A.	F7	124
Rock Creek, stm., Mt., U.S.	D13	136
Rock Creek, stm., Nv., U.S.	C9	134
Rock Creek Butte, mtn., Or., U.S.	F8	136
Rockdale, Il., U.S.	C9	120
Rockdale, Tx., U.S.	D11	130
Rockefeller Plateau, plat., Ant.	D27	81
Rockenhausen, Ger.	G3	16
Rockford, Il., U.S.	C8	120
Rockford, Oh., U.S.	D1	114
Rockford, Tn., U.S.	B15	122
Rockglen, Sk., Can.	E8	124
Rockhampton, Austl.	D8	76
Rockhampton Downs, Austl.	C7	74
Rock Hill, S.C., U.S.	B4	116
Rockingham, N.C., U.S.	B6	116
Rockingham Bay, b., Austl.	B6	76
Rock Island, Il., U.S.	C7	120
Rocklake, N.D., U.S.	F14	124
Rockland, On., Can.	C14	112
Rockland, Id., U.S.	H14	136
Rockland, Me., U.S.	F7	110
Rocklands Reservoir, l., Austl.	K3	76
Rockledge, Fl., U.S.	H5	116
Rocklin, Ca., U.S.	E4	134
Rockmart, Ga., U.S.	D13	122
Rockport, In., U.S.	G10	120
Rockport, Ky., U.S.	G11	120
Rockport, Ma., U.S.	B15	114
Rockport, Mo., U.S.	D2	120
Rock Port, Mo., U.S.	D2	120
Rock Rapids, Ia., U.S.	H2	118
Rock River, Wy., U.S.	F6	126
Rocksprings, Tx., U.S.	B7	132
Rockstone, Guy.	B6	84
Rock Tombs see Speos, hist., Egypt	K1	58
Rock Valley, Ia., U.S.	H2	118
Rockville, In., U.S.	I2	112
Rockville, Md., U.S.	E8	114
Rockwall, Tx., U.S.	E2	122
Rockwell, Ia., U.S.	B4	120
Rockwell, N.C., U.S.	A5	116
Rockwell, Me., U.S.	I7	
Rockwood, Pa., U.S.	I10	112
Rockwood, Tn., U.S.	I13	120
Rocky Cape National Park, p.o.i., Austl.	n12	77a
Rockyford, Ab., Can.	E17	138
Rocky Ford, Co., U.S.	C5	128
Rocky Mount, N.C., U.S.	I8	114
Rocky Mount, Va., U.S.	H5	114
Rocky Mountain, mtn., Mt., U.S.	C14	136
Rocky Mountain House, Ab., Can.	D16	138
Rocky Mountain National Park, p.o.i., Co., U.S.	G7	126
Rocky Mountains, mts., N.A.	D6	106
Rocky Mountain Trench, val., N.A.	G15	138
Rocky Point, c., Bah.	K8	116
Rodalben, Ger.	G3	16
Rodbār, Afg.	C9	56
Rødbyhavn, Den.	I4	8
Rodeo, Arg.	E3	92
Rodeo, Mex.	C6	100
Rodeo, N.M., U.S.	L7	132
Roderick Island, i., B.C., Can.	D2	138
Rodewisch, Ger.	F8	16
Rodez, Fr.	E8	18
Roding, Ger.	G8	16
Rodino, Russia	G21	8
Rodney, On., Can.	F7	112
Rodney, Cape, c., Ak., U.S.	D6	140
Rodniki, Russia	H19	8
Ródos (Rhodes), Grc.	G11	28
Ródos (Rhodes), i., Grc.	G10	28
Rodrigues, i., Mrts.	K9	142
Roebourne, Austl.	D3	74
Roebuck Bay, b., Austl.	C3	74
Roeland Park, Ks., U.S.	E3	120
Roermond, Neth.	C14	14
Roeselare, Bel.	D11	14
Roes Welcome Sound, strt., Nu., Can.	C13	106
Roff, Ok., U.S.	C2	122
Rogačevo, Russia	D20	10
Rogaguna, Laguna, l., Bol.	B3	90
Rogaguado, Laguna, l., Bol.	B3	90
Rogaland, state, Nor.	G2	8
Rogaška Slatina, Slvn.	D12	22
Rogers, Ar., U.S.	H3	120
Rogers, Tx., U.S.	D10	130
Rogers, Mount, mtn., Va., U.S.	H4	114
Rogers Lake, l., Ca., U.S.	H8	134
Rogers Pass, p., B.C., Can.	E13	138
Rogersville, N.B., Can.	D11	110
Rogersville, Tn., U.S.	C11	122
Rogersville, Tn., U.S.	H3	114
Roggewein, Cabo, c., Chile	e30	78l
Rogliano, Fr.	G15	18
Rognedino, Russia	G16	10
Rogue, stm., Or., U.S.	H2	136
Rohri, Pak.	D2	54
Rohtak, India	D6	54
Roi Et, Thai.	E6	48
Roi Georges, Îles du, is., Fr. Poly.	E12	72
Roilianka, Ukr.	C16	26
Rojas, Arg.	G7	92
Rojo, Cabo, c., Mex.	E9	100
Rojo, Cabo, c., P.R.	C1	104a
Rokan, Indon.	C2	50
Rokan, stm., Indon.	C2	50
Rokel, stm., S.L.	H2	64
Rokiškis, Lith.	E8	10
Rokycany, Czech Rep.	G9	16
Roland, Mb., Can.	E16	124
Roland, Ia., U.S.	B4	120
Rôlandia, Braz.	D6	90
Roldanillo, Col.	E3	86
Rolfe, Ia., U.S.	B3	120
Roll, Az., U.S.	K2	132
Rolla, Mo., U.S.	G6	120
Rolla, N.D., U.S.	F14	124
Rolling Fork, Ms., U.S.	E8	122
Rolling Fork, stm., Ky., U.S.	G12	120
Rollingstone, Austl.	B6	76
Rollins, Mt., U.S.	C12	136
Rolvsøya, i., Nor.	A10	8
Roma, Austl.	F7	76
Roma, Leso.	F8	70
Roma, Tx., U.S.	H8	130
Romagna, hist. reg., Italy	F9	22
Roman, Rom.	C13	26
Romanche Gap, unds.	I12	144
Romang, Pulau, i., Indon.	G8	44
Romania, ctry., Eur.	D11	26
Roman Nose Mountain, mtn., Or., U.S.	G3	136
Romano, Cape, c., Fl., U.S.	K4	116
Romano, Cayo, i., Cuba	A9	102
Romans-sur-Isère, Fr.	D10	18
Romanzof Mountains, mts., Ak., U.S.	C11	140
Romblon, Phil.	D4	52
Rome see Roma, Italy	I9	22
Rome, Ga., U.S.	C13	122
Rome, N.Y., U.S.	E14	112
Romeo, Mi., U.S.	B2	114
Romilly-sur-Seine, Fr.	F12	14
Romney, W.V., U.S.	E7	114
Romny, Ukr.	D4	32
Romont, Switz.	D3	22
Romorantin-Lanthenay, Fr.	G10	14
Rompin, stm., Malay.	K6	48
Romsey, Eng., U.K.	J11	12
Ron, Mui, c., Viet.	C8	48
Rona, i., Scot., U.K.	D7	12
Rona, i., Scot., U.K.	B7	12
Ronan, Mt., U.S.	C12	136
Roncador, Banco see Roncador, Cayos de, unds., Col.	F7	102
Roncador, Cayos de, unds., Col.	F7	102
Roncador, Serra do, plat., Braz.	F7	84
Roncador Bank see Roncador, Cayos de, unds., Col.	F7	102
Ronda, Spain	H5	20
Ronda, Serranía de, mts., Spain	H5	20
Rondane Nasjonalpark, p.o.i., Nor.	F3	8
Ronde, Pointe, c., Dom.	i5	105c
Rondônia, state, Braz.	F5	84
Rondonópolis, Braz.	G7	84
Rong, stm., China	I3	42
Rong'an, China	I3	42
Rongcheng, China	C10	42
Ronge, Lac la, l., Sk., Can.	D10	106
Rongelap, at., Marsh. Is.	B7	72
Rongjiang, China	I3	42
Rongkop, Indon.	H7	50
Rongshui, China	I3	42
Rongxian, China	J4	42
Rønne, Den.	I6	8
Ronneby, Swe.	H6	8
Ronne Ice Shelf, ice, Ant.	C34	81
Ronse, Bel.	D12	14
Ronuro, stm., Braz.	F7	84
Roodhouse, Il., U.S.	E7	120
Rooiboklaagte, stm., Nmb.	B5	70
Roorkee, India	D6	54
Roosendaal, Neth.	C13	14
Roosevelt, Mn., U.S.	C3	118
Roosevelt, Ok., U.S.	G9	128
Roosevelt, Ut., U.S.	C6	132
Roosevelt, stm., Braz.	E5	84
Roosevelt Campobello International Park, p.o.i., N.B., Can.	F10	110
Roosevelt Island, i., Ant.	C24	81
Root, stm., Mn., U.S.	H7	118
Ropaži, Lat.	C7	10
Roper, N.C., U.S.	I9	114
Roper, stm., Austl.	B6	74
Roper Valley, Austl.	B6	74
Ropesville, Tx., U.S.	H6	128
Roque, Braz.	B3	88
Roquefort, Fr.	E5	18
Roraima, state, Braz.	F11	86
Roraima, Mount, mtn., S.A.	E11	86
Røros, Nor.	E4	8
Rosa, Lake, l., Bah.	B11	102
Rosales, Mex.	A6	100
Rosalia, Wa., U.S.	C9	136
Rosamond, Ca., U.S.	I7	134
Rosamond Lake, l., Ca., U.S.	I7	134
Rosario, Arg.	F7	92
Rosário, Braz.	B3	88
Rosario, Mex.	D5	100
Rosario, Mex.	B4	100
Rosario, Para.	C6	92
Rosario, Ur.	G9	92
Rosario, Bahía del, b., Mex.	G4	98
Rosario, Islas del, is., Col.	B4	86
Rosario de Arriba, Mex.	F4	98
Rosario de la Frontera, Arg.	B5	92
Rosario de Lerma, Arg.	B5	92
Rosario del Tala, Arg.	F8	92
Rosário do Sul, Braz.	E10	92
Rosário Oeste, Braz.	F6	84
Rosarito, Mex.	K8	134
Rosarito, Mex.	A2	100
Rosas, Mex.	H4	130
Roscoe, S.D., U.S.	B13	126
Roscoe, Tx., U.S.	B7	130
Roscommon, Ire.	H4	12
Roscommon, state, Ire.	H4	12
Roscrea, Ire.	I5	12
Rose, Mount, mtn., Nv., U.S.	D5	134
Roseau, Dom.	j6	105c
Roseau, Mn., U.S.	C3	118
Roseau, stm., N.A.	C2	118
Roseberth, Austl.	E2	76
Roseboro, N.C., U.S.	B7	116
Rosebud, Mt., U.S.	A6	126
Rosebud, S.D., U.S.	D12	126
Rosebud, Tx., U.S.	C11	130
Rosebud, Ab., Can.	E18	138
Rosebud Creek, stm., Mt., U.S.	A6	126
Rosebush, Mi., U.S.	E5	112
Rose City, Mi., U.S.	D5	112
Rosedale, Austl.	E8	76
Rosedale, Ab., Can.	E18	138
Rosedale, In., U.S.	I2	112
Rosedale, Ms., U.S.	D7	122
Rose Hill, N.C., U.S.	B7	116
Rose Hill, Va., U.S.	H2	114
Rose Island, i., Bah.	K8	116
Rosemary, Ab., Can.	F18	138
Rosenberg, Tx., U.S.	H3	122
Rosenheim, Ger.	I8	16
Rosepine, La., U.S.	G5	122
Roses, Golfe de, b., Spain	B14	20
Roses, Golfo de see Roses, Golfe de, b., Spain	B14	20
Roseto degli Abruzzi, Italy	H11	22
Rosetown, Sk., Can.	C6	124
Rosetta see Rashid, Egypt	G1	58
Rosetta Mouth see Rashid, Masabb, mth., Egypt	G1	58
Rose Valley, Sk., Can.	B10	124
Roseville, Il., U.S.	D7	120
Roseville, Mi., U.S.	F7	112
Roseville, Mi., U.S.	F5	118
Rosholt, S.D., U.S.	F2	118
Rosholt, Wi., U.S.	G9	118
Rosica, stm., Blg.	F12	26
Rosiclare, Il., U.S.	G9	120
Rosignol, Guy.	B6	84
Roşiori de Vede, Rom.	E12	26
Roskilde, Den.	I4	8
Roskilde, state, Den.	I5	8
Roslavl', Russia	G15	10
Rosman, N.C., U.S.	A3	116
Rosmead, S. Afr.	G7	70
Ros Mhic Thriúin see New Ross, Ire.	I6	12
Ross, Austl.	o13	77a
Ross, stm., Yk., Can.	C4	106
Ross, stm., Austl.	J6	76
Rossano, Italy	F10	24
Rossano, Italy	E13	10
Rossburn, Mb., Can.	D13	124
Rosseau, Lake, l., On., Can.	C10	112
Rossel, Cap, c., N. Cal.	m16	79d
Rossell y Rius, Ur.	F10	92
Rossford, Oh., U.S.	C2	114
Ross Ice Shelf, ice, Ant.	D23	81
Rossignol, Lake, l., N.S., Can.	F11	110
Ross Island, i., Ant.	C22	81
Ross Lake, res., N.A.	B5	136
Rossland, B.C., Can.	G13	138
Rosslau, Ger.	E8	16
Rosso, Maur.	F1	64
Ross-on-Wye, Eng., U.K.	J10	12
Rossoš', Russia	D5	32
Ross R. Barnett Reservoir, res., Ms., U.S.	E9	122
Ross River, Yk., Can.	C4	106
Ross Sea, s., Ant.	C23	81
Røssvatnet, l., Nor.	D5	8
Rossville, Ga., U.S.	C13	122
Rossville, Il., U.S.	H2	112
Rossville, Ks., U.S.	E2	120
Røst, i., Nor.	C4	8
Rosthern, Sk., Can.	B7	124
Roštkala, Taj.	B11	56
Rostock, Ger.	B7	16
Rostov, Russia	C22	10
Rostov-na-Donu, Russia	E6	32
Rosvinskoe, Russia	C24	8
Roswell, Ga., U.S.	C1	116
Roswell, N.M., U.S.	H3	128
Rota, i., N. Mar. Is.	B5	72
Rotan, Tx., U.S.	B7	130
Rotenburg, Ger.	C5	16
Roth, Ger.	G7	16
Rothaargebirge, mts., Ger.	E4	16
Rothenburg ob der Tauber, Ger.	G6	16
Rothera, sci., Ant.	B34	81
Rotherham, Eng., U.K.	H11	12
Rotherham, N.B., Can.	E11	110
Rothesay, Scot., U.K.	F7	12
Rothsay, Mn., U.S.	E2	118
Rothwell, N.B., Can.	D10	110
Roti, Pulau, i., Indon.	H7	44
Roto, Austl.	I5	76
Rotondella, Italy	D10	24
Rotorua, N.Z.	D7	80
Rottenburg am Neckar, Ger.	H4	16
Rottenburg an der Laaber, Ger.	H8	16
Rotterdam, Neth.	C13	14
Rotterdam, N.Y., U.S.	B11	114
Rottweil, Ger.	H4	16
Rotuma, i., Fiji	E8	72
Roubaix, Fr.	D12	14
Roudnice nad Labem, Czech Rep.	F9	16
Rouen, Fr.	E10	14
Rouge, stm., Can.	E2	110
Rough, stm., Ky., U.S.	G11	120
Rough River Lake, res., Ky., U.S.	G11	120
Rouleau, Sk., Can.	D9	124
Roulers see Roeselare, Bel.	D11	14
Roulette, Pa., U.S.	C7	114
Round Hill Head, c., Austl.	E8	76
Round Lake, Mn., U.S.	H3	118
Round Lake, l., On., Can.	C12	112
Round Mound, hill, Ks., U.S.	C5	128
Round Mountain, Nv., U.S.	E8	134
Round Mountain, mtn., Austl.	H9	76
Round Rock, Tx., U.S.	D10	130
Roundup, Mt., U.S.	A4	126
Roura, Fr. Gu.	C7	84
Rouses Point, N.Y., U.S.	E3	110
Roussillon, hist. reg., Fr.	G8	18
Routhierville, Qc., Can.	B9	110
Rouyn-Noranda, Qc., Can.	F15	106
Rovaniemi, Fin.	C11	8
Rovenskaja Slabada, Bela.	H13	10
Rovereto, Italy	E8	22
Roversi, Arg.	C6	92
Rovigo, Italy	E8	22
Rovuma (Ruvuma), stm., Afr.	C6	68
Rowan Lake, l., On., Can.	B5	118
Rowena, Austl.	G7	76
Rowland, N.C., U.S.	B6	116
Rowley, stm., Nu., Can.	A15	106
Rowley Island, i., Nu., Can.	B14	106
Roxas, Phil.	C4	52
Roxboro, N.C., U.S.	H7	114
Roxborough, Trin.	r13	105f
Roxburgh, N.Z.	G3	80
Roxton, Tx., U.S.	D3	122
Roy, N.M., U.S.	F4	128
Roy, Ut., U.S.	B4	132
Roy, Wa., U.S.	C4	136
Royal Bardiyā Wild Life Reserve, India	D8	54
Royal Canal, can., Ire.	H6	12
Royal Center, In., U.S.	H3	112
Royal Chitwan National Park, p.o.i., Nepal	E10	54
Royal City, Wa., U.S.	D7	136
Royal Gorge, p., Co., U.S.	D10	118
Royal Leamington Spa, Eng., U.K.	I11	12
Royal Natal National Park, p.o.i., S. Afr.	F9	70
Royal Oak, Mi., U.S.	B2	114
Royalton, Mi., U.S.	F4	118
Royal Tunbridge Wells, Eng., U.K.	J13	12
Royan, Fr.	D5	18
Roye, Fr.	E11	14
Royston, Eng., U.K.	I12	12
Royston, Ga., U.S.	B2	116
Rožan, Pol.	D17	16
Rozdestveno, Russia	C20	10
Roždil'na, Ukr.	C17	26
Rozewie, Przylądek, c., Pol.	B14	16
Rožňava, Slov.	H16	16
Roznov, Rom.	C13	26
Roznów, Pol.	G16	16
Roztocze, hills, Eur.	F19	16
Roztoky, Czech Rep.	F10	16
Rrogozhinë, Alb.	C13	24
Rrogozhinë, Alb.	C13	24
Rtiščevo, Russia	D6	32
Ru, stm., China	E6	42
Ruacana Falls, wtfl., Afr.	D1	68
Ruahine Range, mts., N.Z.	D7	80
Ruapehu, Mount, vol., N.Z.	D6	80
Ruapuke Island, i., N.Z.	H3	80
Rubbestadneset, Nor.	G1	8
Rubcovsk, Russia	D14	32
Rubi, stm., D.R.C.	D5	66
Rubio, Ven.	D5	86
Rubondo Island, i., Tan.	E6	66
Ruby, Ak., U.S.	D8	140
Ruby, Mt., U.S.	E14	136
Ruby Dome, mtn., Nv., U.S.	C1	132
Ruby Lake, sw, Nv., U.S.	C1	132
Ruby Mountains, mts., Nv., U.S.	C1	132
Ruby Valley, val., Nv., U.S.	C1	132
Rucheng, China	I5	42
Ruciane-Nida, Pol.	C17	16
Ruda Śląska, Pol.	F14	16
Rudall, stm., Austl.	D4	74
Rudersdorf, Ger.	D9	16
Rudkøbing, Den.	B6	16
Rudna Pristan', Russia	B11	38
Rudnja, Russia	F14	10
Rudnyj see Rūdnyy, Kaz.	D10	32
Rudnyj, Russia	B11	38
Rudnyj, Russia	D6	32
Rudo, Bos.	F6	26
Rudolf, Lake (Turkana, Lake), l., Afr.	D7	66
Rudolf Hǎyk' see Rudolf, Lake, l., Afr.	D7	66
Rudolstadt, Ger.	F7	16
Rudong, China	E9	42
Rudozem, Blg.	H11	26
Rudyard, Mi., U.S.	B5	112
Rue, Fr.	D10	14
Rufá'ah, Sudan	E6	62
Ruffin, S.C., U.S.	C5	116
Rufiji, stm., Tan.	F7	66
Rufino, Arg.	G6	92
Rufisque, Sen.	G1	64
Rufunsa, Zam.	D4	68
Rugao, China	E9	42
Rugby, Eng., U.K.	I11	12
Rugby, N.D., U.S.	F14	124
Rügen, i., Ger.	B9	16
Rugged Mountain, mtn., B.C., Can.	F4	138
Ruhengeri, Rw.	E5	66
Ruhnu, i., Est.	B6	10
Ruhpolding, Ger.	I8	16
Ruhr, stm., Ger.	E3	16
Ruhunu National Park, p.o.i., Sri L.	H5	53
Rui'an, China	H9	42
Ruidoso, N.M., U.S.	H3	128
Ruidoso, stm., N.M., U.S.	H3	128
Ruijin, China	I6	42
Ruiz, Mex.	D6	100
Ruiz, Nevado del, vol., Col.	E4	86
Ruiz de Montoya, Arg.	C10	92
Ruki, stm., D.R.C.	E3	66
Rukwa, Lake, l., Tan.	F6	66
Rule, Tx., U.S.	A8	130
Ruleville, Ms., U.S.	D8	122
Rulo, Ne., U.S.	D2	120
Rúm, i., Scot., U.K.	D6	12
Rum Cay, i., Bah.	C10	96
Rumbek, Sudan	F5	62
Rumford, Me., U.S.	F6	110
Rumia, Serb.	B14	16
Rumigny, Fr.	E13	14
Rumoi, Japan	B14	38
Rumuruti, Kenya	B1	68
Runan, China	C13	14
Runanga, N.Z.	F4	80
Runde, stm., Zimb.	B10	70
Rundēni, Lat.	D10	10
Rundu, Nmb.	D2	68
Runge, Tx., U.S.	F10	130
Rungwa, Tan.	F6	66
Rungwa, stm., Tan.	F6	66
Running Water Draw, stm., U.S.	G6	128
Ruo, Chn., U.S.	C4	36
Ruoqiang, China	D2	36
Ruoxi, China	G6	42
Rupat, Pulau, i., Indon.	C2	50
Rupert, Id., U.S.	H13	136
Rupert, W.V., U.S.	G5	114
Rupert, stm., Qc., Can.	E15	106
Rupert Creek, stm., Austl.	C4	76
Rupununi, stm., Guy.	F12	86
Rur, stm., Eur.	D15	14
Rural Retreat, Va., U.S.	H4	114
Rurrenabaque, Bol.	B3	90
Rurutu, i., Fr. Poly.	F11	72
Rusape, Zimb.	D5	68
Rusayris, Khazzān ar-, res., Afr.	E6	62
Ruse, Blg.	F12	26
Ruse, state, Blg.	F13	26
Rusera, India	F11	54
Rush Center, Ks., U.S.	C9	128
Rush City, Mn., U.S.	F5	118
Rush Creek, stm., Co., U.S.	C5	128
Rushford, Mn., U.S.	H7	118
Rushmore, Mn., U.S.	H3	118
Rushville, Il., U.S.	D7	120
Rushville, In., U.S.	E12	120
Rushville, Ne., U.S.	E9	126
Rusizi, stm., Afr.	E5	66
Rusk, Tx., U.S.	F3	122
Ruskin, Fl., U.S.	I3	116
Rusnė, Lith.	E4	10
Russas, Braz.	C6	88
Russell, Mb., Can.	D12	124
Russell, In., U.S.	H3	112
Russell, Ks., U.S.	C10	128
Russell, Ky., U.S.	F3	114
Russell, Cape, c., N.T., Can.	A16	140
Russell Cave National Monument, p.o.i., Al., U.S.	C13	122
Russell Islands, is., Sol. Is.	e8	79b
Russellkonda, India	I10	54
Russells Point, Oh., U.S.	D2	114
Russell Springs, Ky., U.S.	G12	120
Russellville, Al., U.S.	C11	122
Russellville, Ar., U.S.	B5	122
Russellville, Ky., U.S.	H11	120
Rüsselsheim, Ger.	G4	16
Russia, ctry., Eur.	B18	2
Russian, stm., Ca., U.S.	E2	134
Russiaville, In., U.S.	H3	112
Russkij, Russia	C13	22
Rusti, Aus.	C13	22
Rustavi, Geor.	F7	32
Rustburg, Va., U.S.	G6	114
Rustenburg, S. Afr.	D8	70
Ruston, La., U.S.	E6	122
Rutana, Bdi.	E6	66
Rute, Spain	G6	20
Ruteng, Indon.	H12	50
Ruth, Nv., U.S.	D1	132
Rutherford, Tn., U.S.	H8	120
Rutherfordton, N.C., U.S.	A3	116
Ruthin, Wales, U.K.	H9	12
Ruthven, Ia., U.S.	H4	118
Rutland, B.C., Can.	G11	138
Rutland, N.D., U.S.	A15	126
Rutland, Vt., U.S.	G4	110
Rutledge, Ga., U.S.	C2	116
Rutog, China	B7	54
Rutshuru, D.R.C.	E5	66
Rutter, On., Can.	B9	112
Ruvuma (Rovuma), stm., Afr.	C6	68
Ruwenzori, mts., Afr.	D6	66
Ruwenzori Range see Ruwenzori, mts., Afr.	D6	66
Ruy Barbosa, Braz.	E19	10
Ruza, Russia	E19	10
Ruza, stm., Russia	E18	10
Ruzaevka, Russia	D7	32
Ružany, Bela.	H7	10
Ružomberok, Slov.	G15	16
Rwanda, ctry., Afr.	E5	66
Ryan, Ok., U.S.	G11	128
Ryan Peak, mtn., Id., U.S.	G12	136
Ryback'e, Kaz.	E14	32
Rybačij, poluostrov, pen., Russia	B15	8
Rybinsk, Russia	B21	10
Rybinskoe vodohranilišče (Rybinsk Reservoir), res., Russia	B21	10
Rybinsk Reservoir see Rybinskoe vodohranilišče, res., Russia	B21	10
Rybnik, Pol.	F14	16
Rybnoje, Russia	E7	34
Ryde, Eng., U.K.	K11	12
Ryderwood, Wa., U.S.	D3	136
Rydzyna, Pol.	E13	16
Ryegate, Mt., U.S.	A3	126
Rye Patch Reservoir, res., Nv., U.S.	C7	134
Ryfoss, Nor.	F3	8
Ryley, Ab., Can.	C18	138
Ryl'sk, Russia	D4	32
Rymařov, Czech Rep.	G13	16
Ryōhaku-sanchi, mts., Japan	C9	40
Ryōtsu, Japan	A11	40
Rysy, mtn., Eur.	G15	16
Ryūgasaki, Japan	D13	40
Ryukyu Islands see Nansei-shotō, is., Japan	k19	39a
Ryukyu Trench, unds.	G15	142
Ržanica, Russia	G16	10
Rzeszów, Pol.	F17	16
Rzeszów, state, Pol.	F17	16
Ržev, Russia	D17	10

S

Name	Map Ref.	Page
Sa, Thai.	C5	48
Saale, stm., Ger.	E7	16
Saalfeld, Ger.	F7	16
Saar see Saarland, state, Ger.	G2	16
Saarbrücken, Ger.	G2	16
Saarburg, Ger.	G2	16
Saaremaa, i., Est.	G9	8
Saarijärvi, Fin.	E11	8
Saarland, state, Ger.	G2	16
Saarlouis, Ger.	G2	16
Saavedra, Arg.	H6	92
Šaba, i., Neth. Ant.	B1	105a
Šabac, Serb.	E6	26
Sabadell, Spain	C13	20
Sabae, Japan	D9	40
Sabah, state, Malay.	H1	52
Sabah, hist. reg., Malay.	D6	44
Sabak, Malay.	K5	48
Sabalana, Kepulauan, is., Indon.	G11	50
Sabana, Archipiélago de, is., Cuba	A7	102
Sabana de la Mar, Dom. Rep.	C13	102
Sabana de Mendoza, Ven.	C6	86
Sabanagrande, Hond.	F4	102
Sabana Grande, P.R.	B2	104a
Sabanalarga, Col.	B4	86
Sabana Llana, P.R.	B3	104a
Sabang, Indon.	J2	48
Sabang, Indon.	I1	50
Sabarei, Kenya	D7	66
Sábari, India	C5	53
Sabarmati, stm., India	G4	54
Sab'atayn, Ramlat as-, sand, Yemen	F6	56
Sabbioneta, Italy	E7	22
Šāberī, Hāmūn-e, l., Asia	C9	56
Sabetha, Ks., U.S.	E2	120
Sabhā, Libya	B2	62
Sabidana, Jabal, mtn., Sudan	D7	62
Sabie, S. Afr.	D10	70
Sabiè, stm., Afr.	D10	70
Sabile, Lat.	C5	10
Sabina, Oh., U.S.	E2	114
Sabina, hist. reg., Italy	H9	22
Sabinal, Tx., U.S.	E8	130
Sabinal, stm., Tx., U.S.	E8	130
Sabinas, Mex.	B9	100
Sabinas, Cayo, i., Cuba	B9	102
Sabiñánigo, Spain	B10	20
Sabinas, Mex.	B8	100
Sabinas, stm., Mex.	B8	100
Sabinas Hidalgo, Mex.	B8	100
Sabine, stm., U.S.	G5	122
Sabine Lake, l., U.S.	A17	140
Sabine Lake, l., U.S.	H5	122
Sabine Pass, strt., U.S.	H5	122
Sabinópolis, Braz.	J4	88
Sabiote, Spain	F7	20
Sabla, Blg.	F15	26
Sable, Cape, pen., Fl., U.S.	K4	116
Sable, Cape, c., N.S., Can.	G16	110
Sablūkah, Shallāl as- (Sixth Cataract), wtfl., Sudan	D6	62
Šablykino, Russia	H18	10
Sabor, stm., Port.	C4	20
Sabou, Burkina	G4	64
Sabrina Coast, cst., Ant.	B16	81
Sabyin, Mya.	F5	56
Sabyin, Mya.	C2	48
Sabzevār, Iran	B8	56
Sac, stm., Mo., U.S.	G4	120
Sacaton, Az., U.S.	J5	132
Sac City, Ia., U.S.	B3	120
Săcele, Romania	D12	26
Sachayoj, Arg.	C6	92
Sachsen, state, Ger.	F9	16
Sachsen (Saxony), hist. reg., Ger.	D5	16
Sachsen-Anhalt, state, Ger.	D7	16
Sachs Harbour, N.T., Can.	B14	140
Šack, Bela.	G10	10
Sackets Harbor, N.Y., U.S.	E13	112
Sackville, N.B., Can.	E12	110
Saco, Me., U.S.	G5	110
Saco, Mt., U.S.	F5	126
Sacramento, Braz.	J2	88
Sacramento, Ca., U.S.	E4	134
Sacramento, stm., Ca., U.S.	E4	134
Sacramento Mountains, mts., N.M., U.S.	E10	98
Sacramento Valley, val., Ca., U.S.	D3	134
Sacramento Wash, stm., Az., U.S.	H2	132
Sacred Heart, Mn., U.S.	G3	118
Sádaba, Spain	B9	20
Şa'dah, Yemen	F5	56
Sadao, Thai.	I5	48
Sada Taung, mtn., Mya.	E4	48
Sada-misaki, c., Japan	F4	40
Sada-misaki-hantō, pen., Japan	F5	40
Sadang, stm., Indon.	E11	50
Sadda, Pak.	B3	54
Saddle Mountain, mtn., Co., U.S.	C3	128
Saddle Mountain, mtn., Br.	E5	56
Saddle Peak, mtn., India	F7	46
Sa Dec, Viet.	G7	48
Sādiqābād, Pak.	D3	54
Sadiya, India	C8	46
Sadlers, St. K/N.	C2	105a
Sado, i., Japan	A11	40
Sado, stm., Port.	F2	20
Sadō-kaikyō, strt., Japan	B11	40
Sadowara, Japan	G4	40
Sādri, India	F4	54
Šadrinsk, Russia	C10	32
Sădvaluspen, Swe.	C7	8
Saegertown, Pa., U.S.	C5	114
Saerluojia Hu, l., China	B11	54
Safárikovo, Slov.	H16	16
Säffle, Swe.	G5	8
Saffron Walden, Eng., U.K.	I13	12
Safi, Mor.	C3	64
Safid Koh, Selseleh-ye, mts., Afg.	C9	56
Safonovo, Russia	E16	10
Safonovo, Russia	D22	8
Safranbolu, Tur.	B15	28
Saga, China	D10	54
Saga, Japan	F3	40
Saga, state, Japan	F3	40
Sagae, Japan	A13	40
Sagaing, Mya.	B2	48
Sagaing, state, Mya.	A2	48
Sagamihara, Japan	D12	40
Sagami-nada, b., Japan	D12	40
Saganaga Lake, l., N.A.	C7	118
Saganthit Kyun, i., Mya.	G4	48
Sāgar, India	F7	54
Sāgar, India	D2	53
Sagara, Japan	E11	40
Sagaranten, Indon.	G5	50
Sagavanirktok, stm., Ak., U.S.	C10	140
Sage, Mount, mtn., Br. Vir. Is.	e8	104b
Sage Creek, stm., Mt., U.S.	B16	136
Sagerton, Tx., U.S.	A8	130
Saginaw, Mi., U.S.	E5	112
Saginaw Bay, b., Mi., U.S.	E6	112
Sağlık, Tur.	B4	56
Sagleipie, Lib.	H3	64
Saglek Bay, b., Nf., Can.	F13	141
Sagonar, Russia	D16	32
Şagu, Rom.	C8	26
Saguache, Co., U.S.	C2	128
Saguache Creek, stm., Co., U.S.	C2	128
Sagua la Grande, Cuba	A7	102
Saguaro National Park, p.o.i., Az., U.S.	K5	132
Saguenay, stm., Qc., Can.	B7	110
Sagunt, Sp.	E10	20
Sagunto see Sagunt, Spain	E10	20
Sāgwāra, India	G4	54
Sa'gya, China	D12	54

Name	Map Ref.	Page
Sahagún, Col.	C4	86
Sahagún, Spain	B5	20
Sahalin, ostrov, i., Russia	F17	34
Sahalinskij zaliv, b., Russia	F17	34
Sahara, des., Afr.	E5	64
Sahāranpur, India	C6	54
Saharsa, India	F11	54
Sahel see Sudan, reg., Afr.	E4	62
Sāhibganj, India	F11	54
Sāhīwāl, Pak.	C4	54
Sāhīwāl, Pak.	C4	54
Šahovskaja, Russia	D18	10
Šahrisabz, Uzb.	G11	32
Šahtjorsk, Russia	G17	34
Šahty, Russia	E6	32
Sahuaripa, Mex.	A4	100
Sahuarita, Az., U.S.	L5	132
Sahuayo de José Maria Morelos, Mex.	F7	100
Šahunja, Russia	H22	8
Šahy, Slov.	H14	16
Sai Buri, Thai.	I5	48
Sai Buri, stm., Thai.	I5	48
Saidor, Pap. N. Gui.	b4	79a
Saidpur, Bngl.	F12	54
Saidu, Pak.	C11	56
Saigō, Japan	C6	40
Saigon see Thanh Pho Ho Chi Minh, Viet.	G8	48
Saijō, Japan	F6	40
Saiki, Japan	G4	40
Saim, Russia	B10	32
Saimaa, l., Fin.	F13	8
Sainte Agathe, Mb., Can.	E16	124
Sainte-Agathe-des-Monts, Qc., Can.	D2	110
Saint-Agrève, Fr.	D10	18
Saint Alban's, Nf., Can.	j22	107a
Saint Albans, Eng., U.K.	J12	12
Saint Albans, Vt., U.S.	F3	110
Saint Albans, W.V., U.S.	F4	114
Saint Albert, Ab., Can.	C17	138
Saint Aldhelm's Head, c., Eng., U.K.	K10	12
Saint-Alexis-des-Monts, Qc., Can.	D3	110
Saint-Amand-Mont-Rond, Fr.	H11	14
Saint-André-Avellin, Qc., Can.	E1	110
Saint Andrew, Barb.	n8	105d
Saint Andrew, Mount, mtn., St. Vin.	o11	105e
Saint Andrews, N.B., Can.	E9	110
Saint Andrews, Scot., U.K.	E10	12
Saint Andrews, S.C., U.S.	D5	116
Sainte-Anne, Guad.	h6	105c
Sainte-Anne, Mart.	l7	105c
Sainte Anne, Lac, l., Ab., Can.	C16	138
Sainte-Anne-de-Beaupré, Qc., Can.	C5	110
Sainte-Anne-de-Madawaska, N.B., Can.	C8	110
Sainte-Anne-des-Monts, Qc., Can.	A10	110
Sainte-Anne-du-Lac, Qc., Can.	D1	110
Saint Ann's Bay, Jam.	i13	104d
Saint-Anselme, Qc., Can.	D6	110
Saint Ansgar, Ia., U.S.	H5	118
Saint Anthony, Nf., Can.	j22	107a
Saint Anthony, Id., U.S.	G15	136
Saint Arnaud, Austl.	K4	76
Saint Augustin, Qc., Can.	i22	107a
Saint Augustine, Fl., U.S.	G4	116
Saint Austell, Eng., U.K.	K8	12
Saint-Avold, Fr.	E15	14
Saint-Barthélemy, i., Guad.	B2	105a
Saint-Basile, N.B., Can.	C8	110
Saint Bathans, Mount, mtn., N.Z.	G3	80
Saint Bees Head, c., Eng., U.K.	G9	12
Saint-Boniface-de-Shawinigan, Qc., Can.	D3	110
Saint-Bonnet, Fr.	E11	18
Saint Brides Bay, b., Wales, U.K.	J7	12
Saint-Brieuc, Fr.	F6	14
Saint-Brieuc, Baie de, b., Fr.	F6	14
Saint Catharines, On., Can.	E10	112
Saint Catherine, Mount, vol., Gren.	q10	105e
Saint Catherines Island, i., Ga., U.S.	E4	116
Saint Catherine's Point, c., Eng., U.K.	K11	12
Saint-Céré, Fr.	E7	18
Saint-Chamond, Fr.	D10	18
Saint Charles, Id., U.S.	A5	132
Saint Charles, Il., U.S.	C9	120
Saint Charles, Mi., U.S.	E5	112
Saint Charles, Mn., U.S.	H6	118
Saint Charles, Mo., U.S.	F7	120
Saint Charles Mesa, Co., U.S.	C4	128
Saint Christopher (Saint Kitts), i., St. K./N.	C2	105a
Saint Christopher and Nevis see Saint Kitts and Nevis, ctry., N.A.	C2	105a
Saint Clair, Mi., U.S.	B3	114
Saint Clair, Mo., U.S.	F6	120
Saint Clair, stm., N.A.	B3	114
Saint Clair, Lake, l., N.A.	B3	114
Saint Clair Shores, Mi., U.S.	B3	114
Saint-Claud, Fr.	D6	18
Saint-Claude, Mb., Can.	E15	124
Saint-Claude, Fr.	C11	18
Saint-Claude, Guad.	h5	105c
Saint Cloud, Fl., U.S.	H4	116
Saint Cloud, Mn., U.S.	F4	118
Saint-Côme, Qc., Can.	D5	110
Saint Croix, i., V.I.U.S.	g10	104c
Saint Croix, stm., N.A.	E9	110
Saint Croix, stm., U.S.	G6	118
Saint Croix Falls, Wi., U.S.	F6	118
Saint Croix Island National Monument, p.o.i., Me., U.S.	E10	110
Saint-Cyr, stm., Qc., Can.	A11	110
Saint David, Az., U.S.	L6	132
Saint David's, Wales, U.K.	J7	12
Saint David's Head, c., Wales, U.K.	J7	12
Saint David's Island, i., Ber.	k16	104e
Saint-Denis, Fr.	E11	14
Saint-Denis, Reu.	i10	69a
Saint-Dié, Fr.	F15	14
Saint-Dizier, Fr.	F13	14
Saint-Donat-de-Montcalm, Qc., Can.	D2	110
Saint Edward, Ne., U.S.	F15	126
Saint Elias, Cape, c., Ak., U.S.	E11	140
Saint Elias, Mount, mtn., N.A.	C2	106
Saint Elias Mountains, mts., N.A.	D12	140
Saint-Élie, Fr. Gu.	C7	84
Saint-Étienne, Fr.	D10	18
Saint-Étienne-du-Rouvray, Fr.	E10	14
Saint-Eugène, Fr.	B4	110
Saint-Eustache, Qc., Can.	E3	110
Saint-Fabien, Qc., Can.	B8	110
Saint-Félicien, Qc., Can.	B4	110
Saint-Félix-de-Valois, Qc., Can.	D3	110
Saint-Florent-sur-Cher, Fr.	G11	14
Saint-Flour, Fr.	D9	18
Sainte-Foy, ngh., Qc., Can.	D5	110
Sainte-Foy-la-Grande, Fr.	E6	18
Saint Francis, Ks., U.S.	B7	128
Saint Francis, Wi., U.S.	I11	118
Saint Francis, stm., N.A.	C7	110
Saint Francis, stm., N.A.	I11	118
Saint Francis, stm., U.S.	C8	122
Saint Francis, Cape, c., S. Afr.	I7	70
Saint Francis Bay, b., S. Afr.	I7	70
Saint Francisville, Il., U.S.	F10	120
Saint Francisville, La., U.S.	G7	122
Saint-François, Guad.	h6	105c
Saint-François, stm., Qc., Can.	D4	110
Sainte Marie, Mart.	k7	105c
Saint-François, Lac, l., Can.	E2	110
Saint-François, Lac, res., Qc., Can.	E5	110
Saint-Gabriel, Can.	D4	110
Saint-Gabriel-de-Gaspé, Qc., Can.	B12	110
Saint-Gall see Sankt Gallen, Switz.	C6	22
Saint-Gaudens, Fr.	F6	18
Sainte Genevieve, Mo., U.S.	G7	120
Saint George, Austl.	G7	76
Saint George, Ber.	k16	104e
Saint George, On., Can.	E10	110
Saint George, S.C., U.S.	E9	112
Saint George, Ut., U.S.	F3	132
Saint George, Cape, c., Fl., U.S.	H13	122
Saint George, Point, c., Ca., U.S.	B1	134
Saint George Island, i., Fl., U.S.	H14	122
Saint-Georges, Qc., Can.	D6	110
Saint-Georges, Qc., Can.	D4	110
Saint-Georges, Fr. Gu.	C7	84
Saint George's, Gren.	q10	105e
Saint George's Bay, b., Nf., Can.	j22	107a
Saint Georges Bay, b., N.S., Can.	E15	110
Saint George's Channel, strt., Eur.	J7	12
Saint George's Channel, strt., Pap. N. Gui.	a5	79a
Saint-Gilles-Croix-de-Vie, Fr.	H6	14
Saint Gotthard Pass see San Gottardo, Passo del, p., Switz.	D5	22
Saint Helena, Ca., U.S.	E3	134
Saint Helena, dep., Afr.	H5	60
Saint Helena Bay see Sint Helenabaai, b., S. Afr.	H3	70
Saint Helens, Eng., U.K.	H10	12
Saint Helens, Or., U.S.	E4	136
Saint Helens, Mount, vol., Wa., U.S.	D4	136
Saint Helier, Jersey	E6	14
Saint-Hilaire-du-Harcouët, Fr.	F7	14
Saint-Hyacinthe, Qc., Can.	E4	110
Saint Ignace Island, i., On., Can.	C11	118
Saint Ignatius, Guy.	F12	86
Saint Ignatius, Mt., U.S.	C12	136
Saint-Isidore, N.B., Can.	C11	110
Saint Ives, Eng., U.K.	K7	12
Saint James, Mi., U.S.	C4	112
Saint James, Mn., U.S.	G4	118
Saint James, Mo., U.S.	G6	120
Saint James, Cape, c., B.C., Can.	E4	106
Saint James Islands, is., V.I.U.S.	e7	104b
Saint-Jean, Guad.	B2	105a
Saint-Jean, Lac, res., Qc., Can.	B4	110
Saint Jean Baptiste, Mb., Can.	E16	124
Saint-Jean-d'Angély, Fr.	C5	18
Saint-Jean-de-Luz, Fr.	F4	18
Saint-Jean-de-Maurienne, Fr.	D12	18
Saint-Jean-du-Gard, Fr.	E9	18
Saint-Jean-Port-Joli, Qc., Can.	C6	110
Saint-Jean-sur-Richelieu, Qc., Can.	E3	110
Saint-Jérôme, Qc., Can.	E3	110
Saint Jo, Tx., U.S.	H11	128
Saint Joe, stm., Id., U.S.	C11	136
Saint John, N.B., Can.	E10	110
Saint John, N.D., U.S.	F14	124
Saint John, Wa., U.S.	C9	136
Saint John, i., V.I.U.S.	e8	104b
Saint John, stm., N.A.	E10	106
Saint John's, Antig.	E19	106
Saint John's, Nf., Can.	j23	107a
Saint Johns, Az., U.S.	I7	132
Saint Johns, Mi., U.S.	E5	112
Saint Johns, stm., Fl., U.S.	G4	116
Saint Johnsbury, Vt., U.S.	F4	110
Saint Joseph, Dom.	j6	105c
Saint Joseph, Il., U.S.	D9	120
Saint Joseph, Mi., U.S.	F3	112
Saint Joseph, Mo., U.S.	E3	120
Saint Joseph, Mo., U.S.	E3	120
Saint Joseph, stm., U.S.	G5	112
Saint Joseph, Lake, l., On., Can.	E12	106
Saint Joseph Island, i., On., Can.	B6	112
Saint-Joseph-de-Beauce, Qc., Can.	D6	110
Saint-Jovite, Qc., Can.	D2	110
Saint-Julien-en-Born, Fr.	E4	18
Sainte-Julienne, Qc., Can.	E3	110
Saint-Junien, Fr.	D6	18
Saint Just, P.R.	B4	104a
Saint Kilda, i., Scot., U.K.	D4	12
Saint Kitts see Saint Christopher, i., St. K./N.	C2	105a
Saint Kitts and Nevis, ctry., N.A.	C2	105a
Saint-Lambert, ngh., Qc., Can.	E3	110
Saint Landry, La., U.S.	G6	122
Saint Laurent, Mb., Can.	D16	124
Saint-Laurent (Saint Lawrence), stm., N.A.	B8	110
Saint-Laurent du Maroni, Fr. Gu.	B7	84
Saint Lawrence, Austl.	D7	76
Saint Lawrence (Saint Laurent), stm., N.A.	B8	110
Saint Lawrence, Gulf of, b., Can.	F18	106
Saint Lawrence Island, i., Ak., U.S.	D5	140
Saint-Léandre, Qc., Can.	B9	110
Saint-Léonard, N.B., Can.	C9	110
Saint-Lô, Fr.	E7	14
Saint Louis, Sk., Can.	B8	124
Saint-Louis, Sen.	F1	64
Saint Louis, Mi., U.S.	E5	112
Saint Louis, Mo., U.S.	F7	120
Saint-Louis, Reu.	i10	69a
Saint-Louis, Lac, l., Qc., Can.	E3	110
Saint-Louis-de-Kent, N.B., Can.	D12	110
Saint Louis Park, Mn., U.S.	G5	118
Saint-Loup-sur-Semouse, Fr.	G14	14
Sainte-Luce, Mart.	l7	105c
Saint Lucia, ctry., N.A.	m6	105c
Saint Lucia, Lake, l., S. Afr.	E11	70
Saint Lucia Channel, strt., N.A.	I6	105c
Saint Lucia Game Reserve, S. Afr.	F11	70
Saint Lucie Canal, can., Fl., U.S.	J5	116
Saint Magnus Bay, b., Scot., U.K.	n18	12a
Saint-Malo, Fr.	F7	14
Saint-Malo, Golfe de, b., Fr.	F6	14
Saint-Marc, Haiti	C11	102
Saint-Marc, Canal de, Haiti	C11	102
Saint-Marc-des-Carrières, Qc., Can.	D4	110
Sainte-Marie, Mart.	k7	105c
Sainte Marie, Nosy, i., Madag.	D9	68
Saint Maries, Id., U.S.	C10	136
Saint Marks, stm., Fl., U.S.	F1	116
Saint-Martin (Sint Maarten), i., N.A.	A1	105a
Saint-Martin, Cap, c., Mart.	k6	105c
Saint Martin, Lake, l., Mb., Can.	C15	124
Saint Martins, N.B., Can.	E11	110
Saint Martinville, La., U.S.	G7	122
Saint Mary, Mo., U.S.	G8	120
Saint Mary, stm., N.A.	G18	138
Saint Mary Peak, mtn., Austl.	H2	76
Saint Mary Reservoir, res., Ab., Can.	G17	138
Saint Marys, Austl.	n14	77a
Saint Marys, Ak., U.S.	D7	140
Saint Marys, Ga., U.S.	F4	116
Saint Marys, Ks., U.S.	E1	120
Saint Marys, Pa., U.S.	C7	114
Saint Marys, W.V., U.S.	E4	114
Saint Mary's, i., Eng., U.K.	L6	12
Saint Marys, stm., U.S.	H5	112
Saint Marys, stm., U.S.	F4	116
Saint Mary's Bay, b., Nf., Can.	j23	107a
Saint Marys City, Md., U.S.	F9	114
Saint-Mathieu, Fr.	D6	18
Saint Matthew Island, i., Ak., U.S.	D5	140
Saint Matthews, Ky., U.S.	F12	120
Saint-Maurice, stm., Qc., Can.	D4	110
Sainte-Maxime, Fr.	F12	18
Saint Meinrad, In., U.S.	F11	120
Saint Michael, Ak., U.S.	D7	140
Saint Michaels, Md., U.S.	F9	114
Saint-Michel-des-Saints, Qc., Can.	D2	110
Saint-Mihiel, Fr.	F14	14
Saint Moritz see Sankt Moritz, Switz.	D6	22
Saint-Nazaire, Fr.	G6	14
Saint-Nicolas see Sint-Niklaas, Bel.	C12	14
Saint-Omer, Fr.	D11	14
Saintonge, hist. reg., Fr.	D5	18
Saint-Pacôme, Qc., Can.	C7	110
Saint-Pamphile, Qc., Can.	D7	110
Saint Paris, Oh., U.S.	D2	114
Saint-Patrice, Lac, l., Qc., Can.	B12	112
Saint Paul, Ab., Can.	B19	138
Saint Paul, Reu.	i10	69a
Saint Paul, In., U.S.	E12	120
Saint Paul, Ks., U.S.	G2	120
Saint Paul, Mn., U.S.	G5	118
Saint Paul, Va., U.S.	H3	114
Saint Paul, stm., Lib.	H2	64
Saint Paul, Île, i., Afr.	M10	142
Saint Paul Island, i., Ak., U.S.	E6	140
Saint Paul's, St. K./N.	C2	105a
Saint Pauls, N.C., U.S.	B7	116
Saint Paul's Point, c., Pit.	c28	78k
Saint Peter, Mn., U.S.	G4	118
Saint Peter Port, Guern.	E6	14
Saint Peters, N.S., Can.	E16	110
Saint Peters Bay, P.E., Can.	D14	110
Saint Petersburg see Sankt-Peterburg, Russia	A13	10
Saint Petersburg, Fl., U.S.	I3	116
Saint-Pierre, Mart.	k6	105c
Saint-Pierre, Reu.	i10	69a
Saint-Pierre, St. P./M.	j22	107a
Saint-Pierre, i., Sey.	k12	69b
Saint-Pierre, Lac, l., Qc., Can.	D3	110
Saint Pierre and Miquelon, dep., N.A.	j22	107a
Saint-Pierre-Jolys, Mb., Can.	E16	124
Saint-Pierre-sur-Dives, Fr.	E8	14
Saint-Pol-sur-Ternoise, Fr.	D11	14
Saint-Pons-de-Thomères, Fr.	F8	18
Saint-Prime, Qc., Can.	B4	110
Saint-Prosper-de-Dorchester, Qc., Can.	D6	110
Saint-Quentin, N.B., Can.	C9	110
Saint-Quentin, Fr.	E12	14
Saint-Raphaël, Fr.	F12	18
Saint-Raymond, Qc., Can.	D5	110
Saint Regis Falls, N.Y., U.S.	F2	110
Saint-Rémy-de-Provence, Fr.	F10	18
Saint Robert, Mo., U.S.	G5	120
Saint-Roch-de-Mékinac, Qc., Can.	D3	110
Saint-Romuald, Qc., Can.	D5	110
Sainte-Rose-du-dégelis see Dégelis, Can.	C8	110
Sainte Rose du Lac, Mb., Can.	C14	124
Saintes, Fr.	D5	18
Saint-Savin, Fr.	H9	14
Saint-Siméon, Qc., Can.	C6	110
Saint Simons Island, Ga., U.S.	E4	116
Saint Simons Island, i., Ga., U.S.	E4	116
Saintes-Maries-de-la-Mer, Fr.	F10	18
Saint Stephen, S.C., U.S.	C6	116
Sainte-Thérèse-de-Blainville, Qc., Can.	E3	110
Saint Thomas, On., Can.	F8	112
Saint Thomas, N.D., U.S.	F16	124
Saint Thomas, i., V.I.U.S.	e7	104b
Saint-Tite, Qc., Can.	D4	110
Saint-Trond see Sint-Truiden, Bel.	D14	14
Saint-Tropez, Fr.	F12	18
Saint-Ubalde, Qc., Can.	D4	110
Saint-Urbain-de-Charlevoix, Qc., Can.	C6	110
Saint-Valéry-en-Caux, Fr.	E9	14
Saint-Vallier, Fr.	D10	18
Saint-Véronique, Qc., Can.	D2	110
Saint Vincent, Mn., U.S.	C1	118
Saint-Vincent, St. Vin.	o11	105e
Saint-Vincent, Baie de, b., N. Cal.	n15	79d
Saint Vincent, Gulf, b., Austl.	J2	76
Saint Vincent and the Grenadines, ctry., N.A.	p10	105e
Saint Vincent Passage, strt., N.A.	m7	105c
Saint-Vith, Bel.	D14	14
Saint-Walburg, Sk., Can.	E9	106
Santa Victoria, Mex.	D7	130
Saint-Yrieix-la-Perche, Fr.	D7	18
Saint-Yvon, Qc., Can.	A12	110
Saipan, i., N. Mar. Is.	B5	72
Saiqi, China	H8	42
Saitama, state, Japan	C12	40
Saito, Japan	G4	40
Sai Yok National Park, p.o.i., Thai.	E4	48
Sajama, Nevado, mtn., Bol.	C3	90
Sajanogorsk, Russia	D16	32
Sajat, Turkmen.	B9	56
Sajman, Taj.	B11	56
Sajószentpéter, Hung.	A7	26
Sak, stm., S. Afr.	G5	70
Sa Kaeo, Thai.	F6	48
Sakai, Japan	E8	40
Sakaide, Japan	E6	40
Sakaiminato, Japan	D6	40
Sakakawea, Lake, res., N.D., U.S.	G12	124
Sakala, Pulau, i., Indon.	G10	50
Sakami, Lac, l., Qc., Can.	E15	106
Sakania, D.R.C.	G5	66
Sakaraha, Madag.	E7	68
Sakarya, Tur.	C13	28
Sakarya, state, Tur.	C13	28
Sakarya (Sangarius), stm., Tur.	B13	28
Sakata, Japan	A12	40
Sakchu-ŭp, Kor., N.	D6	38
Sakété, Benin	H5	64
Sakhalin see Sahalin, ostrov, i., Russia	F17	34
Sakhnin, Isr.	F6	58
Sakht Sar, Iran	B7	56
Sakiai, Lith.	E6	10
Sakiet Sidi Youssef, Tun.	H2	24
Sakishima-shotō, is., Japan	G9	36
Sakon Nakhon, Thai.	D6	48
Sakrand, Pak.	E2	54
Saks, Al., U.S.	D13	122
Sakti, India	H9	54
Saku, Japan	C11	40
Sakuma, Japan	D10	40
Sakurai, Japan	E8	40
Sal, i., C.V.	k10	65a
Sal'a, Slov.	H13	16
Sala, Swe.	F7	8
Salaberry-de-Valleyfield, Qc., Can.	E2	110
Salacgrīva, Lat.	C7	10
Sala Consilina, Italy	D9	24
Salada, Laguna, l., Mex.	F5	98
Saladas, Arg.	D8	92
Saladillo, stm., Arg.	G8	92
Saladillo Dulce, Arroyo, stm., Arg.	E7	92
Salado, stm., Arg.	D4	92
Salado, stm., Arg.	G9	92
Salado, stm., Arg.	E7	92
Salado, stm., Arg.	I5	92
Salado, stm., Cuba	B9	102
Salado, stm., Mex.	B9	100
Salado, stm., N.M., U.S.	I9	132
Salaga, Ghana	H4	64
Salal, Chad	E3	62
Salālah, Oman	F7	56
Salālah, Sudan	C7	62
Salamanca, Chile	E2	92
Salamanca, Mex.	E8	100
Salamanca, Spain	D5	20
Salamanca, N.Y., U.S.	F11	112
Salamanca, co., Spain	D4	20
Salamanga, Moz.	E11	70
Salamat, Bahr, stm., Chad	F3	62
Salamina, Col.	E4	86
Salamina, Grc.	F6	28
Salamina, i., Grc.	F6	28
Salaminía, sci., N. Cyp.	C4	58
Salamīyah, Syria	C8	58
Salamonie, stm., In., U.S.	H4	112
Salantai, Lith.	D4	10
Salaqui, Col.	D3	86
Salaquí, stm., Col.	D3	86
Salas, Peru	E2	84
Salas de los Infantes, Spain	B7	20
Salatiga, Indon.	G7	50
Salavat, Russia	D9	32
Salaverry, Peru	E2	84
Salawati, i., Indon.	F9	44
Sala y Gómez, Isla, i., Chile	L28	142
Sala y Gomez Ridge, unds.	L29	142
Salbani, India	G11	54
Šalčininkai, Lith.	F8	10
Salcombe, Eng., U.K.	K9	12
Saldaña, Spain	B6	20
Saldaña, stm., Col.	F4	86
Saldanha, S. Afr.	H3	70
Saldungaray, Arg.	I7	92
Saldus, Lat.	D5	10
Sale, Austl.	L6	76
Sale, Mor.	C3	64
Salé, Mor.	C3	64
Salebabu, Indon.	E8	44
Saled, Teluk, b., Indon.	H10	50
Salehard, Russia	A11	32
Salem, India	F4	53
Salem, Monts.	D3	105a
Salem, Ar., U.S.	H6	120
Salem, Ia., U.S.	D6	120
Salem, Il., U.S.	F9	120
Salem, In., U.S.	F11	120
Salem, Ma., U.S.	B15	114
Salem, Mo., U.S.	G6	120
Salem, N.H., U.S.	B14	114
Salem, N.J., U.S.	E10	114
Salem, N.Y., U.S.	G3	110
Salem, Oh., U.S.	D5	114
Salem, Or., U.S.	F3	136
Salem, S.D., U.S.	D15	126
Salem, Va., U.S.	G5	114
Salem, W.V., U.S.	E5	114
Salemi, Italy	G6	24
Salem Upland, plat., Mo., U.S.	G6	120
Salentina, Penisola, pen., Italy	D12	24
Salerno, Italy	D8	24
Salerno, Golfo di, b., Italy	D8	24
Salers, Fr.	D8	18
Salgar, Col.	D4	86
Salgótarján, Hung.	A6	26
Salgueiro, Braz.	E6	88
Salher, mtn., India	H4	54
Sali, Cro.	G12	22
Salihli, Tur.	E11	28
Salihorsk, Bela.	H10	10
Salima, Mwi.	C5	68
Salin, Mya.	B2	48
Salina, Ks., U.S.	C11	128
Salina, Ut., U.S.	E5	132
Salina Cruz, Mex.	G11	100
Salina Point, c., Bah.	A10	102
Salinas, Braz.	I5	88
Salinas, Ec.	I1	86
Salinas, P.R.	C3	104a
Salinas, Ca., U.S.	G4	134
Salinas, Pampa de las, pl., Arg.	E4	92
Salinas de Hidalgo, Mex.	D8	100
Salinas Pueblo Missions National Monument, p.o.i., N.M., U.S.	G2	128
Salinas Victoria, Mex.	C8	100
Saline, Mi., U.S.	B2	114
Saline, stm., Ar., U.S.	D6	122
Saline, stm., Ar., U.S.	C4	122
Saline, stm., Il., U.S.	G10	120
Saline Bayou, stm., La., U.S.	F6	122
Saline Lake, l., La., U.S.	F6	122
Salines, Cap de, c., Spain	E14	20
Salines, Point, c., Gren.	r10	105e
Salines, Pointe des, c., Mart.	I7	105c
Salinópolis, Braz.	D8	84
Salipolo, Indon.	E11	50
Salisbury, Austl.	J2	76
Salisbury, Eng., U.K.	J11	12
Salisbury, Md., U.S.	F10	114
Salisbury, Mo., U.S.	E5	120
Salisbury, N.C., U.S.	I5	114
Salisbury, Pa., U.S.	E6	114
Salisbury see Harare, Zimb.	D5	68
Salisbury Island, i., Nu., Can.	C15	106
Salisbury Plain, pl., Eng., U.K.	J11	12
Salish Mountains, mts., Mt., U.S.	B12	136
Salitpa, Al., U.S.	F10	122
Salitre, stm., Braz.	E5	88
Salkhad, Syria	F7	58
Salkum, Tur.	A4	56
Sallig (Coral Harbour), Nu., Can.	C14	106
Sallisaw, Ok., U.S.	B4	122
Salluit, Qc., Can.	C15	106
Salmi, Russia	F14	8
Salmo, B.C., Can.	G13	138
Salmon, stm., B.C., Can.	B8	138
Salmon, stm., Id., U.S.	D11	136
Salmon, Id., U.S.	E10	136
Salmon, Middle Fork, stm., Id., U.S.	E12	136
Salmon Arm, B.C., Can.	F11	138
Salmon Falls Creek, stm., U.S.	H12	136
Salmon Gums, Austl.	F4	74
Salmon Peak, mtn., Tx., U.S.	E7	130
Salmon River Mountains, mts., Id., U.S.	F12	136
Salmon Valley, B.C., Can.	B8	138
Salo, Fin.	F10	8
Salò, Italy	E7	22
Salome, Az., U.S.	J3	132
Salomon, Cap, c., Mart.	I6	105c
Salon-de-Provence, Fr.	F11	18
Salonga, Parc National de la, p.o.i., D.R.C.	E4	66
Salonika see Thessaloníki, Grc.	C6	28
Salonika, Gulf of see Thermaïkós Kólpos, b., Grc.	C6	28
Salonta, Rom.	C8	26
Sal Rei, C.V.	k10	65a
Salsacate, Arg.	E5	92
Salsipuedes, Canal, strt., Mex.	A2	100
Sal'sk, Russia	E6	32
Salsomaggiore Terme, Italy	F6	22
Salt, Az., U.S.	J4	132
Salt, stm., Mo., U.S.	E6	120
Salt, Middle Fork, stm., Mo., U.S.	E5	120
Salt, North Fork, stm., Mo., U.S.	E5	120
Salta, Arg.	B5	92
Salta, state, Arg.	D4	90
Saltash, Eng., U.K.	K8	12
Saltcoats, Sk., Can.	C11	124
Salt Creek, stm., Il., U.S.	D8	120
Saltee Islands, is., Ire.	I6	12
Saltfjellet Svartisen Nasjonalpark, p.o.i., Nor.	C6	8
Saltillo, Mex.	C8	100
Saltillo, Tn., U.S.	B10	122
Salt Lake City, Ut., U.S.	C4	132
Salto, Arg.	G7	92
Salto, Ur.	E9	92
Salto del Guairá, Para.	A10	92
Salto Grande, Embalse, res., Ur.	E9	92
Salton City, Ca., U.S.	J9	134
Salton Sea, l., Ca., U.S.	J10	134
Salto Santiago, Represa de, res., Braz.	B11	92
Saltville, Va., U.S.	H4	114
Saluda, Va., U.S.	G9	114
Saluda, stm., S.C., U.S.	B4	116
Salūm, Egypt	A5	62
Salūmbar, India	F5	54
Salur, India	B6	53
Saluzzo, Italy	F4	22
Salvador, Braz.	G6	88
Salvador, El see El Salvador, ctry., N.A.	F3	102
Salvador, Lake, l., La., U.S.	H8	122
Salvatierra, Mex.	E8	100
Salween (Nu) (Khong) (Thanlwin), stm., Asia	E8	46
Salyan, Azer.	B6	56
Salyan, Nepal	D9	54
Salyersville, Ky., U.S.	G2	114
Salzburg, Aus.	C10	22
Salzburg, state, Aus.	C10	22
Salzgitter, Ger.	D6	16
Salzkammergut, reg., Aus.	C10	22
Salzwedel, Ger.	D7	16
Samacá, Col.	E5	86
Samacevičy, Bela.	H14	10
Samagaltaj, Russia	D16	32
Samak, Libya	B3	62
Samal Island, i., Phil.	G5	52
Samalayuca, Mex.	F10	98
Samalga Pass, strt., Ak., U.S.	g25	140a
Samales Group, is., Phil.	G3	52
Samalkot, India	C6	53
Samālūt, Egypt	J1	58
Samana, Cabo, c., Dom. Rep.	C13	102
Samaná, Bahía de, b., Dom. Rep.	C13	102
Samana Cay, i., Bah.	A11	102
Samandağı, Tur.	B7	58
Samangān see Aybak, Afg.	B10	56
Samani, Japan	C15	38
Samar, i., Phil.	D5	52
Samara, Russia	D8	32
Samara, stm., Russia	D8	32
Samarai, Pap. N. Gui.	c5	79a
Samaria Gorge see Samariás, Farángi, p., Grc.	H6	28
Samariás, Farángi (Samaria Gorge), p., Grc.	H6	28
Samarinda, Indon.	D10	50
Samarkand, Uzb.	G11	32
Sāmarrā', Iraq	C5	56
Samastipur, India	F10	54
Samaúma, Braz.	E5	84
Samba Caju, Ang.	B2	68
Sambaíba, Braz.	D3	88
Sambalpur, India	H9	54
Sambar, Tanjung, c., Indon.	E7	50
Sambas, Indon.	C6	50
Sambava, Madag.	C9	68
Sambhal, India	D7	54
Sambhar, India	E5	54
Sambhar Lake, l., India	E5	54
Sambir, Ukr.	G19	16
Sambito, stm., Braz.	D5	88
Samboja, Indon.	D10	50
Sâmbor, Camb.	F7	48
Samborombón, stm., Arg.	G9	92
Samborombón, Bahía, b., Arg.	G9	92
Sambre, stm., Eur.	D12	14
Sambre à l'Oise, Canal de la, can., Fr.	E12	14
Sambrial, Pak.	B5	54
Samch'ŏk, Kor., S.	B2	40
Sam Chom, Khao, mtn., Thai.	H4	48
Sam Ford Fiord, b., Nu., Can.	A16	106
Samfya, Zam.	C4	68
Samka, Mya.	B3	48
Samnangjin, Kor., S.	D1	40
Sam Ngao, Thai.	D4	48
Samoa, ctry., Oc.	g12	79c
Samoa Islands, is., Oc.	h12	79c
Samo Alto, Chile	E2	92
Samobor, Cro.	E12	22
Samoded, Russia	E19	8
Samokov, Blg.	G10	26
Samos, i., Grc.	F9	28
Samoset, Fl., U.S.	I3	116
Samosir, Pulau, i., Indon.	B1	50
Samothrace see Samothráki, i., Grc.	C8	28
Samothráki, Grc.	C8	28
Samothráki (Samothrace), i., Grc.	C8	28
Sampacho, Arg.	F5	92
Sampanahan, Indon.	E10	50
Sampang, Indon.	G8	50
Sampit, Indon.	E8	50
Sampit, stm., Indon.	E8	50
Sampit, Teluk, b., Indon.	E8	50
Sampwe, D.R.C.	F5	66
Sam Rayburn Reservoir, res., Tx., U.S.	F4	122
Samro, ozero, l., Russia	B11	10
Sam Son, Viet.	C7	48
Samsun, Tur.	A4	56
Samsu-ŭp, Kor., N.	D7	38
Samtown, La., U.S.	F6	122
Samuhú, Arg.	C7	92
Samui, Ko, i., Thai.	H5	48
Samundri, Pak.	C4	54
Samut Prakan, Thai.	F5	48
Samut Sakhon, Thai.	F5	48
Samut Songkhram, Thai.	F5	48
San, Mali	G3	64
San, stm., Asia	F8	48
San, stm., Eur.	F18	16
San (Xan), stm., Asia	F8	48
San, stm., China	E8	42
San (Syan), stm., Eur.	F18	16
Sana, stm., Bos.	E2	26
San'ā', Yemen	F5	56
Sana, stm., Bos.	E3	26
Sanaa see San'ā', Yemen	F5	56
Sanabu, Egypt	K1	58
Sanaga, stm., Cam.	D2	66
San Agustín, Arg.	E5	92
San Agustín, Arg.	F5	92
San Agustín, Cape, c., Phil.	G6	52
San Alberto, Mex.	G6	130
San Ambrosio, Isla, i., Chile	H7	82
Sanana, Pulau, i., Indon.	F8	44
Sanandaj, Iran	B6	56
Sānand, India	G4	54
Sanandita, Bol.	D4	90
Sananduva, Braz.	C12	92
San Andrés, Isla de, i., Col.	F7	102
San Andres Mountains, mts., N.M., U.S.	H2	128
Sajcabajá, Guat.	E2	102
San Andrés Tuxtla, Mex.	F11	100
San Andrés y Providencia, state, Col.	F7	102
San Angelo, Tx., U.S.	C7	130
San Antero, Col.	C4	86
San Antonio, Arg.	D5	92
San Antonio, Col.	F4	86
San Antonio, Col.	E9	92
San Antonio, N.M., U.S.	F2	132
San Antonio, Tx., U.S.	E9	130
San Antonio, stm., Tx., U.S.	F10	130
San Antonio, Cabo, pen., Arg.	H9	92
San Antonio, Cabo de, c., Cuba	B5	102
San Antonio, Lake, res., Ca., U.S.	H4	134
San Antonio, Mount, mtn., Ca., U.S.	I8	134
San Antonio, Punta, c., Mex.	B3	100
San Antonio Abad see Sant Antoni de Portmany, Spain	F12	20
San Antonio Bay, b., Tx., U.S.	F11	130
San Antonio de Bravo, Mex.	D3	130
San Antonio de La Paz, Arg.	D5	92
San Antonio de los Baños, Cuba	A6	102
San Antonio de los Cobres, Arg.	B4	92
San Antonio del Táchira, Ven.	D5	86
San Antonio de Tamanaco, Ven.	C8	86
San Antonio de Grande, Mex.	F2	130
San Antonio Mountain, mtn., N.M., U.S.	G2	128
San Antonio Oeste, Arg.	H4	90
Sanatorium, Tx., U.S.	C7	130
San Augustine, Tx., U.S.	F4	122
San Augustin Pass, p., N.M., U.S.	K10	132
Sanaw, Yemen	F7	56
Sanāwad, India	G6	54
San Bartolomeo in Galdo, Italy	C9	24
San Benedetto del Tronto, Italy	H10	22
San Benedetto Po, Italy	E7	22
San Benedicto, Isla, i., Mex.	F3	100
San Benito, Tx., U.S.	H10	130
San Benito, stm., Ca., U.S.	G4	134
San Benito Mountain, mtn., Ca., U.S.	G5	134
San Bernardino, Ca., U.S.	I8	134
San Bernardino Mountains, mts., Ca., U.S.	I9	134
San Bernardino Strait, strt., Phil.	D5	52
San Bernardo, Chile	F2	92
San Bernardo, Islas de, is., Col.	C3	86
San Bernardo del Viento, Col.	C3	86
Sanbe-yama, vol., Japan	D5	40
San Blas, Mex.	B4	100
San Blas, Mex.	D5	100
San Blas, Cape, c., Fl., U.S.	H13	122
San Blas, Golfo de, b., Pan.	H8	102
San Blas, Serranía de, mts., Pan.	H8	102
San Borja, Bol.	B3	90
Sanborn, Ia., U.S.	A2	120
Sanborn, N.D., U.S.	H15	124
San Bruno, Ca., U.S.	F3	134
San Buenaventura, Bol.	B3	90
San Buenaventura, Mex.	B8	100

Name	Map Ref.	Page
San Buenaventura see Ventura, Ca., U.S.	I6	134
San Carlos, Chile	H2	92
San Carlos, Mex.	C9	100
San Carlos, Mex.	A8	100
San Carlos, Nic.	G5	102
San Carlos, Phil.	E4	52
San Carlos, Phil.	C3	52
San Carlos, Ur.	G10	92
San Carlos, Az., U.S.	J6	132
San Carlos, Ca., U.S.	F3	134
San Carlos, Ven.	C7	86
San Carlos, stm., C.R.	G5	102
San Carlos, stm., Ven.	C7	86
San Carlos Centro, Arg.	E7	92
San Carlos de Bariloche, Arg.	H2	90
San Carlos de Bolívar, Arg.	H7	92
San Carlos de Guaroa, Col.	F5	86
San Carlos del Zulia, Ven.	C5	86
San Carlos de Río Negro, Ven.	G8	86
San Carlos Reservoir, res., Az., U.S.	J6	132
San Cataldo, Italy	G7	24
San Cayetano, Arg.	I8	92
Sancha, stm., China	H1	42
Sanchahe, China	B7	38
Sanchenglong, China	B4	38
San Ciro de Acosta, Mex.	E9	100
San Clemente, Italy	E8	20
San Clemente, Ca., U.S.	J8	134
San Clemente Island, i., Ca., U.S.	K7	134
San Cristóbal, Arg.	E7	92
San Cristóbal, Dom. Rep.	C12	102
San Cristóbal, Ven.	D5	86
San Cristóbal, i., Sol. Is.	f9	79b
San Cristóbal, Bahía, b., Mex.	B1	100
San Cristóbal, Isla, i., Ec.	i12	84a
San Cristóbal, Volcán, vol., Nic.	F4	102
San Cristóbal de las Casas, Mex.	G12	100
Sancti Spíritus, Cuba	A8	102
Sancy, Puy de, mtn., Fr.	D8	18
Sand, Nor.	G2	8
Sand, stm., Ab., Can.	B19	138
Sand, stm., S. Afr.	F8	70
Sand, stm., S. Afr.	C9	70
Sandakli, Indon.	D7	50
Sandakan, Malay.	H2	52
Sândän, Camb.	F8	48
Sandarè, Mali	G2	64
Sand Arroyo, stm., U.S.	D7	128
Sanday, i., Scot., U.K.	B10	12
Sandefjord, Nor.	G4	8
Sanderson, Tx., U.S.	D5	130
Sandersville, Ga., U.S.	D3	116
Sandersville, Ms., U.S.	F9	122
Sand Fork, W.V., U.S.	F5	114
Sand Hill, stm., Mn., U.S.	D2	118
Sand Hills, hills, Ne., U.S.	F11	126
Sändi, India	E8	54
Sandia, Peru	F4	84
San Diego, Ca., U.S.	K8	134
San Diego, Tx., U.S.	G9	130
San Diego, Cabo, c., Arg.	J3	90
San Diego Aqueduct, aq., Ca., U.S.	J8	134
Sandıklı, Tur.	E13	28
Sandila, India	E8	54
Sandilands Village, Bah.	m18	104f
Sand Key, i., Fl., U.S.	I3	116
Sand Lake, l., On., Can.	A4	118
Sandnes, Nor.	G1	8
Sandoa, D.R.C.	F4	66
Sandomierz, Pol.	F17	16
Sandoná, Col.	G3	86
San Doná di Piave, Italy	E9	22
Sandovo, Russia	B19	10
Sandoway, Mya.	C2	48
Sandown, Eng., U.K.	K11	12
Sand Point, Ak., U.S.	E7	140
Sandpoint, Id., U.S.	B10	136
Sandringham, Austl.	E2	76
Sandspit, B.C., Can.	E4	106
Sand Springs, Ok., U.S.	A2	122
Sand Springs, Tx., U.S.	B6	130
Sandstone, Austl.	E3	74
Sandstone, Mn., U.S.	E5	118
Sandu Ao, b., China	H8	42
Sandusky, Mi., U.S.	E7	112
Sandusky, Oh., U.S.	C3	114
Sandvika, Nor.	G4	8
Sandviken, Swe.	F7	8
Sandwich, Eng., U.K.	J14	12
Sandwich Bay, b., Nmb.	C2	70
Sandwich, B.C., Can.	G5	138
Sandwip Island, i., Bngl.	G13	54
Sandy, Or., U.S.	E4	136
Sandy, Ut., U.S.	C5	132
Sandy Bay Mountain, mtn., Me., U.S.	E6	110
Sandy Cape, c., Austl.	E9	76
Sandy Cape, c., Austl.	n12	77a
Sandy Creek, stm., Austl.	I5	76
Sandy Hook, Ky., U.S.	F2	114
Sandy Hook, spit, N.J., U.S.	D12	114
Sandykači, Turkmen.	B9	56
Sandy Lake, l., On., Can.	E12	106
Sandy Point, c., Trin.	r13	105f
Sandy Point Town, St. K./N.	C2	105a
Sandy Springs, Ga., U.S.	C1	116
Sandžak, reg., Serb.	F6	26
San Elizario, Tx., U.S.	C1	130
San Enrique, Arg.	G7	92
San Estanislao, Para.	B9	92
San Esteban, Isla, i., Mex.	A2	100
San Esteban de Gormaz, Spain	C7	20
San Felipe, Chile	F2	92
San Felipe, Col.	G8	86
San Felipe, Mex.	E8	100
San Felipe, Mex.	F5	98
San Felipe, Ven.	B7	86
San Felipe, Cayos de, is., Cuba	B6	102
San Felipe Nuevo Mercurio, Mex.	C7	100
San Felipe Pueblo, N.M., U.S.	F2	128
San Feliu de Guixols see Sant Feliu de Guixols, Spain	C14	20
San Félix, Isla, i., Chile	H6	82
San Fernando, Chile	G2	92
San Fernando, Mex.	C9	100
San Fernando, Mex.	F6	130
San Fernando, Phil.	B2	52
San Fernando, Phil.	C3	52
San Fernando, Spain	H4	20
San Fernando, Trin.	s12	105f
San Fernando de Apure, Ven.	D8	86
San Fernando de Atabapo, Ven.	E8	86
San Fernando del Valle de Catamarca, Arg.	D4	92
Sänfjället Nationalpark, p.o.i., Swe.	E5	8
Sanford, Co., U.S.	D2	128
Sanford, Fl., U.S.	H4	116
Sanford, Me., U.S.	G6	110
Sanford, N.C., U.S.	A6	116
Sanford, Tx., U.S.	F7	128
Sanford, stm., Austl.	E4	74
Sanford, Mount, vol., Ak., U.S.	D11	140
San Francisco, El Sal.	F3	102
San Francisco, Ca., U.S.	F3	134
San Francisco, stm., Arg.	B5	92
San Francisco, stm., U.S.	J8	132
San Francisco, Paso de, p., S.A.	C3	92
San Francisco Bay b., Ca., U.S.	F3	134
San Francisco Creek, stm., Tx., U.S.	E5	130
San Francisco de Borja, Mex.	B5	100
San Francisco de Horizonte, Mex.	I4	130
San Francisco del Chañar, Arg.	D5	92
San Francisco del Oro, Mex.	B5	100
San Francisco del Rincón, Mex.	E7	100
San Francisco de Macorís, Dom. Rep.	C12	102
San Francisco de Mostazal, Chile	F2	92
San Gabriel, Ec.	G3	86
San Gabriel Chilac, Mex.	F10	100
San Gabriel Mountains, mts., Ca., U.S.	I8	134
Sangamankanda Point, c., Sri L.	H5	53
Sangamner, India	B1	53
Sangamon, stm., Il., U.S.	D7	120
Sangar, Russia	D14	34
Sangasanga-dalam, Indon.	D10	50
San Gavino Monreale, Italy	E2	24
Sangay, vol., Ec.	I2	86
Sangay, Parque Nacional, p.o.i., Ec.	H3	86
Sange, D.R.C.	F5	66
Sangeang, Pulau, i., Indon.	H11	50
Sanger, Ca., U.S.	G6	134
Sanger, Tx., U.S.	H11	128
Sângha, Mol.	B15	26
Sangerhausen, Ger.	E7	16
San Germán, P.R.	B1	104a
Sangerville, Me., U.S.	E7	110
Sanggan, stm., China	A6	42
Sanggau, Indon.	C7	50
Sangha, stm., Afr.	E3	66
Sanghar, Pak.	E2	54
Sangihe, hrebet, mts., Russia	D17	32
San Gimignano, Italy	G7	22
San Giovanni in Fiore, Italy	E10	24
San Giovanni in Persiceto, Italy	F8	22
San Giovanni Rotondo, Italy	C9	24
San Giovanni Valdarno, Italy	G8	22
Sangiyn Dalay nuur, l., Mong.	B4	36
Sangju, Kor., S.	F8	38
Sangkapura, Indon.	F8	50
Sângkeu, stm., Camb.	F6	48
Sangkulirang, Indon.	C10	50
Sângli, India	C2	53
Sangkuru, stm., D.R.C.	E4	66
Sângole, India	C2	53
Sangolqui, Ec.	H2	86
San Gorgonio Mountain, mtn., Ca., U.S.	I9	134
San Gottardo, Passo del, p., Switz.	D5	22
Sangre de Cristo Mountains, mts., U.S.	E3	128
Sangre Grande, Trin.	s12	105f
Sangro, stm., Italy	H11	22
Sangrur, India	C5	54
Sangsang, China	D11	54
Sangsang, stm., Braz.	F6	84
Sangutane, stm., Moz.	C11	70
Sangya, China	C13	54
San Hipólito, Punta, c., Mex.	B1	100
Sanhu, China	H6	42
Sanhe, China	I1	58
Sanibel Island, i., Fl., U.S.	J3	116
San Ignacio, Arg.	C10	92
San Ignacio, Bol.	B2	100
San Ignacio, Bol.	D3	90
San Ignacio, Mex.	D3	100
San Ignacio, Para.	C9	92
San Ignacio, Isla, i., Mex.	C4	100
San Ignacio, Laguna, b., Mex.	B2	100
San Ignacio de Moxo, Bol.	C4	90
San Ignacio de Velasco, Bol.	C4	90
San Isidro, Arg.	D5	92
San Isidro, Arg.	G8	92
San Isidro del General, C.R.	H5	102
San Jacinto, Col.	C4	86
San Jacinto, Ca., U.S.	J9	134
San Jacinto Peak, mtn., Ca., U.S.	J9	134
San Jaime, Arg.	E8	92
San Javier, Arg.	E8	92
San Javier, Arg.	C10	92
San Javier, Bol.	C4	90
San Javier, Chile	G2	92
San Javier, Mex.	H8	130
San Javier, stm., Arg.	F8	92
Sanjay National Park, p.o.i., India	G8	54
San Jerónimo, Guat.	E2	102
Sanjiang, China	I3	42
Sanjō, Japan	B11	40
San Joaquin, Bol.	B4	90
San Joaquin, Bol.	B4	90
San Joaquin, stm., Ca., U.S.	G4	134
San Joaquin de Omaguas, Peru	D3	84
San Joaquin Valley, val., Ca., U.S.	G5	134
San Jorge, Arg.	E6	92
San Jorge, stm., Col.	C4	86
San Jorge, Bahía de, b., Mex.	F6	98
San Jorge, Golfo, b., Arg.	I3	90
San Jorge, Isla, i., Sol. Is.	e8	79b
San José, C.R.	H5	102
San José, Mex.	E7	130
San Jose, Phil.	E3	52
San Jose, Phil.	C3	52
San José, Ca., U.S.	F3	134
San Jose, Il., U.S.	D8	120
San Jose, N.M., U.S.	F3	128
San José, Ven.	q19	104g
San Jose, stm., N.M., U.S.	I9	132
San José, Cerro, mtn., Mex.	H2	130
San José, Isla, i., Mex.	C3	100
San José, Isla, i., Pan.	H8	102
San José de Buan, Mex.	B3	100
San José de Batuc, Mex.	A3	100
San José de Chiquitos, Bol.	C4	90
San José de Feliciano, Arg.	E8	92
San José de Guanipa, Ven.	C9	86
San José de Jáchal, Arg.	H7	130
San José de las Lajas, Cuba	A7	102
San José del Cabo, Mex.	D4	100
San José del Guaviare, Col.	F5	86
San José de Mayo, Ur.	G9	92
San José de Ocuné, Col.	E6	86
San José de Tiznados, Ven.	C8	86
San José Island, i., Tx., U.S.	G11	130
San Juan, Arg.	E3	92
San Juan, P.R.	B3	104a
San Juan, state, Arg.	E3	92
San Juan, stm., Arg.	F4	92
San Juan, stm., Col.	E3	86
San Juan, stm., Mex.	H8	130
San Juan, stm., N.A.	G5	102
San Juan, stm., U.S.	F6	132
San Juan, stm., Ven.	B10	86
San Juan, Cabeza de, c., P.R.	B4	104a
San Juan, Cabo, c., Arg.	J4	90
San Juan Basin, bas., N.M., U.S.	G8	132
San Juan Bautista, Mex.	H6	130
San Juan Bautista, Para.	C9	92
San Juan Bautista see Sant Joan de Labritja, Spain	E12	20
San Juan Bautista, Ca., U.S.	G4	134
San Juan Creek, stm., Ca., U.S.	H5	134
San Juan de Colón, Ven.	C5	86
San Juan de Guadalupe, Mex.	C7	100
San Juan de la Maguana, Dom. Rep.	C12	102
San Juan del Norte, Nic.	G6	102
San Juan de los Cayos, Ven.	B7	86
San Juan de los Morros, Ven.	C8	86
San Juan del Río, Mex.	E8	100
San Juan del Río, Mex.	C6	100
San Juan del Sur, Nic.	G4	102
San Juan de Micay, stm., Col.	F3	86
San Juan de Payara, Ven.	D8	86
San Juan de Sabinas, Mex.	G6	130
San Juanico, Mex.	B2	100
San Juan Islands, is., Wa., U.S.	B3	136
San Juanito, Isla, i., Mex.	E5	100
San Juan Mountains, mts., Co., U.S.	C9	98
San Juan Nepomuceno, Col.	C4	86
San Juan Nepomuceno, Para.	C9	92
San Justo, Arg.	E7	92
Sankaran, stm., Afr.	G3	64
Sankeshwar, India	C2	53
Sankh, stm., India	G10	54
Sankheda, India	G4	54
Sankosh, stm., Asia	E13	54
San Lázaro, Cabo, c., Mex.	C2	100
San Leandro, Ca., U.S.	F3	134
San Leonardo, Mex.	G3	130
Şanlıurfa (Urfa), Tur.	A9	58
Şanlıurfa, state, Tur.	A9	58
San Lorenzo, Arg.	F7	92
San Lorenzo, Bol.	D8	92
San Lorenzo, Ec.	G2	86
San Lorenzo, Ec.	G2	86
San Lorenzo, Mex.	C7	100
San Lorenzo, P.R.	B4	104a
San Lorenzo, stm., Mex.	C5	100
San Lorenzo, Cabo, c., Ec.	H1	86
San Lorenzo, Isla, i., Mex.	A2	100
San Lorenzo, Monte (Cochrane, Cerro), mtn., S.A.	I2	90
San Lorenzo de la Parrilla, Spain	E8	20
Sanlúcar de Barrameda, Spain	H4	20
San Lucas, Bol.	D3	90
San Lucas, Mex.	D3	100
San Lucas, Cabo, c., Mex.	D4	100
San Luis, Arg.	G5	92
San Luis, Cuba	B10	102
San Luis, Guat.	D3	102
San Luis, Co., U.S.	D3	128
San Luis, Ven.	B7	86
San Luis, state, Arg.	F5	92
San Luis, Lago, l., Bol.	B4	90
San Luis, Sierra de, mts., Arg.	F5	92
San Luis Creek, stm., Co., U.S.	C3	128
San Luis de la Paz, Mex.	E8	100
San Luis Gonzaga, Mex.	C3	100
San Luis Jilotepeque, Guat.	E3	102
San Luis Obispo, Ca., U.S.	H5	134
San Luis Potosí, Mex.	D8	100
San Luis Potosí, state, Mex.	D8	100
San Luis Reservoir, res., Ca., U.S.	F4	134
San Luis Río Colorado, Mex.	E5	98
San Luis Valley, val., Co., U.S.	D3	128
San Manuel, Arg.	H8	92
San Manuel, Az., U.S.	K6	132
San Marcial, stm., Mex.	A4	100
San Marcos, Col.	C4	86
San Marcos, Mex.	G9	100
San Marcos, Tx., U.S.	E9	130
San Marcos, Isla, i., Mex.	B2	100
San Marino, S. Mar.	G9	22
San Marino, ctry., Eur.	G9	22
San Martín, Arg.	D5	92
San Martín, Arg.	F2	92
San Martín, stm., Bol.	B4	90
San Martín, sci., Ant.	B34	81
San Martín (O'Higgins, Lago), l., S.A.	I2	90
San Martín de los Andes, Arg.	H2	90
San Martino di Castrozza, ngh., Italy	D8	22
San Mateo, Mex.	G1	130
San Mateo, Ca., U.S.	F3	134
San Mateo, Fl., U.S.	G4	116
San Mateo, N.M., U.S.	H9	132
San Matías, Bol.	C5	90
San Matías, Golfo, b., Arg.	H4	90
Sanmen, China	G9	42
Sanmenxia, China	D4	42
Sanmenxia, China	D4	42
San Miguel, Ec.	I2	86
San Miguel, El Sal.	F3	102
San Miguel, Pan.	H8	102
San Miguel, stm., Bol.	C4	90
San Miguel, stm., Co., U.S.	E8	132
San Miguel, Golfo de, b., Pan.	H8	102
San Miguel de Allende, Mex.	E8	100
San Miguel de Cruces, Mex.	C6	100
San Miguel, Mount, N.M., Arg.	G8	92
San Miguel del Salcedo, Ec.	H2	86
San Miguel de Tucumán, Arg.	C4	92
San Miguel Island, i., Ca., U.S.	I5	134
Sanming, China	H7	42
San Miniato, Italy	G7	22
Sannär, Sudan	E6	62
Sannicandro Garganico, Italy	I12	22
San Nicolás, Peru	G2	84
San Nicolás, Phil.	A3	52
San Nicolás de los Arroyos, Arg.	F7	92
San Nicolás de los Garza, Mex.	C8	100
San Nicolas Island, i., Ca., U.S.	J6	134
Sanniquellie, Lib.	H3	64
Sannieshof, S. Afr.	E7	70
Sannikova, proliv, strt., Russia	B16	34
Sano, Japan	C12	40
Sanok, Pol.	G18	16
Sânon, stm., Fr.	F15	14
San Pablo, Phil.	C3	52
San Pablo Bay, b., Ca., U.S.	C3	100
San Pascual, Punta, c., Mex.	F8	92
San Pasqual, Phil.	B5	92
San Pedro, Arg.	F8	92
San Pedro, Arg.	B5	92
San Pedro, Chile	F2	92
San-Pédro, C. Iv.	I3	64
San Pedro, Col.	E4	86
San Pedro, Neth. Ant.	A1	105a
San Pedro, state, Para.	B9	92
San Pedro, Mex.	F8	98
San Pedro, stm., Mex.	G2	130
San Pedro, stm., Mex.	D6	100
San Pedro, stm., N.A.	K6	132
San Pedro, stm., U.S.	L7	132
San Pedro, Punta, c., Chile	B2	92
San Pedro, Volcán, vol., Chile	D3	90
San Pedro Carchá, Guat.	E2	102
San Pedro de Jujuy see San Pedro, Arg.	B5	92
San Pedro de las Colonias, Mex.	C7	100
San Pedro del Gallo, Mex.	C6	100
San Pedro del Paraná, Para.	C9	92
San Pedro de Macorís, Dom. Rep.	C13	102
San Pedro de Ycuamandiyú, Para.	B9	92
San Pedro Peaks, mtn., N.M., U.S.	G10	132
San Pedro Sula, Hond.	E3	102
San Pedro Tabasco, Mex.	D2	102
San Pellegrino Terme, Italy	E6	22
San Pietro, Isola di, i., Italy	E2	24
San Pitch, stm., Ut., U.S.	D5	132
Sanquianga, Parque Nacional, p.o.i., Col.	F4	86
San Quintín, Cabo, c., Mex.	F4	98
San Rafael, Arg.	G3	92
San Rafael, Chile	C2	92
San Rafael, Mex.	C8	100
San Rafael, Ca., U.S.	E3	134
San Rafael, N.M., U.S.	H8	132
San Rafael, Ven.	F5	86
San Rafael, stm., Ut., U.S.	E6	132
San Rafael del Norte, Nic.	F4	102
San Rafael Swell, plat., Ut., U.S.	E6	132
San Ramón, Arg.	D5	92
San Ramón, Bol.	B4	90
San Ramón de la Nueva Orán, Arg.	D4	90
San Remo, Italy	G4	22
San Rodrigo, stm., Mex.	F6	130
San Roque, Punta, c., Mex.	B1	100
San Saba, Tx., U.S.	C9	130
San Saba, stm., Tx., U.S.	C9	130
San Salvador, El Sal.	F3	102
San Salvador, i., Bah.	C10	96
San Salvador de Jujuy, Arg.	A5	92
Sansanné-Mango, Togo	G5	64
San Sebastián see Donostia-San Sebastián, Spain	A9	20
San Sebastián, Bahía, b., Arg.	J3	90
Sansepolcro, Italy	G9	22
San Severo, Italy	I12	22
Sansha, China	H9	42
San Simón, Az., U.S.	K7	132
San Simon Wash, stm., Az., U.S.	K4	132
Sanski Most, Bos.	E3	26
San Solano, Arg.	E4	92
Sans-Souci, sci., Haiti	C11	102
Santa, stm., Peru	E2	84
Santa Adélia, Braz.	K1	88
Santa Amalia, Spain	E5	20
Santa Ana, Bol.	B3	90
Santa Ana, El Sal.	E3	102
Santa Ana, Mex.	F7	98
Santa Ana, Ca., U.S.	J8	134
Santa Ana, Ven.	C9	86
Santa Ana del Alto Beni, Bol.	B3	90
Santa Anna, Tx., U.S.	C8	130
Santa Bárbara, Chile	H2	92
Santa Bárbara, Col.	E4	86
Santa Bárbara, Hond.	E3	102
Santa Bárbara, Mex.	B6	100
Santa Bárbara, Ca., U.S.	I6	134
Santa Barbara Channel, strt., Ca., U.S.	I6	134
Santa Barbara Island, i., Ca., U.S.	J7	134
Santa Catalina, Gulf of, b., Ca., U.S.	J7	134
Santa Catalina, Isla, i., Mex.	C3	100
Santa Catalina Island, i., Ca., U.S.	J7	134
Santa Catarina, Mex.	L10	134
Santa Catarina, state, Braz.	C12	92
Santa Catarina, Ilha de, i., Braz.	C13	92
Santa Cecilia, Braz.	C12	92
Santa Clara, Cuba	A7	102
Santa Clara, Mex.	I7	86
Santa Clara, Ca., U.S.	F3	134
Santa Clara, N.M., U.S.	H9	132
Santa Clara, Ut., U.S.	F3	132
Santa Clara, Peru	D3	84
Santa Clara, stm., Ca., U.S.	I7	134
Santa Clotilde, Peru	D3	84
Santa Coloma de Farners, Spain	C13	20
Santa Coloma de Farners see Santa Coloma de Farners, Spain	C13	20
Santa Comba, Spain	A2	20
Santa Cruz, Braz.	C8	88
Santa Cruz, C.R.	G5	102
Santa Cruz, Phil.	D4	52
Santa Cruz, Phil.	C3	52
Santa Cruz, Ca., U.S.	G3	134
Santa Cruz, state, Arg.	I2	90
Santa Cruz, Isla, i., Ec.	i11	84a
Santa Cruz Cabrália, Braz.	I6	88
Santa Cruz de la Sierra, Bol.	C4	90
Santa Cruz del Quiché, Guat.	E2	102
Santa Cruz del Sur, Cuba	B9	102
Santa Cruz de Mudela, Spain	F7	20
Santa Cruz do Capibaribe, Braz.	D7	88
Santa Cruz do Piauí, Braz.	D5	88
Santa Cruz do Rio Pardo, Braz.	L1	88
Santa Cruz do Sul, Braz.	D11	92
Santa Cruz Island, i., Ca., U.S.	J6	134
Santa Cruz Islands, is., Sol. Is.	E7	72
Santa Elena, Arg.	E8	92
Santa Elena, Ec.	I1	86
Santa Elena, Ec.	B7	100
Santa Elena, Bahía de, b., Ec.	H1	86
Santa Eufemia, Spain	F6	20
Santa Eulalia, Spain	D9	20
Santa Eulàlia del Riu see Santa Eulària del Riu, Spain	E12	20
Santa Eulària del Riu, Spain	E12	20
Santa Fe, Arg.	E7	92
Santa Fe, Spain	G7	20
Santa Fe, N.M., U.S.	F3	128
Santa Fe, state, Arg.	D7	92
Santa Fe, stm., Fl., U.S.	G3	116
Santa Fe de Bogotá see Bogotá, Col.	E4	86
Santa Fe de Minas, Braz.	I3	88
Santa Fé do Sul, Braz.	D6	90
Santa Filomena, Braz.	E3	88
Sant'Agata di Militello, Italy	F8	24
Santa Gertrudis, Mex.	G2	130
Santa Helena, Braz.	B3	88
Santa Helena de Goiás, Braz.	G1	88
Santai, China	F1	42
Santa Inés, Braz.	G5	88
Santa Inés, Bahía, b., Mex.	B3	100
Santa Inés, Isla, i., Chile	J2	90
Santa Isabel, Arg.	H4	92
Santa Isabel, P.R.	C3	104a
Santa Isabel, i., Sol. Is.	e8	79b
Santa Isabel, stm., Mex.	F1	130
Santa Isabel, Pico de, mtn., Eq. Gui.	I6	64
Santa Isabel Creek, stm., Tx., U.S.	G8	130
Santa Juliana, Braz.	J2	88
Santal, Baie du, b., N. Cal.	m16	79d
Santa Lucía, Arg.	D10	92
Santa Lucía, Ur.	F9	92
Santa Lucia Range, mts., Ca., U.S.	G4	134
Santa Luzia, Braz.	D7	88
Santa Magdalena, Arg.	G6	92
Santa Magdalena, Isla, i., Mex.	C2	100
Santa Margarita, Ca., U.S.	H5	134
Santa Margarita, Isla, i., Mex.	C2	100
Santa Margherita Ligure, Italy	F6	22
Santa María, Arg.	C4	92
Santa María, Mex.	D10	92
Santa María, Mex.	F6	130
Santa María, i., Vanuatu	j16	79d
Santa María, stm., Mex.	E10	92
Santa María, stm., Mex.	F9	98
Santa María, stm., Az., U.S.	I3	132
Santa Maria, Cabo, c., Ur.	G10	92
Santa Maria, Cabo de, c., Ang.	C1	68
Santa Maria, Cabo de, c., Port.	H3	20
Santa Maria, Isla, i., Chile	H1	92
Santa María, Isla, i., Ec.	i11	84a
Santa María, Laguna de, l., Mex.	F9	98
Santa Maria Asunción Tlaxiaco, Mex.	G10	100
Santa Maria Capua Vetere, Italy	C7	24
Santa María da Boa Vista, Braz.	E5	88
Santa Maria da Vitória, Braz.	G3	88
Santa Maria de Itabira, Braz.	J4	88
Santa María del Oro, Mex.	C6	100
Santa María del Río, Mex.	E8	100
Santa Maria di Leuca, Capo, c., Italy	E12	24
Santa Maria do Suaçuí, Braz.	J4	88
Santa Maria la Real de Nieva, Spain	C6	20
Santa Marinella, Italy	H8	22
Santa Marta, Col.	B4	86
Santa Marta, Cabo de, c., Ang.	C1	68
Santa Marta, Ciénaga Grande, b., Col.	B4	86
Santa Mónica, Mex.	F7	130
Santa Monica, Ca., U.S.	I7	134
Santa Monica Bay, b., Ca., U.S.	J7	134
Santan, Indon.	D10	50
Santana, Coxilha de (Santa Ana, Cuchilla de), hills, S.A.	E10	92
Santana da Boa Vista, Braz.	E11	92
Santana do Ipanema, Braz.	E7	88
Santana do Livramento, Braz.	E9	92
Santander, Col.	F3	86
Santander, Phil.	F4	52
Santander, Spain	A7	20
Santander, state, Col.	D5	86
Santander Jiménez, Mex.	C9	100
Santanghu, China	C3	36
Santaquin, Ut., U.S.	D5	132
Santarcangelo di Romagna, Italy	F9	22
Santarém, Braz.	D7	84
Santarém, Port.	E2	20
Santaren Channel, strt., Bah.	C9	96
Santa Rita, Braz.	D8	88
Santa Rita, Hond.	E3	102
Santa Rita, Mex.	F3	130
Santa Rita, Mt., U.S.	B14	136
Santa Rita, Ven.	B6	86
Santa Rosa, Arg.	H5	92
Santa Rosa, Braz.	C10	92
Santa Rosa, Braz.	H2	88
Santa Rosa, Braz.	F7	86
Santa Rosa, Col.	D2	84
Santa Rosa, Ca., U.S.	E3	134
Santa Rosa, Tx., U.S.	H10	130
Santa Rosa, Ven.	C7	86
Santa Rosa, Ven.	D7	86
Santa Rosa, Mount, hill, Guam	i10	78c
Santa Rosa Beach, Fl., U.S.	G12	122
Santa Rosa de Copán, Hond.	E3	102
Santa Rosa del Conlara, Arg.	F5	92
Santa Rosa de Leales, Arg.	C5	92
Santa Rosa de Osos, Col.	D4	86
Santa Rosa de Sucumbíos, Ec.	G3	86
Santa Rosa de Viterbo, Col.	E5	86
Santa Rosa Island, i., Ca., U.S.	J5	134
Santa Rosalía, Mex.	B2	100
Santa Rosalía, Ven.	H9	130
Santa Rosalía, Ven.	D8	86
Santa Rosa Wash, stm., Az., U.S.	K5	132
Šantarskie ostrova, is., Russia	E16	34
Santa Sylvina, Braz.	C7	92
Santa Teresa, Braz.	J5	88
Santa Teresa, Braz.	C9	100
Santa Teresa, Embalse de, res., Spain	D5	20
Santa Teresa, Fortaleza de, hist., Ur.	F11	92
Santa Uxía, Spain	B1	20
Santa Vitória do Palmar, Braz.	F11	92
Santee, stm., S.C., U.S.	C6	116
Santee Dam, dam, S.C., U.S.	C5	116
Sant'Eufemia, Golfo di, b., Italy	F9	24
Sant Feliu de Guíxols, Spain	C14	20
Santhià, Italy	E5	22
Santhia, Braz.	D10	92
Santiago, Chile	F2	92
Santiago, Pan.	H7	102
Santiago, Para.	C9	92
Santiago, i., C.V.	l10	65a
Santiago, stm., Mex.	C6	100
Santiago, stm., S.A.	D2	84
Santiago, Isla, i., Ec.	i11	84a
Santiago de Compostela, Spain	B2	20
Santiago de Cuba, Cuba	C9	102
Santiago del Estero, Arg.	C5	92
Santiago del Estero, state, Arg.	C5	92
Santiago de los Caballeros, Dom. Rep.	C12	102
Santiago Island, i., Phil.	B2	52
Santiago Ixcuintla, Mex.	E6	100
Santiago Jamiltepec, Mex.	G10	100
Santiago Larre, Arg.	G8	92
Santiago Papasquiaro, Mex.	C6	100
Santiago Peak, mtn., Ca., U.S.	J8	134
Santiago Peak, mtn., Tx., U.S.	E4	130
Santiaguillo, Laguna, l., Mex.	C6	100
Santiam Pass, p., Or., U.S.	F5	136
Säntis, mtn., Switz.	C6	22
Santisteban del Puerto, Spain	F7	20
Sant Joan de Labritja, Spain	E12	20
Sant Jordi, Golf de, b., Spain	D11	20
Santo Amaro, Braz.	G6	88
Santo Amaro, Braz.	B4	88
Santo André, Braz.	L2	88
Santo Ângelo, Braz.	D10	92
Santo Antão, i., C.V.	k10	65a
Santo Antônio, Braz.	D8	88
Santo Antônio, S. Tom/P.	I6	64
Santo Antônio, stm., Braz.	F1	88
Santo Antônio da Patrulha, Braz.	D12	92
Santo Antônio de Jesus, Braz.	G6	88
Santo Antônio de Pádua, Braz.	K4	88
Santo Antônio do Amparo, Braz.	K3	88
Santo Antônio do Içá, Braz.	C11	92
Santo Augusto, Braz.	C11	92
Santo Domingo, Dom. Rep.	C13	102
Santo Domingo, Mex.	I3	130
Santo Domingo, Mex.	D8	100
Santo Domingo, Mex.	C2	100
Santo Domingo, Ven.	D5	86
Santo Domingo de la Calzada, Spain	B7	20
Santo Domingo de los Colorados, Ec.	H1	86
Santo Domingo Pueblo, N.M., U.S.	F2	128
Santo Domingo Tehuantepec, Mex.	G11	100
Santo Domingo Zanatepec, Mex.	G11	100
Santo Estêvão, Braz.	G6	88
Santo / Malo, state, Vanuatu	j16	79d
Santo Onofre, stm., Braz.	G4	88
Santoríni see Thíra, i., Grc.	G8	28
Santos, Braz.	L2	88
Santos Dumont, Braz.	K4	88
Santo Tirso, Port.	C2	20
Santo Tomás, Mex.	L9	134
Santo Tomás, Punta, c., Mex.	L9	134
Santo Tomé, Arg.	E7	92
Santo Tomé, Arg.	D9	92
San Vicente de Alcántara, Spain	E3	20
San Vicente de Baracaldo see San Vicente de Barakaldo, Spain	A8	20
San Vicente del Caguán, Col.	F4	86
San Vincente, Italy	D5	92
San Vincenzo, Italy	G7	22
San Vito, Capo, c., Italy	F6	24
San Vito, i., Italy	L3	42
Sanyati, stm., Zimb.	D4	68
Sanyō, Japan	E4	40
Sanyuan, China	D3	42
Sanzao Dao, i., China	K5	42
Sanza Pombo, Ang.	B2	68
São Benedito do Rio Preto, Braz.	B3	88
São Bento do Norte, Braz.	C7	88
São Bento do Sul, Braz.	C13	92
São Bento do Una, Braz.	E7	88
São Borja, Braz.	D10	92
São Caetano do Sul, Braz.	L2	88
São Carlos, Braz.	L1	88
São Cristóvão, Braz.	F7	88
São Desidério, Braz.	G2	88
São Domingos, Braz.	G2	88
São Domingos, Gui.-B.	G1	64

Name	Map Ref.	Page
São Domingos do Maranhão, Braz.	C3	88
São Felipe, Braz.	H5	88
São Félix de Balsas, Braz.	D3	88
São Francisco, Braz.	H3	88
São Francisco, stm., Braz.	H5	88
São Francisco, stm., Braz.	E6	88
São Francisco, Baía de, b., Braz.	C13	88
São Francisco, Ilha de, i., Braz.	C13	88
São Francisco de Assis, Braz.	D10	92
São Francisco de Goiás, Braz.	H1	88
São Francisco de Paula, Braz.	D12	92
São Francisco do Maranhão, Braz.	D4	88
São Francisco do Sul, Braz.	C13	92
São Gabriel, Braz.	E10	92
São Gabriel, Braz.	F5	88
São Gabriel da Palha, Braz.	J5	88
São Gabriel de Goiás, Braz.	H2	88
São Gonçalo do Sapucaí, Braz.	K3	88
São Gonçalo dos Campos, Braz.	G6	88
Sao Hill, Tan.	F7	66
São Jerônimo, Braz.	E12	92
São Jerônimo da Serra, Braz.	A12	92
São João da Aliança, Braz.	H1	88
São João da Barra, Braz.	K5	88
São João de Boa Vista, Braz.	L2	88
São João de Cortês, Braz.	B3	88
São João Del Rei, Braz.	K3	88
São João do Araguaia, Braz.	C1	88
São João do Jaguaribe, Braz.	C6	88
São João do Piauí, Braz.	E4	88
São João dos Patos, Braz.	D4	88
São Joaquim, Braz.	D12	92
São Joaquim, Parque Nacional de, p.o.i., Braz.	D13	92
São Joaquim da Barra, Braz.	K1	88
São José, Braz.	C13	92
São José, stm., Braz.	J5	88
São José da Laje, Braz.	E7	88
São José das Piranhas, Braz.	D6	88
São José de Anauá, Braz.	G11	86
São José do Cedro, Braz.	C11	92
São José do Egito, Braz.	D7	88
São José do Gurupi, Braz.	A4	88
São José do Mipibu, Braz.	D8	88
São José do Peixe, Braz.	D4	88
São José do Rio Preto, Braz.	K1	88
São José dos Campos, Braz.	L3	88
São José dos Pinhais, Braz.	B13	92
São Leopoldo, Braz.	D12	92
São Lourenço, Braz.	L3	88
São Lourenço, Pantanal de, sw., Braz.	C5	90
São Lourenço do Sul, Braz.	E12	92
São Luís, Braz.	B3	88
São Luís do Curu, Braz.	B6	88
São Luís de Quitunde, Braz.	E8	88
São Luís Gonzaga, Braz.	D10	92
São Manuel, Braz.	L1	88
São Manuel, stm., Braz.	E6	84
São Marcos, stm., Braz.	I2	88
São Marcos, Baía de b., Braz.	B3	88
São Mateus, Braz.	J6	88
São Mateus, Braço Norte, stm., Braz.	I3	88
São Mateus do Sul, Braz.	B12	92
São Miguel, Braz.	D6	88
São Miguel, i., Port.	C3	60
São Miguel do Araguaia, Braz.	F7	84
São Miguel d'Oeste, Braz.	C11	92
São Miguel do Guamá, Braz.	A2	88
São Miguel dos Campos, Braz.	E7	88
São Miguel do Tapuio, Braz.	C5	88
Saona, Isla, i., Dom. Rep.	C13	102
Saône, stm., Fr.	C10	18
Saône-et-Loire, state, Fr.	C10	18
Saoner, India	H7	54
São Nicolau, i., C.V.	k10	65a
São Nicolau, stm., Braz.	C5	88
São Paulo, Braz.	L2	88
São Paulo, state, Braz.	D7	90
São Paulo de Olivença, Braz.	D4	84
São Paulo do Potengi, Braz.	C7	88
São Pedro do Piauí, Braz.	C4	88
São Pedro do Sul, Port.	D2	20
São Raimundo das Mangabeiras, Braz.	D3	88
São Raimundo Nonato, Braz.	E4	88
São Romão, Braz.	I3	88
São Roque, Braz.	L2	88
São Roque, Cabo de, c., Braz.	C8	88
São Sebastião, Braz.	L3	88
São Sebastião, Ilha de, i., Braz.	L3	88
São Sebastião, Ponta, c., Moz.	C12	70
São Sebastião do Paraíso, Braz.	K2	88
São Sepé, Braz.	E11	92
São Simão, Braz.	K2	88
São Simão, Represa de, res., Braz.		
São Timóteo, Braz.	G4	88
São Tomé, Braz.	C7	88
São Tomé, i., S. Tom./P.	I6	64
São Tomé, Cabo de, c., Braz.	L5	88
São Tomé, Pico de, mtn., S. Tom./P.	I6	64
Sao Tome and Principe, ctry., Afr.	I6	64
Saoura, Oued, stm., Alg.	D4	64
São Valério, stm., Braz.	F1	88
São Vicente, Braz.	M2	88
São Vicente, i., C.V.	k9	65a
São Vicente, Cabo de, c., Port.	H1	20
Sapanca, Tur.	C13	28
Sape, Selat, strt., Indon.	H11	50
Sapele, Nig.	H6	64
Sapelo Island, i., Ga., U.S.	E4	116
Sápes, Grc.	B8	28
Sapitwa, mtn., Mwi.	D6	68
Šapki, Russia	A14	10
Sapkina, stm., Russia	C26	8
Sapockin, Bela.	C7	10
Sappa Creek, stm., U.S.	A9	128
Sappa Creek, South Fork, stm., Ks., U.S.	B8	128
Sappho, Wa., U.S.	B2	136
Sapporo, Japan	C14	38
Sap Songkhla, Thale, l., Thai.	I5	48
Saptakoshi Mari, Nepal.	E11	54
Sapudi, Pulau, i., Indon.	G9	50
Sapulpa, Ok., U.S.	A2	122
Sapwe, D.R.C.	G5	66
Saqqâra, Egypt	I2	58
Saqqâra, Pyramides de (Step Pyramid), hist., Egypt	I1	58
Saqqez, Iran	B6	56
Saraana, Baie, b., Qc, Can.	B1	110
Sarāb, Iran	B6	56
Saraburi, Thai.	E5	48
Saracura, stm., Braz.	F4	84
Saraféré, Mali	F4	64
Saragosa, Tx., U.S.	C6	130
Saragossa see Zaragoza, Spain	C10	20
Sarai Naurang, Pak.	B3	54
Saraipāli, India	H9	54
Sarajevo, Bos.	F5	26
Saraji, Austl.	D7	76
Sarakhs, Iran	B9	56
Saraktaš, Russia	D9	32
Saraland, Al., U.S.	G10	122
Saran', Kaz.	E12	32
Saran, Gunung, mtn., Indon.	D7	50
Saranac, Mi., U.S.	F4	112
Saranac Lake, stm., N.Y., U.S.	F3	110
Saranda see Sarandë, Alb.	E13	24
Sarandë, Alb.	E13	24
Sarandi, Braz.	C11	92
Sarandí del Yi, Ur.	F10	92
Sarandí Grande, Ur.	F9	92
Sarangani Bay, b., Phil.	H5	52
Sarangani Islands, is., Phil.	H5	52
Sarangani Strait, strt., Phil.	H5	52
Sārangarh, India	H9	54
Sārangpur, India	G6	54
Saranpaul', Russia	B10	32
Saransk, Russia	D6	32
Saraphi, Thai.	C4	48
Sarapul, Russia	C8	32
Sarāqib, Syria	C7	58
Sarasota, Fl., U.S.	I3	116
Sarata, Ukr.	C16	26
Saratoga, Ca., U.S.	F3	134
Saratoga, Tx., U.S.	G4	122
Saratoga, Wy., U.S.	B10	132
Saratoga Springs, N.Y., U.S.	G2	110
Saratov, Russia	D7	32
Saratov Reservoir see Saratovskoe vodohranilišče, res., Russia	D7	32
Saratovskoe vodohranilišče, res., Russia	D7	32
Sarāvān, Iran	D9	56
Saravan, Laos.	E8	48
Saravena, Col.	D5	86
Saray, Tur.	B10	28
Saraya, Gui.	G2	64
Sarayevo see Sarajevo, Bos.	F5	26
Sarayköy, Tur.	F11	28
Sarayönü, Tur.	E15	28
Sarbāz, Iran	D9	56
Sarcelle, Passe de la, strt., N. Cal.	n16	79d
Sarcidano, reg., Italy	E3	24
Sarcoxie, Mo., U.S.	G3	120
Sārda (Mahākālī), stm., Asia.	D8	54
Sardah, Bngl.	F12	54
Sardārpur, India	G5	54
Sardārshahr, India	D5	54
Sardegna, state, Italy	D4	24
Sardegna (Sardinia), i., Italy	D3	24
Sardinata, Col.	H11	102
Sardinia see Sardegna, state, Italy	D4	24
Sardinia see Sardegna, i., Italy	D3	24
Sardis, Al., U.S.	E12	122
Sardis, Ga., U.S.	D4	116
Sardis, Tn., U.S.	B10	122
Sardis, sci., Tur.	E10	28
Sardis Lake, res., Ms., U.S.	C9	122
Sardis Lake, res., Ok., U.S.	C3	122
Šardonem', Russia	E21	8
Sarek, mtn., Swe.	C7	8
Sareks Nationalpark, p.o.i., Swe.	C7	8
Sar-e Pol, Afg.	B10	56
Sarepta, La., U.S.	E5	122
Sargent, Ga., U.S.	D14	122
Sargent, Ne., U.S.	F13	126
Sargodha, Pak.	B4	54
Sarh, Chad	F3	62
Sārī, Iran	B7	56
Saria, i., Grc.	H10	28
Sangöl, Tur.	E11	28
Sarıkaya, Tur.	E15	28
Sarikei, Malay.	B7	50
Sarina, Austl.	C7	76
Sariñena, Spain	C10	20
Sariska Tiger Reserve, India	E6	54
Sarita, Tx., U.S.	G10	130
Sariwŏn, Kor. N.	E6	38
Sarıyar Baraji, res., Tur.	D14	28
Sarja, Russia	G21	8
Šark, i., Guern.	E6	14
Šarkauščyna, Bela.	E10	10
Şarkikaraağaç, Tur.	E14	28
Şarkışla, Tur.	B3	58
Sárkŏz, Hung.	C5	26
Şarköy, Tur.	C10	28
Sarles, N.D., U.S.	F15	124
Sārlyk, Russia	D9	32
Sarmi, Indon.	F10	44
Sarmiento, Arg.	I3	90
Särna, Swe.	F5	8
Sarnia, On., Can.	F7	112
Sarno, Italy	D8	24
Sarolangun, Indon.	E3	50
Saronic Gulf see Saronikós Kólpos, b., Grc.	F6	28
Saronikós Kólpos, b., Grc.	F6	28
Saronno, Italy	E6	22
Saros Körfezi, b., Tur.	C9	28
Sárospatak, Hung.	A8	26
Sarowbi, Afg.	C10	56
Sarpsborg, Nor.	G4	8
Sarqan, Kaz.	E13	32
Sarralbe, Fr.	E15	14
Sarre (Saar), stm., Eur.	E15	14
Sarrebourg, Fr.	F16	14
Sarreguemines, Fr.	E16	14
Šarscin, Bela.	H14	10
Sartell, Mn., U.S.	F4	118
Sartène, Fr.	H14	18
Sarthe, state, Fr.	G9	14
Sarthe, stm., Fr.	G8	14
Saruhanlı, Tur.	E10	28
Sárvár, Hung.	B3	26
Sárviz, can., Hung.	C5	26
Saryg-Sep, Russia	D17	32
Sarykamyšskoe ozero, l., Asia	A8	56
Saryözek, Kaz.	F13	32
Saryqopa köli, l., Kaz.	C15	32
Saryqopa köli, l., Kaz.	E10	32
Sarysū, stm., Kaz.	E11	32
Sary-Taš, Kyrg.	G12	32
Sarzana, Italy	F7	22
Sasabeneh, Eth.	F8	62
Sasaginnigak Lake, l., Mb., Can.	C17	124
Sasakwa, Ok., U.S.	C2	122
Sasamungga, Sol. Is.	d7	79b
Sāsārām, India	F9	54
Sasayama, Japan	D8	40
Sásd, Hung.	C5	26
Sasebo, Japan	F2	40
Saseginaga, Lac, l., Qc., Can.	A11	112
Saskatchewan, state, Can.	E10	106
Saskatchewan, stm., Can.	E10	106
Saskatoon, Sk., Can.	B7	124
Saskylah, Russia	B11	34
Sasovo, Russia	D6	32
Sasovo, Russia	I21	8
Saspamco, Tx., U.S.	E9	130
Sassafras, Ky., U.S.	G2	114
Sassafras Mountain, mtn., U.S.	A3	116
Sassandra, C. Iv.	I3	64
Sassandra, stm., C. Iv.	I3	64
Sassari, Italy	D2	24
Sassnitz, Ger.	B9	16
Sasso Marconi, Italy	F8	22
Sassuolo, Italy	F7	22
Sasyk, ozero, l., Ukr.	D16	26
Sasyqqöl köli, l., Kaz.	E14	32
Satadougou, Mali.	G2	64
Satah Mountain, vol., B.C., Can.	D6	138
Sata-misaki, c., Japan	H3	40
Satāna, India	H5	54
Sātāo, Port.	D3	20
Sātāra, India.	C1	53
Satara Ruskamp, S. Afr.	D10	70
Satélite, Mex.	C1	130
Satellite Beach, Fl., U.S.	H5	116
Sateņgar, Pulau, i., Indon.	G10	50
Satevó, Mex.	G1	130
Satevó, stm., Mex.	G1	130
Satilla, stm., Ga., U.S.	E4	116
Sátiro Dias, Braz.	F6	88
Satit (Tekezē), stm., Afr.	E7	62
Šatki, Russia.	I20	8
Satluj see Sutlej, stm., Asia	C5	54
Satna, India.	F8	54
Sátoraljaújhely, Hung.	A8	26
Sātpura Range, mts., India	H6	54
Satsuma-hantō, pen., Japan.	H3	40
Satsunan-shotō, is., Japan.	k19	39a
Sattahip, Thai.	F5	48
Satui, Indon.	E9	50
Satu Mare, Rom.	B9	26
Satu Mare, state, Rom.	B10	26
Satun, Thai.	I4	48
Satura, Russia	I18	8
Saturnino M. Laspiur, Arg.	E6	92
Satyamangalam, India.	F3	53
Sauce, Arg.	E8	92
Sauce Corto, Arroyo, stm., Arg.	H7	92
Saucier, Ms., U.S.	G9	122
Saucillo, Mex.	A6	100
Saudárkrókur, Ice.	k30	8a
Saudi Arabia, ctry., Asia	E5	56
Sauerland, reg., Ger.	E4	16
Saueruiná, stm., Braz.	F6	84
Saugatuck, Mi., U.S.	F3	112
Saugeen, stm., On., Can.	D8	112
Saugerties, N.Y., U.S.	B12	114
Saugstad, Mount, mtn., B.C., Can.	D4	138
Saujil, Arg.	D4	92
Sauk, stm., Mn., U.S.	F4	118
Sauk Centre, Mn., U.S.	F3	118
Sauk City, Wi., U.S.	H9	118
Sauk Rapids, Mn., U.S.	F4	118
Saukville, Wi., U.S.	E1	112
Saül, Fr. Gu.	C7	84
Saulieu, Canal de la, can., Fr.	B8	18
Saulgau, Ger.	I5	16
Saulieu, Fr.	G13	14
Sault aux Cochons, stm., Qc., Can.	A7	110
Sault-de-Vaucluse, Fr.	E11	18
Saulteaux, stm., Ab., Can.	B16	138
Sault Sainte Marie, On., Can.	B5	112
Sault Sainte Marie, Mi., U.S.	B5	112
Saumarez Reef, rf., Austl.	C9	76
Saumlaki, Indon.	G9	44
Saumur, Fr.	G8	14
Saunders Island, i., Falk. Is.	J4	90
Saunders Island, i., S. Geor.	K12	82
Sauquoit, N.Y., U.S.	B10	114
Saurimo, Ang.	B3	68
Sausar, India.	H7	54
Sausu, Indon.	D12	50
Sautar, Ang.	C2	68
Sauteurs, Gren.	q10	105e
Sauveterre-de-Guyenne, Fr.	E5	18
Sauwald, for., Aus.	B10	22
Sauzal, Mex.	C1	130
Savalou, Benin.	H5	64
Savanna, Il., U.S.	B7	120
Savanna, Ok., U.S.	C3	122
Savannah, Ga., U.S.	D4	116
Savannah, Tn., U.S.	B10	122
Savannah, stm., U.S.	D4	116
Savannah River Plant, sci., S.C., U.S.	C4	116
Savannah Sound, Bah.	K9	116
Savannakhét, Laos.	D7	48
Savanna-la-Mar, Jam.	i12	104d
Savant Lake, On., Can.	A8	118
Savant Lake, l., On., Can.	A8	118
Sāvantvādi, India	D1	53
Savaştepe, Tur.	D10	28
Savè, Benin.	H5	64
Save (Sabi), stm., Afr.	B11	70
Sāveh, Iran	B7	56
Savelugu, Ghana.	H4	64
Savenay, Fr.	G7	14
Saverne, Fr.	F7	18
Savigliano, Italy	F4	22
Savino-Borisovskaja, Russia	E21	8
Savinskij, Russia	E19	8
Šavissik, Grnld.	B13	141
Šavnik, Serb.	G6	26
Savoie, state, Fr.	D12	18
Savoie, hist. reg., Fr.	D12	18
Savoy see Savoie, hist. reg., Fr.	D12	18
Savona, B.C., Can.	F10	138
Savona, Italy.	F5	22
Savonlinna, Fin.	F13	8
Savoy, Tx., U.S.	D2	122
Savoy see Savoie, hist. reg., Fr.	D12	18
Savran', Ukr.	A17	26
Savusavu Bay, b., Fiji.	p19	79e
Savu Sea see Sawu, Laut, s., Indon.	G7	44
Savu, Pulau, i., Indon.	H7	44
Sawah, Indon.	B9	50
Sawahlunto, Indon.	D2	50
Sawai Mādhopur, India	E6	54
Sawākin, Sudan.	D7	62
Sawahhalok, Thai.	D4	48
Sawara, Japan	D13	40
Sawata, Japan	A11	40
Sawatch Range, mts., Co., U.S.	B2	128
Sawdā', Jabal, mtn., Sau. Ar.	F5	56
Sawdā', Jabal as-, hills, Libya	A4	62
Sawdā', Qurnat as-, mtn., Leb.	D7	58
Sawdirī, Sudan	E5	62
Sawqirah, Oman.	F8	56
Sawqirah, Dawhat, b., Oman	F8	56
Sawtooth National Recreation Area, p.o.i., Id., U.S.	F12	136
Sawu, Laut (Savu Sea), s., Indon.	G7	44
Sawu, Pulau, i., Indon.	H7	44
Sawyer, Mi., U.S.	G3	112
Sawyer, N.D., U.S.	F12	124
Saxby, stm., Austl.	B3	76
Saxon, Wi., U.S.	E8	118
Saxony see Sachsen, state, Ger.	F9	16
Saxony-Anhalt see Sachsen-Anhalt, state, Ger.	D7	16
Saxton, Pa., U.S.	D7	114
Say, Niger	G5	64
Sayan Mountains, mts., Asia.	D17	32
Sayaxché, Guat.	D2	102
Saydā (Sidon), Leb.	E6	58
Saydā, state, Leb.	E6	58
Şayhūt, Yemen	F7	56
Sayil, stm., Mex.	B3	102
Saylac, Som.	B8	66
Saylūn, Khirbat (Shiloh), hist., W.B.	F6	58
Sayram Hu, l., China	F14	32
Sayre, Ok., U.S.	F9	128
Sayre, Pa., U.S.	C9	114
Sayreville, N.J., U.S.	D11	114
Sayward, B.C., Can.	F5	138
Saywūn, Yemen	F6	56
Saza, Japan.	F2	40
Sazan, i., Alb.	D13	24
Sba, Alg.	D4	64
Ščadryn, Bela.	H12	10
Ščučyn, Bela.	G7	10
Scafell Pike, mtn., Eng., U.K.	G9	12
Scalea, Italy.	E9	24
Scammon Bay, Ak., U.S.	D6	140
Scandia, Ks., U.S.	B11	128
Scanlon, Mn., U.S.	E6	118
Scapa Flow, b., Scot., U.K.	C9	12
Scapegoat Mountain, mtn., Mt., U.S.	C14	136
Ščapino, Russia	E20	34
Ščappoose, Or., U.S.	E3	136
Ščara, stm., Bela.	G8	10
Scarborough, St. K./N.	C2	105a
Scarborough, Trin.	r13	105f
Scarborough, Eng., U.K.	G12	12
Scarborough, ngh., On., Can.	E10	112
Scărișoara, Rom.	F11	26
Scarp, i., Scot., U.K.	C5	12
Scawfell Island, i., Austl.	C7	76
Ščedro, Otok, i., Cro.	G13	22
Ščekino, Russia	F20	10
Ščelkovo, Russia	E20	10
Ščerbakovo, Russia	C21	34
Ščerbinka, Russia	E20	10
Schaffhausen, Switz.	C5	22
Schaffhouse see Schaffhausen, Switz.	C5	22
Schärding, Aus.	B10	22
Schefferville, Qc., Can.	E17	106
Scheinfeld, Ger.	G6	16
Schelde, stm., Eur.	C13	14
Schell Creek Range, mts., Nv., U.S.	D2	132
Schenectady, N.Y., U.S.	B11	114
Schenevus Creek, stm., N.Y., U.S.	B11	114
Schertz, Tx., U.S.	E9	130
Schiedam, Neth.	C13	14
Schiermonnikoog, i., Neth.	C2	16
Schiltigheim, Fr.	F16	14
Schio, Italy.	E8	22
Schkeuditz, Ger.	E8	16
Schladming, Aus.	C10	22
Schlater, Ms., U.S.	D8	122
Schleiden, Ger.	F1	16
Schleswig, Ger.	B5	16
Schleswig, Ia., U.S.	B2	120
Schleswig-Holstein, state, Ger.	B6	16
Schlitz, Ger.	F5	16
Schlüchtern, Ger.	F5	16
Schmölln, Ger.	F8	16
Schneeberg, Ger.	F8	16
Schneeberg, mtn., Ger.	F7	16
Schneverdingen, Ger.	C5	16
Schoelcher, Mart.	k6	105c
Schofield, Wi., U.S.	G9	118
Schoharie, N.Y., U.S.	B11	114
Schoharie Creek, stm., N.Y., U.S.	B11	114
Schönebeck, Ger.	D7	16
Schongau, Ger.	I6	16
Schöningen, Ger.	D6	16
Schopfheim, Ger.	I3	16
Schorndorf, Ger.	H5	16
Schouten, Kepulauan, is., Indon.	F10	44
Schouten Island, i., Austl.	o14	77a
Schouten Islands, is., Pap. N. Gui.	a3	79a
Schramberg, Ger.	H4	16
Schreiber, On., Can.	C11	118
Schriever, La., U.S.	H8	122
Schrobenhausen, Ger.	H7	16
Schulenburg, Tx., U.S.	E11	130
Schultz Lake, l., Nu., Can.	C11	106
Schuyler, Va., U.S.	G7	114
Schuylkill, stm., Pa., U.S.	D10	114
Schuylkill Haven, Pa., U.S.	D9	114
Schwabach, Ger.	G7	16
Schwaben, hist. reg., Ger.	H5	16
Schwäbische Alb, mts., Ger.	H5	16
Schwäbisch Gmünd, Ger.	H5	16
Schwäbisch Hall, Ger.	G5	16
Schwandorf, Ger.	G8	16
Schwaner, Pegunungan, mts., Indon.	D8	50
Schwarzach im Pongau, Aus.	C10	22
Schwarzwald (Black Forest), mts., Ger.	H4	16
Schwatka Mountains, mts., Ak., U.S.	C8	140
Schwaz, Aus.	C8	22
Schwechat, Aus.	B13	22
Schweinfurt, Ger.	F6	16
Schweizer Nationalpark, p.o.i., Switz.	D7	22
Schweizer-Reineke, S. Afr.	E7	70
Schwerin, Ger.	C7	16
Schweriner See, l., Ger.	C7	16
Schwyz, Switz.	C5	22
Sciacca, Italy	G7	24
Scicli, Italy	H8	24
Scilly, Isles of, is., Eng., U.K.	L6	12
Scio, Oh., U.S.	D4	114
Scio, Or., U.S.	F4	136
Scioto, stm., Oh., U.S.	E3	114
Šcit, mtn., Bos.	F8	124
Scobey, Mt., U.S.	F8	124
Scone, Austl.	I8	76
Scooba, Ms., U.S.	E10	122
Scordia, Italy.	G8	24
Scoresbysund (Ittoqqortoormiit), Grnld.	C21	141
Scoresby Sund, strt., Grnld.	C21	141
Scotia, N.Y., U.S.	B12	114
Scotia Ridge, unds.	N8	144
Scotia Sea, s.	C21	141
Scotland, On., Can.	E9	112
Scotland, S.D., U.S.	D15	126
Scotland, Tx., U.S.	H10	128
Scotland, state, U.K.	E8	12
Scotland, La., U.S.	G7	122
Scotlandville, La., U.S.	G7	122
Scotrun, Pa., U.S.	G2	114
Scotstown, Qc., Can.	E14	110
Scott, Sk., Can.	B5	124
Scott, Ms., U.S.	D7	122
Scott, Ca., U.S.	B2	134
Scott, Cape, c., B.C., Can.	F2	138
Scott, Mount, mtn., Or.,	H4	136
Scott Base, sci., Ant.	C22	81
Scott City, Ks., U.S.	C8	128
Scott City, Mo., U.S.	G8	120
Scott Coast, cst., Ant.	C22	81
Scott Island, i., Ant.	B23	81
Scott Islands, is., B.C., Can.	F2	138
Scott Peak, mtn., Id., U.S.	F14	136
Scott Reef, rf., Austl.	B4	74
Scottsbluff, Ne., U.S.	F9	126
Scotts Bluff National Monument, p.o.i., Ne., U.S.	F9	126
Scottsboro, Al., U.S.	C12	122
Scottsdale, Austl.	n13	77a
Scottsdale, Az., U.S.	J5	132
Scotts Head, c., Dom.	j6	105c
Scotts Hill, Tn., U.S.	B10	122
Scottsville, Ky., U.S.	H11	120
Scottville, Mi., U.S.	E3	112
Scourie, Scot., U.K.	C7	12
Scout Lake, Sk., Can.	E8	124
Scranton, N.D., U.S.	A9	126
Scranton, Pa., U.S.	C10	114
Screven, Ga., U.S.	E3	116
Scribner, Ne., U.S.	J2	118
Scrub Island, i., Anguilla	A2	105a
Ščučye, Russia	C10	32
Ščučin'sk see Shchūchinsk, Kaz.		
Ščučyn, Bela.	G7	10
Scugog, Lake, l., On., Can.	D11	112
Scunthorpe, Eng., U.K.	H12	12
Scutari, Lake, l., Eur.	H16	22
Ščytkavičy, Bela.	G10	10
Seaford, De., U.S.	F10	114
Seaforth, On., Can.	E8	112
Seahorse Point, c., Nu., Can.	C15	106
Sea Islands, is., U.S.	E5	116
Sea Isle City, N.J., U.S.	E11	114
Seal, stm., Mb., Can.	D11	106
Seal, Cape, c., S. Afr.	I6	70
Sea Lake, Austl.	J4	76
Sealark Channel, strt., Sol. Is.	e9	79b
Seal Cays, is., T./C. Is.	B12	102
Seale, Al., U.S.	E13	122
Sealevel, N.C., U.S.	B9	116
Seal Island, i., N.S., Can.	G10	110
Sealy, Tx., U.S.	H2	122
Seara, Braz.	C11	92
Searcy, Ar., U.S.	B7	122
Searles Lake, l., Ca., U.S.	H8	134
Searsport, Me., U.S.	F7	110
Seaside, Ca., U.S.	G4	134
Seaside, Or., U.S.	D3	136
Seaside Park, N.J., U.S.	E11	114
Seattle, Wa., U.S.	C4	136
Sebago Lake, l., Me., U.S.	G6	110
Se Bai, stm., Thai.	E7	48
Sebakung, Indon.	D10	50
Sebangan, Teluk, b., Indon.	E8	50
Sebangka, Pulau, i., Indon.	C4	50
Sebastian, Tx., U.S.	H10	130
Sebastian, Cape, c., Or., U.S.	A2	134
Sebastián Vizcaíno, Bahía, b., Mex.	A1	100
Sebastopol, Ca., U.S.	E3	134
Sebastopol, Ms., U.S.	E9	122
Sebec Lake, l., Me., U.S.	E7	110
Sebekino, Russia	D5	32
Sebes, Rom.	D10	26
Sebeș Körös (Crișul Repede), stm., Eur.	B8	26
Sebewaing, Mi., U.S.	E6	112
Sebino see Iseo, Lago d', l., Italy	E6	22
Sebnitz, Ger.	F10	16
Sebree, Ky., U.S.	G10	120
Sebring, Fl., U.S.	I4	116
Sebuku, Indon.	A10	50
Sebuku, Teluk, b., Indon.	A11	50
Sebuyau, Malay.	C7	50
Sechelt, B.C., Can.	G7	138
Secchia, stm., Italy	F7	22
Sechura, Peru	E1	84
Sechura, Desierto de, des., Peru	E1	84
Seclantás, Arg.	B4	92
Sečovská Polianka, Slov.	H17	16
Section, Al., U.S.	C13	122
Security, Co., U.S.	C4	128
Seda, China	E5	36
Seda, Lith.	D5	10
Sedalia, Indon.	B4	74
Sedalia, Mo., U.S.	F4	120
Sedan, Fr.	E13	14
Sedanova, Russia	C18	32
Sedayu, Indon.	G8	50
Seddon, N.Z.	E6	80
Seddon, Kap, Grnld.	B14	141
Sedel'nikovo, Russia	C11	32
Sederon, Fr.	E11	18
Sedgwick, Ab., Can.	D19	138
Sedgwick, Co., U.S.	G10	126
Sedgwick, Ks., U.S.	D11	128
Sédhiou, Sen.	G1	64
Sedlčany, Czech Rep.	G10	16
Sedom (Sodom), hist., Isr.	G6	58
Sedro Woolley, Wa., U.S.	B4	136
Sedula, Lith.	E7	10
Seehausen, Ger.	D7	16
Seeheim, Nmb.	E3	70
Seeis, Nmb.	C3	70
Seekoei, stm., S. Afr.	G7	70
Seeley Lake, Mt., U.S.	C13	136
Seelyville, In., U.S.	E10	120
Sées, Fr.	F9	14
Seesen, Ger.	E6	16
Seferihisar, Tur.	E9	28
Segamat, Malay.	A11	50
Segarcea, Rom.	E10	26
Segesta, sci., Italy	G6	24
Segezha, Russia	E15	8
Ségou, Mali	G3	64
Segorbe, Spain	E10	20
Segovary, Russia	E20	8
Segovia, Spain	D6	20
Segovia, co., Spain	C6	20
Segozero, ozero, l., Russia	E15	8
Segre, stm., Eur.	H6	18
Séguédine, Niger	E7	64
Seguí, Arg.	E7	92
Seguin, Tx., U.S.	E9	130
Segundo, Indon.	C10	50
Segura, stm., Arg.	F10	92
Segura, stm., Spain	F9	20
Segura, Sierra de, mts., Spain	F8	20
Sehithwa, Bots.	B6	70
Sehnsa, Pak.	D10	56
Sehwān, Pak.	D10	56
Seibert, Co., U.S.	B6	128
Seikpyu, Mya.	B2	48
Seiland, i., Nor.	A10	8
Seiling, Ok., U.S.	E10	128
Seim, stm., Eur.	D4	32
Seinäjoki, Fin.	E10	8
Seine, stm., Mb., Can.	E17	124
Seine, stm., Fr.	F11	14
Seine, Baie de la, b., Fr.	E8	14
Seine, Bay of the see Seine, Baie de la, b., Fr.	E8	14
Seine-et-Marne, state, Fr.	F12	14
Seine-Maritime, state, Fr.	E9	14
Seixal, Port.	F1	20
Seixas, Ponta do, c., Braz.	D9	88
Sejmčan, Russia	D19	34
Sejny, Pol.	B19	16
Sekayam, stm., Indon.	C7	50
Sekayu, Indon.	E3	50
Sekeladi, Indon.	D8	50
Seki, Japan	D9	40
Şeki, Azer.	A6	56
Sekiu, Wa., U.S.	B2	136
Sekoma, Bots.	D6	70
Sekondi, Ghana	I4	64
Selaginskij, mys, c., Russia	B23	34
Selatan, Tanjung, c., Indon.	F9	50
Selatpanjang, Indon.	C3	50
Selawik, Ak., U.S.	C8	140
Selawik Lake, l., Ak., U.S.	C7	140
Selayar, Pulau, i., Indon.	G12	50
Selayar, Selat, strt., Indon.	F12	50
Selb, Ger.	F8	16
Selbu, Nor.	E4	8
Selby, Eng., U.K.	H11	12
Selby, S.D., U.S.	B12	126
Selbyville, Md., U.S.	F10	114
Sel'co, Russia	G17	10
Sel'co, Russia	E19	8
Selçuk, Tur.	F10	28
Seldovia, Ak., U.S.	E9	140
Selebi-Phikwe, Bots.	C9	70
Selečnja, Russia	D18	32
Selemdža, stm., Russia	F14	34
Selemdžinsk, Russia	F15	34
Selendoma, Russia	F10	34
Selenga, D.R.C.	E3	66
Selenge, stm., Asia	G9	34
Selenicë, Alb.	D13	24
Selennjah, stm., Russia	C16	34
Sélestat, Fr.	F15	14
Seleznëvo, Russia	F13	8
Selfoss, Ice.	l29	8a
Selfridge, N.D., U.S.	A11	126
Sel'gon, Russia	G16	34
Sélibaby, Maur.	F2	64
Seliger, ozero, l., Russia	C15	10
Seligman, Az., U.S.	H4	132
Selihova, zaliv b., Russia	D20	34
Selimbau, Indon.	C8	50
Selinsgrove, Pa., U.S.	D8	114
Selinunte, sci., Italy	G6	24
Selišče, Russia	D16	10
Seližarovo, Russia	D16	10
Selkirk, Mb., Can.	D17	124
Selkirk, Scot., U.K.	F10	12
Selkirk Mountains, mts., N.A.	F13	138
Sellers, S.C., U.S.	B6	116
Sellersburg, In., U.S.	F12	120
Selles-sur-Cher, Fr.	G10	14
Selm, Ger.	E3	16
Selma, Al., U.S.	E11	122
Selma, Ca., U.S.	G6	134
Selma, In., U.S.	H4	112
Selmer, Tn., U.S.	B10	122
Selmont, Al., U.S.	E11	122
Šelon', stm., Russia	B13	10
Selong, Indon.	H10	50
Selva, Arg.	D6	92
Selvagens, Ilhas, is., Port.	C1	64
Selvas, for., Braz.	E8	82
Selway, stm., Id., U.S.	D11	136
Selwyn, Austl.	C3	76
Selwyn, Passage, strt., Vanuatu	k16	79d
Selwyn Lake, l., Can.	D10	106
Selwyn Mountains, mts., Can.	C4	106
Selwyn Range, mts., Austl.	C3	76
Seman, stm., Alb.	D13	24
Semangka, Teluk, b., Indon.	F4	50
Semara, W. Sah.	D2	64
Semarang, Indon.	G7	50
Semayang, Kenohan, l., Indon.	D10	50
Sembé, Congo	D2	66
Semenanjung Malaysia, hist. reg., Malay.	K6	48
Semenov, Russia	H21	8
Semeru, Gunung, vol., Indon.	H8	50
Semey (Semipalatinsk), Russia	D13	32
Semežava, Russia	H10	10
Semichi Islands, is., Ak., U.S.	g21	140a
Semiluki, Russia	D5	32
Semily, Czech Rep.	F11	16
Seminary, Ms., U.S.	F9	122
Seminoe Reservoir, res., Wy., U.S.	A9	132
Seminole, Tx., U.S.	B5	130
Seminole, Ok., U.S.	B2	122
Seminole, Lake, res., U.S.	G14	122
Seminole Draw, stm., U.S.	B5	130
Semiozernoe, Kaz.	D10	32
Semipalatinsk see Semey, Kaz.	D13	32
Semitau, Indon.	C7	50
Semizbughy, Kaz.	D13	32
Semliki, stm., Afr.	D6	66
Semnān, Iran	B7	56
Semois, stm., Eur.	E13	14
Semporna, Malay.	A11	50
Semuda, Indon.	E8	50
Sena, stm., Camb.	F7	48
Sena, Bol.	B3	90
Senador Caneda, Braz.	I1	88
Senador Pompeu, Braz.	C6	88
Senaki, Geor.	F6	32
Sena Madureira, Braz.	E4	84
Senanga, Zambia	D3	68
Senatobia, Ms., U.S.	C8	122
Sendai, Japan	H3	40
Sendai, Japan	A13	40
Sendelingsdrif, Nmb.	F3	70
Sendhwa, India	H5	54
Sendurjana, India	H7	54
Senduruhan, Indon.	D7	50
Seneca, Il., U.S.	C9	120
Seneca, Ks., U.S.	E1	120
Seneca, Mo., U.S.	H3	120
Seneca, S.C., U.S.	B3	116
Seneca, Or., U.S.	F8	136
Seneca Falls, N.Y., U.S.	B9	114
Seneca Lake, l., N.Y., U.S.	B9	114
Senegal, ctry., Afr.	G2	64
Senegal, stm., Afr.	F2	64
Senekal, S. Afr.	F8	70
Senetosa, Capu di (Senetosa, Punta di), c., Fr.	H14	18
Senetosa, Punta di see Senetosa, Capu di, c., Fr.	H14	18
Senftenberg, Ger.	E10	16
Sengés, Braz.	B13	92
Senggi, Indon.	F11	44
Sênggê, stm., China	B8	54
Senhor do Bonfim, Braz.	F5	88
Senica, Slov.	H13	16
Senigallia, Italy	G10	22
Senise, Italy	D10	24
Senj, Nor.	D16	22
Senja, i., Nor.	B7	8
Senkaku-shotō, is., Japan	F7	36
Şenkaya, Tur.	A5	56
Senlis, Fr.	E11	14
Senmonorom, Camb.	F8	48
Senneterre, Qc., Can.	F15	106
Senoia, Ga., U.S.	D14	122
Şenpazar, Tur.	B16	28
Sens, Fr.	F12	14
Senta, Serb.	D7	26
Sentarum, Danau, l., Indon.	C7	50
Sentinel, Ok., U.S.	G9	128
Sentinel Butte, mtn., N.D., U.S.	A8	126
Senyavin Islands, is., Micron.	C6	72
Seo de Urgel see La Seu d'Urgell, Spain	B12	20
Seonāth, stm., India.	H8	54

Name — Map Ref. — Page

Seoni, India — G7 54
Seoni Mālwa, India — G6 54
Seoul see Sŏul, Kor., S. — F7 38
Sepanjang, Pulau, i., Indon. — G9 50
Sepasu, Indon. — C10 50
Sepetiba, Baía de b., Braz. — L4 88
Sepi, Sol. Is. — e8 79b
Sepik, stm., Pap. N. Gui. — a3 79a
Şepopol, Pol. — B17 16
Sept-Îles, Qc., Can. — E17 106
Sepúlveda, Spain — C7 20
Seputih, stm., Indon. — F4 50
Sequatchie, stm., Tn., U.S. — B13 122
Sequillo, stm., Spain — C5 20
Sequim, Wa., U.S. — B3 136
Sequoia National Park, p.o.i., Ca., U.S. — G7 134
Serabad, Uzb. — B10 56
Serafimovič, Russia — E6 32
Seraing, Bel. — D14 14
Seram (Ceram), i., Indon. — F8 44
Seram, Laut (Ceram Sea), s., Indon. — F8 44
Serang, Indon. — G5 50
Serasan, Pulau, i., Indon. — B6 50
Serasan, Selat, strt., Indon. — B6 50
Serayevo see Sarajevo, Bos. — F5 26
Serbeulangit, Pegunungan, mts., Indon. — K3 48
Serbia and Montenegro (Yugoslavia), ctry., Eur. — F6 26
Serdo, Eth. — E8 62
Serdobsk, Russia — D6 32
Séré'ama, Mont, mtn., Vanuatu — i16 79d
Serebrjanye Prudy, Russia — F21 10
Serebryansk, Kaz. — E14 32
Sered', Slov. — H13 16
Seredejskij, Russia — F18 10
Serëdka, Russia — B11 10
Seremban, Malay. — K5 48
Serengeti National Park, p.o.i., Tan. — E6 66
Serengeti Plain, pl., Tan. — E6 66
Serengka, Indon. — D7 50
Serenje, Zam. — C5 68
Seret (Siret), stm., Eur. — A12 26
Sergač, Russia — I21 8
Sergeevka, Kaz. — D11 32
Sergeevka, Russia — C10 38
Sergeja Kirova, ostrova, is., Russia — A6 34
Sergen, Tur. — B10 28
Sergiev Posad, Russia — D21 10
Serginskij, Russia — B10 32
Sergipe, state, Braz. — F7 88
Sergozero, ozero, l., Russia — C17 8
Seria, Bru. — A9 50
Serian, Malay. — C7 50
Seribudolok, Indon. — B1 50
Seridó, stm., Braz. — D7 88
Sérifos, i., Grc. — F7 28
Serik, Tur. — G14 28
Serinyol, Tur. — B7 58
Serio, stm., Italy — E6 22
Serkovo, Russia — A15 32
Serlovaja Gora, Russia — F12 34
Serov, Russia — C10 32
Serowe, Bots. — C8 70
Serpejsk, Russia — F17 10
Serpentine Lakes, l., Austl. — E5 74
Serpents Mouth, strt. — C11 86
Serpuhov, Russia — F20 10
Serra, Braz. — K5 88
Serra Branca, Braz. — D7 88
Serra da Canastra, Parque Nacional da, p.o.i., Braz. — K2 88
Serra da Capivara, Parque Nacional da, p.o.i., Braz. — E4 88
Serra de Outes, Spain — B1 20
Serra do Navio, Braz. — C7 84
Serra do Salitre, Braz. — J2 88
Serra dos Órgãos, Parque Nacional da, p.o.i., Braz. — L4 88
Serrana, Braz. — K2 88
Serrana, Cayo de, unds., Col. — E7 102
Serrana Bank see Serrana, Cayo de, unds., Col. — E7 102
Serrania, Braz. — K2 88
Serranía de la Neblina, Parque Nacional, p.o.i., Ven. — G8 86
Serranilla, Banco see Serranilla, Cayo de, unds., Col. — E8 102
Serranilla, Cayo de, unds., Col. — E8 102
Serranilla Bank see Serranilla, Cayo de, unds., Col. — E8 102
Serrano, Banco see Serrana, Cayo de, unds., Col. — E7 102
Serrano, Braz. — E6 88
Sera Talhada, Braz. — E6 88
Serres, Fr. — E11 18
Sérres, Grc. — B6 28
Serrezuela, Arg. — E5 92
Serrinha, Braz. — F6 88
Serrita, Braz. — D6 88
Sertânia, Braz. — E7 88
Sertãozinho, Braz. — K1 88
Serui, Indon. — F10 44
Serule, Bots. — B8 70
Serutu, Pulau, i., Indon. — J4 48
Sêrxü, China — E4 36
Seryševo, Russia — F14 34
Sesayap, Indon. — B10 50
Sesayap Lama, Indon. — B10 50
Seseganaga Lake, l., On., Can. — A8 118
Sese Islands, is., Ug. — E6 66
Sesfontein, Nmb. — D1 68
Sesheke, Zam. — D3 68
Sesia, stm., Italy — E5 22
Sesibu, Indon. — A10 50
Sessa Aurunca, Italy — C7 24
Sestao, Spain — A7 20
Sestri Levante, Italy — F6 22
Şestroreck, Russia — F14 8
Šešupė, stm., Eur. — F5 10
Šėta, Lith. — E7 10
Sète, Fr. — F9 18
Sete Barras, Braz. — B13 92
Sete Cidades, Parque Nacional da, p.o.i., Braz. — C5 88
Sete Lagoas, Braz. — J3 88
Sete Quedas, Parque Nacional da, p.o.i., Braz. — A11 92
Sete Quedas, Salto das (Guaíra, Salto del), wtfl., S.A. — B10 92
Seth Ward, Tx., U.S. — G7 128
Seto, Japan — D10 40
Seto-naikai (Inland Sea), s., Japan — E5 40
Seton Portage, B.C., Can. — F8 138
Settat, Mor. — C3 64
Setté Cama, Gabon — E1 66
Sette-Daban, hrebet, mts., Russia — D16 34
Settlers, S. Afr. — D9 70
Setúbal, Port. — F1 20
Setúbal, state, Port. — F1 20
Setúbal, Baía de, b., Port. — F1 20
Seul, Lac, l., On., Can. — A6 118
Seul Choix Point, c., Mi., U.S. — C4 112
Seulimeum, Indon. — J2 48

Sevan, Lake see Sevana Lich, l., Arm. — A6 56
Sevana Lich, l., Arm. — A6 56
Sevastopol', Ukr. — G15 6
Ševelevskaja, Russia — F20 8
Seven Persons, Ab., Can. — E3 124
Seven Sisters Peaks, mtn., B.C., Can. — B2 138
Seventy Mile House, B.C., Can. — E9 138
Severn, stm., On., Can. — E12 106
Severn, stm., U.K. — J10 12
Severnaja Dvina (Northern Dvina), stm., Russia — E19 8
Severnaja Osetija, state, Russia — F6 32
Severnaja Sos'va, stm., Russia — B10 32
Severnaja Zemlja, is., Russia — B12 30
Severna Park, Md., U.S. — E9 114
Severnoe, Russia — C13 32
Severnoe uvaly, hills, Russia — C7 32
Severnyj Ural, mts., Russia — B9 32
Severočeský, state, Czech Rep. — F10 16
Severodvinsk (Molotovsk), Russia — D18 8
Severo-Enisejskij, Russia — B16 32
Severo-Kuril'sk, Russia — F20 34
Severomoravský, state, Czech Rep. — G13 16
Severomorsk, Russia — B15 8
Severo-Sibirskaja nizmennost' (North Siberian Lowland), pl., Russia — B6 34
Severoural'sk (Severouralsk), Russia — B9 32
Severo-Zadonsk, Russia — F21 10
Severy, Ks., U.S. — D12 128
Sevettijärvi, Fin. — B13 8
Sevier, stm., Ut., U.S. — D4 132
Sevier, East Fork, stm., Ut., U.S. — F5 132
Sevier Desert, des., Ut., U.S. — D4 132
Sevier Lake, l., Ut., U.S. — D4 132
Sevierville, Tn., U.S. — I2 114
Sevilla, Col. — E4 86
Sevilla (Seville), Spain — G5 20
Sevilla, co., Spain — G5 20
Seville see Sevilla, Spain — G5 20
Seville, Fl., U.S. — G4 116
Sevlievo, Blg. — F12 26
Sewāni, India — D5 54
Seward, Ak., U.S. — D10 140
Seward, Ne., U.S. — G15 126
Seward, Pa., U.S. — D7 114
Seward Peninsula, pen., Ak., U.S. — C7 140
Sessmith, Ab., Can. — A12 138
Sextín, stm., Mex. — B6 100
Seybaplaya, Mex. — C2 102
Seychelles, ctry., Afr. — k12 69b
Seychelles, is., Sey. — k13 69b
Seydişehir, Tur. — F14 28
Seydisfjördur, Ice. — k32 8a
Seyhan (Sarus), stm., Tur. — A6 58
Seymour, Austl. — K5 76
Seymour, S. Afr. — H8 70
Seymour, Ct., U.S. — C12 114
Seymour, In., U.S. — F12 120
Seymour, Mo., U.S. — G5 120
Seymour, Tx., U.S. — H9 128
Seymour, Wi., U.S. — D11 112
Sežana, Slvn. — E10 22
Sézanne, Fr. — F12 14
Sfakía, Grc. — H7 28
Sfântu Gheorghe, Rom. — D12 26
Sfântu Gheorghe, Brațul, b., Rom. — E16 26
Sfântu Gheorghe, Ostrovul, i., Rom. — D16 26
Sfax, Tun. — C7 64
's-Gravenhage (The Hague), Neth. — B13 14
Sha, stm., China — H7 42
Sha, stm., China — E6 42
Shaanxi, state, China — D3 42
Shabeelle (Shebelē Wenz, Wabē), stm., Afr. — D8 66
Shabunda, D.R.C. — E5 66
Shabwah, Yemen — F6 56
Shache (Yarkant), China — B12 56
Shackleton Ice Shelf, ice, Ant. — C28 81
Shackleton Range, mts., Ant. — D2 81
Shady Cove, Or., U.S. — A3 134
Shady Grove, Fl., U.S. — F2 116
Shadyside, Oh., U.S. — E5 114
Shageluk, Ak., U.S. — D8 140
Shag Rocks, r., S. Geor. — J8 90
Shāhābād, India — C3 53
Shāhābād, India — C6 54
Shāhābād, India — D8 54
Shāhāda, India — H5 54
Shah Alam, Malay. — K5 48
Shāhdādpur, Pak. — E2 53
Shahdol, India — G8 54
Shahe, China — J3 42
Shahezhen, China — E8 42
Shāhjahānpur, India — E7 54
Shāh Kot, Pak. — C4 54
Shāhpur, India — C3 53
Shāhpur, Pak. — D2 54
Shāhpur, India — G8 54
Shāhpura, India — E4 54
Shāhpura, India — G8 54
Shāhpura, India — G8 54
Shahr-e Kord, Iran — C7 56
Shaighālu, Pak. — C2 54
Shajapur, India — G6 54
Shakawe, Bots. — D3 68
Shaker Heights, Oh., U.S. — G8 112
Shakespeare Island, i., On., Can. — B10 118
Shakhtinsk, Kaz. — E12 32
Shaki, Nig. — H5 64
Shakopee, Mn., U.S. — G5 118
Shakotan-hantō, pen., Japan — C14 38
Shaktoolik, Ak., U.S. — D7 140
Shala, Lake see Shala Hāyk', l., Eth. — F7 62
Shala Hāyk', l., Eth. — F7 62
Shalalth, B.C., Can. — F8 138
Shaler Mountains, mts., Can. — A8 106
Shallowater, Tx., U.S. — H7 128
Shalqar, Kaz. — E9 32
Shaluli Shan, mts., China — E4 36
Shām, Jabal ash-, mtn., Oman — E8 56
Shamattawa, Mb., Can. — D12 106
Shambe, Sudan — F6 62
Shambu, Eth. — F7 62
Shamli, India — D6 54
Shamokin, Pa., U.S. — D9 114
Shamrock, Fl., U.S. — G2 116
Shamrock, Tx., U.S. — F8 128
Shamva, Zimb. — D5 68
Shan, state, Mya. — B4 48
Shancheng, China — D6 42
Shandan, China — D5 36
Shandi, Sudan — D6 62
Shandong, state, China — C7 42
Shandong Bandao (Shantung Peninsula), pen., China — C9 42

Shand uul, mtn., Mong. — C5 36
Shangani, Zimb. — A9 70
Shangani, stm., Zimb. — D4 68
Shangbahe, China — F6 42
Shangcheng, China — F6 42
Shangch'iu see Shangqiu, China — D6 42
Shangchuan Dao, i., China — K5 42
Shangdu, China — C7 36
Shanggao, China — G6 42
Shanghai, China — F9 42
Shanghai, state, China — F9 42
Shanghai Shih see Shanghai, state, China — I4 38
Shanghang, China — I7 42
Shanghe, China — C7 42
Shangjao see Shangrao, China — G7 42
Shanglin, China — E4 42
Shanglin, China — J3 42
Shangqing, China — I8 42
Shangqiu, China — D6 42
Shangqiu, China — D6 42
Shangrao, China — G7 42
Shangshui, China — E6 42
Shangsi, China — J2 42
Shangxian, China — E3 42
Shangyi, China — A6 42
Shangying, China — B7 38
Shangyou Shuiku, res., China — I6 42
Shangyu, China — F9 42
Shanhaiguan, China — B8 38
Shanhua, China — A8 42
Shanhaikwan see Shanhaiguan, China — A8 42
Shanhetun, China — B7 38
Shankou, China — K3 42
Shannon, Il., U.S. — B8 120
Shannon, Ms., U.S. — C10 122
Shannon, stm., Ire. — I3 12
Shannon Ø, i., Grnld. — B22 141
Shannontown, S.C., U.S. — C5 116
Shanshan, China — C3 36
Shansi see Shanxi, state, China — B5 42
Shantar Islands see Šantarskie ostrova, is., Russia — E16 34
Shantipur, India — G12 54
Shantou, China — J7 42
Shantung see Shandong, state, China — C7 42
Shantung Peninsula see Shandong Bandao, pen., China — C9 42
Shanwei, China — J6 42
Shanxi, state, China — C6 42
Shanxian, China — D7 42
Shanyang, China — E3 42
Shanyin, China — C5 42
Shaoguan, China — I5 42
Shaohing see Shaoxing, China — G9 42
Shaoshing see Shaoguan, China — G9 42
Shaoleng, stm., China — C3 38
Shaowu, China — H7 42
Shaoxing, China — G9 42
Shaoyang, China — H4 42
Shaqqā, Syria — F7 58
Shaqrā', Sau. Ar. — D6 56
Shaqrā', Yemen — G6 56
Shar, Kaz. — E14 32
Shara, gora, mtn., Asia — A5 56
Sharbaqty, Kaz. — D13 32
Shardara, Kaz. — F11 32
Shardara bögeni, res., Asia — A10 56
Shari-dake, mtn., Japan — C16 38
Sharin Gol, Mong. — B6 36
Sharjah see Ash-Shāriqah, U.A.E. — D8 56
Shark Bay, b., Austl. — E2 74
Sharktooth Mountain, mtn., B.C., Can. — D5 106
Sharm ash-Shaykh, Egypt — K5 58
Sharon, N.D., U.S. — G16 124
Sharon, Pa., U.S. — C5 114
Sharon, Tn., U.S. — H9 120
Sharon, Wi., U.S. — B9 120
Sharpe, Lake, res., S.D., U.S. — C12 126
Sharpsburg, Md., U.S. — E8 114
Sharriton, Eth. — F7 62
Shashi, China — F5 42
Shasi see Shashi, China — C3 134
Shasta, Ca., U.S. — C3 134
Shasta, Mount, vol., Ca., U.S. — B2 134
Shasta Lake, res., Ca., U.S. — C3 134
Shāti', Wādī ash-, stm., Libya — B2 62
Shats'k, Ukr. — E19 16
Shats'kyi Pryrodnyi Natsional'nyi Park, p.o.i., Ukr. — E19 16
Shattuck, Ok., U.S. — E9 128
Shaunavon, Sk., Can. — E5 124
Shaw, Ms., U.S. — D8 122
Shawan, China — C2 36
Shawinigan, Qc., Can. — D4 110
Shawinigan-Sud, Qc., Can. — D4 110
Shawnee, Ks., U.S. — E3 120
Shawnee, Oh., U.S. — E3 114
Shawnee, Ok., U.S. — F11 128
Shawneetown, Il., U.S. — G9 120
Shawville, Qc., Can. — C13 112
Shaxian, China — H7 42
Shayang, China — F5 42
Shay Gap, Austl. — D4 74
Shaykh Miskīn, Syria — F7 58
Shaykh 'Uthmān, Yemen — G6 56
Shchūchīnsk, Kaz. — D12 32
She, stm., China — D9 42
Shebelē Wenz, Wabē (Shabeelle), stm., Afr. — C8 66
Sheberghān, Afg. — B10 56
Sheboygan, Wi., U.S. — E2 112
Sheboygan, stm., Wi., U.S. — E1 112
Sheboygan Falls, Wi., U.S. — E1 112
Shechem, sci., W.B. — C6 62
Shediac, N.B., Can. — D12 110
Shedin Peak, mtn., B.C., Can. — B3 138
Sheenjek, stm., Ak., U.S. — C11 140
Sheep Mountain, mtn., Az., U.S. — K2 132
Sheerness, Eng., U.K. — J13 12
Sheet Harbour, N.S., Can. — F14 110
Sheffield, N.Z. — F4 80
Sheffield, Eng., U.K. — H11 12
Sheffield, Al., U.S. — C11 122
Sheffield, Ia., U.S. — B4 120
Sheffield, Pa., U.S. — C6 114
Sheffield, Tx., U.S. — D6 130
Shegaon, India — H6 54
Shehong, China — F1 42
Sheikhpura, India — F10 54
Shekhūpura, Pak. — C5 54
Shekki see Zhongshan, China — J5 42
Shelagyote Peak, mtn., B.C., Can. — D5 106
Shelbina, Mo., U.S. — E5 120
Shelburne, N.S., Can. — G11 110
Shelburne, On., Can. — D9 112
Shelburne Falls, Ma., U.S. — B13 114
Shelby, Ia., U.S. — C2 120
Shelby, Mi., U.S. — E3 112
Shelby, Mt., U.S. — B15 136
Shelby, N.C., U.S. — A4 116

Shelby, Ne., U.S. — F15 126
Shelbyville, Il., U.S. — E9 120
Shelbyville, In., U.S. — E12 120
Shelbyville, Mo., U.S. — E5 120
Shelbyville, Tn., U.S. — B12 122
Shelbyville, Lake, res., Il., U.S. — E8 120
Sheldon, Ia., U.S. — H3 118
Sheldon, Mo., U.S. — G3 120
Shelek, Kaz. — F13 32
Shelekhov, Gulf of see Šelihova, zaliv, b., Russia — D20 34
Shelikof Strait, strt., Ak., U.S. — E9 140
Shell, Wi., U.S. — F7 118
Shellbrook, Sk., Can. — A7 124
Shell Creek, see Ne., U.S. — F15 126
Shelley, B.C., Can. — C8 138
Shellharbour, Austl. — J8 76
Shellman, Ga., U.S. — F14 122
Shellmouth Dam, dam, Mb., Can. — D12 124
Shell Rock, Ia., U.S. — B5 120
Shell Rock, stm., U.S. — I6 118
Shellsburg, Ia., U.S. — B6 120
Shelton, Ct., U.S. — C12 114
Shelton, Ne., U.S. — G14 126
Shemogue, N.B., Can. — D12 110
Shemonaīkha, Kaz. — D14 32
Shemonaikha see Shemonaīkha, Kaz. — D14 32
Shenandoah, Ia., U.S. — D2 120
Shenandoah, Va., U.S. — F7 114
Shenandoah, stm., U.S. — E8 114
Shenandoah, North Fork, stm., Va., U.S. — F7 114
Shenandoah, South Fork, stm., Va., U.S. — F7 114
Shenandoah National Park, p.o.i., Va., U.S. — F7 114
Shenber, Kaz. — E11 32
Shenchi, China — B4 42
Shencottah, India — G3 53
Shendam, Nig. — H6 64
Shenge, S.L. — H2 64
Shengsi Liedao, is., China — I5 38
Shengxian, China — G9 42
Shengze, China — F9 42
Shenjing, China — J5 42
Shenmu, China — B4 42
Shenqiu, China — E6 42
Shensi see Shaanxi, state, China — E3 42
Shenton, Mount, mtn., Austl. — E4 74
Shenxian, China — C6 42
Shenyang (Mukden), China — D5 38
Shenzhen, China — J6 42
Sheoganj, India — F4 54
Sheopur, India — F6 54
Shepherd, Ab., Can. — E17 138
Shepherd, Mi., U.S. — E5 112
Shepherd, state, Vanuatu — k17 79d
Shepherd, Îles, is., Vanuatu — k17 79d
Shepherdstown, W.V., U.S. — E7 114
Shepherdsville, Ky., U.S. — F12 120
Shepparton, Austl. — K5 76
Sheppey, Isle of, i., Eng., U.K. — J13 12
Shô, stm., Japan — C10 40
Shoal, stm., Fl., U.S. — G12 122
Sheqi, China — E5 42
Sherard, Cape, c., Nu., Can. — C10 141
Sherard Osburn Fjord, b., Grnld. — A14 141
Sherborne, Eng., U.K. — K10 12
Sherbro Island, i., S.L. — H2 64
Sherbrooke, Qc., Can. — E4 110
Sherburn, Mn., U.S. — H4 118
Sherburne, N.Y., U.S. — B10 114
Sheridan, Ar., U.S. — C6 122
Sheridan, In., U.S. — H3 112
Sheridan, Or., U.S. — E3 136
Sheridan, Tx., U.S. — E11 130
Sheridan, Wy., U.S. — C6 126
Sherman, Tx., U.S. — D2 122
Sherman Mills, Me., U.S. — E8 110
Sherman Station, Me., U.S. — E8 110
Sherman Mountain, mtn., Ar., U.S. — I4 120
Sherpur, Bngl. — F12 54
Sherpur, Bngl. — F13 54
Sherridon, Mb., Can. — E10 106
Sherstone, Eth. — F7 62
Shertallai, India — G3 53
's-Hertogenbosch, Neth. — C14 14
Sherwood, Ar., U.S. — C6 122
Sherwood, Oh., U.S. — C1 114
Sherwood, Tn., U.S. — B12 122
Sherwood Shores, Tx., U.S. — B2 54
Sherwood Park, Ab., Can. — C17 138
Shetland Islands, is., Scot., U.K. — n17 12a
Shetrunji, stm., India — H3 54
Shexian, China — G8 42
Sheyang, China — E9 42
Sheyenne, N.D., U.S. — G14 124
Sheyenne, stm., N.D., U.S. — H16 124
Sheykhābād, Afg. — A2 54
Shiant Islands, is., Scot., U.K. — D6 12
Shibām, Yemen — F6 56
Shibata, Japan — B12 40
Shibīn el-Kôm, Egypt — H1 58
Shibing, China — H2 42
Shibukawa, Japan — C12 40
Shicheng, China — H7 42
Shickley, Ne., U.S. — G15 126
Shidao, China — C10 42
Shidler, Ok., U.S. — E12 128
Shiëli, Kaz. — F11 32
Shifang, China — E5 36
Shiga, state, Japan — D9 40
Shigatse see Xigazê, China — D6 46
Shiguaigou, China — A4 42
Shihchia-chuang see Shijiazhuang, China — C6 42
Shihkiachwang see Shijiazhuang, China — C6 42
Shihezi, China — C2 36
Shijiao, China — J5 42
Shijiazhuang, China — C6 42
Shijiu Hu, l., China — F8 42
Shikārpur, India — D2 53
Shikārpur, India — E7 54
Shikohābād, India — E7 54
Shikoku, i., Japan — F6 40
Shikoku-sanchi, mts., Japan — F6 40
Shikotsu-ko, l., Japan — C14 38
Shilan, China — I8 42
Shiliguri, India — E12 54
Shiliu see Changjiang, China — L3 42
Shilka, Russia — F13 34
Shilka, stm., Russia — F13 34
Shillington, Pa., U.S. — H13 112
Shillong, India — F13 54
Shiloh, Oh., U.S. — I5 112
Shiloh see Saylūn, Khirbat, hist., W.B. — F6 58
Shilong, China — J5 42
Shimabara, Japan — G3 40
Shimada, Japan — E11 40
Shimane, state, Japan — D5 40
Shimbiris, mtn., Som. — B9 66
Shimen, China — G4 42
Shimizu, Japan — D11 40
Shimla, India — C6 54
Shimoda, Japan — E11 40
Shimodate, Japan — C13 40

Shuyak Island, i., Ak., U.S. — E9 140
Shuyang, China — D8 42
Shwangliao see Liaoyuan, China — C6 38
Shwebo, Mya. — A2 48
Shwegun, Mya. — D3 48
Shwegyin, Mya. — D3 48
Shyghys-Qongyrat, Kaz. — E13 32
Shymkent, Kaz. — F11 32
Shyok, India — A7 54
Shyok, stm., Asia — B4 46
Si, China — D7 42
Sia, Indon. — D9 56
Siahān Range, mts., Pak. — C2 50
Siak, stm., Indon. — C2 50
Siak Sri Indrapura, Indon. — C3 50
Siālkot, Pak. — B5 54
Siam see Thailand, ctry., Asia — E5 48
Siam, Gulf of see Thailand, Gulf of, b., Asia — G5 48
Sian see Xi'an, China — D3 42
Siangtan see Xiangtan, China — H5 42
Šipka Pass see Šipčenski Prohod, p., Blg. — G12 26
Sianów, Pol. — B12 16
Siantan, Pulau, i., Indon. — B4 50
Siapa, stm., Ven. — G9 86
Siargao Island, i., Phil. — F6 52
Siasconset, Ma., U.S. — C15 114
Siasi, Phil. — H3 52
Siasi Island, i., Phil. — H3 52
Siaškotan, ostrov, i., Russia — G19 34
Siau, Pulau, i., Indon. — E7 44
Šiauliai, Lith. — E6 10
Sibaj, Russia — D9 32
Sibayi, Lake, l., S. Afr. — E11 70
Šibenik, Cro. — G12 22
Siberia see Sibir', reg., Russia — C12 34
Siberut, Pulau, i., Indon. — D1 50
Sibi, Pak. — D10 56
Sibigo, Indon. — K2 48
Sibir', reg., Russia — C12 34
Sibircevo, Russia — B10 38
Sibirjakova, ostrov, i., Russia — B4 34
Sibiti, Congo — E2 66
Sibiu, Rom. — D11 26
Sibiu, state, Rom. — D11 26
Sibley, Ia., U.S. — H3 118
Sibley, La., U.S. — E5 122
Sibley, Ms., U.S. — F7 122
Sibley Peninsula, pen., On., Can. — C10 118
Sibolga, Indon. — C1 50
Sibsāgar, India — C7 46
Sibu, Malay. — B7 50
Sibuguey Bay, b., Phil. — G4 52
Sibut, C.A.R. — C3 66
Sibutu Island, i., Phil. — H2 52
Sibutu Passage, strt., Asia — H2 52
Sibuyan Island, i., Phil. — D4 52
Sibuyan Sea, s., Phil. — D4 52
Sicapoo, Mount, mtn., Phil. — B3 52
Siccus, stm., Austl. — H2 76
Sichang see Xichang, China — F5 36
Si Chon, Thai. — H4 48
Sichuan, state, China — E5 36
Sichuan Pendi, bas., China — F1 42
Sichuanzhai, China — A5 48
Sicié, Cap, c., Fr. — F11 18
Sicilia (Sicily), i., Italy — G7 24
Sicilia, state, Italy — F8 24
Sicily see Sicilia, i., Italy — G7 24
Sicily, Strait of, strt. — G5 24
Sicily Island, La., U.S. — F7 122
Sicuani, Peru — F3 84
Sidareja, Indon. — G6 50
Sidas, Indon. — C6 50
Siddhapur, India — G4 54
Siddipet, India — B4 53
Siddipet, India — C4 53
Sidéradougou, Burkina — G4 64
Siderno, Italy — F10 24
Sidéropolis, Braz. — D13 92
Sideros, Ákra, c., Grc. — H9 28
Sidhauli, India — E8 54
Sidhi, India — F8 54
Sidi Barrāni, Egypt — A5 62
Sidi bel Abbès, Alg. — C5 64
Sidi-Ifni, Mor. — D2 64
Siding Spring Mountain, mtn., Austl. — H7 76
Sidirókastro, Grc. — B6 28
Sidi Sālim, Egypt — G1 58
Sidlaghatta, India — E3 53
Sídley, Mount, mtn., Ant. — C28 81
Sidmouth, Eng., U.K. — K10 12
Sidnaw, Mi., U.S. — E10 118
Sidney, B.C., Can. — H7 138
Sidney, Il., U.S. — D9 120
Sidney, Ia., U.S. — D2 120
Sidney, Mt., U.S. — G9 124
Sidney, Ne., U.S. — F10 126
Sidney, N.Y., U.S. — B10 114
Sidney, Oh., U.S. — D1 114
Sidney Lanier, Lake, res., Ga., U.S. — B2 116
Sidon see Şaydā, Leb. — E6 58
Sidon, Ms., U.S. — D8 122
Sidorovsk, Russia — A14 32
Sidra, Gulf of see Surt, Khalīj, b., Libya — A3 62
Sidrolândia, Braz. — D6 90
Siedlce, Pol. — D18 16
Siedlce, state, Pol. — D17 16
Siegburg, Ger. — F3 16
Siegen, Ger. — F4 16
Siemianowice Śląskie, Pol. — F15 16
Siĕmpang, Camb. — E8 48
Siĕmréab, Camb. — F6 48
Siena, Italy — G8 22
Sienyang see Xianyang, China — D3 42
Sieradz, Pol. — E14 16
Sieradz, state, Pol. — E14 16
Sieraków, Pol. — D12 16
Sierpc, Pol. — D15 16
Sierra Blanca, Tx., U.S. — C2 130
Sierra Blanca Peak, mtn., N.M., U.S. — H3 128
Sierra Chica, Arg. — H7 92
Sierra Colorada, Arg. — H3 90
Sierra Gorda, Chile — D3 90
Sierra Leone, ctry., Afr. — H2 64
Sierra Mojada, Mex. — G4 130
Sierra Nevada see Nevada, Sierra, mts., Ca. — F6 134
Sierra Nevada, Parque Nacional, p.o.i., Ven. — C6 86
Sierra Vista, Az., U.S. — L6 132
Siesta Key, Fl., U.S. — I3 116
Sífnos, i., Grc. — G7 28
Sifón Villanueva, Mex. — G7 130
Sig, Russia — D16 8
Sigatoka, Fiji — q18 79e
Sigep, Indon. — D1 50
Sighetu Marmației, Rom. — B10 26
Sighișoara, Rom. — C11 26
Siglan, Russia — E19 34
Sigli, Indon. — J2 48
Siglufjördur, Ice. — j30 8a
Sigmaringen, Ger. — H5 16
Signal Mountain, Tn., U.S. — B13 122
Signal Mountain, mtn., Vt., U.S. — F4 110
Signy, sci., Ant. — B36 81
Sigourney, Ia., U.S. — C5 120
Sigsig, Ec. — D2 84
Siguanea, Ensenada de la, b., Cuba — B6 102
Siguatepeque, Hond. — C8 102
Sigüenza, Spain — B8 20
Siguiri, Gui. — G3 64
Sigulda, Lat. — C7 10

Name	Map Ref.	Page
Sigurd, Ut., U.S.	E5	132
Sigurd Falls, wtfl., Tan.	F7	66
Sihabuhabu, Dolok, mtn., Indon.	B1	50
Sihanoukville see Kâmpóng Saôm, Camb.	G6	48
Sihor, India	H3	54
Sihorā, India	G8	54
Sihote-Alin', mts., Russia	E17	30
Sihtovo, Russia	E15	10
Sihui, China	J5	42
Siirt, Tur.	B5	56
Sija, Russia	E19	8
Sijunjung, Indon.	D2	50
Sikandarābād, India	D6	54
Sikanni Chief, stm., B.C., Can.	D6	106
Sikao, Thai.	I4	48
Sikar, India	E5	54
Sikasso, Mali	G3	64
Sikeston, Mo., U.S.	H8	120
Sikhote-Alin Mountains see Sihote-Alin', mts., Russia	E17	30
Sikiang see Xi, stm., China	J5	42
Siking see Xi'an, China	D3	42
Sikkos, i., Grc.	G8	28
Sikkim, state, India	E12	54
Sikonge, Tan.	F6	66
Sikotan, ostrov (Shikotan-tō), i., Russia	C17	38
Siktjah, Malay.	B13	34
Sikuati, Malay.	G1	52
Sikyón, sci., Grc.	F5	28
Sil, stm., Spain	B3	20
Sila, Thai.	I5	48
Šilalė, Lith.	E5	10
Silao, Mex.	E8	100
Silas, Al., U.S.	F10	122
Silaut, Indon.	E2	50
Silay, Phil.	E4	52
Silchar, India	F14	54
Şile, Tur.	B12	28
Siler City, N.C., U.S.	I6	114
Sileru, stm., India	C5	53
Silesia, hist. reg., Eur.	F13	16
Siletitengiz köli, l., Kaz.	D12	32
Siletz, Or., U.S.	F3	136
Siletz, stm., Or., U.S.	F3	136
Silgadhī, Nepal	D8	54
Silghāt, India	E14	54
Silhouette, i., Sey.	j13	69b
Siliana, Tun.	H3	24
Siliana, Oued, stm., Tun.	I3	24
Silifke, Tur.	B4	58
Siling Co, l., China	C12	54
Silistra, Blg.	E14	26
Šilivri, Tur.	B11	28
Siljan, l., Swe.	F6	8
Šilka, Russia	F12	34
Šilka, stm., Russia	F12	34
Silkeborg, Den.	H3	8
Sillamäe, Est.	A10	10
Sillem Island, i., Nu., Can.	A16	106
Sillian, Aus.	D9	22
Sillon de Talbert, pen., Fr.	F5	14
Šilovići, Russia	E15	10
Silsbee, Tx., U.S.	G4	122
Silton, Sk., Can.	D9	124
Siluas, Indon.	C7	50
Šilutė, Lith.	E4	10
Silvânia, Braz.	I1	88
Silvassa, India	H4	54
Silver, Tx., U.S.	B7	130
Silver Bank Passage, strt., N.A.	B12	102
Silver Bell, Az., U.S.	K5	132
Silver City, N.C., U.S.	B6	116
Silver City, N.M., U.S.	K8	132
Silver Creek, Ms., U.S.	F9	122
Silver Creek, Ne., U.S.	F15	126
Silver Creek, stm., Az., U.S.	I6	132
Silver Creek, stm., Or., U.S.	G7	136
Silverdale, Wa., U.S.	C4	136
Silver Lake, Ks., U.S.	E2	120
Silver Lake, Mn., U.S.	G4	118
Silver Lake, Wi., U.S.	F11	112
Silver Lake, l., Or., U.S.	G7	136
Silver Lake, l., Or., U.S.	G5	136
Silver Spring, Md., U.S.	E8	114
Silver Star Mountain, mtn., Wa., U.S.	B6	136
Silverthrone Mountain, vol., B.C., Can.	E4	138
Silverton, Austl.	H3	76
Silverton, B.C., Can.	G13	138
Silverton, Co., U.S.	F9	132
Silverton, Tx., U.S.	G7	128
Silvi, Italy	H11	22
Silvies, Or., U.S.	G7	136
Silvies, stm., Or., U.S.	G7	136
Šimanovsk, Russia	F14	34
Simao, China	A5	48
Simão Dias, Braz.	F6	88
Simav, China	D11	28
Simav, stm., Tur.	C11	28
Simbach, Ger.	H8	16
Simbo Island, i., Sol. Is.	e7	79b
Simcoe, Ont., Can.	F9	112
Simcoe, Lake, l., On., Can.	D10	112
Simdega, India	G10	54
Simeria, Rom.	D10	26
Simeulue, Pulau, i., Indon.	K2	48
Simferopol', Ukr.	G15	6
Simikot, Nepal	C8	54
Similkameen, stm., N.A.	G10	138
Simiti, Col.	D4	86
Simi Valley, Ca., U.S.	I7	134
Simizu see Shimizu, Japan	D11	40
Simla, Co., U.S.	B4	128
Simmern, Ger.	G3	16
Simmie, Sk., Can.	C15	124
Simnas, Lith.	F6	10
Simoca, Arg.	C5	92
Simões, Braz.	D5	88
Simojärvi, l., Fin.	C12	8
Simojovel, Mex.	G12	100
Simon, Lac, l., Qc., Can.	E1	110
Simonette, stm., Ab., Can.	A12	138
Simonoseki see Shimonoseki, Japan	F3	40
Simonstad see Simon's Town, S. Afr.	I4	70
Simon's Town, S. Afr.	I4	70
Simoom Sound, B.C., Can.	F4	138
Simpang, Indon.	D3	50
Simpang-kiri, stm., Indon.	K3	48
Simplon Pass, p., Switz.	D4	22
Simpson Desert, des., Austl.	D7	74
Simpson Island, i., On., Can.	C11	118
Simpson Peninsula, pen., Nu., Can.	B13	106
Simpson Strait, strt., Nu., Can.	B11	106
Simpsonville, S.C., U.S.	B3	116
Simrishamn, Swe.	I6	8
Simonbaai, Neth. Ant.	A1	105a
Simušir, Malay.	C1	50
Simušir, ostrov, i., Russia	G19	34
Sina, stm., India	B2	53
Sinabang, Indon.	K3	48
Sinabung, Gunung, vol., Indon.	K4	48
Sinai (Sinai Peninsula), pen., Egypt	J4	58
Sinai, Mount see Mūsa, Jebel, mtn., Egypt	J5	58
Sinai, Mount, vol., Gren.	q10	105e
Sinaia, Rom.	D12	26
Sinai Peninsula see Sinai, pen., Egypt	J4	58
Sinajana, Guam	j10	78c
Sinaloa, state, Mex.	C5	100
Sinaloa, stm., Mex.	C5	100
Sinamaica, Ven.	B6	86
Sinan, China	H3	42
Sinanpaşa, Tur.	E13	28
Sinäwin, Libya	A2	62
Sincan, Tur.	D15	28
Sincé, Col.	B2	84
Sincelejo, Col.	C4	86
Sinch'ang-úp, Kor., N.	D8	38
Sin-ch'on, Kor., N.	E6	38
Sinclair, Wy., U.S.	B9	132
Sinclair, Lake, res., Ga., U.S.	C2	116
Sinclair Mills, B.C., Can.	B9	138
Sind, state, Pak.	F2	54
Sind, stm., India	F7	54
Sindangan, Phil.	F4	52
Sindangbarang, Indon.	G5	50
Sindara, Gabon	E2	66
Sindari, India	F3	54
Sindelfingen, Ger.	H4	16
Sindhnūr, India	D3	53
Sindhuli Mārdi, Nepal	E11	54
Sindingale, Mya.	C2	48
Sindor, Russia	B8	32
Sines, Port.	G2	20
Sinfra, C. Iv.	H3	64
Singalamwe, Nmb.	D3	68
Singapore, Sing.	C3	50
Singapore, ctry., Asia	L6	48
Singapore, Strait of, strt., Asia	C4	50
Singaraja, Indon.	H9	50
Sing Buri, Thai.	E5	48
Singen, Ger.	I4	16
Singida, Tan.	E6	66
Singitic Gulf see Agiou Órous, Kólpos, b., Grc.	C6	28
Singkaling Hkämti, Mya.	C8	46
Singkang, Indon.	F11	50
Singkawang, Indon.	C6	50
Singkep, Pulau, i., Indon.	D4	50
Singkil, Indon.	K3	48
Singkuang, Indon.	C1	50
Singleton, Austl.	I8	76
Singleton, Mount, mtn., Austl.	E3	74
Singuédeze (Shingwidzi), stm., Afr.	C10	70
Sining see Xining, China	D5	36
Sinj, Cro.	G13	22
Sinjah, Sudan	E6	62
Sinjai, Indon.	F12	50
Sinjaja, stm., Eur.	D11	10
Sinjaja, stm., Russia	D14	34
Sinjuga, Russia	E12	34
Sinkat, Sudan	D7	62
Sinkiang see Xinjiang, state, China	A5	46
Sinnamahoning, Pa., U.S.	C7	114
Sinnamary, Fr. Gu.	B7	84
Sinnar, India	B2	53
Sinnūris, Egypt	I1	58
Sinnyöng, Kor., S.	C1	40
Sinoie, Lacul, l., Rom.	E15	26
Sinop, Tur.	A4	56
Sinsheim, Ger.	G4	16
Sinsiang see Xinxiang, China	D5	42
Sinskoe, Russia	D14	34
Sintang, Indon.	C7	50
Sint Christoffelberg, hill, Neth. Ant.	p21	104g
Sint Eustatius, i., Neth. Ant.	B1	105a
Sint Helenabaai, b., S. Afr.	H3	70
Sint Kruis, Neth. Ant.	p21	104g
Sint Maarten (Saint-Martin), i., N.A.	A1	105a
Sint Nicolaas, Aruba	p20	104g
Sint-Niklaas, Bel.	C12	14
Sintra, Port.	F1	20
Sint-Truiden, Bel.	D14	14
Sinú, stm., Col.	C4	86
Sinúiju, Kor., N.	D6	38
Sió, stm., Hung.	C5	26
Siocon, Phil.	G4	52
Siófok, Hung.	C5	26
Sion, Switz.	D4	22
Siorapaluk, Grnld.	B12	141
Sioux Center, Ia., U.S.	H2	118
Sioux City, Ia., U.S.	B1	120
Sioux Falls, S.D., U.S.	H2	118
Sioux Lookout, On., Can.	A6	118
Sioux Narrows, On., Can.	B4	118
Sioux Rapids, Ia., U.S.	B2	120
Sipalay, Phil.	F4	52
Sipan, Otok, i., Cro.	H14	22
Sipapo, stm., Ven.	E8	86
Siparia, Trin.	s12	105f
Šipčenski Prohod (Shipka Pass), p., Blg.	G12	26
Šipicyno, Russia	F22	8
Siping, China	C6	38
Sipiwesk Lake, l., Mb., Can.	D11	106
Siple, Mount, mtn., Ant.	C28	81
Siple Island, i., Ant.	C28	81
Si Prachan, Thai.	E4	48
Sipsey, stm., Al., U.S.	D10	122
Sipunskij, mys, c., Russia	F21	34
Sipura, Pulau, i., Indon.	E1	50
Siqueira Campos, Braz.	A12	92
Siquia, stm., Nic.	F5	102
Siquijor, Phil.	F4	52
Siquijor Island, i., Phil.	F4	52
Siquirres, C.R.	H5	102
Šira, India	E3	53
Šira, Russia	D16	32
Sira, stm., Nor.	G2	8
Si Racha, Thai.	F5	48
Siracusa, Italy	G9	24
Sirahā, Nepal	E11	54
Sirājganj, Bngl.	F12	54
Sir Bani Yās, i., U.A.E.	E7	56
Sir Douglas, Mount, mtn., Can.	F15	138
Sir Edward Pellew Group, is., Austl.	C7	74
Siret, Rom.	B12	26
Siret (Seret), stm., Eur.	A12	26
Sirhān, Wādī as-, val., Sau. Ar.	H8	58
Sirik, Tanjong, c., Malay.	B7	50
Sirikit Reservoir, res., Thai.	D5	48
Sirino, Monte, mtn., Italy	D9	24
Sir James MacBrien, Mount, mtn., N.T., Can.	C4	106
Sīrjān, Iran	D8	56
Sirkeli, Tur.	C15	28
Sirocina, Bela.	F13	10
Sirohi, India	F4	54
Širokovo, Russia	F14	34
Sironj, India	F6	54
Sırpsındığı, Tur.	B9	28
Sirri, Jazīreh-ye, i., Iran	D7	56
Sirsa, India	D5	54
Sir Sandford, Mount, mtn., B.C., Can.	E13	138
Sirsi, India	D2	53
Sirsilla, India	B4	53
Sirte, Gulf of see Surt, Khalīj, b., Libya	A3	62
Sir Timothy's Hill, hill, St. K./N.	C2	105a
Širupa, stm., Mex.	G8	98
Širvintos, Lith.	E7	10
Sisaket, Thai.	E7	48
Sisimiut see Holsteinsborg, Grnld.	D15	141
Siskiyou Pass, p., Or., U.S.	A3	134
Sisseton, S.D., U.S.	F1	118
Sīstān, reg., Asia	C9	56
Sister Bay, Wi., U.S.	C2	112
Sisteron, Fr.	E11	18
Sisters, Or., U.S.	F5	136
Sistersville, W.V., U.S.	E5	114
Sit', stm., Russia	B20	10
Sitāmarhi, India	E10	54
Sītāpur, India	E8	54
Siteia, Grc.	H9	28
Siteki, Swaz.	E10	70
Si Thep, sci., Thai.	E5	48
Sithonía, pen., Grc.	C6	28
Sitídgi Lake, l., N.T., Can.	B4	106
Sítio d'Abadia, Braz.	H2	88
Sitka, Ak., U.S.	E12	140
Sitkalidak Island, i., Ak., U.S.	E9	140
Sittard, Neth.	C14	14
Sittee see Sion, Switz.	D4	22
Sittoung, stm., Mya.	C3	48
Sittwe, Mya.	D7	46
Siuri, India	G11	54
Siuslaw, stm., Or., U.S.	G3	136
Sivaganga, India	G4	53
Sivakāsi, India	G3	53
Sivaki, Russia	F14	34
Sivas, Tur.	B4	56
Šiveluč, vulkan, vol., Russia	E21	34
Siverek, Tur.	B4	56
Siverskij, Russia	A12	10
Sivrihisar, Tur.	D14	28
Siwa, Egypt	B5	62
Siwalik Range, mts., India	C6	54
Siwān, India	E10	54
Sixian, China	E7	42
Sixth Cataract see Sablūkah, Shallāl as-, wtfl., Sudan	D6	62
Siyang, China	E8	42
Sizuoka see Shizuoka, Japan	E11	40
Sjælland, i., Den.	I4	8
Sjalec, Bela.	F19	8
Sjamža, Russia	F19	8
Sjarhevičy, Bela.	G10	10
Sjas', stm., Russia	A15	10
Sjas'stroj, Russia	F15	8
Sjenica, Serb.	F7	26
Sjuzikozero, Russia	F17	8
Skærfjorden, b., Grnld.	B22	141
Skaftafell Nasjonalpark, p.o.i., Ice.	k31	8a
Skagafjördur, b., Ice.	j31	8a
Skagen, Den.	H4	8
Skagerrak, strt., Eur.	H3	8
Skagit, stm., N.A.	H8	138
Skagway, Ak., U.S.	E12	140
Skaistkalne, Lat.	D7	10
Skalat, Ukr.	A10	26
Skalka, l., Swe.	C8	8
Skåne, state, Swe.	H5	8
Skärdu, Pak.	B12	56
Skarszewy, Pol.	B14	16
Skarżysko-Kamienna, Pol.	E16	16
Skeena, stm., B.C., Can.	B1	138
Skeena Crossing, B.C., Can.	A3	138
Skeena Mountains, mts., B.C., Can.	D5	106
Skegness, Eng., U.K.	H13	12
Skei, Nor.	F2	8
Skeleton Coast, cst., Nmb.	B1	70
Skellefteå, Swe.	D9	8
Skellefteälven, stm., Swe.	D8	8
Skellytown, Tx., U.S.	F7	128
Skerryvore, r., Scot., U.K.	E5	12
Ski, Nor.	G4	8
Skiatook, Ok., U.S.	H1	120
Skibbereen, Ire.	J3	12
Skidal', Bela.	G7	10
Skiddaw, mtn., Eng., U.K.	G9	12
Skidmore, Tx., U.S.	F10	130
Skien, Nor.	G3	8
Skierniewice, Pol.	E16	16
Skierniewice, state, Pol.	D16	16
Skikda, Alg.	B6	64
Skilak Lake, l., Ak., U.S.	D9	140
Skillet Fork, stm., Il., U.S.	F9	120
Skinnastaðir, Ice.	j31	8a
Skipton, Austl.	K4	76
Skipton, Eng., U.K.	H10	12
Skive, Den.	H3	8
Skjálfandafljót, stm., Ice.	k31	8a
Sklad, Russia	B13	34
Sklov, Bela.	F13	10
Skloŭ, Bela.	F13	10
Skofja Loka, Slvn.	D11	22
Skoganvarre, Nor.	B11	8
Skoganvarri see Skoganvarre, Nor.	B11	8
Skokie, Il., U.S.	F2	112
Skón, Camb.	F7	48
Skópelos, i., Grc.	D6	28
Skopin, Russia	D6	32
Skopje, Mac.	A4	28
Skopje see Skopje, Mac.	A4	28
Skórcz, Pol.	C14	16
Skövde, Swe.	G5	8
Skowhegan, Me., U.S.	F7	110
Skownan, Mb., Can.	C14	124
Skriplivska, Russia	E9	10
Skrudaliena, Lat.	E9	10
Skudeneshavn, Nor.	G1	8
Skukuza, S. Afr.	D10	70
Skull Valley, Az., U.S.	I4	132
Skuna, can., Ms., U.S.	D9	122
Skunk, stm., Ia., U.S.	D6	120
Skuodas, Lith.	D4	10
Skuratovskij, Russia	F20	10
Skvyra, Ukr.	D11	16
Skye, Island of, i., Scot., U.K.	D6	12
Skyland, N.C., U.S.	A3	116
Skyring, Península, pen., Chile	I1	90
Skyring, Seno, strt., Chile	J2	90
Skyros, i., Grc.	E7	28
Slabada, Bela.	G11	10
Slagelse, Den.	I4	8
Slagnäs, Swe.	D8	8
Slamet, Gunung, vol., Indon.	G6	50
Slancy, Russia	A11	10
Slaney, stm., Ire.	H6	12
Slănic, Rom.	D12	26
Slano, Cro.	H14	22
Slaný, Czech Rep.	F10	16
Slater, Ia., U.S.	C4	120
Slater, Mo., U.S.	E4	120
Slatina, Cro.	E14	22
Slatina, Rom.	E11	26
Slaughter, La., U.S.	G7	122
Slaunae, Bela.	F12	10
Slautnoe, Russia	D22	34
Slave Coast, cst., Afr.	H5	64
Slave Lake, Ab., Can.	A16	138
Slavgorod, Russia	D13	32
Slavjanka, Russia	C9	38
Slavjansk-na-Kubani, Russia	E5	32
Slavkovičy, Russia	C12	10
Slavonia see Slavonija, hist. reg., Cro.	E14	22
Slavonija, hist. reg., Cro.	E14	22
Slavonski Brod, Cro.	E15	22
Slavsk, Russia	E4	10
Sławno, Pol.	B12	16
Slayton, Mn., U.S.	G3	118
Sleaford, Eng., U.K.	H12	12
Sledge, Ms., U.S.	C8	122
Sledzjuki, Bela.	G13	10
Sleeper Islands, is., Nu., Can.	D14	106
Sleeping Bear Dunes National Lakeshore, p.o.i., Mi., U.S.	D3	112
Sleepy Eye, Mn., U.S.	G4	118
Slesin, Pol.	D14	16
Slidell, La., U.S.	G9	122
Slide Mountain, mtn., N.Y., U.S.	B11	114
Sliema, Malta	I8	24
Slievekimalta, mtn., Ire.	I4	12
Sligeach see Sligo, Ire.	G4	12
Sligo, Ire.	G4	12
Sligo, Pa., U.S.	C6	114
Sligo, state, Ire.	G4	12
Sligo Bay, b., Ire.	G4	12
Slinger, Wi., U.S.	H10	118
Slíno, ozero, l., Russia	C16	10
Slippery Rock, Pa., U.S.	C5	114
Slīteres Rezervāts, Lat.	C5	10
Sliven, Blg.	G13	26
Sljudjanka, Russia	D18	32
Sloan, Nv., U.S.	H1	132
Slobidka, Ukr.	B16	26
Slobodskoj, Russia	C8	32
Slobozia, Mol.	C16	26
Slobozia, Rom.	E14	26
Slobozia, Rom.	F12	26
Slocan, B.C., Can.	G13	138
Slocan Lake, l., B.C., Can.	G13	138
Slocomb, Al., U.S.	F13	122
Słomniki, Pol.	F15	16
Slonim, Bela.	G8	10
Slough, Eng., U.K.	J12	12
Slovakia, ctry., Eur.	H14	16
Slovak Republic see Slovakia, ctry., Eur.	H14	16
Slovenia, ctry., Eur.	E11	22
Slovenia see Slovenia, ctry., Eur.	E11	22
Slovenské rudohorie, mts., Slov.	H15	16
Slov'ians'k, Ukr.	E5	32
Slovinka, Russia	G20	8
Słowiński Park Narodowy, p.o.i., Pol.	B13	16
Slubice, Pol.	D10	16
Sluč, stm., Bela.	H10	10
Sluck, Bela.	G10	10
Šluknov, Czech Rep.	E10	16
Slupca, Russia	D13	16
Słupca, Pol.	D13	16
Słupsk (Stolp), Pol.	B13	16
Słupsk, state, Pol.	B13	16
Slutsk see Sluck, Bela.	G10	10
Småландsfarvandet, b., Den.	I4	8
Smalininkai, Lith.	E5	10
Smaljavičy, Bela.	F10	10
Smallwood Reservoir, res., Nf., Can.	E18	106
Smalouka, Bela.	E13	10
Smarhon', Bela.	F9	10
Smederevo, Serb.	E7	26
Smeralda, Costa, cst., Italy	C3	24
Smethport, Pa., U.S.	C7	114
Šmidovič, Russia	G15	34
Šmidta, poluostrov, pen., Russia	F17	34
Šmigiel, Pol.	D12	16
Smila, Ukr.	E4	32
Smiley, Sk., Can.	C4	124
Smiley, Tx., U.S.	E10	130
Smiltene, Lat.	C8	10
Smith, stm., Ca., U.S.	A16	138
Smith, stm., Ca., U.S.	B2	134
Smith, stm., Mt., U.S.	C15	136
Smith, stm., Or., U.S.	G2	136
Smith, stm., Va., U.S.	H5	114
Smith Arm, b., N.T., Can.	B6	106
Smith Bay, b., Nu., Can.	B10	141
Smith Bay, b., Ak., U.S.	B9	140
Smith Canyon, p., Co., U.S.	D5	128
Smith Center, Ks., U.S.	B9	128
Smithers, B.C., Can.	B3	138
Smithfield, S. Afr.	G8	70
Smithfield, N.C., U.S.	A7	116
Smithfield, Ut., U.S.	B5	132
Smith Island see Sumisu-jima, i., Japan	E13	38
Smith Island, i., N.C., U.S.	C8	116
Smithland, Ky., U.S.	G9	120
Smith Mountain Lake, res., Va., U.S.	G6	114
Smith Point, c., N.S., Can.	E13	110
Smith River, Ca., U.S.	B1	134
Smiths, Al., U.S.	E13	122
Smiths Falls, On., Can.	D13	112
Smiths Grove, Ky., U.S.	G11	120
Smithton, Austl.	n12	77a
Smithville, Ga., U.S.	E1	116
Smithville, Ms., U.S.	C10	122
Smithville, Tn., U.S.	I12	120
Smithville, Tx., U.S.	D10	130
Smjadovo, Blg.	F14	26
Smoke Creek Desert, des., Nv., U.S.	C6	134
Smokey, Cape, c., N.S., Can.	D16	110
Smoky, stm., Ab., Can.	A12	138
Smoky Cape, c., Austl.	H9	76
Smoky Dome, mtn., Id., U.S.	G12	136
Smoky Hill, stm., U.S.	B7	128
Smoky Lake, Ab., Can.	B18	138
Smoky Hill, North Fork, stm., U.S.	B7	128
Smøla, i., Nor.	E2	8
Smolensk, Russia	F15	10
Smolenskaja-Moskovskaja vozvyšennost', plat., Eur.	F15	10
Smolenskaja oblast', co., Russia	F15	10
Smoljan, Blg.	H11	26
Smoot, Wy., U.S.	H16	136
Smoothrock Lake, l., On., Can.	A9	118
Smorodovka, Russia	C12	10
Smyrna see İzmir, Tur.	E10	28
Smyrna, De., U.S.	E10	114
Smyrna, Ga., U.S.	D14	122
Smyrna, Tn., U.S.	I11	120
Smythe, Mount, mtn., B.C., Can.	D6	106
Snæfell, mtn., Ice.	k32	8a
Snaefell, mtn., I. of Man	G8	12
Snæfellsnes, pen., Ice.	k28	8a
Snag, Yk., Can.	C3	106
Snake, stm., Mn., Can.	B4	106
Snake, stm., U.S.	E5	118
Snake Creek, stm., S.D., U.S.	B14	104
Snake River Plain, pl., Id., U.S.	D3	132
Snake Valley, val., U.S.	D3	132
Snares Islands, is., N.Z.	D4	8
Snåsavatnet, l., Nor.	D4	8
Sneads, Fl., U.S.	G13	122
Sneedville, Tn., U.S.	H2	114
Sneek, Neth.	A14	14
Snežka, mtn., Czech Rep.	F11	16
Sniardwy, Jezioro, l., Pol.	C17	16
Sniatyn, Ukr.	A12	26
Snina, Slov.	G18	16
Snohomish, Wa., U.S.	C4	136
Snoul, Camb.	F8	48
Snoqualmie Pass, p., Wa., U.S.	C5	136
Snøtinden, mtn., Nor.	C5	8
Snov, stm., Eur.	H15	10
Snover, Mi., U.S.	E7	112
Snowbird Lake, l., N.T., Can.	C10	106
Snowdon, mtn., Wales, U.K.	H8	12
Snowdonia National Park, p.o.i., Wales, U.K.	I8	12
Snowflake, Az., U.S.	I6	132
Snow Hill, Md., U.S.	F10	114
Snow Hill, N.C., U.S.	A8	116
Snow Lake, Mb., Can.	E10	106
Snowmass Mountain, mtn., Co., U.S.	D9	132
Snow Mountain, mtn., Ca., U.S.	D3	134
Snowtown, Austl.	I2	76
Snowy, stm., Austl.	K7	76
Snowy Mountain, mtn., N.Y., U.S.	G2	110
Snowy Mountains, mts., Austl.	K7	76
Snowy River National Park, p.o.i., Austl.	K6	76
Snuõl, Camb.	F8	48
Snyder, Ok., U.S.	G10	128
Snyder, Tx., U.S.	B7	130
Soacha, Col.	E4	86
Soalala, Madag.	D8	68
Soap Lake, Wa., U.S.	C7	136
Soavinandriana, Madag.	D8	68
Sobaek-sanmaek, mts., Kor., S.	C1	40
Soběslav, Czech Rep.	G10	16
Sobinka, Russia	I19	8
Sobradinho, Braz.	F22	8
Sobradinho, Represa de, res., Braz.	E5	88
Sobral, Braz.	B5	88
Sobrance, Slov.	H18	16
Sobrarbe, hist. reg., Spain	B10	20
Sochaczew, Pol.	D16	16
Soch'e see Shache, China	B12	56
Soči, Russia	F5	32
Société, Archipel de la (Society Islands), is., Fr. Poly.	E11	72
Society Hill, S.C., U.S.	B6	116
Society Islands see Société, Archipel de la, is., Fr. Poly.	E11	72
Soco, stm., Dom. Rep.	C13	102
Socompa, Paso (Socompa, Portezuelo de), p., S.A.	B3	92
Socompa, Portezuelo de (Socompa, Paso), p., S.A.	B3	92
Soconusco, Sierra de see Madre de Chiapas, Sierra, mts., N.A.	G12	100
Socorro, Col.	D5	86
Socorro, N.M., U.S.	I10	132
Socorro, Tx., U.S.	C10	130
Socorro, Isla, i., Mex.	F3	100
Socotra see Suqutrā, i., Yemen	G7	56
Soc Trang, Viet.	H8	48
Socuéllamos, Spain	E8	20
Soda Creek, B.C., Can.	D8	138
Soda Lake, l., Ca., U.S.	H9	134
Sodankylä, Fin.	C12	8
Soda Springs, Id., U.S.	H15	136
Søderham, Swe.	F7	8
Södermanland, state, Swe.	G7	8
Södertälje, Swe.	G7	8
Sodo, Eth.	F7	62
Sodom see Sedom, hist., Isr.	G6	58
Sodus, N.Y., U.S.	E12	112
Sodwana Bay National Park, p.o.i., S. Afr.	E11	70
Soe, Indon.	G7	44
Soekmekaar, S. Afr.	C9	70
Soest, Ger.	E4	16
Soest, Neth.	B14	14
Sofala, Moz.	B12	70
Sofala, state, Moz.	B12	70
Sofia see Sofija, Blg.	G10	26
Sofia, stm., Madag.	D8	68
Sofija (Sofia), Blg.	G10	26
Sofija, state, Blg.	G10	26
Sofijsk, Russia	F16	34
Sofjanga, Russia	D14	8
Sofronovo, Russia	D20	10
Sogamoso, Col.	E5	86
Sogamoso, stm., Col.	D5	86
Soğanlı, stm., Tur.	C15	28
Sogda, Russia	F15	34
Sognefjorden, b., Nor.	F1	8
Sogn og Fjordane, state, Nor.	F2	8
Sogod, Phil.	E5	52
Sogo Nur, l., China	C5	36
Sogoža, stm., Russia	B22	10
Soguksu Milli Parkı, p.o.i., Tur.	C15	28
Sögüt, Phil.	F12	28
Söğüt Gölü, l., Tur.	F12	28
Söğütlü, Tur.	C13	28
Sog Xian, China	E3	36
Sohâg, Egypt	B6	62
Sohna, India	D6	54
Sohor, gora, mtn., Russia	F10	34
Soignies, Bel.	D12	14
Sointula, B.C., Can.	F4	138
Soira, mtn., Erit.	E7	62
Soissons, Fr.	E12	14
Sojana, Russia	D20	8
Sojat, India	F4	54
Sojna, Russia	D22	8
Sojŏsǒn-man, b., Kor., N.	E6	38
Sokch'o, Kor., S.	A1	40
Söke, Tur.	F10	28
Sokele, D.R.C.	F4	66
Sokodé, Togo	H5	64
Sokol, Russia	G19	8
Sokol, Russia	B14	34
Sokol, Russia	C19	16
Sokolov, Czech Rep.	F8	16
Sokołów Małopolski, Pol.	F18	16
Sokone, Sen.	G1	64
Sokoto, Nig.	G6	64
Sokoto, stm., Nig.	G5	64
Sokyriany, Ukr.	A14	26
Sol, Costa del, cst., Spain	H5	20
Sola, Vanuatu	i16	79d
Solai, Kenya	D7	66
Solan, India	C6	54
Solana, Fl., U.S.	J3	116
Solānki, Phil.	B3	52
Solāpur, India	C2	53
Solca, Rom.	B12	26
Soldier, stm., Ia., U.S.	B2	120
Soldiers Grove, Wi., U.S.	H8	118
Soldotna, Ak., U.S.	D9	140
Soledad, Col.	B4	86
Soledad, Ca., U.S.	G4	134
Soledad, Ven.	C10	86
Soledad Díez Gutiérrez, Mex.	D8	100
Soledade, Braz.	D11	92
Soledad Pass, p., Ca., U.S.	I7	134
Solen, N.D., U.S.	A12	126
Solenzara, Fr.	H15	18
Soleure see Solothurn, Switz.	C4	22
Solginskij, Russia	E19	8
Soligalič, Russia	G19	8
Soligorsk see Salihorsk, Bela.	H10	10
Sol'-Ileck, Russia	D8	32
Solihull, Eng., U.K.	I11	12
Solikamsk, Russia	C9	32
Soliman, Tun.	H4	24
Solingen, Ger.	E3	16
Solís de Mataojo, Ur.	G10	92
Sollefteå, Swe.	E7	8
Sollentuna, Swe.	G7	8
Sóller, Spain	E13	20
Solnečnogorsk, Russia	D19	10
Sologne, reg., Fr.	G10	14
Sologoncy, Russia	C11	34
Solok, Indon.	D2	50
Solomennoe, Russia	F16	8
Solomon, Az., U.S.	K7	132
Solomon, stm., Ks., U.S.	B11	128
Solomon, North Fork, stm., Ks., U.S.	B10	128
Solomon, South Fork, stm., Ks., U.S.	B10	128
Solomon Basin, unds.	J18	142
Solomon Islands, ctry., Oc.	D7	72
Solomon Islands, is., Oc.	d7	79b
Solomon Sea, s., Oc.	D6	72
Solomon's Pools see Sulaymān, Birak, sci., W.B.	G5	58
Solon, China	B9	36
Solon, Ia., U.S.	C6	120
Solon, Me., U.S.	F7	110
Solothurn, Switz.	C4	22
Soloveckie ostrova, is., Russia	D16	8
Solov'evsk, Russia	F12	34
Solov'evsk, Russia	F13	34
Solsona, Spain	C12	20
Šolta, Otok, i., Cro.	G13	22
Soltănābād, Iran	B8	56
Soltau, Ger.	C5	16
Solvang, Ca., U.S.	I5	134
Solvay, N.Y., U.S.	A9	114
Sol'vyčegodsk, Russia	F22	8
Solway Firth, b., U.K.	G9	12
Solwezi, Zam.	C4	68
Solza, Russia	D18	8
Söma, Japan	B13	40
Soma, Tur.	D10	28
Somabhula, Zimb.	D4	68
Somália, ctry., Afr.	D9	66
Somali Basin, unds.	I8	142
Somaliland see Somalia, ctry., Afr.	D9	66
Somali Republic see Somalia, ctry., Afr.	D9	66
Sombo, Ang.	B3	68
Sombor, Serb.	D6	26
Sombrerete, Mex.	D7	100
Sombretillo, Mex.	H7	130
Sombrio, Braz.	D13	92
Sombrio, Lagoa do, l., Braz.	D13	92
Somdari, India	F4	54
Somerset, Austl.	n12	77a
Somerset, Co., U.S.	E9	132
Somerset, Ky., U.S.	G13	120
Somerset, Oh., U.S.	E3	114
Somerset, Pa., U.S.	D6	114
Somerset, Tx., U.S.	E9	130
Somerset East, S. Afr.	H7	70
Somerset Island, i., Nu., Can.	A12	106
Somerset West, S. Afr.	I4	70
Somers Point, N.J., U.S.	E11	114
Somersworth, N.H., U.S.	G5	110
Somerton, Az., U.S.	K2	132
Somerville, N.J., U.S.	D11	114
Somerville, Tn., U.S.	B9	122
Somerville, Tx., U.S.	G2	122
Somerville Lake, res., Tx., U.S.	D11	130
Somes (Szamos), stm., Eur.	B9	26
Sominо, Russia	A17	10
Somme, state, Fr.	D11	14
Somme, stm., Fr.	E11	14
Somme, Baie de la, b., Fr.	D10	14
Sommen, l., Swe.	H6	8
Sömmerda, Ger.	E7	16
Somogy, state, Hung.	C4	26
Somosierra, Puerto de, p., Spain	C7	20
Somosomo, Fiji	p20	79e
Somosomo Strait, strt., Fiji	p19	79e
Somoto, Nic.	F4	102
Somovo, Russia	H17	10
Somport, Col du (Somport, Puerto de), p., Eur.	G5	18
Somport, Puerto de (Somport, Col du), p., Eur.	G5	18
Sompuis, Fr.	F13	14
Son, stm., India	F10	54
Sonāmukhi, India	A5	54
Soná, Pan.	H7	102
Sonāmura, India	G14	54
Sönch'ŏn-ŭp, Kor., N.	E6	38
Sønderborg, Den.	I3	8
Sønderjylland, state, Den.	I3	8
Sondershausen, Ger.	E6	16
Søndre Strømfjord, Grnld.	D15	141
Sonepur, India	H9	54
Song, Nig.	H7	64
Song, Thai.	C5	48
Song Bay Hap, Cua, b., Viet.	H7	48
Song Cau, Viet.	F9	48
Song Da see Black, stm., Asia	D9	46
Songea, Tan.	G7	66
Songe, Nor.	G3	8
Song Hong see Red, stm., Asia	D9	46
Songhua, stm., China	B11	36
Songhua Hu, res., China	C7	38
Songjiang, China	F9	42
Songjiu, Kor., S.	B1	40
Songkhla, Thai.	I5	48
Songkhram, stm., Thai.	C6	48
Songlinba, China	I6	42
Sŏngnam, Kor., S.	F7	38
Sŏngnim, Kor., N.	E6	38
Songpan, China	E5	36
Song Phi Nong, Thai.	E4	48
Songololo, D.R.C.	F2	66
Songxi, China	H8	42
Songxian, China	D4	42
Sonid Zuoqi, China	C7	36
Sonīpat, India	D6	54
Son La, Viet.	B6	48
Sonmiāni, Pak.	D10	56
Sonmiāni Bay, b., Pak.	D10	56
Sonneberg, Ger.	F7	16
Sonningdale, Sk., Can.	B6	124
Sono, stm., Braz.	E1	88
Sono, stm., Braz.	G2	88
Sonora, Ca., U.S.	F5	134
Sonora, Tx., U.S.	D7	130
Sonora, state, Mex.	A3	100
Sonora, stm., Mex.	A3	100
Sonora, Desierto de, des., N.A.	F6	98
Sonoyta, Mex.	F6	98
Sonqor, Iran	C6	56
Sonseca, Spain	E6	20
Sonsonate, El Sal.	F3	102
Sonsorol Islands, is., Palau	D9	44
Sonstraal, S. Afr.	E6	70
Son Tay, Viet.	B7	48
Sonthofen, Ger.	I6	16
Sooke, B.C., Can.	H7	138
Sooner Lake, res., Ok., U.S.	A12	122
Sopchoppy, Fl., U.S.	G14	122
Soperton, Ga., U.S.	D3	116
Sopki, Russia	C13	10
Sopot, Pol.	B14	16

Name	Map Ref.	Page
Sop Pong, Laos.	A6	48
Sopron, Hung.	B3	26
Sopur, India.	A5	54
Sora, Italy.	I10	22
Sorada, India.	I10	54
Sorata, Bol.	C3	90
Sorbhog, India.	E13	54
Sorel, Qc., Can.	D3	110
Sorell, Cape, c., Austl.	o12	77a
Sørfold, Nor.	C6	8
Sorgues, Fr.	E10	18
Soria, Spain.	C8	20
Soria, co., Spain.	C8	20
Soriano, Ur.	F8	92
Sørli, Nor.	D5	8
Sorø, Den.	I4	8
Soro, India.	H11	54
Soro, Monte, mtn., Italy.	G8	24
Soroca, Braz.	L2	88
Sorocaba, Braz.	D8	92
Sorochinsk, Russia.	D8	32
Soroco, P.R.	B4	104a
Sorol, at., Micron.	C5	72
Soron, India.	E7	54
Sorong, Indon.	F9	44
Sororó, stm., Braz.	C1	88
Sorot', stm., Russia.	C12	10
Soroti, Ug.	D6	66
Sørøya, i., Nor.	A10	8
Sorrento, Italy.	D8	24
Sorsa, La., U.S.	G8	122
Sorris-Sorris, Nmb.	B2	70
Sor Rondane Mountains, mts., Ant.	C7	81
Sorsk, Russia.	D16	32
Sorso, Russia.	D2	24
Sorsogon, Phil.	D4	52
Sort, Spain.	B12	20
Sortavala, Russia.	F14	8
Sør-Trøndelag, state, Nor.	E4	8
Sõrve neem, c., Est.	C4	10
Šoša, stm., Russia.	D18	10
Sos del Rey Católico, Spain.	B9	20
Soskovo, Russia.	H18	10
Sosna, stm., Russia.	H21	10
Sosneado, Cerro, mtn., Arg.	G3	92
Sosnogorsk, Russia.	B8	32
Sosnovec, Russia.	D15	8
Sosnovka, Kaz.	D13	32
Sosnovka, Russia.	C19	8
Sosnovo-Ozërskoe, Russia.	F11	34
Sosnovskoe, Russia.	I20	8
Sosnovyj Bor, Russia.	A11	10
Sosnowiec, Pol.	F15	16
Soso, Ms., U.S.	F9	122
Sos'va, Russia.	B10	32
Sotkamo, Fin.	D13	8
Soto, Mex.	F1	130
Soto la Marina, Mex.	D9	100
Soto la Marina, Barra, i., Mex.	C10	100
Sotra see Store Sotra, i., Nor.	F1	8
Sotteville-lès-Rouen, Fr.	E9	14
Souanké, Congo.	D2	66
Soubré, C. Iv.	H3	64
Soudan, Austl.	D7	74
Souderton, Pa., U.S.	D10	114
Soufrière, St. Luc.	m6	105c
Soufrière, vol., Guad.	h5	105c
Soufrière, vol., St. Vin.	o11	105e
Soufrière Hills, vol., Monts.	i13	105a
Souillac, Fr.	E7	18
Sŏul (Seoul), Kor., S.	F7	38
Soulac-sur-Mer, Fr.	D4	18
Sound, The, strt., Eur.	I5	8
Sounding Creek, stm., Ab., Can.	E19	138
Sounding Lake, l., Ab., Can.	B3	124
Sources, Mont-aux- (Phofung), mtn., Afr.	F9	70
Soure, Braz.	D8	84
Sour el Ghozlane, Alg.	H14	20
Souris, Mb., Can.	E13	124
Souris, stm., N.A.	E13	124
Sourlake, Tx., U.S.	G4	122
Sourland Mountain, hill, N.J., U.S.	D11	114
Sousa, Braz.	D6	88
Sousel, Port.	F3	20
Sousse, Tun.	I4	24
Sout, stm., S. Afr.	H6	70
South, stm., N.C., U.S.	B7	116
South America, cont.	G9	4
Southampton, On., Can.	D8	112
Southampton, Eng., U.K.	K11	12
Southampton, N.Y., U.S.	D13	114
Southampton, Cape, c., Nu., Can.	C13	106
Southampton Island, i., Nu., Can.	C14	106
South Andaman, i., India.	F7	46
South Anna, stm., Va., U.S.	G8	114
South Antler Creek see Antler, stm., N.A.	E12	124
South Australia, state, Austl.	E6	74
South Australian Basin, unds.	M15	142
Southaven, Ms., U.S.	B8	122
South Baldy, mtn., N.M., U.S.	J9	132
Southbank, B.C., Can.	C5	138
South Bay, Fl., U.S.	J5	116
South Bay, b., Nu., Can.	C14	106
South Baymouth, On., Can.	C7	112
South Bend, In., U.S.	G3	112
South Bend, Wa., U.S.	D3	136
South Bohemia see Jihočeský kraj, state, Czech Rep.	G10	16
South Borneo see Kalimantan Selatan, state, Indon.	E9	50
South Boston, Va., U.S.	H6	114
Southbridge, N.Z.	F5	80
Southbridge, Ma., U.S.	B13	114
South Brookfield, N.S., Can.	F11	110
South Bruny Island, i., Austl.	o13	77a
South Burlington, Vt., U.S.	F3	110
South Carolina, state, U.S.	B5	116
South Charleston, W.V., U.S.	F4	114
South China Basin, unds.	H14	142
South China Sea, s., Asia.	H15	30
South Dakota, state, U.S.	C12	126
South Downs, hills, Eng., U.K.	K12	12
South East, state, Bots.	D7	70
South East Cape, c., Austl.	o13	77a
Southeast Indian Ridge, unds.	N12	142
Southeast Pacific Basin, unds.	P25	142
South East Point, c., Austl.	L6	76
Southend-on-Sea, Eng., U.K.	J13	12
Southern, state, Bots.	D7	70
Southern see HaDarom, state, Isr.	H5	58
Southern Alps, mts., N.Z.	F4	80
Southern Bug see Pivdennyy Buh, stm., Ukr.	A17	26
Southern Cook Islands, is., Cook Is.	E10	72
Southern Cross, Austl.	F3	74
Southern Ghāts, mts., India.	G3	53
Southern Indian Lake, l., Mb., Can.	D10	106
Southern Ocean.	P8	142
Southern Pines, N.C., U.S.	A6	116
South Esk, stm., Austl.	n13	77a
South Fabius, stm., Mo., U.S.	E6	120
South Fallsburg, N.Y., U.S.	C11	114
Southfield, Mi., U.S.	B2	114
South Fiji Basin, unds.	L20	142
South Foreland, c., Eng., U.K.	J14	12
South Fork, Co., U.S.	F10	132
South Fulton, Tn., U.S.	H8	120
Southgate, Mi., U.S.	B2	114
South Georgia, i., S. Geor.	J9	90
South Georgia and the South Sandwich Islands, dep., S.A.	K11	82
South Grand, stm., Mo., U.S.	F3	120
South Hatia Island, i., Bngl.	G13	54
South Haven, Mi., U.S.	F3	112
South Henderson, N.C., U.S.	H7	114
South Henik Lake, l., Nu., Can.	C11	106
South Hero, Vt., U.S.	F3	110
South Hill Village, Anguilla.	A1	105a
South Holston Lake, res., U.S.	H3	114
South Honshu Ridge, unds.	G16	142
South Houston, Tx., U.S.	H3	122
South Indian Basin, unds.	O12	142
South Indian Lake, Mb., Can.	D11	106
South International Falls, Mn., U.S.	C5	118
South Island, i., N.Z.	G5	80
South Konkan Hills, hills, India.	C1	53
South Korea see Korea, South, ctry., Asia.	G8	38
South Lake Tahoe, Ca., U.S.	E5	134
Southland, Tx., U.S.	H7	128
Southlawn, Il., U.S.	E8	120
South Llano, stm., Tx., U.S.	D8	130
South Loup, stm., Ne., U.S.	F13	126
South Lyon, Mi., U.S.	F6	112
South Magnetic Pole, misc. cult.	B18	81
South Manitou Island, i., Mi., U.S.	C3	112
South Miami, Fl., U.S.	K5	116
South Milwaukee, Wi., U.S.	F2	112
South Moravia see Jihomoravský kraj, state, Czech Rep.	G12	16
South Nahanni, stm., N.T., Can.	C5	106
South Nation, stm., On., Can.	C14	112
South Negril Point, c., Jam.	i12	104d
South Ogden, Ut., U.S.	B5	132
South Orkney Islands, is., Ant.	B36	81
South Paris, Me., U.S.	F6	110
South Pass, p., Wy., U.S.	E4	126
South Pekin, Il., U.S.	D8	120
South Pittsburg, Tn., U.S.	B13	122
South Platte, stm., U.S.	F11	126
South Point, c., Barb.	n8	105d
South Pole, misc. cult., Ant.	D1	81
Southport (Gold Coast), Austl.	F9	76
Southport, Austl.	o13	77a
Southport, Eng., U.K.	H9	12
Southport, In., U.S.	E11	120
Southport, N.C., U.S.	C7	116
South Portland, Me., U.S.	G6	110
South River, On., Can.	C10	112
South Ronaldsay, i., Scot., U.K.	C10	12
South Sandwich Islands, is., S. Geor.	K11	82
South Sandwich Trench, unds.	N11	144
South Saskatchewan, stm., Can.	A8	124
South Shetland Islands, is., Ant.	B35	81
South Sioux City, Ne., U.S.	I2	118
South Skunk, stm., Ia., U.S.	C5	120
South Slocan, B.C., Can.	G13	138
South Sound, b., Br. Vir. Is.	e9	104b
South Spicer Island, i., Nu., Can.	B15	106
South Sulphur, stm., Tx., U.S.	D3	122
South Sumatra see Sumatera Selatan, state, Indon.	E4	50
South Taranaki Bight, b., N.Z.	D5	80
South Tasman Rise, unds.	N17	142
South Thompson, stm., B.C., Can.	F11	138
South Torrington, Wy., U.S.	E8	126
South Uist, i., Scot., U.K.	D5	12
South Umpqua, stm., Or., U.S.	G3	136
South Ventana Cone, mtn., Ca., U.S.	G4	134
South Vietnam see Vietnam, ctry., Asia.	E9	48
South West Africa see Namibia, ctry., Afr.	E2	68
South West Cape, c., Austl.	o12	77a
South West Cape, c., N.Z.	H2	80
South West City, Mo., U.S.	H3	120
Southwest Harbor, Me., U.S.	F8	110
Southwest Indian Ridge, unds.	M8	142
Southwest Miramichi, stm., N.B., Can.	D10	110
Southwest National Park, p.o.i., Austl.	o12	77a
Southwest Pacific Basin, unds.	M23	142
Southwest Point, c., Bah.	K8	116
South Whitley, In., U.S.	G4	112
South Wichita, stm., Tx., U.S.	H9	128
South Windham, Me., U.S.	G6	110
Southwold, Eng., U.K.	I14	12
Soutpansberg, mts., S. Afr.	C9	70
Sovata, Rom.	C11	26
Sovetsk, Russia.	G20	10
Sovetsk, Russia.	E4	10
Sovetskaja Gavan', Russia.	G17	34
Sovetskij, Russia.	F13	8
Sovpole, Russia.	D20	8
Sowa Pan, pl., Bots.	B7	70
Soweto, S. Afr.	E8	70
Sōya-misaki, c., Japan.	B14	38
Soyang-chosuji, res., Kor., S.	F7	38
Sozh, stm., Eur.	B10	10
Sozimskij, Russia.	C8	32
Sozopol, Blg.	G14	26
Spa, Bel.	D14	14
Spain, ctry., Eur.	E7	20
Spalding, Sk., Can.	B9	124
Spalding, Eng., U.K.	I12	12
Spanish, On., Can.	B7	112
Spanish, stm., On., Can.	B8	112
Spanish Fork, Ut., U.S.	C5	132
Spanish Point, c., Ber.	k15	104e
Spanish Sahara see Western Sahara, dep., Afr.	E2	64
Spanish Town, Br. Vir. Is.	e9	104b
Spanish Town, Jam.	i13	104d
Spánta, Ákra, c., Grc.	H6	28
Sparkman, Ar., U.S.	D6	122
Sparks, Nv., U.S.	D6	134
Sparland, Il., U.S.	C8	120
Sparlingville, Mi., U.S.	F7	112
Sparrows Point, Md., U.S.	E9	114
Sparta, Ga., U.S.	C3	116
Sparta see Spárti, Grc.	F5	28
Sparta, Ky., U.S.	H4	114
Sparta, N.J., U.S.	C11	114
Sparta, Tn., U.S.	I12	120
Sparta, Wi., U.S.	H8	118
Spartanburg, S.C., U.S.	B4	116
Spárti, Grc.	F5	28
Spartivento, Capo, c., Italy.	G10	24
Spartivento, Capo, c., Italy.	F2	24
Spas-Klepiki, Russia.	I19	8
Spassk-Dal'nij, Russia.	B10	38
Spearfish, S.D., U.S.	C8	126
Spearville, Ks., U.S.	D9	128
Spednic Lake, l., N.A.	E9	110
Speedway, In., U.S.	I3	112
Speightstown, Barb.	n8	105d
Speikkogel, mtn., Aus.	C12	22
Speke Gulf, b., Tan.	E6	66
Spencer, Ia., U.S.	H3	118
Spencer, In., U.S.	E11	120
Spencer, Ne., U.S.	E14	126
Spencer, W.V., U.S.	F4	114
Spencer, Cape, c., Austl.	G7	74
Spencer, Cape, c., N.B., Can.	E11	110
Spencer Gulf, b., Austl.	F7	74
Spencerville, Oh., U.S.	D1	114
Spences Bridge, B.C., Can.	F9	138
Speos (Rock Tombs), hist., Egypt.	K1	58
Sperryville, Va., U.S.	F7	114
Spétses, i., Grc.	F6	28
Spey, stm., Scot., U.K.	D9	12
Speyer, Ger.	G4	16
Spezia see La Spezia, Italy.	F6	22
Spezzano Albanese, Italy.	E10	24
Sphinx see Abū el-Hul, hist., Egypt.	I1	58
Spickard, Mo., U.S.	D4	120
Spilimbergo, Italy.	D9	22
Spillville, Ia., U.S.	A5	120
Spinazzola, Italy.	D10	24
Spindale, N.C., U.S.	A4	116
Spires see Speyer, Ger.	G4	16
Spirit Lake, Ia., U.S.	H3	118
Spirit Lake, l., Ia., U.S.	D7	106
Spiro, Ok., U.S.	B4	122
Spišská Nová Ves, Slov.	H16	16
Spitsbergen, i., Nor.	B4	30
Spitsbergen Bank, unds.	B5	142
Spittal an der Drau, Aus.	D10	22
Split, Cro.	G13	22
Split Lake, l., Mb., Can.	D11	106
Spokane, Wa., U.S.	C9	136
Spokane, stm., U.S.	C8	136
Spoleto, Italy.	H9	22
Spoon, stm., Il., U.S.	D7	120
Spooner, Wi., U.S.	F8	118
Sporava, Bela.	H8	10
Spornoe, Russia.	D19	34
Spotsylvania, Va., U.S.	F8	114
Sprague, Wa., U.S.	C9	136
Spratly Islands, is., Asia.	D5	44
Spray, Or., U.S.	F7	136
Spree, stm., Ger.	E10	16
Spremberg, Ger.	E10	16
Spring, Tx., U.S.	G3	122
Spring, stm., U.S.	H3	120
Spring, South Fork, stm., U.S.	H6	120
Springbok, S. Afr.	F3	70
Spring City, Tn., U.S.	B14	122
Spring City, Ut., U.S.	D5	132
Spring Creek, stm., Austl.	D3	76
Spring Creek, stm., N.D., U.S.	G11	124
Spring Creek, stm., S.D., U.S.	C8	134
Springdale, Nf., Can.	j22	107a
Springdale, Ar., U.S.	H3	120
Springdale, Ut., U.S.	F4	132
Springe, Ger.	D5	16
Springerville, Az., U.S.	I7	132
Springfield, N.S., Can.	F12	110
Springfield, Co., U.S.	D6	128
Springfield, Fl., U.S.	G13	122
Springfield, Ga., U.S.	D4	116
Springfield, Il., U.S.	E8	120
Springfield, Ma., U.S.	B13	114
Springfield, Mn., U.S.	G4	118
Springfield, Mo., U.S.	G4	120
Springfield, Oh., U.S.	E2	114
Springfield, Or., U.S.	F3	136
Springfield, S.C., U.S.	C4	116
Springfield, S.D., U.S.	E14	126
Springfield, Tn., U.S.	H10	120
Springfontein, S. Afr.	G7	70
Spring Glen, Ut., U.S.	D5	132
Spring Green, Wi., U.S.	A7	120
Spring Grove, Mn., U.S.	H7	118
Springhill, N.S., Can.	E12	110
Springhill, La., U.S.	D5	122
Spring Hope, N.C., U.S.	I7	114
Springhouse, B.C., Can.	E8	138
Spring Lake, N.C., U.S.	A7	116
Springs, S. Afr.	E9	70
Springsure, Austl.	D7	76
Springvale, Austl.	D3	76
Springvale, Me., U.S.	G6	110
Spring Valley, Ca., U.S.	K9	134
Spring Valley, Il., U.S.	J9	118
Spring Valley, N.Y., U.S.	C11	114
Spring Valley, Wi., U.S.	G6	118
Spring Valley, val., Nv., U.S.	D2	132
Springview, Ne., U.S.	E13	126
Springville, Al., U.S.	D12	122
Springville, Ca., U.S.	G7	134
Springville, Ut., U.S.	C5	132
Sproat Lake, l., B.C., Can.	G5	138
Spruce Grove, Ab., Can.	C17	138
Spruce Knob, mtn., W.V., U.S.	F6	114
Spruce Mountain, mtn., Az., U.S.	I4	132
Spruce Pine, Al., U.S.	C11	122
Spruce Pine, N.C., U.S.	I3	114
Spulico, Capo, c., Italy.	E10	24
Spurfield, Ab., Can.	A16	138
Spurger, Tx., U.S.	G4	122
Spurn Head, c., Eng., U.K.	H13	12
Spuzzum, B.C., Can.	G9	138
Squam Lake, l., N.H., U.S.	G5	110
Squamish, B.C., Can.	G7	138
Square Lake, l., Me., U.S.	D8	110
Squatec, Qc., Can.	C8	110
Squaw Cap Mountain, mtn., N.B., Can.	C10	110
Squaw Lake, Mn., U.S.	C12	136
Squilax, B.C., Can.	F11	138
Squillace, Golfo di, b., Italy.	F10	24
Squinzano, Italy.	D12	24
Sragen, Indon.	G7	50
Srbija (Serbia), state, Serb.	D6	26
Srbobran, Serb.	D6	26
Srê Âmběl, Camb.	G6	48
Sredinnyj hrebet, mts., Russia.	E20	34
Sredna Gora, mts., Blg.	G11	26
Srednee Kujto, ozero, l., Russia.	D14	8
Srednekolymsk, Russia.	C19	34
Srednerusskaja vozvyšennost', plat., Russia.	D5	32
Srednesibirskoe ploskogor'e (Central Siberian Uplands), plat., Russia.	C10	34
Srednij Ural, mts., Russia.	C9	32
Srednjaja Olëkma, Russia.	E13	34
Šrem, Pol.	D13	16
Srê Moăt, Camb.	F8	48
Sremska Mitrovica, Serb.	E6	26
Sremski Karlovci, Serb.	D6	26
Srêng, stm., Camb.	F6	48
Srêpôk, stm., Camb.	F8	48
Sretensk, Russia.	F12	34
Sri Aman, Malay.	C7	50
Sri Jayewardenepura Kotte, Sri L.	H4	53
Srīkākulam, India.	B6	53
Sri Kālahasti, India.	E4	53
Sri Lanka, ctry., Asia.	G5	53
Srinagar, India.	A5	54
Srīrampur, India.	B2	53
Srirangam, India.	F4	53
Srivardhan, India.	B1	53
Srivilliputtūr, India.	G3	53
Sroda Śląska, Pol.	E12	16
Środa Wielkopolska, Pol.	D13	16
Sseu-tch'ouan see Sichuan, state, China.	E5	36
Ssup'ing see Siping, China.	C6	38
Staaten, stm., Austl.	C8	74
Stacyville, Ia., U.S.	H6	118
Stade, Ger.	C5	16
Stadlandet, pen., Nor.	E1	8
Stadl-Paura, Aus.	B10	22
Stadskanaal, Neth.	A16	14
Stadtallendorf, Ger.	F5	16
Stadtoldendorf, Ger.	E5	16
Stafford, Eng., U.K.	I10	12
Stafford, Ks., U.S.	D10	128
Stafford Springs, Ct., U.S.	C13	114
Staffordsville, Ky., U.S.	G14	120
Stagen, Indon.	E10	50
Staines, Eng., U.K.	J12	12
Staked Plain see Estacado, Llano, pl., U.S.	H6	128
Stakhanov, Ukr.	E5	32
Stalać, Serb.	F8	26
Stalowa Wola, Pol.	F18	16
Stamford, Austl.	C4	76
Stamford, Eng., U.K.	I12	12
Stamford, Ct., U.S.	C12	114
Stamford, N.Y., U.S.	B11	114
Stamford, Tx., U.S.	B8	130
Stamford, Lake, res., Tx., U.S.	A8	130
Stamps, Ar., U.S.	D5	122
Stanberry, Mo., U.S.	D3	120
Stancionno-Ojašinskij, Russia.	C14	32
Standard, Ab., Can.	E18	138
Standerton, S. Afr.	E9	70
Standish, Mi., U.S.	E6	112
Stanfield, Or., U.S.	E7	136
Stanford, Ky., U.S.	G13	120
Stanford, Mt., U.S.	C16	136
Stanhope, N.J., U.S.	C11	114
Stanislaus, stm., Ca., U.S.	F5	134
Stanley, Austl.	n12	77a
Stanley, N.B., Can.	D10	110
Stanley, Falk. Is.	J5	90
Stanley, N.C., U.S.	A4	116
Stanley, N.D., U.S.	F11	124
Stanley, Wi., U.S.	G8	118
Stanley Falls, wtfl, D.R.C.	D4	66
Stanley Reservoir, res., India.	F3	53
Stanleyville see Kisangani, D.R.C.	D5	66
Stanovoe nagor'e, mts., Russia.	E11	34
Stanovoj hrebet, mts., Russia.	E14	34
Stanovoy Mountains see Stanovoe nagor'e, mts., Russia.	E11	34
Stanthorpe, Austl.	G8	76
Stanton, Ky., U.S.	G2	114
Stanton, Mi., U.S.	E4	112
Stanton, N.D., U.S.	G12	124
Stanton, Tx., U.S.	B6	130
Stantonsburg, N.C., U.S.	A8	116
Stanwood, Wa., U.S.	B4	136
Staples, Mn., U.S.	E4	118
Stapleton, Al., U.S.	G11	122
Stapleton, Ne., U.S.	F12	126
Starków, Pol.	E16	16
Star, N.C., U.S.	A6	116
Starachowice, Pol.	E17	16
Stara Pazova, Serb.	D7	26
Staraja Rudnja, Bela.	H13	10
Stara Zagora, Blg.	G12	26
Starbuck, Mb., Can.	E16	124
Starbuck, Wa., U.S.	D8	136
Star City, Ar., U.S.	D7	122
Star City, Sk., Can.	B9	124
Star City, W.V., U.S.	E6	114
Stargard Szczeciński, Pol.	C11	16
Stargo, Az., U.S.	J7	132
Star Harbour, b., Sol. Is.	f10	79b
Starica, Russia.	D17	10
Stari Grad, Cro.	G13	22
Stari Rjad, Russia.	B17	10
Stari Vlah, reg., Serb.	F7	26
Starke, Fl., U.S.	F3	116
Starkville, Ms., U.S.	D10	122
Starnberg, Ger.	H7	16
Starnberger See, l., Ger.	I7	16
Starodub, Russia.	H15	10
Staroe Rahino, Russia.	B15	10
Starogard Gdański, Pol.	C14	16
Starokozache, Ukr.	C16	26
Starokozache, Ukr.	C16	26
Star Peak, mtn., Nv., U.S.	C7	134
Start Point, c., Eng., U.K.	K9	12
Staryja Darohi, Bela.	G11	10
Staryj Oskol, Russia.	D5	32
Starý Sącz, Pol.	G16	16
Stassfurt, Ger.	E7	16
State College, Pa., U.S.	D7	114
Stateline, Nv., U.S.	E5	134
Staten Island see Estados, Isla de los, i., Arg.	J4	90
State Harbor, N.C., U.S.	H4	114
Statesboro, Ga., U.S.	D4	116
Statesville, N.C., U.S.	I5	114
Staunton, Bela.	H14	10
Staunton, Il., U.S.	E8	120
Staunton, Va., U.S.	F6	114
Staunton see Roanoke, stm., U.S.	H8	114
Stavanger, Nor.	G1	8
Stave Lake, l., B.C., Can.	G8	138
Stavely, Ab., Can.	F17	138
Stavne, Ukr.	A10	26
Stavropol', Russia.	E6	32
Stavroúpoli, Grc.	B7	28
Stawell, Austl.	K4	76
Stawiszyn, Pol.	E14	16
Stayner, On., Can.	D9	112
Steamboat Springs, Co., U.S.	C10	132
Stearns, Ky., U.S.	H13	120
Steele, Mo., U.S.	H8	120
Steele, N.D., U.S.	H14	124
Steele, Mount, mtn., Wy., U.S.	B9	132
Steels Point, c., Norf. I.	y25	78i
Steelville, Mo., U.S.	G6	120
Steensby Inlet, b., Nu., Can.	A15	106
Steenwijk, Neth.	B15	14
Steep Rock, Mb., Can.	C15	124
Stefanie, Lake, l., Afr.	G7	62
Stefansson Island, i., Nu., Can.	A9	106
Ştefan Vodă, Rom.	E14	26
Stege, Den.	B8	16
Stehekin, Wa., U.S.	B6	136
Steiermark, state, Aus.	C11	22
Steinach, Aus.	C8	22
Steinbach, Mb., Can.	E17	124
Steinfurt, Ger.	D3	16
Steinhausen, Nmb.	B4	70
Steinkjer, Nor.	D4	8
Stekljanka, Russia.	G19	8
Stella, S. Afr.	E7	70
Stellarton, N.S., Can.	E14	110
Stellenbosch, S. Afr.	H4	70
Stelvio, Parco Nazionale dello, p.o.i., Italy.	D7	22
Stelvio, Passo dello, p., Italy.	D7	22
Stendal, Ger.	D7	16
Stende, Lat.	C5	10
Stephen, Mn., U.S.	C2	118
Stephens, Ar., U.S.	D5	122
Stephens, Port, b., Austl.	I9	76
Stephens, Cape, c., N.Z.	E7	114
Stephens Creek, Austl.	H3	76
Stephens Lake, res., Mb., Can.	D11	106
Stephenville, Nf., Can.	j22	107a
Stephenville, Tx., U.S.	B9	130
Stepnjak, Kaz.	D12	32
Step Pyramid see Saqqâra, Pyramides de, hist., Egypt.	I1	58
Steptoe Valley, val., Nv., U.S.	D2	132
Sterkstroom, S. Afr.	G8	70
Sterling, Co., U.S.	A5	128
Sterling, Il., U.S.	C8	120
Sterling, Mi., U.S.	D5	112
Sterling City, Tx., U.S.	C7	130
Sterling, Ne., U.S.	D1	120
Sterlington, La., U.S.	E6	122
Sterlitamak, Russia.	D9	32
Šternberk, Czech Rep.	G13	16
Sterzing see Vipiteno, Italy.	D8	22
Stettin see Szczecin, Pol.	C10	16
Stettin Lagoon, b., Eur.	C10	16
Stettler, Ab., Can.	D18	138
Steubenville, Oh., U.S.	D5	114
Stevenage, Eng., U.K.	J12	12
Stevenson, Al., U.S.	C13	122
Stevenson Entrance, strt., Ak., U.S.	E9	140
Stevens Peak, mtn., Id., U.S.	C11	136
Stevens Point, Wi., U.S.	G9	118
Stevensville, Mi., U.S.	F3	112
Stevensville, Mt., U.S.	D12	136
Stewardson, Il., U.S.	E9	120
Stewart, B.C., Can.	D4	106
Stewart, stm., Yu., Can.	C3	106
Stewart, Isla, i., Chile.	J2	90
Stewart, Island, i., N.Z.	H3	80
Stewartstown, Pa., U.S.	E9	114
Stewartsville, Mo., U.S.	E3	120
Stewart Valley, Sk., Can.	D6	124
Stewiacke, N.S., Can.	E13	110
Steyr, Aus.	B11	22
Steytlerville, S. Afr.	H7	70
Stickney, S.D., U.S.	D14	126
Stiene, Lat.	B6	10
Stif, Alg.	B6	64
Stigler, Ok., U.S.	B3	122
Stih, hora, mtn., Ukr.	A10	26
Stikine, stm., N.A.	D4	106
Stikine Ranges, mts., B.C., Can.	D4	106
Stilbaai, S. Afr.	I5	70
Stilfontein, S. Afr.	E8	70
Stillhouse Hollow Lake, res., Tx., U.S.	D10	130
Stillwater, B.C., Can.	G6	138
Stillwater, Mn., U.S.	F6	118
Stillwater, Ok., U.S.	A1	122
Stilwell, Ok., U.S.	I3	120
Stînca-Costeşti, Lacul, res., Eur.	B14	26
Stirling, Ab., Can.	G18	138
Stirling, Scot., U.K.	E9	12
Stirling, Scot., U.K.	D12	112
Stirling City, Ca., U.S.	D4	134
Stirrat, W.V., U.S.	G15	120
Stjernøya, i., Nor.	A9	8
Stobi, sci., Mac.	B4	28
Stockbridge, Ga., U.S.	C1	116
Stockbridge, Mi., U.S.	B1	114
Stockdale, Tx., U.S.	E10	130
Stockerau, Aus.	B13	22
Stockholm, Swe.	G8	8
Stockholm, state, Swe.	G8	8
Stockport, Eng., U.K.	H10	12
Stockton, Ca., U.S.	F4	134
Stockton, Il., U.S.	B8	120
Stockton, Ks., U.S.	B9	128
Stockton, Mo., U.S.	G4	120
Stockton-on-Tees, Eng., U.K.	G11	12
Stockton Plateau, plat., Tx., U.S.	D5	130
Stockton Reservoir, res., Mo., U.S.	G4	120
Stockton Springs, Me., U.S.	F8	110
Stoczek Łukowski, Pol.	D18	16
Stoffberg, S. Afr.	D9	70
Stojba, Russia.	F15	34
Stoke-on-Trent, Eng., U.K.	I11	12
Stokke, Nor.	G4	8
Stokmarknes, Nor.	B6	8
Stolac, Bos.	H14	22
Stolberg, Ger.	F2	16
Stolbovo, Russia.	H17	10
Stolbovoj, ostrov, i., Russia.	C5	114
Stoneboro, Pa., U.S.	C5	114
Stone Harbor, N.J., U.S.	E11	114
Stonehaven, Scot., U.K.	E10	12
Stonehenge, Austl.	E4	76
Stonehenge, hist., Eng., U.K.	J11	12
Stone Mountain, mtn., Vt., U.S.	F5	110
Stoner, B.C., Can.	C8	138
Stoneville, N.C., U.S.	H6	114
Stonewall, Mb., Can.	D16	124
Stony Creek, stm., On., Can.	E10	112
Stonington, Il., U.S.	E8	120
Stonington, Me., U.S.	F8	110
Stony Lake, l., Mb., Can.	D11	106
Stony Lake, l., On., Can.	D11	112
Stony Plain, Ab., Can.	C16	138
Stony Point, N.C., U.S.	I4	114
Stony Rapids, Sk., Can.	D9	106
Stony River, Ak., U.S.	D8	140
Stopnica, Pol.	F16	16
Stora Lulevatten, l., Swe.	C8	8
Storavan, l., Swe.	D8	8
Stord, i., Nor.	G1	8
Storebælt, strt., Den.	I4	8
Store Koldewey, i., Grnld.	B22	141
Støren, Nor.	E4	8
Store Sotra, i., Nor.	F1	8
Storkerson Bay, b., N.T., Can.	B14	140
Storkerson Peninsula, pen., Nu., Can.	A9	106
Storlien, Swe.	E5	8
Storm Bay, b., Austl.	o13	77a
Storm Lake, Ia., U.S.	B2	120
Stornoway, Scot., U.K.	C6	12
Storozhynets', Ukr.	A12	26
Storrs, Ct., U.S.	C13	114
Storsjøen, l., Nor.	F4	8
Storsjön, l., Swe.	E5	8
Storstrøm, state, Den.	I4	8
Storthoaks, Sk., Can.	E12	124
Storuman, Swe.	D6	8
Storuman, l., Swe.	D7	8
Storvindeln, l., Swe.	D7	8
Storvreta, Swe.	F7	8
Story City, Ia., U.S.	B4	120
Stosch, Isla, i., Chile.	I1	90
Stoughton, Sk., Can.	E10	124
Stoughton, Ma., U.S.	B14	114
Stoughton, Wi., U.S.	B8	120
Stoŭng, stm., Camb.	F7	48
Stow, Oh., U.S.	C4	114
Stowe, Vt., U.S.	F4	110
Stowell, Tx., U.S.	H4	122
Stowmarket, Eng., U.K.	I14	12
Stoyoma Mountain, mtn., B.C., Can.	G9	138
Stradella, Italy.	E6	22
Stradečý, Bela.	I6	10
Strahan, Austl.	o12	77a
Strakonice, Czech Rep.	G9	16
Stralsund, Ger.	B9	16
Strand, S. Afr.	I4	70
Stranraer, Scot., U.K.	G8	12
Strasbourg, Sk., Can.	C9	124
Strasbourg, Fr.	F16	14
Strasburg, Ger.	C9	16
Strasburg, N.D., U.S.	A12	126
Strasburg, Oh., U.S.	D4	114
Strasburg, Pa., U.S.	E9	114
Strasburg, Va., U.S.	F7	114
Strășeni, Mol.	B15	26
Stratford, On., Can.	E8	112
Stratford, N.Z.	D6	80
Stratford, Ca., U.S.	G6	134
Stratford, Ct., U.S.	C12	114
Stratford, Ok., U.S.	B2	122
Stratford, Tx., U.S.	C7	122
Stratford, Wi., U.S.	G8	118
Stratford-upon-Avon, Eng., U.K.	I11	12
Strathalbyn, Austl.	J2	76
Strathclair, Mb., Can.	D13	124
Strathgordon, Austl.	o12	77a
Strathlorne, N.S., Can.	D15	110
Strathmore, Ab., Can.	E17	138
Strathmore, val., Scot., U.K.	E9	12
Strathroy, On., Can.	F8	112
Strathy Point, c., Scot., U.K.	C8	12
Stratton, Co., U.S.	B6	128
Stratton, Ne., U.S.	G12	126
Straubing, Ger.	H8	16
Strausberg, Ger.	D9	16
Strawberry, stm., U.S.	H6	120
Strawberry, stm., Ut., U.S.	C6	132
Strawberry Mountain, mtn., Or., U.S.	F8	136
Strawberry Reservoir, res., Ut., U.S.	C5	132
Strawn, Tx., U.S.	B9	130
Stražnice, Czech Rep.	H13	16
Streaky Bay, b., Austl.	F6	74
Streatham, B.C., Can.	C9	138
Streator, Il., U.S.	C9	120
Středočeský, kraj, state, Czech Rep.	G10	16
Stredoslovenský, Kraj, state, Slov.	H15	16
Streeter, N.D., U.S.	A13	126
Streetsboro, Oh., U.S.	C4	114
Streetsville, On., Can.	E10	112
Strehaia, Rom.	E10	26
Strelka-Čunja, Russia.	B18	32
Strel'na, stm., Russia.	C18	8
Strel'skaja, Russia.	G22	8
Strenči, Lat.	C8	10
Strešyn, Bela.	H13	10
Strickland, stm., Pap. N. Gui.	b3	79a
Strimon, Gulf of see Strymonikós Kólpos, b., Grc.	C6	28
Strymonikós Kólpos (Strimon, Gulf of), b., Grc.	C6	28
Strzegom, Pol.	F12	16
Strzelce Krajeńskie, Pol.	D11	16
Strzelce Opolskie, Pol.	F14	16
Strzelecki Creek, stm., Austl.	G3	76
Strzelecki Desert, des., Austl.	G3	76
Strzelecki National Park, p.o.i., Austl.	n13	77a
Strzelin, Pol.	F12	16
Strzyżów, Pol.	G17	16
Stuart, Fl., U.S.	I5	116
Stuart, Ia., U.S.	C3	120
Stuart, Ne., U.S.	E13	126
Stuart, Va., U.S.	H5	114
Stuart, stm., B.C., Can.	B7	138
Stuart Island, i., Ak., U.S.	D7	140
Stuart Lake, l., B.C., Can.	B5	138
Stuarts Draft, Va., U.S.	G6	114
Studen Kladenec, Jazovir, res., Blg.	H12	26
Stung Treng, Camb.	F8	48
Stupino, Russia.	F21	10
Stura di Demonte, stm., Italy.	F4	22
Sturge Island, i., Ant.	B21	81
Sturgeon, stm., On., Can.	B9	112
Sturgeon Bay, Wi., U.S.	D2	112
Sturgeon Bay, b., Mb., Can.	B15	124

Sturgeon Falls – Talaud Islands I • 55

Name	Map Ref.	Page
Sturgeon Falls, On., Can.	B10	112
Sturgeon Lake, l., Ab., Can.	A13	138
Sturgeon Lake, l., On., Can.	A7	118
Sturgeon Lake, l., On., Can.	D11	112
Sturgis, Sk., Can.	C11	124
Sturgis, Ky., U.S.	G10	120
Sturgis, Mi., U.S.	G4	112
Sturgis, S.D., U.S.	C9	126
Štúrovo, Slov.	I14	16
Sturt, Mount, mtn., Austl.	G3	76
Sturtevant, Wi., U.S.	F2	112
Sturt National Park, p.o.i., Austl.	G3	76
Sturt Stony Desert, des., Austl.	G3	76
Stutterheim, S. Afr.	H8	70
Stuttgart, Ger.	H5	16
Stuttgart, Ar., U.S.	C7	122
Stylís, Grc.	E5	28
Styr, stm., Eur.	H9	10
Styria see Steiermark, state, Aus.	C11	22
Šu see Shū, Kaz.	F12	32
Suaçuí Grande, stm., Braz.	J4	88
Suai, Malay.	B8	50
Suaita, Col.	D5	86
Suapure, stm., Ven.	D8	86
Suaqui Grande, Mex.	A4	100
Subah, Indon.	G6	50
Subang, Indon.	G5	50
Subansiri, stm., Asia	D14	54
Subarnarekha, stm., India	G11	54
Sūbāṭ, stm., Sudan	F6	62
Subate, Lat.	D8	10
Subei, China	D3	36
Subeita see Shivta, Horvot, sci., Isr.	H5	58
Subiaco, Italy	I10	22
Sublette, Ks., U.S.	D8	128
Sublett Range, mts., Id., U.S.	H14	136
Subotica, Serb.	C6	26
Sucarnoochee, stm., U.S.	E10	122
Succotah, hist., Egypt	H3	58
Suceava, Rom.	B13	26
Suceava, state, Rom.	B12	26
Suchań, Pol.	C11	16
Suchou see Suzhou, China	F9	42
Süchow see Xuzhou, China	D7	42
Sucio, stm., Col.	D3	86
Sucre, Bol.	C3	90
Sucre, Col.	C4	86
Sucre, state, Col.	C4	86
Sucre, state, Ven.	B10	86
Sucuaro, Col.	E7	86
Sucumbíos, state, Ec.	H3	86
Sucuriju, Braz.	C8	84
Sucuriú, stm., Braz.	C6	90
Sud, state, N. Cal.	m16	79d
Sud, Canal du, strt., Haiti	C11	102
Suda, Russia	A20	10
Suda, stm., Russia	A20	10
Sudan, Tx., U.S.	G6	128
Sudan, ctry., Afr.	E5	62
Sudan, reg., Afr.	E4	62
Sudbišči, Russia	H20	10
Sudbury, On., Can.	B8	112
Sudbury, Eng., U.K.	I13	12
Sudd see As-Sudd, reg., Sudan	F6	62
Sudetes, mts., Eur.	F11	16
Sudogda, Russia	H19	8
Sudomskaja vozvyšennost', plat., Russia	C12	10
Sudost', stm., Eur.	H16	10
Südtirol see Trentino-Alto Adige, state, Italy	D8	22
Suđuroy, i., Far. Is.	n34	8b
Sue, stm., Sudan	F5	62
Sueca, Spain	E10	20
Suez see El-Suweis, Egypt	I3	58
Suez, Gulf of see Suweis, Khalîg el-, b., Egypt	J4	58
Suez Canal see Suweis, Qanâ el-, can., Egypt	H3	58
Suffield, Ab., Can.	D2	124
Suffolk, Va., U.S.	H9	114
Sufu see Kashi, China	B12	56
Sugar City, Id., U.S.	G15	136
Sugar Hill, Ga., U.S.	B1	116
Sugar Island, i., Mi., U.S.	B5	112
Sugar Land, Tx., U.S.	H3	122
Sugarloaf, hill, Oh., U.S.	C4	114
Sugarloaf Mountain, mtn., Me., U.S.	E6	110
Sugarloaf Point, c., Austl.	I9	76
Suğla Gölü, l., Tur.	F14	28
Sugoj, stm., Russia	D20	34
Sugut, stm., Malay.	G1	52
Suhag, Egypt	B6	62
Suhai Hu, l., China	G16	32
Suhana, Russia	C12	34
Ṣuḥār, Oman	E8	56
Sühbaatar, Mong.	A6	36
Suhindol, Blg.	F12	26
Suhiniči, Russia	F18	10
Suhl, Ger.	F6	16
Suhodol'skij, Russia	G21	10
Suhona, stm., Russia	F22	8
Suhoverkovo, Russia	D18	10
Suhumi, Geor.	F6	32
Şuhut, Tur.	E13	28
Suiá-Miçu, stm., Braz.	F7	84
Suichuan, China	H6	42
Suide, China	C4	42
Suifu see Yibin, China	F5	36
Suihua, China	B10	36
Suijiang, China	F5	36
Suileng, China	B10	36
Suining, China	E7	42
Suining, China	F1	42
Suipacha, Arg.	G8	92
Suiping, China	E5	42
Suippes, Fr.	E13	14
Suir, stm., Ire.	I5	12
Suixi, China	E7	42
Suiyang, China	H2	42
Suiyang, China	B9	38
Suiyangdian, China	E5	42
Suizhong, China	A9	42
Suizhou, China	F5	42
Šuja, Russia	H19	8
Šuja, stm., Russia	E15	8
Sujāngarh, India	E5	54
Sujāwal, Pak.	F2	54
Sukabumi, Indon.	G5	50
Sukadana, Indon.	D6	50
Sukadana, Indon.	F4	50
Sukadana, Teluk, b., Indon.	D6	50
Sukagawa, Japan	B13	40
Sukamara, Indon.	E7	50
Sukaraja, Indon.	E7	50
Sukau, Malay.	A11	50
Sukhothai, Thai.	D4	48
Sukhumi see Suhumi, Geor.	F6	32
Sukkertoppen (Maniitsoq), Grnld.	D15	141
Sukkozero, Russia	E14	8
Sukkur, Pak.	E2	54
Sukoharjo, Indon.	G7	50
Sukromlja, Russia	D17	10
Sukses, Nmb.	B3	70
Sukumo, Japan	G5	40
Sukunka, stm., B.C., Can.	A9	138
Sul, Baía, b., Braz.	C13	92
Sula, i., Nor.	F1	8
Sula, stm., Russia	C23	8
Sula, Kepulauan (Sula Islands), is., Indon.	F8	44
Sulaimān Range, mts., Pak.	C3	54
Sula Islands see Sula, Kepulauan, is., Indon.	F8	44
Sulawesi (Celebes), i., Indon.	F7	44
Sulawesi Selatan, state, Indon.	E11	50
Sulawesi Tengah, state, Indon.	D12	50
Sulawesi Tenggara, state, Indon.	E12	50
Sulaymān, Birak (Solomon's Pools), sci., W.B.	G5	58
Sulcis, reg., Italy	E2	24
Sulechów, Pol.	D11	16
Sulęcin, Pol.	D11	16
Sulejówek, Pol.	D17	16
Sulen, Mount, mtn., Pap. N. Gui.	a3	79a
Sulina, Rom.	D16	26
Sulina, Braţul, stm., Rom.	D16	26
Sulingen, Ger.	D4	16
Sulitelma, mtn., Eur.	C7	8
Sullana, Peru	D1	84
Sulligent, Al., U.S.	D10	122
Sullivan, Il., U.S.	E9	120
Sullivan, In., U.S.	E10	120
Sullivan Lake, l., Ab., Can.	E18	138
Sulmona, Italy	H10	22
Sulphur, La., U.S.	G5	122
Sulphur, Ok., U.S.	C2	122
Sulphur, stm., U.S.	D5	122
Sulphur Springs, Tx., U.S.	D3	122
Sulphur Springs Draw, stm., U.S.	H6	128
Sulphur Springs Valley, val., Az., U.S.	L7	132
Sultan, Wa., U.S.	C5	136
Sultan Alonto, Lake, l., Phil.	G5	52
Sultandağı, Tur.	E14	28
Sultanhisar, Tur.	F11	28
Sultan Kudarat, Phil.	G4	52
Sultānpur, India	E8	54
Sulu Archipelago, is., Phil.	H3	52
Sulu Chi, l., China	C11	54
Sulūq, Libya	A4	62
Sulu Sea, s., Asia	F2	52
Sulzbach-Rosenberg, Ger.	G7	16
Šum, Russia	A14	10
Šumadija, reg., Serb.	E7	26
Sumangat, Tanjong, c., Malay.	G1	52
Sumatera (Sumatra), i., Indon.	E3	44
Sumatera Barat, state, Indon.	D2	50
Sumatera Selatan, state, Indon.	E4	50
Sumatera Utara, state, Indon.	K4	48
Sumatra see Sumatera, i., Indon.	E3	44
Sumba, Far. Is.	n34	8b
Sumba, i., Indon.	H11	50
Sumba, Selat, strt., Indon.	H11	50
Sumbawa, i., Indon.	H10	50
Sumbawa Besar, Indon.	H10	50
Sumbawanga, Tan.	F6	66
Sumbe, Ang.	C1	68
Sumburgh Head, c., Scot., U.K.	o18	12a
Sumé, Braz.	D7	88
Sumedang, Indon.	G5	50
Sümeg, Hung.	B4	26
Šumen, Blg.	F13	26
Sumenep, Indon.	G8	50
Šumerlja, Russia	C7	32
Sumisu-jima (Smith Island), i., Japan	E13	36
Šumjači, Russia	G15	10
Summerfield, Fl., U.S.	G3	116
Summerfield, N.C., U.S.	H6	114
Summer Lake, l., Or., U.S.	H6	136
Summerland, B.C., Can.	G11	138
Summerside, P.E., Can.	D13	110
Summersville, Mo., U.S.	G6	120
Summerton, S.C., U.S.	C5	116
Summerville, Ga., U.S.	C13	122
Summerville, S.C., U.S.	C5	116
Summit, S.D., U.S.	F1	118
Summit Lake, B.C., Can.	B8	138
Summit Mountain, mtn., Nv., U.S.	D9	134
Sumner, Ia., U.S.	B5	120
Sumner, Ms., U.S.	D8	122
Sumner, Wa., U.S.	C4	136
Sumoto, Japan	E7	40
Sumpangbinangae, Indon.	F11	50
Šumperk, Czech Rep.	G13	16
Sumpiuh, Indon.	G6	50
Sumqayıt, Azer.	A6	56
Šumšu, ostrov, i., Russia	F20	34
Sumter, S.C., U.S.	C5	116
Sumusta el-Waqf, Egypt	J1	58
Sumy, Ukr.	D4	32
Sumzom, China	F4	36
Sun, stm., Mt., U.S.	C14	136
Sunāmganj, Bngl.	F13	54
Sunbright, Tn., U.S.	H13	120
Sunburst, Mt., U.S.	B14	136
Sunbury, Austl.	K5	76
Sunbury, Oh., U.S.	D3	114
Sunbury, Pa., U.S.	D9	114
Sunchales, Arg.	E7	92
Suncho Corral, Arg.	C6	92
Sunch'ŏn, Kor., S.	G7	38
Sunch'ŏn-ŭp, Kor., N.	E6	38
Sun City, Az., U.S.	J4	132
Suncook, N.H., U.S.	G5	110
Sunda, Selat (Sunda Strait), strt., Indon.	G4	50
Sundance, Wy., U.S.	C8	126
Sundarbans, reg., Asia	H12	54
Sundargarh, India	G9	54
Sunda Shelf, unds.	I13	142
Sunda Strait see Sunda, Selat, strt., Indon.	G4	50
Sundays, stm., S. Afr.	H7	70
Sunde, Nor.	G1	8
Sunderland, Eng., U.K.	G11	12
Sundown, Tx., U.S.	H6	128
Sundridge, On., Can.	C10	112
Sundsvall, Swe.	E7	8
Sunflower, Ms., U.S.	D8	122
Sunflower, Mount, mtn., Ks., U.S.	B7	128
Sungaianyar, Indon.	E10	50
Sungaibuntu, Indon.	F5	50
Sungaidareh, Indon.	D2	50
Sungaiguntung, Indon.	C3	50
Sungai Kolok, Thai.	I5	48
Sungailangsat, Indon.	D2	50
Sungailimau, Indon.	D1	50
Sungaipenuh, Indon.	E2	50
Sungai Petani, Malay.	J5	48
Sungaipinang, Indon.	D8	50
Sungairotan, Indon.	E4	50
Sungaiselan, Indon.	E5	50
Sungari see Songhua, stm., China	B11	36
Sungari Reservoir see Songhua Hu, res., China	C7	38
Sungchiang see Songjiang, China	F9	42
Sungguminasa, Indon.	F11	50
Sungsang, Indon.	E4	50
Sunland Park, N.M., U.S.	L10	132
Sunne, Swe.	G5	8
Sunnynook, Ab., Can.	E19	138
Sunnyside, Ut., U.S.	D6	132
Sunnyside, Wa., U.S.	D7	136
Sunnyslope, Ab., Can.	E17	138
Sunnyvale, Ca., U.S.	F3	134
Sun Prairie, Wi., U.S.	A8	120
Sunrise, Fl., U.S.	J5	116
Sunrise, Wy., U.S.	E8	126
Sunrise Manor, Nv., U.S.	G1	132
Sunset, La., U.S.	G6	122
Sunset, Tx., U.S.	H11	128
Sunset Country, reg., Austl.	J3	76
Sunset Crater National Monument, p.o.i., Az., U.S.	H5	132
Sunshine, Austl.	K5	76
Suntar, Russia	D12	34
Suntar-Hajata, hrebet, mts., Russia	D17	34
Sun Valley, Id., U.S.	G12	136
Sunwu, China	B10	36
Sunwui see Jiangmen, China	J5	42
Sunyani, Ghana	H4	64
Suojarvi, Russia	E15	8
Suomussalmi, Fin.	D13	8
Suō-nada, s., Japan	F4	40
Suordah, Russia	C15	34
Supamo, stm., Ven.	D10	86
Supaul, India	E11	54
Superí see La Merced, Arg.	D5	92
Superior, Az., U.S.	J5	132
Superior, Mt., U.S.	C12	136
Superior, Wi., U.S.	E6	118
Superior, Wy., U.S.	B7	132
Superior, Laguna, b., Mex.	G11	100
Superior, Lake, l., N.A.	B10	108
Supetar, Cro.	G13	22
Suphan Buri, Thai.	E4	48
Suphan Buri, stm., Thai.	E5	48
Suponevo, Russia	G17	10
Supung Reservoir, res., Asia	D6	38
Suqian, China	E8	42
Sūq Suwayq, Sau. Ar.	E4	56
Suquṭrā (Socotra), i., Yemen	G7	56
Ṣūr (Tyre), Leb.	E6	58
Ṣūr, Oman	E8	56
Sur, Point, c., Ca., U.S.	G4	134
Sura, stm., Russia	C7	32
Surabaya, Indon.	G8	50
Surakarta, Indon.	G7	50
Ṣūrān, Syria	C7	58
Šurany, Slov.	H14	16
Surat, Austl.	F7	76
Sūrat, India	H4	54
Sūratgarh, India	D4	54
Surat Thani, Thai.	H4	48
Suraž, Bela.	E13	10
Suraž, Russia	G15	10
Surendranagar, India	G3	54
Surf City, N.J., U.S.	E11	114
Surfers Paradise, Austl.	G9	76
Surgères, Fr.	C5	18
Surgoinsville, Tn., U.S.	H3	114
Surgut, Russia	B12	32
Suriāpet, India	C4	53
Surigao, Phil.	F5	52
Surin, Thai.	E6	48
Surinam, ctry., S.A.	C6	84
Suring, Wi., U.S.	D1	112
Surprise Valley, val., U.S.	B5	134
Surrency, Ga., U.S.	E3	116
Surrey, N.D., U.S.	F12	124
Surry, Va., U.S.	G9	114
Sursee, Switz.	C5	22
Surt, Libya	A3	62
Surt, Khalīj (Sidra, Gulf of), b., Libya	A3	62
Surtanāhu, Pak.	E2	54
Surtsey, i., Ice.	I29	8a
Suru, Pap. N. Gui.	b3	79a
Sürüç, Tur.	A9	58
Suruga-wan, b., Japan	E11	40
Surulangun, Indon.	E3	50
Surumu, stm., Braz.	F11	86
Šuryškary, Russia	A10	32
Susa, Italy	E4	22
Sušac, Otok, i., Cro.	H13	22
Sūsah, Libya	A4	62
Susaki, Japan	F6	40
Susanino, Russia	F17	34
Susanino, Russia	G19	8
Susanville, Ca., U.S.	C5	134
Šušenskoe, Russia	D16	32
Susitna, stm., Ak., U.S.	D9	140
Susleni, Mol.	B15	26
Susoh, Indon.	K3	48
Susong, China	F7	42
Suspiro del Moro, Puerto, p., Spain	G7	20
Susquehanna, Pa., U.S.	C10	114
Susquehanna, stm., U.S.	E9	114
Susquehanna, West Branch, stm., Pa., U.S.	C8	114
Susques, Arg.	D3	90
Sussex, N.B., Can.	E11	110
Sussex, N.J., U.S.	C11	114
Sussex, Va., U.S.	H8	114
Susuman, Russia	D18	34
Susurluk, Tur.	D11	28
Susuzmüsellim, Tur.	B9	28
Šušvė, stm., Lith.	E6	10
Sutak, India	B6	54
Sutherland, S. Afr.	H5	70
Sutherland, Ia., U.S.	A2	120
Sutherlin, Or., U.S.	G3	136
Sutjeska Nacionalni Park, p.o.i., Bos.	F5	26
Sutlej (Langqên) (Satluj), stm., Asia	D3	54
Sutter, Ca., U.S.	D4	134
Sutter Buttes, mtn., Ca., U.S.	D4	134
Sutter Creek, Ca., U.S.	E5	134
Sutton, Ak., U.S.	D10	140
Sutton, W.V., U.S.	F5	114
Sutton, Monts see Green Mountains, mts., N.A.	G4	110
Sutton in Ashfield, Eng., U.K.	H11	12
Sutton West, On., Can.	D10	112
Suttor, stm., Austl.	C6	76
Sutwik Island, i., Ak., U.S.	E8	140
Suure-Jaani, Est.	B8	10
Suur Munamägi, hill, Est.	C9	10
Suur Pakri, i., Est.	A6	10
Suva, Fiji	q19	79e
Suvadiva Atoll, at., Mald.	i12	46a
Suvarlı, Tur.	A8	58
Suvasvesi, l., Fin.	E12	8
Suvorov, Russia	F19	10
Suwa, Japan	C11	40
Suwałki, Pol.	B18	16
Suwałki, state, Pol.	C18	16
Suwannaphum, Thai.	E6	48
Suwannee, stm., U.S.	G2	116
Suwanose-jima, i., Japan	k19	39a
Suwarrow, at., Cook Is.	E10	72
Suweis, Khalîg el- (Suez, Gulf of), b., Egypt	J4	58
Suweis, Qanâ el- (Suez Canal), can., Egypt	H3	58
Suwŏn, Kor., S.	F7	38
Suzaka, Japan	C11	40
Suzdal', Russia	H19	8
Suzhou, China	F9	42
Suzhou, China	E7	42
Suzigou, China	A10	42
Suzuka, Japan	E9	40
Suzuka-sammyaku, mts., Japan	D9	40
Suzu-misaki, c., Japan	B10	40
Suzun, Russia	D14	32
Suzzara, Italy	F7	22
Svalbard, dep., Eur.	B6	30
Svaliava, Ukr.	A10	26
Svapa, stm., Russia	H18	10
Svappavaara, Swe.	C9	8
Svärdsjö, Swe.	F6	8
Svartenhuk, pen., Grnld.	C15	141
Svartisen, ice, Nor.	C5	8
Svataj, Russia	C19	34
Svay Riĕng, Camb.	G7	48
Svėdasai, Lith.	E8	10
Svegssjön, l., Swe.	E5	8
Švėkšna, Lith.	E4	10
Svelvik, Nor.	G4	8
Švenčionėliai, Lith.	E8	10
Švenčionys, Lith.	E9	10
Svendborg, Den.	A6	16
Šventoji, Lith.	D3	10
Šventoji, stm., Lith.	E7	10
Sverdlovsk see Ekaterinburg, Russia	C10	32
Sverdrup, ostrov, i., Russia	B4	34
Sverdrup Channel, strt., Nu., Can.	A6	141
Sverdrup Islands, is., Nu., Can.	B5	141
Sveti Nikole, Mac.	B4	28
Svetlahorsk, Bela.	H12	10
Svetlaja, Russia	B12	36
Svetlogorsk, Russia	F2	10
Svetlograd, Russia	E6	32
Svetlyj, Russia	D10	32
Svetlyj, Russia	F3	10
Svetlyj, Russia	E12	34
Svetogorsk, Russia	F13	8
Svetozarevo, Serb.	F8	26
Svidník, Slov.	G17	16
Svilengrad, Blg.	H13	26
Svínoy, i., Far. Is.	m34	8b
Svir, Bela.	F9	10
Svir', stm., Russia	F16	8
Svirica, Russia	F15	8
Svirsk, Russia	D18	32
Svislač, stm., Bela.	G11	10
Svištov, Blg.	F12	26
Svit, Slov.	G16	16
Svitavy, Czech Rep.	G12	16
Svjacilavičy, Bela.	H14	10
Svjatoj Nos, mys, c., Russia	B18	8
Svjatoj Nos, mys, c., Russia	B17	34
Svobodnyj, Russia	F14	34
Svolvær, Nor.	B6	8
Svratka, stm., Czech Rep.	G12	16
Swabia see Schwaben, hist. reg., Ger.	H5	16
Swain Reefs, rf., Austl.	C9	76
Swainsboro, Ga., U.S.	D3	116
Swains Island, at., Am. Sam.	E9	72
Swakop, stm., Nmb.	C2	70
Swakopmund, Nmb.	C2	70
Swale, stm., Eng., U.K.	G11	12
Swan, stm., Ab., Can.	A15	138
Swan, stm., Can.	B13	124
Swan, stm., Mt., U.S.	C13	136
Swanage, Eng., U.K.	K11	12
Swanee see Suwannee, stm., U.S.	G2	116
Swan Hill, Austl.	J4	76
Swan Hills, Ab., Can.	B15	138
Swan Islands see Santanilla, Islas, is., Hond.	D6	102
Swan Lake, Mb., Can.	E15	124
Swan Lake, l., Mb., Can.	B13	124
Swan Lake, l., Mn., U.S.	G4	118
Swannanoa, N.C., U.S.	I3	114
Swan Peak, mtn., Mt., U.S.	C13	136
Swanquarter, N.C., U.S.	A9	116
Swan Range, mts., Mt., U.S.	C13	136
Swan Reach, Austl.	J2	76
Swan River, Mb., Can.	B12	124
Swansboro, N.C., U.S.	B8	116
Swansea, Austl.	o13	77a
Swansea, Wales, U.K.	J8	12
Swanton, Vt., U.S.	F3	110
Swanville, Mn., U.S.	F4	118
Swart-Mfolozi, stm., S. Afr.	F10	70
Swartz Creek, Mi., U.S.	F6	112
Swarzędz, Pol.	D13	16
Swāt, stm., Pak.	A3	54
Swatow see Shantou, China	J7	42
Swaziland, ctry., Afr.	E10	70
Sweden, ctry., Eur.	E6	8
Swedish Knoll, mtn., Ut., U.S.	D5	132
Swedru, Ghana	H4	64
Sweeny, Tx., U.S.	E12	130
Sweet Briar, Va., U.S.	G6	114
Sweetgrass, Mt., U.S.	A15	136
Sweet Grass Hills, hills, Mt., U.S.	B15	136
Sweet Home, Tx., U.S.	E10	130
Sweet Springs, Mo., U.S.	F4	120
Sweetwater, Tn., U.S.	A1	116
Sweetwater, Tx., U.S.	B7	130
Sweetwater, stm., Wy., U.S.	E5	126
Swellendam, S. Afr.	H5	70
Świdnica, Pol.	F12	16
Świdnik, Pol.	E18	16
Świdwin, Pol.	C11	16
Świebodzice, Pol.	F12	16
Świebodzin, Pol.	D11	16
Świecie, Pol.	C14	16
Świerzawa, Pol.	E11	16
Świętokrzyski Park Narodowy, p.o.i., Pol.	F16	16
Swift Current, Sk., Can.	D6	124
Swift Current Creek, stm., Sk., Can.	D6	124
Swinburne, Cape, c., Nu., Can.	A11	106
Swindle Island, i., B.C., Can.	D2	138
Swindon, Eng., U.K.	J11	12
Swinford, Ire.	H4	12
Świnoujście (Swinemünde), Pol.	C9	16
Switzerland, ctry., Eur.	C14	18
Swords, Ire.	H6	12
Syalah, Russia	C13	34
Syan (San), stm., Eur.	F18	16
Sycamore, Ga., U.S.	E2	116
Sycamore, Il., U.S.	C9	120
Sycamore, Oh., U.S.	D2	114
Syčovka, Russia	E17	10
Sydenham, stm., On., Can.	F7	112
Sydney, Austl.	I8	76
Sydney, N.S., Can.	D16	110
Sydney Bay, b., Norf. I.	y25	78i
Sydney Lake, l., On., Can.	A4	118
Sydney Mines, N.S., Can.	D16	110
Syičy, Bela.	H12	10
Syke, Ger.	D4	16
Sykesville, Pa., U.S.	C7	114
Syktyvkar, Russia	B8	32
Sylacauga, Al., U.S.	D12	122
Sylhet, Bngl.	F13	54
Syloga, Russia	E20	8
Sylt, i., Ger.	B4	16
Sylva, N.C., U.S.	A2	116
Sylvan Grove, Ks., U.S.	C10	128
Sylvania, Ga., U.S.	D4	116
Sylvania, Oh., U.S.	C2	114
Sylvan Lake, Ab., Can.	D16	138
Sylvan Lake, l., Ab., Can.	D16	138
Sylvan Pass, p., Wy., U.S.	F16	136
Sylvester, Ga., U.S.	E2	116
Sylvester, Tx., U.S.	B7	130
Sym, Russia	B15	32
Syme see Sými, i., Grc.	G10	28
Sými, i., Grc.	G10	28
Šymkent see Shymkent, Kaz.	F11	32
Synevir, Ukr.	A10	26
Syowa, sci., Ant.	C9	81
Syracuse, In., U.S.	G4	112
Syracuse, Ks., U.S.	C7	128
Syracuse, Ne., U.S.	D1	120
Syracuse, N.Y., U.S.	A9	114
Syrdarīya see Syr Darya, stm., Asia	F11	32
Syrdarja, Uzb.	A10	56
Syr Darya (Syrdarīya), stm., Asia	F11	32
Syria, ctry., Asia	B4	56
Syriam, Mya.	D3	48
Syrian Desert (Shām, Bādiyat ash-), des., Asia	C4	56
Sýrna, i., Grc.	G9	28
Sýros, i., Grc.	F7	28
Sysmä, Fin.	F11	8
Sysola, stm., Russia	B8	32
Syt'kovo, Russia	D16	10
Syväri, l., Fin.	E13	8
Syzran', Russia	D7	32
Szabolcs-Szatmár-Bereg, state, Hung.	A9	26
Szamos (Someș), stm., Eur.	B9	26
Szamotuły, Pol.	D12	16
Szarvas, Hung.	C7	26
Szczawnica, Pol.	G16	16
Szczecin (Stettin), Pol.	C10	16
Szczecin, state, Pol.	C11	16
Szczecinek, Pol.	C12	16
Szczuczyn, Pol.	C18	16
Szczytno, Pol.	C17	16
Szechwan see Sichuan, state, China	E5	36
Szechwan Basin see Sichuan Pendi, bas., China	F1	42
Szeged, Hung.	C7	26
Szeghalom, Hung.	B8	26
Székesfehérvár, Hung.	B5	26
Szekszárd, Hung.	C5	26
Szentendre, Hung.	B5	26
Szentes, Hung.	C7	26
Szeping see Siping, China	C6	38
Szerencs, Hung.	A8	26
Szob, Hung.	B5	26
Szolnok, Hung.	B7	26
Szombathely, Hung.	B3	26
Szprotawa, Pol.	E11	16
Szubin, Pol.	C13	16
Szypliszki, Pol.	B19	16

T

Name	Map Ref.	Page
Taal, Lake, l., Phil.	D3	52
Tábara, Spain	C5	20
Tabar Islands, is., Pap. N. Gui.	a5	79a
Tabarka, Tun.	H2	24
Tabasco, state, Mex.	D6	96
Tabelbala, Alg.	D4	64
Taber, Ab., Can.	G18	138
Tabernes de Valldigna see Tavernes de la Valldigna, Spain	E10	20
Tabira, Braz.	D7	88
Tablas de Daimiel, Parque Nacional de las, p.o.i., Spain	E7	20
Tablas Island, i., Phil.	D4	52
Tablas Strait, strt., Phil.	D3	52
Tablat, Alg.	H14	20
Table Mountain, mtn., Az., U.S.	K6	132
Table Rock, Ne., U.S.	D1	120
Table Rock Lake, res., U.S.	H4	120
Table Top, mtn., Az., U.S.	K4	132
Tablones, P.R.	B4	104a
Taboi, Mount, hill, St. Vin.	p11	105e
Tábor, Czech Rep.	G10	16
Tabor, Russia	B19	34
Tabor, Ia., U.S.	D2	120
Tabora, Tan.	E6	66
Tabor City, N.C., U.S.	B7	116
Tabou, C. Iv.	I3	64
Tabrīz, Iran	B6	56
Tabuaeran, at., Kir.	C11	72
Tabu-dong, Kor., S.	C1	40
Tabuk, Phil.	B3	52
Tabūk, Sau. Ar.	J7	58
Tabuleiro do Norte, Braz.	C6	88
Tabwémasana, Mont, mtn., Vanuatu	j16	79d
Tacámbaro de Codallos, Mex.	F8	100
Tacaná, Volcán, vol., N.A.	H12	100
Tacañitas, Arg.	D6	92
Taché, Lac, l., N.T., Can.	C7	106
Tacheng, China	B1	36
Tachia, stm., Tai.	I9	42
Tachichitlte, Isla de, i., Mex.	C4	100
Tachie, stm., B.C., Can.	B6	138
Táchira, state, Ven.	D6	86
Tachoshui, Tai.	I9	42
Tacima, Braz.	D8	88
Tacloban, Phil.	E5	52
Taclobo, Phil.	D4	52
Tacna, Peru	G3	84
Tacna, Az., U.S.	K3	132
Tacoma, Wa., U.S.	C4	136
Taconic Range, mts., U.S.	B12	114
Taco Pozo, Arg.	B6	92
Tacuarembó, Ur.	E9	92
Tacuarembó, stm., Ur.	E10	92
Tacuarí, stm., Ur.	F10	92
Tacutu (Takutu), stm., S.A.	F11	86
Tademaït, Plateau du, plat., Alg.	D5	64
Tādepallegūdem, India	C5	53
Tadjemout, Alg.	D5	64
Tadjerouine, Tun.	I2	24
Tadjoura, Dji.	E8	62
Tadotsu, Japan	E6	40
Tadoule Lake, l., Mb., Can.	D11	106
Tadoussac, Qc., Can.	B7	110
Tādpatri, India	D4	53
T'aean, Kor., S.	F7	38
T'aebaek-sanmaek, mts., Asia	F8	38
Taech'ŏn, Kor., S.	F7	38
Taedong-gang, stm., Kor., N.	E6	38
Taegu, Kor., S.	D1	40
Taejin, Kor., S.	C2	40
Taejŏn, Kor., S.	F7	38
Taeng, stm., Thai.	C4	48
Tafahi, i., Tonga	E9	72
Tafalla, Spain	B9	20
Tafanlieh, Tai.	J9	42
Tafassâsset, Oued, stm., Afr.	E6	64
Tafassasset, Ténéré du, des., Niger	E7	64
Taféa, state, Vanuatu	I17	79d
Tafelberg, hill, Neth. Ant.	p22	104g
Tafí Viejo, Arg.	C5	92
Tafo, Ghana	H4	64
Taft, Ca., U.S.	H6	134
Taft, Tx., U.S.	F10	130
Taftān, Kūh-e, vol., Iran	D9	56
Taga, Samoa	g11	79c
Tagajō, Japan	A14	40
Taganrog, Russia	E5	32
Tagânt, reg., Maur.	F2	64
Tagawa, Japan	F3	40
Tagaytay, Phil.	C3	52
Tagbilaran, Phil.	F4	52
Tage, Pap. N. Gui.	b3	79a
Tagish Lake, l., Can.	C3	106
Tagliamento, stm., Italy	E9	22
Taglio di Po, Italy	E9	22
Taguatinga, Braz.	G2	88
Taguke, China	B10	54
Tagula Island, i., Pap. N. Gui.	B10	74
Tagum, Phil.	G5	52
Tagus (Tajo) (Tejo), stm., Eur.	E2	20
Tahakopa, N.Z.	H3	80
Tahan, Gunong, mtn., Malay.	J6	48
Tahat, mtn., Alg.	E6	64
Tahiataš, Uzb.	F9	32
Tahifet, Alg.	E6	64
Tahiryuak Lake, l., N.T., Can.	A8	106
Tahiti, i., Fr. Poly.	v23	78h
Tahiti-Faaa, Aéroport International de, Fr. Poly.	v21	78h
Tahkuna nina, c., Est.	A5	10
Tahlequah, Ok., U.S.	I3	120
Tahoe, Lake, l., U.S.	E5	134
Tahoe City, Ca., U.S.	D5	134
Tahoe Lake, l., Nu., Can.	A8	106
Tahoka, Tx., U.S.	A6	130
Tahoua, Niger	F5	64
Tahquamenon, stm., Mi., U.S.	B4	112
Tahta, Egypt	L2	58
Tahta, Russia	E6	32
Tahta-Bazar, Turkmen.	B9	56
Tahtaköprü, Tur.	D12	28
Tahtamygda, Russia	F13	34
Tahtsa Lake, res., B.C., Can.	C3	138
Tahtsa Peak, mtn., B.C., Can.	C3	138
Tahuata, i., Fr. Poly.	s18	78g
Tahulandang, Pulau, i., Indon.	E7	44
Tahuna, Indon.	E8	44
Tai'an, China	C7	42
Taiarapu, Presqu'île de, pen., Fr. Poly.	w22	78h
Taibai Shan, mtn., China	E2	42
Taibilla, Sierra de, mts., Spain	F8	20
Taibus Qi, China	C8	36
Taicang, China	F9	42
T'aichou see Taizhou, China	E8	42
T'aichung, Tai.	I9	42
Taieri, stm., N.Z.	G4	80
Taigu, China	C5	42
Taihang Shan, mts., China	C5	42
Taihape, N.Z.	D6	80
Taihe, China	H6	42
Taihe, China	E6	42
Taihezhen, China	B5	38
T'aihsien see Taizhou, China	E8	42
Taihu, China	F7	42
Tai Hu, l., China	F9	42
Taikang, China	D6	42
Taikou, China	F4	42
Tailai, China	B9	36
Tai Lake see Tai Hu, l., China	F9	42
Tailem Bend, Austl.	J2	76
Taimba, Russia	B17	32
T'ainan, Tai.	J8	42
Taínaro, Ákra, c., Grc.	G5	28
Taining, China	H7	42
Taiobeiras, Braz.	H4	88
T'aipei, Tai.	I9	42
T'aipeihsien, Tai.	I9	42
Taiping, China	J2	42
Taiping, Malay.	J5	48
Taipingdian, China	E4	42
Taipu, Braz.	C8	88
Tais, Indon.	F3	50
Taisha, Japan	D5	40
Taishan, China	J5	42
Tai Shan see Yuhuang Ding, mtn., China	C9	42
Taishun, China	H8	42
Taitao, Península de, pen., Chile	I2	90
T'aitung, Tai.	J9	42
Taivalkoski, Fin.	D12	8
Taiwan, ctry., Asia	J9	42
Taiwan Strait, strt., Asia	I8	42
Taixian, China	E9	42
Taixing, China	E9	42
Ṭaiyiba, Isr.	F6	58
Taiyuan, China	C5	42
Taizhao, China	D14	54
Taizhou, China	E8	42
Taizi, stm., China	D5	38
Tajbola, Russia	B15	8
Tajga, Russia	C15	32
Tajgonos, mys, c., Russia	D21	34
Tajgonos, poluostrov, pen., Russia	D21	34
Tajikistan, ctry., Asia	B11	56
Tajima, Japan	B12	40
Tajimi, Japan	D10	40
Tajique, N.M., U.S.	G2	128
Tajitos, Mex.	F6	98
Tāj Mahal, hist., India	E7	54
Tajmura, stm., Russia	B18	32
Tajmyr, ozero, l., Russia	B9	34
Tajmyr, poluostrov, pen., Russia	B7	34
Tajšet, Russia	C17	32
Tajumulco, Volcán, vol., Guat.	E2	102
Tajuña, stm., Spain	D7	20
Tak, Thai.	D4	48
Takachu, Bots.	C5	70
Takahagi, Japan	C13	40
Takahashi, Japan	E6	40
Takahe, Mount, mtn., Ant.	C29	81
Takaka, N.Z.	E5	80
Takakkaw Falls, wtfl., B.C., Can.	E14	138
Takalar, Indon.	F11	50
Takamatsu, Japan	E7	40
Takanabe, Japan	G4	40
Takaoka, Japan	C9	40
Takasago, Japan	E7	40
Takasaki, Japan	C11	40
Takatsuki, Japan	E8	40
Ta-kaw, Mya.	B4	48
Takayama, Japan	C10	40
Takefu, Japan	D9	40
Takenake, China	A8	54
Takengon, Indon.	J3	48
Takeo, Japan	F3	40
Take-shima, is., Asia	B4	40
Taketa, Japan	G4	40
Takêv, Camb.	G7	48
Takhatpur, India	G8	54
Takhli, Thai.	E5	48
Takhta-Bazar see Tahta-Bazar, Turkmen.	B9	56
Takijuq Lake, l., Nu., Can.	B8	106
Takikawa, Japan	C14	38
Takla Lake, l., B.C., Can.	A5	138
Takla Landing, B.C., Can.	D5	106
Takla Makan Desert see Taklimakan Shamo, des., China	G14	32
Taklimakan Shamo (Takla Makan Desert), des., China	G14	32
Takolekaju, Pegunungan, mts., Indon.	E11	50
Taksimo, Russia	F10	34
Taku, Japan	F3	40
Takuan, Mount, vol., Pap. N. Gui.	d6	79b
Takum, Nig.	H7	64
Takutea, i., Cook Is.	E11	72
Takutu (Tacutu), stm., S.A.	F11	86
Talačyn, Bela.	F12	10
Talagang, Pak.	B4	54
Talagante, Chile	F2	92
Talaimannar, Sri L.	G4	53
Talāja, India	H4	54
Talak, reg., Niger	F6	64
Tālāla, India	H3	54
Talang, Gunung, vol., Indon.	D2	50
Talangbetutu, Indon.	E4	50
Talangpadang, Indon.	F4	50
Talangrimbo, Indon.	E4	50
Talara, Peru	D1	84
Talas, Kyrg.	F12	32
Talasea, Pap. N. Gui.	b4	79a
Tal'at al-Jamā'ah, Rujm, mtn., Jord.	H6	58
Talata Mafara, Nig.	G6	64
Talaud, Kepulauan (Talaud Islands), is., Indon.	E8	44
Talaud Islands see Talaud, Kepulauan, is., Indon.	E8	44

I·56 Talavera de la Reina – Tervola

Name	Map Ref.	Page
Talavera de la Reina, Spain	D5	20
Talawanta, Austl.	B3	76
Talawdī, Sudan	E6	62
Talayan, Phil.	G5	52
Talbotton, Ga., U.S.	E14	122
Talbragar, stm., Austl.	I7	76
Talca, Chile	G2	92
Talcahuano, Chile	H1	92
Tālcher, India	H10	54
Talco, Tx., U.S.	D3	122
Taldom, Russia	D20	10
Taldykorgan see Taldyqorghan, Kaz.	F13	32
Taldyqorghan, Kaz.	F13	32
Talence, Fr.	E5	18
Talent, Or., U.S.	A3	134
Talgar see Talghar, Kaz.	F13	32
Talghar, Kaz.	F13	32
Talhār, Pak.	F2	54
Taliabu, Pulau, i., Indon.	F7	44
Talibon, Phil.	E5	52
Talibong, Ko, i., Thai.	I4	48
Talica, Russia	C10	32
Talien see Dalian, China	B9	42
Tālīkota, India	C3	53
Taliparamba, India	E2	53
Talisay, Phil.	E4	52
Taliwang, Indon.	H10	50
Talkeetna, Ak., U.S.	D9	140
Talkeetna Mountains, mts., Ak., U.S.	D10	140
Talla, Egypt	J1	58
Talladega, Al., U.S.	D12	122
Tallahala Creek, stm., Ms., U.S.	F9	122
Tallahassee, Fl., U.S.	F1	116
Tallahatchie, stm., Ms., U.S.	D8	122
Tallangatta, Austl.	K6	76
Tallapoosa, Ga., U.S.	D13	122
Tallapoosa, stm., U.S.	E12	122
Tallard, Fr.	E11	18
Tallassee, Al., U.S.	E12	122
Tall as-Sulṭān, sci., Gaza	G6	58
Tall Bīsah, Syria	D7	58
Tallinn, Est.	G11	8
Tallmadge, Oh., U.S.	C4	114
Tall Rif'at, Syria	B8	58
Tallulah, La., U.S.	E7	122
Talmage, Ca., U.S.	D2	134
Talmage, Ne., U.S.	K2	118
Tal'menka, Russia	D14	32
Talnah, Russia	C6	34
Taloda, India	H5	54
Taloga, Ok., U.S.	E10	128
Talok, Indon.	C11	50
Tāloqān, Afg.	B10	56
Talovka, Russia	F7	32
Talquin, Lake, res., Fl., U.S.	G14	122
Talsi, Lat.	C5	10
Taltal, Chile	B2	92
Taltson, stm., N.T., Can.	C8	106
Talu, Indon.	C1	50
Taluk, Indon.	D2	50
Talumphuk, Laem, c., Thai.	H5	48
Talurqjuak, Nu., Can.	B12	106
Talvikjulja, Russia	B13	8
Talwood, Austl.	G7	76
Tama, Arg.	E4	92
Tama, Ia., U.S.	C5	120
Tamalameque, Col.	C5	86
Tamale, Ghana	H4	64
Tamalea, Indon.	E11	50
Tamalpais, Mount, mtn., Ca., U.S.	F3	134
Tamana, Japan	G3	40
Tamana, Mount, hill, Trin.	s12	105f
Tamanaco, stm., Ven.	C9	86
Tamaniquá, Braz.	I9	86
Taman Negara, p.o.i., Malay.	J6	48
Tamano, Japan	E6	40
Tamanquaré, Ilha, i., Braz.	H9	86
Tamapatz, Mex.	E9	100
Tamar, stm., Austl.	n13	77a
Tamarac, stm., Mn., U.S.	C2	118
Tamaroa, Il., U.S.	F8	120
Tamási, Hung.	C5	26
Tamaulipas, state, Mex.	C9	100
Tamazulapan del Progreso, Mex.	G9	100
Tamazunchale, Mex.	E9	100
Tambacounda, Sen.	G2	64
Tambakboyo, Indon.	G7	50
Tamba-kōchi, plat., Japan	D8	40
Tambangsawah, Indon.	E3	50
Tambara, Moz.	D5	68
Tāmbaram, India	E5	53
Tambej, Russia	B3	34
Tambelan, Kepulauan, is., Indon.	C5	50
Tamberías, Arg.	E3	92
Tambo, stm., Austl.	K6	76
Tambohorano, Madag.	D7	68
Tambolongang, Pulau, i., Indon.	G12	50
Tambora, Gunung, vol., Indon.	H10	50
Tamboril, Braz.	C5	88
Tamboryacu, stm., Peru	H4	86
Tambov, Russia	D6	32
Tambre, stm., Spain	B2	20
Tambu, Teluk, b., Indon.	C11	50
Tambunan, Malay.	H1	52
Tambura, Sudan	F5	62
Tâmchekkeṭ, Maur.	F2	64
Tame, Col.	D6	86
Tameapa, Mex.	C5	100
Tâmega, stm., Port.	C3	20
Tamel Aike, Arg.	I2	90
Tamenghest, Alg.	E6	64
Tamenghest, Oued, stm., Alg.	E5	64
Tamga, Russia	B10	38
Tamgak, Adrar, mtn., Niger	F6	64
Tamiahua, Mex.	E10	100
Tamiahua, Laguna de, l., Mex.	E10	100
Tamiami Canal, can., Fl., U.S.	K4	116
Tamil Nādu, state, India	F4	53
Tamiš (Timiș), stm., Eur.	D7	26
Tâmîya, Egypt	I1	58
Tamkūhi, India	E10	54
Tam Ky, Viet.	E9	48
Tammerfors see Tampere, Fin.	F10	8
Tammisaari, Fin.	G10	8
Tamms, Il., U.S.	G8	120
Tampa, Fl., U.S.	I3	116
Tampa Bay, b., Fl., U.S.	I3	116
Tampang, Indon.	F4	50
Tampaon, stm., Mex.	E9	100
Tampere (Tammerfors), Fin.	F10	8
Tampico, Mex.	D10	100
Tampico, Il., U.S.	C8	120
Tampin, Malay.	K6	48
Tamsagbulag, Mong.	B8	36
Tamshiyacu, Peru	D3	84
Tamsweg, Aus.	C10	22
Tamu, Mya.	D7	46
Tamuning, Guam	i10	78c
Tamworth, Austl.	H8	76
Tamworth, Eng., U.K.	I11	12
Tana (Teno), stm., Eur.	B12	8
Tana, stm., Kenya	D8	66
Tana, Lake see T'ana Häyk', l., Eth.	E7	62
Tanabe, Japan	F8	40
Tanabi, Braz.	K1	88
Tana bru, Nor.	A12	8
Tanacross, Ak., U.S.	D11	140
Tanafjorden, b., Nor.	A13	8
Tanaga Island, i., Ak., U.S.	g23	140a
T'ana Häyk', l., Eth.	E7	62
Tanahbala, Pulau, i., Indon.	F2	44
Tanahgrogot, Indon.	D10	50
Tanahjampea, Pulau, i., Indon.	G12	50
Tanahmasa, Pulau, i., Indon.	F2	44
Tanahmerah, Indon.	G10	44
Tanah Merah, Malay.	J6	48
Tanahputih, Indon.	C2	50
Tanakeke, Pulau, i., Indon.	F11	50
Tanakpur, India	D7	54
Tanami Desert, des., Austl.	C5	74
Tan An, Viet.	G8	48
Tanana, Ak., U.S.	C9	140
Tanana, stm., Ak., U.S.	D10	140
Tananarive see Antananarivo, Madag.	D8	68
Tanbar, Austl.	E3	76
Tan Chau, Viet.	G7	48
Tanch'ŏn-ŭp, Kor., N.	D8	38
Tancítaro, Pico de, mtn., Mex.	F7	100
Tanda, Egypt	K1	58
Tānda, India	E9	54
Tānda, India	C5	54
Tandag, Phil.	F6	52
Tandaltī, Sudan	E6	62
Țăndărei, Rom.	E14	26
Tandil, Arg.	H8	92
Tando Ādam, Pak.	F2	54
Tando Allāhyār, Pak.	F2	54
Tandou Lake, l., Austl.	I3	76
Tandula Tank, res., India	H8	54
Tandun, Indon.	C2	50
Tāndūr, India	C3	53
Tanega-shima, i., Japan	I9	38
Tanezrouft, des., Afr.	E4	64
Tang, stm., China	E7	42
Tang, stm., China	E5	42
Tang, stm., China	B6	42
Tanga, Russia	F11	34
Tanga, Tan.	F7	66
Tangail, Bngl.	F12	54
Tanga Islands, is., Pap. N. Gui.	a5	79a
Tanga Langua, c., Gren.	q10	105e
Tanganyika see Tanzania, ctry., Afr.	F6	66
Tanganyika, Lake, l., Afr.	F6	66
Tangarana, stm., Peru	I4	86
Tangarare, Sol. Is.	e8	79b
Tanger (Tangier), Mor.	B3	64
Tangerang, Indon.	G5	50
Tangerhütte, Ger.	D7	16
Tangermünde, Ger.	D7	16
Tanggu, China	B7	42
Tanggulashan, China	A14	54
Tanggula Shan, mts., China	E3	36
Tanggula Shankou, p., China	B13	54
Tanghe, China	E5	42
Tangi, Pak.	A3	54
Tangier, N.S., Can.	F14	110
Tangier see Tanger, Mor.	B3	64
Tangier, Va., U.S.	G10	114
Tangipahoa, stm., U.S.	G8	122
Tangjiagou, China	F7	42
Tangkou, China	F8	42
Tangmai, China	E4	36
Tango-hantō, pen., Japan	D8	40
Tangra Yumco, l., China	C11	54
Tangshan, China	B8	42
Tangtou, China	D8	42
Tangyan, Mya.	A4	48
Tangyin, China	D6	42
Tangyuan, China	B10	36
Tanhoj, Russia	F10	34
Taniantaweng Shan, mts., China	F4	36
Tanigawa-dake, mtn., Japan	C11	40
Tanimbar, Kepulauan, is., Indon.	G9	44
Tanintharyi, state, Mya.	F3	48
Tanis, hist., Egypt	H2	58
Tanjay, Phil.	F4	52
Tanjung, Indon.	H10	50
Tanjung, Indon.	E9	50
Tanjungbalai, Indon.	B1	50
Tanjungbatu, Indon.	C3	50
Tanjungbatu, Indon.	B11	50
Tanjungkarang-Telukbetung see Bandar Lampung, Indon.	F4	50
Tanjunglabu, Indon.	E5	50
Tanjungpandan, Indon.	E5	50
Tanjungpinang, Indon.	C4	50
Tanjungpura, Indon.	K4	48
Tanjungraja, Indon.	E4	50
Tanjungredep, Indon.	B10	50
Tanjungselor, Indon.	B10	50
Tanjunguban, Indon.	C4	50
Tānk, Pak.	B3	54
Tankwa, stm., S. Afr.	H5	70
Tanna, i., Vanuatu	I17	79d
Tannenberg see Stębark, Pol.	C16	16
Tanner, Mount, mtn., B.C., Can.	G12	138
Tannu-Ola, hrebet, mts., Asia	D16	32
Tannūrah, Ra's, c., Sau. Ar.	D7	56
Tanon Strait, strt., Phil.	E4	52
Tanout, Niger	F6	64
Tanquinho, Braz.	G6	88
Tanshui, Tai.	I9	42
Tanta, Egypt	H2	58
Tan-Tan, Mor.	D2	64
Tantoyuca, Mex.	E9	100
Tanuku, India	C5	53
Tanvald, Czech Rep.	F11	16
Tanyang, Kor., S.	C1	40
Tanzania, ctry., Afr.	F6	66
Tao'er, stm., China	B5	38
Taohuazhen, China	A6	42
Taole, China	B2	42
Taonan, China	B5	38
Taongi, at., Marsh. Is.	B7	72
Taormina, Italy	G9	24
Taos, Mo., U.S.	F5	120
Taos, N.M., U.S.	E3	128
Taos Pueblo, N.M., U.S.	E3	128
Taoudenni, Mali	E4	64
Taounate, Mor.	C4	64
Taourirt, Mor.	C4	64
Taoyuan, China	G4	42
Taoyüan, Tai.	I9	42
Tapa, Est.	G11	8
Tapachula, Mex.	H12	100
Tapaga, Cape, c., Samoa	h12	79c
Tapah, Malay.	J5	48
Tapajós, stm., Braz.	D6	84
Tapaktuan, Indon.	K3	48
Tapalqué, Arg.	H7	92
Tapauá, stm., Braz.	E4	84
Tapejara, Braz.	D12	92
Taperoá, Braz.	D7	88
Tapes, Braz.	E12	92
Tapeta, Lib.	H3	64
Taphan Hin, Thai.	D5	48
Taphoen, stm., Thai.	E4	48
Tāpi, stm., India	H4	54
Ta Pi, stm., Thai.	H4	48
Tapiche, stm., Peru.	E3	84
Tapini, Pap. N. Gui.	b4	79a
Taplan National Park, p.o.i., Thai.	E6	48
Tāplejungg, Nepal.	E11	54
Tappen, N.D., U.S.	H14	124
Tapuae-o-Uenuku, mtn., N.Z.	E5	80
Tapuio, stm., Braz.	C3	88
Tapul Group, is., Phil.	H3	52
Tapun, Mya.	C2	48
Tapuruquara, Braz.	H9	86
Taqāṭu' Hayyā, Sudan	D7	62
Taquara, Braz.	D12	92
Taquaras, Ponta das, c., Braz.	C13	92
Taquari, stm., Braz.	D12	92
Taquari Novo, stm., Braz.	C5	90
Taquaritinga, Braz.	K1	88
Tar, stm., N.C., U.S.	I8	114
Tara, Austl.	F8	76
Tara, Russia	C12	32
Tara, stm., Eur.	G16	22
Tara, stm., Russia	C13	32
Taraba, stm., Nig.	H7	64
Tarabuco, Bol.	C3	90
Ṭarābulus (Tripoli), Leb.	D6	58
Ṭarābulus (Tripoli), Libya	A2	62
Ṭarābulus (Tripolitania), hist. reg., Libya	A2	62
Taraclia, Mol.	D15	26
Tarago, Austl.	J7	76
Taraira (Traíra), stm., S.A.	H7	86
Taraju, Indon.	G6	50
Tarakan, Indon.	B10	50
Tarakan, Pulau, i., Indon.	B10	50
Taralga, Austl.	J7	76
Tara Nacionalni Park, p.o.i., Serb.	F6	26
Tārānagar, India	D5	54
Taranaki, Mount (Egmont, Mount), vol., N.Z.	D6	80
Tarancón, Spain	D8	20
Taranto, Italy	D11	24
Taranto, Golfo di, b., Italy	E10	24
Tarapoto, Peru	E2	84
Taraquá, Braz.	G7	86
Tarare, Fr.	D10	18
Tarariras, Ur.	G9	92
Tarāsa Dwīp, i., India	G7	46
Tarascon, Fr.	F10	18
Tarascon-sur-Ariège, Fr.	G7	18
Tarasovo, Russia	C19	32
Tarat, Alg.	D6	64
Tarata, Bol.	C3	90
Taratakbuluh, Indon.	C2	50
Tarauacá, stm., Braz.	E3	84
Taravao, Isthme de, isth., Fr. Poly.	v22	78h
Tarawa, at., Kir.	C8	72
Tarawera, N.Z.	D7	80
Taraz (Žambyl), Kaz.	F12	32
Tarazona, Spain	C9	20
Tarbagataj, hrebet see Tarbagatay, khrebet, mts., Asia	E14	32
Tarbagatay, khrebet, mts., Asia	E14	32
Tarbagatay Shan see Tarbagatay, khrebet, mts., Asia	E14	32
Tarbela Reservoir, res., Pak.	A4	54
Tarbert, Scot., U.K.	D6	12
Tarbes, Fr.	F6	18
Tarboro, N.C., U.S.	I8	114
Tarbū, Libya	B3	62
Tarcoola, Austl.	F6	74
Tardoki-Jani, gora, mtn., Russia	G16	34
Taree, Austl.	H9	76
Tareja, Russia	B7	34
Tärendö, Swe.	C10	8
Tarentum, Pa., U.S.	D6	114
Tarfa, Wadi el-, stm., Egypt	J2	58
Tarfaya, Mor.	D2	64
Targhee Pass, p., U.S.	F15	136
Tărgovište, Blg.	F13	26
Târgoviște, Rom.	E12	26
Târgu Bujor, Rom.	D14	26
Târgu Frumos, Rom.	B14	26
Târgu Jiu, Rom.	D10	26
Târgu Mureș, Rom.	C11	26
Târgu-Neamț, Rom.	B13	26
Târgu Ocna, Rom.	C13	26
Târgu Secuiesc, Rom.	D12	26
Tarifa, Spain	H5	20
Tarifa, Punta de, c., Spain	H5	20
Tarija, Bol.	D4	90
Tarikere, India	E2	53
Tarim, stm., China	F14	32
Tarim Pendi, bas., China	F12	30
Taritatu, stm., Indon.	F10	44
Tarkastad, S. Afr.	G8	70
Tarkio, Mo., U.S.	D2	120
Tarkio, stm., U.S.	D2	120
Tarko-Sale, Russia	B13	32
Tarkwa, Ghana	H4	64
Tarlac, Phil.	C3	52
Tarm, Den.	I3	8
Tarma, Peru	F2	84
Tarn, state, Fr.	F8	18
Tarn, stm., Fr.	F7	18
Tärnaby, Swe.	D6	8
Tarnak, stm., Afg.	B1	54
Târnava Mare, stm., Rom.	C11	26
Târnăveni, Rom.	C11	26
Tarn-et-Garonne, state, Fr.	F7	18
Tarnobrzeg, Pol.	F17	16
Tarnobrzeg, state, Pol.	F17	16
Tarnogród, Pol.	F18	16
Târnova, Mol.	A14	26
Tarnów, Pol.	G16	16
Tarnów, state, Pol.	G16	16
Tarnowskie Góry, Pol.	F14	16
Taro, Sol. Is.	d7	79b
Taro, stm., Italy	F7	22
Taron, Pap. N. Gui.	a5	79a
Tarong, Austl.	F8	76
Taroom, Austl.	E7	76
Taroudannt, Mor.	C3	64
Ta Roun, Co, mtn., Viet.	D8	48
Tarpon Springs, Fl., U.S.	H3	116
Tarquinia, Italy	H8	22
Tarra, stm., S.A.	C5	86
Tarrafal, C.V.	k10	65a
Tarragona, Spain	C12	20
Tarragona, co., Spain	D11	20
Tarraleah, Austl.	o13	77a
Tarrasa see Terrassa, Spain	C13	20
Tàrrega, Spain	C12	20
Tárrega see Tàrrega, Spain	C12	20
Tarsus, Tur.	B5	58
Tartagal, Arg.	D4	90
Tartu, Est.	G12	8
Ṭarṭūs, Syria	D6	58
Ṭarṭūs, state, Syria	D7	58
Tarum, stm., Indon.	G5	50
Tarumirim, Braz.	J5	88
Tarumizu, Japan	H3	40
Tarutao, Ko, i., Thai.	I4	48
Tarutao National Park, p.o.i., Thai.	I4	48
Tarutino, Russia	E19	10
Tarutung, Indon.	B1	50
Tarvisio, Italy	D10	22
Tarzan, Tx., U.S.	B6	130
Taşağıl, Tur.	B2	58
Tasāwah, Libya	B2	62
Tasböget, Kaz.	F11	32
Taseeva, stm., Russia	C16	32
Taseevo, Russia	C17	32
Taseko Lakes, l., B.C., Can.	E7	138
Taseko Mountain, mtn., B.C., Can.	E7	138
Tāsgaon, India	C2	53
Tashi Gang Dzong, Bhu.	E13	54
Ṭashk, Daryācheh-ye, l., Iran	D7	56
Tasikmalaya, Indon.	G5	50
Tåsinge, i., Den.	B6	16
Taškent, Uzb.	F11	32
Taškepri, Turkmen.	B9	56
Taš-Kumyr, Kyrg.	F12	32
Tasman Basin, unds.	N18	142
Tasman Bay, b., N.Z.	E5	80
Tasmania, state, Austl.	n13	77a
Tasmania, i., Austl.	o13	77a
Tasman Peninsula, pen., Austl.	o13	77a
Tasman Sea, s., Oc.	G7	72
Tășnad, Rom.	B9	26
Tassialouc, Lac, l., Qc., Can.	D16	106
Taštagol, Russia	D15	32
Tastiota, Mex.	A3	100
Tata, Hung.	B5	26
Tata, Mor.	D3	64
Tatabánya, Hung.	B5	26
Tatarbunary, Ukr.	D16	26
Tatarija, state, Russia	C8	32
Tatarinka, Russia	E16	10
Tatarsk, Russia	C13	32
Tatarskij proliv, strt., Russia	G17	34
Tatarskoe-Maklakovo, Russia	I21	8
Tatarstan see Tatarija, state, Russia	C8	32
Tatar Strait see Tatarskij proliv, strt., Russia	G17	34
Tate, Ga., U.S.	B1	116
Tate, stm., Austl.	A4	76
Tateyama, Japan	E12	40
Tate-yama, vol., Japan	C10	40
Tathlina Lake, l., N.T., Can.	C7	106
Tatlayoko Lake, B.C., Can.	E6	138
Tatlayoko Lake, l., B.C., Can.	E6	138
Tatlow, Mount, mtn., B.C., Can.	E7	138
Tatnam, Cape, c., Mb., Can.	D12	106
Tatranský Narodny Park, p.o.i., Slov.	G15	16
Tatrzański Park Narodowy, p.o.i., Pol.	G15	16
Tatsuno, Japan	E7	40
Tatsuno, Japan	D10	40
Tatuí, Braz.	L1	88
Tatum, N.M., U.S.	H5	128
Tatum, Tx., U.S.	E4	122
Tat'ung see Datong, China	A5	42
Tatvan, Tur.	B5	56
Tau, Am. Sam.	h13	79c
Tau, Nor.	G1	8
Tau, i., Am. Sam.	h13	79c
Tauá, Braz.	C5	88
Taubaté, Braz.	L3	88
Tauberbischofsheim, Ger.	G5	16
Taujskaja guba, b., Russia	E18	34
Taumarunui, N.Z.	D6	80
Taumaturgo, Braz.	E3	84
Taum Sauk Mountain, mtn., Mo., U.S.	G7	120
Taungbon, Mya.	E3	48
Taungdwingyi, Mya.	B2	48
Taunggyi, Mya.	B3	48
Taungnyo Range, mts., Mya.	E3	48
Taungup, Mya.	C2	48
Taungup Pass, p., Mya.	C2	48
Taunsa, Pak.	C3	54
Taunton, Eng., U.K.	J9	12
Taunton, Ma., U.S.	C14	114
Taupo, N.Z.	D6	80
Taupo, Lake, l., N.Z.	D7	80
Tauragė, Lith.	E5	10
Tauranga, N.Z.	C7	80
Taurianova, Italy	F9	24
Taurisano, Italy	E12	24
Tauroa Point, c., N.Z.	B5	80
Taurus Mountains see Toros Dağları, mts., Tur.	A3	58
Taūshyq, Kaz.	F8	32
Tautira, Fr. Poly.	v23	78h
Tavares, Braz.	D7	88
Tavas, Tur.	F12	28
Tavastehus see Hämeenlinna, Fin.	F10	8
Tavda, Russia	C11	32
Tavda, stm., Russia	C11	32
Tavernes de la Valldigna, Spain	E10	20
Tavernier, Fl., U.S.	K5	116
Taveuni, i., Fiji	p20	79e
Taviano, Italy	E11	24
Tavira, Port.	G3	20
Tavistock, On., Can.	E9	112
Tavistock, Eng., U.K.	K8	12
Tavolara, Isola, i., Italy	D3	24
Tavoliere, reg., Italy	C9	24
Tavor, Har, mtn., Isr.	F6	58
Tavoy Point, c., Mya.	F3	48
Tavşanlı, Tur.	D12	28
Tavua, Fiji	p18	79e
Tawaeli, Indon.	D11	50
Tawakoni, Lake, res., Tx., U.S.	E2	122
Tawas City, Mi., U.S.	D6	112
Tawau, Malay.	A10	50
Tawîla, Gezira, is., Egypt	K4	58
Tawitawi Group, is., Phil.	H3	52
Tawitawi Island, i., Phil.	H2	52
Ṭawkar, Sudan	D7	62
Taxco de Alarcón, Mex.	F8	100
Taxkorgan Tajik Zizhixian, China	B12	56
Tay, stm., Scot., U.K.	E9	12
Tay, Firth of, b., Scot., U.K.	E9	12
Tay, Loch, l., Scot., U.K.	E8	12
Tayabamba, Peru	E2	84
Tayabas Bay, b., Phil.	D3	52
Tayan, Indon.	C7	50
Taylor, Az., U.S.	I6	132
Taylor, Ne., U.S.	F13	126
Taylor, Tx., U.S.	D10	130
Taylor, Mount, mtn., N.M., U.S.	H9	132
Taylors, S.C., U.S.	B3	116
Taylorsville, Ky., U.S.	F12	120
Taylorsville, Ms., U.S.	F9	122
Taylorsville, N.C., U.S.	I4	114
Taylorville, Il., U.S.	E8	120
Taymā', Sau. Ar.	K9	58
Taymouth, N.B., Can.	D10	110
Taymyr Peninsula see Tajmyr, poluostrov, pen., Russia	B7	34
Tay Ninh, Viet.	G8	48
Taytay, Phil.	E2	52
Tayu, Indon.	G7	50
Taz, stm., Russia	A14	32
Taza, Mor.	C4	64
Tazewell, Tn., U.S.	H2	114
Tazewell, Va., U.S.	G4	114
Tazin, stm., Can.	C8	106
Tazin Lake, l., Sk., Can.	D9	106
Tazovskaja guba, b., Russia	A13	32
Tazovskij, Russia	A13	32
Tazovskij poluostrov, pen., Russia	C4	34
Tbessa, Alg.	B6	64
Tbilisi, Geor.	F6	32
Tchaourou, Benin	H5	64
Tchentlo Lake, l., B.C., Can.	A5	138
Tchesinkut Lake, l., B.C., Can.	B5	138
Tchibanga, Gabon	E2	66
Tcho-kiang see Zhejiang, state, China	G8	42
Tchollíré, Cam.	C2	66
Tchula, Ms., U.S.	D8	122
Tczew, Pol.	B14	16
Té, stm., Camb.	F8	48
Teá, stm., Braz.	H9	86
Teaca, Rom.	C11	26
Teaehoa, c., Fr. Poly.	s18	78g
Teague, Tx., U.S.	F2	122
Teahupoo, Fr. Poly.	w22	78h
Te Anau, Lake, l., N.Z.	G2	80
Teapa, Mex.	G12	100
Te Awamutu, N.Z.	C6	80
Teba, Spain	H5	20
Tebakang, Malay.	C7	50
Tebicuary, stm., Para.	C9	92
Tebicuary-mí, stm., Para.	C9	92
Tebingtinggi, Indon.	B1	50
Tebingtinggi, Indon.	E3	50
Tebingtinggi, Pulau, i., Indon.	C3	50
Tébourba, Tun.	H3	24
Téboursouk, Tun.	H3	24
Tecalitlán, Mex.	F7	100
Tecate, Mex.	K9	134
Techirghiol, Rom.	E15	26
Techlé, W. Sah.	E2	64
Techou see Dezhou, China	C7	42
Tecka, Arg.	H2	90
Tecka, stm., Arg.	H2	90
Tecomán, Mex.	F7	100
Tecopa, Ca., U.S.	H9	134
Tecpan de Galeana, Mex.	G8	100
Tecuala, Mex.	D6	100
Tecuci, Rom.	D14	26
Tecumseh, Ok., U.S.	B2	122
Tedžen, Turkmen.	B9	56
Tedžen (Harīrūd), stm., Asia	B9	56
Teec Nos Pos, Az., U.S.	G7	132
Teeli, Russia	D16	32
Tees, stm., Eng., U.K.	G11	12
Teeswater, On., Can.	D8	112
Tefé, Braz.	D5	84
Tefé, stm., Braz.	D4	84
Tefenni, Tur.	F12	28
Tegal, Indon.	G6	50
Tégama, reg., Niger	F6	64
Tegéa, sci., Grc.	F5	28
Tegineneng, Indon.	F4	50
Tegucigalpa, Hond.	E4	102
Tegul'det, Russia	C15	32
Tehachapi, Ca., U.S.	H7	134
Tehachapi Pass, p., Ca., U.S.	H7	134
Tehek Lake, l., Nu., Can.	C12	106
Tehrān (Teheran), Iran	B7	56
Tehrathum, Nepal	E11	54
Tehuacán, Mex.	F10	100
Tehuantepec, Golfo de, b., Mex.	H11	100
Tehuantepec, Gulf of see Tehuantepec, Golfo de, b., Mex.	H11	100
Tehuantepec, Isthmus of see Tehuantepec, Istmo de, isth., Mex.	G11	100
Tehuantepec, Istmo de, isth., Mex.	G11	100
Teignmouth, Eng., U.K.	K9	12
Teixeira, Braz.	D7	88
Teixeira Pinto, Gui.-B.	G1	64
Tejakula, Indon.	H9	50
Tejkovo, Russia	H19	8
Tejon Pass, p., Ca., U.S.	I7	134
Tejupilco de Hidalgo, Mex.	F8	100
Tekamah, Ne., U.S.	C1	120
Tekapo, Lake, l., N.Z.	F4	80
Tekax, Mex.	B3	102
Teke, Tur.	B12	28
Teke Burnu, c., Tur.	E9	28
Tekeli, Kaz.	F13	32
Tekezē (Satīt), stm., Afr.	E7	62
Tekirdağ, Tur.	C10	28
Tekirdağ, state, Tur.	B10	28
Tekkali, India	B7	53
Tekoa, Wa., U.S.	C9	136
Tekonsha, Mi., U.S.	B1	114
Te Kuiti, N.Z.	D6	80
Tel, stm., India	A6	53
Tela, Hond.	E4	102
Telaopengsha Shan, mtn., China	C11	54
Telavi, Geor.	F7	32
Tel Aviv-Jaffa see Tel Aviv-Yafo, Isr.	F5	58
Tel Aviv-Yafo, Isr.	F5	58
Telč, Czech Rep.	G11	16
Teleckoe, ozero, l., Russia	D15	32
Telefomin, Pap. N. Gui.	b3	79a
Telegraph Creek, B.C., Can.	D4	106
Telêmaco Borba, Braz.	B12	92
Telemark, state, Nor.	G3	8
Telembí, stm., Col.	G2	86
Telén, Arg.	H5	92
Telen, stm., Indon.	C10	50
Telenești, Mol.	B15	26
Teleno, mtn., Spain	B4	20
Teleorman, state, Rom.	E12	26
Teleorman, stm., Rom.	E12	26
Telescope Point, c., Gren.	q10	105e
Telese, Italy	C8	24
Telford, Eng., U.K.	I10	12
Télimélé, Gui.	G2	64
Telire, stm., C.R.	H6	102
Teljo, Jabal, mtn., Sudan	E5	62
Telkwa, B.C., Can.	B3	138
Tell Basta, hist., Egypt	H2	58
Tell City, In., U.S.	G11	120
Tell El-Amarna, hist., Egypt	K1	58
Tellel Rub, hist., Egypt	H2	58
Teller, Ak., U.S.	C6	140
Tellicherry, India	F2	53
Tellier, Arg.	I3	90
Tello, Col.	F4	86
Telluride, Co., U.S.	F9	132
Tel Megiddo, sci., Isr.	F6	58
Telmen nuur, l., Mong.	B4	36
Teloloapan, Mex.	F8	100
Telos see Tílos, i., Grc.	G10	28
Telsen, Arg.	H3	90
Telšiai, Lith.	E5	10
Teltow, Ger.	D9	16
Telukbayur, Indon.	D2	50
Telukbayur, Indon.	B10	50
Telukdalem, Indon.	L3	48
Teluk Intan, Malay.	K5	48
Tema, Ghana	H5	64
Temagami, Lake, l., On., Can.	A9	112
Temaju, Pulau, i., Indon.	C6	50
Te Manga, mtn., Cook Is.	a26	78j
Temangga, Indon.	C7	50
Tematangi, at., Fr. Poly.	F12	72
Temax, Mex.	B3	102
Tembeling, stm., Malay.	J6	48
Tembenči, stm., Russia	A17	32
Tembesi, stm., Indon.	D3	50
Tembilahan, Indon.	D3	50
Temblador, Ven.	C10	86
Temblor Range, mts., Ca., U.S.	H6	134
Teme, stm., Eng., U.K.	I10	12
Temecula, Ca., U.S.	J8	134
Temelli, Tur.	D15	28
Temengor, Tasik, res., Malay.	J5	48
Temetiu, mtn., Fr. Poly.	s18	78g
Temir, Kaz.	E9	32
Temirtau, Kaz.	D12	32
Témiscaming, Qc., Can.	B10	112
Témiscamingue, Lac (Timiskaming, Lake), res., Can.	B10	112
Témiscouata, Lac, l., Qc., Can.	C7	110
Tëmkino, Russia	E17	10
Temora, Austl.	J6	76
Temosachic, Mex.	A5	100
Tempe, Az., U.S.	J5	132
Tempe, Danau, l., Indon.	F12	50
Tempino, Indon.	D3	50
Tempio Pausania, Italy	D2	24
Temple, Tx., U.S.	C10	130
Templi, Valle dei, sci., Italy	G7	24
Templin, Ger.	C9	16
Tempoal, stm., Mex.	E9	100
Tempoal de Sánchez, Mex.	E9	100
Tempy, Russia	D20	10
Temuco, Chile	G2	90
Temwen, i., Micron.	m12	78d
Tena, Ec.	H3	86
Tenabo, Mex.	B2	102
Tenaha, Tx., U.S.	F4	122
Tena Kourou, mtn., Burkina	G4	64
Tenāli, India	C5	53
Tenasserim, Mya.	F4	48
Tendaho, Eth.	E8	62
Tende, Col de, p., Eur.	E13	18
Ten Degree Channel, strt., India	G7	46
Tendō, Japan	A13	40
Ténenkou, Mali	G3	64
Ténéré, des., Niger	F7	64
Ténès, Alg.	H12	20
Ténès, Cap, c., Alg.	H12	20
Teng, stm., Mya.	B3	48
Tengah, Kepulauan, is., Indon.	G10	50
Tengchong, China	G4	36
Tenggara, Nusa (Lesser Sunda Islands), is., Indon.	G6	44
Tenggara Celebes see Sulawesi Tenggara, state, Indon.	E12	50
Tenggarong, Indon.	D10	50
Tengger Shamo, des., China	D5	36
Tenghilan, Malay.	G1	52
Tengiz köli, l., Kaz.	D11	32
Tengréla, C. Iv.	G3	64
Tengtiao (Na), stm., Asia	A6	48
Tengxian, China	J4	42
Tengxian, China	D7	42
Tenkāsi, India	G3	53
Tenke, D.R.C.	G5	66
Tenkeli, Russia	B17	34
Tenkiller Ferry Lake, res., Ok., U.S.	B4	122
Tenkodogo, Burkina	G4	64
Tennant Creek, Austl.	C6	74
Tennessee, state, U.S.	D10	108
Tennessee, stm., U.S.	A11	122
Tennille, Ga., U.S.	D3	116
Teno, Chile	G2	92
Teno (Tana), stm., Eur.	B12	8
Tenom, Malay.	A9	50
Tenos see Tínos, Grc.	F8	28
Tenos see Tínos, i., Grc.	F8	28
Tenosique, Mex.	D2	102
Tenryū, Japan	E10	40
Tenryū, stm., Japan	E10	40
Tensas, stm., La., U.S.	F7	122
Tensed, Id., U.S.	C10	136
Ten Sleep, Wy., U.S.	C5	126
Tenterfield, Austl.	G8	76
Ten Thousand Islands, is., Fl., U.S.	K4	116
Tentolomatinan, Gunung, mtn., Indon.	E7	44
Teocaltiche, Mex.	E7	100
Teodelina, Arg.	G7	92
Teófilo Otoni, Braz.	I5	88
Teo Lakes, l., Sk., Can.	C4	124
Teotihuacán, sci., Mex.	F9	100
Tepa, Indon.	G8	44
Tepalcatepec, Mex.	F7	100
Tepebaşı, Tur.	B3	58
Tepehuanes, Mex.	C6	100
Tepehuanes, stm., Mex.	C6	100
Tepeji de Ocampo, Mex.	F9	100
Tepelenë, Alb.	D13	24
Tepic, Mex.	E6	100
Teplice, Czech Rep.	F9	16
Tepoca, Bahía de, b., Mex.	F6	98
Tepoca, Punta, c., Mex.	G6	98
Ter, stm., Spain	B14	20
Téra, Niger	G5	64
Tera, stm., Spain	C4	20
Teradomari, Japan	B11	40
Teraina, i., Kir.	C11	72
Teramo, Italy	H10	22
Terbuny, Russia	H21	10
Terceira, i., Port.	C3	60
Tercero, stm., Arg.	F6	92
Terdal, India	C2	53
Terek, stm., Russia	G18	6
Terempa, Indon.	B5	50
Terengganu, state, Malay.	J6	48
Terengganu, stm., Malay.	J6	48
Terenos, Braz.	D6	90
Teresina, Braz.	C4	88
Teresópolis, Braz.	L4	88
Terespol, Pol.	D19	16
Terevaka, Cerro, mtn., Chile	e29	78l
Tergüün Bogd uul, mtn., Mong.	C5	36
Teriang, stm., Malay.	K6	48
Teriberka, Russia	B16	8
Terihi, i., Fr. Poly.	t19	78g
Terlingua, Tx., U.S.	E4	130
Terlingua Creek, stm., Tx., U.S.	E4	130
Termas del Arapey, Ur.	E9	92
Termas de Río Hondo, Arg.	C5	92
Termez, Uzb.	B10	56
Termini Imerese, Italy	G7	24
Termini Imerese, Golfo di, b., Italy	F7	24
Terminillo, Monte, mtn., Italy	H9	22
Términos, Laguna de, b., Mex.	C2	102
Termoli, Italy	H11	22
Termonde see Dendermonde, Bel.	C12	14
Ternej, Russia	B12	38
Terneuzen, Neth.	C12	14
Terni, Italy	H9	22
Ternitz, Aus.	C12	22
Ternopil', Ukr.	F14	6
Terpenija, mys, c., Russia	G17	34
Terpenija, zaliv, b., Russia	G17	34
Terra Alta, W.V., U.S.	E6	114
Terra Bella, Ca., U.S.	H6	134
Terrace, B.C., Can.	B2	138
Terracina, Italy	C7	24
Terra Cotta Army (Qinshihuang Mausoleum), sci., China	D3	42
Terral, Ok., U.S.	H11	128
Terralba, Italy	E2	24
Terra Santa, Braz.	D6	84
Terrassa, Spain	C13	20
Terrebonne Bay, b., La., U.S.	H8	122
Terre-de-Bas, Guad.	i5	105c
Terre-de-Haut, Guad.	i5	105c
Terre-de-Haut, i., Guad.	i5	105c
Terre Haute, In., U.S.	E10	120
Terrell, Tx., U.S.	E2	122
Terre-Neuve see Newfoundland and Labrador, state, Can.	i23	107a
Territoire du Yukon see Yukon, state, Can.	B3	106
Territoires du Nord-Ouest see Northwest Territories, state, Can.	C6	106
Terry, Ms., U.S.	E8	122
Terry, Mt., U.S.	A7	126
Terschelling, i., Neth.	A14	14
Terskej-Alatau, hrebet, mts., Kyrg.	F13	32
Teruel, Col.	F4	86
Teruel, Spain	D9	20
Teruel, co., Spain	D10	20
Terujak, Indon.	J3	48
Tervola, Fin.	C11	8

Name	Map Ref.	Page
Terzaghi Dam, dam, B.C., Can.	F8	138
Tes, stm., Asia	D16	32
Tescott, Ks., U.S.	B11	128
Teseney, Erit.	D7	62
Teshekpuk Lake, l., Ak., U.S.	B9	140
Teshio, Japan.	B14	38
Teshio, stm., Japan	B15	38
Teslin, Yk., Can.	C4	106
Teslin, stm., Can.	C4	106
Teslin Lake, l., Can.	C4	106
Tēsovo, Russia	E17	10
Tēsovo-Netyl'skij, Russia	B13	10
Tēsovskij, Russia	B13	10
Tessalit, Mali	E5	64
Tessaoua, Niger	G6	64
Testa, Capo, c., Italy	C3	24
Testour, Tun.	H3	24
Tetachuck Lake, res., B.C., Can.	C4	138
Tete, Moz.	D5	68
Tête Jaune Cache, B.C., Can.	D11	138
Tetepare Island, i., Sol. Is.	e7	79b
Teterow, Ger.	C8	16
Tetica, mtn., Spain	G8	20
Teton, Id., U.S.	G15	136
Teton, stm., Id., U.S.	G15	136
Teton, stm., Mt., U.S.	C15	136
Tetonia, Id., U.S.	G15	136
Teton Range, mts., Wy., U.S.	G16	136
Tetouan, Mor.	B4	64
Tetovo, Mac.	A4	28
Tetufera, Mont, mtn., Fr. Poly.	v22	78h
Teuco, stm., Arg.	D4	90
Teulada, Italy	F2	24
Teulada, Capo, c., Italy	F2	24
Teulon, Mb., Can.	D16	124
Teutoburger Wald, hills, Ger.	D4	16
Teuva, Fin.	E9	8
Tevere (Tiber), stm., Italy	H9	22
Teverya, Isr.	F6	58
Te Waewae Bay, b., N.Z.	H2	80
Tewah, Indon.	D8	50
Tewantin-Noosa, Austl.	F9	76
Tewkesbury, Eng., U.K.	I11	12
Texada Island, i., B.C., Can.	G7	138
Texana, Lake, res., Tx., U.S.	F11	130
Texarkana, Ar., U.S.	D4	122
Texarkana, Tx., U.S.	D4	122
Texas, Austl.	G8	76
Texas, state, U.S.	E8	108
Texas City, Tx., U.S.	H4	122
Texel, i., Neth.	A13	14
Texhoma, Ok., U.S.	E7	128
Texico, N.M., U.S.	G5	128
Texoma, Lake, res., U.S.	H11	128
Teyateyaneng, Leso.	F8	70
Teyvareh, Afg.	C9	56
Teziutlán, Mex.	F10	100
Tezpur, India	E14	54
Tezzeron Lake, l., B.C., Can.	B6	138
Tha, stm., Laos	B5	48
Tha-anne, stm., Nu., Can.	C11	106
Thabana-Ntlenyana, mtn., Leso.	F9	70
Thabaung, Mya.	D2	48
Thabazimbi, S. Afr.	D8	70
Thabyu, Mya.	E4	48
Thagyettaw, Mya.	F4	48
Thai Bình, Viet.	B8	48
Thailand, ctry., Asia	E5	48
Thailand, Gulf of, b., Asia	G5	48
Thai Nguyen, Viet.	B7	48
Thak, Pak.	C3	54
Thal, Pak.	B3	54
Thala, Tun.	I2	24
Thal Desert, des., Pak.	C3	54
Thalfang, Ger.	G2	16
Tha Li, Thai.	D5	48
Thalia, Tx., U.S.	H9	128
Thālith, Ash-Shallāl ath- (Third Cataract), wtfl., Sudan	D6	62
Thahwil, Russia	C5	22
Thames, N.Z.	C7	80
Thames, stm., On., Can.	F8	112
Thames, stm., Eng., U.K.	J13	12
Thames, Firth of, b., N.Z.	C6	80
Thamesford, On., Can.	E8	112
Thamesville, On., Can.	F7	112
Thāna, India	B1	53
Thandaung, Mya.	C4	48
Thangoo, Austl.	C4	74
Thangool, Austl.	E8	76
Thanh Hoa, Viet.	C7	48
Thanh Pho Ho Chi Minh (Saigon), Viet.	G8	48
Thanjāvūr, India	F4	53
Thann, Fr.	B12	18
Thap Than, stm., Thai.	E6	48
Tharabwin West, Mya.	F4	48
Tharād, India	F3	54
Thar Desert (Great Indian Desert), des., Asia	D3	54
Thargomindah, Austl.	F5	76
Tharrawaddy, Mya.	D2	48
Tha Sala, Thai.	H4	48
Thásos, i., Grc.	C7	28
Thásos, sci., Grc.	C7	28
Thaton, Mya.	D3	48
Tha Tum, Thai.	E6	48
Thau, Bassin de, l., Fr.	F9	18
Thaungyin (Moei), stm., Asia	D3	48
Thaya (Dyje), stm., Eur.	H12	16
Thayawthadangyi Kyun, i., Mya.	F3	48
Thayer, Ks., U.S.	G2	120
Thayer, Mo., U.S.	H6	120
Thayetchaung, Mya.	F4	48
Thayetmyo, Mya.	C2	48
Thazi, Mya.	B3	48
Thebes see Thiva, Grc.	E6	28
The Bottom, Neth. Ant.	B1	105a
The Cheviot, mtn., Eng., U.K.	F10	12
The Dalles, Or., U.S.	E5	136
Thedford, Ne., U.S.	E12	126
The Father see Ulawun, Mount, vol., Pap. N. Gui.	b5	79a
The Fens, reg., Eng., U.K.	I12	12
The Fishing Lakes, l., Sk., Can.	D10	124
The Granites, hill, Austl.	D6	74
The Hague see 's-Gravenhage, Neth.	B12	14
The Heads, c., Or., U.S.	H2	136
Theinkun, Mya.	G4	48
The Lakes National Park, p.o.i., Austl.	L6	76
The Little Minch, strt., Scot., U.K.	D6	12
Thelon, stm., Can.	C11	106
The Lynd, Austl.	B5	76
The Minch, strt., Scot., U.K.	D6	12
Thenia, Alg.	H14	20
Theodore, Austl.	E8	76
Theodore, Sk., Can.	C10	124
Theodore, Al., U.S.	G10	122
Theodore Roosevelt National Park North Unit, p.o.i., N.D., U.S.	G10	124
Theodore Roosevelt National Park South Unit, p.o.i., N.D., U.S.	G10	124
The Pas, Mb., Can.	E10	106
Thepha, Thai.	I5	48
The Pinnacle, hill, Mo., U.S.	G4	120
The Rand see Witwatersrand, mts., S. Afr.	D8	70
Theresa Creek, stm., Austl.	D6	76
The Rhins, pen., Scot., U.K.	G7	12
Thermaïkós Kólpos (Salonika, Gulf of), b., Grc.	C6	28
Thermopolis, Wy., U.S.	D4	126
Thermopylae see Thermopyles, hist., Grc.	E5	28
Thermopyles (Thermopylae), hist., Grc.	E5	28
The Rock, Austl.	J6	76
The Rockies, mtn., Wa., U.S.	D5	136
The Rope, clf., Pit.	c28	78k
Thesiger Bay, b., N.T., Can.	B15	140
The Slot see New Georgia Sound, strt., Sol. Is.	e8	79b
Thessalía, state, Grc.	D5	28
Thessalía, hist. reg., Grc.	D5	28
Thessalon, On., Can.	B6	112
Thessaloníki (Salonika), Grc.	C6	28
Thessaly see Thessalía, hist. reg., Grc.	D5	28
Thetford, Eng., U.K.	I13	12
Thetford Mines, Qc., Can.	D5	110
Theunissen, S. Afr.	F8	70
The Valley, Anguilla	A1	105a
The Village, Ok., U.S.	F11	128
The Wash, b., Eng., U.K.	I13	12
The Weald, reg., Eng., U.K.	J13	12
Thibodaux, La., U.S.	H8	122
Thief Lake, l., Mn., U.S.	C3	118
Thief River Falls, Mn., U.S.	C2	118
Thiene, Italy	E8	22
Thiers, Fr.	D9	18
Thiès, Sen.	G1	64
Thika, Kenya	E7	66
Thimphu, Bhu.	E12	54
Thingvallavatn, l., Ice.	k29	8a
Thingvellir, Ice.	k29	8a
Thingvellir Nasjonalpark, p.o.i., Ice.	k29	8a
Thio, N. Cal.	m16	79d
Thionville, Fr.	E15	14
Thira, Grc.	G8	28
Thíra (Santoríni), i., Grc.	G8	28
Third Cataract see Thālith, Ash-Shallāl ath-, wtfl., Sudan	D6	62
Thiruvananthapuram (Trivandrum), India	G3	53
Thiruvārūr, India	F4	53
Thistilfjördur, b., Ice.	j32	8a
Thiva, Grc.	E6	28
Thiviers, Fr.	D6	18
Thjórsá, stm., Ice.	k30	8a
Thohoyandou, S. Afr.	C10	70
Thoi Bình, Viet.	H7	48
Thomas, Ok., U.S.	F10	128
Thomas, W.V., U.S.	E6	114
Thomaston, Al., U.S.	E11	122
Thomaston, Ga., U.S.	D1	116
Thomaston, Me., U.S.	F7	110
Thomasville, Al., U.S.	F2	116
Thomasville, Ga., U.S.	F2	116
Thomasville, N.C., U.S.	I5	114
Thompson, Mb., Can.	D11	106
Thompson, Ia., U.S.	H5	118
Thompson, stm., B.C. Can.	F9	138
Thompson, stm., U.S.	E4	120
Thompson Falls, Mt., U.S.	C11	136
Thompson Peak, mtn., Ca., U.S.	B3	134
Thomsen, stm., N.T., Can.	B16	140
Thomson, Ga., U.S.	C3	116
Thomson, Il., U.S.	C7	120
Thomson, stm., Austl.	E4	76
Thongwa, Mya.	D3	48
Thonon-les-Bains, Fr.	C12	18
Thonotosassa, Fl., U.S.	H3	116
Thonze, Mya.	D2	48
Thorhild, Ab., Can.	B17	138
Thorlákshöfn, Ice.	k30	8a
Thorlákshöfn, Ice.	l29	8a
Thornaby-on-Tees, Eng., U.K.	G11	12
Thornbury, On., Can.	D9	112
Thorndale, Tx., U.S.	D10	130
Thornton, Co., U.S.	B4	128
Thornton, Tx., U.S.	F2	122
Thorntonville, Tx., U.S.	C4	130
Thorp, Wi., U.S.	G8	118
Thorsby, Ab., Can.	C16	138
Thorshavn see Tórshavn, Far. Is.	n34	8b
Thórshöfn, Ice.	j32	8a
Thouars, Fr.	H8	14
Thoune see Thun, Switz.	D4	22
Thousand Lake Mountain, mtn., Ut., U.S.	E5	132
Thousand Oaks, Ca., U.S.	I7	134
Thousand Ships Bay, b., Sol. Is.	e8	79b
Thousand Springs Creek, stm., U.S.	B2	132
Thrace, hist. reg., Eur.	H13	26
Thrakikó Pélagos, s., Grc.	C8	28
Three Forks, Mt., U.S.	E15	136
Three Gorges Dam, dam, China	F4	42
Three Hills, Ab., Can.	E17	138
Three Hummock Island, i., Austl.	n12	77a
Three Kings Islands, is., N.Z.	B5	80
Three Mile Plains, N.S., Can.	F12	110
Three Points, Cape, c., Ghana	I4	64
Three Rivers, Mi., U.S.	G4	112
Three Rivers, Tx., U.S.	F9	130
Three Sisters, mtn., Or., U.S.	F5	136
Three Sisters Islands, is., N.Z.	f10	79b
Three Springs, Austl.	E3	74
Thrissur see Trichūr, India	F3	53
Throssel, Lake, l., Austl.	E4	74
Thu, Cu Lao, i., Viet.	G9	48
Thuan Chau, Viet.	B6	48
Thu Dau Mot, Viet.	G8	48
Thuin, Bel.	D13	14
Thule (Qaanaaq), Grnld.	B12	141
Thun, Switz.	D4	22
Thun Chang, Thai.	C5	48
Thunder Bay, On., Can.	C9	118
Thunder Bay, b., On., Can.	C9	118
Thunderbird, Lake, res., Ok., U.S.	F11	128
Thunderbolt, Ga., U.S.	D4	116
Thunder Butte Creek, stm., S.D., U.S.	B10	126
Thunder Creek, stm., Sk., Can.	D7	124
Thuner See, l., Switz.	D4	22
Thung Salaeng Luang National Park, p.o.i., Thai.	D5	48
Thung Wa, Thai.	I4	48
Thüringen, state, Ger.	F7	16
Thüringer Wald, mts., Ger.	F6	16
Thurles, Ire.	I5	12
Thurmont, Md., U.S.	E8	114
Thursday Island, Austl.	B8	74
Thurso, Scot., U.K.	C9	12
Thurston Island, i., Ant.	C31	81
Thusis, Switz.	D6	22
Thylungra, Austl.	F4	76
Thyolo, Mwi.	D5	68
Thysville see Mbanza-Ngungu, D.R.C.	F3	66
Tiachiv, Ukr.	A10	26
Tianchang, China	E8	42
Tiandeng, China	J2	42
Tiandong, China	J2	42
Tian'e, China	I2	42
Tiangang, China	C7	38
Tianguá, Braz.	B5	88
Tianjin (Tientsin), China	B7	42
Tianjin, state, China	B7	42
Tianjun, China	D4	36
Tianlin, China	I2	42
Tian Ling, mtn., China	B8	38
Tianmen, China	F5	42
Tianqiaoling, China	C8	38
Tianshifu, China	D6	38
Tianshui, China	D1	42
Tiantang, China	G9	42
Tiantang, China	J4	42
Tianwangsi, China	F8	42
Tianyang, China	J2	42
Tianzhen, China	A6	42
Tianzhu, China	D5	36
Tianzhu, China	H3	42
Tiarei, Fr. Poly.	v22	78h
Tiaro, Austl.	E9	76
Tiassalé, C. Iv.	H4	64
Ti'avea, Samoa	g12	79c
Tibaji, stm., Braz.	A12	92
Tibal-og, Phil.	G5	52
Tibasti, Sarir, des., Libya	C3	62
Tibati, Cam.	C2	66
Tibbie, Al., U.S.	F10	122
Tiber see Tevere, stm., Italy	H9	22
Tiberias, Lake see Kinneret, Yam, l., Isr.	F6	58
Tibesti, mts., Afr.	C3	62
Tibet see Xizang, state, China	B5	46
Tibet, Plateau of see Qing Zang Gaoyuan, plat., China	B6	46
Tiblawan, Phil.	G6	52
Tibnīn, Leb.	E6	58
Tibooburra, Austl.	G4	76
Tiburón, Cabo, c.	C3	86
Tiburón, Isla, i., Mex.	G6	98
Tíča, Jazovir, res., Blg.	F13	26
Tîcao Island, i., Phil.	D4	52
Tichît, Maur.	F3	64
Ticino, stm., Eur.	D14	18
Tickfaw, stm., La., U.S.	G8	122
Ticonderoga, N.Y., U.S.	G3	110
Ticul, Mex.	B3	102
Tidioute, Pa., U.S.	C6	114
Tidjikja, Maur.	F2	64
Tiébissou, C. Iv.	H3	64
T'iehling see Tieling, China	C5	38
Tiel, Neth.	C14	14
Tieli, China	B10	36
Tieling, China	C5	38
Tielt, Bel.	C12	14
Tiémé, C. Iv.	H3	64
Tienching see Tianjin, China	B7	42
Tien Giang see Mekong, stm., Asia	F9	46
Tien Shan, mts., Asia	F13	32
T'ienshui see Tianshui, China	D1	42
Tientsin see Tianjin, state, China	B7	42
Tien Yen, Viet.	B8	48
Tie Plant, Ms., U.S.	D9	122
Tierp, Swe.	F7	8
Tierra Amarilla, Chile	C2	92
Tierra Blanca, Chile	F10	100
Tierra Blanca, Mex.	G3	130
Tierra Blanca Creek, stm., U.S.	G6	128
Tierra de Campos, reg., Spain	C6	20
Tierra del Fuego, state, Arg.	J3	90
Tierra del Fuego, i., S.A.	J3	90
Tiétar, stm., Spain	E5	20
Tieté, stm., Braz.	L2	88
Tieté, stm., Braz.	D6	90
Tieti, N. Cal.	m15	79d
Tiffany Mountain, mtn., Wa., U.S.	B7	136
Tiffin, Oh., U.S.	C2	114
Tifton, Ga., U.S.	E2	116
Tiga, Île, i., N. Cal.	m16	79d
Tigalda Island, i., Ak., U.S.	F7	140
Tigapuluh, Pegunungan, mts., Indon.	D3	50
Tighina, Mol.	C16	26
Tigil', Russia	E20	34
Tignall, Ga., U.S.	C3	116
Tignish, P.E., Can.	D12	110
Tigoda, stm., Russia	A14	10
Tigre, Col.	F7	86
Tigre, stm., Peru	D2	84
Tigre, stm., Ven.	C10	86
Tigris (Dicle) (Dijlah), stm., Asia	C5	56
Tiguentourine, Alg.	D6	64
Tihany, hist., Hung.	C4	26
Tihert, Alg.	H13	20
Tihookeanskij, Russia	C10	38
Tihoreck, Russia	E6	32
Tihua see Ürümqi, China	C2	36
Tihuatlán, Mex.	E10	100
Tihvin, Russia	A16	10
Tijuana, Mex.	K8	134
Tijuana, stm., N.A.	K8	134
Tijucas, Braz.	C13	92
Tijucas do Sul, Braz.	B13	92
Tijuco, stm., Braz.	J1	88
Tikal, sci., Guat.	D3	102
Tikal, Parque Nacional, p.o.i., Guat.	D3	102
Tikrīt, Iraq	C5	56
Tikša, Russia	D15	8
Tikšeozero, ozero, l., Russia	C14	8
Tiksi, Russia	B14	34
Tiladummati Atoll, at., Mald.	h12	46a
Tilburg, Neth.	C14	14
Tilbury, On., Can.	F7	112
Tilcha, Austl.	G3	76
Tilden, Il., U.S.	F8	120
Tilden, Ne., U.S.	E15	126
Tilden, Tx., U.S.	F9	130
Tilhar, India	D7	54
Tilimsen, Alg.	C4	64
Tilin, Mya.	B2	48
Tillabéri, Niger	G5	64
Tilley, Ab., Can.	F19	138
Tillia, Niger	F5	64
Tillmans Corner, Al., U.S.	G10	122
Tillson, N.Y., U.S.	C11	114
Tillsonburg, On., Can.	F9	112
Tílos, i., Grc.	G10	28
Tilpa, Austl.	H5	76
Tilton, N.H., U.S.	G5	110
Tiltonsville, Oh., U.S.	D5	114
Tima, Egypt	L2	58
Timaná, Col.	G3	86
Timanskij krjaž, hills, Russia	B8	32
Timaru, N.Z.	G4	80
Timbalier Bay, b., La., U.S.	H8	122
Timbaúba, Braz.	D8	88
Timbedgha, Maur.	F3	64
Timbedra Lake, l., U.S.	B11	126
Timbiras, Braz.	C4	88
Timbó, Braz.	C13	92
Timbo, Lib.	H3	64
Timbuktu see Tombouctou, Mali	F4	64
Timétrine, India	F4	64
Timétrine, mts., Mali	F4	64
Timimoun, Alg.	D5	64
Timiris, Râs, c., Maur.	F1	64
Timirjazevo, Russia	E4	10
Timiş, state, Rom.	D8	26
Timiş (Tamiš), stm., Eur.	D7	26
Timiškaming, Lake (Témiscamingue, Lac), res., Can.	B10	112
Timişoara, Rom.	D8	26
Timmendorfer Strand, Ger.	B7	16
Timmins, On., Can.	F14	106
Timmonsville, S.C., U.S.	B6	116
Timms Hill, hill, Wi., U.S.	F8	118
Timna'see Mikhrot Timna', hist., Isr.	I5	58
Timok, stm., Eur.	E9	26
Timon, Braz.	C4	88
Timor, i., Asia	G8	44
Timor Sea, s.	K15	142
Timošino, Russia	H21	8
Timotes, Ven.	C6	86
Timpanogos Cave National Monument, p.o.i., Ut., U.S.	C5	132
Timpton, stm., Russia	E14	34
Timšer, Russia	B9	32
Tims Ford Lake, res., Tn., U.S.	B12	122
Tina, stm., S. Afr.	G9	70
Tina, Khalig el- (Pelusium Bay), b., Egypt.	G3	58
Tinaca Point, c., Phil.	H5	52
Tinambung, Indon.	E11	50
Tinapagee, Austl.	G5	76
Tinaquillo, Ven.	C7	86
Tindivanam, India	E4	53
Tindouf, Alg.	D3	64
Tineba, Pegunungan, mts., Indon.	D12	50
Tineg, stm., Phil.	B3	52
Ting, stm., China	I7	42
Tinggi, Pulau, i., Malay.	K7	48
Tingha, Austl.	G8	76
Tinghert, Hamâdat (Tinghert, Plateau du), plat., Afr.	D7	64
Tinghert, Plateau du (Tinghert, Hamâdat), plat., Afr.	D6	64
Tinghsien see Dingxian, China	B6	42
Tinglev, Den.	B5	16
Tingo Maria, Peru	E2	84
Tingri, China	D11	54
Tingri see Dinggyê, China	D11	54
Tinguiririca, Volcán, vol., Chile	G2	92
Tinharé, Ilha de, i., Braz.	G6	88
Tinh Bien, Viet.	G7	48
Tinian, i., N. Mar. Is.	B5	72
Tinjar, stm., Malay.	B9	50
Tinos, Grc.	F8	28
Tínos, i., Grc.	F8	28
Tinsley, Ms., U.S.	E8	122
Tinsukia, India	C8	46
Tintagel, B.C., Can.	B5	138
Tintina, Arg.	C6	92
Tintinara, Austl.	J3	76
Tio, Erit.	E8	62
Tiobrad Árann see Tipperary, Ire.	I4	12
Tioga, N.D., U.S.	F11	124
Tioman, Pulau, i., Malay.	K7	48
Tionesta, Pa., U.S.	C6	114
Tipasa, Alg.	H13	20
Tipitapa, Nic.	F4	102
Tipperary, Ire.	I4	12
Tipperary, state, Ire.	I5	12
Tipton, Ca., U.S.	G6	134
Tipton, Ia., U.S.	C6	120
Tipton, In., U.S.	H3	112
Tipton, Mo., U.S.	F5	120
Tipton, Ok., U.S.	G9	128
Tipton, Mount, mtn., Az., U.S.	H2	132
Tiptonville, Tn., U.S.	H8	120
Tip Top Mountain, mtn., On., Can.	F13	106
Tiptūr, India	E3	53
Tiputini, stm., Ec.	H4	86
Tira, Isr.	F5	58
Tīrān, i., Sau. Ar.	K5	58
Tirana see Tiranë, Alb.	C13	24
Tiranë, Alb.	C13	24
Tirano, Italy	D7	22
Tiraspol, Mol.	C16	26
Tire, Tur.	E10	28
Tiree, i., Scot., U.K.	E6	12
Tirich Mir, mtn., Pak.	B11	56
Tîrna, stm., India	B3	53
Tirodi, India	H7	54
Tirol, state, Aus.	C8	22
Tiros, Braz.	J3	88
Tirso, stm., Italy	E2	24
Tirthahalli, India	E2	53
Tiruchchirāppalli, India	F4	53
Tiruchengodu, India	F3	53
Tirukkalukkunram, India	E5	53
Tirukkovilūr, India	E4	53
Tiruliai, Lith.	E6	10
Tirunelveli, India	G3	53
Tirupati, India	E4	53
Tiruppattūr, India	F4	53
Tiruppur, India	F3	53
Tirūr, India	F3	53
Tirutturaippūndi, India	F4	53
Tiruvalla, India	G3	53
Tiruvannāmalai, India	E4	53
Tiruvottiyūr, India	E5	53
Tiruvur, India	C5	53
Tisa (Tisza) (Tysa), stm., Eur.	D7	26
Tisdale, Sk., Can.	B9	124
Tishomingo, Ms., U.S.	C10	122
Tisīyah, Syria	F7	58
Tiskilwa, Il., U.S.	C8	120
Tisovec, Slov.	H15	16
Tista (Tisza) (Tysa), stm., Eur.	C7	26
Tisza (Tisa) (Tysa), stm., Eur.	C7	26
Tiszaújváros, Hung.	B7	26
Tiszavasvári, Hung.	A8	26
Titaf, Alg.	D5	64
Tit-Ary, Russia	B14	34
Titicaca, Lake, l., S.A.	G4	84
Titilāgarh, India	H9	54
Titonka, Ia., U.S.	H4	118
Titov Veles, Mac.	B4	28
Titule, D.R.C.	D5	66
Titusville, Fl., U.S.	H5	116
Titusville, Pa., U.S.	C6	114
Tiuni, India	C6	54
Tīvaouane, Sen.	F1	64
Tiverton, Eng., U.K.	K9	12
Tivoli, Italy	I9	22
Tivoli, Tx., U.S.	F11	130
Tīyās, Syria	D8	58
Tizimín, Mex.	B3	102
Tizi-Ouzou, Alg.	H14	20
Tiznit, Mor.	D3	64
Tizmant el-Zawâya, Egypt.	I1	58
Tizoc, Ven.	C2	36
Tjačevo, Pol.	D10	22
Tjukalinsk, Russia	C12	32
Tjul'gan, Russia	D9	32
Tjumen', Russia	C10	32
Tjung, stm., Russia	D13	34
Tjuva-Guba, Russia	B15	8
Tlacotalpan, Mex.	F11	100
Tlacote see TIntonatzin —	—	—
Tlahualilo de Zaragoza, Mex.	B7	100
Tlaltenango de Sánchez Román, Mex.	E7	100
Tlapaneco, stm., Mex.	G9	100
Tlaquepaque, Mex.	E7	100
Tlaxcala, state, Mex.	F9	100
Tlaxcala de Xicohténcatl, Mex.	F9	100
Tłuszcz, Pol.	D17	16
Tmassah, Libya	B3	62
Tňáoč, stm., Camb.	C2	48
Toa Alta, P.R.	B3	104a
Toa Baja, P.R.	B3	104a
Toachí, stm., Ec.	H2	86
Toahayana, Mex.	B5	100
Toamasina, Madag.	D8	68
Toba, Japan.	E9	40
Toba, Danau, l., Indon.	K4	48
Tobago, i., Trin.	r13	105f
Toba Inlet, b., B.C., Can.	F6	138
Toba Kākar Range, mts., Pak.	C10	56
Tobarra, Spain	F9	20
Tobas, Arg.	D6	92
Toba Tek Singh, Pak.	C4	54
Tobelo, Indon.	E8	44
Tobermorey, Austl.	D7	74
Tobermory, On., Can.	C8	112
Tobermory, Scot., U.K.	E6	12
Tobias, Ne., U.S.	G15	126
Tobias Barreto, Braz.	F6	88
Tobin, Mount, mtn., Nv., U.S.	B8	134
Tobique, stm., N.B., Can.	C9	110
Toboalí, Indon.	E5	50
Tobol (Tobyl), stm., Asia	C11	32
Toboli, Indon.	D12	50
Tobol'sk, Russia	C11	32
Toboso, Phil.	E4	52
Tobseda, Russia	B25	8
Tobyhanna, Pa., U.S.	C10	114
Tobyl, Kaz.	D10	32
Tobyl (Tobol), stm., Asia	D10	32
Tobylzhan, Kaz.	D13	32
Tobyš, stm., Russia	C24	8
Tocantínia, Braz.	E1	88
Tocantinópolis, Braz.	D2	88
Tocantins, stm., Braz.	F8	84
Tocantins, stm., Braz.	D1	88
Tocantins, stm., Braz.	F1	88
Tocantinzinho, stm., Braz.	H1	88
Tochcha Lake, l., B.C., Can.	B5	138
Tochigi, Japan.	C12	40
Tochigi, state, Japan	C12	40
Tochio, Japan	B12	40
Toco, Trin.	s13	105f
Tocoa, Hond.	E5	102
Toconao, Chile	D3	90
Tocopilla, Chile	D2	90
Tocuco, stm., Ven.	C5	86
Tocumwal, Austl.	J5	76
Tocuyo, stm., Ven.	B7	86
Tocuyo de la Costa, Ven.	B7	86
Toda Rāisingh, India	E5	54
Todi, Italy	H9	22
Todos os Santos, Baia de, b., Braz.	G6	88
Todos Santos, Bol.	C3	90
Todos Santos, Bahía de, b., Mex.	L8	134
Tofino, B.C., Can.	G5	138
Toga, i., Vanuatu	i16	79d
Toga, Japan	B9	40
Togiak, Ak., U.S.	E7	140
Togian, Kepulauan, is., Indon.	F7	44
Togo, ctry., Afr.	H5	64
Togtoh, China.	A4	42
Togučin, Russia	C14	32
Togur, Russia	C14	32
Togwotee Pass, p., Wy., U.S.	G15	136
Tōhaku, Japan	D6	40
Tohieva, Mont, mtn., Fr. Poly.	v20	78h
Tohopekaliga, Lake, l., Fl., U.S.	H4	116
Tohtamyš, Taj.	B11	56
Toi-misaki, c., Japan.	H4	40
Toiyabe Range, mts., Nv., U.S.	D8	134
Tōjō, Japan	E6	40
Tojtepa, Uzb.	F11	32
Tok, Ak., U.S.	D11	140
Tokachi, stm., Japan	C15	38
Tokachi-dake, vol., Japan	C15	38
Tokaj, Hung.	A8	26
Tōkamachi, Japan	B11	40
Tokara-kaikyō, strt., Japan	j19	39a
Tokara-rettō, is., Japan	k19	39a
Tokat, Tur.	A4	56
Tōkchŏk-kundo, is., Kor., S.	F6	38
Tokelau, dep., Oc.	D9	72
Tokko, Russia	D12	34
Tokma, Russia	C19	32
Tokmak, Kyrg.	F13	32
Tokoro, stm., Japan	C15	38
Tokoroa, N.Z.	D6	80
Tok-to, is., Asia	B4	40
Tokuno-shima, i., Japan	k19	39a
Tokushima, Japan	E7	40
Tokushima, state, Japan	E7	40
Tokuyama, Japan	E4	40
Tokwe, stm., Zimb.	B10	70
Tōkyō, Japan	D12	40
Tōkyō, state, Japan	D12	40
Tokyo Bay see Tōkyō-wan, b., Japan	D12	40
Tōkyō-daigaku-uchūkūkan-kenkyūsho, sci., Japan	H4	40
Tōkyō-wan, b., Japan	D12	40
Tôlañaro, Madag.	F8	68
Tolbo, Mong.	B3	36
Tôle bi, Kaz.	F12	32
Toledo, Braz.	B11	92
Toledo, Col.	D5	86
Toledo, Spain	E6	20
Toledo, Ia., U.S.	I5	118
Toledo, Il., U.S.	E9	120
Toledo, Oh., U.S.	C2	114
Toledo, Or., U.S.	F3	136
Toledo, Montes de, mts., Spain	E6	20
Toledo Bend Reservoir, res., U.S.	F4	122
Tolentino, Italy	G10	22
Toli, China	B1	36
Toliara, Madag.	E7	68
Tolima, state, Col.	E4	86
Tolima, Nevado del, vol., Col.	E4	86
Toljatti, Russia	D7	32
Tolka, Russia	B14	32
Tolna, state, Hung.	C5	26
Tolo, Teluk, b., Indon.	F7	44
Tolosa, Spain	A8	20
Tolstoj, mys, c., Russia	E20	34
Tolti, Pak.	A6	54
Tolú, Col.	C4	86
Toluca, Il., U.S.	C8	120
Toluca, Nevado de, vol., Mex.	F9	100
Toluca de Lerdo, Mex.	F9	100
Tom', stm., Russia.	C14	32
Tomah, Wi., U.S.	H8	118
Tomahawk, Wi., U.S.	F9	118
Tomakomai, Japan.	C14	38
Tomanivi, mtn., Fiji	p19	79e
Tomar, Port.	E2	20
Tomari, Russia	G17	34
Tomás Gomensoro, Ur.	E9	92
Tomasine, stm., Qc., Can.	B13	112
Tomaszów Lubelski, Pol.	F19	16
Tomaszów Mazowiecki, Pol.	E16	16
Tombador, Serra do, plat., Braz.	F6	84
Tomball, Tx., U.S.	G3	122
Tombigbee, stm., U.S.	F10	122
Tombos, Braz.	K5	88
Tombouctou (Timbuktu), Mali	F4	64
Tombstone, Az., U.S.	L6	132
Tombstone Mountain, mtn., Yk., Can.	C3	106
Tombua, Ang.	D1	68
Tom Burke, S. Afr.	C9	70
Tomé, Chile	H1	92
Tomé-Açu, Braz.	B1	88
Tomelilla, Swe.	I5	8
Tomelloso, Spain	E8	20
Tomichi Creek, stm., Co., U.S.	C2	128
Tomini, Indon.	C12	50
Tomini, Teluk, b., Indon.	F7	44
Tomioka, Japan	C11	40
Tommot, Russia	E14	34
Tomo, stm., Col.	E7	86
Tompkins, Sk., Can.	D5	124
Tompkinsville, Ky., U.S.	H12	120
Tompo, Indon.	C12	50
Tom Price, Austl.	D3	74
Tomptokan, Russia	E15	34
Tomsk, Russia	C15	32
Toms River, N.J., U.S.	E11	114
Tonalá, Mex.	G12	100
Tonami, Japan	C9	40
Tonantins, Braz.	I7	86
Tonasket, Wa., U.S.	B7	136
Tonawanda, N.Y., U.S.	B6	114
Tonbo, Mya.	C2	48
Tonbridge, Eng., U.K.	J13	12
Tondano, Indon.	E8	44
Tønder, Den.	B4	16
Tondi, India	G4	53
Tone, stm., Japan	D13	40
Tonekābon, Iran	B7	56
Tonga, ctry., Oc.	E9	72
Tongaat, S. Afr.	F10	70
Tonga Ridge, unds.	K21	142
Tongariro National Park, p.o.i., N.Z.	D6	80
Tongatapu, state, Tonga	o14	78e
Tongatapu, i., Tonga	n13	78e
Tonga Trench, unds.	L21	142
Tongbai, China	E5	42
Tongbai Shan, mts., China	E5	42
Tongbei, China	B10	36
Tongcheng, China	F7	42
Tongchuan, China	D3	42
Tongde, China	D5	36
Tongeren, Bel.	D14	14
Tonggu, China	G6	42
Tongguan, China	D4	42
Tonghai, China	G5	36
Tonghe, China	B10	36
Tonghua, China	D6	38
Tongjiang, China	B11	36
Tongjiang, China	F2	42
Tongjosŏn-man, b., Kor., N.	E7	38
Tongliao, China	C4	38
Tongliao, China	C9	36
Tongling, China	F7	42
Tongling, China	J3	42
Tonglu, China	G8	42
Tongnae, Kor., S.	D2	40
Tongo, Austl.	H4	76
Tongoa, i., Vanuatu	k17	79d
Tongoy, Chile	E2	92
Tongren, China	H3	42
Tongres see Tongeren, Bel.	D14	14
Tongsa Dzong, Bhu.	E13	54
Tongtian, stm., China	E4	36
Tongue, Scot., U.K.	C8	12
Tongue of the Ocean, unds.	C9	96
Tongue, stm., U.S.	B7	126
Tongxian, China	B7	42
Tongxu, China	D6	42
Tongyu, China	B5	38
Tongzi, China	G2	42
Tonj, Sudan	F5	62
Tonk, India	E5	54
Tonkawa, Ok., U.S.	E11	128
Tonkin, Gulf of, b., Asia	A7	48
Tônlé Sab, Boeng, l., Camb.	F6	48
Tonle Sap see Tônlé Sab, Boeng, l., Camb.	F6	48
Tonneins, Fr.	E6	18
Tonopah, Nv., U.S.	E8	134
Tonoshō, Japan	E7	40
Tonosí, Pan.	D1	86
Tonota, Bots.	B8	70
Tons, stm., India	F8	54
Tønsberg, Nor.	G4	8
Tonto National Monument, p.o.i., Az., U.S.	I5	132
Toodyay, Austl.	F3	74
Tooele, Ut., U.S.	C4	132
Toogoolawah, Austl.	F9	76
Toomsboro, Ga., U.S.	D2	116
Toora-Hem, Russia	D17	32
Toowoomba, Austl.	F8	76
Topeka, Ks., U.S.	E2	120
Top Hill, hill, Gren.	q11	105e
Topia, Mex.	C5	100
Topki, Russia	C15	32
Topko, gora, mtn., Russia	E16	34
Topley, B.C., Can.	B4	138
Toplița, Rom.	C12	26
Topocalma, Punta, c., Chile	G1	92
Topol'čany, Slov.	H14	16
Topolobampo, Mex.	B4	100
Topolováțu Mare, Rom.	D8	26
Topozero, ozero, l., Russia	D14	8
Toppenish, Wa., U.S.	D6	136
Topsa, Russia	E20	8
Top Springs, Austl.	C6	74
Torbali, Tur.	E10	28
Torbat-e Heydarīyeh, Iran	B8	56
Torbat-e Jām, Iran	B9	56
Torbrook, N.S., Can.	F12	110
Torch Lake, l., Mi., U.S.	C4	112
Tordesillas, Spain	C10	8
Töre, Swe.	C10	8
Torgau, Ger.	E8	16
Torgay, stm., Kaz.	E10	32
Torghay ūstirti, plat.	D10	32
Torghay zhylgh, reg., Kaz.	D10	32
Torhout, Bel.	C12	14
Toribulú, Indon.	D11	50
Torino (Turin), Italy	E4	22
Torit, Sudan	G6	62
Tormes, stm., Spain	C5	20
Torna, Russia	B20	8
Torna, mtn., India	B1	53

Name	Map Ref.	Page

Torneälven (Tornionjoki), stm., Eur. — C10 8
Torneträsk, l., Swe. — B8 8
Torngat Mountains, mts., Can. — F13 141
Tornillo, Tx., U.S. — C1 130
Tornionjoki (Torneälven), stm., Eur. — C10 8
Tornquist, Arg. — I6 92
Toro, Spain — C5 20
Toro, mtn., Mex. — F6 100
Toro, Lago del, l., Chile — J2 90
Toro, Punta, c., Chile — F1 92
Törökszentmiklós, Hung. — B7 26
Torom, Russia — F16 34
Toronto, On., Can. — E10 112
Toronto, Ks., U.S. — G1 120
Toronto, S.D., U.S. — G2 118
Toropec, Russia — D14 10
Tororo, Ug. — D6 66
Toros Dağları (Taurus Mountains), mts., Tur. — A3 58
Torosozero, Russia — E18 8
Toroume, hill, Cook Is. — b26 78j
Torquay, Sk., Can. — E10 124
Torquay (Torbay), Eng., U.K. — K9 12
Torrance, Ca., U.S. — J7 134
Torrão, Port. — F2 20
Torreblanca, Spain — D11 20
Torre Pellice, Italy — F4 22
Torreperojil, Spain — F7 20
Torres, Braz. — D3 92
Torres, Îles, is., Vanuatu — i16 79d
Torres Islands see Torres, Îles, is., Vanuatu — i16 79d
Torres Strait, strt., Oc. — b3 79a
Torres Vedras, Port. — E1 20
Torrevella, Spain — G10 20
Torrevieja see Torrevella, Spain — G10 20
Torridon, Scot., U.K. — D7 12
Torrijos, Spain — D6 20
Torrington, Ct., U.S. — C12 114
Torrington, Wy., U.S. — E8 126
Torröjen, l., Swe. — E5 8
Torsa (Amo), stm., Asia — E12 54
Torsby, Swe. — F5 8
Tórshavn (Thorshavn), Far. Is. — n34 8b
Tortola, i., Br. Vir. Is. — e8 104b
Tórtolas, Cerro de las (Las Tórtolas, Cerro), mtn., S.A. — D2 92
Tortona, Italy — F5 22
Tortorici, Italy — F8 24
Tortosa, Spain — D11 20
Tortosa, Cap de, c., Spain — D11 20
Tortue, Île de la, i., Haiti — B11 102
Tortuga Island see Tortue, Île de la, i., Haiti — B11 102
P.R. — B2 104a
Toruń, Pol. — C14 16
Toruń, state, Pol. — C15 16
Torup, Swe. — H5 8
Toržok, Russia — C17 10
Toržym, Pol. — D11 16
Tosa, Japan — F5 40
Tosa-shimizu, Japan — G5 40
Tosa-wan, b., Japan — F6 40
Tosca, S. Afr. — D6 70
Toscana, state, Italy — G8 22
Toses, Collada de, p., Spain — B12 20
Tosno, Russia — A13 10
Toson Hu, l., China — D4 36
Tosontsengel, Mong. — B4 36
Tostado, Arg. — D7 92
Tõstamaa, Est. — G10 8
Tosu, Japan — F3 40
Totana, Spain — G9 20
Toteng, Bots. — B6 70
Totiyas, Som. — D8 66
Tot'ma, Russia — F20 8
Totness, Sur. — B6 84
Totoya, i., Fiji — q20 79e
Tottenham, Austl. — I6 76
Tottenham, On., Can. — D10 112
Tottori, Japan — D7 40
Tottori, state, Japan — D8 40
Touba, C. Iv. — H3 64
Toubkal, Jebel, mtn., Mor. — C3 64
Touchet, stm., Wa., U.S. — D8 136
Touchwood Lake, l., Ab., Can. — B19 138
Toudao, stm., China — C6 38
Touggourt, Alg. — C6 64
Touho, N. Cal. — m15 79d
Toul, Fr. — F14 14
Touliu, Tai. — J9 42
Toulon, Fr. — F11 18
Toulon-sur-Arroux, Fr. — H13 14
Toulouse, Fr. — F7 18
Toumodi, C. Iv. — H3 64
Tounassine, Hamada, des., Alg. — D3 64
Toungo, Nig. — H7 64
Toungoo, Mya. — C3 48
Touraine, hist. reg., Fr. — G9 14
Tourcoing, Fr. — D11 14
Tourinan, Cabo, c., Spain — A1 20
Tournai, Bel. — D11 14
Tournon, Fr. — D10 18
Tournus, Fr. — H13 14
Touros, Braz. — C8 88
Tours, Fr. — G9 14
Toussidé, Pic, vol., Chad — C3 62
Touws, stm., S. Afr. — H5 70
Toužim, Czech Rep. — F9 16
Tovar, Ven. — C6 86
Tovarkovskij, Russia — G21 10
Tow, Tx., U.S. — D9 130
Towada, Japan — D14 38
Towanda, Ks., U.S. — D12 128
Towanda, Pa., U.S. — C9 114
Tower, Mn., U.S. — D6 118
Tower Hill, Austl. — D5 76
Tower Hill, Austl. — E9 120
Towerhill Creek, stm., Austl. — C5 76
Towla, Mount, mtn., Zimb. — B9 70
Town and Country, Wa., U.S. — D9 136
Town Hill, hill, Ber. — k16 104e
Townsend, Mt., U.S. — D15 136
Townshend Island, i., Austl. — D8 76
Townsville, Austl. — A6 76
Towson, Md., U.S. — E9 114
Towuti, Danau, l., Indon. — F7 44
Toyah, Tx., U.S. — C4 130
Toyah Creek, stm., Tx., U.S. — D4 130
Toyama, Japan — C10 40
Toyama, state, Japan — C10 40
Toyama-wan, b., Japan — C10 40
Tōyō, Japan — F6 40

Tōyō, Japan — F7 40
Toyohashi, Japan — E10 40
Toyokawa, Japan — E10 40
Toyonaka, Japan — E8 40
Toyooka, Japan — D7 40
Toyosaka, Japan — B12 40
Toyota, Japan — D10 40
Toyoura, Japan — E3 40
Tozeur, Tun. — C6 64
Trabzon, Tur. — A4 56
Tracadie, N.B., Can. — C12 110
Tracy, Qc., Can. — E3 110
Tracy, Ca., U.S. — F4 134
Tracy City, Tn., U.S. — B13 122
Tradewater, stm., Ky., U.S. — G10 120
Traer, Ia., U.S. — B5 120
Trafalgar, Cabo, c., Spain — H4 20
Traill Ø, i., Grnld. — C21 141
Traipu, Braz. — E7 88
Traíra (Taraira), stm., S.A. — H7 86
Trairi, Braz. — B6 88
Trakai, Lith. — F7 10
Tralee, Ire. — I3 12
Trá Lí see Tralee, Ire. — I3 12
Trammel, Va., U.S. — G3 114
Tramperos Creek (Punta de Agua Creek), stm., U.S. — E5 128
Tramping Lake, l., Sk., Can. — B5 124
Tra My, Viet. — E9 48
Trân, Blg. — G9 26
Tranås, Swe. — G6 8
Trancas, Arg. — C5 92
Tranco de Beas, Embalse de, res., Spain — F8 20
Trang, Thai. — I4 48
Trangan, Pulau, i., Indon. — G9 44
Trang Dinh, Viet. — A8 48
Trani, Italy — C10 24
Tran Ninh see Xiangkhoang, Plateau de, plat., Laos — C6 48
Tranqueras, Ur. — E9 92
Transantarctic Mountains, mts., Ant. — D30 81
Transkei, hist. reg., S. Afr. — G8 70
Transylvania, hist. reg., Rom. — C10 26
Transylvanian Alps see Carpaţii Meridionali, mts., Rom. — D11 26
Trapani, Italy — F6 24
Trapper Peak, mtn., Mt., U.S. — E12 136
Traralgon, Austl. — L6 76
Trárza, reg., Maur. — F1 64
Trasimeno, Lago, l., Italy — G9 22
Trois-ïo-Montes, hist. reg., Port. — C3 20
Trat, Thai. — F6 48
Traun, Aus. — B11 22
Traun, stm., Aus. — B11 22
Traunstein, Ger. — I8 16
Travellers Lake, l., Austl. — I4 76
Travelers Lake, res., U.S. — F2 118
Traverse City, Mi., U.S. — D4 112
Tra Vinh, Viet. — H8 48
Travis, Lake, l., Tx., U.S. — D10 130
Travnik, Bos. — E4 26
Trayning, Austl. — F3 74
Trbovlje, Slvn. — D12 22
Trebič, Czech Rep. — G11 16
Trebinje, Bos. — G5 26
Trebišov, Slov. — H17 16
Treblinka, Pol. — D18 16
Trece Martires, Phil. — C3 52
Tregosse Islets, is., Austl. — A8 76
Tregubovo, Russia — B14 10
Treinta y Tres, Ur. — F10 92
Trélazé, Fr. — G8 14
Trelew, Arg. — H3 90
Trelleborg, Swe. — I5 8
Tremadog Bay, b., Wales, U.K. — I8 12
Tremblant, Mont, mtn., Qc., Can. — D2 110
Trembleur Lake, l., B.C., Can. — B5 138
Tremiti, Isole, is., Italy — H12 22
Tremont, Il., U.S. — K9 118
Tremonton, Ut., U.S. — B4 132
Tremp, Spain — B11 20
Trempealeau, Wi., U.S. — G7 118
Trenche, stm., Qc., Can. — B4 110
Trenčín, Slov. — H14 16
Trenel, Arg. — G5 92
Treng, Camb. — F6 48
Trenggalek, Indon. — H7 50
Trenque Lauquen, Arg. — G6 92
Trent, stm., On., Can. — D12 112
Trent, stm., Eng., U.K. — H12 12
Trente et Un Milles, Lac des, l., Qc., Can. — B13 112
Trentino-Alto Adige, state, Italy — D8 22
Trento (Trent), Italy — D7 22
Trenton, N.S., Can. — E14 110
Trenton, On., Can. — D12 112
Trenton, Fl., U.S. — G3 116
Trenton, Ga., U.S. — C13 122
Trenton, Mo., U.S. — D4 120
Trenton, N.C., U.S. — A8 116
Trenton, Ne., U.S. — A8 128
Trenton, N.J., U.S. — D11 114
Trentwood, Wa., U.S. — C9 136
Trepassey, Nf., Can. — j23 107a
Tres Algarrobos, Arg. — G6 92
Tres Arroyos, Arg. — I7 92
Tres Coroados, Arg. — K3 88
Tres Coroas, Braz. — D12 92
Tres de Mato, Braz. — C10 92
Tres Esquinas, Col. — G4 86
Tres Lagoas, Braz. — D6 90
Três Lagos, Arg. — I2 90
Três Lomas, Arg. — H6 92
Três Marias, Braz. — J3 88
Três Marias, Islas, is., Mex. — E5 100
Três Rios, Braz. — L4 88

Trident Peak, mtn., Nv., U.S. — B7 134
Trier, Ger. — G2 16
Trieste (Trst), Italy — E10 22
Trieste, Gulf of, b., Eur. — E10 22
Triglav, mtn., Slvn. — D10 22
Triglavski narodni park, p.o.i., Slvn. — D10 22
Trigueros, Spain — G4 20
Trikala, Grc. — D4 28
Trikora, Puncak, mtn., Indon. — F10 44
Trilby, Fl., U.S. — H3 116
Triman, Pak. — D2 54
Trincheras, Mex. — F7 98
Trincomalee, Sri L. — G5 53
Trindade, Braz. — I1 88
Trindade, Braz. — H12 82
Trinec, Czech Rep. — G14 16
Trinidad, Bol. — B3 90
Trinidad, Col. — E6 86
Trinidad, Cuba — B8 102
Trinidad, Ur. — F9 92
Trinidad, Co., U.S. — D5 128
Trinidad, Tx., U.S. — E2 122
Trinidad, Isla, i., Arg. — I7 92
Trinidad and Tobago, ctry., N.A. — s13 105f
Trinity, Tx., U.S. — G3 122
Trinity, stm., Tx., U.S. — C2 134
Trinity, stm., Tx., U.S. — D13 130
Trinity, Elm Fork, stm., Tx., U.S. — H11 128
Trinity, South Fork, stm., Ca., U.S. — C2 134
Trinity, West Fork, stm., Tx., U.S. — H11 128
Trinity Bay, b., Nf., Can. — j23 107a
Trinity Bay, b., Tx., U.S. — H4 122
Trinity Islands, is., Ak., U.S. — E9 140
Trinity Peak, mtn., Nv., U.S. — C7 134
Trinity Site, hist., N.M., U.S. — H2 128
Trino, Italy — E5 22
Tripa, stm., Indon. — J3 48
Tripoli, Grc. — F5 28
Tripoli see Ṭarābulus, Leb. — D6 58
Tripoli see Ṭarābulus, Libya — A2 62
Tripoli, Ia., U.S. — I6 118
Tripolis, sci., Tur. — F12 28
Tripolitania see Ṭarābulus, hist. reg., Libya — A2 62
Tripura, state, India — G13 54
Tristan da Cunha Group, is., St. Hel. — J4 60
Tristão, Îles, is., Gui. — G2 64
Triste, Golfo, b., Ven. — B7 86
Tri Ton, Viet. — G7 48
Triumph, La., U.S. — H9 122
Trivandrum see Thiruvananthapuram, India — G3 53
Trnava, Slov. — H13 16
Trobriand Islands, is., Pap. N. Gui. — b5 79a
Trogir, Cro. — G13 22
Troia, Italy — C9 24
Troick, Russia — D10 32
Troickoe, Russia — D15 32
Troickoe, Russia — G16 34
Troicko-Pečorsk, Russia — B9 32
Troina, Italy — G8 24
Troisdorf, Ger. — F2 16
Trois-Pistoles, Qc., Can. — B7 110
Trois Pitons, Morne, vol., Dom. — j6 105c
Trois-Rivières, Qc., Can. — D4 110
Trois-Rivières, Guad. — i5 105c
Trojan, Blg. — G11 26
Trojanova Tabla, hist., Serb. — E9 26
Trollhättan, Swe. — G5 8
Trombetas, stm., Braz. — C6 84
Troms, state, Nor. — B8 8
Tromsø, Nor. — B8 8
Trona, Ca., U.S. — H8 134
Tronador, Cerro, mtn., S.A. — H2 90
Trondheim, Nor. — E4 8
Trondheimsfjorden, b., Nor. — E4 8
Troodos, Cyp. — D3 58
Troodos Mountains, mts., Cyp. — D3 58
Troon, Scot., U.K. — F8 12
Trophy Mountain, vol., B.C., Can. — E11 138
Tropic, Ut., U.S. — F4 132
Tropojë, Alb. — B14 28
Troškūnai, Lith. — E7 10
Trosna, Russia — H18 10
Trotuş, stm., Rom. — C13 26
Troup, Tx., U.S. — E3 122
Trout, stm., N.T., Can. — C6 106
Trout, stm., Wi., U.S. — F6 118
Trout Creek, Mi., U.S. — E9 118
Trout Creek Pass, p., Co., U.S. — C3 128
Trout Lake, l., N.T., Can. — C6 106
Trout Lake, l., On., Can. — E12 106
Troutville, Va., U.S. — G6 114
Trouville-sur-Mer, Fr. — E9 14
Trowbridge, Eng., U.K. — J10 12
Troy, Al., U.S. — F13 122
Troy, Id., U.S. — D10 136
Troy, Ks., U.S. — F2 120
Troy, Mo., U.S. — F7 120
Troy, N.C., U.S. — A6 116
Troy, N.H., U.S. — B13 114
Troy, N.Y., U.S. — B12 114
Troy, Oh., U.S. — D1 114
Troy, Pa., U.S. — C9 114
Troy, Tn., U.S. — H8 120
Troy see Truva, sci., Tur. — D9 28
Troyes, Fr. — F13 14
Troy Peak, mtn., Nv., U.S. — E1 132
Trst see Trieste, Italy — E10 22
Trstená, Slov. — G15 16
Truax, Sk., Can. — E8 124
Trubč'evsk, Russia — H16 10
Truchas, N.M., U.S. — E3 128
Truchas Peak, mtn., N.M., U.S. — E3 128
Trucial States see United Arab Emirates, ctry., Asia — E7 56
Truckee, Ca., U.S. — D5 134
Truckee, stm., U.S. — D6 134
Trud, Russia — C16 10
Trujillo, Col. — E3 86
Trujillo, Hond. — E4 102
Trujillo, Peru — E2 84
Trujillo, Spain — E5 20
Trujillo, Ven. — C6 86
Trujillo, stm., Ven. — C6 86
Trujillo Alto, P.R. — B4 104a
Truk Islands see Chuuk, is., Micron. — C6 72
Truman, Mn., U.S. — H4 118
Truman, Ar., U.S. — B7 120
Trumann, N.Y., U.S. — B9 114
Trumbull, Ct., U.S. — C12 114
Trumbull, Mount, mtn., Az., U.S. — G3 132
Trundle, Austl. — I6 76
Trung Phan (Annam), hist. reg., Viet. — D8 48
Trung Khanh, Viet. — A7 48
Truro, N.S., Can. — E13 110
Truro, Eng., U.K. — K7 12
Trusan, stm., Malay. — A9 50
Truscott, Tx., U.S. — H9 128
Truşeni, Mol. — B15 26
Truth or Consequences, N.M., U.S. — J9 132
Trutnov, Czech Rep. — F11 16
Truva (Troy), sci., Tur. — D9 28
Truxton Wash, stm., Az., U.S. — H3 132

Truyère, stm., Fr. — E8 18
Tryduby, Ukr. — A17 26
Tryon, N.C., U.S. — A3 116
Tryon, Ne., U.S. — F12 126
Trzcianka, Pol. — C12 16
Trzciel, Pol. — D11 16
Trzebiatów, Pol. — B11 16
Trzebinia, Pol. — F15 16
Trzebnica, Pol. — E13 16
Tsaagaannuur, Mong. — E15 32
Tsaidam Basin see Qaidam Pendi, bas., China — D3 36
Tsala Apopka Lake, l., Fl., U.S. — H3 116
Tsamkong see Zhanjiang, China — K4 42
Ts'anghsien see Cangzhou, China — B7 42
T'sangwu see Wuzhou, China — J4 42
Tsaratanana, Madag. — D8 68
Tsaratanana, mts., Madag. — C8 68
Tsau, Bots. — E3 68
Tsavo, Kenya — E7 66
Tsayachuz Peak, mtn., B.C., Can. — C4 138
Tsebrykove, Ukr. — B17 26
Tses, Nmb. — D4 70
Tsetserleg, Mong. — B5 36
Tsévié, Togo — H5 64
Tshabong, Bots. — D6 70
Tshane, Bots. — D5 70
Tshela, D.R.C. — E2 66
Tshidilamolomo, S. Afr. — D7 70
Tshikapa, D.R.C. — F4 66
Tshofa, D.R.C. — F5 66
Tshuapa, stm., D.R.C. — E4 66
Tshumbe (Chiumbe), stm., Afr. — B3 68
Tsiafajavona, vol., Madag. — D8 68
Tsiigehtchic, N.T., Can. — B4 106
Tsimlyansk Reservoir see Cimljanskoe vodohranilišče, res., Russia — E6 32
Tsinan see Jinan, China — C7 42
Tsineng, S. Afr. — E6 70
Tsinghai see Qinghai, state, China — D4 36
Tsingkiang see Qingjiang, China — E8 42
Tsingtao see Qingdao, China — C9 42
Tsingyuan see Baoding, China — B6 42
Ts'in-hai see Qinghai, state, China — D4 36
Tsining see Jining, China — D7 42
Tsinling Shan see Qin Ling, mts., China — E3 42
Tsintsabis, Nmb. — D2 68
Tsiombe, Madag. — F8 68
Tsipa see Cipa, stm., Russia — F11 34
Tsiribihina, stm., Madag. — D7 68
Tsiroanomandidy, Madag. — D8 68
Tsitsihar see Qiqihar, China — B9 36
Tsna see Cna, stm., Russia — D6 32
Tsomo, stm., S. Afr. — H8 70
Tsomog, Mong. — B6 36
Tsu, Japan — E9 40
Tsubame, Japan — B11 40
Tsuchiura, Japan — C13 40
Tsugaru-kaikyō, strt., Japan — D14 38
Tsukumi, Japan — F4 40
Tsukushi-sanchi, mts., Japan — F3 40
Tsumeb, Nmb. — D2 68
Tsumkwe, Nmb. — D3 68
Tsuni see Zunyi, China — H2 42
Tsuruga, Japan — D9 40
Tsuruoka, Japan — A12 40
Tsurugi-san, mtn., Japan — F7 40
Tsushima, Japan — E2 40
Tsushima-kaikyō (Eastern Channel), strt., Japan — F2 40
Tsuyama, Japan — D7 40
Tswaane, Bots. — C6 70
Ttruchchendūr, India — G4 53
Tua, D.R.C. — C3 66
Tua, stm., Port. — C3 20
Tua, Tanjung, c., Indon. — F6 50
Tuai, N.Z. — D7 80
Tual, Indon. — G9 44
Tuam, Ire. — H4 12
Tuamotu, Îles, is., Fr. Poly. — E12 72
Tuamotu Archipelago see Tuamotu, Îles, is., Fr. Poly. — E12 72
Tuamotu Ridge, unds. — K24 142
Tuanan, Indon. — D4 50
Tuangku, Pulau, i., Indon. — K3 48
Tuapse, Russia — F5 32
Tuasivi, Cape, c., Samoa — g11 79c
Tuba, Indon. — C18 32
Tuba, stm., Russia — D16 32
Tubac, Az., U.S. — L5 132
Tuban, Indon. — G8 50
Tubarão, Braz. — D13 92
Tūbas, W.B. — F6 58
Tübingen, Ger. — H4 16
Tubruq, Libya — A4 62
Tubuai, i., Fr. Poly. — F12 72
Tubuai, Îles, is., Fr. Poly. — F12 72
Tucacas, Ven. — B7 86
Tucano, Braz. — F6 88
Tucheng, China — G2 42
Tuchów, Pol. — G16 16
Tuckerman, Ar., U.S. — B7 120
Tuckerton, N.J., U.S. — E11 114
Tučkovo, Russia — E19 10
Tucson, Az., U.S. — K5 132
Tucumán, state, Arg. — C5 92
Tucumcari, N.M., U.S. — F5 128
Tucunuco, Arg. — E3 92
Tucupita, Ven. — C11 86
Tucuruí, Braz. — D8 84
Tucuruí, Represa de, res., Braz. — D8 84
Tudela, Phil. — B4 52
Tudela, Spain — B9 20
Tudmur (Palmyra), Syria — D8 58
Tufi, Pap. N. Gui. — b4 79a
Tugela, stm., S. Afr. — F10 70
Tug Fork, stm., U.S. — G3 114
Tuggerah Lake, l., Austl. — I8 76
Tūghyl, Kaz. — E14 32
Tuguegarao City, Phil. — B3 52
Tugur, Russia — F16 34
Tuhai, stm., China — C8 42
Tuhuangda, China — B2 42
Tui, Spain — B2 20
Tuira, stm., Pan. — D3 86
Tujmazy, Russia — D8 32
Tukangbesi, Kepulauan, is., Indon. — G7 44
Tukituki, stm., N.Z. — D7 80
Tukosméra, Mont, mtn., S.A. — i17 79d
Tūkrah, Libya — A4 62
Tuktoyaktuk, N.T., Can. — B4 106
Tukums, Lat. — D6 10
Tukuringra, hrebet, mts., Russia — F14 34
Tukuyu, Tan. — F6 66
Tula, Mex. — D9 100
Tulach Mhór see Tullamore, Ire. — H5 12
Tulaghi, Sol. Is. — e8 79b
Tulancingo, Mex. — E9 100
Tulare, Ca., U.S. — G6 134
Tulare Lake Bed, reg., Ca., U.S. — G6 134

Tulare Lake Canal, can., Ca., U.S. — G6 134
Tularosa, N.M., U.S. — H2 128
Tularosa Valley, bas., N.M., U.S. — E9 98
Tulbagh, S. Afr. — H4 70
Tulcán, Ec. — G3 86
Tulcea, Rom. — D15 26
Tulcea, state, Rom. — D15 26
Tulčyn, Ukr. — A16 26
Tule, Lake, l., Ca., U.S. — B4 134
Tulemalu Lake, l., Nu., Can. — C11 106
Tule Valley, val., Ut., U.S. — D3 132
Tuli, Zimb. — B9 70
Tuliszków, Pol. — D14 16
Tullahoma, Tn., U.S. — B12 122
Tullamore, Ire. — H5 12
Tulle, Fr. — D7 18
Tullibigeal, Austl. — I6 76
Tulln, Aus. — B13 22
Tullos, La., U.S. — F7 122
Tullu, Sudan — E4 62
Tully, Austl. — A5 76
Tulsa, Ok., U.S. — H2 120
Tulsequah, B.C., Can. — D4 106
Tuluá, Col. — E3 86
Tulum, Mex. — B4 102
Tulum, sci., Mex. — B4 102
Tulun, Russia — D18 32
Tulungagung, Indon. — H7 50
Tulungselapan, Indon. — E4 50
Tuma, stm., Nic. — F5 102
Tumacacori National Historical Park, p.o.i., Az., U.S. — L5 132
Tumaco, Col. — G2 86
Tumaco, Rada de, b., Col. — G2 86
Tuman-gang (Tumen), stm., Asia — C8 38
Tumany, Russia — D20 34
Tumanskij, Russia — D24 34
Tumba, stm., Russia — D20 34
Tumbarumba, Austl. — J6 76
Tumbes, Peru — D1 84
Tumbes, Punta, c., Chile — H1 92
Tumbler Ridge, B.C., Can. — A10 138
Tumen, China — C8 38
Tumen, stm. (Tuman-gang), stm., Asia — C8 38
Tumereng, Ven. — D11 86
Tumiritinga, Braz. — J5 88
Tumkūr, India — E3 53
Tumotegi, China — A4 42
Tumpat, Malay. — I6 48
Tumsar, India — H7 54
Tumtum, Wa., U.S. — C9 136
Tumu, Ghana — G4 64
Tumuc-Humac Mountains, mts., S.A. — C6 84
Tumut, Austl. — J7 76
Tun, stm., Thai. — D4 48
Tunapuna, Trin. — s12 105f
Tunari, Cerro, mtn., Bol. — C3 90
Tunas de Zaza, Cuba — B8 102
Tunchang, China — L3 42
Tunduru, Tan. — G7 66
Tundža, stm., Eur. — G13 26
Tungabhadra, stm., India — D3 53
Tungabhadra Reservoir, res., India — D2 53
Tungaru, Sudan — E6 62
Tungchow see Tongxian, China — B7 42
T'ungch'uan see Tongchuan, China — D3 42
Tung Hai see East China Sea, s., Asia — F9 36
T'unghsien see Tongxian, China — B7 42
T'unghua see Tonghua, China — D6 38
Tunghwa see Tonghua, China — D6 38
Tungkal, stm., Indon. — D3 50
Tungku, Malay. — A11 50
Tungla, Nic. — F5 102
T'ungliao see Tongliao, China — C4 38
Tungsha Tao (Pratas Island), i., Tai. — K7 42
Tungshih, Tai. — I9 42
Tungsten, N.T., Can. — C5 106
Tungurahua, state, Ec. — H2 86
Tungurahua, vol., Ec. — H2 86
Tuni, India — C6 53
Tunia, stm., Col. — F4 86
Tunis, Tun. — H4 24
Tunis, Golfe de, b., Tun. — H5 24
Tunis, Gulf of see Tunis, Golfe de, b., Tun. — H5 24
Tunisia, ctry., Afr. — C6 64
Tunisie see Tunisia, ctry., Afr. — C6 64
Tunja, Col. — E5 86
Tunkhannock, Pa., U.S. — C10 114
Tunliu, China — C5 42
Tunnel Hill, Ga., U.S. — C13 122
Tunnelton, W.V., U.S. — E6 114
Tunnsjøen, l., Nor. — D5 8
Tuntum, Braz. — C3 88
Tunu see Østgrønland, state, Grnld. — C18 141
Tununak, Ak., U.S. — D6 140
Tunuyán, Arg. — F3 92
Tunuyán, stm., Arg. — F4 92
Tunxi, China — G8 42
Tuo, stm., China — E7 42
Tuo, stm., China — G1 42
Tuobalage, Russia — D13 34
Tuoji-Haja, Russia — B20 32
Tuoketuo, China — A6 42
Tuolumne, can., Ca., U.S. — F5 134
Tuolumne, stm., Ca., U.S. — F5 134
Tuotuo, stm., China — D6 36
Tupã, Braz. — D6 90
Tupaciguara, Braz. — J1 88
Tuparecê, Braz. — D10 92
Tuparro, stm., Col. — E7 86
Tupelo, Ms., U.S. — C10 122
Tupelo, Ok., U.S. — C2 122
Tupik, Russia — F13 34
Tupinambarana, Ilha, i., Braz. — D6 84
Tupiza, Bol. — D3 90
Tupper Lake, N.Y., U.S. — F2 110
Tupper Lake, l.,

Turfan Depression see Turpan Pendi, depr., China — C2 36
Turginovo, Russia — D18 10
Turgoš, Russia — A18 10
Turgutlu, Tur. — E10 28
Türi, Est. — B8 10
Túria, stm., Spain — D9 20
Túria (Turia), stm., Spain — D9 20
Turiaçu, Braz. — A3 88
Turiaçu, stm., Braz. — B3 88
Turimiquire, Cerro, mtn., Ven. — B10 86
Turin see Torino, Italy — E4 22
Turin, Ab., Can. — F18 138
Turinsk, Russia — C10 32
Turka, Ukr. — G19 16
Turkana, Lake see Rudolf, Lake, l., Afr. — D7 66
Turkestanskij hrebet, mts., Asia — B10 56
Türkeve, Hung. — B7 26
Turkey, ctry., Asia — B3 56
Turkey, stm., Ia., U.S. — I7 118
Turkey Creek, stm., Ne., U.S. — K2 118
Turkish Republic of Northern Cyprus see Cyprus, North, ctry., Asia — C4 58
Türkistan, Kaz. — F11 32
Türkmenabat, Turkmen. — B7 56
Turkmenia see Turkmenistan, ctry., Asia — B8 56
Turkmenistan, ctry., Asia — B8 56
Türkoğlu, Tur. — A7 58
Turks and Caicos Islands, dep., N.A. — A12 102
Turks Island Passage, strt., T./C. Is. — B12 102
Turks Islands, is., T./C. Is. — B12 102
Turku (Åbo), Fin. — F9 8
Turkwel, stm., Kenya — D7 66
Turley, Ok., U.S. — H2 120
Turlock, Ca., U.S. — F5 134
Turmalina, Braz. — I4 88
Turmantas, Lith. — E9 10
Turnagain, stm., B.C., Can. — D5 106
Turneffe Islands, is., Belize — D4 102
Turner, Mt., U.S. — F5 124
Turner, Or., U.S. — F4 136
Turners Falls, Ma., U.S. — B13 114
Turnhout, Bel. — C13 14
Turnov, Czech Rep. — F11 16
Turnu Măgurele, Rom. — F11 26
Turnu Roşu, Pasul, p., Rom. — D11 26
Turočak, Russia — D15 32
Turon, Ks., U.S. — D10 128
Turpan, China — C2 36
Turpan Pendi (Turfan Depression), depr., China — C2 36
Turquino, Pico, mtn., Cuba — C9 102
Turrell, Ar., U.S. — B8 122
Turret Peak, mtn., Az., U.S. — I5 132
Turtle, stm., Mb., Can. — D14 124
Turtle-Flambeau Flowage, res., Wi., U.S. — E8 118
Turtle Islands, is., S.L. — H2 64
Turtle Lake, N.D., U.S. — G13 124
Turtle Lake, Wi., U.S. — F6 118
Turu, stm., Russia — B18 32
Turuhan, stm., Russia — C6 34
Turuhansk, Russia — C6 34
Turvo, Braz. — K1 88
Turvo, stm., Braz. — K1 88
Turwi, stm., Zimb. — B10 70
Turzovka, Slov. — G14 16
Tuscaloosa, Al., U.S. — D11 122
Tuscaloosa, Lake, res., Al., U.S. — D11 122
Tuscany see Toscana, state, Italy — G8 22
Tuscarora Mountain, mts., Pa., U.S. — D8 114
Tuscola, Tx., U.S. — B8 130
Tuscola, Il., U.S. — C11 122
Tuscumbia, Al., U.S. — C11 122
Tuscumbia, Mo., U.S. — F5 120
Tuskegee, Al., U.S. — E13 122
Tustumena Lake, l., Ak., U.S. — D9 140
Tuticorin, India — G4 53
Tutin, Serb. — F7 26
Tutóia, Braz. — B4 88
Tutove, Mount, mtn., N.Z. — G3 80
Tuttle, N.D., U.S. — G14 124
Tuttle Creek Lake, res., Ks., U.S. — B12 128
Tutuala, E. Timor — G8 44
Tutuila, i., Am. Sam. — h12 79c
Tutupaca, Volcán, vol., Peru — G3 84
Tutwiler, Ms., U.S. — C8 122
Tutzing, Ger. — I7 16
Tuva, state, Russia — D16 32
Tuvalu, ctry., Oc. — D8 72
Tuvuca, i., Fiji — p20 79e
Tuwayq, Jabal, mts., Sau. Ar. — E6 56
Tuxford, Sk., Can. — D8 124
Tuxpan, Mex. — E10 100
Tuxpan de Rodríguez Cano, Mex. — E10 100
Tuxtepec, Mex. — F11 100
Tuxtla Gutiérrez, Mex. — G12 100
Túy see Tui, Spain — B2 20
Tuy, stm., Ven. — B8 86
Tuyen Hoa, Viet. — D8 48
Tuyen Quang, Viet. — B7 48
Tuy Hoa, Viet. — F9 48
Tuyun see Duyun, China — H2 42
Tüyür, Burj aṭ, hill, Sudan — C5 62
Tuz, Iraq — C5 56
Tuz Gölü, l., Tur. — B3 56
Tuzigoot National Monument, p.o.i., Az., U.S. — I4 132
Tuzla, Bos. — E5 26
Tuzla, Rom. — D17 26
Tuzly, Ukr. — D17 26
Tvardita, Mol. — C15 26
Tver' (Kalinin), Russia — D18 10
Tver, stm., Russia — D18 10
Tverskaja oblast', co., Russia — C18 10
Tweed, On., Can. — D12 112
Tweed, stm., U.K. — F10 12
Tweed Heads, Austl. — G9 76
Twee Rivieren, S. Afr. — E5 70
Twelve Mile Lake, l.,

Twelve Mile Lake, l., Sk., Can. — E7 124
Twentekanaal, can., Neth. — B15 14
Twentynine Palms, Ca., U.S. — I9 134
Twin Buttes, mtn., Or., U.S. — F4 136
Twin Buttes Reservoir, res., Tx., U.S. — C7 130
Twin City, Ga., U.S. — D3 116
Twin Falls, Id., U.S. — H12 136
Twin Lakes, Ga., U.S. — F2 116
Twin Lakes, l., Ca., U.S. — B9 134
Twinsburg, Oh., U.S. — C4 114
Twisp, Wa., U.S. — B6 136
Twitchell Reservoir, res., Ca., U.S. — H5 134
Twitya, stm., N.T., Can. — C5 106
Two Butte Creek, stm., Co., U.S. — D6 128
Twofold Bay, b., Austl. — K7 76
Two Harbors, Mn., U.S. — D7 118

Name	Map Ref.	Page
Two Medicine, stm., Mt., U.S.	B14	136
Two Rivers, Wi., U.S.	D2	112
Tybee Island, Ga., U.S.	D5	116
Tychy, Pol.	F14	16
Tyczyn, Pol.	G18	16
Tye, Tx., U.S.	B8	130
Tygda, Russia	F14	34
Tyler, Mn., U.S.	G2	118
Tyler, Tx., U.S.	E3	122
Tylertown, Ms., U.S.	F8	122
Tylihul, stm., Ukr.	B17	26
Tylihul's'kyi lyman, l., Ukr.	B17	26
Tym, stm., Russia	C14	32
Tymovskoe, Russia	F17	34
Tynda, Russia	E13	34
Tyndall, S.D., U.S.	D15	126
Tyndaris, sci., Italy	F8	24
Tynemouth, Eng., U.K.	F11	12
Tynset, Nor.	E4	8
Tyre see Şūr, Leb.	E6	58
Tyrifjorden, l., Nor.	F3	8
Tyrma, Russia	F15	34
Tyrma, stm., Russia	F15	34
Tyrnavos, Grc.	D5	28
Tyrone, Ok., U.S.	E7	128
Tyrrell, Lake, l., Austl.	J4	76
Tyrrhenian Sea, s., Eur.	G11	6
Tysa (Tisza) (Tisa), stm., Eur.	A10	26
Tysneseya, i., Nor.	F1	8
Tysse, Nor.	F1	8
Tytuvénai, Lith.	E6	10
Ty Ty, Ga., U.S.	E2	116
Tyva see Tuva, state, Russia	D16	32
Tzaneen, S. Afr.	C9	70
Tzekung see Zigong, China	F5	36
Tzucacab, Mex.	B3	102
Tzukung see Zigong, China	F5	36
Tzupo see Zibo, China	C8	42

U

Name	Map Ref.	Page
Uatumã, stm., Braz.	D6	84
Uaua, Braz.	E6	88
Uaupés, Braz.	H8	86
Uaupés (Vaupés), stm., S. A.	G7	86
Uaxactún, sci., Guat.	D3	102
Ubá, Braz.	K4	88
Ubaidullaganj, India	G6	54
Ubaitaba, Braz.	H6	88
Ubajara, Parque Nacional de, p.o.i., Braz.	B5	88
Ubangi (Oubangui), stm., Afr.	E3	66
Ubatã, Braz.	H6	88
Ubaté, Col.	E5	86
Ubatuba, Braz.	L3	88
Ube, Japan	F4	40
Úbeda, Spain	F7	20
Uberaba, Braz.	J2	88
Uberlândia, Braz.	J1	88
Überlingen, Ger.	I5	16
Ubiña, Peña, mtn., Spain	B4	20
Ubl'a, Slov.	H18	16
Ubly, Mi., U.S.	E7	112
Ubombo, S. Afr.	E11	70
Ubon Ratchathani, Thai.	E7	48
Ubrique, Spain	H5	20
Ubundu, D.R.C.	E5	66
Učaly, Russia	D9	32
Učami, Russia	B17	32
Ucayali, stm., Peru	D3	84
Uchinoura, Japan	H4	40
Uchiura-wan, b., Japan	C14	38
Uchiza, Peru	E2	84
Uchoa, Braz.	K1	88
Uckermark, reg., Ger.	C9	16
Ucon, Id., U.S.	G15	136
Učur, stm., Russia	E15	34
Uda, stm., Russia	F15	34
Uda, stm., Russia	C17	32
Udagamandalam, India	F3	53
Udaipur, India	F4	54
Udalguri, India	E13	54
Udall, Ks., U.S.	D11	128
Udamalpet, India	F3	53
Udankudi, India	G4	53
Udaquiola, Arg.	H8	92
Udayapur, Nepal.	E11	54
Uddevalla, Swe.	G4	8
Uddjaur, l., Swe.	D8	8
Udgir, India	B3	53
Udhampur, India	B5	54
Udimskij, Russia	F21	8
Udine, Italy	D10	22
Udmurtia see Udmurtija, state, Russia	C8	32
Udmurtija, state, Russia	C8	32
Udokan, hrebet, mts., Russia	E12	34
Udomlja, Russia	C17	10
Udon Thani, Thai.	D6	48
Udskaja guba, b., Russia	F16	34
Udskoe, Russia	F15	34
Udupi, India	E2	53
Udža, Russia	B12	34
Ueckermunde, Ger.	C9	16
Ueda, Japan	C11	40
Uele, stm., D.R.C.	D4	66
Uelen, Russia	C26	34
Uel'kal', Russia	C26	34
Uelzen, Ger.	C6	16
Ueno, Japan	E9	40
Uere, stm., D.R.C.	D5	66
Uetersen, Ger.	C5	16
Ufa, Russia	D9	32
Ufa, stm., Russia	C9	32
Uffenheim, Ger.	G6	16
Ugab, stm., Nmb.	E2	68
Uganda, ctry., Afr.	D6	66
Ugarčin, Blg.	F11	26
Ugarit, sci., Syria	C6	58
Ugashik, Ak., U.S.	E8	140
Uglegorsk, Russia	G17	34
Uglekamensk, Russia	C10	38
Uglič, Russia	C21	10
Ugljan, Otok, i., Cro.	F12	22
Ugodiči, Russia	C22	10
Ugodskij Zavod, Russia	E19	10
Ugra, stm., Russia	F18	10
Uherské Hradiště, Czech Rep.	G13	16
Uherský Brod, Czech Rep.	H13	16
Uhlenhorst, Nmb.	C3	70
Uhra, stm., Russia	B22	10
Uhta, Russia	B8	32
Uhta, Russia	F18	8
Uige, Ang.	B1	68
Uinta Mountains, mts., Ut., U.S.	C6	132
Uiraúna, Braz.	D6	88
Uisŏng, Kor.	C1	40
Uitenhage, S. Afr.	H7	70
Uithuizermeeden, Neth.	A15	14
Uj, stm., Russia	D10	32
Ujandina, stm., Russia	C17	34
Ujar, Russia	C16	32
Ujelang, at., Marsh. Is.	C7	72
Újfehértó, Hung.	B8	26
Ujhāni, India	D7	54
Uji, Japan	E8	40
Uji-guntō, is., Japan	H2	40
Ujiji, Tan.	E5	66
Ujjain, India	G5	54
Ujunggandang, Indon.	G12	50
Ujungkulon National Park, p.o.i., Indon.	G4	50
Ujungpandang (Makasar), Indon.	F11	50
Uk, Russia	C17	32
Uka, Russia	E21	34
Ukara Island, i., Tan.	E6	66
Ukerewe Island, i., Tan.	E6	66
Uki Ni N'asi Island, i., Sol. Is.	e9	79b
Ukmergė, Lith.	E7	10
Ukraine, ctry., Eur.	F15	6
Ukui, Indon.	D3	50
Ukyr, Russia	G10	34
Ula, Bela.	E12	10
Ulaanbaatar, Mong.	B6	36
Ulaangom, Mong.	G7	34
Ulan, Austl.	I7	76
Ulan Bator see Ulaanbaatar, Mong.	B6	36
Ulan Buh Shamo, des., China	A2	42
Ulan-Burgasy, hrebet, mts., Russia	F10	34
Ulanhot, China	B9	36
Ulanhów, Pol.	F18	16
Ulansuhai Nur, l., China	A3	42
Ulan-Ude, Russia	F10	34
Ulawa Island, i., Sol. Is.	e9	79b
Ulawun, Mount (The Father), vol., Pap. N. Gui.	b5	79a
Ulchin, Kor., S.	B2	40
Ulcinj, Serb.	H6	26
Ulco, S. Afr.	F7	70
Uldz, stm., Asia	B7	36
Uleåborg see Oulu, Fin.	D11	8
Ulen, Mn., U.S.	D2	118
Ulety, Russia	F11	34
Uležʹ, Alb.	C13	24
Ulhāsnagar, India	B1	53
Ul'ianovka, Ukr.	A17	26
Uliastay, Mong.	B4	36
Ulindi, stm., D.R.C.	E5	66
Ulja, Russia	E17	34
Uljanovo, Russia	G18	10
Uljanovsk, Russia	D7	32
Ul'kan, Russia	C19	32
Ulla, stm., Spain	B2	20
Ulladulla, Austl.	J8	76
Ullin, Il., U.S.	G8	120
Ullűng-do, i., Kor., S.	A10	40
Ulm, Ger.	H5	16
Ulm, Mt., U.S.	C15	136
Ulmarra, Austl.	G9	76
Ulmeni, Rom.	D13	26
Ulónguè, Moz.	C5	68
Ulsan, Kor., S.	D2	40
Ulster, hist. reg., Eur.	G5	12
Ulster Canal, can., Eur.	G5	12
Ulu, Indon.	E8	44
Ulu, Russia	D14	34
Ulúa, stm., Hond.	E3	102
Ulubat Gölü, l., Tur.	C11	28
Uluborlu, Tur.	E13	28
Uluçınar, Tur.	B6	58
Ulukışla, Tur.	A5	58
Ulul, i., Micron.	C5	72
Ulungur, stm., China	B2	36
Ulungur Hu, l., China	B2	36
Ulunhan, Russia	F11	34
Uluru (Ayers Rock), mtn., Austl.	E6	74
Ulverston, Eng., U.K.	G9	12
Ulverstone, Austl.	n12	77a
Ulysses, Ks., U.S.	D7	128
Ulytaŭ zhotasy, mts., Kaz.	E11	32
Uma, China	F13	34
Umán, Mex.	B3	102
Umanak, Grnld.	C15	141
Umanak Fjord, b., Grnld.	C15	141
Umargåon, India	H4	54
Umaria, India	G8	54
Umarizal, Braz.	D7	88
Umarkot, Pak.	F2	54
Umatac, Guam	j9	78c
Umatilla, Fl., U.S.	H4	116
Umatilla, Or., U.S.	E7	136
Umatilla, Lake, res., U.S.	E4	136
Umba, Russia	C16	8
Umbertide, Italy	G9	22
Umboi Island, i., Pap. N. Gui.	b4	79a
Umbria, state, Italy	G9	22
Umbukul, Pap. N. Gui.	a4	79a
Umbuzeiro, ozero, l., Russia	C16	8
Umeå, Swe.	E9	8
Umeälven, stm., Swe.	D8	8
Umfolozi Game Reserve, S. Afr.	F10	70
Umfors, Swe.	C6	8
Umfreville Lake, res., On., Can.	A3	118
Umkomaas, S. Afr.	G10	70
Umm al-Arānib, Libya	B2	62
Umm al-Jimāl, Khirbat, sci., Jord.	F7	58
Umm al-Qaywayn, U.A.E.	D8	56
Umm as-Sa'd, sci., Syria	E7	58
Umm Bel, Sudan	E5	62
Umm Durman (Omdurman), Sudan	D6	62
Umm el Fahm, Isr.	F6	58
Umm Lajj, Sau. Ar.	D4	56
Umm Mitmam, sand, Egypt	H3	58
Umm Omeiyid, Râs, mtn., Egypt	K3	58
Umm Ruwābah, Sudan	E6	62
Umm Sayyidah, Sudan	E6	62
Umnak Island, i., Ak., U.S.	g25	140a
Umpqua, stm., Or., U.S.	G3	136
Umpulo, Ang.	C2	68
'Umrān, Yemen	F5	56
Umraniye, Tur.	D14	28
Umred, India	H7	54
Umreth, India	G4	54
Umtata, S. Afr.	G9	70
Umuarama, Braz.	A11	92
Umzingwani, stm., Zimb.	B9	70
Umzinto, S. Afr.	G10	70
Una, Braz.	H6	88
Una, India	C5	54
Una, stm., Bos.	E13	22
Unac, stm., Bos.	D2	116
Unadilla, Ga., U.S.	D2	116
Unadilla, N.Y., U.S.	B10	114
Unaí, Braz.	I2	88
Unalakleet, Ak., U.S.	D7	140
Unalaska, Ak., U.S.	F6	140
Unalaska Island, i., Ak., U.S.	F6	140
Unare, stm., Ven.	C9	86
'Unayzah, Sau. Ar.	D5	56
Uncia, Bol.	C3	90
Uncompahgre Peak, mtn., Co., U.S.	E9	132
Uncompahgre Plateau, plat., Co., U.S.	E8	132
Unden, l., Swe.	G5	8
Underberg, S. Afr.	F9	70
Undva nina, c., Est.	B8	10
Uneča, Russia	H15	10
Uneiuxi, stm., Braz.	H9	86
Unga Island, i., Ak., U.S.	E7	140
Ungava, péninsule d', pen., Qc., Can.	D16	106
Ungava Bay, b., Can.	D17	106
Ungava Peninsula see Ungava, Péninsule d', pen., Qc., Can.	D16	106
Ungheni, Mol.	B14	26
União, Braz.	C4	88
União dos Palmares, Braz.	E7	88
Unicoi, Tn., U.S.	H3	114
Uniejów, Pol.	D14	16
Unimak Island, i., Ak., U.S.	F7	140
Unimak Pass, strt., Ak., U.S.	F6	140
Unini, stm., Braz.	H11	86
Union, Ia., U.S.	B5	120
Unión, Arg.	G5	92
Unión, Para.	B9	92
Union, La., U.S.	G8	122
Union, Mo., U.S.	F6	120
Union, N.J., U.S.	D11	114
Union, Or., U.S.	E9	136
Union, S.C., U.S.	B4	116
Union, W.V., U.S.	G5	114
Union Bay, B.C., Can.	G6	138
Union City, Ga., U.S.	D14	122
Union City, Mi., U.S.	F4	112
Union City, Oh., U.S.	D1	114
Union City, Pa., U.S.	C6	114
Union City, Tn., U.S.	H8	120
Unión de Reyes, Cuba	A7	102
Unión de Tula, Mex.	E7	100
Union Flat Creek, stm., U.S.	D9	136
Union Grove, Wi., U.S.	F11	112
Union Island, i., St. Vin.	p10	105e
Union Point, Ga., U.S.	C2	116
Union Springs, Al., U.S.	E13	122
Uniontown, Al., U.S.	E11	122
Uniontown, Ky., U.S.	G10	120
Uniontown, Pa., U.S.	E6	114
Unionville, Mi., U.S.	E6	112
United, Pa., U.S.	D6	114
United Arab Emirates, ctry., Asia	E7	56
United Arab Republic see Egypt, ctry., Afr.		
United Kingdom, ctry., Eur.	D8	6
United States, ctry., N.A.	C10	102
Unity, Sk., Can.	B4	124
Universal City, Tx., U.S.	E9	130
University, Ms., U.S.	C9	122
University City, Mo., U.S.	F7	120
University Park, N.M., U.S.	K10	132
University Park, Tx., U.S.	E2	122
Unjha, India	G4	54
Unnão, India	E8	54
Uno, Canal Numero, can., Arg.	H9	92
Unquillo, Arg.	E5	92
Unst, i., Scot., U.K.	n19	12a
Unstrut, stm., Ger.	E7	16
Unža, stm., Russia	G21	8
Unzen-dake, vol., Japan	G3	40
Uong Bi, Viet.	B8	48
Uozu, Japan	C10	40
Upata, Ven.	C10	86
Upemba, Lac, l., D.R.C.	F5	66
Upernavik, Grnld.	C14	141
Upia, stm., Col.	E5	86
Upington, S. Afr.	F5	70
Upland, Ne., U.S.	A10	128
Upleta, India	H3	54
Upolu, i., Samoa	h11	79c
Upolu Point, c., Hi., U.S.	c6	78a
Upper Arlington, Oh., U.S.	D2	114
Upper Arrow Lake, l., B.C., Can.	F13	138
Upper Austria see Oberösterreich, state, Aus.	B10	22
Upper Blackville, N.B., Can.	D10	110
Upper Darby, Pa., U.S.	E10	114
Upper Egypt see El-Sa'īd, hist. reg., Egypt	J2	58
Upper Fraser, B.C., Can.	B8	138
Upper Iowa, stm., U.S.	H7	118
Upper Kapuas Mountains, mts., Asia	C8	50
Upper Klamath Lake, l., Or., U.S.	H5	136
Upper Lake, Ca., U.S.	D3	134
Upper Manitou Lake, l., On., Can.	B5	118
Upper Musquodoboit, N.S., Can.	E14	110
Upper Red Lake, l., Mn., U.S.	C4	118
Upper Sandusky, Oh., U.S.	D2	114
Upper Takutu-Upper Essequibo, state, Guy.	F12	86
Upper Trajan's Wall, misc. cult., Mol.	C15	26
Upper Volta see Burkina Faso, ctry., Afr.	G4	64
Uppsala, Swe.	F7	8
Uppsala, state, Swe.	F7	8
Upshi, India	B6	54
Upton, Ky., U.S.	G12	120
Uraba, Golfo de, b., Col.	C3	86
Uracoa, Ven.	C10	86
Uraj, Russia	B10	32
Urakawa, Japan	C15	38
Ural, stm.	E8	32
Ural Mountains see Ural'skie gory, mts., Russia	C9	32
Ural'sk see Oral, Kaz.	D8	32
Ural'skie gory (Ural Mountains), mts., Russia	C9	32
Urana, Austl.	J6	76
Urandangi, Austl.	D7	74
Urangan, Austl.	E9	76
Urania, La., U.S.	F6	122
Uranium City, Sk., Can.	D9	106
Uraricaá, stm., Braz.	F10	86
Uraricoera, Braz.	F11	86
Uraricoera, stm., Braz.	F11	86
Ura-Tjube, Taj.	B10	56
Uravakonda, India	D3	53
Uravan, Co., U.S.	E8	132
Urawa, Japan	D12	40
Urbana, Il., U.S.	D9	120
Urbana, Oh., U.S.	D2	114
Urbandale, Ia., U.S.	C4	120
Urbania, Italy	G9	22
Urbino, Italy	G9	22
Urcos, Peru	F3	84
Urdinarrain, Arg.	F8	92
Ure, stm., Eng., U.K.	G11	12
Urèčča, Bela.	H10	10
Uren', Russia	H21	8
Ureña, Ven.	D5	86
Ures, Mex.	G7	98
Ureshino, Japan	F2	40
Urewera National Park, p.o.i., N.Z.	D7	80
Urgenč, Uzb.	F10	32
Urho Kekkosen kansallispuisto, p.o.i., Fin.	B12	8
Uriah, Al., U.S.	F11	122
Uriah, Mount, mtn., N.Z.	E4	80
Uribante, stm., Ven.	D6	86
Uribe, Col.	F4	86
Uribia, Col.	B5	86
Urich, Mo., U.S.	F4	120
Urique, stm., Mex.	B5	100
Úritskij, Kaz.	D11	32
Urjung-Haja, Russia	B11	34
Urjupinsk, Russia	D6	32
Urla, Tur.	E9	28
Urlați, Rom.	D13	26
Urlings, Antig.	f4	105b
Urmia, Lake see Orūmīyeh, Daryācheh-ye, l., Iran	B6	56
Uromi, Nig.	H6	64
Urošewac, Serb.	G8	26
Urrao, Col.	D3	86
Ursa, Il., U.S.	D6	120
Uruaçu, Braz.	H1	88
Uruapan, Mex.	L9	134
Uruapan del Progreso, Mex.	F7	100
Urubamba, Peru	F3	84
Urubamba, stm., Peru	F3	84
Urubaxi, stm., Braz.	H9	86
Urucará, Braz.	D6	84
Uruçuí, Braz.	F1	88
Uruburetama, Braz.	B6	88
Urucu, stm., Braz.	D5	84
Uruçuca, Braz.	H6	88
Uruçuí, Serra da, hills, Braz.	E3	88
Urucuia, stm., Braz.	I3	88
Urucurí-preto, stm., Braz.	E3	88
Uruguai (Uruguay) (Uruguay), stm., S.A.	F8	92
Uruguaiana, Braz.	D9	92
Uruguay, ctry., S.A.	F10	92
Uruguay (Uruguai) (Uruguay), stm., S.A.	F8	92
Urumchi see Ürümqi, China	C2	36
Ürümqi, China	C2	36
Urup, ostrov, i., Russia	G19	34
Urupês, Braz.	K1	88
Urutai, Braz.	I1	88
Uruwira, Tan.	F6	66
Ürzhar, Kaz.	E14	32
Urziceni, Rom.	E13	26
Uržum, Russia	C7	32
Usa, stm., Russia	A9	32
Usa, stm., Russia	A9	32
Uşak, Tur.	E12	28
Uşak, state, Tur.	E12	28
Ušaki, Russia	A13	10
Usakos, Nmb.	B2	70
Usborne, Mount, mtn., Falk. Is.	J5	90
Uščerpe, Russia	H14	10
U.S. Department of Energy Hanford Site, sci., Wa., U.S.	D7	136
Usedom, i., Eur.	B10	16
Ushant see Ouessant, Île d', i., Fr.	F3	14
Ushashi, Kaz.	E14	32
Ushashi, Tan.	E6	66
Ushtöbe, Kaz.	E13	32
Ushuaia, Arg.	J3	90
Usingen, Ger.	F4	16
Usinsk, Russia	A9	32
Usk, Wa., U.S.	B9	136
Usk, stm., Wales, U.K.	J9	12
Uslar, Ger.	E5	16
Usman' ezers, l., Lat.	C4	10
Usole, Russia	C9	32
Usole-Sibirskoe, Russia	D18	32
Uspallata, Arg.	F3	92
Uspanapa, stm., Mex.	G11	100
Ussuri (Wusuli), stm., Asia	C11	36
Ussurijsk, Russia	C10	38
Ust'-Barguzin, Russia	F10	34
Ust'-Belaja, Russia	C23	34
Ust'-Bol'šereck, Russia	F20	34
Ust'-Čaun, Russia	C23	34
Ust'-Chorna, Ukr.	A10	26
Ust'-Cil'ma, Russia	D25	8
Uste, Russia	G18	8
Uster, Switz.	C5	22
Ustica, Isola di, i., Italy	F7	24
Ust'-Ilimsk, Russia	C18	32
Ust'-Ilimskoe vodohranilišče, res., Russia	C18	32
Ústí nad Labem, Czech Rep.	F10	16
Ústí nad Orlicí, Czech Rep.	G12	16
Ust'-Išim, Russia	C12	32
Ustja, stm., Russia	F21	8
Ust'-Javron'ga, Russia	E8	10
Ustjužna, Russia	B19	10
Ustka, Pol.	B12	16
Ust'-Kamčatsk, Russia	E21	34
Ust'-Kamenogorsk see Öskemen, Kaz.	E14	32
Ust'-Koksa, Russia	D15	32
Ust'-Kujda, Russia	B16	34
Ust'-Kulom, Russia	B8	32
Ust'-Kut, Russia	C19	32
Ust'-Lyža, Russia	A9	32
Ust'-Maja, Russia	D15	34
Ust'-Man'ja, Russia	B10	32
Ust'-Nera, Russia	D17	34
Ust'-Nijukža, Russia	E13	34
Ust'omčug, Russia	E22	8
Ust'-Ordynskij, Russia	D18	34
Ust'-Ožernoe, Russia	C15	32
Ust'-Pinega, Russia	D19	8
Ust'-Reki, Russia	E22	8
Ust'-Sumy, Russia	D14	32
Ust'-Ulagan, Russia	D15	32
Ust'-Urgal, Russia	F15	34
Ust-Urt Plateau, plat., Asia	F9	32
Ust'-Vyjskaja, Russia	E22	8
Usu, China	C1	36
Usuki, Japan	F4	40
Usulután, El Sal.	F3	102
Usumacinta, stm., N.A.	D2	102
Usumbura see Bujumbura, Bdi.	E5	66
Ušumun, Russia	F14	34
Usvjaty, Russia	E13	10
Utah, state, U.S.	D5	132
Utah Lake, l., Ut., U.S.	C5	132
Utata, Russia	F10	34
Ute, Ia., U.S.	B2	120
Ute Creek, stm., N.M., U.S.	E5	128
Utegi, Tan.	E6	66
Utena, Lith.	E8	10
Utete, Tan.	F7	66
Uthai Thani, Thai.	E4	48
Uthal, Pak.	D10	56
U Thong, Thai.	E4	48
Utiariti, Braz.	F6	84
Utica, Ks., U.S.	C8	128
Utica, Mi., U.S.	F6	112
Utica, Ne., U.S.	G15	126
Utica, N.Y., U.S.	E14	112
Utica, Oh., U.S.	D3	114
Utica see Utique, sci., Tun.	G3	24
Utiel, Spain	E9	20
Utila, Isla de, i., Hond.	D4	102
Utinga, stm., Braz.	G5	88
Utique (Utica), sci., Tun.	G3	24
Uto, Japan	G3	40
Utopia, Tx., U.S.	E8	130
Utorgoš, Russia	B13	10
Utraula, India	E9	54
Utrecht, Neth.	B14	14
Utrecht, S. Afr.	E10	70
Utrera, Spain	G5	20
Utroja, stm., Eur.	D10	10
Utrik, at., Marsh. Is.	B7	72
Utsjoki, Fin.	B12	8
Utsunomiya, Japan	C12	40
Uttaradit, Thai.	D4	48
Uttarakhand, state, India	C7	54
Uttarkāshi, India	C7	54
Uttar Pradesh, state, India	E7	54
Uttoxeter, Eng., U.K.	I11	12
Utuado, P.R.	B2	104a
Utukok, stm., Ak., U.S.	C7	140
Utupua, i., Sol. Is.	E7	72
Uulu, Est.	B7	10
Uva, stm., Col.	F7	86
Uvalda, Ga., U.S.	D3	116
Uvalde, Tx., U.S.	E8	130
Uvarovo, Russia	D6	32
Uvaravičy, Bela.	H13	10
Uvdal, Nor.	F3	8
Uvinza, Tan.	F6	66
Uvira, D.R.C.	E5	66
Uvs Lake see Uvsu-Nur, ozero, l., Asia	F7	34
Uvsu-Nur, ozero, l., Asia	F7	34
Uwajima, Japan	F5	40
Uwa, Japan	F5	40
Uwayl, Sudan	F5	62
Uxbridge, On., Can.	D10	112
Uxmal, sci., Mex.	B3	102
Uyo, Nig.	H6	64
Uyuni, Bol.	D3	90
Uyuni, Salar de, pl., Bol.	D3	90
Uzbekistan, ctry., Asia	E10	30
Uzda, Bela.	G10	10
Uzerche, Fr.	D7	18
Uzgen, Kyrg.	F12	32
Uzhhorod, Ukr.	A9	26
Užice, Serb.	F6	26
Uzlovaja, Russia	F20	10
Üzümlü, Tur.	G12	28
Uzun Ada, i., Tur.	E9	28
Uzunköprü, Tur.	B9	28
Uzunkuduk, Uzb.	F11	32
Užur, Russia	C16	32
Uzventis, Lith.	E5	10

V

Name	Map Ref.	Page
Vaal, stm., S. Afr.	F7	70
Vaaldam, res., S. Afr.	E8	70
Vaalwater, S. Afr.	D8	70
Vaasa (Vasa), Fin.	E9	8
Vabalninkas, Lith.	D7	10
Vác, Hung.	B6	26
Vacaria, Braz.	D12	92
Vacaria, stm., Braz.	I4	88
Vacaville, Ca., U.S.	E4	134
Vaccarès, Étang de, l., Fr.	F10	18
Vache, Île à, i., Haiti	C11	102
Vad, Russia	I21	8
Vadakara see Badagara, India	F2	53
Vădeni, Rom.	D14	26
Vadnagar, India	G4	54
Vado, N.M., U.S.	K10	132
Vado Ligure, Italy	F5	22
Vadsø, Nor.	A13	8
Vaduz, Liech.	C6	22
Vága, stm., Russia	F20	8
Vågåmo, Nor.	F3	8
Vágar, i., Far. Is.	m34	8b
Vaghena Island, i., Sol. Is.	d7	79b
Vah, stm., Russia	B13	32
Váh, stm., Slov.	H13	16
Vahsel, Cape, c., S. Geor.	J9	90
Vaiden, Ms., U.S.	D9	122
Vaigač, ostrov, i., Russia	A9	32
Vaigai, strt., Grnld.	C15	141
Vaijāpur, India	B2	53
Vaikam, India	G3	53
Väike-Maarja, Est.	A9	10
Vail, Co., U.S.	D10	132
Vail, Ia., U.S.	B2	120
Vaimali, Vanuatu	k17	79d
Vaippār, stm., India	G4	53
Vaison-la-Romaine, Fr.	E11	18
Vaitahu, Fr. Poly.	s18	78g
Vākhān, hist. reg., Afg.	B11	56
Valaam, Russia	F14	8
Valadeces, Mex.	H9	130
Valandovo, Mac.	B5	28
Valašské Meziříčí, Czech Rep.	G13	16
Valatie, N.Y., U.S.	B12	114
Vâlcea, state, Rom.	E11	26
Vâlcedrăm, Blg.	F10	26
Valcheta, Arg.	H3	90
Valdagno, Italy	E8	22
Valdai Hills see Valdajskaja vozvyšennost', hills, Russia	C15	10
Valdaj, Russia	B16	10
Valdaj, Russia	E16	8
Valdajskaja vozvyšennost' (Valdai Hills), hills, Russia	C15	10
Valdarno, val., Italy	G8	22
Val-de-Cães, Braz.	A1	88
Valdecañas, Embalse de, res., Spain	E5	20
Valdemarsvik, Swe.	G7	8
Valdepeñas, Spain	F7	20
Valderaduey, stm., Spain	C5	20
Valdés, Península, pen., Arg.	H4	90
Val-des-Bois, Qc., Can.	C14	112
Valdez, Ak., U.S.	D10	140
Valdivia, Chile	G2	90
Valdivia, Col.	D4	86
Valdobbiadene, Italy	E8	22
Val-d'Oise, state, Fr.	E10	14
Val-d'Or, Qc., Can.	F15	106
Valdosta, Ga., U.S.	F2	116
Valdovino see Aviño, Spain	A3	20
Vale, Or., U.S.	G9	136
Valemount, B.C., Can.	D11	138
Valença, Braz.	L4	88
Valença, Braz.	G6	88
Valença, Port.	B2	20
Valença do Piauí, Braz.	D4	88
Valence, Fr.	E10	18
Valencia, Phil.	F5	52
Valencia, Spain	E10	20
Valencia, state, Spain	E10	20
València, co., Spain	E10	20
València, Golf de, b., Spain	E10	20
Valencia, Golfo de, b., Spain	E10	20
Valencia, Lago de, l., Ven.	B8	86
Valencia de Alcántara, Spain	E3	20
Valencia de Don Juan, Spain	B5	20
Valencia Island, i., Ire.	J2	12
Valente, Braz.	F6	88
Valentine, Ne., U.S.	E12	126
Valentine, Tx., U.S.	D3	130
Valenza, Italy	F5	22
Valera, Ven.	C6	86
Valga, Est.	H12	8
Valiente, Península, pen., Pan.	H7	102
Valjevo, Serb.	E7	26
Valkeakoski, Fin.	F11	8
Valkenswaard, Neth.	C14	14
Valladares, Mex.	H7	130
Valladolid, Mex.	B3	102
Valladolid, Spain	C6	20
Valladolid, co., Spain	C6	20
Valle, Lat.	D7	10
Vallecillo, Mex.	H7	130
Valle de Allende, Mex.	B6	100
Valle de la Pascua, Ven.	C8	86
Valle del Cauca, state, Col.	F3	86
Valle de Olivos, Mex.	B5	100
Valle de Santiago, Mex.	E8	100
Valle de Zaragoza, Mex.	B6	100
Valledupar, Col.	B5	86
Vallée d'Aoste see Valle d'Aosta, state, Italy	E4	22
Vallejo, Ca., U.S.	E3	134
Vallejuelo, Dom. Rep.	C12	102
Vallenar, Chile	D2	92
Valle Redondo, Mex.	K9	134
Valletta, Malta	I8	24
Valley, Al., U.S.	E13	122
Valley, Ne., U.S.	C1	120
Valley, Wa., U.S.	B9	136
Valley City, N.D., U.S.	C13	124
Valley East, On., Can.	B8	112
Valley Falls, Ks., U.S.	E2	120
Valley Farms, Az., U.S.	K5	132
Valley Head, Al., U.S.	C13	122
Valley Mills, Tx., U.S.	C10	130
Valley of the Kings, sci., Egypt	B6	62
Valley Springs, S.D., U.S.	H2	118
Valley Station, Ky., U.S.	F12	120
Valleyview, Ab., Can.	A13	138
Valley View, Tx., U.S.	H11	128
Vallimanca, Arroyo, stm., Arg.	H7	92
Vallorbe, Switz.	D3	22
Valls, Spain	C12	20
Valmeyer, Il., U.S.	F7	120
Valmiera, Lat.	C8	10
Valoria la Buena, Spain	C6	20
Valožyn, Bela.	F9	10
Vālpārai, India	F3	53
Valparaíso, Chile	F2	92
Valparaíso, Mex.	D7	100
Valparaiso, Fl., U.S.	G12	122
Valparaiso, In., U.S.	G2	112
Valparaíso, Ne., U.S.	F16	126
Valparaíso, state, Chile	F2	92
Valréas, Fr.	E10	18
Vals, stm., S. Afr.	E8	70
Vals, Tanjung, c., Indon.	G10	44
Valsbaai see False Bay, b., S. Afr.	I4	70
Valtimo, Fin.	E13	8
Valujki, Russia	D5	32
Valverde del Camino, Spain	G4	20
Valyncy, Bela.	E11	10
Vamori Wash, stm., Az., U.S.	L5	132
Van, Tur.	B5	56
Van, Lake see Van Gölü, l., Tur.	B5	56
Vanadzor, Arm.	A5	56
Vanajavesi, l., Fin.	F10	8
Vanavara, Russia	C18	32
Van Bruyssel, Qc., Can.	C4	110
Van Buren, Ar., U.S.	B4	122
Van Buren, Me., U.S.	C8	110
Van Buren, Mo., U.S.	G6	120
Vanceburg, Ky., U.S.	F2	114
Vancouver, B.C., Can.	G7	138
Vancouver, Wa., U.S.	E4	136
Vancouver Island, i., B.C., Can.	G4	138
Vancouver Island Ranges, mts., B.C., Can.	G5	138
Vandalia, Il., U.S.	F8	120
Vandalia, Mo., U.S.	E6	120
Vandalia, Oh., U.S.	E1	114
Vandavāsi, India	E4	53
Vanderbijlpark, S. Afr.	E8	70
Vanderbilt, Tx., U.S.	F11	130
Vanderhoof, B.C., Can.	B6	138
Vanderkloof Dam, res., S. Afr.	F7	70
Vanderlin Island, i., Austl.	C7	74
Vandervoort, Ar., U.S.	C4	122
Van Diemen Gulf, b., Austl.	B6	74
Vandry, Qc., Can.	C3	110
Vandžiogala, Lith.	E6	10
Vanegas, Mex.	D8	100
Vänern, l., Swe.	G5	8
Vänersborg, Swe.	G5	8
Vangaindrano, Madag.	E8	68
Van Gölü, l., Tur.	B5	56
Van Horn, Tx., U.S.	C3	130
Van Horne, Ia., U.S.	B5	120
Vanier, ngh., On., Can.	C14	112
Vanikolo, i., Sol. Is.	E7	72
Vanimo, Pap. N. Gui.	a3	79a
Vanino, Russia	G17	34
Vänivilāsa Sāgara, res., India	E3	53
Vāniyambādi, India	E4	53
Vankarem, Russia	C25	34
Vankleek Hill, On., Can.	E2	110
Van Lear, Ky., U.S.	G3	114
Vanna, i., Nor.	A8	8
Vännäs, Swe.	E8	8
Vannes, Fr.	G6	14
Van Ninh, Viet.	F9	48
Van Phong, Vung, b., Viet.	F9	48
Van Phong Bay see Van Phong, Vung, b., Viet.	F9	48
Van Reenen, S. Afr.	F9	70
Van Rees, Pegunungan, mts., Indon.	F10	44
Vanrhynsdorp, S. Afr.	G4	70
Vansant, Va., U.S.	G3	114
Vansittart Island, i., Nu., Can.	B14	106
Vanskoe, Russia	B19	10
Vanthali, India	H3	54
Vanua Balavu, i., Fiji	p20	79e
Vanua Lava, i., Vanuatu	i16	79d
Vanua Levu, i., Fiji	p19	79e
Vanuatu (New Hebrides), ctry., Oc.	k16	79d
Van Wert, Oh., U.S.	D1	114
Van Wyksdorp, S. Afr.	H5	70
Van Zylsrus, S. Afr.	E6	70
Vao, N. Cal.	n16	79d
Var, state, Fr.	F12	18
Var, stm., Fr.	F13	18
Varada, stm., India	D2	53
Varallo, Italy	E5	22
Vārānasi (Benares), India	F9	54
Varandej, Russia	A9	32
Varangerfjorden, b., Nor.	A14	8
Varangerhalvøya, pen., Nor.	A13	8
Varano, Lago di, l., Italy	I12	22
Varaždin, Cro.	D13	22
Varazze, Italy	F5	22
Varberg, Swe.	H5	8
Vardak, state, Afg.	A2	54
Vardar (Axiós), stm., Eur.	B5	28
Varde, Den.	I3	8
Vardø, Nor.	A14	8
Varel, Ger.	C4	16
Varèna, Lith.	F7	10
Varennes-sur-Allier, Fr.	C9	18
Varese, Italy	E5	22
Vârfurile, Rom.	C9	26
Vargem, Riacho da, stm., Braz.	E6	88
Vargem Grande, Braz.	B3	88
Varginha, Braz.	K3	88
Varkallai, India	G3	53
Varkaus, Fin.	E12	8
Värmeln, l., Swe.	G5	8
Värmland, state, Swe.	G5	8
Varna, Blg.	F14	26
Varna, Russia	D10	32
Varna, state, Blg.	F14	26
Varniai, Lith.	E5	10
Varnjany, Bela.	F9	10
Varnsdorf, Czech Rep.	F10	16
Varnville, S.C., U.S.	D4	116
Varpalota, Hung.	B5	26
Várska, Est.	C10	10
Varvarin, Serb.	F8	26
Várzea, stm., Braz.	C11	92
Várzea Alegre, Braz.	D6	88
Várzea da Palma, Braz.	I3	88

Name — Map Ref. — Page

Várzea Grande, Braz. G6 84
Varzino, Russia B17 8
Vas, state, Hung. B3 26
Vasa see Vaasa, Fin. E9 8
Vasai, India E3 46
Vasalemma, Est. A7 10
Vasco, País see Euskal Herriko, state, Spain A8 20
Vashkivtsi, Ukr. A14 26
Vashkivtsi, Ukr. A12 26
Vashon Island, i., Wa., U.S. C4 136
Vasilevič, Bela. H12 10
Vasilevskij Moh C18 10
Vasiliká, Grc. C6 28
Vasjugan, stm., Russia. C13 32
Vaška, stm., Russia. D21 8
Vaskelovo, Russia. F14 8
Vaslui, Rom. C14 26
Vaslui, state, Rom. C14 26
Vass, N.C., U.S. A6 116
Vassar, Mi., U.S. E6 112
Västerås, Swe. G7 8
Västerbotten, state, Swe. D8 8
Västernorrland, state, Swe. E7 8
Västervik, Swe. H7 8
Västmanland, state, Swe. G7 8
Vasto, Italy H11 22
Västra Götaland, state, Swe. G4 8
Vasvár, Hung. B3 26
Vatan, Fr. G10 14
Vatican see Vatican City, ctry., Eur. I9 22
Vatican City, ctry., Eur. I9 22
Vaticano, Capo, c., Italy F9 24
Vatnajökull, ice, Ice. k31 8a
Vatomandry, Madag. D8 68
Vatra Dornei, Rom. B12 26
Vättern, l., Swe. G6 8
Vatu-i-ra Channel, strt., Fiji p19 79e
Vatukoula, Fiji p18 79e
Vauclin, Montagne du, mtn., Mart. k7 105c
Vaucluse, state, Fr. F11 18
Vaucouleurs, Fr. F14 14
Vaughan, On., Can. E10 112
Vaughn, N.M., U.S. G3 128
Vaukavysk, Bela. G7 10
Vaupés, state, Col. G6 86
Vaupés (Uaupés), stm., S.A. E9 72
Vava'u, i., Tonga H3 64
Vavoua, C. Iv. H3 64
Vavuniya, Sri L. G5 53
Växjö, Swe. H6 8
Vaza-barris, stm., Braz. E6 88
Vazante, Braz. J2 88
Vazuza, stm., Russia E17 10
Vazuzskoe vodohranilišče, res., Russia E16 10
Veazie, Me., U.S. F8 110
Veblen, S.D., U.S. B15 126
Vecht (Vechte), stm., Eur. B15 14
Vechta, Ger. D4 16
Vechte (Vecht), stm., Eur. B15 14
Vecpiebalga, Lat. C8 10
Vecsés, Hung. B6 26
Veddige, Swe. H4 8
Vedea, stm., Rom. F12 26
Vedia, Arg. G7 92
Vednoe, Russia C19 10
Veedersburg, In., U.S. H2 112
Veendam, Neth. A15 14
Veenendaal, Neth. C14 14
Vega, i., Nor. D4 8
Vega Alta, P.R. B3 104a
Vega Baja, P.R. B3 104a
Vegreville, Ab., Can. C18 138
Veguita, N.M., U.S. I10 132
Veinticinco de Mayo, Arg. G7 92
Veiros, Braz. D7 84
Veisiejai, Lith. F6 10
Vejle, Den. I3 8
Vela Luka, Cro. H13 22
Velas, Cabo, c., C.R. G4 102
Velázquez, Ur. G10 92
Velden, Ger. H8 16
Veleka, stm. G14 26
Veležčina, Bela. F11 10
Vélez, Col. D5 86
Vélez-Málaga, Spain H6 20
Vel'gija, Russia B17 10
Velhas, stm., Braz. I3 88
Velikaja, stm., Russia. C11 10
Velikaja, stm., Russia. D23 34
Velikaja Kema, Russia B12 38
Velika Morava, stm., Serb. E8 26
Velike Luki, Russia D13 10
Velikij Ustjug, Russia F21 8
Veliki Vitorog, mtn., Bos. E4 26
Velikoe, Russia G17 8
Velikoe, ozero, l., Russia C19 10
Velikonda Hills, hills, India. D4 53
Veliko Tărnovo, Blg. F12 26
Velikovisočnoe, Russia C25 8
Veli Lošinj, Cro. F11 22
Velingara, Sen. G2 64
Veliž, Russia E14 10
Vel'ké Kapušany, Slov. H18 16
Velké Meziříčí, Czech Rep. G12 16
Vella Gulf, strt., Sol. Is. d7 79b
Vella Lavella, i., Sol. Is. d7 79b
Vellār, stm., India. F4 53
Velletri, Italy I9 22
Vellore, India E4 53
Velma, Ok., U.S. G11 128
Vel'sk, Russia F20 8
Velten, Ger. D9 16
Velva, N.D., U.S. F13 124
Velyka Mykhailivka, Ukr. B16 26
Velykodolyns'ke, Ukr. C16 26
Velykoplos'ke, Ukr. C16 26
Velykyi Bychkiv, Ukr. B11 26
Velykyi Kuialnyk, stm., Ukr. B17 26
Venadillo, Col. E4 86
Venado Tuerto, Arg. F6 92
Venafro, Italy C8 24
Venâncio Aires, Braz. D11 92
Vence, Fr. F13 18
Venda, hist. reg., S. Afr. C10 70
Vendas Novas, Port. F2 20
Vendée, state, Fr. C4 18
Vendéen, Bocage, reg., Fr. C4 18
Vendôme, Fr. G10 14
Vendrell see El Vendrell, Spain C12 20
Venetie, Laguna, b., Italy E9 22
Venetie, Ak., U.S. C10 140
Veneto, state, Italy E8 22
Venev, Russia F21 10
Venèzia (Venice), Italy E9 22
Venezia, Golfo di, b., Italy E9 22
Venezuela, ctry., S.A. B4 84
Venezuela, Golfo de, b., S.A. A3 84
Venezuela, Gulf of see Venezuela, Golfo de, b., S.A. A3 84
Venezuelan Basin, unds. G7 144
Vengerovo, Russia C13 32
Vengurla, India D1 53
Veniaminof, Mount, vol., Ak., U.S. E8 140
Venice see Venèzia, Italy E9 22
Venice, Fl., U.S. I3 116
Venice, La., U.S. H9 122
Venice, Gulf of, b., Eur. E9 22
Vénissieux, Fr. D10 18
Venlo, Neth. C15 14
Venosa, Italy D9 24

Ventersdorp, S. Afr. E8 70
Venterstad, S. Afr. G7 70
Ventimiglia, Italy G4 22
Ventotene, Isola, i., Italy D7 24
Ventspils, Lat. C4 10
Ventuari, stm., Ven. E8 86
Ventura, Ca., U.S. I6 134
Venturia, N.D., U.S. B13 126
Venustiano Carranza, Mex. G12 100
Venustiano Carranza, Presa, res., Mex. B8 100
Vera, Arg. D7 92
Vera, Spain G9 20
Vera, Cape, c., Nu., Can. B8 141
Veracruz, Mex. F10 100
Veracruz, state, Mex. F10 100
Veranópolis, Braz. D12 92
Veraval, India H3 54
Verbania, Italy E5 22
Verbano see Maggiore, Lago, l., Eur. C14 18
Verbeek, Pegunungan, mts., Indon. E12 50
Verbilki, Russia D20 10
Vercelli, Italy E5 22
Vercors, reg., Fr. E11 18
Verde, stm., Braz. D4 90
Verde, stm., Braz. F4 88
Verde, stm., Braz. H1 88
Verde, stm., Braz. J1 88
Verde, stm., Braz. F6 84
Verde, stm., Mex. E7 100
Verde, stm., Az., U.S. J5 132
Verde, Cape, c., Bah. A10 102
Verde Grande, stm., Braz. H4 88
Verden, Ger. D5 16
Verden, Ok., U.S. F10 128
Verde Pequeno, stm., Braz. H4 88
Verdi, Nv., U.S. D5 134
Verdigre, Ne., U.S. E14 126
Verdigris, stm., U.S. H13 128
Verdon, stm., Fr. F12 18
Verdun, ngh., Qc., Can. E3 110
Verdun-sur-Garonne, Fr. F7 18
Verdun-sur-Meuse, Fr. E14 14
Vereeniging, S. Afr. E9 70
Veregin, Sk., Can. C11 124
Vereja, Russia E19 10
Vereščagino, Russia B15 32
Vergemont Creek, stm., Austl. D4 76
Vergennes, Vt., U.S. F3 110
Verhnedneprovskij, Russia E16 10
Verhneimbatsk, Russia B15 32
Verhnemulomskoe vodohranilišče, res., Russia B14 8
Verhneural'sk, Russia D13 34
Verhnevilujsk, Russia E7 34
Verhnij Baskunčak, Russia E7 32
Verhnij Most, Russia C11 10
Verhnij Ufalej, Russia C10 32
Verhnjaja Amga, Russia E14 34
Verhnjaja Angara, stm., Russia E11 34
Verhnjaja Inta, Russia A10 32
Verhnjaja Salda, Russia C10 32
Verhnjaja Tajmyra, stm., Russia B8 34
Verhnjaja Tojma, Russia E21 8
Verhojansk, Russia C15 34
Verhojanskij hrebet (Verkhoyansk Mountains), mts., Russia C14 34
Verhopuja, Russia F19 8
Verhove, Russia H20 10
Verigin see Veregin, Sk., Can. C11 124
Verin, Spain C3 20
Verissimo, Braz. J1 88
Verkhovyna, Ukr. A11 26
Verkhoyansk Mountains see Verhojanskij hrebet, mts., Russia C14 34
Vermelho, stm., Braz. E2 88
Vermilion, Oh., U.S. C3 114
Vermilion, stm., Ab., Can. C19 138
Vermilion, stm., Can. B8 112
Vermilion, stm., Mn., U.S. C6 118
Vermilion Bay, b., La., U.S. H6 122
Vermilion Lake, l., On., Can. A6 118
Vermilion Lake, l., Mn., U.S. D5 118
Vermilion Pass, p., Can. E14 138
Vermillion, stm., S.D., U.S. E15 126
Vermillion, East Fork, stm., S.D., U.S. D15 126
Vermont, Il., U.S. D7 120
Vermont, state, U.S. F4 110
Vernal, Ut., U.S. C7 132
Verndale, Mn., U.S. E3 118
Verneuil, Fr. F9 14
Vernon, B.C., Can. F11 138
Vernon, Fr. E10 14
Vernon, Al., U.S. D10 122
Vernon, Ct., U.S. C13 114
Vernon, In., U.S. F12 120
Vernon, Tx., U.S. G9 128
Vernon, Ut., U.S. C4 132
Vernon, Or., U.S. E3 136
Vernon River, P.E., Can. D13 110
Vero Beach, Fl., U.S. I5 116
Véroia, Grc. C5 28
Verona, On., Can. D13 112
Verona, Italy E8 22
Verona, Ms., U.S. C10 122
Verónica, Arg. G9 92
Versailles, Fr. F11 14
Versailles, Il., U.S. E7 120
Versailles, In., U.S. F13 120
Versailles, Ky., U.S. F5 120
Versailles, Oh., U.S. D1 114
Veršino-Darasunskij, Russia F12 34
Veršino-Šahtaminskij, Russia F12 34
Vertedero, P.R. B3 104a
Vertientes, Cuba B8 102
Verviers, Bel. D14 14
Verwoerd Reservoir see Gariep Dam, res., S. Afr. G7 70
Vescovato, Fr. G15 18
Veseli nad Lužnicí, Czech Rep. G10 16
Veselýj Jar, Russia C11 38
Vesele, Monte, mtn., Italy D9 24
Vesoul, Fr. G15 14
Vespasiano, Braz. J4 88
Vesta, C.R. H6 102
Vest-Agder, state, Nor. G1 8
Vestavia Hills, Al., U.S. D12 122
Vesterålen, is., Nor. B6 8
Vestfjorden, b., Nor. C5 8
Vestfold, state, Nor. G4 8
Vestgrønland (Kitaa), state, Grnld. D16 141
Vestmannaeyjar, Ice. l29 8a
Vestsjælland, state, Den. I4 8
Vestvågøy, i., Nor. B5 8
Vesuvio (Vesuvius), vol., Italy D8 24
Vesuvius see Vesuvio, vol., Italy D8 24
Veszprém, Hung. B4 26
Veszprém, state, Hung. B4 26
Vésztő, Hung. C8 26
Vet, stm., S. Afr. F8 70
Vetapálem, India D5 53
Vetju, Russia E24 8
Vetlanda, Swe. H6 8
Vetluga, Russia H21 8
Vetluga, stm., Russia C7 32
Vetlužskij, Russia G21 8
Vetlužskij, Russia H21 8

Vetrişoaia, Rom. C15 26
Vetschau, Ger. E9 16
Veurne, Bel. C11 14
Vevey, Switz. D3 22
Veynes, Fr. E11 18
Vézère, stm., Fr. D7 18
Viacha, Bol. C3 90
Viadana, Italy F7 22
Viale, Arg. E8 92
Viamão, Braz. E12 92
Viamonte, Arg. F6 92
Vian, Ok., U.S. B4 122
Viana, Braz. B3 88
Viana do Bolo, Spain B3 20
Viana do Castelo, Port. C1 20
Viana do Castelo, state, Port. C2 20
Viangchan (Vientiane), Laos D6 48
Viareggio, Italy G7 22
Vibank, Sk., Can. D10 124
Viborg, Den. H3 8
Viborg, S.D., U.S. D15 126
Viborg, state, Den. H3 8
Vibo Valentia, Italy F10 24
Vic, Spain C13 20
Vicam, Mex. B3 100
Vicebsk, Bela. E13 10
Vicebsk, state, Bela. E11 10
Vicente Guerrero, Mex. D6 100
Vicente Guerrero, Presa, res., Mex. D9 100
Viciejka, Bela. F9 10
Vichadero, Ur. E10 92
Vichra, stm., Eur. F14 10
Vichuquén, Chile G1 92
Vichy, Fr. C9 18
Vici, Ok., U.S. E9 128
Vicksburg, Ms., U.S. E8 122
Viçosa, Braz. K4 88
Viçosa do Ceará, Braz. B5 88
Vic-sur-Cère, Fr. E8 18
Victor, Ia., U.S. C5 120
Victor, Mt., U.S. D15 136
Victor, Mt., U.S. D13 136
Victor Harbor, Austl. J2 76
Victoria, Arg. F7 92
Victoria, B.C., Can. H7 138
Victoria, P.E., Can. D13 110
Victoria, Chile I1 92
Victoria see Labuan, Malay. A9 50
Victoria see Rabat, Malta H8 24
Victoria, Sey. j13 69b
Victoria, Ks., U.S. C9 128
Victoria, Tx., U.S. F11 130
Victoria, Va., U.S. G7 114
Victoria, state, Austl. K4 76
Victoria, Chutes see Victoria Falls, wtfl., Afr. D4 68
Victoria, Lake, l., Afr. E6 66
Victoria, Lake, l., Austl. I3 76
Victoria, Mount, mtn., Mya. B1 48
Victoria, Mount, mtn., Pap. N. Gui. b4 79a
Victoria Falls, wtfl., Afr. D4 68
Victoria Fjord, b., Grnld. A16 141
Victoria Harbour, On., Can. D10 112
Victoria Island, reg., Can. A8 106
Victoria Land, reg., Ant. C20 81
Victoria Nile, stm., Afr. D6 66
Victoria Peak, mtn., Belize D3 102
Victoria Peak, mtn., B.C., Can. F4 138
Victoria River Downs, Austl. C6 74
Victoria, Phil. E4 52
Victoria Strait, strt., Nu., Can. B10 106
Victoriaville, Qc., Can. D4 110
Victoria West, S. Afr. G6 70
Victorica, Arg. H5 92
Victorino, Ven. F8 86
Victorville, Ca., U.S. I8 134
Vicuña, Chile E2 92
Vicuña Mackenna, Arg. F5 92
Vidalia, Ga., U.S. D3 116
Vidalia, La., U.S. F7 122
Vidal Ramos, Braz. C13 92
Videira, Braz. C12 92
Vidigueira, Port. F3 20
Vidin, Blg. F9 26
Vidisha, India G6 54
Vidor, Tx., U.S. G4 122
Vidra, Rom. E13 26
Vidsel, Swe. D9 8
Vidzeme, hist. reg., Lat. C8 10
Viechtach, Ger. G8 16
Viedma, Arg. H4 90
Viedma, Lago, l., Arg. I2 90
Vieille Case, Dom. i6 105c
Viejo, Cerro, mtn., Peru D2 84
Viella, Spain B11 20
Vienna see Wien, Aus. B13 22
Vienna, Ga., U.S. D2 116
Vienna, Il., U.S. G9 120
Vienna, Mo., U.S. F5 120
Vienna, W.V., U.S. E4 114
Vienna see Wien, state, Aus. B13 22
Vienna Woods see Wienerwald, mts., Aus. B13 22
Vienne, Fr. D10 18
Vienne, state, Fr. C6 18
Vienne, stm., Fr. C6 18
Vientiane see Viangchan, Laos D6 48
Vieques, P.R. B5 104a
Vieques, Aeropuerto, P.R. B5 104a
Vieques, Isla de, i., P.R. B5 104a
Vieremä, Fin. E12 8
Vierwaldstätter See (Lucerne, Lake of), l., Switz. D5 22
Vierzon, Fr. G11 14
Viesca, Mex. C7 100
Vieste, Italy I13 22
Vietnam, ctry., Asia E9 48
Viet Tri, Viet. B7 48
Vieux Fort, Qc., Can. i22 107a
Vieux Fort, St. Luc. m7 105c
Vieux-Fort, Pointe du, c., Guad. i5 105c
Vieux-Habitants, Guad. h5 105c
Vievis, Lith. F7 10
Vigala, Est. B7 10
Vigan, Phil. B3 52
Vigevano, Italy E5 22
Vignola, Italy F8 22
Vigo, Spain B1 20
Vigo, Ría de, est., Spain B1 20
Vihari, Pak. D4 54
Vihorevka, Russia C18 32
Vihowa, Pak. C3 54
Vihren, mtn., Blg. H10 26
Viitasaari, Fin. E11 8
Viivikonna, Est. A11 10
Vijapur, India G4 54
Vijayawada, India C5 53
Vikārābād, India C3 53
Viking, Ab., Can. C19 138
Vikna, Nor. D4 8
Vila da Ribeira Brava, C.V. k10 65a

Vila do Bispo, Port. G1 20
Vila do Conde, Port. C2 20
Vila Fontes, Moz. D6 68
Vilafranca del Panadés see Vilafranca del Penedès, Spain C12 20
Vilafranca del Penedès, Spain C12 20
Vila Franca de Xira, Port. F2 20
Vila Gamito, Moz. C5 68
Vilagarcía de Arousa, Spain B1 20
Vilaine, stm., Fr. G7 14
Vilaka, Lat. C10 10
Vilalba, Spain A3 20
Vilanandro, Tanjona, c., Madag. D7 68
Vilāni, Lat. D9 10
Vilankulo, Moz. B12 70
Vila Nova de Famalicão, Port. C2 20
Vila Nova de Gaia, Port. C2 20
Vilanova i la Geltrú, Spain C12 20
Vila Real, Port. C2 20
Vila Real, state, Port. C3 20
Vila Velha, Braz. K5 88
Vila Verde, Port. C2 20
Vilcabamba, Cordillera de, mts., Peru F3 84
Vileiki, Bela. F9 10
Vilelas, Arg. C6 92
Vilhelmina, Swe. D7 8
Vilhena, Braz. F5 84
Vilija (Neris), stm., Eur. F6 10
Viljandi, Est. G11 8
Viľuj, stm., Russia D13 34
Viľujsk, Russia D13 34
Viľujskoe vodohranilišče, res., Russia B20 32
Vilkaviškis, Lith. F6 10
Vil'kickogo, ostrov, i., Russia A19 34
Vil'kickogo, proliv, strt., Russia A9 34
Vilkija, Lith. E6 10
Villa Abecia, Bol. D3 90
Villa Ana, Arg. D8 92
Villa Ángela, Arg. C7 92
Villa Atamisqui, Arg. D6 92
Villa Bella, Bol. B3 90
Villa Berthet, Arg. C7 92
Villablino, Spain B4 20
Villa Bruzual, Ven. C7 86
Villa Cañás, Arg. G7 92
Villa Carlos Paz, Arg. E5 92
Villacarrillo, Spain F7 20
Villacastín, Spain D6 20
Villach, Aus. D10 22
Villacidro, Italy E2 24
Villa Clara, Arg. E8 92
Villa Concepción del Tio, Arg. E6 92
Villa Constitución, Arg. F7 92
Villa de Arista, Mex. D8 100
Villa de Cos, Mex. D7 100
Villa de Cura, Ven. B8 86
Villa del Carmen, Arg. F5 92
Villa del Río, Spain G6 20
Villa del Rosario, Arg. E6 92
Villa del Rosario, Arg. E8 92
Villa del Rosario, Ven. B5 86
Villa de Soto, Arg. E5 92
Villadiego, Spain B7 20
Villa Dolores, Arg. E5 92
Villa Flores, Mex. G12 100
Villa Florida, Para. C9 92
Villafranca de los Barros, Spain F4 20
Villafranca di Verona, Italy E7 22
Villagarcía de Arosa see Vilagarcía de Arousa, Spain B1 20
Village, The, Ok., U.S. F11 128
Villa General Roca, Arg. F4 92
Villa Gesell, Arg. H9 92
Villagrán, Mex. C9 100
Villa Grove, Il., U.S. E9 120
Villaguay, Arg. E8 92
Villa Guerrero, Mex. F9 100
Villa Hayes, Para. B9 92
Villahermosa, Mex. G12 100
Villa Hidalgo, Mex. H3 130
Villa Huidobro, Arg. G5 92
Villa Insurgentes, Mex. C3 100
Villa Iris, Arg. I6 92
Villajoyosa see La Vila Joiosa, Spain F10 20
Villa Juárez, Mex. B3 100
Villa Krause, Arg. E3 92
Villalba, P.R. B3 104a
Villalba see Vilalba, Spain A3 20
Villaldama, Mex. B8 100
Villalon, Phil. E3 52
Villalonga, Arg. I6 92
Villalpando, Spain C5 20
Villa Mainero, Mex. C9 100
Villa María, Arg. F6 92
Villa Media Agua, Arg. E3 92
Villa Mercedes, Arg. F5 92
Villa Montes, Bol. D4 90
Villa Nueva, Arg. E6 92
Villanueva, Col. B5 86
Villanueva, N.M., U.S. F3 128
Villanueva de Córdoba, Spain F6 20
Villanueva de la Serena, Spain F5 20
Villanueva de la Sierra, Spain D4 20
Villanueva de los Infantes, Spain F8 20
Villanueva del Río y Minas, Spain G4 20
Villanueva y Geltrú see Vilanova i la Geltrú, Spain C12 20
Villa Ocampo, Arg. D8 92
Villa Ocampo, Mex. H2 130
Villa Oliva, Para. B8 92
Villa Pérez, P.R. B2 104a
Villapinzón, Col. E5 86
Villarcayo, Spain B7 20
Villa Regina, Arg. G3 90
Villa Reynolds, Arg. F5 92
Villa Rica, Para. B9 92
Villa Santa Rita de Catasura, Arg. C8 92
Villa Serrano, Bol. C4 90
Villasis, Phil. C3 52
Villa Unión, Arg. D3 92
Villa Unión, Mex. D5 100
Villa Valeria, Arg. G5 92
Villavicencio, Col. E5 86
Villaviciosa de Córdoba, Spain F5 20
Villazón, Bol. D3 90
Villefranche-de-Rouergue, Fr. E8 18
Villefranche-sur-Saône, Fr. C10 18
Villena, Spain F10 20
Villeneuve-sur-Lot, Fr. E6 18
Villeneuve-sur-Yonne, Fr. F12 14
Ville Platte, La., U.S. G6 122

Villers-Cotterêts, Fr. E12 14
Villerupt, Fr. E14 14
Villeta, Col. E4 86
Villeurbanne, Fr. D10 18
Villiers, S. Afr. E9 70
Villingen-Schwenningen, Ger. H4 16
Villisca, Ia., U.S. D3 120
Vilmanstrand see Lappeenranta, Fin. F12 8
Vilnius, Lith. F8 10
Vilsbiburg, Ger. H8 16
Viľ'shanka, Ukr. A17 26
Vilshofen, Ger. H9 16
Viluppuram, India. F4 53
Vilvoorde, Bel. D13 14
Vilvoorde see Vilvoorde, Bel. D13 14
Vimmerby, Swe. H6 8
Vimperk, Czech Rep. G9 16
Vina, Ca., U.S. D3 134
Vina, stm., Cam. C2 66
Viña del Mar, Chile F2 92
Vinalhaven, Me., U.S. F8 110
Vinalhaven Island, i., Me., U.S. F8 110
Vinarós, Spain D11 20
Vinaroz see Vinarós, Spain D11 20
Vincennes, In., U.S. F10 120
Vincennes Bay, b., Ant. B15 81
Vincent, Al., U.S. D12 122
Vinces, Ec. H2 86
Vindelälven, stm., Swe. D8 8
Vindhya Range, mts., India. G6 54
Vinegar Hill, mtn., Or., U.S. F8 136
Vineland, N.J., U.S. E10 114
Vinemont, Al., U.S. C12 122
Vineyard Haven, Ma., U.S. C15 114
Vineyard Sound, strt., Ma., U.S. C15 114
Ving Ngün, Mya. A4 48
Vinh, Viet. C7 48
Vinhais, Port. C4 20
Vinh Long, Viet. G8 48
Vinh Yen, Viet. B7 48
Vinita, Ok., U.S. H2 120
Vinkovci, Cro. E15 22
Vinnytsia, Ukr. A16 26
Vinnytsia, co., Ukr. A16 26
Vinson Massif, mtn., Ant. C32 81
Vintilă Vodă, Rom. D13 26
Vinton, Ia., U.S. B5 120
Vinton, La., U.S. G5 122
Vinton, Va., U.S. G6 114
Viola, Il., U.S. C7 120
Vioolsdrif, S. Afr. F3 70
Vipiteno, Italy D8 22
Vir, Otok, i., Cro. F11 22
Vira, Phil. D5 52
Viramgam, India G4 54
Virarājendrapet, India E2 53
Virbalis, Lith. F5 10
Virden, Mb., Can. E13 124
Virden, Il., U.S. E8 120
Virden, N.M., U.S. K8 132
Vire, Fr. F8 14
Virgem da Lapa, Braz. I4 88
Virgenes, Cabo, c., S.A. J3 90
Virgil, Ks., U.S. C13 128
Virgin, stm., U.S. G2 132
Virgin Gorda, i., Br. Vir. Is. e9 104b
Virginia, S. Afr. F8 70
Virginia, Il., U.S. E7 120
Virginia, Mn., U.S. D6 118
Virginia, state, U.S. G7 114
Virginia Beach, Va., U.S. H10 114
Virginia City, Mt., U.S. E14 136
Virginia City, Nv., U.S. D6 134
Virginia Falls, wtfl., N.T., Can. C5 106
Virginia Peak, mtn., Nv., U.S. D6 134
Virgin Islands, dep., N.A. h14 96a
Virgin Islands, is., N.A. e7 104b
Virgin Islands National Park, p.o.i., V.I.U.S. e7 104b
Virgin Passage, strt., N.A. B5 104a
Virihaure, l., Swe. C7 8
Virje, Cro. D13 22
Virojoki, Fin. F12 8
Viroqua, Wi., U.S. H7 118
Virovitica, Cro. E14 22
Virrat, Fin. E10 8
Virserum, Swe. H6 8
Virtaniemi, Fin. B13 8
Virtsu, Est. G10 8
Virú, Peru E2 84
Virudunagar, India G3 53
Virunga, Parc National de, p.o.i., D.R.C. D5 66
Viru-Nigula, Est. A9 10
Virvytė, stm., Lith. D5 10
Vis see Visrivier, stm., Nmb. E3 70
Vis, stm., S. Afr. H4 70
Vis, Otok, i., Cro. G13 22
Visale, Sol. Is. e8 79b
Visalia, Ca., U.S. G6 134
Visayan Islands, is., Phil. E4 52
Visayan Sea, s., Phil. E4 52
Visby, Swe. H8 8
Viscount, Sk., Can. C8 124
Viscount Melville Sound, strt., Can. B11 94
Višegrad, Bos. F6 26
Viseu, Port. D3 20
Viseu, state, Port. D3 20
Vishakhapatnam, India C6 53
Visnagar, India G4 54
Visnieva, Bela. F9 10
Visoko, Bos. F5 26
Visokoi Island, i., S. Geor. K12 82
Visp, Switz. D4 22
Visrivier, stm., Nmb. E3 70
Vista, Ca., U.S. J8 134
Vistula see Wisła, stm., Pol. B14 16
Vistula Lagoon, b., Eur. B16 16
Vita, Mb., Can. E17 124
Vitarte, Peru F2 84
Vite, India C2 53
Vitebsk see Vicebsk, Bela. E13 10
Viterbo, Italy H9 22
Viti Levu, i., Fiji p19 79e
Vitim, Russia E11 34
Vitim, stm., Russia E12 34
Vitimskoe ploskogor'e, plat., Russia F11 34
Vítkov, Czech Rep. G13 16
Vitória, Braz. K5 88
Vitória da Conquista, Braz. H5 88
Vitória de Mearim, Braz. B3 88
Vitorino Freire, Braz. C3 88
Vitré, Fr. F7 14
Vitry-le-François, Fr. F13 14
Vitteaux, Fr. G13 14
Vittória, Italy H8 24
Vittório Veneto, Italy D9 22
Viveiro, Spain A3 20
Vivero see Viveiro, Spain A3 20
Vivi, stm., Russia C6 34
Vivian, La., U.S. E4 122
Vizcaíno, Desierto de, des., Mex. B2 100
Vizcaya see Bizkaia, co., Spain A8 20
Vize, Tur. B10 28
Vizianagaram, India B6 53
Vizille, Fr. D11 18

Vizinga, Russia B7 32
Vjalikaja Maščanica, Bela. G12 10
Vjaliki Radvaničy, Bela. H7 10
Vjaseja, Bela. G10 10
Vjatka, stm., Russia C8 32
Vjatskije Poljany, Russia C8 32
Vjazemskij, Russia G15 34
Vjaz'ma, Russia E17 10
Vjazniki, Russia H20 8
Vjazyn', Bela. F10 10
Vjoses (Aóös), stm., Eur. D13 24
Vladeasa, Vârful, mtn., Rom. C9 26
Vladičin Han, Serb. G8 26
Vladikavkaz, Russia F6 32
Vladimir, Russia H18 8
Vladimirskaja oblast', co., Russia I19 8
Vladimirskij Tupik, Russia. E16 10
Vladivostok, Russia C9 38
Vlasenica, Bos. E5 26
Vlasotince, Serb. G8 26
Vlasovo, Russia B16 34
Vlieland, i., Neth. A13 14
Vlissingen, Neth. C12 14
Vlora see Vlorë, Alb. D13 24
Vlorë, Alb. D13 24
Vltava (Moldau), stm., Czech Rep. F10 16
Vnukovo, Russia E20 10
Vöcklabruck, Aus. C10 22
Vo Dat, Viet. G8 48
Vodla, stm., Russia F17 8
Vodlozero, ozero, l., Russia E16 8
Vodosalma, Russia D14 8
Voël, stm., S. Afr. H7 70
Voghera, Italy F6 22
Voh, N. Cal. m15 79d
Vohimena, Tanjona, c., Madag. F8 68
Vohipeno, Madag. E8 68
Võhma, Est. G11 8
Voi, Kenya E7 66
Voinești, Rom. B14 26
Voiron, Fr. D11 18
Voitsberg, Aus. C12 22
Vojmsjön, l., Swe. D6 8
Vojnica, Russia D14 8
Vojvodina, co., Serb. D7 26
Volcán, Pan. H6 102
Volcano, Hi., U.S. d6 78a
Volcano Islands see Kazan-rettō, is., Japan G18 30
Volčiha, Russia D14 32
Volda, Nor. E2 8
Volga, S.D., U.S. G2 118
Volga, stm., Russia E7 32
Volga-Baltic Canal see Volgo-Baltijskij kanal, can., Russia G17 8
Volgino, Russia B16 10
Volgo, ozero, l., Russia C16 10
Volgo-Baltijskij kanal, can., Russia G17 8
Volgodonsk, Russia E6 32
Volgograd, Russia E6 32
Volgograd Reservoir see Volgogradskoe vodohranilišče, res., Russia E7 32
Volgogradskoe vodohranilišče, res., Russia D7 32
Volhov, Russia A15 10
Volhov, stm., Russia G14 8
Volissós, Grc. E8 28
Völkermarkt, Aus. D11 22
Völklingen, Ger. G2 16
Volksrust, S. Afr. E9 70
Voločanka, Russia B7 34
Voločisk, Ukr. D11 32
Voloe, Russia F17 10
Vologda, Russia A22 10
Vologda, stm., Russia A22 10
Vologodskaja oblast', co., Russia G19 8
Volokolamsk, Russia D18 10
Volonga, Russia C22 8
Vólos, Grc. D5 28
Vološka, Russia F19 8
Volosovo, Russia A12 10
Volot, Russia C13 10
Volovo, Russia D7 32
Vol'sk, Russia D7 32
Volta, stm., Ghana H5 64
Volta Blanche (White Volta), stm. G4 64
Volta Lake, res., Ghana H4 64
Volta Noire (Black Volta) (Mouhoun), stm., Afr. G4 64
Volta Redonda, Braz. L3 88
Volterra, Italy G7 22
Vol'teva, Russia D21 8
Voltri, ngh., Italy F5 22
Volturno, stm., Italy C8 24
Völvi, Límni, l., Grc. C6 28
Volyn', co., Ukr. E10 32
Volžsk, Russia C7 32
Volžskij, Russia E7 32
Vonavona Island, i., Sol. Is. e7 79b
Vondanka, Russia C13 32
Vondrozo, Madag. E8 68
Von Frank Mountain, mtn., Ak., U.S. D8 140
Vopnafjörður, Ice. k32 8a
Vopnafjörður, b., Ice. k32 8a
Vorarlberg, state, Aus. C6 22
Vorderrhein see Rein Anterius, stm., Switz. D6 22
Vordingborg, Den. I4 8
Vóreio Aigaío, state, Grc. D8 28
Vóreioi Sporades, is., Grc. D6 28
Vóreion Evvoïkós, b., Grc. E6 28
Vorkuta, Russia A10 32
Vormsi, i., Est. G9 8
Voroncovo, Mol. B16 26
Voronec, Russia D7 32
Voronezh, Russia D5 32
Voronežskaja oblast', co., Russia H21 10
Voronovo, Bela. H8 10
Vorsma, Russia H20 8
Vorpommern, hist. reg., Ger. C9 16
Voskresensk, Russia E21 10
Voskresenskoe, Russia B21 10
Voss, Nor. F2 8
Vostočno-Sibirskoe more, s., Russia B20 34
Vostočnyj Sajan, mts., Russia D17 32
Vostok, i., Kiri. E11 72
Vostok, sci., Ant. C15 81
Votice, Czech Rep. G10 16
Votkinsk, Russia C8 32
Votuporanga, Braz. D7 90
Vouga, stm., Port. D2 20
Vouziers, Fr. E13 14
Voyageurs National Park, p.o.i., Mn., U.S. C6 118

Name	Map Ref.	Page
Voyeykov Ice Shelf, ice, Ant.	B17	81
Vože, ozero, l., Russia	F18	8
Vozega, Russia	F19	8
Voznesene, Russia	F16	8
Vozroždenija, ostrov, i., Asia	E9	32
Vraca, Blg.	F10	26
Vradyivka, Ukr.	B17	26
Vrancea, state, Rom.	D13	26
Vrangelja, ostrov (Wrangel Island), i., Russia	B24	34
Vranje, Serb.	G8	26
Vratsa see Vraca, Blg.	F10	26
Vrbas, Serb.	D6	26
Vrbas, stm., Bos.	E4	26
Vrbovec, Cro.	E13	22
Vrchlabí, Czech Rep.	F11	16
Vrede, S. Afr.	E9	70
Vredenburg, S. Afr.	H3	70
Vredenburgh, Al., U.S.	F11	122
Vredenburg-Saldanha see Vredenburg, S. Afr.	H3	70
Vredendal, S. Afr.	G4	70
Vriddhāchalam, India	F4	53
Vrindāvan, India	E6	54
Vršac, Serb.	D8	26
Vrútky, Slov.	G14	16
Vryburg, S. Afr.	E7	70
Vryheid, S. Afr.	E10	70
Vselug, ozero, l., Russia	C14	10
Vsetín, Czech Rep.	G13	16
Vsevidof, Mount, mtn., Ak., U.S.	F6	140
Vučitrn, Serb.	G7	26
Vukovar, Cro.	E16	22
Vulcan, Ab., Can.	F17	138
Vulcan, Rom.	D10	26
Vulcăneşti, Mol.	D15	26
Vulcano, Isola, i., Italy	F8	24
Vulsino see Bolsena, Lago di, l., Italy	H9	22
Vung Tau, Viet.	G8	48
Vunidawa, Fiji	p19	79e
Vunisea, Fiji	q18	79e
Vuohijärvi, l., Fin.	F11	8
Vuyyūru, India	C5	53
Vyāra, India	H4	54
Vyborg (Viipuri), Russia	F13	8
Vyčegda, stm., Russia	B7	32
Vyčegodskij, Russia	F22	8
Východočeský, state, Czech Rep.	F11	16
Východoslovenský Kraj, state, Slov.	H17	16
Vygoniči, Russia	G16	10
Vygozero, ozero, l., Russia	E16	8
Vyksa, Russia	I20	8
Vylkove, Ukr.	D16	26
Vynohradiv, Ukr.	A10	26
Vypolzovo, Russia	C16	10
Vyrica, Russia	A13	10
Vyšgorodok, Russia	C11	10
Vyškod', Russia	C13	10
Vyškov, Czech Rep.	G12	16
Vyšneol'šanoe, Russia	H20	10
Vyšnevolockoe vodohranilišče, res., Russia	C16	10
Vyšnij Voločok, Russia	C17	10
Vyšní Mýto, Czech Rep.	G12	16
Vysokiniči, Russia	F20	10
Vysokoe, Russia	D17	10
Vysokogornyj, Russia	G16	34
Vysokovsk, Russia	D19	10
Vytebet', stm., Russia	G18	10
Vytegra, Russia	F17	8
Vyzhnytsia, Ukr.	A12	26

W

Name	Map Ref.	Page
Wa, Ghana	G4	64
Waal, stm., Neth.	C14	14
Waalwijk, Neth.	C14	14
Wabag, Pap. N. Gui.	b3	79a
Wabakimi Lake, l., On., Can.	A8	118
Wabamun, Ab., Can.	C16	138
Wabamun Lake, l., Ab., Can.	C15	138
Wabana, Nf., Can.	j23	107a
Wabasca, stm., Ab., Can.	D7	106
Wabasca-Desmarais, Ab., Can.	D8	106
Wabash, In., U.S.	H4	112
Wabash, stm., U.S.	F9	120
Wabasha, Mn., U.S.	G6	118
Wabasso, Mn., U.S.	G3	118
Wabeno, Wi., U.S.	F10	118
Wabera, Eth.	F8	62
Wabowden, Mb., Can.	E11	106
Wabrzeźno, Pol.	C14	16
Wabu Hu, l., China	E7	42
Waccamaw, stm., U.S.	C7	116
Waccamaw, Lake, l., N.C., U.S.	B7	116
Wachapreague, Va., U.S.	G10	114
Wachau, reg., Aus.	B12	22
Wacissa, Fl., U.S.	F2	116
Waco, Tx., U.S.	C10	130
Waco Lake, res., Tx., U.S.	C10	130
Waconda Lake, res., Ks., U.S.	B10	128
Wadayama, Japan	D7	40
Wad Bandah, Sudan	E5	62
Wadbilliga National Park, p.o.i., Austl.	K7	76
Waddenzee, strt., Neth.	A14	14
Waddington, N.Y., U.S.	D14	112
Waddington, Mount, mtn., B.C., Can.	E5	138
Wadena, Sk., Can.	C10	124
Wadena, Mn., U.S.	E3	118
Wadesboro, N.C., U.S.	B5	116
Wādī as-Sīr, Jord.	G6	58
Wādī Halfā', Sudan	C6	62
Wadley, Al., U.S.	D13	122
Wadley, Ga., U.S.	D3	116
Wad Madanī, Sudan	E6	62
Wadowice, Pol.	G15	16
Wadsworth, Nv., U.S.	D6	134
Wadsworth, Oh., U.S.	C4	114
Wafangdian, China	B9	42
Wageningen, Neth.	C14	14
Wager Bay, b., Nu., Can.	B13	106
Wagga Wagga, Austl.	J6	76
Wagin, Austl.	F3	74
Waging am See, Ger.	I8	16
Wagner, S.D., U.S.	D14	126
Wagoner, Ok., U.S.	I2	120
Wagon Mound, N.M., U.S.	F4	128
Wagontire Mountain, mtn., Or., U.S.	G7	136
Wagrien, reg., Ger.	B6	16
Wagrowiec, Pol.	D13	16
Waha, Libya	B4	62
Wahai, Indon.	F8	44
Wah Cantonment, Pak.	B4	54
Wahiawā, Hi., U.S.	b3	78a
Wahpeton, N.D., U.S.	E2	118
Wahran (Oran), Alg.	B4	64
Wai, India	B1	53
Waialua, Hi., U.S.	b3	78a
Wai'anae, Hi., U.S.	b3	78a
Waiau, N.Z.	F5	80
Waiau, stm., N.Z.	G2	80
Waiau, stm., N.Z.	F5	80
Waiblingen, Ger.	H5	16
Waidhofen an der Thaya, Aus.	B12	22
Waidhofen an der Ybbs, Aus.	C11	22
Waigeo, Pulau, i., Indon.	E9	44
Waihi, N.Z.	C6	80
Waikabubak, Indon.	H11	50
Waikato, stm., N.Z.	C6	80
Waikelo, Indon.	H11	50
Waikerie, Austl.	J2	76
Wailuku, Hi., U.S.	c5	78a
Waimate, N.Z.	G4	80
Waimea, Hi., U.S.	a2	78a
Wainganga, stm., India	H7	54
Waingapu, Indon.	H12	50
Waini, stm., Guy.	D12	86
Wainunu Bay, b., Fiji	p19	79e
Wainwright, Ab., Can.	B3	124
Wainwright, Ak., U.S.	B7	140
Waipukurau, N.Z.	E7	80
Wairarapa, Lake, l., N.Z.	E6	80
Wairau, stm., N.Z.	E5	80
Wairoa, N.Z.	D7	80
Wairoa, stm., N.Z.	B6	80
Waïsisi, Vanuatu	l17	79d
Waitaki, stm., N.Z.	G4	80
Waitara, N.Z.	D6	80
Waitemata, N.Z.	C6	80
Waite Park, Mn., U.S.	F4	118
Waitotara, N.Z.	D6	80
Waitsburg, Wa., U.S.	D8	136
Waiwo, Indon.	F9	44
Wajima, Japan	B9	40
Wajir, Kenya	D8	66
Waka, D.R.C.	D4	66
Waka, Eth.	F7	62
Wakarusa, In., U.S.	G3	112
Wakasa-wan, b., Japan	D8	40
Wakatipu, Lake, l., N.Z.	G3	80
Wakaw, Sk., Can.	B8	124
Wakayama, Japan	E8	40
Wakayama, state, Japan	F8	40
Wakeeney, Ks., U.S.	B9	128
Wakefield, Eng., U.K.	H11	12
Wakefield, Ks., U.S.	B11	128
Wakefield, Ne., U.S.	E15	126
Wakefield, Va., U.S.	H8	114
Wake Forest, N.C., U.S.	I7	114
Wake Island, dep., Oc.	B7	72
Wake Island, at., Wake I.	H19	142
Wakema, Mya.	D2	48
Waki, Japan	E7	40
Wakis, Pap. N. Gui.	b5	79a
Wakita, Ok., U.S.	E10	128
Wakkanai, Japan	B14	38
Wakomata Lake, l., On., Can.	B6	112
Wakonda, S.D., U.S.	E15	126
Waku Kungo, Ang.	C2	68
Walane, hist. reg., Rom.	E11	26
Walawe, stm., Sri L.	H5	53
Walbrzych, Pol.	F12	16
Walbrzych, state, Pol.	F12	16
Walcha, Austl.	H8	76
Walcott, Ia., U.S.	C7	120
Walcott, N.D., U.S.	E1	118
Walcott, Lake, res., Id., U.S.	H13	136
Waldbröl, Ger.	F3	16
Walden, On., Can.	B8	112
Walden, Co., U.S.	C10	132
Waldheim, Sk., Can.	B7	124
Waldkirchen, Ger.	H9	16
Waldmünchen, Ger.	G8	16
Waldoboro, Me., U.S.	F7	110
Waldorf, Md., U.S.	F9	114
Waldport, Or., U.S.	F2	136
Waldron, Sk., Can.	D11	124
Waldron, Ar., U.S.	C4	122
Waldron, In., U.S.	E12	120
Waldshut-Tiengen, Ger.	I4	16
Waldviertel, reg., Aus.	B12	22
Wales, state, U.K.	I9	12
Wales Island, i., Nu., Can.	B13	106
Walewale, Ghana	G4	64
Walgett, Austl.	G6	76
Walgreen Coast, cst., Ant.	C30	81
Walhachin, B.C., Can.	F10	138
Walhalla, N.D., U.S.	F15	124
Walhalla, S.C., U.S.	B2	116
Walhalla, hist. reg., Ger.	G8	16
Walker, Ia., U.S.	B6	120
Walker, stm., Nv., U.S.	D7	134
Walker Bay, b., S. Afr.	I4	70
Walker Lake, l., Nv., U.S.	E7	134
Walkerton, On., Can.	D8	112
Walkerton, In., U.S.	G3	112
Walkertown, N.C., U.S.	H5	114
Walkerville, Mt., U.S.	D14	136
Wall, S.D., U.S.	D10	126
Wallace, Id., U.S.	C11	136
Wallace, N.C., U.S.	B7	116
Wallace, Ne., U.S.	G11	126
Wallaceburg, On., Can.	F7	112
Wallal Downs, Austl.	C4	74
Wallam Creek, stm., Austl.	G6	76
Wallangarra, Austl.	G8	76
Wallaroo, Austl.	F7	74
Wallasey, Eng., U.K.	H9	12
Walla Walla, Wa., U.S.	D8	136
Wallingford, Ct., U.S.	C13	114
Wallingford, Vt., U.S.	G4	110
Wallis, Tx., U.S.	H2	122
Wallis, Îles, is., Wal./F.	E9	72
Wallis and Futuna, dep., Oc.	E9	72
Wallisville, Lake, res., Tx., U.S.	H4	122
Wallowa, Or., U.S.	E9	136
Wallowa, stm., Or., U.S.	E9	136
Walls of Jericho National Park, p.o.i., Austl.	n13	77a
Walnut, Ia., U.S.	C2	120
Walnut, Il., U.S.	C8	120
Walnut, Ms., U.S.	C10	122
Walnut, N.C., U.S.	I3	114
Walnut, stm., Ks., U.S.	D11	128
Walnut Canyon National Monument, p.o.i., Az., U.S.	H5	132
Walnut Cove, N.C., U.S.	H5	114
Walnut Creek, stm., Ks., U.S.	C9	128
Walnut Grove, Mn., U.S.	G3	118
Walnut Grove, Ms., U.S.	E9	122
Walnut Ridge, Ar., U.S.	H7	120
Walnut Springs, Tx., U.S.	B10	130
Walpole, Austl.	G3	74
Walpole, N.H., U.S.	G4	110
Walsall, Eng., U.K.	I11	12
Walsenburg, Co., U.S.	D4	128
Walsh, Austl.	C8	74
Walsh, Ab., Can.	E3	124
Walsh, stm., Austl.	A5	76
Walsrode, Ger.	D5	16
Walterboro, S.C., U.S.	D5	116
Walters, Ok., U.S.	G10	128
Waltershausen, Ger.	F6	16
Walthall, Ms., U.S.	D9	122
Walthill, Ne., U.S.	B1	120
Walton, In., U.S.	H3	112
Walton, N.Y., U.S.	B10	114
Walvisbaai see Walvis Bay, Nmb.	C2	70
Walvis Bay (Walvisbaai), Nmb.	C2	70
Walvis Bay, b., Nmb.	C2	70
Walvis Ridge, unds.	K14	144
Walworth, Wi., U.S.	B9	120
Wamba, D.R.C.	D5	66
Wamba, Nig.	H6	64
Wamba (Uamba), stm., Afr.	F3	66
Wampsville, N.Y., U.S.	A10	114
Wampú, Hond.	E5	102
Wampú, stm., Hond.	E5	102
Wampum, Pa., U.S.	D5	114
Wamsutter, Wy., U.S.	B9	132
Wan'an, China	H6	42
Wanapa, Neth. Ant.	p23	104g
Wanapitei, stm., On., Can.	B9	112
Wanapitei Lake, l., On., Can.	B8	112
Wanbaoshan, China	B6	38
Wanbi, Austl.	J3	76
Wanchese, N.C., U.S.	I10	114
Wandel Hav, s., Grnld.	A22	141
Wandering, stm., Ab., Can.	A18	138
Wanfoxia, China	C4	36
Wang, stm., Thai.	D4	48
Wanganui, N.Z.	D6	80
Wanganui, stm., N.Z.	D6	80
Wangaratta, Austl.	K6	76
Wangcun, China	C7	42
Wangdu Phodrang, Bhu.	E12	54
Wangiwangi, Pulau, i., Indon.	G7	44
Wang Noi, stm., Thai.	E5	48
Wangpan Yang, b., China	F9	42
Wangqing, China	C8	38
Wangtai, China	H7	42
Wangyehmiao see Ulanhot, China	B9	36
Wanhedian, China	E5	42
Wanhsien see Wanxian, China	F3	42
Wani, India	A4	53
Wanie-Rukula, D.R.C.	D5	66
Wanigela, Pap. N. Gui.	b4	79a
Wanipigow, stm., Can.	C18	124
Wankaner, India	G3	54
Wanneroo, Austl.	F3	74
Wannian, China	H7	42
Wanning, China	L4	42
Wanparti, India	C4	53
Wantan, China	F4	42
Wanxian, China	F3	42
Wanzai, China	G6	42
Wapakoneta, Oh., U.S.	D1	114
Wapanucka, Ok., U.S.	C2	122
Wapato, Wa., U.S.	D6	136
Wapello, Ia., U.S.	C6	120
Wāpi, India	H4	54
Wapiti, stm., Can.	A12	138
Wappingers Falls, N.Y., U.S.	C12	114
Wapsipinicon, stm., U.S.	J8	118
War, W.V., U.S.	G4	114
Warangal, India	B4	53
Wārāseoni, India	H7	54
Waratah, Austl.	n12	77a
Waratah Bay, b., Austl.	L5	76
Warburg, Ger.	E4	16
Warburton, Austl.	K5	76
Warburton Bay, b., N.T., Can.	C8	106
Ward, stm., Austl.	E6	76
Wardha, India	H7	54
Wardha, stm., India	H7	54
Ward Hill, hill, Scot., U.K.	C9	12
Wardlow, Ab., Can.	F19	138
Wardner, B.C., Can.	G15	138
Wardswell Draw, stm., U.S.	B5	130
Waremme, Bel.	D14	14
Waren, Ger.	C8	16
Waren, Indon.	F10	44
Warenai, stm., Indon.	F10	44
Warenda, Austl.	D3	76
Warendorf, Ger.	E3	16
Ware Shoals, S.C., U.S.	B3	116
Wargla, Alg.	C6	64
Wariāba, Austl.	G8	76
Warin Chamrap, Thai.	E7	48
Warkworth, On., Can.	D11	112
Warman, Sk., Can.	B7	124
Warmandi, Indon.	F9	44
Warmbad, Nmb.	F4	70
Warmbad, S. Afr.	D9	70
Warm Baths see Warmbad, S. Afr.	D9	70
Warminster, Pa., U.S.	D10	114
Warm Springs, Ga., U.S.	E14	122
Warm Springs, Mt., U.S.	D14	136
Warm Springs, Or., U.S.	F5	136
Warnemünde, ngh., Ger.	B7	16
Warner, Ab., Can.	G18	138
Warner, N.H., U.S.	G5	110
Warner Lakes, l., Or., U.S.	H6	136
Warner Mountains, mts., U.S.	B5	134
Warner Peak, mtn., Or., U.S.	A6	134
Warner Robins, Ga., U.S.	D2	116
Warnow, stm., Ger.	B7	16
Warra, Austl.	F8	76
Warracknabeal, Austl.	K4	76
Warragul, Austl.	L5	76
Warrawagine, Austl.	D4	74
Warrego, stm., Austl.	G5	76
Warren, Ar., U.S.	D6	122
Warren, In., U.S.	H4	112
Warren, Mi., U.S.	B2	114
Warren, Mn., U.S.	C2	118
Warren, Oh., U.S.	C5	114
Warren, Pa., U.S.	C6	114
Warren, Tx., U.S.	G4	122
Warrendale, Mo., U.S.	F4	120
Warrensburg, N.Y., U.S.	G3	110
Warrenton, S. Afr.	F7	70
Warrenton, Mo., U.S.	F6	120
Warrenton, N.C., U.S.	H7	114
Warrenton, Or., U.S.	D2	136
Warri, Nig.	H6	64
Warrington, Eng., U.K.	H10	12
Warrington, Fl., U.S.	G11	122
Warrnambool, Austl.	L4	76
Warroad, Mn., U.S.	C3	118
Warrumbungle National Park, p.o.i., Austl.	H7	76
Warsaw see Warszawa, Pol.	D16	16
Warsaw, Il., U.S.	D6	120
Warsaw, In., U.S.	G4	112
Warsaw, Ky., U.S.	F13	120
Warsaw, Mo., U.S.	F4	120
Warsaw, N.C., U.S.	A7	116
Warsaw, N.Y., U.S.	B7	114
Warspite, Ab., Can.	B18	138
Warszawa (Warsaw), Pol.	D16	16
Warszawa, state, Pol.	D16	16
Warta, Pol.	E14	16
Warta, stm., Pol.	D11	16
Wartburg, Tn., U.S.	H13	120
Wartrace, Tn., U.S.	B12	122
Warud, India	H7	54
Warwick, Austl.	G9	76
Warwick, Eng., U.K.	I11	12
Warwick, R.I., U.S.	C14	114
Warwick Channel, strt., Austl.	B7	74
Wasaga Beach, On., Can.	D10	112
Wasagu, Nig.	G6	64
Wasatch Range, mts., Ut., U.S.	C5	132
Wasbank, S. Afr.	F10	70
Wascana Creek, stm., Sk., Can.	D9	124
Wasco, Ca., U.S.	H6	134
Wasco, Or., U.S.	E6	136
Waseca, Mn., U.S.	G5	118
Washademoak Lake, l., N.B., Can.	E11	110
Washburn, Il., U.S.	D8	120
Washburn, N.D., U.S.	G12	124
Washburn, Wi., U.S.	E7	118
Washburn, Mount, mtn., Wy., U.S.	F16	136
Washburn Lake, l., Nu., Can.	A9	106
Wāshīm, India	H6	54
Washington, D.C., U.S.	F8	114
Washington, Ga., U.S.	C3	116
Washington, Ia., U.S.	C6	120
Washington, Il., U.S.	D8	120
Washington, In., U.S.	F10	120
Washington, La., U.S.	G6	122
Washington, Mo., U.S.	F6	120
Washington, N.C., U.S.	A8	116
Washington, N.J., U.S.	D5	114
Washington, Tx., U.S.	G2	122
Washington, Ut., U.S.	F3	132
Washington, Va., U.S.	F7	114
Washington, state, U.S.	C6	136
Washington, Mount, mtn., N.H., U.S.	F5	110
Washington Court House, Oh., U.S.	E2	114
Washington Island, i., Wi., U.S.	C3	112
Washington Land, reg., Grnld.	A12	141
Washington Terrace, Ut., U.S.	B5	132
Washita, stm., U.S.	G12	128
Washow Bay, b., Mb., Can.	C17	124
Washpool National Park, p.o.i., Austl.	G9	76
Washtucna, Wa., U.S.	D8	136
Wasian, Indon.	F9	44
Wasilków, Pol.	C19	16
Wasior, Indon.	F9	44
Waskada, Mb., Can.	E13	124
Waskaganish, Qc., Can.	E15	106
Waskahigan, stm., Ab., Can.	B13	138
Waskom, Tx., U.S.	E4	122
Waspam, Nic.	E5	102
Wassenaar, Neth.	B13	14
Wasserfangen, Ger.	H6	16
Wassy, Fr.	F13	14
Watampone, Indon.	F12	50
Watamsopeng, Indon.	F11	50
Watatic, Mount, mtn., Ma., U.S.	B14	114
Waterberge, mts., S. Afr.	D8	70
Waterbury, Ct., U.S.	C12	114
Wateree Lake, res., S.C., U.S.	B5	116
Waterford (Port Lairge), Ire.	I5	12
Waterford, Ca., U.S.	F5	134
Waterford, Pa., U.S.	C6	114
Waterford, Wi., U.S.	B9	120
Waterford, state, Ire.	I5	12
Waterhen Lake, l., Mb., Can.	B14	124
Water Island, i., V.I.U.S.	e7	104b
Waterloo, Bel.	D13	14
Waterloo, On., Can.	E9	112
Waterloo, Qc., Can.	E4	110
Waterloo, Ia., U.S.	B5	120
Waterloo, Il., U.S.	F7	120
Waterloo, Wi., U.S.	A9	120
Waterman, Il., U.S.	C9	120
Waterproof, La., U.S.	F7	122
Watersmeet, Mi., U.S.	E9	118
Waterton-Glacier International Peace Park, p.o.i., N.A.	B13	136
Waterton Lakes National Park, p.o.i., Ab., Can.	G16	138
Watertown, N.Y., U.S.	E14	112
Watertown, S.D., U.S.	C15	126
Watertown, Wi., U.S.	A9	120
Waterval Boven, S. Afr.	D10	70
Water Valley, Ms., U.S.	C9	122
Waterville, N.S., Can.	E12	110
Waterville, Me., U.S.	F7	110
Waterville, Oh., U.S.	C2	114
Waterville, Wa., U.S.	C6	136
Watervliet, N.Y., U.S.	B12	114
Watford, Eng., U.K.	J12	12
Watford City, N.D., U.S.	G10	124
Wathena, Ks., U.S.	E2	120
Watkins Glen, N.Y., U.S.	B9	114
Watkinsville, Ga., U.S.	C2	116
Watling Island see San Salvador, i., Bah.	C10	96
Watonga, Ok., U.S.	F10	128
Watrous, Sk., Can.	C8	124
Watsa, D.R.C.	D5	66
Watseka, Il., U.S.	H2	112
Watsikengo, D.R.C.	E4	66
Watson, Sk., Can.	B9	124
Watson Lake, Yk., Can.	C5	106
Watsonville, Ca., U.S.	G4	134
Watt Mountain, vol., Dom.	j6	105c
Watts Bar Lake, res., Tn., U.S.	B14	122
Watts Mills, S.C., U.S.	B4	116
Wattwil, Switz.	C5	22
Watubela, Kepulauan, is., Indon.	F9	44
Watzmann, mtn., Ger.	I8	16
Waubay, Lake, l., S.D., U.S.	B15	126
Wauchope, Austl.	D6	74
Wauchula, Fl., U.S.	I4	116
Wauconda, Wa., U.S.	B7	136
Waugh, Mb., Can.	B3	118
Waukara, Bukit, mtn., Indon.	D11	50
Waukaringa, Austl.	I2	76
Waukarlycarly, Lake, l., Austl.	D4	74
Waukegan, Il., U.S.	A9	120
Waukesha, Wi., U.S.	A9	120
Waukon, Ia., U.S.	H7	118
Waunakee, Wi., U.S.	A8	120
Wauneta, Ne., U.S.	G11	126
Waupaca, Wi., U.S.	H10	118
Waupun, Wi., U.S.	H10	118
Waurika, Ok., U.S.	G11	128
Waurika Lake, res., Ok., U.S.	G10	128
Wausa, Ne., U.S.	E15	126
Wausau, Wi., U.S.	G9	118
Wauseon, Oh., U.S.	C1	114
Wautoma, Wi., U.S.	G9	118
Wauwatosa, Wi., U.S.	E1	112
Wauzeka, Wi., U.S.	A7	120
Wave Hill, Austl.	C6	74
Waverly, Ia., U.S.	B5	120
Waverly, Mo., U.S.	E4	120
Waverly, Ne., U.S.	D1	120
Waverly, N.Y., U.S.	B9	114
Waverly, Oh., U.S.	E2	114
Waverly, Tn., U.S.	H10	120
Waverly, Va., U.S.	G8	114
Waverly Hall, Ga., U.S.	E14	122
Wāw, Sudan	F5	62
Wawa, On., Can.	F14	106
Wawanesa, Mb., Can.	E14	124
Waxahachie, Tx., U.S.	B11	130
Waxhaw, N.C., U.S.	B5	116
Way, Lake, l., Austl.	E4	74
Waya, i., Fiji	p18	79e
Waycross, Ga., U.S.	E3	116
Wayland, Ia., U.S.	C6	120
Wayland, Ky., U.S.	G3	114
Wayland, Mi., U.S.	F4	112
Waylyn, S.C., U.S.	D6	116
Wayne, Ab., Can.	E18	138
Wayne, Mi., U.S.	B2	114
Wayne, Ne., U.S.	E15	126
Wayne, N.J., U.S.	D11	114
Wayne, Oh., U.S.	C2	114
Wayne, W.V., U.S.	F3	114
Wayne City, Il., U.S.	F9	120
Waynesboro, Ms., U.S.	F10	122
Waynesboro, Tn., U.S.	B11	122
Waynesboro, Va., U.S.	F6	114
Waynesville, Il., U.S.	D8	120
Waynesville, N.C., U.S.	A3	116
Waynoka, Ok., U.S.	E10	128
Wāzah Khwāh, Afg.	B2	54
Wazirābād, Pak.	B5	54
Wda, stm., Pol.	C14	16
Wē, N. Cal.	m16	79d
We, Pulau, i., Indon.	J2	48
Weatherford, Ok., U.S.	F10	128
Weatherford, Tx., U.S.	B10	130
Weatherly, Pa., U.S.	D10	114
Weaubleau, Mo., U.S.	G4	120
Weaver Lake, l., Mb., Can.	B17	124
Weaverville, Ca., U.S.	C3	134
Weaverville, N.C., U.S.	I3	114
Webb, Sk., Can.	D5	124
Webb, Ms., U.S.	D8	122
Webbwood, On., Can.	B7	112
Weber, stm., Ut., U.S.	B5	132
Weber City, Va., U.S.	H3	114
Webster, Ab., Can.	A12	138
Webster, Fl., U.S.	H3	116
Webster, Ma., U.S.	B14	114
Webster, S.D., U.S.	B15	126
Webster City, Ia., U.S.	B4	120
Webster Springs, W.V., U.S.	F5	114
Weda, Indon.	E8	44
Weddell Island, i., Falk. Is.	J4	90
Weddell Sea, s., Ant.	B36	81
Wedderburn, Austl.	K4	76
Wedel, Ger.	C5	16
Wedgeport, N.S., Can.	G11	110
Wedowee, Al., U.S.	D13	122
Weed, Ca., U.S.	B3	134
Weems, Va., U.S.	G9	114
Weenen, S. Afr.	F10	70
Weeping Water, Ne., U.S.	D1	120
Weert, Neth.	C14	14
Wee Waa, Austl.	H7	76
Wegorzewo, Pol.	B17	16
Węgrów, Pol.	D17	16
Wei, stm., China	C8	42
Wei, stm., China	C6	42
Wei, stm., China	D3	42
Weichang, China	C2	38
Weichuan, China	D6	42
Weida, Ger.	F8	16
Weiden in der Oberpfalz, Ger.	G7	16
Weifang, China	C8	42
Weihai, China	C10	42
Weihaiwei see Weihai, China	C10	42
Weihe, China	B8	38
Weilburg, Ger.	F4	16
Weilmoringle, Austl.	G6	76
Weimar, Ger.	E7	16
Weimar, Tx., U.S.	E11	130
Weinan, China	D3	42
Weinheim, Ger.	G4	16
Weipa, Austl.	B8	74
Weippe, Id., U.S.	D11	136
Weir, Ks., U.S.	D14	128
Weir, stm., Austl.	G8	76
Weirton, W.V., U.S.	D5	114
Weiser, Id., U.S.	F10	136
Weiser, stm., Id., U.S.	F10	136
Weishan Hu, l., China	D7	42
Weishi, China	D6	42
Weisner Mountain, mtn., Al., U.S.	C13	122
Weissenburg in Bayern, Ger.	G7	16
Weissenfels, Ger.	E7	16
Weiss Lake, res., U.S.	C13	122
Weisswasser, Ger.	E10	16
Weitra, Aus.	B11	22
Weixi, China	F4	36
Weixian, China	C6	42
Weiz, Aus.	C12	22
Wejherowo, Pol.	B14	16
Wekoewa Punt, c., Neth. Ant.	p23	104g
Welaka, Fl., U.S.	G4	116
Welch, Ok., U.S.	H2	120
Welch, Tx., U.S.	B5	130
Welch, W.V., U.S.	G4	114
Weldiya, Eth.	E7	62
Weldon, Sk., Can.	A8	124
Weldon, Il., U.S.	D9	120
Weldon, N.C., U.S.	H8	114
Weleetka, Ok., U.S.	B2	122
Welk'īt'ē, Eth.	F7	62
Welkom, S. Afr.	E8	70
Welland, On., Can.	F10	112
Welland, stm., Eng., U.K.	I12	12
Wellborn, Fl., U.S.	F3	116
Wellesley Islands, is., Austl.	C8	74
Wellingborough, Eng., U.K.	I12	12
Wellington, Austl.	I7	76
Wellington, On., Can.	E12	112
Wellington, N.Z.	E6	80
Wellington, Eng., U.K.	K9	12
Wellington, S. Afr.	H4	70
Wellington, Co., U.S.	G7	126
Wellington, Ks., U.S.	D11	128
Wellington, Mo., U.S.	E4	120
Wellington, Oh., U.S.	C3	114
Wellington, Ut., U.S.	D6	132
Wellington, Isla, i., Chile	I2	90
Wellington Channel, strt., Nu., Can.	B7	141
Wellman, Ia., U.S.	C6	120
Wellman, Tx., U.S.	A5	130
Wells, Mn., U.S.	H5	118
Wells, Nv., U.S.	B1	132
Wells, N.Y., U.S.	G2	110
Wells, Tx., U.S.	F3	122
Wells, Lake, l., Austl.	E4	74
Wells, Mount, hill, Austl.	C5	74
Wellsboro, Pa., U.S.	C8	114
Wellsburg, W.V., U.S.	D5	114
Wellsford, N.Z.	C6	80
Wells-next-the-Sea, Eng., U.K.	I13	12
Wellston, Oh., U.S.	E3	114
Wellsville, Ks., U.S.	F2	120
Wellsville, Mo., U.S.	E6	120
Wellsville, N.Y., U.S.	B8	114
Wellsville, Oh., U.S.	D5	114
Wellsville, Ut., U.S.	B5	132
Wellton, Az., U.S.	K2	132
Wels, Aus.	B10	22
Welsford, N.S., Can.	E10	110
Welshpool, Wales, U.K.	I9	12
Welwyn Garden City, Eng., U.K.	J12	12
Wema, D.R.C.	E4	66
Wembere, stm., Tan.	E6	66
Wemindji, Qc., Can.	E14	106
Wenatchee, Wa., U.S.	C6	136
Wenatchee Mountains, mts., Wa., U.S.	C6	136
Wenchang, China	L4	42
Wenchi, Ghana	H4	64
Wenchow see Wenzhou, China	G9	42
Wenchuan, China	E5	36
Wendell, Id., U.S.	H12	136
Wenden, Az., U.S.	J3	132
Wendeng, China	C10	42
Wendover, Ut., U.S.	C2	132
Weng'an, China	H2	42
Wenling, China	G9	42
Wenlock, stm., Austl.	B8	74
Wenquan, China	E14	32
Wenshan, China	A7	48
Wenshang, China	D7	42
Wenshui, China	C4	42
Wenshui, China	G2	42
Wensleydale, val., Eng., U.K.	G11	12
Wentworth, Austl.	J3	76
Wentworth, S.D., U.S.	G2	118
Wenxi, China	D4	42
Wenxian, China	D5	42
Wenzhou, China	F9	36
Wepener, S. Afr.	F8	70
Werda, Bots.	D7	70
Werdau, Ger.	F8	16
Werder, Ger.	D8	16
Werl, Ger.	E3	16
Werne, Ger.	E3	16
Werra, stm., Ger.	E5	16
Werribee, Austl.	K5	76
Werrikimbe National Park, p.o.i., Austl.	H9	76
Werris Creek, Austl.	H8	76
Wertheim, Ger.	G5	16
Wesel, Ger.	E2	16
Weser, stm., Ger.	C4	16
Weslaco, Tx., U.S.	C7	128
Weslemkoon Lake, l., On., Can.	C12	112
Wesley, Dom.	i6	105c
Wesleyville, Pa., U.S.	B5	114
Wessel, Cape, c., Austl.	B7	74
Wessel Islands, is., Austl.	B7	74
Wessington, S.D., U.S.	C14	126
Wessington Springs, S.D., U.S.	C14	126
West, Ms., U.S.	D9	122
West, Tx., U.S.	C10	130
West Allis, Wi., U.S.	B9	120
West Antarctica, reg., Ant.	D30	81
Westbank, B.C., Can.	G11	138
West Bank, dep., Asia	F6	58
West Bay, b., Tx., U.S.	E12	130
West Bend, Ia., U.S.	B3	120
West Bend, Wi., U.S.	E1	112
West Bengal, state, India	G11	54
West Blocton, Al., U.S.	D11	122
West Bohemia see Západočeský kraj, state, Czech Rep.	G9	16
West Borneo see Kalimantan Barat, state, Indon.	D7	50
West Branch, Ia., U.S.	C6	120
Westbridge, B.C., Can.	G11	138
West Bromwich, Eng., U.K.	I11	12
Westbrook, Me., U.S.	G6	110
Westbrook, Mn., U.S.	G3	118
Westbrook, Tx., U.S.	B6	130
West Burlington, Ia., U.S.	D6	120
West Burra, i., Scot., U.K.	n18	12a
Westby, Austl.	J6	76
Westby, Wi., U.S.	H8	118
West Cache Creek, stm., Ok., U.S.	G10	128
West Caicos, i., T./C. Is.	B11	102
West Cape, c., N.Z.	G2	80
West Cape Howe, c., Austl.	G3	74
West Carlisle, Tx., U.S.	H6	128
West Caroline Basin, unds.	I16	142
West Chester, Pa., U.S.	E10	114
Westchester Station, N.S., Can.	E13	110
Westcliffe, Co., U.S.	C3	128
West Columbia, S.C., U.S.	B4	116
West Columbia, Tx., U.S.	H3	122
West Des Moines, Ia., U.S.	C4	120
West Dolores, stm., Co., U.S.	F8	132
West Elk Peak, mtn., Co., U.S.	E9	132
West End, Ar., U.S.	C6	122
West End, N.C., U.S.	A6	116
Westerland, Ger.	B4	16
Westerly, R.I., U.S.	C14	114
Western, state, Sol. Is.	e7	79b
Western Australia, state, Austl.	D4	74
Western Cape, state, S. Afr.	H5	70
Western Channel, strt., Asia	E2	40
Western Desert, des., Egypt	B5	62
Western Division, state, Fiji	p18	79e
Western Dvina (Daugava) (Zahodnjaja Dzvina) (Zapadnaja Dvina), stm., Eur.	D7	10
Western Ghāts, mts., India	E3	46
Westernport, Md., U.S.	E7	114
Western Sahara, dep., Afr.	E2	64
Western Samoa see Samoa, ctry., Oc.	g12	79c
Western Sayans see Zapadnyj Sajan, mts., Russia	D16	32
Western Shore, N.S., Can.	F12	110
Westerschelde, est., Neth.	C12	14
Westerstede, Ger.	C3	16
Westerville, Oh., U.S.	D3	114
Westerwald, mts., Ger.	F3	16
West European Basin, unds.	D12	144
West Falkland, i., Falk. Is.	J4	90
West Fargo, N.D., U.S.	E1	118
Westfield, In., U.S.	H3	112
Westfield, Ma., U.S.	B13	114
Westfield, N.J., U.S.	D11	114
Westfield, N.Y., U.S.	B6	114
Westfield, Pa., U.S.	C8	114
Westfield, Wi., U.S.	H9	118
West Fork, Ar., U.S.	I3	120
West Frankfort, Il., U.S.	G9	120
West Friese Eilanden (West Frisian Islands), is., Neth.	A14	14
West Frisian Islands see West Friese Eilanden, is., Neth.	A14	14
Westgate, Austl.	F6	76
West Grand Lake, res., Me., U.S.	E8	110
West Hamlin, W.V., U.S.	F3	114
West Hartford, Ct., U.S.	C13	114
West Haven, Ct., U.S.	C13	114
West Helena, Ar., U.S.	C8	122
Westhoff, Tx., U.S.	E10	130
Westhope, N.D., U.S.	F12	124
West Indies, is.	C7	82
West Java see Jawa Barat, state, Indon.	G5	50
West Jefferson, N.C., U.S.	H4	114
West Jordan, Ut., U.S.	C4	132
West Kettle, stm., B.C., Can.	G11	138
West Kingston, R.I., U.S.	C14	114
West Lafayette, In., U.S.	H2	112
Westlake, La., U.S.	G5	122
Westland National Park, p.o.i., N.Z.	F3	80
West Laramie, Wy., U.S.	F7	126
West Lebanon, In., U.S.	H2	112
West Liberty, Ia., U.S.	C6	120
West Liberty, Ky., U.S.	G2	114
West Lorne, On., Can.	F8	112
Westmeath, state, Ire.	H5	12
West Memphis, Ar., U.S.	B8	122
Westminster, Co., U.S.	B3	128

Name	Map Ref.	Page
Westminster, Md., U.S.	E9	114
West Monroe, La., U.S.	E6	122
Westmoreland, Ks., U.S.	B12	128
Westmoreland, Tn., U.S.	H11	120
Westmorland, Ca., U.S.	J10	134
West Nicholson, Zimb.	B9	70
West Nishnabotna, stm., Ia., U.S.	C2	120
West Nueces, stm., Tx., U.S.	E7	130
West Nusa Tenggara see Nusa Tenggara Barat, state, Indon.	G10	50
Weston, Mo., U.S.	E3	120
Weston, Oh., U.S.	C2	114
Weston, Or., U.S.	E8	136
Weston, W.V., U.S.	F5	114
Weston-super-Mare, Eng., U.K.	J9	12
West Orange, N.J., U.S.	G5	122
Westover, Tn., U.S.	B10	122
West Palm Beach, Fl., U.S.	J5	116
West Palm Beach Canal, can., Fl., U.S.	J5	116
West Pensacola, Fl., U.S.	G11	122
West Plains, Ks., U.S.	F2	120
West Plains, Mo., U.S.	H6	120
West Point, Ga., U.S.	E13	122
West Point, Ia., U.S.	D6	120
West Point, Ky., U.S.	F11	120
West Point, Ms., U.S.	D10	122
West Point, Ne., U.S.	J2	118
West Point, N.Y., U.S.	C11	114
West Point, Va., U.S.	G9	114
West Point Lake, res., U.S.	D13	122
West Poplar (Poplar, West Fork), stm., N.A.	F8	124
Westport, N.S., Can.	F10	110
Westport, On., Can.	D13	112
Westport, Ire.	H3	12
Westport, Ct., U.S.	C12	114
Westport, In., U.S.	E12	120
Westport, Or., U.S.	D3	136
Westport, c, Aruba	o19	104g
West Quoddy Head, c, Me., U.S.	F10	110
Westray, i., Scot., U.K.	B9	12
West Richland, Wa., U.S.	D7	136
West Road, stm., B.C., Can.	C7	138
West Rutland, Vt., U.S.	G3	110
West Salem, Il., U.S.	F9	120
West Salem, Oh., U.S.	D3	114
West Shoal Lake, l., Mb., Can.	D16	124
West Siberian Plain see Zapadno-Sibirskaja ravnina, pl., Russia	B12	32
West Slovakia see Západoslovenský Kraj, state, Slov.	H14	16
West Spanish Peak, mtn., Co., U.S.	D4	128
West Sumatra see Sumatera Barat, state, Indon.	D2	50
West Terre Haute, In., U.S.	E10	120
West Union, Ia., U.S.	B6	120
West Union, Oh., U.S.	F2	114
West Unity, Oh., U.S.	C1	114
West Valley City, Ut., U.S.	C4	132
West Vancouver, B.C., Can.	G7	138
Westville, N.S., Can.	E14	110
Westville, In., U.S.	G3	112
West Virginia, state, U.S.	F5	114
West Walker, stm., U.S.	E6	134
West Warwick, R.I., U.S.	C14	114
West Webster, N.Y., U.S.	E12	112
Westwold, B.C., Can.	F11	138
Westwood, Ca., U.S.	C5	134
Westwood Lakes, Fl., U.S.	K5	116
West Wyalong, Austl.	I6	76
West Yellowstone, Mt., U.S.	F15	136
Wetar, Pulau, i., Indon.	G8	44
Wetar, Selat, strt., Asia	G8	44
Wetaskiwin, Ab., Can.	C17	138
Wete, Tan.	E7	66
Wethersfield, Ct., U.S.	C13	114
Wetmore, Ks., U.S.	E2	120
Wetumpka, Al., U.S.	E12	122
Wetzlar, Ger.	F4	16
Wewahitchka, Fl., U.S.	G13	122
Wewak, Pap. N. Gui.	a3	79a
Wewoka, Ok., U.S.	B2	122
Wexford, Ire.	I6	12
Wexford, state, Ire.	I6	12
Weyburn, Sk., Can.	E10	124
Weymontachie, Qc., Can.	C3	110
Weymouth, N.S., Can.	F10	110
Weymouth, Eng., U.K.	K10	12
Weymouth, Ma., U.S.	B15	114
Whakatane, N.Z.	C7	80
Whangarei, N.Z.	B6	80
Whapmagoostui, Qc., Can.	D15	106
Wharfe, stm., Eng., U.K.	H11	12
Wharton, W.V., U.S.	G4	114
Wharton Basin, unds.	K12	142
Wharton Lake, l., Nu., Can.	C10	106
Whataroa, N.Z.	F4	80
What Cheer, Ia., U.S.	C5	120
Whatley, Al., U.S.	F11	122
Wheatland, Ca., U.S.	D4	134
Wheatland, Ia., U.S.	C7	120
Wheatley, Ar., U.S.	C7	122
Wheaton, Il., U.S.	C9	120
Wheaton, Md., U.S.	E8	114
Wheat Ridge, Co., U.S.	B3	128
Wheeler, Ms., U.S.	C10	122
Wheeler, Tx., U.S.	F8	128
Wheeler, stm., Qc., Can.	D17	106
Wheeler Lake, res., Al., U.S.	C11	122
Wheeler Peak, mtn., N.M., U.S.	E3	128
Wheeler Peak, mtn., Nv., U.S.	D2	132
Wheeling, W.V., U.S.	D5	114
Wheelwright, Ar., U.S.	F7	92
Wheelwright, Ky., U.S.	G3	114
Whidbey Island, i., Wa., U.S.	B4	136
Whiskey Peak, mtn., Wy., U.S.	E5	126
Whistler, B.C., Can.	F8	138
Whitakers, N.C., U.S.	H8	114
Whitby, On., Can.	E11	112
Whitby, Eng., U.K.	G12	12
Whitchurch, Eng., U.K.	H10	12
Whitchurch-Stouffville, On., Can.	E10	112
White, Ga., U.S.	C14	122
White, stm., N.A.	C2	106
White, stm., N.A.	C2	106
White, stm., In., U.S.	J6	132
White, stm., In., U.S.	F10	120
White, stm., Nv., U.S.	H7	128
White, stm., U.S.	F3	136
White, stm., U.S.	D13	126
White, stm., U.S.	C7	122
White, East Fork, stm., In., U.S.	F10	120
White, Lake, l., Austl.	D5	74
White Bay, b., Nf., Can.	i22	107a
White Bear Lake, Mn., U.S.	F6	118
White Bluff, Tn., U.S.	H10	120
White Butte, mtn., N.D., U.S.	A9	126
White Castle, La., U.S.	G7	122
White City, Ks., U.S.	C12	128
White Cliffs, Austl.	H4	76
Whitecourt, Ab., Can.	B15	138
White Deer, Tx., U.S.	F7	128
Whiteface Mountain, mtn., N.Y., U.S.	F3	110
Whitefield, N.H., U.S.	F5	110
Whitefish, Mt., U.S.	B12	136
Whitefish Bay, Wi., U.S.	A10	120
Whitefish Bay, b., On., Can.	B4	118
Whitefish Bay, b., N.A.	B5	112
Whitefish Lake, l., Ab., Can.	B18	138
Whitefish Lake, l., N.T., Can.	C9	106
Whitefish Point, Mi., U.S.	B4	112
Whitefish Point, c., Mi., U.S.	B4	112
White Hall, Ar., U.S.	C6	122
White Hall, Il., U.S.	E7	120
Whitehall, Mi., U.S.	G3	110
Whitehall, N.Y., U.S.	G7	118
Whitehall, Wi., U.S.	G9	12
Whitehaven, Eng., U.K.	C4	106
Whitehorse, Yk., Can.	C4	106
White House, Tn., U.S.	H11	120
Whitehouse, Tx., U.S.	E3	122
White Island, l., Nu., Can.	B13	106
White Island, i., N.Z.	C7	80
White Lake, S.D., U.S.	D14	126
White Lake, l., On., Can.	C13	112
White Lake, l., La., U.S.	H6	122
Whitemark, Austl.	n13	77a
White Mountain Peak, mtn., Ca., U.S.	F7	134
White Mountains, mts., N.H., U.S.	F5	110
Whitemouth, stm., Mb., Can.	E18	124
Whitemouth Lake, l., Mb., Can.	E18	124
Whitemud, stm., Mb., Can.	D15	124
White Nile (Abyad, Al-Bahr al-), stm., Afr.	E6	62
White Oak, Tx., U.S.	E4	122
White Oak Creek, stm., Tx., U.S.	D3	122
White Otter Lake, l., On., Can.	B6	118
White Pigeon, Mi., U.S.	G4	112
Whitepine, Mt., U.S.	C11	136
White Pine, Tn., U.S.	H2	114
White Plains, N.C., U.S.	H5	114
White Plains, N.Y., U.S.	C12	114
Whiteriver, Az., U.S.	J6	132
White River, S.D., U.S.	D12	126
White River Junction, Vt., U.S.	G4	110
White Rock, S.D., U.S.	G8	138
White Russia see Belarus, ctry., Eur.	E14	6
Whitesail Lake, res., B.C., Can.	C3	138
Whitesand, stm., Sk., Can.	C11	124
White Sands National Monument, p.o.i., N.M., U.S.	B1	130
Whitesboro, Tx., U.S.	D2	122
White Sea see Beloe more, s., Russia	D18	8
White Settlement, Tx., U.S.	B10	130
White Springs, Fl., U.S.	F3	116
White Sulphur Springs, Mt., U.S.	D16	136
White Sulphur Springs, W.V., U.S.	G5	114
Whitesville, Ky., U.S.	G11	120
Whiteville, N.C., U.S.	B7	116
Whiteville, Tn., U.S.	B9	122
White Volta (Volta Blanche), stm., Afr.	G4	64
Whitewater, Mt., U.S.	F6	124
Whitewater, Wi., U.S.	B9	120
Whitewater, stm., U.S.	E13	120
Whitewater Baldy, mtn., N.M., U.S.	J8	132
Whitewater Creek, stm., N.A.	F6	124
Whitewater Lake, l., Mb., Can.	E13	124
White Woman Creek, stm., U.S.	C7	128
Whitewood, Austl.	C4	76
Whitewood, Sk., Can.	D11	124
Whitewood, S.D., U.S.	C9	126
Whithorn, Jam.	i12	104d
Whithorn, Scot., U.K.	G8	12
Whiting, Ia., U.S.	B1	120
Whiting, Ks., U.S.	E2	120
Whitley City, Ky., U.S.	H13	120
Whitman, Ma., U.S.	B15	114
Whitmire, S.C., U.S.	B4	116
Whitmore Mountains, mts., Ant.	D31	81
Whitney, On., Can.	C11	112
Whitney, Lake, res., Tx., U.S.	C10	130
Whitney, Mount, mtn., Ca., U.S.	G7	134
Whitney Point, N.Y., U.S.	B9	114
Whitsunday Island, i., Austl.	C7	76
Whitsundiep, can., Neth.	C7	66
Whittemore, Ia., U.S.	A3	120
Whittemore, Mi., U.S.	D6	112
Whittle, Cap, c., Qc., Can.	i22	107a
Whittlesea, Austl.	K5	76
Whittlesey, Mount, hill, Wi., U.S.	E8	118
Whitwell, Tn., U.S.	B13	122
Wholdaia Lake, l., N.T., Can.	C9	106
Whyalla, Austl.	F7	74
Whycocomagh, N.S., Can.	E15	110
Wiang Phan, Thai.	B4	48
Wiarton, On., Can.	D8	112
Wichian Buri, Thai.	E5	48
Wichita, Ks., U.S.	D11	128
Wichita, stm., Tx., U.S.	G10	128
Wichita Falls, Tx., U.S.	H10	128
Wick, Scot., U.K.	C9	12
Wickenburg, Az., U.S.	J4	132
Wickepin, Austl.	F3	74
Wickett, Tx., U.S.	C5	130
Wickham, Austl.	D3	74
Wickiup Reservoir, res., Or., U.S.	G5	136
Wickliffe, Ky., U.S.	H8	120
Wicklow, Ire.	H6	12
Wicklow, state, Ire.	H7	12
Wicklow Head, c., Ire.	I7	12
Wicklow Mountains, mts., Ire.	H6	12
Widgiemooltha Creek, stm., Austl.	F6	76
Więcbork, Pol.	C13	16
Wieleń, Pol.	D12	16
Wieliczka, Pol.	F16	16
Wielkopolska, reg., Pol.	D13	16
Wielkopolski Park Narodowy, p.o.i., Pol.	D12	16
Wien (Vienna), Aus.	B13	22
Wien, state, Aus.	B13	22
Wiener Neustadt, Aus.	C13	22
Wienerwald, mts., Aus.	B13	22
Wieprz, stm., Pol.	E18	16
Wieprza, stm., Pol.	B12	16
Wieprz-Krzna, Kanal, can., Pol.	E19	16
Wierden, Neth.	D2	16
Wiergate, Tx., U.S.	F5	122
Wieruszów, Pol.	E14	16
Wierzyca, stm., Pol.	B14	16
Wiesbaden, Ger.	F4	16
Wiesloch, Ger.	G4	16
Wigan, Eng., U.K.	H10	12
Wiggins, Co., U.S.	A4	128
Wiggins, Ms., U.S.	G9	122
Wight, Isle of, i., Eng., U.K.	K11	12
Wigtown, Scot., U.K.	G8	12
Wilbur, Wa., U.S.	C8	136
Wilburton, Ok., U.S.	C3	122
Wilcannia, Austl.	H4	76
Wilcox, Sk., Can.	D9	124
Wilcox, Pa., U.S.	C8	114
Wilcox, Az., U.S.	A9	128
Wild Coast, cst., S. Afr.	H9	70
Wilder, Id., U.S.	G9	136
Wilderness of Judea (Midbar Yehuda), des., Asia	G6	58
Wildhay, stm., Ab., Can.	C13	138
Wildhorse Creek, stm., U.S.	G10	126
Wild Horse Lake, l., Mt., U.S.	B17	136
Wild Rice, stm., Mn., U.S.	D2	118
Wild Rice, stm., N.D., U.S.	H17	124
Wildrose, N.D., U.S.	F10	124
Wild Rose, Wi., U.S.	G9	118
Wildwood, Ab., Can.	C15	138
Wildwood, N.J., U.S.	F11	114
Wilge, stm., S. Afr.	E9	70
Wilhelm, Mount, mtn., Pap. N. Gui.	b3	79a
Wilhelmina Gebergte, mts., Sur.	C6	84
Wilhelmshaven, Ger.	C4	16
Wilhelmstal, Nmb.	B3	70
Wilkerson Pass, p., Co., U.S.	B3	128
Wilkes-Barre, Pa., U.S.	C10	114
Wilkesboro, N.C., U.S.	H4	114
Wilkes Land, reg., Ant.	C16	81
Wilkie, Sk., Can.	B5	124
Willacoochee, Ga., U.S.	E2	116
Willamette, stm., Or., U.S.	E4	136
Willamette, Middle Fork, stm., Or., U.S.	G4	136
Willamina, Or., U.S.	E3	136
Willandra Billabong Creek, stm., Austl.	I5	76
Willandra National Park, p.o.i., Austl.	I5	76
Willapa Bay, b., Wa., U.S.	D2	136
Willard, Mo., U.S.	G4	120
Willard, Oh., U.S.	C3	114
Willard, Ut., U.S.	B4	132
Willard, Punta, c., Mex.	A2	100
Willcox, Az., U.S.	K7	132
Willcox Playa, l., Az., U.S.	K7	132
Willemstad, Neth. Ant.	p22	104g
Willeroo, Austl.	C6	74
William, Mount, mtn., Austl.	K4	76
William "Bill" Dannelly Reservoir, res., Al., U.S.	E11	122
Williams, Az., U.S.	H4	132
Williams, Ia., U.S.	I5	118
Williams, Mn., U.S.	C3	118
Williams, stm., Austl.	C3	76
Williamsburg, Ia., U.S.	C5	120
Williamsburg, Ky., U.S.	H1	114
Williamsburg, Va., U.S.	G9	114
Williams Lake, B.C., Can.	D8	138
Williamson, N.Y., U.S.	E12	112
Williamson, W.V., U.S.	G3	114
Williamson, stm., Or., U.S.	H5	136
Williamson, Mount, mtn., Ca., U.S.	G7	134
Williamsport, Pa., U.S.	C8	114
Williamston, Mi., U.S.	F5	112
Williamston, N.C., U.S.	I8	114
Williamston, S.C., U.S.	B3	116
Williamstown, Ky., U.S.	F1	114
Williamstown, N.J., U.S.	E11	114
Williamstown, W.V., U.S.	E4	114
Willikies, Antig.	f4	105b
Willimantic, Ct., U.S.	C13	114
Willingboro, N.J., U.S.	D10	114
Willis, Tx., U.S.	G3	122
Willis Group, is., Austl.	C10	74
Williston, Fl., U.S.	G3	116
Williston, N.D., U.S.	F10	124
Williston, S.C., U.S.	C4	116
Williston Lake, res., B.C., Can.	D6	106
Willits, Ca., U.S.	D2	134
Willmar, Mn., U.S.	F3	118
Willoughby, Oh., U.S.	C4	114
Willoughby Bay, b., Antig.	f4	105b
Willow, Ak., U.S.	D10	140
Willow, stm., B.C., Can.	C8	138
Willowbrook, Sk., Can.	C10	124
Willow Bunch, Sk., Can.	E8	124
Willow Bunch Lake, l., Sk., Can.	E8	124
Willow Creek, Ca., U.S.	C2	134
Willow Creek, Mt., U.S.	E15	136
Willow Creek, stm., Ab., Can.	F17	138
Willow Creek, stm., Or., U.S.	F9	136
Willow Creek, stm., Or., U.S.	E7	136
Willow Lake, l., N.T., Can.	C7	106
Willowmore, S. Afr.	H6	70
Willowra, Austl.	D6	74
Willow Reservoir, res., Wi., U.S.	F9	118
Willows, Ca., U.S.	D3	134
Willow Springs, Mo., U.S.	H6	120
Willowvale, S. Afr.	H9	70
Wills Creek, stm., Austl.	D2	76
Wills Point, Tx., U.S.	E2	122
Wilmar, Ar., U.S.	D6	122
Wilmer, Al., U.S.	G10	122
Wilmer, Tx., U.S.	E2	122
Wilmette, Il., U.S.	F2	112
Wilmington, De., U.S.	E10	114
Wilmington, N.C., U.S.	B7	116
Wilmington, Oh., U.S.	E2	114
Wilmington, Vt., U.S.	H4	110
Wilmore, Ky., U.S.	G13	120
Wilmot, S.D., U.S.	F2	118
Wilpattu National Park, p.o.i., Sri L.	G4	53
Wilsall, Mt., U.S.	D16	136
Wilson, Austl.	H2	76
Wilson, La., U.S.	G7	122
Wilson, N.C., U.S.	I8	114
Wilson, N.Y., U.S.	E11	112
Wilson, Ok., U.S.	G11	128
Wilson, stm., Austl.	F4	76
Wilson, Cape, c., Nu., Can.	B14	106
Wilson, Mount, mtn., Ca., U.S.	I7	134
Wilson, Mount, mtn., Co., U.S.	F8	132
Wilson Lake, res., Al., U.S.	C11	122
Wilson Lake, res., Ks., U.S.	C10	128
Wilson's Promontory, pen., Austl.	L6	76
Wilsons Promontory National Park, p.o.i., Austl.	L6	76
Wilsonville, Ne., U.S.	A8	128
Wilton, Eng., U.K.	J11	12
Wiluna, Austl.	E4	74
Wimauma, Fl., U.S.	I3	116
Wimberley, Tx., U.S.	D9	130
Winamac, In., U.S.	H2	112
Winburg, S. Afr.	F8	70
Winchendon, Ma., U.S.	B13	114
Winchester, On., Can.	C14	112
Winchester, Eng., U.K.	J11	12
Winchester, Il., U.S.	E7	120
Winchester, In., U.S.	H5	112
Winchester, Ky., U.S.	G1	114
Winchester, Tn., U.S.	B12	122
Winchester, Va., U.S.	E7	114
Wind, stm., Yk., Can.	B3	106
Wind Cave National Park, p.o.i., S.D., U.S.	D9	126
Winder, Ga., U.S.	B2	116
Windermere, B.C., Can.	F15	138
Windermere, Eng., U.K.	G10	12
Windfall, Ab., Can.	B14	138
Windhoek, Nmb.	C3	70
Windigo, stm., Qc., Can.	C3	110
Windom, Mn., U.S.	H3	118
Windorah, Austl.	E4	76
Window Rock, Az., U.S.	H7	132
Wind River Peak, mtn., Wy., U.S.	E3	126
Wind River Range, mts., Wy., U.S.	D3	126
Windsor, Austl.	I8	76
Windsor, N.S., Can.	E12	110
Windsor, On., Can.	F6	112
Windsor, Qc., Can.	E5	110
Windsor, Eng., U.K.	J12	12
Windsor, Co., U.S.	E3	134
Windsor, Ct., U.S.	C13	114
Windsor, Mo., U.S.	F4	120
Windsor, N.C., U.S.	I9	114
Windsor, Va., U.S.	H9	114
Windsor Forest, Ga., U.S.	E4	116
Windsor Locks, Ct., U.S.	C13	114
Windthorst, Tx., U.S.	H10	128
Windward, Gren.	p11	105e
Windward Islands, is., N.A.	k6	105c
Windward Passage, strt., N.A.	C11	102
Windy Peak, mtn., Co., U.S.	C2	128
Winfield, Al., U.S.	D11	122
Winfield, Ks., U.S.	D12	128
Winfield, Mo., U.S.	E7	120
Winfield, W.V., U.S.	F4	114
Wing, N.D., U.S.	G13	124
Wingate, N.C., U.S.	B5	116
Wingham, Austl.	H9	76
Wingham, On., Can.	E8	112
Wingo, Ky., U.S.	H9	120
Winisk, On., Can.	D13	106
Winisk, stm., On., Can.	E13	106
Winisk Lake, l., On., Can.	E13	106
Wink, Tx., U.S.	C4	130
Winkana, Mya.	D3	48
Winkelman, Az., U.S.	K6	132
Winkler, Mb., Can.	E16	124
Winlock, Wa., U.S.	D3	136
Winneba, Ghana	H4	64
Winnebago, Mn., U.S.	H4	118
Winnebago, Ne., U.S.	B1	120
Winnebago, Lake, l., Wi., U.S.	H5	118
Winneconne, Wi., U.S.	G10	118
Winnemucca, Nv., U.S.	B8	134
Winnemucca Lake, l., Nv., U.S.	C6	134
Winner, S.D., U.S.	D13	126
Winnetka, Il., U.S.	F2	112
Winnett, Mt., U.S.	H5	124
Winnibigoshish, Lake, l., Mn., U.S.	D4	118
Winnie, Tx., U.S.	H4	122
Winning, Austl.	D2	74
Winnipeg, Mb., Can.	E16	124
Winnipeg, stm., Can.	E11	106
Winnipeg, Lake, l., Mb., Can.	E11	106
Winnipeg Beach, Mb., Can.	D17	124
Winnipegosis, Mb., Can.	C13	124
Winnipegosis, Lake, l., Mb., Can.	B13	124
Winnipesaukee, Lake, l., N.H., U.S.	G5	110
Winnsboro, La., U.S.	E7	122
Winnsboro, S.C., U.S.	B4	116
Winnsboro, Tx., U.S.	E3	122
Winnsboro Mills, S.C., U.S.	B4	116
Winona, Mn., U.S.	G7	118
Winona, Ms., U.S.	D9	122
Winona, Mo., U.S.	G6	120
Winooski, stm., Vt., U.S.	F4	110
Winschoten, Neth.	A15	14
Winschoterdiep, can., Neth.	A15	14
Winsen, Ger.	C6	16
Winslow, Az., U.S.	H6	132
Winslow, In., U.S.	F10	120
Winslow, Me., U.S.	F7	110
Winsted, Ct., U.S.	C13	114
Winston, Fl., U.S.	H3	116
Winston, Or., U.S.	G3	136
Winston-Salem, N.C., U.S.	H5	114
Winter Garden, Fl., U.S.	H4	116
Winter Harbor, Me., U.S.	F8	110
Winter Harbour, B.C., Can.	F2	138
Winterhaven, Ca., U.S.	K2	132
Winterset, Ia., U.S.	C4	120
Wintersville, Oh., U.S.	D5	114
Winterswijk, Neth.	B15	14
Winterthur, Switz.	C5	22
Winterville, Ms., U.S.	D7	122
Winterville, N.C., U.S.	I9	114
Winthrop, Me., U.S.	F7	110
Winthrop, Mn., U.S.	G4	118
Winthrop Harbor, Il., U.S.	F2	112
Wintinna, Austl.	E6	74
Winton, Austl.	D4	76
Winton, N.Z.	H3	80
Winton, N.C., U.S.	H8	114
Wirāṭnagar, Nepal	E11	54
Wīrganj, Nepal	H2	54
Wisbech, Eng., U.K.	I12	12
Wiscasset, Me., U.S.	G7	110
Wisconsin, state, U.S.	G9	118
Wisconsin, stm., Wi., U.S.	I8	118
Wisconsin Dells, misc. cult., Wi., U.S.	H9	118
Wisconsin Rapids, Wi., U.S.	G8	118
Wise, Va., U.S.	H3	114
Wiseman, Ak., U.S.	C9	140
Wishek, N.D., U.S.	A13	126
Wishram, Wa., U.S.	E5	136
Wisła, Pol.	G14	16
Wisła (Vistula), stm., Pol.	B14	16
Wiślany, Mierzeja, spit, Eur.	B15	16
Wisłok, stm., Pol.	F17	16
Wisłoka, stm., Pol.	G17	16
Wisner, La., U.S.	F7	122
Wisner, Ne., U.S.	C15	126
Wisznice, Pol.	E19	16
Witbank, S. Afr.	D9	70
Witdraai, S. Afr.	E5	70
Witham, stm., Eng., U.K.	H12	12
Withlacoochee, stm., U.S.	F2	116
Witney, Eng., U.K.	J11	12
Wit Nossob, stm., Nmb.	C4	70
Witsand, S. Afr.	I5	70
Witt, Il., U.S.	E8	120
Wittenberg, Wi., U.S.	G9	118
Wittenberg, Ger.	E8	16
Wittenberge, Ger.	C7	16
Wittenoom, Austl.	D3	74
Wittingen, Ger.	D6	16
Wittlich, Ger.	G2	16
Wittmund, Ger.	C3	16
Wittstock, Ger.	C8	16
Witu Islands, is., Pap. N. Gui.	a5	79a
Witvlei, Nmb.	C4	70
Witwatersrand, mts., S. Afr.	D8	70
Witzenhausen, Ger.	E5	16
Wiżajny, Pol.	B18	16
Wkra, stm., Pol.	C15	16
Wleń, Pol.	E11	16
Włocławek, Pol.	D15	16
Włocławek, state, Pol.	D14	16
Włoszczowa, Pol.	F15	16
Woburn, Ma., U.S.	B14	114
Wodonga, Austl.	K6	76
Wodzisław Śląski, Pol.	G14	16
Wokam, Pulau, i., Indon.	G10	44
Woking, Eng., U.K.	J12	12
Wokingham Creek, stm., Austl.	C4	76
Wolbrom, Pol.	F15	16
Wolcott, In., U.S.	D10	120
Wolcott, N.Y., U.S.	E13	112
Wolcottville, In., U.S.	G4	112
Woleai, at., Micron.	C5	72
Wolf, stm., Ms., U.S.	G9	122
Wolf, stm., Wi., U.S.	B9	122
Wolf, Volcán, vol., Ec.	h11	84a
Wolfach, Ger.	H4	16
Wolf Creek, Or., U.S.	H3	136
Wolf Creek, stm., Mt., U.S.	C17	136
Wolf Creek, stm., U.S.	E9	128
Wolf Creek Pass, p., Co., U.S.	F10	132
Wolf Creek Reservoir, res., Ks., U.S.	B12	128
Wolfeboro, N.H., U.S.	G5	110
Wolfen, Ger.	E8	16
Wolfenbüttel, Ger.	D6	16
Wolfenden, Mount, mtn., B.C., Can.	F3	138
Wolfforth, Tx., U.S.	H6	128
Wolfhagen, Ger.	E4	16
Wolf Lake, Mi., U.S.	E4	112
Wolf Lake, l., Ab., Can.	B20	138
Wolf Point, Mt., U.S.	F8	124
Wolfratshausen, Ger.	I7	16
Wolf Rock, r., Eng., U.K.	L7	12
Wolfsberg, Aus.	D11	22
Wolfsburg, Ger.	D6	16
Wolfville, N.S., Can.	E12	110
Wolgast, Ger.	B9	16
Woliński Park Narodowy, p.o.i., Pol.	C10	16
Wollaston Lake, l., Sk., Can.	D10	106
Wollaston Peninsula, pen., Can.	B7	106
Wollemi National Park, p.o.i., Austl.	I7	76
Wollongong, Austl.	J8	76
Wołomin, Pol.	D17	16
Wołów, Pol.	E12	16
Wolseley, Sk., Can.	D10	124
Wolsey, S.D., U.S.	C14	126
Wolverhampton, Eng., U.K.	I10	12
Wolverton, Eng., U.K.	I11	12
Wonarah, Austl.	C7	74
Wondai, Austl.	F8	76
Wonderland, Ca., U.S.	A3	42
Wonewoc, Wi., U.S.	H8	118
Wonogiri, Indon.	G7	50
Wonosari, Indon.	H7	50
Wonosobo, Indon.	G6	50
Wŏnsan, Kor., N.	E7	38
Wonthaggi, Austl.	L5	76
Wood, S.D., U.S.	D12	126
Wood, stm., Ne., U.S.	G13	126
Wood, Mount, mtn., Mt., U.S.	E17	136
Woodall Mountain, hill, Ms., U.S.	C10	122
Woodbine, Ga., U.S.	F4	116
Woodbine, Ia., U.S.	C2	120
Woodbridge, Eng., U.K.	I14	12
Woodbridge, Va., U.S.	F8	114
Woodburn, Or., U.S.	E4	136
Woodbury, Ga., U.S.	D14	122
Woodbury, N.J., U.S.	E10	114
Woodbury, Tn., U.S.	I11	120
Woodlake, Ca., U.S.	G7	134
Woodland, Ca., U.S.	E4	134
Woodland, Me., U.S.	E9	110
Woodland, Me., U.S.	H8	110
Woodland, Wa., U.S.	D4	136
Woodland Park, Co., U.S.	C3	128
Woodridge, Mb., Can.	E17	124
Wood River, Il., U.S.	F7	120
Wood River, stm., Ne., U.S.	G14	126
Woodroffe, Mount, mtn., Austl.	E6	74
Woodruff, Az., U.S.	I6	132
Woodruff, S.C., U.S.	B3	116
Woodruff, Wi., U.S.	F9	118
Woods, Lake, l., Austl.	C6	74
Woods, Lake of the, l., N.A.	B3	118
Woodsboro, Tx., U.S.	F10	130
Woodsfield, Oh., U.S.	E4	114
Woods Hole, Ma., U.S.	C15	114
Woodside, Austl.	L6	76
Woodson, Tx., U.S.	A8	130
Woodstock, Austl.	D3	76
Woodstock, N.B., Can.	D9	110
Woodstock, On., Can.	E9	112
Woodstock, Eng., U.K.	J11	12
Woodstock, Ga., U.S.	C1	116
Woodstock, Il., U.S.	B9	120
Woodstock, Va., U.S.	F7	114
Woodstock, Vt., U.S.	G4	110
Woodsville, N.H., U.S.	F4	110
Woodville, Al., U.S.	C12	122
Woodville, Ms., U.S.	F7	122
Woodville, Tx., U.S.	G4	122
Woodward, Ok., U.S.	E9	128
Woody, stm., Can.	B12	124
Woody Head, c., Austl.	G9	76
Woolmarket, Ms., U.S.	G9	122
Woomera, Austl.	F7	74
Woonsocket, R.I., U.S.	B14	114
Woonsocket, S.D., U.S.	C14	126
Wooramel, stm., Austl.	E2	74
Wooramel, Austl.	E2	74
Wooster, Oh., U.S.	D4	114
Worcester, S. Afr.	H4	70
Worcester, Eng., U.K.	I10	12
Worcester, Ma., U.S.	B14	114
Worden, Il., U.S.	E8	120
Wörgl, Aus.	C9	22
Workington, Eng., U.K.	G9	12
Worksop, Eng., U.K.	H11	12
Worland, Wy., U.S.	C5	126
Worms, Ger.	G4	16
Worthing, Eng., U.K.	K12	12
Worthington, In., U.S.	E11	120
Worthington, Mn., U.S.	H3	118
Worthington, Oh., U.S.	D3	114
Worthington Peak, mtn., Nv., U.S.	E1	132
Wosi, Indon.	F8	44
Wotho, at., Marsh. Is.	B7	72
Wotje, at., Marsh. Is.	C8	72
Wotu, Indon.	E12	50
Wouhnta, Nic.	F6	102
Wounded Knee, S.D., U.S.	D10	126
Wounded Knee Creek, stm., S.D., U.S.	D10	126
Wowan, Austl.	D8	76
Wowoni, Pulau, i., Indon.	F7	44
Woy Woy, Austl.	I8	76
Wrangel Island see Vrangelja, ostrov, i., Russia	B24	34
Wrangell, Ak., U.S.	E13	140
Wrangell, Cape, c., Ak., U.S.	g21	140a
Wrangell Mountains, mts., Ak., U.S.	D11	140
Wrath, Cape, c., Scot., U.K.	C8	12
Wrens, Ga., U.S.	C3	116
Wrentham, Ab., Can.	G18	138
Wrexham, Wales, U.K.	H10	12
Wright, Mount, mtn., B.C., Can.	B14	136
Wright City, Mo., U.S.	F6	120
Wright Patman Lake, res., Tx., U.S.	D4	122
Wrightson, Mount, mtn., Az., U.S.	L6	132
Wrightstown, Wi., U.S.	D1	112
Wrightsville, Ga., U.S.	D3	116
Wrightsville Beach, N.C., U.S.	B8	116
Wrigley, N.T., Can.	C6	106
Wrigley, Tn., U.S.	I10	120
Wrocław (Breslau), Pol.	E13	16
Wrocław, state, Pol.	E13	16
Wrong Lake, l., Mb., Can.	B17	124
Wrottesley, Cape, c., N.T., Can.	B15	140
Wroxton, Sk., Can.	C12	124
Września, Pol.	D13	16
Wschowa, Pol.	E12	16
Wu, stm., China	H3	42
Wu, stm., China	G7	42
Wu, stm., China	G2	42
Wu, stm., China	I5	42
Wu, stm., China	H4	42
Wubu, China	C4	42
Wuchang, China	B7	38
Wuchang see Changzhou, China	F8	42
Wuchang Hu, l., China	F7	42
Wuchow see Wuzhou, China	J4	42
Wuchuan, China	J4	42
Wuchuan, China	K4	42
Wuchuan, China	A4	42
Wuchung see Wuzhong, China	C2	42
Wuda, China	B2	42
Wudaoliang, China	D3	36
Wudi, China	C7	42
Wuding, China	F5	36
Wuding, stm., China	C4	42
Wudu, China	E5	36
Wufeng, China	F4	42
Wugang, China	H4	42
Wugong, China	D2	42
Wugong Shan, mts., China	H5	42
Wuhai, China	B2	42
Wuhan (Hankow), China	F6	42
Wuhsi see Wuxi, China	F9	42
Wuhsing see Huzhou, China	F9	42
Wuhu, China	F8	42
Wuhu, China	J6	42
Wuhuanchi, China	C4	38
Wüjang, China	B7	54
Wujia, China	H2	42
Wujiadu, China	D3	36
Wujiang, China	F8	42
Wukari, Nig.	H6	64
Wukeshu, China	B7	38
Wulateqianqi, China	A3	42
Wulatezhongqi, China	A3	42
Wuliang Shan, mts., China	G5	36
Wulong, China	G2	42
Wuluhan, Indon.	H8	50
Wulumuchi see Ürümqi, China	C2	36
Wuluo, China	H3	42
Wuming, China	J3	42
Wundwin, Mya.	B2	48
Wunnummin Lake, l., On., Can.	E13	106
Wunstorf, Ger.	D5	16
Wupatki National Monument, p.o.i., Az., U.S.	H5	132
Wuppertal, Ger.	E3	16
Wuppertal, S. Afr.	H4	70
Wuqi, China	C3	42
Wuqia, China	B12	56
Wuqiao, China	B6	42
Wuqing, China	B6	42
Wurno, Nig.	G6	64
Würzburg, Ger.	G5	16
Wurzen, Ger.	E8	16
Wushan, China	F2	42
Wusheng, China	F2	42
Wushenqi, China	B3	42
Wushi, China	J4	42
Wusih see Wuxi, China	F9	42
Wusuli (Ussuri), stm., Asia	B11	36
Wutai, China	B5	42
Wutai Shan, mtn., China	C5	42
Wutong, China	I3	42
Wutongqiao, China	F5	36
Wutsin see Changzhou, China	F8	42
Wut'ung'ch'iao see Wutongqiao, China	F5	36
Wutungqiao see Wutongqiao, China	F5	36
Wuvulu Island, i., Pap. N. Gui.	a3	79a
Wuwei, China	D5	36
Wuwei, China	F7	42
Wuxi, China	F9	42
Wuxi, China	F2	42
Wuxiang, China	C5	42
Wuyang, China	E5	42
Wuyi, China	G8	42
Wuyi Shan, mts., China	H7	42
Wuyuan, China	A4	42
Wuyuan, China	G7	42
Wuzhai, China	B4	42
Wuzhi Shan (Wuzhi Peak), mtn., China	L3	42
Wuzhong, China	C2	42
Wuzhou, China	J4	42
Wyaconda, stm., Mo., U.S.	D6	120
Wyandotte, Mi., U.S.	B2	114
Wyandra, Austl.	F5	76
Wyangala, Lake, res., Austl.	J7	76
Wyatt, Mo., U.S.	H8	120
Wycheproof, Austl.	K4	76
Wye, stm., U.K.	J10	12
Wyk, Ger.	B4	16
Wylie, Lake, res., U.S.	A4	116
Wymark, Sk., Can.	D6	124
Wymore, Ne., U.S.	K2	118
Wyndham, Austl.	C4	74
Wyndmere, N.D., U.S.	E1	118
Wynne, Ar., U.S.	B8	122
Wynnewood, Ok., U.S.	G11	128
Wynniatt Bay, b., Can.	A8	106
Wynona, Ok., U.S.	E1	122
Wynot, Ne., U.S.	E15	126
Wynyard, Sk., Can.	C9	124
Wyodak, Wy., U.S.	C7	126
Wyoming, On., Can.	F7	112
Wyoming, Mi., U.S.	F4	112
Wyoming, Mn., U.S.	F5	118
Wyoming, state, U.S.	E5	126
Wyoming Peak, mtn., Wy., U.S.	H16	136
Wyong, Austl.	I8	76
Wyperfeld National Park, p.o.i., Austl.	J3	76
Wyszków, Pol.	D17	16
Wyśmierzyce, Pol.	E16	16
Wysokie Mazowieckie, Pol.	D18	16
Wytheville, Va., U.S.	H4	114

Name	Map Ref.	Page

X

Xaafuun, Raas, c., Som...... B10 66
Xábia, Spain............... F11 20
Xaidulla, China........... A4 46
Xainza, China............ C12 54
Xai-Xai, Moz............. D11 70
Xalapa (Jalapa), Mex..... F10 100
Xalin, Som............... C9 66
Xam (Chu), stm., Asia..... B7 48
Xambioá, Braz............ D1 88
Xambrê, stm., Braz........ A11 92
Xam Nua, Laos.......... B7 48
Xá-Muteba, Ang.......... B2 68
Xan (San), stm., Asia..... E8 48
Xangongo, Ang.......... D2 68
Xankändi, Azer........... B6 56
Xánthi, Grc.............. B7 28
Xanxerê, Braz............ C11 92
Xapecó, stm., Braz........ C11 92
Xapuri, Braz............. F4 84
Xar Moron, stm., China... C3 38
Xàtiva, Spain............ F10 20
Xau, Lake, pl., Bots...... B7 70
Xavantina, Braz.......... D6 90
Xaxim, Braz............. C11 92
Xcalak, Mex............. C4 102
X-Can, Mex.............. B4 102
Xelva, Spain............. E9 20
Xenia, Oh., U.S.......... E2 114
Xepenehe, N. Cal......... m16 79d
Xhumo, Bots............. B7 70
Xi, stm., China.......... J5 42
Xiachuan Dao, i., China... K5 42
Xiagaixin, China......... A5 48
Xiamen (Amoy), China.... I7 42
Xi'an (Sian), China....... D3 42
Xianfeng, China......... G3 42
Xiang, stm., China........ G5 42
Xiangcheng, China........ E5 42
Xiangfan, China.......... F4 42
Xianggang (Hong Kong), China............... J6 42
Xiangkhoang, Laos....... C6 48
Xiangkhoang, Plateau de (Tran Ninh), plat., Laos.. C6 48
Xiangning, China......... D4 42
Xiangride, China......... D4 36
Xiangshan, China........ G9 42
Xiangtan, China......... H5 42
Xiangxiang, China........ H5 42
Xianyin, China.......... G5 42
Xianyuan, China......... D3 42
Xiangzhou, China........ J3 42
Xianju, China........... G9 42
Xianshui, stm., China..... B9 46
Xiantao, China.......... F5 42
Xianyang, China......... D3 42
Xianyang, China......... G8 42
Xianyou, China.......... I8 42
Xiao, stm., China........ G8 42
Xiaochengzi, China....... C5 38
Xiaogan, China.......... F5 42
Xiaoguai, China......... B1 36
Xiao Hinggan Ling (Lesser Khingan Range), mts., China............... B10 36
Xiaojin, China.......... E5 36
Xiaojiu, China.......... B7 38
Xiaoluan, stm., China.... D2 38
Xiaopingyang, China..... J3 42
Xiaoshan, China......... F9 42
Xiaoxian, China......... D7 42
Xiaoyi, China........... C4 42
Xiapu, China........... H9 42
Xiawa, China........... D4 42
Xiaxian, China.......... D4 42
Xibo, stm., China........ D3 38
Xichang, China.......... F5 36
Xichong, China.......... F1 42
Xicoténcatl, Mex......... D9 100
Xiè, stm., China......... G8 86
Xifei, stm., China........ E7 42
Xifeng, China........... H2 42
Xifeng, China........... C6 38
Xigazê, China........... D12 54
Xihan, stm., China....... D1 42
Xihe, China............ F5 42
Xiheying, China......... B6 42
Xihua, China........... E6 42
Xiji, China............ C5 38
Xiliao, stm., China....... C5 38
Xilin, China............ D11 54
Xilinhot, China......... C2 38
Ximakou, China......... F5 42
Ximalin, China.......... A6 42
Ximiao, China.......... C5 36
Xin, stm., China........ G7 42
Xin'an, China........... C6 38
Xin'anjiang Shuiku, res., China............... G8 42
Xinavane, Moz.......... D11 70
Xin Barag Youqi, China... B8 36
Xin Barag Zuoqi, China... B8 36
Xinbin, China.......... D6 38
Xincai, China........... E6 42
Xinchang, China......... G9 42
Xincheng, China......... B6 42
Xincheng, China......... G6 36
Xindu, China........... I4 42
Xinfeng, China......... I6 42
Xinfeng Shuiku, res., China. J6 42
Xing'an, China......... A9 42
Xinguo, China.......... H6 42
Xinghai, China......... D4 36
Xinghe, China.......... A5 42
Xinghua, China......... E8 42
Xinglong, China........ D1 42
Xingren, China......... F6 36
Xingrenbu, China....... C1 42
Xingtai, China......... C6 42
Xingtang, China........ B6 42
Xingu, stm., Braz........ D7 84
Xingxian, China........ B4 42
Xinhe, China........... F5 36
Xinhua, China.......... H4 42
Xinhui, China.......... J5 42
Xining, China.......... D5 36
Xinji, China........... C6 42
Xinjiang, China........ D4 42
Xinjiang, state, China.... A5 46
Xinjin, China.......... E5 36
Xinjin, China.......... B9 42
Xinjiulong (New Kowloon), China............... J6 42
Xinkai, stm., China...... C5 38
Xinlin, China.......... B7 38
Xinlitun, China........ D5 38
Xinmin, China......... C5 38
Xinning, China........ H4 42
Xinshao, China........ H4 42
Xintian, China......... I5 42
Xinwen, China......... D7 42
Xinxian, China......... B5 42
Xinxiang, China....... C5 42
Xinxiang, China....... D5 42
Xinxing, China........ C8 38
Xinyang, China........ E6 42
Xinye, China........... E5 42
Xinyi, China........... D8 42
Xinyu, China.......... H6 42
Xinzhou, China........ B5 42
Xiongyuecheng, China... A9 42
Xiping, China.......... E6 42
Xiping, China.......... G8 42
Xiqing Shan, mts., China.. E5 36
Xique-Xique, Braz....... F4 88
Xırdalan, Azer.......... A6 56
Xishanqiao, China....... F8 42
Xisha Qundao (Paracel Islands), is., China..... B5 50
Xishui, China.......... F6 42
Xiti, China............ B9 54

Xiu, stm., China......... G6 42
Xi Ujimqin Qi, China..... B2 38
Xiushui, China......... A10 42
Xiuyan, China......... A10 42
Xiva, Spain........... E10 20
Xixabangma Feng, mtn., China............... D10 54
Xixi, China............ H8 42
Xixian, China.......... E6 42
Xixiang, China......... E2 42
Xixona, Spain.......... F10 20
Xiyang, China......... C5 42
Xizang (Tibet), state, China. B5 46
Xizi, China............ D3 38
Xochicalco, sci., Mex..... F9 100
Xochistlahuaca, Mex...... G9 100
Xu, stm., China......... H7 42
Xuancheng, China........ F8 42
Xuan'en, China.......... F3 42
Xuang, stm., Laos........ B6 48
Xuanhan, China......... F2 42
Xuanhua, China......... A6 42
Xuanwei, China......... F5 36
Xuchang, China........ D5 42
Xun, stm., China........ J4 42
Xungru, China.......... D10 54
Xunwu, China.......... I6 42
Xupu, China........... H4 42
Xüguer see Jücar, stm., Spain............... E10 20
Xuwen, China.......... K4 42
Xuyi, China........... E8 42
Xuyong, China......... G1 42
Xuzhou, China......... D7 42
Xylókastro, Grc......... E5 28

Y

Yaak, Mt., U.S.......... B11 136
Yaan, China............ E5 36
Yaapeet, Austl.......... J3 76
Yablonovy Range see Jablonovyj hrebet, mts., Russia.......... F11 34
Yabluniv, Ukr........... A12 26
Yabrin, Sau. Ar........ E6 56
Yabucoa, P.R.......... B4 104a
Yabuli, China.......... B8 38
Yacambu, Parque Nacional, p.o.i., Ven... C7 86
Yacata, i., Fiji......... p20 79e
Yacheng, China......... L3 42
Yachi, stm., China....... H2 42
Yaco see Iaco, stm., S.A... F4 84
Yacuíba, Bol.......... D4 90
Yacyretá, Isla, i., Para.... C9 92
Yādgīr, India.......... C3 53
Yadkin, stm., N.C., U.S... H4 114
Yadkinville, N.C., U.S..... H5 114
Yadong, China......... E12 54
Yafran, Libya.......... A2 62
Yagoua, Cam.......... B3 66
Yagradagzê Shan, mtn., China.......... D4 36
Yaguajay, Cuba........ A8 102
Yaguarón (Jaguarão), stm., S.A.......... F11 92
Yaguas, stm., S.A....... I6 86
Yahe, China........... B9 38
Yahk, B.C., Can........ G14 138
Yahualica, Mex........ E7 100
Yai, Khao, mtn., Thai..... E4 48
Yainax Butte, mtn., Or., U.S.. A4 134
Yaita, Japan.......... C12 40
Yaitopya see Ethiopia, ctry., Afr.......... F7 62
Yaizu, Japan.......... E11 40
Yajiang, China........ E5 36
Yakacık, Tur........... B7 58
Yakeshi, China........ B9 36
Yakima, U.S........... D6 136
Yakima, stm., Wa., U.S... D7 136
Yakmach, Pak......... D9 56
Yako, Burkina......... G4 64
Yakoma, D.R.C........ D4 66
Yakumo, Japan........ C14 38
Yaku-shima, i., Japan.... I9 38
Yakutat Bay, b., Ak., U.S.. E11 140
Yakutia see Jakutija, state, Russia........ D14 34
Yala, Thai............ I5 48
Yalahau, Laguna de, b., Mex............... B4 102
Yale, B.C., Can........ G9 138
Yale, Mi., U.S......... E7 112
Yale, Ok., U.S......... A2 122
Yale, Mount, mtn., Co., U.S... C2 128
Yalgoo, Austl.......... E3 74
Yalinga, C.A.R........ C4 66
Yalobusha, stm., Ms., U.S.. D9 122
Yalong, stm., China..... F5 36
Yalova, Tur.......... C12 28
Yalpuh, ozero, l., Ukr.... D15 26
Yalu (Amnok-kang), stm., Asia............... D7 38
Yalu, stm., China....... D6 38
Yalvaç, Tur........... E14 28
Yamaga, Japan........ F3 40
Yamagata, Japan...... A13 40
Yamagata, state, Japan... A13 40
Yamaguchi, Japan...... E4 40
Yamaguchi, state, Japan.. E4 40
Yamal Peninsula see Jamal, poluostrov, pen., Russia......... B2 34
Yamanaka, Japan...... C9 40
Yamanashi, state, Japan.. D11 40
Yamasaki, Japan...... D7 40
Yamaska, stm., Qc., Can.. E4 110
Yamatengwumulu, China.. D4 36
Yamba, Austl.......... G9 76
Yambio, Sudan........ G5 62
Yamdena, Pulau, i., Indon.. G9 44
Yame, Japan.......... F3 40
Ya Men, b., China...... J5 42
Yamethin, Mya........ B3 48
Yamma Yamma, Lake, l., Austl............... F3 76
Yamoussoukro, C. Iv..... H4 64
Yampa, stm., Co., U.S.... C8 132
Yampil', Ukr.......... A15 26
Yamsay Mountain, mtn., Or., U.S.......... H5 136
Yamuna, stm., India..... F8 54
Yamzho Yumco, l., China.. D13 54
Yan, stm., China....... C4 42
Yan, stm., Sri L....... G5 53
Yanac, Austl.......... K3 76
Yanagawa, Japan...... F3 40
Yanai, Japan.......... F5 40
Yanam, India.......... C6 53
Yan'an, China......... D3 42
Yanbu' al-Baḥr, Sau. Ar... E4 56
Yanceyville, N.C., U.S.... H6 114
Yancheng, China....... C3 42
Yancheng, China....... E9 42
Yanchi, China......... C2 42
Yanco Creek, stm., Austl... J5 76
Yanda Creek, stm., Austl... H5 76
Yandama Creek, stm., Austl............... G3 76
Yandé, Île, i., N. Cal..... m14 79d
Yandina, Sol. Is........ e8 79b
Yandoon, Mya........ D2 48
Yanfolila, Mali........ G3 64
Yang, stm., Thai....... D7 48
Yangambi, D.R.C....... D4 66
Yan'gang, China....... I7 42
Yangbajain, China...... C13 54
Yangcheng, China...... D5 42
Yangchiang see Yangjiang, China..... K4 42

Yangchou see Yangzhou, China............... E8 42
Yangchow see Yangzhou, China............... E8 42
Yangch'üan see Yangquan, China..... C5 42
Yangchun, China....... J4 42
Yangdachengzi, China.... B6 38
Yanggao, China........ A5 42
Yanghexi, China........ G3 42
Yangjiang, China....... K4 42
Yangki see Taiyuan, China.. C5 42
Yangliuqing, China...... B7 42
Yangon (Rangoon), Mya... D2 48
Yangon, state, Mya...... D3 48
Yangpingguan, China.... E1 42
Yangquan, China....... C5 42
Yangriwan, China...... F4 42
Yangsan, Kor., S....... D2 40
Yangshan, China....... I5 42
Yangshuo, China....... I4 42
Yangtze see Chang, stm., China............... F8 36
Yangtze see Jinsha, stm., China.......... F5 36
Yangxian, China....... E2 42
Yangxin, China........ G6 42
Yangyang, Kor., S....... A1 40
Yangyuan, China....... A5 42
Yangzhou, China....... E8 42
Yanhe, China.......... G3 42
Yanji, China.......... C8 38
Yanji, China.......... C8 38
Yanjiadian, China...... B9 42
Yankeetown, Fl., U.S..... G3 116
Yankton, S.D., U.S...... E15 126
Yanqi, China.......... C2 36
Yanqing, China........ A6 42
Yanshou, China........ B8 38
Yantabulla, Austl....... G5 76
Yantai, China......... C9 42
Yantan, China......... C9 42
Yantongshan, China.... C6 38
Yanyuan, China....... F5 36
Yanzhou, China....... D7 42
Yao, Chad............ E3 62
Yaoundé, Cam......... D2 66
Yaoxian, China........ D3 42
Yao Yai, Ko, i., Thai..... I4 48
Yap, i., Micron........ C4 72
Yapacana, Parque Nacional, p.o.i., Ven.... F8 86
Yapacani, Bol......... C4 90
Yapen, Pulau, i., Indon... F10 44
Yapen, Selat, strt., Indon.. F10 44
Yappar, stm., Austl...... B4 76
Yaque del Norte, stm., Dom. Rep........ C12 102
Yaqui, stm., Mex....... G8 98
Yaracuy, state, Ven...... B7 86
Yaraka, Austl......... E5 76
Yardımcı, Tur......... A10 58
Yardımcı Burnu, c., Tur... G13 28
Yarí, stm., Col......... H5 86
Yariga-take, mtn., Japan.. C10 40
Yarim, Yemen......... G5 56
Yaring, Thai.......... I5 48
Yaritagua, Ven........ B7 86
Yarkand see Shache, China.. B12 56
Yarkand see Yarkant, stm., China....... G13 32
Yarkant see Shache, China.. B12 56
Yarkant, stm., China.... G13 32
Yarloop, Austl......... F3 74
Yarmouth, N.S., Can..... G10 110
Yarmouth, Me., U.S..... G6 110
Yarmu, Pap. N. Gui..... a3 79a
Yarram, Austl......... L6 76
Yarraman, Austl....... F8 76
Yarrawonga, Austl...... K5 76
Yarumal, Col......... D4 86
Yasawa Group, is., Fiji... p18 79e
Yashiro-jima, i., Japan... F5 40
Yasinia, Ukr......... A11 26
Yasothon, Thai........ E6 48
Yass, Austl........... J7 76
Yasugi, Japan......... D6 40
Yasun, stm., Ec........ H3 86
Yasuni, Parque Nacional, p.o.i., Ec.......... H4 86
Yata, stm., Bol....... B3 90
Yatağan, Tur......... F11 28
Yaté, N. Cal.......... n16 79d
Yates City, Il., U.S...... D7 120
Yathkyed Lake, l., Nu., Can... C11 106
Yatsuo, Japan......... C10 40
Yatsushiro, Japan...... G3 40
Yatsushiro-kai, b., Japan.. G3 40
Yatuá, stm., Ven....... G8 86
Yauca, Peru.......... F3 84
Yauco, P.R........... B2 104a
Yautepec, Mex........ F9 100
Yavari (Javari), stm., S.A... D3 84
Yavaros, Mex......... B4 100
Yavatmāl, India........ H7 54
Yaví, Cerro, mtn., Ven.... E9 86
Yavita, Ven.......... H9 102
Yavoriv, Ukr.......... G19 16
Yauzeli, Tur.......... A8 58
Yaw, stm., Mya........ B2 48
Yawatahama, Japan..... F5 40
Yaxchilán, sci., Mex..... D2 102
Yayladağı, Tur........ C7 58
Yayuan, China......... D7 38
Yazd, Iran........... C7 56
Yazoo, stm., Ms., U.S.... E8 122
Yazoo City, Ms., U.S..... E8 122
Ybbs an der Donau, Aus... B12 22
Yding Skovhøj, hill, Den... I3 8
Ydra (Hydra), i., Grc..... F6 28
Ye, Mya............. E3 48
Yebyu, Mya.......... E4 48
Yecheng, China........ B12 56
Yech'ŏn, Kor., S....... C1 40
Yecla, Spain.......... F9 20
Yedashe, Mya......... C3 48
Yedi Göller Milli Parkı, p.o.i., Tur....... B14 28
Yedseram, stm., Nig..... G7 64
Yeeda, Austl......... C4 74
Yeghegnadzor, Arm..... B6 56
Yei, Sudan........... G6 62
Yei, stm., Sudan....... F6 62
Yela Island, i., Pap. N. Gui............... B10 74
Yelarbon, Austl....... G8 76
Yell, i., Scot., U.K...... n18 12a
Yellandu, India........ C5 53
Yellow see Huang, stm., China............... D8 36
Yellow, stm., Wi., U.S.... F7 118
Yellow, stm., Wi., U.S.... H6 114
Yellow Grass, Sk., Can.... E9 124
Yellowhead Pass, p., Can.. D12 138
Yellow House Draw, stm., Tx., U.S........ H3 122
Yellowknife, N.T., Can.... C8 106
Yellowknife, stm., N.T., Can.. C8 106
Yellow Sea, s., Asia..... B5 108
Yellowstone, stm., U.S.... B7 126
Yellowstone, Clarks Fork, stm., U.S..... B3 126
Yellowstone Falls, wtfl., Wy., U.S..... F16 136
Yellowstone Lake, l., Wy., U.S.......... F16 136
Yellowstone National Park, p.o.i., U.S...... F16 136

Yellowtail Dam, dam, U.S............... B4 126
Yellville, Ar., U.S....... H5 120
Yelverton Bay, b., Nu., Can... A9 141
Yemen, ctry., Asia...... F6 56
Yenagoa, Nig......... H6 64
Yenangyaung, Mya...... B2 48
Yenanma, Mya........ C2 48
Yen Bai, Viet......... B7 48
Yench'eng see Yancheng, China..... E9 42
Yenchi see Yanji, China... C8 38
Yenda, Austl......... J6 76
Yendéré, Burkina...... G4 64
Yendi, Ghana.......... H4 64
Ye-ngan, Mya......... B3 48
Yengisar, China....... B12 56
Yengo National Park, p.o.i., Austl....... I8 76
Yenice, Tur.......... A6 58
Yenice, state, Fr....... B15 28
Yenicekale, Tur....... A7 58
Yenierenköy, N. Cyp..... C5 58
Yenimehmetli, Tur...... D15 28
Yenipazar, Tur........ C13 28
Yenişehir, Tur........ C12 28
Yenisey see Enisej, stm., Russia............ C6 34
Yenshuichen, Tai....... J9 42
Yentai see Yantai, China.. C9 42
Yeola, India.......... H5 54
Yeo Lake, l., Austl...... E4 74
Yeo, Kap, c., Grnld..... B12 141
Yeovil, Eng., U.K....... K10 12
Yepachic, Mex........ A5 100
Yeppoon, Austl....... D8 76
Yerevan (Erivan), Arm.... A5 56
Yerington, Nv., U.S..... E6 134
Yerköy, Tur.......... B3 56
Yerlisu, Tur.......... C9 28
Yermo, Ca., U.S........ I9 134
Yerupaja, Nevado, mtn., Peru............... F2 84
Yerushalayim (Jerusalem), Isr... G6 58
Yesa, Embalse de, res., Spain............. B9 20
Yeşildere, Tur......... A4 58
Yeşilköy, Tur.......... C11 28
Yeşiltepe, Tur......... A3 58
Yeso, N.M., U.S....... G4 128
Yetman, Austl......... G8 76
Yetti, reg., Afr........ D3 64
Yeu, Île d', i., Fr....... H6 14
Yevlax, Azer......... A6 56
Yexian, China......... E5 42
Yexian, China......... B3 48
Yeywa, Mya.......... B3 48
Ygatimí, Para.......... B10 92
Yguazú, stm., Para...... B10 92
Yhú, Para........... B10 92
Yi, stm., China........ D5 42
Yi, stm., China........ E6 42
Yi, stm., Ur.......... F10 92
Yi'allaq, Gebel, mtn., Egypt........ H4 58
Yibin, China.......... F5 36
Yibug Caka, l., China.... B11 54
Yicheng, China........ F5 42
Yichuan, China........ D5 42
Yichuan see Yinchuan, China............... C3 42
Yichun, China......... B10 36
Yichun, China......... H6 42
Yidie, China.......... C4 42
Yidu, China.......... C8 42
Yidu, China.......... F4 42
Yifeng, China......... G6 42
Yigilca, Tur.......... C14 28
Yilan, China.......... B10 36
Yilaxi, China......... C7 38
Yiliang, China........ F5 36
Yilong, China......... F2 42
Yin, stm., Mya........ B2 48
Yinchuan, China....... C3 42
Ying, stm., China...... E6 42
Yingcheng, China...... F5 42
Yingcheng see Yingchengzi, China... B6 38
Yingchengzi, China..... B6 38
Yingde, China......... I5 42
Yingjin, stm., China..... C3 38
Yingkou, China........ A10 42
Yingkou, China........ A9 42
Yingpan, stm., China.... I2 42
Yingshang, China...... E6 42
Yingshouyingzi, China... A7 42
Yingtan, China........ G7 42
Yining, China........ F14 32
Yining see Yanji, China... C8 38
Yinkeng, China....... H6 42
Yinmatu, stm., China.... D2 38
Yinnyein, Mya........ D3 48
Yin Shan, mts., China.... C6 36
Yi'ong, stm., China..... E3 36
Yirga 'Alem, Eth....... F7 62
Yirol, Sudan......... G6 62
Yishan, China......... I3 42
Yishui, China......... D8 42
Yisuhe, China......... H5 42
Yitong, stm., China..... C6 38
Yitulihe, China........ A9 36
Yiwu, China.......... G8 42
Yiwu, China.......... C3 36
Yixian, China......... D4 38
Yixing, China......... F8 42
Yixun, stm., China..... D2 38
Yiyang, China........ D4 42
Yiyang, China........ G7 42
Yiyang, China........ C8 42
Yizhang, China........ I5 42
Yli-Kitka, l., Fin....... C13 8
Ylivieska, Fin......... D11 8
Ymer Ø, i., Grnld...... C21 141
Ynykčanskij, Russia..... D16 34
Yoakum, Tx., U.S...... E10 130
Yocona, stm., Ms., U.S... C9 122
Yog Point, c., Phil...... C5 52
Yogyakarta, Indon...... G7 50
Yogyakarta, state, Indon... H7 50
Yoho National Park, p.o.i., B.C., Can..... E14 138
Yōka, Japan.......... D7 40
Yokadouma, Cam...... D2 66
Yokkaichi, Japan...... D9 40
Yoko, Cam.......... D2 66
Yokoate-jima, i., Japan... k19 39a
Yokohama, Japan..... D12 40
Yokosuka, Japan...... D12 40
Yokote, Japan........ E14 38
Yola, Nig............ H7 64
Yolombo, D.R.C....... E4 66
Yom, stm., Thai....... D5 48
Yonago, Japan........ D6 40
Yoncalla, Or., U.S...... G3 136
Yonezawa, Japan...... B12 40
Yong'an, China........ I7 42
Yongchang, China...... D5 36
Yongch'ŏn, Kor., S..... D1 40
Yongchuan, China...... G1 42
Yongchun, China...... I7 42
Yongding, China....... I6 42
Yongding, stm., China... A6 42
Yŏngdŏk, Kor., S....... C2 40
Yongdong, Kor., S...... F7 38
Yongfeng, China....... H6 42
Yonggi, Kor., S........ C1 40
Yongi, China......... C7 38

Yŏngil-man, b., Kor., S... C2 40
Yŏngju, Kor., S........ C1 40
Yongkang, China....... H5 42
Yongle, China......... H5 42
Yongnian, China....... C6 42
Yongning, China...... J3 42
Yongning, China...... B1 42
Yongping, China...... F4 36
Yongren, China....... F5 36
Yongshan, China...... D2 42
Yongshou, China...... D2 42
Yongtai, China....... I8 42
Yongxing, China...... H5 42
Yongxing, China...... B4 42
Yongxiu, China....... G6 42
Yongzhou, China..... H4 42
Yonibana, S.L......... H2 64
Yonkers, N.Y., U.S...... D12 114
Yonne, state, Fr....... G12 14
Yonne, stm., Fr....... F12 14
Yopal, Col........... E5 86
Yopurga, China....... B12 56
York, Austl.......... F3 74
York, Eng., U.K........ H11 12
York, Al., U.S......... E10 122
York, N.D., U.S....... F14 124
York, Pa., U.S........ E9 114
York, S.C., U.S........ A4 116
York, Cape, c., Austl.... B8 74
York, Kap, c., Grnld.... B12 141
Yorke Peninsula, pen., Austl............. F7 74
Yorketown, Austl...... G7 74
York Factory, Mb., Can... D12 106
Yorkshire Dales National Park, p.o.i., Eng., U.K... G10 12
York Sound, strt., Austl... B4 74
Yorkton, Sk., Can...... C11 124
Yorktown, Tx., U.S..... E10 130
Yorktown, Va., U.S..... G9 114
Yorkville, Il., U.S....... J10 118
Yorkville, N.Y., U.S..... E14 112
Yoro, Hond........... E4 102
Yoron-jima, i., Japan.... l19 39a
Yosemite National Park, p.o.i., Ca., U.S...... F6 134
Yosemite Village, Ca., U.S... F6 134
Yoshino, stm., Japan.... E7 40
Yōsōbulang see Altay, Mong... B4 36
You, stm., Mya........ A2 48
Yŏsu, Kor., S.......... G7 38
You, stm., China....... G6 36
You, stm., China....... G4 42
Youanmi, Austl....... E3 74
Youghal, Ire.......... J5 12
Young, Austl......... J7 76
Young, Sk., Can....... C8 124
Young, Ur........... F9 92
Young, Az., U.S....... I5 132
Younghusband Peninsula, pen., Austl......... K2 76
Young Island, i., Ant.... B21 81
Youngs Rock, r., Pit..... c28 78k
Youngstown, Ab., Can... C2 124
Youngstown, N.Y., U.S... E10 112
Youngstown, Oh., U.S... C5 114
Youngsville, La., U.S.... G6 122
Youngsville, N.C., U.S... H7 114
Yountville, Ca., U.S.... E3 134
Youssoufia, Mor....... C3 64
Youxian, China....... H5 42
Youyang, China...... G3 42
Yŏyang-ni, Kor., S...... B1 40
Yozgat, Tur.......... B3 56
Ypres see Ieper, Bel..... D11 14
Ypsilanti, Mi., U.S...... B2 114
Yreka, Ca., U.S........ B3 134
Yrghyz, Kaz......... E10 32
Ysabel Channel, strt., Pap. N. Gui....... a4 79a
Ystad, Swe.......... I5 8
Ystäborg, Swe......... E6 8
Ytterhogdal, Swe...... E6 8
Yuam, stm., Thai...... J3 42
Yuam see Red, stm., Asia... D9 46
Yuan, stm., China...... H6 42
Yuan, stm., China...... G4 42
Yuanling, China....... F5 36
Yuanmou, China....... F5 36
Yuantan, China....... G5 42
Yuanyang, China...... G9 42
Yuasa, Japan......... E8 40
Yuba City, Ca., U.S..... D4 134
Yuba, stm., Ca., U.S.... C15 38
Yubari, Japan........ C15 38
Yucaipa, Ca., U.S..... I8 134
Yucatán, state, Mex..... B3 102
Yucatán, Península de (Yucatan Peninsula), pen., N.A....... C3 102
Yucatan Channel, strt., N.A... A4 102
Yucatan Peninsula see Yucatán, Península de, pen., N.A....... C3 102
Yucca, Az., U.S....... I2 132
Yucca Mountain, mtn., Nv., U.S....... G9 134
Yucca Valley, Ca., U.S... I9 134
Yucheng, China....... C7 42
Yuci, China.......... C5 42
Yudu, China.......... I6 42
Yuechi, China........ F2 42
Yueqing, China....... G9 42
Yuexi, China......... F5 36
Yueyang, China....... G5 42
Yufa, China.......... B7 42
Yugan, China........ G7 42
Yugoslavia see Serbia and Montenegro, ctry., Eur... F6 26
Yuhebu, China....... C3 42
Yuhuan Dao, i., China.. G9 42
Yuhuang Ding, mtn., China... C6 42
Yizhang, China....... F11 128
Yukon, Ok., U.S....... B3 106
Yukon, state, Can..... C11 140
Yukon, stm., N.A...... D1 140
Yukon Flats, sw., Ak., U.S.. C11 140
Yukuhashi, Japan...... F3 40
Yūli, Tai............ J9 42
Yulin, China.......... B3 42
Yulin, China.......... J3 42
Yuma, Az., U.S........ K2 132
Yuma, Co., U.S....... A6 128
Yuma, Bahía de, b., Dom. Rep........ C13 102
Yumare, Ven......... B7 86
Yumbel, Chile........ H1 92
Yumbo, Col.......... E4 86
Yumen, China........ D4 36
Yumt uul, mtn., Mong... B3 36
Yun, stm., China...... F5 42
Yun, stm., Dom. Rep... C13 102
Yunak, Tur.......... E14 28
Yunan, China......... J4 42
Yuncheng, China...... C4 42
Yuncheng, China...... D6 42
Yungchi see Jilin, China.. C7 38
Yungchia see Wenzhou, China............... F9 36
Yungki see Nanning, China............... J3 42
Yunkai Dashan, mts., China.. J4 42
Yun Ling, mts., China... F4 36
Yunling, stm., China.... A6 42
Yunmeng, China...... F5 42
Yunnan, state, China.... F5 36
Yunnanfu see Kunming, China............... F5 36
Yunta, Austl......... H2 76
Yunwu Shan, mtn., China.. A7 42
Yunxi, China......... E4 42

Yunxian, China....... E4 42
Yunxiao, China....... I7 42
Yunyang, China....... F3 42
Yunyang see Yunxian, China.. E4 42
Yunzalin, stm., Mya.... D3 48
Yuping, China........ H3 42
Yuqing, China........ H2 42
Yurimaguas, Peru..... E2 84
Yuriria, Laguna de, l., Mex.. E8 100
Yuruá see Juruá, stm., S.A... D4 84
Yurubí, Parque Nacional, p.o.i., Ven........ B7 86
Yurungkax, stm., China.. A5 46
Yuscarán, Hond....... F4 102
Yūsef, Bahr (Yūsuf, Bahr), can., Egypt....... K1 58
Yushan, China........ G8 42
Yü Shan, mtn., Tai..... J9 42
Yushanzhen, China.... G3 42
Yushu, China......... E4 36
Yushu, China......... B7 38
Yutian, China........ A5 46
Yutian, China........ B7 42
Yuty, Para........... C9 92
Yützu see Yuci, China... C5 42
Yuxian, China........ B5 42
Yuxian, China........ D5 42
Yuyao, China........ F9 42
Yuzawa, Japan....... E14 38
Yvelines, state, Fr...... F10 14
Yverdon-les-Bains, Switz.. D3 22
Ywathagyi, Mya...... A2 48

Z

Zaandam see Zaanstad, Neth............... B13 14
Zaanstad, Neth....... B13 14
Zabalac', Bela......... G7 10
Zabălţ, Rom......... C8 26
Zabīd, Yemen........ G5 56
Žabinka, Bela........ H6 10
Ząbkowice Śląskie, Pol... F12 16
Žabljak, Serb........ F6 26
Zabno, Pol.......... F16 16
Zābol, Iran.......... C9 56
Zābol, state, Afg...... C1 54
Zabolotiv, Ukr....... A12 26
Zabor''e, Bela........ E12 10
Zabory, Russia....... F15 10
Zabrze, Pol......... F14 16
Zabykčanne, Bela..... G14 10
Zacapa, Guat........ E3 102
Zacapu, Mex......... F8 100
Zacatecas, Mex....... D7 100
Zacatecas, state, Mex... D7 100
Zacatlán, Mex....... F10 100
Zacoalco de Torres, Mex.. E7 100
Zacualtipan, Mex...... E9 100
Zadar (Zara), Cro...... F12 22
Zadetkale Kyun, i., Mya.. G3 48
Zadetkyi Kyun, i., Mya... H3 48
Zadoi, China........ B8 46
Za'farāna, well, Egypt... I3 58
Zafer Burnu, c., N. Cyp... C5 58
Zafirovo, Blg......... F13 26
Zafra, Spain......... F4 20
Żagań, Pol.......... E11 16
Žagarė, Lith......... D6 10
Zagazig, Egypt....... H2 58
Zaghouan, Tun....... H4 24
Zaghouan, Jebel, mtn., Tun............... H4 24
Zagora, Mor......... C3 64
Zagórz, Pol......... G18 16
Zagreb, Cro......... E12 22
Zagros, Kūhhā-ye, mts., Iran.. C7 56
Zagros Mountains see Zāgros, Kūhhā-ye, mts., Iran............ C7 56
Za'gya, stm., China.... B13 54
Zāhedān, Iran....... D9 56
Zahirābād, India...... C3 53
Zahlah, Leb.......... D7 58
Zahnitkiv, Ukr....... A15 26
Zahrebetnoe, Russia.... B17 8
Zaire see Congo, Democratic Republic of the, ctry., Afr... E4 66
Zaire see Congo, stm., Afr... F2 66
Zajsan see Zaysan, Kaz... E14 32
Zajsan, ozero see Zhaysang köli, l., Kaz... E14 32
Zaka, Zimb.......... B10 70
Zakamensk, Russia..... F9 34
Zakarpattia, co., Ukr.... A10 26
Zakhidnyi Buh (Bug), (Buh), stm., Eur.... D17 16
Zakho, Iraq......... B5 56
Zakliczyn, Pol....... G16 16
Zakopane, Pol....... G16 16
Zakouma, Chad...... E3 62
Zakroczym, Pol...... D16 16
Zakynthos, i., Grc..... F3 28
Zakynthos, i., Grc..... F3 28
Zala, state, Hung..... C3 26
Zala, stm., Hung..... C3 26
Zalaegerszeg, Hung.... C3 26
Zalamea de la Serena, Spain............. F5 20
Zalantun, China...... B9 36
Zalari, Russia........ D18 32
Zalaszentgrót, Hung... C4 26
Zalău, Rom......... B10 26
Zalese, Russia....... F4 10
Zalim, Sau. Ar....... E5 56
Zalingei, Sudan...... E4 62
Žaludok, Bela....... G7 10
Zama, Ms., U.S....... E9 122
Zamakh, Yemen...... F6 56
Zamanti, stm., Tur..... A6 58
Zambeze, stm., Afr.... D3 68
Zambezi, Zam........ C3 68
Zambezi, stm., Afr..... D4 68
Zambezi Escarpment, clf., Zimb........ D4 68
Zambia, ctry., Afr...... D4 68
Zamboanga, Phil...... G3 52
Zamboanga Peninsula, pen., Phil.......... G3 52
Zambrów, Pol........ C18 16
Zambyl see Taraz, Kaz... F12 32
Zamęžnaja, Russia..... D24 8
Zami, stm., Mya...... D4 48
Zamora, Ec.......... D2 84
Zamora, Spain........ C5 20
Zamora de Hidalgo, Mex... F7 100
Zamość, Pol......... F19 16
Zamość, state, Pol..... F19 16
Zanaga, Congo....... E2 66
Záncara, stm., Spain.... E8 20
Zanda, China........ C8 54
Zanesville, Oh., U.S.... E3 114
Zanjan, Iran......... B6 56
Zanjón, Iran......... B6 56
Zannettü, ostrov, i., Russia... A20 34
Zante see Zákynthos, i., Grc............. F3 28
Zanthus, Austl....... F4 74
Zanzibar, i., Tan....... F7 66
Zanzibar, i., Tan....... F7 66
Zanzibar Channel, strt., Tan............... F7 66
Zaostrovje, Russia.... F14 8
Zaō-zan, vol., Japan.... A13 40
Zaozërnyj, Russia..... C16 32
Zaozhuang, China..... D7 42
Zap, N.D., U.S....... G12 124
Zapadnaja Dvina, Russia.. D15 10

Name	Map Ref.	Page
Zapadna Morava, stm., Serb.	F8	26
Zapadno-Sibirskaja ravnina (West Siberian Plain), pl., Russia.	B12	32
Zapadnyj hrebet, mts., Russia	F17	34
Zapadnyj Sajan, mts., Russia	D16	32
Západočeský kraj, state, Czech Rep.	G9	16
Západoslovenský kraj, state, Slov.	H14	16
Zapala, Arg.	G2	90
Zapata, Tx., U.S.	H8	130
Zapata, Península de, pen., Cuba	A7	102
Zapatosa, Col.	D5	86
Zapatosa, Ciénaga de, l., Col.	C5	86
Zapljuse, Russia	B12	10
Zapole, Russia	B12	10
Zapoljarnyj, Russia.	B14	8
Zapopan, Mex.	E7	100
Zaporizhzhia, Ukr.	E5	32
Zapovednyj, Russia	C10	38
Zaprudnja, Russia	D20	10
Zaqatala, Azer.	A6	56
Zaragoza, Mex.	A8	100
Zaragoza, Mex.	C1	130
Zaragoza (Saragossa), Spain.	C10	20
Zaragoza, co., Spain	C9	20
Zarajsk, Russia	F21	10
Zaranj, Afg.	C9	56
Zarasai, Lith.	E9	10
Zárate, Arg.	G8	92
Zarautz, Spain	A8	20
Zarauz see Zarautz, Spain	A8	20
Zaraza, Ven.	C9	86
Zareče, Russia	E21	8
Zarečensk, Russia	C14	8
Zarghon Shahr, Afg.	C10	56
Zaria, Nig.	G6	64
Żarki, Pol.	F15	16
Żarma see Zharma, Kaz.	E14	32
Zărneşti, Rom.	D12	26
Zarubino, Russia	C9	38
Zarumilla, Peru.	D1	84
Żary, Pol.	E11	16
Zarzaïtine, Alg.	D6	64
Zarzal, Col.	E4	86
Zasa, Lat.	D8	10
Záskár, stm., India	B6	54
Záskár Mountains, mts., Asia	B7	54
Zaslawye, Bela.	F10	10
Zastava, Russia	G22	8
Zasule, Russia	D22	8
Žatec, Czech Rep.	F9	16
Zatyshshya, Ukr.	B16	26
Zavalla, Tx., U.S.	F4	122
Zave, Zimb.	D5	68
Zavet, Blg.	F13	26
Zavodoukovsk, Russia.	C11	32
Zavodovski Island, i., S. Geor.	K12	82
Zavolžsk, Russia	H20	8
Zawadzkie, Pol.	F14	16
Zawiercie, Pol.	F15	16
Zāwiyat al-Mukhaylá, Libya	A4	62
Zaysan, Kaz.	E14	32
Zaysan, Lake see Zhaysang köli, l., Kaz.	E14	32
Zayü, stm., China	C8	46
Zayzan see Zaysan, Kaz.	E14	32
Zaza, stm., Cuba	B8	102
Zaza, Presa, res., Cuba	B8	102
Zbąszynek, Pol.	D11	16
Zbraslav, Czech Rep.	G10	16
Žďár nad Sázavou, Czech Rep.	G11	16
Žďiar, Slov.	G16	16
Zduńska Wola, Pol.	E14	16
Zearing, Ia., U.S.	B4	120
Zeballos, B.C., Can.	G4	138
Zebedelia, S. Afr.	D9	70
Zebulon, Ga., U.S.	C1	116
Zedang, China	D13	54
Zeebrugge, Bel.	C11	14
Zeehan, Austl.	n12	77a
Zeeland, Mi., U.S.	F4	112
Zeeland, N.D., U.S.	B13	126
Zeerust, S. Afr.	D7	70
Žefat, Isr.	F6	58
Zehdenick, Ger.	C8	16
Zehlendorf, Ger.	D6	74
Zeist, Neth.	B14	14
Zeitz, Ger.	E8	16
Zeja, Russia	F14	34
Zeja, stm., Russia	F14	34
Zejskoe vodohranilišče, res., Russia	F14	34
Zelee, Cape, c., Sol. Is.	e9	79b
Zelenoborskij, Russia.	C14	8
Zelenogorsk, Russia	F13	8
Zelenograd, Russia	D20	10
Zelenogradsk, Russia.	F3	10
Zelenokumsk, Russia	F6	32
Železnodorožnyj, Russia	B8	32
Železnodorožnyj, Russia	F4	10
Železnogorsk, Russia	H18	10
Železnogorsk-Ilimskij, Russia	C18	32
Zelienople, Pa., U.S.	D5	114
Zella-Mehlis, Ger.	F6	16
Zell am See, Aus.	C9	22
Zell am Ziller, Aus.	C8	22
Zel'va, Bela.	G7	10
Želva, Lith.	E8	10
Žemaitijos nacionalnis parkas, p.o.i., Lith.	D4	10
Zembin, Bela.	F11	10
Zembra, Ile, i., Tun.	G4	24
Zémio, C.A.R.	C4	66
Zempoala, sci., Mex.	F10	100
Zemun, Serb.	E7	26
Zeng, stm., China	J5	42
Zenon Park, Sk., Can.	A10	124
Zentsūji, Japan	E6	40
Zenza do Itombe, Ang.	B1	68
Zephyr, Tx., U.S.	C9	130
Zephyrhills, Fl., U.S.	H3	116
Zepu, China	B12	56
Zeravšan, stm., Asia	B10	56
Zeravšanskij hrebet, mts., Asia	B10	56
Zerbst, Ger.	D8	16
Żerków, Pol.	D13	16
Zerqan, Alb.	C14	24
Žešart, Russia	E23	8
Zeulenroda, Ger.	F7	16
Zeven, Ger.	C5	16
Zevenaar, Neth.	E2	16
Zeydābād, Afg.	A2	54
Zeytinbağı, Tur.	C11	28
Zêzere, stm., Port.	E2	20
Zgierz, Pol.	E15	16
Zgorzelec, Pol.	E11	16
Zhabuchaka Hu, l., China	C9	54
Zhakou, China.	F5	42
Zhaltyr, Kaz.	D12	32
Zhambyl see Taraz, Kaz.	F12	32
Zhang, stm., China	I6	42
Zhang, stm., China	C5	42
Zhangaözen, Kaz.	F8	32
Zhanga Qalqotan, Kaz.	D11	32
Zhangaqazaly, Kaz.	E10	32
Zhangatas, Kaz.	F11	32
Zhangbei, China.	A6	42
Zhangguangcai Ling, mts., China	B8	38
Zhanghuang, China.	K3	42
Zhangjiakou, China.	A6	42
Zhangping, China	I7	42
Zhangpu, China.	I7	42
Zhangqiu, China.	C7	42
Zhangshuping, China	F4	42
Zhangwu, China.	C5	38
Zhangye, China.	D5	36
Zhangzhou, China.	I7	42
Zhānibek, Kaz.	E7	32
Zhanjiang, China	K4	42
Zhanyu, China.	B5	38
Zhao'an, China.	J7	42
Zhaodong, China.	A7	38
Zhaojue, China.	C9	46
Zhaoping, China.	I4	42
Zhaoqing, China.	J5	42
Zhaotong, China.	F5	36
Zhaoxing, China.	B11	36
Zhaoyuan, China.	B10	36
Zhari Namco, l., China	C10	54
Zharkent, Kaz.	F13	32
Zharma, Kaz.	E14	32
Zharsuat, Kaz.	E14	32
Zhaxi Co, l., China	B10	54
Zhaxigang, China	C5	54
Zhaysang köli, l., Kaz.	E14	32
Zhayylma, Kaz.	D10	32
Zhayyq see Ural, stm.	E8	32
Zhecheng, China	D6	42
Zhegu, China.	D13	54
Zhejiang, state, China	G8	42
Zhelezinka, Kaz.	D13	32
Zhelin, China.	F9	42
Zhem see Embi, stm., Kaz.	E9	32
Zhenbeikou, China.	B2	42
Zheng'an, China.	G2	42
Zhengding, China.	B6	42
Zhenghe, China.	H8	42
Zhenglan Qi, China.	C8	36
Zhengning, China.	D3	42
Zhengyang, China.	E5	42
Zhengzhou, China.	D5	42
Zhenhai, China.	G9	42
Zhenjiang, China.	E8	42
Zhenlai, China.	B9	36
Zhenning, China.	H1	42
Zhenping, China.	E5	42
Zhentou, stm., China	E6	42
Zhenxiong, China.	F5	36
Zhenyu, China.	H9	42
Zhenyuan, China	H3	42
Zhenyuan, China.	D2	42
Zherong, China.	H8	42
Zhetiqara, Kaz.	D10	32
Zhezdi, Kaz.	E11	32
Zhezqazghan, Kaz.	E11	32
Zhijiang, China.	H3	42
Zhixia, China.	G8	42
Zhob, stm., Pak.	C2	54
Zhob, Pak.	C2	54
Zhok", stm., Pak.	C10	56
Zholymbet, Kaz.	D12	32
Zhongba, China.	C5	46
Zhongdian, China.	F4	36
Zhongning, China.	C1	42
Zhongpingchang, China	F3	42
Zhongshan, China.	J5	42
Zhongshan, China.	I4	42
Zhongshan, sci., Ant.	B12	81
Zhongtiao Shan, mts., China	D4	42
Zhongwei, China.	C1	42
Zhongxian, China.	F3	42
Zhongxiang, China.	F14	34
Zhosaly, Kaz.	E10	32
Zhoucun, China.	C7	42
Zhouning, China.	H8	42
Zhoushan Dao, i., China	F9	42
Zhoushan Qundao, is., China	F10	42
Zhouzhi, China.	D3	42
Zhuanghe, China.	B10	42
Zhuanglang, China.	D1	42
Zhuantöbe, Kaz.	F11	32
Zhucang, China.	H2	42
Zhucheng, China.	D8	42
Zhuhe, China.	G5	42
Zhuji, China.	G9	42
Zhujia Jian, i., China	G10	42
Zhujiang Kou, est., Asia.	J5	42
Zhumadian, China	E5	42
Zhuolu, China.	A6	42
Zhuozhou, China.	B6	42
Zhuozi, China.	A5	42
Zhushan, China.	E4	42
Zhuxi, China.	E3	42
Zhuzhou, China.	H5	42
Zhympity, Kaz.	D8	32
Zhytomyr, Ukr.	E14	6
Zi, stm., China	C8	42
Zi, stm., China	G4	42
Ziārat, Pak.	C10	56
Zibo, China.	C8	42
Zichang, China.	C3	42
Ziębice, Pol.	F13	16
Zielona Góra, Pol.	E11	16
Zielona Góra, state, Pol.	D11	16
Zierikzee, Neth.	C12	14
Ziesar, Ger.	D8	16
Zifta, Egypt	H2	58
Žigalovo, Russia	D19	32
Zigansk, Russia	C13	34
Zigong, China.	F5	36
Zigui, China.	F4	42
Ziguinchor, Sen.	G1	64
Zihuatanejo, Mex.	G8	100
Ziiyang, China	E3	42
Zijin, China.	J6	42
Žilaja Tambica, Russia	E17	8
Žilina, Slov.	G14	16
Žilino, Russia	F4	10
Zillah, Libya	B3	62
Zillertaler Alpen (Aurine, Alpi), mts., Eur.	C8	22
Zilupe, Lat.	D11	10
Zilwaukee, Mi., U.S.	E6	112
Zima, Russia	D18	32
Zimapán, Mex.	E9	100
Zimbabwe, ctry., Afr.	D4	68
Zimbabwe Ruins, sci., Zimb.	B10	70
Zimi, S.L.	H2	64
Zimnicea, Rom.	F12	26
Zimonino, Russia	G14	10
Zinder, Niger	G6	64
Zinga Mulike, Tan.	F7	66
Zinnik see Soignies, Bel.	D12	14
Zion, Il., U.S.	F2	112
Zion National Park, p.o.i., Ut., U.S.	F4	132
Zionsville, In., U.S.	I3	112
Zipaquirá, Col.	E5	86
Zirbitzkogel, mtn., Aus.	C11	22
Žirnatino, Russia	G16	10
Žirovnice, Czech Rep.	G11	16
Zitong, China.	F1	42
Zittau, Ger.	F10	16
Ziway, Lake see Ziway Hāyk', l., Eth.	F7	62
Ziway Hāyk', l., Eth.	F7	62
Zixi, China.	G7	42
Ziya, stm., China	B7	42
Ziyuan, China.	I4	42
Žizdra, stm., Russia	F19	10
Zizhong, China.	G1	42
Zizhou, China.	C3	42
Žižica, Russia	D14	10
Žižickoe, ozero, l., Russia	D14	10
Zlaté Moravce, Slov.	H14	16
Zlatoust, Russia	C9	32
Zlatoustovsk, Russia	F15	34
Zlín, Czech Rep.	G13	16
Zlītan, Libya	A2	62
Žlobin, Bela.	H13	10
Złoczew, Pol.	E14	16
Złotów, Pol.	C13	16
Złynka, Russia	H14	10
Zmeinogorsk, Russia	D14	32
Žmigród, Pol.	E12	16
Zmíinyi, ostriv, i., Ukr.	D17	26
Znamenka, Russia	F17	10
Znamensk, Russia	F4	10
Znamenskoe, Russia	C12	32
Znin, Pol.	D13	16
Znojmo, Czech Rep.	H12	16
Zoar, S. Afr.	H5	70
Zodziņa, Bela.	F11	10
Zoétélé, Cam.	D2	66
Zogang, China	F4	36
Žohova, ostrov, i., Russia	A19	34
Zohreh, stm., Iran	D7	56
Zolotaja Gora, Russia	F14	34
Zomba, Mwi.	D6	68
Zonguldak, Tur.	B14	28
Zonguldak, state, Tur.	B15	28
Zonza, Fr.	H15	18
Zorita, Spain	E5	20
Zorra, Arroyo de la, stm., Mex.	E6	130
Zouar, Chad	C3	62
Zouérat, Maur.	E2	64
Zoug see Zug, Switz.	C5	22
Zouxian, China.	D7	42
Zovka, Russia	B11	10
Zrenjanin, Serb.	D7	26
Zuata, stm., Ven.	C9	86
Zuaydīyah, Jabal az-, mtn., Syria	E8	58
Zubovo, Russia	F17	8
Zudáñez, Bol.	C4	90
Zuera, Spain	C10	20
Zufar (Dhofar), reg., Oman	F7	56
Zug, Switz.	C5	22
Zugdidi, Geor.	F6	32
Zuger See, l., Switz.	C5	22
Zugspitze, mtn., Eur.	I6	16
Zújar, stm., Spain	F5	20
Žukopa, Russia	D15	10
Žukovka, Russia	G16	10
Žukovskij, Russia	I7	32
Zuli, stm., China	D1	42
Zulia, state, Ven.	C5	86
Zulia, stm., S.A.	C5	86
Zululand, hist. reg., S. Afr.	F10	70
Zumbo, Moz.	D5	68
Zumbrota, Mn., U.S.	G6	118
Zungeru, Nig.	H6	64
Zunhua, China.	A7	42
Zuni, stm., U.S.	I7	132
Zuni Pueblo, N.M., U.S.	H8	132
Zunyi, China.	H2	42
Zuo, stm., China	J2	42
Zuodeng, China.	J2	42
Zuomuchedong Hu, l., China	D12	54
Zuoyun, China.	A5	42
Zuwayzā, Jord.	G6	58
Zvenigorod, Russia	E19	10
Zvezdec, Blg.	G14	26
Zvezdnyj, Russia	C19	32
Zvishavane, Zimb.	B9	70
Zvolen, Slov.	H15	16
Zwedru, Lib.	H3	64
Zweibrücken, Ger.	G3	16
Zweisimmen, Switz.	D4	22
Zwickau, Ger.	F8	16
Zwierzyniec, Pol.	F18	16
Zwoleń, Pol.	E17	16
Zwolle, Neth.	B14	14
Zwolle, La., U.S.	F5	122
Żyrardów, Pol.	D16	16
Zyrjanka, Russia	C19	34
Zyrjanovsk, Kaz.	E14	32
Zyrjanskoe, Russia	C15	32
Zyryan see Zyryanovsk, Kaz.	E14	32
Zyryanovsk, Kaz.	E14	32
Zyryanskoe, Russia	C15	32
Žytkaviči, Bela.	H10	10
Żywiec, Pol.	G15	16